ENCYCLOPEDIA
OF
PSYCHOLOGY

Volume 1 ◇ A-K

ENCYCLOPEDIA OF PSYCHOLOGY

H. J. EYSENCK is Professor of Psychology and Director of the Department of Psychology at the University of London. A leading exponent of rigorous scientific psychology, he is best known for his experimental personality research; also for his concern to advance scientific knowledge in order to solve persistent individual and social problems. He has contributed over three hundred articles to the literature, and has written or edited more than twenty major books, which include not only standard works on abnormal psychology, personality, crime, politics, and drugs, but some of the most lucid and widely read popular expositions of scientific psychology.

WILHELM ARNOLD is Professor of Psychology at the University of Würzburg in West Germany. One of the leading exponents of character and personality psychology, he is best known for his research into educational psychology. His work *Person, Character and Personality* is in its third edition.

RICHARD MEILI is Professor of Psychology at the Psychological Institute of the University of Berne, Switzerland, and is an internationally respected expert in the field of psychological testing. His *Handbook of Psychological Diagnostics* is now in its fifth edition.

ENCYCLOPEDIA OF PSYCHOLOGY

Volume 1 ⋄ A-K

Editors
H. J. Eysenck
W. Arnold
R. Meili

FONTANA/COLLINS
in association with Search Press

First published by Search Press 1972
First issued in Fontana 1975

Copyright © 1972 by Herder KG, West Germany

Printed in Great Britain by
Richard Clay (The Chaucer Press) Ltd., Bungay, Suffolk

Executive editor John Cumming

Any patents, trade marks or trade names, of pharmaceutical preparations, psychological tests and so on, which appear in this Encyclopedia, are cited only by way of example. The presence or absence of any manufacturer's name or that of any product, or the order of appearance of any cited, is no indication of any judgment passed on the same, and does not show that any substance, formula or test etc. is free.

FOREWORD

This two-volume *Encyclopedia of Psychology* is an international venture, both in the sense that the authors for the definitions and articles have been drawn from many different countries and also because it is being published in English, German, French, Spanish, Portuguese and Italian. Entries in this Encyclopedia are of two kinds. First there are the ordinary definitions, occupying a line or two, which can be found in most dictionaries; second, there are articles covering important terms and concepts, specially written by well-known authorities, ranging in length up to 4,000 words, and containing suitable bibliographies for further study. This combination seemed particularly suitable for a readership which would include professional psychologists as well as students, and also psychiatrists, sociologists, educators, social workers, anthropologists and quite generally anyone interested in modern psychology, its achievements, its theories and its problems.

Such an ambitious venture must stand or fall by the quality of the people writing the articles and definitions. We have been exceptionally lucky in obtaining the co-operation of well-known experts in all the fields covered; a brief mention of just a few of these will give the reader some idea of the quality of the authorship.

From the United States, Anne Anastasi has written on Differential Psychology and A. Bandura on Socialization; L. Berkowitz on Aggression; I. Bilodeau on Motor Skills and Practice; J. E. Birren on Aging and Gerontology; H. R. Blackwell on Decision Processes; J. Brozek on Soviet Psychology; R. B. Cattell on Factor Analysis; E. R. Hilgard on Behaviorism; A. L. Irion on Reminiscence; H. A. Murray on Need; J. Zubin and F. Schumer on Projective Tests. From Britain, H. J. Butcher has written on Questionnaires; C. Cherry on Communication; Alan and Anne Clarke on Mental Defect; D. Furneaux on Hypnosis; H. G. Jones on Habit; R. Lynn on Arousal; Irene Martin on Emotion and Stress; P. McKellar on Imagination and Fantasy; Ian Oswald on Sleep and Dreams; S. Rachman on Behavior Therapy and Aversion Therapy; H. Tajfel on Prejudice; P. E. Vernon on Personality; and A. Yates on Conflict and Frustration. From the Soviet Union, A. R. Luria has written on Aphasia and Localization of Psychological Functions, the Frontal Lobes, and Soviet Psychology; E. N. Sokolov on the Orienting Reflex and A. N. Sokolov on Thinking and Inner Speech. In addition there are many German, French and Japanese authors who may not be so well known to English-speaking readers, but who are regarded as international experts in their fields. The list given above is only a random sample of well-known contributors; many others could have been named in addition or instead of those actually mentioned.

It is our hope that this Encyclopedia will be found useful by those for whom it is intended; we also hope that it will play a part in making our science more truly international than it has been hitherto, by helping to standardize terms and information, drawing attention to work done in other countries, and generally making people more aware of the international character of modern psychology.   *H. J. Eysenck*

PREFATORY NOTE

This Encyclopedia for the most part presents psychology as increasingly understood and accepted in the English-speaking world; nevertheless, some entries represent views that now occur predominantly in the literature of other linguistic and cultural areas. An international work with contributors from twenty-two countries which takes into account the standard divisions and nomenclature of the university departments and institutes of the countries to which it is addressed, offers a unique opportunity to compare and obtain information on the diverse views and methods of the theoreticians and practitioners of a still young science; it necessarily includes some concepts which diverge significantly from their English analogues.

The bibliographies appended to each major article, and to many shorter entries, in most cases list the sources of the author's references to the essential Anglo-American literature, but in areas where theory and research have been written up largely in other languages, the appropriate books and articles are recorded. Unless the author has referred specifically to the original or current foreign-language edition, or the English version differs in some pertinent respect from the edition cited, only English translations are given. In the case of un-Englished Russian works, French or German translations are cited whenever possible. Editions later than the first are indicated by a number before the date (e.g. [2]1971). It is hoped that the sometimes extensive (though always selective) bibliographies will prove one of the most valuable features of the Encyclopedia.

A list of the main articles and contributors is provided at the beginning of this first volume, together with a key to the initials of the authors of the shorter entries. Short, unsigned definitions are the work of a group of psychologists and lexicographers in the Herder Lexicographical Institute.

Wherever it seems appropriate, headwords are followed by the main synonymous (or approximately equivalent) terms. In the case of pharmaceutical preparations, however, complete lists of the corresponding trade names for even the English-speaking countries would be beyond the scope of this Encyclopedia; nevertheless, examples of such products on the market during the preparation of this work are usually cited. Less common synonyms are sometimes given at the end of an entry. The main abbreviations to be found in the Encyclopedia are listed in these preliminary pages; other abbreviations, too numerous to be listed initially, appear in context.

A number of people, ranging from specialist advisers to translators, have helped to produce this edition of the Encyclopedia. They will be acknowledged in the second volume.

J.C.

AUTHORS OF SHORTER ARTICLES
KEY TO INITIALS

A.A.	A. Anastasi	D.G.	D. Görlitz
A.B.	A. Broadhurst	D.P.	D. Pfau
A.Ba.	A. Bandura	D.V.	D. Vaitl
A.Be.	A. Bellebaum	D.Vo.	D. Vormfelde
A.B.K.	A. B. Kristofferson	E.D.	E. David
A.D.B.C.	A. D. B. Clarke	E.F.-K.	E. Furch-Krafft
A.E.B.	A. E. Bergin	E.G.W.	E. G. Wehner
A.E.L.	A. E. Lányi	E.H.	E. Heineken
A.E.M.	A. E. Maxwell	E.J.	E. Jorswieck
A.F.	A. Friedemann	E.L.	E. Lehmann
A.G.	A. Gubser	E.L.H.	E. L. Hartley
A.H.	A. Hajos	E.M.	E. Mittenecker
A.Hi.	A. Hicklin	E.M.-L.	E. Müller-Luckmann
A.J.Y.	A. J. Yates	E.N.-N.	E. Noelle-Neumann
A.K.	A. Karsten	E.N.S.	E. N. Sokolov
A.L.	A. Lang	E.R.	E. Rausch
A.N.S.	A. N. Sokolov	E.R.H.	E. R. Hilgard
A.R.	A. Rausche	E.U.	E. Ullrich
A.R.L.	A. R. Luria	E.W.	E. Wehner
A.R.-S.	A. Rocheblave-Spenlé	F.B.	F. Bomio
A.S.-M.	A. Schmidt-Mummendey	F.Bu.	F. Buggle
A.T.	A. Tanda	F.-C.S.	F.-C. Schubert
A.Th.	A. Thomas	F.H.	F. Haeberlin
A.V.	A. Vergote	F.J.	F. Jodelet
A.W.	A. Wellek	F.K.	F. Keller
A.W.-F.	A. Weill-Fassima	F.Ki.	F. Kiener
A.Y.	A. Yates	F.Kl.	F. Klix
B.B.	B. Brooker	F.K.I.	F. K. Illyés
B.H.	B. Heinze	F.M.	F. Merz
B.J.U.	B. J. Underwood	F.Ma.	F. Mattejat
B.L.	B. Louis	F.N.	F. Novak
B.R.	B. Rollett	F.S.	F. Süllwold
B.S.	B. Schmidt	F.Sch.	F. Schumer
B.Sp.	B. Spiegel	F.W.	F. Wesley
B.T.	B. Tschanz	G.A.	G. Arnold
B.W.	B. Wittlich	G.B.	G. Bachmair
C.B.	C. Brinkmann	G.B.T.	G. B. Trasler
C.Bü.	C. Bühler	G.C.M.	G. C. Mialaret
C.C.	C. Cherry	G.D.	G. Debus
C.D.F.	C. D. Frith	G.D.W.	G. D. Wilson
C.G.	C. Guttmann	G.E.	G. Erdmann
C.G.H.	C. G. Hoyos	G.G.	G. Guttmann
C.M.	C. Münkel	G.H.	G. Huber
C.N.	C. Nahoum	G.J.	G. Jones
C.S.	C. Scharfetter	G.K.	G. Kaulfush
D.B.	D. Bartussek	G.Ka.	G. Kanizsa
D.E.	D. Eaves	G.Ki.	G. Kaminski
D.E.B.	D. E. Berlyne	G.K.S.	G. K. Stürup
D.F.	D. Furneaux	G.L.	G. Lischke

ix

MAIN ABBREVIATIONS USED IN THIS WORK

AA	= Achievement age
abb.	= abbreviation
ACh	= Acetylcholine
ACTH	= Adrenocorticotrophic hormone
AL	= Adaptation level
Am.	= American
ANS	= Autonomic nervous system
ant.	= antonym
anthropol.	= anthropological
A.P.A.	= American Psychological Association
AQ	= Achievement quotient
b.	= born
biol.	= biological
CA	= Chronological age
c.	= *circa* = about
cc	= cubic centimeter (centimetre)
cf.	= *confer* = compare
ch., chs	= chapter(s)
CFF	= Critical flicker frequency
chem.	= chemical
CNS	= Central nervous system
cps	= cycles per second
CR	= Conditioned response
CS	= conditioned stimulus
d.	= died
db	= decibel
d.f.	= degrees of freedom
DNA	= Desoxyribonucleic acid
E., Es	= Experimenter(s)
EA	= Educational age
Ed., Eds	= Editor(s)
ed. cit.	= edition cited
EEG	= Electroencephalogram
e.g.	= *exempli gratia* = for example
EKG	= Electrocardiogram
Eng.	= English
EQ	= Educational quotient
ERG	= Electroretinogram
esp.	= especially
ESP	= Extrasensory perception
et al.	= *et alii* = and others
etc.	= *et cetera* = and so forth

et seq.	= *et sequens, sequentia* = and the following
ex., exs	= example(s)
f., ff.	= and the following
FFF	= Flicker-fusion frequency
fig., figs	= figure(s)
fn.	= footnote
Fre.	= French
GABA	= Gamma-amino-butyric acid
GAS	= General adaptation syndrome
Ger.	= German
Gr.	= Greek
GSR	= Galvanic skin response
Hz.	= Hertzian wave = cps
Ib.	= *ibidem* = in the same place
Id.	= *idem* = the same person(s)
i.e.	= *id est* = that is
introd.	= introduction by
IQ	= Intelligence quotient
IRM	= Innate releasing mechanism
It.	= Italian
IU	= Interval of uncertainty
j.n.d.	= Just-noticeable difference
Lat.	= Latin
loc. cit.	= *loco citato* = in the place (passage) cited
m.	= meter (metre)
MA	= Mental age
math.	= mathematical
med.	= medical
min.	= minute
mm.	= millimeter (millimetre)
n.d.	= no date
No., Nos	= number(s)
n.p.	= no place of publication
n.s.	= new series
NS	= Nervous system
O	= Observer
op. cit.	= *opere citato* = in the work cited
o.s.	= old series
OT	= Occupational therapy
p	= probability
p., pp.	= page(s)

PE	= Probable error	SD	= Standard deviation
philol.	= philological	SE	= Standard error
philos.	= philosophical	sec.	= second(s)
phys.	= physical	sect.	= section
physiol.	= physiological	ser.	= series
PR	= Percentile rank	S-R	= Stimulus-response
pref.	= preface	stat	= statistical
q.v.	= *quod vide* = which see	syr	= synonym
R	= Response	TAT	= Thematic Apperception Test
REM	= Rapid eye movement	TE	= Trial-and-error learning
resp.	= respectively	trans.	= translation
rev.	= revised by	UR	= Unconditioned response
RI	= Retroactive inhibition	US	= Unconditioned stimulus
RNA	= Ribonucleic acid	V	= volt
rpm	= revolutions per minute	vol.	= volume
RS	= Reinforcing stimulus	VTE	= Vicarious trial and error
RT	= Reaction time	WHO	= World Health Organization
S	= Stimulus		
S., Ss	= Subject(s)		

MAIN ARTICLES

Catecholamines (Janke, W., Giessen, W. Germany)

Character (Arnold, W., Würzburg, W. Germany)

Child Psychology (Yule, W., London, England)

Clinical Psychology (Schraml, W., Freiburg, W. Germany)

Cognitive Orientation (Kreitler, H. & Kreitler, S., Tel Aviv, Israel)

Color Blindness (Plattig, K. H., Erlangen, W. Germany)

Color Perception (Kanizsa, G., Trieste, Italy)

Color Vision (Plattig, K. H., Erlangen, W. Germany)

Communication (Cherry, C., London, England)

Comparative Psychology (Holland, H. C., Beckenham, England)

Conditioning, Classical & Operant (Holland, H. C., Beckenham, England)

Conflict (Yates, A., Nedlands, Australia)

Conscience (Trasler, G., Southampton, England)

Consciousness (Pongratz, L.; Arnold, W., Würzburg, W. Germany)

Consciousness, Disorders of (Ehrhardt, H., Marburg, W. Germany)

Construct Validity (Horn, J. L., Denver, USA)

Correlational Techniques (Maxwell, A. E., London, England)

Creativity (Kaulfush, G., Hamburg, W. Germany)

Credibility (Topič, O., Karlovy Vary, Czechoslovakia)

Criminality (Trasler, G., Southampton, England)

Crowd Behavior (Jodelet, F., Nancy, France)

Cybernetic Education (Frank, H., West Berlin, Germany)

Cybernetics and Psychology (Klix, F., Berlin, German Democratic Republic)

Decision Processes (Blackwell, H. R., Columbus, USA)

Defiance (Meister, H., Saarbrücken, W. Germany)

Depression (Sattes, H., Würzburg, W. Germany)

Depth Psychology (Miles, T. R., Bangor, Wales)

Development (Oerter, R., Augsburg, W. Germany)

Differential Psychology (Anastasi, A., New York, USA)

Dream (Oswald, I., Edinburgh, Scotland)

Drive (Bolles, R. C., Seattle, USA)

Drug Dependence (Teasdale, J. D., London, England)

Ear (Monje, M., Kiel, W. Germany)

Educational Guidance (Illyés, F. & Lányes, A. E., Budapest, Hungary)

Educational Psychology (Mialaret, G. C., Caen, France; Pelzer, K. E., Würzburg, W. Germany)

Educational Science (Husén, T., Stockholm, Sweden)

Ego (Meili, R., Berne, Switzerland; Pawlik, K., Hamburg, W. Germany; Toman, W., Erlangen, W. Germany)

Emotion (Martin, I., London, England)

Encephalopathy (Engels, H. J., Bonn, W. Germany)

Energy, Psychic (Toman, W., Erlangen, W. Germany)

Existence Analysis (Boss, M. & Hicklin, M., Zürich, Switzerland)

Experiment (Merz, F., Marburg, W. Germany)

Experimental Esthetics (Berlyne, D. E., Toronto, Canada)

Exploration (Nahoum, C., Vanves, France)

Expression (Kirchhoff, R., West Berlin, Germany)

Eye (Monjé, M., Kiel; Rix, R., Erlangen, W. Germany)

Factor Analysis (Cattell, R. B., Champaign, USA)

Family (Toman, W., Erlangen, W. Germany)

Fantasy (McKellar, P., Dunedin, New Zealand)

Fatigue (Gubser, A., W. Germany)

Feedback System (Rohracher, H., Vienna, Austria)

Folk Psychology (Schmidbauer, W., Feldafing, W. Germany)

Forensic Psychology (Müller-Luckmann, E., Brunswick, W. Germany)

Frequency Distributions (Mittenecker, E., Graz, Austria)

Frontal Lobes (Luria, A. R., Moscow, USSR)

Frustration (Yates, A. J., Nedlands, Australia)

Ganzheit, Gestalt, Structure (Metzger, W., Münster, W. Germany)

Geisteswissenschaftliche Psychologie (Novak, F., Würzburg, W. Germany)

General Psychology (McKellar, P., Dunedin, New Zealand; Müller, P., Neuchâtel, Switzerland)

Genital Stage (Toman, W., Erlangen, W. Germany)

Geometrical-optical Illusions (Rausch, E., Frankfurt, W. Germany)

Gerontology (Birren, J. E., Los Angeles, USA)

Gonadotropic Hormones (Maisch, H., Hamburg, Germany)

Grammar (Abraham, W., W. Germany)

Graphology (Pokorny, R., Tel Aviv, Israel; Novak, F., Würzburg, W. Germany)

Group Dynamics (Braun, P., Würzburg, W. Germany)

Group Formation (Schmidt-Mummendey, A., Mainz, W. Germany)

Guilt (Ehrhardt, H., Marburg, W. Germany)

Habit (Jones, H. G., Leeds, England)

Hermaphroditism (Maisch, H., Hamburg, W. Germany)

History of Psychology (Wesley, F., Portland, USA; Wehner, E., Würzburg, W. Germany)

Homeostasis (Vormfelde, D., West Berlin, Germany)

Homosexuality (Maisch, H., Hamburg, W. Germany)

Hormones (Janke, W., Giessen, W. Germany)

Humanistic Psychology (Cohen, J., Manchester, England; Bühler, C., Los Angeles, USA)

Humor (Victoroff, D., Paris, France)

Hypnosis (Furneaux, D., Uxbridge, England)

Id (Lischke, G., Freiburg, W. Germany)

Identical Retinal Points (Rix, R., Erlangen, W. Germany)

Identification (Toman, W., Erlangen, W. Germany)

Imagery, Mental (Süllwold, F., Frankfurt)

Impression (Kiener, F., West Berlin, Germany)

Imprinting (Tschanz, B., Diemerswil, Switzerland)

Incest (Maisch, H., Hamburg, W. Germany)

Incubation (Ramsay, R. W., Amsterdam, The Netherlands)

Industrial Psychology (Wilson, G. D., London, England)

Infancy (Malrieu, P., Toulouse, France)

Information (Weltner, K., Wiesbaden, W. Germany)

Information, Psychology of (Frank, H., West Berlin, Germany)

Information Theory (Weltner, K., Wiesbaden, W. Germany)

Inhibition (Blöschl, L., Düsseldorf; Spreng, M., Erlangen; Schönpflug, W., Bochum, W. Germany)

Inner Speech (Sokolov, A. N., Moscow, USSR)

Instinct (Broadhurst, P. L. & Wilcock, J., Birmingham, England)

Instructional Technology (Glaser, R., Pittsburgh, USA)

Intelligence (Meili, R., Berne, Switzerland)

Intelligence Tests (Steck, P., Würzburg, W. Germany)

Interview (Bellebaum, A., Freiburg, W. Germany)

Language (Kaminski, G., Tübingen, W. Germany)

Latency (Toman, W., Erlangen, W. Germany)

Laterality (Ullmann, J. F., Bonn, Germany)

Leadership (Marschner, G. R. W., Bardenberg, W. Germany)

Learning (Metz, F., Marburg, W. Germany)

Learning Curves (Bartl, M., Augsburg, W. Germany)

Learning Theory (Foppa, K., Berne, Switzerland)

Libido (Toman, W., Erlangen, W. Germany)

Life History (Bühler, C., Los Angeles, USA)

Literature, Psychology of (Cumming, J., London, England)

Localization of Psychological Functions (Luria, A. R., Moscow, USSR)

Logical Reasoning (Wason, P. C., London, England)

Longitudinal Studies (Meili, R., Berne, Switzerland)

Mania (Sattes, H., Würzburg, W. Germany)

Manipulation (Autrum, H.-J., Munich; Haas, H., Mannheim, W. Germany)

Mathematical Psychology (Faverge, J.-M. F., Brussels, Belgium)

Maturation; Maturity (Engels, H. J., Bonn, W. Germany)

Meditation (Lotz, J. B., Rome, Italy; Dumoulin, H., Tokyo, Japan)

Memory (Underwood, B. J., Evanston, USA; Schubert, F. C., Würzburg, W. Germany)

Mental Defect (Clarke, A., Hull, England)

Mental Hygiene (Friedemann, A., Bienne, Switzerland)

Methods of Psychology (Traxel, W., Kiel, W. Germany)

Military Psychology (Mitze, G., Bonn, W. Germany)

Mind–Body Problem (Pongratz, L., Würzburg, W. Germany; Rohracher, H., Vienna, Austria)

Models (Tack, W., Hamburg, W. Germany)

Motivation (Nuttin, J. R., Louvain, Belgium)

Motor Skills (Bilodeau, I., New Orleans, USA)

Music, Psychology of (Lundin, R. A., Sewanee, USA)

Music Therapy (H.-N. Genius, Würzburg, W. Germany)

Need (Murray, H. A., Cambridge, Mass. USA)

Neuroanatomy (Bosque, P. G., Valladolid, Spain)

Neuropsychology (Guttmann, G., Vienna, Austria)

Neurosis (Wolpe, J., Philadelphia, USA)

Nervous System (Guttmann, G., Vienna, Austria)

Non-parametric Tests (Lienert, G. & Sarris, V., Düsseldorf, W. Germany)

Objective Tests (Wilson, G. D., London, England)

Occupational Psychology (Leplat, J., Paris, France)

Oedipus Complex (Toman, W., Erlangen, W. Germany)

Operational Definition (Buggle, F., Hamburg, W. Germany)

Opinion Polls (Noelle-Neumann, E., Allensbach, Germany)

Orienting Reflex (Sokolov, E. N., Moscow, USSR)

Pain (Sternbach, R. A., San Diego, USA)

Parapsychology (Beloff, J., Edinburgh, Scotland)

Perception (Droz, R., Lausanne, Switzerland)

Perseveration (Mittenecker, E., Graz, Austria)

Person (Arnold, W., Würzburg, W. Germany)

Personality (Vernon, P. E., Calgary, Canada; Takuma, T., Tokyo, Japan)

Personnel Selection (Marschner, G. R. W., Bardenburg, W. Germany)

Perversions (Broadhurst, A., Birmingham, England)

Phenomenology (Rudert, J., Heidelberg, W. Germany)

Philosophy and Psychology (Braun, P., Würzburg, W. Germany)

Physiology (Plattig, K. H., Erlangen, W. Germany)

Physiological Psychology (Plattig, K. H., Erlangen, W. Germany)

Physiology of Behavior (Grossmann, K., Freiburg, W. Germany)

Political Psychology (Baeyer-Katte, W., Heidelberg, W. Germany)

Practice (Bilodeau, I., New Orleans, USA)

Prejudice (Tajfel, H., Bristol, England)

Probability Theory (Maxwell, A. E., London, England)

Prognosis (Schneider, H.-J., Hamburg, W. Germany)

Programmed Instruction (Frank, H., West Berlin, Germany)

Projection (Toman, W., Erlangen, W. Germany)

Projective Techniques (Zubin, J. & Schumer, F., New York, USA)

Psychagogy (Schmidbauer, W., Feldafing, W. Germany)

Psychoanalysis (Ancona, L., Rome, Italy)

Psychodiagnostics (Meili, R., Berne, Switzerland)

Psycholinguistics (Kaminski, G., Tübingen, W. Germany)

Psychopathy (Hare, R. D., Vancouver, Canada)

Psychopathy: a Psychoanalytic View (Toman, W., Erlangen, W. Germany)

Psychopharmacology (Janke, W., Giessen, W. Germany)

Psychophysics (Stevens, S. S., Cambridge, USA)

Psychoses (Lorr, M., Washington, USA)

Psychosomatics (Hamilton, M., Leeds, England)

Psychotechnics (Thomas, A., Münster, W. Germany)

Psychotherapy (Bergin, A. E., New York, USA)

Punishment (Church, R. M., Providence, USA)

Questionnaires (Butcher, H. J., Sussex, England)

Reaction Timers (Thomas, A., Münster, W. Germany)

Regression (Toman, W., Erlangen, W. Germany; Mikula, G., Graz, Austria)

Reinforcement (Bolles, R. C., Seattle, USA)

Religion, Psychology of (Keilbach, W., Munich, W. Germany; Spinks, G. S., Bury, England; Vergote, A., Louvain, Belgium)

Reminiscence (Irion, A. L., St Louis, USA)

Restitution of Mental Processes (Luria, A. R., Moscow, USSR)

Repression (Toman, W., Erlangen, W. Germany)

Retention Curve (Hofer, M., Marburg, W. Germany)

Retina (Rix, R., Erlangen, W. Germany)

Risk Taking (Kogan, N., Princeton, USA)

Rôle (Rocheblave-Spenlé, A., Paris, France)

Satiation (Karsten, A., Frankfurt, W. Germany)

Scaling (Eyferth, K., Darmstadt, W. Germany)

Schizophrenia (Cooper, J. E., London, England)

School Readiness (Mandl, H., Augsburg, W. Germany)

Semantics (Bar-Hillel, J., Jerusalem, Israel)

Sensation (Plattig, K. H., Erlangen, W. Germany)

Sense Organs (Monjé, M., Kiel, W. Germany)

Sexuality (Broadhurst, A., Birmingham, England)

Sexuality in Childhood (Thomas, K., West Berlin, Germany)

Sign and Symbol (Kreitler, S. & Kreitler, H., Tel Aviv, Israel)

Simulation (Drösler, J., Brunswick, W. Germany)

Skin Diseases (Vaitl, D., Münster, W. Germany)

Sleep (Oswald, I., Edinburgh, Scotland)

Socialization (Bandura, A., Stanford, USA)

Social Perception (Pagès, R. C., Paris, France)

Social Psychology (Hartley, E. L., Green Bay, USA; Victoroff, D., Paris, France)

Social Scale (Schmidt-Mummendey, A., Mainz, W. Germany)

Sociogram (Schmidt-Mummendey, A., Mainz, W. Germany)

Soundness of Mind (Topič, O., Karlovy Vary, Czechoslovakia)

Soviet Psychology (Brožek, J., Bethlehem, USA; Luria, A. R., Moscow, USSR)

Space Perception (Pick, H., Minneapolis, USA)

Sport, Psychology of (Schilling, G., Magglingen, Switzerland)

Statistics (Faverge, J.-M., Brussels, Belgium)

Stereotactic Methods (Adler, M., West Berlin, Germany)

Stereotype (Schenk, J., Würzburg, W. Germany)

Strata Theory (Wellek, A., Mainz, W. Germany)

Stress (Martin, I., London, England)

Suicide (Thomas, K., West Berlin, Germany)

Surface and Source Traits (Hundleby, J. D., USA)

Synapses (Spring, M., Erlangen, W. Germany)

Taboo (Lindner, I., Frankfurt, W. Germany)

Taxis (Lindner, I., Frankfurt, W. Germany)

Teaching Machines (Zemanek, H., Vienna, Austria)

Test Design (Bauer, W., Freiburg, W. Germany)

Test Norms (Lienert, G. & Sarris, V., Düsseldorf, W. Germany)

Test Theory (Horn, J. L., Denver, USA)

Thinking (Sokolov, A. N., Moscow, USSR; Jorswieck, E., West Berlin, Germany)

Time (Lang, A., Berne, Switzerland)

Time, Experience of (Wittkowski, J., Würzburg, W. Germany)

Topological Psychology (Wehner, E., Würzburg, W. Germany)

Traffic Psychology (Hoyos, C., Munich, W Germany)

Traits (Eysenck, H. J., London, England)

Transfer (Hofer, M., Marburg; Thomas, A., Münster, W. Germany)

Transference (Toman, W., Erlangen, W. Germany)

Twin Studies (Zazzo, R., Paris, France)

Type (Eysenck, H. J., London, England)

Unconscious (Toman, W., Erlangen, W. Germany)

Validity (Pfau, D., Würzburg, W. Germany)

Verbal Behavior, Establishment and Modification of (Sapon, S., Rochester, USA)

Verstehende Psychologie (Mierke, K., Kiel, W. Germany)

Vigilance (Haider, M., Vienna, Austria)

Visual Illusions (Rausch, E., Frankfurt, W. Germany)

Visual Perception (Oyama, T., Chita, Japan)

Vocational Guidance (Arnold, W., Würzburg, W. Germany)

Will (Mierke, K., Kiel, W. Germany)

Youth (Oerter, R., Augsburg, W. Germany)

A

Abasement. A general term for behavior indicative of submission to, e.g., aggression or punishment. See *Appeasement gestures.*

Abasia. The inability to walk, in the absence of nerve lesions or disorders of the muscular apparatus, i.e. of apparent organic causation. Abasia is recognized in a condition of mental conflict which would seem to inhibit further vocal and other protest in the individual affected. Occurs mainly in neurotic disorders, especially as a symptom of hysteria. *Astasia* is the inability to stand, similarly without recognizable organic cause; *astasia-abasia,* the combination of both afflictions.   *A.H.*

Aberration. 1. See *Chromatic aberration.* 2. *Spherical aberration:* Marginal rays bend more than those refracted by the inner surface of the lens; i.e. focal points on the optical axis are not identical.   *R.R.*

Abience. Tendency to avoid or withdraw from a stimulus. Hence *abient behavior* or *response,* behavior withdrawing the organism from the stimulus, or negating or even cancelling the stimulus in some way.   *J.G.*

Abilities: a psychometric account. Many modern psychologists, particularly in America, have given up the use of the term "intelligence" in the technical sense, and prefer to use terms like "human abilities"; "intelligence", if it is retained at all, is used to denote a particular area of inquiry. At the same time, doubt is being thrown on the usefulness of the IQ, and preference is often given to "ability profiles". The British school (Burt, Vernon, Eysenck) considers the concepts of "general intelligence" and "special abilities" as complementary, and continues to use the concept of IQ as well as that of ability profiles. The arguments employed by protagonists reach back into the past, and a brief account of the development of these divergent notions is essential, if only because the facts have often been misrepresented. The concept of "intelligence", very much as used later by more experimentally-oriented writers, owes its inception to Spencer and Galton; Binet constructed his tests very much along the lines of their expressed views. The crucial step toward quantitative testing of theories, as opposed to simple quantification or measurement, was taken by Spearman, who used the techniques of correlational analysis and factor analysis (q.v.), both of which had been developed by Pearson, in relation to the scores obtained by groups of children on various intelligence tests. He was concerned to test the theory that these correlations were due entirely to a general intellective factor, "g"; in addition to this he recognized specific factors, "s" factors, which were specific to particular tests. Essentially his point was that under these conditions matrices of intercorrelations between tests should be of rank one; he did not use matrix algebra himself, but his formulas are the equivalent of more modern versions.

Thurstone generalized Spearman's methods and formulas, translated them into matrix algebra, and carried out large-scale studies, using as many as fifty-seven tests on one group of subjects; on the basis of these studies he concluded that Spearman was wrong in postulating a single "g" factor, and that an alternative description in terms of several "primary abilities" fitted the data much better. The main factors he discovered were S (spatial ability), P (perceptual speed), N (numerical ability), V (verbal meaning), M (memory), W (verbal fluency), and R (inductive reasoning). There are several reasons why this apparent conflict between the two systems is much less real than appears at first. Spearman had laid down two main conditions under which he said his "g" would be found. The first related to populations sampled; he worked with random samples of the population (usually children), and while very low IQs would probably be missing in these groups (being confined to mental defective colonies or special schools for the educationally subnormal), nevertheless the range of IQs would be approximating to 100 points. Thurstone contravened this first rule by working only with students, and with specially selected students at that; all his subjects had IQs around the 95th percentile! By thus reducing the range of "g" to less than 10 per cent, he naturally reduced his chances of discovering traces of it in his experiment. The second difference between Spearman and Thurstone relates to choice of tests. Spearman had stated explicitly that tests should not be too similar to each other; if they were, then the "s" factors would overlap and cause additional correlations which would emerge as separate factors and disturb the unit rank of the matrix. Thurstone used groups of tests which were very similar, often almost identical, and consequently his study could certainly not be considered as a test of Spearman's hypothesis.

Thurstone later on recognized the force of these objections, particularly as a consequence of his work with children. Having originally elaborated a system of rotation of axes based on the principle of "simple structure", he found that with random samples of the population he could no longer keep his factors orthogonal (independent) and yet retain simple structure; accordingly he gave up orthogonality and allowed his factors to be correlated. These correlated factors correspond quite well to the types of tests Spearman had called for, and indeed Thurstone found that when the matrix of intercorrelations between his factors was analyzed, a single "g" factor was indeed found. This suggests a hierarchical structure of intellect, with "g" at the top, and the "primary abilities" (whose intercorrelations necessitated the postulation of "g") at a lower level; the actual tests used, whose intercorrelations gave rise to the "primary abilities", would of course be at a lower level still. The agreement between Spearman and Thurstone is almost perfect, and it should also be noted that in his work Spearman had also found evidence of group or "primary" factors, such as verbal ability and fluency, which could not be explained entirely in terms of similar "s" factors.

More recently, Guilford has suggested a model of human intellect which takes Thurstone's set of factors even further, and which admits no "g" at all. Guilford postulates four types of mental contents (figural, symbolic, semantic, and behavioral), upon which five types of operations can be performed: cognition, memory, evaluation, divergent production and convergent production. This leads to one or more of six products: units, classes, relations, systems, transformations, or implications. Thus we have 120 possible combinations of these three classes of variables, and Guilford points out that examples of most of these are already in existence in the mental testing literature; he himself and his students have added many of the missing ones. Psychometrically, Guilford's work is subject to several criticisms. He has concentrated most of his studies on populations with a restricted range of intelligence, thus reducing the scope of "g"; and he has used orthogonal methods of rotation, thus ignoring the correlations between "simple structure" factors which would have emerged only if he had used an oblique method of rotation. Certainly the scores on his tests, when administered to random samples of the population, are highly correlated, even though they come from different parts of his three-dimensional "box"; an appropriate analysis of the intercorrelations would almost certainly give rise to some form of hierarchical system. In spite of these criticisms, Guilford's long-continued work has certainly been useful in producing a whole range of novel tests, and in linking mental testing much more firmly than was previously the case with experimental and theoretical psychology. Of more practical importance is the criticism that Guilford's factors are so narrow and specialized that they have little value in prediction, as in educational and vocational guidance. This is almost certainly true; knowledge of a child's "g" and a few of the broader "primary abilities" is probably as predictive as any amount of further testing and probing.

While there are still many points of detail on which experts disagree, on the whole most would probably now agree on some form of hierarchical model, although they might not be at one in assessing the practical importance of "g" as opposed to "primary abilities". Fortunately such decisions are seldom needed; in most practical situations tests would provide information on both types of factors. Furthermore, the problem is an empirical one, and in due course enough information should be available to make a decision possible.

The division of "intellect" into these various factors is not the only kind that is possible; Cattell, for instance, has suggested that we should distinguish "fluid" from "crystallized" ability, i.e. potentiality for

intellectual achievement from acquired knowledge. Jensen has suggested a division between level 1 (associative ability) and level 2 (reasoning ability), measured by tests of rote learning and of the education of relations respectively. A thorough discussion of these and other schemes is given by Butcher; like all descriptive systems there is no one "true" scheme which must prevail, but different schemes may serve different purposes. Objections to any form of analysis, on the grounds that the mind "acts as a whole", are not very useful; scientific understanding is predicated upon analysis, and analysis has proved extremely useful already. Other criticisms of such concepts as "intelligence" and "primary abilities" suggest that they imply "reification"; intelligence is not a thing, but an abstraction. Exactly; scientific concepts like gravitation, electricity and intelligence are abstract in that they relate to certain properties of the data. No psychologist has ever publicly talked about "intelligence" as a reified unity; it is a hypothetical concept having certain mathematical properties the presence or absence of which can be tested in relation to data from given samples of tests and subjects. This is precisely the purpose of most of the experimental work done in this field.

Other criticisms have been made of these factorial studies of mental abilities, and these are more difficult to answer. What is normally correlated is the score on one test with the score on another; these scores may be derived in quite different ways from different subjects, yet be identical for all of them. Consider subject A who gets twenty answers right, working straight through from the easiest to the twentieth, and then fails to get the twenty-first or any more difficult ones right; compare him with subject B who gets only twelve right out of the first twenty (perhaps because he hurries and does not bother to check his wrong answers), but goes on to get another eight right out of the more difficult problems succeeding number 20. Both get the same score, namely 20, but they have behaved in a very dissimilar fashion, and have solved quite different problems in many cases. Or consider subject C, who gives up easily, but does not make any errors; he too may solve twenty problems, but those solved by him may only overlap very partly with those solved by A or B. In what sense can we say that these three subjects, although having the same score, are equivalent for the purpose of statistical analysis? Eysenck has suggested that the unit of analysis should be the individual problem; this can be attempted and solved correctly; attempted and solved erroneously; attempted and given up before any solution becomes apparent; or not attempted at all. Furneaux has taken up this suggestion and provided an analysis of intellect in terms of such concepts as mental speed, error-checking mechanism, and continuance (or persistence); he has shown that these are relatively independent of each other. Only the first of these may be regarded as a proper "ability"; the other two are probably related to personality (e.g., extraverts are known to be quicker and more prone to error than introverts). Analysis along these lines is as yet relatively novel, but in due course it should throw much light on the problem of mental abilities. Certainly the customary failure of psychometrists to take into account personality differences in analyzing intelligence tests is a source of weakness; the fact that there are few overall correlations between total scores on tests and personality traits does not prove that there is not considerable interaction, and it even seems that the very nature of the factors found in a given sample may be affected by the personality make-up of the subjects involved.

Little use has hitherto been made of electrophysiological recording in work on mental abilities. Ertl has demonstrated repeatedly that when evoked potentials on the EEG are compared for bright and dull subjects, marked differences can be observed; the records of the bright subjects (as measured by IQ tests) are characterized by EEG patterns which suggest the speedy transmission of information. This finding may link up with Furneaux's isolation of mental speed as the main (perhaps the only) truly cognitive factor in intelligence test performance. This type of work has not yet touched on the different "primary abilities", but has been concerned entirely with "g"; its extension to other problems will be awaited with interest. In particular it seems that the inclusion of such electrophysiological tests in a factorial study should facilitate the identification and interpretation of "g". It also seems likely that such tests would throw much light on the hereditary nature of "g"; no tests of this kind have as yet been carried out on uniovular and binovular twins.

Racial differences in human abilities have been frequently studied, and the evidence has been reviewed by Eysenck; most of the work has been done on American Negroes. Results seem to show that when Negroes are compared with whites, the Negroes have IQs some 15 points lower than the whites; this is true whether testing is carried out by white or black testers. Contrary to the belief that these differences are due to poorer environment, it is found that when working-class whites are compared with middle-class Negroes, differences in favor of the whites still persist; it is also found that differences are largest in respect to "fluid" intelligence, as measured by relatively "culture free" tests, and least with respect to "crystallized" ability, as measured by tests involving culture-transmitted knowledge. Orientals in California, although inferior to whites in socio-economic status, are somewhat superior on tests of "fluid" ability, suggesting innate racial differences. American Indians, although as much below Negroes with respect to socio-economic status as Negroes are below whites, are equal to Negroes on IQ tests. Maoris, though inferior to whites in IQ, are superior to them on verbal fluency. There are many detailed findings which suggest that there are important racial differences between different populations, but much work remains to be done before any worthwhile generalizations become possible. See *Differential Psychology.*

Bibliography: Burt, C.: The evidence for the concept of intelligence. Brit. J. Educ. Psychol., 1955, *25*, 158–77. **Butcher, H. J.:** Human intelligence. London, 1968. **Cattell, R. B.:** Theory of fluid and crystallized intelligence: a critical experiment. J. Educ. Psychol., 1963, *54*, 1–22. **Ertl, J. P. & Schafer, E. V. F.:** Brain response correlates and psychometric intelligence. Nature, 1969, Vol. 223, 421–2. **Eysenck, H. J.:** Intelligence assessment: a theoretical and experimental approach. Brit. J. Educ. Psychol., 1967, *37*, 81–98. **Id.:** Race, intelligence and education. London, 1971. **Furneaux, W. P.:** Intellectual abilities and problem-solving behavior. In: **Eysenck, H. J.** (Ed.): Handbook of abnormal psychology. London, 1960. **Guilford, J. P.:** The nature of human intelligence. New York, 1967. **Jensen, A. R.:** Environment, heredity, and intelligence. Harvard, Reprint Ser. No. 2, 1969. **Id.:** Hierarchical theories of mental ability. In: **Dockrell, W. B.** (Ed.): On intelligence. London, 1970. **Spearman, C.:** The abilities of man. London, 1927. **Thurstone, L. L. & Thurstone, T. G.:** Factorial studies of intelligence. Psychometric Monogr., 1941, No. 2. **Vernon, P. E.:** The measurement of abilities. London, 1956.   *H. J. Eysenck*

Abilities: a conceptual account. Some other notions (*"Begabung"*, q.v., "talent" and "capacity"—the latter no longer being in common use) are virtually synonymous with "ability"; there is no clear distinction between these concepts. Linguistic overlap occurs in a number of languages, and contradictions may be found in a single dictionary. A given word may have different meanings in different languages: while the word "apti-tude" as used in the English literature (*Eignung* in German) signifies the "ability" to exercise a profession or acquire certain forms of knowledge or skill, the French word *"aptitude"* corresponds to the English term "ability", designating ability in the narrower sense as it is used in empirical research—although unfortunately not in general practice. Here ability means *all the psychological conditions needed to perform an activity.* Ability is therefore operationally defined by the activity with which it is

associated; in this sense, e.g., even the ability "intelligence" (q.v.) is frequently defined today as that which is measured by an intelligence test. It follows from this definition of the term ability that there are as many different abilities as there are activities, and that the question as to the number and nature of abilities is meaningless. The word is therefore primarily an abbreviation for "all the psychological conditions needed to perform an activity". It should, however, be noted that ability includes only the necessary conditions; some influences which might facilitate the activity, such as interest, degree of activation, practice and certain experiences are therefore excluded. This does not, however, mean that ability is reduced to innate conditions, as was frequently the case in the past and as applies to the word *Begabung.* Some of the conditions may well be explained by experience and general learning processes. It has been generally recognized that it is empirically impossible to make a reliable distinction between acquired and innate conditions of psychological phenomena.

Activities and the abilities normally associated with them may be quite specific: e.g. knitting, adding, writing advertising slogans, and so on; or complex, such as manual crafts, trades, mechanical engineering, and so on. It is necessary to distinguish between complex abilities and those which are more general and cover a group of relatively similar activities. (See *Attention; Memory.*)

Empirical findings and conclusions. The decisive change brought about by empirical research into the notion of ability is that abilities are no longer considered—as were "capacities"—as innate, uniform and clearly distinct "powers", but (in a much less precise manner) as a *set of conditions*. This attitude has been motivated primarily by research into the relations between abilities, using correlational techniques (q.v.). Correlations may be determined between performances in a variety of cognitive problems (i.e. highly specialized ability) or between performances in different school subjects (e.g. mathematics and languages), or between intelligence and motor abilities (skills) (e.g. drawing). These studies have shown that there are very many relations within the range of intellectual abilities, and that, e.g., mathematical aptitude is not so very different from linguistic aptitude as is often assumed; indeed, it has even been shown that there is a definite correlation between manual skill and intelligence. It follows that many abilities (not only those which are specialized or relatively complex) overlap partially; this means that the basic conditions for different abilities are sometimes the same.

The age-old debate between those who assumed a central capacity in man and those who believed in several, or a wide range of, capacities has therefore finally been settled by empirical research. We now know that the conditions on which performance is based are complex, even in the case of specialized activities; in other words there are several conditions for performance, none of which can be attributed to any individual achievement.

Factor analysis (q.v.) provides a method of determining and defining basic conditions (factors) common to different activities. It therefore becomes possible to determine the inner structure of an ability defined with reference to an activity. Through this research we have come to realize above all that the conventional classification of ability into intelligence, memory, attention, motor skills and sensorimotor activities is extremely superficial and has little basis in the light of psychological principles. The correlations are sometimes very slight between different feats of intelligence, and almost wholly absent between memory and motor skills, etc.

Nevertheless the notion of ability is still used today in connection with such activities or ranges of activity. Since ability is no longer viewed as a uniform, clearly defined capacity, we come up against the question of the meaning of general or complex ability.

Two answers are given: (*a*) the conditions which are common to a group of partial abilities; (*b*) the totality of the conditions effective in all of them. If we define intelligence by the general factor "g", as Spearman has suggested, we will opt for the first concept; but if we measure intelligence by a complex test such as the Binet–Simon intelligence scale, intelligence is then defined by the total set of conditions for the different tasks.

The concept of ability is primarily important in applied psychology, in the case of all types of aptitude test. At first, unsuccessful attempts were made to subdivide the ability proper to a certain profession into partial abilities such as intelligence, motor skills, perception, etc. Later, the emphasis was placed on testing specific activities approximating most closely to those of the vocation in question. Recently, attempts have been made to use aptitude tests to determine the basic factors of vocational achievement; but it has been found that many factors other than ability play a part in vocational success and in school achievement.

Bibliography: Cox, J. W.: Mechanical aptitude. London, 1928. **Id.:** Manual skill: its organization and development. Cambridge, 1934. **Meili, R.:** Lehrbuch der psychologischen Diagnostik. Berne, ⁵1965. **Piéron, H.** *et al.*: L'utilisation des aptitudes. Paris, 1954. **Révész, G.:** Talent und Genie. Berne, 1952. **Vernon, P.:** The structure of human abilities. London, 1950.   *R. Meili*

Ability grouping. In many countries series of tests have been devised to select those suitable for secondary (or even tertiary) education, and to divide them into relatively homogeneous groups according to their presumed general, or specialized, scholastic ability. Syn. *Homogeneous grouping.* Only the intellectual aspect of suitability can be covered since effort and so on vary greatly and depend on external circumstances. See *Abilities.*   *R.M.*

Ability research. Branch of psychological research dealing with questions of ability.

It clarifies, e.g., what the prerequisites for some particular activity are, and whether and to what degree anyone possesses them and hence can participate in this activity. Still currently engaging most attention is the elucidation of the intellectual prerequisites. See *Abilities*.   *H.-J.A.*

Ability to dissociate. See *Spaltbarkeit*.

Abklingen (Ger.). Fading out. The slow cessation of a tone, emotional process or sensation.

Ablation. 1. The surgical removal of an organ or bodily part (*Amputation*). **2.** The separation of one organ from another. **3.** The removal, interruption or weakening of a psychic relationship or dependency (e.g. of children and parents) during or for psychic maturation, especially in the case of the displacement of affect, i.e. *transference*, in psychoanalysis (q.v.).

Ablation experiments: term for animal experiments in which—after acquisition of a certain behavior—cerebral tissues are excised, and the relation between the extent of excision (*Extirpation*, q.v.) and location (neural centers and pathways) on the one hand and the functional loss on the other is observed. Lashley's (q.v.) experiments (c. 1929) were important in this field: rats which had learnt to negotiate a maze retained their orientation there even after extirpation of specific motor centers and cutting of pathways. **Bibliography:** Lashley, K. S.: Nervous mechanisms in learning. In: Murchison, C. (Ed.): The foundation of experimental psychology. Worcester, Mass., 1929. **Id.:** Brain mechanisms and intelligence. Chicago, 1929.   *F.S.*

Ablösung (Ger.). The dissolution of a psychic bond between two individuals, or of the dependence of one on the other. Used in European psychoanalysis for the termination of a psychotherapeutic reliance (transference,

q.v.) of the analysand (q.v.) on the analyst, and deemed requisite before treatment can be said to have come to an end.   *H.N.G.*

Abnormal psychology is the study of "abnormal behavior" or "abnormal personality", i.e. "abnormalities" of sensory perception, of psychomotor function, of cognitive, motivational and other psychological functions; abnormalities of personality including psychoses, neuroses, psychosomatic disorders, character disorders, mental deficiencies, etc.; abnormalities of social behavior such as crime or delinquency, drug addiction and other sociopathic behavior.

1. *Concept of abnormality.* The word "abnormal" is used in several different senses and also in various combinations of them. The major dimensions of differentiation are: (*a*) whether it is defined as deviation from the ideal norm or as the statistical unusuality; (*b*) whether the definition of abnormality is to be universal or to differ according to the culture; (*c*) whether it is based on objective characteristics of behavior, or on the fact that a person is objectionable to himself or to others, or calls forth sanctions from others.

Satisfactory definition of the discipline also depends on and is made problematic by studies of the development and health of personality, of cultural norms, of the reaction of individuals and society to deviant behavior, and so on.

2. *Mental illness* (general and classificatory approach). Scientific approaches to mental illness have been developed since the end of the eighteenth century by Pinel, Mesmer, Esquirol, Bernheim, Charcot and several others. Janet (1895–1947) saw the neurotic process as the reduction of the energy level, and distinguished two principal types: psychasthenia and hysteria. Kraepelin (1856–1926) regarded certain symptoms of mental illness which tended to appear in clusters as manifestations of specific types of mental illness. His contribution to the

description of "*dementia praecox*" (later elaborated as schizophrenia by Bleuler) and manic-depressive illness introduced an epoch in psychiatry. The description of abnormal character developed by K. Schneider and others has stimulated biopsychological studies of criminals and other sociopaths.

Recently, statistical methods have been used in classification. For example, Jenkins and his colleagues found three major syndromes of children's behavior problems: over-inhibited, unsocialized-aggressive, and socialized-delinquent. Eysenck, using factor analysis, found three independent variables: introversion–extraversion, neuroticism and psychoticism.

Classification and description depend also on the researcher's view of the origin and treatment of abnormalities. There are biological, behavioristic, psychodynamic, sociodynamic and other theories. From an eclectic viewpoint, Meyer evaluated the influence of the inherited structures and tendencies of life experiences and of environmental stress. The present classification of the American Psychiatric Association distinguishes two classes: "disorders caused by or associated with impairment of brain tissue function", and "disorders of psychogenic origin or without clearly defined physical cause of structural change in the brain". The latter category includes psychotic, psychophysiological, autonomic and visceral, psychoneurotic, personality, and transient situational personality disorders. See also *Psychiatry, Clinical psychology, Psychoses, Psychoneurosis, Mental defect, Psychopathology, Delinquency, Drug dependence*.

3. *Biological approaches*. The inheritance of abnormal tendencies has been studied by family investigation and other more sophisticated methods. Observations of monozygotic twins, especially in comparison with dizygotic twins, have been reported with psychotics, neurotics and sociopaths (Lange, Rosanoff, Kallmann, Salter, Yoshimasu, Inoue). The genetics of some psychological factors, e.g. intelligence, motor skills, neurotic

tendencies, has also been studied. (See *Heredity*.) In a constitutional approach to the problem, Kretschmer described physical types which he correlated with psychotic disorders and their pre-morbid personality patterns. More recently, Sheldon's system of somatotypes, Lindegard's method, factor analysis method and other new techniques have been employed in constitutional approaches (see *Traits*).

4. *Experimental approaches*. Jackson's hierarchical model of the dissolution of function stimulated the early experimental studies. Pavlov's experiments in conditioning and induced neurosis have been highly influential. Conflict between neural excitation and inhibition was regarded by Pavlov as the precipitating factor of neurosis. Many studies of aggression, fixation and other maladaptive habits of animals have been reported (Lashley, Liddel, Maier, Masserman). (See *Aggression, Animal psychology*.) Effects of early experiences have been studied in animals (Denenberg, Levine, Thompson, Harlow). Some studies have dealt with abnormalities of human behavior in such experimentally induced situations as sensory deprivation. Laboratory techniques with psychiatric patients have been developed (Luria, Malmo, Eysenck). These techniques are used also as objective tests in clinical practice. From experimental evidence and behavioral theory, Eysenck, Wolpe and others developed behavior therapy (q.v.).

The effects of drugs have been studied experimentally and clinically. (See *Psychopharmacology, Hormone*.) Neurophysiological studies on brain damage have been developed by direct observation or by means of neurological techniques such as EEG. (See *Neuropsychology, Brain pathology*.) Biochemical studies have tried to determine the chemical causes of mental disorders or to clarify a chemical process under abnormal mental conditions. (See *Psychopharmacology, Neuropsychology*.)

5. *Psychodynamic approaches*. Since Freud, a number of psychoanalytic and other

psychodynamic studies have been reported, based on orthodox Freudian theory, Jungian, Adlerian, neo-Freudian theories, or other eclectic theories (see *Psychoanalysis*). In the field of child psychiatry (q.v.) or clinical-educational psychology, since Healy and others, the psychodynamic approach has become especially dominant in diagnostic and therapeutic practice. Related to this field are many observations of children under certain environmental conditions, and especially under abnormal home conditions (Bowlby, Goldfarb, Spitz). Experimental and clinical observations of the dynamics of personality have also been attempted. They include the recording of dreams, imagery and other characteristic phenomena. Behavioral theories and other theories based on the experimental approaches have been synthesized using psychodynamic concepts (Mowrer and Kluckhorn, Dollard and Miller, Maier). Although psychodynamics has been faulted for its lack of objective clarity (Eysenck), the psychodynamic approach is dominant in projective diagnosis and psychotherapy (q.v.) in the clinical field.

6. *Socio-cultural approaches.* Much anthropological research related to socio-psychological approaches in psychoanalysis has been carried on into the "abnormal psychology" of primitive societies (Fortune, Benedict, Mead, Malinowski). (See *Anthropology*.) Comparative studies have been made of personality and behavior disorders in different modern countries, and among different ethnic or social groups. There have been many ecological (or epidemiological) studies of mental disorders (Hollingshead, Redlich, *et al.*), of crime and delinquency (Shaw, McKay, *et al.*) and other behavior disorders. (See *Criminality*.) Deviant acculturation or group reference is emphasized even in individual clinical practice, especially in the case of crime and delinquency (Jenkins, Mizushima). Group dynamics (q.v.) and other socio-psychological theories have been evaluated and adopted in social therapy (q.v.). Socio-cultural approaches have also influenced the recent development of community psychiatry, community psychology, social work and other related practices. But there are as yet few systematic studies of the historical sociodynamics of abnormal behavior and societal reaction to it.

7. *Ontological approaches.* In the European tradition of psychiatry, Jaspers' "*Verstehende Methode*" has had a great influence. More recently, Binswanger, Von Gebsattel, Minkowski, Boss and others have developed "existential analysis" (q.v.), based on the existential philosophies. The "existential analyst" rejects the objective orientation of psychodynamics and tries to understand the patient in the context of his subjective world and its meaning. Related to this are such new approaches as Frankel's "*Logotherapie*" or clinical applications of Eastern thought (Yoga and Zen). Rogers' self theory, Gestalt theories, and some organismic theories, with their emphasis on the phenomenal world, and the totality and uniqueness of a person, occasionally approximate to the "existential" tendency.

8. *Summary.* As an objective science, abnormal psychology uses biological, physiological, behavioral, psychodynamic, sociocultural, and other experimental and observational approaches to statistically unusual or deviant behavior. It is related to diagnostic and therapeutic psychiatry, clinical psychology and other scientific approaches to mental health, in which subjective and artistic methods are included or integrated.

Bibliography: Arieti, S. (Ed.): American handbook of psychiatry. New York, 1959. **Binswanger, L.:** Schizophrenie. Pfüllingen, 1957. **Eysenck, H. J.** (Ed.): Behaviour therapy and the neuroses. London, 1960. **Id.** (Ed.): Handbook of abnormal psychology. New York, 1961. **Fenichel, O.:** The psychoanalytic theory of neurosis. New York, 1945. **Hunt, J. McV.** (Ed.): Personality and the behavior disorders. New York, 1944. **Jaspers, K.:** Allgemeine Psychopathologie. Berne, 1913. **Kraepelin, E.:** Lehrbuch der Psychiatrie. Leipzig, 1883–1927. **Kanner, L.:** Child psychiatry. Springfield, Ill., 1935. **Lemert, E. M.:** Social pathology. New York, 1951. **Pavlov, I. P.:** Selected works. Moscow, 1955. **Ullman, L. P. & Krasner, L.:** A psychological approach to abnormal behavior. Englewood Cliffs, N.J., 1969. *K. Mizushima*

Abortion. In the strict medical usage, synonymous with *miscarriage*, i.e. the interruption of pregnancy either through natural processes or artificial induction. Non-technically, however, "abortion" is often used to refer only to the intentional termination of pregnancy as a method of *birth control* (q.v.) (still illegal in many parts of the world), while "miscarriage" is reserved for naturally occurring rejections of the fetus. *G.D.W.*

Spontaneous abortion is the natural expulsion of an abnormally developing fetus; *therapeutic abortion* is the term used to describe a (usually surgically) induced termination which satisfies the medico-legal conditions of the particular country or state: these usually require that continuation of pregnancy would endanger the mother's life, or her physical or psychic health, but vary considerably.

Criminal abortion describes a termination which does not satisfy such conditions. Abortion can be followed by more or less severe feelings of deprivation in the mother. Most vaginal terminations for psychiatric reasons are therefore carried out in the first three months.

Abortifacient: an agent which produces abortion (syn. *Abortient*).

Bibliography: Baker, A. A.: Psychiatric disorders in obstetrics. Oxford, 1967. Clark, M. *et al.*: Sequels of unwanted pregnancy. Lancet, 1968, No. 2, 501ff. Tredgold, R. F.: Psychiatric indications for termination of pregnancy. Lancet, 1964, No. 2, 1251ff.

Abreaction. A term used in psychiatry, and especially in psychoanalysis, to describe the more or less rapid discharge of long pent-up affects (tension). The process is unconscious—unlike, say, the working off of "actualized", or relived, repressed contents of experiences (though the word is used, less precisely, in this sense). Popular abuse of the term has tended to rob it of any consistent value outside the early literature. See *Cathartic method. R.Hä.*

Absence. 1. A form of *petit mal* (q.v.); term for the attack characteristic of children. The consciousness is clouded for 5–15 sec., and the sufferer is wholly or largely immobile (e.g. exhibits only eye movements). This form of attack gives a typical 3/sec. spikes and waves EEG pattern. Absence can be so transient that the child is unconscious of it, and it is subsumed into the total process of movement or speech. Such "absences" are to be distinguished from attacks of psychomotor epilepsy (temporal lobe epilepsy), which are sometimes called "pseudo-absences". **2.** "Absence" is also encountered in the (Freudian) psychoanalytic literature as descriptive of a fleeting loss of consciousness in hysteria, or even sexual orgasm. *C.S.*

Absolute error. The observed value plus or minus the true value; the true value being most probably the mean of the measurements.

Absolute pitch. 1. The generally recognized definition of the standard pitch of A as 440 vibrations a second, internationally adopted in 1960, and therefore the new "concert pitch". **2.** A special sense for actual pitch (as opposed to relative pitch). This special ability is very rare and occurs mostly among musicians (placed by Wellek at 8·8% and by G. Revesz at 3·4%).

Absolute pitch in this sense is not necessarily an accompaniment of musical ability. Wellek distinguishes three types of absolute pitch recognition according to criteria of retroactive experience (relation of new sounds to retained experience of a sound), and the tendency to confusion (in the "polar" type within the 4th and 5th, in the less common "linear" type within the chromatic note-row—Am. tone-row).

Bibliography: Neu, D. M.: A critical review of the literature on "absolute pitch". Psychol. Bull., 1947. Wellek, A.: Das absolute Gehör und seine Typen. Leipzig, 1938.   B.S.

Absolute threshold. See *Threshold*.

Absolute value. A numerical value $(-X)$ whose negative sign becomes positive: i.e. a number without regard to its sign. See *Scale*.
                                                        W.H.B.

Absorption. When light (radiation) quanta pass through a medium, as a rule they divide into three parts. One part is *reflected*, one is *absorbed* (transduced, or transformed into heat), and one is *transmitted*. Taking light as a whole as 1, the relationship is: reflection + absorption + transmission $= 1$. The graphic representation of absorption as a function of the wavelength of light is an *absorption curve* (absorption coefficient); and, analogously, we have a reflection curve and a transmission curve. *Absorptivity* is the ratio of the amount of radiation absorbed to the amount incident, and, as a, stands in the following relationship to e (the emissivity, or constant to which the rate of emission of radiation is proportional): $e = a$ (Kirchoff's relation, or law). The absorption curve decides the color of the surface in question (see *Color mixture*). For a *black body* the absorption for all wavelengths is uniformly 1 (i.e. $a = 1$, since a black body absorbs all radiation incident on it); for a *grey body* the absorption for all wavelengths is uniform, i.e. less than 1.

Bibliography: Eisberg, R. M.: Fundamentals of modern physics. New York, 1961. Weale, R. A.: Photochemistry and vision. In: Photophysiology, Vol. 4. New York, 1968.   A.H.

Abstinence. Voluntary self-deprivation of a substance, or the act of refraining from some action. Used in psychoanalysis to refer to sexual restraint (occasionally in something like the sense of "chastity"): i.e. refraining from, e.g., masturbation (q.v.), petting (q.v.), coitus (q.v.). Abstinence in this sense is often bound up with the proscriptions of a sexual ethics in which reproduction is seen as the overriding aim of sexuality, and which permits and even legalizes sexual relations only within marriage (e.g. Christianity, Islam). Abstinence is also used to describe the action of the voluntary drug-abstainer, whose restraint may, of course, be ritual (a temporary return to "drug virginity") or a planned tolerance-reductive measure.   J.F.

Abstraction. 1. The process of developing a concept. A distinction is made between abstraction as *generalization, isolation,* and *idealization.* In generalization, the apparently essential characteristics of things, classes and their relations are ideally separated from the apparently inessential by considering them under one particular aspect. In isolation, the characteristics, relations and so on are considered independently: i.e. individuals are classed according to a common feature. In idealization, ideal models are constructed. The ability to abstract is possessed only by man, characterizes a stage of mental development (Piaget), and is thought of as a mark of adult "normality".   V.M.

2. A general term for introspection (q.v.), emphasizing inattention to or obliviousness of the external world. **3.** A pejorative term for an intellectual construct that has suppressed properties deemed essential to any discussion of the individuals thus classed.

Bibliography: Piaget, J.: The psychology of intelligence. London, 1950.

Absurdity test. A task in which discovery of the contradiction or incongruity of a picture or story is the objective. Syn. *Absurdities test*.

Abulia. Abnormality of volition characterized by extreme apathy and indecisiveness.

Often subjectively described as a total absence of will-power or drive and accompanied by feelings of automatism in which the person experiences himself only as "reacting to" rather than "operating on" the environment and is completely unable to direct his own thoughts or behavior. *P.W.B.*

Acalculia. Inability to calculate mathematically as the result of the loss of the capacity for numerical ideation (damage to the left parietal area in right-handed people) or as one of the presenting symptoms of an *aphasia* (q.v.).   *C.S.*

Acceleration. An increase in the speed of the development process. Bodily growth and maturation are out of step. Acceleration shows itself primarily in an increase in body size and weight; early growth of the milk teeth and the permanent teeth, and an earlier start to puberty (particularly significant in girls) are also symptomatic. Acceleration has been observed in all civilized nations since the first half of the last century. The phenomenon has increased in frequency in the last few decades. Attempts have been made to explain acceleration as consequent on environmental changes leading to a rise in pituitary hormone production (changes in nutrition, excessive stimulus, added stress in urban life, general changes in the conditions of life and work). Investigations which show the number of accelerates in the above sense to be much higher in urban than in agricultural areas would seem to confirm the relation between environmental influences and acceleration. See *Retardation; Maturation; Development.*

Bibliography: Carmichael, L. (Ed.): Manual of child psychology. New York, ²1954. Günther, H.: Säkulare umweltbedingte Variationen der Körpergestalt des Menschen. Endokr., 1951, *28.* Id.: Die säkulare Progression der Körpergrösse des Menschen. Münchner Med. Wschr., 1954, *96.* Hathaway, M. L.: Heights and weights of children and youth in the United States. U.S. Dept. Agr. Home Econ. Res.

Rpt. (Washington), No. 2, 1957. Id. & Ford, E. D.: Heights and weights of adults in the United States. U.S. Dept. Agr. Home Econ. Res. Rpt. (Washintgon), No. 10, 1960. Martin, W. E. & Stendler, C. B.: Child development: the process of growing up in society. New York, ²1959. Stott, L. H.: Child development. New York & London, 1957. Tanner, J.: Education and physical growth. London, 1961. Tanner, J. M.: Growth at adolescence. Oxford, ²1962. Thomae, H.: Längsschnittuntersuchungen zum Problem der Beziehungen zwischen körperlicher und seelischer Entwicklung. Z. exp. angew. Psychologie, 1957, *4.*   *G.S.*

Acceptance. See *Rejection.*

Accident proneness. The theory of accident proneness implies a personal predisposition which makes some people more liable to accidents than others. As accidents present a serious social problem, this concept is an important field of psychological research. Unfortunately it has also become so fertile a field for psychological controversy that, even after fifty years, the validity of the concept is still questioned. Some of this disbelief is caused by the difficulty of substantiating the concept by statistical means; or to the rigid way in which it is so often defined. But some of it can also be traced to the natural reluctance of certain behaviorists to accept a concept implying the existence of deep-seated personality traits. In view of this controversial thinking, it is very advisable for any student or would-be researcher to study the literature; although it would be surprising if a truly objective assessment of this did not convince him that there is ample research support for the concept, if viewed in a realistic manner.

Accident proneness is by no means a simple phenomenon. It can be caused by any number of human failings or maladjustments and will therefore show itself in different ways in different people, and to different degrees. A person could be more prone to one type of accident than to another; he could have the skill to cope with one task but not another; or he could be motivated to behave carefully in one sphere and recklessly in another. And not only do people change both physically and psychologically as they develop, but their behavior can be modified by factors like experience or discipline, or the pressures of social opinion. It is therefore essential to view accident proneness as a multi-dimensional problem of complex human beings functioning in a complex environment; failure to appreciate this has been one of the main reasons for the rather poor quality of much of the research in this field, and the confusion over the validity of the concept.

For the better-planned experimental studies have demonstrated that people display markedly different accident rates and that these differences are associated with recognizable personal characteristics. A recent major study on road accidents has shown that it is possible to lower the accident rate substantially in a transport company by using psychological tests (which have been subjected to repeated cross validation) to screen out the bad accident risks on the basis of their intelligence, psychomotor functions, personality, social attitudes and interpersonal relations. Findings like these emphasize the important practical implications of differential liability to accidents.

Bibliography: Arbous, A. G. & Kerrich, J. E.: Accident statistics and the concept of accident proneness, 1951, Biometrics, 7, 340–432. Shaw, L. & Sichel, H. S.: Accident proneness. London & New York, 1970. Walbeehm, T. B.: The accident-prone driver. London, 1960.   *Lynette Shaw*

Accident research. Accidents are the greatest killer of our modern age and therefore provide an extremely important field of psychological research. But it is by no means a homogeneous one where the same causes are operative or the same preventative measures applicable. Accidents occur among people of very different ages, and in the course of activities which make very different demands on their capabilities or serve very different psychological needs. Accidents in different spheres of life are therefore best regarded as fields of specialized research.

1. *Methods and results.* There are various research approaches: studying the causes of individual accidents or the characteristics of accident offenders; exploring the value of psychological tests as accident predictors; studying the efficacy of preventative measures such as training, therapy, discipline, or safety propaganda, or the influence of such factors as morale or social opinion. As in many other branches of behavioral research, greater attention has been paid to the causative than to the preventative factors, since it is easier to determine the causes of human behavior than to find ways of modifying it. But accident research has suffered from another common bugbear of psychologic complaint, namely the conflict between the rival doctrines of dynamic psychology and behaviorism (q.v.) (especially the American behavioristic doctrine of "specificity", where conduct is believed to consist of specific and almost unrelated S-R bonds or habits). This clash has resulted in two widely divergent schools of thought: (*a*) that accidents are virtually unpredictable as they are predominantly situation-dictated events, and (*b*) that accidents can be predicted as they are often the outcome of a relatively consistent pattern of behavior dictated by dynamic personality traits. This controversy, which has at times been a very heated one (as over the question of accident proneness), is most unfortunate; for research has shown that although there is something to be said for both points of view, there is nothing to be gained by too rigid an adherence to either; accidents have many causes, some environmental and some person-centered, and the only realistic way to study the problem is in this context.

But this very complexity presents great methodological difficulties, and is really the main reason for rather slow progress, especially in the field of experimental research, where it is virtually impossible to control all the independent variables. Failure to appreciate this complexity has also led to many of the misleading statements found in the research literature, where the low correlations between accidents and single characteristics have been repeatedly cited as evidence that such factors as intelligence and personality have little or nothing to do with accidents—findings which have been refuted by the better studies, where adequate controls and a more realistic multivariate approach have yielded very positive results. But these controlled experimental studies are possible only with such subjects as professional drivers or factory workers engaged on a particular task. With the general public, or with children, often the best one can do is to compare groups with high/low accident rates to see whether they display different characteristics. However, this somewhat crude method has proved very productive, for findings of these studies have displayed remarkably consistent trends. Most of these comparative studies have been done on traffic accidents, and on factors related to personality; and very different research methods have been used: personality inventories, projective techniques, attitude scales, clinical interviews, and studies of home background and personal history. In the psychological studies, the high-accident groups have displayed marked anti-social attitudes and a number of distinctive personality characteristics, such as immaturity, irresponsibility, impulsiveness, aggressiveness, emotional instability, or neurotic anxiety. Of course the characteristics differ from person to person, but in each case they are indicative of personality imbalance. In the sociological studies, these groups have contained a preponderance of people with histories of crime, drunkenness, traffic offenses, debt, and other manifestations of social maladjustment. Findings like these are very compatible with three controlled experimental studies: in one it was possible to predict future accident rates on the basis of a comprehensive personality rating derived

from projective tests; in the second, a factor analysis (q.v.) of personality traits revealed two higher-order factors of extraversion and neuroticism which correlated significantly with a graded accident criterion; and in the third, the accident offenders displayed a number of psychomotor malfunctions such as hasty and impulsive movements, or shock reactions, all indicative of personality disturbances.

But it is also very interesting to note that similar findings have emerged from studies of industrial and childhood accidents, showing that accidents in any sphere are one manifestation of personal and social maladjustment. But different circumstances will undoubtedly impose different controls on accident-producing behavior. The rather similar personality traits (especially those of extraversion) found in accident-prone children and adult traffic offenders, indicates that this sort of acting-out behavior must fulfill rather similar psychological needs. But in the industrial working context there is stronger evidence of the neurotic traits, and the extravert ones seem to be under better control—possibly because of stricter supervision, or because the consequences of extraverted behavior are more readily appreciated. It seems possible that the people who are liable to industrial accidents are, on the whole, more deeply maladjusted, and that their accidents are often associated with personality functions not under conscious control.

Whereas the relationship between personality and accidents is largely a linear one (i.e. the more pronounced the defects the higher the accident potential) the effects of other psychological factors cannot be measured in this way. Group studies on experience show a pronounced learning curve, starting with a high accident rate which soon levels off. The effects of intelligence and skill seem to follow the same curvilinear trend, though the curve is less steep in a complex operation like driving, where lack of intelligence often accentuates the personality defect. (For example, it is dangerous enough for a person's driving behavior to be motivated by exhibitionism or aggression; it is doubly so when he is too stupid to appreciate the consequences of his action, or to think quickly in a crisis.) The age factor, on the other hand, shows a U-shaped curve, with the young and the old as the worst offenders. But these are only general trends, as liability to accidents has proved to be a very individual matter—so much so that the only reliable way of predicting it is to assess each person individually, on his own merits.

2. *Preventative measures.* Controlled studies of the efficacy of preventative measures are still rare, but several studies of traffic accidents have shown that accident rates can be reduced by: (*a*) thorough training to improve driving skills, (*b*) eliminating the people with bad accident records; (*c*) using comprehensive psychological tests to screen out potential offenders, (*d*) enforcing discipline, and (*e*) as in one unusual study, by combining discipline with propaganda aimed at changing the image of reckless driving from "clever" to "psychologically sick" behavior. But there are formidable difficulties in applying some of these methods on a large scale and to the general public. The whole question of translating research findings into prevention policies, which are both practicable and socially acceptable, offers a tremendous challenge to psychological research.
Bibliography: Brody, L.: Human factors research in occupational accident prevention (Am. Soc. Safety Engineers). Chicago, 1962. Haddon, W., Suchman, E. A. & Klein, D.: Accident research. New York, 1964. Hakkinen, S.: Traffic accidents and driver characteristics (Finland's Inst. of Technology). Helsinki, 1958. Shaw, L. & Sichel, H. S.: Accident proneness. London & New York, 1970. U.S. Pub. Health Serv.: A review of mental health in industry. Washington, D.C., 1958. Viteles, M. S.: Industrial psychology. New York, 1932.   *Lynette Shaw*

Accommodation. Adaptation: changes take place in the curvature of the lens of the eye in order to accommodate variations of distance. The curvature of the anterior surface of the lens is adjusted more than that of the posterior surface by the action of the ciliary muscle. The lens is kept flat for distant objects, and is made to bulge—become spherical—for near ones. The *near point* (nearest point at which something can be seen distinctly) and *far point* (the most distant point at which something can be seen distinctly when accommodation is relaxed) are limit points for the accommodative power of the eye. Accommodative failure occurs in old age with increasing loss of elasticity of the lens. Accommodation of 14 diopters (q.v.) when young is reduced to 2 diopters in old age. *Absolute accommodation:* accommodation of one eye; *binocular accommodation:* of both eyes at once.
Bibliography: Campbell, F. W. & Gubisch, R. W.: Optical quality of the human eye. J. Physiol., 1966, *186*, 558–78. Weale, R. A.: From sight to light. London, 1968.   *R.R.*

Accommodation of information. The adjustment of the subjective expectation of the probability of events or signals to their actual probability of occurrence. The subjective information (q.v.) of the *receiver* is reduced to accord with the objective information of the *sender*; the necessary apperception and reaction times are minimized. Accommodation of information (i.e. of surprisal value) occurs unconsciously, but can be influenced by conscious processes. The average speed of the process increases up to app. twenty years of age and then gradually decreases. The process is speeded up by an increase in motivation.
Bibliography: Riedel, H.: Psychostruktur. Quickborn, 1967.   *H.R.*

Acculturation. A term originating in American ethnology (q.v.) for processes of cultural change arising through intensive and continuous contact or influence between two or more culturally distinctive groups. The specific cultural features of the other group or groups are assimilated to, and in a more or less altered form adopted by, or rejected eventually but for a few characteristics by, the other group or groups. In the case of a mutual exchange of features between groups, the result of acculturation can be a novel, widely influential form of culture or even civilization which then becomes the dominant form for all groups participating in the process. The original use of this now somewhat too inclusive and non-specific term referred only to unilateral influences: e.g. the influence on "primitives" and their traditions of the customs of the "civilized majority", leading to the adoption of these customs. See *Assimilation.*   *W.D.F.*

Bibliography: Carlton, P. L.: Cholinergic mechanisms in the control of behavior. In: Efron, D. (Ed.): Psychopharmacology 1957–1967, Washington, 1968. Koelle, G. B. (Ed.): Cholinesterases and anticholinesterases. Hdb. d. exp. Pharmakol. Vol. 15. Berlin, 1963. Reeves, C.: Cholinergic synaptic transmission and its relationship to behavior. Psychol. Bull., 1966, 65, 321–35. Rosenzweig, M. R., Krech, D. & Bennett, E. L.: A search for relations between brain chemistry and behavior. Psychol. Bull., 1960, 57, 476–492. Id.: Brain chemistry and adaptive behavior. In: Harlow, H. F. & Woolsey, C. N. (Eds): Biological and biochemical bases of behavior. Madison, 1965. Russell, R. W.: Neurophysiological and biochemical correlates of effects of drugs on behavior: The acetylcholine system. In: Steinberg, H. (Ed.): Animal behavior and drug action. London, 1964.   *W.J.*

Acetoxycycloheximide. See *Antibiotics.*

Acetylcholine (abb. ACh). A nerve hormone traditionally thought to be the chemical transmitter substance in the parasympathetic system, which it activates. It is now known that ACh is a transmitter substance (*a*) in all postganglionic fibers of the parasympathetic division of the autonomic nervous system, and in a few postganglionic fibers of the sympathetic division (e.g. sweat glands), (*b*) in the preganglionic fibers of the parasympathetic *and* sympathetic divisions, (*c*) in the motor nerves of the skeletal muscles. Recently the function of ACh in the central nervous system has been recognized, which has given rise to many hypotheses in regard to the connection between ACh and behavior, and especially learning and sleep (see *Psychopharmacology*). High concentrations of ACh are found in particular in the cortex, nucleus caudatus, hypothalamus, thalamus, midbrain, and corpus callosum. ACh is difficult to identify since it occurs only in minute quantities, and is very speedily inactivated by cholinesterase (ChE) (q.v.). However, inhibition of ChE (see *Cholinesterase inhibitors*) allows of indirect opportunities for studying relations between ACh and behavior.

Achievement. 1. General term for the successful attainment of some goal requiring a certain effort. **2.** The degree of success attained in a task, e.g. solving a test. **3.** The result of a certain intellectual or physical activity defined according to individual and/or objective (organizational) prerequisites: i.e. proficiency.   *G.R.W.M.*

Achievement age. The chronological age at which a specific level of achievement is usually attained.

Achievement, assessment of. There are various methods designed to measure (an) individual achievement against a specific achievement norm (standard): e.g. achievement batteries (groups of tests covering several areas of academic performance), achievement quotient (q.v.), Thematic Apperception Test (q.v.), and so on. See *Abilities.*   *G.R.W.M.*

Achievement curve. A graphic representation of the process of achievement over a period of time (performance in a specific area, test values, etc.).   *G.R.W.M.*

Achievement motive; achievement motivation. A hypothetical construct designed to explain inter- and intra-individual differences in the orientation, intensity and consistency of achievement behavior. In terms of content, achievement motivation may be characterized as the tendency to maintain and increase individual proficiency in all areas in which a standard of quality is taken as binding (Heckhausen, 1963). Research into achievement motivation was established on the basis of a recently-developed theory of motivation (McClelland & associates, 1953, 1969). According to McClelland, the basic principle for *definition* of a motive is the connection (dependent on experience) of an expected change in affect with specific key conditions; and, for *delimitation* of different motives, the particular class of content of expectations. In the case of achievement motivation, these expectations of positive or negative affective changes refer to the attainment or non-attainment of the individual standard of quality. According to whether *hope of success* or *fear of failure* is provoked by a situation, adient or abient behavior will result; a conflict can arise when expectations are equally intense. On this theoretical base, McClelland (1953) developed a special thematic apperception test (q.v.) to measure achievement motivation. On the basis of new results, J. W. Atkinson and (in Germany) Heckhausen have further developed the theory and methods of measurement.

A large number of experimental and cultural investigations have been carried out for construct validation (see *Construct validity*) of achievement motivation, which has been demonstrated as relatively constant as an individual characteristic in the course of diverse achievement situations and of time. Childhood experiences especially, i.e. the nature of early independence training, are positively related to achievement-orientation in adult life. According to Heckhausen, the average correlation between scholastic achievement and achievement motivation is $r = 0.40$; if scholastic knowledge, anxiety and so on are taken into account, it can be $r = 0.60$.

On the whole, success-motivated individuals show an average, and the failure-motivated an unrealistically high or very low degree of risk-taking behavior and aspiration level. The significance of achievement motivation for national economic development was shown by McClelland and associates in a number of studies and a program for alteration of motive in this regard.

Bibliography: Atkinson, J. W. (Ed.): Motives in fantasy, action, and society. Princeton, N.J., 1958. Heckhausen, H.: Hoffnung und Furcht in der Leistungsmotivation. Meisenheim, 1963. McClelland, D. C., Atkinson, J. W., Clark, R. A. & Lowell, E. L.: The achievement motive. New York, 1953. McClelland, D. C. & Winter, D. G.: Motivating economic achievement. New York, 1969.   *H.-J.K. & C.M.*

Achievement quotient (abb. AQ). The ratio between the expected and the actual measured level of performance in school. Chronological age (CA) or mental age (MA) may be used to estimate the theoretical performance, and achievement or educational age to measure the actuality.   *J.M.*

Achievement society (*Achieving society*). A model of advanced industrial societies in which the individual achievement in the work process determines status in the work organization and also the predominant range of possible life-satisfactions as defined by that society. As a societal model, it is opposed to privilege as a principle governing the distribution of income, prestige, and so on, and therefore derives from egalitarian theory; yet, as a normative principle, it supports the legitimization of inequality.

Bibliography: McClelland, D. C.: The achieving society. Princeton, N.J., 1961.   *C.B.*

Achievement tests. In general, measures of the effect of a special training. School performance tests form the most popular category. There are also vocational achievement tests, e.g. for skills such as those involved in stenography and so on, which are used both to check success in learning and (to some extent in conjunction with aptitude tests) for selection purposes.   *R.M.*

Achromatic lens. Lens corrected for reduction of chromatic *aberration* (q.v.), which cannot be wholly compensated. Lenses of different materials with different focal powers are combined one behind the other in order partly to correct an eye's inability simultaneously to bring to a single focus light of all relevant wavelengths.   *R.R.*

Achromatop(s)ia. Complete color blindness: no colors but only degrees of luminosity—shades of grey—can be distinguished. Partial color blindness is *color anomaly*: e.g. *anomalous dichromatism*—only two colors are seen; *anomalous trichromatism*—abnormal ratios of primary color mixtures (usually red-green).   *R.R.*

Ach-Vygotsky method. A method used by Ach (1921) to study concept formation. Nonsense words were attached to stereometric objects of varying size and weight for which there was no ready concept and word. For example, *gatsun* indicated "large and heavy". After a short time with these blocks, the initially meaningless word came to mean something for S. (*gatsun* gradually came to *mean* "large and heavy"). S. formed the concept *gatsun,* and subsequently used it as a general term for large, heavy objects. Rimat varied the method to study concept formation in adolescents; it was modified by Vygotsky, who describes (1962) its implications, one of which is that concept formation is a creative process, and not a passive one based on mechanical associative connections.

Bibliography: Ach, N.: Über die Begriffsbildung. Bamberg, 1921. **Rimat, F.:** Intelligenzuntersuchungen anschliessend an die Ach'sche Suchmethode. Göttingen, 1925. **Vygotsky, L. S.:** Thought and language. Cambridge, Mass., 1962 (Orig. Russ., Moscow-Leningrad, 1934).   *H.J.A.*

Acoustics. A division of psychology concerned with the nature and investigation of sound. It includes the physics of sound or noise, the physiology of the ear and the psychology of hearing. See *Auditory perception.*

Bibliography: Békésey, G. von: Experiments in hearing. New York, 1960. **Hirsh, I. J.:** The measurement of hearing. New York, 1952. **Kryter, K. D.:** The effects of noise on man. J. Speech Hear. Disorders. 1960, Monogr. Supp., No. 1. **Rodda, M.:** Noise and society. London, 1967. **Wever, E. G.:** Theory of hearing. New York, 1949.   *V.M.*

Acoustic type. A type who perceives and remembers above all acoustically. Belongs among the *sense types* (q.v.).

Acquiescence (syn. *Acquiescence tendency*). Originally the term for a *response set* (q.v.) or bias in answering personality inventories: the subject tends, regardless of the content of the test-item, to answer "Yes", "Correct", "Right" rather than "No", "Incorrect", "Wrong", and so on (*acquiescent response set*—L. J. Cronsbach). In the course of the debate on the traits of the "authoritarian personality" (q.v.) classifiable as "acquiescence", the concept was "socio-psychologized": in this sense, the *acquiescence tendency* is a characteristic of authoritarian, conformist behavior or an aspect of a more general personality syndrome (Couch & Keniston, 1960). Although a conceptual distinction is usually made between formal and social acquiescence, high positive correlations have been obtained (e.g. Couch & Keniston, Overall Agreement Score; B. M. Bass, Social Acquiescence Scale).

Bibliography: Bass, B. M. & Berg, I. A.: Objective approaches to personality assessment. Princeton, 1959. **Berg, I. A.** (Ed.): Response set in personality assessment. Chicago, 1967. **Couch, A., & Keniston, K.:** Yeasayers and naysayers: agreeing response set as a personality variable. J. abnorm. soc. Psychol., 1960, 60, 151–74. **Messick, S., & Jackson, D. N.:** Acquiescence and the factorial interpretation of the MMPI. Physchol. Bull., 1961, 58, 299–304.   *H.D.S.*

Acquired responses. Behavior primarily learned through experience; as opposed to *innate responses*, behavior primarily ascribed to inheritance. The distinction does not imply an absolute separation between environmentally learned and inherited behaviors, whereas popular usage tends to such absolutism and therefore to devalue the terms.

Acromegaly (*Acromegalia*). Unusual growth of the "acral" (or extreme peripheral) parts of the face, such as nose, ears and malar bones, and of fingers and toes. This enlargement is caused by hypersecretion of the growth hormone somatotrop(h)in in the anterior lobe of the pituitary body, and is usually a sign of pituitary adenoma, which is frequently accompanied by disturbances of other glands (q.v.), e.g. the thyroid gland (q.v.) and sexual glands. Mechanical pressure of this adenoma on nearby nerves and parts of the brain can lead to disorders of vision and psychic changes. Acromegaly in children can lead to gigantism, or overgrowth of the long skeletal bones.   *E.D.*

Acrophobia. An exaggerated or abnormal dread of being in (very) high places.

Act. See *Act psychology*.

ACTH (abb. for *Adrenocorticotrophic hormone*) (corticotrophin; corticotropin). A glandotropic hormone produced from the anterior pituitary, which stimulates the output of corticosteroids (q.v.) in the adrenal gland. The production of ACTH is regulated (*a*) by the level of corticosteroid circulating in the blood (negative feedback), (*b*) by the corticotrophin-releasing factor (CRF) via the pituitary, and (*c*) by the level of adrenalin(e) (q.v.) (epinephrine) circulating in the blood. The relative value of the three control factors has not yet been determined.

ACTH is available in a number of forms for therapeutic application. An overdose of ACTH can have quasi-psychotic effects. Little is known about the psychic effects of physiological doses of ACTH. Euphoric effects are most often noticed in patients, but it is not clear whether these are anything other than mere accompaniments of successful therapeutic effects. The small number of investigations carried out on healthy testees show no evidence of any stronger psychic effects. ACTH plays a special role in response to stress. According to H. Selye, all stressors (psychically and physically effective) induce increased production of ACTH via the sympathetic nervous system, hypothalamus and anterior pituitary.

Bibliography: Hodges, J. R.: The control of pituitary corticotrophic function. J. Psychosom. Res., 1965, *9*, 63–6. Malitz, S., Hamburg, D. A. & Modell, S.: Effects of ACTH on mental function. J. nerv. ment. dis., 1953, *118*, 315–31.   *W.J.*

Acting out. The attempt of the patient in psychotherapy or psychoanalysis, who is afraid of his unconscious conflicts, not to allow them to become conscious. Instead he tries to transfer, displace, or "act them out" by finding immediate, illusive, "real" solutions. For instance, a girl who is afraid of men because of some traumatic family experience, but who refuses to face up to the extent of the trauma during psychotherapy because of increasing fear of it, will begin suddenly to flirt with a number of men. In this way she "proves" to herself and the therapist that she is not afraid of men and therefore does not really need to discover any cause of her fear. The opposite to acting out is *reality-testing*, which is the attempt to find genuine explanations for the consciously realized conflicts. Reality-testing usually takes place toward the end of, and after, psychotherapy, whereas acting out comes usually in mid-course.

Bibliography: Toman, W.: An introduction to the psychoanalytic theory of motivation. London & New York, 1960.   *W.T.*

Actinomycin. See *Antibiotics*.

Action. 1. Intentional behavior. **2.** A unified series of behaviors. **3.** A change brought about by force or a natural agency. **4.** A deliberative act of will with some external sign or result, particularly change. **5.** The process of change. **6.** A physiological or mechanical process. **7.** The movement or function of the body or one of its parts. **8.** Performance. See *Activity*.   *J.M.*

Action potential (syn. *Action current*). In general, this is the term for any change in electrical potential during intense physiological activity of functional units (nerves and muscles) in organisms.

Stimulation causes, e.g., nerve cells to be influenced so that the functional membrane surrounding the cell is locally depolarized, and the resting potential due to the differential permeability of the cell membrane to sodium and potassium ions is reduced. There is a local reversal of potential in response to above threshold stimulus: i.e. if the stimulus exceeds a certain minimum intensity, spontaneous activation of the entire cell occurs with complete depolarization of the membrane, and a much greater action potential is established. Once the membrane is depolarized, resting potential, or polarization, is reestablished.   *M.S.*

Activation. Nowadays the term is used mostly when referring to the functions of the ascending reticular activating system (ARAS) (q.v.). This system regulates the level of general attention in relation to environmental stimuli on the one hand, and cerebral processes on the other. In consequence, the organism is continually in varying states of activation, or in an "activation continuum". The organism reaches its highest activation level at an average stimulus intensity, whereas the level of activation via the ARAS remains low at very intense and very weak stimulation. Sleep, of course, is not simply consequent upon cessation of activation, but is an active process in this sense. Activation level can be determined in terms of brain cell potential, breathing and pulse rate, and galvanic skin response (q.v.). See *Arousal*.

Bibliography: Lindsley, D. B.: Psychophysiology and motivation. Nebraska Symposium on Motivation, 1957, 44–104. Id.: Attention, consciousness, sleep and wakefulness. In: **Field, J.,** et al. (Eds): Handbook of physiology. Sect. 1, Vol. 3. Washington, D.C., 1960, 1553–94.   *R.Hd.*

Activation pattern. The activation pattern of the EEG (q.v.) indicates desynchronization, or suppression of alpha waves (q.v.), in favor of low-voltage fast activity when the individual suddenly engages in visual activity (e.g. opens his eyes to look at a presented object). *Diffuse* (affecting all areas of both cerebral hemispheres) and *localized* (affecting only certain cortical areas) forms have been distinguished; together with a *tonic* (long-term wakefulness), and a *phasic* (short-term shifts of attention to presented modulations of stimuli) form. Syn. *Alpha blocking; Arousal reaction*.

Bibliography: Morrell, L. K.: Some characteristics of stimulus-provoked alpha activity. Electroencephalog. Clin. Neurophysiol., 1966, *21*, 552–61.   *J.C.*

Active hypnosis, gradual. A psychotherapeutic technique forming part of the "dual standard approach" (E. Kretschmer). After a "basic practice" consisting of the "weight" and "heat" stages of autogenic training (q.v.), an autohypnotic state is induced and deepened. In clinical practice, gradual active hypnosis is always coupled with a parallel analysis. The method attempts a combination of two psychotherapeutic approaches: analysis and a form of "conditioning".

Bibliography: Kretschmer, E.: Über gestufte Aktivübungen und den Umbau der Hypnosetechnik. Dtsch. med. Wschr., 1946, *71*, 281–83.   *H.N.G*

Active therapy. Therapy in which the therapist makes some kind of active intervention rather than passively recording and interpreting information from the patient. In active therapy an attempt is usually made to break up a neurotic habit by forcing the patient to act against his symptoms, e.g. making the drug addict go through withdrawal, or forcing the phobic patient to confront the situation which he fears in the hope that he will become accustomed to it and overcome it. In psychoanalysis, active therapy is usually employed in order to break down a *resistance.*   *G.D.W.*

Activity. In psychology, activity is either a behavior (movement) of an organism or of a human individual which is directly released by inner conditions, or the readiness or capacity to behave, when the term "arousal" (q.v.) or "activation" is usual. The term is applied to psychological and physiological phenomena. It does not imply that the process in question has no external initial stimulus, but only that it can be traced to an energy peculiar to the individual in question. In this sense, a response to an environmental stimulus is also conceivable as an active process, insofar as the stimulus releases energy resulting in a determinate, specific answer on the part of the organism.

The concept of activity has a long history in psychological thought, and might be said to be conterminous with that of the conception of the "psyche", or "soul", as possessing not only cognitive ability but the capacity for aspiration and effort. Only the rigorous variety of association psychology (q.v.) wholly neglected the aspect of activity. Other schools paid more or less attention to this moment of the psychological process (in the nineteenth century, for example, the theories of Herbart, Fechner, Brentano and Wundt), and it was a basic principle of all divisions of dynamic psychology (q.v.).

More recently, conceptions of activity have tended to the *arousal* (q.v.) or *activation*

(q.v.) model. Especially since the findings of Woodworth & Schlosberg (1954), activity is conceived as a psychophysical variable which on the one hand is expressed in specific physical symptoms as a level of readiness of the organism or of individual functional systems to behave, or expend energy, and on the other can appear in individual experience as tension release or excitation. Accordingly, the living organism always manifests a specific *activation level* which is very low in deep sleep (q.v.), but significantly higher in the relaxed waking state. A high activation level corresponds to an emotional state (released, e.g., by an organic need or an external situation), whereas an even higher one is characteristic of a strong affective state (such as rage). Activation level therefore can also be seen as comprising a dimension of emotional or motivational behavior.

The relation between activation (arousal) and achievement has often been investigated. It is assumed that there is a curvilinear relation between these two variables. This implies that a medium activation level is most favorable for performance, whereas both a very low and very high activation level reduces performance.

Bibliography: Duffy, E.: Activation and behavior. New York & London, 1962. **Fahrenberg, J.:** Psychophysiologische Persönlichkeitsforschung. Göttingen, 1967. **Heckhausen, H.:** Activierung und Leistung. 25th Cong. of German Psychological Society, 1966. Göttingen, 1967. **Lindsley, D. B.:** Emotion. In: **Stevens, S. S.** (Ed.): Handbook of experimental psychology. New York & London, 1951. **Schönpflug, W.** (Ed.): Methoden der Aktivierungsforschung. Berne, 1969. **Traxel, W.:** On the scaling of activation. 16th International Psychology Congress, 1960. Amsterdam, 1962. **Id.:** Gefühl und Gefühlsausdruck. In: **Meili, R. & Rohracher, H.** (Eds) Lehrbuch der experimentellen Psychologie. Berne, ²1968. **Woodworth, R. S. & Schlosberg, H.:** Experimental psychology. New York & London, ²1954.   *W. Traxel*

Activity bed. Specially devised bed used to register, e.g., nocturnal restlessness in psychiatric patients, and thus, e.g., to study the effects of drug therapy.

Activity cage. A device used by Campbell & Sheffield to measure general activity level in rats: the revolving drum records the distance run by the rat. There are many similar devices, including the spring-suspended cage. Activity (restless activity) is closely related to motivation (q.v.); measurements of activity can therefore be used as indirect evidence for determining motivation.

Bibliography: Campbell, B. A. & Sheffield, F. D.: Relation of random activity to food deprivation. J. comp. physiol. Psychol., 1953, *46*, 320–22. Foppa, K.: Lernen, Gedächtnis, Verhalten. Cologne, 1968.

V.M.

Activity quotient (syn. *Action quotient*). Busemann's formal index of the linguistic style typical of a certain age-group. The ratio of the number of verbs (activity words) to adjectives (qualitative words, or qualifiers) is the activity quotient, which varies according to age. Throughout an individual's life, Busemann found there was a rhythmic alternation of "actional" (high a.q.) and "qualitative" phases (low a.q.). A high activity quotient indicated emotional lability and a relatively low achievement level for the specific age-level.

Bibliography: Busemann, A.: Die Sprache der Jugend als Ausdruck der Entwicklungsrhythmik: Sprachstatistische Untersuchungen. Jena, 1925. *S.Kr.*

Activity-specific potential (syn. *Action-specific potential;* abb. ASP). The potential that must be reached for a specific activity. ASP is essentially distinct from all those factors which, however necessary for a certain activity, take effect non-specifically. *R.Hä.*

Actone. 1. H. A. Murray's term for an act or pattern of action examined as specific to the individual, or in regard to the specificity of the act and therefore without regard to its effects, e.g. on others. **2.** A simple reflexlike response considered in isolation. *J.G.*

Act psychology. A view of psychology represented by Franz Brentano (q.v.) (1838–1917), and later mainly by his pupil Carl Stumpf (1848–1936), emphasizing "psychical phenomena" as "intentionally containing an object in themselves". This fundamental "intentionalism" derives from a long tradition (Aristotle, Philo of Alexandria, Anselm, Thomas Aquinas, Sir William Hamilton, etc.), with the emphasis on Aristotelian-Scholastic philosophy. The viewpoint of act psychology is opposed to that of empiricism (q.v.) and sensationalism, and in regard to the development of the particular complex of problems it represents, belongs to the pre-history of Husserl's phenomenological psychology and Dilthey's cultural science psychology.

Brentano classifies the subject-matter of psychology as distinct from that of the natural sciences. It is exclusively concerned with "inner perception", as a category of phenomena whose specific nature is elicited by analytic description as "intending" some object.

The essence of psychical phenomena is their "intentionality". They are "acts" whose mode of existence is "being for an *other*", i.e. an object which they themselves, as acts, are not. Neo-scholastic philosophy calls this the "intentional (or mental) *inexistence* of an object". In the visual modality, for example, one "intends" the actual object seen, which then "inexists" (immanently) in the act of seeing.

In Brentano's view, ideas are the "fundamental principle of other psychical phenomena", and to that extent act psychology is a psychology of consciousness. Two further classes of psychical phenomena are distinguished, and, together with ideas, comprise all possible psychological events. They are characterized by the specific way in which they realize the intentional inexistence of objects: namely, ideating and judging; i.e. rejecting or recognizing and feeling; i.e. *loving* or *hating*. The three kinds of acts and classes of mental phenomena are: *ideas judgments* and *feelings* (movements of the heart, or *Gemüt*).

In this view, the concept of experience means the apprehension ("directly" and "evidently" experienced by "inner perception" in analytic description) of acts of consciousness (q.v.). For act psychology, the individual—in accordance with his general nature as a vehicle of consciousness—is the subject of and ground for the possibility of intentional acts. It sees psychology as concerned with the analysis and description of the general nature of conscious processes in order to establish a fundamental discipline for the human sciences (*Geisteswissenschaften*). See *Philosophy and psychology*.

Bibliography: Brentano, F.: Psychologie vom empirischen Standpunkt (Vol. 1), Ed. O. Kraus. Hamburg, ⁶1955. Id.: Von der Klassifikation der psychischen Phänomene (Vol. 2), Ed. O. Kraus. Leipzig, ²1925. Id.: Vom sinnlichen und noetischen Bewusstsein (Vol. 3), Ed. O. Kraus. Leipzig, 1928.   *P. Braun*

Actual anxiety. According to Freud, the anxiety which occurs as a result of frustrations or interruptions of, or inadequate, sexual excitement or satisfaction.

Actual neuroses are, in Freud's terminology, neuroses (q.v.) whose symptoms, contrary to those of transference neuroses, derive from inadequate satisfactions, particularly in sexual activity.

Bibliography: Freud, S.: Introductory lectures on psycho-analysis. London, ²1929.   *W.T.*

Actual genesis. A term from gestalt psychology (F. Sander). An initially diffuse, undifferentiated pre-gestalt can, under favorable conditions, develop into a gestalt. The subject can actively forward these conditions by bringing the object under observation closer, scrutinizing it more carefully, and so on. "Actual genesis" also refers to typical processes of productive thought (q.v.) in which a "gestalt" evolves from an imprecise idea. See *Ganzheit*.   *V.M.*

Actuality of emotions. A term used by

Külpe (q.v.) for the phenomenon that emotions cannot be remembered or conceived without the simultaneous recurrence of all associated phenomena. Hence it is impossible to have an "image" of an emotion; instead it recurs, or becomes actual, in itself.

Bibliography: Külpe, O.: Outlines of psychology: based upon the results of experimental investigation. New York, 1895.   *R.Hä.*

Actualization. The process by which memory contents become conscious and actual. A distinction is made between active searching for memory contents and their sudden coming to mind (without the active participation of the individual). This actualization occurs variously according to the conscious or unconscious association with it of certain occasions or fragmentary memories.

Bibliography: Selz, O.: Zur Psychologie des produktiven Denkens und des Irrtums. Bonn, 1922.
    H.-J.A.

Actual neurosis. See *Actual anxiety.*

Acuity, visual. Sensitivity of sight, particularly the ability to resolve minute spatial detail in the visual field. Tested either by the familiar letter chart or by more sophisticated laboratory displays, and commonly stated as a ratio between the distance at which the subject can make a given discrimination and the normal distance for that discrimination. The best-known index uses a constant numerator of 20, so that 20/15 is better than average vision, and 20/40 is rather worse than average. Acuity is affected adversely by many factors, including *myopia*, *diplopia*, and *astigmatism*.   *G.D.W.*

Adaptation. The adaptation of the activation of a sense cell to a prolonged stimulus. In general, sensory adaptation (see *Sense organs*) implies that absolute threshold is raised and the responsiveness of sensory function is decreased.   *J.G.*

Adaptation level (abb. AL). **1.** H. Helson found (1947) that after responding to a number of stimuli, Ss could say which stimulus was "in the middle", i.e. from what point of magnitude they could describe the stimulus as "big" or "small". Such reference points (i.e. neutral points) occur on every dimension of perception, either in the course of experience (hence we characterize a play as good or bad) or in regard to a situation (an object remains bright in the evening). Our perceptual apparatus adapts to the situation, and this simultaneously ensures constant and sensitive perception.   *V.M.*

2. According to Helson (e.g., 1959), AL is the frame of reference by which the colors seen are determined according to different light stimuli. Under strongly colored lighting, objects with an albedo (q.v.) higher than the AL are inclined to appear under the hue of the lighting, those with a lower albedo to assume the hue complementary to that of the lighting, and those with an albedo approximating that of the AL to appear gray.   *G.K.*

3. A general term for emotional equilibrium or neutrality.

Bibliography: Helson, H.: Adaptation level as frame of reference for prediction of psychophysical data. Amer. J. Psychol., 1947, *60*, 1–29. Id.: Adaptation level theory. In: S. Koch (Ed.): Psychology. A study of a science. Vol. 1. New York, 1959.

Adaptation, social. See *Adjustment, social.*

Adaptation syndrome. See *Stress.*

Adaptive system. The quantity of possible behaviors of an adaptive system changes in accordance with the influences of the system's environment, in such a way that it maintains its distinctive function. In the simplest case this is due to a control system (q.v.) depending on a fixed, programmed connection between system inputs and outputs. In complex instances adaptation occurs

by alteration of the system itself. Examples are: changes in the retina during adaptation to darkness; changes in human behavior as the result of learning.   *K.-D.G.*

Addition theorem. 1. The addition theorem of *probability* (q.v.): if $A_1, A_2, \ldots, A_n$ are exclusive events (q.v.) in a random sample, then in this sample $P(A_1 + A_2 \ldots A_n) = P(A_1) + P(A_2) + \ldots P(A_n).P(A_1 + A_2 + \ldots A_n)$ represents the probability that either A_1 or A_2 or $\ldots A_n$ will occur. If A and B are random events with the probability $P(A)$ or $P(B)$, then in a random sample the event $A + B$ has the probability $P(A + B) = P(A) + P(B) - P(AB)$. **2.** The addition theorem for *means*: the arithmetic mean of a number of random variables whose means exist, is equal to the sum of these means, $E(X_1 + X_2 + \ldots + X_n) = E(X_1) + \ldots E(X_n)$. Here $E(X_1)$ represents the expected value of the random variables X_1. **3.** The addition theorem for *distributions* (see *Frequency distributions*): the sum of a specific distribution of a series of values corresponds to this distribution. See *Deviation.*   *W.H.B.*

Adiadochokinesis. A symptom of acute diseases of the cerebellum, presenting as the inability to carry out alternating movements, e.g. alternate extension and bending of the fingers. Together with other coordination disturbances such as intention tremor and nystagmus, adiadochokinesis is a complex of cerebellar asynergies, and is often coupled with myasthenia. It does not appear in chronic cerebellar prolapse when parts of the cerebrum take over cerebellar function. It can be improved by optical control and practice.   *E.D.*

Adience. Tendency to approach or increase exposure to a stimulus. Hence *adient behavior* or *response*, behavior leading the organism to, or prolonging, the stimulus in some way.

Adjustment. 1. A state in which the needs of the individual on the one hand and the claims of the environment on the other are fully satisfied. Harmony between the individual and the objective or social environment. **2.** The process by which this harmonious relationship can be attained. The state is of course expressible only in theoretical terms, since in practice no more than a relative adjustment is reached in the sense of optimal satisfaction of individual needs and untroubled relation to the environment. Adjustment takes the form of variation of the environment and variation in the organism through the acquisition of responses appropriate to the situation; the variation in the organism may be biological (see *Phylogenesis*).   *R.Hä.*

Adjustment, social. A process, or state resulting from that process, of physical, socio-systemic or organizational changes in group-specific behavior or relations, or a specific culture. In a functionalist perspective, the meaning and purpose of such a process depend on an improvement in individual or group survival prospects, or in the mode of attaining to significant goals. The biological connotations of the concept show its close relation to the theory of evolution (q.v.). The adaptive character of behavior modifiable through learning is also part of the total problematics of social adjustment, and owes its introduction into the debate above all to H. Spencer. The term is also used to indicate the process by which an individual or a group reaches a state of social equilibrium in the sense of experiencing no *conflict* (q.v.) with the milieu (ant. *Social maladjustment*).   *W.D.F.*

Adler, Alfred. B. 7/2/1870 in Vienna; d. 28/5/1937 in Aberdeen. Graduated in medi-

cine, Vienna, 1895. Began work as an ophthalmologist in Vienna in 1897, later practiced as an internist. First meeting with Freud 1899–1900. Adler defended Freud's ideas at the Viennese School of Medicine, in local medical circles and in the press. From 1902 he took part in the small discussion circle at Freud's home. Wrote *The Doctor as Educator* (1904). His first decision to break with the circle was withdrawn at Freud's request. In 1907 he published his monograph on organ inferiority (Eng. trans.: *Study of Organ Inferiority and its Psychical - Compensation.* Washington, 1917). Lecture in Vienna, 1908: "The Instinct of Aggression". In 1910 he became the president of the Viennese branch of the Psychoanalytic Association. Co-editor with Freud and Stekel of the *Zentralblatt für Psychoanalyse.* In January and February 1911, he gave four lectures forming "A Critique of Freud's Sexual Theory of Mental Life". After the fourth lecture the majority of Freud's supporters present decided (despite Stekel's objection) to make the "justification for remaining a member of our Society dependent on acceptance of Freud's sexual theory". Adler and seven other doctors left the meeting. In August 1911, in Vol. I, No. 10/11 of the *Zentralblatt für Psychoanalyse*, Adler announced his resignation from the Editorial Board. *The Neurotic Constitution* was published in 1912 (Eng. trans.: New York, 1917); Adler saw this work as establishing "Individual Psychology" (i.e. the theory of the unity of the individual: indivisible, free, goal-directed, responsible for his actions, whole in himself) as the basis of a new form of psychotherapy (q.v.). Other works: *The Practice and Theory of Individual Psychology*, 1920 (Eng. trans.: New York & London, 1927); *Understanding Human Nature*, 1928–30 (Eng. trans.: New York & London, 1928); *The Education of Children*, 1929 (Eng. trans: New York & London, 1930); *Superiority and Social Interest.* London, 1965. After World War I, he organized child-guidance clinics in Vienna. In 1926–7

Adler made a lecture tour in the U.S.; and another in 1928. In 1927 he was appointed Visiting Professor at Columbia University. From 1932 to 1937 he was Visiting Professor of Psychiatry at Long Island College of Medicine (New York).

Through a widespread misunderstanding, Adler's theory of neurosis has been taken to be the Adlerian psychology of normality. In fact, he describes neurosis as the sum of *social maladjustments* whose common characteristic is an *egocentricity* of experience and behavior. The contrasting, normal state is centered on the *group* in its "community feeling", "social interest" and social goals, and is directed to a striving for perfection in the accomplishment of social ideals. Normality is the experiential knowledge that personal happiness ("fulfillment") can never be won at the expense of others and of the task benefiting all, but only together with others, and is most accessible for the individual who does not pursue it too avidly and who does not make egocentric claims. The purpose of Individual Psychology is to convince the neurotic of the desirability of this normal state and to help him to see clearly the modalities of his self-centeredness and possible will-to-power, and, if necessary, to help to unify the unique psyche by means of social tasks and interpersonal relationships.
Bibliography: Ansbacher, H. L. & R. R.: The individual psychology of Alfred Adler. London, 1955. Bottome, P.: Alfred Adler: a biography. New York, 1939 (Alfred Adler: Apostle of freedom. London, 1947). Orgler, H.: Alfred Adler: the man and his work. New York, ²1948. Rom, P.: Alfred Adler und die wissenschaftliche Menschenkenntnis. Frankfurt a.M., 1966. Sperber, M.: Alfred Adler, oder das Elend der Psychologie. Vienna, 1970. Way, L.: Alfred Adler: an introduction to his psychology. Harmondsworth, 1956. *W.M.*

Adolescence. The post-pubertal period in which individual self-responsibility is established. The characteristics of physical maturity are already present. The psychic phenomena of puberty (q.v.) are gradually discarded. A search for freedom, and increasing self-confidence and self-consciousness, are characteristic of this phase of development (q.v.). In the literature, the beginning of adolescence is sometimes equated with that of puberty. The age-ranges conventionally associated with adolescence are 12–21 years for girls, and 13–22 for boys.
Bibliography: Bühler, C.: Das Seelenleben des Jugendlichen. Jena, 1929. Id.: From birth to maturity. London, 1935. Carmichael, L.: Manual of child psychology. New York, ²1954. Erikson, E. E.: The challenge of youth. Garden City, N.Y., 1965. Henry, N. B. (Ed.): Adolescence. Yearbook Nat. Soc. Stud. Educ., 43(I), 1944. Hoffman, M. L., & Hoffman, L. W. (Eds.): Review of child development research. Vols. 1 & 2. New York, 1964; 1966. Jersild, A. T.: The psychology of adolescence. New York, 1957. Kay, W.: Moral development. London, 1968. Stolz, H. R., & Stolz, L. M.: Somatic development of adolescent boys. New York, 1951. Strang, R.: The adolescent views himself. New York, 1957. Tanner, J. M.: Growth at adolescence. Oxford, 1962. Wattenberg, W. W.: The adolescent years. New York, 1955. *K.E.P.*

Adrenal glands. The *glandulae suprarenalis*, suprarenal glands, or adrenal glands, are two endocrine glands weighing app. 11–18 g. and situated above the kidneys. Each consists of a firmer, yellowish-brown cortex outside, and a softer, reddish-brown medulla inside. The *adrenal cortex*, consisting of three histologically distinctive layers, produces *steroids* (*cortisone*, q.v.; hydrocortisone). According to effect, the "corticosteroids" can be divided into three groups: (*a*) the *mineralocorticoids* and aldosterone, as regulators of the mineral metabolism; (*b*) the *glucocorticoids* and cortisol (q.v.), which influence the carbohydrate and sugar supply to produce an increase in blood sugar, and inhibit non-specific reactions of the body (e.g. in allergies); and (*c*) the *androcorticoids*, which co-determine post-pubertal body-growth and the development of female secondary sexual characteristics. The *adrenal medulla*, deriving historico-developmentally from the sympathetic nervous system, produces the hormones *adrenalin(e)* (q.v.) (epinephrine) and *noradrenalin(e)* (q.v.) (norepinephrine). *E.D*

Adrenalin(e) (*Epinephrine; Suprarenine*). A natural hormone of the adrenal medulla and a derivative of pyrocatechin (catechol). It was prepared in 1901 by T. B. Aldrich, H. Fürth and J. Takamine as 1-(3·4 di-hydroxy-phenyl-)-2-methylamino-ethanol. Its effects mimic those of stimulation of the sympathetic nervous system (it is a sympathetic transmitter substance). Like *noradrenalin(e)* (norepinephrine), it raises blood pressure by constriction of peripheral blood vessels and increasing heart activity, but inhibits, e.g., intestinal peristalsis, bronchial muscular contraction, and sweat secretion. In particular, by catabolism of liver and muscle glycogen, unlike insulin (q.v.), it increases the blood sugar level, and thereby promotes metabolic activity, physical and mental capacity, and performance readiness. Since additional natural adrenaline is released under stress, anxiety and fright, and psychic behavior is altered in consequence, it is counted among the psychogenic hormones (see *Catecholamines; Hormones*). **E.D.**

Adrenergic. 1. A term used to characterize the effects of chemical substances which mimic the effects of adrenalin (q.v.). **2.** Descriptive of nerve fibers or nervous systems in which noradrenalin or adrenalin functions as a transmitter substance (q.v.). Adrenergic activity patterns are peripheral-vegetative expressions of sympathetic activation. The once conventional equation of sympathicomimetic and adrenergic is inaccurate, as "adrenergic" is also used to refer to the central nervous system (q.v.) insofar as adrenalin, noradrenalin or related substances act as transmitter substances (see *Catecholamines; Biogenic amines*). **W.J.**

Adrenergics (*Adrenergic substances*). Substances which have the same effects as, or similar effects to, adrenalin (q.v.) or noradrenalin (q.v.) in the nervous system. **W.J.**

Adrenocorticotrop(h)ic hormone. See *ACTH*.

Adultomorphism. The attempt to interpret children's behavior in terms proper to adults. (Syn. *Enelicomorphism*; ant. *Pedomorphism*). **K.E.P.**

Adult psychology. A dimension of developmental psychology. The psychology of adults has only recently come to be considered as a separate area of research. It is necessary to divide development into several, largely independent dimensions. Adult psychology must be distinguished from juvenile psychology and gerontology (see *Aging*). Biological factors and various socio-cultural considerations must be taken into account in determining the dimension of adulthood, therefore a clear and uniform distinction is difficult to arrive at; in general the time span lasting from the third decade of life to the commencement of old age (about the sixth decade of life) ███████ into consideration. In the opini██ ██████ authors, this time span contain█ ███████ abilities (e.g. C. Bühler) (see, on ███ █████ hand, *Abilities; Intelligence; Intelligence tests*). The relation of age to productivity, performance, creativity, and so on; problems of development in marital life; problems of retirement and leisure activities: these are among the various research areas which might be considered parts of adult psychology.

Bibliography: Breckinridge, E. L.: Effective use of older workers. Chicago, 1953. Bühler, C.: Der menschliche Lebenslauf als psychologisches Problem. Göttingen, ²1957. Id., & Masserick, F.: Lebenslauf und Lebensziele. Stuttgart, 1969. Dennis, W.: Variations in productivity among creative workers. Sci. Mon., 1955, 80, 277–8. Id.: The age decrement in outstanding scientific contributions: Fact or artifact? Amer. Psychologist., 1958, 13, 457–60. Harris, D. B. (Ed.): The concept of development. Minneapolis, 1957. Kleemeier, R. W. (Ed.): Aging and leisure: A research perspective into the meaningful use of time. New York, 1961. Lehman, H. C.: Age and achievement. Princeton, 1953. Id.: The age decrement in outstanding scientific creativity. Amer. Psychologist., 1960, 15, 128–34. Pressey, S. L., & Kuhlen, R. G.: Psychological development through the life span. New York, 1957. **F.C.S.**

Advantage by illness. Psychologically, the subjective benefit or degree of relative satisfaction which the sick person gains from his sickness. Freud made a distinction between primary (*paranosis*) and secondary (*epinosis*) advantage by illness. The primary variety is the reduction of anxiety or anxiety-aggression that has arisen through the withdrawal of possible satisfaction or by reason of inadequate defense (q.v.) mechanisms. The secondary variety is an environmental gain enjoyed because of the sickness.
Bibliography: Freud, S.: Collected papers, Vol. 1. London, 1924–25.   *W.T.*

Advertising psychology. See *Marketing psychology*.

Aesthesiometer. See *Esthesiometer*.

Aesthetics. See *Esthetics*.

Aetiology. See *Etiology*.

Affect. A term that is not defined uniformly. In general, it is used to characterize a feeling-state of particular intensity. Sometimes an "affect" is characterized as a state brought about by actions almost wholly devoid of intentional control in accordance with moral and objective viewpoints. The term is also found in the literature as practically synonymous with "emotion" in certain senses. See *Emotion; Depth psychology*.   *R.M.*

Affect, displacement of. The change of the object of an affect in the course of the duration or recurrence of that affect. E.g. a boy might express his acute anger at his father in ill-treatment of his dog; a girl might displace the affective element of her fear of her father onto a teacher, and therefore express it as fear of the teacher. (Syn. *Transposition of affect*.)   *W.T.*

Affect, flattening of. Acute inability to give an emotional response. Usually the result of two contradictory "affects" (anger, joy), motives or behavioral tendencies. Stupor is a variant of flattening of affect. See *Ambivalence*.   *W.T.*

Affect, projection of. The perception of one's own affective states in other individuals or groups who (in the judgment of neutral observers) show no signs of any such states. One's own affective state is suppressed or occurs in isolation, either being experienced unconsciously or as not appertaining to oneself. See *Projection*.   *W.T.*

Affection. 1. A general term for emotion (q.v.) or feeling. **2.** A general term for tenderness or love. **3.** Influence or alteration of a psychic state or constitution by the environment; the state of being affected by something external. **4.** An obsolete synonym for disposition, inclination, trait.   *R.Hä.*

Affective logic; affective reasoning. Propositions or sequences of propositions which appear to have a logically exact, unambiguous, and regular structure but, when analyzed, are seen to proceed by emotional transitions peculiar to an individual, and therefore to have no intersubjective validity. See *Logical reasoning*.   *J.M.*

Affective psychoses. Psychoses in which the primary disturbance is an alteration of mood and the ensuing alterations in thought and behavior are secondary processes. They include involutional melancholia and illnesses of the manic-depressive continuum. The illness is regarded as functional although biochemical and genetic factors play a part. Affective disorders in which etiological factors are predominantly environmental are usually milder and do not amount to an illness of psychotic intensity.   *D.E.*

non-specialist is apt to view much of the controversy as a dispute between those whose biological orientation stresses the role of innate determinants (here he probably will think of orthodox psychoanalysis and European ethology), and those who emphasize the role of learning and experience (such as, most notably, American psychologists and social scientists), the major arguments really center upon endogenous versus exogenous causation. Writers such as Freud (1948), Storr (1968), and Lorenz (1963), trace the mainsprings of aggression primarily to internal sources, and assume that man has a spontaneously engendered drive impelling him to attack and even destroy other persons; they maintain that this energy must be discharged (whether by direct aggression, the observation of violence, the destruction of inanimate objects, participation in competitive sports, or achieving positions of dominance and mastery), if uncontrolled explosions of violence and perhaps even suicide are not to occur. However, some critics of this reasoning have also expressed a strong biological emphasis while still disputing the idea of an internally generated aggressive drive. The zoologist, J. P. Scott (1958), for example, holds that fighting behavior develops under the influence of a variety of genetic and environmental factors, but says the hereditary determinants affect the organism's predisposition to aggression rather than create a spontaneously produced instigation. Scott points out that an animal or human being can live satisfactorily for a long period of time without engaging in fights, unless external conditions stimulate aggressive reactions. Proponents of the endogenous causation thesis have accused their opponents of "naive optimism" about human nature, but still lack adequate evidence for their own position.

Also highly questionable is the Freudian–Lorenzian conception of a unitary aggressive drive that supposedly powers a wide variety of non-aggressive as well as aggressive actions. In agreement with many other students of animal behavior, Scott insists that there is no single instigation to aggression. Fighting serves a number of different functions and has a multiplicity of causes. Moyer (1968) has presented a list of different kinds of aggression (predatory, inter-male, fear-induced, irritable, territorial defense, maternal, and instrumental), and suggests that each type has a somewhat different basis in physiological mechanisms and eliciting stimuli. At the human level, Berkowitz (1962, 1970c) maintains that instrumental aggression, which is governed by anticipated rewards, must be differentiated from impulsive aggression which is evoked by situational cues in a manner akin to conditioned responses. The unitary aggressive-drive conception is highly dubious, and, by leading investigators to neglect or deny the operation of many different casual factors, may even be an impediment to more adequate formulations, as R. A. Hinde (1959) has argued in his discussion of unitary drive theories.

In addition to using gross analogies, extremely speculative leaps of inductive reasoning, and highly selective documentation (see Montagu, 1968; Berkowitz, 1969a), endogenous-causation theorists often refer to indications of appetitive aggression. As has been demonstrated in a number of experiments (e.g., Azrin et al., 1965; Lagerspetz, 1964; Ulrich, 1966), animals at times exhibit a clear preference for aggressive activity. Instead of regarding this preference as an expression of a spontaneously generated drive, however, the opportunity for aggression is better viewed as a reinforcer, with the reinforcing quality of aggression being limited to certain conditions and functioning much like other reinforcers.

Nor is the apparent generality of aggressive behavior adequate support for the unitary-aggressive-drive theory. A hostile person may display certain other traits, but the correlation between hostility and these other characteristics is no proof that one trait had caused the others. Furthermore, the unitary-drive idea of energy flowing from one type of behavior to another must be differentiated from the more precisely defined response-generalization concept developed by experimental psychologists. Research has shown that reinforcements provided for a certain reaction can strengthen other, similar responses. Rewarding one class of aggressive responses, such as hostile remarks, can increase the likelihood of other kinds of aggressive behavior. The reinforcement influence generalizes from one act to the others because they have something in common; perhaps the aggressor regards all of these as hurting someone. Whatever the exact meaning of the various aggressive actions, it is theoretically unparsimonious to interpret response generalization as an energy transfer from one response channel to another.

As discussed by some of its proponents, the frustration-aggression hypothesis (frequently seen as the major alternative to the Freudian–Lorenzian conception) also seems to posit a "built-in" influence on aggression. Dollard, Doob, Miller, Mowrer & Sears (1939) had said that they took no position on this issue, but many readers believed that their classic presentation of the frustration-aggression doctrine implied an innate connection between an antecedent stimulus event, the frustration, and the subsequent aggression. The Yale group had maintained that a frustration, defined as "an interference with the occurrence of an instigated goal response at its proper time in the behavior sequence", will universally arouse an instigation to aggression. Some American psychologists (e.g., Bandura & Walters, 1963) have questioned this thesis by citing demonstrations of learned modifications of frustration reactions as evidence of the inadequacy of the frustration-aggression hypothesis. However, the presence of learning does not necessarily exclude the possibility of innate behavioral determinants; built-in behavior patterns may be modifiable by

learning but can still play a crucial role in motivating action. The frustration-aggression relationship may be learnable without being entirely learned. Experiments with animals (see Ulrich, 1966) have shown that thwartings can produce aggression even without prior learning, and what holds for other species may also be true for man.

Some other criticisms of this traditional social science doctrine can also be answered readily (see Berkowitz, 1962, 1969b). It is especially important to distinguish between frustrations and mere deprivations. As the Dollard, Doob et al. formulation clearly indicates, if the individual is to be regarded as frustrated, he must be performing anticipatory goal responses (i.e. must be anticipating the satisfaction to be gained from reaching his goal), and then be prevented from achieving adequate consummation. This blocking can have a number of consequences, as Dollard and his colleagues had recognized, and some of these may be stronger than the instigation to aggression, but as the frustration (in the present limited sense of the term) continues, the likelihood of aggression presumably increases. All in all, Berkowitz (1962, 1969b) has proposed two alterations of the frustration-aggression hypothesis while still accepting its basic validity: (a) contrary to the 1939 discussion, every aggressive action does not necessarily rest on a prior frustration: aggressive behavior can be learned much as other modes of conduct are learned; (b) the linkage between frustration and aggression may be weaker than was assumed by the Yale group, and may not be revealed in overt behavior unless there are appropriate situational conditions, such as external stimuli associated with aggression, which facilitate the occurrence of aggression.

Along with other writers (see Ulrich, 1966), Berkowitz (1969b) has also suggested that the frustration-aggression relation may be a special case of the connection between aversive stimuli and aggression. Thwartings are noxious events in important respects, and pain is a reliable stimulus to fighting (see

Ulrich, 1966). In this regard, Scott believes social fighting has evolved from defensive reactions to pain. We should note, however, that the aversive stimulus also produces a heightened arousal state which can increase responsivity to the dominant aggressive cues in the environment.

2. *The control of aggression.* Followers of the Freudian–Lorenzian conception generally advocate "discharging" one's supposedly pent-up aggressive drive in various aggressive or even non-aggressive activities. Simple though this prescription seems to be, the findings uncovered by experimental research are far more complex than this reasoning would have us expect and are better explained by standard experimental-psychological analyses (Berkowitz, 1970a, b).

Engaging in, or even seeing, aggressive behavior frequently increases the probability of further aggression. In many cases, according to recent research, angry people do feel better and may even experience a temporarily reduced inclination to attack their tormentors upon learning that these persons have been hurt. Their aggressive goal has been reached and they are gratified. The long-term consequences may be very different, however. The information about the injury inflicted on the intended target is also a reinforcement, and as such, can heighten the likelihood that aggression will occur again in the future (Patterson, Littman & Bricker, 1967). Moreover, those people who believe they did not have adequate justification for their aggression are later apt to invent reasons to show their behavior was indeed appropriate and proper (Brock & Pallak, 1969). These rationalizations can also increase the chances of further aggression. Then, too, the injured party may retaliate, thereby provoking yet another attack. For many reasons, aggression is all too likely to lead to still more aggression.

This does not mean that all violent actions should be excused or that every effort should be made to avoid all frustrations. Extreme permissiveness can also heighten the chances

of aggressive behavior, and people should learn to react constructively and non-aggressively to the thwartings they inevitably will encounter in life. Punishment conceivably could be employed as a means of controlling aggression (see Berkowitz, 1970b). Evidence suggests that punishment can be effective if it is employed early in the disapproved-behavior sequence, is carried out consistently, is combined with reasoning, and if the punished individual has readily discriminated the attractive alternative responses available to him. Nevertheless, punishment is also painful and may give rise to aggressive responses, especially if other people with aggressive stimulus properties are nearby.

Effective control of aggression requires that we avoid reinforcing this behavior without re-instigating it. Extreme permissiveness may also be hazardous since the aggressor may believe other people tacitly approve of his action when they fail to condemn it. With children, at least, it may be better to remove them quickly and temporarily from the provoking situation when they become violent rather than ignore their aggression, and then permit them to return only when they have quieted down. This "time out" procedure can be combined with explanations to show why the disapproved behavior is wrong. Aggression can also be lessened by minimizing the number of aggression-evoking stimuli in the environment, and by teaching people to act in ways that are incompatible with aggression when they do encounter stimulation to violence. They should not be encouraged to attack someone or some object, or to express their anger in the hope that they will drain some hypothetical energy reservoir. This notion of hostility catharsis is, in its traditional form, an outmoded theoretical conception lacking adequate empirical support; it also has potentially dangerous social implications. Aggression ultimately produces more aggression.

Bibliography: Azrin, N. H., Hutchinson, R. R. & McLaughlin, R.: The opportunity for aggression as an operant reinforcer during aversive stimulation.

Journal of Experimental Analysis of Behavior, 1965, 8, 171-80. Bandura, A. & Walters, R. H.: Social learning and personality development. New York, 1963. Berkowitz, L.: Aggression: a social psychological analysis. New York, 1962. Id.: Simple views of aggression. American Scientist, 1969a, 57, 372-83. Id.: The frustration-aggression hypothesis revisited. In: Berkowitz, L. (Ed.): Roots of aggression: a re-examination of the frustration-aggression hypothesis. New York, 1969b. Id.: Experimental investigations of hostility catharsis. Journal of Consulting and Clinical Psychology, 1970a. Id.: The control of aggression. In: Caldwell, Bettye & Ricciuti, H. (Eds): Review of Child Development Research, Vol. 3. New York, 1970b. Id.: The contagion of violence. In: Page, M. (Ed.): Nebraska symposium on motivation, 1970. Lincoln, Nebr. 1970c. Brock, T. C. & Pallak, M. S.: The consequences of choosing to be aggressive. In: Zimbardo, P. G. (Ed.): The cognitive control of motivation. Glenview, Ill., 1969, 185-202. Dollard, J., Doob, L., Miller, N., Mowrer, O. Sears, R.: Frustration and aggression. New Haven, 1939. Freud, S.: Beyond the pleasure principle. London, 1948. Hinde, R. A.: Unitary drives. Animal Behavior, 1959, 7, 130-41. Lagerspetz, K.: Studies on the aggressive behaviour of mice. Helsinki, 1964. Lorenz, K.: Das Sogenannte Böse. Vienna, 1963. Eng. trans.: On aggression, New York & London, 1966. Montagu, M. F. A. (Ed.): Man and aggression. New York, 1968. Moyer, K. E.: Kinds of aggression and their physiological basis. Communications in Behavioral Biology, 1968, 2, 65-87. Patterson, G. R., Littman, R. A. & Bricker, W.: Assertive behavior in children: a step toward a theory of aggression. Monographs of Society for Research in Child Development, 1967, 32, 5, 1-43. Scott, J. P.: Aggression. Chicago, 1958. Storr, A.: Human aggression. New York, 1968. Ulrich, R.: Pain as a cause of aggression. American Zoologist, 1966, 6, 643-62.

L. Berkowitz

Aggressiveness; aggressivity. 1. The tendency to display aggression (q.v.). **2.** The quality of a will to dominance, or even achievement.

Aging, psychology of. The psychology of aging is concerned with the explanation of changes in behavior over the adult phase of the life span—app. three-fourths of the average length of life. The subject-matter includes the changes that occur in capacities such as perception, memory, learning, intelligence, thinking and problem solving. It also embraces age changes in skills and patterns of behavior such as those involved in emotions, and interpersonal relationships. Since many of the behavior changes with age are not easily subjected to experiment, much of the basic information available in the psychology of aging has been descriptive, although experimental studies are coming to be more frequent.

The psychology of aging has a biological and a social orientation, since genetic and other biological factors determine the limits set upon behavior by the capacities of the nervous system, as well as other organ systems, and our habits and social roles are determined by the nature of the group or society in which we have grown up and grown old. For example, chronological age is an important factor in determining how members of society relate to one another. The characteristics of age status systems of a society are not as yet fully known, but social psychologists are increasingly concerned with the social status and roles of different age levels.

Specialists emphasize different aspects of the psychology of aging; different weight is given to the importance of the biological limitations of aging, or to the importance of the social environment, much as in child psychology. Similarly, the psychology of aging tends to be concerned with whether man ages because of "nature" or "nurture". At present, few formal theories of the psychology of aging have been proposed. Those offered in the past have mostly been borrowings from or derivatives of theories developed in some other area of psychology such as brain damage, learning, personality, or psycho-pathology.

The psychological theory of aging is directed toward systematic explanation of age differences in the behavior and capacities of adults. Because each of the many aspects contain such dissimilar observed facts it is not likely that there will be any single theory of aging that will prove universally serviceable for all psychologists.

1. *History.* One of the first scientists to be concerned with the empirical aspects of aging was a Belgian, Quetlet (1835). His concept of the "average man" took into account a central tendency around which extremes, both positive and negative, were distributed. He evidently believed that there are marked individual differences in man's longevity and in his behavior with age, and that the characteristics of aging are partly a function of the environment in which the individual lives. The English psychologist Francis Galton was also concerned with the aging of various behavioral capacities. His work in the second half of the nineteenth century, while pioneering in many respects, was not directly followed up by other scientists, and the field lay relatively dormant. The first psychologist systematically to review the literature and facts of the psychology of aging was G. S. Hall (1922). His book *Senescence* reflected a developmental psychological point of view of the whole life span, reminiscent of his earlier work on adolescence. On retirement, he addressed himself directly to the processes of aging. Hall saw the superficiality of regarding aging merely as a regression toward an earlier stage of life, and emphasized the high degree of variability among older persons, as well as the point that aging is not an inverse process of earlier development. The question of individual differences increasing with age is often discussed, but as yet insufficient data prevent postulation of a law in this regard.

Following World War II, a number of laboratory investigators began an accelerated phase of investigation into the psychological processes of aging. The work of Kallmann & Jarvik and their colleagues (1959) suggests that aging is indeed multivariate. Studies of one-egg twins over the age of sixty-five suggests that monozygotic twins show more similar patterns of aging in appearance, intelligence and cause of death than do fraternal twins and siblings. There is thus a continuing genetic influence on late-life similarities, as seen earlier in one-egg children. Therefore the patterns of aging are to some extent genetically determined.

2. *Life span differentiation.* The adult, like the child, appears to evolve toward greater differentiation. Differentiation in both child and adult is brought about by social as well as biological processes. At each age level or phase of life, individuals are presented with characteristic tasks that require resolution. In this sense there is as much dynamic quality in the life of the seventy-year-old as there is in the fifty-year-old or in the adolescent. In part, the tasks facing individuals at characteristic ages give life a pattern. Some, such as Bühler (1951), have inferred there is a basic tempo or rhythm to adult life. Analysis of biographical information has led Bühler to opine that there are demarcated phases of construction, combination and reduction. In terms of social behavior, individuals as they grow older are thought to change from a pattern of achievement orientation and striving to a withdrawal from life and reduction of activity. This pattern, while not universally accepted as normal or typical, has been described as a process of "disengagement" (Cumming & Henry, 1961). The concept behind the term is that individuals as they grow older undergo a reduction in energy and become willing accomplices in the gradual loss of an active role in society.

The extent to which an individual shows high motivation in later life must depend to some degree on the state of his nervous system. Insufficient information is available about the anatomical and biochemical changes in the nervous system with age, to predict detailed behavioral consequences. But there is little doubt that the nervous system is in a key position to influence aging in the rest of the body. Not only is the nervous system critical in integrating behavior but it also mediates the vegetative processes of the body, and can presumably distribute the influences of its aging capacities. Nerve cells have a particular significance since they are fixed post-mitotic cells; that is, they do not divide after their origins in embryonic life. The cells of the nervous system are of great importance not only in the organization of behavior, but as a limiting factor in the ability to survive and function. It is not surprising that, unlike studies of childhood, studies of aging have more frequently involved measured aspects of the biological capacities of the organism along with observed behavior characteristics.

3. *Theories of behavior and aging.* Behavior of the older adult, whether perceptual, associative, or motor, tends to be slower than might be expected in a young adult. The basis for this has been given considerable attention, since evidence suggests that all behavior mediated by the central nervous system tends to be slow in the aging organism. Whereas young adults are quick or slow to respond in their behavior in accordance with their estimation of the demands of the environment, older adults may show a generalized slowness of behavior. One likely explanation is the known gradual loss of nerve cells that occurs diffusely in the nervous system with advancing age. Other explanations have involved reduced neural excitability, physical-chemical changes at the synapse that limit transmission speed, and a lowering of subliminal excitation of the nervous system. In addition, two functional hypotheses have been advanced to explain the slowness, the *neural noise hypothesis* and the *excitability hypothesis*.

The neural noise hypothesis postulates that with advancing age there is increased random neural activity, or neural noise, against which background any signal must be distinguished; the signal-to-noise ratio is assumed to be reduced with advancing age because of an increase in the noise level. Among factors contributing to such an increase might be spontaneous firing of hyper-irritable neurons, or perhaps local conditions of irritation produced by dying cells. Crossman & Szafran (1956), interpreting their data on visual and somaesthetic discrimination, have suggested that the

nerve impulses conveying signals along the sensory pathways occur against a background of ambient neural activity that increases with age. It should follow that differential thresholds are likely to be relatively less affected by aging than are absolute thresholds. Some evidence in favor of this contention is to be found in a study of tachistoscopic recognition thresholds, in which a comparison of information-transfer functions, with and without distorted input, revealed no consistent decline with age among professional pilots (Szafran, 1966). Similarly, the older pilots did not show the traditionally expected more severe change of the effective threshold in the presence of white masking noise input to the contralateral ear. A preference of the older adult for guidance in his skilled activities by the largest possible picture of the immediate environment could also be ascribed to a decrease in the signal-to-noise ratio. Seeking additional sensory cues may indicate a need for stronger input, required perhaps to effect the intermediate processes between perception and action (Szafran, 1951; 1955).

Statistical decision theory, as applied to perception, should make it feasible to determine experimentally whether the observed decrement in performance with age is due entirely to a decrement in sensitivity or at least in part to a change in response criterion (Green & Swets, 1966). As yet there have been very few experiments of this nature, although F. I. M. Craik (1969) has reported no evidence of any substantial age differences in the estimates of the relative signal strength, and some tendency for the older subjects to adopt a more cautious criterion under one of the experimental conditions employed. From the theory, one would also predict that the human observer of faint or very brief signals can vary in confidence about his judgments, and that shifts in the criterion which he must use to arrive at a decision may be promoted by training and further enhanced by experience. A study of the effectiveness of increased sensory thresholds under unfavorable circumstances, using pilots as subjects, suggests that an important change of "strategy" in detecting distorted signals may occur as a result of prolonged experience, and that this strategy change can be relatively immune to the adverse effects of aging (Szafran, 1968).

Although many older adults may be able to minimize the very subtle relative functional losses in perceptual input by using efficiently stored hypotheses or information, there is evidence that perceptual identification may be impaired to some extent in later life (Birren, 1955; Wallace, 1956; Welford, 1958; Birren & Riegel, 1962). Older subjects have been reported to be less able than the younger to detect simple designs embedded in more complex ones (Axelrod & Cohen, 1961). Since an explanation merely in terms of known changes in the sensory input is obviously unsatisfactory in these cases, the observations provide some support for the view that with advancing age the ability to shift from one perceptual hypothesis to another may be reduced (Welford, 1958; Birren, 1964).

The other hypothesis of a functional character assumes that the excitability or arousal of the older nervous system is low. In this view, readiness to rapid response is low because neurons are not in a high state of subliminal excitation such as might result from a relative sensory deprivation of the older person, and perhaps an inherent lessening of activity of the reticular activating system. The finding of increased response time in relation to increasing task difficulty does not preclude an alternative interpretation along the lines of delayed synaptic transmission. Hence, if the single synapse takes longer for transmission with advancing age, the greater the number of synapses involved in any complex behavior the greater will be the time of response in the older adult. The lengthening of the time need not be a linear function of the time delay at any single unit, but may grow as a power function of the number of synapses, as the excitation spreads over a network.

It was pointed out earlier that slowness of behavior is not only associated with advancing age, but is seen in subjects with brain damage, mental retardation and certain forms of psychosis. Whether the same mechanism underlies the slowness shown in all four groups, is to be questioned. This assumes, for purposes of discussion, that behavioral slowing is a general factor: slowness of all behavior mediated by the central nervous system (Birren, 1965). It is possible that there is a basis in the nervous system for a generalized slowing consisting of the extra-pyramidal centers, midbrain and reticular formation with rostral and caudal connections. The structure likely to influence the elements of the speed of complex behavior is the reticular activating system of the brain stem. In turn, the extra-pyramidal system functions in cooperation with the reticular formation. Hassler (1965) emphasized the control of the extra-pyramidal system on slowness of behavior. The loss of cells in the extra-pyramidal structures of the nervous system could contribute substantially to the slowness of behavior seen with advancing age. Such an anatomic point of view is of course related to an activation hypothesis which in effect says that the tonic influences on the older nervous system diminish and result in a lower preparedness to respond or to organize responses.

4. *Information theory and "intelligence theory"*. Evidence has been collected by Szafran (1966) and others that with advancing age the nervous system can process fewer units of information per unit time. Information theory lends itself to an explanation of such age changes. One unresolved issue is the constancy of the *bit* of information, particularly when dealing with complex stimuli. Rabbitt (1965), for example, showed that when irrelevant information is introduced into the stimulus, older persons will take a longer time to respond. The amount of information in a stimulus would appear to depend upon the subject's purpose in responding to it. There is always more

information in the environment than we are responding to. How then, with age, does the subject ignore or handle the massive amount of information from which he is withholding response? One implication of research by Rabbitt is that older subjects find increasing amounts of irrelevant information a distraction. This may reflect what some researchers regard as a weak set, or others as weak inhibitory processes, attention or vigilance.

Increased conceptual organization of information may permit the older subject to process fewer bits, but larger chunks of information per unit time. This would increase the total effectiveness of his behavior by allowing him to deal with larger chunks of information through the formation of concepts, although at the same time a decrease in processing time per unit may be observed.

Results of standardized intelligence tests (Guilford, 1969) suggest that certain functions rise in scores with advancing age. Results of vocabulary measurement show, for example, that the healthy adult will generally know more words after an increase in age: that is, with advancing age the individual accumulates more experience. If each element of experience remained as an isolated bit, the individual would be searching an increasingly large store of information and his performance would probably slow down. Concomitant with rises in stored information with age shown on intelligence test scores, other measures—such as speed on decoding tests—show a decrease. Thus the aging nervous system contains an increasing mass of stored information to process, yet seems to have a slower processing mechanism. How does the middle-aged and older adult maintain effectiveness? Tentatively, it would seem that an explanation might lie in the fact that, with increasing experience, verbal and other information is reorganized conceptually and need neither exist nor be retrieved as isolated bits.

A study of successful middle-aged individuals carried out at the University of Chicago (Birren, 1969) suggests that successful middle-aged professionals tend to concentrate on crucial aspects of a situation, whereas the young professional person must deal with more information since he doesn't know what crucial information to look for. With additional experience, the individual forms concepts and can classify categories of crises, clients, or interpersonal relations according to their assumed nature. Though this increases his effectiveness, in a limited sense he may be processing fewer bits of information than he did as a young professional; nevertheless, as an older person, he can use his larger mass of experience and retrieve it in larger chunks or concepts.

Consequently the effectiveness of the older man in adapting to a technological environment is not necessarily indicated directly by the number of bits of information he can process per unit time. Possibly, his experience or information may be organized so that he can deal with larger chunks of information or experience acquired with age. Effectiveness, in response to a complex environment, is a joint function of the conceptual organization of the individual's experience and his processing time. At some age this joint function may result in declining effectiveness, but it would appear to occur later in life than our curves of choice-reaction time with age would imply. One cannot extrapolate directly to effectiveness of behavior from either a simple curve of information processing of bits of information per second, or from total information stored as in a vocabulary test. As suggested, the "bit" itself may not be a constant quantity. Studies of isolated elements of experience do not tell us how they are grouped under concepts and hence available to the retrieval mechanisms of the nervous system. In this view, aged individuals are more or less efficient in terms of the organization of their retrieval mechanisms and concepts as well as their processing time.

5. *Major problems.* There has been a tendency in the social psychology of aging to regard older persons as constituting a

minority group. In general, social surveys indicate that older persons tend to be disadvantaged with regard to income, services and prestige in society. But there is little substantial evidence that older persons identify with others of the same age as constituting their reference group. This would be necessary were older persons really to constitute a minority group within societies. However, access to study populations has often been limited; therefore the literature on aging appears to be concerned with institutionalized adults available and amenable to investigation. The literature is biased in suggesting high levels of dependency and incapacity, for such characteristics reflect the nature of the populations institutionalized rather than the characteristics of older individuals leading an independent life in society. Because of the lack of easy access to older members of the population for study of these and other topics, little detailed information is usually available about the factors influencing the life satisfaction and functioning of older adults independently living in society. Therefore psychologists have tended to revert to points of view about the development of children. As research explores the details of aging with the same enthusiasm and effort that has been given to child psychology, much more should be revealed about the conditions that lead to optimum life satisfaction and functioning throughout the life span, including old age.

Bibliography: Axelrod, S. & Cohen, L. D.: Senescence and embedded-figure performance in vision and touch. Percept. Motor Skills, 1961, *12*, 283–8. Birren, J. E.: Age changes in speed of simple responses and perception and their significance for complex behavior. In: Old age in the modern world. London, 1955, 235–47. Id.: The psychology of aging. Englewood Cliffs, New Jersey, 1964. Id.: Age changes in speed of behavior; its central nature and physiological correlates. In: Welford, A. T. & Birren, J. E. (Eds): Behavior, aging, and the nervous system. Springfield, Ill., 1965, 191–216. Id.: Age and decision strategies. In: Welford, A. T. & Birren, J. E. (Eds): Decision making and age. Basle and New York, 1969, 23–6. Birren, J. E. & Riegel, K.: Lights, numbers, letters, colors, syllables, words and word relationships. In: Tibbitts, C. & Donahue, W. (Eds): Social and psychological aspects of aging. New York, 1962, 751–8. Bühler, Charlotte: Maturation and motivation. Personality, 1951, *1*, 184–211. Craik, F. I. M.: Applications of signal detection to studies of aging. In: Welford, A. T. & Birren, J. E. (Eds): Decision making and age. Basle, 1969. Crossman, E. R. F. W. & Szafran, J.: Changes with age in the speed of information intake and discrimination. Experientia, Suppl., 1956, *4*, 128–35. Cumming, M. Elaine & Henry, W. E.: Growing old; the process of disengagement. New York, 1961. Green, D. M. & Swets, J. A.: Signal detection theory and psychophysics. New York, 1966. Guilford, J. P.: Intellectual aspects of decision making. In: Welford, A. T. & Birren, J. E. (Eds): Decision making and age. Basle, 1969. Hall, G. S.: Senescence. New York, 1922. Hassler, R.: Extrapyramidal control or the speed of behavior and its change by primary age processes. In: Welford, A. T. & Birren, J. E. (Eds): Behavior, aging, and the nervous system. Springfield, Ill., 1965, 284–306. Quetlet, A.: Sur l'homme et le développement de ses facultés, 2 vols. Paris, 1835. Rabbitt, P. M. A.: Age and discrimination between complex stimuli. In: Welford, A. T. & Birren, J. E. (Eds): Behavior, aging, and the nervous system. Springfield, Ill., 1965, 35–53. Szafran, J.: Changes with age and with exclusion of vision in performance at an aiming task. Quart. J. Exp. Psychol., 1951, *3*, 111–18. Id.: Experiments on the greater use of vision by older adults. In: Old age in the modern world. London, 1955, 213–35. Id.: Age differences in the rate of gain of information, signal detection strategy and cardiovascular status among pilots. Gerontologia, 1966, *12*, 6–17. Id.: Psychophysiological studies of aging in pilots. In: Talland, G. A. (Ed.): Human aging and behavior. New York, 1968, 37–74. Wallace, J. G.: Some studies of perception in relation to age. Brit. J. Psychol., 1956, *47*, 283–97. Welford, A. T.: Ageing and human skill. London, 1958.

J. E. Birren

Agnosia. A disorder of recognition despite intact functioning of the sense organs, intelligence, and consciousness. A perceived object is not recognized, i.e. is not identified by reference to memory content. (*a*) *Optical* or *visual agnosia* can affect optical-spatial orientation and recognition, and identification of the outward appearance of individual objects (lesion of the upper parieto-occipital region); recognition of characteristic features of objects or persons (injury to the visual cortex of the occipital lobe); or knowledge of the (acquired) significance of colors (parieto-occipital lesion). (*b*) *Acoustic* or *auditory agnosia* might be described as a sensory *aphasia* (q.v.) extended to the entire acoustic field, and consists of a disorder of the recognition of noises, melodies (sensory amusia), etc. Localization of the lesion: temporal lobes of the dominant hemisphere. (*c*) *Tactile agnosia* (*stereoagnosis, astereognosis*): inability to recognize an object by touch despite the retention of sensitivity. Tactile agnosia was at one time thought to be caused by a parietal lesion, whereas the occurrence of an isolated tactile agnosia is now thought doubtful. *C.S.*

Agonistic behavior. A collective term for behavior in social confrontations; it includes attacks (offensive and defensive), threats, fighting, evasion, subjection, appeasement gestures (q.v.), flight. This group of behaviors forms a unity for theorists who attempt to explain aggressive behavior as arising out of the conflict between tendencies to attack and to flight. Neurophysiological findings would seem to support this hypothesis. Electrical stimulation of the midbrain reveals transitions between attack, threat behavior and flight.

Bibliography: Holst, E. von & St Paul, U.: Vom Wirkungsgefüge der Triebe. Naturwiss., 1960, *47*, 464–76. Hunsperger, R. W.: Affektreaktion auf elektrische Reizung im Hirnstamm der Katze. Helvet. physiol. acta., 1956, *14*, 70–92. *R.S.A.*

Agoraphobia. An exaggerated or abnormal dread of traversing or being in open spaces.

Agrammatism. Ungrammatical speech. Each word is correctly formed and pronounced but the order is wrong, or there is an incorrect conjugation of verbs, declension of nouns, and comparison of adjectives and adverbs. Parts of speech (say, a verb or preposition) may be omitted. If the message is present to a minor degree, it may be possible to decipher it. More severe cases speak nonsense. Often accompanied by perseveration or stereotypy (q.v.). Syn.: (in organic states) *jargon* or *syntactical aphasia*; (in functional states) *incoherence, drivelling.* *B.B.*

Agraphia. An inability to write consequent upon injury to a specific cerebral area. With a lesion in the area of the (in the right-handed, left) parietal lobe, as "apractic" (or apraxic) or ideokinetic agraphia, it forms part of an *apraxia* (q.v.). It is to be distinguished by the site of the lesion in Broca's area (q.v.) from the "aphasic" agraphia that accompanies *aphasia* (q.v.). *C.S.*

Agreement coefficient. A measure of the degree of agreement among rankings.

$$CA = 100 \left[1 - \frac{\Sigma T - \Sigma B}{\frac{N}{2(H-L)}} \right]$$

where $CA =$ coefficient of agreement, $T =$ the top 50% of rankings, $B =$ the bottom 50% of rankings, $H - L =$ the highest less the lowest possible ranking, and $N =$ the number of cases. *J.M.*

Aha experience (*Ah-ah experience*). The experience of direct understanding or insight that announces or accompanies the sudden occurrence of a solution (often only illusive) in a thought process. *H.-J.A.*

Alalia. Not in common use now, the term means without the ability to talk. This meaning is now carried by *aphasia*, which is divided into many sub-categories; these in turn have no completely accepted system of classification. If it is ever to be of use, the term must be restricted to those mute (aphonic) patients who have no peripheral disturbance of articulation (anarthria), and yet appear to be able to formulate ideas and can communicate them in some other way, such as writing. However, this disorder is at present commonly called *motor aphasia*, or when present in a lesser degree, *verbal aphasia* (see *Aphasia*).   *B.B.*

Alarm function. Function ascribed to the ascending reticular activating system (q.v.). It effects the transition from the relaxed waking condition to a state of general attention (q.v.).   *R.H?*

Alarm reaction(s). 1. (syn. *Alarm calls*). Varying calls elicited in certain species by the presence of a predator, and serving to communicate danger: e.g. "mobbing" calls in birds. **2.** An emergency reaction in the initial phase of general adaptation.   *J.G.*

Albedo. The albedo of a surface is the reflective power of that surface: i.e. the ratio of reflected to incident light. *Albedometer:* a device for measuring albedo.
Bibliography: Berlyne, D. E.: The influence of the albedo and complexity of stimuli on visual fixation in the human infant. Brit. J. Psychol., 1958, *49*, 315–18.   *G.K.*

Alcoholism. No one discipline has yet found any conclusive evidence to indicate the etiology of alcoholism. Physiological study, psychiatric appraisal, psychoanalytic interpretation, and socio-cultural formulation all yield divergent opinions (Yates, 1970, pp. 305ff.). Several additional factors contribute to the equivocation: the variety of disciplines each viewing the topic primarily from its own vantage point; the failure to discover any underlying common premorbid personality structure; the lack of agreement with respect to therapeutic goals and criteria for their evaluation; controversy over whether alcoholism is a disease *per se*, symptom of malaise or product of socio-psychological aberration; and diverse estimates of incidence, depending upon the criteria adopted.

Many non-behavioral scientists (not to mention members of Alcoholics Anonymous) hold that there is some physiologically based deficiency or predisposition to become an alcoholic. This implies that alcoholism is some form of disease entity which a person carries with him until he is cured, a paradigm so far unsubstantiated. Other scientists retain a functional definition of sickness but reject the necessity for a physiological basis. Alcoholism as a disease is then viewed in socio-psychological terms. Certain learning theorists (e.g. Ullmann & Krasner, 1969, pp. 498ff.) totally reject the disease concept and view alcoholism entirely in terms of learning theory. For the psychoanalytically oriented, alcoholism is often a symptom of some underlying infantile fixation to be treated by psychodynamic means. Sometimes it is argued that alcoholism is a symptom which has also become a disease. Others attempt to combine these diverse views into a multi-variate omnibus approach. But, to date, no general factors have emerged that would encompass the hypothesized psychological, behavioral, social, genetic and physiological components of the alcoholism syndrome. It may well be that the concept of alcoholism is little more than a convenient— if misleading—reification.

It is within the above context that the following definition of alcoholism is offered: "Alcoholism is a chronic behavioral disorder manifested by repeated drinking of alcoholic beverages in excess of the dietary and social uses of the community and to an extent that interferes with the drinker's health or his social or economic functioning" (Keller, 1958). But such a definition is by no means universally accepted. Many would object to the emphasis on description and symptomatology at the expense of etiology (for instance, Zwerling & Rosenbaum).

Regardless of orientation, it is necessary to know more about the physiological and socio-psychological effects of alcohol. Naïveté rather than scientific rigor has marked most of the earlier studies in this area (see reviews by Carpenter, 1962; Lester, 1966). More recent investigations (see Franks, 1970) challenge hitherto generally accepted conclusions, such as that of Jellinek & MacFarland (1940) to the effect that the use of alcohol consistently brings about a deterioration in mental performance and that the effect of alcohol is a simple linear function of the amount ingested. Too many studies suffer from being predicated upon single dosages rather than sustained alcohol intake. Although individuals do not differ widely in their brain tissue tolerance to alcohol, there are wide differences among them in their subjective and manifest reactions to alcohol: these cannot yet be satisfactorily accounted for in theoretical terms despite several attempts to do so (Eysenck, 1957; Franks, 1967).

Despite a wide variety of approaches there is hardly more reason now to be optimistic about therapy than there was in the 'forties. The present trend seems to be toward greater sophistication in the conceptualization and execution of treatment models, and recognition of the need to develop multiple interdisciplinary programs, each geared toward different patient populations (see Pattison, 1966; Blum & Blum, 1967). But adequate scientific standards and criteria for program evaluation and comparison are still lacking.

The behavioral approach to alcoholism, with its assumption that deviant drinking behavior is, in part, a conditioned response subject to the same learning principles that determine any other form of behavior, has its clinical origins in the naïve and now outmoded aversive conditioning procedures of the 'forties. Later, experimental psychologists came to the forefront, advocating a scientifically rigorous but clinically not very successful S-R regimen which focused largely upon the drinking per se. Gradually, a more integrative approach developed which extended itself to pertinent aspects of the patient's total life style, including behavioral, biogenetic, developmental and socio-environmental influences (Lazarus, 1965).

If alcohol-drinking behavior is reinforced by its tension-reducing effect, then it becomes necessary to develop other and more acceptable devices for reducing tension, including direct environmental manipulation. Much needed research into the drinking patterns of alcoholics and the rewarding effects of alcohol in a variety of settings is under way (e.g. Mello et al., 1968; Nathan et al., 1970; Vogel-Sprott, 1970).

Behavior is malleable; therefore it is sometimes argued that it should be possible to teach selected ex-alcoholics to engage in limited social drinking with no adverse consequences. This unlikely contention, contrary to generally accepted practice and opinion, has yet to be validated. Perhaps prophylaxis is of greater importance. Prevention can occur at various levels: direct treatment of the alcoholic; early detection of the potential alcoholic with a view to changing the processes in his life that seem likely to lead to alcoholism; and a more general reduction of the personal and societal tensions that, in a complex society, lead to a variety of aberrations, of which alcoholism is but one.

Little is known with confidence about the kind of alcoholic most likely to respond to a particular type of therapeutic regimen. Techniques for sustaining motivation in the recovered alcoholic, and the establishment of alcoholism-training programs for therapist specialists and the technicians who can be trained for much of the work, require attention in the future. Computerized longitudinal studies of potential alcoholic populations through health and sickness, and into the post-sickness stages when appropriate, are desirable.

Investigation of any aspect of alcoholism is now facilitated by the existence of a continually updated documentation program duplicated throughout the world (Keller, 1964).

Bibliography: Blum, E. M. & Blum, R. H.: Alcoholism: modern psychological approaches to treatment. San Francisco, 1967. Carpenter, J. A.: Effects of alcohol on some psychological processes: a critical review with special reference to automobile driving skill. Quart. J. Stud. Alc., 1962, *23*, 274–314. **Eysenck, H. J.:** Drugs and personality. 1: Theory and methodology. J. Ment. Sci., 1957, *103*, 119–31. **Franks, C. M.:** The use of alcohol in the investigation of drug-personality postulates. In: **Fox, Ruth** (Ed.): Alcoholism—behavioral research, therapeutic approaches, 55–79. New York, 1967. **Franks, C. M.:** 1970 Alcoholism. In: **Costello, C. G.** (Ed.): Symptoms of psychopathology: a handbook. New York, 1970, 448–80. **Jellinek, E. M. & MacFarland, R. A.:** Analysis of psychological experiments on the effects of alcohol. Quart. J. Stud. Alc., 1940, *1*, 272–371. **Keller, M.:** Alcoholism: nature and extent of the problem. Ann. Amer. Acad. Polit. Soc. Sci., 1958, *315*, 1–11. **Id.:** Documentation of the alcohol literature. Quart. J. Stud. Alc., 1964, *25*, 725–41. **Lazarus, A. A.:** Towards the understanding and effective treatment of alcoholism. S. Afr. Med. J., 1965, *39*, 736–41. **Lester, D.:** Self-selection of alcohol by animals, human variation, and the etiology of alcoholism: a critical review. Quart. J. Stud. Alc., 1966, *27*, 394–438. **Mello, Nancy K., McNamee, H. B. & Mendelson, J. H.:** Drinking patterns of chronic alcoholics: gambling and motivation for alcohol. Psychiatric Research Report No. 24, American Psychiatric Association, March 1968, 83–118. **Nathan, P. E., Title, N. A., Lowenstein, L. D., Solomon, P. & Rossi, M.:** Behavioral analysis of chronic alcoholism: interaction of alcohol and human contact. Arch. Gen. Psychiat., 1970. **Pattison, E. M.:** A critique of alcoholism treatment concepts with special reference to abstinence. Quart. J. Stud. Alc., 1966, *27*, 49–71. **Ullmann, L. P. & Krasner, L.:** A psychological approach to abnormal behavior. Englewood Cliffs, N.J., 1969. **Vogel-Sprott, Muriel:** Alcoholism and learning. In: Biology and Alcoholism (Chapter 10), 1970, *11*. **Yates, A. J.:** Behavior therapy. New York, 1970. **Zwerling, I. & Rosenbaum, M.:** Alcohol addiction and personality (non-psychotic conditions). In: **Arietti, S.** (Ed.): American Handbook of Psychiatry, Vol. 1, New York, 1959, 623–44.

C. M. Franks

Aldosterone. An adrenal hormone (see *Corticosteroids*) which is one of the so-called mineralocorticoids and is by far the most potent natural hormone in view of its effect on electrolyte concentration. Detailed knowledge of the effective mechanism of aldosterone is not yet available. The amount of aldosterone in urine probably varies according to emotional stress. Little is known of the psychic effects of this hormone in healthy individuals.

Bibliography: Baulien, E. E. & Potel, R.: Aldosterone. Oxford, 1964. **Laragh, J. H. & Kelly, W. G.:** Aldosterone: its biochemistry and physiology. In: **Levine, R. & Luft, R.** (Eds): Advances in metabolic disorders. New York, 1964. **Mason, J. W., Jones, J. A., Ricketts, P. T., Brady, J. V. & Tolliver, G. A.:** Urinary aldosterone and urine volume responses to 72-hr avoidance sessions in the monkey. Psychosom. Med., 1968, *30*, 733–45. **Nowakowski, H.:** Aldosterone. Berlin, 1963.

W.J.

Alexia. Caused by a lesion in a specific cortical area (angular gyrus of the left temporal lobe in the right-handed), alexia is an inability to read because the affected individual has lost any understanding of written or printed characters. Word blindness = sensory alexia. "Aphasic alexia", on the other hand, refers to a loss of expressive speech. See *Aphasia*.   *C.S.*

Algedonic. Concerning the pleasure-pain dimension. The algedonic is one of the three dimensions of the emotions in the typology of W. Wundt (q.v.).   *R.Hä.*

Algesia (syn. *Algesis*). Sense of, or sensitivity to, pain. Subject to considerable variations (subjective attitude, earlier experiences, etc.). Certain diseases and the surgical reduction of nerve fibers can lead to a higher or lower pain threshold (see *Hypalgesia; Hyperalgesia; Pain*).   *M.S.*

Algesimeter (syn. *Algesiometer*). An instrument for measuring sensitivity to pain by means of defined mechanical (calibrated pressure needle, etc.), thermal (heat radiation), or electrical pain stimuli.   *M.S.*

Algolagnia. Sexual arousal by administering or suffering pain. *Active algolagnia:* sadism (q.v.); *passive algolagnia:* masochism (q.v.).   *G.L.*

Algometer. An instrument for recording pain sensitivity in certain individuals. Defined pain stimulation is applied, e.g. by electrical current, and the pain response is determined subjectively by question and answer, or objectively by measuring reflexes or EEG variations. A very problematical method because of the considerable differences in pain evaluation. See *Pain.*   *E.D.*

Algopareunia. See *Dyspareunia.*

Algorithm. An unambiguous, fixed, step-by-step system of operations for solving a class of problems. The sequence of operations is specified in the simplest case. The next operation is usually made to depend on the result of the previous one.   *H.R.*

Alienation. 1. A term in social psychology and clinical psychoanalysis for states causing conflict (self-alienation, loss of a sense of identity, a feeling of depersonalization), the cause of which is traced back to some environmental pressure (e.g. the excessive demands of social or performance standards). As *Entfremdung*, the concept originated with Hegel, who used it to denote the distance between mind and reality.   *W.D.F.*

2. In the Marxian sense, the objectification of labor is the loss of the object of labor, and bondage to it; it is alienation inasmuch as "the more powerful labor becomes, the more powerless becomes the laborer" (Marx, 1964). An ambitious theoretical attempt to reconcile this view with the Freudian theory of the negation of the pleasure principle is to be found in Marcuse (1955), who also offers an analysis of a more progressive stage of alienation under technological rationality, in which alienation masquerades as fulfillment (1964). Skinner's fictional *Walden Two* envisions a proficiently socialized "non-alienated" society of the kind that Marcuse would classify as "pure alienation".

Bibliography: Bensmen, J. & Rosenberg, B.: The meaning of work in bureaucratic society. In: Stein, M. R. (Ed.): Identity and anxiety. New York, 1960. Marcuse, H.: Eros and civilization. Boston, 1955. Id.: One-dimensional man. Boston, 1964. Marx, K.: The economic and philosophic manuscripts of 1844. New York, 1964. Schacht, R.: Alienation. New York & London, 1971. Shepard, J. M.: Automation and alienation. Cambridge, Mass., 1971. Skinner, B. F.: Walden two. New York, 1948.   *J.C.*

Allele (syn. *Allelomorph*). Either of two genes located at one chromosome locus and controlling alternative (Mendelian) characters. In diploid (q.v.) organisms, both alleles can be in the same cell. In characteristics one allele can dominate (dominant-recessive inheritance, e.g. brown or blue eyes dominate in man), or else the characteristic is expressed in an intermediate form (pink pea-flowers in the case of alleles for white and red).

Multiple allele: any of more than two different genes for the same characteristic (e.g. human blood groups).   *H.S.*

Allergy. An abnormal tendency to react to specific stimulus objects and situations which is conditioned by physical (and possibly psychic) hypersensitivity. Among the allergies are hay-fever, asthma, and certain skin irritations. See *Psychosomatics.*   *K.E.P.*

Allochthonous dynamics. According to Gutjahr (1959), in an actualization process, a distinction must be made between motivational (allochthonous, according to R. Bergius) and autochthonous (individual-specific) dynamics. Allochthonous dynamics represents powers which occur as a result of active searching by the individual. Bergius (*Handbuch der Psychologie*, Vol. 1/2, 209) sees autochthonous dynamics as consisting "of the forces occurring through the functional interaction of the limbs". According to Gutjahr, autochthonous dynamics can occur "only in a behavioral process released by a specific motivation". Autochthonous dynamics is subject to the individual behavioral process. For example, all memories that "come suddenly to mind" without any conscious searching are actualized autochthonously.

Bibliography: Gutjahr, W.: Zur Psychologie des sprachlichen Gedächtnisses. II. Über Aktualisierungsdynamik. Z. Psychol., 1959, *163*, 1–108.

H.-J.A.

Allolalia. Meaning a different, unusual or abnormal state of speech. More specific words for particular varieties of speech disorder are favored now. B.B.

Allopreening. One adult bird preens another in answer to preening invitation postures. This social preening among certain families of birds may be compared with similar behaviors in mammals in which one adult cleans another as if attending to its young. Allopreening has the effect of checking aggression, or acting as a form of greeting or courtship, especially in pairing. Tongueplay and so on in humans can be interpreted as derived from analogous mutual preening actions. V.P.

All-or-none law (syn. *All-or-nothing principle*). A functional unit subject to the all-or-none law within the organism reacts to every above-threshold stimulation with a potential ungraded in relation to the stimulus size or intensity. Stimulation produces a maximal response or none at all. The validity of the law in the case of excitable functional units (neurons) in the organism depends on the electrical processes of excitation. The functional membrane surrounding every excitable cell is at first locally depolarized by every stimulus not occurring within the refractory period. This local depolarization, or reduction of resting potential, is reversed by metabolic processes (the sodium-potassium "ion pump") during below-threshold stimulation, but during above-threshold stimulation brings about a considerable ungraded (in relation to stimulus intensity) increase in membrane permeability, and thus a further locally unrestricted depolarization which very quickly leads to a complete (reversible) reversal of membrane potential (see *Action potential*). Examples where the law applies are cardiac muscle contraction and the frequency coding of stimulus-intensity information conveyed to sensory nerves with a uniform amplitude.

Bibliography: Grossman, S. P.: A textbook of physiological psychology, New York, 1967. M.S.

Allport, Gordon Willard. B. 11/11/1897, in Montezuma (Indiana), d. 7/10/1967 in Cambridge (Mass.). An American psychologist specializing in the study of personality who studied at Harvard, Berlin, Hamburg and Cambridge (Eng.) Universities, and returned to teach at Harvard in the Psychology Department, and in the School of Social Relations (from 1924 to 1930, social ethics; and from 1930 to 1966, psychology). For twelve years he edited the *Journal of Abnormal and Social Psychology*. In addition to personality theory and research, Allport concerned himself with diagnostic psychology and prejudice (*The Nature of Prejudice*, 1954). In his main works *Personality: A Psychological Interpretation* (1937), and *Becoming* (1955), he emphasized the individuality, individual world and uniqueness of personality, and represented an image of man dominated neither by the pleasure-pain principle nor by the stimulus-response schema. At the same time Allport recognized the importance of biology and the study of traits. His theory of "functional autonomy" stresses the present moment and the relative unimportance of antecedent (e.g. genetic) explications of behavior. The uniqueness of motives in the adult is emphasized at the expense of the instincts, etc., from which they derive. Allport distinguishes between individual and interindividual, or common, traits (which are, however, only *more like* those of other individuals). Of ultimate importance is the forward striving of the individual self—the "*proprium*" ("propriate striving", "propriate functions")—to ideal self-realization, and the categories of maturity, organization, the new, development, and self-dynamic activity.

Main works: Personality: a psychological interpretation. New York, 1937. ABCs of scapegoating, 1944. The use of personal documents in psychological science. New York, 1947. The nature of prejudice. Reading, Mass., 1954. Becoming: basic considerations for a psychology of personality. New Haven, Conn., 1955. Personality and social encounter, Boston, 1960. A study of values: a scale for measuring the dominant interests in personality (with P. E. Vernon & G. Lindzey). Boston, ³1960. Pattern and growth in personality. New York, 1961.

Bibliography: Allport, Gordon W.: In: Boring, E. G. & Lindzey, G. (Eds): A history of psychology in autobiography, Vol. 5, New York, 1967, 3–25. Hall, C. S. & Lindzey, G.: Theories of personality. New York, 1957.   *G.S.*

Alpha-methyldopa (syn. *Aldomet; Methyldopa; Hydromet*—with hydrochlorothiazide). A substance which leads to the formation of false transmitter substances in adrenergic nervous systems. Alpha-methyldopa inhibits decarboxylase in the conversion of dopa (q.v.) into the noradrenaline precursor dopamine (q.v.), and probably brings about substitution of the natural neurotransmitter noradrenaline by the false transmitter (alpha-) methylnoradrenaline. As a result of this substitution, the CNS and ANS tissues are deprived of noradrenaline. Alpha-methyldopa causes a fall in blood pressure and is used therapeutically against hypertension. The psychic effects of alpha-methyldopa are not clearly established, although depression has sometimes been reported.

Bibliography: Acheson, G. H. (Ed.): Second symposium on catecholamines. Pharmacol. Rev., 1966, *18*, 1–804. Thoenen, H.: Bildung und funktionelle Bedeutung adrenerger Ersatz-transmitter. New York, 1969.   *W.J.*

Alpha movement (syn. *Alpha motion*). M. Wertheimer's term for an illusion of movement: the perception of a change in size when objects otherwise alike are rapidly presented and one object appears to grow or diminish. See *Motion, apparent.*   *V.M.*

Alpha waves (syn. *Alpha rhythm; Berger rhythm*). Slow wave-form variations in potential (0·1–40 Hz) which can be recorded at the cerebral cortex or scalp (electroencephalogram: EEG) by means of electrodes, and which represent the temporal-spatial integral of slow postsynaptic impulses of the cortical cells. EEG waves in the 8–12 Hz (8–12 c/s) frequency range are characterized as alpha waves. When the adult subject is inactive these waves occur predominantly at occipital locations. Alpha waves are inhibited by sensory stimuli and intellectual activity and are replaced by *beta waves* (q.v.) of a lower amplitude. Their frequency drops with a diminution of the level of cerebral excitation (sleep).   *M.S.*

Alternate forms. Two collections of test items so similar that they are taken to be not different tests but versions of the same one.

Alternating method. A term sometimes applied to the use of programmed instruction (q.v.) together with conventional methods.   *H.I.*

Alternative (syn. *Alternative hypothesis*). In statistical hypothesis testing: an hypothesis which represents an alternative to the hypothesis (H_0) which is to be tested. See *Statistics.*   *W.H.B.*

Alternative reinforcement. Reinforcement (q.v.) by fixed temporal intervals between, or a fixed ratio of, responses, according to a *reinforcement schedule.*

Altruism. Unselfish behavior. A collective term for all modes of behavior directed to the advantage of others and not to one's own profit. The conditions for the occurrence and acquisition of altruism have been investigated in recent years. Positive correlations between various tests for unselfishness would seem to indicate the existence of a general personality trait that would accord with the above definition.

Bibliography: Krebs, D. L.: Altruism: an examination of the concept and a review of the literature. Psychol. Bull., 1970, *73*, 258–302. Hartshorne, H., *et al.*: Studies in the nature of character. II: Studies in service and self-control. New York, 1929.   *D.B.*

Amaurotic idiocy. Also known as cerebromacular degeneration or Tay-Sach's disease, this is a rare condition at one time thought to occur only in Jewish families. A degenerative disease of the central nervous system due to a recessive gene. The child is normal at birth and develops normally until the onset of the disease. Symptoms are arrested mental development, muscular weakness and rapidly developing blindness (amaurosis). Death occurs within two years of onset.
                                                               V.K.J.

Ambidexterity. Equal dexterity, or skill, with both hands. How skilled hands are depends, among other factors, on heredity, education and imitation. Usually the right hand is the guiding hand and the left the helping. By practice one can train both hands equally. In work processes requiring a different performance from each hand, ambidexterity proves to be of little use, since rhythmic action is disturbed and there is the danger of accidents. Adj. *Ambidextrous.* See also *Handedness.*   *W.S.*

Ambivalence. The existence of two (possibly contradictory) values, goals or directions. The term was introduced into psychology by E. Bleuler to indicate the simultaneous occurrence of two antagonistic emotions (q.v.) (e.g. inclination and disinclination, hate-love). Affective ambivalence is a general characteristic of schizophrenia (q.v.). *R.Hä.*

Ambivalent behavior. Often the same behavioral situation releases different responses alternating in conflict (q.v.). For instance, if a female wrasse (*Labridae*) appears at a male's nest, this means "strange fish in my preserve" and at first releases attack behavior, until there is an increasing alternation between attack and courtship, and finally the female's readiness for spawning inhibits the male's hostility. The stickle-back's zig-zag dance also arises from ritualized movements indicating both attack and leading-to-the-nest.
Bibliography: Bastock, M., Morris, D. & Moynihan, M.: Some comments on conflict and thwarting in animals. Behav., 1953, *6*, 66–84.   *K.F.*

Amblyopia. Functional dimness of vision in the absence of organic defect. It occurs, e.g., in squinting (strabismus). To avoid double images, the image from one eye is suppressed. This can affect vision in the suppressed eye; if the condition is allowed to persist, it can prove irreversible.   *R.R.*
Toxic amblyopia: a reduction in vision associated with excessive consumption of tobacco, alcohol and certain drugs.

Amenorrh(o)ea. The condition in which a woman's menstrual periods are missed. A distinction is made between *primary* and *secondary* amenorrhea. In the first case, menstruation has never occurred since the beginning of sexual maturation, e.g. because of hypofunction of the primary sex glands (ovaries) or thyroid gland. In the second case, menstruation *has* occurred before cessation, which is normal during pregnancy as a result of placental hormone production and uterine changes, but also occurs as a result of a specific method of birth control using slowly absorbed and long-term effective sexual hormones. Amenorrhea also occurs after cessation of ovarian function during the menopause. In all three cases, secondary amenorrhea is physiological and not indicative of any disease. Secondary amenorrhea may be termed pathological if it is caused by lesions of the pituitary gland, the thyroid gland, or the ovaries. A disturbance of gonadotrophin production (essential for menstruation) by the anterior pituitary can also be psychically conditioned. Amenorrhea is often observed in cases of depression (q.v.), schizophrenia (q.v.), extreme psychological stress (q.v.), and as a result of sexual neuroses and abstinence from sexual intercourse.

Bibliography: Hamburg, D. A. *et al.*: Studies of distress in the menstrual cycle and the post-partum period. In: Michael, R. P. (Ed.): Endocrinology and human behaviour. London, 1968. Sturgis, S. H. *et al.*: The gynaecological patient: a psycho-endocrine study. London, 1962. *G.L.*

Amentia. Synonymous with "oligophrenia", "mental defect", "mental deficiency", "mental subnormality". Tredgold defined amentia as a condition in which the mind has failed to reach complete or normal development. The term is no longer used and since the introduction of the British Mental Health Act (1959) has been replaced by the terms "subnormality" and "severe subnormality". In German the term is sometimes used to designate subacute delirious states. *V.K.J.*

Ametropia. Defective vision resulting from a pathological change in the refractive mechanism of the eye or a non-physiological distance between retina and lens. (See *Myopia; Hyperopia; Astigmatism.*) Not to be confused with *Presbyopia.* *R.R.*

Amnesia. Strictly speaking, the term refers to a complete loss of memory for past events. In practice it is used to refer to a general impairment of memories previously acquired, due to some temporary or permanent pathological process which may be organic or functional. It is not used to refer to an inability to recall past events, the memory for which has faded with time. *R.H.*

Amnesic syndrome. This embodies impairment of memory for recent past events and a marked impairment of the ability to learn new material. Intellectual ability is not otherwise affected, nor are perception and clarity of consciousness. Confabulation can also occur in some cases. Possible causes are alcoholic Korsakoff psychosis, bitemporal lesions, encephalitis and severe head injury, and there may be damage to deep cortical and sub-cortical structures, particularly the mesial aspects of the temporal lobes, hippocampus and mammillary bodies. *R.H.*

Amodal. In contradistinction to *modal completion* (i.e. amplification, gestalt completion, or dynamic gestalt activity), A. E. Michotte defines amodal completion as that with no underlying sensory equivalence between the gestalt to be completed and the completing part. Hence, e.g., the perceived half of a ball is completed to become a total form as the "whole ball". Without amodal completion our limited capacity for perception would not allow us to adjust adequately to our environment. See *Ganzheit.*

Bibliography: Metzger, W. (Ed.): Handbuch der Psychologie, Vol. 1/1. Göttingen, 1966. *V.M.*

Amok. A rare psychiatric disturbance which occurs specifically in Malays, although it has counterparts in other cultures. Patients run wild and become homicidal, the hyperactive state persisting until exhaustion occurs. It may be of epileptic origin or arise from chronic intoxication with cannabis. *D.E.*

Amorphous type. An unemotional, inactive, unobtrusive character.

Amphetamines. Stimulant drugs (psycho-motor stimulants) used therapeutically to combat listlessness, and formerly in clinical use as anti-depressants: e.g. as amphetamine sulfate (Benzedrine), methamphetamine (Methedrine), and dextroamphetamine (dex-amphetamine; Dexedrine) (very often used in psychopharmacological investigations). The amphetamines have peripheral sym-pathicomimetic (e.g. in raising pulse rate and blood pressure) and central effects in the sense of increased arousal of the reticular formation. *Psychic effects:* a feeling of subjective alertness (usually before objective changes in performance), in most cases a positive influence on mood, increase of vigilance (q.v.), often a reduction in reaction times, higher results in clerical tests, and certain simple and complex motor skills tests (e.g. pursuit rotor, q.v.). Effects on motor endurance in certain respects have been demonstrated in soldiers and athletes ("doping"). The effect is dependent on initial condition. The most favorable effects were reported after sleep deprivation and extended psychic stress. Side effects observed are tremor, irritability, loss of appetite, and sleep disorders. Chronic recourse to large doses can produce habituation, dependence and addiction, and even psychotic states (*Amphetamine psychoses*).

Bibliography: Cole, S.: Experimental effects of amphetamine. Psychol. Bull., 1967, *68*, 81–90.

K.-D.S.

Amphetamine-barbiturate mixtures. Compounds which, through the addition of barbiturates, can add physical addiction to psychic drug dependence. Drinamyl ("purple hearts") is one such mixture widely used or abused, especially among the social groups of housewives and teenagers, being (in the United Kingdom) generally legally pre-scribed for the former, and illegally obtained by the latter.

Bibliography: Legge, D. & Steinberg, H.: Actions of a mixture of amphetamine and barbiturate in man. Brit. J. Pharmacol., 1962, *18*, 490–500.

Ampliation. A. E. Michotte has carried out experiments toward an explanation of the perception · of causality. When a self-propelled object *A* begins to move, a pre-viously immobile object *B* is set in motion in such a way that both movements are per-ceived as identical. Ss then assert that *B*'s movement is caused by *A*, even though there is actually no causal relation. Michotte calls this illusion *ampliation*, and postulates an *ampliation structure* underlying the per-ception of causality.

Bibliography: Metzger, W. (Ed.): Handbuch der Psychologie., Vol. 1/1. Göttingen, 1966.   V.M.

Amplification. A psychotherapeutic method (C. G. Jung, q.v.) which—in contradistinction to the Freudian method of *reductio in primam figuram* by free association—attempts to extend and enrich dream-contents in analysis and interpretation by directed associations and by comparison of individual dream motifs with analogous material in the form of images, symbols, legends, myths, and so on. In this way dream-contents are supposed to be revealed in all possible nuances of meaning and in their various aspects.   H.N.G.

Amusia. Loss of the ability of musical expression (*expressive amusia*), or also of the ability to apprehend, remember, and recognize melodies (*receptive amusia*), as a result of a lesion in the cerebral centers (usually the left parietal lobe in right-handed people) responsible for this function.   C.S.

Amylobarbitone (*Amytal; Sodium Amytal*). A barbiturate synthesized in 1923. A hypno-sedative or minor tranquilizer which in animals reduces certain aggressive behaviors and is highly anticonvulsant. Used clinically to treat certain disorders featuring fear and conflict.

Bibliography: Miller, N. E.: The analysis of moti-vational effects illustrated by experiments on amylo-barbitone sodium. In: Steinberg, H., *et al.* (Eds):

Animal behavior and drug action. London, 1964, 1-18.

Amytal. See *Amylobarbitone*.

Anaglyphs. Pictures composed of two similar views partly superimposed as to simulate the *retinal disparity* relationships in normal binocular vision. When viewed through spectacles which allow only one image to be presented to each eye, a *stereoscopic* effect is obtained.   *G.D.W.*

Anagogic. In psychoanalytic psychiatry, the term pertains to moral ideals, or to the spiritual or profound significance of dreams, thoughts, and other behavior. More specifically, C. G. Jung employed the term to denote those tendencies of the unconscious which are morally uplifting (opposite to the Freudian concept of *id*).   *G.D.W.*

Analeptics. Substances which excite or stimulate the control centers of the ANS, or the CNS. If psychic effects are in question, the term *psychoanaleptics*, or *stimulants*, is sometimes used. Among other applications, analeptics are used therapeutically in the case of intoxication from hypnotics (q.v.), or of overdoses of narcotics (q.v.). Some important analeptics are caffeine (q.v.), pentamethylene tetrazol (Cardiazol, Metrazol, Pentetrazol), nikethamide (Coramine), strychnine (q.v.), camphor.
Bibliography: Hahn, F.: Analeptics. Pharmacol. Rev., 1960, *12*, 447-530.   *W.J.*

Anal eroticism (syn. *Anal erotism*). Sensuous preoccupation with defecation and particularly with feces and the gaining of pleasure from the manipulation of feces. See *Anal stage*.   *T.W.*

Analgesia. Insensitivity to pain while in possession of the other senses. Analgesia is always present as well in cases of anesthesia (q.v.). Localized analgesia occurs with mechanical or pharmacological treatment of corresponding pain nerves, or generalized analgesia after the administration of pain-killing drugs (see *Analgesics*). To some extent analgesia can be induced by distraction by means of, or the superimposition of, powerful sensory stimuli such as light or sound, or by the temporary elimination of certain brain centers. Analgesia is often the aim of non-specific pain therapy. However, analgesia is symptomatic of illness when caused by organically perceptible nervous, or psychic, changes.   *E.D.*

Analgesics (syn. *Analgetics*). Psychotropic substances used therapeutically to relieve or remove pain. Narcotics (q.v.) and local anesthetics are not counted among the analgesics. Functional distinctions between the actions of analgesics, say between those affecting central (hypothalamus and thalamus) and peripheral (origin and conduction of pain afference) areas are possible only to a very limited extent, since the etiology of pain (q.v.) and of the interactions of peripheral and central structures are as yet unclear. Among the centrally effective analgesics are the so-called *narcotic analgesics*, which can produce drug addiction or dependence (q.v.): opium alkaloids such as morphine (q.v.) and its natural derivatives methyl morphine (see *Codeine*), dihydrocodeine, diamorphine (see *Heroin*), thebacodone, hydromorphone, etc., and the synthetic opiates (q.v.) pethidine, methadone, propoxyphene, levorphanol, etc. The morphine antagonists nalorphine and pentazocine are analgesics, but are not addictive. The so-called *peripheral analgesics* include the non-addictive and also anti-pyretic and antirheumatic pyrazol derivates (amidopyrine, phenylbutazone), the salicylates (salicylic acid, acetylsalicylic acid) and the aniline derivative phenacetin. In addition to increased stimulation of receptors, psychic factors (as expectations, affects, cognitions) are also involved in the experience of pain. The action of many analgesics consists in the alteration of sensory and psychic elements of pain. When tranquilizers (q.v.) and neuroleptics (q.v.) are used as analgesics, psychic elements are probably affected for the most part. The testing of analgesics in animals centers upon threshold determinations and measurements of the latency and duration of reactions: spinal reflexes, vocalization during (medullar) and after stimulation (thalamic reflexes) serve as pain indicators. Electrical and thermic stimuli are mainly used. In analgesics testing in animals, in addition to post-operative, mainly experimentally induced, states of pain are used: e.g. mechanical stimuli, heat radiation, electrical stimulation of epidermis of tooth pulp, and chemical stimulation (e.g. bradykinin injection). Control substances used for comparison are usually morphine (q.v.) or acetylsalicylic acid. In addition to recording pain waves, physiological (e.g. breathing and heart rates) and psychological variables (e.g. symptom and characteristic word lists, reaction time) are used to test efficacy. Most analgesics can induce a slight drowsiness.

Bibliography: Desstevens, G. (Ed.): Analgetics. New York, 1965. Grimlund, K.: Phenacetin and renal damage at a Swedish factory. Acta med. Scand. (Supp.), 1963, *405*, 1–26. Mellett, L. B. & Woods, L. A.: Analgesia and addiction. In: Jucker, E. (Ed.): Fortschritte der Arzneimittelforschung. Vol. 5. Basle, 1963. Soulairac, A., Cahn, J. & Charpentier, J. (Eds): Pain. New York, 1968. See also under *Morphine*.   *W. Boucsein*

Analgesimeter. A device for measuring the intensity of pain. Marked frontal areas are subjected to short-term heat radiation resulting in pain. Wolf developed a pain scale on the basis of his measurements of such pain waves, with the *dol* (Lat. *dolor*, pain) as the unit (a dol is one tenth of the scale covering the pain sensation induced by the least perceptible stimulus to that at which a further increase in

stimulation induces no further increase in pain). These measurements are used to confirm the effects of analgesics. See *Pain. V.M.*

Anal intercourse. Anal stimulation can have a strongly erotic effect and occasionally induce orgasm. The physiological and psychological mechanisms concerned approximate those of other erotic responses. Novel recording methods have permitted the confirmation of previously unrecognized rhythmic contractions of the external anal sphincter during sexual stimulation (Masters & Johnson, 1966). Individual differences in anal response are due to intensity of varying nerve supply and psychological impressionability. Anal techniques are used in heterosexual intercourse, in sexual play among children, in male homosexual intercourse, as a form of masturbation, or as additional stimulation during normal vaginal intercourse.

Bibliography: Masters, W. H. & Johnson, V. E.: Human sexual response. Boston, 1966.   *G.L.*

Analogy. 1. Analogous behavior is functionally like but genetically different. Morphological and behavioral structures are probably analogous if they occur in species of the same form of life. Very similar patterns of behavior in closely related types are termed *homologous* (see *Homology*). *Analogue:* an organ or structure having an analogous or corresponding function in different species.   *K.F.*

2. Mathematical proportion, or the equality of ratios. *Analogy of Pythagoras:* the proportion between the lengths of strings affording the distinct though concordant notes of the musical scale. **3.** The inferring of further similarities between two things similar in one respect from that one similarity. See *Problem-solving*.

Analogy test (syn. *Analogies test*). A form of test used mainly in intelligence testing. E.g.: *Bird* is to *air*, as *fish* is to ? . . . The testee must find the missing word or select it from a list in order to establish the analogy between the two sets of terms. Such tasks can also use pictures, geometrical figures or numbers. *R.M.*

Anal-sadistic stage. Equivalent to anal stage (q.v.). The term "sadistic" refers to the destructive possibilities increasingly available to a child with the refinement of motor skills and understanding of conditions of power in the environment, but normally less and less invoked by him. *W.T.*

Anal stage. According to Freud, the phase of child development in which the expulsion of feces and the manipulation of the child's own body are of primary interest. On average, the anal stage includes the second and third years of age. In the early part of the stage, the interests of the oral stage (q.v.) are increased by interest in locomotion, and in bodily and manual activity. Among the physical activities is defecation, a function that a child at first performs relatively without control, and on impulse. In social relations, the power aspects of his parents and his own power begin to be perceived and exercised in an all-or-nothing form. In the later anal stage, locomotion and body and hand movements are refined. Defecation comes under the control of the child himself and of his parents. A distinction is made between the exercise of power toward the child's parents, and the perception of their power. In this stage, the child learns to work, to cooperate, to emulate, and to resist. According to Freud, K. Abraham, and Fenichel, regression to the early anal stage can lead to paranoia, masochistic perversions and pregenital conversion neuroses, and fixation; and later regression to the late anal stage can lead to compulsive neuroses, sadistic perversions, and milder forms of pregenital conversion neuroses. Instead of specific neurotic symptoms, a certain deformation of

personality—the "anal character"—can result. Freud includes pedantry, stinginess and frugality among the characteristics of this disordered personality.

Bibliography: Abraham, K.: Selected papers on psychoanalysis. London, 1927. Freud, S.: Three essays on the theory of sexuality. London, ²1962. Id.: Introductory lectures on psycho-analysis. London, ²1929. Id.: Collected papers, Vol. 2. London, 1924-5. Fenichel, O.: The psychoanalytic theory of neuroses. New York, 1945. Toman, W.: An introduction to psychoanalytic theory of motivation. London & New York, 1960. *W.T.*

Analysand. An individual undergoing psychological analysis or psychoanalytic therapy. See *Psychoanalysis.*

Analysis of Reading Ability. Graded tests by M. D. Neale consisting of oral reading passages and three diagnostic tests. Word recognition, comprehension, auditory discrimination, sound production, syllable recognition as well as reading. For 6 to 13 years.

Bibliography: Neale, M. D.: Analysis of reading ability. London, ²1966. *J.M.*

Analysis of variance. See *Variance, analysis of.*

Analytical Intelligence Test (abb. AIT). A group of six primarily non-verbal tests. One of the first group tests (q.v.) designed to determine the intelligence profile for vocational and school counseling. Two forms for use from 12 and 15 years.

Bibliography: Meili, R.: Der analytische Intelligenztest. Berne, 1967. *R.M.*

Analytical psychology. Generally, an approach to the subject-matter of psychology which emphasizes reduction to its elements. Specifically (and more usually), the school of psychoanalytic psychiatry associated with Jung (q.v.), as opposed to that of Freud. Jung's theory of personality is less deterministic than that of Freud, more mystical and sometimes even religious, and he lays much less stress on the role of sex and aggression. In addition to the *personal unconscious*, Jung postulated a *collective unconscious* which contains the latent memories inherited from man's evolutionary past, and is manifested in universal symbols and myths called *archetypes*. Thus the aim of Jungian analysis and dream interpretation is not just to bring memories of personal experiences into consciousness, but to release the creative potential of the collective unconscious. The term is sometimes used to refer to any psychological method which might be termed "analytic".   *G.D.W.*

Analytic(al) situation. The socio-dynamic process between the analyst (therapist) and analysand (patient), which is largely dependent on psychoanalytic techniques. It is based on the following factors: (*a*) The fundamental rule of analysis (the "analytic contract") requires the patient to declare everything that occurs to him during analysis (free association, q.v.), even though he may find it irrelevant, meaningless, painful or impolite; the analyst guarantees absolute discretion and expert assistance. This should produce an asymmetry of verbal communication. (*b*) The analyst tries to eliminate from the therapy all elements regarding his own private sphere, thus enabling the patient to transfer to the analyst his earlier emotional relations and expectations from specific individuals. Of course, in this process the analyst can provide only an approximation to neutrality in the shape of freedom from any "individual valuation". (*c*) The so-called rule of abstinence requires that the patient's wishes—either real (e.g. drugs) or arising out of transference (i.e. those directed onto the analyst and emanating from early childhood) —are not actually satisfied by the analyst. The analyst cannot and should not exert any influence on the actual situation (e.g. in marriage or vocation). This abstinence, or non-fulfillment of wishes by the analyst,

raises affective pressure and hence therapeutic potential during analysis. (*d*) The patient's position on the couch enables the analyst to register every deviation from the agreed posture, and also from verbal communication, as special behavior, or acting-out (q.v.). Lying on a couch also helps induce the regression (q.v.), or return to childhood, which is requisite for analysis. Historically, this phase derives from the carthartic phase, during which hypnosis is used. Modern methods of analysis, which are adapted to the type of analysand, or the particular social situation of the analysis, involve technical modifications (parameters) deviating from the classical analytic situation (analyses of children, adolescents, delinquents or psychotics; analytic group therapy, minor analysis). See *Psychoanalysis*.

Bibliography: Becker, A. M.: Die Behandlungstechnik der Psychoanalyse. In: Schraml, W. J. (Ed.): Klinische Psychologie. Berne, 1970. **Freud, S.:** Standard edition of the complete psychological works. Vols. 1, 5, 16, 17. **Id.:** Group psychology and the analysis of the ego. London, ²1959. **Id.:** Introductory lectures on psycho-analysis. London, ²1929. **Id.:** New introductory lectures on psycho-analysis. London, 1933. **Id.:** An outline of psychoanalysis, ²1959. **Greenson, R.:** The technique and practice of psychoanalysis. New York, 1967. **Glover, E.:** The technique of psychoanalysis. London, 1955.   *W.J.S.*

Anamnesis. 1. All the information regarding an individual's life collected by questioning him or by some other means. The anamnesis is often neglected by psychologists. Developmental psychology, however, would seem unmistakably to show that test results can only be correctly interpreted in conjunction with an anamnesis.   *R.M.*

2. Recollection. In Platonic philosophy, the soul's gradual rediscovery of all that it experienced in a previous existence. Learning as the eliciting of innate knowledge, or its implications.

Anancasm. A compulsive, repetitive behavior pattern.

Anancastia. The anancastic reactive type (or compulsive or obsessive character) is the counterpart of the hysteric reactive type. Anancastia represents a possible initial stage of compulsion neurosis, and is characterized by scrupulosity, minutely ordered, pedantic control over self and others, obsessive cleanliness, fear of loss, hypochondria, obsessive anxieties at inappropriate moments. A rigid form of reaction.

Bibliography: Kretschmer, E.: Der sensitive Beziehungswahn. Berlin, ⁴1966. Id. & Kretschmer, W.: Medizinische Psychologie. Stuttgart, ¹³1970. *W.K.*

Androgen(e)s. Male sexual hormones (steroid hormones) mostly produced in the testes (see *Gonads; Hormones*), and to a lesser extent (where the biological significance is not wholly clear) in the adrenal cortex (see *Corticosteroids*). The most important of the androgens produced by the testes are (in order of significance): testosterone, Δ^4-androstenedione, dehydroepiandrosterone (DHEA: androsterone). Primarily the two last-mentioned hormones are produced by the adrenal cortex, in larger quantities than by the testes. Androgens break down in a complex series of stages to form primarily the biologically inactive 17-ketosteroids (q.v.). Unmodified testosterone (q.v.) is excreted in the urine only in very small amounts.

Bibliography: Dorfman, R. L. & Shipley, K A.: Androgenes. New York, 1956. Rose, R. M.: Androgen excretion in stress. In: Bourne, P. G. (Ed.): The psychology and physiology of stress. New York, 1969. Tonutti, E., Weller, O., Schuchardt, E. & Heinke, E.: Die männliche Keimdrüse, Stuttgart, 1960. *W.J.*

Androgyny. A term for a certain historically and ideologically conditioned conception of a mixture of male and female characteristics: Physically and psychically men and women exhibit characteristics thought proper to the other sex. Androgyny is to be distinguished from *hermaphroditism* (q.v.), which is a somatic dual sexuality, and from *pseudo-*

hermaphroditism, which is characterized by abnormal development of the external sex organs. In androgyny the generative glands are those of a specific sex. More usually a distinction is made between androgyny and *gynandry* (q.v.), in which the former refers to the condition of a male exhibiting female characteristics, and the latter to a female exhibiting male characteristics. Adj. *androgynous*; n. *androgyne.* *D.V.*

Andromania (syn. *Nymphomania*). Pathologically excessive sexual desire (for men) in women with occasional limitation of consciousness (M. Bleuler). *D.V.*

Andropause. Cessation of male sexual activity at some time after sixty years of age. Since the investigations of Kinsey *et al.*, however, it is known that such a definite postulate is untenable. Male sexuality gradually wanes (a process beginning after the culmination point at approximately age sixteen), while its manifestations alter and become more dependent on stimuli. In addition there is a considerable increase in the interindividual variability of frequency of sexual behavior. The problem of the "andropause" is part of the psychology of *aging* (q.v.). See *Aged, sexuality in the.*

Bibliography: Kinsey, A. C., Pomeroy, W. B. & Martin, C. E.: Sexual behavior in the human male. Philadelphia & London, 1948. *G.L.*

Anencephalia. In this condition the cranial vault is deficient and practically the entire brain is missing, with the exception of some nervous tissue at the base of the posterior cranial fossa. Among the possible explanations of this condition are irradiation of the fetus or maternal malnutrition. This condition is incompatible with life. *V.K.J.*

Anesthesia. Insensitivity to all sensory stimuli. Includes loss of pain and skin sensitivity.

Occurs in a generalized form during narcosis (q.v.) and is usually accompanied by loss of consciousness. A result of medical treatment of specific skin areas with novocaine, etc. (*local anesthesia*), or agents to block nerve pathways. *Anesthesiology* is the special branch of medicine concerned with anesthesia and *anesthetics* (or agents producing anesthesia), which first made modern surgery possible; it is practised by qualified specialists.   *E.D.*

Anesthetic type (syn. *Anesthetic*). Insensitive pole of the schizoid marginal temperament according to E. Kretschmer: "Indifferent, frigidly nervous", some "eccentrics", "coldly despotic", "irascible", "fanatic", coldly calculating, egocentric. "Indolent, apathetic, dull loafers"; "loss of immediacy between emotional stimulus and motor response". In individual cases it is arguable whether sympathy is permanently absent or is only masked and responsive to specific motivation. Bibliography: Kretschmer, E.: Physique and character. London, 1925.   *W.K.*

Angiotensin. A tissue hormone (see *Hormones*) with powerful vasoconstrictive action, which raises blood pressure more than any other known substance. Angiotensin leads to increased production of catecholamines (q.v.) from the adrenal medulla and of aldosterone (q.v.) from the adrenal cortex. It is assumed that angiotensin plays a part in the causation of essential hypertonia. A distinction is made between angiotensin I and angiotensin II, the latter being produced biosynthetically from the former.
Bibliography: Page, I. H. & Bumpus, F. M.: Angiotensin. Physiol. Rev., 1961, *41*, 331–90. Peart, W. S.: The rentin-angiotensin system. Pharmacol. Rev., 1965, *17*, 143–182.   *W.J.*

Angle illusion. A more general name for those geometric illusions which induce the perceptual distortion of angles, e.g. *Poggendorf illusion, Lipps illusion* (q.v.).   *C.D.F.*

Anhedonia. An absence of pleasure or pleasantness, usually together with lifelessness—when it is known as the "anhedonic-apathetic" syndrome. Anhedonia in situations which are usually pleasurable can appear as a symptom of depressions (q.v.) of various causation.   *C.S.*

Anima. In Jung's analytical psychology, the *anima* and *animus* represent the opposed personified characteristics and tendencies of the two sexes, which everyone has but to a considerable extent represses from the self-image, and masks with (male or female) sex stereotypes. The anima is one of the archetypes (q.v.) and is the supraindividual soul-image of the woman in the unconscious of the man; according to Jung it is inherited from primordial origins, appears in fantasies or in dreams (see *Dream*), or in a fantasy- or emotionally-conditioned reality, and becomes clear for the individual in the process of individuation (q.v.). Unconscious projection of the anima (or animus) on the female (or male) partner can disarrange the relationship between man and woman by preventing confrontation with the true personality of the other person.   *H.N.G.*

Animal psychology. Nowadays animal psychology is, in some quarters, unjustly considered to be an antiquated study. Ethology, or comparative psychology (q.v.), is the favored objective approach. Various animal psychologists have in recent years more or less suddenly become ethologists. In fact, ethology is not so novel a science as some would think; the term appeared even in 1920 in the zoological dictionary edited by Knottnerus-Mejer, where it was defined as "the theory of animal life and behavior" (Hediger, 1963). Heinroth, the founder of modern ethology, published his fundamental work "Contributions to biology: the ethology and psychology of the Anatidae" in 1910. It is significant that in 1969, i.e. in its twenty-sixth year of publication, the *Zeitschrift für Tierpsychologie* (Journal of Animal Psychology), began to appear with the English sub-title, "Journal of Comparative Ethology". The last major comprehensive work on animal psychology was that of Hempelmann (1926), or, in the Anglo-American world, Maier & Schneirla (1935)—which came out in a new, enlarged edition in 1964. Of course, their *Principles of Animal Psychology* is concerned more with behaviorism (q.v.), the dominant approach in Britain and the U.S.A. for many years, which considers animal or man as a more or less complex stimulus-response mechanism.

Animal psychology has not undergone a harmonious, unilinear development: its two extreme approaches were largely determined by, on the one hand, Cartesianism (the mechanical conception of the animal put forward by Descartes, 1596–1650), and, on the other hand, an excessive anthropomorphization of animals. Even the so to speak "anecdotal" phase of animal psychology which survived until the first half of the twentieth century was characterized by a strong anthropomorphic tendency. This largely subjective trend was then replaced by an experimental, objective method, interested only in measurable behavior.

A dominant tendency at present is to consider man merely as an animal (Hill, 1957; Morris, 1967), and thus to make him part-object of a general ethological approach which discards all interest in subjective, mental phenomena (Eibl–Eibesfeldt, 1967), and ultimately sees him purely in neurophysiological and mechanistic terms (Tinbergen, 1951). The separation of animal and human psychology which was once conventional has disappeared in favor of a comparative psychology. The many achievements of anatomical research and physiology, of the study of problems such as aggression, learning, stress, frustration, etc., have in no small way resulted from comparative studies. The pioneers in the field were Scheitlin (1840) and C. G. Carus (1866). "It is only a step

from comparative anatomy to comparative psychology"; Carus took this step. This method investigates the analogies and homologies, but also the essential differences, between the individual groups.

The history of animal psychology may be seen largely as the history of the struggle against anthropomorphization. Humanization led to such extremes as the ascription to the spider of a high degree of (human) intelligence on account of its web, and to the police dog of something like a sense of duty in the pursuit of criminals, and so on. The anthropomorphic tendency is a persistent source of erroneous judgments, and has its equivalent in animals in zoomorphism. This assimilative tendency results in the consideration, and consequently the treatment, of different species as the same. Hence the circus lion zoomorphizes the tamer, and the dog its master, who in turn anthropomorphizes his dog, gives it a human name, and even talks to it as if it were human, and so on. Anthropomorphism often leads to overevaluation (and just as often to underevaluation) of animal behavior. In order to avoid such errors, at the height of the anecdotal and anthropormorphic stage of animal psychology, Lloyd Morgan's canon was established, which held that an animal act such as the construction behavior of the bee was not to be interpreted in terms of higher mental abilities (intelligence) if it was possible to interpret it in a less complex fashion (e.g. as instinctive- or drive-activity). Bierens de Haan (1935) found it necessary to emphasize, however, that it was not so much a matter of explaining animal behavior as economically as possible, as of searching for the *correct* explanation. Economy of interpretation is advisable not only in the explication of animal behavior, but in situations where it might be said that animals are too often placed in complex experimental devices before their normal behavior has been adequately assessed. Ethology requires a behavioral catalog (or "ethogram": Eibl–Eibesfeldt, 1967) for each species, but no really adequate example has been forthcoming. The two headwords "instinct" and "intelligence" characterize a trend in animal psychology which—especially in Europe—has specified the major points of debate for half a century. The anecdotes used to defend the concept of animal intelligence were justly rejected, but on the other hand modes of behavior were declared to be mythical which were later shown to be actual, as, e.g., in the case of parent beavers carrying their young in their arms (Hediger, 1970). There was an increasing tendency for untrue conceptions (such as the idea that the ostrich sticks its head in the sand) to lead to overcompensation in the form of a complete rejection of any study of animal behavior that might in any way be classed as "anecdotal". The classic example of this process is that of the so-called "thinking" horses and dogs which caused a worldwide sensation before, during and after World War I (Krall, 1914). These seemed to be animals which were able to express human thoughts and complex calculations by tapping. Of course, all these apparent achievements could be attributed to signals from the experimenter. Instead of this highly interesting finding becoming the object of intensive research, the negative conclusion was drawn that human influence should be as far as possible excluded from all experiments which were to be recognized as scientifically responsible. Significantly, it was Koehler (1937) who required that all contact between researcher and animal during the experiment was to be strictly excluded, and that the animal was "to make its own free decisions". In some experiments, Koehler would even read intensively in order to avoid any suspicion of "thought transference". But of course this did not exclude the specifically human element from the experimental situation. Indeed, it is doubtful whether this could be achieved at all, since experimental animal and experimenter are to be conceived of not only as two partners in the action–reaction sense, but as two systems which influence one another in a multitude

of ways. Communications (q.v.) research and semiotics (q.v.) (Osgood & Sebeok, 1965) require us to re-examine the relations between animal and experimenter with all the instrumental and conceptual means now at our disposal. In this regard, the important experiments of Rosenthal (1966) require attention: very often the experimenter finds exactly what he (perhaps unconsciously) expected of the experiment. This applies to some extent to the maze experiments which have been so popular for some decades, and which have been used mainly for the study of intelligence, or learning behavior and orientation. The Dutch animal psychologist Bierens de Haan (d. 1958) declared in 1936: "Since Small's experiments (c. 1900) thousands and thousands of creatures—from children to toads and cockroaches—have negotiated . . . innumerable mazes. In the process, animals have been made to starve and go thirsty, their nerves have been severed and their sense organs extirpated, they have been poisoned and deprived of vitamins, and their memory and ability to transfer what has been learnt to other mazes have been studied. In the U.S.A., especially, in the course of the years the labyrinth has become almost a standard apparatus for all research into animal psychology . . ." . Fischel (1932) has opined that "the results obtained in this way have not been worth the immense time and trouble expended". The multitudinous variations on the maze experiment owe their existence to the desire objectively to measure and compare the psychic performance and capabilities of the most varied individuals and species. The Skinner box (q.v.) (Ferster & Skinner, 1957) is in principle devoted to the same end. Both devices are used essentially to obtain directly comparable, quantitative results. The directly measurable, that which can be represented in terms of scores and curves, is also to the fore in ethology and even approaches the condition of the only valid object of study, even though—as at times in psychiatry—considerable interest is attached to the individual, special case, or exception. Ethology is concerned more with the average, species-specific behavior, and not with the behavior of isolated individuals, which, on the other hand, the animal psychologist makes it his concern (and the zoologist his duty) to understand as far as possible. Ethology is concerned with an understanding of the causes of mechanisms, and applies itself not to individual "personalities" but to innate, average behavior. Tinbergen (1951) understands by "behavior" all the movements of the healthy, undamaged animal. The animal psychologist, however, is also concerned with sick, injured animals and those subjected to extraordinary situations. He believes he is able in a certain sense to achieve a certain "empathy" with the situation of an individual animal, with, of course, the aid of ethological data and precise information about the specific environment—the key to which was provided by von Uexküll (1928). In this sense, the animal psychologist's approach can be quite free from any anthropomorphism, and is wholly subject to critical control. On the basis of his biologically grounded "empathy", he has to be able to offer behavioral prognoses for every animal in every situation. The justness of these predictions is open to precise verification. If in the past the comparative assessment of intelligence, of acquired behavior or learning ability, was in the foreground, in the last few decades the emphasis has been on innate, instinctive, behavior (see *Instinct*). Some special forms of learning occurring as imprinting (q.v.) within quite short periods of time, and which are possibly decisive for the entire later life of the individual concerned, have remained the objects of comprehensive investigations (Thorpe, 1956; Lorenz, 1967; Sluckin, 1964).

The problem of the abovementioned "dichotomous" oppositions of innate and acquired behaviors, i.e. of instinct and intelligence, has been stressed particularly by Lehrman (1953). Instinctive activities were thought of as rigid; learning as plastic. Instinctive behaviors are therefore allowed

taxonomic significance in something like the same sense as morphological characteristics. This idea has to some extent been overstressed. Ultimately, even bones and other organs are not absolutely "rigid", but just as subject to evolution (Hediger, 1963).

For some time, (especially European) behavior researchers (among whom one may number ethologists and animal psychologists) have been divided to some extent into two camps. Bierens de Haan (1940) defended the thesis that instinct and instinctive activities are in a certain sense plastic, whereas the ethologists kept to the idea of absolute rigidity. A kind of compromise was reached by ethologists—especially Lorenz and Tinbergen—in the division of the individual instinctive actions into appetitive behavior and "end" behavior. According to this idea, e.g., the bird's selection of a nesting place and material depends on a plastic appetitive behavior which takes account of specific conditions. The special kind of nest construction, the end activity, on the other hand, is wholly fixed; it occurs in accordance with fixed, innate patterns. Schneirla (Maier & Schneirla, 1964, 643) believes that it is possible to see this decisive dichotomy of rigid innate and plastic acquired behavior as analogous with computer performance: in the inherited ability to carry out a specific behavior, and in the actual behavior in a particular situation, he finds an analogy to what the computer has stored and the task that it has to perform at a particular moment. Contrary conceptions are also proposed currently in view of the human position— for man is to be taken into account in comparative psychology or ethology. The characteristics shared by men and animals were (under Darwin's influence) overemphasized for a long time, whereas whatever separates them was overlooked or belittled.

For centuries, spiritual (intellectual) characteristics were ascribed to animals (even bees). If one is to see the "spirit" as comprising language, history, religion, art, and so on, clearly there are significant and fundamental differences between animal and man. For example, it has never been possible to teach the creatures closest to man, the anthropoid apes, more than three words; they are without the decisive speech center in the brain. Accordingly attempts have been made recently to circumvent this difficulty by using ASL (American Sign Language)— a "deaf-and-dumb" language (Gardner, 1969). However, apart from the area of the human spirit, there are other profound differences between animal and man: e.g. the use of fire. Here there are no transitional stages: either one makes and uses fire, or one has no control over it. A halfway house is inconceivable. The exclusive use of fire has been of fundamental importance in human development.

Lorenz (1967) has recently reaffirmed the spiritual aspect as a human monopoly, and rejected the idea of chance as dominant in the phylogenesis of animals and man. Previously, random mutations and selection were held to be solely responsible for all evolution. Now Lorenz too has stated, in opposition to the assumption of a supreme randomness in biological events: "It is a misconception to believe that 'pure chance' rules over the development of organisms."

Bibliography: Bierens de Haan, J. A.: Die tierpsychologische Forschung, ihre Wege und Ziele. Leipzig, 1935. Id.: Labyrinth und Umweg. Leyden, 1937. Id.: Die tierischen Instinkte und ihr Umbau durch Erfahrung. Leyden, 1940. Carus, C. G.: Vergleichende Tierpsychologie. Vienna, 1866. Eibl-Eibesfeldt, I.: Grundriss der vergleichenden Verhaltensforschung. Munich, 1967. Ferster, C. B. & Skinner, B. F.: Schedules of reinforcement. New York, 1957. Fischel, W.: Methoden zur psychologischen Untersuchung der Wirbeltiere. Handbuch biol. Arbeitsmethoden. Sect. 6. Part D. Leipzig, 1932. Gardner, R. A. & Gardner, B. T.: Teaching sign language to a chimpanzee. Science, 1969, 165, 664–72. Hediger, H.: Wild animals in captivity: an outline of the biology of zoological gardens. London, 1950. Id.: Studies of the psychology and behavior of captive animals in zoos and circuses. London, 1955. Id.: Tierpsychologie im Zoo und im Zirkus. Basle, 1961. Id.: Tierpsychologie und Ethologie. Schweiz. Arch. Neurol. Neurochir. u. Psychiatrie. (Festschrift for M. Bleuler), 1963, 91, 281–90. Id.: Verstehens- und Verständigungsmöglichkeiten zwischen Mensch und Tier. Schweiz. Z. Psychol., 1967, 26, 234–55. Id.: Zum Fortpflanzungsverhalten des Kanadischen Bibers. Forma et Functio, 1970, 2, 336–51. Heinroth, O.: Beiträge zur Biologie, namentlich Ethologie und Psychologie der Anatiden. Vortr. 5. Intern. Ornithol. Congr. Berlin, 1910. Hempelmann, F.: Tierpsychologie vom Standpunkte des Biologen. Leipzig, 1926. Hill, O. W. C.: Man as an animal. London, 1957. Knotterus-Mejer, T.: Zoologisches Wörterbuch. Leipzig & Berlin, 1920. Koehler, O.: Die "zählenden" Tauben und die "zahlsprechenden" Hunde. Der Biologe 1. Munich, 1937. Krall, K.: Denkende Tiere. Leipzig, 1914. Lehrman, D.: A critique of Konrad Lorenz's theory of instinctive behavior. The Quarterly Rev. Biol., 1953, 28, 337–63. Lorenz. K.: On aggression. London, 1966. Id.: Die instinctiven Grundlagen menschlicher Kultur. Die Naturwiss., 1967, 54, 377–88. Id.: Studies in animal and human behavior, Vol. 1. London, 1970. Maier, N. R. F. & Schneirla, T. C.: Principles of animal psychology. New York, ²1964. Morris, D.: The naked ape. London, 1967. Osgood, C. E. & Sebeok, T. A.: Psycholinguistics. Indiana, 1965. Rosenthal, R.: Experimental effects in behavioral research. New York, 1966. Scheitlin, P.: Versuch einer vollständigen Thierseelenkunde. Stuttgart & Tübingen, 1840. Sluckin, W.: Imprinting and early learning. London, 1964. Thorpe, W. H.: Learning and instinct in animals. London, 1956. Tinbergen, N.: The study of instinct. Oxford, 1951. Id.: Social behavior in animals. London, 1953. Id.: On aims and methods of ethology. Z. Tierpsychol., 1963, 20, 404–33. Uexküll, J. von: Theoretische Biologie. Berlin, 1928. Id. & Kriszat, G.: Streifzüge durch die Umwelten von Tieren und Menschen. Frankfurt, 1971.

H. Hediger

Animism. The view that ascribes anthropomorphic behavior (see *Anthropomorphism*) to objects and natural phenomena: i.e. the attribution to inanimate objects of such conditions of human activity as life, thought, free decision, by projecting them outward from the human state. Piaget has described an animistic phase in the development of human intelligence. In E. B. Taylor's anthropological studies of religion, animism in so-called primitive societies is seen as a form of "understanding of the supernatural".

A.T.

Animosity. Strong enmity, hatred or hostility which may be covert or manifest.   G.D.W.

Animus. 1. An intention or objective, or the effort directed toward that end. **2.** A characteristic approach or "animating" principle. **3.** Inspiration. **4.** Hostility—usually deep-set—or animosity. **5.** Jung's term for the archetypal masculinity component of the soul-image: "a very feminine woman has a masculine soul" (see *Anima*). On the whole, "animus" is an imprecise term, and one to be avoided in exact discourse.   *J.M.*

Anisometropia. Unequal sight: the result of inequality of refractive power.   *R.R.*

Anisotropy. Unequal evaluation. We perceive space in a different way from so-called Euclidean space. E.g.: a vertical is often taken as being longer than a horizontal which is objectively of the same length.   *V.M.*

Anklingen (Ger.). The slow entry or occurrence of an emotional process or sensation.
R.Hä.

Anlage (Ger.). *Anlage:* fundamental disposition or arrangement. *Anlagen* are the first recognizable bases of a morphological or functional differentiation toward a specific organ, or a specific characteristic of a self-developing organism. One may speak of the *anlage* of the optic vesicle, etc., but also, in the sense of *disposition*, of an "*anlage* to", say, confirmed rational or emotional behavior. The term is now more usually met with in the German literature in the sense of the first recognizable accumulation of cells basic to a specific developmental process.

In all self-developing individuals of a species (apart from special cases of defective development) the same *anlagen* always appear in the same spatial and temporal sequence. This organizational plan and the spatio-temporal arrangement of further *anlagen* differentiation or development into organs, systems of organs, functions and functional systems, together with the point in time, kind and extent of the interaction of self-developing systems, and the point in time, kind and extent of the influence of external factors on development and its outcome, are passed on from generation to generation by means of elementary, material information units.

The bearers of the specific items of information are known as *genes* (q.v.), though, of course, a gene is an abstraction and the *actual* carriers are *chromosomes* (q.v.); the totality of characteristics transmitted by an individual form of life is known as a *genotype* (q.v.). The totality of structures and functions produced by the interaction of genotype, cytoplasm ("cellsap") and environment is known as the *phenotype* (q.v.). The branch of science concerned with the investigation of the process of reaction chains from the gene to the ultimate, perceptible characteristic is known as *phenogenetics*. *Cytogenetics* (itself a combination of experimental cytology and genetics) is concerned with the structures within the living cell which are bearers and transmitters of inherited information, and with their possible variations. Phenogenetics and cytogenetics now compose the additional study of *molecular genetics*. Genes "mutate" within a population of individuals of the same species at a rate (alteration or loss of function of a gene = gene mutation) which stays the same so long as conditions of life do not change essentially. Therefore every population contains a specific number of *mutations*, or mutant genes (see *Allele*): a result of natural selection. With a change in the environment, therefore, new selection pressures favorable to the preserved mutant forms find already present and "waiting" in the population the allelomorphic material necessary for corresponding, harmonious total alteration of the particular organism.

The question of *innate* and *acquired* characteristics (also in behavior and experience) does not directly concern the nature of the *anlage(n)*, but the phenotypes developing from its (their) interaction with the environment. The dominant phylogenetic selection pressures determine whether a component observable feature of a phenotype will behave in an ontogenetically environment-stable or environment-labile manner. Since selection (q.v.) can directly affect only the phenotype and not the genotype, the degree of environmental stability of a phenotype component is independent of the complexity or relative simplicity of its genetic basis.

Bibliography: Gerking, S. D.: Biological systems. London, 1969. Loewy, A. G. & Siekevitz, P.: Cell structure and function. New York, 1969. Oparin, A. I.: Genesis and evolutionary development of life. New York, 1968. Sinnott, E. W., Dunn, L. C. & Dobzhansky, T.: Principles of genetics. New York & London, ⁵1958.

P. Leyhausen

Anomaloscope. A device (W. Nagel, 1907) for presenting color mixtures in order to measure color sense and deficiency. The instrument consists essentially of a drum and a scale of 73 gradations. The test color is sodium yellow (light), which may be varied in intensity and is compared with the color mixtures in two approximate fields. If 40 gradations of lithium red are mixed with 33 gradations of mercury green (Rayleigh equation) in one field, and this mixture is set against 14 gradations of sodium yellow in the other field, a subject with normal vision will experience no difference in color and intensity.   R.R.

Anonymization. The process of reification (objectification) and reduction of the intensity of socio-emotional interpersonal contacts which is characteristic of modern highly-organized, bureaucratized industrial societies under the division of labor. Anonymization is characterized by a loss of individual distinctiveness and by a feeling of personal alienation in view of the increasing urbanization that accompanies intensified horizontal and vertical mobility of the population.   W.N.

Anop(s)ia. Blindness even though the retina is intact: caused by damage to the optic pathway. A lesion of the *fasciculus opticus* (between the retina and the optic chiasm) leads to unilateral anopia; a lesion of the optic tract (between the optic chiasm and the optic cortex) leads to hemiopia (q.v.), or blindness in half of the visual field.   R.R.

Anorexia nervosa. A term (proposed by Sir William Gull, 1874) for a syndrome the main feature of which is a considerable reduction or a loss of appetite and hunger. A neurotic or psychosomatic symptom, especially in adolescent girls though it also occurs as a reaction in poor eaters among children. No primary organic findings, but frequently secondary disturbances of inner secretory organs.   F.-C.S.

Anorgasmy (syn. *Anorgasmia*). Absence of the orgasmic phase in the sexual reaction cycle. Primary anorgasmy can occur in any form of physical sexual stimulation capable of leading to orgasm, including masturbation (q.v.) and anal intercourse (q.v.), both in heterosexual and homosexual activity. Primary anorgasmy seldom occurs in men but quite frequently in women. Apart from anatomical and neurophysiological defects, incompatible sexual attitudes in the partners and/or faulty imprinting (q.v.) and/or socio-cultural conditioning may be responsible.

Physiological pain accompanying anorgasmy, sometimes after coitus interruptus (q.v.), or in the woman after premature ejaculation in the man, has been reported.

G.L.

Anosmia, Absence of the sense of smell after traumatic brain damage, in tumors of the frontal lobes, the olfactory sulcus and the sellar region, also after diseases of the peripheral olfactory apparatus.   R.R.

Anosognosia. Non-recognition of a state of sickness or disease in one's own body (e.g. a patient does not recognize that he is paralyzed on one side). Anosognosia occurs in a combination of any cerebral locus with a diffuse brain lesion and is diagnostically non-specific. It is often psycho-dynamically interpreted as a defense mechanism (q.v.), in the sense of a refusal to recognize actuality.
C.S.

Anoxemia, cerebral. A reduced supply of oxygen to the brain caused by anoxemia = an oxygen deficiency in the arterial blood. The brain (q.v.) is the most sensitive organ in terms of reaction to oxygen deprivation, so that even slight general oxygen deficiency in the blood can lead to deprivation symptoms such as lassitude, loss of discriminative ability, euphoria and loss of restraint. High-degree anoxemia leads to loss of consciousness, and after approximately 3 to 5 minutes to irreversible brain damage.
Anoxia: deficient supply of blood to the tissues. See *Brain pathology.*   *E.D.*

Antagonists (syn. *Antagonistic muscles*). Every physical movement represents a play of agonists and antagonists, an interaction controlled by the pyramidal system. The antagonist of an extensor would be a flexor, and vice versa.   *E.D.*

Anterior cerebrum. See *Forebrain.*

Anthropocentrism. A doctrine or theory which elevates man as the center of the world and sees the well-being of humanity as the ultimate purpose of things. This idea is related to the geocentric view of the universe, as represented by, say, Ptolemy, the Fathers of the Church, and Scholasticism. Since the Renaissance, however, thinking has concentrated more upon man himself than upon his relation to the supernatural. The anthropocentrism of

the Italian philosopher Vico (1668–1744) and that of the French materialists of the eighteenth century were the forerunners of anthropology (q.v.). With Ludwig Feuerbach and Karl Marx, man became the only object and goal of philosophy. Scheler, Jaspers, Heidegger and Sartre are essentially concerned with man, the midpoint of their philosophies. Man is the absolute, even though imperfect and difficult to conceive adequately; hence the interplay between the investigation of his essence (nature) and the elucidation of his existence (freedom).   *M.R.*

Anthropology. Anthropology studies man as a living, social being with certain habits, who exists in a context of human interrelations, makes tools, institutions and laws, forms values and beliefs, strives for cultural identity, and is subject to forces beyond his control. In order to attain to the status of a scientific discipline (i.e. in order to apprehend its object systematically, and to describe and explain it by means of appropriate concepts), anthropology must clearly determine the area of application of its methods, and its possible systems of reference. It includes a variety of fields of research, which (except for morphological anthropology) have as their common concern the observation of man in an optimally inclusive and direct fashion in all the complexity of his actual existence, while concentrating on differences and variations rather than on human identity as such.

Although anthropology is as old as philosophy, it has used scientific methods only since the nineteenth century; its present individual areas of research have been distinct fields only since the turn of the century. These areas are related by the common pursuit of objectivity and a more exact understanding of human existence as a whole whose every part functions in conjunction with all other parts, and not as a mere sum of component elements.

The dominant theory in nineteenth-century anthropology was that of evolution,

63 ANTHROPOLOGY, PSYCHOLOGICAL

which tended to ascribe to every human society a unified form of development on the Western model. This doubtful simplification nevertheless led to a concern for scientifically respectable explication (Herbert Spencer; E. B. Taylor). Similarly, the various diffusionist theories compensated for their excessive atomism with highly proficient observations (H. Graebner; W. Schmidt). At quite an early stage in modern anthropology, a primary distinction was made between natural-scientific, or morphological, and social or cultural anthropology (q.v.), which arose from the difference in perspectives (man as a biological "life-form" as distinct from man as a "social being") and in the methods used (comparative/differential; extensive/intensive).

Natural-scientific anthropology studies man's origin and the causation and mechanisms of his biological development—his "specificity"; and tries—using morphological, genetic and environmental criteria—proficiently to define the notion of "race" (q.v.), geographically conditioned variations, and so on.

Social and *cultural anthropology* (and also ethnology), as developed in the twentieth century, is a theoretical discipline which assimilates the evidence of ethnography (monographic and empirical representation of the specific nature of individual and, particularly, archaic social forms), palaeontology, archaeology and history, and attempts the extremely difficult task of a comparative study of these discrete materials. In a search for greater clarity, modern ethnology examines the structure and function of social systems and constructs models for this purpose. Two main tendencies are apparent: (*a*) that orientated to *sociology* (social anthropology), which examines human interrelations in the context of social structures (functionalist and structuralist tendencies: E. Evans-Pritchard; A. R. Radcliffe-Brown; B. Malinowski; E. Durkheim; M. Mauss; C. Lévi-Strauss); (*b*) that orientated to *psychology* (cultural anthropology), which studies the

different manifestations of culture in regard to the relation between the individual and cultural schemata (R. Benedict; M. Mead; A. Kardiner). It distinguishes between "culture" as a number of collective and unified schemata of behavior and belief) and "society" (as a special form of cultural schematization) when studying its object in its dynamic course of development (cultural variations, acculturations: R. Linton; M. Herskovits; E. Lebach; G. Balandier).

Bibliography: Balandier, G.: Phénomènes sociaux totaux et dynamique sociale. Cahiers d'histoire mondiale, 1961, 6, No. 3. Benedict, R.: Patterns of culture. Boston, 1934. Comas, J.: Manual of physical anthropology. Springfield, 1960. Durkheim, E. & Mauss, M.: Primitive classification. London, 1963. Evans-Pritchard, E. E.: Nuer religion. Oxford, 1956. Herskovits, M. J.: The economic life of primitive people. New York, 1940. Kardiner, A.: The individual and his society. New York, 1939. Leach, E. R.: Rethinking anthropology. London, 1961. Lévi-Strauss, C.: Structural anthropology. New York, 1963. Lowrie, R. H.: An introduction to cultural anthropology. New York, 1940. Mauss, M.: Manuel d'ethnologie. Paris, 1947. Radcliffe-Brown, A. R.: Structure and function in primitive society. London & Glencoe, Ill., 1952. *M.-J. Borel*

Anthropology, psychological. Anthropology attempts a summary approach to the various aspects of human reality: *synchronically*, at a given moment; and *diachronically*, in their process of development. The pertinent problems can be considered from a *positive* viewpoint which takes into account man's physical, biological, psychological, social and cultural characteristics. But a *philosophical* viewpoint is also possible which, according to Scheler, takes up a position midway between the natural sciences and metaphysics, and studies the nature and meaning of man and culture.

Anthropology in its physical, social, cultural and philosophical aspects was enriched in the nineteenth century by the addition of psychological anthropology, which emerged from the development and mutual influence and interpenetration of general psychology, social psychology, sociology, cultural anthropology, and social anthropology. Its field is the *relations between personality and culture*, which are the object of multifarious investigations. These are concerned with the interdependences between (*a*) differences in the areas of perception, emotion, motivation, intellect, and above all the various aspects of psycholinguistics and nurture and education, in the development of attitudes, essential traits and structures of temperament, character and personality, and (*b*) different cultures, societies and institutions, especially in regard to language, myths, stereotypes, beliefs, sexual life, and social and familial structure, and the nature and modes of child care and treatment. Numerous examples may be found in Hsu (1961), who was the first to use the term "anthropological psychology", and other authors (see bibliography).

Social and cultural anthropology (q.v.) have always shown interest in psychological themes—as is apparent, e.g., in the studies that came from the Torres Strait expedition of 1898 and later investigations (B. Malinowski, F. Boas, M. Mead, E. Sapir, etc.). The attempts (above all those of a psychoanalytical bent) to ground a theory of man in the psychological processes of ego formation and in the unconscious elements of personality, or at least to give a psychological basis to the origin of various beliefs, rites, customs and institutions, are well known. A related effort is that of R. Benedict, who sees the particular aspects of a national culture as determined by the personality characteristics of a nation.

The reverse attitude is more frequently met with: i.e. that which stresses the formative influence of a national culture on the personality of its component individuals. The thesis of R. Linton and A. Kardiner is important in this regard: Each culture determines a *basic* or *modal* personality, which then becomes the field of operation of further individual differences. The decisive influence of cultural patterns in the various stages of development in the course of which personality is constituted, is the central theme of modern psychological anthropology, especially in its psychoanalytical and structuralist emphases.

The strongest tendency in psychological anthropology is a concern to use empirical, and as far as possible experimental, methods to examine the interdependences between psychological and anthropological variables. It takes two main directions: (*a*) the intercultural verification of psychological hypotheses; (*b*) the development of theories of human behavior, which in an *empirically verifiable* way integrate the psychological, sociological and historical aspects of human social behavior within a community.

The anthropological perspective of psychology proper should also be mentioned. Even in the first treatise on psychology, the *De Anima* of Aristotle, the psychic is defined as the psychosomatic behavior of the *whole man* (403 a). One of the first texts in which the word "psychology" occurs is entitled "Anthropological Psychology" (*Anthropologische Psychologie*, by O. Casmann. Hanau, 1594). This trend is emphasized nowadays. Even after the split between the physical and the psychic (Descartes), retained in the theoretical parallelism and methodological introspectionism of the first stage of experimental psychology, the interest in anthropology was still apparent (e.g. the folk psychology (q.v.) of W. Wundt). Contemporary psychology has once again made human *behavior* its object.

Bibliography: Benedict, R.: Patterns of culture Boston, 1934. Hsu, L. K.- Psychological anthropology Homewood, Ill., 1961. Hunt, R.: Personalities and cultures: Readings in psychological anthropology. New York, 1967. Kardiner, A., *et al.*: The psychological frontiers of society. New York, 1945. Kluckhohn, C., Murray, H. A. & Schneider, D.: Personality in nature, society and culture. New York, 1953. Kroeber, A. L.: Anthropology today. New York, 1965. Lindzey, G. (Ed.): Handbook of social psychology. Cambridge, Mass., 1954; ²1968. Tyler, S. A.: Cognitive anthropology. New York, 1969. *M. Yela*

Anthropometry. The scientific method of comparative measurement of the skull, externally and internally (craniometry), of individual bones (osteometry), and other structures of the human body. Used to some extent in anthropology.   *M.S.*

Anthropomorphism. The tendency to interpret the manifestations of the animate and inanimate environment analogously to human behavior and experience. Anthropomorphism is not only a feature of mythic thinking (see *Myth*), but in the history of science played a part in animal psychology, and was only overcome by the proficient methodology of comparative psychology (q.v.) and behaviorism (q.v.).   *W.Sc.*

Antibiotics. Substances derived as natural products of various micro-organisms (bacteria, molds), and which more or less selectively inhibit or block the growth of other micro-organisms. They are used in the treatment of infectious diseases. The best-known antibiotics are penicillin and streptomycin. Antibiotics have become of especial interest to psychologists since the discovery of the significance of ribonucleic acid (RNA) (q.v.) for learning and retention, and of the way in which antibiotics affect the synthesis of RNA and protein. Animal experiments (rats, goldfish) would seem to show that, e.g., actinomycin D, puromycin and acetoxycycloheximide block long-term memory, whereas learning and short-term memory remain unaffected. The way in which antibiotics act in influencing retention is not yet clear. In particular it is still questionable whether it is a question of specific disturbances of retention or of reproduction. Investigations in which disturbances of retention caused by puromycin were removed by other substances would seem to support the disturbed reproduction theory.

Bibliography: Agranoff, B. W., Davis, R. E., Lim, R. & Casola, L.: Biological effects of antimetabolics used in behavioral studies. In: Efron, D. (Ed.): Psychopharmacology 1957–1967. Washington, 1968.

Deutsch, J. A.: The physiological basis of memory. Ann. Rev. Psychol. 1969, *20*, 85–104.   *W.J.*

Anticholinergics. Substances which block the action of acetylcholine (q.v.) and hence (peripherally and autonomically) parasympathetic activity (parasympathicolytic). The most important substances with an anticholinergic effect are atropine (q.v.) and scopalamine (q.v.). Many psychopharmaceutical drugs which are used for therapeutic purposes, for instance against depressions (see *Antidepressives*) or spasms (see *Spasmolytics*), have unpleasant side-effects (e.g. dryness of the mouth). Anticholergic drugs are frequently used as experimental stimuli in investigations of learning in animals, in which they retard habituation to new stimuli.
Bibliography: Bignami, G.: Anticholinergic agents as tools in the investigation of behavioral phenomena. In: Brill, H. (Ed.): Neuro-psycho-pharmacology. Amsterdam, 1967. Carlton, P. L.: Cholinergic mechanisms in the control of behavior. In: Efron, P. (Ed.): Psychopharmacology 1957–1967. Washington, 1968.
                                                     W.J.

Anticholinesterase agents. See *Cholinesterase inhibitors.*

Anticipation. 1. Mental adjustment to a coming event, etc. **2.** A schematic presemblance of the solution in problem solving (Selz).   *H.-J.A.*

Anticipation error (syn. *Anticipatory error*). A term of C. L. Hull's. In serial learning experiments, Ss have learned a series of nonsense syllables. The fact that they repeat some syllables prematurely, i.e. before the right syllables according to the series, is ascribed by Hull to anticipation of the later syllables. In general, if a response in serial learning occurs earlier than it should, it is an anticipation error which confirms the existence of an *anticipation response.*
Bibliography: Hull, C. L.: Essentials of behavior. New Haven, Conn., 1951.   *V.M.*

Anticipation neurosis. In Kraepelin's theory, excessive anxiety about the outcome of a future experience is said to disturb the normal mental attitude to that experience, or in the case of certain basic activities such as speech, writing, and so on—to produce a partial response, or even to block the intended response. The latter is usually known as an *anticipation* (or *anticipatory*) *response*. *J.M.*

Anticonvulsives. Agents which reduce or prevent convulsions. In high doses hypnotics and tranquilizers can act as anticonvulsant drugs in tetanus and status epilepticus.

Bibliography: Irwin, S.: Anti-neurotics: practical pharmacology of the sedative-hypnotics and minor tranquilizers. In: Efron, D. H. (Ed.): Psychopharmacology 1957–1967. Washington, 1968. *E.L.*

Antidepressives (syn. *Antidepressants*). The antidepressive drugs are used to treat depressions (q.v.) of varying etiology. Chemically, antidepressives are divided primarily into the tricyclic iminodibenzyl derivatives (e.g. imipramine [G22355, Tofranil], q.v.; desipramine [Pertofran]; trimipramine [Surmontil]), the dibenzocycloheptene derivatives (e.g. amitriptyline [Tryptizol, Laroxyl, Elavil]; nortryptaline [Aventyl, Allegron]), and the dibenzodiazepine derivatives (e.g. dibenzazepine), which may be classed together as thymoleptics in the narrower sense in contrast to the thymeretics—represented mainly by the monoamine oxidase inhibitors (q.v.) (MAO inhibitors: e.g. iproniazid [Marsalid]; nialamide [Niamid]; isocarboxazid [Marplan]). Lithium is also used for prophylaxis of phasic endogenous depressions. The therapeutic effects of antidepressives are broadly classed as alleviation of mood, increase of drive and removal of anxiety or reduction of agitation. Anxiety-reductive and stimulant effects are largely excluded in the case of only one agent (Pöldinger), whereas improvement of mood can be brought about in combination with the other two aims (thymoleptic or thymeretic effect). The mechanism by which these effects are obtained is as yet inadequately explained. Animal experiments with the tricyclic antidepressives, which are particularly relevant clinically, showed symptoms of central inhibition as well as central excitation (Sigg). Biochemically, anticholinergic and noradrenaline-potentiating effects are to be observed simultaneously in this group. MAO inhibitors effect a rise in the concentration of intraneuronal *biogenic amines* (q.v.). Substances which have only anticholinergic or noradrenaline-potentiating effects are shown to be unsuitable for reduction of depressive moods (Davis *et al.*). Lithium also affects noradrenaline concentration, though on another level: mania can be alleviated at the same time as phasic depressions are prevented (Schou). The differentiation of biochemical action and indication of different types of preparations permit conclusions to be drawn on the biochemical basis and the etiological differentiation of depressions (Davis *et al.*). Tests of the specifically antidepressive action of antidepressant agents on healthy individuals are difficult to carry out, since the requisite initial emotional conditions are not so obviously present, or cannot be induced. Nevertheless, it would seem possible to demonstrate differences in effect dependent on habitual tendencies to depression (recorded by means of questionnaires). Information on effects in healthy individuals obtained by controlled experiments are available only for imipramine (q.v.). Overdosage with the tricyclic antidepressives can produce a form of delirium (q.v.).

Bibliography: Davis, J. M., Klerman, G. L. & Schildkraut, J. J.: Drugs used in the treatment of depression. In: Efron, D. H. (Ed.): Psychopharmacology 1957–1967. Washington, 1968. Pöldinger, W.: Vergleichende Untersuchungen antidepressiv wirkender Psychopharmaka an gesunden Vpn. In: Bente, D. & Bradley, P. B. (Eds): Neuro-Psychopharmacology. Amsterdam, 1965. Schou, M.: Lithium in psychiatry—a review. In: Efron, D. H. (Ed.): Psychopharmacology 1957–1967. Washington, 1968. Sigg, E. B.: Tricyclic thymoleptic agents and some newer antidepressants. In: Efron D. H. (Ed.): Psychopharmacology 1957–1967. Washington, 1968. *P.D.*

Antiemetics. Drugs used to treat the tendency to vomit (hyperemesis), and motion and sea sickness (nausea). The various antiemetics have little in common apart from the intended therapeutic effect. Many of them are anticholinergics (q.v.) (e.g. scopalamine, q.v.), antihistamines (q.v.), or phenothiazines (q.v.). The psychic effects of antiemetics vary according to their chemical structure; however, most of them have a sedative effect and can influence performance.

Bibliography: Brand, J. J. & Perry, W. L. M.: Drugs used in motion sickness. Pharmacol. Rev., 1966, *18*, 895–924.   *W.J.*

Antihistamines. Substances which block or reduce the effects of *histamine* (q.v.). The antihistamines are not entirely histamine-antagonizing (especially questionable in the CNS); they are for the most part substances which reduce or inhibit allergic and anaphylactic reactions and the fall in blood pressure after the application of histamine. This occurs with most antihistamines by means of a blocking of the histamine receptors; with others by means of an inhibition of biosynthesis or a biological inactivation of histamine (e.g. potentiation of the enzymes which inactivate histamine). Chemically and pharmacologically, the antihistamines belong to different groups: ethanolamine (e.g. diphenhydramine [Benadryl]), ethyldiamine (e.g. tripelenamine [Pyribenzamine]) and propylamine (e.g. pheniramine). Antihistamines with other primary therapeutic applications are, e.g.: anticholinergics (q.v.) (scopalamine, q.v.), spasmolytics (q.v.), phenothiazine (q.v.) (e.g. piomethazine), and drugs used to control Parkinsonism. Most antihistamines have central effects. Sedative effects occur even with therapeutic doses. Influences on performance are difficult to demonstrate (reaction time, concentration tests).

Bibliography: Handbuch der experimentellen Pharmakologie. Vol. 18. Part 1: Histamine. Its chemistry, metabolism and physiological and pharmacological actions. Berlin, 1966. Wagner, H. J.: Überprüfung des Leistungsverhaltens unter dem Einfluss verschiedener Antihistaminica. Arzneimittel-Forsch. (Drug Res.), 1962, *12*, 1065–1070. Turk, J. L.: Immunology in clinical medicine. London, 1969.   *W.B.*

Antihypertensives. Antihypertensive drugs are substances which reduce blood pressure (hypertension). There are several agents which can be called antihypertensive; they bring about a fall in blood pressure (q.v.) by means of very different physiological mechanisms (e.g. peripheral, central). In addition to their required specific action, most antihypertensive drugs have numerous other effects, e.g. on the CNS, with the corresponding psychic changes (subjective sedation and influence on performance). Many antihypertensives belong to the sympathicolytics (q.v.), the ganglionic blocking agents (q.v.), or the reserpine (q.v.) group; some are also parasympathicomimetics (q.v.).

Bibliography: Green, A. F.: Antihypertensive drugs. Advances in pharmacology, 1962, *1*, 161–225. Schlittler, E.: Antihypertensive agents. New York, 1967.   *W.J.*

Anti-Semitism. Dislike of Jews. Measured by (among other rating techniques) the Anti-Semitism Scale reported on by Adorno and others (See *Authoritarian personality*). Underlying trends of the anti-Semitic ideology would seem to be: stereotypy; rigid adherence to middle-class values; high moral estimation of one's own group; desire for the power and dominance of one's own group; fear of sensuality and immorality, of overthrow and victimization; a desire to strengthen group-divisive phenomena. The connection between (anti-Semitic) prejudice and emotional instability has been confirmed. See *Authoritarianism; Prejudice; Stereotype.*
                                                          J.G.

Anxiety. *Origins of the concept.* Like its Latin original *anxietas*, anxiety commonly connotes an experience of varying blends of uncertainty, agitation and dread. The

Latin usage included a suggestion of strangulation which is sometimes implied in the present-day connotation. The term was introduced into psychology when Freud (1894) described the anxiety neurosis as a syndrome distinct from neurasthenia. But its acceptance in the discipline did not become general until more than forty years later. May (1950) has noted that, outside the publications of psychoanalytic writers, anxiety was not even listed in the indexes of psychological books written before the late 1930s.

In his earliest formulations, Freud considered anxiety to be the outcome of repressed somatic sexual tensions (*libido*, q.v.). He believed that libidinal images that were perceived as dangerous were repressed; and that the libidinal energy was cut off from normal expression and transformed into anxiety. He later replaced this notion with the much broader conception of anxiety as a signal for danger; distinguishing now between objective anxiety (fear) and neurotic anxiety, depending on whether the danger came from the outside world or from internal impulses (Freud, 1936). Freud's followers in the course of the years proposed many modifications of his views. For example, May (1950) characterized anxiety as "the apprehension cued off by a threat to some value the individual holds essential to his existence as a personality", and Sullivan (1953) referred to it as the state of tension arising from the experience of disapproval in interpersonal relations.

2. *An operational definition.* All the foregoing formulations, and many others like them, seem to be attempts to capture the essence of an assumed "entity" called anxiety. But no yardstick is available to indicate which, if any, of them is "right". In any event, none of them is precise enough to be of use in scientific investigation. Only by an operational definition can such objections be circumvented. According to one fairly widely used definition, anxiety is the autonomic response pattern characteristic of a particular individual organism after the administration of a noxious stimulus (Wolpe, 1952). The pattern varies from one individual to the next. A *noxious stimulus* is an extrinsic agent (such as an electric current) that produces local tissue disturbance which the subject may report as pain, and which, if strong enough, can produce tissue damage. The unconditioned response to noxious stimulation generally has both motor and autonomic components. Unconditioned autonomic responses similar to those produced by noxious stimulation can also be evoked by other agents; for example, by very intense auditory stimuli and by ambivalent stimulus situations—which are situations in which strong and incompatible action-tendencies are simultaneously aroused. Fonberg (1956) has impressively demonstrated the essential similarity between the effects of ambivalent stimulation and those of noxious stimulation.

When unconditioned anxiety responses are evoked they can be conditioned to "neutral" stimuli that impinge on the organism at about the same time. The conditioned generally resembles the unconditioned anxiety response, though exceptions have been noted (Hein, 1969). The anxiety that conditioned stimuli evoke is in turn conditionable to other stimuli. Because of serial conditionings, most organisms, and certainly most human beings with "normal" histories, come to have anxiety evocable by a great many conditioned stimuli before reaching adulthood. However, the extent of such conditioning is controlled by various innate factors (Eysenck, 1957). The operational definition demands in every case a specification of the antecedents of the emotional response. If this is done, there is clearly little point in the distinction proposed by Freud between fear and anxiety—especially since the determination whether the controlling stimuli come from within or without must often be left to the subject. In any case, to vary the name of the response according to its antecedents can only lead to confusion. Another distinction between fear and anxiety that is commonly promulgated is that the former is episodic and the latter chronic. For this to be operationally usable, a temporal dividing line would have to be established; but the inevitable arbitrariness of this would severely limit its usefulness.

3. *The topography of anxiety responses.* The autonomic events that make up an anxiety response are predominantly functions of the sympathetic division of the autonomic nervous system. Common manifestations of the sympathetic response are: increased heart rate, raised blood pressure, increased respiratory rate, sweating of the palms, dilatation of the pupils, and dryness of the mouth. Some parasympathetic responses may also participate in the anxiety pattern; common ones are diarrhea, nausea, vomiting, and frequency of urination. Studies by Hess (1947) suggest the additional occurrence of diffuse autonomic effects manifested by increased general irritability. This is possibly related to the general rise in muscle tension that is ordinarily so constant an accompaniment of anxiety (Jacobson, 1938). Whereas the combination of autonomic events constituting the anxiety response varies greatly from one individual to the next, it is quite consistent within individuals. Nevertheless, it may change for the individual if he is subjected to new conditioning events that add new components to the constellation, or through selective operant conditioning (Miller Banuazizi, 1968) that may change the balance of response elements already present. At least some autonomic responses are subject to operant conditioning; that is, they can be strengthened by arranging for them to be followed by rewards, and weakened by withdrawing the rewards. In one set of experiments (DiCara & Miller, 1968), cardiac acceleration was conditioned in one group of animals, and cardiac deceleration in another, by relating the given response to the "reward" of escape or avoidance of shock.

The autonomic responses characteristic of anxiety have been the subject of steadily increasing research efforts in recent years. This has been inspired by the intrinsic interest of the subject as well as by the central role of anxiety in most neuroses. It has been shown in both animal and human subjects that anxiety responses can be specifically conditioned to selected stimuli, and deconditioned. Deconditioning is usually accomplished by counter-conditioning, which depends on inhibiting the anxiety by a response incompatible with it. (See *Neuroses*.)

4. *Unadaptive ("pathological") anxiety responses.* Anxiety responses conditioned to stimulus situations objectively associated with danger are judged *adaptive*. Anxiety responses to stimuli without relation to danger are *unadaptive*. Persistent unadaptive conditioned habits are called *neurotic*. Under certain circumstances a low degree of anxiety may enhance such functions as performing on stage (the Yerkes–Dodson Law); but if the level is considerable it interferes with the effective performance of many classes of behavior. The generalized rise in muscle tension impairs coordination of movement. Mental concentration, the ready flow of associations, and the registration of impressions may all be diminished. There may be reduced efficiency at work, impaired social functioning, or inadequate sexual behavior—manifested as impotence in males and frigidity in females.

Unadaptive anxiety can also result from physiological pathology. Generalized anxiety is a feature of severe cases of Vitamin B1 deficiency (beri-beri), and apparently results from a widespread lowering of the thresholds of sympathetic synapses. Anxiety without determinable stimulus antecedents, and presumably of organic origin, is frequently observed in cases of schizophrenia. Other organic sources of anxiety are the hypoglycemic syndrome, thyrotoxicosis, tumors of the adrenal medulla (pheochromocytoma), and limbic lobe seizures.

Bibliography: DiCara, L. V. & Miller, N. E.: Longterm retention of instrumentally learned heart-rate changes in the curarized rat. Comm. behav. biol., 1968, *2*, 19–23. Eysenck, H. J.: The dynamics of anxiety and hysteria. London, 1957. Fonberg, E.: On the manifestation of conditioned defensive reactions in stress. Bull. Soc. sci. lettr. lodz. class III. Sci. math. natur., 1956, 7, 1–10. Freud, S.: 1894. Quoted in Jones, E., The life and work of Sigmund Freud. New York, 1961. Id.: The problem of anxiety. New York, 1936. Hein, P. L.: Heart rate conditioning in the cat and its relationship to other physiological responses. Psychophysiol., 1969, 5, 455–64. Hess, W. R.: Vegetative Funktionen und Zwischenhirn. Basle, 1947. Jacobson, E.: Progressive relaxation. Chicago, 1938. May, R.: The meaning of anxiety. New York, 1950. Miller, N. E. & Banuazizi, A.: Instrumental learning by curarized rats of a specific visceral response, intestinal or cardiac. J. comp. physiol. psychol., 1968, 65, 1–7. Sullivan, H. S.: The interpersonal theory of psychiatry. New York, 1953. Wolpe, J.: Experimental neuroses as learned behavior. Brit. J. psychol., 1952, 43, 243–68. Yerkes, R. M. & Dodson, J. D.: The relation of strength of stimulus to rapidity of habit formation. J. comp. neurol. psychol., 1908, 18, 459–82. *J. Wolpe*

Anxiety scales. Inventories for measurement of the specific reaction or set of *anxiety* (q.v.): e.g. J. A. Taylor's Manifest Anxiety Scale, MAS, 1953; children's version, CMAS; IPAT Anxiety Scale Questionnaire, 1957–63; Sarason's Test Anxiety Scale for children and students. *F.K.*

Apathetic type. An unemotional, inactive, listless and indirect character.

Apathy: an absence of feeling. *Disorganization apathy:* mass despair or loss of morale.

Aperture color. A vague, soft, texture-free expanse of color seen through an opening in a neutral screen.

Aphasia. A speech disorder which occurs as a result of localized brain lesions, especially in the so-called *speech areas* of the dominant cerebral hemisphere (in right-handed people the left hemisphere).

Aphasic speech disorders are distinguished from other, more elementary, speech disorders in that they disturb speech in the sense of a complex form of symbolic activity, whereas in the more elementary forms only the motor components of speech (dysarthria), the phonation processes (dysphonia), or the fluid innervation of the act of speaking (stuttering, q.v.) are disturbed.

Aphasia can take various forms depending on the localization of the lesion of the cerebral cortex. As early as 1861, P. Broca reported that damage to the caudal section of the third (inferior) frontal lobe convolution of the left cerebral hemisphere (*Broca's area*, q.v.), while causing no functional disorders of lip or tongue movement, could impair "motor speech", and therefore lead to an inability to speak actively and expressively (*motor aphasia*), even though the spoken matter might remain relatively comprehensible. In 1873, C. Wernicke confirmed that injury to the posterior part of the superior temporal convolution of the left hemisphere could lead to the reverse: a disorder of "sensory speech", causing impaired comprehension of spoken matter, even though acoustic perception of non-articulated sounds might be retained. This form of speech disorder, known as *sensory aphasia*, is not accompanied by any impairment of articulated speech, although the patient's active speech can be incorrect and agrammatical. In addition to these two basic forms of aphasia, an amnesic aphasia was distinguished in which both comprehension of spoken matter as well as the ability to articulate are retained, but the names of objects or people are forgotten (*nominal aphasia*). The localization of the brain damage causing nominal aphasia has not yet been established, although many authors have postulated its connection with injury to the inferior parietal area of the left hemisphere, which has been seen as the cortical area responsible for concept formation.

Attempts to trace the different aphasias to lesions of specific areas of the cerebral cortex did not, however, offer a scientific explanation of disorders of speech in the sense of complex forms of symbolic activity. Consequently, a number of authors maintained that brain injuries led to a disturbance of complex "abstract" or "categorized" behavior, and that every lesion of highly complex areas of the cerebral cortex must lead to a disorder of highly complex "symbolic" forms of activity depending on holistic operations of the entire brain (K. Goldstein *et al.*). However, the mechanisms of extremely complex forms of symbolic behavior were still unexplained; consequently, asphasia began to be viewed as a disorder of the highest mental processes whose anatomical and physiological basis was taken as largely unknown. A conflict arose between mechanistic attempts to derive speech disorders from precisely localized brain lesions, and holistic views of speech as a holistic symbolic activity which could be examined without reference to its cerebral substrate.

Progress in modern neuroanatomy, neurophysiology (q.v.) and neuropsychology (q.v.) permitted much more accurate analyses of speech disorders, and a more satisfactory explanation of aphasic symptoms.

It was demonstrated that damage to each of the abovementioned areas of the cerebral cortex eliminated one of the factors essential to speech activity, and led to partial forms of aphasic speech disorder.

Damage to the posterior sections of the upper temporal area of the left hemisphere (the secondary sections of the auditory area) leads to impairment of complex forms of sound analysis, makes it impossible to differentiate similar phonemes, and leads to acoustic (sensory) aphasia, which is shown in an inability to comprehend phrases (which are perceived with insufficient acuity), to difficulty in repeating words accurately (with inappropriate sounds within words = *literal paraphasia*; or inappropriate syllables within words = *verbal paraphasia*), and to an inability to give accurate spoken descriptions of objects, together with inaccurate analysis of word-sounds, necessary for writing.

Damage to the secondary cortex of the sensorimotor area of the dominant hemisphere (especially of the inferior sections of the post-central and pre-motor area) does not directly impair the auditory analysis of spoken sounds, but can lead to a significant disturbance of expressive (articulated) speech.

Damage to the secondary sections of the inferior part of the post-central area (central fissure) leads to a disturbance of the kinesthetic afference of speech movements, causing diminished accuracy of articulated speech and confusion of similar articulemes: e.g. the lip consonants *b–m*, and the point consonants *d–l–n* (tongue and gums). In the worst cases, this makes clearly articulated speech impossible and leads to ("afferent" or "kinesthetic") motor aphasia, evidenced both in speech and in a characteristic disorder of written language.

Damage to the inferior sections of the *pre-motor region* of the left hemisphere produces a marked impediment in denervation of resultant articulations, and impairment of "kinetic melodies", and leads to an "efferent" (or kinetic) aphasia, which becomes evident in a major disturbance of speech flow and in a pathological persistence of specific verbal stereotypies in speaking and in writing.

The abovementioned forms of speech disorder are partial disturbances of speech activity which occur because the lesion eliminates major factors essential to the act of speech.

Damage to individual sections of the cerebral cortex is not in itself a sufficient explanation of disturbances of complex verbal behavior; an important part of the total explanation is provided by analysis of the *pathophysiological changes* which occur in the activity of the damaged regions of the cerebral cortex.

An injury of the posterior parts of the cortex of the left (dominant) hemisphere inevitably leads to a pathological condition in these cortical areas, evident especially in a disturbance of normal concentration of neural processes and in characteristic "phasic" inhibitions of the cortex, in the course of which stimuli producing the traces of various systems are assimilated to one another in intensity, thus lose their selectivity (q.v.), and are easily confused with one another. The result is that attempts to find the appropriate word produce an uncontrolled mass of equally probable associations, and that the normal process of selecting the required (descriptive) verbal terms is disturbed. A pathophysiological mechanism of this kind produces the typical symptoms of "amnesic" (nominal) aphasia, or paraphasias (q.v.) (confusions of words).

On the other hand, injuries to specific regions of the cerebral cortex of the left (dominant) hemisphere can lead to a significant impairment of the plasticity of neural processes, causing neural stereotypies that have occurred once to become pathologically stable. This can easily disturb the formation of new and mobile reference systems and affect the process of constant switching from one set of verbal references to others (i.e. the basic prerequisite for all verbal behavior), and result in an inability to produce active, detailed speech. This kind of pathological condition of the cerebral cortex (and especially of the cortex of the anterior sections of the "speech area") is often the prime cause of those forms of speech disorder which manifest themselves in disturbances of spontaneous speech.

Bibliography: Brain, R.: Speech disorders. London, 1961; ²1965. Conrad, K.: New problems of aphasia. Brain, 1954, 77, 491–509. De Reuck, A. V. S. & O'Connor, M. (Eds): Disorders of language. London, 1964. Goldstein, K.: Language and language disorders. New York, 1948. Head, H.: Aphasia and kindred disorders of speech, Vols 1, 2. Cambridge, 1926. Landsell, H.: Laterality of verbal intelligence in the brain. Science, 1962, 135, 922–3. Luria, A. R.: Higher cortical functions in man. New York & London, 1966. Id.: Traumatic aphasia. The Hague, 1970. Ombredane, A.: L'aphasie et l'élaboration de la pensée explicite. Paris, 1951. Piercy, M. F.: The effects of cerebral lesions on intellectual function: a review of current research trends. Brit. J. Psychiat., 1964, 110, 310–52.   A. R. Luria

Aphemia. Loss of the ability to enunciate; generally used in the sense of a loss only of the ability to proceed from thought to verbal enunciation. See *Aphasia.*

Aphrasia. Inability to utter (expressive aphrasia), or understand (sensory aphrasia), phrases. Single words are understood or can be used correctly. It is one of the group of aphasias, none of which is sharply delineated from another. The comprehension by a patient of a word sequence will depend upon his emotional state and its emotional significance as well as the length of the phrase, its construction or subtlety of meaning. In this wider sense it is common in both organic and functional states. It is rare if restricted to patients limited to the use or comprehension of single words.   *B.B.*

Aphrodisiacs. Pharmaceutical compounds to increase sexual reactivity, sexual hormones, and various folk medicines, all of disputed efficacy. Some serve to prolong orgasm (e.g. yohimbine) by inhibition of the sympathetic nerve. There are sometimes unpleasant aftereffects. See *Anorgasmy.*   *G.L.*

Aplasia. The failure of organs and tissues to develop.

Apollonian type. In accordance with the mythological conception of the Greek god Apollo, the Apollonian type represents striving for order, measure, harmony and form. The opposite is the Dionysian type; in accordance with the Greek god Dionysus, this is the dynamic, creative and passionate type. Schelling postulated the combination of the two as ideal: "To be simultaneously inebriated and sober is the secret of true poetry". Nietzsche adopted and developed the conceptual opposition in his *The Birth of Tragedy.*

Bibliography: Klein, O.: Das Apollinische und Dionysische bei Nietzsche und Schelling. Stuttgart, 1935.   *W.K.*

Apparent motion; apparent movement. See *Motion, apparent.*

Apparition. Hallucinated figure. Often associated with spontaneous ESP (q.v.), e.g. in connection with a telepathic communication from a person in distress (= "crisis apparition"), or in connection with a haunt (q.v.) (= ghost). A phantom or phantasm.   *J.B.*

Appeasement gestures. Certain species exhibit effective aggression-inhibitory, ritualized behavior. For instance, they make themselves appear as small as possible, flatten hair or feathers, or retract limbs, and withdraw combat-releaser weapons such as teeth or bill from the superior adversary (gulls elicit inhibition by looking away and down). Immobility often accompanies these wholly submissive attitudes. The victor is inhibited. In the mating season (q.v.), appeasement gestures play an important role and bring male combat to an end.

Bibliography: Carthy, J. D. Ebling, F. J. (Eds): The natural history of aggression. London, 1964. Lorenz, K.: On aggression (Eng. trans.). London, 1966. Tinbergen, N.: Einige Gedanken über Beschwichtigungsgebärden. Z. Tierpsychol., 1959, *42*, 651–65.   *K.F.*

Apperception. According to Wundt, a process by which a mental (psychic) content is recognized, or *clearly* perceived. Apperceptive perception is characterized in that physical stimuli are not perceived in isolation but in an "apperceptive mass" from which we select the contents that are meaningful for us.

Bibliography: Wundt. W.: An introduction to psychology. London, 1912.   *V.M.*

Apperception categories. W. Stern distinguishes the following phases of apperception (q.v.) through which a child normally passes in the course of mental development: (*a*) substance stage (0–8 years); (*b*) action stage (9–10 years); (*c*) relation stage (11–13 years); (*d*) quality stage (from 14 years).

Bibliography: Stern, W.: Allgemeine Psychologie auf personalistischer Grundlage. The Hague, ²1950.
          K.P.

Appetitive behaviors. Modes of behavior with for the most part an inherited base, which continue instinctively (and without their normal specific releaser) in order to maintain psycho-physiological equilibrium. Appetitive behaviors may therefore be seen as instincts (q.v.), or "appetitive drives", produced endogenously and without a releasing stimulus. But see *Aggression*; *Drive; Instinct; Emotion; Sexuality.*

Bibliography: Craig, W.: Appetites and aversions as constituents of instincts. Biol. Bull., 1918, *34*, 91–107.
          H.S.

Applied psychology. The application of psychological knowledge and research to tasks arising out of the needs of life. The fundamentals of applied psychology are *general psychology* (q.v.) and *characterology* (q.v.) or *personality* (q.v.) assessment as a special aspect of the theory of human behavior. Applied psychology is, therefore, the useful, practical application of scientific knowledge. When specific empirical principles are used in order to assist men to direct their lives in various ways, one speaks of *practical psychology.* Scientific psychology adopts a proficient methodological approach, and is concerned to establish adequate modes of classification and verifiable results, whereas "pre-scientific" psychology approaches its objects in ways that might be classed as exclusively intuitive (see *Intuition*).

1. *Psychology as a profession.* A man or woman who intends to become a practicing psychologist must combine a basic scientific attitude, a desire to gain and add to knowledge, with a measure of social dedication and a basic desire to help others out of common humanity. It is not only a question of applying scientific knowledge already verified and established, but of the possibility of

discovering new methods. Essential prerequisites for the practice of psychology—as for that of every other profession requiring a rigorous academic training—are an above average intellectual ability, and mature judgment in the sense of being able clearly to distinguish contradictory opinions and estimate the value of different viewpoints. It is also essential that a practical psychologist should not be of a wavering or unstable disposition.

2. *Basic principles of applied psychology.* More, almost, than in any other profession, the ethical aspects of applied psychology require constant and careful consideration. Professional dangers specific to the psychologist would seem to be above all of a psychic nature: disturbances of mental equilibrium, and concerns affecting acuity of thought, moral sensitivity, and dedication to and joy in life and work, which tend to affect human relations.

Profit ought not to be a basic consideration in the practice of psychology; power-seeking and competitiveness are also essentially foreign to its aims. Excessive egotism, self-assertion and envy, and any form of aggressive tendency can obviously affect adversely any relationship between psychologist and client.

Just as the medical practitioner is bound by the Hippocratic oath, the psychologist is bound to help any who come to him for advice and assistance. Principles for an international code of ethics for psychologist have been proposed by F. Baumgarten (*Revue internationale d'éthique professionelle*, 1953, and *Psychologie und Praxis*, 1961). The German Psychological Association has also made proposals in this regard (G. Kaminsky, 1965). The definitive work on questions of professional ethics is, however, the American Psychological Association's *Casebook on Ethical Standards of Psychologists* (1968). Developments in research methods have given rise to the question of experiments on human beings, both in diagnosis and therapy. Experiments on supposedly less valuable

human beings, the mentally deficient, or prisoners, are of course inhuman and unjustifiable. The boundaries of applied psychology are defined by injury to one's fellow men.

Problematical areas in this regard are certain psychologists' and psychiatrists' recommendations for treatment of mental disorders with drug therapy (see *Psychopharmacology*), narcoanalysis (q.v.) and the use of "lie detectors" (q.v.). Similar possibilities of interfering with the liberty of one's fellow men exist in the field of advertising psychology ("subliminal perception" and stimuli producing unconscious reactions). Tape-recordings, film records, television observation and one-way-screen observations essentially presuppose the agreement of the person recorded or observed. All diagnoses, consultations and treatments are concerned with individual human beings whose *dignity* must be respected. In addition the psychologist must allow the matter in hand, and not extraneous factors such as inappropriate sympathy and antipathy, to direct his degree of concern.

Whenever psychologists have reason to expect that situations of conflicting responsibility might arise (e.g. in educational or vocational guidance), they must remember that they are bound by *professional secrecy* in regard to the testee or client in question. The possibility of withdrawal from a client relationship must also be ensured, especially if there is any possibility of complex transference. Client relations within one's own family, or one's own circle of friends and acquaintances, should be avoided. The professional duty of discretion of course also includes proficient discrimination: the obligation of secrecy on the psychologist is lifted where the client would otherwise be endangered.

The psychologist is also bound to maintain standards in his professional activity that are qualitatively as high as possible. Therefore he is bound to abandon activities which cannot be humanly justified. For instance, the independent psychologist employed by an organization or business concern is bound to carry out his duties as required by the employer; but where this involves him in a conflict of interests, he is also bound by the general rule that the interests of the *individual* in question must take precedence over those of, say, an industrial concern or government agency.

3. *Methods of applied psychology.* Proficient judgments require the determination of symptoms (test results, modes of behavior) and their logical classification according to psychological categories (syndromes, etc.), and the careful confirmation and presentation of findings. Where the observation or judgment of a man as a whole (in terms of achievement and character traits) is concerned, test methods, questionnaires (q.v.), and interviews (q.v.) are not the only methods to be applied. The psychologist must also practice adequately the arts of personal encounter and expression, and be proficient in exploration (q.v.), behavioral observation, and analysis of expression, according to the specific case. Special attention must also be given to *social conditions* (for example, parents or teachers often see children only in one aspect of their lives). See *Abilities.*

Psychologists required to give evidence regarding an individual must remember the possibility of this being taken as applying to that individual in all life situations, and should therefore take into account the temporal limits to the relevance of their findings.

Since psychology implies service to the individual, a psychological diagnosis made in connection with a report is never permissible in the total absence of the patient or subject. Even though some diagnostic methods that do not require the subject's presence can be of help, they should never be used alone. In the actual individual case, *typological systems* can only afford valuable assistance to the diagnostician. *Typology* (q.v.) has to be supplemented by an individual diagnosis in the sense of differential psychology (q.v.),

which is concerned to observe and describe a person in terms of his individual characteristics with regard to inter-individual and intra-individual differences. Frequently the psychologist has to call on other experts for assistance. Team work (see *Team*) and the rating system are invaluable, for the checking of ratings by several diagnosticians can help to overcome the possibility of subjective assessments. The psychologist also has to take into account the internal and external conditions of his work situation as they may affect the client, his partner in the work, and the assessment. This includes not only his degree of obvious motivation and concern, but conditions such as a quiet atmosphere in suitable premises and the avoidance of such disturbances as a window opening on to a noisy street—both positive and negative factors of influence must always be considered. Finally, as regards methodology, it must be stressed that as full a range as possible of proven techniques must be invoked in the description and assessment of human personalities.

Characterological analysis is a construct analysis: i.e. the interpretation of a specific character trait, e.g. aggressivity, depends on the nomothetic nexus of relations governing the concept in question. At the beginning of every character analysis, the intuitive approach forms a hypothesis which must be confronted with the results of scientific procedure, i.e. the phenomenologically intuitive process requires verification by operational and statistical criteria. The particular trait must be determined in relation to other traits (q.v.).

4. *Reports.* A report, where there is no prescribed model, can take the form of a rating, a personality profile, advice as the result of counseling, or a predictive summary. A report commissioned by, say, a prospective employer might consist of a statement of the terms of reference, followed by a short description of the rating method and process used. Reports can include a description of aptitude, performance, intelligence, special

abilities, essential traits, motivation, emotivity, sociability, development, professional achievement, social conditions, and even the attitude to and estimate of self of the person concerned—all according to situation and purpose. Various models are possible: (a) a description of fixed traits (static personality model); (b) an analysis based on behavior determinants; (c) a causal analysis tracing the grounds, causes and motives of behavior (dynamic model); (d) the behavior of a personality in regard to development; (e) the possible meaning and purpose of a specific behavior or behavior pattern.

5. *Tasks and fields of application.* The tasks proper to applied psychology focus in general on the determination of character traits. A frequent task is to ascertain the ability and aptitude of an individual in order to advise him accordingly (school and educational counseling, vocational guidance, therapeutic counseling—e.g. advice on learning problems; psychologists co-operating in rehabilitation and resocialization). The psychologist is required to present his findings in various—usually documentary—forms, which differ from country to country. See *Vocational guidance.*

One of the most pressing fields of application is the area of *work and vocation.* Industrial psychology (q.v.) can be technically oriented, and concern itself principally with human behavior during work and the discovery of optimal working conditions (workplace conditions; light, color, temperature, noise, human factors research, and so on); but work can also occupy psychologists with problems of vocational aptitude and inclination, occupational mobility, labor market prospects, and socio-political motivation. Questions of working atmosphere and morale, industrial relations, and modes of rationalization intended to make labor more humane, belong to the wide range of tasks that require the expertise and research potential of industrial psychologists.

Educational counselors are concerned with the varied field of mental defects and various problems met with by young people, such as legasthenia, stuttering, lack of concentration, sexual problems, neglect. They are required to diagnose, counsel, apply therapy, and on occasion have recourse to the specialized methods of clinical psychology (q.v.). Educational psychologists also play an important part in teacher training, and research into new educational methods (e.g. in programmed instruction, q.v.). A distinction is sometimes made between educational psychologists and *school* psychologists, whereby the latter are those particularly concerned with testing, rating, remedial measures, and conflict situations among schoolchildren.

Forensic, or legal, *psychology* (q.v.) is sometimes thought of as ancillary to the administration of justice. Testimonies and evidence, the credibility of witnesses and defendants, and the fitness of individuals to stand trial, can come within the competence of the forensic psychologist, who can, in some countries, be called on to act as a graphologist and attest to the genuineness of or identify a sample of handwriting. He can also be asked to confirm psychological disturbances in cases of suspected diminished responsibility or guilt. Psychologists also play an important part in the links between courts, schools and probation officers, and in reform institutions and the prison service.

Psychopharmacology (q.v.) is concerned with the effects of chemical substances (e.g. narcotics, stimulants, sedatives) on human drives, emotions, perception, ideation, behavior, expression, character, development and culture, and so on, and such phenomena as the effects of hallucinogens and addiction to medically prescribed drugs. The use of psychopharmaceutical compounds is properly reserved to psychotherapists with a medical training or to psychiatrists. Questions proper to the psychologist are reactions and dangers dependent on personality, e.g. in traffic psychology (behavior of drives under the influence of alcohol) or in sport (doping), and any unjustifiable use of drugs to manipulate human beings.

Traffic psychology includes anthropological and objective tasks. Behavior in traffic, driving capability and accident proneness are related to personality. Technical possibilities in traffic psychology (e.g. simulators) still require psychological elucidation.

Management psychology and related fields present major problems for the psychologist: group relations and leadership, risks and security, administration problems and management training, and teamwork planning are among them.

Advertising, publicity, market research and opinion polls are related areas requiring psychologists to estimate, e.g., appropriate ways of sampling or influencing large numbers of people. (See Marketing.)

Military psychology dates back to the experiences of American psychologists in World War I. Officer selection and pilot selection and training are only two of the many sub-fields in this regard.

Among the fields of application under development at present is *political psychology* (q.v.), which embraces, e.g., the psychological suasions of government and social justice, peace research, the causes of authoritarianism and prejudice (q.v.), the treatment of refugees, and problems of developing nations.

The psychology of *religion* (q.v.) examines the principles of religious experience. The psychology of *sport* (q.v.) offers assistance in training, learning processes, and the selection of appropriate techniques. The conditions for adequate performance, attitude to success and failure, personal experiences leading to depression or euphoria, are psychological questions as important for, e.g., the athlete, as is technical proficiency in the particular pursuit.

In view of unrest in universities, the contribution of psychologists to university life is essential, particularly in guidance on study problems. Here the psychologist has to deal not only with performance problems but with particular neuroses and even suicidal tendencies.

There are many other areas of applied psychology that come under the above heads, ranging from statistics to counseling, not the least important of which are of course, marriage guidance and individual vocational advice. See *Occupational psychology*.

Bibliography: Anastasi, A.: Fields of applied psychology. New York, 1964. Argyle, M.: Psychology and social problems. London, 1964. Arnold, W.: Person und Schuldfähigkeit. Würzburg, 1965. Id.: Angewandte Psychologie. Stuttgart, 1970. Dorsch, F.: Geschichte und Probleme der angewandten Psychologie. Berne, 1963. Dudycha, G. J.: Applied psychology. New York, 1963. Eysenck, H. J. (Ed.): Handbook of abnormal psychology. London, 1961. Fraser, J. M.: Industrial psychology. New York, 1962. Fryer, D. H. & Henry, D. R. (Eds): Handbook of applied psychology. New York, 1950. Gray, J. S.: Psychology applied to human affairs. New York, ²1954. Guilford, J. P.: Fields of psychology. New York, ²1950. Joyce, C. R. B. (Ed.): Psychopharmacology: Dimensions and perspectives. London, 1968. Koch, S. (Ed.): Psychology, a study of a science, Vols. 1–6. New York, 1959–66. Webb, W. B.: The profession of psychology. New York, 1962.

W. Arnold

Apport. Object supposed to have been paranormally transported into a closed room during a *séance* (q.v.) or during a *poltergeist* (q.v.) disturbance. *J.B.*

Apprehension. 1. The act of becoming aware. Apperception (q.v.). Conscious central processing of newly received perceptions and ideas on the basis of the existing experiential matrix. In developmental psychology, the transition from holistic to analytic apprehension is important in the 7–8 years range. **2.** Anxiety (q.v.).

Apprehension span: Measured by the number of objects that can be correctly apprehended at one exposure. See *Attention*.

Bibliography: Miller, G. A.: The magical number seven plus or minus zero. Psychol. Rev., 1956, *63*, 81–97. *K.E.P.*

Approach-approach conflict. A term used by K. Lewin (q.v.) for a conflict situation in which the individual has to choose between two equally attractive alternatives: e.g. the fable of the ass who starved because it could not choose between two bundles of hay.

Approach-avoidance conflict: A goal is as attractive as it is unattractive, hence the situation that arises is often called an *ambivalence conflict.* Some visits to the dentist might be classed here.

Double approach-avoidance conflict: Two or more aspects of the goal are simultaneously as attractive as they are unattractive.

Avoidance-avoidance conflict: An individual is asked to choose between two equally unattractive alternatives. *Leaving-the-field* (q.v.) may be the result. See *Conflict.*

Bibliography: Lewin, K.: Principles of topological psychology. New York, 1936. Id.: Field theory and learning. Yearb. nat. Soc. Stud. Educ., 1942, *41,* 215–42. Miller, N. E.: Experimental studies in conflict. In: Hunt, J. McV.: Personality and the behavior disorders (ch. 14). New York, 1944. *R.Hä*

Approach gradient. See *Gradient.*

Approximative consciousness. According to C. G. Jung (q.v.), when ego-activity is diminished a quasi- or near-conscious state can exist intermediate to the conscious and unconscious. The contents of this allegedly highly-complex state are said to manifest themselves occasionally in dreams as *scintillae,* or sparks of light.   *J.G.*

Apraxia (syn. *Dyspraxia*). Impairment of learned purposeful movements which is not attributable to paralysis, disorders of coordination, sensibility, language comprehension or apprehension (intelligence, consciousness).

1. *Ideational apraxia:* disturbance of the conception of a movement. The volitional impulse is incorrect (e.g. the patient puts the match and the cigarette in his mouth). Occurs with diffuse brain lesions which are the cause of simultaneous dementia.

2. *Motor apraxia:* Awkwardness in executing certain movements as a result of damage to the corresponding limb center, which does not lead to paralysis but to disturbance of kinesthetic memory images.

3. *Ideomotor (ideokinetic) apraxia:* Confused execution of an act as a result of interruption of the connection between the ideational and limb centers (e.g. the patient nods when asked to make a threatening gesture with his fist). The very simplest minor movements can be performed successfully, since they are controlled from the limb centers alone.   *C.S.*

Aptitude might be thought of as potential ability. Traits (q.v.) are determined and assessed with regard to certain future ends (e.g. work) without considering underlying talent and its development. An attempt is made simultaneously to predict *future ability* to hold down a job, and to examine, e.g., capability, achievement motivation, reliability, and responsibility. See *Abilities; Objective tests.*   *W.S.*

Aptitude tests. Tests of aptitude for some activity or occuptation. H. Münsterberg (1863–1916) was one of the first to suggest such tests, which were used during World War I for pilots and lorry drivers and then in industry. Today combinations of several tests (test batteries) are usually administered; one part is not designed to measure any specific activity but aims at assessing more general and above all intellectual performance. Special aptitude tests have been constructed, e.g., for algebra, engineers, dentists, musicians, office staff. The success of these methods depends very much on careful psychological analysis of the relevant activities.   *R.M.*

ARAS. Abb. for *Ascending reticular activating system* (q.v.).

Archetypes. Primeval images and ideas which are said to be genetically inherited and to be common to all men (C. G. Jung, q.v.). They are contained in the racial unconscious or "collective unconscious" (whereas the personal or individual unconscious contains the feeling tones, or affective components). These primordial symbols are said to have been meaningful at all times and for all races, and are found in many forms, especially in fairy tales, myths, religion and art. In the language of the unconscious, which is pictorial discourse, these archaic images reappear in a personified or symbolic form. The notion of the archetype is, of course, a hypothetical construct. See also *Mandala*.

Bibliography: Jung, C. G.: Introduction to the science of mythology. London, 1951.   *H.N.G.*

Area sampling. A survey method making for more accurate sampling than quota sampling (q.v.), and ensuring random sampling (q.v.). The given area to be sampled is divided into districts, and the districts into dwelling units. Specific dwelling units are selected and specific respondents within them. Repeated calls are necessary to ensure the interviewing of all respondents in the total area. An expensive method used by official bodies.

Bibliography: Cantril, H.: Gauging public opinion. Princeton, 1947.

Arecolin(e). Alkaloid obtained from betel (q.v.) or areca nut. It has a cholinergic action. Peripheral-autonomic effects are weaker than with the pharmacological substances muscarine (q.v.) and pilocarpine (q.v.). Arecoline excites the reticular formation; in low to medium doses it can produce subjective stimulation and euphoria.

Bibliography: Herz, A.: Wirkungen des Arecolins auf das Zentralnervensystem, Naunyn-Schmiedebergs Arch. exp. Path. Pharmacol., 1962, *242*, 414–19.
                                                    W.J.

Areflexia. Absence of reflexes in state of profound unconsciousness; a sign of absence of spinal function.

Argyll-Robertson pupil. The pupil does not respond to light (or negligibly), whereas accommodation (q.v.) is retained. Occurs in neuro-syphilitic disorders (CNS).   *A.Hi.*

Arithmetic mean. A statistical measure of the central tendency of a distribution:

$$\bar{X} = \frac{\Sigma X_i}{N}$$

The mean value is defined by $\Sigma(X_i - \bar{X}) = 0$.
                                                    W.H.B.

Armchair psychology. E. W. Scripture's term (usually pejorative) for psychological theories conceived and propagated wholly without experimental verification.   *H.-J.A.*

Army Alpha Test. Developed by a number of leading American psychologists for group testing of intelligence on the entry of the U.S.A. into World War I. The test consists of various series of tasks, such as sequences of instructions, counting, arranging words in sentences, analogies. The Army Alpha provided an impetus for the use of tests in American schools.   *R.M.*

Army Beta Test. A test developed at the same time as the Army Alpha, but designed for illiterates and those unable to understand English. The constituent tests are non-verbal and the instructions have to be given without any use of language.   *R.M.*

Army General Classification Test (abb. AGCT). A test designed for U.S. army use in World War II and given to more than ten million individuals; made available for civilian use after the war. The test contains an equal number of word-recognition, numerical reasoning, and block counting tests (perceptual relations). The crude score is converted into an IQ. This test series was later replaced by the Army Qualification Test (AFQT).   *R.M.*

Arousal. In its most limited meaning, arousal refers to the increase in frequency and decrease in amplitude of EEG rhythms (desynchronization) which occur as a result of stimulation. The animal is then said to show an increase in arousal. The term *activation* is also used more or less synonymously.

The stimulation may take a number of forms. Any novel or intense external stimulus will produce an increase in arousal, but with repetition the stimulus has less and less effect, and finally none at all. Certain internal stimuli can also increase arousal. In a classical experiment, Moruzzi & Magoun (1949) showed that arousal increases as a result of electrical stimulation of the brain stem reticular formation by means of implanted electrodes. Under this stimulation neural impulses are transmitted from the brain stem to the cerebral cortex, thus producing the EEG desynchronization. It is now generally accepted that the brain stem reticular formation plays a vital role in the maintenance of arousal levels.

The other area of the brain principally involved in the maintenance of arousal is the thalamic reticular formation. The brain stem and thalamic divisions of the reticular formation operate in different ways. Stimulation of the brain stem reticular formation produces a relatively long-lasting increase in arousal, possibly lasting for several hours in the case of a subject awoken from sleep. This is known as the generalized arousal reaction. It produces activation over the whole of the cerebral cortex and takes a relatively large number of trials to habituate. In contrast, stimulation of the thalamic reticular formation produces the "localized reaction", which lasts for a shorter period, is confined to the particular area of the cortex served by the thalamic nucleus concerned, and is relatively quickly habituated in something of the order of ten trials.

EEG desynchronization is not the only physiological manifestation of an increase in arousal. Other effects are the activation of the sympathetic nervous system, leading to the acceleration of heart rate and respiration rate, the psychogalvanic reaction, and pupil dilation. There is also an increase in the sensitivity of the sense organs and a speeding up of reaction times. Pavlov called this group of reactions the *orientation reaction*, which is used synonymously with the *arousal reaction*.

The concept of arousal has interested psychologists for five principal reasons. Firstly, it appears to provide the physiological basis for the concept of a general activation drive, which many have postulated without understanding the physiological mechanisms involved. Such a concept has been assumed in various guises, including "excitation" (Duffy), "general emotional state" (Cannon) and "drive" (q.v.) (Hull). With the discovery of the physiology of arousal the postulation of these drive states seems to have been vindicated.

Secondly, arousal seems to provide the physiological basis for certain personality differences. There are several similarities between arousal and the personality characteristic of anxiety, since both involve an abnormally high level of sympathetic reactivity. Eysenck (1967) has suggested that his two personality dimensions of neuroticism (q.v.) and introversion—extraversion (q.v.) are, respectively, functions of the strength of the two divisions of the arousal system, the thalamic and the brain stem. Hence introverts behave in many respects as if they were chronically highly aroused. For instance, they have greater reactions to pain, habituate slowly and have faster EEG rhythms.

Thirdly, some of the baffling problems of mental illness may be explicable in terms of malfunctions of the arousal system. There is much evidence that neurotics are characterized by overreactive arousal systems. The evidence relating psychosis to disturbance of the arousal system is less strong, but there is support from various sources for the view that the majority of chronic hospitalized psychotics are under-aroused. There is probably also a smaller group of acute psychotics who are hyper-aroused (Gellhorn, 1957; Lynn, 1966).

Fourthly, it has been suggested by Berlyne (1960) that many human activities can be understood as a search for increases in arousal. For these he has coined the term "arousal jags". Such popular human activities as gambling, sports competitions, adventure enjoyed either in reality or vicariously through fiction or television, drug taking and esthetic experiences frequently involve increases in arousal. This theory, however, has yet to make the impact on psychologists which it seems to deserve.

Fifthly, arousal has proved a useful concept to those working on the psychological effects of drugs. These may be classified broadly into those which increase arousal and those which decrease it. The stimulants, amphetamines and hallucinogens appear to increase arousal, whereas the depressants, sedatives and tranquilizers decrease it. This formulation gives the investigator a framework in which to consider the details of the site and mode of action of a particular drug.

Arousal is now generally regarded as a scale. At the lowest level is the state of coma, then deep and light sleep, and drowsiness. From the middle of the scale upwards are the states of relaxation, alertness, excitement, anxiety and finally terror. Many stimulus situations shift the individual from one of these states to another according to the intensity with which the stimulus is applied. For instance, being driven in a car slowly can induce drowsiness, but as the speed increases one may be taken through all the stages on the scale, right up to terror. This scale of states of consciousness seems to reflect an underlying physiological scale of the extent of neural activity in the reticular formation. Hence a considerable degree of synthesis between psychological and physiological states has been achieved in this field.

Bibliography: Berlyne, D. E.: Conflict, arousal and curiosity. London, 1960. Eysenck, H. J.: The biological basis of personality. Illinois, 1967. Gellhorn, E.: Autonomic imbalance and the hypothalamus. Minneapolis, 1957. Lynn, R.: Attention, arousal and the orientation reaction. Oxford, 1966. Moruzzi, G. & Magoun, H. W.: Brain stem reticular formation and activation of the EEG. EEG Clin. Neurophysiol. 1949, 1, 455–73.   R. Lynn

Arrangement. A term used by A. Adler to refer to an unconscious organization of attitudes, symptoms, behavior, etc., which mediates between the *striving for superiority*, and the limitations of reality discovered through experience, in determining the *life plan* of the patient. Also used more generally to describe a pattern of ideas which is developed by the patient in order to account for, or justify, his neurotic behavior. Cf. the defense (q.v.) mechanism of *rationalization*.

                                                                                        G.D.W.

Arthur Scale. A performance test for children of 5 to 15 years. A test battery formed from the best performance tests (1930), using concrete materials (e.g. S. C. Kohs' mosaic test). A slightly different form has been in use since 1947.   *R.M.*

Articular sensations. See *Organic sensations.*

Articulation. 1. The movements effectively producing or modifying speech sounds. The production of such sounds. 2. The production of consonantal sounds. 3. Clarity of speech. 4. A joint between bones or cartilages. 5. Interrelation or clarification: e.g. of items or ideas.   *D.G.*

Artifact (artefact), statistical. An error (q.v.) resulting from incorrect assessment of parameters (q.v.), or the use of inadequate or inaccurate experimental methods. *W.H.B.*

Artificial intelligence. See *Simulation.*

Art, primitive. The very term is symptomatic of the problems confronting the anthropological psychologist studying contacts between cultures. The esthetic question of "primitive" art was first raised when its various forms were measured against European conceptions of art, and attempts were made to accommodate more magical-religious artifacts (see *Ethnology; Folk psychology*). The psychology of art studies the occurrence in archaic art-forms of typical structures that are clearly partly determined by the holistic (gestalt) nature of human perception.

Bibliography: Smith, M. W. (Ed.): The artist in tribal society. London, 1961.   *W.S.*

Art, psychology of. In a wider perspective, the psychology of art forms an important part of the general theory and science of art, and, according to its founder M. Dessoir, is to be distinguished as an objective science from esthetics (see *Experimental esthetics*, however), which is an evaluative science. More precisely, the psychology of art is the psychology of the *visual arts*, and in this narrower sense forms, together with the psychology of *literature* (q.v.) and the psychology of *music* (q.v.), an essential component of an inclusive psychology of culture (see *Cultural anthropology*). Instead of the psychology of sound or auditory phenomena and psychophonetics, the psychology of visual perception is essentially important in regard to the visual arts, together with the study of the sense of touch and form for sculpture. Spatial sensitivity is, of course, a major theme here. The questions of comprehensibility of content and empathy are also posed somewhat differently, say in the matter of allegorical painting and sculpture, where the problems of form and content, etc., are materially different to those arising in music and literature. Because of their basic geometric and architectonic contents, the visual arts became the essential, paradigmatic object of gestalt psychology (see Sander, 1932, 1967; Arnheim, 1954).

More general psychological and sociological contributions to the study of "modern" abstract or non-objective art are to be found in Malraux (1949), and particularly in the works of the psychiatrist Winkler (1949) and the sociologist and philosopher Gehlen

(1960, ²1965). Gehlen examines (among other questions) such special areas of psychological interest as the *eidetic* and *kinesthetic* ability of the painter Kandinsky. Wellek (1966) provides a summary discussion of this theme. The interpretation of such phenomena and the connections between artistic intention and objective reception offer many problems for discussion, and not only in the field of so-called modern art. Siddig and Thieme (1969) carried out an investigation in which art experts and laymen were used experimentally to analyze the lack of correlation between painters' declared intentions and the actual judgments of observers. What R. Francès calls "L'age esthétique d'un sujet", i.e. the maturity of esthetic judgment in the individual, can be measured by the yardstick of the *consensus* of opinion obtained among those of supposedly mature judgment, the experts. There is a considerable amount of statistical information on musical taste in this regard. Burt (1924, 1933) followed up C. Spearman in attempting a factorial analysis of questions of taste; the work was extended by R. W. Pickford and H. J. Eysenck. These investigators postulate a "general factor of esthetic ability" in Spearman's sense, which (according to Pickford) aims at a balance between "emotional expressiveness" and "harmony of form", and therefore *implicitly* justifies an "esthetics of *form and expression*" (cf. Wellek). In addition to this general factor, all the types of painting, music and literature investigated exhibit a *bipolar* factor, showing an opposition of the more colorful, emotionally expressive, emotionally impressionistic or expressively distorted types of art to those which are less colorful, and so on. The first group is usually preferred by extraverted and the second group by introverted types (see *Type; Traits*); often the contrast is between the more and less modern, or between romantic and classical (Pickford, 1967, esp. p. 926). In principle, these findings recall Wölfflin's contrasts in his *Principles of Art History* (Eng. trans., London, 1932), and Wellek's *Typologie der Musikbegabung*

(1939). Psychology (especially since H. Prinzhorn) has shown more interest in the art-
products of the psychologically disturbed
than in their verse and music (up to Jakáb,
1956; Pickford, 1967; Plokker, 1969);
recently drawing and painting under hypnosis
have awakened interest. In addition, the viewpoint of comparative developmental psychology as represented by Krueger (1915) and
Werner ([2]1948) is particularly fruitful in this
area, not least of all with regard to the theory
of art itself. There is a vast amount of literature devoted to children's art (cf. summary
in Mühle, 1967); Westrich (1968) has produced a developmental psychology of drawing
during the puberal phase. As early as 1934,
Münz (a teacher of the blind) and the
psychologist V. Löwenfeld made an interesting survey of sculpture by the blind and produced a comparative-psychological analysis
(cf., for a more general view, Révész, 1950).

A survey of the British and American views
and literature can be found in the collection of readings edited by Hogg (1969) and
the summary account in Schrickel ([2]1968).
(See also: *Literature; Music; Ganzheit*).

Bibliography: Arnheim, R.: Art and visual perception.
New York, 1954. Burt, C.: The psychology of art.
In: Burt, C. (Ed.): How the mind works. London,
1933. Gehlen, A.: Zeit-Bilder. Frankfurt & Bonn,
[2]1965. Hogg, J. (Ed.): Psychology and the visual arts.
Harmondsworth, 1969. Jakáb, I.: Zeichnungen und
Gemälde der Geisteskranken. Budapest & Berlin, 1956.
Krueger, F.: Über Entwicklungspsychologie. Leipzig,
1915. Malraux, A.: Psychology of art. New York,
1949-50. Morgan, D. N.: Psychology and art today.
In: Aesth. Art Critic., 1950, *9*. Mühle, G.: Entwicklungspsychol. des zeichnerischen Gestaltens. Munich, [2]1967. Munro, T. M.: Methods in the psychology
of art. In: Aesth. Art Critic., 1948, *6*. Münz, L. &
Löwenfeld, V.: Plastische Arbeiten Blinder. Brünn,
1934. Odgen, R. M.: The psychology of art. New
York, 1938. Perrer, S. C.: Principles of art appreciation. New York, 1949. Pickford, R. W.: Studies
in psychiatric art. Springfield, Ill., 1967. Plokker,
J. H. & Wiesenhütter, E.: Zerrbilder. Schizophrene
Gestalten. Stuttgart, 1969. Prinzhorn, H.: Bildnerei
der Giesteskranken. Darmstadt, [2]1970. Reitman, F.:
Psychotic art. London, 1950. Révész, G.: Psychology
and art of the blind. London, 1950. Sander, F.:
Elementarästhetische Wirkungen zusammengesetzter
geometrischer Figuren. Wundts Psychol. Stud., 1913,
9. Id.: Gestaltpsychol. und Kunsttheorie. Neue
Psychol. Stud., 1932, *4*. Id.: Gestaltpsychologisches
zur modernen Kunst. In: Mühlher R. & Fischl, J.
(Eds): Gestalt und Wirklichkeit. Festschrift für Wein-
hand. Berlin, 1967. Schrickel, H. G.: Psychology of
art. In: Roback, A. A. (Ed.): Present-day psychology.
New York, [2]1968. Siddig, A. & Thieme, T.: Die
verlorenen Botschaften. Über die Urteilsstruktur bei
Künstlern . . . Z. f. expt. u. angew. Psychol., 1969, *6*.
Vándor, T.: Visuelle Erlebnisse in Hypnose. Meisenheim, 1969. Wellek, A.: Das Farbenhören und seine
Bedeutung für die Bildende Kunst. Palette (Basel),
1966, *23*; Exakte Ästhetik (Frankfurt a. M.), 1966,
3-4. Werner, H.: Comparative psychology of mental
development. Chicago, [2]1948. Westrich, E.: Die
Entwicklung des Zeichnens während der Pubertät.
Frankfurt a. M., 1968. Winkler, W.: Psychol. der
modernen Kunst. Tübingen, 1949.   *A. Wellek*

Ascendance-submission. A bipolar continuum
from complete dominance to complete submission in interpersonal relations.

*Allport Ascendance-Submission Reaction
Study* (A–S Reaction Study): an inventory to
measure the individual's location on this
continuum; one of the first self-evaluation
scales in which the individual must choose the
behavior appropriate to him in a certain
situation.   *R.M.*

Ascending reticular activating system (ARAS).
A non-specific sensory system located in the
reticular formation (q.v.). The ARAS is fed by
primary afferent and cortico-reticular fibers.
Activation (i.e. arousal) of the ARAS effects a
general activation of the organism. It would
seem to be responsible for the transition from
a state of wakefulness to one of general attention. See *Alarm function*.   *R.H.*

Asceticism. A voluntary renunciation of "all"
sensuous gratification, sometimes in an
attempt to train the will to endure enforced
deprivation of pleasure. Usually associated
with the fulfillment of the ideal way of life
postulated by certain religious and even
political systems.   *J.G.*

Asexual. 1. A term descriptive of an individual wholly without secondary sexual characteristics, and who possesses only rudimentary sex organs. **2.** Term for a process of reproduction (e.g. spore formation) without the union of individuals or cells of different sexes: asexual generation; asexual reproduction.

G.L.

As if (Ger. *als ob*). A term deriving its currency from Hans Vaihinger's *Die Philosophie des Als Ob* (1911; Eng. trans.: *The Philosophy of "As If"*. New York & London, 1925) and referring to reality-enhancing, non-verifiable hypotheses or "guiding fictions". Whereas Vaihinger conceived of man's knowledge (classes, categorizations, concepts, and so on) as largely a network of such "as if" strategies, the term is also applied less inclusively to suppositions deliberately assumed in order to judge the consequences of such a situation. Adler (q.v.) applied Vaihinger's relativist conception to, e.g., the incorporation of novel experience and ideas into one's "scheme of apperception": the new is treated "as if" it were (or were not) the individually known, and thus assimilated by relation. The unified individual acts "as if" he knew his goal; and so on. *J.C.*

Asphyxia. Arrested breathing. The CO_2 content of the blood responsible for breathing control rises above a partial pressure of 56 mm Hg and poisons the breathing center; consequently artificial respiration is necessary. Asphyxia occurs in the newborn during birth either as a blue, non-dangerous, or a white, dangerous form. It results from blocking of the respiratory passages or lesions of the brain resulting from birth trauma. *E.D.*

Aspiration level. The level of aspiration is the possible goal (score) an individual sets himself in his performance. Hoppe (1930) traced personal achievement to the experience of success and failure: a specific action only becomes success or failure because of its relation to a momentary goal or norm which can serve as a yardstick for the action considered in the sense of achievement. In experiments with different tasks Hoppe observed an increase in aspiration level after repeated success in the same achievement, and a decrease after repeated failure, which he described as typical shifts in aspiration level. An atypical shift would be an increase after failure and a decrease after success. Hoppe used the term *ego level* for the attempt to keep one's self-image as high as possible by a high standard of achievement. In experiments with children (10 to 15 years) and adults, Jucknat used two series of tasks: a success series (ten cards with solvable maze tests and a scale of increasing difficulty) and a failure series (ten similiar though insoluble tasks). Measurement of the choice time for the task in a decision conflict (i.e. the time from the start of the problem-solving process to decision taking) revealed the following: a final decision for a specific, easy or difficult, task is made only after a more or less protracted period of consideration and trying of several tasks. After successful solution of a task, on average the time taken to select the new task constantly decreases. After success, encouragement is shown not only in the increase of aspiration level but in the speed of selection and in immediate application to more difficult tasks. After failure, the average selection time either remains approximately the same, or even increases. The drop in self-estimation is expressed not only in the decrease in aspiration level but in considerable fluctuation or a slow, lingering process of selection.

1. *Aspiration level and achievement motivation.* Confrontation with a standard of excellence is a central theme of achievement motivation (q.v.) (D. C. McClelland, J. W. Atkinson, H. Heckhausen, etc.). The personality-specific expression of achievement motivation decisively influences the aspiration level preferred by the individual. Not only its intensity but above all its orientation

plays a part in achievement motivation, whether hope of success or fear of failure is predominant (Heckhausen, 1963). Jucknat and others trace the formation of an aspiration level to the interaction of momentary achievement, longstanding achievement confidence, momentary achievement impulse, seriousness of the situation and type of subject. Heckhausen indicates that social situations, e.g. the presence, prestige and behavior of onlookers, also influence aspiration level. The goal discrepancy of subjects, i.e. the difference between the level of aspiration and the level of achievement attained previously, would seem to be an indicator of individual achievement motivation. It is constantly evident that those confident of success prefer an aspiration level somewhat above the actual achievement, whereas those concerned with the possibility of failure prefer an aspiration level far above or far below their actual capacity. Sears found that the average positive discrepancy in children after failure is greater than after success. This would indicate that estimation of ability is more realistic after success than after failure. Confident, realistically adjusted children behave reasonably in regard to aspiration level. Socially maladaptive children showing disturbed performance are mainly characterized by their affective wishes in regard to aspiration level. After protracted success-and-failure experiments with school and college students, Nuttin recorded effects on perception, learning and memory. In comparisons of normal and manic-depressive subjects, cumulative occurrences of success and failure often result in destructive deformations and traumatic operations of judgment. Both successes and failures are experienced as stress situations by children with speech defects.

2. *Aspiration level and group achievement.* When a group of individuals are faced with the task of deciding between goals of varying degrees of difficulty, one problem is how a common group goal is established from the individual goals set. It has been shown that group members with a high desire for group achievement chose tasks of average difficulty, whereas members with a low desire for group achievement chose either very difficult or very easy tasks (Zandér, Medow *et al.*). Differences in the estimation of subjects' own individual performance were found among members with a central or peripheral position in the group (Zander & Medow). Members with a central position evaluated their own performance after failure at a level lower than that at which members with a peripheral position judged theirs; but after success there was hardly any difference in self-evaluations. With failure, group members evaluated the group result at a lower level than their personal performance ($X = 3·21$ or $4·67$). With success, on the other hand, they evaluated their personal and the group performance at approximately the same high level ($X = 5·09$). With success and failure, the group performance is usually judged more favorably by those with a central position in the group than by those with a peripheral position. E. Mayo has indicated positive effects of success on the climate of work (see *Industrial psychology*). Harmonious understanding, a feeling of responsibility and recognition of individual importance are features of a harmonious work group. Although failure can stimulate enthusiasm for work, it will often be a dogged or bitter rather than happy enthusiasm.

Research into the relations between performance (achievement) and aspiration level, and into the dynamic processes of success and failure, has become increasingly significant since Hoppe's classical investigation, and is carried out in widely varying fields: in psychology, education, sociology, economics and politics.

Bibliography: Atkinson, J. W.: Motivational determinants of risk-taking behavior. Psychol. Rev., 1957, *64*, 359–372. **Id. & N. T. Feather:** A theory of achievement motivation. New York, 1966. **Festinger, L.:** Wish, expectation, and group standards as affecting level of aspiration. J. abnorm. soc. Psychol., 1942, *37*, 184–200. **Heckhausen, H.:** Hoffnung und Furcht in der Leistungsmotivation. Meisenheim/Glan,

1963. Id.: Allgemeine Psychologie in Experimenten. Göttingen, 1969. Hilgard, E. R., Sait, E. M. & Margaret, G. A.: Level of aspiration as affected by relative standing in an experimental social group. J. exp. Psychol., 1940, 27, 411–21. Hoppe, F.: Erfolg und Misserfolg. Psychol. Forsch., 1930, 14, 1–62. Jucknat, M.: Leistung, A. und Selbstbewusstsein. Psychol. Forsch., 1937, 22, 89–179. Lewin, K.: Feldtheorie in den Sozialwissenschaften. Berne, 1963. Lewin, K., Dembo, T., Festinger, L. & Sears, P.: Level of aspiration. In: J. McV. Hunt (Ed.): Personality and the behavior disorders, Vol. 1. New York, 1944, 333–378. Mayo, E.: The human problems of an industrial civilization. Cambridge, Mass., 1933. Id.: The social problems of an industrial civilization. Cambridge, Mass., 1945. Medow, H. & Zander, A.: Aspirations for the group chosen by central and peripheral members. J. Pers. soc. Psychol., 1965, 1, 224–28. Nuttin, J.: Tâche, réussite et échec. Théorie de la conduite humaine. Louvain, 1953. Zander, A. & Medow, H.: Individual and group levels of aspiration. Human Relations, 1963, 16, 89–105.

A. Karsten

Assignment therapy. Psychotherapeutic treatment by assigning to an appropriate play, work or discussion group. See *Group therapy*.

Assimilation. 1. Generally, the process of incorporation of some aspect of the surrounding environment into the self or whole. Among the variety of uses in psychology is that of the distortion of new facts and stimuli to accord with expectations based on previous experience. Thus the details of a rumor are modified in accordance with one's prejudices before being transmitted to others. In perceptual psychology, assimilation phenomena (the accentuation of stimulus similarities) are opposed to *contrast* phenomena (the accentuation of stimulus differences). *Cultural assimilation*, also called *acculturation* (q.v.), is the process of becoming like the social environment in some respects, e.g. adopting the prevailing attitudes of that society.

G.D.W.

2. In the *biological* sense, assimilation is the conversion by living organisms (with the aid of sunlight and chlorophyll) of simple, low-energy chemicals into more complex, energy-rich compounds. H.Sch.

3. *Physiologically*, assimilation is the formation of substances proper to the body from basic chemical substances, ultimately absorbed from food and directly from the intermediary metabolism. In E. Hering's color theory, assimilation refers to the building-up of the three color-sensitive substances in the retina (q.v.) (corresponding to the antagonistic colors green-red, blue-yellow and black-white) under light stimulation. Assimilation and dissimilation (q.v.) take place to varying degrees at the same time; the resulting color sensation depends on the dominance of one or the other process. R.R.

Assimilation-contrast theory. A theory of information processing (Yale group). Information which falls within the tolerance of one's own opinion is accepted and "processed" by reciprocal approximation of divergent viewpoints. Information diverging from one's own viewpoint is rejected. In extreme cases, the receiver of the information puts forward his own opinion even more radically in opposition to the viewpoint received by him ("boomerang effect").

H.-J.A.

Associate chain theories. See *Associative chain theory*.

Association. Thunder has always been connected with lightning and such associations probably go back to the beginning of human thought. Various types and degrees of associations have been postulated whenever man began to reflect more systematically about the nature and the origin of his knowledge, thoughts, images and ideas. The *Psychological Abstracts* indicate "learning" as a cross-reference for "association" and list studies in conditioning, verbal learning, sensation, memory, recall, and so on, under this combined category.

1. *History of associationism.* The concept of associationism appears first in Plato's

Phaedo where it is pointed out that the mere sight of a lover's lyre or gown will bring thoughts and feelings similar to those caused by the lover himself. Aristotle, in *On Memory and Reminiscence*, established several principles of association which influenced much later psychology. He thought that we recall an object because it is either similar or dissimilar to the one in our present thought, or because the two objects were originally perceived by us closely in time and space. These Aristotelian principles of association became known as the laws of similarity, contrast, and contiguity. Aristotle thought that repetition, emotion, attention, and certain forms and shapes of objects also influence the formation of associations.

For Aristotle, association implied that thoughts are environmentally determined and not "god-given". This was not acceptable to the Scholastic philosophers, and speculations about association lay dormant for about 2000 years, until they were revived as "associationism" or the "doctrine of associationism" by the British empirical philosophers Hobbes, Locke, Hume, Hartley, Bain and others. As summarized by Esper (1964), these writers closely followed Aristotle's laws of association in postulating that all mental life stems from sensory stimulation, and that similar experiences may later occur as ideas or as mental elements in the absence of the original stimulation. Hartley extended the laws of association to include muscular movements and suggested certain neurophysiological rules as the basis for associationism. Bain proposed the additional principles of pleasure and pain, and pointed out that those associations which lead to pleasure will be repeated, and those which lead to pain will not.

The experimental basis of associationism was established mainly by Sechenov. In *Reflexes of the Brain* (1863), he explained certain mental and purposive acts in terms of neurological mechanisms which had been demonstrated in laboratories.

Sechenov's work paved the way for Pavlov who spent many years investigating the circumstances under which animals and humans learn or form associations between new and previously known stimuli and responses. Pavlov (1934) maintained that there was no difference between the psychologist's term "association" and the psychologist's terms "conditioning" (q.v.) or "temporary nervous connections". Pavlov's work has influenced much of present psychology, in theory as well as in practice.

2. *Modern associationist theories.* Modern psychology encompasses many areas, and associationistic principles play an important part in several of them. Developmental psychology (q.v.) has been strongly influenced by Watson's behaviorism (1919). Watson demonstrated that Pavlov's findings apply equally well to human infants, as many of their fears and desires can be conditioned by direct or indirect associations with physical pain or pleasure. Watson's classical conditioning procedures have been augmented by Skinner's (1953) operant conditioning methods. These methods use the naturally occurring behavior fluctuations, and reward those which approach "wanted" behavior, and neglect those which are not wanted. Many of the principles of conditioning and their experimental studies pertaining to sucking, feeding, toilet training, and other child-rearing problems, are currently reported in the *Journal of Experimental Child Psychology*.

The psychology of learning (q.v.) leans most heavily on associationistic principles. Robinson (1932) listed the following laws of association as important to learning theorists: contiguity, assimilation, frequency, intensity, duration, context, acquaintance, and so on. Various theorists, however, have investigated and emphasized different aspects necessary for the establishment of associations. As pointed out by Hilgard Bower (1956), Guthrie stressed mere time or contiguity, Hull the reduction of physiological needs, and Tolman the formation of mental patterns. Congruent with current trends of specialization, research in learning has examined more discrete problems of association. As frequently reported in the *Journal of Verbal Learning and Verbal Behavior*, investigators seek to understand the mechanisms of learning by examining specialized problems such as whole vs. part learning, massed vs. distributed practice, interference of retention, perceptual generalization, unlearning, inhibitions, and so on.

The social implications of modern associationistic theories are perhaps most evident in the areas of education, counseling, and clinical psychology, where they have found many practical applications. Eysenck (1968) has pioneered the investigation and description of procedures which uncondition or desensitize socially undesirable behavior. A homosexual, for instance, may be given an electric shock while looking at pictures of men; an alcoholic may be given a drug which will cause nausea at his next intake of alcohol; and so on. Behavior modification techniques based on Skinnerian operant conditioning are also expanding rapidly into fields of education, juvenile delinquency, psychopathology, and into other areas where retraining is an issue.

Pongratz (1967; pp. 58, 173) has pointed out that associationism has been criticized by gestalt psychology and other phenomenological approaches. Psychoanalytic views have also been opposed to knowledge gained through the investigation of association, because they hold that human thought and conduct cannot be dissected into elements and laws of association. Despite these various counter-currents, associationism has occupied much of psychology's theory and practice and is likely to make many further contributions to the understanding of human behavior. See *Conditioning*.

Bibliography: Esper, E. A.: A history of psychology. Philadelphia & London, 1964. Eysenck, H. J.: Fact and fiction in psychology. London, 1965. Hilgard, E. R. & Bower, G. H.: Theories of learning. New York, ³1956. Jowett, B.: The Republic of Plato (trans.) Oxford, ³1908. Pavlov, I. P.: Selected works. Moscow, 1955. (Original publication, 1934). Pongratz, L. J.: Problemgeschichte der Psychologie. Berne & Munich,

1967. Robinson, E. S.: Association theory to-day. N.Y., 1932. Ross, W. D. (Ed.): The works of Aristotle. Oxford, 1908-1931. Sechenov, I.: Reflexes of the brain. Cambridge, Mass., 1965 (originally publ. in: Meditsinsky Vestnik, Nos. 47 & 48, 1863). Skinner, B. F.: Science and human behavior. New York, 1953. Watson, J. B.: Psychology from the standpoint of a behaviorist. Philadelphia, 1919.   *F. Wesley*

Association coefficient. A term for forms of measurement of the degree of relationship between two alternative characteristics within a fourfold table.   *H.-J.S.*

Association, free. The non-purposefully linked course, trend or flow of thoughts, ideas and memories that arises in dreams (q.v.), daydreaming, and free fantasy, in psychotherapy (q.v.) and psychoanalysis. The subject or the observer (the psychotherapist) is said to be able to discern in free associations the motives and wishes which control these associations without his agency or volition.

Bibliography: Freud, S.: The interpretation of dreams. London, 1955. Jung, C. G.: Studies in word association. London, 1969.   *W.T.*

Association, induced. Related thoughts, ideas or memories induced or directed by stimulus or orienting ideas, goals or motives. In everyday life, associations may occur in the context of searching for a name, or a technique to solve a specific task; in psychology as divergent thought (under an overall theme); and in psychotherapy as the working out of a theme, a relationship with a certain person, or a traumatic event—when the orienting ideas are examined to uncover motives and wishes.   *W.T.*

Association, laws of. Since Aristotle, the following psychological laws governing association have been postulated with minor variations: *similarity* (two similar memory-contents are linked); *contrast* (two contrasted elements are linked with one another);

contiguity in space and time (two simultaneous or immediately successive elements are linked together). See *Association*. H.-J.A.

Association pathways. The neural association pathways in the cerebral cortex (intracortical pathways) are distinguished from those which pass largely beneath the cerebral cortex (subcortical pathways). The former represent mainly tangential connections of neighboring nerve cells (ganglionic cells, q.v.); the latter, in the form of nerve fibers (axons, q.v.) transmitting resting and action potential (q.v.), link cortical areas to their hemisphere. The *fibrae arcuatae cerebri* (bow-shaped nerve fibers) connect the convolutions on the surface of the cortex (see *Gyrus*). The *fasciculus longitudinalis superior* extends between the frontal and occipital lobes of the cerebrum. The *fasciculi intersegmentales* connect nerve cells of the same side with different spinal segments.

Association areas: The term sometimes used for the largest cortical areas, the frontal association area (in the frontal lobe) and parietal-temporal-occipital association area (PTO), which overlaps the parietal, the temporal, and the occipital lobes.

Bibliography: Braus, H. & Elze, E.: Anatomie des Menschen. Berlin, 1960. Grossman, S. P.: Physiological psychology. New York, 1967. Teitelbaum, P.: Physiological psychology. Englewood Cliffs, N.J., 1967.   G.A.

Association psychology. A school or trend in psychology seeking to explain all mental states and processes in terms of associations (see *Association*). The founders and principal proponents of this theory of mental organization might be said to be Hobbes, Hume, Hartley, James Mill, J. S. Mill, and A. Bain. The term is often used to refer only to psychology before the second half of the nineteenth century. Association psychology still plays a not insignificant role in learning (q.v.) theory.   H.-J.A.

Association-sensation ratio. Ratio of mass of total association cortex to total sensory cortex. Sometimes used to indicate learning ability.

Association test. The subject is required to respond with association to stimuli, usually words. The method is used in psychoanalysis to uncover repressed complexes, and sometimes in forensic psychology (in certain countries) to confirm evidence. It is, of course, applied in marketing psychology to determine reactions to a brand name and so on. Occasionally, an attempt is made to decide the degree of "originality" of the subject by comparing his associations with those typical in the population.   V.M.

Associative chain theory. The postulate that one act in a series is caused by (causes) another.

Associative fluency. In divergent thinking: a factor assessed by tests in which, e.g., as many synonyms as possible have to be given for a predetermined word, or sentences must be completed with adjectives, or words must be made out of one initial word.   M.A.

Associative inhibition. See *Memory*.

Astasia; astasia-abasia. See *Abasia*.

Asthenic type. According to E. Kretschmer's typology, a long, lean and dysplastic version of the leptosome (q.v.) constitution (physique), with a similar tendency to psychic disturbances. According to K. Conrad, the hypoplastic pole of the "secondary variant" body-build types. E. Kretschmer assesses the asthenic character as simply submissive under stress, and featuring no particular defense reactions: "weak-willed, thin-skinned natures which suffer the stresses of life without being able to defend themselves from them, neither hating nor showing anger".

Bibliography: Kretschmer, E.: Der sensitive Beziehungswahn. Berlin, ⁴1966. Id.: Physique and character. London, 1925. Conrad, K.: Der Konstitutionstyp. Berlin, ²1963.   W.K.

Astigmatism. The refractive surfaces of the eye, cornea and lens can feature irregularities, or variable degrees of refraction in varying visual fields. Usually the variations of refraction extend to 0·5 diopters, but more extensive irregularities are experienced as disturbances of vision and classed as astigmatism. Astigmatic lenses are used to correct the deviation. Corneal astigmatism is usually predominant.
                                                                    R.R.

Astigmometer (syn. *Astigmatometer*). A device for measuring the degree of astigmatism of the eye's refractive system in different visual fields. First described by Hemlholtz (1855); various modifications since—e.g. by E. Javal and H. Schiötz.   R.R.

Asymmetry. Asymmetry (the opposite of symmetry) refers to the *skewness* (q.v.) of distributions. An asymmetrical frequency distribution is one without a mean value $\bar{X}$ to which $f(X - \bar{X})$ is applicable. In mathematics and logic, asymmetry means that a relation R, which is applicable for xRy, is not applicable for yRx.   W.H.B.

Ataractic drugs. See *Tranquilizer*.

Atavistic regression (*Atavism*). A throw-back or *reversion* to a more primitive ancestral form. In genetics, the reappearance in an organism of a character or trait which has not manifested itself for several generations. Also used more loosely to refer to primitive modes of behavior in general.   G.D.W.

Ataxia (syn. *Ataxy*). Incoordination of the groups of muscles responsible for movement, with the result that both oriented movements (e.g. reaching out for an object), sequential movements (e.g. walking or talking), and the equilibrium of trunk and limbs in a certain position, are disturbed. Ataxic movements tend to overshoot the goal.

The causes of ataxia are not located in the corresponding muscle group but in the spinal and cerebral centers responsible for control of movement.

Spinal ataxia: In disorders of the conductors responsible for depth sensitivity (e.g. in polyneuritis), or the nerve roots or ganglia of the spinal cord, e.g. in *tabes dorsalis*, or locomotor *ataxia* (ataxy), usually a sequel of syphilis. The tabetic patient generally sways or even falls if asked to stand upright with eyes closed (Romberg's sign, q.v.).

Cerebellar ataxia: Occurs during nonfunctioning of certain areas of the cerebellum as the result of tumors, atrophy, and so on; here, too, the patient sways when asked to stand with eyes closed (astasia) or to walk (abasia, q.v.).

Cerebral ataxia: Occurs with lesions of frontal, temporal and parietal lobes, of the thalamus and mesencephalon. Loss of coordination is not so pronounced as with cerebellar ataxia.   D.V.

Ataxiameter. A device which records and measures all an individual's involuntary movements, when he is trying to stand upright and motionless, with eyes closed. The ataxiameter is often used in experimental investigations of suggestibility (q.v.).   F.-C.S.

Athletic type. Robust physique, massive or slim. The locomotor apparatus (bones, muscles, etc.) is well developed, and there is occipital protuberance. Solid, high-set head with abundant hair and thick skin. Affinity to the barykinetic (q.v.) temperament, schizophrenia, epilepsy.

Bibliography: Kretschmer, E.: Physique and character. London, 1925. Id. & Kretschmer, W.: Medinische Psychologie. Stuttgart, [13]1970.   W.K.

Atmosphere effect. Woodworth & Sells observed (1935) that in a syllogism affirmative premisses tended to induce a positive formulation of the conclusion, even when the conclusion was logically false. Negative premisses tended to induce negative conclusions. This suggestive effect exerted by the "atmosphere" or context of the premisses, they termed an "atmosphere effect". E.g.: All these candies are chocolate-creams.

All these candies are delicious.

Chocolate-creams are delicious.

Bibliography: Woodworth, R. S. & Sells, S. B.: An atmosphere effect in formal syllogistic reasoning. J. exp. Psychol., 1935, *18*, 451–60.   H.-J.A.

Atomism. 1. *Atomistic psychology* tries to obtain insight into psychological processes or mental states by reducing them to their elements or discrete components, and is therefore opposed to gestalt psychology (see *Ganzheit*, etc.). Gestaltist theoreticians sometimes use the term pejoratively to characterize association psychology (q.v.), sensualism (q.v.) and extreme forms of neobehaviorism (q.v.). **2.** *Logical atomism* is the philosophical view that certain entities are ultimately unanalyzable, related only contingently, or wholly independent: e.g. there are unanalyzable atomic propositions from which other propositions are generalized.   *H.-J.A.*

Atonia (syn. *Atony*). The absence of all normal muscular tension. In the smooth tissue musculature this can lead to circulatory collapse; in the gastro-intestinal tract, to ileus (cessation of bowel peristalsis); and in the pregnant uterus to a dangerous arrestation of the birth process.   *E.D.*

Atrophy. Decrease in volume and loss of function in organs or parts of organs, usually as the result of inactivity or a lack of oxygen or nourishment.   *E.D.*

Atropine (*Hyoscyamine*). A parasympathetic-inhibiting substance found together with the other belladonna drug hyoscine (scopalamine, q.v.) in deadly nightshade and similar plants. Main physiological effects in small doses (0·5–5 mg): dilatation of pupils, paralyzed accommodation, inhibition of aqueous humor flow, reduction of sweat and saliva (increase in skin resistance, dryness of the mouth), antispasmodic effect (especially in gastro-intestinal area), peristalsis inhibition, rapid pulse (but slows down heart rate with very low doses, up to 0·5 mg). In the CNS there is slow electrocortical activity (5–8 Hz), and reduction of the arousal reaction of the reticular formation under stimulation (e.g. light). The main psychic effects (several hours) with low doses (0·5–5 mg administered orally): subjective deactivation; performance non-uniform but largely affected. At higher doses (10 mg): activation. Hallucinations occasionally with very high doses. In numerous animal investigations (some in animals reacting differently from men) symptoms of sedation at lower dosage seem less pronounced than in men. The EEG behavior dissociation described by A. Wikler (EEG retardation unaccompanied by deactivation) is theoretically significant. No satisfactory explanation is as yet forthcoming for the coexistence of activating and deactivating symptoms, both in animals and in man. It is extremely probable that many psychic effects are not "centrally" but "peripherally" conditioned by the considerable autonomic effects (unusual vegetative sensations). There are numerous substances related to or derived from atropine (e.g. naltropine, homatropine, scopalamine). Their effects are to some effect quite different to those of atropine, especially in the relations between central and autonomic action. Several of these drugs have relatively slight peripheral-physiological effects, but more powerful central effects (e.g. naltropine).

Bibliography: Longo, V. G.: Behavioral and electro-encephalographic effects of atropine and related compounds. Pharmacol. Rev., 1966, *18*, 965–96. Soyka, L. F. & Unna, K. R.: A comparison in man of the autonomic and behavioral effects of N-Allylnoratropine with atropine. Psychopharmacologia. 1964, *6*, 453–61. *W.J.*

Attention. There are several concepts of attention. Knowledge concerning attention is developing rapidly, especially in cognitive-perceptual psychology, physiological psychology, psychophysics, and behavior theory. But these developments proceed independently to a great extent; different meanings of the term are found in the different fields as well as within each field. It is possible to discern some continuity with historical meanings of attention in most cases.

In the older literature, attention was defined in terms of conscious awareness and played crucial roles in the great theories of consciousness. Structural psychology and functional psychology each made use of the term and two quite different conceptions emerged.

Structural psychology associated attention with the clearness of items in consciousness. Wundt described consciousness as consisting of a clear core or focus and a less-clear periphery, and considered attention to be the process by which items in peripheral consciousness are brought into the focus of consciousness. Attention transforms perception into apperception and imparts clarity (Boring, 1929). Titchener went further, implying a continuum of clearness produced by attention and giving clearness the status of a dimension of sensation which he called "attensity". Attensity, along with intensity, extensity, duration and others, became a fundamental dimension of the structure of consciousness (Boring, 1929).

Rather than placing attention "within" consciousness, as the structuralists appeared to do, William James (1890), representing the functionalists, located it prior to consciousness and described attention as a process

of selection among items not yet in consciousness: a selection of some items to enter consciousness while other items remain excluded. James argued that attention is a necessary condition for conscious clearness but he specifically denied that it is sufficient; additional cognitive operations are also required. Hence James emphasized the importance of attention in the relationship between an organism and its environment. Through the selective action of attention a psychological environment is created out of the physical environment and thereby attention gains adaptive significance. But James did not confine attention only to selection among stimuli. He recognized intellectual as well as sensorial attention, and volitional as well as passive attention.

Few references to attention are to be found in the literature of gestalt psychology, behaviorism and psychoanalysis, and for many years the concept was ignored. Its revival was heralded by an influential book by Donald Hebb (Hebb, 1949). Citing new evidence for spontaneous central neural activity, Hebb posited attention as an autonomous central process acting as a reinforcement of sensory processes and strongly influenced by learning. Attention determines perceptual organization and the selection of a response, given a particular sensory input. Response selection rather than stimulus selection is emphasized, and a similarity between attention and set is apparent.

A book by Broadbent (1958) proposed a new theory of attention, couched in the terminology of information theory and based on stimulus selection. This event marks the beginning of modern attention theory in cognitive-perceptual psychology. Broadbent's theory was based on the results of extensive experiments of two kinds: "listen-and-answer" and "split memory span". In the former, subjects listen to several speech messages simultaneously and then are interrogated about the messages. Broadbent showed how limited one is in performing such a task, and worked out some of the factors involved.

In the split-span experiment, immediate memory for digits is tested with successive pairs of digits presented dichotically, i.e., one member of each pair to the right ear, the other to the left ear. The main finding was that subjects organize their responses according to ear rather than according to order of presentation when the number of pairs is small and they are presented rapidly.

Broadbent's theory is most like the position taken by William James. The function of attention is to prevent overloading of the individual's information-processing capacity. The cognitive structure (P-system, in Broadbent's terms) has an information-processing capacity which is much less than the total entering the organism by the sensory pathways; attention serves as a gate to admit some and exclude the remainder: it is a "filter" interposed between sensory input and P-system. The filter is all-or-none, admitting the contents of one input channel at a time and completely blocking the remainder, but it can switch rapidly between channels, and the boundaries of channels are flexible, being in part a function of the amount of information in the sensory pathways.

This filter theory of selective attention stimulated many experiments which have led to several modifications of the theory. These have recently been reviewed (Swets & Kristofferson, 1970; Moray, 1969). A dominant experimental method in this work is the shadowing technique, in which two different messages of continuous speech are presented simultaneously, one to each ear, and the subject follows one of the messages by repeating it as he hears it. The message which is not being repeated conveys little information to the subject although under certain conditions it does convey some. If, for example, it contains the subject's own name, there is some chance that it will be heard. Such findings have been taken to mean that there must be some interpretation of sensory input prior to attention, and several more recent theories differing from Broadbent in various ways on this point have been proposed (Moray, 1969).

The idea of selective attention as a sensory filter has been studied in psychophysics (q.v.) for some years, and several methods have been developed for the quantitative investigation of some aspects of attention. For example, the probability of detecting a weak stimulus is higher if the subject knows in advance the identity of the sensory channel in which the signal will occur. This literature, particularly that which relates attention to signal detection theory, has been reviewed recently (Swets & Kristofferson, 1970).

Initial presentation of a novel stimulus is likely to produce a complex response pattern which has behavioral, central-neural and autonomic components. This "orienting reflex" (q.v.) habituates rapidly and may reappear if the stimulus is changed slightly. It is interpreted as a state of heightened attentiveness and has been studied extensively (Sokolov, 1963): both physiologically (Lindsley, 1960), where it is related to activation or arousal (q.v.), and behaviorally (see Jerison, 1968, for a brief summary). As behavior, it is related to observing responses, such as eye-movements, which are often used to indicate attending, and to instrumental and classical conditioning.

The importance of observing responses in learning has been recognized by behavior theorists for many years, especially by those who study discrimination learning. The sufficiency of observing responses as attentional mechanisms is now being questioned and learning theorists are turning to hypothetical constructs of selective attention in the analysis of discrimination learning (Trabasso & Bower, 1968).

The arousal systems of the brain are being mapped out. Their response to external stimuli is observed as a desynchronization of the electroencephalogram (q.v.) and the relationships among attentiveness, arousal and levels of consciousness are being determined. There is some evidence that the arousal systems are involved in selective attention through inhibition and facilitation of sensory inputs (Lindsley, 1960).

94

Attention enters into certain areas of applied psychology. In engineering psychology, for example, attention sets limits on the design of those information-processing systems which include human operators. Of particular importance are limits on the ability to receive information simultaneously from multiple sources and to sustain attention for long periods of time. Much research has been done on the latter under the heading of "vigilance" (q.v.) (Swets & Kristofferson, 1970). Another example is the considerable recent literature on attentional deficits associated with various pathological conditions, particularly schizophrenia.

Bibliography: Boring, E. G.: A history of experimental psychology. New York & London, 1929. Broadbent, D. E.: Perception and communication. Oxford, 1958. Hebb, D. O.: The organization of behavior. New York & London, 1949. James, W.: The principles of psychology. New York, 1950 (1890). Jerison, H. J.: Attention. Int. Encycl. Soc. Sci., 1968, 444–9. Lindsley, D. B.: Attention, consciousness, sleep and wakefulness. Vol. 3, 1553–1593, in Am. Physiol. Soc., Handbook of Physiology. Section 1: Neurophysiology. Ed. Magoun, H. W. et al., Baltimore, 1960. Moray, N.: Attention. Selective processes in vision and hearing. London, 1969. Sokolov, E. N.: Perception and the conditioned reflex. New York, 1963. Swets, J. A. & Kristofferson, A. B.: Attention. Ann. Rev. of Psychol., 1970, 21, 339–66. Trabasso, T. & Bower, G. H.: Attention in learning: Theory and research. New York-London-Sydney, 1968.

A. B. Kristofferson

Attention, distributive. Attention distributed over several processes or objects. See *Attention.*

Attention, fluctuation of. Attention (q.v.) cannot be given with the same intensity to a single process or object after a certain period of time, but is subject to fluctuations or periodic changes evidenced in fluctuating performance. H. Rohracher postulates a cause in regeneration of the ganglionic cells.

H.-J.A.

Attention span. The number of objects (e.g. random digits) which can be grasped in one short presentation.

Attention theories. 1. *Physiological:* G. E. Müller believed that certain processes increased the stimulability of certain areas of the brain, thus leading to improved receptivity. H. Ebbinghaus and E. Dürr derived attention from effects occurring in the nerve pathways of the brain, and assumed that impulses passing through certain frequently-used pathways must lead to more precise perception ("*Bahnungstheorie*").

More modern theories treat attention for the most part physiologically, and refer to increased activation by the ARAS (see *Ascending reticular activating system; Alarm function*).

2. *Psychophysiological:* H. Henning's "sensibilization" theory sees attention as the result of a sensitization of the sense organs and neural pathways brought about by external and internal stimuli. Similarly, H. Rohracher sees attention as an activation of individual mental functions, provoked by powerful external stimuli or by drives, interests and volition. These theories are based on stimulation; P. K. Hofstätter explains attention in terms of the "suppressor-fields" which lead to a "reduction in the effective stimulation of the environing field".

3. *Psychological:* B. Erdmann sees attention as psychic energy pure and simple which cannot be derived more accurately. Mach and Wundt (like Kant) view attention as a consequence of volitional activity.

4. *Mechanical model:* D. E. Broadbent (1957): see *Attention.*

Theories of attention are largely determined by the fundamental conception of attention itself.

Bibliography: Broadbent, D. E.: A mechanical model for human attention and immediate memory. Psychol. Rev., 1957, 64, 205–15. *H.-J.A.*

Attention types. Experimental investigations (especially those of O. Vollmer), both with visual and acoustic stimuli, showed the existence of two attention types which can be categorized according to Kretschmer's constitutional typology. Schizothymes (q.v.)

showed a narrow attention span: their attention was detailed and their perception more objective. Cyclothymes (q.v.) featured a broad attention span; their attention tended to fluctuate, and perceived the whole in a more subjective manner.

Bibliography: Vollmer, O.: Die sogenannte Aufmerksamkeitstypen und die Persönlichkeit. Suppl. Vol. 14. Leipzig, 1929.   *W.K.*

Attitude. An *attitude* is normally defined as a perceptual orientation and response readiness in relation to a particular object or class of objects. Some qualifications must be added however:

(*a*) Attitudes are reasonably *enduring*, thus distinguishing them from *sets* and *expectations* which normally refer to more temporary states of readiness. This does not mean that attitudes can never change (for attitude change is a very important field in social psychology), just that they are extremely resistant to alteration.

(*b*) Attitudes must show *variation* between individuals and between cultures, i.e. they relate to issues upon which people disagree. In this way they are distinguished from various other concepts referring to response predispositions and characteristic behavior, such as *instinct* (q.v.) and *habit* (q.v.). As Sherif *et al.* (1965, 19) point out, "the fact that we customarily walk downstairs instead of tumbling down does not require explanation in terms of an attitude, nor does the characteristic response of eating when a hungry person is offered food". This fact of variance within and between cultures is often taken to mean that attitudes are *learned* through experience. Although this appears to be true in the main, it seems likely that certain genetic predispositions, e.g. aggressiveness, (which also show variance in the population) may be partial determinants of certain attitudes (McGuire, 1969).

(*c*) Possibly the most important distinguishing feature of attitudes is that they are necessarily *evaluative* or *affective*. Beliefs may be constituents of attitudes ("Negroes

are dirty"), or they may be largely unrelated to attitudes ("Negroes are tall").

(*d*) The attitude concept in psychology has the scientific status of a *hypothetical construct*. It cannot be directly observed, but must be inferred from observable behavior such as verbal statements of *opinion*, physiological changes due to exposure to the attitude object, or overt acts in relation to the object. None of these observables may be equated with attitudes; they can only be used as indicators, measures, or "operational definitions".

1. *Measurement.* Attitudes are most commonly measured through analysis of patterns of response to questionnaires and other *self-report* techniques. These fall into two major groups: (*a*) *Scales which present directional statements of opinion* (e.g. "Homosexuals ought to be publicly whipped"), to which S responds with some amount of agreement or disagreement. Among the best-known scales of this kind are the *F-Scale* (Adorno, Frenkel-Brunswik, Levinson & Sanford, 1950), the *Dogmatism Scale* (Rokeach, 1960), and the *Social Attitudes Inventory* (Eysenck, 1954). (*b*) *Scales which present non-directional concepts* (e.g., "Father", "death penalty") and require the respondent to evaluate them. The *Semantic Differential* (Osgood, Suci & Tannenbaum, 1957), and the *Conservatism Scale* (Wilson & Patterson, 1968) are scales of this kind. When applicable, the latter item format would seem to be preferable on a number of counts. It is economical, less susceptible to acquiescence response bias, eliminates certain sources of ambiguity (e.g. differences in the perceived point of emphasis in the opinion statement), and avoids algebraic addition problems for the subject (e.g. having to disagree with a negatively worded statement).

Of the various techniques for selecting scale items, most of the traditional methods (e.g. those of Thurstone and Guttman) were concerned with the construction of *unidimensional* scales (Scott, 1969). With the advent of the computer, the mathematical models upon which they are based have been largely

8

superseded by the technique of *factor analysis*, which permits the development of *multi-dimensional* attitude scales.

In addition to the self-report technique, various *disguised* measures of attitudes have also been investigated, on the argument that they are less contaminated by various inhibitory factors (such as "social desirability") which might lead to faking. Actually, this problem is not very insistent in the area of attitude measurement because of the evaluative nature of attitudes themselves. Whereas with variables such as intelligence and neuroticism there is considerable agreement as to which end of the scale is desirable, an individual's own position in relation to an attitude object is by definition perceived as good.

Nevertheless, attitudes can be measured without the subject's awareness in terms of their effects upon memory and perceptual processes (e.g. recall thresholds, binocular resolution), or performance on certain tasks involving materials relevant to the attitude object (e.g. classifying opinion statements as favorable or unfavorable toward an issue instead of indicating one's own agreement). Several physiological measures of attitudes have also been used, especially autonomic measures such as the GSR (Cook & Selltiz, 1964). Apart from the fact that they are very cumbersome by comparison with questionnaires, the major disadvantage of most physiological measures is that they indicate only the *intensity* of an attitude response, not its *direction*. The recent hope that pupil size might constitute a measure of direction as well as intensity (Hess, 1965) now appears to be subsiding (McGuire, 1969).

2. *Structure*. There is widespread agreement amongst researchers that attitudes relating to various areas of social controversy (religion, politics, art, sexual behavior, race, and so on) tend to be intercorrelated, forming a *general factor* in social attitudes. This major dimension has been variously called fascism, authoritarianism, dogmatism, and rigidity, but is probably best described as *conservatism*, a tendency to resist change (Wilson, 1970). The extreme or "ideal" conservative is characterized by the following attitude clusters: religious dogmatism, right-wing political orientation, intolerance of minority groups, insistence on strict rules and punishments, anti-hedonistic outlook (the tendency to regard pleasure as bad), preference for conventional art, clothing, and institutions, and opposition to scientific progress. The individual opposite in each of these groups of attitudes would be described as *liberal*. See *Authoritarian personality*.

Eysenck (1954) has shown that, particularly in the field of political attitudes, it is also useful to study variation along a second, independent dimension which he called *toughmindedness-tendermindedness*. The toughminded individual is characterized by attitudes that are realistic, worldly, and aggressive (and tends to be an extraverted personality type), while the tenderminded individual has attitudes which are idealistic, moral, and submissive (and tends to be introverted). See *Traits; Type*.

3. *Functions*. McGuire (1969) discusses four types of adaptive functions which might be served by holding certain attitudes. These are not regarded as either mutually exclusive or exhaustive.

(*a*) *Utilitarian functions*—Attitudes may dispose us toward objects and paths that are instrumental in achieving valued goals, e.g. adopting the attitude of a group in order to gain acceptance within that group.

(*b*) *Economy functions*—Like all categories and generalizations, attitudes provide a simplification of the complex world and give guidance as to appropriate behavior in a new situation, e.g. holding a "stereotyped" image of a natural group enables one to treat all members of that group alike.

(*c*) *Expressive functions*—Attitudes may have self-assertive and cathartic functions, and may be adopted to bolster or justify one's behavior. The theory of *cognitive dissonance* (Festinger, 1957) draws attention to the fact that a change in attitude often follows rather than precedes a change in behavior, apparently serving a supportive function.

(d) *Ego-defense functions*—Some attitudes may be held not because of any characteristics of the object in question, but because they help to resolve certain inner conflicts, cf. the notion that anti-Semitism originates as a defense mechanism to facilitate the repression of oedipal hostility toward an authoritarian father (Adorno *et al.*, 1950).

McGuire notes that attitudes may be extremely resistant to change because they serve several or all of these functions at once. For example, a racial prejudice originating for ego-defensive reasons would soon be bolstered by a network of supportive attitudes and become a preferred way for the individual to assert himself and give meaning to his world. It would be a basis of selecting friends and would thus have utility as a means of remaining acceptable to the group. The difficulty in changing such an attitude is apparent.

4. *Attitude change.* In discussing the history of the attitude concept, McGuire (1969) notes that in the early part of this century it was so central to social psychology that it was often equated with it. After passing through an era in the 1950s when it was overshadowed by studies of group dynamics, the attitude concept has regained its dominant status within social psychology, and this has been largely through the work of Hovland, Festinger, Sherif, and others, on the variables and processes involved in attitude change. While it would be impossible to summarize the findings in this vast field here, it may be worthwhile to list some examples of fairly well-established findings.

(a) The extent to which a communication is effective in changing attitudes depends upon the perceived *credibility* of the source (e.g. the prestige of the communicator).

(b) Certain *personality* characteristics, e.g. low self-esteem and general passivity, dispose an individual toward high persuasibility.

(c) There are advantages in having both the first say (*primacy*) and the last say (*recency*)

in persuading an audience. These variables have relevance to the fair conduct of political debates and trial by jury.

(d) Attitudes which are close to those already held by the audience are likely to be *assimilated*, while those which are very far removed are likely to result in a reaction away from the communicator (*contrast effect*).

(e) Communications which present *both sides* of an argument while favoring one, are more effective than one-sided communications.

(f) Presenting and dismissing the opposite side of an argument ("*inoculation*") results in a greater resistance against later counter-communications.

(g) Establishing conditions favorable to *cooperation toward common goals* is an effective means of reducing intergroup hostility (the "common enemy" approach).

Bibliography: Adorno, T. W., Frenkel-Brunswik, E., Levinson, D. J. & Sanford, R. N.: The authoritarian personality. New York, 1950. Cook, S. W. & Selltiz, C.: A multiple-indicator approach to attitude measurement. Psychol. Bull., 1964, *62*, 36–55. Eysenck, H. J.: The psychology of politics. London, 1954. Festinger, L.: A theory of cognitive dissonance. Stanford, 1957. Hess, E. H.: Attitude and pupil size. Sci. Amer. 1965, *212*, 46–54. McGuire, W. J.: The nature of attitudes and attitude research. In: Lindzey, G. & Aronson, E. (Eds): Handbook of social psychology 2nd ed. Vol. 3. London, 1969. Osgood, C. E., Suci, G. J. & Tannenbaum, P. H.: The measurement of meaning. Urbana, Illinois, 1957. Rokeach, M.: The open and closed mind. New York, 1960. Scott, W. A.: Attitude measurement. In: Lindzey, G. & Aronson, E. (Eds.): Handbook of social psychology, 2nd ed., Vol. 2, London, 1969. Sherif, C. W., Sherif, M. & Nebergall, R. E.: Attitude and attitude change. Philadelphia, 1965. Wilson, G. D.: Is there a general factor in social attitudes? Evidence from a factor-analysis of the Conservatism Scale. Brit. J. Soc. Clin. Psychol., 1970. Wilson, G. D. & Patterson, J. R.: A new measure of conservatism. Brit. J. Soc. Clin. Psychol., 1968, 7, 264–9.   *G. D. Wilson*

Attitude change. A process in which an attitude (or an opinion, a judgment, etc.) is changed (see *Attitude*).

From a socio-psychological viewpoint, an attitude is a dependent variable of a process of social influence. The independent variables conditioning it are elements of a communication process: source variables, message variables, channel variables, receiver variables and destination variables. The more adequately these variables, and in particular their general mode of operation as well as their significance for a specific situation, are known, the easier it is to predict the direction and degree of a change of attitude.

Attitude change as a dependent quantity is regarded as a stochastic process in which the individual (the recipient) has to pass in turn through the stages of attention, comprehension, yielding, retention, and action, if the communication process is to effect a change in attitude.

In order to forecast and explain changes of attitude (and also changes of opinion and judgment), a series of models (attitude change theories) has been produced. Among these, consistency models regard such changes as subserving the restoration of a state of equilibrium (the principle of homeostasis) (see *Dissonance, cognitive*). There are also models with a greater psychophysical orientation, and "functional" models which stress the role of needs. See *Communication*.

Bibliography: Insko, C. A.: Theories of attitude change. New York, 1967. Rosenberg, M. J. & Hovland, C. J.: Attitude organization and change. New Haven, Conn., 1960.   *H.D.S.*

Attitude types. According to Jung's classification these are *introverts* and *extraverts*, and determine *function types* (q.v.). Introversion (q.v.) and extraversion (q.v.) indicate the nature of the probable reaction, of "expectation", and "direction" or "orientation". See *Type*.

Bibliography: Jung, C. G.: Psychologische Typen. Zürich, ⁰1960. (Eng. tran.: Psychological types. In: Contributions to analytical psychology. London, 1928. But see: Collected works, Vol. 6, in preparation).   *W.K.*

Attributes. 1. Any quality, property, character (usually elementary) of a subject or his behavior, or of a spiritual or material substance, that is deemed indispensable to the nature and therefore to any conception of the phenomenon in question. **2.** That which is predicated of the subject of a proposition. **3.** An invariant (discriminatory) response. **4.** Sometimes used loosely for *traits* (q.v.). In general, a term more appropriate to metaphysics than to exact psychology.   *J.G.*

Atypical. A marked deviation from the typical, e.g. in an individual differing from the social or group norm, or in a test-score.

Aubert-Förster phenomenon. At the same visual angle, objects that are nearer (e.g. letters) are recognized more easily than those that are more distant. The objects that are nearer take up a larger area of the retina.
                    V.M.

Aubert phenomenon. When an illuminated vertical line has been fixated in a dark room for some time, if the head is tilted to one side one has the impression that the line is displaced in the direction opposite to the tilting. The center of equilibrium alone is insufficient for full spatial orientation. *V.M.*

Audile (syn. *Auditive type; Auditory type*). A type whose ideas are affected by auditory stimulation, by the passing of time, and by movements. T. Kiefer in particular distinguishes between the visual and audile imagery types.

Bibliography: Kiefer, T.: Der visuelle Mensch. Munich & Basle, 1956.   *W.K.*

Audiogram. The result of an audiometric investigation (see *Audiometry*), it represents the loss of auditory sensitivity as the function of amplitude of a just perceptible sound. The unit of measurement is given in dB.
                    M.B.

Audiology. The theory of testing and investigating auditory acuity in order to diagnose and treat hearing disorders. The most important area of examination is *audiometry* (q.v.). In testing hearing the patient's own impressions of his auditory acuity (problem of *simulation*, q.v., child audiometry) are usually necessary; therefore an audiological examination or experiment can suffer from the usual sources of error that beset all psychological experimentation (fatigue, monotony, background noises, and so on). Problems also arise in regard to the subject's tonal adaptation and sensitization.   *M.B.*

Audiometer. A device for determining auditory acuity. The acumeter (Politizer's version) is an instrument producing a noise of constant intensity. The distance at which the noise can just be heard is taken as the auditory threshold. The basic audiometer is a device generating sounds of different frequencies (discrete or continuous); the tones can also be varied in intensity (discretely in 5 dB stages, or continuously). The amplifier is graduated in dB, and is fitted with earphones and usually has a loudspeaker too. There are various other forms of noise generator (e.g. for above-threshold audiometry).   *M.B.*

Audiometry. The measurement of auditory acuity by means of electro-acoustic noise generators (see *Audiometer*). The result of an audiometric investigation is usually recorded as an audiogram (q.v.). In addition to basic audiometry (diagnosis of disorders of the outer and inner ears, and combined disturbances), audiometry is also concerned with above-threshold audiometry (the differential diagnosis of the impairment of auditory acuity of the inner ear); speech audiometry (suitability of hearing aids; counting and word-recognition tests, etc.). There are various other divisions, ranging from child audiometry to objective audiometry (psycho-galvanic skin reaction, etc.).   *M.B.*

Audio-visual aids. Means of presenting information during instruction, which is directed to the eye and ear. This definition would cover wall-charts and maps as well as the more modern media, such as slides, loops, films, gramophone records, tapes, radio, and television. Audio-visual aids are intended to make the material of the lesson more "actual", and clearly apprehensible, and to stimulate the pupil's attention and motivation. In programmed instruction (see *Instructional technology*), and particularly in machine learning (q.v.), audio-visual techniques are no longer mere aids but integral components of the instructional process.
Bibliography: Lumsdaine, A. A. & Glaser, R.: Teaching machines and programmed learning. Vol. I. Washington, 1962. The following journals, among others, provide information on a fast-moving field: Programmed Learning and Educational Technology (U.K.); Audio-Visual Communication Review (U.S.A.).   *H.I.*

Audition colorée. See *Colored hearing*.

Auditory acuity. See *Auditory perception*.

Auditory ossicles (syn. *Ossicular chain*). The three bones (hammer, anvil and stirrup) of the middle ear. Part of the mechanical transmission system between the external auditory canal and the cochlea of the inner ear, the ossicles increase the force but reduce the amplitude of the transmitted vibration (adaptation of 26 dB). The hammer (manubrium and malleus), which is connected to the drum, transmits the mechanical vibrations by way of the anvil (incus) and the stirrup (stapes) to the oval window of the cochlea.   *M.S.*

Auditory perception. The decoding by the central nervous system of certain stimuli processed physiologically by the sense of hearing. As in all the sensory modalities, a distinction must be made between *perception* and *sensation*. Auditory perception is far more complex than auditory sensation, since it leads to the identification (recognition) of composite sound stimuli (sound patterns) or elements. Auditory sensation is brought about by the stimulation of specific elements in the ear, and is the elementary form of nervous response to sound stimuli. *Sound* is the adequate stimulus. The objective, physical parameters for sound are *frequency* (audible range from about 16 to 22,000 c/s) and *amplitude*. In the case of frequencies under 16 c/s, one speaks of *infrasonic* waves (which produce vibratory or "fluttering" sensations); in the case of frequencies over 30,000 c/s, of *ultrasonic* waves. *Pitch* is closely related to frequency but may vary with intensity. *Intensity* (known as *loudness* in subjective terms) depends on the amplitude of the oscillations, which are measured in phons or decibels (dB). Auditory sensitivity varies with frequency. It is greatest (lowest absolute auditory threshold; threshold of audibility) in the middle frequency range (1000 to 3000 c/s). The sensitivity of hearing is good in regard to variations in intensity and frequency (see *Sense organs*). The measurement of auditory thresholds and the determination of hearing defects are the functions of *audiometry* (q.v.).

See *Sense organs: the ear* for detailed information on sound; the reception of stimuli (external ear to ear drum); mechanical amplification by the middle ear; transformation into nervous impulses in the cochlea; sensitivity to frequencies; measurement of loudness, and adaptation; auditory range and localization; and estimation of the distance of a sound source.

1. *Auditory perception* is very complex and depends on many factors; it allows the following possibilities: specific judgments of sound sensations; determination of the spatial location of sound sources; separation of several different simultaneous sound stimuli (a specific type of sound can be recognized accurately in the presence of other sounds); and comprehension of language and all the precise distinctions of intonation (we recog-

nize an individual by his speech). Finally, auditory perception has many important functions in speech. Auditory perception relies on a series of operations in the higher centers of the central nervous system (q.v.), starting from information received (sensations); it is essentially based on the availability of all previous experience (mnemic traces stored in the memory); on conditioning, on associations, and on (for the most part) unconscious cognitive and affective operations (music).

2. *The subjective characteristics of sound* (auditory phenomena). Depending on its individual nature, sound may be perceived as pleasant, neutral or unpleasant. The "auditory area" consists of more than 300,000 distinguishable qualities; this allows perception of the most finely-nuanced language and music. The subjective qualities of auditory perception are either directly dependent on frequency, e.g. "light" (high frequencies) and "dark" sounds (low frequencies), or they are produced by physically defined sound qualities. A distinction may be made between:

(a) *Tone*, consisting of sound made up of harmonic partial vibrations (oscillations).

(b) *Noise*, stimulated by mixed vibrations (partial vibrations associated in an irregular frequency ratio).

(c) *Surface noise*, a persistent, monotonous sound free from fluctuations in intensity.

(d) *Excessive noise*, defined by the subjective characteristic of excessive loudness.

(e) *Timbre*, the characteristic quality which enables us to distinguish between different (musical) tones which have the same fundamental frequency (or pure tone) but a different "spectral" composition (overtones). It is dependent on the relative intensity of the overtones contained in its "spectrum", or group of frequencies. The tone impression can be analyzed by frequency analyzers (spectrum analyzers), spectrometers or resonators.

3. *Space orientation.* Auditory perception plays a major part in spatial orientation,

which is based on the synergic operation, or coordination, of several senses. Hearing provides information on distant, intangible, inaccessible and invisible objects. Estimation of the distance of a sound source and directional hearing are important here (see *Sense organs: the ear*). Acoustic estimation of distance is highly accurate up to a distance of about one meter. The assumption that the distance of the sound source could be determined by the pressure difference between the two ears was refuted by von Békésy. In reality several factors are involved: one factor is loudness (the louder sound is heard as the nearer one); a second, the frequency spectrum. It is possible to estimate the distance of noise and speech more accurately than that of pure tones.

The absolute auditory directional threshold is estimated at about 3°, but is in reality 8–12°; the direction of relatively complex sound sources can be determined quite adequately. The very old (and initially very vague) assumption that the direction of a sound source could be determined from the difference in *acoustic pressure* (since the head acts as an obstacle to sound) has been precisely investigated in recent years (Trendelenburg, 1950) and is taken into account in telecommunications engineering and stereophony. Von Hornbostel's and Wertheimer's temporal theory of acoustic localization is based on the measurable retardation of sound impinging on the ear facing away from the sound source (localization to right and left of the median plane) (see *Differential running time*). Recent experimental research based on "trade" tests and ablation experiments has proved that both theories are justified; temporal difference comparison is primarily effective up to a sound level of 60 dB, while the comparison of intensity gives optimal results in the high frequency and intensity range. The phase difference between the two ears allows directional hearing at low and middle frequencies (up to about 1000 c/s), whereas intensity difference comes into play at higher frequencies. The

difference in arrival time at the two ears is also important (e.g. in the case of loud reports).

Bibliography: Békésy, G. von: Experiments in hearing. New York, 1960. Chocholle, R.: Das Qualitätssystem des Gehörs. In: Metzger, W. (Ed.): Handbuch der Psychologie, Vol. 1. Göttingen, 1966. Davis, H. Psychophysiology of hearing and deafness. In: Stevens, S. S. (Ed.): Handbook of experimental psychology. New York, 1951. Hirsh, I. J.: The measurement of hearing. New York, 1952. Ranke, O. F. & Lullies, H.: Gehör, Stimme, Sprache. Lehrbuch der Physiologie in zusammenhängenden Einzeldarstellungen. Berlin, 1953. Stevens, S. S., & Davis, H.: Hearing; its psychology and physiology. New York, 1938. Stevens, S. S.: Handbook of experimental psychology. New York, 1951. Trendelenburg, F.: Akustik. Berlin, ²1950. Wever, E. G.: The theory of hearing. New York, 1949. Zwicker, E. & Feldkeller, R.: Das Ohr als Nachrichtenempfänger, Stuttgart, ²1967.

R. Chocholle

Auditory type. See *Audile*.

Aura. Kind of halo believed by spiritualists (see *Spiritualism*) to envelop the human body and to be visible to a suitably trained sensitive (q.v.) who may infer from its coloration facts about the mental state of the person. Sometimes used of normal field-forces of an electromagnetic nature surrounding the body.   *J.B.*

Aura, epileptic. A direct premonition of the convulsive attack occurring in approximately half of all epileptics. It is variously constituted, and can be emotional (anxiety, happiness); proportional (e.g. altered color sense, illusions of sense); occur in thinking (e.g. rapidity, retardation, compulsive thinking, confusion); or as sweating, cold, warmth, flushing, and so on. An aura is seldom experienced without a subsequent attack.

C.S.

Ausdruck. See *Expression*.

Austrian school. A school of psychology founded by F. Brentano (q.v.) at the end of the nineteenth century. In contrast to W. Wundt (q.v.), Brentano conceived of psychology as concerned not with psychic *contents*, but with psychic *acts* (see *Act psychology*). The representatives of the Graz School are considered to belong to this group of psychologists. The most important are C. von Ehrenfels (q.v.), the precursor of gestalt psychology (see *Ganzheit*), A. Meinong (q.v.) and his pupils S. Witasek (1870–1915) and V. Benussi (1878–1927). In a broader sense, the Austrian school also includes C. Stumpf (q.v.), T. Lipps (q.v.), H. Cornelius (1893–1947), and E. Mach (q.v.), O. Külpe (q.v.), and A. Messer (1867–1937).

Bibliography: Boring, E. G.: A history of experimental psychology. New York, ²1957. Pongratz, L.: Problemgeschichte der Psychologie. Berne, 1967. *F.M.*

Authoritarianism (syn. *Authoritarian attitude*). A collective term for various anti-democratic and potentially fascist social attitudes, which are seen as constituting one of the main components of the authoritarian personality (q.v.).

Authoritarian attitudes are commonly characterized by: (*a*) *conventionalism* (q.v.): ossified or rigid attachment to traditional middle-class norms and values; (*b*) *authoritarian submission:* a submissive and uncritical attitude to the idealistically viewed moral authorities of one's own reference group; (*c*) *authoritarian aggression:* the tendency to look out for, despise, condemn, penalize and punish those who offend against traditional and conventional values; (*d*) rejection of more individual and personal inventive or creative attitudes, and of "soft-hearted" and "subjective, psychological, human approaches to personal and social problems" (*anti-intraception*); (*e*) *superstitious and stereotyped behavior:* belief in mystical powers determining individual human destiny, and the disposition to think in rigid categories; (*f*) a preference for positions of *power*, and "toughness": a preoccupation with dimensions such as dominance-submission, strong-weak, leader-followers; identification with

those in positions of power, excessive emphasis on one's own power, strength and toughness; (*g*) *destructiveness and cynicism:* a generalized hostility and readiness to vilify other men and the human; (*h*) *projectivity;* the projection of unconscious emotional impulses on the environment; (*i*) an exaggerated concern with *sexual* "goings-on" in society. (See *Attitude*.)

Adorno *et al.* developed the F scale, or fascism scale, which consists basically of the above variables, and is still used (in the modified form resulting from various methodological critiques—e.g. Christie & Jahoda, 1954) to measure fascistic tendencies.

Bibliography: Adorno, T. W., *et al.*: The authoritarian personality. New York, 1950. Christie, R. & Jahoda, M. (Eds): Studies in the scope and method of "The authoritarian personality". New York, 1954.

A.S.-M.

Authoritarian personality (syn. *Antidemocratic personality*). Numerous characteristics form a syndrome or major pattern in certain individuals whose personalities might be defined as "potentially fascist" according to the research carried out by Adorno *et al.* (1950) using attitude scales, interviews and projective techniques. The authors also distinguish typical variations within the pattern (critique by Pettigrew, 1958).

The most important characteristics of the authoritarian mentality are: (*a*) *anti-Semitism* as a stereotype composed of negative attitudes to Jews, who are viewed as personally offensive, socially threatening, too assimilative, too seclusive, too intrusive, and generally "other than" non-Jews; (*b*) *ethnocentrism* (q.v.), in the sense of a stereotyped, relatively consistent attitude of rejection of alien groups (non-Jewish foreigners or strangers, those of different skin pigmentation, culturally unlike societies) to whom the individual in question may in fact be positively disposed rather than hostile; (*c*) *fascism* (q.v.) (or authoritarianism); (*d*) politico-economic *conservatism*, i.e. right-wing conservative ideas regarding the value of property and possessions (both one's own and in general), money and work; a positive attitude toward social inequality arising from economic competition—a supposed relation between efficiency/worthiness and riches.

In addition to the distinction between social attitudes characteristic of the authoritarian and non-authoritarian types, the authors describe differing cognitive styles. Authoritarians are classed as cognitively more rigid and intolerant in regard to equivocal situations (intolerance of ambiguity) than are non-authoritarians.

A relation is also postulated between characteristics of the authoritarian personality and specific experiences in early childhood and the parental home situation, and an attempt is made to explain this by recourse to the psychoanalytic model.

Bibliography: Adorno, T. W., Frenkel-Brunswik, E., Levinson, D. J. & Sanford, R. N.: The authoritarian personality. New York, 1950. Christie, R. & Jahoda, M. (Eds.): Studies in the scope and method of "The authoritarian personality". New York, 1954. Pettigrew, T. F.: Personality and sociocultural factors in intergroup attitudes: A cross-national comparison. T. confl. Resol., 1958, 2, 29–42.   A.S.-M.

Authority. A person's status in a relationship between two or more individuals, which allows him to influence and to dominate the opinions, judgments, valuations and decisions of the other or others in this relationship or group. (See *Group dynamics*.)

Individuals are granted authority formally or informally by reason of their group role (e.g. a teacher in the classroom, a father in a family, an officer, and so on), or because of their expertise in some group-relevant field (e.g. specialist knowledge, superior general education, or special physical aptitudes). Such persons are granted, or tacitly acknowledged as having, authority, inasmuch as they signify the possibility of satisfying, or manifest the ability to satisfy, the needs of the other group members. Authority is usually bound up with the social power of the individual.

Adams & Romney (1959) have attempted a model analysis of the relationship and behavior apparent between those who are invested with authority and those who acknowledge it in them.

Bibliography: Adams, J. S. & Romney, A. K.: A functional analysis of authority. Psychol. Rev., 1959, 66, 234–51. Homans, G. C.: Social behavior: Its elementary forms. New York, 1961.   A.S.-M.

Autism. 1. *History.* Much confusion and misunderstanding surround the word "autism". In lay language autism (from the Greek *autos*, self) implies preoccupation with one's thoughts and daydreams. The superficial relationship between this usage and autism as used in such expressions as "infantile autism", and "the autistic child", is highly misleading. The term "autism" was applied by Leo Kanner in 1944 to a very rare and unique type of childhood psychosis, first described by him in a classic paper published a year earlier. A striking characteristic of the children with "Kanner's syndrome" was their pensive, totally absorbed facial expression, which resembled that of a normal person who was daydreaming or "lost in thought". For this reason, and because it was difficult to attract the attention of, or communicate with, these children, Kanner entitled his second paper "Early Infantile Autism". As a result of uncritical thinking, Kanner's loose analogy with adult autism has been misconstrued; therefore it is unfortunately widely believed that infantile autism involves a more or less voluntary rejection of the real world in favor of fantasy. Needless to say, such an interpretation is unwarranted. Kanner has insisted that infantile autism is "inborn", and has repudiated the idea that it is caused by faulty child rearing. Others, notably Bettelheim, insist that autism is psychologically caused.

2. *Specificity.* Further confusion results from the widespread use of the term "autistic" to refer to almost any young child with a profound behavior disorder who shows some of the symptoms of Kanner's syndrome. Kanner has stated that only ten per cent of children diagnosed by others as autistic proved to be true cases when seen by him. The writer's experience confirms this: of the nearly 1,800 cases of severely disordered children for whom I have collected detailed diagnostic information, only about 150 show the striking configuration of symptoms described by Kanner. My data also confirm Kanner's complaint that the diagnosis of autism has been applied indiscriminately to children who resemble the true autistic only superficially. Of 346 psychotic children in my files whose case histories contain at least two diagnoses, 169 had autistic listed as the first diagnosis, and 107 had autistic as the second diagnosis. Of these children, only 43 were diagnosed as autistic on both occasions, the remaining "autistic" children being reclassified as schizophrenic, retarded, emotionally disturbed, brain damaged, and so on.

3. *Incidence.* Studies by Lotter in England and by Treffert in the USA have established an incidence of about four psychotic children per 10,000 births. Since true autism seems to represent about ten per cent of children loosely called autistic, about one child in 25,000 would be a realistic estimated incidence of classical autism.

4. *Description.* The onset of classical autism is usually at birth (or before), although a few cases appear normal till the thirtieth month. In no case is the onset later than thirty-six months.

The child with infantile autism is usually attractive and well-proportioned, and is often described as having the appearance of high intelligence. Unless the mother is experienced she will not realize her infant is abnormally unresponsive and fails to adapt himself to her body when held. Most parents report early concern that the child may be deaf, but the child's intense interest in music, and often his extraordinary ability to reproduce it by singing or humming, belies deafness. Sudden onset of walking, with little prior crawling, is common. About half of autistic children never develop speech—these are the children who tended to be quiet

and passive infants. Those autistics who later develop speech tend to be very alert and sensitive, though not socially responsive, as infants. When speech occurs it is of an unusual sort and is not used for communication. The child merely repeats what he has heard. The voice is puppet-like, and has a hollow, monotonic quality. The words "Yes" and "I" are not used until the child is seven or eight years old. "Yes" is expressed by repeating the question, and "I" is expressed by saying "You". Kanner has termed these speech characteristics "affirmation by repetition" and "pronominal reversal". He has also identified and named several other unique speech patterns.

Two of the most significant symptoms are "autistic aloneness"—the child is socially inaccessible or (apparently) self-isolated; and what Kanner has termed "obsessive insistence on the preservation of sameness". The latter refers to the child's extreme agitation when his physical environment is changed—the arrangement of furniture or playthings, position of window blinds, route taken to grandmother's house, utensils or containers used in feeding, and so on. Strong eccentricities in feeding are common, such as drinking only milk, or no milk, or refusing foods that require chewing. Excellent finger dexterity is common, and is often manifested by spinning small objects. Autistic children are very agile and graceful, and are skilful climbers. They rarely fall or hurt themselves accidentally, although insensitivity to pain is common. They are fascinated by mechanical objects or appliances, in contrast to their antipathy toward humans or pets. Idiot savant abilities in arithmetic, memory, music, calendar skills, and sometimes art, are common among true cases of autism.

5. *Prognosis* has been closely tied to speaking ability. Those who have some meaningful speech by age $5\frac{1}{2}$ have a fifty per cent likelihood of at least partial recovery. Prognosis has been very poor for the mute children, but recent biochemical discoveries may change this picture. Among the few

cases who have recovered spontaneously are several gifted composers and mathematicians.

6. *Causation.* Cause is unknown. Kanner's original report that parents of true autistic children showed unusual drive and intelligence were at first discounted, but later reports by Rimland, Lotter, and Treffert, in which Kanner's diagnostic criteria were heeded, have confirmed his finding. Rimland regards autism as a crippling genetic deviation from high intelligence. Recent blood serotonin studies of accurately diagnosed cases of autism have revealed a serious metabolic defect. Further research promises to remove much of the mystery surrounding classical autism.

Bibliography: Bettelheim, B.: The empty fortress. New York, 1967. Boullin, D. J., Coleman, Mary & O'Brien, R. A.: Abnormalities in platelet 5-hydroxytryptamine efflux in patients with infantile autism. Nature, 1970, *226*, 371–2. Eisenberg, L.: The autistic child in adolescence. Amer. J. Psychiat., 1956, *112*, 606–12. Kanner, L.: Autistic disturbances of affective contact. Nerv. Child, 1943, *2*, 217–50. Id.: Early infantile autism. J. Pediat., 1944, *25*, 211–17. Id.: The specificity of early infantile autism. Ztschr. f. Kinderpsychiat., 1958, *25*, 108–13. Kanner, L. & Lesser, L. I.: Early infantile autism. Pediat. Clinics N. Amer., 1958, *5*, 711–30. Lotter, V.: Epidemiology of autistic conditions in young children. II: Some characteristics of the parents and children. Soc. Psychiat., 1967, *1*, 163–73. Rimland, B.: Infantile autism: The syndrome and its implications for a neural theory of behavior. New York, 1964. Id.: On the objective diagnosis of infantile autism. Acta Paedopsychiat., 1968, *35*, 146–61. Treffert, D. A.: The epidemiology of infantile autism. Arch. of Gen. Psychiat., 1970, *25*, 431–8.

J. Rimland

Autobiography. A special version of the biographical method (q.v.) in personality research. The autobiographer is both observer and the subject-matter of the observation.

G.K.

Autochthonous action. The precursor of displacement activity or, more generally, an action originating within the individual, as opposed to allochthonous actions, or instinctive movements activated by an external source.

Bibliography: Kortlandt, A.: Wechselwirkung zwischen Instinkten. Arch. Neerl. Zool., 1940, 10, Suppl. 2, 64–78.   *K.F.*

Autochthonous dynamics. See *Allochthonous dynamics.*

Autochthonous ideas. A term which refers to ideas which occur independently of the prevailing stream of thought. They are experienced by the subject as being foreign to his normal mode of thinking. This is an obscure term which may include such diverse phenomena as obsessional thinking, the experience of thought insertion and primary delusions. It is of little descriptive value.   *R.H.*

Autoeroticism. Sexual activity directed to one's own self or one's own body. Sometimes used as synonym for masturbation (q.v.). See also *Narcissism.*

Autogenic training. A technique developed by the Berlin nerve specialist J. H. Schultz on the basis of experience with hypnosis; it is applicable in individual and group therapy. It is essentially a form of self-hypnosis. Exercises induce a hypnotic state and a form of relaxation. The basic stage consists of six individual exercises: experience of weight (muscular decontraction); experience of warmth (decontraction of tissues); heart exercise; breathing exercise; control of abdominal area; adjustment of head (feeling of frontal coolness). Some meditative and contemplative processes are connected with the technique, which should be acquired only under medical supervision. In addition to therapeutic possibilities in the case of functional irregularities of organs, etc., the technique can prove extremely invigorating, intellectually and physically, in healthy subjects.

Bibliography: Schultz, J. H.: Das autogene Training. Stuttgart, [13]1970.   *H.N.G.*

Autohypnosis. A hypnosis (q.v.) induced by autosuggesion, in contradistinction to hetero-hypnosis, which is induced by another person. Although autohypnosis is induced by the subject himself, it depends on certain conditions such as repeated, simple optical, acoustic, or sensory stimuli.

Self-hypnotic practices are age-old (yoga techniques). One of the best-known auto-hypnotic techniques used today in medical therapy (in certain countries) is autogenic training (q.v.). *H.N.G.*

Autokinetic effect (syn. *Autokinetic illusion; Autokinetic phenomenon*). If one watches a fixed point of light in a dark room, the point eventually appears to move. After some time the eye musculature becomes tired and causes a slight eye movement. Although the movement is compensated, because of the darkness, the perception-processing system has no points by which it can judge to what extent the movement on the retina (q.v.) is caused by the movement of the eye. The experiment has been used in social psychology to determine suggestibility. *V.M.*

Automata theory. The theory of automata is concerned with the classes and principles of possible abstract automata. Applications are the mathematical construction of cyber-netic systems and, e.g., teaching and learning systems. *K.-D.G.*

Automatic writing. A psychological pheno-menon in which a person's hand writes spontaneously and produces meaningful sen-tences, but without that person being con-sciously aware of what is being written. Usually associated with mediumship (q.v.).
J.B.

Automation in education. The use of modern technology to solve the various problems of mass instruction of students of varying abi-lity, the planning of curricula and timetables, and even the use of mass media (especially radio and television) in the classroom. See *Instructional technology; Learning; Machine learning.*

Automatism. Locomotor movements are not the result of chain reflexes but of rhythmic, automatic activation. The fins of a fish manifest distinctive rhythms; if one dominates, the result is superposition. The most stable is absolute coordination 1:1. In relative coordination the phasic relations vary. *K.F.*

Automatisms. In psychology and psychiatry, "automatisms" are actions performed with-out conscious control. Most catatonic symp-toms (see *Catatonia*) may be described as automatisms. Compulsive acts also usually take this form. *R.Hä.*

Automatist. Person, usually a medium (q.v.), who produces automatic writing (q.v.). *J.B.*

Automatization. Process of developing an activity or behavior until it is performed wholly or virtually without conscious control. An automatized activity usually takes place uniformly. *H.-J.A.*

Automatograph. An instrument for measure-ment of involuntary (e.g. arm) movements, which records the process graphically.

Automaton, abstract. Mathematical models of learning, and, more generally, the relation between the organism and the environment, can be represented in terms of automata theory. The environment and organism may be viewed as abstract automata which exist in interaction. As a mathematical system, an abstract automaton requires no concrete form. *K.O.G.*

Autonomic balance. The postulated balance between the antagonistic functions of the sympathetic (adrenergic) and parasympathetic (cholinergic) nervous systems. M. A. Wenger (1941, 1942, 1948, 1957) extracted a factor which he termed "autonomic imbalance", and which could be phasic or chronic, or obtain for either system: "Autonomic imbalance, when measured in an unselected population, will be distributed continuously about a central tendency . . . autonomic balance." Other authors have disagreed, reporting reliable patterns of autonomic activation. Lacey (1958) termed this autonomic response specificity, "autonomic response-stereotypy": "For a given set of autonomic functions, Ss tend to respond with an idiosyncratic pattern of autonomous activation in which maximal activation is shown, whatever the stress."

Bibliography: Eysenck, H. J.: The biological basis of personality, London & Springfield, 1967. **Lacey, J. I. & Lacey, B. C.**: Verification and extension of the principle of autonomic response-stereotypy. Amer. J. Psychol., 1958, *71*, 50–73. Wenger, M. A.: Pattern analysis of autonomic variables during rest. Psychosom. Med., 1957, *19*, 240–244.   *D.B.*

Autonomic nervous system (Abb. ANS). Also known as the *vegetative*, or *visceral, nervous system*, the ANS consists of all nerve fibers of the central nervous system (CNS) and peripheral nervous system (PNS) mediating involuntary functions. Its activation is mainly unconscious. Its preganglionic (sympathetic and parasympathetic) fibers are myelinated, whereas its postganglionic fibers (extending from sympathetic ganglia) are not myelinated. These fibers convey impulses slowly at speeds of 5 to app. 20 m/sec. The ANS controls and coordinates the functions of all internal organs, such as the heart, lungs, blood vessels, stomach, intestine, gallbladder, urogenital system, and glands. Through innervation of all smooth muscle fibers and the internal sense organs known as enteroceptors, the ANS plays an important role in the transmission of information for the regulation

of blood pressure (q.v.), heart activity, breathing, water balance, blood sugar, and so on. It is divided into the *sympathetic* (thoraciolumbar division) with an ergotrophic function in stimulating physical activity, and a *parasympathetic* (cranial-sacral division) with a tropotrophic activity for refreshment, alimentation, and elimination of waste. The vagus (or tenth cranial nerve) belongs to the parasympathetic.   *E.D.*

Autonomy, functional. According to Allport's principle of functional autonomy, means originally used to attain to a specific end continue to be used even when the original goal has long since been reached: i.e. motives can become independent of their origins: e.g. capital is acquired for its own sake rather than for the life-enhancing things it once provided.

Bibliography: Allport, G. W.: Personality. New York, 1937.   *R.Hä.*

Autosuggestion. Self-suggestion through the largely unconscious, but also conscious, influence of one's own ideas and judgments (*Heterosuggestion* is suggestion by others). A frequent phenomenon in that emotional expectations, wishes and fears can condition certain views, convictions and attitudes. When used as a conscious method, autosuggestion can, within certain limits, help to control affectivity. E. Coué demonstrated an autosuggestive method of strengthening the unconscious will in order to lead the patient to health and a sense of well-being (see *Couéism*). See also *Autogenic training*.

H.N.G.

Auxiliary ego. In psychodrama (q.v.), a participant who assists or substitutes for the "ego", i.e. the patient, whose conflicts are portrayed in dramatic form. In this way the sick person learns possible rational ways of mastering his conflicts, that he can put into practice later. Either the psychotherapist himself or a specially trained assistant enacts the part.   *W.Sc.*

Average. A general term for measures of the central tendency of a distribution (see *Frequency distribution*). But average usually refers to the arithmetic mean.   *W.H.B.*

Average deviation. See *Deviation*.

Average error. An old measure of the variability (q.v.) of test data caused by error, and = ±0·6745 of standard error. Sometimes called *probable error* (PE). See *Deviation*.
W.H.B.

Aversion therapy is one of the methods of behavior therapy (q.v.). The purpose of aversion therapy is to produce an association between an undesirable behavior pattern and unpleasant stimulation *or* to make the unpleasant stimulation a consequence of the undesirable behavior. In either case, it is hoped that an acquired connection between the behavior and the unpleasantness will develop. There is a further hope that the development of such a connection will be followed by a reduction of the target behavior. Ideally, the therapeutic program includes attempts to foster alternative, acceptable behavior. Aversion therapy is used predominantly for the treatment of those behavior disorders (e.g. alcoholism and sexual deviations) in which the patient's conduct is undesirable but nevertheless self-reinforcing. The appetitive characteristics of these disorders frequently involve the therapist in problems concerning the introduction of other, suitable forms of satisfying behavior. Sometimes it is not sufficient only to eliminate the unsuitable behavior: the therapist should attempt to foster alternate forms of behavior which are incompatible with the unacceptable behavior. A variety of unpleasant (aversive) stimuli have been employed in this form of treatment, but the most widely used are electrical or chemical forms of aversion.

In the electrical form of treatment, the therapist administers a mildly painful shock to the patient whenever the undesirable behavior, or its imaginal equivalent, is elicited. In the chemical method, the patient is given a nausea-producing drug (emetine or apomorphine), and is then exposed to the deviant stimulus, or required to carry out the deviant act when the drug produces its maximal effect. The chemical method has found its widest application in the treatment of alcoholism, and the electrical method is used predominantly in the treatment of sexual disorders. The advantages and disadvantages of these two techniques are discussed by Rachman (1965), who recommended the preferential use of electrical aversion on several grounds, including the fact that this method allows for increased control over the treatment situation, closer definition of the treatment process and increased theoretical clarity.

Aversion therapy is based on a conditioning paradigm, the basis of which is to be found in Pavlov's work (1927). The earliest clinical application of aversion therapy appears to have taken place in Russia some forty years ago. One of the earliest Western accounts of aversion therapy was provided in 1935 by Max, who described the treatment of a patient with a homosexual fixation by the administration of electrical shocks. During the late 'thirties and 'forties, however, chemical aversion therapy was widely employed—predominantly in treating alcoholics. The resurgence of interest in this form of therapy occurred as a result of the increasing interest in behavior therapy from 1950 onwards. During the past decade it has been adopted fairly widely in Britain, and to a lesser extent on the Continent and in the United States. In current practice the electrical form of treatment is more widely employed and the disorders which are most frequently chosen for this type of treatment are alcoholism and sexual disorders. Although there is now sufficient evidence to conclude that the treatment is an effective procedure (Rachman & Teasdale, 1969), it is also recognized that the technique requires refinement, and the underlying theory is only partially satisfactory.

The explanation of aversion therapy which is based on a classical conditioning model can still be used to encompass many of the phenomena encountered with this form of treatment. It has become increasingly clear, however, that the classical conditioning theory is limited, and that greater importance must be attached to the cognitive factors which are part of this or any other form of treatment. This theoretical development is paralleled by the exploration of a new form of aversion therapy based largely on cognitive manipulations. Covert sensitization, like aversion therapy proper, attempts to build up an association between an undesirable activity and an unpleasant effect. However, this treatment is carried out entirely at the imaginal level—the patient is required to imagine the deviant activity or stimulus and *then* to imagine some extremely undesirable consequence, such as nausea, shame, pain and so forth. Although research on this form of cognitive treatment is still at the rudimentary stage (Rachman & Teasdale, 1969) it coincides with, and indeed is part of, the shifting emphasis from a purely conditioning approach to a more sophisticated view of aversion therapy. It seems probable that aversion therapy, both practically and theoretically, will combine conditioning theory and cognitive variables.

Bibliography: Blake, B.: The application of behavior therapy to the treatment of alcoholism. Behav. Res. Ther., 1967, 5, 78–85. Cautela, J.: Covert sensitization. Psychol. Reports, 1967, 20, 459–68. Eysenck, H. J. & Rachman, S.: The causes and cures of neurosis. London, 1965. Feldman, M. P.: Aversion therapy for sexual disorders. Psychol. Bulletin, 1966, 65, 65–79. Lemere, G. & Voegtlin, W.: An evaluation of the aversion treatment of alcoholism. Quart. J. Stud. Alcohol., 1950, 11, 199–204. Rachman, S. & Teasdale, J.: Aversion therapy and the behavior disorders. London, 1969.   S. Rachman

Aviation psychology (syn. *Aeronautical psychology*). A branch of applied psychology (q.v.). Aviation psychologists investigate the special conditions to which human behavior is subjected in aviation; among their practical concerns are aspects of the selection and training of pilots, stewardesses, maintenance personnel, and so on, the avoidance of possible accidents, and the construction of adequate instruments and displays, etc. See also *Motor skills; Accident research; Stress.*

Bibliography: Aitken, R. C. B.: Prevalence of worry in normal aircrew. Brit. J. Med. Psychol., 1969, 42, 283–6. Cartellieri, D.: Einführung in die Luftfahrtpsychologie. Schriftenreihe der HTS der deutschen Luftwaffe, 1965. Gourney, A. B.: Psychological measures in aircrew. Aerospace Med., 1970, 41, 18–91. Miller, R. B. et al.; Survey of human engineering needs in maintenance of ground electronics equipment. Pittsburgh, 1954. Sells, S. B. & Berry, C. A. (Eds): Human factors in jet and space travel: a medical-psychological analysis. New York, 1961. Whiteside, T. C. D.: Problems of vision in flight at high altitude. London, 1957.   F.M.

Avitaminosis. A deficiency or complete absence of one or more vitamins, marked by specific symptoms. Beri-beri, for example, presents as inflammations of the motor nerves together with disturbed gait and movement, and cardiovascular disease; it is caused by a lack of vitamin B_1. Beri-beri is unknown among peoples with a mixed diet but is found in those with an exclusive diet of, e.g., polished rice. Scurvy is a vitamin C deficiency disease, and in the past occurred on sailing ships which were without fresh citrus fruit and green vegetables: a characteristic symptom was degeneration of the teeth and gums. Rickets is a disease of small children who lack adequate sunlight and therefore cannot convert the first stage of vitamin D into its active form, and who because of calcium deficiency develop irregular bone formation and softening. These and all other genuine avitaminoses can be prevented or cured by correcting dietary deficiencies or, in certain cases, by injecting special vitamin preparations. See *Vitamins.*   E.D.

Avoidance-avoidance conflict. See *Approach-approach conflict; Conflict.*

Avoidance behavior (syn. *Aversive behavior*). Abient behavior, or withdrawal, liable to increase distance between the subject and a goal (a physical object, a social partner or a situation). Barriers on the way to the goal play a part in avoidance. The intensity of the avoidance behavior is a function of the distance to the goal (*avoidance gradient*). Avoidance can be a learned reaction to specific situations. It is also to a certain extent explicable as instinctive activity derivable from the "innate releasing mechanism". It is displayed in the motor phenomena of flight (escape) and defense, but is also interpreted as an inner ego-protective process (Freud), as an inner process for removal of possibly threatening cognitive patterns (Lazarus), of specially tabooed words, etc. (*perceptual defense*, subliminal perception), and for protection against painful and persistent stimulation (J. M. Sokolov). Avoidance in thinking and perception is usually known as *defense* or *defensive behavior*. The disposition to avoidance or defensive behavior differs from individual to individual and is mainly diagnosed by the use of *projective techniques* (q.v.). See *Gradient*.

Bibliography: Campbell, B. A. & Church, R. M. (Eds.): Punishment and aversive behavior. New York, 1969. Lazarus, R. S.: Psychological stress and the coping process. New York, 1966.   *W.Sch.*

Avoidance gradient. See *Gradient*.

Avoidance reaction. See *Conditioning, classical and operant*.

Awareness (*Bewusstheit*). A concept used by N. Ach (Würzburg school). In his experiments Ach instructed the testees to perform some activity, e.g. adding, upon an agreed signal. Ss performed the action after the signal without consciously realizing the instruction. In this way, Ach showed that Ss were in a psychic state which he called "task-awareness", or "readiness". He defined several kinds of awareness in this sense, which was connected with the Würzburg school's theory of *Bewusstseinslagen*, or "conscious" attitudes, which could not be separated into sensory or imaginal contents. See *Consciousness; Thinking*.

Bibliography: Humphrey, G.: Thinking. London, 1951.   *V.M.*

Axial gradient. A gradient (q.v.) or change in metabolic activity along, e.g., the primary axis of the body.

Axiom. An axiom, or axiomatic system, in contrast to a theorem, is an *unproved* proposition. The older philosophic systems (as even today non-technical thinking) conceived an axiom as a proposition whose truth-content is self-evident. The development of mathematics after the mid-nineteenth century led to an abandonment of the idea of self-evident truth, since when an axiomatic system for a specific theory has been understood as a collection of *elementary* unproved postulates known as axioms, which are *taken as* given, and from which all other propositions, or theorems, of the theoretical system are then deduced. The only restriction on the choice of axioms is that they are non-contradictory, when the system is known as consistent.   *J.B.G.*

Axis cylinder (syn. *Axis cylinder process; Axite; Neuraxis; Neurite*). The central core of an *axon* (q.v.); also used synonymously with "axon". The basic components of the core itself are axolemma, neuronemes and axoplasma.

Bibliography: Chévremont, M.: Notions de cytologie et d'histologie. Liège, 1960.   *G.A.*

Axon(e). Nerve cells (*neuron(e)s*) consist of a cell body, a number of dendrites (or fibers) branching off from the cell body, and an elongated part leading from the cell body to the specific organ or to other neurons: the conducting core, or axis cylinder, of this longer section is known as an *axon*, which divides into several *end feet*, or synaptic knobs (see *Synapses*). In lower animals these nerve fibers have practically no medullary sheath (or fatty layer or *myelin*) insulating them from surrounding tissue, but only a thin covering (*endoneurium*) and a cellular layer (sheath of Schwann); they show continuous conductivity (i.e. the impulse proceeds continuously along the fiber) and therefore conduct slowly (app. 1 m/sec). Most vertebrate axons have an insulating myelin sheath which is interrupted at app. 1 mm intervals by the nodes of Ranvier,

points at which the cell membrane is laid bare. The primary nerve impulse (depolarization) proceeds only from node to node along the nerve fiber and therefore travels faster (5 to 100 m/sec), since between the nodes (*internodium*) conductivity does not depend directly on chemical processes and relatively slow stimulation by and displacement of sodium ions, but on a spreading *electrochemical* disturbance. An axon can extend to a length of 1 m; the diameter of non-medullar nerve fibers in vertebrates is between 1–2 μ and of those with myelin sheaths between 3–20 μ.   *M.S.*

B

Babinski reflex. This reflex was recorded by the Paris neurologist J. F. Babinski in 1901 as a pathological reflex in organic nervous diseases in the region of the spinal cord and the pyramidal tract (upper motor neurons). It is produced by stroking the sole of the foot and manifests itself in dorsiflexion (upward extension) of the big toe instead of a normal plantar flexion (contraction). Its occurrence in infancy is physiological, and normal, as long as the pyramidal tract has not yet fully matured. Syn. *Babinski sign.*   *E.D.*

Bahnung (Ger.). See *Attention theories.*

Balance, loss of. An objective or subjective disorder of control over equilibrium while standing and/or walking (swaying, staggering, tendency to fall) resulting from the loss of labyrinthine sense in the inner ear of one or both sides of the head (often accompanied by vertigo and nausea); or from a disorder of the central vestibule (e.g. in diseases of the CNS, q.v.), or of the *archicerebellum* (with typical cerebellar *ataxia*, q.v.; spontaneous nystagmus). See *Equilibrium.*   *F.C.S.*

Balanced experiment. If a measurement is repeated in such a way that the first observation sometimes takes place under the one experimental condition and the second under the other (e.g. control), a systematic error (q.v.) must be expected (dependence of measurements, q.v.). To prevent this, one half of the whole sample is always observed under the one experimental condition and then under the other or vice versa (experimental planning, q.v.). This arrangement is known as a balanced experiment. *Balancing* refers to this technique and, more generally, to all measures to ensure that the variation of the extraneous variable in each repetition is the same for all conditions of the independent variable.   *W.H.B.*

Ball-and-field test. A Stanford–Binet test (q.v.) item: the testee is asked to show by drawing how he would look for, e.g., a ball in a large field.

Ballard (-Williams) phenomenon. "Reminiscence": described by Ballard (1913), confirmed by O. Williams (1926). Phenomenon that what has been learnt is remembered (reproduced) better after several days than after the termination of the learning period. However, this increment is only observed when between this period and the test certain activities are practiced which have some connection with what has been learnt. These activities (in the case of Ballard, e.g., a retention test) themselves offer another opportunity for learning. Therefore the phenomenon is—as C. J. Hovland has demonstrated—an artifact.

Bibliography: Ballard, P. B.: Obliviscence and reminiscence. Brit. J. Psychol. Monogr. Suppl. 1, 1913, *2.*   *H.-J.A.*

Bandwag(g)on effect. To withhold one's opinion, then vote in accordance with the majority view once that view is known, is in popular usage to "hop (or get, climb, etc.) on the bandwagon". The *bandwagon effect* is a noticeable result of public opinion polls, and is observable, e.g., during voting for political parties or at revival meetings, and refers to the increasing tendency to associate with or even switch to the dominant view. A bandwagon was a railroad (railway) pay car in the USA.   *J.C.*

Barany test. A test, especially in the selection of pilots, to record nystagmus (q.v.) after rotation of the subject about the three axes of the vestibule, i.e. the semicircular canals of the inner ear. A special chair is used.
                                                          A.L.

Barbiturates. Salts of barbituric acid or malonylurea. Psychotropic group of substances discovered in 1862, and homologous with the hypnotics (q.v.). In chemical terms, barbiturates are cycloureids. Since the first clinical use of barbitone (barbital) (1903), more than 2500 barbiturates have been synthesized, and are used as sedatives (q.v.), anticonvulsants (q.v.), narcotics (q.v.) for the purpose of narcoanalysis (q.v.), but chiefly as hypnotics. Depending on the varying speed of precipitation the barbiturates are divided into those slow to take effect and those of long duration (barbitone, phenobarbitone); those of intermediate duration of action (amylobarbitone, cyclobarbitone, pentobarbitone, secobarbitone); and those of ultra-short duration of action (hexobarbitone, thipentone). Their effects are very similar qualitatively. They produce a general and central sedation with increased dosage. This is shown, e.g., in a lowered flicker-fusion frequency (q.v.), shorter duration of afterimage, underestimation of time, poorer performance in vigilance tests, increased bodily unsteadiness, reduced conditionability, decreased intellectual perform-

ance and some loss of motor skill. There is also a reduction of anxiety and an increase in extravert behavior. Sleep induced by barbiturates is distinguished in various ways from that not due to medication: electrophysiologically (e.g. inhibited peripheral and central electrocortical arousal response— blocked EEG arousal); and in behavior (diminished proportion of paradoxical sleep-phases and reduced bodily movement). Chronic use of barbiturates leads to tolerance and physical and psychic dependence, and also to withdrawal symptoms ("withdrawal sickness") when weaning from drug dependence (q.v.).

Bibliography: Adams, B. G., *et al.*: Patients receiving barbiturates in an urban general practice. J. Coll. gen. Practitioners, 1966, *57*, 24–31. Black, P. (Ed.): Drugs and the brain. Baltimore, 1969. Maynert, E. W. Sedatives and hypnotics II. In: Di Palma, J. R. (Ed.): Drills pharmacology in medicine. New York, 1965, 188–209.   *E. Lehmann*

Bar diagram (syn. *Bar chart*). **1.** A graphic representation of magnitudes by means of narrow rectangles of a uniform width but varying lengths, the lengths corresponding to the magnitudes. **2.** A graphic representation of a whole so divided as to display the relation between its parts.   *J.M.*

Barrier (*Barrière*). Concept from K. Lewin's vector or topological psychology (q.v.). "Barrier" is used by Lewin to denote factors inhibiting behavior in the "life space": i.e. everything that hinders or prevents a course of action corresponding to the forces at work in the field. The "barrier" itself also exerts forces counteracting those in existence. In daily life every obstacle that has to be circumvented or overcome represents a barrier.   *H.-J.A.*

Bartlett, Sir Frederick Charles. B. 20/10/1866 at Stow-on-the-Wold (*England*). Studied at St. John's College, Cambridge, and London University. Professor of Experimental

Psychology and Director of the Psychological Laboratory, Cambridge. Worked in the field of experimental psychology, investigated thinking, perception, memory. He related the function and nature of memory to social psychology, and also worked in the area of military psychology. Bartlett's researches led to a rejection of the "storage" conception of memory, and emphasized remembering as a "construction" (i.e. "schemata" used to absorb new information), and therefore an active process of reinterpretation. Editor and co-editor of the British Journal of Psychology; Mind; Psychological Abstracts; Journal of General Psychology.

Works include: An experimental study of some problems of perceiving and imaging, *Brit. J. Psychol.*, 1916; Feeling, imaging and thinking, *Brit. J. Psychol.*, 1925; with Myers, C. S.: Text book of experimental psychology, Part 2, 1925. Remembering: A study in experimental and social psychology, 1932. Thinking: An experimental and social study, 1958.

Bibliography: Boring, E. G.: A history of experimental psychology. New York, 1950. Murchison, C.: A history of psychology in autobiography, Vol. 3. Worcester, 1936. Id.: The psychological register. Worcester, 1929.   W. S.

Bartlett test. A simultaneous test (named after S. Bartlett, 1932) of the statistical significance (q.v.) of more than two variant samples. It is sometimes used to check the homogeneity of variance (q.v.) in an analysis of variance (q.v.). See *Mathematical psychology; Statistics.*   *W.H.B.*

Barykinetic type. Temperament related to the athletic in which the entonic proportion (q.v.) of fluidity (q.v.) is prominent: the reactions are characterized by "heaviness", no matter whether they seem to be rather clumsy or rather supple (simultaneous, antagonistic application of tension). Moderate adaptability. Dull expression of emotions. Apparent imperturbability, often however

concealing sensitiveness and lability of mood. Intense emotional reactions are at first held back and then compressed into one moment with a consequent abrupt or explosive effect. Genially sociable or dysphorically mistrustful, constant and reliable. Introverted and extraverted characteristics seem to be counterbalanced.

Bibliography: Kretschmer, E.: Physique and character. New York, 1931. Kretschmer, E. & W.: Medizinische Psychol. Stuttgart, ¹³1970. Kretschmer, E. & Enke, W.: Die Persönlichkeit der Athletiker. Stuttgart, 1936.
                                                   W.K.

Basal ganglia. The term *ganglia* (q.v.) is here used exceptionally for masses of nerve cells in the subcortex with an identical or similar function within the central nervous system (q.v.). The following are among the basal ganglia: *corpus striatum* (striate body), *globus pallidus*, *corpus amygdaloideum*, and *claustrum*.   *G.A.*

Basal text. An extremely brief formulation of the subject-matter of a lesson which is to be given directly or in a teaching program. In cybernetic education the target of a program is usually defined with the aid of a basal text.   *H.F.*

Basedow's disease. Described in 1840 by K. A. von Basedow; due to enlargement and overactivity of the thyroid gland. It is characterized by exophthalmic (protuberant) eyes, struma (soft, frequently pulsating enlargement of the thyroid gland), tachycardia (heart rate increased up to 160 per minute), raised basal metabolic rate, ready sweating, tremors, motor disturbance, subfebrile temperatures, diarrhea, emaciation, reduced virility, and menstrual disorders, but especially by nervousness and psychic hyperexcitability. Its etiology is largely unexplained. In addition to hereditary predisposition, various factors may act as "triggers" and provoke its onset. Treatment is not uniform and extends to radiation and surgical excision of parts of the thyroid gland. Syn. *Exophthalmic goiter; Graves' disease; Hyperthyroidism, Parry's disease; Thyreotoxicosis.*   E.D.

Basilar membrane. The coiled, fluid-(perilymph-)filled, inner auditory canal (cochlea) is divided into two halves by the basilar membrane, which carries the organ of Corti (q.v.) with its four rows of hair cells. Longitudinally, the basilar membrane features continuously changing mechanical properties; it is set in motion when mechanical sound impulses are transmitted via the auditory ossicles and the oval window; and, together with the organ of Corti, enables the cochlea to function as a transducer which translates these mechanical into electrical impulses. It is assumed that the sound frequency is transmitted by maximum deformation of different parts of the membrane, leading to maximum stimulation of groups of hair cells in different places (dispersion): i.e. there is a distribution of low to high frequencies along the membrane.   M.S.

Batterie de tests d'aptitude scolaire (abb. BASC). Intelligence tests (q.v.) of scholastic ability; four parallel series, each with different tests, agree in their factorial structure.
Bibliography: Cardinet, J. & Rousson, M.: Etudes factorielles de tests d'aptitudes scolaires. Schweiz. Z. Psychol. Anwend., 1967, *26*, 256–70; *27*, 362–80.
                                    R.M.

Bayes' theorem. An inferential statistical model representing an alternative to the classical testing of hypotheses. Instead of single decisions in favor of H_0 or H_1 on the basis of the results of individual samplings, it permits a successive revision of the probabilities of the hypotheses which are to be compared. Syn. *Bayes' principle.*
Bibliography: Lindley, D. V.: Introduction to probability and statistics. Cambridge, 1965.   W.H.B.

Beat. The periodical reinforcement of two simultaneously sounded, and therefore simultaneously heard, notes (tones) which are near to one another in vibration frequency.

Bed wetting. See *Enuresis.*

Begabung. (Ger. = Ability). *Begabung* may be defined as the whole range of innate abilities to achieve qualified performances in various cultural fields. In this view, "ability" is an *endogenous fact* which, however, is realized in the achievements and creations of actual life. Therefore the specific experiential context of achievement is very important: it can crucially motivate, innervate, promote, repress, hinder or even arrest individual fulfillment. *Begabung* is revealed in achievement characteristics; modes of behavior and even attitudes are involved, since every achievement can result only from a behavior, and this only from a certain attitude. (See *Abilities.*)

This definition of ability has a substantial basis in the psychophysical constitution of the human *person* (q.v.). It is multidimensional, for it includes cultural factors (general ability, e.g.: vitality, emotional capacity and the will, motor skills and so on; and special abilities such as linguistic or numerical thinking). It also includes personal constitutional causative factors, and ability types and capacities (theoretical and practical; nature, talent, genius; normal and subnormal ability) that are graduated (and therefore measurable) in terms of cultural dimensions differentiated according to number and especially quality. Dynamic plasticity (q.v.) is one of the features of ability defined as a multidimensional, graduated, substantial datum. Ability in this sense can both be developed and unfold. The nucleus of ability can grow; it can be differentiated in greater or smaller, stronger or weaker branches.

Begabung is more comprehensive than *intelligence* (q.v.) which is essentially the capacity to produce and understand meanings, relationships and significant contexts.

Begabung is genetically conditioned; its unfolding depends on environment.

Ability as defined here and *aptitude* (q.v.) can be established diagnostically by analyses of achievement and performance; the following at least are factors in all achievement: intelligence, personal temperament, adaptability, and capability of practice. Mental and moral considerations, positive and negative, cannot be disregarded in research into ability. *Begabung* is conceived more inclusively from the standpoint of *characterology* (q.v.), which sees each individual's achievement, despite its situational determination, as dependent just as much on essential *traits* (q.v.)—displayed in sentiments and attitudes—as on *anlagen* (q.v.).

Begabung, therefore, is also the special capability of exerting a personal influence on the environment in action and reaction (objectively, and in personal, spiritual modes). This definition makes it possible to speak also of ability in regard to emotion, thinking, imagination, memory, fantasy, and mind ("spirit").

Intelligence has been identified with ability. Ziehen used the special term *"Beanlagung"* to define ability as the "general nature of the more important psychical processes of the individual in so far as it does not depend on practice but on the innate or very early acquired organization of the brain". By *Beanlagung*, he understands ability in the narrower sense, i.e. in regard to active achievement and the special and individual value of its various manifestations. Such a division of the concept is no longer tenable.

Klages includes the qualities of ability in the sense of *Begabung* in his *Stoff des Charakters*, or "character material". By this he understands quantitative traits, as distinguished from directive characteristics (type and motivation of the character). He sees differences in abilities or capacities from one person to another; a greater or lesser degree of "ability" qualifies the "character" (q.v.). A Wenzl, in his *Theorie*

der Begabung (1934), adhered to the view of ability as intelligence.

A recent denaturizing tendency has interpreted ability as a process of learning (Roth, 1970). The question must arise whether such a process can be effected insubstantially, without any need for a human agent. A person, i.e. a unity of body, soul and mind, is always individually furnished with natural gifts. Every person can be supplied by his milieu with further gifts, but the natural gifts (dispositions) are prerequisites for the exogenous process of unfolding and education. It is disastrous if strained and artificial constructions cause ability to be interpreted as a "gift from without", and if a theoretical construct eliminates the real, factual disposition which has always been present in each individual, and will be in future. The concept would be too narrow and unilateral if it were restricted solely to the capacity for learning. "Ability" also means independent *creativity* (q.v.). In current linguistic usage *gift* is used not only in the sense of "gift received", but in the sense of "innate attributes, or talent".

Whereas *Begabung* is actualized as the basis of achievements in a definite sociocultural area, *talent* (q.v.) extends beyond normal, average qualities and surpasses them in its achievements. *Genius* (q.v.) is supreme ability which the mind inspires and impregnates.

2. *Methodology of research.* It seems inadmissible to try to define the phenomenon of ability solely from the operational standpoint (E. L. Thorndike), just as it is onesided to try to elucidate the problem in a purely "humanistic" (*geisteswissenschaftlich*) way (e.g. Seeberger, 1966). The operational technique of factor analysis has produced a general intelligence factor ("g" factor). The following individual ability factors were determined: memory, linguistic ability, logical thinking, technical thinking, spatial thinking, arithmetical abilities (Thurstone, 1938; W. Arnold found corresponding factors in 1960). Ability research is chiefly directed to distinguishing between operating numerically and

scientifically, and thinking logically with words. In our time there has also been a noticeable shift of emphasis in regard to ability and aptitude, in the socio-political and educational-political spheres, to the creation and development of specialist colleges and even universities to encourage special abilities in predominantly economic and technical subjects.

Bibliography: Arnold, W.: Begabung und Bildungswilligkeit. Munich & Basle, 1968. Klages, L.: The science of character. London, 1928. Mierke, K.: Bildung, Bildsamkeit. Stuttgart, 1963. Roth, H. (Ed.): Begabung und Lernen. Stuttgart, 1970. Seeberger, W.: Begabung als Problem. Stuttgart, 1966. Thurstone, L. L.: Primary mental abilities. Chicago, 1938. Wenzl, A.: Theorie der Begabung. Heidelberg, ^{2}1957.

W. Arnold

Begriff. See *Concept*.

Behavior. 1. The activity of an organism. 2. The observable activity of a specific organism. 3. The measurable activity of a specific organism. 4. The responses of an individual, species or group to stimuli. 5. A specific response of a specific organism. 6. A part-response of a response pattern. 7. Movement or a movement. 8. The total activity, subjective and objective, non-observable and observable, of an individual or group.

The above definitions represent only a small number of the existing views of the object of psychology. For more detailed expositions of differing viewpoints see, e.g.: *Act psychology; Behaviorism; Comparative psychology; General psychology; History of psychology*. For specific aspects, see, e.g.: *Aggression; Drive; Habit; Learning*.

Behavioral. Methods, theories and phenomena which are determined by behavior are termed behavioral, and are thus distinguished from those which are physiological or determined by experience. Also used in a general sense to characterize an objective as opposed to a subjective approach. Must not be

confused with *behaviorist* and *behavioristic* (q.v.).   *R.H.*

Behavior, animal. See *Animal psychology; Comparative psychology; Drive; Instinct*.

Behaviorism is a radical form of objective ‚psychology in which all references to introspection and consciousness are rejected in favor of a discussion of psychologically relevant events primarily in terms of stimulus and response. This radical form was first proposed in America by John B. Watson (1878–1958) in a paper entitled "Psychology as the behaviorist views it" (1913). His position, although repeatedly under attack, gained favor in America. Less popular in other parts of the world than in the United States, related views are prominent in the U.S.S.R. and Eastern Europe (though there more commonly thought of as physiology), and a belated recognition has come to behaviorism in England (e.g., Broadbent, 1961).

1. *Precursors of behaviorism*. The definition of psychology as the study of consciousness, with introspection as the preferred method, was widely accepted in the late nineteenth century and early twentieth century. Cattell (1904), McDougall (1908), and others sought to extend the domain of psychology to cover behavior, while retaining consciousness and introspection. This was not radical enough for Watson.

More radical objectivisms had also emerged, such as that of Sechenov in Russia, followed by the observations of Pavlov and Bekhterev. Germany produced Loeb with his doctrine of tropisms (he emigrated to America and taught at Chicago while Watson was a student there); objective views like his were promulgated in Germany by Beer, Bethe, and von Uexküll. Throughout the world students of animal activities carried out objective studies of behavior.

Philosophers, too, had begun to raise doubts about consciousness and introspection as ways to get at the fundamental nature of mind. E. A. Singer (1911) influenced E. R. Guthrie (1886-1959), an American psychologist important in promoting behaviorism. In France there had been the mechanistic conception of La Mettrie and, later, Comte's positivism.

It is not surprising to find that others created a fertile soil for Watson's doctrines, but this does not detract from his originality, boldness, and personal influence.

2. *Watsonian behaviorism.* The central tenet of behaviorism is, of course, the objectivity of the data to be accepted by science. The facts of observation are to be limited to those of any other science: observable events that can be recorded by an experimenter, often with the aid of precision instruments. The events to be included are, first of all, the antecedent stimuli, and then the consequent responses of muscles and glands. Muscles and glands are the only effectors; there is no additional "mental activity". The behaviorist was also interested in the *products* of behavior, which can also be objectively measured. Verbal responses, although produced by muscular movements, are really products of movement, quite as much as words typed on a page or checkmarks on a psychological test. This interest in the products of behavior saved behaviorism from becoming a "muscle-twitch" psychology —an unfavorable description mentioned by Watson in the preface to his *Psychology from the Standpoint of a Behaviorist* (1919), and often attributed to Tolman (1932, p. 5), who was merely repeating something that Watson had said he had been charged with (and denied) much earlier. The acceptance of verbal responses as behavior also freed behaviorism from restrictions that would otherwise have been imposed: for instance, it permits the study of dreams, without calling this introspection.

Watson did not wish only to eliminate imprecision and subjectivity. There were at least three more aspects of this theory as it developed: associationistic atomism, peripheralism, and extreme environmentalism.

The search for an analytic unit led first to the central concept of habit; it became the core systematic concept until the *conditioned reflex* (q.v.) doctrine took its place. In theoretical terms, the conditioned reflex was an analytical unit, serving his system in much the same way as the sensation in the introspective psychology that he was opposing. The attacks by the gestalt psychologists on behaviorism and sensationism focussed on this "molecular" or "atomistic" feature. Despite Watson's great interest in the brain (his 1919 chapter on the neurophysiological basis of action contains no less than 26 diagrams of the brain and cord and neurones, apart from numerous diagrams of sense organs and effectors in other chapters) he gradually came to espouse what is called a *peripheralism*—by contrast with a centralism. The centralist believes that thinking takes place in the brain; Watson had it take place in the vocal cords, as the thinker talks to himself. The emotions, too, might be thought of as having central representation, but Watson was more interested in what happened in the body, and defined the emotions accordingly. This is an aspect of Watsonian behaviorism from which modern students have diverged, particularly as newer methods for studying brain activity have developed. For example, the notion that hunger depends upon stomach contractions (a peripheralist view) is generally modified now to the belief that it depends on something happening in the hypothalamus (a centralist view).

The third additional Watsonian dogma was that of *extreme environmentalism*, to which he came gradually. It is something of a surprise to find a chapter on instincts in his 1919 book, after his behaviorism was well established; although he then believed the role of innate tendencies was chiefly to provide a background for habit formation, he did not deny innateness. Later he became bolder, and rejected hereditary potentials in man in favor of a learning basis for individual differences (Watson, 1925).

The essence of behaviorism lay in its

emphasis upon making psychology an objective science; the associationistic atomism, peripheralism, and environmentalism were not essential to the position, but at the height of Watson's influence they had an important impact upon psychology (and other social sciences) in America.

3. *Tolman's purposive behaviorism.* Early in his career, Edward C. Tolman (1886–1959) became fascinated by Watson's behaviorism, but critical of it, and he soon began to develop his independent position, first in a paper entitled "A new formula for behaviorism" (1922), and later in his major book, *Purposive Behavior in Animals and Men* (1932). His system is most simply characterized by three statements:

(*a*) It is a *behaviorism* in that it rejects introspection as a method. Although a subjective vocabulary is sometimes used (e.g. "inventive ideation"), such conceptual formulations are always considered to be *inferences* from observed behavior. The data are behavioral.

(*b*) It is characterized as a *molar* behaviorism by contrast with Watson's *molecular* behaviorism. An act of behavior has distinctive properties of its own, to be identified and described irrespective of the underlying muscular, glandular, or neural processes.

(*c*) It is a non-teleological *purposivism.* This means only that behavior is organized and regulated in accordance with objectively determinable goals, often a matter of expectations (probabilistic outcomes) based on prior experience.

An important concept of Tolman's, accepted later by Hull, but rejected by Skinner, is that of an *intervening variable.* A stimulus response psychology, modeled after the simple reflex arc, was not acceptable to Tolman; very much takes place between stimulus and response to modify the stimulus-response correlation: any careful account of behavior must respect the prior history of the organism, its present drive state, etc., in addition to the present stimulating conditions.

4. *Hull's behavior system.* Clark L. Hull (1884–1952), greatly impressed by Pavlov's *Conditioned Reflexes* (1927), began a series of theoretically guided experimental studies that seemed to him to fulfill the work left undone by Watson. Although he continued later to contribute to theory and experiment, the system reached its height of confidence in *Principles of Behavior* (1943). Instead of assuming that a chain of conditioned reflexes provided a simple explanation of habit, Hull developed an elaborate model in which the triggering stimulus was the first term of a complicated set of events which resulted in the response as the end term. Between stimulus and response there were many intervening variables (as made familiar by Tolman, but not with Tolman's content). These included tendencies to respond acquired in the past, stimulus generalization, drives based on physiological deprivation or noxious stimulation, and other features, both associative and non-associative, affecting the actual evoked response. One important intervening variable which served to integrate many forms of behavior was the fractional anticipatory (or antedating) goal response (r–G), which became in his system a surrogate for ideational processes. The presence of these complex intermediaries distinguished his system from Watson's. Otherwise, in spirit, it was equally behavioristic, and essentially peripheralist. Despite the prominence of Hull's system for some twenty years, the emergence of other kinds of mathematical models, more sophisticated than his empirical curve-fitting, led to its rapid decline in influence in the 1960s, despite the strong discipleship of Kenneth W. Spence (1907–67) and others.

5. *Skinner's experimental analysis of behavior.* B. F. Skinner (b. 1904) kept a strict behaviorism alive in the midst of a climate of opinion rather antithetical to it, and if there was any "school" of psychology in the United States in the early 1970s it was that associated with his approach to behavior. His followers developed a society of their

own, a central journal (*Journal of the Experimental Analysis of Behavior*), and some satellite journals; and those close to Skinner's position spoke a common language of operant conditioning, schedules of reinforcement, and shaping of behavior, and shared common taboos of the kind associated with earlier radical behaviorism, as against any inner processes not describable in behavioral terms. By contrast with Tolman and Hull, intervening variables or other inferential terms were felt to be unnecessary excesses.

Skinner views his standpoint as essentially a powerful technology, rather than a scientific system; it is indeed a very radical behaviorism (Skinner, 1938; 1952; 1959). The basic terms and relationships can be learned quickly. There is, to begin with, an *operant level*, according to which any organism behaves in a given environment. This is the "entering behavior", and one need not ask if it is innate or acquired, species-specific or culturally derived. It is this behavior which presents itself for modification and control. It is controlled by manipulating the discriminatory stimuli and the stimuli serving as reinforcements (rewards). The teaching or training process is one of *shaping* the behavior by *reinforcing* (rewarding) any shifts in the desired direction and *extinguishing* (by non-reinforcement or non-reward) any shifts in the undesired direction. The method can be used to produce *discriminations* between stimuli, and *differentiation* of response patterns. This is all the information that is needed to apply Skinner's technology to various individual and social problems. There are of course more complex aspects having to do with intermittent reinforcements of various kinds, with secondary reinforcements, with chaining of responses—but these are accessory details. The important result is that behavior is brought under the control of the stimulus, and hence can be managed.

The successes of the method are readily documented: in animal training (as in the various "marine-lands" in America in which dolphins and killer whales perform remark-able tricks to the delight of the audience, after being "shaped" by Skinner's methods); in programmed instruction, which Skinner invented as a form of teaching that made use of his principles; and in various forms of psychotherapy. Therefore Skinner has come nearer than anyone to achieving what Watson set out to do: to predict and control behavior, without reference to subjective processes or states.

6. *The permanent contributions of behaviorism to general psychology.* The success of Skinner's technology has led to its acceptance by his disciples as an ultimate psychology, but many other psychologists, who have no hesitation about accepting its successes, and even making use of its methods, do not believe it to be the final answer to psychology's understanding of man. It glosses over the problems of the biological bases of behavior (heredity, hormonal control, and so on), the subjective states represented by dreams and hallucinations (as well as imagining and planning), and dismisses the possibilities of systematic science (e.g. hierarchical organization; mathematical models with interchangeable constants). Some of these reservations have to do with Skinner's personal preferences, rather than with the possibility of a behaviorism, but some alternative methods of dealing with subjective processes still seem plausible to many, if not most, contemporary psychologists. In expressing these doubts, some essentially behaviorally oriented writers have described their position as a "subjective behaviorism" (Miller, Galanter & Pribram, 1960, 211–14).

The major contribution of behaviorism may have been to give confidence to students of human and animal nature that they were dealing with a subject-matter sufficiently like that of other sciences to place them in the tradition of Darwin, Mendel, Newton and Einstein. Having gained the new perspective that behaviorism provided, and the new scientific status that it enhanced, they have found that the positives of behaviorism can now be incorporated into modern psychology without its negatives.

Bibliography: Bergmann, G.: The contributions of John B. Watson. Psychol. Rev., 1956, 63, 265–76. Broadbent, D. E.: Behaviour. London, 1961. Broadhurst, P. L.: John B. Watson, Int. Ency. Soc. Sciences, 1968, 16, 484–7. Cattell, J. McK.: The conceptions and methods of psychology. Pop. Sci. Mo., 1904, 46, 176–86. Hull, C. L.: Principles of behavior. New York, 1943. McDougall, W.: Introduction to social psychology. London, 1908. Miller, G. A., Galanter, E. & Pribram, K. H.: Plans and the structure of behavior. New York, 1960. Pavlov, I. P.: Conditioned reflexes. London, 1927. Singer, E. A.: Mind as an observable object. J. Phil. Psychol. sci. Meth., 1911, 8, 180–86. Skinner, B. F.: The behavior of organisms. New York, 1938. Id.: Science and human behavior. New York, 1953. Id.: Cumulative record. (Rev. ed.) New York, 1961. Id.: Behaviorism at fifty. Science, 1963, 140, 951–9. Tolman, E. C.: A new formula for behaviorism. Psychol. Rev., 1922, 29, 44–53. Id.: Purposive behavior in animals and men. New York, 1932. Watson, J. B.: Psychology as the behaviorist views it. Psychol. Rev., 1913, 20, 158–77. Id.: Psychology from the standpoint of a behaviorist. Philadelphia & London, 1919. Id.: Behaviorism. New York, 1925. Woodworth, R. S. & Sheehan, M. R.: Contemporary schools of psychology. New York, ³1964.   E. R. Hilgard

Behaviorism, descriptive. 1. B. F. Skinner's learning theory (q.v.), which explains behavior largely in terms of linguistically formulated observations and their relations to one another and thus dispenses with mathematical constructs, intervening (theoretically necessary) variables and formal representations. **2.** Descriptive behaviorism is also used as a collective term for the techniques of operant conditioning by which operants, or emitted responses, are examined without necessary reference to originating rather than reinforcing stimuli.   *R.Hä. & J.C.*

Behaviorism, molar. Term used for the learning theory of E. C. Tolman (q.v.) who does not start from the smallest possible elements of behavior but instead considers the holistic, purposive units or aspects. *Molar behavior:* one of these units. Syn. *Purposive behavior (ism); Molarism.*   *R.Hä.*

Behaviorism, molecular. Behaviorism is called molecular when it seeks to explain all behavior as built from the smallest possible units (e.g. the concept of J. B. Watson, q.v.). C. L. Hull (q.v.) does not consider his theory molecular because he reserves the notion for physiological behavior theories. See *Behaviorism.* (Syn. *Molecularism.*) *R.Hä.*

Behaviorist; behavioristic. Appertaining to behaviorism (q.v.). The concept is used both to denote the method, and in a pejorative sense by, e.g., authors who reject operational definitions and deny the relevance of animal experiments—often carried out by behaviorists—for human psychology. *Behaviorist* (n.) indicates a practitioner or adherent of behaviorism.   *R.Hä.*

Behavior, physiology of. See *Physiology of behavior.*

Behavior rating. 1. Observing, scoring and measuring a specific behavior or class of behaviors. **2.** (also *Behavior-rating schedule*). An alternative-choice questionnaire on behavior in a range of situations.

Behavior sampling. A record of an individual's behavior (possibly a specific behavior) during a certain period of time.

Behavior therapy is a term used to describe a number of therapeutic methods developed in recent years. Although the actual procedures vary from desensitization to aversion treatment they share certain theoretical conceptions. The rationale adapted by practitioners of behavior therapy is that neurotic behavior and other types of disorder are predominantly acquired. If neurotic behavior is acquired, then it should be subject to the established laws of learning. Knowledge about the learning process concerns not only the acquisition of new behavior patterns, but the reduction or elimination of existing behavior patterns. Behavior therapy derives its impetus from experimental psychology and is essentially an attempt to apply the findings and methods of this discipline to the disorders of human behavior. The aspect of experimental psychology with the most immediate and obvious value for therapy is the study of learning; the literature on this subject provides a valuable starting-point for the development of scientific methods of treatment.

Although some of the ideas used in the theory and practice of behavior therapy have a long history, the subject was firmly established less than twenty years ago. The most important stages in development can be attributed to the work of Wolpe, Eysenck and Skinner. Historically, major influences on the course of development of behavior therapy are found in the works of Pavlov and of Watson. Their approach to abnormalities of behavior, in conjunction with the rapid growth of learning theory, provided a suitable climate for the development of behavior therapy. This form of therapy grew partly as a consequence of growing dissatisfaction with depth psychotherapy. Wolpe's research made a timely appearance in the early 1950s and was supported and developed by the work of Eysenck and his colleagues. Skinner's contribution to the subject can be traced to 1953 with his interest in the shaping of behavior of chronic psychotic patients. This work was continued and developed by Lindsley and by Ayllon, who made the first systematic attempt to apply the techniques of operant conditioning in a psychiatric ward. This research has mushroomed and the establishment of psychiatric and other special facilities for the psychological management of abnormal behavior has undergone rapid expansion during the past five years. Most of these research and treatment programs are described as "token economy" projects. Desirable and constructive behavior is shaped and reinforced by therapists and nurses. Rewards are often given in the form of tokens to be exchanged for special privileges or items. Currently, behavior therapy is being developed and investigated extensively in Britain, the U.S., and various European countries. At present the most widely used therapeutic methods are desensitization for anxiety conditions, aversion therapy for deviant behavior, and operant conditioning for deficit behavior.

Broadly speaking, problems of behavior can arise in two ways. If the person fails to acquire a necessary, adaptive form of behavior this deficit can constitute a problem (e.g. enuresis, q.v.). Most neurotic disorders in adults are, however, essentially surplus reactions: the patient has acquired a persisting unadaptive form of behavior (e.g. anxiety, phobic states, etc.). The learning and un-learning techniques which have been used for therapeutic purposes include the following: (a) Desensitization (Wolpe, 1958; Eysenck & Rachman, 1965; Marks, 1969); (b) Aversion therapy (q.v.) (Rachman & Teasdale, 1969; Feldman, 1966); (c) Operant conditioning (q.v.) (Ayllon & Azrin, 1968; Ullman & Krasner, 1968; Sloane & Macaulay, 1968); (d) Negative practice (q.v.) (Yates, 1970); (e) Special techniques— bell and pad conditioning treatment for enuresis, feedback procedures for stuttering (Turner, Young & Rachman, 1970; Yates, 1970).

Behavior therapy has been successfully used in the treatment of a variety of neurotic conditions including, most notably, the phobias, and sexual, obsessional, children's speech and other disorders. It has also been of considerable value in the rehabilitation of severely ill patients with deficit disorders or inadequate behavior. The most significant advances to date have been made in the treatment of phobic disorders (Marks, 1969). Encouraging successes have also been obtained in the treatment of sexual disorders and alcoholism (Rachman & Teasdale, 1969). The use of conditioning procedures in the rehabilitation of chronic schizophrenics is described by Ayllon & Azrin (1968). Other applications of operant conditioning procedures are described by Sloane & Macaulay (1968) and by Ullman & Krasner (1968). General accounts of the clinical effectiveness of these methods are provided by Meyer & Chesser (1970) and by Yates (1970).

The methods of behavior therapy have also been the subject of a large number of experimental investigations. In particular, desensitization treatment has been studied extensively (Rachman, 1967). Much of this experimental work has been carried out on non-psychiatric volunteers who have an excessive, irrational fear of some object or situation. The experimental findings are virtually unanimous in showing that the treatment is capable of producing significant and lasting reductions in fear. It has also been shown that the two major components of the treatment, relaxation and graded imaginal presentations of the fearful stimulus, contribute to therapeutic effectiveness. They appear to act in combination. After the patient has been trained to obtain deep relaxation, he is asked to imagine scenes of increasing fearfulness. Successive repetitions of these imaginal presentations are given until the patient reports decreasing anxiety. Eventually he is able to tolerate the imaginal fearful situations with tranquility, and this change generally transfers to the real-life situation without difficulty. Wolpe's (1958) original theory, on which this and other forms of treatment are based, has received a fair degree of support but is not entirely unchallenged. Wolpe's theory proposed that the main basis for the therapeutic effect was the development of condition inhibition and that this could best be achieved by eliciting the anxiety reaction and then superimposing upon it an antagonistic and incompatible response (e.g. relaxation).

Both the clinical and experimental evidence show that significant and lasting reductions in anxiety can be achieved by desensitization;

furthermore, it appears to be unnecessary for the therapist or patient to undertake extensive exploration into the possible origins, since deeper significant reductions in fear obtained with this form of treatment are not followed by the appearance of new or substitute symptoms.

Aversion therapy is based on a conditioning paradigm and involves the repeated association of stimuli which provoke some form of undesirable behavior and aversive stimuli (chemical or electrical). This form of treatment has been used predominantly in the treatment of sexual disorders and alcoholism (q.v.).

The operant conditioning techniques derive largely from the work of Skinner and rest on the central concept of reinforcement (q.v.). Behavior which produces satisfying consequences is strengthened, but behavior which produces unsatisfactory consequences is weakened. In order to generate and maintain behavior, the reinforcing or satisfying consequences must be made contingent on the responses in question. In speech training, e.g., the correct enunciations are followed by reinforcing consequences (e.g. praise, rewards). Similar principles are used in the management and rehabilitation of chronic psychotic patients in whom encouraging advances have been recorded (Ayllon & Azrin, 1968). The overall clinical effectiveness of the operant procedures is still under investigation.

A number of special treatment techniques have also been developed: the two most prominent are used for the management of enuresis and of stuttering. The enuresis treatment was developed by Mowrers in 1938 and was based on a classical conditioning model. The aim was to produce a conditioned connection between the interoceptive stimuli preceding urination and an alarm bell which would awaken the child and prevent or interrupt urination. Lovibond (1964) proposed an alternative theory based on avoidance conditioning. However, the theory and its deductions have recently been queried

(Turner *et al.*, 1970). Clinically, this technique is highly effective in arresting bed-wetting, but relapses remain a problem.

Some important theoretical advances have already been attained. Significant improvements in neurotic and other types of abnormal behavior can be achieved with behavioral methods even in the absence of deep exploratory psychotherapy. The reduction or elimination of abnormal behavior is rarely followed by the development of substitute symptoms. These, and related findings, are of significance not only for behavior therapy but have wider implications for our understanding and explanations of behavioral abnormalities in general.

Progress has been rapid and encouraging but there is still a great need for large-scale field trials and intensive experimental investigations of the theory and methods of behavior therapy.

Bibliography: Ayllon, T. & Azrin, N.: The token economy. New York, 1968. Eysenck, H. J. & Rachman, S.: The causes and cures of neurosis. London, 1965. Feldman, M. P.: Aversion therapy for sexual deviations. Psychological Bulletin, 1966, *65*, 65–79. Lovibond, S.: Conditioning and enuresis. Oxford, 1964. Meyer, V. & Chesser, E.: Behaviour therapy in clinical psychiatry. London, 1970. Marks, I.: Fears and phobias, London, 1969. Rachman, S.: Systematic desensitization, Psychological Bulletin, 1967, *67*, 93–103. Rachman, S. & Teasdale, J.: Aversion therapy and the behaviour disorders. London, 1969. Sloane, H. & Macaulay, B.: Operant procedures in remedial speech and language training. Boston, 1968. Turner, R. K., Young, G. & Rachman, S.: Treatment of nocturnal enuresis by conditioning. Behav. Res. Therapy, *8*, 1970. Ullman, L. & Krasner, L.: A psychological approach to abnormal behavior. New York, 1968. Wolpe, J.: Psychotherapy by reciprocal inhibition. Stanford, 1958. Yates, A.: Behavior therapy. New York, 1970. *S. Rachman*

Bekhterev, Vladimir M. B. 22/1/1857 in Vjatka, d. 24/12/1927 in Leningrad; Professor of psychiatry at Kazan; later Professor of psychology and neurology in St. Petersburg (at the Army Medical School). Ranks with Pavlov (q.v.) as the founder of *objective psychology* (q.v.) (later known as *reflexology*,

q.v.; conditioned reflexes, q.v.). Worked on problems of the central nervous system, of the spine (Bekhterev's disease) and on "associative reflexes". Bekhterev's emphasis on the physiological approach (which extended also to thought processes) and his pioneer work on "motor responses" make him one of the precursors of behaviorism.

Works: Die Bedeutung der Suggestion im sozialen Leben, 1905. Objektive Psychologie. Leipzig, 1907. (La psychologie objective. Paris, 1913.) Die Funktionen der Nervenzentra. Jena, 1908–11. General Principles of human reflexology, New York, 1932.

Bibliography: Boring, E. G.: A history of experimental psychology, New York, [2]1950. Schniermann, A. L.: Bekhterev's reflexological school. In: Murchison, C.: Psychologies of 1930. Worcester, 1930, 221–42.

W.S.

Belief-value matrix. In E. C. Tolman's *Purposive Behaviorism*, the system of *expectancies* (including classifications and categorizations) and *valences* (value judgments) which the individual brings to any new situations and which partly determine his response to the environment. *G.D.W.*

Bell Adjustment Inventory. A personality questionnaire measuring emotionality, social, domestic and other adjustments, and yielding higher emotionality scores for females than for males in high school, college and delinquent groups.

Bibliography: Bell, H. M.: The theory and practice of personal counseling. Stanford, 1939. *J.G.*

Belladonna alkaloids. Psychotropic substances occurring in numerous plants, especially in the genus *solanum* (deadly nightshade, thorn apple). Belladonna alkaloids have been known for centuries. The most important are *atropin(e)* (q.v.) and *scopolamin(e)* (q.v.). There is a wide range of natural, semi- and wholly synthetic related preparations. They have strong anticholinergic and CNS effects.

125   BESTIALITY

In stronger doses they have psychosomimetic effects. See *Psychosomimetics*.   *W.J.*

Bell–Magendie law (syn. *Bell's law*). The principle laid down by the Scottish physiologist C. Bell (1811) that the anterior (ventral) roots of the nerves of the spinal cord are motor, the posterior (dorsal) roots sensory.   *F.-C.S.*

Bell's palsy. A phenomenon named after the Scottish anatomist C. Bell (1774–1842): owing to a peripheral paralysis of the facial nerve, the eyeball moves upward under the upper lid of the paralyzed half of the face.   *D.V.*

Bender Gestalt Test. A widely used procedure for testing gestalt comprehension and reproduction. The person tested must copy nine geometrical figures. The test has been used to determine the level of intelligence in the range of 5 to 10 years, and as an aid in evaluation for the projective method of personality diagnosis; the spatial errors made have also been invoked in the diagnosis of brain damage. The validity (q.v.) of several evaluation formulas is guaranteed by a large number of investigations on a rough selection basis.
Bibliography: Tolor, A. & Schulberg, H. C.: An evaluation of the Bender Gestalt Test. Springfield, Ill., 1963.   *A.L.*

Bennett tests. 1. *College Qualification Test* (1955–61): six-category intelligence group test: verbal, numerical, science information, social studies information, total information, total. **2.** *Differential Aptitude Test:* for school grades 8 to 12: verbal, numerical, abstract, and mechanical reasoning; spatial relations; clerical speed and accuracy; language usage (spelling and sentences). **3.** *Hand-tool Dexterity Test* (1946): manual dexterity test using screw and screwdriver. **4.** *Short Employment Tests* (1951–56): clerical, numerical, verbal tests for management and

professional grades. **5.** *Tests of Mechanical Comprehension* (1940–55): high-school and adult mechanical aptitude tests with several difficulty levels. Mathematical and technical drawings requiring right-wrong-better judgment.   *J.G.*

Benton Test. A procedure similar to the Bender–Gestalt test but using different models and instructions designed to test gestalt comprehension and reproduction from recent memory.   *A.L.*

Berdache. A sexual role among the Sioux Indians of North America. The Sioux consider a berdache to be both male and female. The role is formally assigned by the medicine man after the youth has told him certain dreams. A berdache dresses like a woman, takes no part in military expeditions and is often a kind of jester (or even teacher). He is said to take no interest in sexual activities with women. Yet he is not necessarily homosexual. Now that the Indians have to a large extent adopted the sex roles of Western civilization, that of the berdache is no longer assigned.
Bibliography: Erikson, E. H.: Observations on Sioux education. J. Psychol., 1939, 7, 101–56.   *G.L.*

Berger rhythm. See *Alpha rhythm*.

Bernoulli distribution. See *Binomial distribution*.

Beschreibung. See *Introspection; Description method*.

Bestiality. Sexual contact between humans and animals. Most societies condemn or ridicule this behavior, but it is not infrequent in some, e.g. Copper Eskimos, Hopi Indians, Masai. Kinsey estimates the frequency of bestiality as 8% for males and 3·6% for females in his sample. Syn. *Erotic zoophilia, Zoophilia.* *P.Le.*

Beta movement. According to M. Wertheimer, apparent movement during which an impression is created that an object is moving from one place to another. If, e.g., in a dark room a small lamp is allowed to flash at a place A and a second small lamp at a place B, alternately, Ss perceive the "movement" of a small lamp from A to B and back. See *Motion, apparent.* *V.M.*

Beta rhythm; beta waves. EEG waves in the frequency range 13 to 30 c/s which appear predominantly when there is a high level of cerebral activation (sensory stimulation, mental activity). See *Alpha rhythm.* *M.S.*

Betel. The betel nut, or kernel of the betel palm: chewed as a stimulant when ground and mixed with (or wrapped in) betel leaves together with burnt coral paste: i.e. a *masticatory stimulant*, especially in India and the Far East. See *Arecolin; Intoxicants.* *J.G.*

Betz cells. Large pyramid(al) cells in the motor cortex.

Bewusstheit. See *Awareness.*

Bezold-Brücke phenomenon. The greater visibility of red and green under reduced light intensity, and the predominance of yellow and blue when the intensity is heavily increased. A similar effect occurs with changes in the spatial dimensions of the stimuli: when the angle of vision is reduced, it becomes more difficult to distinguish between yellow and blue than between red and green. See *Tritanopia; Purkinje effect.* *G.Ka.*

Bias. A term used in statistics to denote a systematic error (q.v.). Random samples with bias can no longer be regarded as representative of all the cases in question. The reasons for this are not due to the intended experimental variation. *W.H.B.*

Bibliotherapy. Making use of reading for therapeutic gain. Books may be prescribed by the therapist for many different reasons: to help the patient understand the terminology of therapy, to remedy deficiencies in knowledge, to give vicarious satisfactions not available in reality, to facilitate vocational rehabilitation, and so on. *G.D.W.*

Bifactor method. The extraction first of a factor general to all the tests, and then the extraction of more limited group factors among test clusters. See *Factor analysis.*

Bilingualism. 1. The ability to speak fluently and as "mother tongues" two languages learned at approximately the same time. Known as *coordinate* bilingualism when the learning situations are distinct (e.g. one language from one parent, one from the other), and the sets of meaning responses in each language are independent. **2.** The ability to speak fluently two languages one of which is learned later than the first. Known as *compound* bilingualism, when the set of meaning responses is common to both languages. Successful second-language learning has been thought to approximate more to the coordinate model, and various educational strategies are used to provoke original responses in the new language. Chomskyian models, however, have been influential recently. No *conclusive* evidence of general adverse effects on mental development has been shown in bilingual children. (But see, e.g., Arsenian, 1945; Darcy, 1946; Leopold, 1948; Macnamara, 1966; Smith, 1949; Thompson, 1952.) IQ, socio-economic situation, and parents' attitude are important factors.

Polyglottism, the ability and will to acquire fluency in several languages, has been variously assessed, the Adlerian school judging it favorable as an outgoing tendency (e.g. Brachfeld, 1932), some psychoanalytic commentators finding it neurotic, and the polyglot a "linguistic Don Juan" (see Vereecken, 1966).

The problem of bilingualism (and polyglottism) is best considered in the context of abilities (q.v.) and the family, as well as in terms of the language-and-mind debate, i.e. especially between the idea of universal grammar as an innate schematism (Chomsky) and the Skinnerian concept of language acquisition in terms of reinforcement—a debate which can hardly be said to have been concluded). See *Differential psychology; Grammar; Language.*

Bibliography: Arsenian, S.: Bilingualism in the postwar world. Psychol. Bull., 1945, *42*, 65–86. Brachfeld, O.: Zur Individualpsychologie des Sprachenerlernens. Int. Z. Ind. Psychol., 1932, *10*, 201–7. Chomsky, N.: Language and mind. New York, 1968. Darcy, N. T.: The effect of bilingualism upon the measurement of the intelligence of children of preschool age. J. Educ. Psychol., 1946, *37*, 21–44. Elwert, Th.: Das zweisprachige Individuum. Akad. Wiss. Lit., 1959, 267–344. Fisher, J. A.: Readings in the sociology of language. The Hague, 1968. Leopold, W. F.: The study of child language and infant bilingualism. Word, 1948, *4*, 1–17. Macnamara, J.: Bilingualism and primary education. Edinburgh, 1966. Skinner, B. F.: Verbal behavior. New York, 1957. Smith, M. E.: Measurement of vocabulary of young bilingual children in both of the languages used. J. Genet. Psychol., 1949, *74*, 305–10. Thompson, G. G.: Child psychology. Boston, 1952. Vereecken, J. L. T. M.: Quelques considérations sur le polyglottisme. Psychother. Psychosom., 1966, *14*, 66–77.   J.C.

Bimodal. A term used for a distribution with two peaks (maxima, or modes). See *Frequency distributions.*

Binary digit (*Bit*). A measure introduced by C. E. Shannon for the information unit H. It is defined as the number of information units necessary in order to be able to make a decision between two equally probable or two unequally probable alternative outcomes. The magnitude H depends on the number of alternatives (N), which are available for selection, and on the probability (p_i) of the single alternatives. With two equally probable possibilities one needs an information unit ($H = 1$ bit) in order to make a decision. With four such possibilities two information units are needed; and so on. In general terms, the following formula holds good: $2^H = N$, or more simply: $H = \log 2 N$, where logarithms to the base 2 are used. It has been calculated on the basis of answers given that the information units at the expert's disposal are in the order of magnitude 10^6.

If unequal probabilities are the two alternatives (A,B) for selection, E. B. Newman's law is used: condition $p_A = p_B$

$$H = -p_A \log 2p_A - p_B \log 2p_B$$
$$\stackrel{L}{=} \log 2\,2 = 1.$$

The value lies between 1 and 0 and follows the curve calculated by Newman. If there are more than two possibilities, the law can be generalized:

$$H = -\frac{\Sigma}{N} p_i \log 2p_i$$

See *Communication; Information theory. W.S.*

Binary system. In mathematics, the use of only two symbols, a zero and a digit, to construct a system of numbers. By using 0 and 1 we get for the numbers 0 to 9 of the decimal system: 0, 1, 10, 11, 100, 101, 110, 1000, 1001. The importance of the binary system is its application in fields such as computer calculation (Boolean algebra), data processing, and information theory (q.v.).

K.E.P.

Binet, A. B. 11/7/1857 in Nice; d. 18/10/1911 in Paris. An important representative of classical experimental psychology in France. After studying law, medicine and biology, together with Henri Beaunis he founded in 1889 the first psychology laboratory in France, at the Sorbonne, and in 1894 became its director.

He published much of his research in the first French psychological journal *L'année psychologique*, which appeared in 1895, and which he founded and edited. Binet's main field was research into "higher mental processes" in children and adults. In answer to a request from the French Ministry of Education, he devised his first standardized test to discover defective primary-school children in collaboration with T. Simon. The test was developed from intelligence scales for the investigation of normally gifted and subnormal children, which were extended to become an intelligence test for the age range 3 to 15. First published in 1905, it was revised in 1908 and 1911. The 1911 version offered more accurate assessments of general ability and was the model for countless imitations. Each of the tests in a series of increasing difficulty accords with a specific developmental level. There is a revised American version by L. Terman (Stanford Revision).

Works: La psychologie du raisonnement. Paris, 1886. Les altérations de la personalité. Paris, 1891, L'étude expérimentale de l'intelligence. Paris, 1903. Le développement de l'intelligence chez les enfants. L'année psychologique, 1908 (Eng .trans.: Binet, A. & Simon, T.: The development of intelligence in children. London, 1916). Les idées modernes sur les enfants. Paris, 1909.

Bibliography: Claparède, E.: A. Binet. Archives Psychologiques, 1911, *11*, 376–88. Simon, T.: A. Binet. L'année psychologique, 1912, *18*, 1–14.   *G.S.*

Binet-Simon Scale. Historically the most influential procedure for examining intellectual ability, the first intelligence test was developed in 1905 on behalf of the French Ministry of Education by A. Binet and Th. Simon to select children of defective intelligence for transfer to special schools. To begin with, it consisted of thirty verbal, perceptive and manipulative tasks in a series of increasing difficulty. In the decisive revision of 1908 the mental age principle was introduced: those tests which were

almost always done correctly by ⅔ to ¾ of a representative sample of children of a certain age, but only seldom by younger children and almost always by older ones, were grouped into test levels typical for respective ages. The Binet–Simon test contains levels at which normal children can pass for each year between 2 and 13; later procedures employ partly differentiated age scales and widen the age range downwards (see *Development tests*), and upwards to include adults. The sum of all the tasks which a testee can do indicates the level of his development on an intelligence age scale (abb. MA; see *Mental age; Intelligence quotient:* IQ).

Typical of all tests conforming to the Binet–Simon principle is the grouping of tasks of a heterogeneous nature (as regards task standard, material, assumptions about knowledge, solution processes, etc.) into a global measure of intelligence. The MA scale and the IQ concept quickly spread everywhere. They signified a decisive breakthrough in the measurement of abilities (q.v.); on the other hand they were the reason—at least in practice—why a differentiated consideration of the forms and structure of intellectual achievements was delayed and made difficult.

Adaptations, revisions and modifications of IQ tests on the mental age-level principle were published at an early date in many countries. Some influential examples were those of E. Claparède and A. Descoeudres in French-speaking Switzerland, O. Decroly in Belgium, C. Burt in Britain, G. H. Jaederholm in Sweden and W. Stern, O. Bobertag, P. Chotzen and E. Hylla in Germany. One of Burt's major contributions was the substitution (1911) of paper-and-pencil Yes–No and cross-out or underlining responses to printed tests for Binet's *verbal* tests and responses. It was Wundt (1912) who introduced the IQ index. In the U.S.A., after the first adaptations of H. H. Goddard, F. Kuhlmann and others, the new and carefully developed Stanford–Binet test (q.v.), by L. M. Terman & M. A. Merrill, 1937 and 1960, became one of the most widely used intelligence tests. In German-speaking countries importance was attached especially to the "*Binetarium*" of I. Norden as well as to the comprehensive Viennese development test series by Ch. Bühler, H. Hetzer and others; those in use today also include the test series for Swiss children by H. Biäsch, the J. Kramer's intelligence test, and an adaptation of the Stanford–Binet by H.-R. Lückert. In French-speaking countries, the Stanford–Binet test has been revised as the Terman–Binet test, and is widely used. *A.L.*

Binocular fusion; binocular integration. The fusion of the two separate retinal images as the two eyes function in unison.

Binocular rivalry. Radically different colors or figures presented simultaneously to corresponding areas of the two eyes are not usually combined. If, for example, a red and a green square are presented the observer sees each of these squares alternately rather than a single brown square. The rate of alternation of the two percepts and the prevalence of one or the other are determined by factors such as light intensity and the content of the stimuli.   *C.D.F.*

Binomial distribution. If an alternative event A in any experiment has a probability B, the probability is that this event will occur x times in N experiments:

$$_Np_x = \binom{N}{x} \cdot [P^x \cdot (1 - P)^{N-x}]M,$$

This is the binomial distribution, or Bernoulli distribution. The expression for $_Np_x$ consists of the probability of a certain sequence of alternative events the aggregate result of which $f(A) = x$ in N experiments has a probability of $p^x \cdot (1 - P)^{n-x}$, as well as of the number of all possible sequences of

the length N all of which lead to the result $f(A) = x, \binom{N}{x}$.

Bibliography: Maxwell, A. E.: Basic statistics in behavioural research. Harmondsworth, 1970, 62–72.
                                                        W.H.B.

Biocenosis. The living community in which an animal or a plant species exists, i.e. all the organisms of a biotope (see *Ecology*), among which there is often a range of direct or indirect relationships. For example, in a beech wood the principal organic factor is the copper-beech; this tree is responsible for the conditions of light and humidity that determine which other plants will occur there (e.g. wild anemones). Certain kinds of worm, beetle and slug in turn live on beech leaves; certain spiders on the slugs; and certain birds on the beetles; and so on.   *H.S.*

Bioclimatics. 1. The branch of biology dealing with the influence of climate (weather, air temperature, air humidity, etc.) on living creatures. **2.** The way in which an organism interrelates with climate. Syn. *Bioclimatology*.   *K.E.P.*

Biodynamics. 1. The physiology of the active relations between organisms and their environment. **2.** The name given to a theory associated with J. H. Masserman, in which an ambitious attempt is made to combine the basic principles of psychoanalysis, behaviorism, and so-called "psychobiology".

Biogenetic law. A principle postulated by E. Haeckel: ontogeny recapitulates phylogeny: i.e. the individual development of any kind of organism is a brief recapitulation of its phylogeny, or stages of species-specific evolutionary development. This is not an actual law, as the repetition does not necessarily take place, but can be demonstrated in very many cases. In the human embryo, the pharyngeal arches, homologous to the gill bars of lower vertebrates (fish), and the primary hair of the fetus may serve as examples. Such instances of the law offer clear evidence for the accuracy of Darwin's theory of evolution. *H.S.*

Biogenic amines. A group of biologically active substances which are main, intermediate or end products in cellular metabolism and have a number of physiological functions, especially in the nervous system. In part, biogenic amines act as *transmitter substances* (q.v.). The term "biogenic amine" refers in its most restricted sense to substances which are obtained from aromatic aminoacids as decarboxylation products (separation of CO_2 from the carboxyl group [COOH]).

Substance	Conversion into next substance under influence of enzyme	Enzyme activity disturbed by	Effects
Phenylalanine	Hydroxylase	Inborn error of metabolism	Phenylketonuria
Tyrosine	Tyrosine hydroxylase	α–methyl–tyrosine	Reduction of endogenous noradrenaline concentration
Dopa	Dopa decarboxylase	α–methyldopa	Replacement of noradrenaline by α–methyl–noradrenaline (false transmitter)
Dopamine	Dopamine–β–hydroxylase	Adrenalone, Arterenone, Disulfiram	Decrease in noradrenaline concentration
Noradrenaline	(a) Catechol–o–methyl transferase (COMT)	COMT–inhibitors	
(a)	(b) Monoamine oxidase (MAO)	MAO–inhibitors (e.g. Iproniazid)	Increase in noradrenaline concentration in brain
Normetanephrine (b)			
3, 4–Dehydroxymandelic acid			

(left margin, vertical: biosynthesis ↑, decomposition ↓)

Biosynthesis and decomposition of natural noradrenaline, and some possible pharmacological effects.

The most important of these substances are the neurohormones *histamine* (q.v.) (from histidine), *tryptamine* (q.v.) (from tryptophane), *serotonin* (q.v.) (from 5-hydroxytryptophane) and *tyramine* (q.v.) (from tyrosine). From other (basic and aliphatic) amino-acids the following are derived by decarboxylation: *cadaverine, putrescine, agmatine* (all three constituents of ribosomes), *propanolamine, cysteamine, β-alaline* and *γ-aminobutyrate*

(GABA, q.v.), which plays a part in brain metabolism.

In the wider sense, biogenic amines also include substances which are not obtained by decarboxylation, especially the *catecholamines* (q.v.) (e.g. *noradrenaline*, q.v., and *dopamine*, q.v.].

Biogenic amines have been at the center of pharmacological, biochemical and clinical-therapeutic research since 1950. It is often assumed that the biosynthesis and decomposition of the biogenic amines are disturbed in psychiatric illnesses (depression, schizophrenia). In particular, numerous studies discuss the pathogenetic significance of the metabolism of noradrenaline and serotonin (the catecholamine and serotonin hypothesis of mental illnesses). The main starting-points for these discussions are the possibilities of pharmacological intervention, and morbid (inborn) errors of the biosynthesis and decomposition of the biogenic amines. Some possible pharmacological effects are indicated, using noradrenaline as an example (see tabular summary).

Bibliography: Brune, G. G.: Biogenic amines in mental illness. International Review of Neurobiology, 1965, *8*, 197–220. **Euler, U. S. von, Rosell, S. & Uvnäs, B.** (Eds): Mechanisms of release of biogenic amines. Oxford, 1966. **Franzen, F. & Eysell, K.:** Biologically active amines found in man: their biochemistry, pharmacology and pathophysiological importance. Oxford, 1969. **Guggenheim, M.:** Die biogenen Amine. Basle, 1961. **Himwich, H. E.** (Ed.): Amines and schizophrenia. Oxford, 1967. *W.J.*

Biographical methods in personality research. These consist mostly of a life-history analysis in order to obtain as full and well-rounded a picture as possible of the structure and dynamics of some personality (q.v.). Since the conclusions drawn often owe much to inexpert observations and documents, errors are usually rife. *G.K.*

Bio information. Corresponds largely to the term ESP (q.v.). Used often in Warsaw Pact countries. *H.H.J.K.*

Biology and psychology. As the "science of life", psychology might be considered part of biology. As a discipline in its own right, psychology studies specifically human problems transcending anatomy, physiology, (phylo)genetics and molecular biology. When it relinquishes the objective methods of an experiential science in studying forms of existence and change, it approximates to philosophy (see *Philosophy and Psychology*). The principal founders of empirical psychology were biologists and natural scientists: H. L. F. von Helmholtz, E. H. Weber, G. T. Fechner, W. Wundt, E. Hering, G. E. Müller, and so on. Since then, scientific psychology has been closely allied with biological research in numerous areas: e.g. the physiology of the senses, nerves, brain, metabolism, and development; electrophysiology; endocrinology (q.v.), ecology, molecular biology, etc. Comparative psychology, the psychology of learning, and motivational psychology overlap research into evolution, behavioral physiology, ethology and biocybernetics. Psychological statistics is closely related to biometry. The application of purely biological methods to the study of human behavior and experience is called "biologism", and the over-stressing of psychological principles "psychologism".

Psychology is most obviously distinct from biology in the areas where social and cultural influences on the basis of individual differences and experiences (learning in the broadest sense) produce behavioral differences, restrictions and combinations: e.g. socialization, group behavior, the development of "internal modes of behavior control" (often called "character", "personality", or—in their partial aspects—"motives", "traits", etc.). The increasing influence of biological anthropology and comparative psychology (q.v.) can be noticed here. A psychology of learning oriented solely toward environmental influences is being replaced by research into learning processes which are broader in scope and based on biology: the RNA-DNA system now enters into ontogenetic considerations; and the biological analysis of behavioral potentials—

in, say, human and population genetics— is helping to extend our knowledge of the causes of behavior.

Bibliography: Hess, W. R.: Psychologie in biologischer Sicht. Stuttgart, 1968. Lorenz, K.: Evolution and modification of behavior. Chicago & London, 1965. Tembrock, G.: Grundriss der Verhaltenswissenschaften. Jena, 1968.   *K. E. Grossman*

Biometry. The application of quantitative methods to research into biological phenomena.

Biorhythm. Life rhythm. The rhythmic course of the life processes of organisms, e.g. corresponding to the day or season, or according to the rhythms inherent in the organism (endogenous rhythm). The biorhythmic phenomena which manifest themselves psychically in man have scarcely been explored but they appear in the female periodic cycle as well as in the phases of juvenile growth. Some ingenuously precise suppositions (such as that of W. Flies that the life of a man moves in rhythmic phases of 23 days, that of a woman in phases of 28, and that the life span can be subdivided into seven year phases) are confirmed neither biographically nor statistically.   *F.-C.S.*

Biotic experiment (K. Gottschaldt). An experiment in a real-life situation, but without the awareness of the subject; hence disturbing field forces that might come from the test situation are excluded. It is distinguished from pure behavioral observation because the facts to be observed have been deliberately contrived by the experimenter.

The quasi-biotic experiment also takes place without S's awareness, but the situation is not quite true to life. Disturbing field forces are nevertheless excluded since S., while aware that he is taking part in an experiment, knows neither his own role nor the object of the test. This situation is achieved by inserting the critical phase, i.e. the actual test, in an extended framework from which it differs considerably in theme, thereby assuming a "biotic" character (e.g. S., according to instructions, experiences the critical phase only as a preparatory action for a subsequent task which he thinks will be the real test).

Bibliography: Spiegel, B.: Über die Notwendigkeit biotischer Versuchsansätze in der Verhaltensforschung. Bericht über den 24. Kongress der Deutschen Gesellschaft für Psychologie, Göttingen. 1965, 409–13.

B.Sp.

Biotonus. M. Verworn's (1863–1921) (initially wholly physiological) term for the potential life energy of an individual in regard to the physiological processes of an organism. Biotonus depends on the quality and rate of the metabolism and determines the functional rate and intensity of all organs. It is in equilibrium when the synthesizing and decomposing forces are balanced; high when the synthesizing forces are stronger, low when the decomposing forces are stronger. G. Ewald (b. 1883) extended the term to a man's total state of tension, which is bound up with his temperament, and made biotonus the basic concept of a typology (q.v.): biotonus is said to condition the intensity of mental events, mental alertness and the tonality of the vital emotions (temperament, q.v., vitality, q.v.). Biotonus varies from the melancholic (with a "limp" biotonus) to the circumspect type (in whom it is "average") and to the hypomanic (with a "taut" biotonus).

Bibliography: Ewald, G.: Temperament und Charakter. Berlin, 1924.   *F.-C.S.*

Bipolarity of traits. Personality traits whose extreme degrees of expression represent opposites (e.g. dominance-submission; extraversion-introversion, q.v.). The zero point of the scale indicating the lowest degree of expression does not coincide with the end of the scale (unipolar trait), but is at the (qualitatively neutral) mid-point between the two opposites. See *Traits*.   *K.P.*

Birth order. Adler was the first psychologist to describe the psychological features of specific birth order. Toman has systematized his observations: A family of two children may consist of two brothers, two sisters, or one brother and one sister (sibs, or siblings); in the last case either the boy or the girl is older. Families of three children give eight possibilities, and of n children 2^n possibilities, if only the sex and age sequence vary. The birth order of a given person is one of $n2^{n-1}$ possibilities. If there are only two children, one boy may be the elder or younger brother of a brother or sister. The same applies to a girl in a family of two children. There are therefore eight types of birth orders or sibling relationships. These eight types form the basis of all more complex family constellations. An only child does not have a birth order or sibling relationship.

Studies of children in permanent social contacts outside the family with persons of similar age have shown a preference (based on experience in their original families) for leadership and responsibility roles by the oldest brother or sister of a family and for dependence and opposition roles among the youngest members. Persons with siblings of the opposite sex were more successful in exercising this role toward non-family members of the opposite than of the same sex. Persons with siblings of the same sex only, tended to exercise these roles toward persons of the same rather than of the opposite sex.

Mixed birth orders (e.g. the elder brother of a sister and brother; a sister who has an older and younger brother as well as an even younger sister) are built up from the principal types of birth orders and sibling relationships. Their tendencies in social behavior are therefore correspondingly mixed. Twins generally acquire seniority and juniority characteristics from their environment, while both assume characteristics of their birth position in relation to their brothers and sisters. An only child is distinguished from other only children according to the sib position of the parent of the same sex. Only children always show a need for personal relations in which the partner assumes the role of a father or mother. See *Family*.

Bibliography: Ansbacher, H. L. & Ansbacher, R. R.: The individual psychology of Alfred Adler. New York, 1956. Dechêne, H. Ch.: Geschwisterkonstellation und psychische Fehlentwicklung. Munich, 1967. Toman, W.: Family constellation. New York, ²1969.   *W.T.*

Birth trauma. Considered by Rank to be the original ontogenetic form of anxiety determining future anxiety reactions in the individual. Birth transfers the individual from an intra-uterine state of uninterrupted satisfaction of his requirements (warmth, soft contact, food and oxygen supply through the mother's bloodstream) to a state of global deprivation (coldness, physical pressure, breathing problems, unfamiliar effects of light and sound, hunger).

However, Rank made no serious attempt to study the effects of the act of birth on birth anxiety and subsequent anxiety reactions as well as individual susceptibility to anxiety. It is probable, too, that the particular characteristics of a birth (easy or difficult) also depend on the social and mental circumstances of the mother's life (e.g. happy marriage, illegitimate birth, first or *n*-th birth), and that the continuation of these circumstances after birth and the mother's attitude to them have a more significant influence on the development of the child and its susceptibility to anxiety than does the more physical act of birth.

Bibliography: Rank, O.: The trauma of birth. New York, 1929. Toman, W.: Motivation, Persönlichkeit Umwelt. Göttingen, 1968.   *W.T.*

Biserial correlation. A correlation measurement for the degree of frequency of the common occurrence of the classes of a quantitatively and an alternatively measured (dichotomous) continuous variable. The *point-biserial correlation* is applied when, instead of the dichotomous, there is a genuine alternative variable. See *Correlational techniques*.   *W.H.B.*

Bisexual. A term applied to women and men who show both homo- and heterosexual behavior. According to psychoanalytic theory, everyone is bisexual. Precise evidence is not yet available, but it can be concluded at least indirectly from material presented by Kinsey and others that bisexual desires are very often met with.   *G.L.*

Bit. Abbreviation for binary digit (q.v.; number in the binary system). In information theory, the amount of information which will reduce known alternative possibilities by one half. See *Communication*.

Bivariate distribution. In contrast to a one-dimensional (univariate) variable, a two-dimensional variable (X_1, X_2) constitutes a bivariate distribution which (for a continuous case) can be expressed as

$$dF = (x_1, x_2)\, dx_1 dx_2$$

In the case of discrete data or such as are comprised in classes, there is a bivariate *frequency distribution* (q.v.) or a *correlation table* (q.v.). The *correlation coefficient* (q.v.) is a measurement for the degree of statistical dependence of the variables of this distribution.   *W.H.B.*

Blacky pictures. A projective method developed by G. S. Blum (1946) for diagnosing psychosexual development according to psychoanalytical concepts, using twelve scenes in the life of a family of dogs—the leading character is the little black dog Blacky. The child invents stories about the cartoons and answers questions. The reliability (q.v.) and validity (q.v.) of the method (which suggests, e.g., family conflict situations such as the Oedipus conflict) have been questioned; there is less argument about its clinical utility.   *A.L.*

Bleuler's syndrome. The "psycho-organic syndrome" described in 1916 by E. Bleuler

(1857–1939), the Swiss psychiatrist whose main work *Dementia Praecox or the Group of Schizophrenias* appeared in 1911 (Eng. trans.: New York, 1950); later this was called the "organic psychosyndrome", equated with the amnes(t)ic syndrome and finally, as "diffuse cerebral", contrasted with a "cerebrally local" or "endocrine" psychosyndrome (M. Bleuler). It always refers to those psychic combinations of symptoms which can be recorded descriptively and phenomenologically (in the sense of Jaspers' psychopathology) and which are to be found in chronic and diffuse cerebral disorders of a primary and secondary nature, in which disturbances of perception and memory, emotionally hyperesthetic debility, and other impairments of efficiency due to organic brain lesions can be demonstrated. See *Psychoses.*

Bibliography: Bleuler, E.: Lehrbuch der Psychiatrie. (Ed. M. Bleuler) Berlin, ¹¹1969. (Textbook of psychiatry. New York, 1924.) O.S.

Blind analysis. The evaluation of data without any contact with the subject. Hence it is not influenced by any subjective impression, yet cannot draw on any information that might be derived from direct observation. On the whole, the tendency is to make the diagnosis solely from the objective data. Comparative investigations have shown that, given good tests, on average blind analysis produces no worse results. R.M.

Blind, education of the. In the education of the blind, attempts are made to compensate by systematic training for difficulties in personality development caused by the total or partial loss of sight (such as dependence on strangers' help, restricted possibilities of cognition, inability to conceive esthetic values in the visual modality); and to enable the blind or partially-sighted child, as he grows up, to share in our cultural or intellectual heritage as a full member of the

community. The greater dependence of such children has to be considered in the structure and conditions of their education; and the cause of the absence or defect of vision (blindness at birth, early in life or later) influences the choice of teaching methods, which (with such aids as braille, tape libraries, and defect-specific devices) try to make full use of even the least degree of sight. H.S.

Blind experiment (syn. *Blind test*). A control procedure designed to exclude undesired variables from the experiment. Testees are diagnosed without the experimenter being able to speak to them, etc.; i.e. the diagnosis is made solely by tests.

Double blind test. In this form of the blind test the experiment is conducted without the person in charge or the testee having any knowledge of the variables. E.g. drugs are administered to one group of testees, whereas another group receive placebos. The research director then determines the effect without knowing to which group the testees belonged. V.M.

Blind, psychology of the. A branch of psychology concerned with the effects of the absence of sight on the sensory, motor, intellectual and personality traits of the blind person, and with research into measures for rehabilitation of the blind in general.

Differences between the sighted and the blind in regard to the discrimination of tactile and auditory signals derive from the additional practice blind people have had. The sense of touch is especially important for reading and the differentiated apprehension of environmental phenomena. Hearing is important for communication and for moving about.

Disablement due to blindness is especially noticeable in motor skills (q.v.), peculiarities in blind children, and difficulties in moving about in the street (recognition of objects: obstacles, traffic signs; see *Orientation*).

There is no difference in intellectual performance between the sighted and the blind. There are more cases of extreme variants among the blind in the lower distribution range (multiple damage: blindness and deafness, blindness and brain damage, etc.).

In regard to specific personality traits, how the blind person comes to terms with his affliction is of major interest. Resignation and adaptation by compensation (q.v.) are assumed. Psychologically important distinctions among the blind are the degree of blindness and when it happened, and the age and sex of the blind person.

The partially sighted seem to have more difficulties in performance and achievement than the totally blind. Investigations to see whether people who have lost their sight profit from their visual experience have yielded no uniform results. Studies dealing with the question (important in cognition theory) of the spatial awareness of those born blind arrive at different conclusions: no primary spatial notions (von Senden, 1932) versus the different nature of tactile-kinesthetic space (Juurmaa, 1966).

Rehabilitation measures are directed primarily to adapting technological advances for the blind (the development of automatic reading appliances, electronic appliances for guiding the blind, light prostheses, etc.).

Bibliography: Research Bulletin: Publication of the American Foundation for the Blind. New York (quarterly). Juurmaa, J.: An analysis of the ability for orientation and operations with spatial relationships. Work—Environment—Health, 1966, *2*, 45–52. Révész, G.: Psychology and art of the blind. London, 1950. Senden, M. von: Raum- und Gestaltauffassung bei operierten Blinden vor und nach der Operation. Leipzig, 1932. Zahl, P. A. (Ed.): Blindness: modern approaches to the unseen environment. Princeton, 1950.   *M. Brambring*

Blind spot. The point where the optic nerve leaves the eyeball. It corresponds to the *papilla nervi optici* and is situated 12 to 18 degrees on the nasal side of the *fovea centralis*. There are no light receptors here.   *R.R.*

Blocks (*Blocking*). The terms *block* and *blocking* are often used synonymously in psychology and physiology for an inhibition, barrier, obstacle or an interrupted action. In hierarchical function models (as, e.g., in reflex and instinct theory, Tinbergen, 1951), blocking is adduced to explain prepotent reflexes (q.v.).

The usual applications of the terms: (*a*) in physiology: *synaptic blocking, anodic blocking, depolarization* and *hyperpolarization blocking, heart blocking*, all of which are terms to denote obstructions of the transmission of electrical impulses in nerve fibers and cells. *Ganglionic blocks:* chemical substances in vegetative ganglia; their effect is to inhibit excitation. *Alpha-wave blocking:* the suppression of the alpha-wave activity in the electroencephalogram. (*b*) In psychology and psychopathology: *mental block:* see below. *Memory block:* a name or concept normally easy to recall cannot at the moment be brought to mind. *Affective block:* psychopathological obstruction of the emotional capacity for experience and response; to be distinguished from "*emotional block*": an inhibition of perceiving, thinking or acting as a result of emotional arousal, e.g., caused by examination anxiety or stage fright. (*c*) In the experimental sense, a block can also be: an external obstacle which obstructs the realization of some reaction (e.g. a barrier in a maze). In the planning of experiments (block design): the smallest responsive group of contiguous experimental lots (or subjects), to which the different experimental conditions are allotted at random or systematically. Since Bills (1931), "*psychic*" or "*mental*" blockings have come to mean brief interruptions of thought processes or continuous stimulus-response activities where no specific external stimulus or subjectively perceptible motive (q.v.) can be made responsible.

Subjective accompaniments of blocks are: a "mental vacuum", "sensory dissociation" in the perception of stimuli or in the train of thought, as well as momentary motor inability to give the response which until a very short time before had been given correctly. There are significant colloquial expressions for the phenomenon, such as: "short circuit", "losing the thread", "breaking off one's train of thought", "on the tip of my tongue", etc.

From the standpoint of behavioral psychology, blocks are best observed during continuous behaviors with relatively homogeneous stimulus- and activity-structures (e.g. during the continuous naming of colors, or the continuous addition of digits). They appear then as relatively long interruptions of the activity (duration of a block is between app. 0·5 and 10 sec., and in rare cases even as much as 1 min. or more). In continuous activities, e.g. the numbers $2 + 3$ suddenly cannot be added ("the answer won't come"), or the figures appear as unintelligible characters ("like hieroglyphs"), or the testees recognize, e.g., the color green, but are momentarily unable to pronounce the associated word "green". A few seconds later the specific response is given quite normally once more. Blocks can appear in series, and can be announced by responses which become longer and longer but which also frequently appear with extreme suddenness in the midst of the response activity. Blocks can also disappear with the same suddenness. Blocks cannot voluntarily be prevented from appearing. Fatigue and anxiety states especially can give rise to intensified blocking.

There is as yet no satisfactory theoretical explanation for blocking. Bills regarded it as a defensive inhibition of fatigue (*refractory period theory*).

Mental blocking is related to several psychological phenomena of attention, thought, activity and motivation, as well as certain psychopathological effects (e.g. the interruption of a thought process in schizophrenic thought disorders, etc.).

Bibliography: Bäumler, G.: Statistische, experimentelle und theoretische Beiträge zur Frage der Blockierung bei fortlaufenden Reaktionstätigkeiten (Dissertation). Würzburg, 1967. Bills, A. G.: Blocking: a new principle of mental fatigue. American Journal of Psychology, 1931, 43, 230–45. Tinbergen, N.: The study of instinct. Oxford, 1951.

G. Bäumler

Blood-brain barrier (BBB). A term coined by Stern & Gautier (1921) to denote the fact that most chemical substances pass with relatively greater difficulty from the blood into the tissues of the central nervous system than into other bodily tissues. The barrier is conceived as a system regulating the passage of substances present in the blood into the CNS. It cannot be clearly delineated either anatomically or physiologically and biochemically, but has the character of an intervening variable in the sense of a collection of numerous factors. The extent to, and speed with which different substances pass the barrier depend on their chemical and physical properties (e.g. molecular size, fat solubility). Gases pass with especial ease (e.g. O_2; inhalant narcotics); many hormones pass with difficulty, or not at all, e.g. adrenalin(e).

Bibliography: Dobbing, J.: The blood-brain barrier. Physiological Review, 1961, 41, 130–88. Lorenzo, A. V.: Mechanism of drug penetration in the brain. In: P. Black (Ed.): Drugs and the brain. Baltimore, 1969.

W.J.

Blood pressure. The prevailing pressure in the blood vessels, which can be measured physically. It can be measured directly with a manometer introduced into the vessel, or indirectly (according to S. Riva-Rocci) with an inflated sphygmomanometer strapped round the arm. There are two components, one hydrostatic and the other hemodynamic. The latter is the consequence of the heart's activity, serves to overcome resistance to flow and decreases continuously in the circulatory system in the direction of the blood flow (from 120 mmHg via the aorta, via 35 mmHg in the capillary circulation to 0 in the veins near the heart). In the arteries it fluctuates with the rhythm of the heart beat between a systolic (120 mmHg) and a diastolic (80 mmHg) value.

These fluctuations of pressure appear as the pulse and can be recorded as a sphygmogram. The mean blood pressure is regulated by the vasomotor center in the brain stem by way of pressure points in the blood vessels and heart activity, as well as vascular contractile power. (For morbid changes of the blood pressure see under *Hypertonia* and *Hypotonia*).   *E.D.*

Blumenfeld illusion (syn. *Blumenfeld alley*). If Ss are given the task of making two parallel rows with small gas lamps in a dark room, they will arrange the lamps other than when they are asked to take the corresponding lamps in pairs to the same distance in depth. This optical illusion (see *Geometric-optical illusions*) is an argument against the "parallel axiom" (or "parallel postulate" of Euclid's geometry) in space perception. See *Visual perception.*   *V.M.*

Body build index (syn. *Body type index*). According to H. J. Eysenck, the body may be considered as a rectangle in terms of two independent dimensions: height and width. Height is measured by length of arms, of leg, total height, etc.; width by chest width, and chest or hip circumference. General, total body size is calculated by height multiplied by width (i.e. transverse chest width). Body build, or shape (whether the body is relatively long or relatively squat), is calculated by dividing the height by the width (or one hundred times the height divided by six times the transverse chest width = IB). Macrosomatics, mesosomatics and microsomatics are descriptive terms for body size 1 SD above, within ±SD of, and 1 SD below the mean of the population respectively (SD = % standard deviation). Eurymorphs, mesomorphs and leptomorphs

are descriptive terms for body build, similarly determined.

Bibliography: Rees, L. & Eysenck, H. J.: A factorial study of some morphological and psychological aspects of human constitution. J. ment. Sci., 1945, *91*, 8–21.   *J.C.*

Body concept. See *Body image.*

Body ego. An aspect of the "ego" (q.v.) concept: all ego-experiences in regard to one's own body. Equivalent to L. Kleist's "somatopsyche".   *H.-J.A.*

Body image (syn. *Body schema*). In general, a spatial idea of one's own body which changes according to information received from one's body and the environment; in this image the parts of the body have a different appearance. Schilder (1935) and Head (1926) described the distortion of the body image from a neurological and psychiatric angle, and extended their findings to the field of normality. (*a*) The change of the body image through each new position and movement of the body; (*b*) the development of the body image depends on social contact. The body image mainly operates unconsciously, and is used as a standard by which all positions, movements and perceptions of the body are compared before there is any response.

Bibliography: Fisher, S. & Cleveland, S. E.: Body image and personality. New York & London, 1958. Head, H.: Aphasia and kindred disorders of speech. London, 1926. Schilder, P.: The image and appearance of the human body. London, 1935.   *J.O.*

Body size. See *Body build index.*

Body Sway Test of Suggestibility. A test for primary (motor) suggestibility from Eysenck's battery. Basically, the Hull Body Sway Test is used: the subject listens to a record while standing upright; the degree of movement on being told that he is falling forward is measured.

Body temperature. Organisms which are poikilothermic, i.e. with a variable body temperature, adapt it to the environment and may reach even higher levels than man (e.g. the lizard when the sun is very hot). Homoiothermic (warm-blooded) creatures such as man maintain a uniform *interior body* temperature in the cranial, pulmonary and abdominal cavities. The rectal temperature varies between approximately 36·2 and 37·5°C, being at its lowest at about 6 a.m., and at its highest at about 6 p.m. In the outer body, which in man may also be described as poikilothermic, the temperature as the skin is approached drops more or less to that of the environment. Body temperature is subject to a complicated biocybernetic process controlled by centers—a "cooling center" in the rostral hypothalamus and a "heating center" at the back of the hypothalamus. The control value is the temperature of the arterial blood, any rise in which after transmission through corresponding hypothalamic or even spinal points produces vasodilation, sweating, and a feeling of heat; any drop in arterial blood temperature leads to vasoconstriction, and an increase in the metabolic rate, shivering and numbness. Fever may be regarded as a change in the normal values of the hypothalamic control centers.   *K.H.P.*

Bone conduction. The conduction of sound through the skull bones to the cochlea. (Air) sound waves above 800 Hz create cranial vibrations and their oscillation nodes, or nodal points, pass through the petrosal bone and compress the cochlea according to the sound rhythm. Because of the unequal elasticity of the two (oval and round) windows (Békésy's compression theory) each bulges to a different degree and there is thus displacement of fluid in the two scalae (lymphatic canals in the cochlea). Since the fluid mass of the semicircular canals is also joined to one of the two scalae (von Ranke's mass coupling theory), the asymmetry of the scalae (and hence the displacement of fluid) is further intensified. The associated vibration of the basilar membrane separating the two scalae leads to the excitation of auditory cilia, and thus the sound is perceived.   *E.D.*

Bonhoeffer's syndrome. Karl Bonhoeffer (1868–1948) described in 1912, in an article on psychoses and infections and other diseases (in: Aschaffenburg, G.: *Handbuch der Psychiatrie*. Leipzig & Vienna, 1912) the "acute exogenous reaction-type". Under this term he grouped all the acute psychic concomitant symptoms of physical (i.e. not just primarily cerebral) illnesses. M. Bleuler and K. Conrad have done much to develop the concept. See *Psychoses; Psychosomatics*.

Bibliography: Bleuler, M., Willi, J. & Buehler, H. R. *et al.*: Akute psychische Begleiterscheinungen körperlicher Krankheiten. Stuttgart, 1966. Conrad, K.: Die symptomatischen Psychosen. In: Gruhle, H. W., Jung, R., Mayer-Gross, W. & Müller, M. (Eds): Psychiatrie der Gegenwart, Vol. 2, 369–436.   *O.S.*

Boredom. A psychological condition associated with environmental monotony and characterized by negative affect, loss of interest, wandering attention, low arousal and impaired working efficiency. In its extreme form boredom may give rise to symptoms ranging from depression to agitation and hallucinations, and is being held increasingly responsible for many social problems including delinquency, suicide and marital unhappiness.   *G.D.W.*

Bovarism (syn. *Bovaryism*). Holding an unreal, glamorized conception of oneself to the extent that one fails to distinguish between romance and reality. Also: such a conception. From Emma Bovary in Flaubert's novel *Madame Bovary*.

Bowel training (syn. *Cleanliness training; Toilet training*). According to Freudian theory, exceptionally severe or too early anal training in regularity of stool, etc., can result in later abnormal orderliness, obstinacy and stinginess. Attempts have been made to test the hypothesis of the existence of an anal trait and some evidence has been obtained, but the relation to coercive or speedily-completed bowel training has not been demonstrated.

Bibliography: Barnes, C. A.: A statistical study of the Freudian theory of levels of psychosexual development. Genet. Psychol. Monogr., 1952, *45*, 105–24. Beloff, H.: The structure and origin of the anal character. Genet. Psychol. Monogr., 1957, *55*, 141–72.
J.G.

Brace Scale of Motor Ability. A test to estimate ability to learn motor skills. Useful for determining gross motor coordination difficulties. The scale can be applied throughout the age-range of 5 to 18 years and contains thirty-nine tasks testing motor abilities (e.g. agility). Revisions by McClory & Young (1954) and Vickers *et al.* (1942) are available: Iowa–Brace Scale.

Bibliography: Brace, D. K.: Measuring motor ability. A scale of motor ability tests. New York, 1927. McCloy, C. H. & Young, N.: Tests and measurements in physical education. New York, ³1954. Vickers, V. *et al.*: The Brace used with young children. Res. Quart., 1942, *13*, 299–302.
J.M.

Bradykinesia (*Bradykinesis; Hypokinesis*). A motor disorder. Slowness of movement as a result of central organic disturbance.

Bradykinin. A polypeptide contained in the tissues the significance of which is as yet unexplained. Pain of limited duration can be produced by the injection of bradykinin into arteries leading to the extremities or to the intestines, or by use on skin blisters. Hence bradykinin is used for the experimental induction of pain and for testing, *inter alia*, analgesics (q.v.). In therapy bradykinin is used as a peripheral vasodilator, when it brings about a considerable fall in blood pressure.

Bibliography: Erdös, E. G.: Structure and function of biologically active peptides: bradykinin, kallidin, and congeners. Annals of the New York Academy of Science, 1963, *104*, 1–464. Lim, R. K. S. & Gurman, F.: Manifestations of pain in analgesic evaluation in animals and man. In: Soulairac, A., Cahn, J. & Charpentier, J. (Eds): Pain. New York, 1968. *W.B.*

Bradyphrasia (syn. *Bradyarthria; Bradylalia; Bradyphasia; Bradyglossia*). An organically conditioned speech disorder. Retardation of speech by drawing out the syllables, and by pauses of varying length as a result of central organic disturbance: in lesions of the cerebellum and associated structures, especially in multiple sclerosis; often combined with other motor disorders.   *F.-C.S.*

Bradyphrenia (syn. *Hypophrenia*). Retardation of the mental functions through a lack of inner drive consequent upon central organic disturbance, e.g. encephalitis (q.v.).
F.-C.S.

Brain. Conscious processes cannot occur without a properly functioning brain: every experiential content depends on the activation of specific nerve cells. If these cells are activated by specific stimuli (see *Neuropsychology*), the related psychological processes occur; if the nerve cells are destroyed, the mental processes dependent on them are irrevocably lost: the totality of neuronal activity in our brain represents our individual world.

Even in simply organized forms of life, the nerve cells are associated in larger groups which receive stimuli from the sense cells or transmit corresponding information to the effectors. This tendency to centralization is particularly marked in all the vertebrates. These have a central nervous system (brain and spinal cord) in which the mass of brain substance dominates that of the spinal cord with an increasing level of differentiation.

The cell bodies of the neuron(e)s (grey matter) are either combined in nuclei embedded deep in the brain in the fibrous masses of other nerve cells (white matter), or form a superficial cell layer with many transverse connections, i.e. the (cerebral) cortex. In the primates there is a very substantial multiplication of cells in the anterior section of the brain (the endbrain, or telencephalon, q.v.), and in particular in the main cerebral cortex (covering the hemispheres of the endbrain) in which the terminals of all specific, sensory stimuli are located and the pathways for control of the voluntary motor system originate. The caudal brain sections adjoining the endbrain, i.e. the interbrain (diencephalon, q.v.) and midbrain (mesencephalon, q.v.), which still play a dominant part in controlling the behavior of the lower vertebrates, are much less important in all the higher vertebrates (especially in man), and are almost completely covered by the hemispheres of the endbrain. This structural principle led to the assumption that the "higher" parts of the brain which developed later took over the functions of their phylogenetic precursors in a differentiated form (hierarchical function model). In this assumption, the cerebral cortex, as the most recent differentiation in brain development, is thought to be the highest central nervous unit on whose activity the control of all more complex behavioral processes and the occurrence of psychic (mental) processes depend. This view has been revised more recently with the discovery of a cell system which extends as a functional unit in the longitudinal axis of the brain, through all the hierarchical levels, and on the activity of which the activation level of the living being is dependent at any given time. This *non-specific activation system* includes a group of multiform nerve cells in the midbrain and in the hindmost section of the brain, the hindbrain (rhombencephalon, q.v.), with many transverse links, by reason of which it is known as the reticular formation or substance (*formatio reticularis*). It continues, without any clear demarcation, into

the interbrain (thalamus: non-specific thalamic projection system), and—functionally at least—into the endbrain (*limbic system*). Stimulation of the non-specific activation system controls the activity of the cerebral cortex and hence all experience and behavior. If this stimulation is blocked (by pathological processes or interventions in animal experiments) the organism falls into a state of permanent coma even though the cortex remains intact; the activity of the cerebral cortex determines the specific content of a conscious process, whereas the non-specific activation system determines the kind of awareness and the experiential (emotional or motivational) background for this process.

The changes in electrical potential which accompany stimulation of the cortical neurons (see *Nervous system*) can be amplified and recorded from the scalp without surgical intervention (see *Electroencephalogram*). Specific intervention has recently allowed stimulation components fundamental to a specific conscious content to be isolated from all other simultaneous stimulation, and to be observed separately, even though their current amounts to only a few millionths of a volt (see *Neuropsychology*). This advance into the region of just measurable cerebral phenomena has given initial access to an objectively observable correlate for heterogeneous psychic phenomena.

Bibliography: Crosby, E. C., Humphrey, T. & Lauer, E. W.: Correlative anatomy of the nervous system. New York, 1962. Ferner, H.: Anatomie des Nervensystems und der Sinnesorgane des Menschen. Munich & Basle, 1970.   G. Guttmann

Brain pathology. The branch of medicine concerned with the analysis of changes (especially in mental processes) which occur in the event of brain damage.

Brain damage may be of two kinds: *organic* and *dynamic*. Organic damage to cerebral activity is associated with irreversible destruction of the nerve cells (ganglionic cells) or pathways (nerve fibers). This damage may be caused by hemorrhage or circulatory disorders in the brain, lesions resulting from injury, brain tumors or inflammatory processes. It may be local or affect the whole brain; the involvement of the entire brain occurs quite often in the event of vascular weakness or atrophic processes resulting from defective development, or aging. The second type of brain damage consists of dynamic lesions which are either perifocal (on the limits of the pathological focus) or at points which are linked functionally with the focus. This damage is based on a temporary inhibition of functions which occurs primarily in connection with a disturbance of the synaptic conductivity of stimuli due to disturbance of the chemical equilibrium between acetylcholine (a chemical substance—transmitter-substance—carrying nerve impulses) and cholinesterase (an enzyme which inactivates acetylcholine). Dynamic damage to brain activity is sometimes referred to as "diaschitis" (K. von Monakow). The main problem in brain pathology is to determine the basic mechanisms of functional disorders (above all disturbance of mental functions) in the event of focal damage to the brain.

The traditional approach to this problem was based on the assumption that each brain section (or each group of brain cells) had a specific function, simple in one case and complex (mental) in another. The proponents of this classical theory (of "narrow localization") believed that in addition to the sections of the cerebral cortex with sensation or motor functions there were also cortical areas specifically concerned with the highest mental functions (ideation, conceptualization, speech, writing, calculating, etc.); injury to these cortical areas would therefore result in the failure of the associated functions. This was the theory of Gall, who established the "science" of phrenology (q.v.) early last century: this located the most complex "abilities" in certain limited brain "centers"; this opinion was shared by Broca who believed the inferior frontal gyrus of the left cerebral hemisphere to be the "motor verbal imagery center"; the same

theory was held by O. and C. Vogt and in particular by K. Kleist who introduced the term "brain pathology" and believed that functions such as the understanding of words or sentences, calculation, or even the "personal, social or. religious ego" were located in specific parts of the brain. He therefore believed that destruction of the corresponding brain sections would lead to the isolated cessation of these specific functions.

Clinical practice has not confirmed these theories; it has shown that a given function (e.g. writing) can be disturbed by brain injury in various, different areas, whereas the destruction of a single, limited section of the brain may give rise to a whole range of disturbances of mental functions (e.g. cortical injury to the left temporal lobe—in a right-handed person—can affect the understanding of words, naming of objects, writing, and so on).

These facts have led a number of scientists to the opposite assumption: namely, that the human brain always works as a whole, and that the complex mental processes are not localized in specific areas of the brain, but are a function of the whole cortex. This theory of "anti-localization" was propounded by F. L. Goltz, and has been supported more recently by K. S. Lashley, K. von Monakow, and, to some extent, by K. Goldstein. These researchers consider that a disturbance of the complex forms of rational (or categorial) activity depends on the extent of the injury rather than on the particular area of the brain which it affects.

Neither of the two theories outlined above has stood the test of time. While the "localizationists" worked from the incorrect assumption that the highest mental functions were innate abilities which could not be broken down into component parts and could be traced to the functions of individual nerve cells, the "anti-localizationists" considered (wrongly as it turned out) that the highest mental processes were categories of intellectual life which could not be subjected to detailed analysis and were in some undefined manner dependent on the brain as a whole.

Recent scientific developments have led to a thorough revision of the notion of "function", and to a radical reappraisal of the nature of disturbances of mental functions in the event of brain damage.

Scientists now assume that there are two completely different interpretations of the term "function": it may be understood on the one hand as the activity of a tissue (e.g. the photosensitive functions of the retina, or the secretory functions of the glands); and on the other hand as a complex adaptive activity designed to carry out a specific task (e.g. the function of digestion, of breathing, or of locomotion). In the latter case, the "function" is complex and consists of a complicated functional system which works toward a permanent (invariable) goal with varying means. Breathing, which primarily involves the muscles of the diaphragm, may be taken over by the intercostal muscles if the diaphragm muscles are damaged; if the former are damaged, it can be performed by swallowing air; and so on. Most biological "functions" consist of such complex functional systems involving the joint activity of a wide range of nerve mechanisms located to some extent on different planes. All the higher psychological "functions" enjoy the same complex nature. Unlike the biological "functions", these are even more complex functional systems whose origins are socio-historical, while their structure is heterogeneous (dependent on a range of aids), and their method of functioning voluntary (i.e. they are subject to self-control).

It is therefore clear that these "functions" cannot be carried out by isolated cell groups, but are dependent on the common activity of all the different brain areas, each of which makes a specific contribution to the performance of these "functional systems". The process of writing, for example, can only take place if the cerebral cortex is in a certain state (which is guaranteed by sub-cortical structures); and a further condition is precise phonematic analysis of the sound content of the words to be written (this is ensured by the mechanisms of the temporal-auditory cortex); a simultaneous kinesthetic (articulatory) analysis of the sounds (by the apparatus of the post-central, kinesthetic cortex) is essential, and can only take place if the spatially organized visual patterns of the letters to be written (governed by the visual parietal areas of the cortex) are unimpaired. The following are also requisite for writing: a continuous sequence of movement impulses and the implementation of fluid "kinetic" functions (functions of the pre-motor areas of the cortex), and maintenance of initial intentions with a continuous check on performance of the corresponding actions (which would be impossible without participation of the frontal lobes).

The complex "function" may therefore be disturbed by damage to almost any brain area, but the disturbances will always differ, depending on the contribution of the particular zone to the structure of the functional system as a whole.

This idea has completely changed the orientation of brain pathology. The function of the research worker is no longer to determine which function is disturbed in the event of a limited (local) brain lesion, but rather to isolate the main factor whose failure led to the disturbance of the whole functional system; and to show how the given "function" is disturbed in the event of local brain injury.

This trend—the search for the primary damage which occurs in the event of a local brain lesion, and analysis of the secondary (system-dependent) damage which occurs as a consequence of the primary damage—is the main orientation of modern brain pathology or neuropsychology. The aim is first to describe meticulously the disorder of mental activity which occurs in the event of local brain injury and then to "qualify" the symptom, i.e. to detect its cause and isolate the factor whose failure has led to the disturbance, after which the secondary "system disturbances" can be determined; only when all this has been done is it possible to carry out a local ("topical") analysis of the injury. Brain pathology, or neuropsychology, is of fundamental importance to psychology as a whole. It allows an analysis to be made oj the factors which constitute complex psychological processes, and permits more accurate research into the psychophysiological structure and brain mechanisms of these factors. It therefore provides criteria for differentiation between "functions" which appear externally similar but are in reality fundamentally different, and vice versa: it establishes an inner system of links between "functions" which may at first sight appear completely disparate. The auditory perception of music and that of language (phonematic perception) may seem to be related processes, but the fact that a lesion of the left temporal lobe leads to impairment of phonematic hearing, whereas musical hearing remains unaffected, proves that they are in fact very different. On the other hand, processes such as spatial orientation, calculation, and the comprehension of complex logico-grammatical structures are completely different forms of activity; however, the fact that injuries to the lower parietal areas of the cortex leads to disturbance of *all* these processes suggests that they are all dependent on a single region. Research into brain damage (neuropsychological analysis) can therefore be of great significance for psychology, because it investigates the detailed inner structure of psychological processes and their mechanisms in the brain.

Bibliography: Ajusioguerra, J. & Hécean, H.: La cortex cérébrale. Paris, 1966. Ivanov-Smolenski, A. G.: Grundzüge der Pathophysiologie der höheren Nerventätigkeit. Berlin, 1954. Kleist, K.: Gehirnpathologie. Leipzig, 1934. Luria, A. R.: Higher cortical functions in man, New York, 1966. Id.: Traumatic aphasia. The Hague, 1970. Monakow, K. von: Die Lokalisation im Grosshirn und der Abbau der Funktionen durch lokale' Herde. Wiesbaden, 1964.   A. R. Luria

Brain stem. The part of the brain (q.v.) left after the exclusion of the cerebrum and cerebellum.

Brainwashing. The subjection of an individual to conditions of physical and even psychic duress in order to persuade him to disclose secrets, bear false witness, or alter his political viewpoint or moral convictions, or otherwise to "convert" him to a desired viewpoint or action. Measures used (usually in exceptional situations, e.g. imprisonment), which eventually bring about intellectual and emotional disorganization, are, e.g.: deprivation of food and sleep, excessive physical stress, refusal of medical attention, isolation. Syn. *Menticide; Coercive persuasion.*
Bibliography: Biderman, A. D. & Zimmer, H.: The manipulation of human behavior. New York, 1961. Eysenck, H. J.: Crime and personality. London, 1964. Lifton, R. J.: Thought reform and the psychology of totalism. New York, 1961. Schein, E. H., Schneier, I. & Barker, C. H.: Coercive persuasion. New York, 1961.   M.A.

Branching. A technique in the construction of teaching programs: one or several subprograms are linked to a main program. These alternative learning paths either offer complements to and elucidations of the main program, or afford an opportunity for repetition. On the basis of his replies to a criterion unit the learner is guided into one of these pre-programmed learning paths according to his individual knowledge or ability; he may be taken to a remedial frame: when he has finished it, he will be taken back into the main program or sequence of frames: e.g. each step ends with a multiple-choice question; the answer chosen decides the next step taken. This is the multiple path or branching program technique originated by Norman Crowder. See *Instructional technology; Machine learning; Programmed learning.*   L.J.I.

Bravais–Pearson correlation coefficient. This coefficient gives the correlation (q.v.) of two continuous *normal distributions* (q.v.). It is not identical with the product-moment correlation (q.v.), but can be satisfactorily estimated from it. *W.H.B.*

Breeding and parental care. Certain creatures take or plan measures in advance which serve directly to protect their offspring, such as placing the nests in protected spots, making protective covers and supplying their progeny with food (e.g. the breeding pellets, or spherical dung-balls in which eggs are laid, of the *Scarabaeus sacer* and Spanish Copris beetles and other members of the Scarab family). Parental care serves indirectly to look after the nests and the young who are watched over and supplied with oxygen or food. *External parental care:* some pipe-fish (e.g. *Nerophis ophidion*), the midwife toad (*Alytes obstetricans*), leeches, crabs, spiders and bugs carry the eggs around with them. *Internal parental care:* those which incubate in body cavities are certain cichlids (in the mouth), needle-fish and sea-horses (in pockets); the frog *Rhinoderma darwinii* even carries its offspring in the sound vesicles. Viviparous creatures: in ovoviparous species the young are still in the egg case at birth. Apart from the egg-laying Greenland Shark, sharks develop a yolk-sack placenta. Cloacal mammals, while laying eggs, have neither placenta nor nipples but lacteal areas. Marsupials give birth to living young but usually have no placenta, and premature young grow together with the nipples. The eutheria have a placenta which enables gas and food to pass between the embryo and the mother. Insessores have a short (rabbits 28 days), autophagi a long gestation (porpoises 63 days). There is prolongation of pregnancy with embryonic development arrested temporarily. E.g. roe-deer and badgers have a prolonged gestation period with temporarily arrested embryonic development.

Bibliography: Hesse, R. & Doflein, F.: Tierbau und Tierleben, Vol. 2. Jena, 1943. *K.F.*

Brentano, Franz. B. 16/1/1838 in Marienberg near Boppard on the Rhine; d. 17/3/1917 in Zürich. 1864 ordained priest, 1866–73 *Privatdozent* (lecturer), and later Professor of philosophy at Würzburg, 1874–80 Professor at Vienna University, and until 1895 a lecturer in Vienna. His philosophy was neo-Aristotelian in origin, and his psychology was descriptive. Brentano opposed the analysis of consciousness into contents. His theory of the intentionality of psychic phenomena, and his "empirical", rationally argumentative account of mind and experience as a mode of acting, make him the founder of act psychology (q.v.). His recognition of the importance of the intentional orientation of all psychic phenomena to some inner "given" entitles him to rank as a forerunner of phenomenology (q.v.) (see *Husserl*). His understanding of inner perception as prerequisite for all psychology, and his distinction between psychic acts and non-psychic contents influenced (among others) A. Meinong (q.v.) and C. von Ehrenfels (q.v.).

Works: Die Psychologie des Aristoteles, insbesondere seine Lehre vom *nus poetikòs*. Mainz, 1867 (reprinted: Darmstadt, 1967). Psychologie vom empirischen Standpunkt, Ed. O. Kraus. Leipzig, 1924–28. Vom Ursprung sittlicher Erkenntnis. Leipzig, 1907. Von der Klassifikation der psychischen Phänomene. Leipzig, 1911.

Bibliography: Barclay, J. R.: Franz Brentano and Sigmund Freud, J. Existentialism, 1964, *5*, 1–36. Brett, G. S.: Associationism and "act" psychology. In: Murchison, C. (Ed.): Psychologies of 1930. Worcester, Mass., 1930, 39–55. Kraus, O.: Franz Brentano. Zur Kenntnis seines Lebens und seiner Lehre. Munich, 1919. Utitz, E.: Franz Brentano. Kantsstudien, Vol. 22. Cologne, 1918. *K.E.P*

Brentano's illusion. If in the first of two adjacent pictures we have a circle, and in the second a circle of equal size but surrounded by a larger, concentric circle, the circle in the second picture appears larger than the circle in the first picture which, objectively, is of the same size. See *Delboeuf's illusion; Geometrical-optical illusions.*   *V.M.*

Breton's law. A new formulation of Weber's law (q v.): the relation between the stimulus and the smallest just-noticeable stimulus difference is parabolic.   *V.M.*

Brightness. The luminous intensity experienced in visual perception is defined as brightness. A distinction is made between photometric brightness (=luminous intensity) and the specific brightness characteristic of colors (yellow and green being brighter than violet and red). G. T. Fechner assumed that brightness is proportional to the logarithm of light intensity (luminous intensity, retinal illumination). Depending on the duration of exposure to light, Aiba & Stevens (1964) found power functions with different exponents.

Bibliography: **Aiba, T. S. & Stevens, S. S.:** Relation of brightness to duration and luminance under light and dark adaptation, Vis. Res., 1964, *4*, 391–401).
                       A.H.

Broca's area. The inferior frontal gyrus of the left cerebral hemisphere (in the right-handed). It is particularly important as the location of the motor language center (but see *Aphasia; Brain pathology*) in the dominant hemisphere.   *C.S.*

Bundle hypothesis. Gestalt theorists' term (pejorative) for the view that a whole is only the sum of its parts.

Bühler–Hetzer test. A test for pre-school children (1932); see *Development tests.*
Bibliography: **Bühler, C. & Hetzer, H.:** Testing children's development from birth to school age. London, 1935.

Bühler, Karl. B. 27/5/1879 at Meckesheim (Baden); d. 24/10/1963 in Pasadena (Calif.); M.D. 1903, Ph.D. 1904; 1907–09 one of the most important researchers of the Würzburg school (q.v.); worked in Bonn from 1909, in Munich from 1913, in Dresden from 1918, and finally in Vienna from 1922 to 1938 (the high point of his academic activity). He was arrested by the Nazis, and sought refuge in Oslo in the autumn of 1938. He went to St Paul (Minn., U.S.A.) in 1940, and lived from 1945 in Los Angeles. His contributions to the psychology of thought belong to his Würzburg period: he defended his method of observation under experimental conditions against W. Wundt (q.v.), G. E. Müller (q.v.), etc. The results of his research work into types of thought are recorded in his articles "Über Gedanken" (1907), "Über Gedankenzusammenhänge" (1908), "Über Gedankenerinnerungen" (1908), and in "Tatsachen und Probleme zu einer Psychologie der Denkvorgänge" (Archiv der Gestaltpsychologie, 1907, *9* and 1908, *12*). These articles also contributed to the defeat of the elementarism (q.v.) and sensualism (q.v.) of classical psychology, and to the recognition of the *Ganzheit* (q.v.) principle. The holistic view of psychic processes was the explicit theme of his *Die Gestaltwahrnehmungen* (Stuttgart, 1913) and, once again, of his last work: *Das Gestaltprinzip im Leben des Menschen und der Tiere* (Berne & Stuttgart, 1960). Bühler gained lasting merit with his book *Die Krise der Psychologie* (Jena, ²1927), in which he endeavors by his theory of aspects to rescue the unity of psychology from the controversies of the schools. His books *Ausdruckstheorie* (Jena, 1933) and *Sprachtheorie* (Jena, 1934) have considerable significance for social psychology. In 1962 his theory of language, and particularly the functions and phenomena of spoken language, formed the central topic of a semantics (q.v.) congress in Indiana; the newly-developing psycholinguistic research (see *Psycholinguistics*) cannot disregard it. Finally, with his *Die geistige Entwicklung des Kindes*

(Jena, 1918; Eng. trans.: *The Mental Development of the Child*. New York & London, 1930), Bühler gave a decisive impetus to developmental psychology. His fundamental, far-reaching and spirited works make Bühler one of the basic personalities of modern psychology.

Bibliography: Festschrift für K. Bühler. In: Zeitschrift für experimentelle und angewandte Psychologie, 1959, *6*, 1–118. Wellek, K.: K.B. 1879–1963. Archiv der Gestaltpsychologie, 1964, *116*, 3–8.   *L.J.P.*

Burt, Sir Cyril Lodowic. B. 3/3/1883; d. 10/10/1971 in London; studied at Christ's Hospital, London, and at Oxford and Würzburg. Read natural science and psychology, and was a disciple of W. McDougall (q.v.) and O. Külpe (q.v.).

1907–12: taught experimental psychology and physiology at Liverpool University, where he carried out research into the measurement of intelligence; 1913–32 official educational psychologist to the London County Council; 1924–31 Professor of Education in the University of London; 1931–51 Professor of Psychology at University College, London; 1951: Professor Emeritus, University of Oxford. Investigations into and publications on problems of general intelligence, methods of testing intelligence and mental differences between individuals; some of the best standard intelligence tests. Burt also investigated backwardness in children, and delinquency. In the nineteen thirties, he developed the use of factor analysis in England, and the view of factors as classifications of consistent correlations between different test results (the multi-level view of ability—see *Abilities*).

Works: Joint editor of the *British Journal of Psychology, Pedagogical Seminary and Journal of Genetic Psychology, Genetic Psychology Monographs;* Ed. *British Journal of Statistical Psychology*. His publications include: Experimental tests of general intelligence, *Brit. J. Psychol.*, 1909. The distribution and relations of educational abilities, 1917. Mental and scholastic tests, 1921; ⁴1949. Handbook of tests for use in schools, 1923. The mental differences between individuals, Brit. Ass. Presidential address, 1923. The young delinquent, 1925. The backward child, 1937. The factors of the mind, 1940. Intelligence and fertility, 1946. The structure of the mind—a review of the results of factor analysis, *Brit. J. Educ. Psychol.*, 1949, *19*, 110–11, 176–99. The evidence for the concept of intelligence, *Brit. J. Educ. Psychol.*, 1955, *25*, 158–77. Intelligence and heredity, *Irish J. Educ.*, 1969, *3*.

Bibliography: Boring, E. G.: A history of experimental psychology. New York, ²1950. Burt, C.: Cyril Burt. In: Boring, E. G. (Ed.): History of psychology in autobiography. Vol. 4. Worcester, Mass., 1952, 53–73. Murchison, C.: The psychological register. Worcester, Mass., 1929.   *W.S.*

Butyrophenones. Chemical subgroup of the neuroleptics (q.v.). Clinically important derivatives are haloperidol, meperone, fluanisone, trifluperidol, fluoropipamide, droperidol, benperidol and pimozide. The butyrophenones are related pharmacologically and clinically to the phenothiazines (q.v.). There have been hardly any psychological investigations. Some results indicate situationally dependent effects. See *Haloperidol*.

Bibliography: Goldstein, B. J., Clyde, D. J. & Caldwell, J. M.: Clinical efficacy of the butyrophenones as antipsychotic drugs. In: Efron, D. H. (Ed.): Psychopharmacology 1957–1967. Washington, 1968. Janke, W. & Debus, G.: Double-blind psychometric evaluation of pimozide and haloperidol versus placebo in emotionally labile volunteers under two different work load conditions. Psychopharmacologia, 1970, *18*, 162–83. Lehmann, H. E. & Ban, T. A.: The butyrophenones in psychiatry. First North American Symposium on the butyrophenones. Quebec, 1964.   *G.D.*

C

CA. See *Chronological age*.

Cadre formation. 1. The training and further training of executive staff in all areas of an organization. **2.** The training or indoctrination of theoretically aware and wholly trustworthy key members of a (revolutionary) political party. See *Leadership; Management*.
G.R.W.M.

Caffeine. A psychopharmacological drug (which is chemically identical with *theine*) to be found in coffee, tea, cola, maté, etc. It ranks as a stimulant (q.v.). Since the end of the last century, caffeine has been frequently studied in psychopharmacological experiments (in doses up to approximately 500 mg). It is less stimulating than the amphetamines and has relatively strong side-effects (e.g. tremor). As a rule (after about 30 min.) caffeine induces a feeling of increased wakefulness although no positive changes in performance can be detected.
Bibliography: Weiss, B. & Laties, V.: Enhancement of human performance by caffeine and the amphetamines. Pharmacol. Rev., 1962, *14*, 1–36. K.D.S.

Calibration. Calibration of a random sample of raw values is standardization (q.v.), i.e. determining distribution standards and checking how far they are representative. The term calibration is used especially in connection with the standardization of a newly constructed test (test calibration). The raw value distribution of the previous test is checked by using the calibration sample to see if it agrees with the distribution (see *Frequency distribution*) of the test values in the population (q.v.). If that is not the case, the necessary correction is made. Subsequently the raw values are transformed into standard values in conformity with a standard criterion.
W.H.B.

California Test of Personality. Personality questionnaires dealing with personal and social adjustment. Five different scales from the nursery-school to the adult level with percentile grading norms for sixteen personality variables such as self-confidence, self-esteem, nervous symptoms, social and total adjustment, antisocial tendencies, etc.
Bibliography: Thorpe, L. P., Clark, W. W. & Tiegs, E. W.: California Test Bureau, 1942–1953. Monterey, Calif. R.M.

Call. In parapsychology: subject's response at a given trial in a card-guessing test. J.B.

Calorie (*Calory*). 1. In physics: the amount of heat at 1 atm required to raise the temperature of one gram of water from 14·5 to 15·5°C (1000 cal = 1 kcal.). **2.** In physiology: a value for measuring energy or heat production.
G.R.W.M.

Canalization 1. A general term for a process in human development involving the *consolidation* of certain kinds of behavior from a range of many developmental possibilities.

2. In a narrower sense, according to G. Murphy, the consolidation and thus the preference of definite means of drive satisfaction from among several initially possible choices. The canalization process is discussed mainly in connection with socialization (q.v.).

W.D.F.

Cancellation tests. B. Bourdon was the first to have a set of letters cancelled as a test of attentiveness. To exclude habituation to letters, E. Toulouse and H. Piéron have used symbols, and some other tests of this kind have been suggested. Since memory can play a part in the use of symbols, Meili has constructed a "non-model" cancellation test.

Bibliography: Meili, R.: Lehrbuch der psychol. Diagnostik. Berne, ⁶1965. Id.: Durchstreichtest ohne Modell. Berne, 1956.   *R.M.*

Cannabis. A variety of hemp, *cannabis indica v. sativa*. Parts of the female hemp plant, after various modes of preparation, are eaten, drunk or smoked for their narcotic effects. A number of hemp products are met with; their pharmacological efficacy depends in large measure on their composition and the conditions under which they have been grown. The best known are hashish (q.v.), or Indian hemp, which comes from India, and marihuana (q.v.), from South America. The active elements in cannabis have been identified as tetra(hydro)cannabinols which are contained especially in the resin of the female plant. See *Narcotics; Psychotomimetics.*

Bibliography: Bewley, T. H.: Heroin and cocaine addiction. Lancet, 1965, No. 1, 808–10. Isbell, H. *et al.*: Effects of 1-△⁹-*trans*-tetrahydrocannabinol in man. Psychopharmacol., 1967, *11*, 184–8. Wholstenhome, G. E. W. & Knight, J. (Eds): Hashish: its chemistry and pharmacology. Boston & London, 1965.   *G.E.*

Cannon emergency function. An adaptation process in the organism as a reaction to sudden serious mental or physical stress, especially to meet some danger, i.e. in an emergency; the process was described by W. B. Cannon after extensive experiments. By temporarily shifting the autonomic balance toward sympathicotonia the organism prepares for a quick release of energy for the purpose of fight or flight, thereby reducing the restitutive processes. Onset and control are set in train by the hypophyseal-midbrain system; and this leads to an increased release of adaptive hormones from the hypophysis and adrenal medulla (especially adrenalin). This induces a fairly stereotyped series of reactions in three stages: the alarm-reaction stage (with hypotonia, increased blood flow, increased permeability, hypothermia and other symptoms of shock, which partly revert in the "counter shock" phase, i.e. when the adaptation begins); the resistance stage (defense phase; release of energy, and adaptation); the exhaustion stage. See *Emotion.*   *F.-C.S.*

Bibliography: Cannon, W. B.: Bodily changes in pain, hunger, fear and rage. New York, ²1929.

Capacity. 1. A general term for the retentiveness, or storage capacity, of *memory* (q.v.). Information theory (q.v.) attempts to provide a measurement of capacity in terms of the amount of information retained (bit, q.v.). *Flow capacity* is the amount of information which can be absorbed in a unit of time (bit/sec.).

2. A general term for ability (see *Abilities*).

E.H.

Capillary. One of the capillaries, or smallest blood vessels. The capillary wall is a single layer of endothelial cells allowing the passage of liquid nutrients and metabolic waste.

H.L.

Cardiac neurosis. Imprecise designation for the varied complex of symptoms in an organ neurosis involving cardiac disorders: e.g. heart pains, irregular or rapid heart beat, a sensation of pressure or constriction in the area of the heart, and feelings of anxiety. No objective demonstrable symptoms of an organic heart condition are present. These functional heart disorders are generally the result of repressed mental conflict situations. See *Conversion neurosis*.   *A.-N.G.*

Cardiazol shock. A general convulsive reaction produced by cardiazol, a central analeptic (q.v.).

Cardinal point; cardinal value. The point or value, according to Fechner, in a quantitative series of sensations at which *difference threshold* (q.v.) begins to increase in proportion to stimulus.

Case history method. The use of case histories (histories of psychotherapeutic and psychiatric cases, reports on education and the home, forensic documents, biographies and autobiographies) in the "anthropological" disciplines (psychoanalysis, psychiatry, psychology, pedagogy, sociology, ethnology, and criminology). This biographical method was developed and refined predominantly by the proponents of psychoanalysis (q.v.) as an instrument of research; to the analysis of the life they added the investigation of experience. Case histories can be interpreted either qualitatively or quantitatively. The qualitative interpretation corresponds to the research approach of the psychology of "understanding" (*Verstehende Psychologie*), and thus psychoanalysis or depth psychology (q.v.) too; the quantitative calculation of solid data (birth, family details, school, occupation, etc.) corresponds to the Ideal of an exact natural or social science. Numerous concepts and hypotheses are based on case histories: psychoanalysis owes much to Freud's and Breuer's Anna case, and four cases of hysteria: "little Hans", the wolf man, the rat man, and the famous Dora; child psychology employs parents' (Darwin,

W. & C. Stern, E. & G. Scupin) and adolescent diaries (C. Bühler, W. Küppers); cultural-anthropological field research uses studies of "primitive" cultures (M. Mead, P. Parin). Individual emphases and a variety of information on the one hand, and quantitative evaluation on the other will always to some extent remain the bases of conflicting approaches.

Bibliography: Allport, G. W.: The use of personal documents. Psychological science. Social Science Research Council Bulletin, New York, 1942, 49. Dollard, J.: Criteria for the life history. New Haven, 1935. Schraml, W. J.: Die Psychoanalyse und der menschliche Lebenslauf. Psyche, 1965, *19*, 250–68. Thomae, H.: Die biographische Methode in den anthropologischen Wissenschaften. Studien Gen. 1952, *5*, 163–77.   *W.J.S.*

Case study. A method of personality psychology which aims to define the "qualitatively unique" individual character of a human being (G. W. Allport). The case study requires a highly detailed study (often continued over a lengthy period) of the individual in the course of which all available data on this person are collected and processed (results of psycho-diagnostic tests, anamnestic-biographical details, creative performance, etc.). The case study is used in ideographic personality research and above all in clinical psychology for practical and diagnostic purposes.

Bibliography: Allport, G. W.: Pattern and growth in personality. New York, 1961. Anastasi, A.: Psychological testing. New York, 1961. Gathercole, C. E.: Assessment in clinical psychology. Harmondsworth, 1968. Hetherington, R. R. *et al.*: Introduction to psychology for medical students. London, 1964. *K.P.*

Caspar Hauser complex (also *Kasper–Hauser*). Alexander Mitscherlich used the name Caspar Hauser (a compulsive impostor who died in 1833 from self-inflicted injuries, and allegedly a foundling who had grown up in complete solitude) to designate a "complex" (q.v.) characteristic of the inner loneliness and emotional atrophy of city dwellers (inability to make contacts).   *W.Sc.*

Caspar Hauser experiments. A method in comparative psychology (q.v.): animals are reared under optimum experience deprivation (care has to be taken that no organic injury is inflicted on the animal). The aim is to separate genetically conditioned from acquired behavioral components. *W.Sc.*

Castration. Removal of the sexual glands (in males the testicles, in females the ovaries), thus changing the organism's hormonal function and sterilizing the person. Male castration has occurred as a cultic or religious practice, or as a punishment, for thousands of years. Castration can also be accidental or therapeutic. Female castration is only used therapeutically in cases of physical disease in or around the ovaries. Castration before physical development is complete (i.e. about twenty years of age) results in inhibition of the development of the sexual organs, prolongation of bone growth, "babyface"-change, as well as changes in the body's metabolic processes. In adults (when growth is complete) therapeutic castration is used to diminish libido. Psychic changes and general fatness seldom occur. A change in fat-distribution to more fat on the breasts and hips is common. Therapeutic castration has been used since 1892 in Switzerland, and is now also employed in several other countries. The first law permitting therapeutic castration was passed in 1929 (Denmark). When used in cases whose sexual drive involves them in considerable psychic sufferings or social devaluation, and when supplemented with psychiatric help, the results are excellent. 3,186 cases have been reported: 2% have relapsed into criminal sexual activity.

Bibliography: Langelüddeke, A.: Die Entmannung von Sittlichkeitsverbrechern. Berlin, 1963. Stürup, Georg K.: Treatment of sexual offenders in Herstedvester, Denmark. Copenhagen, 1968. *G.K.S.*

Castration complex. According to Freud, a boy's anxiety that he may lose his sexual organs; or the alleged fear experienced by a girl who, after recognizing that she does not have a (male) sexual organ, is afraid that she may lose other parts of her body as well. This castration complex is said to appear in the early genital phase (q.v.) in connection with the prevention of, and threats against, masturbation or heterosexual genital interest in members of the same family. Castration anxiety is the mildest of infantile fears. In the anal phase (q.v.) the child develops the fear that he might be seriously mutilated or even crushed to pieces and killed; in the oral phase (q.v.) there is the fear of being eaten up, swallowed or dissolved.

In association with developmental disorders in the early genital phase the castration complex is said to persist into adulthood, and is claimed to be the cause of a neurotic inability to make love, involving in particular fear of the opposite sex, symptoms of impotence in a man and frigidity (q.v.) in a woman, and even resulting in perversions (q.v.). *W.T.*

Catalepsy. Preservation of posture for an inordinately long period of time. This posture itself may or may not be abnormal and may be spontaneous or induced by an observer. Some writers include in this group only those whose postures have been imposed by an observer or by fortuitous events, reserving the term catalepsy for them only. In this restricted group the postures are preserved without reason but are not again assumed spontaneously by the patient. This restricted form is often associated with *flexibilitas cerea* (waxy flexibility), and may be due to heightened suggestibility. However, this restriction of the group is not logically or practically defensible. As well as in schizophrenia, catalepsy is found in organic brain disease, epilepsy, disturbed personalities and hysterical and subnormal people. *B.B.*

Catamnesis. 1. That part of a case history reporting on the effect of therapy (or counseling) and the rehabilitation of the patient (or client). The report is based on external observation of, or on self-observation by, the patient, and deals with this condition and behavior (usually some considerable time) after the termination of the therapy or counseling.

2. A case history from onset of a problem or sickness to, or even including, admission to a clinic or hospital.   *F.-C.S.*

Cataplexy. Transient attacks of powerlessness triggered off by emotional experience, most commonly by laughter but also by anxiety, annoyance or anger. This may be partial or complete both in distribution or degree. The condition may coexist with *narcolepsy* (q.v.), both conditions resulting from the same cause.   *J.P.*

Catathymia. A psychic change brought about by the influence of some affect. It occurs in prelogical and magical thought, in primitive everyday thinking and also in mental illness: e.g. thunder is heard and shortly afterwards somebody falls down dead. The two events are linked by the affect (fright) accompanying them. Catathymia is significant in the study of the falsification of memory.   *A.Hi.*

Catathymic amnesia: Transient amnesia.

Catatonia. See *Schizophrenia*, in which catatonic symptoms are prominent. These embrace a number of predominantly motor deviations: catalepsy (*flexibilitas cerea:* waxy flexibility), stupor, hyperkinesis, etc. Acute and chronic forms are observed. Symptoms of intense arousal, tension and anxiety are found in *pernicious* catatonia which, if not treated, soon proves fatal.   *A.Hi.*

Catecholamines. A group of hormones (q.v.) at the center of interdisciplinary psychophysiological research. The most important are adrenalin(e) (q.v.) and noradrenalin(e).

Most of the catecholamines are formed in the adrenal medulla (q.v.), adrenaline and noradrenaline being approximately in the ratio 3:1 but varying according to the nature of the "stimuli". They can be measured in blood plasma or urine and used as dependent variables in psychological experiments. Catecholamines are also produced in the central and autonomic nervous systems (sympathetic NS), where noradrenaline is predominant. The significance of adrenaline in the central nervous system is not yet clear. Direct evidence of catecholamines in the central or autonomic nervous system cannot readily be established in humans *in vivo*. Psychophysiological catecholamine research concentrates on three groups of problems: (*a*) catecholamines as CNS transmitter substances; (*b*) catecholamines as objective indicators of emotional and motivational arousal; (*c*) their administration in order to induce non-specific or specific excitation.

(*a*) Catecholamines certainly act as transmitter substances in the central nervous system. The presence of noradrenaline in the brain (particularly concentrated in the hypothalamus, q.v.), and that of dopamine (a natural precursor of noradrenaline) have been demonstrated. The biosynthesis and decomposition of noradrenaline are of great importance in elucidating the processes by which psychoactive drugs (q.v.), and especially antidepressives, take effect. It is assumed that the biosynthesis of noradrenaline is disturbed in cases of depression (Schildkraut, 1965). Concentrated noradrenaline is biologically inactivated either inside the cell by monoamine oxidase (see *Monoamine oxidase inhibitors*), or outside it at the receptors by means of catechol-*o*-methyl transferase. Noradrenaline is synthesized in four stages (several enzymes are involved; see *Biogenic amines*). This synthesis can be blocked specifically by certain substances (e.g. by alpha-methyl tyrosine, or biogenic amines). Adrenaline is synthesized from noradrenaline by splitting off the methyl group CH_3.

(b) Numerous experiments in recent years have demonstrated the relations between the secretion of catecholamines (urine or plasma) and emotions. In particular, research teams led by U. S. von Euler, Elmadjan, L. Levi and M. Frankenhäuser demonstrated that stressors (such as flying, parachute jumps, examinations, exciting films, stress interviews, threats of electric shocks, sensory deprivation), as well as pleasant affects, caused catecholamines to *be released in larger quantities*. There is an unvarying relation between the mean values of scaled emotions or stimulus intensities and the release of catecholamines. Adrenaline release is usually the more sensitive indicator. It is not yet clear to what extent there are interactions between the ratio of noradrenaline to adrenaline and emotional qualities. Hypotheses according to which anxiety corresponds to the release of adrenaline, and annoyance (anger) to that of noradrenaline (Ax, 1953; Funkenstein *et al.*, 1957), do not as yet have adequate experimental support. However, it has been proved that there is a relatively greater release of noradrenaline in the case of physical, and of adrenaline in that of mental, stress. Intraindividually, the release of catecholamines is only moderately constant, and catecholamine detection is not reliable enough for individual determinations; especially when measuring the concentration in urine, several factors, e.g. meals, must be kept constant. There are as yet no proven correlations between the release of catecholamines and constant personality traits.

(c) Adrenaline and noradrenaline exist in synthetic forms, and can be administered intravenously. As neither drug will penetrate the blood-brain barrier, any direct action in the central nervous system is ruled out. Physiological doses of both substances in healthy subjects induce symptoms of sympathetic excitation with varying patterns of effect. With increased dosage, adrenaline leads to subjective excitation, and a feeling of general arousal. This emotional and motor excitation is usually experienced as slightly unpleasant. According to the situation (S. Schachter) the "non-specific" excitation resulting from small doses of adrenaline can be "transformed" into specific emotions (unpleasant, e.g. anxiety, annoyance; and possibly even pleasant, e.g. joy). There is little effect on performance. Speed tests (q.v.) sometimes show quantitative improvements; low doses also have a negative effect on motor constancy. Small amounts of noradrenaline have only an insignificant, if any, psychic effect. Animal experiments show that both substances directly activate the reticular formation (q.v.). It is not yet known how infused catecholamines, or those detectable in the blood or urine, relate to central catecholamine variations.

Bibliography: Anden, N.-E., Carlsson, A. & Häggendal, J.: Adrenergic mechanisms. Ann. Rev. Pharmacol., 1969, *9*, 119–34. Ax, A. F.: The physiological differentiation between fear and anger in humans. Psychosom. Med., 1953, *15*, 433–42. Breggin, P.: The psychophysiology of anxiety: With a review of the literature concerning adrenaline. J. nerv. ment. dis., 1964, *139*, 558–68. Chessick, R. D., Bassan, M. & Shattan, S.: A comparison of the effect of infused catecholamines and certain affect states. Amer. J. Psychiatr., 1966, *123*, 156–65. Euler, U. S. von.: Noradrenaline. Illinois, 1956. Frankenhäuser, M.: Biochemische Indikatioren der Aktiviertheit: Die Ausscheidung von K.n. In: W. Schönpflug (Ed.): Methoden der Aktivierungsforschung. Berne, 1969. Funkenstein, D. H., King, S. H. & Drolette, M. E.: Mastery of stress. Harvard, 1957. Kroneberg, G. & Schümann, A. J. (Eds) New aspects of storage and release mechanisms of catecholamines. Berlin, 1970. Landis, C. & Hunt, W. A.: Adrenaline and emotion. Psychol. Rev 1932, *39*, 467–85. Levi, L.: Biochemische Reaktionen bei verschiedenen experimentell hervorgerufenen Gefühlszuständen. In: P. Kielholz (Ed.): Angst. Berne, 1967. Marley, E.: Behavioral and electrophysiological effects of catecholamines. Pharmacol. Rev., 1966, *18*, 753–68. Mason, J. W.: A review of psychoendocrine research in the sympathetic adrenal medullary system. Psychosom. Med., 1968, *30*, 631–53. Schachter, S. & Singer, J.: Cognitive, social and physiol. determinants of emotional states. Psychol. Rev., 1962, *69*, 379–99. Schildkraut, J. J.: The catecholamine hypothesis of affective disorders: a review of supporting evidence. Amer. J. Psychiatr., 1965, *122*, 509–22. Wurtman, R. J.: Catecholamines. Boston, 1966. *W. Janke*

Category. In general usage, categories are classes, kinds or types offering the necessary subdivisions of conceptual systems for ordering objects in the environment. The concept of category is essential to a theory of judgment; for example, Aristotle distinguished ten categories of predicates (substance, quantity, quality, relation, place, time, position, state, action, passion) which may be asserted of any object, while Kant proposed a number of classes of "transcendental concept", or conditions necessary for judging experience.

In his theory of types, Bertrand Russell tried to provide a non-paradoxical concept of class and predicate. Ryle's category theory, based on his analysis of the use of concepts in natural language, is intended to determine the conditions for sound predication.   *M.J.B.*

Cathartic method. A psychotherapeutic technique used by Breuer and Freud to treat neurotic symptoms, and intended to produce a "catharsis" (purging, or release). Hypnosis is used to arouse (by hypermnesia, q.v.) memories of repressed affective experiences thought to be originally responsible for the neurotic disorder. The therapeutic efficacy of this process is thought to reside in the abreaction of the affects repressed until then (see *Repression*), a process which takes place during hypnosis or in the course of the accompanying dialogue.   *H.-N.G.*

Cathexis (syn. *Cathection*). In psychoanalytical terminology cathexis signifies a concentration or investment of mental energy or libido (q.v.) in a certain direction: e.g. toward some object or person.   *J.L.I.*

Cattell, James McKeen. B. 25/5/1860 in Easton (Pa.), d. 20/1/1944 in Garrison (N.J.). Studied under H. Lotze and W. Wundt (q.v.) and at the universities of Göttingen Leipzig, Paris and Geneva. 1887: lecturer at the University of Pennsylvania; 1888: lectured at Cambridge, England; 1888–91: Professor of psychology at Pennsylvania; 1891–1917: Professor at Columbia University; 1929: President of the International Congress of Psychologists held for the first time in America. Cattell introduced exact experimental psychology into America. He encouraged research into reaction times and associations (q.v.). He gave much time to the rank-order method for pair comparison (see *Psychophysics*). His main interest was the diversity of human nature and human abilities (differential psychology). He developed mental tests and was the first to use the term.

In 1921, Cattell founded the Psychological Corporation, whose object was primarily to bring psychological discoveries to the notice of the public and the administration, and to promote applied psychology.

Works: 1894–1940: Editor and manager of numerous journals, such as the *Psychological Review*, and the *American Naturalist*. Publications include: The inertia of the eye and brain, *Brain*, 1885, *8*, 295–312. Mental tests and measurements, *Mind*, 1890, *15*, 373–81. With C. S. Dolley: On reaction-times and the velocity of the nervous impulse, *Psy. Rev.* 1896. The conceptions and methods of psychology, *Pop. Sci. Mo.*, 1904, *46*, 176–86. The interpretation of intelligence tests, *Scient. Mo.*, 1924. Some psychological experiments, I, II, *Science*, 1928. Psychology in America, *Scient. Mo.*, *30*, 1930, 114–26.

Bibliography: Boring, E. G.: A history of experimental psychology. New York, ²1950. Garrett, H. E.: Great experiments in psychology. New York, 1930. Murchison, C.: The psychological register. Worcester, 1929. Poffenberger, A. T. (Ed.): James McKeen Cattell: Man of science. Vol. 1: Psychological research; Vol. 2: Addresses and formal papers. Lancaster, 1947. Woodworth, R. S.: James McKeen Cattell, 1860–1944, Psychol. Rev., 1944, *51*, 201–9.
                                                                 W.S.

Cattell's factorial theory of personality. See *Personality*.

Caudal. In animals with a recognizable head region the end of the body opposite this head region is known as *caudal* (Latin, *cauda:* tail region). Ant.: frontal (Latin, *frons:* forehead; cephalic). H.S.

Caudate nucleus. Mass of grey matter in the subcortical area of the cerebral hemispheres; part of the *corpus striatum* (q.v.).

Causality. An asymmetrical relationship between two terms, the antecedent being known as the *cause,* and the consequent as the *effect.* The terms can be events, phenomena, or objects. The relation itself is such that the effect necessarily follows on the occurrence of the cause, and the cause always precedes the effect. The *cause* of a phenomenon is often distinguished from its *condition* (or "necessary cause"), the cause ("sufficient cause") being *sufficient* for its production, whereas the condition is *necessary.*

Principle of causality: the postulate that every phenomenon has a cause. "Nothing ever happens without a cause or at least a determining reason; that is, without something affording an *a priori* reason why something exists rather than does not exist, and why it exists in this and not in any other way" (Leibniz, *Theodicy*). J.B.G.

Ceiling effect. If a task or a test is too easy, and many testees who obtain the highest score ought to obtain one still higher according to the factual criteria, then one speaks of a so-called ceiling effect, which influences standard deviation (q.v.) and correlation (q.v.). W.H.B.

Censorship. According to Freud (*The Ego and the Id*, first German edition, 1923), censorship is a functional sphere which checks forbidden impulses (motives), or those which can no longer be satisfied; or modifies them before their gratification or partial gratification in such a way that they are no longer directly recognizable as those forbidden or no longer gratifiable motives. In his later structural theory of the psyche, Freud ascribed this function of censorship (objective counter-cathexis, inner defense or repression, q.v.) on the one hand to the ego (q.v.). But the ego was said to be concerned with the organization of gratifications of permissible or at least not forbidden impulses. On the other hand, the super-ego (q.v.) also includes certain aspects of censorship among its functions.

Bibliography: Freud, S.: Introductory lectures on psycho-analysis. London, ²1929. Id.: The ego and the id. London, ²1962.

Centile (*Percentile*). A standard measure frequently used in psychology, especially in the calibration (q.v.) of diagnostic instruments. The whole area of a frequency distribution (q.v.) of raw values is divided into 100 sections. Hence exactly 1% of all cases occurs in a centile area. *Centile rank:* the relative rank of a score in a distribution. W.H.B.

Central convolution (syn. *Central gyrus*). The anterior central convolution (*Gyrus precentralis*) is the rearmost convolution of the frontal lobe, and is separated by the central fissure or sulcus (*Sulcus centralis*) from the posterior central convolution (*Gyrus postcentralis*). The anterior central convolution contains the representational fields for the motor behavior of the striate musculature. G.A.

Central nervous system (abb. CNS). All the nervous elements, cells and conducting pathways within the brain (q.v.) and spinal cord (q.v.). This system is responsible for the entire nervous control of the activity of the living organism. All afferent sensory nerve paths receiving information from the sense organs (q.v.) regarding the state of the environment end in the CNS, where, in terms of reflexes, reactions, behavior patterns and volitions, this information is processed and conveyed once more by means of efferent motor nerve fibers to the motor effectors, and hence to the environment. The CNS has a hierarchical construction. See *Nervous system; Neuroanatomy.*   *E.D.*

Centrifugal nerves (syn. *Centrifugal neuron(e)s*). Nerve fibers of the peripheral system which conduct information from the periphery of the body to the brain and spinal cord. Since they for the most part conduct sensory information from the eye, ear, vestibule, the organs of smell and taste, the cutaneous sense points, and the enteroceptors, they are also known as sensory nerve fibers. See *Sense organs.*   *E.D.*

Centroid method (*Center of gravity method*). A factor-analytical method developed by C. L. Burt (q.v.) and L. L. Thurstone (q.v.) to extract factors (q.v.) from intercorrelation matrices. The variables (e.g. tests) can be represented as vectors in a certain space. A common factor of these tests can be represented as a vector (q.v.) passing through the "centroid" of the end points of the variable vectors.   *W.H.B.*

Cephalic. Forming part of, or appertaining to, the head (ant. *Caudal*, q.v.).

Cephalization. The formation of a head at the frontal end of higher animals, especially with regard to the nervous system, which localizes a relay and control center in the head (see *Brain*), thus making possible a biologically meaningful coordination of all the vital processes in an individual.   *H.S.*

Cerebellum. The smaller main part of the brain; it is noticeably wrinkled, and is situated in the lower part of the occiput close to the cranial bone. It consists of three parts, the *archi-, paleo-,* and *neocerebellum.* The first has developed from the vestibulary nuclei, helps to maintain the balance and is responsible for seasickness. The other two parts help to maintain muscular tonus and to coordinate all muscular movement in response to the information coming from the sense organs. Therefore the cerebellum has fibrous links with all the sensory channels, with the cerebrum (q.v.), and with the extrapyramidal motor system. Acute disturbance seriously affects balance, and movement and coordination; in cases of slow deterioration or congenital defect the cerebrum partly takes over the function of the cerebellum.

Bibliography: Eccles, J. C.: The physiology of synapses. Berlin, 1964.   *E.D.*

Cerebral arteriosclerosis (*Diffuse sclerosis; group of leucodystrophies*). Generic name for a group of rare sclerotic processes affecting the cerebrum. The condition (which leads very quickly to death) is classed as a hereditary disorder of the metabolism with tissue degeneration (hereditary-degenerative diseases). Three principal symptoms are common to all forms of this disease: spasticity on both sides, blindness on both sides (caused by atrophy of the optical nerve), and dementia.   *G.A.*

Cerebral cortex (*Cortex cerebri*). The grey layer of nerve cells which is only a few mm thick and is situated directly below the surface of the cerebrum. According to location on the cerebral cortex, individual areas are distinguished by the architectural structure of the nerve-cell layers. While the anatomical division into frontal, parietal, temporal and occipital lobes does not indicate any functional units, the cortical projection areas are functionally uniform. Broca's area in the temporal lobe would seem to be connected with the active formation of speech (see *Brain pathology*), the precentral gyrus (as the origin of the pyramidal tract) with voluntary motor activity, and the primary optical cortical projection field in the occipital lobe with image recognition (if it is destroyed, there is visual amnesia). While those of some other areas are known, the functions of most parts of the cortex are unexplained, but it is supposed that they can selectively assume different tasks. *E.D.*

Cerebral nerves. The brain (q.v.; see *Encephalon*) consists of the forebrain, midbrain and hindbrain. The twelve pairs of cerebral nerves originate in the encephalon and run through the base of the skull to the head, while others branch off into other parts of the body. The *corpus pineale* is a continuation of the midbrain. The *cortex cerebri* (cerebral cortex) consists of grey matter and mainly contains nerve cell bodies. The brain stem is the midbrain, hindbrain and *pons*.
G.A.

Cerebral palsy. A traumatic condition resulting from intrauterine brain lesions of extremely varied genesis, i.e. birth injuries or injuries suffered during early infancy, such as cerebral malformations, congenital syphilis, toxoplasmosis, encephalitis, etc. It usually presents as a spastic (q.v.) paralysis (spasticity) of one or both sides of the body; the latter form is known as Little's disease (q.v.). Frequent accompaniments are defective intelligence, tremor, and choreatic movements of the affected limbs. Cure is usually impossible; treatment is restricted to alleviation of the symptoms. *E.D.*

Cerebral stimulation. The electrical release of behavior patterns in animals allowed to move freely; this is done by implanting micro-electrodes in the brain. The method of auto-stimulation in which the experimental animal actuates a contact of its own accord gives valuable results. Indifferent stimulus

centers were stimulated about 25 times per hour and positive centers with a reward effect between 200 to 7000 times per hour; habituation symptoms were noted. The position of the electrode tip is marked by micro-electrolysis, electro-coagulation or Berlin blue reaction, histologically fixed, and entered on brain charts.

Bibliography: Olds, J. & Olds, M. E.: The mechanisms of voluntary behavior. In: Heath, R. G. (Ed.): The role of pleasure in behavior. New York, 1964, 23–53. *K.F.*

Cerebration. See *Encephalization*.

Cerebrospinal system. The human nervous system is divided into the central and autonomous nervous systems. In the CNS the central nervous system proper, consisting of the cerebrum and spinal cord, is distinguished from the peripheral nervous system. The latter includes the two major groups of the brain and spinal nerves. The ANS comprises the (largely antagonistic) sympathetic and parasympathetic systems. *G.A.*

Cerebrotonia. According to Sheldon's constitutional theory of personality, cerebrotonia is a temperamental quality correlated with ectomorphic (q.v.) bodily components: characteristic traits are postural restraint, sensitivity, expressive inhibition, and difficulty of adaptation.
Bibliography: Sheldon, W. H.: The varieties of temperament. New York, 1942. *W.K.*

Cerebrum (*Telencephalon* and *Diencephalon*). It represents the main mass of the brain (q.v.) and consists of the *pallium*, the brainstem ganglia, the olfactory brain, the *corpus callosum*, the *fornix* and the *septum pellucidum*. It is divided almost completely into two parts by a longitudinal fissure. Its histological structure is characterized by a grey substance containing cells and a white substance containing fibers. The *cortex cerebri* or cerebral cortex (q.v.), and the basal ganglia form part of the grey substance, while the mass of fibrous links between the nerve cells belongs to the white substance. The function of the cerebrum is very complex and has scarcely been investigated in detail; in addition to the mental functions which can be recognized even in animals, it especially includes those which distinguish man from animals, such as recognizing (q.v.), abstracting, learning (q.v.), thinking (q v.), criticizing, speaking (q.v.), and artistic creation, but also *drive* (q.v.) and the processes of the consciousness (q.v.).

Bibliography: Pribram, K. H.: Brain and behavior (4 vols). Harmondsworth, 1969.   *E.D.*

CFF. Abb. for *Critical flicker frequency* (q.v.).

Chain behavior. See *Chain reflex.*

Chaining. See *Conversational chaining.*

Chain reflex (syn. *Chain behavior; Chain reaction*). A number of individual responses linked to one another so that the same sequence is always maintained. Presumably the effects of preceding links act as cues for the release of the next. Chain reflexes in any existing form are always learnt.   *H.Ro.*

Chain theory (Ger. *Kettentheorie*). Metzger's term (1954) for the perception theories of association psychology. Chain theory is opposed to the explanations of gestalt psychology.

Bibliography: Metzger, W.: Psychologie. Darmstadt, ²1954.   *R.Hä.*

Channel. The channel is that part of a communications system (communications unit) which transmits signals (q.v.) from an input (sender) to an output (receiver). According to the kind of signals, a distinction is made between discrete and continuous channels. The transmission system interferes with (distorts) the signals to a greater or lesser extent.

Channel capacity: the maximum amount of information which can be transmitted through a channel per unit of time (measured in bit/sec.).   *B.R.*

Character. The word comes from the Greek *kharakter* (meaning: an engraved or stamped mark). In current usage, it has two different basic meanings: the first denotes the purely factual characteristics of a thing or a person as distinguished from other things or persons. The second refers to the purely psychic distinctiveness of a living creature. In this second sense, *being a person is the foundation for developing a character*. In regard to man, the concept of character also has an ethical content. If the concept of *person* (=self) refers to the individual being of man, character denotes the *specific thus-ness* of man.

Since antiquity, character has been a subject for research. Theophrastus wrote character studies which have come down to us. Aristotle investigated the polarity and the affinity of character traits, and postulated a basic structure of character. Kant introduced the concept of the "empirical" character to mean man now, at this moment, and in his special "thus-ness". Empirical character is dependent on age, educational and environmental influences, climate, nutrition, whereas the fundamental character is hardly affected by these influences.

In the natural-scientific mode of the nineteenth century, J. Bahnsen saw a man's character as derived from the general characteristics of all those things which have to be brought into action for their distinctive features to be recognized. This attitude made him a precursor of systematic research. According to A. Pfänder, character has its foundations in a primal drive (the instinct of self-development). The empirical character is the creation (self-expression) of the fundamental character. For A. Gehlen, character is a product of education: it is the total expression of stable habits and views by virtue of which a person prefers certain things to others. Accordingly, character would be a form of behavior with an invariant value-tendency: a product of cultivation by the society in which man lives and of its particular division of interests.

G. Kerschensteiner speaks of an "instinctive character"—a predisposition restricted to life in terms of the emotions, instincts and impulses. Out of this instinctive and emotional life there develop intellectual life and a capacity for experience. In this view, the concept of character would also comprise mind. Hence the concept of character would lie between that of natural dispositions and that of ethical values. For Le Senne, character is elementally tripartite: the "innate", the "firm", and the "lasting" are the three structural aspects of the inner life. (See *Drive; Instinct.*)

Characterology in the wider sense deals with the ways in which man develops, specializes, compensates and responds to his natural dispositions. Layer models allow characterologists some theoretical foundation (P. Lersch, A. Wellek).

Characterology in the narrower sense was originally developed mainly in German-speaking countries. Its concerns are in many ways identical with those of personality research in Britain and America.

The notion of character cannot be divided into elements conceivable in isolation; it has to be grasped as a whole. It is an objective unity.

As every character behaves in a peculiarly distinctive way, there are many modes of individual expression for observation and diagnosis. This is the theoretical point of departure for the psychology of *expression* (q.v.).

For character diagnosis, *typologies* (q.v.) are used (e.g. those of E. Kretschmer, H. W. Sheldon, G. Ewald, E. R. Jaensch, C. G. Jung, E. Spranger), together with the methods of general *personality diagnosis* and psychometric *factor analysis* (q.v.) (R. B. Cattell). In research into the vital part played by character inheritance, use was made of longitudinal *genealogy* (F. Galton) and twin studies (K. Gottschaldt). The central theme of this work is *abilities* (q.v.). Character is further molded in the development of fundamentals (i.e. basic experiences): *emotions* (q.v.), *thinking* (q.v.), *intelligence* (q.v.), *memory* (q.v.), *attention* (q.v.), and *will* (q.v.).

Summary: Character is the indivisible, individual distinctiveness of a person (more precisely, of a *self*), which is exhibited in certain modes of individual experience and experiencing; these modes are organized as wholes and are subject to change, but they persist in essence. Character is the *form* of a person, and a stage in the forming, or development, of his personality. See *Personality; Traits; Type.*

Bibliography: Allport, G. W.: Pattern and growth in personality. New York, 1961. Arnold, W.: Person. Charakter, Persönlichkeit. Göttingen, ³1970. Hebb, D. O.: A textbook of psychology. Philadelphia, Pa., 1958. Klages, L.: Grundlagen der Charakterkunde. Bonn, ¹³1966. Lersch, Ph.: Aufbau der Person. Munich, ¹⁰1966. Rohracher, H.: Kleine Charakterkunde. Munich, ¹²1969. Rostand, J.: L'Hérédité humaine. Paris, 1966. Wellek, A.: Polarität im Aufbau des Charakters. Munich, ³1966.

W. Arnold

Characteropathy. An irreversible, *abnormal* change (absence, deficiency, excess or faulty structure of the emotional-volitional possibilities of action and reaction) as the result of a disease that can be clearly shown to have been somatic, or of a condition that followed the illness.

Such a genesis must be sharply divided from marked inherited inadequacies or defects of feeling and volition (see *Psychopathy*), from character disturbances due to harmful social or environmental influences, and from endogenously and episodically conditioned behavioral disorders.

Characteropathy occurring after damage to the brain (see *Encephalopathy*) is usually an ensuing abnormal change in the quantity and structure of the basic mental disposition or of the persistency in experiencing and acting which are determinative of and significant for the individual's attitude.

H.-J.E.

Charpentier-Koseleff illusion. Also known as the *size-weight illusion*. Of two objects which are of the same weight but of different sizes, the smaller will be considered the heavier. Analogously, a mistake is made in regard to volume when two objects of identical dimensions but of different weights are presented. The heavy object appears smaller.

Bibliography: Koseleff, P.: Eine Modifikation des Charpentier-Effektes. Psychol. Forschung, 1936, *21*, 142–5. Usnadze, D.: Über die Gewichtstäuschung und ihre Analoga. Psychol. Forschung, 1931, *14*, 366–79.

P.S.

Charpentier's bands. A series of alternate light (white) and dark (black) stripes perceived as the afterimage (q.v.) of an illuminated (white) sector rotated on a black background. Named after A. Charpentier (1852–1916).

Charpentier's illusion. The apparent movement of a small point of light in a darkened room. See *Autokinetic effect*.   K.E.P.

Charpentier's law. A. Charpentier (1852–1916): the product of the object's light intensity and of the stimulus or image area (size of the retina, dependent on the angle of vision) is a constant for the magnitude of the threshold value of light sensitivity (optical threshold stimulus).

Bibliography: Graham, C. H. (Ed.): Vision and visual perception. New York & London, 1965.

F.-C.S.

Chemoreceptors. The sense organs (q.v.) which are affected by a change in the chemical environment (e.g. taste, smell).

Chemotaxis. See *Chemotropism* 2.

Chemotropism. 1. A spatially orientated growth movement of plants in response to a chemical stimulus source. **2.** More generally, orientation of a cell or organism at any stage of development in relation to a chemical stimulus.   H.H.

Chiasm, optic. The point where the optic nerves cross behind the anterior cranial fossa in front of the hypophysis (q.v.). Here the fibers of the nasal retina halves cross over to the contralateral *tractus opticus* (q.v.), whereas the fibers of the temporal retina halves

From: Pauli & Arnold, *Psychologisches Praktikum* (Stuttgart, [6]1957).

continue on the same side. The fibers of the *macula lutea* (yellow spot, q.v.) cross in part, so that the point where visibility is sharpest is represented in both parts of the brain. Because of this crossing over, there is synchronization of both eyes. Pathological processes in the area where the crossing over takes place cause hemiano(p)sia (q.v.).   R.R.

Child guidance. A method originating in the U.S.A. and England which embraces the diagnosis and treatment of behavioral, performance (learning), and psychosomatic disturbances in children, and parent-counseling.

The *child-guidance clinic* is the basic institutional unit. The approach depends on the team-work of psychiatrist, psychologist and social worker (or psychiatric social worker). The psychiatrist examines and treats the child; psychological diagnosis and test administration are the responsibilities of the psychologist; and the social worker interviews the parents to obtain the life history and offer advice. The training which combines all three subjects (dynamic psychiatry, psychology and sociology) and underlies the child-guidance method has become a model for child psychiatric and psychotherapeutic institutions, although in many places all three professions are represented in the team, and the emphasis is not always the same. Child guidance is a basis for all preventive work. See *Psychohygiene*.

Bibliography: Bordin, E. S.: Psychological counseling. New York, 1955. Harms, E.: Handbook of child guidance. New York, 1947. Hopmann, W.: Zur Bedeutung und Entwicklung der psychoanalytischen Psychotherapie und child guidance clinics in den USA. Prax. Kinderpsychol., 1952. Jones, M.: Social psychiatry. London, 1952. Id.: Social psychiatry in practice. Harmondsworth, 1968. O'Connor, N. & Franks, C. M.: Childhood upbringing and other environmental factors. In: Eysenck, H. J. (Ed.): Handbook of abnormal psychology. London, 1960. Seebohm Report: Government Report of the Committee on Local Authority and Allied Personal Services (H.M.S.O.). London, 1969. Savage, R. D.: Psychometric assessment of the individual child. Harmondsworth, 1968.　　　*W.H.S.*

Childhood. Childhood proper might be said to begin with the first "defiance" period at the age of 3 to 4. Its first phase (approximately from 4 to 7) is characterized by a form of realism colored by fantasy and magic. Then comes a phase of naïve realism (from 7 to 10) in which analytical thought and the first signs of abstract thought develop. Childhood ends with a short phase of somewhat "critical" realism (from the age of 9 to 10 until the beginning of puberty) when a second period of defiance leads into youth. But the term is often used for the whole period from birth to puberty. See *Child psychology; Concept formation; Piaget.*
　　　　　　　　　　　　　　　　M.Sa.

Childhood experiences. Psychoanalysis (q.v.) has called attention to the (traumatic) effects which early childhood experience can have on the entire development of an individual and his character. Such experiences may be episodic, and isolated events. But "chronic" forms (e.g. bowel training) are also said to occur.　　　　　　*M.Sa.*

Child, only. Growing up in a family situation where there are no brothers or sisters must have definite consequences for a child's development, but empirical investigations of the subject seem to offer, contradictory evidence on intelligence and school work, and certain personality traits. A fairly consistent finding would seem to be that only children seek the supportive company of others (and particularly others in a similar situation) when unhappy or under anxiety stress (Lewis; Schachter).

Bibliography: Lewis, H.: Deprived children. London, 1954. Schachter, S.: Psychology of affiliation. Stanford, Cal., 1959.　　　　　　*K.E.P.*

Child psychiatry. Psychiatry (q.v.) as applied to mental disorders in children.

Child psychology is concerned with the development of psychological processes in the child from birth and before, through infancy and childhood to adolescence and maturity. All the processes of interest to psychologists in general are studied, but in developing as opposed to mature organisms.

1. *History and methods.* Interest in child development is as old as recorded history. The study of children is only now breaking away from the realm of sentimental mythology and entering the domain of objective science. Early theories of child development range from William James's empiricist view of the infant as being aware of only a "big,

booming, buzzing confusion", to the nativist view of Gestaltist psychologists that the infant can make sense of his world at birth. Freud regarded the infant as a bundle of instincts whereas Watson eschewed such speculation and studied only what was directly observable. He overemphasized the environmental influences of children's development, at the expense of ignoring genetically determined individual differences.

Naturalistic observations play an important part in the methodology of child psychology. Early studies of children relied on observations of varying quality. The baby diaries written by people such as Charles Darwin were not so productive as those of Jean Piaget, but such records can only serve as starting-points for more controlled study of representative samples.

Direct, controlled observations of children's behavior in both natural and laboratory settings have been fruitful when the usual requirements of the reliability of observation have been met. Tests and questionnaires have dominated child psychology, particularly in the area of intellectual development and educational attainment. In the field of personality testing, very few tests measure up to the minimum psychometric requirements, and projective techniques have proven to be of as little value as with adults.

In recent years, the experimental method has been applied to child psychology with renewed vigor. Conditioning techniques, in particular, have allowed more systematic study of the pre-linguistic child's repertoire of behavior.

The cross-sectional studies pioneered by such workers as Gesell served to establish broad norms of development. However, they tended to overemphasize the importance of chronological age and to underplay the importance of social and environmental influences. They also championed the concept of discrete stages of development, while underemphasizing individual differences in the rate of development. Currently, the methodology of cross-sectional studies has

been influenced by the epidemiological model, and greater sophistication is evident in sampling and measuring techniques.

Longitudinal studies are the most appropriate for answering the many questions about the later effect of particular events in childhood and, conversely, about the antecedents of later deviant development. The best-known such study is probably the Berkeley Growth Study associated with the name of Nancy Bayler. Kagan (1964) described ten American longitudinal studies, and in Britain the National Survey and the National Child Development Study have extended the methodology by studying large-scale national samples, in the case of Douglas, for over twenty-one years.

2. *Neonatal period and early experience.* The newborn child is not a *tabula rasa* on which can be written the desires of his parents. Both Watsonian "behaviorism" and psychoanalysis conspired to ignore the genetic and biological predispositions of infants and concentrated instead on the effects on the child of its environment, and particularly on the effects of parental child-rearing practices. However, recognition of biologically determined individual differences forces the child psychologist to adopt an interactionist rather than a solely genetic or environmental position in seeking explanations for the development of behavior (Berger, 1971).

In fact, studies of the effects of child-rearing practices on children's later development have been singularly unproductive. Yarrow attempted to replicate some of the major studies, including the oft-quoted Sears, Maccoby & Levin, *Patterns of Child Rearing*, which had related dependency and aggression in children to specific patterns of maternal practices. Yarrow was forced to conclude from her own study that the "compelling legend of maternal influences on child behavior that has evolved does not have its roots in solid data".

Studies of delinquents have implicated "inconsistent" parental discipline, showing a correlation between that and antisocial behavior. However, most such studies can only be regarded as suggestive since they are retrospective and not based on direct, concurrent observation. Experimental studies of behavior modification techniques have demonstrated a causal relationship between adult management practices and children's behavior, so that a methodology is now available to examine this in the context of the parent-child interaction.

3. *Personality*. Starting from a multiplicity of theoretical positions, studies of personality in children are in broad agreement in isolating two major dimensions: extraversion and neuroticism (Rachman, 1969). The evidence is in favor of there being a continuity in the growth of personality. However, much of the evidence is based on self-rating inventories such as the Junior Eysenck Personality Inventory, or Cattell's HSPQ. Since the child must have a reading age of about eight years to be able to complete these satisfactorily, this effectively limits their use. Observational studies of children as young as four years have yielded factors closely similar to the E and N dimensions. What is needed is to relate self-ratings with objective behavioral measures, as has been done profitably in adults.

Extraverted children are scholastically superior to introverted children. The relationship between attainment and neuroticism is less clear-cut, since there are interactions between neuroticism, extraversion and sex. There is some suggestion that introverts tend to develop more slowly than extraverts, but this needs confirming in longitudinal studies.

It has now been established that in the neonatal period there are stable patterns of behavior, both in the type of behavior shown and in its manner or formal characteristics. Hence, whatever the behavior, some infants will display it at greater intensities than others. Some will be more regular than others in its emission. Such characteristics have been labeled "temperamental factors"; in the New York Longitudinal Study,

Thomas has reliably identified nine temperamental characteristics. Bridger views temperamental factors in terms of excitatory and inhibitory processes in the central nervous system. This ties in well with the Eysenckian two-dimensional model of personality (q.v.) structure.

The New York Longitudinal Study has shown that temperamental characteristics tend to cluster together, and they have identified three types of children: *difficult* ones who are characterized as being irregular in function and who react at high levels of intensity; *easy* children who are regular and react at low levels of intensity; and children who are *slow to warm up* to new situations. In this follow-up study, they found that proportionately many "difficult" children later presented with behavioral and adjustment difficulties. Although this work needs to be replicated, it has helped to shift the focus of interest in the area of children's behavior disturbances from mere consideration of parental mishandling to an appraisal of the significance of biologically based individual differences between children, and the interaction between the child management and the child's characteristics.

4. *Cognitive development*. One of the strongest influences on research into cognitive development has been the Swiss psychologist, Jean Piaget. Stemming from his interest in "genetic epistemology" (the origin and growth of knowledge), he has stimulated much research into children's thinking. His own early work suggested that there were fixed sequences of "stages" in the growth of thought. He also believed that thinking at one stage is qualitatively different from thinking at another.

Piaget has described the three main stages of intellectual development as: (*a*) Sensory motor intelligence (from birth to 18 months); (*b*) concrete operations: (i) the pre-operational stage (from 18 months to 7 years); (ii) concrete operations (7 years to 12 years); (*c*) formal operations (from 12 years onwards).

Perhaps his most influential work has been that concerned with the attainment of object permanence and the conservation of liquids and solids. Methodologically, Piaget's own early work was very weak, but his major findings have been broadly confirmed in large-scale replication projects. Most importantly for his theories, it has been shown that infants rarely acquire the responses said to be characteristic of a later stage of intellectual development, without having attained those of earlier stages. Bruner's work has demonstrated that it is possible to accelerate the child's progress through the Piagetian stages provided appropriate teaching methods are used. Currently, research is needed to find the limits of such procedures.

5. *Perception.* Fantz has demonstrated that form perception exists in young infants. They show preference for pattern over uniform surfaces from birth, and there is some evidence for the preference of the human face over other objects.

Using operant conditioning procedures, Bower has demonstrated that as early as two months, infants have a limited visual memory. He has also shown that size constancy is present at a very early age. It is not until about six months however that most infants are capable of discriminating novel stimuli from familiar ones, and it is at this age that attachments to familiar people become most apparent.

6. *Language.* The 1960s saw the growth of psycholinguistics (q.v.), and its influence is now felt in developmental psychology. The sterile description of vocabulary growth so common in the 1920s has been replaced by studies of children's grammar. Chomsky, Lenneberg and Roger Brown have made their mark, but as yet no normative studies of language development analyzed in their terms have appeared. (See *Grammar.*)

The psycholinguists emphasize the structure of a child's grammar rather than its content. Somewhere in the second year of life, most children acquire a grammar utilizing simple two-word combinations of "pivot words" such as "see" or "all-gone", which can be combined with other single words to form novel, telegraphic sentences. There are large social-class differences in the way in which parents expand these simple sentences, with middle-class parents extending not only the grammatical complexity but also the range of ideas expressed by the child. It is probable that this is one of the reasons for the middle-class child's advantage in the area of language development.

7. *Intelligence.* Intelligence tests are used for both descriptive and predictive purposes. The older tests yielding global estimates of intelligence are being replaced by tests describing different cognitive processes in greater detail. However, the global IQ score is still useful in making predictions within certain limits.

Concern has been expressed about the stability of the IQ measures. There are difficulties over basing predictions on Developmental Scale scores obtained on infants largely because of the different content of the test and the different functions measured. But psychometric assessments are more useful than clinical judgments in predicting children who will develop atypically.

Much work has revolved around the question of the relative hereditary and environmental contributions to intelligence. This has been ably reviewed by Jensen, who concluded that 80% of the variance measured in IQ scores is attributable to genetic rather than environmental influences. Clearly, any individual's actual functioning depends on the interaction between his inheritance and the environment in which he finds himself.

8. *Social—emotional.* Following the Spitz, Goldfard & Bowlby work on the effects of institutionalization and separation from the mother, the attachment behavior of young children has been subjected to much intensive study. The main methodological and theoretical shifts have been away from psychodynamic formulations toward the study of psychological processes such as perception underlying the attachment. Separation is

no longer viewed as a unitary phenomenon having all-or-none effects on emotional development. The effects of the breaking of an existing attachment are now differentiated from the consequences of institutional placement. It is also recognized that short, intense separations may have immediate effects without any long-term consequences. Nowhere in child psychology has the influence of ethology been so much in evidence, as can be seen in Bowlby's most recent work.

The family, peer groups and the school as socializing influences continue to be studied. The most important development in this area has been the increase in direct observational studies, coupled to the increase in experimentation. Bandura's work on the learning of social behavior by imitation commands an important place.

9. *Educational.* Much of the laboratory work on learning remains divorced from actual teaching practices in the classroom. This was clearly shown in the failure of programmed learning (q.v.) to be implemented more generally. One reason for its failure was that the assumption that success was self-rewarding appears not to hold for all children. They have to learn that success is a positive experience.

There have been relatively few studies of pupil-teacher interaction in the classroom situation. Most have been done by those interested in behavior modification techniques for modifying disruptive, aggressive behavior.

Concern over the educational failure of the underprivileged led to mass social intervention in the form of compensatory educational programs. Many attempted to raise the level of attainment by first boosting general intelligence, and these largely failed in their aims. Those which tackled the problems directly and used specific structured techniques met with more success.

Reading failure has been the subject of many studies. Depending on the definitions employed, anything from 5% to 25% of ten-year-old children are identified as having reading problems. There is now a large consensus that few of these cases are "dyslexic" in the sense of having one particular neurological syndrome. Quality of teaching, motivational factors and the influence of the home are equally important factors in the etiology of reading difficulties.

10. *Abnormal behavior.* Research into children's disorders has tended to concentrate on neurotic behavior, despite the evidence that such disorders largely remit without treatment and carry no risk of later disturbance in adulthood. Knowledge of the genesis and treatment of antisocial disorders, apart from the work on delinquency, is much more limited. Yet antisocial disorders are notoriously difficult to treat and often lead to gross problems in adulthood, as the thirty-year follow-up study of Robins showed.

Epidemiological studies have established the prevalence of disturbance in the middle years of childhood as being at least 6%. Many more boys than girls are affected. Examining possible etiological processes, it has been shown that boys react more adversely than girls to stresses within the family. Research now needs to be structured so that intra-familial processes can be directly observed.

The problems of treatment of disturbances in childhood differ from those in adulthood, in that the aim is more frequently to build up patterns of behavior which have not developed, rather than to break abnormal patterns. Developmental disorders such as language delays are peculiar to this period. Traditional treatment methods based on psychoanalytic techniques have not proved useful. In contrast, behavior modification techniques, including operant conditioning and modeling techniques, are being successfully applied in an ever-increasing variety of problem behaviors. Careful evaluation studies of these powerful techniques are required to establish their limits.

The field of child psychology is vast, and this review has touched only on some of the more important growth points. Premature theorizing is being replaced by empirical observation and experimentation. The next decade should see the appearance of empirically based theories of child development.

Bibliography: Bandura, A.: Principles of behavior modification. New York, 1969. Becker, W. C., Madsen, C. H., Arnold, R. & Thomas, D. R.: The contingent use of teacher attention and praise in reducing classroom behavior problems. J. spec. Educ., 1967, *1*, 287–307. Berger, M.: Early experience and other environmental factors: An overview. In: Eysenck, H. J. (Ed.): Handbook of abnormal psychology. London, 1971. Bowlby, J.: Attachment and loss, in: Attachment, Vol. 1. London, 1969. Bruner, J. S., Olver, R. R. & Greenfield, P. M.: Studies in cognitive growth. New York, 1966. Clarke, A. M. & Clarke, A. D. B. (Eds): Mental deficiency: the changing outlook. London, 1965. Douglas, J. W. B., Ross, J. M. & Simpson, H. R.: All our future. London, 1968. Elkind, D. & Flavell, J. H. (Eds): Studies in cognitive development: Essays in honor of Jean Piaget. London, 1969. Eysenck, H. J. & Eysenck, S. B. G.: Personality structure and measurement. London, 1969. Fantz, R. L. & Nevis, S.: Pattern preferences and perceptual-cognitive development in early infancy. Merrill-Palmer Quarterly, 1967, *13*, 77–108. Flavell, J. H. & Hill, J. P.: Developmental psychology. Ann. Rev. Psychol., 1969, 1–56. Foss, B. M. (Ed.): Determinants of infant behavior, Vols 1–4, 1963–69. Hess, R. D. & Shipman, V. C.: Cognitive elements in material behavior. In: Hill, J. P. (Ed.): Minnesota Symposia on Child Psychology, Vol. 1. Minneapolis, 1967. Hoffman, M. L. & Hoffman, L. W. (Eds): Review of child development research, Vols 1 & 2. New York, 1964 & 1966. Jensen, A. R.: How much can we boost I.Q. and scholastic achievement? Harvard Educ. Rev., 1969, *39*. Kagan, J.: American longitudinal research on psychological development. Child Devel., 1964, *35*, 1–32. McNeill, D.: Developmental psycholinguistics. In: Smith, F. & Miller, G. A. (Eds): The genesis of language. Cambridge, Mass., 1966. Mussen, P. H. (Ed.): Handbook of research methods in child development. New York, 1960. Newton, R. & Levine, S. (Eds): Early experience and behavior. Springfield, Ill., 1968. Pringle, M. L. K., Butler, N. & Davie, R.: 11,000 seven-year-olds. London, 1966. Rachman, S.: Extraversion and neuroticism in childhood. In: Eysenck & Eysenck, *op. cit.*, 1969. Robins, L. N.: Deviant children grown up. Baltimore, 1966. Rutter, M., Tizard, J. & Whitmore, K. (Eds): Education, health and behaviour, London, 1970. Thomas, A., Chess, S., Birch, H. G., Hertzig, M. E. & Korn, S.: Behavioral individuality in early childhood. London, 1964. Thomas, A., Chess, S. & Birch, H. G.: Temperament and behavior disorders in children. London, 1968. Thomas, H.: Some problems of studies concerned with evaluating the predictive validity of infant tests. J. child Psychol. Psychiat., 1967, *8*, 197–205. Tizard, J.: New trends in developmental psychology. Brit. J. educ. Psychol., 1970, *40*, 107. Yarrow, M. R., Campbell, J. D. & Burton, R. V.: Child rearing. San Francisco, 1968.   *W. Yule*

Children as witnesses. From antiquity until the last century, children's statements remained suspect as evidence. Only when experimental research into testimonies began in the early years of this century were those of children thought to merit psychological examination. The first findings of forensic psychology in this regard were reported by Stern (1903). For some time after that the testimony of pre-adolescent girls was considered unreliable, partly because of medical prejudice (Möbius, 1908; *et al.*). Since World War II, more attention has been given to children's evidence because of new approaches in psychological testing. Although legal conditions vary in different countries and states, the evidence of minors in cases of sexual assault and so on is often considered.
Bibliography: See *Forensic psychology*.   *M.M.*

Chirognomics. A pseudoscientific theory about the expressiveness of the shape and nature of the hand. Certain sections (e.g. the fingers) and parts (e.g. joints) are made to refer symbolically to character traits, although there is no proof of such a connection. The degree of definition in the shape of the hand and its parts is taken to be the expression of symbolically analogous character traits (e.g. the thumb as a symbol of power; a strong thumb as a sign of violence). The hand may be thought of as expressive in the sense mainly of "constitutional" psychology: E. Kretschmer, W. H. Sheldon. Medical diagnostics also attaches importance to the state of the hand.
Bibliography: Bürger, M.: Die Hand des Kranken. Munich, 1956. Kretschmer, E.: Physique and character. London, 1925. Sheldon, W. H.: The varieties of human physique. New York & London, 1963. *P.K.*

Chirology. The art of reading the hand, originating in ancient chiromancy; the art of prophesying from the shape and the lines of the hand, which were thought to relate to the stars (in imitation of astrology) or to organs of the body. Chirology has renounced its mantic purpose and now concerns itself with the interpretation of character (q.v.) from the shape, state and lines of the hand, but its findings have no validity: in the main they are based on unjustified and empirically unfounded analogies or metaphorical generalizations. In addition to chirology, there is scientific research into the lines of the hand and the patterns of callosities.

Bibliography: Kiener, F.: Hand, Gebärde und Charakter. Munich, 1962.   F.K.

Chi-square distribution (χ^2-*distribution*). A random distribution of magnitudes which represent functions of observation values (e.g. frequencies). It is used to test statistical hypotheses and is therefore sometimes called a test distribution. The function

$$C = \left[\left(\frac{r-2}{2}\right)! \cdot 2\frac{r-2}{2}\right]^{-1}$$

gives the functional value of χ for a specific r (number of independent, normally distributed random variables). This allows calculation of the probability $d\Phi(\chi^2)$ that an observed χ^2 lies between the values χ^2 and $d(\chi_1^2)$.   *W.H.B.*

Chi-square test (χ^2 test). An inferential-statistical test based on the chi-square distribution (q.v.). Probably the most frequent application is the random testing of deviations (q.v.) of observed values (e.g. frequencies) from the values of a random spot-check expected on the basis of the χ^2 distribution (test for the validity of the adaptation). In addition, the χ^2 test is used to test the randomness of deviations between observed and hypothetical variances (q.v.) as well as in the combination of significance tests (see *Significance*).   *W.H.B.*

Chlordiazepoxide (syn. *Librium*). A tranquilizer (q.v.) with which, after meprobamate (q.v.), a new class of chemical substances, the benzodiazepines (*inter alia:* diazepam [Valium], oxazepam [Serax]), were introduced into pharmacotherapy; they have anti-neurotic, but minor sedative, effects over a wide dosage range. In therapeutic doses, chlordiazepoxide has a central effect, predominantly in the limbic system. Large doses induce sleep but are not narcotic. Autonomic effects are largely non-existent. The effects on healthy persons have been tested in numerous experimental investigations. The effects in daily life depend on habitual personality characteristics and situational conditions (see *Differential psychopharmacology*). Emotional relaxation can occur with doses of up to 60 mg., and will be greater with the emotionally unstable and those under emotional stress. Under certain conditions (e.g. mental stress) paradoxical arousal is possible. At up to 30 mg., scarcely any influence on performance can be shown. Impairments of performance are most noticeable in speed tests of perception and cognition. When the dose is increased to more than 30 mg., there is more likelihood of subjective sedation and impairment of performance.

Bibliography: Janke, W. & Debus, G.: Experimental studies on anti-anxiety agents with normal subjects: methodological consideration and review of the main effects. In: Efron, D. H. (Ed.): Psychopharmacology 1957–1967. Washington, 1968. See also *Tranquilizers.*   G.D.

Chloroform. A narcotic (q.v.) in use since 1847, very potent in a limited area of narcosis, with undesirable toxic effects on the myocardium and liver parenchyma. Now little used for humans.   *E.L.*

Chlorpromazine (syn. *Amargil, Largactil, Megaphen, Thorazine*). Clinically the best-known neuroleptic (q.v.) of the phenothiazine (q.v.) derivatives, it has been widely used since J. Delay & P. Deniker (1952) described its beneficial effects in psychiatric therapy. Among the phenothiazines, chlorpromazine affords a comparatively medium neuroleptic effect with moderate extrapyramidal but stronger autonomic side-effects (circulation) in large doses. In healthy persons, chlorpromazine (up to 200 mg.) has an effect on performance independently of the nature of the tests; it is not emotionally relaxing, but in isolated cases increases tension and as a rule is sedative. A reduction of experimentally induced anxiety could not be demonstrated positively. Paradoxal sleep is prolonged by small doses, and shortened by large ones. See *Dream.*

Bibliography: **Brodie, C. M.**: Chlorpromazine as anxiety-reducer: effects on complex learning and reaction time. J. exp. Res. Pers., 1967, *2*, 160–67. **Hartlage, L. C.**: Effects of chlorpromazine on learning. Psychol. Bull., 1965, *64*, 235–45. **Janke, W. & Debus, G.**: Experimental studies in anti-anxiety agents with normal subjects: methodological considerations and review of the main effects. In: **Efron, D. H.** (Ed.): Psychopharmacology 1957–1967, Washington, 1968. **Lewis, S. A. & Evans, J. I.**: Dose effects of chlorpromazine on human sleep. Psychopharmacologia, 1969, *14*, 342–8.   *G.D.*

Choice reaction (syn. *Choice experiment*). Choice reactions are all those reactions in which Ss have to respond variously to several, different stimuli. E.g. they must press a button with the left hand in response to a red light, with the right hand in response to a blue light, and with both feet in response to a white light. In such experiments, Ss are primarily required to apply sensory discrimination and appropriate motor coordination. In choice experiments, reaction times are significantly longer than in other reaction situations.   *A.T.*

Choleric type. According to medieval tradition an irascible, vehement temperament; an emotionally active, direct personality.   *W.K.*

Cholinergic. 1. Characteristic of the effect of chemical substances comparable to that of acetylcholine (q.v.). **2.** Nerve fibers or nervous systems in which acetylcholine or acetylcholine-related substances function as transmitters (q.v.). To equate cholinergic with parasympathetic is incorrect, since "cholinergic" is used in connection with the central nervous system when acetycholine functions as a transmitter. According to many authors, cholinergic nervous systems are of fundamental importance for learning. See *Psychopharmacology.*   *W.J.*

Cholinergics. Substances with a cholinergic effect.

Cholinesterase (abb. ChE) (syn. *Acetylcholinesterase*, abb. AChE). An enzyme under the influence of which the acetylcholine (q.v.) released in the organism is inactivated within a very short time (in the region of milliseconds).   *W.J.*

Cholinesterase inhibitors. Substances which block or delay the rapid enzyme decomposition of acetylcholine (q.v.). In consequence the effect of acetylcholine at the receptor is strengthened and/or prolonged. Important cholinesterases are neostigmine (prostigmin) (q.v.), physostigmine (q.v.), pyridostigmine, edrophonium (Tensilon). Certain substances (organic phosphates, e.g. diisopropylfluorophosphate [isofluorophate; Fluoropryl], DFP) inhibit cholinesterase irreversibly, and cause death by convulsions and impairment of the breathing and circulation. Some of these substances are used as insecticides (e.g. nitrostigmine). Some substances related to DFP have been considered for use in chemical warfare as "nerve poisons" (e.g. sarine, somane, tabune). Small doses of cholinesterase inhibitors impair the performance of healthy persons; large doses create symptoms resembling psychosis. Cholinesterases are used extensively to investigate the relations between acetylcholine and behavior. See *Psychopharmacology.*

Bibliography: Koelle, G. B.: Cholinesterases and anticholinesterase agents. In: Hdb. d. exp. Pharmakol. Vol. 15. Berlin, 1963. See also *Acetylcholine; Anticholinergics.*   *W.J.*

Chorea. An extrapyramidal (see *Pyramidal tract*) motor disorder in the form of constantly repeated spasms of particular muscles or groups of muscles. The intention to move, together with emotional excitement, increases the disturbance of movement. The following are distinguished: (*a*) *Chorea minor* (Sydenham's chorea; St Vitus' dance) as the result of a rheumatic cerebral inflammation, a childhood disease; (*b*) *Huntington's chorea:* a dominant inherited, degenerative complaint in which there is cellular atrophy in the *caudatum* and *putamen*, i.e. the *corpus striatum.* In addition to the motor disturbance (and often preceding this), there is psychic damage in the sense of increasing "coarsening of the personality", loss of restraint, and dementia (q.v.). (N.B.: This chorea, with its cerebral pathological causation, must not be confused with *chorea major*, a term once used for serious hysterical attacks.)   *C.S.*

Choriongonadotrophine (syn. *Chorionic gonadotrophin*). An extrahypophyseal gonadotrop(h)ic hormone (protein hormone), which is formed during pregnancy in the trophoblast and later in the fetal section of the placenta. Biological significance and effect: prevents cyclic modification of the *corpus luteum* (yellow body) in the follicle, which it stimulates to further growth during the first months of pregnancy, thus maintaining its function. Choriongonadotrophine therefore mainly has a luteinizing action similar to that of gonadotrophic hormone. The placenta begins to produce choriongonadotrophine some four to five weeks after fertilization, and reaches the maximum value in about the sixth week of pregnancy: this facilitates early diagnosis of pregnancy, since large quantities of choriongonadotrophine are detectable in the urine and blood plasma.

H.M.

Chromatic. In general, "chromatic" means colored. (*a*) Visual perception: *monochromatic* and *polychromatic light stimuli; monochromatic* refers to radiation with one wavelength. *Polychromatic light stimuli* are radiation composed of several wavelengths. The color of mono- and polychromatic light can be the same. Afterimages are *homochromous* (*homochromatic*) when they show the same color as the primary stimulus, and *heterochromous* (*heterochromatic*) when they show a different color. (*b*) In music, the twelve-part scale is called chromatic in contrast to the seven-part scale, which is diatonic. (*c*) *Chromatisms:* see *Synesthesia. Chromatopsia:* morbid varicolored vision due to many different reasons such as a cataract operation, poisoning, etc.   *A.H.*

Chromatic aberration. In optics: a chromatic image-forming defect. In a convex lens the rear focal point for short-wave light rays (blue) is in front of the rear focal point for long-wave light rays (red). If one examines the image of a point source in the focal plane (retina), it is seen to feature colored (chromatic) rings, or chromatic *dispersion circles.* Since in the human eye, too (with the exception of the retinal layer in the narrow foveal area), all optic media have a convex effect, these produce a chromatic aberration (color deviation). Although, as a rule, nothing of this considerable degree of chromatic aberration is noticed in perception, we do see colored dispersion circles immediately the chromatic aberration of the eye is artificially increased or diminished. It is not yet known how chromatic aberration in the human eye is corrected or suppressed for the purpose of perception.   *A.H.*

Chromatic adaptation. Reduction of the hue and saturation of a color when fixated.

Chromatoptometer. Light rays which are perceived as different colors are distinguished physically by their wavelengths. Since the angle of refraction as the ray passes from one optic medium to another depends on the wavelength, rays of different wavelengths unite in the eye at different points on the optic axis. The point of union (focal point) of light-blue rays is nearer to the cornea than the focal point of red rays (see *Chromatic aberration*). The chromatoptometer makes use of this chromatic aberration: when the emmetrope (see *Emmetropia*) looks at an electric lamp (bulb) through an interposed cobalt glass (which transmits red and blue light only), he sees violet; the myope (see *Myopia*) sees red with a blue edge; the hyperope (see *Hyperopia*) sees blue with a red edge.   *R.R.*

Chromomeres. When cells begin to divide, small nodules known as chromomers, become recognizable on the strands from which chromosomes are formed. They are considered to be the beginning of a spiralization.
H.S.

Chromesthesia. See *Color hearing; Synthesia*.

Chromosomal aberration. A chromosomal anomaly, discovered in 1959 (Lejeune, Gautier, Turpin), which consists of either a missing or an additional gene; there are somatic and psychic consequences. Trisomia 21 (chromosome 21 according to the Denver nomenclature) is the cause of Down's disease (see *Mongolism*). The XO aberration (instead of XX) brings about the Turner syndrome (q.v.) (gonadal dysgenesia), the XXY aberration (instead of XY) causes the Klinefelter syndrome (q.v.) (men with a marked feminine aspect); men with the XYY aberration are usually tall with disturbed social behavior. There are other forms of chromosomal aberration which all cause brain disturbances.
Bibliography: Züblin, W.: Chromosomale Aberrationen und Psyche. Basle & New York, 1969. *F.Ki.*

Chromosomes. Minute, thin strands with a fibrous, rod-like structure in the cell nucleus whose number remains constant with the species (forty-six in humans); as a rule they are only recognizable by refined spectroscopic techniques when a cell divides, and they each split into two. Each chromosome is a DNA (desoxyribonucleic acid) molecule (for structure of DNA helix, see Watson, 1968); the chromosome theory of heredity holds that the genes strung along the molecule are fundamentally responsible for the transmission of inherited characteristics. Some inheritance processes and changes can be traced to the molecule responsible.
Bibliography: Watson, J. D.: The double helix. London, 1968. Id.: Molecular biology of the gene. London, 1969.   *H.S.*

Chronaxie. A characteristic dimension in testing nerve function: an index of tissue excitability calculated in terms of the reaction time for stimulation with a current double the threshold intensity.

Chronograph. Usually an electronic appliance with the help of which (e.g. in continuous reaction experiments) the smallest periods of time can be measured and recorded. See *Chronoscope*.   *K.E.P.*

Chronological age (abb. CA). The subject's age from his birth to a specific point.

Chronoscope. Term used for an accurate stop-watch (capable of measuring 1/1000 sec.). Inventors: C. Wheatstone & M. Hipp.

Cinema. See *Film*.

Circuit processes. Processes which, as they take place, retroact on their initial conditions, e.g. the changes in a river bed caused by water pouring over it. The functional principle underlying circuit processes is known as *feedback* (q.v.).   *K.-D.G*

Circular psychosis. French psychiatrists in the 1850s (Falret & Bailarger) described *folie circulaire* as an episodic illness with normal intervening periods, each episode being characterized either by extreme cheerfulness or depression. Because of variations in associated disorders of movement and thought, classifications multiplied until Kraepelin subsumed all such illnesses under *manic depressive psychosis* (q.v.). Since then, other attempts have been made to separate discrete types of circular illness according to their patterns of mood, behavior, thought and perceptual symptoms; these are labeled variously periodic psychosis, cycloid psychosis, recoverable schizophrenia, schizophreniform psychosis and schizoaffective psychosis. The field is variously charted and overlaps with that of the recoverable psychoses, i.e. those mentioned above, together with degeneration psychosis, reactive psychosis, psychogenic psychosis and acute psychosis. See *Psychoses.*   *B.B.*

Circulation response. A response by the organism to a change in internal or external conditions. Cardiac and circulation responses are observed during physical exertion, e.g. muscular work, passive rotation or tilting of the body, in experiences with a strong emotional content, or in cases of physical trauma (shock), but also as a phenomenon accompanying changes in arousal, e.g. emotions and stress, and also as a consequence of simple sensory stimuli (orienting reflex). These reactions are not only demonstrable in cardiac activity (pulse, beat, EKG), but in the arterial system (systolic and diastolic blood pressure, pulse wave velocity, peripheral resistance and volume) and in venous pressure, vein condition and capillary circulation. The cardio-circulatory system is able to adjust in many, interdependent regulating circuits to changing requirements; a general distinction must be made between an ergotropic (sympathetic) and trophotropic, vagotonic functional condition (autonomic system). See *Arousal.*

Because of the close, neurovegetative connections, mental stress and emotive excitation primarily influence the cardio-circulatory system: blushing, loss of color, pulse acceleration, blood pressure reaction, etc. The pulse frequency and systolic blood pressure are used most commonly as activation indicators because they can still be measured relatively simply, and generally vary in direct relation to the degree of physical effort and mental stress. It has not yet been possible to demonstrate specific patterns of circulation response during individual emotions (see *Emotion*). See *Psychophysiological methods.*

Bibliography: Donat, K.: Herz und Kreislauf. In: Bartelheimer, H. & Jores, A. (Eds): Klinische Funktionsdiagnostik, Stuttgart, *3,* 1967. Legewie, H.: Indikatoren von Kreislauf, Atmung u. Energieumsatz. In: Schönpflug, W. (Ed.): Methoden der Aktivierungsforschung. Berne, 1969.   *J.Fa.*

Circumcision. The partial or total medicosurgical or ritual removal of the prepuce. In depth psychology, circumcision is often described as a ritualized approximation to, or threat of, castration (castration complex, q.v.); in some cultures it forms part of an initiation ritual (see *Initiation*). Even today circumcision is sometimes used as a "therapy" and (or) punishment for infant masturbation (q.v.), but is usually a form of treatment for phimosis (chronic contraction of the prepuce). Circumcision is often indicated or rationalized —according to the point of view—as a measure to intensify sexual hygiene. A comparison of large social groups in which circumcised men form a minority or a majority, shows that at any moment the minority is regarded as sexually more effective, both in respect to the auto- and the stereotype. This heightened effectiveness is supposed to result from a more than average ability to control ejaculation (q.v.), based in the circumcised on a diminished sensitiveness of the glans penis, in the non-circumcised on decreased stimulation by the vagina during intercourse, since the glans penis is extensively protected by the prepuce. Both views seem to be refuted by neurological and sexological investigations.

There are three main kinds of circumcision: (a) *Incision:* only the *frenulum* is incised. (b) *Circumcision:* the entire foreskin is removed (e.g. among Jews and Arabs). The above statements refer to this form. (c) *Subincision:* the urethra is cut open to the root of the penis (New Guinea and Melanesia).   *G.L.*

Clairvoyance. A form of ESP (q.v.) where the information acquired by the subject is assumed to derive directly from an external physical source, not from the mind or brain of another person as in telepathy (q.v.).   *J.B.*

Clairvoyant. Person with special ability for clairvoyance (q.v.). Must not be confused with its colloquial usage where it refers to a fortune-teller.   *J.B.*

Clang. A term for the acoustic phenomenon produced by the superimposition of harmonic partials. The latter, which comprise the fundamental tone and its overtones, represent the simplest periodic sound vibrations, the frequencies of which rise in the ratio of whole numbers. The number, choice and intensity of the individual partials basically determine the *timbre*, while the pitch is fixed by the fundamental tone even if it is not heard. Other features of clang are its loudness and duration.

In clang analysis, both partials and clang are distinguished qualitatively and quantitatively with respect to pitch and intensity. This can be done by the human ear alone or by means of resonators, interference valves, electric filters, Fourier analysis. See *Music, psychology of.*
Bibliography: Wellek, A.: Musikpsychologie und Musikästhetik. Frankfurt, 1963.   *B.S.*

Claparède, Edouard. B. 24/3/1873, d. 29/9/1940, in Geneva. Doctor and psychologist; professor at Geneva where in 1912 he founded the "Institut J.-J. Rousseau". Devoted himself to comparative psychology, especially to child psychology, and is considered to be the co-founder of applied psychology; advanced the development of industrial psychology, and put forward proposals for the use of psychology in medicine. Claparède considered psychological processes from the standpoint of their biological utility. See *Functionalism.*

Works. Psychologie de l'enfant et pédagogie expérimentale, 1905. Psychologie judiciaire (in: *Année psychol.*), 1906. L'éducation fonctionelle, 1931. Le développement mental, ²1946. 1901: founded the "Archives de Psychologie" (with Flournay).
Bibliography: Claparède, E.: Edouard Claparède. In: Murchison, C. (Ed.): A history of psychology in autobiography, Vol. 1. Worcester, Mass., 1930, 63–97.   *F.-C.S.*

Classification. The operation of dividing into classes the elements of a group of objects with the aid of some *common characteristic* (relation of equivalence or similarity). Each object thus classified belongs to one class only. The term also denotes the result of the process. In traditional logic, classification was dichotomous and culminated in a "tree" structure (Tree of Porphyry, c. 232 to 301 A.D.). It progressed in each case in accordance with the next, higher generic concept (*genus proximum*) and the difference constituting the species (*differentia specifica*). The concept of "grouping" (Piaget) shows that the concrete thinking of the child also progresses according to a "tree-structure" classification. See *Concept.*   *M.-J.B.*

Classification methods are used to group events in categories or classes. According to the nature of the characteristics classified, qualitative may be distinguished from quantitative classification.

Classification tests are either those in which a testee is asked to classify objects, or those used to classify a group of people according to some predetermined set of categories (e.g. "streaming" by IQ, etc., in schools).   *G.M.*

Class, social. A term used in sociology and social psychology (q.v.) in regard to social stratification; it is applied to individuals or small groups (families) in a given society or community who show relative similarities in regard to certain possibilities: choice of vocation, and/or income, and/or living conditions and standards, and/or social prestige (vocational group); there are many other modes of division, or "classes"—e.g. linguistic usage. Empirical research is constantly concerned to establish the characteristics of new social strata in the process of formation. In general, the *Marxist* concept of class (but see Lukàcs, 1971) differs in postulating that ownership or non-ownership of the means of production and of the products (property or no property) is sufficient to develop *class consciousness*, expressed as a form of solidarity among members of a class. In the first case, class is defined in terms of the complex of characteristics relevant at a given time, place, and so on; in the second case, in terms of economic circumstances and the resulting emotions.

Bibliography: Barber, B. & E. G.: European social class: stability and change. New York, 1965. Bendix, R. & Lipset, S. M. (Eds): Class, status and power. New York, ²1966. Bergel, E. E.: Social stratification. New York, 1962. Brandis, W. & Henderson, D. (Eds): Primary socialisation, language and education, Vol. 1: Social class, language and communication. London, 1969. Bronfenbrenner, V.: Socialization and social class through time and space. In: Maccoby, E. E., *et al.* (Eds): Readings in social psychology. New York, 1958. Centers, R.: The psychology of social classes. New York, 1949. Lukàcs, G.: History and class-consciousness. London, 1971.   *W.D.F.*

Classical conditioning. See *Conditioning, classical and operant.*

Claustrophilia. A desire to be confined or to withdraw to a small, enclosing space. *Claustrophobia:* a fear of such confinement or withdrawal.

Cleanliness. See *Bowel training.*

Client-centered therapy. A form of psychotherapy or counseling developed by C. Rogers. The approach is *non-directive*, involving no attempts to diagnose, interpret or persuade, the aim being to provide a climate of *warmth, empathy*, and *acceptance* in which the *client* will be free to gain insight into his unique *self* enabling him to mobilize his potentialities in the solution of his own problems. The job of the therapist is to communicate his sincere feeling that the client is a person of *unconditional self-worth*, of value regardless of his attitudes, ideas, and behavior, and to reflect what the client is saying in such a way as to clarify his thoughts and make it clear that his feelings are fully understood. The method has gained widespread popularity, particularly in the U.S.A., and is the basis of the group technique called *sensitivity training* or *T-groups.*   *G.D.W.*

Climate of work. This comprises factors in the social structure of a factory which lie outside the worker but influence him. Among them are good factory organization, communication facilities between worker and employer and between the workers themselves, some voice in affairs, direct and indirect recognition, group relationships, etc.

An unfavorable atmosphere decreases productivity and individual activity, and quantities produced, and finds expression, e.g. in discontent, work-shyness and increased absenteeism. See *Industrial psychology; Occupational psychology.*

Bibliography: Friedmann, G.: The anatomy of work. Glencoe, Ill., 1961. Davison, J. P. *et al.*: Productivity and economic incentives. London, 1958. Gouldner, A. W.: Wildcat strike. London, 1955. Sayles, L. R.: Behavior of industrial work groups. New York, 1958. Winn, A.: The laboratory approach to organization development: a tentative model of planned change. J. manag. Stud., 1969, *6*, 155–66. Zalezinik, A., *et al.*: The motivation, productivity and satisfaction of workers: a predictive study. Harvard, 1958.   *W.S.*

Climax (*Orgasm*). The peak of excitement during sexual intercourse or masturbation.

Normally corresponding with ejaculation in the male, and ideally, vaginal contractions immediately following ejaculation for the female. (See also *Clitoral orgasm.*) In medicine, the height of a fever or disease process.

G.D.W.

Clinical psychology. 1. *Definition.* There is no single generally accepted definition of clinical psychology. We can therefore do no more than outline the main trends of thought on the subject: (*a*) Clinical psychology is the activity of the psychologist in a clinic or hospital, confined normally to diagnosis and, within certain limits, to advice (Meyerhoff, 1959). (*b*) Clinical psychology is a *special method* (exploration and observation) which was first introduced into child psychology by Jean Piaget. (*c*) Clinical psychology is the application of the results and methods of all the basic psychological disciplines (general, developmental, differential, social, and dynamic psychology or psychoanalysis), and related disciplines such as comparative psychology (q.v.), sociology and methodology in the "clinical sector" (Schraml, 1970; Wolman, 1965). Clinical psychology is also understood as the application in the clinical sphere of psychology stemming from a unified conception (e.g. learning theories or C. R. Rogers' conception); depending on the interpretation concept which is adopted, emphasis is placed on individual sectors (e.g. social aspects or learning disorders) (e.g. Sundberg & Taylor, 1963). Definition (*c*) is stressed here because clinical psychology is an applied, i.e. a pragmatic, discipline.

2. *Historical background.* Three phases can be distinguished in the development of clinical psychology. (*a*) During and after World War I, methods of psychological examination developed in the laboratory were used to evaluate brain damage caused by injury or accident (W. Poppelreuther, O. Lippmann). A psychological laboratory already existed at the time in the clinic run by the famous psychiatrist E. Kraepelin. Clinical psychology combined experimental laboratory psychology, hospital psychology and industrial psychology, and was a precursor of rehabilitation methods. (*b*) A new trend developed with the introduction of psychoanalysis in psychology and psychiatry, primarily in the English-speaking countries. Whether psychoanalysis is used in the strict sense of the word, or of an eclectic use of procedures borrowed from many different psychological systems, or of the results of learning theories combined with those of dynamic psychology or psychoanalysis (O. H. Mowrer), the clinical psychologist is not merely a diagnostician but an adviser and therapist. This situation developed with some speed in the U.S.A. after World War II, when the hospitals of the Veterans' Administration were set up. (*c*) In a final phase of development, clinical psychologists have begun to work in psychiatric, psychosomatic, psychotherapeutic, pediatric, neurological and orthopedic establishments as diagnosticians, therapists (especially in group therapy, q.v.) and consultant social workers, or counseling psychologists. The function of the psychologist as a methodological expert in clinical research is almost entirely novel. Since the average doctor has no training in quantitative methods, a new sphere of clinical psychology has developed.

3. *Applications.* According to internationally accepted terminology, the clinical sector not only covers fixed establishments for the care of patients (hospitals, clinics) but also out-patient departments and the whole range of guidance centers (educational or child guidance, vocational guidance, marriage, family, geriatric, and alcohol and drug addict guidance as well as guidance for suicide risks), and remand establishments, old people's homes and psychiatric establishments and hospitals. In addition, clinical psychologists act in an advisory capacity in the education and health planning institutes of advanced countries and international organizations.

4. *Clinical social psychology.* Clinical social psychology has developed considerably in

the last decade; the boundaries between social psychiatry, psycho-hygiene, social education and clinical social psychology are fluid, but in this sector, too, the activities of social psychiatrists, social workers, sociologists, social education experts and psychologists are often identical. The work is therefore determined by function and method rather than by professional disciplines. (*a*) *Prevention:* (i) Information through mass media (press, radio, television) on mental disorders and how to treat and prevent them (e.g. sex education, child nurture and training). Advice in planning new housing developments, kindergartens, schools and old people's homes, etc. (ii) Participation in the training of all types of educators, social workers and hospital staff by imparting psychological knowledge and by sensitivity training, etc., in dynamic group therapy. (iii) Institutional preventive therapy in all establishments for preventive care. (*b*) *Study and improvement of the social structure of clinical establishments:* (i) Group relations in hospitals (doctors, nurses, administrative staff, specialists and patients). (ii) Group relations in educational establishments and remand homes: educators, psychologists, teachers and pupils. (iii) Social structure in clinics, old people's homes and psychiatric establishments. (*c*) *Rehabilitation and resocialization:* (i) Help in integrating children born with physical or mental defects into society (together with special educational methods). (ii) Reintegration of persons physically handicapped as a result of accidents or disease (examination, retraining and mental rehabilitation). (iii) Reintegration and mental care of the chronically sick. (iv) Reintegration of psychiatric patients and persons who have been in hospital for long periods. (v) Resocialization of delinquents (overlap with the education and rehabilitation of criminals, and with criminal psychology, q.v.).

5. *Clinical diagnosis.* (*a*) As in medicine, a *case history* is compiled to study the previous development of patients or third parties (biological, sociological or biographical data).

(*b*) *Exploration:* As in psychiatry, the intellectual and psychic state of the patient is determined by observing his verbal and para-verbal responses to stimuli. (*c*) The clinical *interview* used primarily in the early stages of psychotherapy (q.v.), psychosomatics (q.v.), and similar areas, allows the patient to speak freely and therefore enables the basis of a conflict and possibilities of interaction to be clarified by association.

6. *Clinical test diagnosis.* A distinction must be made between integrated psychodiagnosis, which is an inseparable part of the clinical process, and purely cooperative psychodiagnosis, which makes results available for clinical practice. The methods (tests) can usefully be divided up according to intention, method and sphere of application. (*a*) *Intention:* intelligence, aptitude and interest studies; *methods:* psychometric; *application:* child psychiatry and educational guidance; neurology and rehabilitation. (*b*) *Intention:* determination of normal or pathological personality structure by projective methods (q.v.); *method:* interpretative, with some measurements; *application:* psychiatry, child psychiatry and educational guidance; psychotherapy and guidance. (*c*) *Intention:* individual conflict, biographical genesis and social relations by thematic methods (e.g. TAT, CAT for children, Four-Picture test); *application:* early stages of psychotherapy and psychosomatics; child psychiatry and educational guidance; guidance centers. (*d*) *Intention:* classification of patients by personality inventories (e.g. MPPI, MPI); *methods:* metric, quantitative; *application:* in hospitals and out-patient departments to classify patients for therapeutic methods. (*e*) *Intention:* analysis of the relation of personalities to individual psycho-physical or physiological data; *method:* experimental, quantitative; *application:* in clinical research.

7. *Psychological guidance, treatment and care.* In most instances, an eclectic, pragmatic method of clinical psychology adapted to the specific situation is used. However, the clinical psychologist must be acquainted

175

with the principles of all the methods listed below; if he does not have the necessary training himself he must at least be able to refer patients for the appropriate special treatment. (*a*) *Guidance and counseling:* (i) informational guidance, i.e. explanation of research results and general knowledge (e.g. from group and development psychology); (ii) guidance based on knowledge of the case history but with a strong directive emphasis (e.g. referral to different guidance centers); guidance of patients who are not accessible to introspective treatment aimed at clarifying the conflict (e.g. certain psychiatric patients). (*b*) *Symptom-oriented methods:* (i) physiotropic or organismic methods: including hypnosis (q.v.), narcosis-hypnosis, suggestion and relaxation methods (autogenic training, q.v., progressive relaxation according to E. Jacobsen, etc.); in these methods the therapists use verbal stimuli to contact the organism directly, either to cure the symptom or to change the responses; (ii) behavior or aversive therapy: the aim is either to eliminate negative stimulus-response associations (e.g. systematic desensitization, aversion therapy, q.v.), or to build up necessary stimulus-response associations which have not yet been acquired (see *Conditioning*). (*c*) *Psychodynamic and conflict-oriented methods:* (i) psychoanalysis (q.v.): attempts are made to cure symptoms by changing the psychodynamic personality structure, gaining insight into the unconscious conflict process, and studying social relationships; derivatives of psychoanalysis (parameters) in child therapy, psychoses and delinquency and all forms of short-term therapy; (ii) deviations from psychoanalysis (changes in the theoretical concept: K. Horney, E. Fromm, H. Schultz-Hencke & H. Sullivan; the early depth-psychology schools of A. Adler & C. G. Jung); and existential analysis (less important from the standpoint of clinical psychology); (iii) non-directive psychotherapy, or client-centered (discussion) therapy (q.v.) according to C. R. Rogers, in which *non*-specific conflict is assumed (suitable for relatively

minor conflicts). (*d*) *Group psychotherapy:* (i) all forms of non-analytical group psychotherapy: e.g. play and constructive groups with children and adolescents, directive discussion groups, psycho-drama (J. L. Moreno) rehabilitation groups for former psychiatric patients and alcoholics; (ii) analytical group psychotherapy; important here are multilateral transference and specific forms of catharsis (q.v.). (*e*) *Clinical* (psychological) *exploitation of other methods* such as rhythm, work and occupational therapy. See *Group therapy.*

8. *Research in clinical psychology.* Primarily progress control and study of the success rate of psychotherapeutic methods, psychopharmacology (q.v.), and psychophysiology (q.v.).

Bibliography: Bulletin de Psychologie. Numéro Spécial: Psychologie Clinique, 1968, *21*, 15–19. Benton, A. L. (Ed.): Contributions to clinical neuropsychology. Chicago, 1970. Gathercole, C. E.: Assessment in clinical psychology. Harmondsworth, 1968. Lubin, B. & Levitt, E. (Eds): The clinical psychologist. Chicago, 1967. Meyerhoff, H.: Leitfaden der Klinischen Psychologie. Munich & Basle, 1959. Schraml, W. J. (Ed.): Hdb. der Klinischen Psychologie. Berne & Stuttgart, 1970. Stern, E. (Ed.): Hdb. der Klinischen Psychologie, Vols 1 & 2. Zürich, 1954/58. Sundberg, N. D. & Tyler, L. E.: Clinical psychology. London, 1963. Wolman, B. B. (Ed.): Handbook of clinical psychology. New York, 1965. Wolpe, J.: The practice of behavior therapy. New York, 1969.

W. J. *Schraml*

Clisis. According to Monakow, the investment of some object of a drive or instinct with *positive emotional qualities.* Investment with *negative* emotional qualities is *ecclisis.*

W.T.

Clitoral orgasm. 1. A pattern of changes in the *clitoris* (the penis analogue in the female) involving tumescence and retraction, which are believed to be associated with sexual climax in the female during intercourse or masturbation. **2.** Sexual climax in the female achieved through physical stimulation of the clitoris rather than the inside of the vagina.

G.D.W.

Closure. A principle proposed by gestalt psychologists to explain how stable percepts can be achieved by the subjective closing of gaps and the completion of incomplete figures to form wholes. See *Ganzheit*.   *C.D.F.*

Closure Faces Test. C. M. Mooney's test of visual perception, used, e.g., to examine the long-term effects of temporal lobectomy.
Bibliography: Mooney, C. M.: Closure with negative afterimages under flickering light. Canad. J. Physiol., 1956, *10*, 191–9. Id.: Closure as affected by configural clarity and contextual consistency. Canad. J. Physiol., 1957, *11*, 80–8.

Cluster. An accumulation of elements (points, observations) relative to the environment; e.g. an accumulation of points in part of the coordinate system. R. C. Tryon's cluster analysis is a method related to factor analysis (q.v.), and used for the grouping of variables on the basis of intercorrelations (e.g. in a correlation table).   *W.H.B.*

Cocaine. An alkaloid synthesized from ecgonine and obtained from leaves of South American coca shrubs (*Erythroxylon coca*), chewed by the Andean Indians on account of their stimulating, invigorating and intoxicating effects. The effect of cocaine on the central nervous system is at first exciting and then inhibiting. It inhibits monamine oxidase (q.v.) and thus increases the effect of the catecholamines (q.v.) present in the body. By blocking conduction in the peripheral nerves it has a strong local anesthetic effect. Acute cocaine intoxication passes through several phases: a euphoric phase, in which there is a feeling of enhanced physical and mental power, is replaced by an intoxicated phase in which the mood is anxious and irritable and there are acoustic and microoptic hallucinations (q.v.); the final phase is depressive. Cocaine use can be addictive. It has little significance nowadays in medical use.
Bibliography: See *Drug dependence; Narcotics.* *G.E.*

Co-consciousness. A term coined by Rohracher for those items of knowledge and information that people are not consciously aware of, but which can be retrieved instantly without effort of memory or verbalization, e.g. one's name, address, etc.   *C.D.F.*

Code. A system of symbols, or a specification for the unambiguous arrangement ("coding") of the symbols of a (relatively large) array and those of another (relatively small) array.
A large number of special codes have been developed for the different areas of information processing (q.v.), which are studied in information theory (q.v.). Existing codes can be classified according to different criteria, e.g. the degree of redundancy (q.v.).
Computer code (syn. *Machine code*): a system of symbols for the operations built into a computer.   *P.-B.H.*

Codeine (*Methyl morphine*). A psychotropic (q.v.) substance, contained in opium (q.v.), related chemically and pharmacologically to morphine (q.v.), but a weaker analgesic than the latter. Only small amounts of morphine occur as a decomposition product, therefore withdrawal symptoms cease in cases of morphine addiction; codeine itself scarcely causes addiction. It inhibits the "cough center"; large doses impair breathing. It acts centrally, as does morphine. Codeine has a mild sedative effect.
Bibliography: Kay, D. C., Gorodetsky, C. W. & Martin, W. R.: Comparative effects of codeine and morphine in man. J. Pharmacol. exp. Therap. 1967, *156*, 101–6.   *W.B.*

Coding. See *Code*.

Coeducation. The joint education or training of boys and girls. Full segregation of the sexes during primary, and even secondary, education is tending to disappear in Western culture, and in certain countries is more often associated with religious or socially privileged educational systems.

Coefficient. 1. In mathematics: a constant value by which another value is multiplied. **2.** In statistics: a value expressing the degree to which an information characteristic occurs under certain conditions. Some coefficients, e.g. the correlation coefficients (q.v.), are so defined that they assume values between 0 and 1.   *G.M.*

Cognition. 1. An expression for every *process* by which a living creature obtains knowledge of some object or becomes aware of its environment. Cognition processes are: perception, discovery, recognition, imagining, judging, memorizing, learning, thinking, and often speech. **2.** Knowing as distinct from volitional or emotional processes. **3.** The product of cognizing, or knowing; the knowledge acquired.   *H.W.*
    4. Like the word "knowledge", "cognition" refers to a human activity which is intellectual and communicable. The many varied meanings of the word can be reduced to two principal ones: (*a*) the representation or grasping in conceptual terms of a (concrete or abstract) object by perception, imagination or conceptualization; (*b*) understanding or explanation: the understanding of an object as specific because it fits into a system of relationships which justifies it by its very nature. In both meanings, the cognitive action determines the object as such, and differentiates between that which is known and the person who has cognizance of it. Cognition therefore contrasts with the pure subjectivity of the states of consciousness,

feeling and belief, because it merely aims at revealing the truth. Problems in regard to cognition concern its origin (reason, experience), nature (intuitive, discursive), and range (phenomenal, absolute). See *Epistemology; Empiricism.*   *M.-J.B.*

Cognition theory (*Theory of knowledge;* Ger., *Erkenntnistheorie*). A collective term for philosophical theories which seek to explain the nature, mechanisms and value of cognition by studying the general relationship between subject and object, thought and world. The term *Erkenntnistheorie* was first used by K. L. Reinhold (*Attempt at a New Theory of Human Ideation*, Jena, 1789) but the problem is as old as philosophy itself. Historically speaking, the first explanations were *dogmatic:* (*a*) there is an object outside thought which is conceived by the latter (*realism, idealism, rationalism,* q.v., *empiricism,* q.v.); (*b*) there is no object outside thought (*phenomenalism*); (*c*) if there is an object, it cannot be known (*skepticism,* q.v.). Later explanations were *critical:* the question of the existence of objects outside thought was replaced by an inquiry into the conditions for cognition, which were looked for at its source, i.e. in the structure of the "cognizing" or "knowing" subject. Finally *dialectical* explanations developed: it is not the type of elements which determines the relationship between cognition and subject; on the contrary, subject and object form a unity in which elements are determined reciprocally. See *Epistemology.*   *M.-J.B.*

Cognitive map (syn. *Cognitive schema*). The picture built up by an organism on the basis of experiences, e.g. the image of a maze constructed by an animal, or an individual's image of an organization.

Cognitive orientation. According to the CO theory, cognitive processes, such as recognition, combination and elaboration of meaning, are necessary conditions for the elicitation of orienting reflexes and the acquisition of conditioned reflexes (q.v.), and determine the direction and course of human molar behavior. It suggests a model of cognitive processes intervening between stimulation and behavior: Interaction between the stimulus representation and CO components (beliefs about goals, norms, self and world) creates a CO cluster which produces a goal-directed behavioral intention, actualized in behavior when implemented by inherited, learned or *ad hoc* adapted plans. Conflicts appear when simultaneously several CO clusters and hence several behavioral intentions arise, or when several plans are activated for implementation of one behavioral intention. Experiments show that CO clusters, measured by questionnaires, correlate highly with behavior (e.g. level and course of achievement after success and failure, acted-out defense mechanisms, and so on) when plans are held constant. Studies reveal that schizophrenics (q.v.) have abnormal CO clusters, whose change by clinical means is followed by a decrease in symptoms. Concerning the genesis of CO it was found that children of four to six years already have differentiated CO clusters referring to various aspects of behavior.

Bibliography: Kreitler, H. & S.: Die weltanschauliche Orientierung der Schizophrenen. Munich & Basle, 1965. Id.: Die kognitive Orientierung des Kindes. Munich & Basle, 1967. Id.: Cognitive orientation: a model of human behavior. ETS, Princeton, N.J., RM 23, 1969. Id.: The cognitive antecedents of the orienting reflex. Schweiz. Z. Psychol. Anwend., 1970, 29, 37–44. Id.: Cognitive orientation and behavior. New York, 1971. *H. & S. Kreitler*

Coherence, coherence factors. Müller proposed coherence factors to explain the formation of "*Gestalten*". These factors included: spatial vicinity, identity, similarity, symmetry and contour (i.e. differentiation of figure from ground). Such factors produce coherence between different parts of the stimulus array, that is, the parts hang together and form a unit. *C.D.F.*

Cohesion (syn. *Cohesiveness*). A term for the forces which induce the individual to remain a member of a group. In general, cohesion is equated with the *attractiveness* of a group, which depends especially on: (*a*) The degree to which the interaction within a group possesses positive qualities for the individual members (the cohesion is greater when interaction produces a greater reward for group members); (*b*) the extent to which group activities are rewarding for each individual (e.g. the recreative effect of leisure activities available in the group); (*c*) the degree to which membership of a group can be used as a means for attaining individual objectives.

The cohesion and attractiveness of a particular group depend also on the value of possible alternatives outside the particular group (the group affords a comparison level for alternatives). The cohesion of a group and the conformity (q.v.) of its members are directly related; the greater the cohesion, the stronger the possible negative sanctions against the non-conforming behavior of an individual without the latter leaving the group. See *Group dynamics*.

Bibliography: Cartwright, D. & Zander, A.: Group dynamics: research and theory. New York, ²1960. *A.S.-M.*

Coital foreplay (syn. *Pre-coital techniques; Foreplay*) consists of techniques used by one or both partners for stimulation before heterosexual intercourse proper (coitus, q.v.) and to induce readiness for penetration. Methods vary within Western culture according to individual and socio-moral factors: kissing, tongue-play, manual or oral stimulation of the woman's breasts, manual stimulation of the male or female genitals, oral-genital stimulation (see *Cunnilingus; Fellatio*), mutual manual-genital stimulation, genital apposition without introduction of the penis into the vagina, intercrural intercourse. If foreplay does not culminate in coitus, it is usually known as "petting". Some of these techniques (especially fellatio and cunnilingus) are still erroneously held to be "abnormal" or even "perverted" in our culture, even though since Kinsey's findings (1948–53) there has been widespread public awareness of the "normal", widespread use of such methods. The reasons for the persistence of such disapproval would seem to be largely moral and religious.

Recent research in Western Germany (Schmidt & Sigusch, 1970) has confirmed the social-class correlation of foreplay as recorded by Kinsey & Masters in the U.S.A. It is practiced in the form of manual-genital contacts, cunnilingus and fellatio more frequently by upper and middle-class than by lower social groups, where sexual activity more often consists of simple coitus. It is worthy of note that foreplay is more frequently prolonged (eleven minutes to one hour) and used (73% compared with 53%) more before than after marriage. Kinsey & Masters (1953) draw attention to the fact that the findings certainly do not support a widely-held assumption that premarital coitus is necessarily quicker and consequently less satisfying than coitus when married.

Whatever form it takes, coital foreplay fulfills the important task of increasing sexual excitement before, and readiness for, coition.
Bibliography: Ford, C. S. & Beach, F. A.: Patterns of sexual behavior. London, 1952. (See *Coitus* for additional literature.)   *H.M.*

Coitus. Heterosexual intercourse, the most common form of sexual behavior among the majority of adults in all known societies, but very rarely indeed the *sole* form of sexual activity. Preference for certain *positions in coitus* depends on a particular culture; the "active male" and "passive female" roles in coitus are not dependent on "nature" and have nothing to do with a biological pattern of "male" and "female". The duration of coitus depends on the speed with which the man reaches orgasm. When such activity begins depends very much (in Western societies) on social class (Kinsey, 1948; 1953); this applies just as much to males as to females:

workers of both sexes first engage in coitus about four years before students of both sexes (Schmidt & Sigusch, 1970); this seems to result not from greater sexual freedom but from earlier material independence, and the earlier age at which workers marry. Greater *mobility of partners* (i.e. number of partners in coitus) for men is frequently written about (Kinsey, 1964; Schofield, 1968, and others), but this also seems to depend to a large extent on class (a greater tendency to change partners is found among workers and not among students, Schmidt & Sigusch, 1970). The average *frequency of coitus* depends on experience and decreases gradually both with men and women as they grow older; this is not a result of any decrease in a woman's capacity to respond sexually as she ages but of physiological processes taking place in the man; yet healthy males have "a capacity for sexual performance that frequently may extend beyond the eighty-year age level" (Masters & Johnson).
Bibliography: Brecher, R. & E.: An analysis of "Human sexual response." New York & London, 1967. Kinsey, A. C. *et al.*: Sexual behavior in the human male. Philadelphia & London, 1948. Id.: Sexual behavior in the human female. Philadelphia & London, 1953. Masters, C. & W. H.: Human sexual response. Boston, 1966. Schmidt, G. & Sigusch, V.: Sexuelle Verhaltensmuster bei jungen Arbeiter und Studenten. In: Schmidt, G. *et al.* (Eds.): Tendenzen des Sexualforschung. Stuttgart, 1970. Schofield, M.: The sexual behaviour of young people. Harmondsworth, 1968.   *H.M.*

Coitus interruptus. A coital technique: after insertion into the vagina, the penis is removed shortly before ejaculation of the semen. Together with condoms and oral contraceptives, it is the most used technique of contraception. Freud's supposition that frequent coitus interruptus could bring on anxiety neuroses is disputed.   *J.F.*

Coitus reservatus. A confusing term since it is used to refer to coitus interruptus (q.v.), to the intentional inhibition of the male orgasm until orgasm has commenced in the female, and to full, intentional inhibition of the male orgasm in coitus. The third denotation is preferred.

Cold, paradoxical. See *Paradoxical cold and warmth.*

Collective idea (syn. *Collective image*). G. E. Müller was foremost in trying to explain the genesis of idea or image complexes as the effect of a collective idea. In the collective idea, successive elements of a learning sequence (e.g. nonsense syllables) are all grasped simultaneously, detached from the mass of available impressions, and associated to form a group, whether the elements are presented uniformly one after the other, or simultaneously. The elements of such a complex are bound together by extremely strong associations (q.v.) and when they become conscious tend to reproduce the entire complex from the beginning (initial reproduction tendency). Two forms may be distinguished: collective ideas of simultaneous, and those of successive, impressions. According to G. E. Müller (1924) mental images of common words and known musical signals depend on the collective idea.
Bibliography: Müller, G. E.: Abriss der Psychologie. Göttingen, 1924.   *F.-C.S.*

Collective unconscious. A form of the unconscious postulated by C. G. Jung (q.v.) and considered by him to be distinct from the "personal" unconscious. The collective part of the unconscious does not include the contents which are specific to our individual ego (q.v.) or which arise from personal experience, but is said to be the powerful spiritual inheritance of human development, reborn in each individual brain-structure. The contents of the collective unconscious are the so-called archetypes (q.v.), which are universally human and enjoy a supra-personal validity. They are supra-individual forms into which the personal

element of the individual enters as content, and they are said to be passed on like instincts.   *H.-N.G.*

Color antagonists. Color pairs with maximum dissimilarity of hue. When they are mixed together, color antagonists (red-green, yellow-blue) produce dull colors (white or grey). Illogically, the term *complementary wavelength* has become usual in colorimetry instead of *compensatory wavelength.* This term denotes the wavelengths (or bands) which are perceived as color antagonists. See *Complementary colors; Ideal colors. A.H.*

Color blindness. Defective physiological color vision with intact perception of form. May be total (= achromatop(s)ia, achromatism) or partial as in "anomalous trichromatism" (all three receptor pigments present in the retina, q.v., but all or some with unphysiologically lower efficacy); and "dichromatism", in which two of the pigments are effective but the third is absent. Depending on whether the first pigment (yellow), the second (green) or the third (blue-violet) of the trichromatic theories of color vision (q.v.) is affected, use is made of the prefixes "proto", "deutero" or "trito". Protanomaly, deuteranomaly and tritanopia or tritanopsia indicate lack of perception of the colors in question. Dichromatism and anomalous trichromatism are congenital conditions and, save for the extremely rare cases of autosomal tritanopia (q.v.), sex-linked, usually recessively. They therefore affect both the eyes and all retinal parts in the same degree.

Color blindness is diagnosed with the aid of pseudoisochromatic charts (q.v.), e.g. those designed by J. Stilling–E. Hertel (see *Stilling color charts*) or by S. Ishihara (see *Ishihara test*) on which numbers and letters are made up of points differing in color but of the same brightness; or, better still, with a color mixer that produces spectral colors (see *Anomaloscope*). In addition to this

Table. Characteristics of color-vision defects and their distribution among the inhabitants of Europe and North America (Kalmus, p. 147, Klein & Franceschetti, pp. 121ff. and Pschyrembel, p. 355).

	Men	Women
Protoforms		
Anomaly: Restricted sensitivity to red. Dark red confused with black, green with white or grey, violet with blue.	0.7%	0.03%
Anopia: No sensitivity to red (red blindness). Red, yellow, green and brown confused with each other; also violet with blue, dark red with black.	1.1%	0.01%
Deuteroforms		
Anomaly: Restricted sensitivity to green. Green confused with yellow, brown and grey.	4-5%	0.35%
Anopia: No sensitivity to green (green blindness). Confusion of colors practically the same as in protanopia, although dark red can be better distinguished from black.	1.8%	0.35%
Tritoforms (very rare)		
Anomaly: Restricted sensitivity to blue. Green confused with blue, delicate pink with pale yellow, light blue with grey.	0.01%	0.01%
Anopia: No sensitivity to blue (blue blindness). Red confused with orange, blue with green, greenish yellow with grey and violet, light yellow with white.	0.01%	0.01%

genetically determined *innate* color blindness, there is *acquired* color blindness caused by traumatic or toxic damage to the optic sensory path (detached retina, scotoma, q.v., atrophy of the optic tract or of the sclerotic coat), often in the form of *circumscribed* color-blindness (affecting only parts of the visual field). Occasionally such disorders of the optic tract lead to total color-blindness (see *Achromatop(s)ia*).   *K.H.Plattig.*

Color blindness tests. Used to determine the various kinds and degrees of color blindness (q.v.). In the widely used pseudoisochromatic charts developed by J. Stilling, S. Ishihara and others, dots of various hues (q.v.) are so arranged that different shapes (letters, numbers) are distinguished by Ss, depending on whether they have good color vision or suffer from varying degrees of color blindness. The Holmgren test (q.v.) involves the matching for hue of differently colored skeins of wool. Deuteranopia and protanopia can be clearly distinguished with E. H. Nagel's anomaloscope (q.v.) which makes it possible to determine the exact components of monochromatic red and green light, which, in additive mixture, are perceived as standard yellow. By plotting a chromaticity diagram, color vision defects can be accurately diagnosed. See *Color vision.*   *A.L.*

Color circle. See *Color square.*

Color constancy. See *Color vision.*

Color contrast, simultaneous. See *Simultaneous contrast.*

Color contrast, successive. When a large number of white, black or colored strips, disks, etc., are laid on a grey or colored background, normal simultaneous contrast (q.v.) gives way to equalization of brightness and hue. The white strips lighten the background, the black ones darken it, the yellow ones add a yellow component to it, and so on. This phenomenon was first noted by W. von Bezold and thoroughly investigated by C. Musatti.

Bibliography: Musatti, C.: Luce e colore nei fenomeni del contrasto, della costanza e dell'eguagliamento. Archivio di Psicologia, Neurologia e Psicologia, 1953, 5.   *G.Ka.*

Colored smelling. See *Synesthesia.*

Color hearing. Tones are often associated with specific colors. Slow music, e.g., conjures up a blue hue; a rapid tempo is connected with red; high-pitched tones evoke light colors, low-pitched tones dark colors. Beyond these associations, rare cases occur of actual synesthesia (q.v.), i.e. individuals who hear tones and simultaneously "see" colors. This phenomenon, probably based on inherited tendencies, has not yet been satisfactorily explained.   *G.Ka.*

Color mixer. A disk with colored angular sectors the width of which can be varied as desired. When the disk is rotated fast enough (over 60 rev/sec) the colors fuse. The result is an additive mixture in which each color component is present in proportion to the width of the corresponding sector. Rotating the disk at a speed below that necessary for the colors to fuse (flicker fusion frequency) produces the phenomenon of *flicker*, i.e. the rotating disk is animated by an irregular pulsation of colored lights.   *G.Ka.*

Color mixture. The coincidence of rays emitted or reflected by two or more objects, either in space or in time. In the first case, rays issuing from several sources simultaneously excite the same area of the retina. In the second, the various light stimuli strike the same point of the retina in rapid succession, with the result that what is perceived is not the individual colors but a product of fusion

(see *Color mixer*). The two processes result in an additive color mixture. A subtractive color mixture is obtained by superposing two or more transparent colored plates. In this case the absorption coefficients coincide in such a way as to produce a new color different from that of any of the individual plates on its own. See *Pigment color mixture.*   *G.K.*

Color perception. Colors can be defined from the viewpoints of physics, physiology and psychology.

1. For physics, colors are specific instances of radiant energy, i.e. nothing but different wavelengths of the electromagnetic spectrum ranging from c. 380 to 750 mμ. In addition to wavelength (or frequency), there are two further properties of radiated light of importance to color vision, namely, the amplitude (or intensity) of the wave and the composition of the spectrum (or purity) of the radiation.

2. As an experienced phenomenon, however, color is not the direct registering of a property of physical radiation but the end-product of physiological processes inside the organism. Although the physiological level is crucial for rounding off these processes and for understanding color sensations, it must be admitted that our physiological knowledge is still far from advanced, so closely are the various processes interwoven and so enormous is the difficulty presented by experimental research in this field. We are faced more with a profusion of theories (e.g. Goethe's theory of color) than with firmly established and generally accepted facts. The theories still thought highly of today are the *three-color theory* of T. Young and H. Helmholtz, and the *four-color theory* of E. Hering and J. Müller, recently improved upon by L. M. Hurvich and D. Jameson. The three-color theory postulates that all that is necessary to make any color appear is to mix the wave-

lengths corresponding to red, green and blue (primary colors), carefully adjusting their intensity. Similarly, the theory assumes the existence on the *retina* (q.v.) of three types of receptor, each specifically sensitive to one of the main wavelengths. Even though each of the three visual pigments reacts in a specific way to the rays of all wavelengths, its reaction is at a maximum for one of the three main rays, and each of the possible combinations of the specific reactions of the spectrum sets in train a physiological process to which corresponds one of the 200–250 hues distinguished by the human eye. According also to the four-color theory or the theory of "antagonistic color pairs", all color-vision phenomena are explained once the existence of three visual substances is admitted. The course of events according to this model, however, greatly differs from that of Young and Helmholtz. It postulates a light-sensitive red-green substance, a yellow-blue substance and a white-black substance. With the dissimilation processes set in motion by specific wavelengths (see *Dissimilation*), it is claimed that such substances are associated with visual perception of red, yellow and white, whereas green, blue and black are seen as a result of the assimilation processes (see *Assimilation*) of the same substances on exposure to other wavelengths. In addition to the above theories, there are many others which are for the most part modifications of the two theories mentioned, or attempts to embody them into a single system capable of accounting for all normal and pathological color phenomena. None of these attempts has so far yielded a satisfactory result. Consequently, interest in physiological theories has today greatly diminished.

3. For psychology, the problems presented by colors arise in connection with: (*a*) suitably classifying our color impressions; (*b*) ascertaining regular correlations between color phenomena and the variable quantity of the stimuli; (*c*) the meanings and aspects of color sensations. In ordering colors, account is taken of three basic properties, i.e. *hue* (q.v.), *brightness* (q.v.) and *saturation* (q.v.), which show a fairly regular correlation with wavelength and amplitude and spectral composition of the radiated light. Of the countless combinations that can be obtained by mixing these three physical variables in different proportions, the human eye can distinguish only about 350,000 color qualities, each of which exhibits a unique mixture of hue, brightness and saturation. All these qualities are classified in diagrams or stereometric models of "color geometry", which illustrate how the various colors are related to each other on the phenomenal plane. These classifications are rounded off by taking into account the "modes of appearance" of colors. With these in mind, colors can be arranged by *surface colors* (q.v.), *film colors* (q.v.), *color volume* and *transparent colors*. In addition, the modes of appearance are distinguished by gloss, glitter, sparkle and direct light sources. One of the key problems of color vision arises from the relative "*constancy*" (q.v.) of the color and the brightness of the objects. "Constancy" is in turn ensured by an outstanding performance on the part of the visual system, i.e. by the phenomenal separation of a single color event into the color of the object and its illumination. *Two* physical variables (intensity and spectral composition on the one hand, and degree of reflection and absorption of the object on the other) are represented by a *single* physical stimulus (intensity and spectral composition of the reflected light) which sparks off a *single* sensory process. To this, in the sphere of sensation, correspond *two* perceptual factors (color of object and light to which it is exposed) which reflect the duality of the physical situation fairly closely. This problem has been tackled by some of the best-known investigators of perception, and has given rise to a literature rich in experimental observations, discussions and theories. (See Gelb, 1929, Katz, 1911 for the history of the problems.) It widely held that "constancy" is the effect of "transformation" exercised by central processes on peripheral processes to make them correspond to external reality. The biological function of color constancy, like other cases of constancy of perception, is to enable us to move about with certitude in a world of familiar objects whose appearance is not constantly changing. Some well-known experiments by Gelb, Kardos and Wallach have shown, however, that the phenomenal separation of light reflected from a surface can take place in such a way that constancy phenomena may be accompanied by cases of inconstancy that are just as conclusive. This suggests that "constancy" is a special effect and not necessarily bound up with phenomenal separation which, on the other hand, appears to obey precise general laws of perception (q.v.). The known facts do not yet permit us to define these laws with certainty. There appears, however, to be a widespread conviction that the phenomena of "constancy" are the result of field factors: the colored appearance of a zone of the visual field is believed to depend on the *relationship* that exists between an area of stimulation and the adjoining areas.

Bibliography: Boring, E. G.: Sensation and perception in the history of experimental psychology. New York, 1942. Committee on Colorimetry, O.S.A.: The science of color. New York, 1953. Evans, R. M.: An introduction to color. New York, 1948. Gelb, A.: Die Farbenkonstanz der Sehdinge. Handbuch der normalen und pathologischen Physiologie, Vol. 12/1. Berlin, 1929. Helmholtz, H.: Handbuch der physiologischen Optik. Hamburg, 1909–11; Eng. trans.: Handbook of physiological optics. London, 1924–5. Hering, E.: Grundzüge der Lehre vom Lichtsinn. Berlin, 1920. Hurvich, L. M. & Jameson, D.: Theorie der Farbwahrnehmung. Handbuch der Psychologie, Vol. 1. Göttingen, 1966. Kanizsa, G.: Die Erscheinungsweise der Farben. Handbuch der Psychologie, Vol. 1. Göttingen, 1966. Kardos, L.: Ding und Schatten. Zeitschrift Psychol. Erg., 1934, 23. Katz, D.: Die Erscheinungsweisen der Farben. Zeitschrift Psychol. Erg., 1911, 7. Le Grand, Y.: Light, color and vision. New York, 1957. Segal, J.: La mécanisme de la vision des couleurs. Paris, 1953. Wallach, H.: Brightness constancy and the nature of achromatic colors. Journal of Experimental Psychology. 1948, 38.

G. Kanizsa

Color perception types. R. Scholl & O. Kroh distinguish between color perception and shape perception types. The two types were found by Scholl (in children) and by Kroh (in adults) to have distinct personalities. *Color perception types:* (a) children are lively and wide-awake; (b) adults are responsive, vivacious, communicative, rarely self-critical and not always thoroughgoing. *Shape perception types:* (a) children are bashful, nervous, anxious, cautious and taciturn; (b) adults reserved, self-controlled, critical, ambitious, composed, inadaptable.

Bibliography: Spieth, R.: Der Mensch als Typus. Stuttgart, 1949. W.K.

Color pyramid. A well-known three-dimensional system of "color geometry". On the central axis, which joins up the two vertices of the double pyramid, are arranged all hueless colors ranging from white to black (brightness). The common base of the two pyramids forms the color square (q.v.) whose angles represent the full colors red, yellow, green and blue. On the lateral area all full colors are arranged in accordance with a given gradation of brightness. As saturation (q.v.) diminishes with an increase or decrease of brightness (q.v.) the distance from the central grey axis is also reduced in the upward and downward directions, so that a model in the form of a double pyramid is obtained. See *Color square.*

Bibliography: Ebbinghaus, H.: Grundzüge der Psychologie. Leipzig, 1902. G.K.

Color pyramid test. A process for assessing personality developed by M. Pfister (1942),

R. Heiss & H. Hiltman (1951). The subject chooses from among a batch of small plates in twenty-four (more recently fourteen) different hues, and is required to build a number of pyramids each comprising fifteen fields. In the main it is the color-choice frequency that is evaluated, together with the structure of the pyramids and the color-selection procedure. Some doubt exists as to the validity of the findings concerning the subject's affectivity (response, regulation, disposition, introversion–extraversion, mal-adjustment).

Bibliography: Schaie, K. W. & Heiss, R.: Color and personality. Berne, 1964.   A.L.

Color sense. See *Color vision.*

Color square. The various hues can be arranged along the sides of an ideal square whose angles form the four basic colors (red, yellow, green and blue). On each side are arranged the hues which are experienced as lying between two adjacent basic colors. The colors can be visualized as being arranged on a circle instead of a square (color circle).
                                                                 G.K.

Color stimulus test. A psychophysical method of measuring the color stimulus in order to establish a system for grading colors, on the basis of which laws expressing relations between certain properties of stimuli and the responses of an "average receiver" can be determined under strictly uniform conditions. This technique is based on the circumstance that in any visual situation each color stimulus can be equated with a single combination of three different suitably chosen colors.

Bibliography: Committee on Colorimetry: The Science of Color. New York, 1953.   *G.K.*

Color symbolism. From time immemorial, colors have possessed symbolic significance, especially in ceremonial rites (e.g. color of clothing or special symbolic objects) and in paintings with a religious or mythical content. No uniform significance, however, is attached to color by various cultures, epochs and liturgies.

The following classification is often made: *red* = activity, excitement, passion, courage, will to win; *yellow* = love of change, mobility, salvation and release, intuition, speech, faith; *green* = acceptance of emotion and experience, sense of reality, joy; *blue* = coldness, intellectuality, truth, security, loyalty; *white* = purity, loneliness, barrenness; *black* = mourning, mysterious power. See *Color vision.*

Bibliography: Berkusky, H.: Zur Symbolik der Farben. Zeitschrift des Vereins für Volkskunde, 1913, *23.* Bopst, H.: Color and personality. New York, 1962. Gutter, A.: Märchen und Märe. Solothurn, 1968.   *F.-C.S.*

Color tests. Used to evaluate favorable and adverse judgments on colors in assessing personality, e.g. color-choice test (M. Lüscher, 1949), color pyramid test (q.v., M. Pfister & R. Heiss). The color symbolism and characterological significance of the colors on which both these tests are based are without empirical verification, and are ambiguous. The re-test reliability of the color choices is also limited.   *A.L.*

Color theory. See *Color vision.*

Color triangle. The different saturation rates of a hue can be so arranged as to cover a triangle whose base is determined by the range of degrees of brightness. A triangle is used because, while the highest saturation rate for each color is reached at a medium degree of brightness, saturation goes on falling steadily, regardless of whether brightness increases or decreases, until the color component completely disappears and the brightness corresponds with that of white or black.   *G.K.*

Color variator. A color mixer (q.v.) the width of whose sectors can be varied while it is rotating.

Color vision. The optic tract (eye with connected neural conducting and processing elements) is a system highly sensitive to color and light. It can, in suitably coded form, display hue, i.e. the wavelength of the light stimulus (between 400 and 800 nm.) and call up a corresponding sensation. *Color coding theories:* (a) Trichromatic theory of color vision (three-receptor hypothesis, three-color theory, three-component theory) put forward by Th. Young (1802) and H. von Helmholtz (1852) is based on the possibility of color mixing, on the laws of color blindness (q.v.), and on the successful isolation of various receptor substances (rhodopsin, iodopsin, cyanopsin, porphyropsin) by G. Wald and co-workers (Nobel Prize 1967) among others. (b) Dominator-modulator theory represented by R. Granit (1943, Nobel Prize 1967). (c) Complementary color theory (four-color theory) of E. Hering (1874).

(a) Young & Helmholtz postulated for the retina three types of light receptors, each excited to the maximum by a particular wavelength. With the incidence of monochromatic or mixed-chromatic light, in every case all three types of receptor are excited, though in varying degrees (see Fig. a); and a clear excitation correlative is obtained, by mixing the individual spectral components, for each of the approximately 160 hues distinguishable by man. This three-receptor theory is in close agreement with the findings obtained with color vision defects. Although these led to the view that the three primary colors of the human eye must be the same as those which enable all the hues to be composed in color printing and television—i.e. red, yellow and blue—visual pigments with the following sensitivity maxima were isolated from the cones (q.v.) of primates: (i) 577 nm. (yellow), (ii) 540 nm. (green) and (iii) 447 nm. (blue-violet) (E. F. MacNichol, jr., 1964).

With these pigments all hues can also be represented, as shown in Fig. b.

(b) Granit's dominator-modulator theory is likewise trichromatic and amplifies the Young–Helmholtz three-color theory. It assumes the dominator system to be made up of broad-band ON-elements in the retina, i.e. receptors that are briefly excited by a broad

The spectral sensitivity or absorptivity of the three retinal color receptors postulated by T. Young and H. L. F. von Helmholtz (a) and of the retinal pigments recently isolated from the cones of monkeys' eyes (b). The common abscissa gives the light wavelength in nm; the hues perceived are given below. The lower ordinate refers to percentage of maximal absorption of the particular pigment; the upper ordinate uses arbitrary absorption units. The actual spectral sensitivity and absorption maxima (though not measured in humans) show a shift toward the short wavelengths in comparison with those originally put forward by Young and Helmholtz.

frequency band (without distinct maxima) at the start of stimulation, and the modulators to consist of narrow band elements for particular frequencies or wavelengths that correspond to the receptor pigments described under (a).

(c) Hering, in the light of psychological investigations, also postulates three visual substances with four colors forming two complementary pairs, i.e. red-green, yellow-blue and, in addition, black-white. Assimilation (q.v.) and dissimilation (q.v.) processes

A state of *un-
the individual
pears when there
ctrolytic balance,
ning and disease.
tal, and its treat-
linical diagnosis.
esis, comas are
physiological re-
diminished reflex
ain lesions (coma
U.H.S.

possible arrange-
rent elements. A
n permutations,
s. The theory of
asis in probability
etric (q.v.) opera-
G.M.

nal tones which
more tones are
ference tone is
to the difference
es sounded. The
frequency equal
ncies sounded.
C.D.F.

racts connecting
or the two sides
aining the com-
hese conduction
analogous areas
tem (q.v.). The
the largest com-
pulses conduct
on one side to
rsa.
Hamilton, G. F. &
nan body. London,
G.A.

he total variance
des with other

variables in a given set. The com...
a variable is equal to the sum of s...
factor loadings. Communality ...
understood as the *squared multipl*...
of the factors with the variable...
analysis.

Communication is a subject which...
increased attention within many...
World War II; for example, in...
psychology, sociology, interna...
tions, epistemology, and in art...
and labor relations. This is perh...
of an increasing awareness of na...
dependences, in trade, defen...
travel, culture, broadcasting an...
institutions. A major force in th...
has been technology, especially...
bal communication and air-tra...
computers.

Communication is therefore...
unified subject, to any degree, b...
within many academic disciplin...
ways. There seems no likelihood...
ing scientific theory with direct re...
fields emerging within the forese...

1. *Philosophy of communicati*...
to discuss this wide subject ration...
guide to setting up experime...
psychology, some consistent gui...
ing—some philosophy—is advisa...
ject is on the one hand practi...
munication, computers, automa...
on, which have developed the...
scientifically, as yet), and on the...
concerns people, their thoughts...
ledge, and their individual and so...
To unite these aspects in di...
writer has found most useful th...
of Charles Sanders Peirce (18...
one-time teacher of William Jam...
called *pragmatism* (see Peirc...
Gallie, 1952; Cherry, 1957; M...
Peirce set up, in particular, a the...
edge which was perhaps fifty ye...
its time. This theory was essenti...
on practical outcomes (observa...

variables in a given set. The communality of a variable is equal to the sum of squares of its factor loadings. Communality may also be understood as the *squared multiple correlation* of the factors with the variable. See *Factor analysis*. G.M.

Communication is a subject which has received increased attention within many fields since World War II; for example, in technology, psychology, sociology, international relations, epistemology, and in art, advertising and labor relations. This is perhaps one sign of an increasing awareness of national interdependences, in trade, defense, science, travel, culture, broadcasting and our many institutions. A major force in this movement has been technology, especially that of global communication and air-travel, and of computers.

Communication is therefore still not a unified subject, to any degree, but is studied within many academic disciplines, in various ways. There seems no likelihood of any unifying scientific theory with direct relevance to all fields emerging within the foreseeable future.

1. *Philosophy of communication*. In order to discuss this wide subject rationally, and as a guide to setting up experiments in, say, psychology, some consistent guide to thinking—some philosophy—is advisable. The subject is on the one hand practical (telecommunication, computers, automation, and so on, which have developed the subject most scientifically, as yet), and on the other hand concerns people, their thoughts and knowledge, and their individual and social behavior. To unite these aspects in discussion, the writer has found most useful the philosophy of Charles Sanders Peirce (1839–1914, the one-time teacher of William James), which he called *pragmatism* (see Peirce, 1931–35; Gallie, 1952; Cherry, 1957; Mead, 1934). Peirce set up, in particular, a theory of knowledge which was perhaps fifty years ahead of its time. This theory was essentially based upon practical outcomes (observables, behavior,

and so on), but enabled him to define such value terms as *know, think, true*. Pragmatism relates the traditionally separate worlds "outside" us and "inside" us, by starting with the concept of *signs* (language, diagrams, icons, tokens, gestures, and so on). The worlds of "mind" and "matter" no longer remain a dualism, because knowledge exists only by virtue of signs, signification, significance: what "exists" is that which has any practical outcome which can then be signified.

2. *Pragmatism and human communication*. Communication proceeds by signs. It is always social, whether between people or when talking to oneself (or "thinking"). Hence it always involves relationships. There are two broad classes of sign: (*a*) linguistic signs (e.g. English, German, Italian, and so on), which are culturally dominant; and (*b*) sign-systems, invented, or needing definitions and rules (e.g. road signs, coinage, mathematics, and so on). Both raise the question: what *is* a sign? Do all perceptions, all *Gestalten*, constitute signs?

In order to distinguish one percept, or concept, from any other, it must be signified. Otherwise there is no logical distinction. A new concept requires a new sign; they cannot be separated. In its most primitive form, the sign may be an icon or "picture" of some new perception (e.g. we can distinguish between a table and a chair either by using these names, or by visualizing the objects). Perception, knowledge and communication all rest upon sign-usage, a usage within some systems, based upon cultural habits (e.g. language) or upon defined rules of a specific system (road-signs, mathematics, and so on).

3. *Observation and communication*. For such logical reasons, our question can be answered: all perceptions do indeed constitute signs, but we should be careful to distinguish between two, quite different, situations of their usage. These are in (*a*) observation (e.g. looking at a tree *as* "a tree"), and in (*b*) communication. Situation (*a*) is non-social, or an I/it situation; situation (*b*) is social, or an I/thou situation. And it is the

lead to displacements of the balance of excitation and therefore to color coding. This complementary color theory clearly does not hold for retinal receptor substances but does apply to "code conversion" in the nervous controls of the retina (q.v.).

Bibliography: MacNichol, E. F., jr.: Three-pigment color vision. Scientific American, 1964, *211*, 48–56.

                                        K. H. Platlig

Color weakness. See *Color blindness*.

Color-word test. Used in differential psychology for investigating "cognitive style"; suggested in 1935 by Stroop under the influence of E. R. Jaensch. Performance in naming colored words ("red", "blue", etc.) printed in colors other than those to which they refer, is poorer than in naming colored dots because the tendency to read the words interferes (see *Interference*).

Bibliography: Hörmann, H.: Konflikt und Entscheidung. Experimentelle Untersuchungen über das Interferenzphänomen. Göttingen, 1960.   *A.L.*

Colored hearing. See *Color hearing*.

Colored shadows. An effect of simultaneous contrast (q.v.) brought about by illumination. When a wall is illuminated by two suitably spaced light sources (one white, one red) and a small opaque screen is interposed, two shadows will appear on it. The shadow caused by interception of the white light will appear red because it is illuminated by the red lamp (the background is pink because it receives white and red light simultaneously). It might be expected that the shadow resulting from interception of the red light would be white, since only white light reaches it. In fact, it appears *green* as a result of antagonistic induction caused by the pink background.

                                        G.K.

Coma. 1. An optical aberration of spherical lenses which occurs when light strikes the lens at a specific angle. **2.** A state of *unconsciousness* from which the individual cannot be wakened. It appears when there are serious changes in the electrolytic balance, and in various kinds of poisoning and disease. A coma may not prove fatal, and its treatment demands complex clinical diagnosis. Depending on their genesis, comas are accompanied by varying physiological reactions, by increased or diminished reflex activity, delirium, and by brain lesions (coma in hypoglycemia).   *U.H.S.*

Combination. Study of the possible arrangements of a number of different elements. A distinction is made between permutations, combinations and variations. The theory of combinations provides the basis in probability theory for many non-parametric (q.v.) operations.   *G.M.*

Combination tones. Additional tones which are heard when two or more tones are sounded together. The *difference tone* is heard at the frequency equal to the difference in frequency between the tones sounded. The *summation tone* is heard at a frequency equal to the sum of the two frequencies sounded.   *C.D.F.*

Commissures. Nerve fiber tracts connecting the hemispheres of the brain or the two sides of the spinal cord and containing the commissural fibers or neurons. These conduction tracts coordinate bilaterally analogous areas of the central nervous system (q.v.). The *corpus callosum* represents the largest commissural tract; in it, impulses conduct information from the cortex on one side to that on the other and vice versa.

Bibliography: Lockhart, R. D., Hamilton, G. F. & Fyfe, F. W.: Anatomy of the human body. London, 1965.   *G.A.*

Communality. That part of the total variance of a variable which coincides with other latter, communication, which is dominant upon us, and the main source of all our knowledge of the world as it seems today, and of the whole of history. We each build up our own, individual, models of the world *not* so much through our direct observation but very largely by being taught: by parents, schools, books, newspapers, radio and TV, and hosts of other social institutions which form our culture. Knowledge is socially derived, for even our most personal and "original" thoughts we have been led to through our language, our sign-systems, and all our social institutions (Mead, 1934).

4. *Communication: the self and society*. The great sociologist Emile Durkheim (1858–1917) was the first to show clearly the dualism between a person and society (Bierstedt, 1966). In brief, when one was born one formed part of one's mother, who taught one self-awareness, and one's earliest concepts. Admittedly this broad statement can raise questions about "instincts" and various innate or chromosomic constraints. Nevertheless one's knowledge (knowing *what, who, that*, and so on) derives from acquisition of verbal and other signs. Therefore, argued Durkheim, nobody can know anything, even that he exists, without society. Conversely, society cannot exist without persons. The person and his society form an inseparable dualism (see Mead, Bierstedt).

It is essential to bear this in mind in all discussion about "international communication" or "understanding". One is largely as one has been taught, through the many institutions of a society; and one can understand other countries' peoples only through the eyes of one's own institutions. Understanding emerges most clearly only when institutions are shared in common (Mangore, 1954; Europa Year Book, 1967) (e.g. of science, of language, of sports, of trade, and so on). Communication is only possible with common habits—not only of language and word usage, but essentially other institutional customs as well. The global spread of telecommunication, news services, cheap travel and tourism, etc., since the end of World War II has therefore raised acutely certain problems in the minds of millions of people (in both the industrial and in the developing countries) who were previously protected. That old cliché "Knowledge is power" has become inverted to read: "Knowledge is an increasing sense of helplessness".

Therefore it is not surprising that studies of "communication" have entered into the academic fields of political philosophy and sociology (Pye, 1963), nor that we are witnessing many challenges today for reappraisal of the purposes, values and methods of education. The technology of communication, globally spread within one generation, has presented us with a great dilemma: how can we adjust ourselves to this overwhelming body of news-items, rumours of changing national images, and partial truths, when we still have emotional capacities more suited to communities of village size? Some writers have predicted a future in which we all carry our personal radio-telephones in our pockets, and are "instantly able to communicate with anyone else in the world". This cannot possibly be the case; one person can have acquaintance, or dealings, at a personal level, with only a relatively small number of people. He can only generalize about the other thousands of millions, and speak of them as "*the* Chinese", "*the* Africans", "*the* Arabs", and so on. In this writer's opinion, what is more likely to happen will be a great improvement in standards of journalism, play-writing, films, and in many other forms of *intermediaries*, or *interpreters* or *mediators* at a first-class professional level —an improvement that will be demanded by coming generations of better-educated people.

International law is another mediator which has greatly improved since World War II, not because we are better people but because it can now be far better *defined* (Mangore, 1954). The existence of global communication (telephones, telegraphy, airways), of computers and many other *information technologies*, is rendering this increasingly and practically possible. The explosive growth of the international organizations since World War II is one source of evidence (see Mangore, 1954; Europa Year Book, 1967).

5. *Pragmatic theory of meaning* (see Peirce, 1931–35; Gallie, 1952; Cherry, 1966; Mead, 1934). Peirce argued that a sign, standing alone, cannot be said to have any meaning. Its meaning results from somebody's response to it. "Meaning" is not a property of the sign itself, in linguistic sign-usage, but the relation between the sign and the person hearing or seeing (responding to it). Furthermore, the nature of that meaning does not emerge (to any observer) until the responder makes *his* sign, in reply. In simplest terms, if someone says "Good morning", one may respond in several ways, thereby showing that this remark was perceived *as* a sign and that it had a certain meaning *to oneself*. Thus one might reply: "Good morning, George!" (meaning a greeting), or "Go to hell!" (meaning aggravation), or one could totally ignore it (meaning what? Conceit, deafness, rudeness, embarrassment . . . or? Nobody can say). In this pragmatic, or psychological sense, "meaning" involves triadic relations between *sign*, *sign-user* and *concept* signified (see Peirce, Gallie; Morris, 1946).

Peirce then observed that *conversation* involved a continual series of stimulus signs and response signs, each successive one interpreting the preceding one; and, therefore, that it was in the nature of conversation that it need never end. It is always possible to add a further, relevant, remark. Fortunately, conversations are ended by some kind of ritualistic sign (for instance, "Goodbye!").

This pragmatic view of meaning is as relevant to psychology as the semantic view is to linguistics. Linguists are concerned with the customary usages of language by whole populations, rather than with momentary use by individuals. They speak of "meaningful sentences", and even of "meaningless sentences" (e.g. Noam Chomsky's example: "Colorless green ideas sleep furi-

ously") (Smith, 1966). The two views of meaning are not to be confused.

6. *Communication: syntactics, semantics and pragmatics.* The theory of knowledge, as it has descended from the early empiricists in particular, has evolved into the science today called "*semiotics*", largely under the guidance of Charles Sanders Peirce (Morris, 1946). It is convenient to divide this field into three related branches.

(a) *Syntactics.* Signs, themselves, their classifications and their orderings, without reference to meaning.

(b) *Semantics* (q.v.). The formal relations between signs and their designata (signified concepts as in mathematics, logic, linguistic theory, and so on).

(c) *Pragmatism.* Signs and their varied usage, by specific persons, in specific situations. This latter branch (c) concerns psychology especially. Semantics is more the interest of logicians, linguists and others less concerned with specific persons and events. Syntactics is the branch which has received the most elaborate scientific and mathematical attention, which is to be outlined next.

7. *Information theory.* The global strategy of World War II, with its fluid fronts, was greatly dependent upon communication. It forced attention upon two fields of technology, later taken up by industrial needs of post-war conditions: (a) systems of communication capable of handling great quantities of information, at high speeds; and (b) the possibility of machines which could adapt their actions to changing conditions, using "information", and so to carry out seemingly human-like tasks (cybernetics) (Wiener, 1961) which evolved eventually into the practical realizations of the computer control of processes. Both offered challenges to mathematicians to define "information" (Shannon, 1949).

As it has evolved, information theory is a part of syntactics (Cherry, 1966; Shannon, 1949). It concerns only signs, their encoding, their frequencies, and errors in transmission. It is most strictly relevant to well-defined technical systems of telecommunication such as teleprinters. How do such systems "send information"? First, there is an identical keyboard at both ends, having a number of keys N. When in use, some human being presses these keys, one at a time, in sequence, each time sending a coded signal which causes the right key to be selected at the receiving-end machine. The first question answered by the theory is (Shannon, 1949): what are the *conceivably possible* simplest and fewest signals needed to convey the message correctly? It is adequate here to illustrate by using a very reduced keyboard of only $N = 8$ letters, shown below.

	A	B	C	D	E	F	G	H
1st Selection	1	1	1	1	0	0	0	0
2nd Selection	1	1	0	0	1	1	0	0
3rd Selection	1	0	1	0	1	0	1	0

The letters here are in an agreed order. When any letter is selected, the coded signal must first indicate whether it lies to the left or right of the dividing line, by using one of two signs (binary digits; one or nought or, in computer tape, hole or no-hole, and so on). A second selection is then needed, thereby quartering the alphabet A . . . H; then a third selection. Each code-group of three digits here uniquely identifies any one of the keys. (E.g. the code 101 selects C, etc.).

From simple mathematics, the fact that three binary selections are needed arises from the equation $3 = \log_2 8$. If now there are N keys, or letters, the number of 1, 0s (binary digits) needed for each code group would be n, where $n = \log_2 N$.

In practice, however, the various keys or letters are not used with equal frequency. In English, for example, the letter A is used most often, followed by T, E . . . Z. A letter used very frequently is said to convey less information content than a rare one (because it could be *guessed* correctly, more often). The idea of probability (q.v.) is therefore brought in. Suppose these letter probabilities are assembled, and denoted by $p(A)$, $p(B)$

. . . $p(x)$ . . . $p(Z)$, and so on. Then it may be shown that *on an average* (i.e. statistically) the least number of binary signals is H, where

$$H = \text{average of } \log_2 \frac{I}{p(x)} = -\Sigma p(x) \log p(x)$$

binary digits per letter.

Again, in practice, all channels of communication are affected by disturbances known as *noise*, and often the statistical properties of this can be assessed too. In this case, the disturbed signals at the receiving end become distorted and do not specify uniquely the letter selected by the sender; they give only *evidence*. The mathematical theory of inference may then be used, in order to compute the *true* rates of information.

One great contribution made by information theory is guidance to those who are concerned with *coding*, for it is possible to compare and measure the efficiencies of various codes. More advanced treatment of the theory does not concern us here.

8. *Information theory. Relevance to psychology.* The first publications, in the early 1950s, regarding information theory aroused great interest in many fields of social science, including psychology and linguistics, and a burst of applications followed (Jackson, 1953; Cherry, 1966). In particular, it seemed directly relevant to choice-reaction time experiments, and to others where *rates of information* within the human subject were of interest. To a great extent, however, this early promise was not maintained, and indeed it misled a number of workers. For the theory is applicable *numerically* only where the set of signs N and their probabilities are defined and known, and this is true in few fields outside technology. There has been very little development of information theory since the early 1950s, apart from applications to coding theory.

Nevertheless, it would be false to say that the theory is irrelevant to psychology, for it does have some relevance to experimental method, by clarifying certain concepts. Without the greatest care, it may not be very useful as a measuring tool (Broadbent, 1958). For example, the probabilities of signs (letters, words, keys, etc.) *to* a person are subjective probabilities—perhaps rank-ordered but not known numerically. Perhaps the most valuable contributions to psychology have been the stimulus the theory gave to new ideas and experiments and, above all, the means it offered for bringing together, in some better understanding, scientists in several disciplines whose traditional boundaries it has overstepped (Cherry, 1966). See *Cybernetics and psychology: Information theory*.

Bibliography: Bierstedt, R.: Emile Durkheim (includes selected bibliography). London, 1966. Broadbent, D. E.: Perception and communication. London, 1958. Cherry, E. C.: On human communication. Cambridge, Mass. & London, 1957 (2nd ed. 1966). Europa Year Book 1967. London, 1967, etc. Gallie, W. B.: Peirce and pragmatism. Harmondsworth, Middx., 1952. Jackson, W.: Proc. symp. on information theory (London). New York, 1953. See also: Proceedings of three later London symp. (Ed. Colin Cherry). London, 1952, 1955 and 1961. Mangore, G. J.: A short history of international organizations. New York, 1954. Mead, G. H.: Mind, self and society. Chicago, 1934. Morris, C.: Signs, language and behavior. New York, 1946. Peirce, C. S.: The collected papers of Charles Sanders Peirce. Vols. 1 to 6, ed. C. Hartshorne & P. Weiss, Harvard, 1931–35. Pye, L. W. (Ed.): Communications and political development. Princeton, N.J., 1963. Shannon, C. E.: The mathematical theory of information. Illinois, 1949. Smith, A. G. (Ed.): Communication and culture. New York, 1966. Wiener, N.: Cybernetics. New York, ²1961. C. Cherry

Communications, animal. These can be acoustic, olfactory, optical or tactile. They can take place between species or be confined to one. When understood, communication signals can change the behavior of the animal or animal group. Animal communications are used in sexual activity, mating and group formation as well as in the establishment of territory ownership. The courtship songs and dances of birds and insects, the particular odor of social insects (q.v.), the re-establishment of territory by song, e.g. in birds, or by the depositing of excrement or urine by dogs are well known. See *Comparative psychology.*
V.P.

Communication(s) systems. "Communications" is generally taken to mean the interaction of systems by the exchange of signs (q.v.) and signals (q.v.). Communications theory and research study the exchange and processing of information in living creatures, especially man. Information theory (q.v.) as science deals with the quantitative aspect, as engineering with the technical aspect. Communication often involves the interposing of technical systems (telephone, radio). Schematically, it is represented as a chain consisting of input (sender; transmitter), (transmission) channel, interference source and output (receiver). See *Communication.*
K.W.

Communicator. In spiritualism (q.v.): the deceased person who is said to be communicating with the sitter (q.v.) at a séance (q.v.) through the medium (q.v.). J.B.

Community. A term applied by F. Tönnies to social systems and their genesis. The word community denotes social groups which, through firm bonds between their members (cohesion, cohesiveness, q.v.) seek spontaneously to achieve common objectives, which frequently have emotional overtones (e.g. family, religious groups). Society is a more complex form which develops from communities. W.D.F.

Community feeling (syn. *Communal spirit*). In Adler's individual psychology the force counteracting the egotistic desire for power; community feeling maintains the individual's ties with the community (F. Tönnies): recent research in developmental psychology (R. A. Spitz, J. Bowlby) points to its origins in the mother-child relationship (basic trust).

Bibliography: Bowlby, J.: The nature of the child's role to his mother. Int. J. Psychoanal., 1958, *39*, 350–73. Spitz, R. A.: The smiling response: a contribution to the ontogenesis of social relations. Genet. Psychol. Monogr., 1946, *34*, 57–125. W.Sc.

Comparative judgment. See *Judgment, comparative.*

Comparative psychology. Students of human behavior in increasing numbers are making use of the greater tractability of non-human species in order to make credible comparisons with problems of human organization and conduct. They do so, whether their essential motivation is practical, therapeutic, or frankly academic, in order to further knowledge and to increase the comfort of men. From reports appearing in the literature, it can be seen that there is a continual re-working of old ground and a ceaseless confirmation of past work, in addition to the daily advance of comparative methods into new fields of research.

The use of animal subjects to further understanding about human beings, though historically old, is at best a compromise; like all compromise solutions it has both advantages and disadvantages. Its advantages lie directly in the basic genetic and environmental controls that can be exercised, the animals providing the investigator with subjects of known heredity and nurture, and possessing homogeneity of those elements, features and functions under examination. They are exemplars of types suitable for analysis which would be unlikely to be found by accident; it is possible to produce in them characteristics which it would be ethically improper (on any criterion of moral action) to produce in humans. The price paid, however, is high, for no matter how expert he may become, the comparative practitioner cannot communicate directly with the subject of his study. Imperfect though it may be, language is the pre-eminent form of human communication, and no equivalent facility is found among the forms of communication (zoosemiotics) available to infra-human species (see, however, Drewe *et al.*, 1970; Goodall, 1965; Thorpe, 1967). To a limited extent, the inability to communicate is compensated for by elaborate investigatory methodologies (common to all studies of behavior) which

give credence to conclusions derived from assumptions about the motivation, purpose and intention of observable and measurable action.

Space does not permit anything but the briefest outline of the use made of animals in all branches of biology and in those areas of research whose development would be greatly impaired without their unique contribution (Fox, 1968; Lane-Petter, 1963). Likewise, lack of space does not allow descriptions of the history or origins of comparative psychology found in ethology (Lorenz, 1970), ecology (Scott, 1958), comparative anatomy (e.g. neuroanatomy) (Zeman & Innes, 1963), and so on. Subjects such as animal husbandry (Lane-Petter, 1963), experimental methodology (Gay, 1968), biometrics and instrumentation must be thought of as subjects in their own right. It is hoped that the few topics it is possible to indicate will serve to illustrate the breadth of the subject and the difficulties of including a discussion of its participation in areas like dentistry and organ transplants which at first sight appear to be particularly and almost exclusively "human". For example: knowledge of *maternal behavior* in humans has benefited considerably from observation of both the epimeletic (care-giving) and et-epimeletic (care-seeking) behavior of animals (Fox, 1968; Grota & Ader, 1969). It is within the orbit of this initial relationship, and largely out of the interactions of mother and offspring, that the vital determining characteristics of the individual's adult social and physical behavior are established (Fox, 1968; Levine, 1966). Although social behavior is clearly discriminable from maternal behavior, there is at least a temporary overlap between the two when the nuclear family (with or without the fathering male) has a structure which arises from the interactions of its members, and can be said to constitute a social group with a greater cohesion within it than there is outside it (Dimond, 1970). The family ties determining the group grow progressively less strong as the offspring mature, or are rejected by the mother, and the interactions between individuals widen to include not only the immediate peer group but members of other families. At this point intra- as well as inter-group play (Jewell & Loizos, 1966) appear to cause the animal to become aware of its physical capacities as well as the behavioral characteristics of its play objects.

Perhaps the greatest use of animal subjects is in the study of the effects of drugs (Kumar et al., 1970; Steinberg, 1965; Steinberg et al., 1964; Thompson & Schuster, 1968), particularly in the study of those chemicals which affect such biological processes as (preferred) food and water intake, fear reactions (Wilson & Dinsmoor, 1970) and other functions which arise within a behavioral repertoire instead of in a straightforward physiological context. In recent years these studies have been exemplified and epitomized by comparative investigations outlining the effects of the so-called psycho-active and psycho-tropic drugs. The study of sedation, memory and learning at all levels, whether by a progressive or consensus approach (Miller, 1964), requires the use of (and in many cases the sacrifice of) many individuals and species. Despite the anthropomorphic implications and ultimate application of the research, the infra-human species plays an indisputably primary role in this context. Animals, too, figure largely in studies of nutrition. Although it is not true to say (and never has been) that "an animal is what an animal eats" (Lat, 1969), there is no doubt that the physical, neurological and behavioral characteristics of an organism can be altered by dietary manipulation (Brozek, 1962; Lat, 1969; Worden, 1968). The existing and encroaching imbalances of human ecology add an urgent necessity to the systematic appraisal of this kind of work. In the field of genetic research, though it is not confined to animals, it is in the interaction of the genotype with its environment that many exciting applications are to be found. The credibility of the basic laws of inheritance is increased by the study

of organisms whose genetic expression is modifiable and whose behavior repertoire contains an element of volition or choice. Genetics is acquiring a profound influence in all branches of biology where the homogeneity of material, referred to in the opening paragraph, is proving to be vital. The efficient way of obtaining such "pure" stocks is by the techniques of special breeding and selection and these methods cannot be used with, or on, humans.

It is necessary, also, to consider the vast contribution made by infra-human species to the semi-permanent modifications of conduct called learning. The largest single application of comparative psychology (if one is to judge from reports) is in behavioral modifications of all kinds, from simple habituation to the habit complexities of primate intelligence. The classical conditioning experiments of Pavlov and his colleagues, the recent successful and developing operant procedures of the Skinnerians and the hybrid paradigms of the behavior therapists (Davison, 1968; Eysenck & Rachman, 1965; Stampfl, 1966; Wolpe, 1958) have all established the fundamental principles of their systems by direct experiments on animals, and it is likely that crucial differences between them will be resolved in a like manner.

Animals are used in numerous forms of research for many reasons, some of which are good because they enhance the knowledge of humans about themselves and lead to an understanding of problems and malfunctions which it would be impossible to clarify without their analogous contribution. Apart from those subjects already referred to, there are many others in comparative psychology which have a particular human relevance. For instance, there are the studies of isolation stress, immobilization stress (Mikhail & Broadhurst, 1965), and punishment (Bandura, 1970) which have an immediate application in penology, in the study of institutionalization and in all forms of aversive treatment. Associated with penology, discipline and social control is the study of the behavioral factors involved in addictive processes (Nicholls, 1963) and in deviancy of all kinds, either of which may involve immediate or postponed gratification (Eysenck, 1963). There is also the area of frustration and drive energization (Amsel, 1962), the abnormal concomitant of which may be self-directed or externalized aggression (Fox, 1968; Lorenz, 1970). Another form of investigation lies in those studies whose psychological/behavioral component is not so clear. In some of these, non-physiological factors appear to combine with structural elements to produce pathologies of anatomy which are, in turn, associated with deteriorations in the functional efficiency of behavior. This type of study is most clearly illustrated within the hybrid discipline of psychosomatics, e.g. ulcer studies, anorexia studies (Russell, 1969) and even tumour studies (Matthes, 1963), where researchers employ animal subjects chosen or pre-treated on a basis which emphasizes and permits evaluation of the contribution made by their functional rather than by their physical capabilities.

The foregoing emphasizes, and the few examples illustrate, that research in comparative psychology assumes a relationship between man and animals. Such an assumption, which requires only that man be located on a phylum appropriate to him and to his progenitors, has dangers, not the least of which lies in the reciprocal errors of under- and over-generalization. These include the easy assumption of complete behavioral similarity between human and non-human species, and also the misleading anecdotes which evaluate animal behavior within a man-orientated anthropomorphic, mentalistic and self-relevant system. All must be avoided if investigations employing non-human subjects are to make an effective contribution to what is advanced as "the proper study of mankind".

Finally, a caution: an informed and ceaseless vigilance is necessary to ensure that a balance is maintained between the needs of science, the health of mankind and the inalienable dignity of the infra-human species. If the first and second can be achieved only at the cost of the third plus a loss in the humanity of those using them, comparative psychology and its practitioners may well share in scientific advance and benefit to the world of men, but may, in the process, lose something more precious than they gain.

Bibliography: Amsel, A.: Frustrative nonreward in partial reinforcement and discrimination learning: Some recent history and a theoretical extension. Psychol. Rev., 1962, 69, 306–28. Bandura, A.: Principles of behavior modification. London, 1970. Brozek, J.: Soviet studies on nutrition and higher nervous activity. Anns. N.Y. Acad. Sci., 1962, 93, Art. 15, 665–714. Davison, G. C.: Systematic desensitization as a counterconditioning process. J. Abnormal Psychol., 1968, 73, 91–9. Dimond, S. J.: The social behaviour of animals. London, 1970. Drewe, E. A., Ettlinger, G., Milner, A. D. & Passingham, R. E.: A comparative review of the results of neuropsychological research on man and monkey. Cortex, 1970, VI, 129–63. Eysenck, H. J.: Emotion as a determinant of integrative learning: an experimental study. Behav. Res. Therap., 1963, 1, 197–211. Id. & Rachman, S. J.: The causes and cures of neurosis. San Diego, Calif., 1965. Fox, M. W.: Abnormal behavior in animals. Philadelphia, 1968. Gay, W. L.: Methods of animal experimentation, Vols. 1, 2 & 3. New York, 1968. Goodall, J.: Chimpanzees of the Gombe Stream Reserve. In: De Vore, I. (Ed.): Primate behavior, New York, 1965. Grota, L. J. & Ader, R.: Continuous recording of maternal behaviour in Rattus Norvegicus. Anim. Behav., 1969, 17, 722–9. Jewell, P. A. & Loizos, C. (Eds): Play, exploration and territory in mammals. London, 1966. Kumar, R., Stolerman, I. P. & Steinberg, H.: Psychopharmacology. Ann. Rev. Psychol. 1970, 21. Lane-Petter, W. (Ed.): Animals for research. London, 1963. Lat, J.: Nutrition, learning and adaptive capacity. In: Kare, M. R. & Maller, O. (Eds): The chemical senses and nutrition. Baltimore, 1967. Id.: Some mechanisms of the permanent effect of short-term, partial and total overnutrition in early life upon the behaviour in rats. Proc. VIII, International Congress of Nutrition, Prague, 1969, Symposium on Nutrition and Behaviour. Levine, S.: Infantile stimulation and adaptation to stress. In: Endocrines and the Central Nervous System. Association for Research in Nervous and Mental Disease. Baltimore, 1966. Lorenz, K.: Studies in animal and human behaviour, Vol. 1. London, 1970. Matthes, T.: Experimental contribution to the question of emotional reactions on the growth of tumours in animals. Proc. Eighth Anti-Cancer Congress, 1963, 3, 1617. Mikhail, A. A. &

Broadhurst, P. L.: Stomach ulceration and emotionality in selected strains of rats. J. Psychom. Res., 1965, *8*, 477. Miller, N. E.: The analysis of motivational effects illustrated by experiments on amylobarbitone sodium. In: Steinberg, H., de Reuck, A. V. S. & Knight, J. (Eds): Animal behaviour and drug action, London, 1964, 1–18. Nicholls, J. R.: A Procedure which produces sustained opiate-directed behavior (morphine addiction) in the rat. Psychol. Rep., 1963, *13*, 895–904. Russell, G. F. M.: Metabolic, endocrine and psychiatric aspects of anorexia nervosa. Scientific Basis of Medicine, Annual Reviews, London, 1969, 236–55. Scott, J. P.: Animal behavior. Chicago, 1958. Stampfl, T. G.: Implosive therapy: The theory, the subhuman analogue, the strategy and the technique. In: Armitage, S. G. (Ed.): Behavior modification techniques in the treatment of emotional disorders. V. A. Publication, Battle Creek, Michigan, 1966. Steinberg, H.: Methods of assessment of psychological effects of drugs in animals. In: Marks, J. & Pare, C. M. B. (Eds): The scientific basis of drug therapy in psychiatry. Oxford, 1965. Id., de Reuck, A. V. S· & Knight, J. (Eds): Animal behaviour and drug action. London, 1964. Thompson, T. & Schuster, C. R.: Behavioral pharmacology. Englewood Cliffs, New Jersey, 1968. Thorpe, W. H.: Animal vocalization and communication. In: Millikan, J. & Darley, F. (Eds): Brain mechanisms underlying speech and language. New York, 1967. Wilson, E. H. & Dinsmoor, J. A.: Effect of feeding on "fear" as measured by passive avoidance in rats. J. comp. physiol. Psychol., 1970, *70*, 431–6. Wolpe, J.: Psychotherapy by reciprocal inhibition. Stanford, 1958. Worden, A. N.: Nutritional factors and abnormal behavior. In: Fox, M. W. (Ed.): Abnormal behavior in animals. Philadelphia, 1968. Zeman, W. & Innes, J. R. M.: Craigie's neuroanatomy of the rat. New York, 1963.

H. C. Holland

Compensation. Covering up, or making up for conscious or unconscious inferiority or insecurity in regard to social, family and individual ideals. First described by A. Adler (q.v.) as a dynamic process resulting from innate "organ inferiority", and later extended by C. G. Jung to cover the relation of the unconscious (q.v.) to the conscious (q.v.), and of dreams to waking life in general. In personality psychology, Lersch distinguishes *direct compensation* ("of the first order")— which corresponds to Adler's concept— from the compensation of the *next chance* ("of the second order"), which G. W. Allport terms "substitution". Unsuccessful compensation or "as-if compensation" ("of the third order") occurs when the adjustment is made possible by a secondary advantage by illness (q.v.) with neurotic symptoms. Recent research classifies compensation among the general biological control processes.

Bibliography: Lersch, P.: Aufbau der Person. Munich, ⁸1962. Orgler, H.: Alfred Adler: the man and his work. London, 1947. Menninger, K.: Regulatory devices of the ego under major stress. Int. J. Psychoanal., 1954, *35*, 1–14.   *W.Sc.*

Complementary colors. The hues which do not produce any intermediate colors when they are mixed but only different degrees of saturation of one of the members of the pair and—in corresponding proportions— an achromatic or grey color. In general those colors are complementary which lie at the extremities of any diameter in the Hering or Ostwald color circles, in particular the color pairs red and green, and yellow and blue.

G.K.

Complementary phenomena. A collective concept for the phenomenon that incomplete visual groups of stimuli are restructured into totalities. In contrast to the purely physiological stimuli images on the retina, there are complementary phenomena such as the "filling up", enlarging and completing of the perceptual field: e.g. the completion of the blind spot (q.v.), of the visual field in hemianopsia (q.v.), in modal phenomena, and in the overlapping of opaque images. The phenomenon of perceptual reliability is explained by gestalt laws such as pregnance, compactness, similarity, proximity, etc. (see *Ganzheit*). Familiarity of experience also plays a part.

Bibliography: Metzger, W.: Figural-Wahrnehmung. In: Hdb. der Psychol., Vol. 1/1, Göttingen, 1966, 693–744. Michotte, A., Thinès, G. & Crabbe, G.: Die amodalen Ergänzungen von Wahrnehmungsstrukturen. In: Hdb. der Psychol., Vol. 1/1. Göttingen, 1966, 978–1002.   *P.S. & R.S.*

Completion test. A variety of task in which a unit has to be completed: e.g. a gap in a sentence, word or picture; the missing part of a sentence or a story; missing numbers, figures or pictures, in a series, etc. The factorial significance of such tests varies according to whether completion occurs as a result of logical reflection, of imagination or of learned mechanisms.   *R.M.*

Complex. 1. In the older psychology of thought, a complex is a group of memory contents which are especially strongly associated, and originate during learning, e.g. when individual components of a series are apprehended as a group.   *R.Hä.*
2. Something (e.g. a theory) possessing distinguishable parts structurally related so as to allow the whole a certain unity.
3. A concept introduced by C. G. Jung (q.v.) into psychoanalytical terminology, and later extended to other fields. It is used to indicate the presence of ideas and thoughts which are repressed and have a strong emotional charge. It is because of this emotional charge that complexes which remain in the unconscious influence a person's behavior. Other writers speak of complexes when they merely wish to indicate overemphasized ideas, without necessarily referring to the supposition that a complex only has some effect when it has been repressed into the unconscious.   *J.L.I.*

Complex psychology. C. G. Jung called his own psychoanalytical approach a "psychology of complexes". The most important differences between this and the psychoanalysis (q.v.) of Freud are: the assumption of a collective unconscious, the process of individuation (q.v.) in a person's development, the assumption of general psychic energy instead of psychosexual energy (see *Libido*) as in the case of Freud, and also the use of compensatory and complementary relations to explain the development of the ego (q.v.).   *J.L.I.*

Complex qualities. A term used by Krueger (Leipzig school, q.v.) with reference to wholes which do not possess a readily partitioned structure. The term is particularly applied to emotions.   *C.D.F.*

Complication experiment. A classical experiment designed to illustrate the so-called *law of prior entry*, which states that of two simultaneous stimuli the one which is being attended to will be perceived as having occurred first. In the complication experiment the task was to read the position of a rotating clock hand (or pendulum) at the moment a bell was sounded. The reading apparently differs measurably according to whether attention is directed to the visual or auditory stimulus.   *G.D.W.*

Comprehension test. 1. A test which requires the testee to answer a number of questions set on a (usually short) text in order to show quality, speed and extent of understanding of the subject-matter, or to test various other factors which the text is designed to correspond with. 2. A test in which the testee is asked to describe his response to a given situation.

Compulsive neurotic. A person who is prone to *obsessions* (q.v.) which compel him to perform certain thought rituals or overt actions such as hand-washing, in an attempt to reduce the anxiety level engendered by the unpleasant obessional thoughts. Such people usually score highly on both introversion and neuroticism scales. The term *anancast* is sometimes used synonymously.   *R.H.*

Computational linguistics (syn. *Mechanolinguistics*). The use of automata theory and/or computers themselves to aid research into the structure of language, or to study specific tasks such as the possibilities of machine translation between a pair of natural languages.

Bibliography: Gross, M.: On the equivalence of models of language used in the fields of mechanical translation and information retrieval, Infor. Storage and Retrieval, 1964, *2*, 43–57. Lamb, S. M.: The digital computer as an aid to linguistics. Language, 1961, *37*, 382–412. Turner, G. J. & Mohan, B. A.: A linguistic description and computer program for children's speech. London, 1970.   *J.C.*

Computer, electronic. A program-controlled, information-storing and processing device. A primarily electrical and electronic system which permits the input and output of data from peripheral appliances (e.g. magnetic tape units) and their processing in a central processor. The latter comprises the computing and control mechanism and storage facilities for data and programs. Computer programs are coded instructions which have to be written in program language (a computer or machine code). Computers are outstanding for their high speed in processing, immense storage capacity, extensive operational range and variable planning possibilities. They are used whenever large amounts of information have to be processed rapidly and frequently, e.g. in evaluating experiments, commercial accounts and process controls. See *Communication; Cybernetics and psychology.*

Bibliography: Cluley, J. C.: Electronic computers. London, 1967.   *K.D.G.*

Computer language. See *Machine language.*

Conation. 1. A term (A. Ward, W. McDougall) for purposive mental drive or striving toward action. Conative forces can appear as "blind impulse" or as purposeful effort. **2.** Voluntary activity.   *I.L.*

Concentration. 1. A special form of attention (q.v.); according to Mierke (1966) disciplined organization and fixation of subjective attention on the grasping and shaping of matter containing meaning and value. The following outward aspects may be observed: vital force, and energy impulses in the person concerned, maturity and practice in paying attention (Mierke); volitional control (N. Ach); conscious restriction of the field of attention (W. Wundt, N. Ach); focusing motive forces by determination and structuring (*Gestaltung*) (A. Wellek); aiming for an excellent, well-planned performance, and finding functional links to develop the idea or thoughts (Mierke). Concentration is dependent on physiological factors such as fatigue (E. Kraepelin), state of satiation (D. Katz), hormone balance (G. Venzmer), and sound functioning of the central nervous system (E. Kleist), as well as on mental and other factors such as interest, general outlook and tradition (E. Spranger), or situation (Mierke). The concept of concentration is taken from educational psychology, where it represents the requisite condition for optimal cognitive achievement. Concentration is prominent in techniques in which the field of consciousness is closely restricted: e.g. in hypnosis (q.v.) and autogenic training (q.v.), which I. H. Schultz calls "concentrative relaxation". In yoga (q.v.), concentration is the first stage leading to meditation (q.v.) and profound contemplation. See *Concentration tests.*

Bibliography: Mierke, K.: K. fähigkeit und K. schwäche. Berne-Stuttgart, 1966.   *E.U.*

2. In Pavlovian theory, "concentration" (i.e. of excitation, indifferent stimulations, inhibition, etc.) refers to the limitation of certain neural processes to a certain area of the cortex. Pavlov speaks in this connection of a "law of concentration of excitation": "the irradiated excitation gathers along certain lines and toward certain foci".

Bibliography: Pavlov, I. P.: Lectures on conditioned reflexes. Vol. 1. New York & London, 1928.

Concentration tests. Methods generally classified as performance tests, and designed to measure concentration, as a rule demand continuous and sustained attention in dealing with optical or acoustical material, and are characterized—at least in theory—by their independence from intelligence (q.v.). The study of the dependence of concentration on the kind of stimulus field on the one hand and on intrapsychic factors on the other is the object of perception experiments. Three kinds of concentration tests can be distinguished: 1. *Exercises in addition* (KLT, KBT, Pauli test); 2. *Cross-out tests* of letters (d2, Bourdon test), figures, or meaningless symbols (Meili); 3. *Selection* and *sorting* exercises (KVT).

Apart from the Pauli test, the *concentration performance test* (KLT) developed by Düker and standardized by Lienert (1959) represents the best-known method. In it 250 simple additions and subtractions have to be completed in thirty minutes. The evaluation based on the number done, quality, the percentage of errors and their quotient is economical and objective. Standard values (age, sex, employment and school) are available for reference. Reliability criteria and validity (q.v.) were checked several times and proved satisfactory. In contrast with KLT, the *concentration-stress* test developed by Kirsch (1959) and used for assessing the ability of future pilots consists of arithmetical exercises with *coded* figures. In the *concentration-time test* (KVT) devised by Abels (1954), sixty cards have to be sorted into four groups. Scoring the test involves the evaluation of time and errors taken together, distinguishing between different kinds of errors and recording the point at which they were made. Reliability and validity checks made so far show that the method can be recommended (Bartenwerfer, 1966). Among the *cross-out tests*, the "d2" by Brickenkamp (1962) is the most important. Letters with certain reference marks have to be crossed out. Evaluation criteria are total number of exercises worked, number and percentage of errors, their distribution, and the range of variation shown. Standards are available for four age groups from 15 to 59. The coefficients of stability, equivalence and inner consistency have proved very

satisfactory; the validity of the method was established in several studies made by the writer.

Bibliography: Abels, D.: Konzentrations-Verlaufstest (KVT). Handweisung. Göttingen, [2]1961. Bartenwerfer, H.: Allgemeine Leistungstests. In: R. Heiss (Ed.): Hdb. der Psychol., Vol. 6. Göttingen, [2]1966, 385–410. Brickenkamp, R.: Aufmerksamkeitsbelastungstest (d2). Handanweisung. Göttingen, 1962. Düker, H. & Lienert, G. A.: Konzentrations-Leistungstest (KLT). Handanweisung. Göttingen, 1965.   G.P.

Concept (Ger., *Begriff*). The "categorization of objects and events on the basis of features and relationships which are either common to the objects perceived or are judged to be so by the individual" (K. Foppa). Features essential to the concept are termed "relevant", those which are unimportant, "irrelevant". Usually a concept is given a symbol (q.v.), a name. The word, therefore, is not the concept itself but only a symbol.

Concept formation as a process of development from childhood to adolescence takes place by way of "qualitative new acquisitions" (Vygotsky). Various phases can be distinguished. Vygotsky (1962) describes three (each of which is divided into stages): (*a*) The child unites diverse concrete objects in groups under a common "family name" and on the basis of external relationship. (*b*) He forms "potential concepts" by establishing objective relationships and connections, "uniting and generalizing single objects", "singling out certain common attributes". This is objective and connective thinking. (*c*) He considers the elements "outside the actually existing bond" between objects, "detaches", "abstracts" and "isolates the individual elements". He then attains to the formation of genuine concepts. Words are integral to the first two developing processes and maintain their guiding function in the third. Similar phases are found in Piaget's schema of concept development. The term is also applied to the process of abstraction and generalization of qualities or properties in any individual conceptualization. See *Child psychology; Piaget.*

Concept centers: areas of the cerebral cortex in which the concepts are said by some to be "localized". (*Conceptual nervous system*, however, refers to a hypothetical model or construct used to study the neural system.)

Bibliography: Bruner, J. S., Goodnow, J. J. & Austin, G. A.: A study of thinking. New York, 1956. Vygotsky, L. S.: Thought and language. Cambridge, Mass., 1962.

H.-J.A.

Concept progress (abb. *v*). The (median) number of added concepts per teaching *step* (q.v.) occurring in the basal text (q.v.) (basal concepts) along a teaching path in a teaching program (q.v.). If z is the median number of basal concepts which appear in a teaching step, then v/z is called the concept concision, $1-v/z$ the concept redundancy. The magnitudes v and z can be illustrated by the Anschütz-diagram.

Bibliography: Anschütz, H.: Über die Verteilung der semantischen Information in Lehrprogrammtexten. GrKG 1965, *6*, 1–10.   *H.F.*

Conceptual model. See *Model thought.*

Concert pitch. An international standard of pitch used by musicians based on the "normal-a" of 440 Hz.   *C.D.F.*

Condensation. In psychoanalysis, the term refers to the fusion of two or more ideas in the unconscious giving rise to a single idea in the conscious mind. This process is supposed to occur particularly in dreams, where several elements in the *latent content* are represented by a single detail in the *manifest content*, e.g. a character appearing in the conscious part of a dream may be derived from the fused memories of several different people, real and fictional. Thus the dream itself is thought to be meager by comparison to the vast complex of unconscious ideas which are presumed to underlie it, and the analysis of a dream lasting only a few minutes

may take many hours. Certain *neologisms* and distorted words such as "alcoholidays" are also described in terms of condensation.

G.D.W.

Conditioned inhibition (syn. *Inhibitory potential*). According to the hypothesis put forward by C. L. Hull in his "mathematico-deductive" theory of learning, stimuli and stimuli traces which are associated with the reduction of reactive inhibition (q.v.), i.e. with the termination of some activity (the cessation of a response), themselves acquire the tendency to produce some inhibition. The inhibition learnt in this way is said to be conditioned (*SIR*). The reactive and conditioned inhibition together form the inhibition potential (*IR*).

Bibliography: Hull, C. L.: Principles of behavior. New York, 1943.   *L.B.*

Conditioned reflex. See *Conditioning, classical and operant.*

Conditioned response. See *Conditioning, classical and operant.*

Conditioning, classical and operant. At all phylogenetic levels, behavioral acts occur without a specific genetic or physiological background; they have biological utility and rely entirely on a particular sensory event. These acts, or segments of performance, are called *reflexes;* and the systematic way these are brought under alternative stimulus control forms the subject-matter of learning (q.v.)—perhaps the cardinal problem of psychology.

One method of accomplishing control, and of describing the data of such modification of behavior on conceptual and physical levels, is conditioning. Conditioning was and, although theoretically sophisticated, still is an experimental procedure for bringing natural reflexes within experimental manipulation. It can be shown that, by pairing a reflex with a neutral intra-organismic event or exteroceptive stimulus, it is possible to establish the capacity of the latter with the capabilities of the former. When evoked by the "normal" stimulus, the reflex is called an "unconditioned reflex"; when elicited by a provided (i.e. not "normal") stimulus it is called a "conditioned reflex": more generally, the term "reflex" having fallen from fashion, the outcome is known as a "conditioned response". Both the procedure and the terminology stem from the work of Pavlov (q.v.), whose experimental methods are standard and definitive (classical) and whose conceptualizations remained unquestioned for several decades.

Responses within the repertoire of many species may be conditioned by the classical method (Hilgard, 1940), but it has limitations apart from the response capacity of the organism. Once established, not only is the CR an imperfect replication of the UCR but it is subject to interference by a number of factors. Its evocation, e.g., is dependent upon the temporal contiguity of the CS and the UCS, the bond which is hypothesized to exist between them being reinforced (strengthened) by some aspect of their association. On the other hand, the reaction is progressively weakened by inhibition of stimulus and response, by stimulus equivalences and the unfavorable biochemical or physiological status of the organism, until extinction (cessation) ensues: although the phenomenon of "spontaneous recovery" suggests that the established bond may persist beyond its elicitability. Classical conditioning appears to be largely confined to reactions which originate in the autonomic nervous system (ANS), and is difficult to demonstrate in "spinal reflexes" and those cases which require a high degree of mediation. There are also inter-individual differences in several of the parameters of the response which make "differential conditionability" a meaningful concept. A feature of the conditioned response is generalization. A response made to a particular CS will be partially elicited by stimuli dimensionally similar to it. Such stimulus generalization is both a boon and a curse; without it perception of the world would be limited (stimuli and events are rarely, if ever, identical) but, alternatively, omnipresent fear would be absent. Indeed, a number of treatments (Wolpe & Lazarus, 1966) of people (victims of severely traumatic occurrences, coupled with the endowment of a labile nervous system) possess rationales based upon generalization. The gradients of responses which emerge from generalization can be understood by an appeal to the principles involved, and their employment in the removal (i.e. extinction) of pathological symptoms is a corollary. The way in which uncontrolled generalization is limited is due to discrimination. Initially emerging from the classical situations of Pavlov (within the context of a method of contrasts), with whom it is therefore historically linked, the nature and use of discrimination and its effects on the shape of generalization, have recently received attention within the context of operant conditioning (see Gilbert & Sutherland, 1969).

1. Instrumental conditioning. The shortcomings and constraints of the classical procedure with its dependence upon experimenter-controlled programs of reinforcement, led to the first deviation from the paradigm of Pavlov. Called instrumental conditioning, and historically associated predominantly with Bekhterev, it differed from the classical form only insofar as the reinforcement, upon which the conditioned bond rested, occurred after the response had been made. Because of this order, the response was said to be "instrumental" in obtaining the reinforcement. The instrumental response could be strengthened in one or admixtures of four different ways: by positive reward, by escape, by avoidance, or by higher order training; the first two represent primary reinforcements, and the second two, secondary.

2. Operant conditioning. This form of learning which, as a theory or principle of learning,

has existed for a bare thirty years (see, however: Bitterman, 1969; Skinner, 1938, 1948a, 1950, 1966), differs from classical conditioning in a number of important ways (Hoffman, 1966). It does not differ, except methodologically, as distinctly from instrumental conditioning (Honig, 1966); although a true Skinnerian (Skinner being the principal exponent of the method), while allowing that operant conditioning deals with instrumental behavior in the overall sense, would deny any useful similarity between them. Operant conditioning examines the consequences of largely voluntary and unprompted actions; consequences which are evaluated by the vigor of the action after it has been associated with reinforcement. Vigor of action (strength of learning) is characterized by the rate of elicitation of the behavior being studied, and the reinforcement which leads to its increase. Likewise, a contingent event is said to be non-reinforcing or punishing (Azrin, 1966) if it leads to a decrease in response rate. The terminology of operant conditioning lies in the language of behavioral response (the operant[s]) rather than of the reflex, and it is primarily concerned with those acts which are mediated by the central nervous system. The data of the technique are the rates of responding, and the changes which occur in them, produced by the organism within a response frame of reference set by itself and its physiological limitations. Responding can be varied by arranging that reinforcement conform to schedules dependent upon fixed or changeable intervals of time, or permanent or temporary ratios of action (Ferster & Skinner, 1957). By these "fixed" or "variable" intervals and ratios, their combination into sequential or concurrent assemblies ("multiple schedules"), the experimenter can produce and maintain behavior of specific dimensionality, and permit analysis of it to a fine degree.

One of the costs of the freedom of operant conditioning is the phenomenon of superstition. "Superstition" is the term given to the behavior, usually transient, which occurs under conditions of its consistent correlation with reinforcement. It is usually the terminal behavior of adventitious or arbitrary reinforcement contingencies; whether they be primary or secondary, positive or negative. It is likely to be thought a stereotyped act when no explanation or purpose is apparent. The reader is referred to Herrnstein (1966) for the way in which human superstitions are formed and transmitted, and the way in which animal superstitions differ (speech in the former case circumventing the ordinary process of conditioning) (Honig, 1966).

A number of supporters of the principles of operant conditioning and the views of Skinner (1950) have been attracted by the way in which "statistics" and "the planned experiment" are questioned, and the "wasteful" process of formal hypothesizing is abjured, as principles of planning. In operant conditioning, flexibility is emphasized, and the manipulation of variables in a developing situation is encouraged. Skinner's views on methodology are at once a credo of scientific method, a sensitive means of studying the individual, and an answer to his critics who complained that (by emptying it) he has degraded the organism to the level of the machine. The limitations of the single response datum (rate) are discussed by Honig (1966).

3. *Similarity with a difference.* The essential similarity between classical and operant conditioning has led students to pose questions about the parsimony or necessity of more than one principle to account for this type of learning. It has been suggested that instrumental conditioning can account for most of the facts of operant conditioning. The Skinnerian denial of this viewpoint remains unconvincing: Skinner argues that behavior "operates" on the environment to *produce* reinforcement and, therefore, that the term "operant" conditioning is appropriate.

But, despite the similarities outlined, differences are considerable. Many forms of "operant" conditioning are only effective after the response in question has first been established by classical methods. An example of this type is seen in the escape/avoidance paradigm, in which avoidance takes place only after the administration of the aversive stimulus and its association with the conditioned stimulus. See Sidman (1966) and Herrnstein (1969) for a discussion of the two-factor theory advanced by Mowrer (1946) to account for aversive learning. Whereas there is no difficulty in establishing most autonomic responses by a simple process of temporal contiguity with an ineffective CS, it is virtually impossible (without deliberate or accidental chaining [Kelleher, 1966]) to do this with ordinary reinforcement in an operant situation.

The differences between operant and classical conditioning appear to give the basis of an answer to the question "What is the difference between conditioning and learning?" It would seem possible to work backwards from classical conditioning to the simpler forms of behavior modification, including habituation and adaptation, and forwards from operant conditioning to mediated responsiveness at all levels of sophistication. (Honig, 1966 et al.; Skinner, 1948b). The view taken of the degree to which the procedures overlap, the different predictions which stem from their acceptance, and the manner in which one may be more heuristic in generating explanations of a comprehensive theory of behavior may depend more on the affiliations and philosophies of the assessor than on true differences in outcome.

Bibliography: Azrin, N. H. & Holz, W. C.: Punishment. In: Honig, W. K. (Ed.): Operant behavior, Ch 9. New York, 1966. Bekhterev, V. M.: Objective Psychologie. Leipzig & Berlin, 1913. Bitterman, M. E.: Thorndike and the problem of animal intelligence. Amer. Psychologist, 1969, 24, 444–53. Evans, R. I.: B. F. Skinner, the man and his ideas. New York, 1968. Ferster, G. B. & Skinner, B. F.: Schedules of reinforcement. New York, 1957. Gilbert, R. M. & Sutherland, N. S.: Animal discrimination learning. London, 1969. Herrnstein, R. J.: Superstition: a corollary of the principles of operant conditioning. In: Honig, W. K. (Ed.): Operant behavior, Ch. 2. New York, 1966. Id.: Method and theory in the study of avoidance. Psychol. Rev. 1969, 76, 49–69. Hilgard, E. R. & Marquis, D. G.: Conditioning and learning. New York, 1940. Hoffman, H. S.: The analysis of discriminated avoidance. In: Honig, W. K. (Ed.): Operant behavior, Ch. 11. New York, 1966. Honig, W. K.: Operant behavior—areas of research and application. New York, 1966. Kelleher, R. T.: Chaining and conditioned reinforcement. In: Honig, W. K. (Ed.): Operant behavior, Ch. 5. New York, 1966. Mednick, S. A.: Learning. Englewood Cliffs, N.J., 1964. Mowrer, O. H. & Lamoreaux, R. R.: Fear as an intervening variable in avoidance conditioning. J. Comp. Psychol. 1946, 39, 29–50. Pavlov, I. P.: The reply of a physiologist to psychologists. Psychol. Rev., 1923, 39, 91–127. Id.: Conditioned reflexes. London, 1927. Sidman, M.: Avoidance behavior. In: Honig, W. K. (Ed.): Operant behavior, Ch. 10. New York, 1966. Skinner, B. F.: The behavior of organisms. New York, 1938. Id.: "Superstition" in the pigeon. J. exp. Psychol., 1948a, 38, 168–72. Id.: Walden Two. New York, 1948b. Id.: Are theories of learning necessary? Psychol. Rev., 1950, 57, 193–216. Id.: Operant behavior. In: Honig, W. K. (Ed.): Operant behavior, Ch. 1. New York, 1966. Watson, J. B.: The place of the conditioned-reflex in psychology. Psychol. Rev. 1916, 23, 89–116. Wolpe, J. & Lazarus, A. A.: Behavior therapy techniques. Oxford, 1966.   H. C. Holland

Conduction. 1. The transmission of nervous impulses through neuron(e)s (see *Axon*). **2.** The transmission of (sound) waves. **3.** The transmission of energy.

Conduction unit. Thorndike's term for the supposed neural mechanism or action system responsible for a specific adaptive behavior.

Conductivity. The capacity for conduction.

Cones. Receptors within the retina which transform light energy into nervous impulses. See *Eye; Visual perception.*

Confact. Behavior acquired as the result of some learning process for a certain situation is transferred to another situation (see *Generalization; Transfer*). According to

Symonds, however, this only happens when both situations contain identical elements.

Bibliography: Symonds, P. M.: The dynamics of human adjustment. New York, 1946.   K.E.P.

Confidence limits (syn. *Fiducial limits*). A term used to define that area round a statistical value of a sample distribution, in which there is a certain probability that the corresponding parameter (q.v.) of the population (q.v.) is to be found. The size of this area, or distance between its limits, is known as a *confidence interval* (q.v.), and is determined by the standard error.   G.M

Conflict. 1. *Definition of conflict*. Conflict has often been defined as present in an organism when two drives (q.v.) (e.g. hunger and thirst) are simultaneously present. As Haner & Brown (1955) have pointed out, this is illogical, since drive states will conflict only when alternative possibilities of action exist (for instance, water and food are both present, but only one may be chosen). Conflict may more logically be defined as "any pattern of stimulation presented to an organism which has the power to elicit two or more incompatible responses, the strengths of which are functionally equal" (Maher, 1966, p. 138).

2. *The work of Luria*. The first serious experimental study of conflict was carried out by Luria (1932) who devised many conflict situations, both experimental and real-life. For example, he made use of Jung's word-association technique by requiring the subject to give a part response to a generic stimulus (e.g. house-room) and then suddenly introducing an "impossible" stimulus (e.g. moon—?). The existence of conflict was indexed by an increase in reaction time. More generally, he devised the "Luria technique" of the "combined motor method" in which both voluntary and involuntary motor responses, as well as verbal reaction-time, were measured. He distinguished three major

types of conflict, arising respectively from the prevention of excitation from issuing into action ("conflicts of the setting"); from lack of preparedness for reacting ("conflicts of defection"); and from the diversion of suppressed activity into central processes.

3. *The work of Lewin*. The contribution of Luria was overshadowed by the simultaneous work of Lewin (1935) who defined conflict as "a situation in which oppositely directed, simultaneously acting forces of approximately equal strength work upon the individual" (Lewin, 1935, p. 122). He described three basic types of conflict situation (Type I: approach-approach; Type II: approach-avoidance; and Type III: avoidance-avoidance). His major contribution was to apply these notions to the interpretation of the effects of rewards and punishments on behavior. Hence, he distinguished situations involving command with threat of punishment (Type III conflict); command with prospect of reward (Type II); prohibition with threat of punishment (Type II); and prohibition with prospect of reward (Type I).

Lewin's work was extended by Hovland & Sears, who made use of a board with one or two lights of different colors placed in each corner of the board diagonally opposite a start point placed in the middle of the near edge. The subject's task was to move a pointer toward a positive light or away from a negative light. With this apparatus, Hovland & Sears were able to demonstrate Lewin's three types of conflict situation and their effect on motor behavior, as well as the effect of a fourth type of conflict situation (double-approach avoidance, in which positive and negative lights appeared simultaneously in each corner) (Hovland & Sears, 1938; Sears & Hovland, 1941). They demonstrated four kinds of conflict resolution (single, double, or compromise reactions; and blocking of response). Interest in this technique has recently been revived by studies by Epstein and associates.

4. *The work of Miller*. The most complete account of Miller's work on conflict may be

found in Miller (1959). He based his analysis of conflict mainly on the work of Brown (1948) with rats. Brown demonstrated empirically gradients of approach and avoidance in rats running in straight alleys; showed that the heights of the approach and avoidance gradients are modified by the strength of appetitive and noxious drives respectively (as well as other factors); and claimed that the slope of the avoidance gradient is steeper than that of the approach gradient. Thus, conflict between approach and avoidance tendencies will be maximized at the point of

Fig. 2. Parallel gradients of approach and avoidance. (Source: Maher, B.A., The application of the approach-avoidance conflict model to social behavior. *J. Conflict Res.*, 1964, 8, 287–91.)

Fig. 1. A three-dimensional model of conflict and displacement. (Source: Murray, E. J., and Berkun, M. M., Displacement as a function of conflict. *J. abnorm. soc. Psychol.*, 1955, **51**, 47–56.)

intersection of the gradients. From this model, Miller deduced that an approach response would be displaced from the original goal object to an alternative one. Murray & Berkun (1955) extended the analysis of conflict by using a three-dimensional model of conflict to predict displacement (Figure 1). The model involves strength of behavioral tendency, degree of similarity between original and displaced goal, and nearness to original and displaced goal. By means of a three-alley straight maze, they were able to demonstrate displacement as a result of conflict.

5. *Extensions of conflict theory*. Hull (1938)

reinterpreted Lewin's model of conflict to account for the behavior of children, and later (1952) extended Miller's model to account for conflict behavior in free space, regarding detour behavior as a special case of approach-avoidance behavior. Many of the novel predictions made by Hull (1938, 1952) have never been tested.

Williams (1959) and, more recently, Delhees (1968) have made use of Cattell's dynamic calculus model in which conflict is defined as a situation in which opposite attitudes are evoked to statements which have positive loadings on one factor and negative loadings on another, both factors being represented in a particular statement. Attitude (q.v.) strength in such a situation may be measured by various indices (reaction time, number of times each attitude is chosen, and so on).

Maher (1964) has distinguished between spatial and temporal gradients of approach and avoidance and has experimentally demonstrated temporal gradients (Maher *et al.*, 1964). He has also stressed the importance of distinguishing strength of response from probability of response as a dependent variable. Most importantly, he has suggested an alternative model involving parallel rather than intersecting gradients of approach and avoidance, and defined a "zone of conflict", as shown in Figure 2, from which many novel predictions may be made.

Worrell (1963) has related degree of

conflict to intra-individual variability. The person in a state of conflict will possess nearly equally strong response tendencies to a given stimulus situation, and his actual response will therefore vary from one occasion to another even though the stimulus situation is identical. Worrell has stressed the effects of prior experience of conflict in producing conflicting response dispositions which will manifest themselves in a wide range of situations, including objectively non-conflict situations, such as simple reaction time.

Epstein (1962) has produced a modified version of Miller's conflict model in which approach is stronger at the goal than avoidance (the net approach increment, however, declines as the goal is neared). In his model the gradients of approach and avoidance to a simultaneously feared and desired goal refer to drives rather than response tendencies, and the summation of these drive tendencies determines the level of activation. Hence conflict may be indexed by a rise in activation as a function of nearness to the goal, as well as by a decrease in adequacy of performance and a relative increase in strength of approach responses to stimuli of low relevance. Epstein has investigated the validity of his model in real-life conflict situations, such as parachute-jump training and in studies making use of projective techniques (q.v.).

6. *Conflict and psychopathology.* The proposition that experimental neurosis may be produced by demanding more and more difficult discriminations derives, of course, from the original work of Pavlov with dogs; the results of this work have been generalized to explain neurotic behavior in human subjects. A good summary of much of this work will be found in Maher (1966). The so-called "neurotic paradox" (in which behavior persists even though repeatedly punished) has also been explained in terms of conflict theory, involving differential delay of reinforcement and punishment.

7. *Conflict and frustration.* The relationship between conflict and frustration is unclear. Thus, behavior in a frustrating situation has sometimes been explained as resulting from conflict arising in the frustrating situation; whereas it has also been argued that frustration arises as a result of conflict. The differing viewpoints of the relationship have been discussed by Yates (1962, pp. 178–81), who has also proposed a solution to the problem. See *Drive; Frustration; Instinct.*

Bibliography: Brown, J. S.: Gradients of approach and avoidance responses and their relation to motivation. J. comp. physiol. Psychol., 1948, *41*, 450–65. Delhees, K. H.: Conflict measurement by the dynamic calculus model and its applicability in clinical practice. Multivar. behav. Res., 1968 (special issue), 73–96. Epstein, S.: The measurement of drive and conflict in humans: theory and experiment. In: Jones, M. R. (Ed.): Nebraska symposium on motivation. Lincoln, 1962, 127–206. Id. & Fenz, W. D.: Theory and experiment on the measurement of approach-avoidance conflict. J. abnorm. soc. Psychol., 1962, *64*, 97–112. Haner, C. F. & Brown, P. A.: Clarification of the instigation to action concept in the frustration-aggression hypothesis. J. abnorm. soc. Psychol., 1955, *51*, 204–6. Hovland, C. I. & Sears, R. R.: Experiments on motor conflict: I. Types of conflict and their modes of resolution. J. exp. Psychol., 1938, *23*, 477–93. Hull, C. L.: The goal-gradient hypothesis applied to some "field-force" problems in the behavior of young children. Psychol. Rev., 1938, *45*, 271–99. Id.: A behavior system. New Haven, 1952. Lewin, K.: A dynamic theory of personality. New York, 1935. Luria, A. R.: The nature of human conflicts. New York, 1932. Maher, B. A.: The application of the approach-avoidance conflict model to social behavior. J. conflict Resol., 1964, *8*, 287–91. Id.: Principles of psychopathology. New York, 1966. Id., Weisstein, N. & Sylva, K.: The determinants of oscillation points in a temporal decision conflict. Psychon. Sci., 1964, *1*, 13–14. Miller, N. E.: Liberalization of basic S–R concepts: extensions to conflict behavior, motivation, and social learning. In: Koch, S. (Ed.): Psychology: a study of a science. New York, 1959. Murray, E. J. & Berkun, M. M.: Displacement as a function of conflict. J. abnorm. soc. Psychol., 1955, *51*, 47–56. Sears, R. R. & Hovland, C. I.: Experiments on motor conflict: II. Determination of mode of resolution by comparative strengths of conflicting responses. J. exp. Psychol., 1941, *28*, 280–86. Williams, J. R.: A test of the validity of P-technique in the measurement of internal conflict. J. Person., 1959, *27*, 418–37. Worrell, L.: Intraindividual instability and conflict. J. abnorm. soc. Psychol., 1963, *66*, 480–88. Yates, A. J.: Frustration and conflict. New York, 1962.

A. J. Yates

Conflicting behavior. If a stimulus produces two types of behavior simultaneously and if a conflict arises between the two, they can either extinguish one another, alternate (ambivalent behavior), repress or encourage one another, or completely reorientate behavior. If fighting cocks are made simultaneously to want to fight and to run away, they begin to pretend to peck at the ground. See *Instinct; Conflict.*   *V.P.*

Conformity; conformist behavior (conformism versus non-conformism). Behavior or behavioral tendency or attitude which takes its norms, standards, etc., from a reference group. For example, it can be shown even in perception experiments that there is considerably less variance in perceptual judgments among a number of test subjects when interaction is possible.

However, not every approximation of individual behavior to that of a group is conformity. Such adaptation of behavior can, for example, also be explained as *contagion* (imitation of behavior without any pressure from the group), or social facilitation (patterns of behavior, already habitual, are easier to act upon after the observation of models). See *Socialization.*

Conformity also needs to be distinguished from *compliance*, in which an individual yields to behavioral precepts more from obedience. Since different individuals react in varying degrees to the behavior of a reference group, conformity represents a personality variable (see *Group dynamics*). In the case of authoritarian individuals (see *Authoritarian personality*), there is usually more conformity in power-holding groups (see *Group*). Members of minority groups can display conformism in regard to behavioral patterns which, from a general perspective, are non-conformist.

Bibliography: Berg, I. A. & Bass, B. M. (Eds): Conformity and deviation. New York, 1961. Collins, B. E. & Raven, B. H.: Group structure: Attraction, coalitions, communications, and power. In: Lindzey, G. & Aronson, E. (Eds): Handbook of social psychology. Vol. 4, Reading, Mass., 1969.   *H.D.S.*

Congenital. A characteristic originating during the fetal stage or during birth.

Congruence, cognitive. This central term in the interpersonal congruence theory of Secord & Backman (1961) refers to a perceptive-cognitive state which some person desires to reach and maintain and which demands congruence between the following three components: (*a*) a particular point of view relative to the conception which that person has of himself; (*b*) the interpretation of this person's behavior which is relevant to this point of view; (*c*) the opinion of this person about how a second person will behave with regard to the first two components when considering this point of view. It is assumed that the three components are congruent when the behavior of the two persons manifests definitions of the first person's self which imply congruence between the relevant aspects of that conception of the self. The model of cognitive congruence enables predictions to be made about interpersonal attraction. An individual will seek to establish contact with those others who will help him to maintain congruence between the abovementioned components.

Bibliography: Secord, P. F. & Backman, C. W.: Personality theory and the problem of stability and change in individual behavior. An interpersonal approach. Psychol. Rev., 1961, *68*, 21–32.   *A.S.M.*

Connector. A neuron(e) located between other neuron(e)s.

Connotations. Linguistic symbols carry meanings. "Meaning" signifies not only the transmission of neutral subject-matter but the abstract qualities connected with it, e.g. emotional and affective aspects. Hayakawa (1949) used the terms "extensional" and "denotative" for reference to a given subject-matter; he used the terms "intensional" and "*connotative*" for cases where there was conceptual-verbal or emotional resonance ("informative" or "affective" connotations). *Informative* connotations are now usually known as *denotations*, and those which are *affective* are known as *connotations* (Osgood, Suci & Tannenbaum, 1957). By "denotative meaning", Osgood understands that correspondence between non-linguistic and linguistic events which has been established by agreement; and by "connotation" he understands mediating processes as a result of which the meaning of a word loses its firmly defined character and becomes a dynamic process (See *Communication; Semantics.*)

Bibliography: Hayakawa, S. I.: Language in thought and action. New York, 1949; London, 1952. Osgood, C. E. *et al.*: The measurement of meaning. Urbana, Ill., 1957. *H.W.*

Conscience. A term used in several distinct (but related) senses concerning the individual's response to the moral principles and behavioral norms of the social groups of which he is a member, and in particular to refer to "the cognitive and affective processes which constitute an internalized moral governor over an individual's conduct" (Aronfreed, 1968). It may therefore denote *cognitive* processes—awareness of the nature and origin of rules of conduct, and ability to evaluate one's own actions and intentions; avoidance of proscribed behavior, and the tendency to act in ways regarded as meritorious, in the absence of punishment or external reinforcement (the *behavioral* aspect); and *affective* components of morality; that is, feelings of obligation, guilt and remorse. Aronfreed suggests that the term should be restricted to "those areas of conduct where substantial changes of affective (emotional) states have become attached to either actions or their cognitive representations"; in contemporary Western cultures these relate to aggressive and sexual behavior, honesty

cleanliness, truthfulness and respect for authority.

1. *The development of moral values.* Research into the cognitive aspects of conscience has been greatly influenced by Piaget's (1932) studies of the development of morality in children, in which he explored children's attitudes toward the rules of a game (marbles), and also required them to make moral judgments upon social situations presented in the form of stories. Piaget identified two stages of moral development: until he is seven or eight years of age a child regards rules "not only as obligatory, but as inviolable", independent of individuals, and externally imposed by authority. In this phase ("heteronomy"), penalties are seen as the inexorable consequence of infractions of literal rules; the intentions of the offender are not important. This view of morality gradually gives place to a recognition that the justification for rules is the mutual advantage of members of the group and their consent to them ("autonomy"); punishment comes to be regarded as a means of restitution; and the notion of "equity" emerges: i.e. the child tends increasingly to evaluate cases on their merits, taking into account the circumstances and the intentions of the offender; morality is to some extent internalized. Piaget and those who have developed his work (especially Kohlberg, 1969) emphasize maturational processes in moral development linked with (and dependent upon) intellectual development; however, there is evidence of class differences in the attainment of internalization (Harrower, 1934; Lerner, 1937; Aronfreed, 1969), and of substantial individual differences within social-class groups (Morris, 1958).

The psychoanalytic theory of moral development, based mainly on retrospective clinical studies, is in some ways complementary to Piaget's scheme (Peters, 1960), but offers an account of the mechanism of internalization of moral values which emphasizes the role of parent-child interaction; it also attempts to explain why some children develop consciences which are more severe and punitive than those of their parents (Sears *et al.*, 1957).

2. *Behavioral aspects of conscience.* The similarity between the suppression of socially-proscribed behavior (internalization) and passive avoidance conditioning forms the basis of theoretical models intended to explain the mechanism of this form of social learning and the origin of individual differences in the effectiveness of behavioral suppression. It is suggested that avoidance behavior is mediated by conditioned anxiety responses, previously established through the temporal association of forbidden behavior with punishment (Mowrer, 1960). Hence failure to inhibit proscribed behavior may result from resistance to conditioning (Eysenck, 1960), or a more specific inability to form anticipatory responses; alternatively it may result from inadequate socialization. See *Psychopathy; Criminality.*

The schemes proposed by Piaget and Kohlberg, and the psychoanalytic theory of the super-ego, imply the general development, in the individual, of moral values and socially-conforming behavior (Bandura & Walters, 1963). But attempts to demonstrate this have not been very successful. Hartshorne & May (1928) used a battery of tests designed to reflect various forms of dishonesty (particularly lying and cheating) among children of varying ages. The resulting correlations were low, and they concluded that there was no evidence of a general trait of honesty. Although a more sophisticated analysis of their data reveals some degree of generality, a substantial part of the variance of their tests was specific to certain situations (Burton, 1963). Burton offers an explanation in terms of the interaction of two generalization gradients—one relating to stimulus elements, the other to verbal mediation. The extent to which parents promote both forms of generalization by appropriate methods of child training and verbal explanation of moral rules appears to be partly a function of their socio-economic

status and education (Bernstein, 1961; Sears *et al.*, 1957; Trasler, 1970), which may explain the class-related differences in moral development noted above.

Suppression of socially-proscribed behavior cannot always be attributed to previous punishment; evidence relating to mechanisms of imitation, "modeling" and vicarious experience is reviewed in Aronfreed (1969), Berkowicz (1964) and Bandura & Walters (1963).

3. *Affective components of morality.* The emotional states associated with conscience are usually denoted by the terms: fear (or anxiety), guilt and shame. Mowrer's (1960) theory assigns a central role to conditioned fear responses; socially-conforming or moral behavior is the means by which the individual reduces this fear. Mowrer reserves the term *guilt* for the heightened state of fear which follows the completion of an act which (on previous occasions) has attracted punishment; this fear, being no longer reducible by learned avoidance responses, tends to persist. The notion that the need to reduce post-transgressional fear (guilt) may cause the individual to solicit punishment by committing other delinquencies is prominent in psychoanalytic theory (see *Criminality*); severe self-criticism, self-abasement and confession may also be regarded as strategies for reducing guilt.

The term *shame* is commonly employed to denote the unpleasant emotion which attends public revelation of one's wrong-doing or shortcomings. It has been suggested that techniques of socialization which rely upon shame rather than guilt as the major sanction are less effective in securing internalization of moral values; the evidence is equivocal, and in practice the distinction between shame and guilt is difficult to draw (Aronfreed, 1968).

The connection between the affective components of conscience and moral behavior is apparently complex. Kohlberg (1964) was unable to demonstrate any relation between the tenacity with which a child will conform to a behavioral rule and the intensity of the guilt which he exhibits if he is induced to break the same rule.

Bibliography: Aronfreed, J.: Conduct and conscience. New York & London, 1968. Id.: The concept of internalization. In: Goslin, D. A. (Ed.): Handbook of socialization theory and research. Chicago, 1969. Bandura, A. & Walters, R. H.: Social learning and personality development. New York, 1963. Berkowicz, L.: The development of motives and values in the child. New York, 1964. Bernstein, B. B.: Social structure, language and learning. Educ. Research, 1961, 3, 163–76. Burton, R. V.: Generality of honesty reconsidered. Psychol. Rev., 1963, 70, 481–99. Eysenck, H. J.: The development of moral values in children—the contribution of learning theory. Brit. J. Educ. Psychol., 1960, 30, 11–21. Harrower, M. H.: Social status and moral development. Brit. J. Educ. Psychol., 1934, 4, 75–95. Hartshorne, H. & May, M. A.: Studies in deceit. New York, 1928. Kohlberg, L.: Development of moral character and moral ideology. In: Hoffman, M. & Hoffman, L. W. (Eds) Review of child development research, Vol. I. New York, 1964. Id.: Stage and sequence: the cognitive-developmental approach to socialization. In: Goslin, D. A. (Ed.): Handbook of socialization theory and research. Chicago, 1969. Lerner, E.: Perspectives in moral reasoning. Amer. J. Sociol., 1937, 63, 249–69. Morris, J. F.: The development of moral values in children—the development of adolescent value-judgments. Brit. J. Educ. Psychol., 1958, 28, 1–14. Mowrer, O. H.: Learning theory and the symbolic processes. New York, 1960. Peters, R. S.: Freud's theory of moral development in relation to that of Piaget. Brit. J. Educ. Psychol., 1960, 30, 250–8. Piaget, J.: The moral judgment of the child. London, 1932. Sears, R. R., Maccoby, E. E. & Levin, H.: Patterns of child rearing. Evanston, 1957. Trasler, G. B.: Criminal behavior. In: Eysenck, H. J.: Handbook of abnormal psychology. London, ²1970.

G. B. Trasler

Consciousness. 1. It was under the banner of "consciousness" that psychology won its independence round about the middle of the last century. Consciousness was the undisputed subject-matter of "classical" psychology, which investigated mainly the sensory manifestations of consciousness, considering sense-data to be the foundations of all mental life and holding that they were more suitable for the experimental approach than the "higher" contents of consciousness. In later years, the Würzburg school (q.v.) broke with this use of experimentation (which was restricted to "simple" psychic processes), and showed that thought processes and volitions can also be observed under experimental conditions: the complex of methodological problems posed by research into consciousness can be seen to enter in here. Scruples about method also led "objective psychology" to abandon consciousness as the object of psychology in favor of research into behavior "*more physico*". But, as early as the nineteen-thirties, the objectivist taboo on consciousness was removed, and consciousness (according to Tolman, the most real reality which we possess and can desire) was again recognized as an object of psychology. The attempt to bring the data of consciousness to the level of manifest behavior made new definitions imperative. Hence, e.g., differentiation was called a criterion of consciousness. It became possible to record "consciousness" even in animal experiments. On the human plane, the criterion of verbalization accords with the demand for objective data of consciousness. Accordingly, everything is conscious which is communicated or, at least, is communicable. Consciousness in this sense is possessed, e.g., by a baby before it is aware of objects or of itself. Even electrophysiological processes can be shown to be correlates of conscious phenomena; hence the (physiological) body is also an indicator of consciousness. Along with intentionality, the physical nature of consciousness is also stressed by contemporary phenomenologists (see *Phenomenology*). On the basis of an historical survey, L. J. Pongratz (1967) describes consciousness as the cognitive presence of something: i.e. consciousness always implies a more or less clear knowledge of something here and now. See *Depth psychology*.

Bibliography: Abramson, H. S.: Problems of consciousness. New York, 1951–55. Boring, E. G.: Physical dimensions of consciousness. New York, 1933. Ey, H.: La conscience. Paris, 1963. Graumann, C. F.: Bewusstsein und Bewusstheit. In: Handbuch der Psychologie, Vol. 1/1. Göttingen, 1964. Gurwitsch, A.: Théorie du champ de la conscience. Paris, 1957.

Hofstätter, P. R.: Die Psychologie und das Leben. Vienna, 1951. Miller, J. G.: Unconsciousness. New York, 1942. Pongratz, L. J.: Problemgeschichte der Psychologie. Berne & Munich, 1967. Schaefer, H.: Bemerkungen zu einer Theorie des Bewusstseins. Psychologische Beiträge, 1960, 4. Thomae, H.: Bewusstsein und Leben. Archiv ges. Psychologie, 1940, 105. Id.: Das Bewusstseinsproblem in der modernen Psychologie. Der Nervenarzt, 1962, 33. Tolman, E. C.: Purposive behavior in animals and men. New York, 1932. Zutt, J.: Was lernen wir aus den Bewusstseinsstörungen über das Bewusstsein? Der Nervenarzt, 1962, 33, 483.   L. J. Pongratz

2. With the introduction of the natural sciences into the field of psychology, the problem of consciousness came to the fore. Knowledge can only be formed by rational, logical, hence conscious endeavors. To that extent, science must have recourse to consciousness. Whereas, in the early stages of traditional psychology, sensation and perception played the chief role in psychophysics (q.v.), the scientific possibilities of psychology later multiplied, especially in the field of the semi- (sub-)conscious and of the wholly unconscious. By conscious effort, introduced by (purposive) intention and (volitional) concentration, and controlled by the application of attention (from the unconscious via the subconscious to the clearly conscious; to be conceived in the form of three concentric circles), its province is steadily becoming more clearly and sharply defined. In more recent times, especially as a result of Soviet psychology (q.v.), consciousness and the possibilities it offers for methodical observation and criticism, as well as its significance in the activation of behavior, have become steadily more important, while in the West, in depth psychology (q.v.) and psychotherapy (q.v.), attempts are still made to apply the concept of consciousness scientifically (e.g. logotherapy, q.v.).

To this extent, psychology might be said to be developing into a science dealing with the different degrees of clarity of consciousness which are expressed (or are at least noticeable) in physically observable behavior (expression, q.v.; gesture, etc.), as well as in emotional experience. If, finally, one considers that

conscious doing, thinking and acting in man are subject to control, it might be deduced that in the future research into consciousness will become increasingly important, not least in connection with information theory (q.v.) and computer techniques.

Bibliography: Hiebsch, H.: Ergebnisse der sowjetischen Psychologie. Berlin, 1967. Manis, M.: Cognitive processes. Belmont, Calif., 1966. Neisser, U.: Cognitive psychology. New York, 1967. Rubinstein, S. L.: Grundlagen der allgemeinen Psychologie. Berlin 1958. Id.: Das Denken und die Wege seiner Erforschung. Berlin, 1967.   W. Arnold

Consciousness, degrees of. If consciousness is taken to mean wakefulness, its level can be approximately recorded by means of a verbal scale ranging from the state of unconsciousness through dullened states of consciousness (stupefaction, confusion, twilight state) to a condition of optimal clarity of consciousness. See *Arousal*.   *V.M.*

Consciousness, disorders of. From clinical observation we know the kind and degree of very different disorders of consciousness. Yet every attempt to grasp these disorders systematically more or less falls short of the reality, because disturbances of consciousness vary considerably and overlap and interact with other psychic changes. The "highest" degree of disturbed consciousness is unconsciousness (q.v.), the full arrestation of conscious mental processes, which (in certain organic diseases, e.g. diabetes) is a warning symptom of coma. Stupefaction, somnolence, twilight condition (q.v.) characterize restrictions of consciousness, especially of awareness of objects. These are usually disoriented twilight conditions which are often and more advantageously studied in the range of illnesses marked by a rapid onset. Typologically, but with certain limitations, one can distinguish mere restriction of consciousness, stupor (stupefaction), dimming of consciousness and dreamlike or delirious consciousness. Mild twilight states and delirium usually present as a dimming of consciousness. Delirium always contains elements of stupor. In addition, comprehension and all purposive processes are impeded, concepts tend to disintegrate, behavior becomes purely instinctive, ideation incoherent, and the individual undergoes hallucinatory, pseudo-hallucinatory and illusory experiences, together with motor arousal of varying intensity. In pathological disorders of consciousness diminished awareness is rarely absent. Hypnosis (q.v.) (as an experimental disturbance of consciousness) can avoid the stupefaction and dullness. In hypnotic states there is a characteristic splitting of the contents of consciousness or elimination of certain part-contents by the hypnotist. Recently there has also been talk of an "extension of consciousness" by the use of certain hallucinogens. It is doubtful that this could be genuine extension, but there is no doubt that every case is a result of intoxication. "Normal" disorders of consciousness can be caused by intense emotional disturbance. Fear, anger, ecstasy are experienced as intensive and sudden emotional arousals of relatively short duration and considerable though varying intensity. A common symptom is a restriction or darkening of the noëtic horizon, i.e. of the horizon of "clearly ordered perceptions, notions and ideas, by which man organizes his image of the world, comprehends it, and behaves consciously and purposively" (Lersch). Other post-traumatic or "post-hysterical" psychogenic or functional disorders of consciousness arise from affective needs: an actual or supposed advantage is sought more or less consciously. From a differential-diagnostic angle, functional disorders of consciousness can occasionally present considerable difficulties, especially as mixed and superimposed images are not infrequent. The forensic evaluation of non-pathological disorders of consciousness is a special problem; individual cases always require some reference to morbid disorders of consciousness. See *Psychoses; Schizophrenia.*

Bibliography: Bleuler, E.: Textbook of psychiatry. New York, 1924. **Brach, J.:** Conscience et connaissance. Paris, 1957. **Ehrhardt, H.:** Die Schuldfähigkeit in psychiatrisch-psychologischer Sicht. In: **Frey, E. R.:** Schuld-Verantwortung-Strafe. Zürich, 1964. **Ey, H.:** La conscience. Paris, 1967. **Eysenck, H. J.** (Ed.): Handbook of abnormal psychology. London, 1969. **Lersch, P.:** Aufbau der Person. Munich, ⁸1962. **Staub, H. & Thölen, H.** (Eds): Bewusstseinsstörungen. Stuttgart, 1961. **Störring, G. E.:** Besinnung und Bewusstsein. Stuttgart, 1953. **Zutt, J.:** Was lernen wir aus den Bewusstseinsstörungen über das Bewusstsein? Nervenarzt, 1962, *33*, 483. *H. Ehrhardt*

Consciousness, restricted. Only a limited number of contents can enter our consciousness at any given moment, and we can turn our attention in only one direction at any given moment. *V.M.*

Consciousness, threshold of. Concept related to restricted consciousness (q.v.).

Conservatism. The tendency to keep to tradition, the opposite of liberalism or radicalism. Different independent factor analyses (q.v.) of attitude measurements each yielded a factor which was interpreted in this sense. In R. B. Cattell's personality system, the inventory factor "radicalism versus conservatism" which correlates with J. P. Guilford's T factor ("thinking introversion", a tendency toward reflection) describes the degree of independence in the formation of opinion. See *Attitude.*

Bibliography: Eysenck, H. J.: Psychology of politics. London, 1954. *D.B.*

Consistency. 1. *Internal consistency* is the homogeneity of the individual elements of a method of measurement (e.g. of test items), and may be determined by discovering the average intercorrelation between the elements, and the correlation of each with the total score. The *internal consistency coefficient* (which may be calculated by Kuder-Richardson formula 20) is a measure of the reliability (homogeneity) of the score obtained from individual test components.

2. A *statistical* test is called consistent when, as the size of the sample increases, the test covers differences with increasing certainty. *G.M.*

3. A synonym for (behavioral) *reliability* (q.v.).

4. Individual *constancy*, i.e. the degree to which a testee displays identical behavior in different situations, at different times, and when performing different tasks. Consistency also determines the extent to which individual behavior can be predicted. It has not yet been established whether different forms of consistent behavior can be traced back to a common personality factor. *K.P.*

Consonance; dissonance. Terms used of the combination of two or more tones. Because of the structural complexity, consonance and dissonance (q.v.) cannot be defined universally, but only from different points of view: mathematically (frequency, H. von Helmholtz), acoustically (coincidence of overtones, or harmonics, C. Husmann), psychologically (degree of fusion, C. Stumpf), and in regard to sequential form (harmony or melodic line). The notion of consonance and dissonance has constantly changed over the centuries. Wellek (1963) attempted a comprehensive definition in his multiplicity theory. See *Music, psychology of.*

Bibliography: Wellek, A.: Musikpsychologie und Musikästhetik. Frankfurt, 1963. *B.S.*

Constancy. Perceptual compensation by which objects retain constant perceptual properties in spite of objective changes, e.g. objects appear the same size even when seen at different distances and the same color even when seen in different illuminations. *C.D.F.*

Constant stimulus method. A psychophysical procedure for estimating an absolute or differential sensory threshold. One stimulus is held invariant (the standard) while a series of similar stimuli are presented in random order for comparison on the variable in question (e.g. brightness, loudness, thickness). The threshold is computed from the proportion of correct responses given for each comparison stimulus. Syn. *Method of right and wrong cases.* *G.D.W.*

Constants. See *Method of constants.*

Constellation theory. G. E. Müller's attempt to explain why in a specific thought process only concepts appropriate to that process impinge upon the conscious mind. The task acts as an orienting idea encouraging the associative tendencies of certain concepts and inhibiting those of others. This system of advancement and blocking is known as *constellation*, and the complex of unified, associated ideas as *a constellation.*

Bibliography: Müller, G. E.: Zur Analyse der Gedächtnistätigkeit und des Vorstellungsverlaufs. Part 3. Leipzig, 1913. *R.Hä*

Constitution. See *Constitutional theory.*

Constitutional theory. "Constitution" may be understood as human reactive potential and reaction style (form and performance). It is grounded in heredity and *anlagen* (q.v.), or fundamental dispositions and those acquired in early childhood, or more rarely at a later date, and can be determined as a type (q.v.) or an individual constitution. Constitutional theory studies mental and physical principles of the healthy and ailing organism as a whole. It can be thought of as a biological science based on description, measurement and correlational statistics. It uses analytical methods to discover typical elements of character or temperament, organic functional systems, and physical proportions. It throws light on basic mental and physical abilities, tendencies to social deviation, and proneness to disease. See *Criminality; Traits.*

Bibliography: Kretschmer, E.: Physique and character. London, 1925.   W.K.

Constitutional types. Theoretical groupings of psychophysical (occasionally exclusively physical: the "biotype") characteristics which are assembled either by a statistical frequency method or by arbitrary selection. Kretschmer's *physique types:* pyknic (q.v.), leptosomic (q.v.), athletic (q.v.) are derived correlatively from manic depressive and schizophrenic *psychoses* (q.v.), and in turn form the starting-point for statistical elucidation of the cyclothymic (q.v.), schizothymic (q.v.), and barykinetic (q.v.) types. Statistically, Sheldon (1942) found three physical growth variables: endomorphy (q.v.), ectomorphy (q.v.), and mesomorphy (q.v.). These provide a basis for describing the viscerotonic (q.v.), cerebrotonic (q.v.), and somatotonic (q.v.) temperaments (Sheldon's constitutional theory of personality). Conrad (1963), using rough measurements, groups the proportions of the body in series of variations ranging between the extremes *compact-elongated* (pyknomorphic-leptomorphic) and *robust-thin* (athletic-hyperplastic-asthenic-hypoplastic). Types based on age and sex are also recognized as psychophysical constitutional types. See *Body build index; Type.*

Bibliography: Eysenck, H. J.: The structure of human personality. London & New York, ²1960. Kretschmer, E.: Physique and character. London, 1925. Sheldon, W.: The varieties of temperament. New York, 1942. Conrad, K.: Der Konstitutionstyp. Berlin, ²1963.   W.K.

Construct validity. 1. *Origin of the phrase.* The phrase *construct validity* came into widespread use in the behavioral sciences in the nineteen fifties. In an article entitled "Construct validity in psychological tests" that did much to establish this usage, Cronbach & Meehl (1955) trace the origin of the term to the work performed by an APA Committee

on Psychological Tests. According to these authors, "The chief innovation of the Committee's report was the term *construct validity.* This was first formulated by a subcommittee (Meehl and R. C. Challman) . . . and later modified and clarified by the entire Committee (Bordin, Challman, Conrad, Humphreys, Super and the present writers)". As concerns the reasons for introducing the term, Cronbach & Meehl state that although "construct validity calls for no new scientific approach", the concept is needed to more clearly . . . "specify types of research required in developing tests for which conventional views on validation are inappropriate".

2. *Controversy relating to use of the phrase.* Several behavioral scientists, perhaps most notably H. P. Bechtoldt and R. B. Cattell, have expressed serious objections to use of the term construct validity. They have argued cogently that at best it is merely an old wine in a new bottle, and that in some of its formulations it is confusing, misleading and could even support a . . . "non-empirical, non-scientific approach to the study of behavior" (Bechtoldt, 1959). Cattell (1964) has recommended use of the term *concept validity* in place of construct validity, on the grounds that it has the desirable connotations and few of the undesirable connotations of the latter, and because . . . "an empirical construct, in logic and epistemology, is only a particular form of a concept . . . [and] the psychologist is often interested in validity for other kinds of concepts, such as are logically deducible from general postulates" (Cattell & Butcher, 1968). Bechtoldt also argues to the effect that the scientifically accurate connotations of construct validity are well represented by the idea of explication of a concept, as indicated by logical positivism and operational methlology, and that construct validity should . . . "be eliminated from further consideration as a way of speaking about psychological concepts, laws and theories".

But, however compelling these arguments may be, they appear to have had little influence on use: construct validity continues to be a widely-used phrase and a number of writers (e.g. Campbell, 1960) have argued compellingly for its continued use. The fact that space has been made available for it in this reference work probably bespeaks of a reality: use of the phrase has become too well-established to expect that it will be supplemented by another term, or cease to be used, in the near future.

3. *A basis for definition.* Available attempts at definition of construct validity are extended essays considerably longer than this entry. Most have been similar to essays designed to explain theory construction generally, or such aspects of this as model specification, hypothesis testing, operationalism, concept explication, functional unity and intervening variables. This is not to say that the concepts represented by these various labels are indistinguishable from those of construct validity, but merely to alert the reader to similarities, and to the fact that the thrust in each case is toward specifying the necessary and sufficient conditions for establishing credence in science for a concept or set of concepts.

In most attempts to describe construct validation, one central idea is that to validate a construct is to identify the observables which denote it, and to show that these observables vary and co-vary in ways that indicate that all represent the same thing—i.e. form a functional unity (Cattell, 1950). It is generally, if implicitly, agreed that the extreme form of operationalism which requires a different construct—and a different construct name— for every distinguishable operation (however trivial the difference) is not desirable in science or for construct validity. Hence, it is implied that to validate a construct is to designate operationally distinct manifestations of the construct and to show that these are unitary.

But this raises some very knotty problems. On the one hand, it invites confusion of construct validity with internal consistency reliability (see *Test theory*); and on the other

hand it can confuse the validation of a particular set of measurement operations (a test) with the elaborate process of building support for an entire theory. Indeed, these would appear to be extremes along a continuum near the middle of which are the conditions specified for construct validity, the continuum representing convergence of different observations of the same phenomenon or correlation (in a broad sense of this term) among different variables. To break the *tertium quid* implied here, theorists have suggested that reliability be defined as convergence among highly similar kinds of observations, and that theory verification be thought of in terms of interrelationships among different constructs, whence the convergence required for construct validity can be defined as that among operationally quite distinct measures of the same construct. But, clearly, behind this verbal solution lurk some very difficult problems of specifying what it is that makes measurement operations "highly similar", and "quite distinct". Toward a solution to this kind of problem, R. B. Cattell has proposed that the basic observations upon which psychological measurements are built can be classified into mutually exclusive and exhaustive categories of media of observations: Data either derive from observations made by the subject himself, from observations made by others, or from the effects of the subject's behavior on the impersonal environment. Measurements based upon observations made through different media may then be regarded as operationally "quite distinct", and yet indicate the same construct. Reliability is then to be understood in terms of convergence within a particular mode of observation; construct validity can be defined (in part, see below) by convergence in measurements of the same attribute based upon observations through different media; and theory construction can be understood in terms of the broader concerns of interrelationships among different constructs, verification of interacting stimulus-response hypotheses, and so on. There remains in each case a practical problem of specifying the degree of relationship required to support an hypothesis of convergence, but this can be treated as a technical issue. In this regard, too, several theorists have emphasized the need to demonstrate a lack of convergence—i.e. the distinctiveness—among supposedly different constructs (see Campbell & Fiske, 1959; Horn & Cattell, 1965).

To provide truly compelling evidence for construct validity in the sense of what R. B. Cattell has defined as a functional unity, it is necessary to go beyond demonstration of convergence and distinctiveness for the observables which represent the concept, and to show that those observables appear together, disappear together, change together or, in general, interact in one of the many ways in which things can interact when they represent a unitary phenomenon. This means, e.g. that in controlled-manipulative experiments independent variable conditions should produce cohesive effects on all of a set of operationally separable measures of the same construct; that in studies of development it should be found that the construct observables "grow" together in a unitary way; and that in studies of process, an occurrence in one manifestation of a construct should be accompanied by a corresponding occurrence in other manifestations. Construct validity in this sense thus becomes very similar to theory verification. There is a difference in emphasis, however, for in construct validation the focus is on establishing credence for a particular measurement operation, and only incidentally are tests of an entire theory at issue, whereas in theory verification the adequacy of measures of constructs is implicitly assumed and the emphasis is upon showing that several constructs "behave" as specified in the theory.

Clearly, construct validation continues to be one of the more controversial topics in the behavioral sciences.

Bibliography: Bechtoldt, H. P.: Construct validity: a critique. American Psychologist, 1959, 14, 619-29. Campbell, D. T.: Recommendations for APA Test Standards regarding construct, trait, or discriminant validity. American Psychologist, 1960, 15, 546-53. Id. & Fiske, D. W.: Convergent and discriminant validation by the multitrait-multimethod matrix. Psychological Bulletin, 1959, 56, 81-105. Cattell, R. B.: Personality. New York, 1950. Id.: Beyond validity and reliability: some further concepts and coefficients for evaluating tests. Journal of Educational Measurement, 1964, 33, 133-43. Id. & Butcher, J. H.: The prediction of achievement and creativity. New York, 1968. Cronbach, L. J.: Essentials of psychological testing. New York, ³1970. Id. & Meehl, P. E.: Construct validity in psychological tests. Psychological Bulletin, 1955, 52, 281-302. Horn, J. L. & Cattell, R. B.: Vehicles, ipsatization and the multiple method measurement of motivation. Canadian Journal of Psychology, 1965, 19, 265-79. *J. L. Horn*

Consumer research. See *Marketing.*

Contact. By the ability to make contact(s) one understands the speed and facility with which a person can establish a positive social relationship with his fellows. An inability to make contacts can indicate neurotic incapacity or be a sign of self-sufficiency (a preference for one's own company rather than the group). See *Sociability.* *G.K.*

Contact behavior. This can be mainly observed in the care of the young. A grey goose chick remains in acoustical and optical contact with its mother. If this fails, it "cries". Young perch often seek to establish contact with the parent by touch. Contact behavior can easily be produced by dummy sign stimuli (q.v.). *V.P.*

Contagion, psychic. A supposed process by which certain behavior (e.g. rhythmic movement) is rapidly passed from individual to individual to affect a whole group. Also associated with the "ideo-real law" (q.v.) postulated by Hellpach, and, like that hypothesis, ultimately dependent upon very precise confirmation of the modes of mutual interdependence of mental and physical phenomena.   *J.M.*

Contamination. 1. Psychopathologically: mixing or fusing words or parts of words with a usually meaningless resultant. Occurs in normal people in a state of great fatigue or in dreams, but especially in schizophrenia (q.v.) as the result of pathological disorders of speech and thought. **2.** Diagnostically: in shape-interpretation methods, the condensation of two heterogeneous contents to produce a false interpretation (e.g. in the Rorschach test: a combination of specific schizoid or schizophrenic behaviors.) **3.** A subjective interference with any interpretation of scores or analyses.   *G.P.*

Content analysis. According to B. Berelson, a research technique which seeks to describe objectively, systematically and quantitatively the manifest content of communication; according to H. D. Lasswell: "quantitative semantics". The method is used especially in the study of publicity, in social psychology and political science, but also in the study of literature and the psychology of development. Verbally communicated material in particular (newspaper articles, texts of speeches, films, diaries, etc.) can be analyzed quantitatively by determining frequencies or their ratios in defined classifications (categories). More recently, content analysis has come to be used as a means for deciding research hypotheses, and sophisticated applications now demand the use of computers. See *Computational linguistics.*

Bibliography: Holsti, O. R.: Content Analysis. In: Lindzey, G. & Aronson, E. (Eds): Handbook of social psychology, Vol. 2. Reading, Mass., 1968, 596–692.

H.D.S.

Contiguity. The coexistence or proximity, in time or space, of different experiences.

Law of contiguity: When events occur simultaneously or in close proximity, they are then associated, which is a precondition for learning. In the strict sense, the law is often synonymous with contiguity theory: when stimulus and response occur together once, a final and (some claim) non-reinforceable connection is established between them. Principles for explaining phenomena such as association (q.v.) and conditioning (q.v.) are based on this law.

E. R. Guthrie's contiguity theory (Guthrie's contiguous conditioning theory): if a stimulus affects an organism while this is in motion, the stimulus will subsequently release this movement. The formation of associations on the basis of *simultaneity* of stimulus and movement is a necessary and sufficient condition for learning.

Bibliography: Guthrie, E. R.: The psychology of learning. New York, 1935.   *H.W.*

Contingency. 1. The degree to which one variable depends on another variable or other variables. **2.** A term descriptive of the phenomenon that within a whole group of individuals featuring certain characteristics, certain combinations of these are especially frequent. The sets of psychological characteristics that are related are "typical"; and the individuals featuring these sets are "types".

W.Se.

3. *Logical contingency:* a state of affairs which, in regard to the laws of logic, may and also may not be. **4.** *Physical contingency:* a state of affairs which, in regard to the laws of physics, may and also may not be. More loosely, *x* is contingent on *y* if the occurrence of *x* is dependent on the occurrence of *y*, and *y* may or may not occur in accordance with the laws of nature.

Contingency coefficient. The coefficient of a non-parametric correlation method the object of which is to determine the degree of interrelationship between two variables of more than one class.   *G.M.*

Continuity, correction of. Its use is required when with small samples a characteristic which is actually continuous is taken to be discrete, and the theoretical distribution of the statistic is also continuous. *W.H.B.*

Continuous scales. 1. Scales in which all values situated between two limits can occur, at least in theory. In psychology such scales are rare although it is often assumed that variables measured by means of discrete scales are also actually continuous (e.g. memory performance in a test). In general, measurable variables are said to be continuous, those obtained merely from measures representing whole numbers are *discontinuous*, or *discrete*. **2.** Scales of infinitesimal increments of gain. *G.M.*

Contour. See *Figure-ground.*

Contraception. The prevention of conception. Various contraceptive measures in current use are: coitus interruptus (q.v.), the "safe" period, mechanical devices such as condoms (sheaths), or intrauterine coils (although the use of such devices, together with abortion, q.v., is properly classed as birth-prevention *after* conception), and various anti-spermicidal creams, etc. The regular self-administration of hormonal contraceptives is a popular and economic method (the "pill"), although various, even fatal, side-effects with certain types in certain individuals have been recorded. Male and female sterilization is sometimes classed as a contraceptive measure, but the term is usually reserved for methods other than the (usually) irreversible. *U.H.S.*

Contraction. The drawing together of a muscle. In the case of the transversal skeletal muscle a distinction is made between individual contractions lasting 0·1 sec, and *tetanic* contractions the duration of which depends on how long the series of stimuli lasts; between *isometric* (those where there is no change of length but only some development of energy), *isotonic* (where only length and not tension changes), and *auxotonic* contractions (a mixture of isometric and isotonic). The contraction of the heart muscle lasts 0·3 to 0·5 sec., and consists of isometric, auxotonic, isometric, and then isotonic phases. *E.D.*

Contrast. Two juxtaposed surfaces of differing brightness and color influence one another in the sense that each surface tends to produce a complementary color in its neighbor (*simultaneous contrast*). The results are as follows: (*a*) if the two surfaces differ in brightness, the difference is more strongly accentuated (*brightness contrast*); (*b*) if the two surfaces have complementary (q.v.) colors, the saturation increases (a maximum saturation of green occurs when it is placed on a red ground); (*c*) if the two colors are not complementary they change according to the rules of summative color mixing. The following also apply: (*a*) the intensity of the contrast effected is proportional to the area affected (*induction area*, or *surface*); (*b*) the smaller the brightness contrast, the greater the simultaneous color contrast; (*c*) the intensity and direction of the contrast are also influenced by structural (gestalt) factors (Benary, 1924); (*d*) simultaneous color contrast is very strongly accentuated if the reciprocally impinging surfaces are covered with a sheet of flimsy white paper (fluorescent contrast).

Bibliography: Benary, W.: Beobachtungen zu einem Exp. über Helligkeitskontrast. Psychol. Forsch. 1924, 5. *G. Ka.*

Contrectation drive. A term introduced by Moll to denote the contact drive as one of the components of the sex drive. When contact or touch is established, this drive loses its force and the so-called *detumescence* drive is substituted. *G.L.I.*

Control group. A group of Ss in an experiment who are not subjected to any experimental treatment, but are equal to the Ss in the experimental group (q.v.). In general, the control-group results must be compared with those for the experimental group before any pronouncement can be made about the degree and direction of the effect of the experiment.   *G.M.*

Controlled variable. See *Variable.*

Convention. A term for rules of social behavior, or customs which have been formed in the course of time and are not explicitly formulated inside the group but are known to all the members. They are considered not so much as generally binding precepts or norms but rather as matters which are self-evident in social interaction. A particularly rigid and stereotyped adherence to social rules and precepts or conventions which actually do not demand such a degree of submission is known as *conventionalism;* it is considered to be a characteristic of the "authoritarian personality" (q.v.). See *Conformity.*   *A.S.-M.*

Convergence. 1. A position, or a change in position, of the two eyes produced by their force of fusion (fusion reflex, making both retinal images coincide), and by the eye muscles, with the result that the visual axes cross at the fixation point. The angle of convergence is the angle between the lines of regard in the visual plane. *Angle of fusion:* the angle between the line of regard and the parallel position. The opposite of convergence is *divergence.* The general term for both is *vergence.* A distinction is sometimes made between accommodative, fusional and proximal convergence, depending on what induces the convergence movement: state of accommodation, disparate retinal points (q.v.), and apparent decrease in the distance of a seen object. Accommodation (q.v.), convergence and pupillary reaction are interconnected.

2. The term "convergence" is also used

for development processes, etc., when there is a tendency or law for variables to agree with or tend toward one another. (W. Stern's convergence theory: convergence between genotype, q.v. and environment, q.v.)   *A.H.*

Convergent thinking. According to J. P. Guilford, one of the two kinds of productive-thinking operations (see *Divergent thinking*). Convergent thinkers look for the one (predetermined) right, or best, or conventional answer to a problem. Convergent thinking can, in certain respects, be examined by tests with one correct solution.
Bibliography: Guilford, J. P.: Three faces of intellect. Amer. Psychologist, 1959, *14,* 469–79.   *J.G.*

Conversational chaining. A type of non-branching program introduced by J. A. Barlow (see *Branching*) in which the desired answer that will fill the blank space in statement 1 occurs at some point in statement 2, where it is emphasized (e.g. in bold type) in the text. The question in each frame, or step (q.v.), is therefore an incomplete statement. This variation of the linear method has the advantage of appearing more discursive.
Bibliography: Barlow, J. A.: Conversational chaining in teaching machine programs. Psychol. Rep. 1960, *7,* 187–93.   *H.F.*

Conversion. The transformation of a mental conflict into a physical symptom which represents a disguised drive gratification or wish fulfillment, or (more frequently) an inhibition of such a drive gratification or wish fulfillment, or both. Conversions appear in hysteria (q.v.) as anesthesias and paresthesias, as motor paralysis, convulsive attacks, and (in more serious regressive conditions) as pregenital conversion neuroses. In contrast to psychosomatic illnesses (see *Organic neuroses*) which subjectively have no "meaning" for the patient, conversions are "meaningful".

According to Freud, conversion neuroses

are *conversion hysteria* and *pregenital* conversion neuroses (especially tics and stuttering). According to Freud and Fenichel, fixations on the later or early anal stages (q.v.) (depending on the gravity of the symptoms) lie at the root of these illnesses. See *Psychopathology; Psychosomatics.*

Bibliography: Fenichel, O.: The psychoanalytic theory of neurosis. New York, 1945. Freud, S.: Three essays on the theory of sexuality. London, ²1962. Toman, W.: An introduction to psychoanalytic theory of motivation. London & New York, 1960.   *W.T.*

Convulsion. A general, involuntary muscular contraction.

Convulsive therapy. This was first introduced by Ladislas von Meduna (1896–1964) into the treatment of schizophrenia (q.v.) and other psychoses. By intravenously injecting cardiazol, metrazol and other analogous substances, Meduna succeeded in artificially inducing an epileptic state. The idea was based fundamentally on his observation that schizophrenia and epilepsy (q.v.) almost never occur together. He therefore supposed that they were mutually antagonistic. Later, Cerletti and Bini obtained convulsive crises by means of electricity and introduced treatment by electric shock into hospitals. The appearance of psychopharmacological drugs for use in medicine has decreased the frequency with which electric shock treatment is used, especially in cases of depression. Present practice is to use it with intravenous anesthesia, and to combine it with drugs which reduce the violence of the convulsions.

Bibliography: Meduna, L. J.: The convulsive treatment. In: Sackler, A. M. (Ed.): The great physiodynamic therapies in psychiatry. New York, 1956, 76–90.   *J.L.I.*

Cooperation. 1. The manner in, and degree to which an individual's activity is linked with that of others or depends on it, e.g. in shared work places, group therapy, teamwork, and so on, through the influence of the overall organization of group dynamics (q.v.) and of appropriate leadership (q.v.), **2.** Readiness to participate, share a workload, etc., respond to counseling, and so on.
G.R.W.M.

Cooperative School and College Ability Tests (abb. SCAT). Tests which attempt to assess the abilities (q.v.) developed by the school. The calculations comprise a total level and values for verbal and "quantitative" abilities. There are four series for different high-school grades; two series for colleges.

Bibliography: Educational testing service. Princeton, 1955–63.   *R.M.*

Coordination. A function of the central nervous system: bringing the perceptual organs into operation so that certain stimuli can impinge which are required for further responses (e.g. visual-motor coordination); to control the function of antagonistic muscles so that they support one another in regard to the intended behavioral goal instead of impeding or preventing it. The process of coordination can be either innate or acquired, and can operate both consciously and unconsciously. See *Brain.*   *A.Ro.*

Coprophagy. The eating of excrement, which can occur in serious cases of imbecility, and occasionally among the insane.   *C.S.*

Copulation. The process of sexual intercourse. With higher-order animals, copulation is only one aspect of pairing (mating), which also involves care of the brood. The frequent isolation of sexuality in experimental research led for a long time to an underestimation of the general social aspects of mating. For instance, aggression aroused by sexual approach has to be restrained, not only for copulation but for the restitution of friendly contact. This is helped by courtship (q.v.), and presumably by coital after-play—which as yet has scarcely been investigated but can be found among parrots, seagulls and ducks. Syn. *Coition; Coitus* (q.v.).   *R.A.S.*

Cornea. Circumscribes the eye almost spherically at the front, is 1 mm thick, and consists of five layers. Its structure allows rays of visible light to pass; they are refracted on the cornea.   *R.R.*

Corona effect. See *Halo effect.*

Corpus luteum (syn. *Yellow body*). The endocrine organ which forms in the female ovary from the spent follicle, the remains of the ovum which has burst during ovulation. It is here that the *corpus luteum* hormones estrogen and progesterone are formed. The latter transforms the uterine lining (which has grown under the influence of the estrogen) so that the fertilized ovum can establish itself. From the third month of pregnancy the *corpus luteum* degenerates, and the placenta takes over the formation of *corpus luteum* hormones, and with it the maintenance of the uterine lining; it also has a beneficial effect on the uterine musculature. If the burst egg is not fertilized and is passed, the hormone production ceases after about fourteen days and the uterine mucus membrane is evacuated during menstruation (q.v.). See *Hormones.*
                                                                                                   E.D.

Corpus quadrigemina. Part of the mesencephalon, and consisting of two masses of tissue believed to contain visual and auditory reflex centers.

Corpus striatum (syn. *Striate body*). Part of the base of each cerebral hemisphere in the prosencephalon, consisting of the internal capsule and the caudate and lenticular nuclei.

Correlational techniques. 1. *History.* The idea that characteristics of individuals are often related (height and weight, intelligence and achievement, and so on) has long been accepted in civilized societies. Yet no effort was made to express the extent of such relationships in quantitative terms before the

end of the nineteenth century. The first person to tackle the question seriously was Francis Galton. One of the problems he considered (Galton, 1886) was the relationship between the heights of fathers and sons. As a result of his investigations he succeeded in deriving linear equations (or regression lines) for predicting a son's height from that of his father, and, conversely, a father's height from that of his adult son. He also showed that when the variabilities of the two sets of measurements were equated the slopes of the two lines, relative to the horizontal and vertical axis respectively, were equal. This slope, which was now a unit-free measure, became known as the correlation coefficient between the two sets of measurements.

Galton's work was soon extended by other writers, notably Karl Pearson and G. U. Yule. Pearson (1896) developed a formula for the direct calculation of a correlation coefficient—the Pearson product-moment correlation coefficient. He also provided techniques for correlating data when one or both of the variables could be measured only in a qualitative way. Yule (1907) contributed notably to the extension of the theory of correlation and regression to include any number of variables. Early in the present century, too, the value of correlational techniques for psychological experimentation was realized. A leading pioneer in this field was Charles Spearman (1904).

By the end of the first decade of the present century most of the basic work on the derivation of correlation and regression coefficients had been done and attention was being directed to questions concerning the sampling errors of these statistics. At first these proved very intractable. One main difficulty was the fact that the distribution of a correlation coefficient is skew, in particular when its numerical value approaches the limits of plus and minus unity. This major difficulty was largely overcome when Fisher (1921) introduced the *z-transformation* of the correlation coefficient, which has a distribution approaching closely to a normal distribution. The development, also by Fisher, of the methods of analysis of variance and co-variance (Fisher, 1925) contributed greatly to the solution of problems concerned with the general theory of linear and multiple regression, and to the interpretation not only of these techniques but of the correlation coefficient itself. The effect of Fisher's and later work on correlational theory is discussed in detail by Hotelling (1953).

2. *The bivariate normal distribution.* This distribution is basic to correlational theory. It arises when, for a sample of N subjects, we have scores or other measurements on two variables X and Y each of which can be measured on a continuous scale and is normally distributed in the population. This is one of the necessary conditions of a bivariate normal distribution. The other condition is that when the N pairs of scores are plotted in a diagram using orthogonal axes (say the X-axis horizontal and the Y-axis vertical), the scatter of points thus obtained shows an elliptical or circular distribution which decreases consistently in density outwards from the point representing the mean scores of the two variables. The diagram is called a *scatter diagram* or *scattergram.*

The density function for a bivariate normal distribution (see Kendall & Stuart, 1961) requires five constants, or population parameters, to define it. These are the means and standard deviations of the two variables and the correlation coefficient between them. The latter, where the whole population of subjects is concerned, is denoted by the Greek letter ρ. An estimate r of ρ, obtained from the scores of a sample of subjects drawn randomly from this population, is found by the formula

$$r = \frac{\Sigma xy}{\sqrt{(\Sigma_{x^2} \cdot \Sigma_{y^2})}}, \qquad (1)$$

in which Σ_{x^2} is the sum of the squares of the deviations of the N-scores on variable X from their mean. Σ_{y^2} is defined similarly for the Y-scores, while Σ_{xy} is the sum of the products of the N pairs of deviational scores.

Formula (1) is Pearson's product-moment formula for the correlation coefficient. It can be expressed in several equivalent forms.

3. *Regression lines.* In the case of a distribution which is approximately bivariate normal there are two regression lines. If the X-axis is divided into intervals, then for values of X within a given interval the mean of the corresponding Y-scores can be obtained. When this is done for all intervals, the Y-means derived will be found to lie roughly on a straight line. This line can be expressed in the form

$$\hat{Y} = a + bX, \qquad (2)$$

in which b is the slope of the line relative to the X-axis, what is called the *regression coefficient* of Y on X; a is the intercept of the line on the Y-axis and $\hat{Y}$ is the estimated value of Y for a given value of X. The regression line is also called a "least square" line, as the constants a and b are found such that the sum of the squares of the distances of all points in the scattergram (taken parallel to the Y-axis) from the line is a minimum.

A process similar to that just described can also be carried out by dividing the Y-axis into intervals and then calculating the X-means corresponding to each interval of Y. This process will lead to a linear equation of estimating X for given values of Y, namely

$$\hat{X} = a' + b'Y. \qquad (3)$$

When the standard deviations of the X and Y scores are equal it is found that b is equal to b' and each is equal to r.

In cases in which scores on one variable, say the Y variable, are measured on a continuous scale but these scores are ascertained only for certain predetermined values of the X-variable it is customary to consider only the "regression" line of Y on X. If bivariate normality cannot be assumed it may be necessary to test for *linearity of regression* (see McNemar, 1962). If the test indicates a non-linear relationship then a more complicated equation than that given by expression (2) is required. When this is the case, the relationship between the two variables cannot be adequately expressed by a product-moment correlation coefficient but a coefficient called the *eta coefficient*, which is a measure of curvilinearity, may be used.

4. *Other correlational methods.* In psychological investigations it is not always possible to collect data in the form required by expression (1), and other procedures for estimating correlation coefficients then become necessary. The most commonly occurring situations and the coefficients appropriate to each are summarized below. Basic reference books are those by McNemar (1962), Lord & Novick (1968), and Kendall & Stuart (1961, 1966).

(*a*) *Tetrachoric coefficient.* This correlation coefficient may be used in the case of data which basically are distributed in a bivariate normal manner but for which scores on the two continuous variables are not available. Instead it is known for each member of a sample of subjects only whether he lies above or below some given point on each of the variables. Tetrachoric correlations are difficult to calculate without a computer and are generally estimated from nomograms.

(*b*) *Biserial coefficient.* This coefficient gives an estimate of the product moment correlation between two variables which have a bivariate normal distribution, but for one of which scores are available only in dichotomous form (e.g. "alcoholic" and "non-alcoholic").

(*c*) *Point biserial coefficient.* This coefficient gives an estimate of the product-moment correlation between two variables one of which is continuous but the other is truly dichotomous (e.g. "male" versus "female"). Bivariate normality is not assumed.

(*d*) *The fourfold point or phi coefficient.* When both variables are dichotomous in form, the scatter diagram is reduced to a fourfold table. The product-moment correlation for such a table is known as the *phi coefficient*. The coefficient is primarily used for correlating test items but unfortunately it is not independent of item difficulty.

(*e*) *The kappa coefficient.* Fourfold tables also arise when two judges separately interview a sample of subjects and note the presence or absence of some characteristic. A *phi* coefficient might again be used as a measure of agreement between the judges, but a preferable measure is the *kappa coefficient*, which takes possible bias between the judges into account (see Spitzer *et al.*, 1967; Everitt, 1968).

(*f*) *Rank correlation.* When a sample of subjects is arranged in order according to some characteristic which they possess to a varying degree, they are said to be ranked. When rankings exist for the subjects on two separate characteristics, the relationship between the rankings can be determined by the use of rank correlation techniques. The two most commonly used coefficients are Spearman's *rho* and Kendall's *tau*.

(*g*) *Intraclass correlation.* The simplest example of this correlation arises in the comparison of identical twins. If we have a sample of N pairs of twins with scores for each on a single variable, then in arranging the scores it is immaterial which score in a pair is placed first. When correlating the data each pair of scores is entered twice in reverse order so that there are then $2N$ pairs of scores in all.

(*h*) *Partial correlation.* The observed correlation between two variables may be influenced by the fact that one or both are linearly related to other concomitant variables. A partial correlation is the correlation between the two variables after the effect of these extraneous influences has been removed.

(*i*) *Serial correlation or autocorrelation.* Given a series of measurements

$$x_1, x_2, x_3, \ldots, x_i, \ldots, x_t,$$

taken at equal intervals of time, correlations may be obtained between the $(t-1)$ pairs of measurements (x_1, x_2), (x_2, x_3), ..., or between the $(t-2)$ pairs of measurements (x_1, x_3), (x_2, x_4), ..., and so on. The first is known as a serial correlation of *lag one*, the second as a serial correlation of *lag two*, and so on. Examination of the values of the successive correlations may reveal trends in the series. A plot of the correlations for lags of increasing size is known as a *correlogram*.

(*j*) *Multiple linear regression and multiple correlation*. Multiple regression arises when we examine the relationship between one variable, generally referred to as the dependent or criterion variable, and the combined effects, assumed to be linear, of several other variables, generally referred to as the independent or predictor variables. In this case the regression equation takes the form

$$\hat{Y} = a + b_1 X_1 + b_2 X_2 + \ldots + b_p X_p, \quad (4)$$

where $\hat{Y}$ is the estimated value of the dependent variable Y for given values of the p independent variables X_1 to X_p. As with simple regression a is the intercept on the Y-axis, but now b_i is the rate of change in Y as X_i varies and the other dependent variables are held constant at their mean values; the b's are known as *partial regression coefficients*, and they are determined so that the sum of the squares of the discrepancies $(\hat{Y}_i - Y_i)$ for $i = 1, 2, \ldots, N$, is a minimum. The correlation between the N pairs of values $(\hat{Y}_i, Y_i)$ is known as the *multiple correlation*.

(*k*) *Canonical correlations*. Canonical correlational analysis is an extension of multiple regression analysis. It arises when a set of p variables X_1 to X_p can be divided meaningfully into two subsets p_1 and p_2, where $p = p_1 + p_2$. The problem here is to find that weighted sum of the first set which correlates maximally with a weighted sum of the second set. The correlation thus obtained is known as the first *canonical correlation* between the two sets. In general p^* independent sets of weights can be found, where p^* equals p_1 or p_2 whichever is the smaller, so that p^* canonical correlations of successively decreasing magnitude are obtained (Hope, 1968).

Bibliography: Everitt, B. S.: Moments of the statistics kappa and weighted kappa. Brit. J. Math. & Stat. Psychol. 1968, *21*, 97–103. Fisher, R. A.: "On the probable error" of a coefficient of correlation deduced from a small sample, Metron, 1921, *1*, 1–32. Id.: Statistical methods for research workers. Edinburgh, 1925. Galton, F.: Regression towards mediocrity in hereditary stature. Jour. Anthrop. Inst., 1886, *15*, 246–70. Hope, K.: Methods of multivariate analysis. London, 1968. Hotelling, H.: New light on the correlation coefficient and its transforms. J. Roy. Stat. Soc., 1953, *15*, 193–224. Kendall, M. G. & Stuart, A.: The advanced theory of statistics, Vols 2 and 3. London, 1961 and 1966. Lord, F. M. & Novick, M. R.: Statistical theories of mental test scores. Reading, Mass., 1968. McNemar, Q.: Psychological statistics. New York & London, 1962. Pearson, K.: Regression, heredity and panmixia, Phil. Trans. Roy. Soc., 1896, Series A, *187*, 253–67. Spearman, C.: The proof and measurement of association between two things, Amer. J. Psychol., 1904, *15*, 88–103. Spitzer, R. L. *et al.*: Quantification of agreement in psychiatric diagnosis. Arch. Gen. Psychiatry, 1967, *17*, 83–7. Yule, G. U.: On the theory of correlation for any number of variables treated by a new system of notation, Proc. Roy. Soc., 1907, Series A, *79*, 182–93. *A. E. Maxwell*

Correlation coefficient. A statistical value which indicates the degree of relationship between two or more variables. Correlation coefficients (except for contingency coefficients, q.v.) vary between -1.00 and $+1.00$; 0.00 indicates the complete absence of any correlation, while the coefficients -1.00 and $+1.00$ indicate a wholly negative or positive correlation. *G.M.*

Correlation indices. Known also as z' transformations, these are transformed correlation coefficients. As such coefficients cannot normally be distributed, they are frequently transformed into more or less normally distributed correlation indices. The formula for transformation of the product-moment correlation r is:

$$z' = \frac{1}{2} [\log_e (1 + r) - \log_e (1 + r)].$$

Tables of transformed values are available, and are used to carry out significance tests on correlation coefficients. They are distributed more or less normally round zero independently of the sample size. See *Correlational techniques*. *G.M.*

Correlation ratio. A statistical index for the degree of correlation between two variables when the relation is curvilinear. See *Correlational techniques*.   *G.M.*

Correlation table. The frequency table for a bivariate distribution (q.v.) which is used as the basis for calculating a correlation coefficient (q.v.). In a correlation table the values of the two variables are arranged in order of magnitude, horizontally and vertically, so that their quantitative relationship is clear.   *G.M.*

Correspondence, law of. The theory that whatever is true of "molecular" behavior is also true of "molar" behavior, and that a unifying principle can be found. This theory is taken over from physics.   *C.D.F.*

Corresponding (retinal) points. The points in the retina which correspond to one another in both eyes, so that when images are formed on both retinas double vision (q.v.) does not occur, but a single visual image is perceived. If these points are determined geometrically by retinal coordinates, they are called coincident points or *identical* (*retinal*) *points* (q.v.).   *A.H.*

Cortex cerebri. See *Cerebral cortex*.

Cortical. Pertaining to the *cortex cerebri*. In physiological terminology it denotes brain processes which occur rationally and consciously, such as thinking (q.v.), recognizing, abstracting, calculating, etc., in contrast to subcortical brain processes which occur unconsciously.   *E.D.*

Cortical blindness. See *Agnosia*.

Cortical deafness. This term is not much employed nowadays and once referred to a form of receptive aphasia in which sounds were heard but words could not be identified or understood.   *B.B.*

Cortical type. A term introduced by Kraus (1919) for a type of person in whom the intellect is most prominent and whose actions are controlled by the cortex.
Bibliography: Kraus, F.: Allgemeine und spezielle Pathologie der Person (2 vols). Leipzig, 1919–26.
                    W.K.

Corticosteroids. A group of steroid hormones, more than thirty in number, which—with the exception of aldosterone—are stimulated by the secretion of ACTH, and are formed in the adrenal cortex; in contrast to the hormones produced in the adrenal medulla they are essential to life because of their action on the carbohydrate, fat and mineral metabolic functions. The following are distinguished: (*a*) mineral corticoids (e.g. aldosterone, q.v.; 11-desoxycortisone; 11-desoxycorticosterone), which act on renal tubules and cause water and Na retention; (*b*) glucocorticoids, with an extensive effect on carbohydrate and sugar metabolism (e.g. cortisone, q.v., hydrocortisone, q.v., 11-dehydrocorticosterone [corticosterone]); (*c*) hormones concerned with protein metabolism or androgenic cortical hormones (e.g. androsterone, androstenedione) which in addition to promoting protein formation influence sexual behavior. Over- (or under-) activity of the adrenal cortex leads to serious physical and mental disorders (e.g. Addison's disease with under-activity; Cushing's disease and the adreno-genital syndrome, with over-activity). The secretion of corticosteroids varies distinctly according to the time of day (maximum in the early morning, minimum around midnight). In man, about 15–30 mg. are produced each day. Since 1950, numerous synthetic corticosteroids have been available, the most important being prednisone (Deltra, Delta-sone), prednisolone (Delta Cortef, Meti-cortelone) and dexamethasone (Decadron, Deronil). Corticosteroids play an important part in psychology in demonstrating the emotional effect of stress stimuli; hydro-cortisone (q.v.) in particular is a sensitive indicator of emotional tension. It has not yet been proved whether, as Selye maintains, there is a greater non-specific secretion of corticosteroids under all kinds of stress (physical or mental).

Bibliography: Currie, A. R., Symington, T. & Grant, J. K. (Eds): The human adrenal cortex. Baltimore, 1962. Dorfman, R. I. & Ungar, F.: Metabolism of steroid hormones. New York, 1965. Eisenstein, A. B. (Ed.): The adrenal cortex. London, 1967. Hübner, H. J. & Staib, W. H.: Biochemie der Nebennieren-rindenhormone. Stuttgart, 1965. Mason, J. W.: A review of psychoendocrine research on the pituitary-adrenal cortical system. Psychosom. Med., 1968, 30, 576–607. Murphy, B. E. P.: The determination of plasma levels of corticoids and their diagnostic significance. In: Bajusz, E. (Ed.): An introduction to clinical neuroendocrinology. Basle, 1967. Rubin, R. T.: Adrenal cortical activity in pathological emotional states: A review. Amer. J. Psychiat., 1966, 123, 387–400. See also Cortisone.   W.J.

Corticosterone. A hormone secreted by the adrenal cortex (see *Corticosteroids*), serving (as glucocorticoid) to regulate the carbohy-drate metabolism.   *W.J.*

Corticotrop(h)ine. See *ACTH*.

Corticotrop(h)ic hormone. See *ACTH*.

Cortisol. See *Hydrocortisone*.

Cortisone. A natural hormone (q.v.) of the adrenal cortex and prototype of the glucocorti-coids (see *Corticosteroids*). Used (now less often) in the treatment of a number of diseases (e.g. Addison's disease, arthritis, allergies, inflammations). ACTH, or adreno-corticotrophic hormone (q.v.), stimulates the production of cortisone. Exogenous admin-istration of cortisone blocks its natural production in the body. Psychological effects correspond closely to those of ACTH. It has been the object of only a few psycholo-gical investigations. There are no certain effects on performance and subjective con-dition when taken in physiological doses. Nor is there any statistical confirmation of euphoric reactions reported in patients.

Bibliography: Delay, J. *et al.*: Etude expérimentale des modifications psychologiques produites par les traitments à l'ACTH et la cortisone. Encéphale, 1952, *41*, 393–406. Kaiser, H.: Cortisonderivate in Klinik und Praxis. Stuttgart, 1968. Lidz, T., *et al.*: Effects of ACTH and cortisone on mood and mentation. Psychosom. Med., 1953, *14*, 363–77.   *W.J.*

Couéism. A method of psychotherapy by *autosuggestion* employed by E. Coué. The patient is first taught the effects of auto-suggestion by physical exercises such as telling himself he is falling backwards, or that he is unable to release his clasped fingers. He is then instructed to repeat to himself frequently every day a suggestion relating to his symptoms or affect, e.g. that he is be-ginning to feel much better.   *G.D.W.*

Counseling. An interpersonal relationship in which one person (the counselor) attempts to help another (the counselee) to understand and cope with his problems in the areas of education, vocation, family relationships, and so on. The term covers a wide range of pro-cedures, including the giving of advice and encouragement, providing information con-cerning available opportunities, and the interpretation of test results. Counseling differs from psychotherapy in that it is usually applied to help "normals" rather than patients, although the two processes merge imperceptibly on many occasions, as in C. Rogers' *Client-centered therapy* (q.v.). In *non-directive counseling* the counselor merely "lends a friendly ear" to the counselee, perhaps reflecting his thoughts and feelings, and detailing the alternative forms of behavior. A *directive* counselor, on the other hand, is likely to lead the conversation and to try to persuade the counselee (or client) to behave in certain prescribed ways.   *G.D.W.*

Coupling (in genes, q.v.). Some hereditary factors are in most cases coupled when they are transmitted from the parents to their off-spring. This is explained by the chromosome theory of heredity: coupled genes are to be found in the same chromosome (q.v.) which is generally transmitted as a whole so that only those maternal and paternal genes can combine freely which are located in different chromosomes. Coupling can be interrupted by crossing-over (q.v.).   *H.S.*

Courtship behavior. Modes of expression during pairing and the prelude to mating behavior and copulation (q.v.). Courtship includes ritual behaviors such as mating dances and mating song. At this time strikingly showy features are displayed. It cannot always be clearly distinguished from aggressive *displays* (q.v.), etc. Courtship may have numerous functions. It is: (*a*) an indication of presence, serves (i) to attract the sexual partner, (ii) to ward off rivals; it aids recognition of: (*b*) the identity of species (courtship rituals of closely related species in the same location are often different), and (*c*) readiness to pair; it inhibits (*d*) non-sexual activities (especially aggression); it reinforces (*e*) intimacy between mates; and serves especially to (*f*) stimulate the individual, the partner, and synchronization for the act of copulation. That mating fits into a social framework can be seen in subsidiary functions of courtship such as feeding the mate, indicating the nest, and so on.

Bibliography: Bastock, M.: Courtship. London, 1967.
                                                          R.A.S.

Counterprobability is a term used in statistical hypothesis testing. It denotes the probability α of erroneous rejection of the null hypothesis in the case of a (significant) deviation of a sample result from the random expectation.
                                                          W.H.B.

Couvade. A custom according to which the father of a child assumes the mother's role by taking to his bed immediately after the birth, while the mother quickly returns to her usual work. This custom has survived longest in southern France (Béarn) and among the Basques (in Europe at least). The couvade often developed from the ceremony which lent a magic emphasis to fatherhood at the transition from a matrilinear (see *Matriarchate*) to a patrilinear society. In general it reflects the structural principles of exchange and social symmetry demonstrated by Lévi-Strauss (1965) in the rules of exogamy. The man and woman "perform" and suffer the birth in equal measure.

Bibliography: Lévi-Strauss, C.: The elementary structures of kinship. New York, 1965. Id.: The savage mind. London & New York, 1966.   *W.Sc.*

Covariance. The measurement of the tendency of two series to vary concomitantly. Given two normalized series, $x_1, x_2, \ldots x_n$ and $y_1, y_2, \ldots y_n$, their covariance $= \sum_{i=1}^{n} (x_i y_i)/n$.
                                                          C.D.F.

Covariance analysis. An extension of the method of analysis of variance: (*a*) in order to reduce experimental error, (*b*) in order to analyze the effect of independent variables on the covariance of two dependent variables. E.g., the use of covariance analysis is necessary when the effect of two teaching methods on retention performance has to be studied in two groups of differing intelligence, since it can be assumed that intelligence and retention performance are not independent of one another. See *Variance, analysis of. G.M.*

Covariant phenomenon. An illusion of depth perception first described by Jaensch. Three threads are hung in front of the observer in a frontal parallel plane. If one outer thread is moved backward and forward the middle appears to move in the opposite direction forward and backward.   *C.D.F.*

Covariation. The concomitant variation between two or more characteristics (variables). The prerequisite for determining statistical dependence or relation. See *Covariance*.
                                                          G.M.

Covert response. Behavior which cannot be directly established by an observer but must be concluded from measurement values, from the observation of the further behavior of the subject, or from the verbal report obtained by the introspection (q.v.) of the subject. The distinction between *covert* and *overt* (q.v.) responses was at first strongly stressed by behaviorism in deposing the traditional psychology of consciousness, but was finally attenuated by the admission of verbal answers as equally objective data. In programmed instruction (q.v.) the purely mental response procedure offers the advantage of a generally shorter learning period over overt response procedure.   *L.J.I.*

Craniology. See *Phrenology*.

Creative synthesis. Apperception (q.v.): the combination of elements into a significant whole in, e.g., conceptualization.

Creativity. The ability to see new relationships, to produce unusual ideas and to deviate from traditional patterns of thinking. One of the prime objects of psychological research is the analysis of creative personality, the creative process, and the products of the creative process, together with the problem of how to encourage creativity. See *Abilities; Personality*.

Bibliography: Gruber, H. E. *et al.*: Contemporary approaches to creative thinking. New York, 1962. Mooney, R. L. & Razik, T. A. (Eds): Explorations in creativity. Chicago, 1967. Taylor, C. W. & Barron, F.: Scientific creativity: its recognition and development. New York, 1963. Taylor, C. W. (Ed.): Creativity: progress and potential. New York, 1964. Vernon, P. E. (Ed.): Creativity: selected readings. Harmondsworth, 1970.   *G.K.*

Creativity tests. Experiments to measure creativity accurately have been conducted since 1930 (C. Spearman); significant studies however have only been made in recent years (C. W. Taylor, J. P. Guilford). In particular it was Guilford's concept of divergent (q.v.) thinking which led to the construction of serviceable tests. What is required in these tests is essentially the production of as large a number of answers as possible (e.g. as many suitable titles as possible have to be found for some story).

Bibliography: Goldman, R. J.: The Minnesota tests of creative thinking. Educ. Res. 1964, *7*, 3–14. Guilford, J. P.: The nature of human intelligence. New York, 1967. Wilson, R. C., Guilford, J. P. *et al.*: A factor-analytical study of creative thinking abilities. Psychometrika, 1954, *19*, 297–311.   *G.L.*

Credibility (syn. *Trustworthiness*). In the legal sense, a deposition (testimony) is evidence that helps a court (or other body) to establish the facts of a case. The court is obliged to take all depositions into account in arriving at its judgment, and to check each of them for credibility, or probable compatibility with the true facts.

A psychologist can appraise the deposition for prosecution purposes in the light of the following criteria: (*a*) the probability of accurate *perception* of the facts (this depends on corrections of customary errors of perception and estimation, e.g. of time, speed, and number), and the probability of *distortion*, under the influence of strong emotion, of the events perceived; (*b*) the probability of accurate *retention* of remembered incidents, i.e. the distinction between original and subsequent events, between personal experience and the influence of suggestion; (c) the *ability to reproduce* the facts accurately. The ability to give testimony depends upon the whole personality of the person concerned. This calls for careful appraisal, and special account has to be taken of any evidence of character traits that have a special bearing on the deposition made. Accuracy of perception is influenced by a person's intellectual capacity, his state of mind at the time of the act, and motivation control (selectivity of perception). Similar factors also influence suggestibility. Investigation of the possible motivation that might lead to a deposition lacking in credibility helps psychologists to judge whether a statement is credible.

The methods used in assessing credibility are extremely problematic. Agreement has not yet been reached as to the utility of general criteria for its assessment. Most psychologists are trying to establish such criteria and apply them. Some, however, consider that each case is too specific to admit of such general criteria. If, in judicial proceedings, only credibility with respect to a specific case is taken as significant, general credibility, i.e. credibility established in the light of general criteria, would seem to be of doubtful immediate utility.

Bibliography: Abercrombie, M. L. Johnson: The anatomy of judgment. London, 1967. Britt, S. H.: The rules of evidence: an empirical study in psychology and law. Cornell Law Quart., 1940, *25*, 556–80.
                                                                                    O. Topič

Crespi effect. Some increment in learning which appears suddenly and intensely and which is disproportionate to the increased reinforcement (q.v.).

Bibliography: Crespi, L. P.: Quantitative variation of incentive and performance in the white rat. Amer. J. Psychol., 1942, *55*, 467–517.   *K.E.P.*

Cretinism (*Congenital myxedema*). A congenital condition in which there is a complete absence or defective functioning of the thyroid gland (see *Hypofunction*) of unknown

causation. An iodine deficiency, endogenous influences or a goitrous mother have been suggested as responsible for fetal damage in these cases. Cretinism frequently occurs in districts where goiter is endemic. The characteristic features of the cretin are stunted physical growth, disturbances in the development of the central nervous system, the skeleton and the skin, and severe subnormality of varying intensity, and a retardation of metabolism. The cretin presents a bloated appearance with a lack of expression; the nose is flat, the hair thick and bristly, the tongue large, and the fingers short; he is hard of hearing and may even be deaf; speech is retarded; there may be constipation and occasionally goiter. The disease can be prevented by prophylactic iodine therapy of expectant mothers and young babies in districts where goiter is prevalent.   *E.D.*

Criminality. The tendency to exhibit behavior which is contrary to the criminal law; more usually, repeated or persistent commission of criminal offences. The utility of this term as a description of individuals has been questioned on the ground that it defines too heterogeneous a class of people (Wootton, 1959) and that—because the scope and limits of the criminal law vary from time to time and from place to place—it entails an arbitrary and psychologically-irrelevant distinction between criminal acts and other forms of deviant social behavior (Mannheim, 1962). Many actions which fall within the scope of the criminal law escape notice, or cannot be traced to their authors; it follows that the group of persons identified as criminals by reason of conviction in the courts inevitably reflects the biases inherent in police practice (Walker, 1965). These limitations upon the empirical definition of criminality constitute a major obstacle to attempts to develop systematic explanations for these forms of deviant social behavior.

The majority of recorded crimes are offenses against property—mainly thefts of various kinds, but also frauds, embezzlement and robbery (i.e. theft involving personal violence or threat). Assaults, murders, crimes of wounding, and sexual offenses are much less frequent, at least in contemporary Western countries. With the two exceptions of shoplifting and offenses related to prostitution, crime is overwhelmingly a male matter; the ratio of the sexes in respect of criminal convictions in Britain being about six to one, a figure typical of Western states. Crime is also predominantly an activity of the young; the peak incidence of convictions tends to occur a little before the age of leaving school, although there is some evidence that future recidivists start earlier than those offenders whose criminal histories are comparatively brief (Walker, 1965). On the whole (and taking into account the immense differences in the frequency of offenses of different kinds), recidivists are seldom specialists, except for those who commit frauds and crimes of breaking-and-entering; most of those with several convictions have committed crimes of more than one kind (Hammond & Chayen, 1963).

1. *Classical theories of criminality*. The early development of criminological theory was dominated by three schools of thought which have exerted considerable influence upon contemporary research. The positivist and crimino-biological schools (Mannheim, 1965) stressed the belief that persistent criminals were atavistic deviants in the process of man's evolution; this view prompted a search for physical signs of primitivism, and an interest in constitutional correlates of criminality which has its modern counterpart in the study of physique and chromosomal endowment in persistent offenders. A second stream of research has concentrated upon the intellectual characteristics of offenders: the imprudent, unprofitable nature of much crime gave rise to the belief that most criminals were too stupid to understand the consequences of their actions. It now appears that early estimates of the incidence of subnormality in criminal populations were much too high (Woodward, 1955), but the investi-

gation of cognitive characteristics of offenders continues to be an important field of research. The third major source of criminological ideas has been psychoanalysis, whose influence is apparent in two respects. First, it has drawn attention to the irrational nature of much criminal behavior. Freud (1915) described the phenomenon of "criminality from a sense of guilt"—that is, offenses committed in order to provoke punishment which will alleviate guilt originating in the Oedipus complex. The notion that intra-psychic conflicts may be responsible for antisocial actions was further developed by Alexander & Staub (1929) and Friedlander (1947). Contemporary psychoanalytic theory assigns great importance to early parent-child relationships in the development of moral behavior; this has stimulated interest in the childhood experiences of criminals and delinquents (Bowlby, 1946; Glueck & Glueck, 1956).

2. *Contemporary developments*. Central to current thinking in relation to criminality is a learning-theory model, "passive avoidance conditioning". Early attempts to explain criminality in terms of learning emphasized the acquisition of criminal techniques or habits: e.g. Sutherland's principle of differential association (Sutherland & Cressey, 1955). But this is now the central problem; few crimes demand skills beyond the repertoire of most people. What is necessary is to show how normal individuals learn to inhibit socially-proscribed acts which they are able and motivated to perform, and to explain why this learning process is sometimes ineffective. Mowrer (1960a) suggested that the appropriate paradigm was that of passive avoidance conditioning; forbidden actions occurring spontaneously in childhood are punished, and (after several repetitions) these categories of behavior become associated with the aversive state induced by punishment. The contemplation of the forbidden action is thereafter sufficient to elicit resurgence of this aversive emotional state, blocking the consummatory phases of the behavioral sequence.

Mowrer's model has obvious implications for the problem of criminality. Lykken (1957) demonstrated a specific defect in the capacity to acquire conditioned avoidance responses in a group of persistent offenders ("primary sociopaths", selected according to Cleckley's criteria: see *Psychopathy*), a finding replicated by Schachter & Latané (1964). Eysenck (1964) argued that persistent criminality is usually (though not always) the consequence of an inherent unresponsiveness to conditioning procedures of all kinds which—according to his general theory of personality—is largely a function of extraversion. Thus highly-extraverted individuals will tend to become criminals unless they are subjected to particularly intense and efficient training. Whether conditionability is a general trait is still a matter of dispute; however, there is considerable experimental evidence to support Eysenck's theoretical arguments in so far as they relate to criminals.

3. *Constitutional bases of criminality.* Eysenck's theory is one of several recent contributions to criminology discourse which have revived interest in constitutional and genetic factors in the causation of criminal behavior. Several investigators of physical type (body build) have found a marked preponderance of mesomorphic physique among criminals, a discovery which compares interestingly with the known relationship between mesomorphy and extraversion (Eysenck, 1964). There have been many demonstrations of differences in autonomic functioning between those who commit crimes and those who do not (Hare, 1970), indicating the possibility of alternative explanations of the relations between physical type and criminality.

Johannes Lange (1929) furnished striking evidence for the existence of a genetic element in the causation of criminality, based upon a study of thirty pairs of twins, thirteen of which appeared to be uniovular. A number of twin studies (q.v.) conducted during the following three decades also yielded patterns which appeared to indicate the operation of a

genetic mechanism, although (because identical twins tend to experience similar childhood environments) such observations present major problems of interpretation (Slater, 1953). More recently attention has been focussed upon the discovery that chromosomal anomalies occur more frequently in certain groups of criminals than in the population at large. Early studies (using the Barr method of staining for sex-chromatin) showed an excess of individuals with supernumerary X-chromosomes among criminal subnormal men detained in state institutions; subsequent studies, using more sophisticated methods of karotyping, seem to indicate that there is a more direct connection between extra-complementary Y-chromosomes and criminal tendencies, a relation which sometimes occurs as the $XXYY$ pattern, so concealing the real nature of the anomaly (Casey *et al.*, 1966). These observations are peculiarly difficult to interpret; although some writers (such as Slater) offer an explanation in terms of the relation between male sexuality and disposition to commit crimes, others argue that subclinical cortical damage may be a crucial link in the connection (see Trasler, 1970, for references).

4. *Techniques of socialization.* The Mowrer model (like classical psychoanalysis) has directed interest to the interaction of parents and children in the process of socialization (that is, the acquisition of appropriate avoidance responses). There is undoubtedly some connection between family breakdown (the interruption of parent-child interaction) and delinquency, but whether this is to be attributed to "maternal deprivation" (as Bowlby would suggest), to the absence of the father at a critical period of the child's development (Grygier *et al.*, 1969), or merely to suspension of the socialization process, is not clear.

The avoidance-conditioning model has extensive implications concerning the sources of inefficiency in parental techniques for the training of children. The characteristics of conditioning procedures developed in the laboratory—the systematic pairing of conditional and unconditional stimuli, the phenomena of generalization, transfer and discrimination learning—have direct counterparts in the parameters of child-training methods, and constitute promising links between this psychological paradigm and the substantial body of sociological observations of patterns of parental behavior. The conjunction of these apparently disparate areas of criminological science has suggested a number of hypotheses which may help to explain consistent differences between socio-economic classes in the incidence of criminality; they may also have implications for long-term trends in the pattern and frequency of criminal behavior (Trasler, 1971).

In recent years increasing attention has been devoted to the role of language in mediating avoidance conditioning. It is clear that the efficiency of this process (in the Mowrer-Eysenck formulation) depends upon generalization from a few examples of punished wrongdoing, occurring spontaneously in childhood, to an extensive range of adult behaviors which have few features in common with the child analogue (Mowrer, 1960b). It is also apparent that the high resistance to extinction exhibited by social avoidance responses relies upon very effective discrimination cues. Bernstein argues that it is possible to distinguish at least two styles of language employed between parents and child, one of which ("elaborated code") is much better adapted to the task of securing efficient avoidance training than the other (termed "restricted code", q.v.). Ability to make use of the more sophisticated style of verbal interaction is a function of education, and is consequently correlated with the socio-economic status of the parents, an observation which may be relevant to the high incidence of delinquency among children of lower-class families (Lawton, 1968).

Although it is now established that the distribution of intelligence (using non-verbal tests) among criminals is not significantly different from that in the population as a whole, the incidence of serious school failure is very high in delinquent groups, apparently because of a specific handicap in the use of verbal and other symbols (Prentice & Kelly, 1963; Graham & Kamano, 1958). This is consistent with the contention that grasp of language is a condition of effective social avoidance training, and points to the importance of further investigation of the cognitive characteristics of persistent offenders (Trasler, 1971; Hare, 1970).

Contemporary developments in the theory of criminality thus reflect the integration of several major lines of inquiry, each of which (as it happens) has its roots in classical criminology.

Bibliography: Alexander, F. & Staub, H.: Der Verbrecher und seine Richter. Vienna, 1929. Bowlby, J.: Forty-four juvenile thieves. London, 1946. Casey, M. D., Blank, C. E., Street, D. R. K., Segall, L. J., McDougall, J. H., McGrath, P. J. & Skinner, J. L.: YY chromosomes and antisocial behaviour. Lancet, 1966, 859–60. Eysenck, H. J.: Crime and personality. London, 1964. Freud, S.: Some character-types met with in psycho-analytic work. Imago, Vol. 4, 1915. Friedlander, K.: The psycho-analytical approach to juvenile delinquency. London, 1947. Glueck, S. & Glueck, E. Physique and delinquency. New York, 1956. Graham, E. E. & Kamano, D.: Reading failure as a factor in the WAIS subtest patterns of youthful offenders. J. clin. Psychol. 1958, 14, 302–5. Grygier, T., Chesley, J. & Tuters, E. W.: Parental deprivation: a study of delinquent children. Brit. J. Criminol., 1969, 9, 209–53. Hammond, W. H. & Chayen, E.: Persistent criminals. London, 1963. Hare, R. D.: Psychopathy—theory and research. New York, 1970. Lange, J.: Verbrechen als Schicksal. Leipzig, 1929. Lawton, D.: Social class, language and education. London, 1968. Lykken, D. T.: A study of anxiety in the sociopathic personality. J. abnorm. soc. Psychol., 1957, 55, 6–10. Mannheim, H.: The study of crime. In: Welford, A. T. (Ed.): Society. London, 1962. Id.: Comparative criminology. London, 1965. Mowrer, O. H.: Learning theory and behavior. New York, 1960a. Id.: Learning theory and the symbolic processes. New York, 1960b. Prentice, N. M. & Kelly, F. J.: Intelligence and delinquency—a reconsideration. J. soc. Psychol., 1963, 60, 327–37. Schachter, S. & Latané, B.: Crime, cognition and the autonomic nervous system. In: Jones, M. R. (Ed.): Nebraska symposium on motivation. Lincoln, 1964. Slater, E.: Psychotic and neurotic illness in twins London, 1953. Sutherland, E. H. & Cressey, D. R.: Principles of criminology. Chicago, 1955. Trasler,

G. B.: The explanation of criminality. London, 1962.
Id.: Criminal behaviour. In: **Eysenck, H. J.** (Ed.): Handbook of abnormal psychology. London, ²1971. **Walker, N. D.**: Crime and punishment in Britain. Edinburgh, 1965. **Woodward, W. M.**: Low intelligence and delinquency. London, 1955. **Wootton, B.**: Social science and social pathology. London, 1959.

G. B. Trasler

Criminal psychology. Criminal psychology is concerned with the causes of criminality (q.v.), and tries to discover the factors which make an individual a criminal. Criminal psychology is to be distinguished from forensic psychology (q.v.), which is a branch of applied psychology, and comprises two directions of research, one orientated to constitutional psychology, and the other to social psychology.

Bibliography: Conger, J. J. & Miller, W. C.: Personality, social class and delinquency. New York, London & Sydney, 1966. **Glueck, S. & Glueck, E.**: Five hundred criminal careers. New York, 1930. **Lombroso, C.**: Crime, its causes and remedies. Boston, 1911. **Rosebuck, J. B.**: Criminal typology. Springfield, Ill., 1967.

F.M.

Criminology. There is only general agreement that criminology is criminal etiology, i.e. that it deals with the causes or factors producing crime. The most important areas of criminology are: (*a*) the observation, description, analysis and classification of crimes and criminals (criminal sociology); (*b*) research into factors producing crime which can be traced back to the organism, or to personality factors (criminal biology and psychology); (*c*) research into the significance of hereditary factors for criminality (criminological research into heredity); (*d*) the prognostication of criminality and recidivism (prognostic research); (*e*) victimology; (*f*) the sociological and sociopsychological study of prison communities. All these tasks are shared by different branches of empirical science: sociology, psychology, psychiatry, and the medical sciences adjacent to criminology; legal sociology, psychology and psychiatry. In addition to the above, further aspects of

criminology studied in the U.S.A. are *prophylaxis* and *penology*.   *H.M.*

Crisis. The term came into psychology from medicine; Hippocrates used it for the sudden cessation of a state which was gravely endangering life (in contrast to the slow *lysis*). Analogously, a crisis is thought of as being a dramatic decision, or coming to terms with mental conflicts.   *W.Sc.*

Criterion. 1. A *decisive* characteristic with which other characteristics are compared. A criterion (e.g. in a validity test) is an indisputable or undisputed measurement of what a test is required to measure. **2.** *Critical values* are said to be criteria when, after they have been reached or exceeded, an alternative decision changes into its opposite (e.g. passing an examination—not passing it).

Criterion group: a reference group with known characteristics used to test validity.
G.M.

Critical flicker frequency; critical flicker fusion. The rate at which the flicker, or rapid change in perception resulting from change in the stimulus, is replaced by a smooth fusion. See *Flicker photometry*.

Critical ratio. The ratio of a difference between two statistics, or of a statistic, to the *standard error* (q.v.) of that difference, or of that statistic.

Critical theory (Ger. *Kritische Theorie*). The name applied to the body of theory emanating from the Frankfurt school of sociology (the Institut für Sozialforschung), and mainly associated with T. W. Adorno, Max Horkheimer, Herbert Marcuse and, in recent years, Jürgen Habermas. Critical theory combines insights of Marxist and Freudian thought in its examinations of the various ways in which "interest" affects knowing, and has produced valuable studies of prejudice in areas ranging from family and education to epistemology, the best known of which in the English-speaking world is *The Authoritarian Personality*. Recently, critical theorists have concerned themselves with the attempts of (positivistic) scientists to establish an inter-subjectively binding language of factual statement in the social sciences.

Bibliography: Adorno, T. W. *et al.*: The authoritarian personality. New York, 1950. Habermas, J.: Erkenntnis und Interesse. Frankfurt, 1968. Horkheimer, M. & Adorno, T. W.: Dialectic of enlightenment. New York, 1972. Wellmer, A.: Critical theory of society. New York, 1971.   *J.C.*

Criticism, compulsive. An irresistible yet subjectively unconscious urge to find fault with (almost) everything. It is often an expression of inner discontent; there is an absence of self-criticism in the affected subject.

H.J.A.

Cross-cultural studies. The comparison and combination of certain cultures to see if similar behavior in different environments occurs under certain common conditions; or to see if certain results are produced by certain emphases (e.g. in learning or the use of folk remedies) that do not occur but might be valuable in the base culture; and so on. The field of research is vast and ranges from pioneering general studies (e.g. Mead, 1937) to cross-cultural studies of alcohol use (e.g. Child, Bacon & Barry, 1965). See *Anthropology; Social psychology*.

Bibliography: Child, I. L., Bacon, M. K. & Barry, H A cross-cultural study of drinking. Quart. J. Stud. Alc., 1965, Supp. 3. Mead, M. (Ed.): Cooperation and competition among primitive peoples. New York, 1937.   *J.G.*

Crossing-over. An "exchange of factors", or exchange of segments of two of the four homologous chromatids during meiosis, i.e. the reductive division of a diploid cell, part of which process is the splitting of each chromosome (q.v.) into two chromatids.

Bibliography: Loewy, A. G. & Siekeritz, P.: Cell structure and function. New York, 1969. Sinnott, E. W. *et al.*: Principles of genetics. New York & London, ⁶1958.   *I.M.D.*

Cross-section(al) method (syn. *Cross-section(al) investigation*). In contrast to the longitudinal method (q.v.), a means of investigating a large number of variables as they are found at a given period of time.

Crowd behavior. Crowd psychology (mass psychology) was one of the first areas of debate and investigation in social psychology, especially in France (Le Bon, 1895; Tarde, 1890). The development of interest in group dynamics, however, eventually took precedence. Recently, various types of event (demonstrations and conventions among the young, "violent" strikes, disasters—whether technical or military, and so on) have re-awakened interest in crowd studies. If we define a "*small group*" as a collection of individuals who are "face to face", we may think of a *crowd* as a collectivity whose members are "side by side": i.e. unorganized, temporary, irregular assemblies featuring a certain activity (which serves to distinguish them from *aggregations*, or collections of people without a common purpose, and "passive" public assemblies or totalities, e.g. *audiences*). The activity in question is categorized according to purpose and outcome: aggression (riots, lynchings), appropriation (occupation of buildings or localities, looting), avoidance or flight (reactions to disasters), and "expression" and play (festivals). Recent research (e.g. Cantril, R. Brown) is still more or less indebted for initial inspiration to Le Bon's descriptive schema (homogeneity of behavior and attitudes in crowds; the emotivity and irrationality which inspire them), and retains his hypothesis of unconscious tendencies freed from a certain form of social control in the anonymous context of the crowd (a point developed later by Freud), though of course it rejects

Le Bon's theory of a "spirit of the race" giving rise to the "crowd soul", or "collective mind". Nowadays research is directed toward explaining how the absence of any regulative interaction between individuals in such an assembly produces in them an illusion of power and of "universality": a kind of contagion allowing a transition to action and a collective "leveling" of manifest behaviors on the basis of a relative similarity of latent predispositions and, ultimately, of processes of emotional fusion and leader-identification. Analyses are also made of the various degrees of "implication" of the individual in the crowd, which can differ considerably according to personality and the occasion. See *Le Bon, G.*

Bibliography: Brown, R.: Social psychology. New York, 1965. Cantril, H.: The psychology of social movements. New York, 1941. Id.: The pattern of human concerns. New Brunswick, N.J., 1965. Le Bon, G.: La psychologie des foules. Paris, 1895. Sprott, W. J. H.: Human groups. Harmondsworth, 1958. Tarde, G.: Les lois de l'imitation. Paris, 1890. Id.: L'Opinion de la foule. Paris, 1901.   *F. Jodelet*

Crude score (syn. *Raw score*). In contrast to a *derived score*, an original, statistically unanalyzed or non-transformed score, or observational value.

Cryptesthesia. An assumed hyperacuity of the senses sometimes invoked as an explanation of alleged ESP (q.v.).   *J.B.*

Cryptomnesia. Recall without recognition. A buried memory for some fact; sometimes invoked to explain an apparent paranormal awareness.   *J.B.*

Cryptorchism. The failure or retardation of descent of one or both testes into the scrotum; instead, they remain in the body cavity or in the inguinal canal. For sperm to be produced normally and to make procreation possible, the testes must descend into the scrotum before puberty, or there is a danger

of malignant degeneration. If descent has not occurred at puberty, hormone therapy is usually necessary, though surgery may be recommended. Mental disturbance must be avoided, e.g. by careful explanation of the condition and treatment.   *K.-D.N.G.*

Cue appreciation, recognition. See *Sign learning.*

Culpability. See *Conscience; Guilt.*

Cult. In modern cultural anthropology (q.v.), a cult or rite is regarded as an activity—as distinct from a myth, which summarizes and interprets the spiritual or intellectual content of cults. Myth and cult are inseparably linked. After some years of religious-phenomenological analysis of "primitive" cults (Jensen, 1960), attention is now being devoted to their (group) psychotherapeutic function.

Bibliography: Durkheim, E.: The elementary forms of the religious life. London, 1915. Eliade, M.: Patterns in comparative religion. London & New York, 1958. Jensen, A. E.: Mythos und K. bei Naturvölkern. Wiesbaden, 1960. Schmidbauer, W.: Psychohygienische und (gruppen)psychotherapeutische Aspekte "primitiver" Riten. Jb. Psychol. Psychother, med. Anthropol. 1970, *18*, 238–57.
                                                            W.Sc.

Cultural anthropology. 1. Whereas *ethnology* (q.v.) is chiefly concerned with the analysis of so-called "primitive" societies, cultural anthropology uses comparative methods to study intercultural possibilities in order to establish typical conceivable patterns of human behavior, both individual and social. It works in close alignment with ethnology (see *Ethnopsychology*) and social psychology on the one hand, and with comparative psychology (q.v.) (research into animal, and especially primate behavior), on the other hand. From the methodological point of view, this comparative approach provides answers to questions which cannot be studied experimentally; it was on such grounds that W. Wundt based his somewhat too extensive separation of experimental from ethnological psychology (see *Folk psychology*). *W.Sc.*

2. In the sense of *cultural sociology*, cultural anthropology is concerned with the analysis of expectations, norms and symbols, the ways in which they are passed from generation to generation (see *Socialization*), and their effects on the structuring of individual existence and the shaping of (individual) life styles. The last is the particular study of cultural anthropology and the psychology of culture in a narrower sense. See *Social anthropology; Culture, psychology of*.

Bibliography: Kroeber, A. L.: The nature of culture. Chicago, Ill., 1952. Malinowski, B.: A scientific theory of culture. Chapel Hill, N.C., 1944. Mühlmann, W. E. & Müller, E. W. (Eds): Kulturanthropologie. Cologne & Berlin, 1966. Znaniecki, F.: Cultural sciences. Urbana, Ill., 1952. *W.D.F.*

Cultural determinants. Factors, mostly norms and ideals, with a unifying influence which determine events and actions for groups of people (such as ways of perceiving, thinking and acting) but also control diversity and differentiation (e.g. the distribution of roles, and their mutual adjustment and complementation as the case may be). Language (q.v.) is one of the most important cultural determinants.

Bibliography: Child, I. L.: Personality in culture. In: Borgatta, E. F. & Lambert, W. W. (Eds): Handbook of personality theory and research. Chicago, 1968, 82–145. *M.A.*

Cultural lag. A term introduced in connection with cultural change and with the analysis of disturbances of an existing cultural system (e.g. by industrialization); it indicates a falling-behind, or a period of time between the point when some technological goal is reached and the point when the attainment of that goal has been absorbed by society. In general, the reason is a discrepancy between set norms and the state of society at the time

when the norms are accepted. It is assumed that social planning will help to avoid such discrepancies, or reduce the intervals of time. *W.D.F.*

Cultural neurosis. Although neuroses (q.v.) are ubiquitous, in their genesis they are often structurally related to the cultural medium in which they make their appearance. At present, one hears much about "neuroses" developing in contemporary society and it is implied that the same dynamics are active as in neuroses proper. This phenomenon might lead to the conclusion that the anxiety-ridden constitution of man is more manifest now than at other times. The secularization of modern life, the transformation of sex into merchandise, and the toleration of aggressiveness are some of the underlying problems. See *Aggression; Alienation*.

Bibliography: Horkheimer, M. & Adorno, T. W.: The dialectic of enlightenment. New York, 1972. Marcuse, H.: One dimensional man. Boston, 1964. *J.-L.I.*

Cultural puberty. A distinction is made between *primitive* puberty and *cultural* puberty according to the significance of the sexual drive. Whereas the former refers to the uninhibited, the latter corresponds to the inhibited form. Spiritual, inward values are prominent and their acquisition is preferred to sexual interests. Young people look for a purpose in life. Intellectual affinity and common interests determine friendships with the opposite sex.

Bibliography: Busemann, A.: Pädagogische Jugendkunde. Frankfurt, 1953. *M.Sa.*

Cultural science psychology. See *Geisteswissenschaftliche Psychologie*.

Culture-free intelligence tests. Constructed at the Institute of Personality and Ability Testing under the direction of R. B. Cattell. They have to be as independent *as possible* of any cultural influences, and therefore contain only exercises with figures (series, classification, matrices and overlapping figures).

Bibliography: Cattell, R. B. & Cattell, A. K. S.: IPAT Culture Free Intelligence Test. Inst. Pers. Abil. Test. Champain, Ill., 1950–59.   *R.M.*

Culture, psychology of. Founded by W. Dilthey; a mode of interpreting individual areas of culture in the past or present by *understanding* them. The tasks of the psychology of culture have now to a large extent been taken over by cultural anthropology (q.v.), as a comparative approach allows of much more sensitive analyses of cultural elements and biological determinants.

W.Sc.

Cumulation. A term in statistics for a method of calculation in which every value of a distribution is added to the sum of the lower values. It occurs in the representation of frequency distributions (q.v.).   *G.M.*

Cumulative frequency. A term for the sums of frequencies of a distribution which are calculated by the successive addition of score or class frequencies in order of magnitude. The total number of cases is determined up to a certain point of a distribution. A graphic representation of the arrangement is known as a *cumulative frequency curve.*

G.M.

Cunnilingus. Oral contact with female genitals (*cunnus*), largely taboo in Jewish-Christian cultural areas. Historical tradition shows that cunnilingus was accepted in many older cultures. Ethology (q.v.) shows that oral-genital contacts are widespread among mammals. The use of cunnilingus correlates quite positively with the level of education. As a masturbation (q.v.) technique, cunnilingus in female homosexual relationships (see *Homosexuality*) is not so widespread as fellatio (q.v.) in those between males. In heterosexual relationships, cunnilingus is more often requested by the male than permitted by the female partner, by reason of the taboo.

Bibliography: Kinsey, A. *et al.:* Sexual behavior in the human female. New York, 1953.   *G.L.*

Curare. A collective name for arrow-poisons (of a strychnine-like kind) obtained from plants by South- and Central-American Indians. Curare contains several alkaloids with a similar pharmacological effect. The most important substances isolated are *d*-tubocurarine and toxiferine. Numerous substances have curare-like effects and are produced semi- or wholly synthetically (e.g. gallamine) and included with curare in the group of curare-like ganglion blocking agents. Curare blocks the transmission of acetylcholine (q.v.) to the muscles (neuro-muscular junction), so that the result is muscular paralysis, and in larger doses death from cessation of breathing. Some substances related to curare are used as spasmolytics (q.v.). There are very few central and autonomic effects from curare-like substances; as they do not pass the blood-brain barrier (q.v.), the central and autonomic effects which have occasionally been observed are apparently conditioned by a reduction in the adrenalin released in the adrenal medulla and by the release of histamine (q.v.). *D*-tubocurarine is used in experimental research on the emotions to explore the relationship between proprioceptive feedback and emotion, especially anxiety. Doses of *d*-tubocurarine reduce anxiety under aversive stimuli.

Bibliography: Davison, G. C.: Anxiety under total curarization: Implications for the role of muscular relaxation in the desensitization of neurotic fears. J. nerv. ment. dis., 1966, *143*, 443–8. De Ruek, A. v. S.: Curare and curare-like agents. London, 1962. Solomon, R. L. & Turner, L. J.: Discriminative classical conditioning in dogs paralyzed by curare can later control discriminative avoidance responses in the normal state. Psychol. Rev., 1962, *69*, 202–19. Thomas, K. B.: Curare: its history and usage. London, 1964.   *W.J.*

Curriculum. The meaning has been widened to include nowadays the unity of the subjects taught, teaching methods and aims. Proficient research endeavors to formulate curricula which fit teaching methods to the particular exigencies of individual subjects or intersubject aims (e.g. moral education). Nowadays curriculum planning is of increasing importance in regard to the organizational restructuring of schools and educational institutions in order to cater for varying abilities (q.v.), but at the same time to foster a spirit of democratic equality. Strategies have to be developed locally or nationally in accordance with legal requirements, dominant socio-cultural norms, national economic requirements, the distribution of intelligence in a population or area, and availability of trained teachers and counselors. See *Educational science*. *G.B.*

Curvature illusion. A class of illusions involving the misperception of curvature. An example is provided by *Hering's illusion* (q.v.), in which straight lines appear curved and by the illusion below in which the two central lines are of equal curvature, but appear to be different by contrast with their surroundings. *C.D.F.*

Curve fitting. The use of, e.g., the least-square method (q.v.) to discover the curve most appropriate to the data.

Cutaneous resistance. See *Skin resistance*.

Cutaneous sense. Cutaneous sensitivity is aroused by the stimulation of different nerve ends, or skin receptors. It allows of three modalities of cutaneous feeling: *mechanical* (pressure, vibration), *thermic*, and *pain-induced*. Sensitivity varies according to the part of the body. The hands, soles of the feet, lips and sexual organs are most sensitive; the back and buttocks least sensitive. *V.M.*

Cybernetic education (*Educational cybernetics*). Problems, suggested solutions and results which come under both cybernetics *and* education. It replaces holistic-intuitive methods by methods of calculation which have proved successful in the modern natural sciences; in cybernetic education, mathematical methods are used not only (as in non-cybernetic education) for statistical analyses, but for the development of workable and verifiable models. The aim of cybernetic education is to objectify teaching by the use of technical systems such as teaching machines (*cybernation*).

Cybernetic education is divided into three stages of increasing complexity. At the *first stage* the six components ("dimensions") of instruction are analyzed separately and interpreted in mathematical terms; at the *second stage* their interdependence, and at the *third stage* their dependence on the socio-cultural environment and feedback to it comprise the object of cybernetic research.

The six cybernetico-educational disciplines at the first stage (basic educational sciences) are as follows: (*a*) theory of subject-matter (information); (*b*) theory of media (in particular teaching machines and computer-assisted instruction); (*c*) psychostructural theory (see *Information, psychology of*); (*d*) sociostructural theory (programs); (*e*) theory of teaching aims; (*f*) theory of instructional algorithms. Information theory (q.v.) enables quantitative statements to be made on subject-matter and connected with learning ability. Abstract machine (automata) theory forms the cybernetic basis of the theory of media and instructional algorithms.

The second-stage disciplines are "didactic". In all, there are sixty-two possible combinations of these disciplines. They consider specific instances ("conditional fields") in the context of the six dimensions referred to above, and determine which didactic decisions are compatible with these instances in the remaining dimensions ("decision fields"). For example, the didactic method of programmed instruction (q.v.) tries to establish instructional algorithms (decision field) which will enable given information to be imparted by a given medium to a psychologically defined group of learners under the influence of certain statistically predictable socio-cultural conditions, in accordance with a given target-criterion (five condition fields).

The third-stage cybernetico-educational disciplines include, e.g., educational economics, instructional organization, the history and geography of education (to be expressed in mathematical terms), and educational and futurology research based on all these concepts.

Cybernetico-educational theory has developed specific methods of programmed instruction, based on information psychology, and using computers to produce instructional algorithms. See *Instructional technology.*

Bibliography: Atkinson, R. C. & Wilson, H. A.: Computer-assisted instruction: A book of readings. New York, 1969. Coulson, J. E. (Ed.): Programmed learning and computer-based instruction. New York, 1962. Frank, H.: Kybernetische Grundlagen der Pädagogik. Baden-Baden, ²1969. Hickey, A. E. & Newton, J. N.: Computer-assisted instruction: A survey of the literature. Newburyport, Mass., 1966. Holtzman, W. (Ed.): Computer-assisted instruction, testing and guidance. New York, 1970. Mager, R. F.: Preparing instructional objectives. Palo Alto, Cal., 1962. Pask, G.: An approach to cybernetics. London, 1961. Smallwood, R. D.: A decision structure for teaching machines. Cambridge, Mass., 1962. Unwin, D. & Leedham, J.: Aspects of educational technology. London, 1967.   *H. Frank*

Cybernetic organism. An information-processing system which can fulfill at least the following functions: perception, motivated operational thinking and outward-directed activity. In this sense, every adult human is a cybernetic organism. Cybernetics endeavors to construct technical simulation models of such organisms.

Bibliography: Stachowiak, H.: Denken und Erkennen im kybernetischen Modell. Heidelberg, 1965.
                                    K.-D.G.

Cybernetics and psychology. 1. *The terms of reference of cybernetics and the interrelation of cybernetics and psychology.* Cybernetics is a *cross-sectional science* in which general laws (regularities) are developed from different individual sciences, examined, and formulated on a suitable level of abstraction. Formal means of representation have been developed for this purpose within the framework of the mathematical sciences. These enable relationships and interactions between complex systems or part-systems to be expressed. A universal characteristic of complex, highly organized systems is the ability to record, process and transmit information. In the present state of scientific development, *research into the structure and functions of data (information) processing systems* has emerged as the specific sphere of study of cybernetics. The research methods of cybernetics are directed toward the presentation and analysis of, and its research objective is, the synthesis and optimization of data-processing systems. Systems of this kind, which are treated in abstract terms in the context of cybernetics, are found in different branches of science: e.g. in physiology (receptor systems, sensorimotor coordination processes, nerve cells functioning as information storage-systems, and nerve networks); in genetics (specification of inherited information, coding and transmission of this information from one generation to another); in operational research (organization of the exchange of information within and between groups); in technological control (development of self-optimizing, technical systems which are capable of "learning"); and in communications and information (optimization of data transmission, self-adapting receiver and sign-recognition systems). One area of experimental psychology which is closely related with this subject is concerned with the analysis of cognitive structures and functions (in particular those of perception, learning, concept formation, thought and speech). These processes are specifically dependent on emotional and affective influences or on differing inner activation levels, while at the same time influencing these conditions. Precise analysis of these processes is therefore concerned with more than a mere description of their own structural laws. It relates them to problems of personality research and clinical psychology.

All the *cognitive* processes in man are very closely related to the exchange of information between the organism and its environment: the laws of perception are based on the modes of data processing by the receptor and analyzer systems; the strategies of concept formation are based on procedures of information generation and utilization (formation and testing of hypotheses). Learning processes are expressed in behavioral changes to the extent that they occur as a consequence of individual data processing; thought processes such as those involved in problem-solving are based on specific interactions between classification and transformation processes, which form a basic algorithmic structure. This applies right up to the level of heuristic processes as the potentially most effective and at the same time most dangerous strategies for the human acquisition of information. Linguistic competence (as an internal, cognitive linguistic structure) and language use (as the ability to form comprehensible sentences) are the bases of linguistic communication as the most advanced form of information exchange between living beings. To the extent that psychophysical processes are essentially processes of information acquisition and processing, they are the object of research by both experimental psychologists and cyberneticians. Research into the structure and function of such complex system-characteristics can help to enrich the theory and construction of cybernetic models; at the same time, cybernetic methods and means of representation can assist psychological research.

2. *The development of cybernetics.* The current means of representation and research in cybernetics are characterized by four independent discoveries, although cybernetics existed even before these advances: (*a*) The discovery that stable system-behavior in the presence of unpredictable causal disturbances (noise interference) can be achieved by feedback of the instantaneous error if the error value (or its dynamic pattern) is used as a correction parameter (Wiener, 1948). In technology this principle has led to the development of control theory; analogies can be drawn with biological control processes: the self-stabilization of homeostatic functions (Ashby, 1956), eye movement, the regulation of muscular tension and sensorimotor coordination are all subject to the same principle (Küpfmüller, 1959). (*b*) The discovery that the information conveyed by a signal (q.v.) can be expressed, and that information content can be measured in physical terms (Shannon & Weaver, 1949). The coding principle of information theory, the capacity of an information-conveying system (channel capacity, q.v.), and the influence of disturbances ("noise") on the reliability of recognition, are all fundamental in the characterization of the capacity of organismic receptor systems ("perceptrons") (Rosenblatt, 1958; Arkadjew & Brawermann, 1966). (*c*) The discovery that transmission structures of the type represented by nerve networks are able to maintain the reliability of recognition of *transformed* input signals or signs (McCulloch & Pitts, 1943; von Neumann, 1958). (*d*) The discovery that information-processing systems can be represented in a theoretically self-contained form with unified means (Gluschkow, 1963). This has contributed in large measure to the development of the theory of abstract automata (Starke, 1969), of higher programming and algorithmic languages, and of the simulation of problem-solving behavior (Feigenbaum & Feldmann, 1963) on computers. *Control theory, information theory, algorithm and automata theory* now constitute the fundamental disciplines of cybernetics,

and in turn lead to specific developments such as learning systems, semantic information theory, formal language theory, and artificial intelligence. All three basic disciplines have resulted in greater knowledge in experimental psychology.

3. *Application and results of cybernetic research methods in experimental psychology.* (a) The methods and means of presentation of control theory have been used in the analysis of highly practiced and learning-dependent, sensorimotor coordination processes (e.g. tracking; motor skills, q.v.). The basic approach may be represented thus

$$\frac{x(t)}{x(s)} \rightarrow \boxed{\frac{h(t)}{H(S)}} \rightarrow \frac{y(t)}{y(s)}.$$

We assume a continuous input function $x(t)$ (on which stochastic disturbances may be superimposed), and the consequential movement $y(t)$ as the output function. We then look for the internal system-structure $h(t)$ which simulates the transmission behavior characteristic of the system under investigation:

$$h(t) = \frac{x(t)}{y(t)}.$$

It has been shown (E. S. Krendel, D. T. McRuer, etc.) that the communicative behavior characteristic of man under specific, limited input conditions can be described by the following equation:

$$A(S) = \frac{e^{-T_o{}^{(S)}}(\alpha T_1 s + 1)}{(T_2 s + 1)(T_3 s + 1)} K(\sigma),$$

in which T_o is the reaction time, dependent on the input signal. T_1 are time constants, and s shows that the input and output functions are transmitted in the range of Laplace transforms. The second component of the numerator is a differential component. It describes the anticipatory content of the transfer system, or the ability of the human being to anticipate processes from specific input functions. The denominator contains two linear first-order time-elements. They describe the adaptability of the system

behavior to changes in the state of the input functions. (The factor K includes non-linearities.) The same approximation is also possible if the input and output signals are stochastically disturbed. The adaptation is then formed through the performance spectra of the input and output functions. (The performance spectrum of a signal is the Fourier transform of the auto- or cross-correlational function.) This approach has been generalized and extended (Schweizer, 1968). The aim of this process is to optimize certain work or control actions. In particular it is necessary to design optimal man-machine systems (q.v.) of the kind studied in human engineering. It has been shown that if sensorimotor demands are inadequately adapted to human transfer behavior, highly-skilled individuals (e.g. pilots in supersonic aircraft simulators) show worse performance than unskilled test subjects in optimized systems. To analyze the optimal design of a man-machine system, the phase characteristic is determined and the range with good compatibility proposed to the designers for preparation of the machine system. Similar methods have also been developed for the analysis of sensorimotor learning behavior.

4. *Methods, and means of representation, of information theory* have been used primarily in the analysis of signal recognition processes, in choice reaction experiments, in processes of complex pattern identification (organismic sign recognition), and in connection with problems of language generation and linguistic communication in psychology. We may take as an example findings made in connection with recognition performance in choice reaction experiments. One basis is Shannon's (1949) measure of information. According to this assumption, the information content $I(x_i)$ of an event is inversely proportional to the logarithm (to base 2) of the probability of its occurrence:

$$I(x_i) = 1d\frac{1}{p(x_i)} = -\log_2 p(x_i).$$

The mean information content of a source X

with the elementary events (x_i) is determined by the entropy $H(X)$:

$$H(X) = -\sum_X p(x_i) \log_2 p(x_i).$$

It was found that the recognition time (measured in reaction times R_i) is proportional to the mean information content of a source event:

$$R_t = K \cdot H(X) + C,$$

if $H(X)$ exhausts the maximum information content of the elementary events. H_{max} $(X) \ldots \log_2(n)$ for all x_i values with $i = 1 \ldots n. O \ldots H(X) \ldots \log_2(n)$. The values between O and $\log_2(n)$ determine the redundancy R of an information source:

$$\left(R = 1 - \frac{H(X)}{\log_2(n)} \right).$$

If the information source is redundant, the recognition time is in non-linear dependence on $H(X)$. Learning processes enable the mean probability of the source events to be assimilated. Changes in the recognition times depend on expectations or attitudes formed on the basis of conditional probabilities between the symbols (or signs). They determine the reciprocal information content between the elementary events. Perception structures are formed by utilizing the redundancy between elementary events. Specific source structures (Markoff sources; syntactic information sources in which the sequence of symbols is determined by fixed rules) lead to special (inner or cognitive) recognition algorithms. They are not only found in language recognition; recognition performance related to specific concepts has a similar basic structure: an object is recognized as an element in a class if it is the vehicle of a special (learnt) association of features. The resulting association with fixed memory content seems to be the basic principle of recognition processes. The formation of perception structures, and in particular higher-level recognition processes, exhibit an extraordinary reduction in the stimuli transmitted by the senses. The filtering out of behavior-relevant environmental data is the cognitive principle for testing behavioral decisions. The statistical definition of information-content is not sufficient for its analysis. *Semantic* characteristics (i.e. the dependence of an item of information on a context and the effect of that context on behavioral attitude) and *pragmatic* characteristics (i.e. the evaluation of an item of information according to its instantaneous significance for a behavioral decision) must be drawn on to extend classical information theory, in order to make proficient predictions in regard to emotionally codetermined or achievement-motivated behaviors. Relevant research is in progress in many institutes today.

5. *The application of automata theory and algorithms* is mainly focussed on the simulation of perception-, thought- and (especially) problem-solving processes in man, and on computer simulation of these processes (see *Simulation of mental processes*). "Simulation" in the cybernetic sense means genuine experimentation with psychological data on computers. The aim is to use the results of computer programs to decide the reliability of research into laws (regularities) and performance characteristics of cognitive (mental) processes. Special importance attaches to sign-recognition algorithms, classification algorithms and problem-solving algorithms. In the simulation of sign-recognition processes we are concerned with the structural simulation of the recognition of (stochastically disturbed, or even geometrically distorted) samples. These objects must be identified as class elements on the basis of characteristic features. The basis for such identification is provided by the functional properties of organismic recognition processes. In the structure of classification algorithms we are concerned with the computer simulation of concept formation processes. Objects are assigned to specific categories on the basis of characteristic features and their association. Learning algorithms for class formation and inductive recognition algorithms have

been developed (Klix, 1971). The development of algorithms for problem-solving is becoming particularly important. These are means of recognition for analysis of the components of complex strategies for human information processing, including heuristic techniques—which are man's most sophisticated forms of data processing. Their increasing practical significance resides in the synthesis of mental performance, e.g. for the automation of production-planning processes, or for programmed instruction specifications in learning psychology.

Cybernetic disciplines (including cybernetico-psychological research) have now reached a high degree of theoretical development through progress in algebra (structural theory, category theory: Klix & Krause, 1969). They comprise means and methods of representation in control, information, and automation theory. See *Communication; Instructional technology*.

Bibliography: Arkadjew, A. G. & Brawermann, E. M.: Zeichenerkennung und maschinelles Lernen. Munich, 1966. Ashby, W. R.: An introduction to cybernetics. New York, 1956. Feigenbaum, E. A. & Feldman, J. (Eds): Computers and thought. New York, 1963. Gluschkow, W. M.: Theorie der abstrakten Automaten. Berlin, 1963. Klix, F.: Information und Verhalten. Einführung in die naturwiss. Grundlagen der Allgemeinen Psychologie. Berlin, 1971. Id. & Krause, B.: Zur Definition des Begriffs "Struktur", seine Eigenschaften und Darstellungsmöglichkeiten in der Experimentalpsychologie. Berlin, 1969. Neumann, J. von: The computer and the brain. New Haven, Conn., 1958. Rosenblatt, F.: The perceptron. Psychol. Rev. 1958, 65. Id.: Principles of neurodynamics. New York, 1961. Shannon, C. & Weaver, W.: The mathematical theory of communication. Urbana, 1949. Schweizer, G.: Probleme und Methoden zur Untersuchung des Regelverhaltens des Menschen. Friedrichshafen, 1967. Wiener, N.: Cybernetics, or control and communication in the animal and the machine. New York, 1948. Id.: Cybernetics. New York, 1961. Id.: God and golem, inc. New York, 1964.   D.Klix

Cycloid. A cycloid personality is one featuring relatively marked alternations of mood within the range defined as normal.

Cyclopropane. A highly effective narcotic (q.v.), both acting and subsiding rapidly, and with parasympathicomimetic side-effects.
E.L.

Cyclothymia. Irregular alternations of elation or excitement and sadness or depression. Abnormal alternations of mood. See *Psychoses; Source traits; Traits*.

Cytoarchitecture. A term for the cytoarchitectural organization of the cerebral cortex, or the fiber lamination, cellular structure and spatial characteristics of cortical areas.

Cytoplasm. What remains of the cell (i.e. a clear solution) after removal by centrifugation of the nuclei, mitochondria and microsomes. The cytoplasm contains enzymes, sodium, potassium and phosphate ions and certain other constituents.

D

Daedaleum. A term for the simplest form of stroboscope invented by J. F. Horner. See *Stroboscope*.

Daltonism. Red-green blindness. John Dalton, the English physicist, described (1798) this defect from which he himself suffered.

Dancing language. On the basis of von Frisch's and Lindauer's theories and experiments (e.g. with a glass hive and paint-marked bees) it has been established that bees convey information regarding, e.g., distance, direction, kind of food, energy required for the flight, to one another by means of elaborately described figures or "dances", which sometimes continue in darkness within the hive. Various researchers have postulated innate and/or acquired characteristics as responsible for this communications system. It has been noted that tempo differs from race to race; one researcher (Steche) has succeeded in artificially instructing bees. Lindauer showed that bees decide where to go to found a new nest by a process of "debate" in terms of repeated inspection of various sites, and danced reports, until unanimity is reached. Haldane characterized the bees' dance as a highly ritualized intention movement, and (in Russell and Whitehead's terminology) as "a propositional function with four variables: 'There is a source of food with smell A at a distance B in direction C requiring D workers.'"

Bibliography: Chauvin, R.: Animal societies. London, 1968. **Frisch, K. von:** Der Farbensinn und Formensinn der Biene. Zool. Jahrb. Allg. Zool. Physiol., 1914, *35*, 1–188. **Id.:** Aus dem Leben der Bienen. Heidelberg, *1953. **Haldane, J. B. S.:** Communication in biology. In: Studies in communication. London, 1955, 29–43. **Ribbands, C. R.:** The behaviour and social life of the honey bee. London, 1950. *J.C.*

Danger-from-without situation. General term introduced by R. A. Stamm (*Behavior*, 1962, *19*, 22) for situations where a social community or its possessions are threatened. The threat may come from members of the same species, ecological competitors, predators, the sudden appearance of unfamiliar objects, loud noises, etc. The reaction to all such situations is similar. The partners close their ranks to counter the danger. They are found to move closer together, make more contact movements, and synchronize and coordinate their subsequent behavior. *R.A.S.*

Dark adaptation (syn. *Scotopic adaptation*). Adaptation of the visual system to dark surroundings; more accurately: an increase of sensitivity to light intensity when the general illumination drops from a higher to a lower level. The opposite process, when there is an increase of general illumination, is *light adaptation* (q.v.) (decrease of sensitivity to light intensity). Dark and light adaptation designate both the process of adaptation and the state of the visual system (the eyes adapted to darkness or light). When there is a sudden change from light to dark, or vice versa, all visual performance is noticeably reduced (functional blindness, glare). As dark or light adaptation increases, visual performance increases, but with the dark-adapted eye, it does not reach the same level as with the light-adapted eye (static characteristics of visual sensitivity as against dynamic characteristics). With a dark-adapted eye the ability to distinguish between colors is absent (see *Duplicity theory*). In the process of adaptation, immediate adaptation (adaptation of the cones, duration three to ten minutes) is distinguished from prolonged adaptation (adaptation of the rods which has not terminated after some hours).

Adaptation range: the range of light intensity between just-perceptible light intensities and the light density which, despite the light-adaptation time, produces glare (according to some writers, from 10^{-9} to 10 lamberts, or units of luminance). See *Glare*.

Bibliography: Bridges, C. D. B.: Bio-Chemistry of visual processes. Compreh. Biochem., 1967, *27*, 31–78. Davson, H. (Ed.): The eye, Vol. 2. New York & London, 1962. Graham, C. H. (Ed.): Vision and visual perception. New York & London, 1965, 185ff Hamburger, F. A.: Das Sehen in der Dämmerung. Vienna, 1949.   *A.H.*

Darwinism. Charles Darwin's theory of the origin of species by (means of) natural selection (1859). In the struggle for existence only those species and individuals can hold their ground whose organisms are able to adapt themselves to environmental conditions. Essential factors are considered to be the structure of the genes (conditioned also by mutation) and the ability to respond to the pressure of selection with suitable behavior. In addition, the phylogenetic aspect (see *Phylogenesis*) of Darwinism stressed the relationship between man and animal and so gave new life to many departments of psychology. There now seemed, for example, to be more justification for comparing the behavior, development, expression, etc., of men and animals, and taking the results of animal psychology into account in human psychology. Recently, because of additional factors (e.g. culture and tradition), the findings of animal psychology (q.v.) are applied to human psychology only when the connection is equivalent. See *Comparative psychology*.

Bibliography: Barnett, S. A.: A century of Darwin. London, 1958. Darlington, C. D.: Darwin's place in history. London, 1959. Darwin, C.: On the origin of species. London, 1859. Id.: The descent of man and selection in relation to sex. London & New York, 1871. Id.: The expression of the emotions in man and animals. London, 1872. Id.: A biographical sketch of an infant. Mind, 1877, *2*, *2*, 285–94. Smith, S.: The origin of "The Origin", Advancement of Sci., 1960, *64*, 391–401.   *P.S. & R.S.*

Daseinsanalyse. See *Existential analysis*.

Dating. Making an appointment or engagement with a person of the opposite sex. This, especially in the U.S.A., is a complex behavioral pattern of unmarried young persons in search of a marriage partner; the relationship to the person "dated" or "dating" is not binding. The number of dates (in the sense either of escorts or occasions) is often regarded as the mark of a girl's prestige.

Bibliography: Coleman, J. S.: The adolescent society. New York, 1961.   *J.F.*

Day blindness. See *Nyctalopia*.

Daydream (syn. *Waking dream; Waking vision*). In daydreams, the individual surrenders to more or less hypertrophied fantasies which he finds pleasurable in some way. They occur frequently in adolescents and children, and can continue to appear throughout some individuals' lives. Daydreams usually serve to fulfill specific wishes.   *J.L.I.*

Day residues. According to Freud, day residues—together with an individual's early and unconscious wishes—operate to produce a dream. They are memories of events of the past day, in which wishes similar to the early unconscious wishes were activated and as a rule could not be gratified. The daytime situation, from which the day residue derives, has already been apprehended by the dreamer (while awake) analogously to early temptation and denial situations. The more recent, though often insignificant, daytime frustration (q.v.) activates, during the dream, more primitive forms of such wishes and frustrations, which are then metamorphosed by the secondary dreamwork into the manifest dream-content (see *Dream*).

Bibliography: Freud, S.: The interpretation of dreams. London, 1955.   *W.T.*

Deafferentation. Separation of the spinal cord from the sensory components by severing the dorsal roots. Used to demonstrate the spontaneity of locomotor movements (see *Automatism*). Complete deafferentation prevents coordinated swimming in sharks and *teleostei* but not in toads. In the tench, *Tinca tinca*, two, and in the pricked dogfish, *Squalus acanthus*, three pairs of intact sensory spinal-cord roots suffice for organized swimming after contact stimuli. Toads make coordinated movements even with one intact sensory root.

Bibliography: Holst, E. V.: Erregungsbildung und Erregungsleitung im Fischrückenmark. Pflüger's Arch., *235*, 345–59. Gray, J.: Animal locomotion. London, 1968.   *K.F.*

Deaf-mute blindness. Blindness and deafness together with dumbness or high-degree speech loss. Multiple defects usually arise from disease (cerebral infection), but in rare cases are wholly congenital. Dumbness is often a consequence of deafness (see *Deaf-mutism*). There is a high mortality rate as a result of extensive brain damage, and increased accident proneness as a result of multiple loss of sense of distance.   *F.-C.S.*

Deaf-mutes, education of. Deaf children become dumb after the babbling stage. The

absence of linguistic communication impairs the general mental, and especially intellectual, development. Special remedial education, undertaken as early as possible, attempts to develop a non-acoustic or substitute sign-language. Pictures, writing, finger language and lip reading are taught to compensate for the absence of spoken language. In addition, it is technically possible to convert spoken language into vibrations applied to the skin, or into visual signs. In this way speech can be apprehended by means of non-acoustic sensory channels.

G.B.

Deaf-mute speech. A deaf person cannot acquire linguistic competence in the usual way if hearing is lost before language acquisition begins. Even after appropriate training, the speech of deaf-mutes is still imprecise by normal standards, despite the increased emphasis on articulation. Proficient vowel formation is hardly possible when hearing is absent; pitch is frequently too high; and volume varies inappropriately. Deaf-mute speech is generally unmelodious.   *H.B.*

Deaf-mutism. Dumbness, or high-degree loss of speech capacity, as a result of congenital deafness, or deafness occurring before or during language (speech) acquisition. Deafness does not bring about any defect of the speech mechanism, and is to be distinguished from mutism accompanied by normal hearing, the various forms of aphasia (q.v.), and spasmodic speech disorders. The absence of speech may be viewed as the specific cause of the many psychological and social inadequacies and disorders of deaf-mutes.   *F.-C.S.*

Deafness. Considerable or complete absence or loss of the ability to hear as a result of (recessive) inheritance, perinatal injury, disease or injury, and sometimes also hysterical conditioning. Defects in the sound-conduction mechanism, and/or in the neutral area (nerve fibers, ganglionic cells in the organ of Corti and/or the cortical hearing center) are met with (see *Sense organs: the ear*). Deafness can also lead to certain alterations of expressed personality (paranoid traits have been reported).   *F.-C.S.*

Death instinct (syn. *Death drive; Death impulse; Thanatos instinct*). According to Freud, the "counterpart" of the life instinct or love instinct (or libido, q.v.). Freud postulates that the organism has an innate tendency to revert to its initial state. This instinct, which would lead to self-destruction, has to be diverted outward by the developing organism. The death instinct contradicts the pleasure principle, and is controlled by the compulsion to repetition. The death instinct may be characterized as more neutral than the aggressive instinct (e.g. Hartmann, Rapaport), and hence represents one of the two major classes of drives and motives, which—for psychoanalysts—comprise all motivational processes. Toman has characterized aggression (q.v.) as representing more primitive forms of motive gratification, which hinder the gratification of other's motives to a greater extent than is requisite for the average gratification of an individual. The distinctions between "libidinous" and aggressive gratifications are fluid, and the assumption of two classes of drive is only a rough division. See *Drive; Instinct*.

Bibliography: Freud, S.: Beyond the pleasure principle. London, ²1959. Hartmann, H., Kris, E. & Loewenstein, R. M.: Notes on the theory of aggres-, sion. Psychoanalytic Study of the Child, 1949, *3-4*, 9-36. Rapaport, D.: The structure of psychoanalytic theory: a systematizing attempt. In: Koch, S. (Ed.): Psychology: a study of a science, Vol. 3. New York, 1959, 55-183.   *W.T.*

Decerebration. The removal of (an animal's) cerebrum; the subject is then known as a *decerebrate*.

Decision processes have been studied most extensively in connection with human sen-

sory discriminations, where the stimulus is best known and controlled. A distinction first suggested by Fechner, as reported by Boring (1942), is appropriate to a description of the present status of this concept. Fechner differentiated between outer and inner psychophysics to describe the interfaces between physical stimuli and physiological correlates on the one hand, and physiological and psychological correlates on the other. In the present context, this distinction implies separate consideration of the transfer function relating physiological correlate to physical stimulus, and the decision process used to derive a sensory discrimination. Use of two-stage models for sensory discrimination is merely an explanatory convenience, and need not imply that such stages actually exist and occur in sequence.

Four models of sensory decision processes will be described in terms of two-stage analysis. Stimulus conditions will be standardized as follows: There is considered to be an extended field of uniform luminance, L. Three decision processes will be used to describe the detection of a luminance increment, ΔL, added briefly to a portion of the field. The fourth will describe judgments of relative magnitude of luminances L' substituted briefly for L over a portion of the field.

1. *Temporal variability of sensory effects.* According to Boring (1929), Fechner first reported variability among successive measures of sensory discrimination, believing them to be due to measurement error. Separately, Urbantschitsch (1875) reported temporal fluctuations in the sensory magnitude resulting from a steady stimulus. Marbe (1895) suggested that these two phenomena were dual evidence of a fundamental variability in sensory effects, a concept supported by the work of Guilford (1927) and many others. All decision processes to be considered here ascribe a key role to such time-varying sensory effects.

2. *The neural quantum model.* Boring (1926) first suggested that sensory magnitudes should reflect the discreteness of peripheral receptive elements by exhibiting small steps

or sensory quanta. Evidence for sensory quanta in discriminatory data obtained from the auditory modality was presented by von Bekesy (1930, 1936). A general model of sensory decision processes known as the neural quantum model has been developed in these terms. Descriptions of the model and experimental data in support of it have been

Fig. 1. Representation of the Neural Quantum Model. Upper left: distribution of effect E from steady luminance L, with quantum steps shown by tick-marks. At a moment, m, level of E exceeds quantum step T_1 by residual r. For detection of ΔL, E must increase by two quantum steps and $\Delta E + r = 2Q$, where Q is the difference in E between quantum steps. Upper right: linear transfer function of ΔL to ΔE. Lower right: predicted variation in probability p of detecting ΔL as a function of ΔL.

reported by Stevens & Davis (1938); Stevens & Volkman (1940); Stevens, Morgan & Volkman (1941); Flynn (1943); and Miller & Garner (1944).

According to this model, the effect E due to a steady prevailing luminance L will be represented by the normal frequency distribution shown in the upper left portion of Figure 1. The magnitude of E, due to L, is

time-varying, and different values are obtained with different frequencies during any sampling period. Momentary changes in E are continuous, E varying from one level to another by passing through all values between the two. Values of E are, however, quantized into the relatively few discrete levels or steps shown by the tick-marks, each quantum step being of essentially the same size. Since E varies continuously, only a one-quantum jump can occur from L alone. The residual r is defined as the difference between m, a momentary value of E, and T_1, the level of the quantum step it just exceeds. The addition of a luminance increment ΔL produces an increment effect ΔE which is added to the momentary value of r. Detection of ΔL requires that $(\Delta E + r)$ reach a criterion value. One such criterion is that $(\Delta E + r)$ must be sufficient to produce a two-quantum jump in E, a sensory change unachievable from momentary changes in E due to L alone. Thus, $(\Delta E + r) = 2Q$, where Q is the size of a quantum step in E.

The value of ΔE required to produce the two-quantum jump will vary from trial to trial, depending upon the value of r existing when ΔL is added; and the distribution of ΔE will depend upon the distribution of r. All values of r from 0 to Q will occur with equal frequency, provided the total range of variability in E covers a fairly large number of quantum steps. If r varies from 0 to Q in this manner, ΔE will vary from Q to $2Q$ in accordance with a rectilinear frequency distribution.

Assume that ΔE is linearly related to ΔL as shown in the upper right portion of the figure. Then, values of p, the probability of detecting ΔL, will be related to the magnitude of ΔL as shown in the lower right portion of the figure. The value of p is zero until $\Delta L = 0.3$, assumed to be the value at which $\Delta E = Q$. Then, p increases linearly until it reaches unity when $\Delta L = 0.6$, at which value $\Delta E = 2Q$. Experimental data have been reported which apparently verify these predictions.

3. *The fixed criterion model.* According to the model proposed by Blackwell (1952, 1963), the effect produced by a steady luminance L is time-varying in accordance with the normal frequency distribution shown in the upper-left portion of Figure 2. This distribution of E is time-sampled and a criterion level E_c is selected which occurs from L only a few per cent of the time at most. Addition of a luminance increment ΔL gives rise to a distribution of E due to $(L + \Delta L)$, with mean value greater by ΔE than the distribution of E due to L alone. The magnitude of ΔE is linearly related to ΔL, as shown in the upper right portion of the figure. Distributions of E due to L or $(L + \Delta L)$ have essentially equal values of σ.

Detection of the presence of ΔL occurs whenever the value of E produced by $(L + \Delta L)$ reaches or exceeds the criterion level of E_c. Then, the relation between p, the probability of detection, and ΔL will be described by the normal ogive shown in the bottom right portion of the figure labeled $S = 0$.

When detection probability is inferred from Yes-No responses, spurious Yes responses may occur, as revealed by blank trials. Assuming independence, the total probability of a Yes response is:

$$p' = p + (1 - p)S,$$

where S is the proportion of Yes responses when $\Delta L = 0$.

The curves in the lower right portion of the figure labeled $S = 0.25$ and $S = 0.50$ represent predictions from two levels of spurious Yes responses. Experimental data have been reported which apparently verify these predictions.

4. *The variable criterion model.* The model reported by Tanner & Swets (1954), and by Green & Swets (1966), also assumes that the effect E produced by L is time-varying in accordance with a normal frequency distribution, and that distributions of E produced by the addition of different values of

ΔL to L are normal also with approximately equal σ, as shown in the upper left portion of Figure 3. However, it is assumed that ΔE, the difference between means of the distributions of E produced by L and $(L + \Delta L)$, is related to ΔL by the non-linear transfer

Fig. 2. Representation of the Fixed Criterion Model. Upper left: distributions of effect E from steady luminance L and from L plus each of two values of ΔL. The distribution of E from L is time-sampled and a criterion value E_c selected to have low probability of occurrence from L alone. Detection occurs whenever E from $(L + \Delta L)$ equals or exceeds E_c. Upper right: linear transfer function of ΔL to ΔE. Lower right: predicted variation in probability p' of responding Yes as a function of ΔL for different levels of spurious Yes responses, S.

function $\Delta E = 5 \cdot 9 \Delta L^{2.7}$ shown in the upper right portion of the figure.

Different criterion levels of E, $E_{c1} \ldots E_{c_n}$, may be selected corresponding to different ratios of two classes of response error, false alarms when Yes responses are given to L alone, and detection failures when No responses are made to $(L + \Delta L)$. Selection of one or another value of E_c depends upon the values assigned to the two-error classes, and reflects an approach to response optimization.

The relation between p, the probability of a Yes response, and ΔL will depend upon the value of $E_{c'}$ as shown in the bottom-right portion of the figure. Experimental

Relative frequency

Fig. 3. Representation of the Variable Criterion Model. Upper left: distributions of effect E from steady luminance L and from L plus each of two values of ΔL. Criterion values of E, E_{c_1} .... E_{c_n}, may be set corresponding to different ratio of false alarms and correct detections of ΔL. Upper right: non-linear transfer function in which $\Delta E = 5.9 \, \Delta L^{2.7}$. Lower right: predicted variation in probability p of responding Yes as a function of ΔL for different criterion values of E.

data have been reported which apparently verify these predictions.

5. *The phi-gamma model.* Müller (1904) and Urban (1909) described a generalized model of sensory discrimination based upon the assumption that temporal variability in human sensory systems is normally distributed. Boring (1917), and Brown & Thomson (1925), postulated normal distributions of factors considered favorable or unfavorable

to discrimination, and assumed that smaller stimulus magnitudes require more of the factors to be favorable than do larger magnitudes. Thurstone (1927) employed the model to describe experimental situations involving judgments of the relative magnitude of two stimuli, each of which was assumed to produce time-varying effects. We shall consider this form of the phi-gamma model, drawing upon the description given by Guilford (1936).

For a stimulus magnitude comparison experiment, the stimulus situation must be altered slightly as follows: The steady prevailing luminance L is momentarily replaced by a field of non-uniform luminance having a small central area of luminance L' either greater or less than L, with the remainder of the field having luminance L. The value of L' is varied from trial to trial. Judgments are made of the relative magnitude of L' with respect to L on each trial, with only the responses Greater and Less being permitted.

As shown in the upper-left portion of Figure 4, L and each value of L' produce separate time-varying normal distributions of effect E. These normal distributions have approximately equal values of σ. Mean values of the distributions of E produced by L and L' are separated by ΔE. This quantity is linearly related to ΔL, the difference between L' and L taken without regard to sign, as shown in the upper-right portion of the figure. Temporal variability of the effects due to L and L' is uncorrelated from trial to trial, and values of E do not change during the duration of a stimulus exposure.

Discrimination is infallible, each judgment correctly reflecting whether or not the sample drawn from the distribution of E produced by L' had greater or less magnitude than the sample drawn from the distribution of E produced by L. Then, the probabilities of response, p_g for Greater and p_1 for Less, will be related to the magnitude of L' as shown in the lower-right portion of the figure. Experimental data have been reported which apparently verify these predictions.

6. *Additional models.* Alternative decision-process models have been described by Atkinson (1963), Luce (1963), Broadbent (1966), Krantz (1969), and many others, with experimental data supporting each. Clearly, there can be no single model describing decision processes in human sensory systems.

Relative frequency

Relative L'

Fig. 4. Representation of the Phi-Gamma Model. Upper left: distributions of effect E from standard luminance L and from two values of comparison luminance L'. Evaluation of the relative magnitude of L' with respect to L involves drawing pairs of samples from uncorrelated distributions of effect due to L and L', with infallible judgment of relative magnitude. Upper right: linear transfer function of ΔL to ΔE. Lower right: predicted variation in judgments p_l (lesser) and p_g (greater) as a function of L'

Rather, the stimulus and response conditions of an experiment will determine the decision process used in making the discrimination.

Bibliography: Atkinson, R. C.: A variable sensitivity theory of signal detection. Psychol. Rev., 1963, 70, 91–106. von Bekesy, G.: Über das Fechnersche Gesetz und seine Bedeutung für die Theorie der akustischen Beobachtungsfehler und die Theorie des Hörens. Ann. d. Phys., 1930, 7, 329–59. Id.: Über die Hörschwelle und Fühlgrenze langsamer sinusförmiger Luftdruckschwankungen. Ann. d. Phys., 1936, 26, 554–66. Blackwell, H. R.: Theory and measurement of psychophysical thresholds. Ann

Arbor, 1952. Id.: Neural theories of simple visual discriminations. J. Opt. Soc. Amer., 1963, 53, 129–60. Boring, E. G.: A chart of the psychometric function. Amer. J. Psychol., 1917, 28, 465–70. Id.: Auditory theory with special reference to intensity, volume, and localization. Amer. J. Psychol., 1926, 37, 157–88. Id.: A history of experimental psychology. New York 1929. Id.: Sensation and perception in the history of experimental psychology. New York, 1942. Broadbent, D. E.: Two-state threshold model and rating scale experiments. J. Acous. Soc. Amer., 1966, 40, 244–5. Brown, Wm. & Thomson, G. H.: The essentials of mental measurement. London, 1925. Flynn, B. M.: Pitch discrimination: The form of the psychometric function and simple reaction time to liminal differences. Arch. Psychol. N.Y., 1943, 280, 1–41. Green, D. M. & Swets, J. A.: Signal detection theory and psychophysics. New York, 1966. Guilford, J. P.: Fluctuations of attention with weak visual stimuli. Amer. J. Psychol., 1927, 38, 534–83. Id.: Psychometric methods. New York, 1936. Krantz, D. H.: Threshold theories of signal detection. Psychol. Rev. 1969, 76, 308–24. Luce, D. R.: A threshold theory for simple detection experiments. Psychol. Rev. 1963, 70, 61–97. Marbe, K.: Schwankungen der Gesichts, empfindungen. Phil. Stud., 1895, 10, 620–41. Miller, G. A. & Garner, W. R.: The effect of random presentation on the psychometric function; implications for a quantal theory of discrimination. Amer. J. Psychol., 1944, 57, 451–67. Müller, G. E.: Die Gesichtspunkte und die Tatsachen der psychophysischen Methodik. Wiesbaden, 1904. Stevens, S. S., & Davis, H.: Hearing: its psychology and physiology. New York, 1938. Stevens, S. S., Morgan, C. T. & Volkman, J.: Theory of the neural quantum in the discrimination of loudness and pitch. Amer. J. Psychol., 1941, 54, 315–35. Stevens, S. S. & Volkman, J.: The quantum of sensory discrimination. Science, 1940, 92, 583–5. Tanner, W. P. Jr. & Swets, J. A.: A decision-making theory of visual detection. Psychol. Rev., 1954, 61, 401–9. Thurstone, L. L.: Psychophysical analysis. Amer. J. Psychol., 1927, 38, 368–89. Urban, F. M.: Die psychophysischen Massmethoden als Grundlagen empirischer Messungen. Arch. ges. Psychol., 1909, 15, 261–355. Urbantschitsch, U.: Über eine Eigentümlichkeit der Schallempfindungen geringster Intensität. Centralbl. f. d. med. Wiss., 1875, 23, 625–8.

H. R. Blackwell

Decortication. The removal of (an animal's) cerebral cortex; the subject is then known as a *decorticate.*

Deculturation. A term from American ethnology, which concentrates on cultural changes within the frame of a dynamic anthropology (q.v.). In general it represents the negative aspect of *acculturation* (q.v.). Both terms denote mechanisms of acceptance, rejection or reorganization of cultural characteristics, institutions or behavioral patterns within one society in contact (or conflict) with another. These phenomena have appeared in, e.g., the integration of the American minorities into American society (Herskovits, Linton). Recently similar phenomena have appeared in the states of Asia and Africa which as a result of decolonialization have to struggle for their own identity (Balandier, Leach).

Bibliography: Herskovits, M. J. (Ed.): Acculturation. New York, 1938. Linton, R.: Acculturation in seven. American Indian tribes. New York, 1940. See also *Cultural anthropology*. *A.T.*

Deduction. The analytical transition from one or several propositions (premises) to one proposition (conclusion). Deduction as a process of transition from the general to the particular is often contrasted with induction, where the opposite occurs. By *transcendental deduction*, Kant understands the application of *a priori* principles to experience. *J.B.G.*

Defect, mental. See *Mental defect*.

Defemination. This appears in a woman, e.g., as the result of a tumor in the *zona reticularis* of the adrenal cortex. The term *virilism* (q.v.) is also used. The secondary sexual characteristics change and become more like those of the male. The voice becomes deeper, a beard begins to grow, and the most reliable diagnostic sign is that the upper limit of the pubic hair changes toward the male form. There is partial atrophy (q.v.) of the external and internal sexual organs. The changes disappear after the removal of the tumor, or estrogen therapy. Contrary to a widely held view, psychological changes do not always follow on defemination. *G.L.*

Defense; defence. In depth psychology, the inner, automatic inhibition of the satisfaction of an impulse that was once possible for the individual, but from a certain point in development was prevented by others or checked by the threat of "punishment". Defense aims at avoidance or control.

Defense-mechanisms are distinctive means of exercising this control, and include: repression, projection, introjection or identification, reaction formation, sublimation, regression, isolation, denial of reality, identification with the aggressor, rationalization, conversion (reversion), and the specific neurotic defense-mechanisms, which play a part in the so-called "defense psychoneuroses".

Defense-psychoneuroses can be, e.g., phobias, conversions, compulsive actions, compulsive ideas, tics, stuttering, and are mental illnesses of those for whom the usual defense-mechanisms prove inadequate and who have to adopt additional neurotic means of warding off the "instinctive impulse". See also *Regression; Psychopathology*.

Bibliography: Fenichel, O.: The psychoanalytic theory of neurosis. New York, 1945. Freud, A.: The ego and the mechanisms of defence. London, 1937. Freud, S.: New introductory lectures on psycho-analysis. London, 1933. Id.: The ego and the id. London, ²1962. Id.: Inhibitions, symptoms and anxiety. London, ²1936. O'Connor, N. & Franks, C. M.: Childhood, upbringing and other environmental factors. In: Eysenck, H. J. (Ed.): Handbook of abnormal psychology. London, 1960. *W.T.*

Defensive reflex (syn. *Defense reflex; Protective response*). An automatic (reflexive) response in answer to a dangerous or painful stimulus.

Defiance, age of (syn. *Obstinacy*). In the older (German) developmental psychology, the period from three to five years of age was defined as the "first phase of defiance", and that from twelve to fifteen as the "second phase of defiance". In these periods one can observe an increase in behaviors characterized by strongly affective and motor

resistance reactions to individuals and things (stamping, crying, refusal to obey, fits of anger, sulking, silences, passivity, "negative attitudes"). Such behaviors are interpreted in the literature as "intrinsic volition"; the first emergence of the ego from the non-ego; an experimental breaking of the physiognomic barrier; first emotional crises; lability of mood as a result of adjustment processes in the internal secretory organs; compensation of inferiority feelings in regard to female characteristics, parental authority, or the restriction of gratification by society; and so on. Systematic investigations of defiance in early infancy carried out by Kemmler (1957) would seem to indicate that it is not primarily a general, endogenously conditioned phenomenon; not every child manifestly experiences a phase of defiance, and there are considerable interindividual variations in extent. The frustration of needs (e.g. for independence and self-sufficiency), and the experience of a discrepancy between what was previously allowed and one's own desire to experiment, together with an inability adequately to master the situation, can primarily condition defiance (as a kind of panic reaction). "Defiance" can be reinforced by parental reactions (see *Reinforcement*), and thus become an acquired form of domination. The child's experiences in such situations are relevant for the entire development of the personality.
Bibliography: Kemmler, L.: Untersuchungen über den frühkindlichen Trotz. Psychol. Forsch., 1957, *25*, 279–338.   H.M.

Deficiency, mental (syn. *Mental defect; Amentia: Feeblemindedness: Oligophrenia*). Mental deficiency (now used only in clinical practice) is the older term for mental subnormality or mental retardation. This and the term feeblemindedness are sometimes used for the least degree of what, according to the (British) Mental Health Act of 1959, is now generally known as subnormality (i.e. not amounting to *severe subnormality*). It might be thought of as a condition in

which there is a minus variation, or some slight form of retardation conditioned by heredity, or a mental disability resulting from brain damage, such as a pre- or postnatal cerebral inflammation, or after injury from cerebral hemorrhage, or some traumatic experience. Sometimes the condition is equated with an IQ of 50–70, but the correspondence is unsatisfactory in the case of adults. An inherited or acquired deficiency in ability is expressed as retarded intellectual maturity, difficulty in acquiring knowledge and dealing with unusual situations. The range of interests is restricted, apprehension is limited, thinking is basically concrete and skill in abstracting is only developed to a slight degree.

It is precisely in regard to this mental subnormality that the aspect of character which is independent of intelligence is decisively significant; with children suffering from mental deficiency it is vitally important to prevent any harmful development of character: an attempt may be made in this direction by employing suitable therapy, avoiding isolation in the family and the environment, and appropriately developing and training existing abilities. Mental deficiency can, but need not, imply a marked absence of personality. It must not be equated with infantilism or primitivism. In general, the treatment is therapeutic (counseling).

N.B. The WHO classification recommends that a distinction be made between the *mentally defective* (organically damaged) and the *mentally retarded* individual (suffering from a learning disability). In general, the term "mental deficiency", though not so evidently negative as some older designations, is best avoided outside a clinical situation in which it is the specifically defined usage of a certain practitioner. See *Mental defect; Autism.*
Bibliography: Benda, C. E.: Die Oligophrenie (Entwicklungsstörungen und Schwachsinnszustände). In: Psychol. der Gegenwart, Vol. 2. Berlin, 1960. Clarke, A. M. & Clarke, A. D. B.: Mental deficiency: the changing outlook. London, ²1965. Masland, R. L., Sarason, S. B. & Gladwyn, T.: Mental subnormality.

New York, 1958. Tredgold, R. F. & Soddy, K.: Mental retardation. London, 1969.   *H.Sa.*

Deficiency motivation (syn. *Deficit motivation*). If motivation is understood as a phenomenon resulting from certain conditions of the organism, deficiency motivation is the result of some disturbance in the sense of the homeostatic principle. Such disturbing stimuli which may be conditioned by a lack of food, liquid, etc., cause the individual to seek ways and means of removing the deficit and restoring equilibrium. In his system, Maslow contrasts "deficiency motives" with "growth motives" (abundancy motivation).

Bibliography: Maslow, A. W.: Deficiency motivation and growth motivation. Lincoln, Neb., 1955.
                                                       P.S. & R.S.

Definition. A statement which either makes clear what one is talking about (real definition) or the way in which one is talking about something (nominal definition). A real definition puts the concept requiring definition into the framework of a classification system. In the simplest cases, the next higher genus (*genus proximum*) and the specific difference (*differentia specifica*) are shown: e.g. "A rhombus is an equilateral parallelogram". "Parallelogram" is the next higher genus, "equilateral" the specific difference. A nominal definition shows which word denotes a concept assumed to be known. Thus it is conventional and serves mostly to abbreviate discourse: e.g. "UNO = df. United Nations Organization". The sign = "df." means "equal *per definitionem*"; the new notation on the left is the *definiendum*; the known term for which it will stand, on the right, is the *definiens*. In formal systems frequent use is made of inductive definitions. These consist of three propositions: (*a*) initial proposition, (*b*) inductive proposition, (*c*) final proposition; e.g.: "(*a*) nought is a number, (*b*) if *n* is a number, *n'* is a number, (*c*) nothing is a number unless it agrees with (*a*) and (*b*)". These definitions make it pos-

sible to elicit gradually all the elements (and only those) of a class. See *Deduction*.
                                                            J.B.G.

Deflation. A state of negative affect (e.g. disappointment) marking a relatively sudden return to the *status quo* (or lower) following some cause for and feeling of elation. For example, one is likely to feel deflated when the winning horse one has backed is later disqualified.   *G.D.W.*

Defloration. The piercing of the vaginal hymen during the first coitus. An intact hymen (*virgo intacta*) is even today a highly-valued attribute in a bride. It is sometimes asserted that a woman feels specially dependent on the man who has deflowered her. In various civilized cultures defloration was a privilege (*jus primae noctis*) of certain persons of standing.   *U.H.S.*

Degeneration in the CNS. If an axon (q.v.) is severed and thus separated from the proximo-distal flow from the perikaryon (cell body) of the nerve cell (neuron), the proximal portion undergoes retrograde degeneration, and the distal continuation secondary, or Waller's, degeneration. In myelin fibers, the myelin sheath first of all undergoes fatty degeneration and can be stained black with osmium tetroxide (Marchi's method); later the axons fragment. Retrograde degeneration leads to chromatolysis of the Nissl bodies in the perikaryon (soma). Transneuronal degeneration sets in when a neuron is cut off from a considerable part of its afferent connections, since the synapses converging on it are affected by terminal degeneration.

Bibliography: Singer, M. & Schade, J. P. (Eds): Degeneration patterns in the nervous system. Progress in Brain Res., *14*, Amsterdam, 1965.   *K.F.*

Degrees of freedom. In a set of k observations, $k - 1$ values can be freely chosen within a system, the last value being fully determined.

The number of degrees of freedom (df) is therefore $k - 1$. For example, the statistic $\Sigma(X_i - X)^2$, the sum of the squared deviations of a sample (q.v.) of N elements, has $N - 1$ degrees of freedom, since, given the definition of the mean ($\Sigma x = 0$), the last value can no longer be freely chosen. The number of degrees of freedom is of prime importance in determining the critical values of test distributions.   *W.H.B.*

Déjà vu experience. Sometimes called *fausse reconnaissance:* an illusion of memory which occasionally occurs in healthy people in a state of exhaustion, but more frequently in neurotics and psychotics. A new situation is experienced for a moment as already known. This an illusion not of the senses but of a paradoxical emotional experience. The following explanations of the phenomenon have been suggested: (*a*) continuance of an emotional state from the preceding situation: the feelings undergo no immediate new orientation because of fatigue or some psychological defect; (*b*) associations of the perceived stimuli with repressed memories; (*c*) partial similarity of certain features, or cues, of the situation to those of a former one, which is then completed on the "part-for-the-whole" principle.   *P.S.*

Delayed conditioning. If a pause occurs between a conditioned and an unconditioned stimulus (see *Conditioning*), this is known as delayed conditioning.

Delayed reaction (syn. *Delayed response*). A reaction to certain stimuli after some delay.

Delayed reaction test. To test memory, Hunter carried out a delayed-response experiment which consisted of leaving the subject (an animal) without access to the incentive for some time after presentation. A concealing shield was withdrawn after the delay, and the accuracy of the animal's choice of the object's location served to indicate acuity of memory. It is doubtful whether this is an adequate way of assessing biologically significant memory. According to Baerends, the sand wasp *Ammophilia* is capable of a "delayed reaction" of up to fifteen hours. In the morning, on its first visit of inspection to all the nests, it decides what activities it will carry out on each one throughout the day.

Bibliography: Baerends, G. P.: Fortpflanzungsverhalten und Orientierung der Grabwespe Ammophilia campestris. Jur. Tijdschr. Entomol., 1941, *84*, 68–275. **Hunter, W. S.:** The delayed reaction in animals and children. Behav. Monogr., 1913, *2*, 21–30.   *K.F.*

Delboeuf's illusion. Large circles which objectively are equally large seem to be different in size when other concentric circles are added to them, whether inside or outside. See *Brentano's illusion*.   *K.E.P.*

Delinquency and personality. In numerous investigations—chiefly of juvenile behavior—only moderate correlations were observed between personality traits and delinquent or criminal behavior (see *Criminality*). Delinquency would seem to correlate most reliably with aggressiveness (see *Aggression*), hostility, impulsiveness, neuroticism (q.v.), and (in agreement with Eysenck's theory) extraversion (q.v.). There are problems of method, principally in regard to the unreliability of criteria for delinquency, and the separation of pre-delinquent expressions of traits from those which are relatively conditioned (e.g. by imprisonment).

Bibliography: Eysenck, H.-J.: Crime and personality. London, 1964. **Quay, H. C.:** Personality and delinquency. In: Quay, H. C., (Ed.): Juvenile delinquency. Princeton, 1965, 139–66.   *M.A.*

Delirium. An exceptional mental state with partial or complete disorientation (q.v.), hallucinations (q.v.), delusions and usually general restlessness. It occurs in the acute exogenous reaction-type during serious somatic illnesses and intoxications affecting the CNS. *Delirium tremens* is probably the best-known variety; it is related to chronic *alcoholism* (q.v.).   *A.Hi.*

Delta movement. This is an apparent movement (q.v.): the position of an object seems to change when the lighting is changed.

Delusion. See *Paranoia; Schizophrenia.*

Delusions of reference. These are said to occur when a person unjustifiably believes that others are talking about him, slandering him and spying on him. He may believe that passages in the newspapers or programs on television are referring to him. Such experiences occur in schizophrenia and in severe depression. In the latter case the person believes that such persecution is justified by his wickedness.   *R.H.*

Dementia. An acquired defect of intelligence, usually accompanying the final stage of an endogenous or exogenous psychotic change; often the result of cerebral traumata and infectious diseases of the brain. Congenital mental subnormality, or that acquired at a very early age, is sometimes referred to as *oligophrenia* (q.v.). See *Psychoses; Psychopathology.*   *U.H.S.*

Dementia, arteriosclerotic. Arteriosclerosis is one of the two common causes of dementia in the elderly. Fairly distinct from senile dementia, the underlying cause is a thickening of the medium-sized arteries of the brain, resulting in diminished blood flow. Deterioration takes place in a step-wise fashion, usually following a series of strokes. Personality is preserved to a late stage, memory loss often being the first sign. Life expectancy is considerably reduced.   *D.E.*

Dementia praecox. A term of only historical interest. A synonym for schizophrenia. Morel in 1860 coined the term *démence precoce*, or premature dementia, to describe severe intellectual deterioration in an adolescent. In 1873 Kraepelin grouped together the syndromes *dementia praecox*, hebephrenia, catatonic and *dementia paranoides* and called the group the *psychological degeneration processes*. In 1899 he changed the name of this group to *dementia praecox* because the illnesses led to intellectual deterioration and usually occurred with young people. Hence the term no longer referred to a specific clinical state. Confusion arose over the implication of youth and permanent dementia until, in 1911, E. Bleuler coined the term *schizophrenia* (q.v.) for this group.   *B.B.*

Dementia, presenile. Pick described in 1892 a dementing state associated with aphasia, now known to be a distinct pathological entity inherited as a Mendelian dominant. Occurring before the age of 60, the progressive dementia is accompanied by brain atrophy which is particularly marked in the frontal and temporal lobes. Special features are early emotional changes, but memory is retained until a late stage. Deterioration is usually rapid.   *D.E.*

Democracy (syn. *Democratic atmosphere*). A decision-making or discussion atmosphere characterized by freedom of expression, tolerance of individual and minority viewpoints, respect for the worth of each group member, and equal opportunity to contribute to the group decision or activity.

Democratic leadership: A democratic group leader not only informs the group of aims in advance and allows them to be discussed, but is open to the discussion changing those aims.

Bibliography: Berkowitz, L.: Sharing leadership in small, decision-making groups. J. Abnorm. soc. Psychol., 1953, *48*, 231–8. Fetscher, I.: Die Demokratie. Stuttgart & Berlin, 1970. Haythorn, W.: The effects of varying combinations of authoritarian and equalitarian leaders and followers. J. Abnorm. soc. Psychol., 1956, 55, 210–19. **Maier, H. R. F. & Solem, A. R.:** The contribution of a discussion leader to the quality of group thinking: the effective use of minority opinions. Hum. Relat., 1952, 5, 277–88.

J.C.

Demography. In the narrower sense, demography means the statistical assessment and description of a population by means of such variable characteristics as sex, age, income, size of family, etc.: the so-called demographic variables. In a wider sense, the term refers to the study of the natural and social structures of a population, and the causes and consequences of its changes.   *A.Hä.*

Demoor's illusion. A defective estimation of weights, especially among the mentally subnormal: the normal overestimating of larger weights and underestimating of smaller weights occurs with gross miscalculation of the proportion of size to weight, or vice versa.   *F.-C.S.*

Demoscopy. The terms "demoscopy", "survey" and (public) "opinion poll" denote a method of investigation based on the statistical analysis of (random) samples, and on inquiries, which enables large numbers of people to be observed and analyzed in regard to some specific attitude, etc. The word "demoscopy" arose from a suggestion (1946) made by the American sociologist S. C. Dodd, and at first it was only adopted in Germany (the Allenbach Institute for Demoscopy was founded in 1947), but recently its use has spread increasingly to other countries. In Britain surveys or opinion polls are used.

The term "demoscopy" was introduced because the use of the word "opinion" gives the misleading impression that inquiries were used only or chiefly to ascertain opinions. In fact, the subjects investigated cover a much wider field; the sampling method is used also to investigate facts (e.g. demographic charac-

teristics or housing conditions), knowledge, behavior, attitudes, effects and the connections between these factors. Even the word "demoscopy" is too narrow in one respect: demoscopy investigates not only "people", but groups of every kind (e.g. doctors or teachers), and not only individuals but also bodies (aggregates), such as neighborhoods, school classes, military units, and government agencies. For the method of demoscopy see *Opinion polls.*   *E.N.-N.*

Demythologization. 1. The liberation of a myth (q.v.) from its magical character and supernatural features. An attempt is made to divest the myth of its sacred character and ritual function by reducing it to purely human phenomena of a historical, rational, scientific, linguistic (Max Müller) and sociological (see *Cultural anthropology*) nature. A process that occurred in numerous primitive societies during cultural changeovers.

2. In existential and religious-anthropological usage: the elucidation of the essence of a myth in a form that will make its relevance immediately clear to modern man.

M.R.

Dendrites. Nerve cells (neurons) consist of a cell body, several dendrites branching from it, and the axon (q.v.), the extended nerve fiber leading to the effector, or to other nerve cells. Numerous nerve fibrils coming from other nerve cells end at synapses (q.v.), or junctions between them and the relatively short dendrites, thus enlarging the extent of impulse conduction into the nerve cell.

Bibliography: Eccles, L. C.: The physiology of nerve cells. Baltimore, 1957.

M.S.

Denial. See *Reality, denial of.*

Density mean. A measurement for the central tendency of a distribution (see *Frequency* *distribution*). It is the value on the score continuum of a single-peak distribution which shows the greatest frequency ($f'(x) = 0; f''(x) < 0$). In the case of a distribution with several peaks there are several density means; it is a measure of the central tendency in this special case only for the section of the distribution between the two adjacent minima. The density mean has weaknesses, especially in regard to samples (q.v.).

W.H.B.

Dependence. In the measurement of probability, dependence of events (q.v.) means that the probability (q.v.) of the occurrence of these events is influenced by the occurrence or non-occurrence of other events:

$$P(A) = P(A|B) \quad \text{and} \quad P(B) = P(B|A).$$

The probability of the common occurrence of events A and B in the case of stochastic dependence is $P(AB) = P(A)P(B)$. See *Mathematical psychology; Statistics.*   W.H.B.

Dependence, social; dependency. The state of an individual when economically, emotionally or otherwise dependent on other individuals. Also used to refer to the relation of the immature child to those who care for or guide it.

In socialization (q.v.), dependence of the child on a person to whom it can relate (mother or parents, and so on) is the necessary premiss for the social imitation (q.v.) of different behavior patterns and for the internalization of social norms and values.

A condition for the development of the child's dependence on, or trust in, its parents is the presence of an appropriate person to whom it can refer and with whom it can identify. If such a person is not available, partly irreversible damage can result in all areas of child development (e.g. hospitalism, q.v.) (see Spitz, 1945).

A possible explanation for the origin of dependent behavior in the child is the principle of *secondary reinforcement* (Mowrer,

1950). The behavior of the persons to whom it refers takes on reinforcing (reward) qualities for the child, through repeated association with the satisfaction of primary or bodily needs by these persons. The reinforcement value is transferred to all aspects of those persons' behavior: the child learns to place a positive value on their presence and attention. Dependence is also intensified by an upbringing and education oriented to warmth and love (see Sears *et al.*, 1957).

See, e.g., Bronfenbrenner (1961) for the relation of dependence to the child-rearing conventions of different social classes, to children's sex, or to family structure.

Bibliography: Bronfenbrenner, U.: The changing American child: A speculative analysis. J. soc. Issues, 1961, *17*, 6–10. Mowrer, O. H.: Learning theory and personality dynamics. New York, 1950. Sears, R. R., Maccoby, E. E. & Levin, H.: Patterns of child rearing. New York, 1957. Sears, R. R., Rau, L. & Alpert, R.: Identification and child rearing. London, 1966. Spitz, R.: Hospitalism: An inquiry into genesis of psychiatric conditions in early childhood. The Psychoanalytic Study of the Child, 1945, *1*, 53–74.

A.S.-M.

Dependent distribution. When the relative frequency of the simultaneous occurrence of events X and Y is unequal to that calculated according to $F(x) . F(y)$, the distribution of these dependent random variables is a "dependent distribution". The degree of dependence (q.v.) can be expressed, e.g., in the form of a correlation coefficient (q.v.). See *Mathematical psychology; Statistics.*   W.H.B.

Dependent samples. In contradistinction to independent samples, dependent (correlational) samples are obtained either by parallelization (q.v.) according to control characteristics, or by the repetition of measurements on the same objects. In the case of parallel samples, the sampling error (q.v.) will decrease with the increase in covariance (q.v.) between the pretest variables and the dependent variables to be tested. In the case of repeated measurements, the sampling error will be smaller than with random samples, and will correspond to the extent of the correlation between the measurements.   *W.H.B.*

Dependent variables. In connection with analyses of dependence (regression analyses, q.v.), dependent variables represent the variable to be measured. Dependent variables are examined to see whether, how and to what extent they are covariant with the systematically changing independent variables. In general terms, X and Y are dependent random variables in a two-dimensional distribution

$$f(x, y) = f_1(x) \cdot F^2(y)$$

where F_1 and F^2 are the marginal distributions of X and Y.   *W.H.B.*

Depersonalization. The feeling of a patient that he has lost his identity. The clear awareness that everything one feels, says or does comes from oneself is partially or entirely missing. This occurs especially in cases of *schizophrenia* (q.v.) or serious *depression* (q.v.).   *A.Hi.*

Depression. The term "depression" is used for a complex of symptoms: a "depressed", despondent condition, unresponsiveness and loss of drive, motor and mental inhibition, typically depressive ideas and definite somatic disorders. One most significant variety is endogenous depression, which is constitutionally grounded, dependent on heredity, and tends to manic-depressive illness. E. Kraepelin distinguished it from *schizophrenia* (q.v.). The characteristic symptoms of *endogenous depression* are a groundless, deeply-felt sadness (melancholia), anxiety (q.v.), or excitement, and typical, sometimes imaginary, ideas of impoverishment; self-accusation, a conviction of sinfulness, as well as depersonalization (q.v.), with a tormenting loss of emotional life. In addition

there is an inadequacy which is experienced mentally and physically as hypochondria, as well as pathognomonic somatic disorders in the form of insomnia, periodical fluctuations of emotional condition with a morning "low", loss of appetite and weight, and vegetative disorders.

Forms of depression. According to the symptoms, there are *inhibited depressions* in which the inhibition can be intensified and become stupor (q.v.); agitated, i.e. anxiously *excited, depressions; hypochondriac depressions*, which are felt entirely somatically and occur within the area of physical feeling and the related anxieties. *Paranoiac depressions* are characterized by imaginary feelings of guilt and ideas of injury; *anancastic* depressions are determined by compulsive notions. In *vegetative depressions*, as in other forms, actual melancholia may be quite absent. In manic-depressive psychoses (q.v.), approximately half of all cases experience the various phases in the form of depressions; in a quarter of the cases there are both depressive and manic phases; and in another quarter there are only manic phases. There is an essential danger of suicide (q.v.) in endogenous depressions. It is rare for the thought of suicide not to occur, and in 10–15 per cent of the cases the patient actually attempts to take his own life. The condition runs in phases, with an average duration of six months. The single phase does not lead to any change in personality, in contrast to the schizophrenic shift.

Unlike the endogenous depression, in a *reactive depression* the depressive resentment remains more or less explicable on normal psychological grounds, as a quantitative increase of normal sadness; it thus appears as an adequate reaction to stressful events of an acute or chronic nature, whose contribution to the causation of the depression can be recognized by the patient too. *Exhaustion depressions* are also largely to be understood in a normal psychological sense, as cases of depressive reactions to chronic somatic and mental over-strain. *Neurotic depressions* are said to arise from unresolved conflicts (q.v.)

in the unconscious; they are more or less repressed and mostly of a chronic nature, and frequently derive from childhood. They often feature aggressive, hysterical and demonstrative characteristics which are not found as a rule in endogenous depressions. A causative factor in *symptomatic depressions* is temporary exogenous or endogenous somatic damage linked to some cerebral injury (infectious diseases, chronic circulatory disturbances, cerebral poisoning from drugs and medicines, disorders of internal secretions, etc.). *Organic depressions* (P. Kielholz) are also due to cerebral damage, e.g. to organic processes in the brain and to cerebral sclerosis. Hence these depressions also feature organic disturbances of reasoning processes which are not found in depressions without any somatic cause, or in endogenous depression. In contrast to these endogenous and symptomatic depressive moods, which can be limited in time, in depressive psychopaths (see *Psychopathy*) there is a very deeply-rooted and lasting depressive mood without enjoyment of life or confidence, and a tendency to treat everything with pessimism. In this group of psychopathic personalities, the constitutionally melancholy take everything to heart and yet often have very strong emotions, and have to be distinguished from others in whom the basic depressive mood is bound up with bitter resignation and contempt for any enjoyment of life. The pathophysiology of endogenous depressions is still unexplained, although it is undoubtedly somatic in origin.

Psychiatry in the English-speaking world (see Kendall, 1968) does not distinguish as rigorously as traditional psychiatry between the individual depressions. The treatment of depressions is oriented by etiology, and is therefore either psychopharmacological or psychotherapeutic. See *Antidepressives; Psychoses, functional; Schizophrenia*.

Bibliography: Coppen, A. & Walk, A.: Recent developments in affective disorders. Brit. J. Psychiat., Special publ., No. 2, 1968. Hill, D.: Depression: disease, reaction, or posture. Am. J. Psychiat., 1968, 25, 37ff. Hippius, H. & Selbach, H.: Das depressive Syndrom. Munich, 1969. Kendall, R. E.: The classification of depressive illnesses. London, 1968. Lange, J.: Die endogenen und reaktiven Gemütserkrankungen und die manisch-depressive Konstitution. Hdb. der Geisteskrankheiten, Vol. 6, Berlin, 1928. Murphy, H. B. M. *et al.*: Cross-cultural factors in depression. Transcultural Psychiat. Res., 1964, 1, 5–21. Schulte, W. & Mende, W.: Melancholie in Forschung, Klinik und Behandlung. Stuttgart, 1969. Tellenbach, H.: Melancholie. Berlin, 1961. Weitbrecht, H. J.: Depressive und manisch-endogene Psychosen. In: Psychiatrie der Gegenwart, Berlin, 1960. Wolpe, J.: The practice of behavior therapy. New York, 1969.

H. Sattes

Deprivation experiments. Experiments in which animals or humans are placed in situations in which desired objects are absent or needs are not gratified. Experiments of this kind are carried out, e.g., in motivation research, when food, sleep, etc., are withheld.

Bibliography: Brozek, J., Guetskow, H. & Baldwin, M. V.: A quantitative study of perception and association in experimental semistarvation. J. Pers., 1951, 19, 245–64. Epstein, S.: The measurement of drive and conflict in humans. In: Jones, R. J. (Ed.): Nebraska Symposium on Motivation. Lincoln, Neb., 1962.

K.E.P.

Deprivation, social. Social isolation affecting individual well-being and capacity, personality, development and the socialization process (see *Socialization*). The effect of social deprivation on work has been shown by investigation to depend on personality traits. Developmental psychology draws on animal experiments, case studies of feral children, and studies of institutionalized or hospitalized children, for data concerning social deprivation. Social deprivation leads to disturbances of development and behavior. See *Child psychology; Depth psychology*.

Bibliography: Anastasi, A.: Fields of applied psychology. New York, 1964. Id.: Differential psychology. New York, ³1958.

D.B.

Deprivation symptoms. See *Withdrawal symptoms*.

Depth perception. The localization of perceived objects in phenomenal (perceived) space in regard to the distance between the objects of perception and the individual (egocentric depth localization, or absolute depth localization), or in regard to the distance between objects of perception (relative). Depth perception can occur in various modalities, though most precisely in the visual modality (the term often means only one's awareness of the distance between one and the visually perceived object); it also occurs in hearing (loudness, frequency spectrum) and by means of the tactile-haptic system (see *Sense organs*). In contrast to some animals, in man the sense of smell plays hardly any part in depth localization. Although different senses can be implicated, a unified impression of phenomenal distance is obtained (unified phenomenal or perceived space, and also active space). See *Space perception.*   *W.P.*

Depth psychology. 1. *Introductory.* "Depth psychology" (Ger. *Tiefenpsychologie*) is a term which has been used extensively on the continent of Europe in the last sixty years but less frequently in American and British writings. Some authors simply equate it with "psychoanalysis" (q.v.) (see, e.g., Rycroft, 1968); others, however, give it a wider meaning: thus English & English (1958, p. 145) characterize it as "any psychology that postulates dynamic psychic activities that are unconscious", while Wyss (1966), under the title *Depth Psychology*, surveys not only the work of Freud but that of Adler, Rank, Fromm, Binswanger, and many others. On this showing the term appears to be roughly coextensive with "psychodynamics"—a word which is currently used to refer to the study of unconscious wishes and conflicts without implying any particular theory, Freudian or otherwise, about their nature or origin. Here, consideration will be given to a variety of ways in which these "deeper" aspects of human personality have been studied.

Perhaps the key point in the notion of

"depth" is that of surface appearance in contrast with what lies "within" or "beneath". Just as we may be misled by the surface appearance of, e.g., a box or a pond, so a person may seem friendly or aloof at a "superficial" level, but may manifest quite different behavior if intimate details of his life are under discussion, his deeper feelings sometimes "erupting" in conditions of stress. Sometimes the contrast is between "inside" and "outside", as in the phrase "innermost feelings", while often there is the suggestion that it is the *real* personality which lies below or within, with the implication that one can be misled if one considers only what is at the surface. The spatial analogy should not, of course, be pressed too far. The notion of "distance away" from the findings of common-sense observation is not without value, but clearly any reference to actual units of measurement would be quite out of place, and one needs to be aware both of the limitations and of the value of this kind of language. A helpful critique of the notion of "depth" in clinical psychology is given by Levy (1963).

2. *Methods of investigation.* (*a*) One of the main methods of investigation has been the *therapeutic interview.* Under this heading may be included not only full-scale psychoanalysis as practiced by Freud (1856–1939) and his close followers, but also the methods of treatment adopted by those who deviated to a greater or lesser extent from the original Freudian tradition, e.g. C. G. Jung (1875–1961), A. Adler (1870–1937), Karen Horney (1885–1952), and Melanie Klein (1882–1960). (For samples of their work see Freud, 1922; Jung, 1954; Adler, 1925; Horney, 1946; Klein, 1932.) "Depth" interpretations are sometimes made even when there is no full-scale psychotherapy, as has been shown by Malan (1963) and by some psychiatric social workers, e.g. Irvine (1956). In all these cases, particular pieces of behavior on the part of the patient (e.g. verbal remarks about present and past difficulties of adjustment) are commented upon by the therapist,

who attempts to indicate what seems to him to be their deeper emotional significance. Criteria for the correctness of interpretations have been discussed by many writers, e.g. Isaacs (1933) and Farrell (1962). There are largely the same procedures in group therapy (see, e.g., Foulkes & Anthony, 1957), except that up to about nine patients are present with the therapist simultaneously. Other types of depth-orientated work with groups have been described by Balint (1957), Bion (1961), and Rice (1965).

(b) A second method of investigating these "deeper" aspects of personality is by means of *projective tests* (q.v.). The earliest and best known is the Rorschach inkblot test (see Klopfer & Davidson, 1962). Here the subject or patient (the setting is usually a clinical one) is presented with a series of cards containing patterns resembling ink-blots, and is required to say "what he sees" there. From a consideration of how he uses the various features of the blots in his successive responses, testers try to reconstruct the unconscious feelings and attitudes which appear to be influencing his life-style. The procedure is basically similar in the case of Murray's Thematic Apperception Test and Bellak's Children's Apperception Test (for a discussion of both see Bellak, 1954), except that in these two tests the cards do not contain meaningless shapes, but pictures of humans and animals in lifelike situations. Phillipson's Object Relations Test (Phillipson, 1955) has been specially constructed on the assumption that the subject's past and present experiences of human relationships will play an important part in determining his responses

(c) Thirdly, attempts have been made to study "below-surface" tensions in the industrial situation. The pioneer worker here has been Jaques (see, especially, Jaques, 1961). He describes his role as that of "social analyst", and his basic method has been to sit in on industrial committee meetings and discussions and to examine with those present the deeper significance of their remarks and emotional displays. For example, when there were wrangles over payment, this often appeared to reflect underlying discontent or insecurity over status. In addition Jaques suggests that, with suitable safeguards, the formula "length of time over which responsibility is carried" (or "time-span") can be used as a basis for paying people a salary or wage which they themselves will inwardly feel to be equitable.

(d) Fourthly, use has been made of the method of systematic record-keeping, particularly in respect of the behavior of children. From many possible examples, two will be given by way of illustration. (i) Isaacs (1948) has recorded samples of the social behavior of children at a nursery school, most of them aged between three and six; and she claims that these records provide evidence of "the deeper sources of love and hate", such as children's fantasies of oral and anal aggression and their feelings of guilt at their own "bad" impulses (see, especially, *op. cit.*, pp. 280 *seq.*). (ii) Bowlby (1966) has collated a large amount of evidence purporting to show the effects on young children of maternal deprivation; and on the basis of this evidence he asserts that "the prolonged deprivation of the child of maternal care may have grave and far-reaching effects on his character and so on the whole of his future life" (*op. cit.*, p. 46).

(e) Finally, mention should be made of a group of more speculative pronouncements involving in various ways the notion of "depth". Examples include the application by Money-Kyrle (1951) of depth principles to the study of political behavior, the use of the "depth interview" for advertising purposes, as described by Packard (1957), and attempts to understand the "deeper" sources of artistic creation, as in Freud's study of Leonardo da Vinci (Freud, 1963). The basic principle in all these cases is that of applying ideas derived from clinical procedures to situations of everyday life.

3. *A scientific critique.* Accurate evidence in this whole area is not easy to come by. It

is arguable, however, that the "deeper" aspects of personality are of such fundamental importance and interest that even poorly controlled experiments are of more value than rigorous experiments on more trivial matters. On the other hand, there are special dangers if far-reaching claims are made by those inadequately trained in evaluating evidence; in particular, ingenious though doubtful speculations, if passed from one person to another, may come to acquire the cachet of established fact when they are nothing of the kind.

(a) A detailed account of psychoanalysis is given elsewhere in this encyclopedia, and the present discussion will be limited to some general remarks about the evaluation of evidence derived from all forms of psychotherapy. For scientific purposes it is necessary to isolate those factors in the stimulus-situation which, in conjunction with earlier stimuli, are influencing a particular response. Thus if an interpretation in terms of aggressive wishes is put forward, it could be that the interesting behavioral changes which result are due not to the patient's recognition of these aggressive wishes for what they are, but to the fact that the therapist is showing that he can tolerate them and that they are not fatally destructive. In general it is arguable that a re-description of the therapy situations in the language of "operant conditioning" (q.v.) would be very advantageous: firstly, it would force investigators to take seriously the problem of analyzing the stimulus-situation into its components; secondly, interesting parallels would immediately be suggested with laboratory findings, and fuller theoretical understanding would be possible as to why particular interpretations given in a particular context have a particular effect. Since laboratory studies have conclusively shown that verbal comments such as "good" and "mm hm" can sometimes act as reinforcers (see, e.g., Greenspoon, 1962), therapists would be forced to make sure that they themselves were not *unwittingly* reinforcing certain types of behavior (e.g. responses relating to sexual matters in a Freudian analysis); also they would be in a position to exert more rational control over the number and timing of particular kinds of interpretation in the light of what is known about reinforcement in other contexts. What is required, in this view, is not replacement of psychotherapy by therapies based on conditioning principles, but a synthesis as a result of which experts in these different fields can learn from each other (compare Skinner, 1956, and Miles, 1966).

(b) The scientific status of projective tests remains a matter of dispute. It seems safe to say that test results can sometimes contribute in a distinctive way to the making of appropriate practical decisions; but the theoretical justification for the term "projection" is more questionable, and the claim that these tests enable us to investigate the "depths" of personality is by no means universally accepted.

(c) The industrial work of Jaques (1961) could well turn out to be important, and there is no dearth of testable hypotheses (see, e.g., pp. 142 *seq*. and pp. 216 *seq*.). Validation on a large scale, however, has not so far been attempted.

(d) Isaacs' work (1948) exemplifies the value of natural history methods when properly used. The quality of the evidence adduced in studies of maternal deprivation has been called in question (see, e.g., Wootton, 1959, Chapter IV, Andry in Bowlby, *op. cit.*, pp. 223–35, and Munro, 1966), but it is hard to avoid the conclusion that maternally deprived children are at risk.

(e) The main difficulty in the more speculative ideas described under (e) above is the lack of any clear procedure for evaluation. It is not that evaluation is intrinsically impossible, as has been shown by Farrell in his interesting commentary on Freud's Leonardo da Vinci (Freud, 1963, pp. 11–18); but what counts for or against particular claims is sometimes a matter for dispute, and the evidence in these areas is insufficient to permit any assured verdict.

In general, the function of the term "depth psychology" may be said to be that of orienting and steering; it commends certain areas in the study of personality as being worth special investigation and emphasizes the danger of "superficiality" if these areas are ignored. Even if in the future the loose metaphor of "depth" becomes supplanted by more precise and literal formulations, this warning will remain pertinent.

Bibliography: Adler, A.: Individual psychology, tr. P. Radin. London, 1925. Andry, R. G.: see Bowlby, op. cit. Anthony, E. J.: see Foulkes & Anthony, op. cit. Balint, M.: The doctor, his patient, and the illness. London, 1957. Bellak, L.: The TAT and CAT in clinical use. New York, 1954. Bion, W. R.: Experience in groups and other papers. London, 1961. Bowlby, J. et al.: Maternal care. New York, 1966. Davidson, H. H.: see Klopfer & Davidson, op. cit. English, H. B. & English, A. C.: A comprehensive dictionary of psychological and psychoanalytic terms. New York & London, 1958. Farrell, B. A.: The criteria for a psychoanalytic explanation. Aristotelian Society, 1962, Suppl. Vol. 36, 77–100. Id.: see Freud, op. cit. (1963). Foulkes, S. H. & Anthony, E. J.: Group psychotherapy. Harmondsworth, 1957. Freud, S.: Introductory lectures on psychoanalysis, tr. Joan Rivière. London, 1922. Id.: Leonardo da Vinci and a memory of his childhood, tr. Alan Tyson. Harmondsworth, 1963. Greenspoon, J.: Verbal conditioning and clinical psychology. In: Bachrach, A. J. (Ed.): Experimental foundations of clinical psychology. New York, 1962, 510–53. Horney, K.: Our inner conflicts. A constructive theory of neurosis. London, 1946. Irvine, E. E.: Transference and reality in the casework relationship. Brit. J. Psychiat. Soc. Work, 1956, III, 1–10. Isaacs, S.: Social development in young children. London, 1933. Id.: Childhood and after. London, 1948. Jaques, E.: Equitable payment. London, 1961. Jung, C. G.: The practice of psychotherapy, tr. R. F. C. Hull. Collected works, Vol. 16. London, 1954. Klein, M.: The psychoanalysis of children, tr. Alix Strachey. London, 1932. Klopfer, B. & Davidson, H. H.: The Rorschach technique: an introductory manual. New York, 1962. Levy, L. H.: Psychological interpretation. New York, 1963. Malan, D. H.: A study of brief psychotherapy. London, 1963. Miles, T. R.: Eliminating the unconscious. Headington, 1966. Money-Kyrle, R. E.: Psychoanalysis and politics: A contribution to the psychology of politics and morals. London, 1951. Munro, A.: Parental deprivation in depressive patients. Brit. J. Psychiat., 112, 1966, 443–57. Packard, V.: The hidden persuaders. London, 1957. Phillipson, H.: The object relations technique. London, 1955. Rice, A. K.: Learning for leadership: interpersonal and intergroup relations. London, 1965. Rycroft, C.: A critical dictionary of psychoanalysis. London, 1968. Skinner, B. F.: Critique of psychoanalytic concepts and theories. In: The foundations of science and the concepts of psychology and psychoanalysis. Minnesota, 1956, 77–87. Wootton, B.: Social science and social pathology. London, 1959. Wyss, D.: Depth psychology. A critical history, tr. Gerald Onn. London, 1966.

T. R. Miles

Derma (syn. *Dermis; Corium; Cutis*). The inner, sensitive mesodermic layer of the skin beneath the epidermis, containing sensory receptors.

Dermal sense. The sensitivity of the sensory receptors in the derma.

Dermatographia. Signs written on the skin with a blunt object become visible after a few seconds as a reddening and possibly as a swelling (welts). This physiological reaction is caused by expansion of the dermal capillaries after mechanical irritation; when excessive (hyperirritability), it is thought to be a sign of morbid vegetative hyperexcitability (*Urticaria factitia*). *E.D.*

Description (method). The subject describes his own experiences without interpreting them. See *Introspection*.

Descriptive psychology. The academic psychology which came into being in Germany at the beginning of this century. In contrast to experimental psychology, it is concerned with the description and understanding (see *Intuitive understanding psychology*) of psychic phenomena, and does not try to explain them causally and mechanically. Its founders were F. von Brentano (q.v.) and W. Dilthey. Other prominent representatives are K. Jaspers, E. Spranger.

Bibliography: Brentano, F. von: Psychologie. 2 vols, Leipzig, 1924. Dilthey, W.: Gesammelte Schriften, Vol. 1. Leipzig & Berlin, 1922. *P.S.*

Desexualize. 1. To sublimate (see *Sublimation*) by diverting attention or energy from sexual to other goals. **2.** To deprive an object or communication medium of sexual associations, reference, or symbolism. **3.** To castrate (see *Castration*).

Desmolysis. H. Schultz-Hencke's term for the psychotherapeutic dissolution of unconscious inhibitions, inappropriate to the age-group of the subject, which are thought to prevent the development of personality.

De(s)oxyribonucleic acid (abb. DNA). The hereditary substance. Together with protein (which consists of amino acids), the nucleic acids are the principal chemical constituents of chromosomes (q.v.) (fibrous strands in the cell nucleus which can be seen by electron microscope during cell division, and of which there is a characteristic number for each species of animal and plant). DNA consists of very large molecules (macromolecular chains), each molecule having a weight in the order of tens of millions, and consisting of nucleotides combined from a sugar (de(s)oxyribose), a phosphate group, and the four bases adenine, guanine, cytosine and thymine. The DNA helix according to Watson and Crick consists of two DNA chains latched together through these bases: an adenine on chain 1 opposite a thymine on chain 2; and the same for guanine and cytosine. The nucleic acids are the carriers of heredity characteristics, whose information code is distinguished by the different arrangement of the nucleotides in the molecular structure. DNA would appear to be the prime carrier of heredity.
Bibliography: Watson, J. D.: The double helix. London, 1968.   *E.D.*

Destruction (syn. *Destructive instinct; Destrudo*). Destruction is best defined psychologically (i.e. psychoanalytically) as the human frustration of the satisfaction (gratification) of human needs (motivation).

Destruction sought for or attained is the more serious according to the degree of individual frustration, its duration, and its extension to others. The complete frustration of human motivation is synonymous with death. The complete frustration of one's own motivation is self-destruction.

Freud considered the destructive instinct as the second energy source of human motives and human behavior after libido (q.v.). Others (Hartmann, Lorenz) conceive it as a large class of motives (see *Death instinct; Aggression*). Destructive behavioral tendencies can also appear in response to frustration (q.v.).
Bibliography: Freud, S.: Beyond the pleasure principle. London, ²1959. Hartmann, H., Kris, E. & Loewenstein, R. M.: Notes on the theory of aggression. Psychoanalyt. Study of the child, 1949, *3/4*, 9–36. Lorenz, K.: On aggression. London, 1966. Toman, W.: Introduction to psychoanalytic theory of motivation. London & New York, 1960.   *W.T.*

Desublimation. The removal of libidinal objectifications, which—according to H. Marcuse—result from the failure of repressive social institutions. Desublimation is achieved by the self-sublimation of all sexual part-instincts in the eros under a non-repressive reality principle free from authoritarianism, and is the basis of a utopian, free society.
Bibliography: See *Alienation*.   *U.H.S.*

Detail response. In the Rorschach test: the observation of and response to larger (*D*) or smaller (*d*) partial areas of the whole inkblot.   *K.E.P.*

Deterioration. Progressive impairment of physical or mental function. See also *Aging; Gerontology.*

Determinants. 1. In a biological sense: heredity factors (*anlagen*, q.v.). **2.** In psychology: (*a*) in general: factors determining some process or development; (*b*) in depth psychology: "boundaries of individual possibilities"

(Schottlaender); (c) in psychoanalysis: the decisive aspects of a dream; (d) in the Rorschach test: inkblot qualities which settle the testee's answer (i.e. image perceived: e.g., color, shape); (e) in general: limiting factors or terms, e.g. in activity, postulation, diagnosis. See *Traits*. K.E.P.

3. Causative or limiting factors. The entire science of psychology is based upon the assumption that thoughts, feelings, and behavior are predictable on the basis of previous conditions, i.e. that they are not random, but *determined*. For example, Freud argued that many apparently meaningless phenomena such as dreams and slips of the tongue are largely determined by unconscious motivational processes. G.D.W.

Determination, coefficient of (syn. *Index of determination*). The square of the product-moment correlation (q.v.) of two variables, r_{xy}^2. The term indicates that the coefficient (q.v.) expresses the proportion of variance of the dependent variable Y, which is "determined" by the independent X, i.e. which it has "in common" with X. See *Correlation; Statistics*. W.H.B.

Determining tendency (syn. *Set*). A term introduced by N. Ach for the idea that the course our consciousness takes is partly determined by and dependent on our consciously or unconsciously operative conceptions of a goal or aim. The course of a thought process is definitely directed by a predisposing set formed by the expected result.

Bibliography: Ach, N.: Über die Begriffsbildung. Bamberg, 1921. Watt, H. J.: Experimentelle Beiträge zu einer Theorie des Denkens. Arch. ges. Psychol., 1905, *4*, 289–436. K.E.P.

Determinism. 1. All the conditions (determinants) which are necessary for the appearance of a phenomenon. The same phenomena can, however, be caused by different "determinisms": biological, social, geographical, etc. **2.** In a philosophical sense: the doctrine

that the phenomena (facts) of the universe depend so closely on those preceding them that they represent their sole effect. **3.** In the Aristotelian theory of causality determinism denotes the concept of "*efficient cause*", i.e. that producing an effect, as distinct from *material cause* (from which something arises), *formal cause* (which decides that a thing should come to be), and *final cause* (purpose). It is, however, sometimes used of formal cause. **4.** Any doctrine which (analogously to the physical world) interprets psychic life as dependent solely on (largely physiological) preconditions (*material*, or *mechanistic*, determinism). **5.** Loosely, any theory which denies freewill when postulating that all phenomena are directed by law. M.-J.B. & J.M.

Detour action. A detour action or behavior is the attainment of a goal not directly but by indirect routes: by means of behaviors which are not essentially connected with the goal. W. Köhler showed in chimpanzees, and K. Bühler in children, that when instinctive equipment, previous knowledge and situation give no direct indications regarding goal-getting, a detour is frequently sought and found which leads to the goal in question. According to K. Lewin, it is not connected to the direct appeal (valence) of the situation, but is controlled by the ego (q.v.); it presupposes control of drive, or leads as a substitute activity to an equivalent substitute goal; it is comparable to judicious behavior in an adult. Detour actions in the broadest sense comprise a large part of all adult actions. H.W.

Deuteranop(s)ia. Green blindness. The medium range of the color spectrum is not perceived. See *Color blindness; Color vision*. R.R.

Development. 1. *The concept.* The term "development" refers to a sequence of changes in organisms (animal or human), groups of organisms (e.g. nations), cultural fields (e.g. art), and dead matter (e.g. geological development). The concept was used by psychology in its early stages to denote the development of embryonic possibilities. In general, development extends from the origin (the beginning of mental or biological life) to the end of individual existence (death or extinction). Animal and human development comprises the whole course of life, although special attention is paid to child development. There is a dual relationship between development and learning: learning is a general term for development if the latter is considered as a special form of the former (long-term, irreversible, differential and structural), and the laws of learning are regarded as the general principles of human behavior. From another angle, development can be taken as the broader concept, not only for a comprehensive definition (such as the one above), but also in view of the processes of maturation and growth which take place in the organism and are independent of learning.

2. *Special interpretations*. Different theoretical conceptions led to two main areas of definition. On the one hand, development is regarded as growth and described as a quantitative increase (L. Carmichael, U. Undeutsch); on the other, it is understood as a qualitative change taking place in phases or stages (O. Kroh, O. Tumlirz, C. Bühler), leading (spirally) to higher developmental forms (A. Gesell), or comprising the superimposition of higher on lower layers (H. Rothacker, Ph. Lersch). A third approach to a definition considers the decisive factors of development such as the "principle of convergence" of *anlage* (q.v.) (natural endowment) and environment (W. Stern), development as *anlage* unfolding according to some plan (K. Bühler), or the combined effects of endowment, environment and personal activity (self-formation and self-realization) of the individual (G. W. Allport, q.v.). Today the question of a conceptual clarification of development is of secondary importance.

3. *History*. The roots of the psychology (or the concept) of development are to be found in Greek philosophy. Heraclitus taught that there was an eternal becoming; Empedocles explained that life originated in abiogenesis. For Aristotle, growth was development from potentiality to action. His principle of being as the realization of essence (entelechy, q.v.) has influenced German developmental psychology up to the present day. The same is true of the influence of Leibniz, who ascribed development and change to the spontaneous activity of "windowless" monads (i.e. elementary units containing the principle of their own changes). Development as learning can be traced back to Locke's empiricism. Darwin established the theory of heredity (q.v.), which explains the origin and development of animal species as arising from selection and mutation. This theory derives from phylogenetic sources not only the physical development of man but his experience and behavior. On the other hand, the concept of development was given a more humanistic interpretation in the nineteenth century. Its use in the philosophy of history was often directly transferred to individual development (ascending spirally toward some final end). The study of history led W. Dilthey to an intuitive characterization of human life as a mental process. W. Preyer's book of 1882 was an important landmark in the evolution of developmental psychology as a branch of objective science. In Germany the work of William and Clara Stern, and Karl and Charlotte Bühler soon took the theory of development to one of its peaks. Other important authors were Hildegard Hetzer, O. Kroh, O. Tumlirz, A. Busemann, especially H. Werner, but also F. Krueger (genetic psychology of totality), Freud (development of sexuality, importance of childhood for the genesis of personality traits) and C. G. Jung (development as active self-formation from the viewpoint of depth psychology). In the U.S.A. research into the psychology of development began at an early date with Stanley Hall and

J. M. Baldwin; in France with A. Binet, O. Decroly and E. Claparède. The most important influence even now is J. Piaget (q.v.), whose work is only just coming to be more widely known outside Europe.

4. *Methods.* There are the following *methods of compiling and interpreting data:* (a) systematic observation without prompting: studies of families and observation in the domestic situation, collection of data from a random sample of situations (e.g. play, meals, in school, etc.), and times during the day; in the optimum case the ethological method (see *Ethology*); (b) systematic observation with prompting: recourse to physical data (e.g. measurement of strength and speed, of reaction time, compilation of physiological data), psychometric techniques, experimentation (q.v.) (in the narrower sense). Specific possibilities in research into development are the evaluation of diary entries and the use of play to gain insight into children's behavior.

Research into the course of development: (a) Comparison of different age levels: longitudinal studies (observation of the same sample over prolonged periods of time), cross-sectional methods (comparison of representatives of different age groups at a given time); when considering the generation effect and test-retest effect, sequential models are used which couple longitudinal and cross-sectional studies; (b) simulation of development: control of conditions which seem to be important in "natural" development by using them as an independent variable and studying their short-term effects (over days or months).

5. *Present state of research.* (a) *Cognitive development.* The study of the development of intelligence was dominated for a long time by the conception of a rapid growth until the end of the second decade, followed by a slow decline in achievement. Often this growth curve obtained by cross-sectional studies could not be confirmed by longitudinal studies, which tended to show a progressively slow rise until old age (Bayle & Oden). As age increases, so does the number

of intelligence factors (differentiation hypothesis of intelligence: H. E. Garrett, C. Burt). H. A. Witkin classifies mental development in terms of field-dependence and field-independence and differentiation: as age increases, there is greater ability to perceive embedded figures (q.v.), i.e. to detach elements (units) from the surrounding field. The development of "field articulation" is subject to fluctuations which may have physiological and social causes. Problem-solving strategies likewise change with age. H. H. Kendler concludes from his results that for young children the simple reinforcement model is still applicable, but with older children the explanation of performance in novel learning situations requires representative variables (concepts) (see *Apperception categories*). The development of thought strategies passes from primitive stereotyped practices (M. W. Weir) to methods which employ only positive examples of a concept, and from there to strategies which can make use of positive and negative information (S. Nadiraschwili). Piaget's approach to the description of cognitive development is being taken further and revised in very different circles. Assimilation and accommodation as component processes of adaptation in the first two years of life develop into sensorimotor intelligence, which coordinates perception and movement sequences. With the elaboration of basic schemata, thinking begins to develop, and moves from the preoperational stage (beginning with the symbolic function) to concrete operational thought, and finally to formal operational thought, when the adolescent is able to think reflectively about the logical operations themselves and use them systematically (e.g. in mathematics). Characteristic progress to higher levels of thought which is associated with age depends on the nature of the exercises set. For the whole of cognitive development *curiosity and exploration* seem to be decisive. This behavior has its roots in the orienting reflex (q.v.) and in the affective excitation released by conflict situations (D. E.

Berlyne). See *Language; Conflict; Child psychology.*

(*b*) When considering *human development as a process of socialization* (see *Socialization*), the assumption of adult and sex roles is most important. Learning cultural standards can be described as the development of value judgments. The basic values of our culture are taken over at an early age but undergo revision in the second decade of life when the child or adolescent is strongly influenced by peer group culture. Norms are assimilated largely by imitative learning, said to include the establishment of the super-ego (q.v.) by the introjection of libidinal objects (parents) and their punitive energy. Classical conditioning (see *Conditioning; Conscience; Criminality*) can be adduced to explain the appearance and operation of the "bad conscience" (H. J. Eysenck).

(*c*) *Development of personality.* Here an increase of cognitive control seems to be generally characteristic of the development of personality traits. The complex interaction of the many components in each person's life leads to a result which is in every case unique. See *Personality; Character.*

(*d*) *Physical development.* This can be characterized by growth curves. On an average, there is a negative acceleration rate for entire body size and weight as well as for many individual organs. In physical development there is rapid growth of the brain, which possesses its full complement of cells even before birth and has already reached 80 per cent of its final weight at the age of four. J. Tanner speaks of a "skeletal age", a "dental maturity age" and a "morphological age". The speed at which maturity is reached is largely genetically programmed but there are environmental influences (acceleration, q.v., of total growth since the previous century), influences of nutritional standards, and dependence on social conditions (children from large families and underprivileged classes tend to be smaller and weigh less). During puberty there is a general advance in growth, and many physiological changes can

be noticed (blood pressure, pulse and basal metabolism). See *Aging.*

6. *Explanatory principles.* Inherent in the concept of development is a sense of "unfolding from within"; this led to a descriptive model of development as *growth and maturation.* This view is very important in explaining the development of animal organisms, but is also applied to human psychological development when discussing physical and mental correlations (U. Undeutsch, F. Steinwachs, W. Arnold, C. Burt). Sequences of changes in experience and behavior are interpreted here as processes of maturation (q.v.). But the modern emphasis in human development is on learning processes. To describe the development of habits (see *Habit*), affective states, and the conditions underlying motivation, the model of classical and instrumental conditioning is useful (though not completely satisfactory). The process of socialization as incorporation of an asocial, uncultured being into the cultural community requires imitative learning as an additional explanatory principle. Neither of the two principles is adequate for the characterization of cognitive development, which requires a description and interpretation of learning as a process of organization and structuralization.

Independently of the dichotomy of learning and maturation, the two concepts differentiation and centralization are still used (H. Werner). With the progressive change of the organism, parts appear which were not visible in the undifferentiated whole. This process of differentiation may be observed in physiological as well as in phylogenetic development (development of the brain, q.v., in the animal world). The individual areas become independent insofar as they fulfill specific tasks; but they do not function independently because, as differentiation increases, central control sources increasingly take care of the coordination, inhibition and activation of the individual areas. As a whole, the principle of centralization enables distant aims to be set and approached; in specific instances, it allows control of motor impulses, selection and structuring in perception, and control of emotional excitation.

7. *Development as a science.* Like other branches of psychology, developmental psychology is changing from a purely descriptive into an "exact" science which endeavors to explain its statements with the aid of theories or at least of *models* (q.v.). Hence the scientific aim of developmental psychology is not primarily educational (to help and protect man), but to elucidate psychological phenomena by examining their genesis. It therefore serves general psychology. The use of the findings of developmental psychology for educational, political and religious ends is a value-oriented application of what is properly a scientific discipline.

Bibliography: Arnold, W.: Begabung und Bildungswilligkeit. Munich, 1968. **Baldwin, J. M.:** Mental development in the child and in the race: Methods and processes. New York, 1895, ³1906. **Baltes, P.:** Sequenzmodelle zum Studium von Altersprozessen: Querschnitts- und Längsschnittssequenzen. In: Report of 25th German Psychology Association Congress. Göttingen, 1966, 423–30. **Bayley, N. & Oden, M. H.:** The maintenance of intellectual ability in gifted adults. J. Ger., 1955, *10*, 91–107. **Binet, A.:** Les idées modernes sur les enfants. Paris, 1932. **Bruner, J. S., Oliver, R. R., Greenfield, P. M.** *et al.*: Studies in cognitive growth. New York, 1966. **Bühler, C.:** From birth to maturity. London, 1935. **Bühler, K.:** Abriss der geistigen Entwicklung des Kindes. Leipzig, ⁷1949. **Burt, C.:** The differentiation of mental ability. Brit. J. educ. Psychol., 1954, *24*, 76–90. **Id.:** Intelligence and heredity. In: The Irish Journal of Educat., 1969, *3*, No. 2. **Carmichael, L.:** Manual of child psychology. New York & London, ²1954. **Claparède, E.:** Psychologie de l'enfant et pédagogie expérimentale. Geneva, 1926. **Eysenck, H. J.:** The development of moral values in children. VII—The contribution of learning theory. Brit. J. educ. Psychol., 1960, *30*, 11–21. **Garrett, H. E.:** A developmental theory of intelligence. Amer. Psychologist, 1946, *1*, 372–8. **Gesell, A.:** The ontogenesis of infant behavior. In: **Carmichael, L.** (Ed.): Manual of child psychology. New York & London, ²1954. **Id.:** The first five years of life. New York, 1941. **Id.:** The mental growth of the pre-school child. New York, 1925. **Id.:** Biographies of child development. New York, 1935. **Id. & Ilg, F. L.:** Child development: an introduction to the study of human growth. New York, 1949. **Hetzer, H.:** Kind und Schaffen.

Jena, 1931. **Kagan, J. & Moss, H. A.:** Birth to maturity. New York, 1962. **Kendler, H. H. & Kendler, T. S.:** Vertical and horizontal processes in problem solving. Psychol. Rev., 1962, *59*, 1–16. **Kroh, O.:** Entwicklungspsychologie des Grundschulkindes. Langensalza, 1944. **Krueger, F.:** Entwicklungspsychol. der Ganzheit. Rev. der Psychol., 1939/40, *2*. **Lersch, Ph.:** Aufbau der Person. Munich, ⁹1964. **Merz, F. & Kalveran, K. T.:** Kritik der Differenzierungshypothese der Intelligenz. Arch. ges. Psychol. 1965, *117*, 287–95. **Nadiraschwili, S.:** Über die Modellierung von Verallgemeinerungsprozessen. Z. Psychol., 1965, *171*, 196–203. **Oerter, R.:** Moderne Entwicklungspsychologie. Donauwörth, ⁸1969. **Piaget, J.:** The psychology of intelligence. London, 1950. **Preyer, W.:** Die Seele des Kindes. Leipzig, 1882. **Rothacker, E.:** Die Schichten der Persönlichkeit. Bonn, ⁴1952. **Stern, W.:** Psychol. der frühen Kindheit bis zum sechsten Lebensjahre. ⁵1928. **Tanner, J.:** Education and physical growth. London, 1962. **Thomae, H.** (Ed.): Entwicklungspsychologie. Handbuch der Psychologie, Vol. 3. Göttingen, 1959. **Tumlirz, O.:** Einführung in die Jugendkunde. Leipzig, 1927. **Undeutsch, U.:** Das Verhältnis von körperlicher und seelischer Entwicklung. Handbuch der Psychologie, Vol. 3. Göttingen, 1959, 329–57. **Weir, M. W.:** Development changes in problem solving strategies. Psychol. Rev., 1964, *71*, 473–90. **Werner, H.:** Einführung in die Entwicklungspsychologie. Leipzig, ²1933. **Witkin, H. A., Dyk, R. B., Faterson, H. F., Goodenough, D. R. & Karp, S. A.:** Psychological differentiation. New York, 1962.

R. Oerter

Developmental age. The sum of all the items (multiplied by certain time values) which have been solved by the testee at any age from (theoretically) the first month of life. In the "normal" child this sum is equal to the age. The term and concept were first used in 1926 by Furfey and (quite independently) Penning.

Bibliography: Furfey, P. H.: Some preliminary results on the nature of developmental age. Sch. Soc. 1926, *23*, 183–4. **Penning, K.:** Das Problem der Schulreife in historischer und sachlicher Darstellung. Leipzig, 1926.

S.Kr.

Development tests (syn. *Development scales*). A collective name for methods used to assess developmental age and progress in comparison with average development (development quotient), especially for infants and pre-school children. Various aspects of achievement

271

(performance: perception, psychomotor, language, socialization) are usually recorded separately by observation in standardized play situations and by questioning persons in charge. The results are presented as a development profile, and a developmental age and development quotient are established. Despite the easy transition to intelligence tests proper (e.g. the Binet-Simon Test, q.v.), longitudinal studies show only very slight correlations between the DQ in the first year of life and the IQ later. The practical value of these methods is to be found in the diagnosis of developmental disturbances. The best-known tests of this kind come from A. Gesell, Ch. Bühler and H. Hetzer, N. Bayley, P. S. Cattell, O. Brunet and I. Lézine.

Bibliography: Stott, L. H. & Ball, R. S.: Infant and pre-school tests: review and evaluation. Monographs of the Society for Research in Child Development. 1965, *30*, 1–151.   A.L.

Deviation. 1. *Average deviation* (abb. AD), also known as *average variation*, or simply *deviation*, is the average value of the absolute deviations or departures of measures from their arithmetic means,

$$AD = \frac{\Sigma |X - \bar{X}|}{N}.$$

But this is seldom used, since the application of absolutes is disadvantageous in many cases. The *median deviation*, $\frac{x_i}{N}$, is a measurement for the central tendency of deviations $x_i = X_i - B$, where B can be any desired value. If a systematic error k is made in each individual observation, the median deviation will be k. If B is identical with the arithmetic mean, the median deviation will be zero.
                                                      W.H.B.

2. Any departure from a norm.

Deviation, sexual. A deviation from the cultural norm in the selection and/or the arrangement of the stimulus situation helping the attainment of orgasm. Also some dis-

agreement with this norm in relation to the frequency of sexual activity and avoidance of orgasm. See *Perversion.*   *U.H.S.*

Dewey, John. B. 20/10/1859 in Burlington (Vermont); d. 2/6/1952 in New York. Social philosopher and educator. Educated at Vermont and Johns Hopkins universities. He first taught psychology at Michigan, and was later Professor in Chicago and Columbia, New York. Taking Hegel as his starting-point, Dewey helped to develop an empirical biological philosophy, functionalism, which emphasized consciousness and thinking as at the service of action and thus of habit formation, and the study of function as fundamental to psychology. Although Dewey made a significant contribution to the branch of American pragmatism known as "instrumentalism" and helped the advance of scientific psychology, his most lasting monument (apart from the multifarious influences of his democratic and ethical theories) has been the extension of child-centered techniques in Anglo-American education and the inspiration of countless teachers and educators to a new respect for cooperative approaches and classroom techniques.

Some Works: Psychology. New York, 1886. The reflex arc concept in psychology. Psychol. Rev., 1896, *3*, 357–70. How we think, N.Y.,1910. Democracy and education. N.Y., 1916. Essays in experimental logic. N.Y., 1916. Human nature and conduct. N.Y., 1922. Experience and nature, N.Y., 1925. Characters and events, 2 vols, N.Y., 1929. Problems of men. N.Y., 1946.

Bibliography: Boring, E. G.: John Dewey: 1859–1952. Amer. J. Psychol., 1953, *66*, 145–7. Roback, A. A.: A history of American psychology. New York & London, 1964. Schilpp, P. A. (Ed.): The philosophy of John Dewey. Evanston, 1940.   F.-C.S.

Dexterity test. An individual test or a battery component which assesses manual speed and accuracy. See *Motor skills; Manual dexterity.*

Dextrality. See *Laterality*.

Diagnostics. See *Psychodiagnostics*.

Diagram. A schematic representation of essential (e.g. spatial) relations between parts or variables.

Diastole. A phase of inactivity during a cardiac cycle in which the heart muscle relaxes, and the ventricle dilates. It alternates rhythmically with the *systole* (contraction of the heart muscle) and lasts, according to the heart rate, 0·3 to 0·8 seconds. During this time the pressure of both ventricles sinks to its minimal value of about 0 mm Hg so that blood can flow from the auricles and adjacent veins into the ventricles.   *E.D.*

Diathesis. Constitutional disposition or predisposition to some disease of the whole organism or of certain systems of the organism. A number of diatheses are distinguished according to the nature of the disease: e.g. *angiospastic diathesis* with vasolability, rapid fluctuations of blood pressure, loss of color and blushing, fainting fits and migraine; *exudative diathesis* with a congenital tendency in children's organisms to various diseases of the skin and the mucous membrane; *hemorrhagic diathesis*, with a tendency to persistent bleeding.   *E.D.*

Diathetic proportion. Prominent scales of temperament with the cyclothymic and cycloid constitutions. An individual can pass through the stages, or experience one as a permanent temperamental emphasis.
  Cyclothymic: elevated (cheerful, impulsively irascible), syntonic (easy-going, genial), subdued (quiet, melancholic).
  Cycloid: hypomanic (excessively jolly, angry, mobile), sub-depressive (dejected, lacking in drive).   *W.K.*

Diatonic. In music: the diatonic scale is the seven-tone major scale consisting of seven whole tones, and two semitones between the third and the fourth and the seventh and eighth intervals.   *P.S. & R.S.*

Dichotomy. 1. The division into two of a population or a sample (distribution) according to an external criterion. **2.** The doctrine or theory that man consists of two parts: soma and psyche, body and soul.

Dichromatopsia (syn. *Dichromatism; Dichromatic vision*). Partial color blindness in which the person affected can only distinguish yellow from blue (red-green blindness) or only green from red (yellow-blue blindness). In the first case green and red are mistaken for one another and for grey; in the second case the person affected cannot distinguish a blue tone from a yellow but sees them both as two different tones of grey. See *Color blindness*.   *G.Ka.*

Diction. Style of verbal presentation, particularly the clarity and precision of words and phrases spoken or sung.   *G.D.W.*

Didactics. In educational theory the branch dealing with the formulation of aims in teaching, the choice of subjects to be taught, and the appropriate teaching method(s); however, the term is usually applied to instructional methodology.
  Didactic analysis: an instructional psychoanalysis undergone by a prospective analyst.   *G.B.*

Diencephalon (syn. *Betweenbrain; Interbrain*). Situated between the telencephalon (q.v.) and mesencephalon (q.v.), and consisting of the hypothalamus (q.v.), the thalamus (q.v.), and metathalamus and epithalamus. The metathalamus contains the geniculate bodies (*corpus geniculatum laterale* and *corpus geniculatum mediale*) which act as synaptic centers in the visual and auditory pathways. The pineal body is part of the epithalamus. (See *Pineal gland.*)

Bibliography: Gardner, E., Gray, D. J. & Orahilly, R.: Anatomy. Philadelphia, 1969.   *G.A.*

Dietetics. The science of regulating food intake for reasons of health.   *G.D.W.*

Difference tone. If two pure tones (primary tones) differing in pitch are sounded simultaneously, a third tone is heard in addition, the frequency of which is equal to the difference in frequency between the two primary tones.   *P.S. & R.S.*

Differential Aptitude Test (abb. DAT). A test devised for educational and vocational guidance (q.v.); the subtests produce eight part-results (verbal reasoning, number ability, abstract reasoning, spatial relations, mechanical reasoning, clerical speed and accuracy in office work, language use: orthography and syntax), which are not differentiated factorially. Widely used in the U.S.A. (especially for grades 8 to 12).

Bibliography: Bennet, G. K., Seashore, H. G. & Wesman, A. G.: Differential Aptitude Tests. Psychol. Corp. N.Y., 1947–59.   *R.M.*

Differential diagnosis. A diagnosis made in order to decide between different groups, e.g. clinical profiles, or occupations.   *R.M.*

Differential inhibition. See *Inhibition, internal.*

Differential psychology is concerned with the nature and origins of individual differences in psychological traits. Such differences are not limited to man, but occur throughout the animal scale. Psychological studies of animals, from one-celled organisms to anthropoid

apes, reveal wide individual differences in learning, emotionality, motivation, and other behavioral characteristics. So large are these differences within each species, that the ranges of performance overlap even when widely separated species are compared. When examined with the same learning task, the brightest rat in a group may excel the dullest monkey.

Although in popular descriptions persons are often put into distinct categories, such as dull or bright, and excitable or calm, actual measurement of any psychological trait shows that individuals vary in degree along a continuous scale. In most traits, the distribution approximates the bell-shaped normal probability curve, with the greatest clustering of cases near the center of the range and a gradual decrease in numbers as the extremes are approached. First derived by mathematicians in their study of probability, the normal curve is obtained whenever the variable measured results from a very large number of independent and equally weighted factors. Because of the extremely large number of hereditary and environmental factors that contribute to the development of most psychological traits, it is reasonable to expect that such traits should be distributed in accordance with the normal curve.

1. *Heredity and environment. (a) Concepts.* The origins of individual differences are found in the innumerable and complex interactions between each individual's heredity and his environment. Heredity comprises the genes transmitted by each parent at conception. If there is a chemical deficiency or imbalance in the genes, a seriously defective organism may result, with physical anomalies as well as severely retarded intelligence. Except for such pathological extremes, however, heredity sets very broad limits to behavior development. Within these limits, what the individual actually becomes depends upon his environment.

Environment includes the sum total of stimuli to which the individual responds from conception to death. It comprises a vast multiplicity of variables, ranging from air and food to educational facilities and the attitudes of one's associates. Environmental influences begin to operate before birth. Nutritional deficiencies, toxins, and other chemical or physical conditions of the prenatal environment may exert a deep and permanent effect upon both physical and mental development. Hence conditions present at birth, often loosely designated as innate or congenital, are not necessarily hereditary. Similarly, organic conditions need not be hereditary. Mental retardation resulting from brain injury in infancy, for example, has an organic but not a hereditary origin.

The relationship between heredity and environment can best be described in terms of interaction. Such interaction implies that a given environmental factor will exert a *different influence* depending upon the specific hereditary material upon which it operates. For example, the number and quality of symphonic recordings available in the home will exert a significant influence upon the musical development of a hearing child but none upon that of a deaf child. Conversely, any given hereditary factor will operate differently under different environment conditions. Two identical twins will differ markedly in body weight if one is systematically over-fed for six months and the other kept on a semi-starvation diet.

(*b*) *Methodology.* The methods used to investigate the operation of hereditary and environmental factors in behavior development may be subsumed under three major approaches: selective breeding, experiential variation, and statistical studies of family resemblances. Selective breeding for behavioral characteristics has been successfully applied to several species. From a single initial group of rats, for example, it proved possible to breed two strains representing "bright" and "dull" maze-learners, respectively. Another investigation on such selectively bred strains provided a good example of the interaction of heredity and environment. When reared in restricted environments,

both strains performed almost as poorly as did the genetically "dull" rats reared in a natural environment. On the other hand, an enriched environment, providing a variety of stimulation and opportunities for motor activity, improved the performance of the "dull" strain; both groups now performed at about the level of the "brights" in a natural environment.

A second approach to the study of heredity and environment is concerned with the behavioral effects of systematic variations in experience. Experimental investigations of this question either provide special training or prevent the normal exercise of a particular function. Through such experiments, many activities formerly regarded as completely unlearned or "instinctive", such as nest-building and the care of the young by rats, have been found to depend upon prior experiences. A series of experiments with monkeys demonstrated the effects of training upon learning ability itself. Through the formation of learning sets, the animals were able to learn the solution of complex problems because of their prior experience in solving simpler problems of a similar nature. Some studies of young children have used the method of co-twin control, in which one identical twin is given intensive training in, e.g., stair climbing, while the other serves as the control. Others have compared the development of children reared in culturally deprived or restricted environments, such as orphanages, with that of children reared in more nearly average environments. Considerable retardation has been found in deprived environments, the retardation becoming more severe with increasing age. There is some evidence, however, that appropriate educational programs, particularly when introduced in early childhood, may counteract the detrimental effects of such environments on intellectual development.

The third approach uses statistical analyses of family resemblances and differences. In general, the closer the hereditary relation, the more similar will test scores be. On most intelligence tests, for example, identical twin correlations are close to 0·90; fraternal twin correlations cluster around 0·70; and siblings yield correlations around 0·50, as do parents and children. It should be noted, however, that a family is a cultural as well as a biological unit. The more closely two persons are related by heredity, in general, the greater will be the similarity of their environments and the extent of their influence upon each other. Investigations of foster children and of identical twins reared apart permit some isolation of hereditary and environmental factors, but several uncontrolled conditions in these studies preclude definitive conclusions.

3. *Nature of intelligence*. (*a*) *Composition*. Intelligence has been identified with the intelligence quotient (IQ) obtained in an intelligence test. Such tests do reflect at least partly the concept of intelligence prevalent in the culture in which they were developed. Most current intelligence tests measure chiefly scholastic aptitude, or that combination of abilities required for school achievement. Modern intelligence testing originated with Alfred Binet's development of a test to assess intellectual retardation among school children. Intelligence tests have frequently been validated against such academic criteria as school grades, teachers' ratings of intelligence, promotion and graduation data, and amount of schooling completed. In content, most intelligence tests are predominantly verbal, with some inclusion of arithmetic skills, quantitative reasoning, and memory. (See *Abilities*.)

With the increasing participation of psychologists in vocational counseling and personnel selection came the realization that supplementary tests were needed to measure aptitudes not covered by traditional intelligence tests. As a result, so-called special aptitude tests were developed for mechanical, clerical, and other functions. At the same time, basic research on the nature of intelligence was being conducted by the techniques of factor analysis. Essentially these techniques involve statistical analysis of the inter-correlations among test scores in order to discover the smallest number of independent factors that can account for their interrelations. Among the aptitudes or "factors" thus identified are verbal comprehension, word fluency, arithmetic skills, quantitative reasoning, perceptual speed, spatial visualization, and mechanical comprehension. Through factor analysis, the functions measured by intelligence tests were themselves identified as relatively independent verbal and numerical aptitudes, and these aptitudes, in combination with some of those underlying special aptitude tests, now provide a more comprehensive picture of human abilities.

(*b*) *Intellectual deviates*. The mentally retarded and the gifted represent the lower and upper extremes of the distribution of intelligence. Because the distribution is continuous, there is no sharp separation between these groups and the normal. In terms of intelligence-test performance, mental retardation is customarily identified with IQs below 70, covering about two to three per cent of the general population. Decisions regarding the disposition and treatment of individual cases are based not only upon the IQ, but also upon a comprehensive study of the individual's intellectual development, educational history, social competence, physical condition and familial situation. Although a few rare forms of mental retardation result from defective genes, many varieties can be traced to environmental factors operating before or after birth and including both physical and psychological conditions. (See *Mental defect*).

At the other end of the scale, children with IQs above 140, falling in the upper one per cent of the general population, have been found to be typically healthy, emotionally well adjusted, successful in school, and characterized by a wide range of interests. As they grow into maturity, these gifted children as a whole maintain their superiority in adult achievements. Other research on the intellectually gifted includes case studies of living scientists and an analysis of records of eminent men of the past. Since the 1950s, research on the nature and sources of creativity has expanded rapidly. The concept of intelligence has thereby been broadened to include a number of creative aptitudes, which have also been identified through factor-analytic studies.

(c) *Growth and decline.* Longitudinal studies of age changes in performance on traditional intelligence tests reveal a slow rise in infancy, followed by more rapid progress and eventual slowing down as maturity is approached. It should be noted, however, that intelligence tests measure a combination of several traits and that the nature of this composite differs with age. In infancy the IQ is based largely upon sensorimotor development, while in childhood it depends increasingly on verbal and other abstract functions.

Intelligence-test performance continues to improve at least into the twenties. Among intellectually superior persons, especially university graduates and those engaged in relatively intellectual occupations, such improvement may continue throughout life. In more nearly average samples, tested abilities tend to decline beyond the thirties, the drop being greatest in tasks involving speed, visual perception, and abstract spatial relations. Older persons can learn nearly as well as younger, but are more seriously handicapped when the task conflicts with well-established habits. Cross-sectional studies, utilizing different samples at different age levels, may give misleading results because of lack of comparability of groups in education, cultural milieu, and other conditions.

3. *Group differences.* (a) *Sex differences.* Psychological test surveys show that men as a group excel in speed and coordination of gross bodily movements, spatial orientation, mechanical comprehension, and arithmetic reasoning, while women excel in manual dexterity, perceptual speed and accuracy, memory, numerical computation, verbal fluency, and other tasks involving the mechanics of language. Among the major personality differences are the greater aggressiveness,

achievement drive, and emotional stability of the male, and the stronger social orientation of the female. Sex differences in aptitudes and personality traits depend upon both biological and cultural factors. The influence of biological conditions may be quite direct, as in the effect of male sex hormone upon aggressive behavior. Or it may be indirect, as in the social and educational effects of the more rapid development of girls as compared to boys. The contribution of culture is illustrated by the wide differences in sex roles found in contemporary cultures and in different historical periods.

(b) *Racial and cultural differences.* If individuals are classified with regard to such categories as social class, occupational level, urban-versus-rural residence, or nationality, significant group differences are often found in child-rearing practices, sexual behavior, emotional responses, interests, and attitudes, as well as in performance on many aptitude tests. In all such comparisons, the direction and amount of group difference depends upon the particular trait investigated. Because each culture or subculture fosters the development of its own characteristic pattern of aptitudes and personality traits, comparisons in terms of such global measures as IQ or general emotional adjustment can have little meaning.

Races are populations that differ in the relative frequency of certain genes. They are formed whenever a group becomes relatively isolated, for either geographic or social reasons, so that marriage among its members is more frequent than marriage with outsiders. Since isolation fosters cultural as well as racial differentiation, the contributions of biological and cultural factors to race differences are difficult to separate. Although available data are inconclusive, studies using special experimental designs point more strongly to cultural than to biological causes of existing racial differences in psychological traits.

In racial comparisons as in all group comparisons, average differences between groups are far smaller than the range of individual differences within each group. Consequently the distributions of the groups overlap to a marked degree. Even when the averages of two groups differ by a large amount, individuals can be found in the low-scoring group who surpass individuals in the high-scoring group. Hence an individual's group membership is a poor guide to his standing in any psychological trait.

Bibliography: Anastasi, A.: Differential psychology. New York, [8]1958. Id.: Psychological testing. New York, [3]1968. Id. (Ed.): Individual differences. New York, 1965. Cooper, R. & Zubek, J.: Effects of enriched and restricted early environments on the learning ability of bright and dull rats. Canad. J. Psychol., 1958, 12, 159–64. Dreger, R. M. & Miller, K. S.: Comparative psychological studies of negroes and whites in the United States: 1959–1965. Psychol. Bull. Monogr. Suppl., 1968, 70 (3, pt. 2), 1–58. Fuller, J. L. & Thompson, W. R.: Behavior genetics. New York, 1960. Garai, J. E. & Scheinfeld, A.: Sex differences in mental and behavioral traits. Genet. Psychol. Monogr., 1968, 77, 169–299. Guilford, J. P.: The nature of human intelligence. New York, 1967. Hebb, D. O.: Heredity and environment in mammalian behavior. Brit. J. anim. Behav., 1953, 1, 43–7. Hirsch, J.: Behavior-genetic analysis. New York, 1967. Hunt, J. McV.: Intelligence and experience. New York, 1961. Maccoby, E. (Ed.): The development of sex differences. Stanford, Calif., 1966. Oden, M. H.: The fulfillment of promise: 40-year follow-up of the Terman gifted group. Genet. Psychol. Monogr., 1968, 77, 3–93. Scheinfeld, A.: Your heredity and environment. Philadelphia, 1964. Sears, R. R., Maccoby, E. & Levin, H.: Patterns of child-rearing. Evanston, Ill., 1957. Tyler, L. E.: The psychology of human differences. New York, [3]1965. Vandenberg, S. G.: Contributions of twin research to psychology. Psychol. Bull., 1966, 66, 327–52.   *A. Anastasi*

Differential psychopharmacology. A branch of psychopharmacology (q.v.) concerned with the description and elucidation of inter- and intra-individual differences in psychological effects of psychopharmaceutical agents. Central areas of research in differential psychopharmacology are: (a) dependence of the effects of pharmaceutical agents on relatively constant, psychological personality and other characteristics of the testees. Such factors have been found to include: sex, age, race, neuroticism, psychoticism, extraversion,

achievement motivation, type of constitution, innate metabolic dysfunction; (b) dependence of the effects of pharmaceutical drugs on actual personality characteristics. It has been shown that there are differential effects, *inter alia*, dependent on emotional arousal and attitudes to the experiment and the experimenter; (c) dependence of drug effects on situational factors such as the nature of the tests, behavior of the experimenter, whether group or individual test. As yet there is no comprehensive theory of the effective mechanism of factors (a) to (c) listed above. In particular, it is still an open question to what extent the covariation of the effects of pharmaceutical agents and relatively constant personality traits can be explained in the sense of individual differences in neuro-physiological (e.g. Eysenck, 1963) and bio-chemical reactions, or with the aid of varying modes of assimilation (e.g., DiMascio, 1968; Janke, 1964) with different personality structures. The marked intraindividual inconstancy of psychopharmaceutical effects proves that there is always a significant participation of situation-adaptive processing mechanisms.

Bibliography: DiMascio, A. & Shader, R. I.: Behavioral toxity. In: Efron, D. (Ed.): Psychopharmacology 1957–1967. Washington, 1968. Eysenck, H. J. (Ed.): Experiments with drugs. Oxford, 1963. Janke, W.: Über die Abhängigkeit der Wirkung psychotroper Substanzen von Persönlichkeitsmerkmalen. Frankfurt, 1964. Janke, W. & Debus, G.: Experimental studies on antianxiety agents with normal subjects. Methodological considerations and review of the main effects. In: Efron, D. (Ed.): Psychopharmacology 1957–67. Washington, 1968. Legewie, H.: Persönlichkeitstheorie und Psychopharmaka. Meisenheim, 1968. Rickels, K. (Ed.): Non-specific factors in drug therapy. Springfield, Ill., 1968.   *W.J.*

Differential running time. The left-right localization of sound depends upon the time difference with which the sound strikes the two ears (Hornbostel). Localization occurs toward the ear struck first, the angle of the apparent source depending on the amount of precession. The ability to localize sounds indicates that people can discriminate time intervals in this way down to 0·015 seconds. *C.D.F.*

Differential sensibility. Ability to distinguish one sensory quality or intensity from another, as indexed by the *differential threshold*, or *just noticeable difference* (j.n.d.). *G.D.W.*

Differential threshold. See *Threshold*.

Differentiation. In psychology the concept of differentiation is used to refer both to differentiation as a basic process in organic and psychological development, and differentiation as a cognitive process.

In developmental psychology differentiation denotes the course taken by the organism from relatively simple to highly structured forms of behavior. Differentiation is necessarily accompanied by integration (q.v.) which incorporates each newly acquired behavioral unit into the totality of the organism in order to avoid any disorganization of behavior. The purpose of differentiation as developmental psychology sees it is to be found especially in an increase of adaptive capability. In conjunction with that, differentiation helps individuality to evolve.

Differentiation in the cognitive sense should be understood as enabling an individual to distinguish two or several environmental stimuli or to react differently to them. In learning theory, differentiation is thus the opposite of generalization (q.v.).
Bibliography: See *Child psychology; Development*.
P.S.

Differentiation inhibition. See *Inner inhibition*.

Differentiation theory of intelligence. The supposition that the development of the intelligence from childhood to adulthood is subject not only to the well-known quantita-

tive but especially to qualitative changes in the sense of a differentiation of initially global capacities into aspects of intellectual performance which become increasingly independent.
Bibliography: Pawlik, K.: Dimensionen des Verhaltens. Berne & Stuttgart, 1968, 350–54. *M.A.*

Difficulty level. The level of an (intelligence) test item assigned to it in relation to the proportion of a sample successfully solving it. See *Abilities; Decision processes; Problem solving*.

Dilatation. The morbid enlargement of hollow organs such as heart, stomach or bladder. In the case of the heart one speaks of myogenous or tonogenous dilatation, depending on whether the muscular mass is hypertrophied (enlarged) from overstrain or overexpanded because of the increased residual volume. In both cases the total mass of the heart is larger and can be seen in an X-ray photograph of the thorax as the *cor bovinum* ("ox heart"). *E.D.*

Dimension. The term denotes a characteristic (usually physical) which enables one to locate some phenomenon in a series. It has also been admitted into psychological terminology with this general meaning. Every psychological measurement embraces one or several dimensions of experience or behavior. W. Stern's theory of personality emphasized the concept of dimension. Recently "dimension" has been used with increasing frequency by some personality researchers in place of the traditional terms *characteristic* and *trait*. Behind this change in terminology is an attempt to determine personality quantitatively by establishing its positions numerically on prescribed bipolar continua, that is dimensionally. Hence the term "dimension" now refers to a construct of personality theory. See *Personality; Traits; Type*.

Bibliography: Arnold, W.: Person, Charakter, Persönlichkeit. Göttingen, ³1970. Eysenck, H. J.: Dimensions of personality. London, 1947. Graumann, C. F.: Eigenschaften als Problem der Persönlichkeitsforschung. In: Handbuch der Psychologie, Vol. 4. Göttingen, 1960, 87–149. Stern, W.: Allgemeine Psychologie, Vol. 1, The Hague, 1935.   *P.S.*

Dimension, psychological-personalistic theory of. An element in W. Stern's theory of personality. According to this conception, personal dimensions are directions and time processes within which a person realizes himself. The concept of dimension is thus understood not formally but dynamically. The basic dimension of any person is the polarity *within/without*. On this basis two groups of personal dimensions can be distinguished: *individual* and *world dimensions*.
Bibliography: Stern, W.: Allgemeine Psychologie. Vol. 1. The Hague, 1935.   *P.S.*

Diminishing returns, law of. Improvement gradually decreases with each successive increment of application.

Dionysian type. See *Apollonian type*.

Diopter. A unit of measurement for the refractive power of an optical system, measured in m^{-1}. The refractive power is the reciprocal value of the focal distance.

Diplacusis. Diplacusis or unilateral displacement to one side of pitch sensitivity can be caused by changes in the perilymph (protein content, viscosity) or by metabolic disorders (e.g. by deafness) in the hair cells. See *Basilar membrane; Organ of Corti*.   *M.S.*

Diploid. Possessing two pairs of chromosome sets. The genetic substance thus exists in duplicate. One chromosome (q.v.) always comes from the father, and one from the mother.

Diplopia. Seeing double. Diplopia in one eye is caused by a refractive defect. Diplopia in both eyes occurs when their visual axes are not focussed during fixation so that the image falls on identical retinal points (q.v.).   *R.R.*

Dipsomania. A form of alcoholism (q.v.) considered to be rare. Described initially by von Bruhl-Cramer as "*die periodische Trunksucht*" which he said was distinct from "*die intermittende Trunksucht*". In the latter, intermittent, form the periods of abstinence were as little as three days, whereas in periodic alcoholism or dipsomania the sufferer remained abstinent for weeks or months. A prodromal phase of irritability and depression followed by a small intake of alcohol and a short period of sobriety is said to precede the phase of heavy pathological drinking, which is short-lived. The term may cover a number of etiological and symptomatological states. Syn. *Periodic alcoholism; Epsilon alcoholism*.   *R.P.S.*

Directive therapy. Psychotherapy in which the therapist assumes a large amount of responsibility in controlling the course of the treatment and in deciding what is best for the patient. See also *Active therapy*.   *G.D.W.*

Directivity (syn. *Directiveness; Directive method; Strictness*). One of the two principal dimensions (directivity vs. permissiveness and warmth and acceptance vs. coldness and rejection) with which the behavior of teachers and parents can be characterized in active teaching and upbringing. The distinguishing features of directivity are frequent orders, instructions, rebukes and questions as well as the irreversibility of judgments. It usually results in little cooperation, interruption of teaching, receptive and unoriginal behavior. See *Child psychology; Punishment*.

Bibliography: O'Connor, N. & Franks, C. M.: Childhood upbringing and other environmental factors. In: Eysenck, H. J. (Ed.): Handbook of abnormal psychology. London, 1960. Riesman, D. et al.: The lonely crowd. Yale, 1950. Sears, R. R., Maccoby, E. E. & Levin, H.: Patterns of child rearing. New York, 1957.   *G.K.*

Direct vision (syn. *Foveal vision*). Optic perception by way of the *fovea centralis;* fixation on an object.

Disappointment. An emotional phenomenon accompanying *frustration* (q.v.), which occurs when expectation is not fulfilled or when a need is not gratified.   *P.S.*

Discrete measure. A discrete measure makes it possible to carry out a discontinuous measurement of a possibly continuous quantitative variable. Such a variable is called a *discrete variable*.   *W.H.B.*

Discriminated operant. B. F. Skinner's term for what, in his system, corresponds to a generalized response. See *Conditioning, classical and operant*.

Discrimination tests. A common method for studying learning, particularly with non-human species, is systematically to reward the subject's choice of one stimulus against another. For example, although rats are relatively non-visual in orientation, under suitable conditions they are able to learn to discriminate horizontal stripes from vertical stripes (i.e. react differently to them). Discrimination problems may of course be used to study perceptual as well as learning phenomena.   *G.D.W.*

Discriminative learning. See *Learning, discriminative*

Discriminatory analysis. A statistical method for classifying individual values in one of several populations (q.v.) or for separating different populations. It is essential that the classification or separation should take place on the basis not of one but of several criteria. If, for example, an individual has to be classified on the basis of a score for one of *x* populations, this is done by discriminatory analysis so that the error (q.v.) on average is minimal. There must be (*a*) several scores for the individual to be classified and (*b*) the corresponding scores for other individuals whose classification with respect to the populations is known or has also to be ascertained. Knowledge of the scores for the members of the basic groups enables a discriminant function to be obtained.   *W.H.B.*

Disease. See *Sickness*.

Disengagement, theory of. This concerns the social and mental processes at work in a diminution of engagement in the social environment. Henry stresses the close connection between aging and disengagement, but other factors, such as variables (cultural values, attitudes, mode of life, economic and social conditions) play a part.

Bibliography: Henry, W. E.: The theory of intrinsic disengagement. Proc. Internat. Gerontology. Copenhagen, 1963.   *P.S. & R.S.*

Disillusion. To disenchant; dispel illusions; bring an individual or group face to face with reality, no matter how discomforting this may be to them.

Disinhibition. 1. This denotes the removal of those factors which prevent a reaction.

2. In a narrower sense, the cessation of the regulative functions of the cerebral cortex (q.v.) under the influence of alcohol or drugs.

K.E.P.

Disintegrated type. See *Integrated type.*

Disintegration. See *Integration.*

Disjection. A splitting of the feeling of personality in dreams; one plays a double role, being simultaneously actor and spectator.

F.-C.S.

Disorientation. People are normally aware of who they are, where they are in time and space, and have a clear perception of their body image—especially in terms of the right-left orientation. When this awareness breaks down the person is said to be disorientated. Occurs in organic conditions which produce clouding of consciousness and/or amnesia; in mental disorders which produce delusions and/or hallucinations; and in neurotic disorders such as hysterical fugues which produce memory loss.

R.H.

Dispersion. The scatter (q.v.), or degree of difference, of individual scores in a population (q.v.) (see *Sample*). The usual statistics are either standard deviations (q.v.) from a central value, such as the mean variation mV (the sum of the absolute deviations divided by N) and the variance (q.v.) (mean value of the squared deviations), or positional parameters as, for example, the quartile deviation.

W.H.B.

Displacement in ESP is an unconscious phase shift by the subject between the sequence of calls (q.v.) and targets (q.v.). If this shift is of a fairly definite order, e.g. mainly by one trial over a large number of trials, evidence for ESP can be obtained through the analysis of displacement.

Forward displacement: The intended targets run ahead of the calls by a certain number of trials, i.e. the subject aims his, say, tenth call at the eleventh target, e.g. if the displacement is by one trial.

Backward displacement: The intended targets limp behind the calls by a certain number of trials, i.e. the subject aims his, say, tenth call at the seventh target, e.g. if the displacement is by three trials.

H.H.J.K.

Displacement activity (syn. *Irrelevant activity; Sparking over*). If the normal course of an instinctive activity (see *Instinct*) is disturbed by the absence of the releasing situation, or the occurrence of a conflict (q.v.) between irreconcilable drives, the drive energy can be "abreacted", or discharged, by means of a behavior which is "irrelevant" or inappropriate to the situation, but appropriate to another instinct. E.g.: for the stickleback, when a rival appears at the border of its territory, a conflict arises between fight and flight motives, which releases the displacement activity of sand-digging (part of nest-digging behavior). By ritualization, displacement activities can acquire specific significance as releasing actions, e.g. the sand-digging, originally an outlet, becomes a threat movement.

I.L.

Display-control relations. In ergonomics, the relationship between control or regulative processes (and particularly directed motion) and, e.g., moving-scale instruments. See *Motor skills.*

Displays. Coordinated movements and postures in the functional sphere of agonistic (fight and flight) and sexual behavior, which appear frequently, serve as signals for attraction or intimidation, and are often in themselves sufficient to decide the outcome of incipient conflicts. See *Appeasement gestures; Courtship; Threat behavior.*

Bibliography: Marler, P. R. & Hamilton, W. J.: Mechanisms of animal behavior. Chichester, 1966. Tinbergen, N.: Social behaviour in animals. London, ²1965.   *K.F.*

Disposition. A theoretical concept to explain the probabilities (which vary between individuals but are relatively constant) that certain forms of behavior, symptoms and other individual traits will appear. A distinction is made between innate and acquired dispositions. In Allport's personality theory the term "personal disposition" is synonymous with "trait" (q.v.).

Bibliography: Allport, G. W.: Pattern and growth in personality. New York, 1961.   *D.B.*

Dissimilation. 1. The breaking up of energy-rich compounds which are obtained by assimilation (q.v.). **2.** Adaptation of an individual to something other than himself. See *Assimilation*.   *H.S.*

Dissociation. A process by which some thoughts, attitudes, or other psychological activities lose their normal relationship to others, or to the rest of the personality, and split off to function more or less independently. In this way logically incompatible thoughts, feelings and attitudes may be held concurrently and yet conflict between them averted. A chronic state of dissociation is usually regarded as pathological. Some behaviors and phenomena which have been described in terms of dissociation include multiple or "split" personality, somnambulism (sleep-walking), automatic writing, certain delusional symptoms, hypnotism, and hysterical amnesia.   *G.D.W.*

Dissociation of sensation. A specific collection of symptoms indicating a lack of response when half the spinal cord has been destroyed. In addition to other symptoms (loss of muscular response in the corresponding half of the body and, on both sides, a diminution of sensitivity to pressure), there is a dissociated paralysis of sensation: a feeling of pain, cold and warmth can be produced on the paralyzed side but no longer on the sound side.   *P.S. & R.S.*

Dissonance. 1. Music: the simultaneous production of two sounds at a distance of a second and a seventh, or what is found unpleasant in our cultural sphere. **2.** Psychology: the disturbance caused by two irreconcilable cognitions (see *Dissonance, theory of*).

Bibliography: Neisser, U.: Cognitive psychology. New York, 1967.   *P.S. & R.S.*

Dissonance, cognitive. The central concept in L. Festinger's theory of cognitive dissonance, which endeavors to explain or predict changes in attitude (q.v.), and especially the connection between attitudes and behavior. Cognitive dissonance exists when there is a dissonant relation between two or more cognitive elements (i.e. knowledge, an opinion or an attitude concerning any objects, oneself or one's own behavior). Such a case arises when—if the elements are considered separately—one of them could be deduced from the opposite of the other. In addition, the relation between the elements must be relevant for there to be dissonance (q.v.) or consonance (q.v.).

According to Festinger, cognitive dissonance is experienced as unpleasant by the individual and creates pressure directed toward the reduction of the dissonance or toward consonance. The strength of this pressure to reduce dissonance depends on the strength of the existing dissonance, which in turn is a function of the relation between the importance and number of the dissonant elements on the one hand and the consonant elements on the other.

Fundamentally, three possibilities of dissonance reduction are described: (*a*) the changing of one's own behavior as a cognitive element; (b) the changing of the environment as a cognitive element; (c) the addition of a new cognitive element to lessen the weight of the dissonant as compared with that of the consonant models. See *Homeostasis*.

Bibliography: Festinger, L.: A theory of cognitive dissonance. New York, 1957. Chapanis, N. P. & Chapanis, A.: Cognitive dissonance: Five years later. Psychol. Bull., 1964, *61*, 1–22.   *A.S.-M.*

Dissonance, theory of. A theory of motivation propounded by L. Festinger according to which the motive for human action results from the dissonance (q.v.) of two cognitive elements. There is a case of dissonance when the two elements mutually exclude one another. From this disagreement comes pressure to restore the harmony which has been disturbed.   *P.S.*

Distal. Considered away from the body's axis; outward; turned toward the environment. Ant.: *proximal*. For example, the upper arm is in the proximal position, the lower arm in the distal position relative to the elbow.   *H.Sch.*

Distance hearing. See *Differential running time; Hearing, localized.*

Distance, social. A variable derived from the attempt to describe group structures, social positions and interactive behavior among members of a group, or of groups among one another, in categories which are spatially analogous. By social distance, one means the relative accessibility of a person or group or the degree of desired contact with a second person or group. It depends on the spatial distance between two individuals, but also on the similarity of their social attitudes, their interests and preferences, occupations, aims, etc. The greater social distance is, the more the likelihood of contact between individuals or groups diminishes, and the more probable it is that negative or hostile attitudes will interpose themselves between them, and vice versa. The possibility of diminishing social distance by creating common interests, spatial proximity, etc., is seen as a way of reducing negative attitudes, prejudices and hostile actions between individuals or groups. Methods for measuring social distance are offered by the different forms of sociogram (q.v.) (Moreno, 1953; Lindzey & Borgatta, 1954), or the social distance scale according to Bogardus (1928).

Bibliography: Bogardus, E. S.: Immigration and race attitudes. Boston, 1928. Lindzey, G. & Borgatta, E. T.: Sociometric measurement. In: Lindzey, G. (Ed.): Handbook of social psychology, Vol. 1. Reading (Mass.), 1954. Moreno, J. L.: Who shall survive? New York, ²1953.   *A.S.-M.*

Distance vision. Seeing, or discrimination of relative distance of, an object more than twenty feet away from the subject.

Distinctiveness. A variable of cues or learned signals, related not only to their appearance but to situational variables, influencing visual discrimination and choice: clarity of outline.

Distorted room. A location suitably designed for the purpose of demonstrating spatial and optical illusions: objects within the room are distorted.

Distributed practice. See *Distribution of practice*.

Distribution. A graphic representation or table of the functional values (scores) of a variable. See *Frequency distribution*.

Distribution of practice (syn. *Distributed practice*). The spacing out of periods of practice (learning) as widely as the total time allows.

Disulfiram (syn. *Tetraethylthiuram disulphide; Antabuse; Aversan; Abstinyl; Refusal*). A substance which is used as an adjunct in the treatment of chronic alcoholism. If administered before alcohol is taken, disulfiram causes pronounced vegetative disturbances (vertigo, vomiting, headache, etc.).

W.J.

Divergent lines illusion. One of the geometric illusions whose effect is achieved in the same way as *Hering's illusion* (q.v.). The parallel lines appear to diverge where they cross the radiating lines.

C.D.F.

Divergent thinking. According to Guilford's intelligence-structure model, a part of intelligence. With divergent thinking the object is not, as with the traditional tests of general ability, to find a single correct solution but to record the variety and originality of the answers as well as the abundance of ideas and restructuring. It is assessed in terms of the factors of verbal and expressive fluency, and the factors of flexibility of thinking. Its definition coincides largely with that of creativity (q.v.).

Bibliography: Guilford, J. P.: The structure of intellect. Psychol. Bull., 1956, *53*, 267–93. Id.: Personality. New York, 1959. Haddon, F. A. & Lytton, H.: Teaching approach and the development of divergent thinking abilities in primary schools. Brit. J. educ. Psychol., 1968, *38*, 171–80. *G.K.*

Diversification quotient. See *Type-token ratio*.

Divining rod. See *Dowsing*.

Dizygotic twins. Twins from two separate eggs, as opposed to monozygotic twins. See *Twin studies*.

DNA. See *Desoxyribonucleic acid*.

Dogmatism. The term for a general tendency to rely strongly on "closed" in contrast to more "open" cognitions or frames of thought ("closed-mindedness" versus "open-mindedness", according to M. Rokeach). The more "closed" a system of opinions, attitudes, convictions is, the less an individual can perceive a multiplicity of different, relevant aspects in a situation. Flexibility of opinions and attitudes is rendered difficult; changes of opinion and attitude are only possible when the whole frame of thought is changed. This can encourage social attitudes like race-centeredness, authoritarianism (q.v.), intolerance, etc. "Dogmatism" is also used as a collective term for the cognitive aspect of such attitudes. See *Attitude*.

With his "dogmatism" scale M. Rokeach (1956) endeavored to formalize more distinctly the concept of authoritarianism and to free it from alleged one-sidedness. This, according to critics of the Adorno group (see *Authoritarian personality*), consists in the fact that scales to record "authoritarian", "anti-democratic", attitudes chiefly measure corresponding tendencies of those who lean to the right in politics. Connections between scales for "authoritarianism" and "dogmatism" mostly prove to be slightly positive. That members of the political left show just as high values with respect to "dogmatism" as do the "authoritarians on the right" has not been refuted. See *Conservatism*.

Rokeach (1960) deals with the problem of ideology from the sociopsychological angle when he defines dogmatism as "resistance to change" appearing in the shape of cognitive totalities of ideas and notions which are organized into relatively closed systems. Dogmatism is thus opposed to rigidity (q.v.) in the sense that a certain adaptation is not ruled out if the system itself can be maintained.

Bibliography: Livson, N. & Nichols, T. F.: Assessment of the general stability of the E, F and PEC scales. Psychol. Rep., 1957, 3, 413–20. Rokeach, M.: Political and religious dogmatism: an alternative to the authoritarian personality. Psychol. Monogr., 1956, 70, No. 18. Id. & Fruchter, B.: A factorial study of dogmatism and related concepts. J. abnorm. soc. Psychol., 1956, 53, 356–60. Rokeach, M.: The open and closed mind. New York, 1960.

H.D.S. & M.-H.B.

Dolichocephalus. A technical term for long-headedness. The skull index (ratio of length to width of skull) is increased. It is used both as a characteristic of individuals and to distinguish supposed racial characteristics. *E.D.*

Dominance. A personality factor approximating to extraversion (q.v.); a striving for self-assertion and independence. See *Authoritarian personality*; *Dominance, will to*.

Dominance ranking (syn. *Dominance hierarchy*). 1. The interindividual relations of dominance and submission in a group of animals or humans. 2. A ranked series of behaviors.

Dominance, will to (syn. *Dominance; Will to dominate*). The disposition (q.v.) to rule in interpersonal relations. The striving for dominance has also appeared in personality research as an independent dimension (q.v.) which can to some extent be checked by factor analysis. The following may be regarded as indicative of an aspiration to dominate: positive, self-convinced, stern, imperious, masterful and power-seeking modes of behavior. A. Adler in his mono-thematic drive theory gives this striving central importance as the *will to power*.

P.S. & R.S.

Dominant. In heredity theory, "dominant" denotes the heredity factor essential for the phenotype (q.v.). Ant. *Recessive. K.E.P.*

DOPA. An abbreviation for dihydroxyphenyl-analine, an intermediate substance formed in the body during the biosynthesis of cate-cholamine (see *Biogenic amines*). DOPA is formed in the adrenal gland, in the sympathetic network and in the brain. In contrast to noradrenaline, dihydroxyphenyl-analine passes the blood-brain barrier (q.v.). It can therefore be injected extra-cerebrally (e.g. intravenously). When small doses are given, after only a few minutes a striking increase in activity, an intensification of alertness and possibly euphoria appear. Little is known about the duration of effect of a single dose. The early hope that it could be used successfully in depression therapy has not been realized. However, it removes depressive states after large doses of reserpine (q.v.). Probably, when it is administered, the effective substance is not dihydroxyphenyl-analine itself, but the natural final stage, noradrenaline. This is suggested by investigations in which the transformation of DOPA into the next stage (see *Dopamine*) is inhibited by decarboxylase inhibitors (see *Alpha-methyldopa*).

Bibliography: Acheson, G. H.: Second symposium on catecholamines. Pharmacol. Rev., 1966, 18, 1–804.

W.J.

Dopamine. A direct precursor in the bio-synthesis of noradrenaline (see *Catechol-amines*). Dopamine can be traced in the brain. It is only partially converted into noradrenaline, and partially reduced to other end-products. The conversion of dopamine into noradrenaline can be inhibited by a number of substances (e.g. by disulfiram = Anta-buse). It can be detected unchanged in human urine. Therefore dopamine excretion can be used as a dependent variable in experiments. The few existing psychological investigations show that the excretion of dopamine decreases steadily from wakefulness through activated to non-activated sleep.

Bibliography: Baekeland, F., Schenker, V. S., Schenker, A. C. & Lasky, R.: Urinary excretion of epinephrine, dopamine and tryptamine during sleep and wakefulness. Psychopharmacologia, 1969, *14*, 359–70. Hornykiewicz, O.: Dopamine (3-hydroxy tyramine) in brain function. Pharmacol. Rev., 1966, *18*, 925–64.
                                                                W.J.

Doppler effect (syn. *Doppler's principle*). A change in the frequency of sound or light waves in relation to an observer; the pitch of the sound or the hue of the light source appears to shift as it recedes from or approaches the observer.

Dorsal. The half containing the back is called dorsal in animals with only one symmetrical plane and a side with abdomen and back which is defined by the position of the nervous system in relation to the intestinal tract. Ant. *Ventral*. In vertebrates the nervous system is dorsal with respect to the intestines, in arthropods it is ventral.   *H.Sch.*

Double-effect theory. See *Mind-body*.

Double images. Double images of an object appearing in binocular vision. They are either longitudinal or transverse, depending on whether the disparate condition is longitudinal (q.v.) or transverse (q.v.). Whereas longitudinal double images in practice appear only pathologically or optically (prisms), transverse double images appear in normal binocular vision also if sufficient attention is paid. If the point of fixation is in front of the object of the double image, there are homonymous or uncrossed double images (the double image in the right eye is to the right of the object of fixation, in the left eye to the left). If the object of fixation is behind the object

of the double vision, there are non-homonymous or crossed double images. In cases of squinting there are pathological uncrossed double images if the squinting is inward and crossed if the squinting is outward. Double images are suppressed when binocular vision is corrected, occasionally they result from binocular rivalry, but are usually ignored. In spite of double images and image inhibition, an impression of depth is given by the object which is seen double.   *A.H.*

Double organs. This refers to the symmetric organs existing in pairs, especially the eyes and ears.   *K.E.P.*

Double vision. Also called *diplopia* (q.v.), it exists when one object can be seen twice. Diplopia can be either *functional* (see *Double images*) or *pathological*. Pathological *binocular* diplopia appears when there are positional anomalies of the eyes, due to squinting after paralysis, etc. *Monocular* diplopia may appear as a result of pathological changes of the eye media (see *Lens; Cornea*). There are also cases of polyopia. Binocular diplopia may also appear because of fatigue of the eye muscles or the effects of drugs (alcohol).
                                                                A.H.

Down's disease (syn. *Down's syndrome; Langdon-Down syndrome; Imbecility; Mongolism*, q.v.; *Trisomia-21*). A frequent form of imbecility which is combined with distinctive physical characteristics. The basic cause is a chromosomal anomaly as a result of which there are three chromosomes instead of the chromosome pair 21.

Symptoms: usually serious imbecility together with a lively, sociable nature; retarded development; stature below normal; mongoloid slanting of the eyes with epicanthic folds of the eyelids; changes in connective membrane and iris, cataract frequently developing; brachycephalic skull; snub nose; tongue large and fissured; mouth usually open; fingers and hands misshapen, and malformations of the internal organs (heart and skeleton). Etiopathogenetically, three forms are distinguished nowadays: (a) the classical trisomia-21; (b) translocation-mongolism, in which the supernumerary chromosome is attached to another autosomal chromosome; (c) mosaic mongolism: different sets of chromosomes side by side in the same individual. With form (a) the mother is frequently no longer young and the risk of a repetition is slight. On the other hand, with form (b) there is the danger of a repetition of mongolism in the family.   *C.S.*

Dowsing. The practice of attempting to locate underground water or other minerals, or some hidden object, by using a pendulum or "divining rod" (such as a forked twig) or similar instrument. The "dowser" traverses the target area until his instrument reveals by its movement the correct position. Possibly a form of clairvoyance (q.v.) that exploits a motor-automatism. Also known as "water-divining".   *J.B.*

Draw-a-Man Test. Sometimes abbreviated to DAM, this test published by Goodenough in 1926 uses drawing to assess intelligence. Goodenough gave norms for children aged 3 to 13, W. E. Hinrichs (1935) and C. A. Oakley (1940) extended the scale up to the age of 18. The best drawing of a human produced by the testee is evaluated according to a standardized list (fifty-one items), and an IQ is calculated. Reliability $r = 0.80$ to 0.90; validity: correlations with the Stanford-Binet test resulted in determination coefficients (q.v.) lying between $r^2 = 0.17$ and $r^2 = 0.58$; correlation with the teacher's assessment: $r = 0.44$ (Goodenough).

In the drawing test by Goodenough & Harris (1963), three drawings, a man, a woman and a self-portrait, have to be completed, from them a mean IQ is calculated which the authors consider to be more reli-

able than the result of evaluating only one drawing.
Bibliography: Goodenough, F. L.: Measurement of intelligence by drawings. New York, 1926. Id. & Harris, D. B.: Drawing test. New York, 1963.
                                                                    I.M.D.

Draw-a-Person Test (syn. *Machover Test;* Abb. DAP). A projective test in which the testee (from two years) is asked to draw a person and then tell a story about the sketch. The postulated projection of the child's body image (q.v.) to some extent determines analysis.   *J.M.*

Dream. A dream is an experience during sleep and forms part of a fantasy life. It is generally distinguished from a hypnagogic hallucination on the grounds that the latter is a brief sensory experience during drowsiness in which the subject feels he is a non-participating observer. All sense modalities, unspoken communications, moods and feelings contribute to a dream. Those who have never experienced one sense modality (e.g. the congenitally blind) have dreams that are normal except for the missing modality. Whether a fantasy is called a dream depends upon the individual. Some subjects will call only bizarre experiences "dreams", and prefer to use the term "thinking" for sleep experiences which, though far removed in space and time from their beds, are internally consistent.

1. *History and methods.* For thousands of years before Sigmund Freud (1856–1939), dreams were interpreted in order to foretell the future. In dream symbolism, Freud saw a means of understanding the individual's motives. Unconscious impulses from the id (q.v.), together with memories which were unconscious owing to repression (q.v.), gave rise to the *latent dream*, which was itself wish-fulfilling. The efforts of the ego, exerted through the *dream-work*, resulted in the *manifest dream*. The *dream-distortion* meant that the dream was rendered less reprehensible and less anxiety-provoking, so that sleep

20

was not disrupted. In this way, dreams served as the *guardians of sleep*, which role they also served by disguising external stimuli as dream components. The forces of repression were considered to be somewhat relaxed during the dream, enabling it to contain features (for instance, of an incestuous nature) which were only thinly disguised or even openly expressed. The psychoanalyst, interpreting the dream as a whole, sought for its latent content.

Freud also believed that dreams contained material which was part of the *archaic heritage* deriving from the experiences of the patient's ancestors. The latter notion was analogous to the belief of C. G. Jung (1875–1961) that in dreams certain specific symbols or *archetypes* (e.g. of re-birth), which were representatives of the *collective unconscious*, frequently revealed themselves, as they also would in world-wide art forms, in myths and in the waking thoughts of the schizophrenic. The study of dreams proved a source of inspiration for both Freud and Jung, and their writings have had a profound influence on modern literature and art.

The clinical interpretation of dreams has been mainly based on day-time recall, but a number of psychologists about the end of the nineteenth century were awakening themselves by alarm clocks during the night in order to catch the freshly-experienced dream; in the 1950s a new technique enabled nocturnal awakenings to become a reliable proposition. Aserinsky and Kleitman observed recurrent periods of sleep with low voltage EEG, facial movements, and rapid conjugate eye movements, and suggested that during these periods dreaming was taking place. Dement and Kleitman later found 80 per cent dream recall from these rapid eye movement periods (paradoxical sleep) and only 7 per cent dream recall from non-rapid eye movement sleep (orthodox sleep). See *Sleep*.

2. *The present state of research.* It became clear that dreaming, like paradoxical sleep, must occupy at least a quarter of the sleep time. Old ideas were swept away: for example,

that extended dreams occur in a flash of time, that brain injuries abolished dreams, that color is not usually experienced in dreams, that some people did not dream. Everyone, if awakened at the right times, will describe dreams.

Mental life of a less "dream-like" and more "thought-like" nature is described after awakenings from orthodox sleep, though in orthodox sleep, at the onset of sleep typical dream adventures are often experienced. Nightmares can be experienced in either kind of sleep. The profusion or number of rapid eye movements in a given time during paradoxical sleep is related to the dream content. The greater the profusion, the more active the events of the dream adventure. Barbiturate drugs reduce the eye movement profusion *and* the vividness of the dreams.

Dement conducted "dream deprivation" experiments in which he woke subjects for several nights whenever they began a period of paradoxical sleep. On a subsequent, undisturbed night of sleep, the subjects spent more than a normal proportion of time in paradoxical sleep, yet this did not happen if the awakenings had been made during orthodox sleep. The selective deprivation of paradoxical sleep is followed by dreams of enhanced vividness, accompanied by a greater profusion of rapid eye movements. The original claim that psychological abnormalities resulted from the selective awakenings has not been substantiated. It is now generally agreed that there is a need for paradoxical sleep, and that compensation will follow its loss, but no experiments have yet demonstrated a purely psychological need for dreams.

The environment influences dream content. When anxiety-provoking films are seen before sleep there is a greater profusion of eye movements during the paradoxical sleep periods, and the dreams contain more anxiety and incorporate elements from the films. Dreams elicited in the laboratory tend to be restrained in their content compared with home dreams. Times of general life anxiety, or depression, are associated with dreams containing themes of anxiety or depression. Anxiety in waking life is accompanied by adrenaline secretion, and in anxious dreams the level of free fatty acids, liberated into the blood by the action of adrenaline, is raised. The penile erections that normally accompany each period of male paradoxical sleep are diminished where dream anxiety is high. Penile tumescence increases sharply prior to seminal emission during sexual dreams. The time of menstruation is characterized by a greater degree of sexual and aggressive dream themes. Sensory stimuli presented without causing awakening during paradoxical sleep tend to become woven into the dream content on the basis of assonance, e.g. in the controlled experiments of Berger, the English girl's name "Sheila" led to a dream report about a "book by Schiller".

The extent of the dream narrative is greater when recall is made near the end of a period of paradoxical sleep, and is much reduced if awakening is delayed until orthodox sleep has just begun again. Dreams described immediately after night awakenings are only poorly recalled the next day, especially if sleep was quickly resumed or if rapid eye movement profusion was low. The successive dreams of a single night show some degree of continuity in their content.

The increased interest in dreams has led to many refinements in the scoring of such themes as anxiety, aggression or sexuality in the dream content. Particular mention should be made of the dream content analysis techniques of Hall and Van de Castle.

In delirium following withdrawal of alcohol or barbiturates from addicts, there is great intensification of paradoxical sleep, which often interrupts wakefulness. There is reason to believe that the experiences of delirium are, in essence, dreams. Despite the similarities in mental life between the dream and schizophrenic mental life, modern evidence has failed to reveal links between schizophrenia and any abnormality of paradoxical sleep. Paradoxical sleep, intoxication by such drugs as cannabis, mescaline or amphetamine, or even simple waking reverie, are states of altered consciousness during which there is thinking divorced from reality, to which such terms as dream-like, autistic, fantasy, or dream, may properly be applied without attempt at rigid distinction.

Bibliography: Abt, L. E. & Riess, B. F. (Eds): Progress in clinical psychology, Vol. 8; Dreams and dreaming. New York & London, 1968. Baekeland, F. & Lasky, R.: The morning recall of rapid eye movement period reports given earlier in the night. J. nerv. ment. Dis. 1968, 147, 570–79. Berger, R. J.: Experimental modification of dream content by meaningful verbal stimuli. Brit. J. Psychol., 1963, 109, 722–40. Id. & Oswald, I.: Eye movements during active and passive dreams. Science, 1962, 137, 601. Bonime, W.: The clinical use of dreams. New York, 1962. Carroll, D., Lewis, S. A. & Oswald, I.: Barbiturates and dream content. Nature (Lond.), 1969, 223, 865–6. Dement, W. C.: The effect of dream deprivation. Science, 1960, 131, 1705–7. Id. & Kleitman, N.: The relation of eye movements during sleep to dream activity, an objective method for the study of dreaming. J. exp. Psychol. 1957, 53, 339–46. Dement, W. C. & Wolpert, E. A.: The relation of eye movements, body motility and external stimuli to dream content. J. exp. Psychol. 1958, 55, 543–53. Fisher, C.: Psychoanalytic implications of recent research on sleep and dreaming. J. Amer. psychoanal. Ass., 1965, 13, 197–303. Id.: Dreaming and sexuality. In: Schur, M., Solnit, A., Lowenstein, R. M. & Newman, L. (Eds): Psychoanalysis—a general psychology. New York, 1966, 537–69. Foulkes, D.: The psychology of sleep. New York, 1966. Hall, C. & Van de Castle, R.: The content analysis of dreams. New York, 1966. Karacan, I., Goodenough, D. R., Shapiro, A. & Starker, S.: Erection cycle during sleep in relation to dream anxiety. Arch. gen. Psychiat., 1966, 15, 183–9. Kramer, M. (Ed.): Dream psychology and the new biology of dreaming. Springfield, Ill., 1969. Oswald, I.: Sleeping and waking: physiology and psychology. Amsterdam, 1962. Id.: Sleep. Harmondsworth, Middlesex, 1970. Pivik, T. & Foulkes, D.: "Dream deprivation": effects on dream content. Science, 1966, 153, 1282–4. Swanson, E. M. & Foulkes, D.: Dream content and the menstrual cycle. J. nerv. ment. Dis., 1968, 145, 358–63.   I. Oswald

Dream analysis (syn. *Dream interpretation*). The interpretation of dreams is a part of psychotherapeutic measures designed to help elucidate unconscious motives in the patient (see *Psychoanalysis*). When unconscious motives activated in sleep cannot be warded off or repressed by the impaired inner control or censorship mechanism of the sleeper, they are converted into manifest dream-content, their partial gratification is attempted in dreams (q.v.), and (according to Freud) the state of sleep is thereby generally maintained. The account the dreamer gives of his dream is taken to be the manifest dream-content. By means of the patient's conceptions of the individual manifest dream-contents, the therapist and patient try to discover the unconscious motives (the latent dream-content) and, if possible, their ontogenetic origin, thus helping the patient to acquire better control over them.

Bibliography: Freud, S.: The interpretation of dreams. London, 1955. Toman, W.: Motivation, Persönlichkeit, Umwelt. Göttingen, 1968.   W.T.

Dream censor(ship). See *Censorship*.

Drill. The acquisition of skills and knowledge by the repetition of some activity. As a result, mental and physical performance is increased as there is extensive automatization (q.v.) (subordinate part processes are excluded from the conscious operation of the will). Drill is dependent on fatigue (q.v.), general alertness and condition. See *Practice*.
W.Sp.

Drill theory (syn. *Practice theory;* Ger. *Einübungstheorie*). K. Groos's theory of children's play: play primarily subserves the development of existing natural talent and is also an exercise preparatory to that vital activity which will later be required of the adult. See *Play theory*.

Bibliography: Groos, K.: Die Spiele des Menschen. Jena, 1899.   P.S.

Drive. Certain physiological states, such as food deprivation, tend to increase animals' behavioral output. A number of early animal experiments showed that, in comparison with satiated rats, hungry rats would run more in activity wheels, and would explore more in a novel situation. These effects were commonly assumed to be unlearned and to be general with respect to the source of physiological disturbance, the kind of behavior affected, and the situation in which the effects occurred. The animal was believed to be inert unless motivated by some disturbance or threat to its well-being. Motivation was supplied by a hypothetical force or energy designated "drive".

The word "drive" was first used to describe this hypothetical force or energy by Woodworth in 1918, but the German equivalent *Trieb* had been used in essentially the same way by Freud in 1915. Within a few years, virtually everyone came to believe in some form of the drive concept. The concept was extended to include non-physiological sources of motivation, to give learned drives, social drives, higher drives, and so on. There were no convincing explanations of how learned drives were learned, but there was little doubt about the validity or usefulness of this kind of approach. The drive concept was applied as readily to human social behavior as to instinctive behavior in the lower animals.

These ideas were eventually combined, systematized and made explicit by Hull (1943) and Brown (1961). Hull emphasized the generality of drive. While there were many potential sources of drive, he said, they contributed alike to the total pool of energization. The resulting drive (D) gave energy to behavior, but did not direct it; direction came from the habits operating in a given situation, and D merely multiplied the strongest habit. D contrasts with another motivational concept, incentive, which Hull had introduced earlier. Drive was unlearned, general, and had a presumed physiological basis. By contrast, incentive depended upon prior learning, was specific to particular reinforcers and occurred in particular situations, and lacked any discernible physiological basis.

The fundamental question was: how much of the total motivation in a given situation could be attributed to drive and how much to incentive? One recent review of the relevant experimentation (Bolles, 1967) indicates that, in comparison with incentive, drive is relatively unimportant. Many of the unlearned and general motivational effects predicted by Hull's theory have turned out to be neither unlearned nor general. For example, the early discovery that hungry rats run more in activity wheels can now be discounted because of recent findings that this effect is relatively specific to the rat, to hunger and to the activity wheel. Other animals, in other situations, and under other kinds of deprivation conditions, may show increased activity, decreased activity, or no change (Campbell, et al., 1966).

Many other hypotheses which drive theorists had proposed to bolster the drive concept have not been confirmed experimentally. Different sources of drive, such as food and water deprivation, are not intersubstitutable, and do not summate to give increased performance. The idea that the energy from one source of motivation can spill over to activate an irrelevant kind of behavior (i.e. displacement) has not been supported in laboratory experiments. The mechanistic philosophy which underlay the original drive concept is now outmoded. The idea that an animal is inert and has to be driven into activity is no longer popular. The drive concept does not fit the facts, even in the cases it was designed to handle—e.g. that of the hungry rat.

Most psychologists have abandoned the hope of explaining social motives in terms of acquired drives. A serious attempt was made to interpret learned fears as acquired drives, but the evidence favoring this interpretation was not very compelling, and there were always alternative explanations. Some psychologists prefer to explain behavior in terms of its intended aims, or its prior reinforcement history, rather than its motives. Others emphasize the importance of associative factors in what is called motivated behavior. The concept of motivation itself seems much less important than it once did. Therefore, we

appear to be entering an era in which virtually no one believes in the concept of drive.

The word "drive" continues to be used, however; it will probably continue in use for some time, as it was originally; i.e. to describe the existence or operation of some motivation system with a physiological basis. This is poor usage, mainly because it lacks descriptiveness. Nothing is really conveyed by referring to a rat's "hunger drive" that is not implied by saying the rat is hungry.

Bibliography: Bolles, R. C.: Theory of motivation. New York, 1967. Brown, J. S.: The motivation of behavior. New York, 1961. Campbell, B. A., Smith, N. F., Misanin, J. R. & Jaynes, J.: Species differences in activity during hunger and thirst. J. Comp. Physiol. Psychol., 1966, 61, 123–7. Freud, S.: Instincts and their vicissitudes. In: Collected Papers, IV. New York, 1959. Hull, C. L.: Principles of behavior. New York, 1943. Woodworth, R. S.: Dynamic psychology. New York, 1918.   R. C. Bolles

Drive theory. In general, the postulating of fundamental or elementary drives or "instincts" in human or animal behavior, and the establishment of criteria for differentiation or development. Freud (q.v.) was the first theorist to postulate that the sexual drive was the sole source of motivation; he later added the self-preservation or ego instincts and finally, in place of them, the two classes of libido (the life or love drive) on the one hand, and the death instinct, on the other. Jung (q.v.) assumed that libido was the basic drive, but emphasized progressive desexualization of libido in the course of individual development. Adler (q.v.) suggested that the power instinct or the search for security was the basic drive. See Drive; Instinct.

W.T.

Dropout. An individual who gives up before reaching his goal, particularly a student who does not complete a course, but also any individual who, either from sickness, lack of specific abilities, or for ethical reasons, attempts to opt out of a particular society or group within a society.

Drug. A product of natural (plant) origin in contrast to a synthetic substance. As a result of the widespread use of the word for medicines in English-speaking countries it has also become increasingly a synonym for natural and synthetic substances.   *G.D.*

Drug addiction. See *Drug dependence.*

Drug dependence is "a state, psychic and sometimes also physical, resulting from the interaction between a living organism and a drug, characterized by behavioral and other responses that always include a compulsion to take the drug on a continuous or periodic basis in order to experience its psychic effects, and sometimes to avoid the discomfort of its absence. Tolerance may or may not be present. A person may be dependent on more than one drug" (World Health Organisation Expert Committee, 1969, p. 6).

   1. *Physical dependence* is a state where the organism requires the presence of the drug for maintenance of bodily homeostasis; a definite, characteristic and self-limited abstinence syndrome occurs when the drug is withdrawn. The WHO definition implicates psychic (psychological) factors in all forms of drug dependence. However, some workers restrict the terms psychic, psychological, and psychogenic to states of dependence where the organism takes drugs for reasons other than the relief of the abstinence syndrome of physical dependence.

   2. *Tolerance* describes a progressive decrease in the effects obtained from a given dose of drugs, and, conversely, the need to use larger doses to obtain the same effect with continued use of some drugs.

   The drugs of dependence now mainly causing concern are grouped in six types, according to their similarity to morphine, barbiturates, alcohol, amphetamines, cocaine and cannabis; some would add LSD and other hallucinogens. Only the first three produce

marked physical dependence, but a physiological withdrawal syndrome can be demonstrated in other classes using sensitive measures: for instance, the electroencephalogram in amphetamine withdrawal (Oswald, Evans & Lewis, 1969). The term "drug dependence" supersedes the previous terms *drug addiction* and *drug habituation*, which attempted—unsuccessfully—to distinguish between, respectively, more and less intense degrees of drug dependence. Research has investigated drug dependence in animals and man.

   3. *Animal studies*. These have been reviewed by Schuster & Thompson (1969) and Teasdale (1971). It has been shown that most drugs abused by humans can serve as reinforcers for the establishment of operant habits in monkeys and rats. Such habits may be very persistent, and it can be said that the animals exhibit drug dependence. "Relapse" back to morphine-reinforced habits can occur long after animals have been withdrawn from the drug, and is more likely to occur in situations previously associated with drug consumption. Younger rats show more dependence-proneness than older ones. There is evidence to suggest genetically based individual variation in dependence-proneness. The drug reinforcement appears to consist either of relief of an unpleasant withdrawal state in physically dependent animals, or of a direct primary reinforcement effect of the drug. Secondary reinforcement can be established by pairing neutral stimuli with drug reinforcement, and the symptoms of the withdrawal state can be classically conditioned to neutral stimuli. The effect of variations in reinforcement schedule and size of reinforcement on drug-reinforced behavior has been investigated. These studies have demonstrated the existence of powerful behavior factors maintaining drug consumption. Such factors presumably operate in the same way in human addicts, in addition to whatever problems of personality, and so on, they may have. Wikler (1968) discusses the relevance of the animal studies to humans.

4. *Human studies.* Before becoming dependent on a drug, the individual must have experience of the drug; their availability among his friends seems an important determinant of exposure to drugs (Chein *et al.*, 1964; de Alarcon, 1969). The effects of drugs on the individual are not simply a function of the drug but depend on the quantity he takes, how often he takes it, and the route of administration; on his personality, his previous experience and present state; and on the social setting in which he uses the drug. The effects of drugs on man have been reviewed by Trouton & Eysenck (1960).

Haertzen (1965) has studied the subjective effects of addictive drugs and shown considerable overlap in the effects of pharmacologically distinct drugs. Oswald, Evans & Lewis (1969) have shown that addictive drugs cause a suppression of paradoxical (rapid-eye-movement) sleep (see *Sleep*), and a rebound increase on withdrawal. Weil, Zinberg & Nelsen (1968) have compared experimentally the effects of cannabis on naïve subjects and experienced users, and suggest the importance of prior experience in determining the drug reaction.

5. *Personality.* There seems to be no unique "addictive personality" common to all drug users, and distinct from other diagnostic groups. Tests such as the Minnesota Multiphasic Personality Inventory have been used to demonstrate the existence of a number of types (e.g. sociopathic, neurotic) within the addict population, some similar to types seen in criminals, delinquents and alcoholics (Hill, Haertzen & Davis, 1962). Von Felsinger *et al.* (1955) demonstrated the importance of personality differences in determining the nature of response to addictive drugs, comparing addicts with non-addicts, and groups within the normal subjects. There is evidence that drug use may be a form of self-medication in some drug users. Chein *et al.* (1964) offer psychodynamic descriptions of the personalities of the addicts they studied, and relate these to their family background.

Most workers have implicated personality

defect in the etiology of drug dependence, but Dole & Nyswander (1967) have argued this is an effect rather than cause of drug use, which they attribute to metabolic abnormality. However, Vaillant (1969) presents evidence of maladjustment in addicts prior to drug use.

6. *Treatment.* Most forms of treatment have been aimed at reducing the addict's personality problems and re-integrating him in the community, and have generally included milieu therapy, psychotherapy, and other rehabilitative procedures. Results have generally been poor (e.g. Vaillant, 1969), with the exception of therapeutic communities run by ex-addicts (e.g. Rosenthal, 1969), for which considerable success is claimed, though good evidence is lacking. Other treatment programs (e.g. Dole & Nyswander, 1967) have included measures aimed more directly at the drug-taking itself and appear quite successful. Parole supervision in the community is associated with favorable outcome (Vaillant, 1969). Cessation of drug use with increasing age appears to occur in a proportion of addicts (Vaillant, 1969).

Bibliography: Chein, I., Gerard, D. L., Lee, R. S. & Rosenfeld, E.: Narcotics, delinquency and social policy: The road to H. London, 1964. de Alarcon, R.: The spread of heroin abuse in a community. Bulletin of Narcotics, 1969, *21*, 17–22. Dole, V. P. & Nyswander, M. E.: Heroin addiction—a metabolic disease. Arch. Internal. Med., 1967, *120*, 19–24. Haertzen, C. A.: Subjective drug effects: a factorial representation of subjective drug effects on the Addiction Research Center Inventory. J. nervous and mental Disease, 1965, *140*, 280–89. Hill, H. E., Haertzen, C. A. & Davis, H.: An MMPI factor analytic study of alcoholics, narcotic addicts, and criminals. Quart. J. Stud. Alcohol, 1962, *23*, 411–31. Oswald, I., Evans, J. I. & Lewis, S. A.: Addictive drugs cause suppression of paradoxical sleep and withdrawal rebound. In: Steinberg, H. (Ed.): Scientific basis of drug dependence. London, 1969. Rosenthal, M. S.: The Phoenix House therapeutic community: an overview. In: Steinberg, H. (Ed.): Scientific basis of drug dependence. London, 1969. Schuster, C. R. & Thompson, T.: Self-administration of and behavioural dependence on drugs. Annual Rev. Pharmacology, 1969, *9*, 483–502. Steinberg, H. (Ed.): Scientific basis of drug dependence. London, 1969. Teasdale, J. D.: Drug dependence. In: Eysenck, H. J. (Ed.): Handbook of abnormal psychology London, ²1971

Trouton, D. & Eysenck, H. J.: The effects of drugs on behaviour. In: Eysenck, H. J. (Ed.): Handbook of abnormal psychology. London, 1960. Vaillant, G. E.: The natural history of urban drug addiction—some determinants. In: Steinberg, H. (Ed.): Scientific basis of drug dependence. London, 1969. Felsinger, J. M. von, Lasagna, L. & Beecher, H. K.: Drug-induced mood changes in man: 2. Personality and reaction to drugs. J. American Medical Association, 1955, *157*, 1113–9. Weil, A. T., Zinberg, N. E. & Nelsen, J. M.: Clinical and psychological effects of marihuana in man. Science, 1968, *162*, 1234–42. Wikler, A. (Ed.): The addictive states. Association for Research in Nervous and Mental Disease, Volume XLVI. Baltimore, 1968. Wilner, D. M. & Kassebaum, G. G. (Eds): Narcotics. New York, 1965. World Health Organisation Expert Committee on Drug Dependence: Sixteenth Report. WHO Technical Report Series, No. 407, 1969.

J. D. Teasdale

Drug dependence, theories of. Various psychological theories are adduced to explain the genesis of drug dependence. After psychoanalysis, learning theory has recently put forward explanations according to which the consequences of drug taking are regarded as reinforcers of a conditioning process (q.v.). (In animal experiments the method of drug self-administration is used to demonstrate the reinforcer effect.) However, most theories can only cover partial aspects of drug dependence, and a comprehensive explanation would have to take into account the complex interaction of physiological, psychological and sociocultural factors in the genesis of drug dependence.

Bibliography: AMA.: Committee on alcoholism and addiction and council on mental health. Dependence on barbiturates and other sedative drugs. Jama, 1965, *193*, 673. Ausubel, D. P.: Drug addiction: physiological, psychological, and sociological aspects. New York, 1966. Collier, H. O. J.: A general theory of the generics of drug dependence by induction of receptors. Nature, 1965, *9*, 181. Eddy, N. B., Halbach, H., Isbell, H. & Seevers, M. H.: Drug dependence: its significance and characteristics. Psychopharm. Bull., 1966, *3*, 1–12. Essig, C. F.: Addiction to non-barbiturate sedative and tranquilizing drugs. Clin. Pharmacol. Therap., 1964, *5*, 334. Isbell, H. & Fraser, H. F.: Addiction to analgetics and barbiturates. Pharmacol. Rev., 1950, *2*, 355–97. Murray, J. B.: Drugs and drug dependency. The American Ecclesiastical Review, 1967, *157*, 12–28. WHO: Scientific Group on the Evaluation of Dependence-Producing Drugs: WHO Technical Report Series No. 287, 1964. *H.K.*

Drug habituation. See *Drug dependence*.

Drug postulate, Eysenck's. The hypothesis that CNS depressant drugs (e.g. alcohol and sodium amytal) increase inhibitory potential yet decrease excitatory potential, tending to extraverted behavior; and that CNS stimulant drugs (e.g. caffeine and dexedrine) decrease inhibitory potential yet increase excitatory potential, tending to introverted behavior. The postulate has been supported by experiments, and has proved extremely valuable in personality factor research.

Drug self-administration. A method in behavioral pharmacology (see *Psychopharmacology*) by which animals can administer drugs to themselves. Techniques for oral, intraperitoneal, intravenous, intracerebral administration and inhalation are available. The most common technique is oral administration, when a choice has usually to be made between an active and a dummy substance. Administration frequently takes place under conditions of stress (e.g. electric shocks). In certain situations the animals take increased quantities of alcohol, opiates, barbiturates, tranquilizers (such as chlordiazepoxide), and stimulants. Certain products are rejected after investigation (chlorpromazine, pemoline). The test animals are usually rats and monkeys. Localized intracerebral administration is especially important. It corresponds to the technique of electrical self-stimulation devised by J. Olds. Drug experiments offer findings which are expecially relevant to the problem of drug dependence (q.v.).

Bibliography: Schuster, C. R. & Thompson, T.: Self-administration of and behavioral dependence on drugs. Ann. Rev. Pharmacol., 1969, *9*, 483–502.

W.J.

Drunken driving. See *Traffic psychology.*

Drunkenness. See *Alcoholism.*

Dual effect theory. See *Mind-body problem.*

Dualism. A religious, cosmogonic, philosophical or metaphysical doctrine which takes as its starting-point the existence of two independent basic principles. In psychology, dualism postulates the twofold nature of physical and mental phenomena (psychophysical *parallelism*, q.v.); in philosophy, dualism postulates that both "mind" and "matter" are present in being (e.g. Descartes: extended substance [*extensio*] and thinking substance [*cogitatio*]); hence dualism is contrasted with monism and pluralism. *F.B.*

Dual morality (syn. *Double morality; Double moral standards*). The existence of double standards, chiefly in sexual morality, allowing one of the sexes greater freedom than the other. Especially in Europe and in the U.S.A., the sexual morality in question depends on supposed biological differences, and/or those sanctioned by religion, which allow men to indulge in pre-marital and extra-marital sexual contacts but expect abstinence from women. In his classification of sexual standards Reiss has characterized the attitude which allows men to have sexual contacts, especially extra-marital intercourse, but considers them reprehensible in women, as an "orthodox double standard". In the course of the last century, partly because of the emancipation of women, a "transitional double standard" has developed, which considers extra-marital sexual contacts permissible for women if they are in love or engaged to be married.
Bibliography: Reiss, I. L.: Premarital sexual standards in America. Glencoe, Ill., 1960.   *J.F.*

Dual sensation. See *Synesthesia.*

Dual vision theory. See *Duplicity theory.*

Dummy sign stimuli. Used by K. Lorenz and N. Tinbergen to determine the key sign stimulus for the chick's pecking of regurgitated food from the bill of the herring gull. The bill of the adult bird is yellow and has a red spot on the lower mandible. Before they were fed, the chicks were systematically presented with dummy bills and heads varied in all dimensions. In this way it was possible to determine that the red color of the spot (at which the chick pecks) was the stimulus actually releasing the pecking and that, e.g., the color of the head and bill played no part. The technique is used above all in comparative psychology, but sometimes in human psychology. It is essential that S. should be presented not with natural environmental phenomena, but models of them that can be easily modified in order to discover the stimulus or combination of stimuli-releasing specific behavior patterns.
Bibliography: Harlow, H. F.: Love in infant monkeys. Frontiers of psychological research. San Francisco & London, 1959. Lorenz, K.: Der Kumpan in der Umwelt des Vogels. J. Ornithol. 1935, *83*, 137–215, 289–413. Tinbergen, N.: De functie van de rode vlek op de snavel van de zilverneeuw. Bijdragen tot de Dierkunde, 1949, *28*, 452–65. Id. & Perseck, A. C.: On the stimulus situation releasing the begging response in the newly hatched herring gull chick. Behaviour, 1950, *3*, 1–38.   *R.Hä.*

Duncan Test. A special form of Student's Test. With the help of this procedure it is possible to compare pairs of median values when the results of more than two independent samples are available (e.g. in connection with an analysis of variance to identify the experimental condition[s] "responsible" for a possibly significant result). For this purpose the median values of the samples are ranked according to numerical magnitude. The adjacent median values can be tested for significance with the t test (q.v.), and all the others with the Duncan test. See *Statistics*.

W.H.B.

Duplicity theory (syn. *Duplicity principle*). This theory assigns different functional roles to the cones (q.v.) and the rods (q.v.), the photoreceptors, which are morphologically more or less distinct. The cones are said to be responsible for daylight vision and hence for color perception (q.v.). The rods are for seeing in faint or half-light. Cones and rods are also referred to as brightness and darkness receptors. The duplicity theory is supported by numerous morphological and functional facts. For example: nocturnal animals have a retina consisting of rods, those active by day a retina of cones or a mixed retina (cones and rods). Different visual functions (spectral sensitivity function, visual acuity, flicker fusion frequency, etc.; cf. Studnitz, 1952) have different corresponding parts for day or night vision, or differ for day or night vision (see, e.g., *Purkinje phenomenon*). In addition to rod substance (*rhodopsin*, q.v.), Studnitz (1952) identified *iodopsin* (the cone substance). Electron microscope investigations have revealed morphological differences between the cones (fibrous structure) and the rods (locular structure).

Bibliography: Graham, C. H. (Ed.): Vision and visual perception. New York & London, 1965. **Studnitz, G. V.:** Physiologie des Sehens. Leipzig, 1952. *A.H.*

Dynamic-effect law. Attention and responses become habitualized to the degree to which they help an individual to reach a goal. A postulate of R. B. Cattell's.

Dynamic personality factors. In personality research based on factor analysis, dynamic personality factors refer to differences in the field of motivation, interests, attitude and adaptation to conflict. Whether an independent personality area exists, as is usually presupposed, is not yet clear. Five occupational interest factors seem to be established (science or scholarship, economics, social life, art, office work). Among extra-occupational interests, adventurousness versus desire for security, diversion and change were confirmed. No connections with aptitude factors have yet been demonstrated.

Bibliography: Guilford, J. F.: Personality. New York, 1959. *B.H.*

Dynamic psychology. An approach which stresses the importance of energetics, or fundamental energy, in psychic life, as contrasted with the older, purely static conception (see *Association psychology*). The phenomena of psychic life are no longer understood as static conditions but as dynamic events, and research is conducted in this sense. Following suggestions from various schools of psychology (especially the effects of the ideas of Freudian psychoanalysis, q.v., as well as depth psychology as a whole, and the influence of Dilthey's ideas), the idea of dynamics found its way into scientific psychology in a twofold aspect: in the sense of change, and alteration, of the fluidity of mental life, and in the stress laid on the forces, drives and needs, i.e. the motivations, conditioning this constant change. It was especially in the hormic psychology (q.v.) of McDougall and the field theory (q.v.) of K. Lewin that the aspect of dynamic psychology was fundamentally emphasized. But great significance is also attached to dynamic thinking in the personality theories of G. W. Allport, S. L. Rubinstein, R. Heiss and H. Thomae. See *Depth psychology; Drive; Instinct.*

Bibliography: Allport, G. W.: Pattern and growth in personality. New York, 1961. **McDougall, W.:** Die energies of men. London, 1932. **Heiss, R.:** Die Lehre vom Charakter. Berlin, ²1949. **Lewin, K.:** A dynamic theory of personality. New York, 1935. **Rubinstein, S. L.:** Grundlagen der allgemeinen Psychologie. Berlin, 1958. **Thomae, H.:** Persönlichkeit: Eine dynamische Interpretation. Bonn, ²1955. **Woodworth, R. S.:** Dynamic psychology. New York, 1918. *K.E.P.*

Dynamics. 1. In physics: a division of mechanics, which deduces tne processes of motion from effective forces. **2.** In general psychology: a construct which explains the observable variability of psychic phenomena by means of dynamic factors such as drive, need, aspiration, instinct, etc. This approach was evident in the psychology of perception (gestalt laws, actual- or dynamo-genesis); in motivational psychology in the drive theories of A. Adler, W. McDougall, W. Stern and others; and in the psychology of thought (see *Würzburg School*). See *Dynamic psychology*.   *P.S. & R.S.*

Dynamic stereotype. Pavlov's term for a specific response pattern according to learned experience. One of a set of stimuli in different modalities may reproduce the characteristic responses of the other stimuli.

Dynamometer. An appliance with which the intensity of a physical response, e.g. manual pressure, can be determined.

Dysarthria. *Dysphasia* (q.v.) caused by brain lesions, especially CNS disease.

Dyscolia. See *Posodynics*.

Dysesthesia. The term designates diminished, increased or poorly-adapted sensitivity to pain, and abnormal sensations. See *Pain*.

Dysfunction. A disturbance of the normal functioning of organs, parts of an organ or of the body.

Dyshormia. Disturbed, unharmonious drive and motor behavior (e.g. shyness). Extremely pathological in catatonia.

Dyslalia. A disturbance in, but not absence of, the ability to talk. (See *Alalia*.) It is in use but its meaning and use vary, and its distinction from dysarthria (q.v.) is sometimes not made. Commonly used as a lesser degree of the condition defined under *alalia* in the sense of a motor aphasia. Syn. *Verbal aphasia; Verbal apraxia*.   *B.B.*

Dyslexia. Disturbed ability to read, i.e. a disturbed comprehension of what is read, ranging from minor or fluctuating disability to a complete and permanent inability to read which is at odds with the individual's apparent intelligence and socio-economic background. The disability may include words and not letters, figures and not letters, and so on. Comprehension after finger tracing has been described. Causes are acquired brain damage or congenital disability. Special reading instruction can benefit some children with congenital or developmental dyslexia, thus demonstrating its protean nature.   *B.B.*

Dysmelia. A defect in the embryonic development of the limbs. It is often the result of harmful exogenous factors such as oxygen, medicines or radiation during the period of limb formation in the fourth to sixth week of pregnancy, and appears as an absence or atrophy of the medullated bones with shortening and faulty positioning of the legs and arms.   *E.D.*

Dysmenorrhea. A menstrual dysfunction. See *Amenorrhea; Hypermenorrhea; Hypomenorrhea; Oligomenorrhea*.

Bibliography: Moon, A. A.: Dysmenorrhoea and the climacteric: psychosomatic assessment and treatment. Med. J. Austral., 1950, *1*, 174. **Wittkower, E. D. & Wilson, A.**: Dysmenorrhoea and sterility: personality studies. Brit. Med. J., 1940, No. 2, 586.

Dyspareunia. A lack of harmony between couples; used especially when one of two sexual partners is frequently or habitually dissatisfied. In addition to psychosocial reasons (e.g. impotence, frigidity or vaginismus), anatomical factors are often implicated which may cause pain during intercourse (e.g. phimosis, or inadequate vaginal lubrication). When some method of contraception other than oral contraceptives is used, there may be varying physiological intolerance of the method employed, which may result in chronic dyspareunia. The word originally denoted insufficient participation by the woman during coitus. *U.H.S.*

Dysphasia. Strictly means difficulty in speaking. It would seem more logical to use this term for the group of speech disorders now grouped under aphasia (q.v.), because few of them are actually without speech of any kind, as the term aphasia implies. It is now used loosely to describe a patient whose abnormal speech is awaiting a more specific label. *B.B.*

Dysphoria. See *Euphoria*.

Dysplastic type. A form of growth which is unharmonious or abnormal, and deviates from genuine biotypes (in proportions and superficial structure). The following are distinguished: malformations, intersexual dysplasia, retarded or accelerated dysplasia. The dysplastic type is not a uniform natural type, but a complex collective term embracing negative characteristics of structure or organization. Conceptually, it is quite different from the basic physical types, despite some schematic points of resemblance.
Bibliography: Kretschmer, E.: Physique and character. London, 1925. *W.K.*

Dysthymia. Originally meant an unpleasant mood state, with *autonomous dysthymia* being synonymous with endogenous depression. Currently used by Eysenck and most British psychologists to denote "the neurotic syndrome characterized by anxiety, reactive depression and/or obsession-compulsion features". The nearest term to this in former use was *psychasthenia*. People with dysthymia are usually introverted neurotics.
Bibliography: Eysenck, H. J.: The dynamics of anxiety and hysteria. London, 1957. *R.H.*

Dysthymic type. An imprecisely defined personality variant: introverted, slow to adapt to stress and tending therefore to protracted dysphoria. For ant.: see *Hysterical type*.
Bibliography: Franks, C. M.: Conditioning and personality. J. abn. and soc. Psychol., 1956, 52, 143. *W.K.*

Dystonia. A disturbance of the normal condition of muscular tonus, especially of the vascular muscles. *Autonomic*, or *vegetative*, *dystonia* refers to an abnormal reaction of the parasympathetic and sympathetic nervous system. The results are circulatory weakness, disorders in blood distribution, cardiac activity, breathing, and the functioning of internal organs, with palpitation, restlessness, insomnia, irregularity of temperature, sweating, vertigo, stomach pains and headache. *E.D.*

Dystrophy. Malnutrition; an inability to assimilate food; used chiefly of infants. It may be a congenital dysfunction or due to an intestinal infection or incorrect feeding. The term dystrophy is also applied to individual organs and, when accompanied by dehydration and loss of weight, often indicates a possible transition to atrophy (q.v.). *E.D.*

E

Ear. See *Organs of sense.*

Ebbinghaus, Hermann. B. 24/1/1850 in Barmen, d. 26/2/1909 in Halle. Professor at Breslau and Halle. One of the pioneers and founders of experimental psychology. The first to carry out experimental investigations into the processes of learning and memorizing, beginning with numerous experiments on himself in which he had to learn neutral elements (nonsense syllables). For the speed at which things are forgotten he obtained the Ebbinghaus curve of retention (q.v.): what has been learnt is forgotten, at first quickly but progressively more slowly; and, for the ratio between quantity of matter to be learnt and time taken to learn it, he established the Ebbinghaus Law: if the quantity of matter to be learnt is increased slightly, the time taken to learn it increases considerably. He engaged in controversy with W. Dilthey about the methodological bases of psychology, and defended experimental psychology against the psychology of understanding (*Verstehende Psychologie*).

Works: Uber das Gedächtnis, 1885 (Eng. trans.: Memory: a contribution to experimental psychology. New York, [2]1964). Grundzüge der Psychologie, 2 vols, [4]1919. Abriss der Psychologie, [8]1922.

Bibliography: Boring, E. G.: A history of experimental psychology. New York & London, [2]1957. Misiak, H. & Sexton, V. S.: History of psychology. New York & London, 1966. Shakow, D.: Hermann Ebbinghaus. Amer. J. Psychol., 1930, *42*, 505–18. Woodworth, R. S.: Hermann Ebbinghaus, J. Phil., 1909, *6*, 253–56.   *F.-C.S.*

Ebbinghaus Law. This law states that an increase in the quantity of matter to be learnt necessitates a disproportionate increase in the time required to learn it. According to Ebbinghaus six or seven meaningless syllables will be reproduced without a mistake after having been presented once, twelve syllables after 16·6 sec., fifteen syllables after 30 sec., and so on.   *H.H.*

Ecclesiogenic neuroses. These, according to E. Schaetzing (1955), are disorders in coping with experience due to a strict, precise, pseudo-Christian upbringing such as is common in ecclesiastical communities, especially in those with Nonconformist or pietistic leanings. The exclusion of certain subjects from discussion, prohibitions, and threats of punishment, lead to the body being despised and cause inhibitions (especially sexual), psychic castration and marital disasters.

40% of the neurotics I have treated for depression (elsewhere 10% to 20%) suffer from ecclesiogenic neuroses. In my experience, when a person finds a natural relationship with a member of the opposite sex blocked as being allegedly sinful, he often becomes a pervert (50% become homosexuals) or impotent (which includes frigidity). 90% of the 1,000 patients I have so far treated with these symptoms, or scruples about masturbation, were suffering from such neuroses.

Whereas genuine piety prevents neuroses, can cure marginal neuroses and acts as a protection against suicide, ecclesiogenic neuroses make it more likely that the sick will be driven to commit suicide in order to escape from the contradiction between the id (q.v.) and the super-ego (q.v.).   *K.T.*

Echolalia. Repetition of the speech of another, especially when this occurs in the setting of an illness producing mental symptoms, e.g. schizophrenia, or brain disease. The same phenomenon can occur as a personality mannerism or in anxious individuals. Syn. *Echophrasia; Echospeech.*   *B.B.*

Echopraxia. Repetition of the movements of another, i.e. imitation of actions (echokinesis) and gestures (echomimia). The term is reserved for describing patients with brain disease or functional psychosis who repeatedly imitate others.   *B.B.*

Ecological representativeness (K. Lewin, E. Brunswik). A term for the presence of organisms appropriate to the conditions of the environment.

Ecology. The study of the relationship between organisms and their environment (living or inanimate). A distinction can be made between autoecology and synecology. Autoecology denotes the relationships between a type of organism and its environment (e.g. dependence on temperature, humidity, soil characteristics, food organisms, enemies, food competitors, etc.). Synecology covers the mutual relationships which prevail within a specific area (e.g. meadow, tree, pool, sea coast), each such area having in turn a relationship with other areas.   *H.S.*

Economic principle. The principle formulated in the psychoanalytically-oriented psychosomatic research conducted by Alexander (1959): the non-sexual mental energy follows

the principle of inertia or energy, while sexual energy follows the surplus principle according to which non-qualified surplus sexual stimulation can be directed by the sexual apparatus into outlet channels, while this is not the case with non-sexual energy.

Bibliography: Alexander, F.: Psychosomatische Medizin, Grundlagen und Anwendungsgebiete. Berlin, 1959.   *D.V.*

Economic type. One of E. Spranger's ideal types which he includes in his "forms of life": a man who views the world from the standpoint of expediency; in extreme cases the means to an end may become an end in itself, e.g. money. This type is a creator rather than an enjoyer. He has little contact with esthetics or religion and much more with power. Sub-types: entrepreneur, speculator, saver, miser.   *W.K.*

Economizing method. Method introduced by H. Ebbinghaus for quantitative determination of memory capacity. Material to be learnt is repeatedly presented to the subject; memory capacity is measured by the number of elements in this material which are retained without repetition, i.e. can be "economized".   *P.S.*

Ecphoric inhibition. See *Inhibitions of memory.*

Ecphory. A term used by R. Semon to designate the activation of a memory trace or *engram*, resulting in a partial repetition of the original psychological event or experience (*ecphoria*).   *G.D.W.*

Ecstasy. 1. A state of rapture characterized by a decrease of self-control, an exuberance of feeling (q.v.) and often excessive movement. Primary forms can be seen in fits of rage and in the orgasm (q.v.); secondary and derived forms appear in mass-psychological phenomena (see *Crowd behavior* and in certain forms of delirium the origin of which may be spontaneous and religious (*unio mystica*) or spontaneous and pathological; it could also be due to the use of narcotics (q.v.). **2.** In the form "ec-stasy", J. P. Sartre (*Being and Nothingness*) uses the term to denote the following: "The distance to the self which constitutes the for-self, which at the same time is not what it is" (it is not its past), "is what it is not" (it has to be its future), "in the oneness of a constant reference backwards is what it is not and is not what it is" (the present).   *P.M.*

Ectoderm. A term for the outer cell-layer created during gastrulation (see *Gastrula*) and all tissues and organs which are formed subsequently by the further differentiation of this cell-layer (in vertebrates, e.g. the nervous system).   *H.S.*

Ectomorph(ic type). A growth dimension (somatotype). The main characteristics are "linearity and leanness". The bones and musculature are deficient in strength. Sheldon elaborated this type for statistical emphasis, correlating it with the cerebrotonic (q.v.) character and approximating it to the leptosomic (q.v.) type.

Bibliography: Sheldon, W. H.: Varieties of human physique. New York, 1940.   *W.K.*

Ectoplasm. Substance exuded from the mouth, nose or other orifices of a materializing medium assumed to be of a paranormal nature. See *Materialization; Medium.*   *J.B.*

Educability. 1. A person's educational potentiality, or disposition to benefit from education as the combined result of innate and environmental factors. A unilateral attribution of significance to "talent" or environment leads to pedagogic pessimism (nativism, q.v.) or optimism (empiricism, q.v.). The irreconcilable antithesis of ineducability and hyper-educability is confuted by the convergence principle (W. Stern): a person is educable when "talent" and environmental factors converge. Of course, not only ability and environment are involved but the adequacy of both and the personal decisions of the individual. The cooperation of the person concerned is required to realize educability, for which both the emotional and linguistic aspects of inter-human communication are important. Educability is also related to the inner (spontaneous) cooperation of the pupil with the external educational aim. Educability always involves problems of spontaneity, one's own activity and receptivity to the environment.   *H.Schr.*

2. To define educability as the ability to be educated is not very useful; it is more proficient to determine the form and level of ineducability, in order to establish a precise definition and define possible therapeutic measures and teaching methods.

Forms. There are several possible classifications. In a psychological perspective, they are (apart from severe subnormality of intelligence): (*a*) subnormality not amounting to severe subnormality, and susceptible to medical treatment and special training; (*b*) general but temporary incapacities; educators would include in this category asocial types who can improve, given certain pedagogic presuppositions; (*c*) partial or localized inabilities, e.g. those related to sense defects. *Level:* educability is directly related to IQ. An IQ below 40 makes it impossible to acquire even fundamental school knowledge (e.g. reading). For an exact diagnosis, other factors would have to be considered: family background, which is or is not favorable to primary-school education; character and motor skills, linguistic competence, timeliness of remedial measures already take, etc. See *Abilities; Autism; Learning.*   *G.C.M.*

Educational cybernetics. See *Cybernetic education*.

Educational guidance is dependent on education itself and therefore differs according to age, nationality, culture, economic conditions, philosophy, ethical considerations, human ideals of society and even family and personal factors—just as the objectives of education themselves differ. In the non-professional sense educational guidance has always existed. Intentional, planned, objective and scientifically based guidance with an expert orientation did not develop until the twentieth century. To some extent the two world wars drew attention to the problem of education; at the same time the difficulties of education were only fully recognized when the results of research in child psychology (q.v.) became available. Education based on parental and pedagogic authority changed and the emphasis shifted to the personality of the child. The conditions of life and work are becoming increasingly complex and requirements are growing: the problems and difficulties of education have therefore become one of the major concerns of society.

1. In the broad, comprehensive, sense. educational guidance designates generally valid indications and assistance for persons active in the educational process in order to achieve optimal control over and influence on the physical, intellectual and moral development of the normal child. The fundamental principles of education are those of love, patience, respect for the personality of the developing child, acceptance of otherness, a progression of demands, regularity, rewards and punishment, etc. Education is also of vital importance as a means of promoting independence and self-discipline. Education with these aims in mind can only be achieved if the environment of the child is calm, harmonious, honest and regular and provides an example which is worthy of imitation. There are periods in the life of a normal child and youth (phases of defiance, puberty, youth) when parents must frequently turn to the expert for guidance. The main task of educational guidance in the future will be to prevent educational conflicts.

2. In the narrower sense, educational guidance signifies carefully planned remedial measures for individual educational difficulties that are not normal problems. This is particularly important in the case of children who are handicapped or whose personality development is disturbed. (*a*) *Educational problems of handicapped children* (blind or suffering from defective vision, mute, deaf, mentally defective, physically handicapped, suffering from speech defects) are dependent on the specific defect. The perception processes, emotionality, and reactions to the outside world may be disturbed, mental development may deviate from the average, and the personality may have undergone a specific change. These children are characterized by failures, inhibitions, fear, distrust, isolation, a lack of self-confidence, anxiety, inability to work and social maladjustment. Parents adopt two extreme attitudes: such children are either spoilt and pampered or neglected and rejected. Parents therefore require expert advice at an early stage in order to prevent or reduce secondary personality problems. This will also facilitate compensation, correction and rehabilitation and influence those around the handicapped child to accept him as he is and view him objectively. (*b*) In the case of a number of other *defects in the development of the personality*, educational guidance again has an important part to play. A uniform taxonomy of these disturbances is not yet available. Reasons, symptoms or the degree of severity may be emphasized from case to case. Behavior problems, learning difficulties, character faults, social maladjustment, defective affective relations, impaired development, damage caused by the environment, etc., are characteristics of the exceptional problem child. The symptoms are varied and range from difficulties in learning to theft, from dyslexia (q.v.) to enuresis (q.v.) and from agressivity to inhibition in widely varying

forms. Systems and methods of guidance in this sphere have reached an advanced level of development.

Institutional facilities. In average cases, educational guidance can be given to the parents by teachers, a school psychologist or any other expert appointed under the school system. There are an increasing number of institutions which study and guide problem children (youth agencies, guidance centers, child neurological or psychological observation centers, child guidance clinics, mental hygiene centers, *centres médico-psycho-pédagogiques, centres d'accueil,* etc.). Because of the range of examinations and treatment involved, educational guidance is generally a team responsibility: depending on the specific problems, specialist doctors, psychologists, orthopedagogic experts or remedial experts, social workers, lawyers, logopedic specialists, psychagogues, psychotherapeutic and physiotherapeutic experts, etc., may be called in. Psychological and psychiatric educational guidance centers, as well as centers run by youth offices, are available, depending on the special emphasis in any individual case.

Form and methods of the examination. Before he can give advice, the specialist must get to know the referred child thoroughly: (*a*) special characteristics and deviations in age-dependent features; (*b*) life history (life history analysis); (*c*) characteristics of changes caused by the handicap; (*d*) features due to environment and disposition; (*e*) positive characteristics and abilities (q.v.); (*f*) interpersonal relations, etc. Individual guidance must take all these aspects into account and therefore requires many different examinations: personal details, anamnesis, exploration (games, drawing, observations of movement, speech and behavior), intelligence tests, personality investigation with different methods and tests; examination of individual ability, investigation of family and environmental conditions, expert medical examination. The findings are then worked out and evaluated, a diagnosis is prepared

and recommendations compiled in a detailed consultation. The consultant himself must have certain specific personality features: sympathy, self-awareness, independence, objectivity, ability to create trust, good ability to cooperate, expert knowledge and experience of psychotherapy and guidance. Guidance is generally given to the parents, or at least one parent, and if necessary to the child's teacher or guardian. The recommendations must be realistic and feasible.

Therapy. Therapy is as varied as the problems encountered. In the case of children or youths who are difficult to educate, it is essential to do more than merely change certain individual characteristics: by eliminating the causes as far as possible, the whole personality must be reeducated. Generally, transfer to a different school or a new environment will be desirable. Treatment methods include play therapy, promotion of psychomotor development, aptitude development, speech education, artistic training, music therapy and other forms of psychotherapy as well as the methods of depth psychology. Educational guidance centers often examine abilities and give vocational guidance.

Educational guidance is extremely important: if it is successful it may not only solve difficult problems but also prepare the way for a balanced life. See *Child psychology; Educational psychology; Remedial education; Autism; Mental defect.*

Bibliography: Aichhorn, A.: Erziehungsberatung und Erziehungshilfe. Berne & Stuttgart, 1959. Bach, H.: Schulische Erziehungsberatung. Hannover, 1960. Fischer, G.: Eltern abnormaler Kinder, Prax. Kinderpsychol., 1960, *9*, 12ff. Katz, H.: Parents of the handicapped. Springfield, 1961. Lückert, H. R. (Ed.): Hdb der Erziehungsberatung. Munich & Basle, 1964. Rassekh-Ardjomand, M.: L'enfant problème etsa rééducation. Neuchâtel, 1962. Rubinstein, J. H.: Role of the diagnostic clinic in the care of the mentally retarded. Amer. J. ment. def., 1962, *66,* 544ff. Werner, R.: Das Verhaltensgestörte Kind. Berlin, 1967.

                                        F. K. Illyés & A. E. Lányi

Educational psychology. I. *Conceptions.* **1.** *Definitions.* The following are three of the most important denotations of the term "education": (*a*) education as a social reality, seen in terms of a network of interrelated political, economic, philosophical, historical, technical and demographic problems; (*b*) education as the end product of a process; (*c*) education as a behavior pattern by means of which an individual or a group influences one or more individuals.

Under (*a*), educational psychology represents all the investigations of institutions, strategies, curricula and teaching methods, and component structures of schools considered as organizations, which are carried out from a psychological viewpoint. In this perspective, educational psychology is a psychology of educational systems.

In sense (*b*), educational psychology is a psychology of the educable and educated, which is still in the course of development: as yet, the classification of the behavioral variables which distinguish (variously educated) individuals has hardly begun.

But educational psychology is usually understood in sense (*c*); it can be defined as the investigation of the psychological components of actual educational situations: as the investigation of the psychological processes actuated or produced by various methods and techniques. A distinction may be made between two forms of educational psychology: a static-descriptive and a dynamic-active form. In the second case, the scientific research work of educational psychology is necessarily "active", since the psychologist is investigating ongoing and changing scholastic situations. In this case, of course, scientific method does not reach the level of realization possible for scientific research in a static educational psychology.

Nevertheless, all forms of educational psychology must have recourse to scientific methods of investigation, both in order to confirm facts and to organize experiments. In certain cases the psychologist will base his work more on documentation (curricula and so on); in others, he will investigate educational reality with the methods and

instruments of clinical and experimental psychology and psychometrics (q.v.).

2. *Areas of educational psychology.* (*a*) Different educational situations and their variants can be classified according to various aspects: (i) age or scholastic levels (pre-school, nursery or kindergarten, primary or infants and junior, secondary or middle and upper school, and tertiary education; or by numbered grades); (ii) educational content (the scholastic situation is not the same in, say, the teaching of mathematics as it is in second or third language instruction); (iii) educational methods and techniques (compare the psychological situation of a child at a teaching machine with that of one discovering his environment as a member of a group); (iv) learning and educational aims (learning situations, adult education, infant education).

(*b*) But it is also possible to investigate the general psychological and sociopsychological laws and determinants of situations and psychological situations in relation to the typical behavior variables of the individuals concerned. In the latter case we may speak of something approaching a *differential* educational psychology. In any case, comprehensive insight into the various perspectives of educational psychology requires the findings of genetics and differential psychology to be taken into account.

(*c*) The educational situation can also be considered in terms of the individuals who take part in it. Apart from the individual who is to be educated, there are three other categories to be studied: Educators proper; adults who do not participate in education itself but form part of the total situation (doctors, psychologists, etc.); and parents. These categories have been made the objects of important investigations, in which increasing stress has been laid on the interaction between them.

(*d*) The psychological effects of the educational institutions themselves also have to be investigated. Every scholastic situation gives rise to certain phenomena of adaptation. Educational psychology investigates the consequences of selective and non-selective systems (streaming, etc.). Educational counseling or guidance has to do with the entire complex of educational processes, and takes various forms according to the structure of the individual school. The structure of the school as an organization also brings about a specific structuring of time in the pupil's life: problems of time distribution (and its consequences) also belong to the area of educational psychology.

3. *Psychology of educational processes.* Educational psychology is particularly concerned with educational behavior in itself; this is a field in which there is much work still to be done.

(a) A taxonomy of educational activities has still to be developed. Nevertheless it is possible to distinguish the essentially important areas of such a classification in the fundamental terms of the individuals concerned: the adult (teacher, parents); adults (all those who influence the child, considered as a totality); the pupil (as an individual); pupils (the totality of pupils as a group, class or school). On the basis of these four elements it is possible to examine all possible interactive combinations.

(b) Educational processes can also be considered in regard to their content. Most frequently, an educational process depends initially on a content determined by the educator (the outcome is foreseen by the teacher); however, the content is not always the starting-point or the goal of the educational process; this is so in research and discovery situations, where the content is not on every occasion that predicted by the teacher. An educational process can also have a change in behavior as its aim (B. F. Skinner). Finally, the emphasis may be on an imprinting factor, when it is a matter not so much of the rational as of the affective, i.e. of an effect in depth. In this case, educational psychology is concerned with the investigation of the emotions (q.v.) and the affective life.

(c) If the basic approach is essentially that of a psychology of emotional behavior, various aspects may be taken into consideration: e.g. that of the teacher and that of the student. In order to investigate incipient communication processes, an initial consideration is the view an educator has of his pupils. It is essential that the educator realizes the role played in the communication process by the methods and techniques applied. Psychologists have begun directly to analyze the educational situation in this regard, by measuring the extent of verbal interventions, i.e. of the exchange of information between pupils, and the communication processes themselves. In regard to the pupils, the reception of information by schoolchildren, students and adults is an object of research. The image the pupil has of his teacher, and the positive and negative factors affecting his receptivity (to the teacher's strategies) are also important. Finally, the analysis of all the difficulties encountered by pupils forms part of educational psychology.

4. *Applications of educational psychology.* (a) Piéron defines educational psychology as a form of educational science deriving from child psychology (q.v.). B. F. Skinner believes that instruction can be defined as that arrangement of reinforcement conditions which bring about changes in behavior (see Ferster & Skinner, 1957). Under these conditions the process of education becomes applied science. (b) Educational psychology can be a research area of general psychology. (c) Educational psychology has a decisive part to play in the formation of educators of all kinds. See also *Educational science.*

G. C. Mialaret

II. *The tasks of educational psychology.* An examination of the existing literature in search of a summary definition of the tasks confronting educational psychology discloses various approximations to "a scientific investigation of the psychic aspect of education" (Fischer); in practice, empirical research into the psychology of education has tended to go beyond this (for some authors) restricted conception (Smedslund, 1969; Warburton, 1962; Weinert, 1966), but without abandoning it as an essential concern. At present there is something more approaching unanimity regarding the themes proper to research work in educational psychology (to judge by practice, at least), than might be expected in view of the difficulties experienced in any attempt to define it as a scientific specialism (see, for a general presentation of the field of educational studies, Tibble, 1966; of educational psychology, McFarland, 1971).

One of the important tasks of educational psychology is the investigation and theoretical elucidation of learning processes. Today the significance of the biological and constitutional bases of learning processes is generally accepted; findings such as those of C. Burt (1949), Newman, Freeman & Holzinger (1937) and others, have determined the approaches of educational psychology in this area (genetics and environment; abilities, q.v.; educability, q.v.). The elucidation of the individual state of development, of personal capacity at a particular moment of time, plays an important part in the investigation of human learning processes (McGeoch & Irion, [2]1952; Gagné, 1967). Stimuli for novel research work are offered in the postulates of Gagné (1967), who opines that human learning—as far as it can be independent of variable conditions—occurs in various forms, whose interrelations can be expressed by a hierarchical ratio of interdependence. An emphasis on the human aspects of learning processes is accompained in more recent educational research by an emphasis on their social context (Backman & Secord, 1968). The variables influencing learning which derive from societal processes and class structure (Ruppert, [3]1957; Deutsch, 1949; Trow et al., 1970) are now under consideration. Bernstein (1961, 1965, 1969) reports findings in regard to the socio-cultural determinants of learning (see also Grammar; Language; Psycholinguistics; Verbal behavior). Many of the motiva-

tional factors conditioning learning can be better understood in the light of social interactions and presuppositions. Investigations such as those of McClelland (1967), Atkinson (1965), Maslow (1954), Heckhausen (1966) offer information on the interdependence of successful learning and motivation. Variables such as level of aspiration, hope of success, anxiety about failure, etc. (see Aspiration level; Motivation), and, e.g., the dependence of successful learning on set (Harlow, 1949), and that of praise and blame on attitude and achievement (Johannesson, 1967), or the effects of willingness to learn, are important. In addition to the analysis of learning processes, research into the conditions for and functions of teaching is a primary area of educational psychology. In this regard, researchers are concerned both with general instructional methodology (Bloom, 1956, 1964) and the analysis of styles of teaching and the roles of educators (Aebli, 1961; Herrmann, 1966). Investigations of the effects of specific dimensions of teacher behavior (Tausch & Tausch, 1965), or of the interaction of teaching style and learning performance are examples of a current direction of research in this area. The effects of education on motivation (Heckhausen, 1966), the optimal arousal of interest by specific teacher strategies, the extensive field of curriculum studies (Achtenhagen & Meyer, 1971; Bruner, 1960, 1966), and instructional technology (q.v.) (Skinner, 1968) are also important areas of investigation. The number of tasks for research in this complex of areas (Travers, 1969) shows how significant the development and adequate provision of educational aids, and methodically established instructional strategies (see Instructional technology), and research into teaching methods, have become in present-day educational psychology as a research discipline. Available findings would seem to show that it is possible to plan methodologies that are functionally more proficient (Bloom, 1964; Skinner, 1968).

Another important area of educational

psychology depends upon the differential psychological approach. Attention to individual personality profiles and predictions of performance, etc., play a major part in practical educational psychology and the planning of future (national) strategies. (For examples of the kind of problem involved, see Deutsch *et al.*, 1968; Eysenck, 1971). (See also *Abilities; Intelligence; Personality; Traits; Educational guidance*). Of course, personality studies in this regard are not restricted to child studies; the differential diagnosis of the educator (Tausch & Tausch, 1965; Weinert, 1966) is also a prerequisite for proficient research into the interaction, and effects of the interaction, of teacher and pupil (see *Educator, personality of*). A further task of educational psychology might be termed "development aid", in the sense of counseling and remedial education, and the treatment (as far as possible) of learning disabilities and scholastic problems (see *Mental defect; Juvenile delinquency*) (Allport, 1937; Maslow, 1962). The educational possibilities of the "self-realization" approach (Allport, 1937, 1961; Maslow, 1962) are above all evident in educational and vocational guidance (q.v.) (Rogers, 1939; Siegfried, 1969).

Another area of educational psychology, as of educational theory, might be seen as that definable in terms of concepts such as educational objective and values, and moral education (Bantock, 1965, 1967; Buber, 1937, 1962; Brezinka, 1969; Kay, 1968; Peters, 1963, 1966; Skinner, 1948; Wilson *et al.*, 1967). See *Child psychology; Conscience.*

Bibliography: Achtenhagen, F. & Meyer, H. L. (Eds): Curriculum-revision: Möglichkeiten und Grenzen. Munich, 1971. Aebli, H.: Grundformen des Lehrens. Stuttgart, 1961. Allport, G. W.: Personality. New York, 1937. Id.: Pattern and growth in personality. New York, 1961. Atkinson, J. W.: An introduction to motivation. Princeton, 1965. Backman, C. W. & Secord, P. F.: A social psychological view of education. New York, 1968. Bantock, G. H.: Education and values. London, 1965. Id.: Education, culture and the emotions. London, 1967. Bernstein, B.: Social class and linguistic development: a theory of social learning. In: Halsey, A. H. *et al.* (Eds): Education, economy and society. New York, 1961, 288–314.

Id.: A socio-linguistic approach to social learning. In: Gould, J. (Ed.): Social science survey. Harmondsworth, 1965. Id.: A socio-linguistic approach to socialization: with some reference to educability. In: Gumperz, J. J. & Hymes, D. (Eds): Directions in sociolinguistics. New York, 1969. Bloom, B. S. (Ed.): Taxonomy of educational objectives. The classification of educational goals, 2 vols. New York, 1956–64. Id.: Stability and change in human characteristics. New York, 1964. Brezinka, W.: Über Absicht und Erfolg der Erziehung. Constance, 1969. Bruner, J. S.: The process of education. New York, 1960. Id.: Toward a theory of instruction. New York, 1966 Id.: Learning about learning. Washington, 1966. Buber, M.: I and thou. Edinburgh & New York,1937. Id.: Das dialogische Prinzip. Heidelberg, 1962. Burt, C.: Mental and scholastic tests. London, ⁶1949. Deese, J. & Hulse, S. H.: The psychology of learning. New York, 1966. Deutsch, M.: An experimental study of the effects of cooperation and competition upon group process. Human relations, 1949, *2*. Deutsch, M., Katz, I. & Jensen, A. R. (Eds): Social class, race and psychological development. New York, 1968. Ellis, E.: The transfer of learning. New York, 1965. Eysenck, H. J.: Race, intelligence and education. London, 1971. Ferster, C. B. & Skinner, B. F.: Schedules of reinforcement. New York, 1957. Fischer, A.: Über Begriff und Aufgabe der pädagogischen Psychologie. Z.f. päd. Psychol. u. exp. Päd., 1917, *18*, 5–13, 109–18. Frank, H.: Kybernetische Grundlagen der Pädagogik. Baden-Baden, 1962. Gage, N. L. (Ed.): Handbook of research on teaching. Chicago, 1963. Gagné, R. M.: Learning and individual differences. Columbus, 1967. Halsey, A. H., Floud, J. E. & Anderson, C. A. (Eds): Education, economy and society. New York, 1961. Harlow, H. F.: The formation of learning sets. Psychol. Rev., 1949, *56*, 51–65. Heckhausen, H.: Einflüsse der Erziehung auf die Motivationsgenese. In: Herrmann, T. (Ed.): Psychologie der Erziehungsstile. Göttingen, 1966. Hilgard, E. R.: Theories of learning and instruction. Chicago, 1964. Johannesson, I.: Effects of praise and blame. Stockholm, 1967. Kay, W. F.: Moral development. London, 1968. Lipsitt, L. P. & Spiker, C. C. (Eds): Advances in child development and behavior, 2 vols. New York, 1963–5. Lovell, K.: Team teaching. Leeds, 1967. McClelland, D. C.: The achieving society. New York, 1967. McFarland, H. S. N.: Psychological theory and educational practice. London, 1971. McGeoch, J. A. & Irion, A. L.: The psychology of human learning. New York, 1952. Maslow, A. H.: Motivation and personality. New York, 1954. Id.: Toward a psychology of being. Toronto, 1962. Newman, H. H., Freeman, F. N. & Holzinger, K. J.: Twins, a study of hereditary and environment. Chicago, 1937. Passow, A. H. (Ed.): Education in depressed areas. New York, 1963.

Peters, R. S.: Authority, responsibility and education. London, 1963. Id.: Ethics and education. London, 1966. Piaget, J.: The psychology of intelligence. London, 1947. Rogers, C. R.: The clinical treatment of the problem child. Boston, 1939. Roth, H.: Pädagogische Anthropologie, 2 vols. Hanover, 1970-1. Ruppert, J. P.: Sozialpsychologie im Raume der Erziehung. Weinheim, 1957. Siegfried, K.: Erziehungsberatung und Schulpsychologie. Stuttgart, 1969. Skinner, B. F.: Walden two. New York, 1948. Id.: Cumulative record. New York, 1961. Id.: The technology of teaching. New York, 1968. Sluckin, W.: Imprinting and early learning. London, 1964. Smedslund, J.: Educational psychology. Ann. Rev. Psychol., 1969, 15, 251-76. Stenhouse, L.: Culture and education. London, 1967. Strom, R. D.: Psychology for the classroom. Englewood Cliffs, 1969. Tanner, J. M. & Inhelder, B.: Discussions on child development, Vols 1-4. London, 1971. Tausch, R. & Tausch, A.: Erziehungspsychologie. Göttingen, ²1965. Tibble, J. W. (Ed.): The study of education. London, 1966. Travers, R. M. W.: Educational psychology. In: Encyclopedia of educational research, Vol. 4. Toronto, 1969. Trow, C. W. et al.: Psychologie des Gruppenverhaltens: Die Klasse als Gruppe. In: Weinert, F. (Ed.): Pädagogische Psychologie. Cologne, ²1970. Vernon, P. E.: Intelligence and cultural environment. London, 1969. Warburton, F. W.: Educational psychology. Ann. Rev. Psychol., 1962, 13, 371-414. Weinert, F.: Erziehungsstile in ihrer Abhängigkeit von der individuellen Eigenart des Erziehers. In: Herrmann, T. (Ed.): Psychologie der Erziehungsstile. Göttingen, 1966. Wilson, J., Williams, N. & Sugarman, B.: Introduction to moral education. Harmondsworth, 1967. Wiseman, S.: Education and environment. Manchester, 1964.   K. E. Pelzer

Educational quotient (abb. EQ). The educational age (EA: measured by achievement tests) divided by chronological age (q.v.).

Educational reform. In the history of education, educational reform has always been very strongly demanded when people began to examine the educational process from a new critical viewpoint. Educational reform at any time seeks to adapt practical educational activity to new discoveries made by science (pedagogy, psychology, didactics) and to the existing state of the technical and cultural development of society. In the course of educational reforms the content and form of educational work have always changed.   *H.Sch.*

Educational science. 1. *Education as a field of inquiry.* The educative process consists of three stages: (*a*) the formulation of objectives: (*b*) the organization of learning opportunities; and (*c*) the appraisal, control and interpretation of the results of learning, all summed up under the term "evaluation".

(*a*) All educational activity takes place in order to attain certain objectives: that is, it is governed by certain values or notions about what is desirable and worth striving for. This means that educational theory, which includes the *philosophy of education*, forms an important branch of study in this discipline. The school is one of the institutions of society, and interacts in terms of both organization and practices with society at large. *Educational sociology* studies the school as an institution. Upbringing and instruction have their *history*. An historical approach to the study of educational problems can illuminate them; it can prove especially fruitful if the comparative method is used, that is, if an attempt is made to see how historical, social and economic factors in different countries have helped to shape current educational systems. This field of inquiry is called *comparative education*.

The three fields of philosophy of education, history of education and comparative education are the humanistic branches of education as a discipline. As a rule these branches do not use empirical or experimental methods. The word "empirical" is reserved for those branches of educational research which use methods based on some form of systematized observation. Empirical education would then denote the type of research which collects data by a systematic study of the educational process.

(*b*) The second phase of the educative process consists in organizing learning opportunities. In terms of instruction, this means: knowing the subject-matter which is to be communicated, *and* mastering the methodology that promotes appropriate communication of the subject-matter. The prerequisite for an appropriate methodology, however, is familiarity with the nature of the objects of educational activity, namely the pupils. No two pupils are alike in respect of their innate abilities. They develop in accordance with individual patterns. They do not behave in groups in the way they do as individuals. For subject-matter to be communicated, it will not suffice to know the individual pupils. One must also know the principles and conditions under which learning takes place. These principles, together with knowledge of individual differences, maturity and development, are taught by *educational psychology* (q.v.), a field which borders on general and experimental psychology and scientifically relates to it in fruitful interaction.

The theory of how learning opportunities ought to be organized forms the core of what has traditionally been called "didactics".

(c) The third and last stage of the educative process was designated above by the appraisal of the didactic measures, the attempt to assess how far the objectives formulated have been achieved. These measures are usually described in educational terminology by the word *evaluation*. This term is concerned in part with examining, testing and grading. However, evaluation does not pertain solely to the more tangible and cognitive results of education, but also to affective results, such as values, attitudes and esthetic taste. The aim of educational research is to measure the results of the educational process. For this reason, the theory of testing and measurement is an important branch of educational psychology. Of basic relevance in this connection is the construction of achievement tests, which are used to measure comprehensively the acquisition of knowledge and skill. Attempts are also made to construct instruments in order to assess more subtle qualities in the moral and esthetic sphere, that is valuative, attitudinal and similar qualities of education.

Remedial education (q.v.), a sector not accounted for in the above itemization of education as a discipline, is also closely related to educational psychology. It is concerned with negative deviations: with pupils who, because of intellectual retardation, find it hard to keep up with their classmates: with pupils beset by reading and writing disabilities; with emotionally disturbed pupils, and so on. It stands to reason that this branch of education has many ties with psychiatry and psychopathology.

Summing up, we can say that education as a discipline consists of the following branches: (a) philosophy of education; (b) history of education; (c) comparative education (which comprise educational theory); and of: (d) educational sociology; (e) educational psychology cum didactics; (f) remedial education (which comprise empirical education).

Education as a discipline is clearly very heterogeneous, not so much in its problems as in its theories and methods. One and the same problem may be treated from many different angles. The question of grouping in school provides an example: should pupils be grouped according to their varying scholastic ability? If so, when and how? This problem has strong political and social value implications. But we cannot understand the substance and the intensity of the commitments involved in the issue of school structure and grouping practices unless we study the historical and social background of the problem. The relationship between the general elementary school for the common people and the "learned" or Latin schools for the social élite has assumed different forms from one country to another, depending upon the degree of social heterogeneity and economic development. The International Project for the Evaluation of Educational Achievement (IEA) (Husén *et al.*, 1967) might be cited as one example of an empirically oriented study whereby advantage is taken of cross-national differences in both independent and dependent variables. Important aspects of school structure can thus be put in a deeper perspective than is possible in a study within the national confines.

Since the practical problems radiate into all branches of education as a discipline, methods can vary sharply between these branches. The study of the history of education requires a quite different research training than when statistical methods and educational tests are used to investigate, for example, the structure of ability, the accretions of knowledge and teacher-pupil interaction. In the last case one must be conversant with scientific method in the so-called behavioral sciences, such as psychology and sociology.

2. *Education as a research discipline.* Science had a long history before the assumptions and methods of education were subjected to systematic study. The first university chairs were not established until the end of the eighteenth century. The first professor of education (which also included philosophy) was appointed at Halle in Germany. This link between education and philosophy set the pattern for future university chairs in several European countries. This meant that the inquiry concentrated mainly on the "humanistic" aspects, or *objectives*, of education.

Not until the arrival of experimental psychology was the basis laid for educational psychology. The United States took the lead during the 1880s and 1890s. American psychologists who had received their experimental schooling in Germany, began to make systematic observations, conduct experiments in perception, and carry out studies in developmental psychology in order to illuminate educational problems. Mention can be made of Stanley Hall, who did pioneering work in child and adolescent psychology, and who introduced Freudian psychoanalysis into the U.S. at the beginning of this century: and of J. McKeen Cattell, who in 1890 made the first attempt to construct a so-called intelligence test (q.v.), whose primary applications were intended for the schools. In 1905 Alfred Binet, commissioned by the French Ministry of Education, constructed the first practicable intelligence test.

William James, the father of pragmatic philosophy, also made a name for himself as a psychologist. During the 1890s he held a series of lectures (published in 1899 under the title, *Talks to Teachers of Psychology*).

The same decade also witnessed the pioneering attempt at "evaluation", carried out by the American physician, Joseph M. Rice, in order to measure the results of school instruction. He travelled to schools in different parts of the country, and devised the first purely educational test, concerned with spelling.

A dissertation on the learning behavior of animals was presented at the end of the 1890s by Edward Lee Thorndike, who was to become a leading figure in American educational psychology virtually throughout the ensuing half-century. In his dissertation he expounded his law of effect. The first edition of his famous *Educational Psychology* appeared in 1903; over a long period of successive revisions its contents have greatly influenced the training of teachers.

In Germany, Ernst Meumann published in 1907 the first of his three massive volumes of *Vorlesungen zur Einführung in die experimentelle Pädagogik*, whose wide-ranging scope included developmental psychology, individual differences, scholastic ability, the psychology and hygiene of school work, and the problems encountered in teaching different subjects.

In Britain, the problem of individual differences was first studied by anthropologists and statisticians, most notably by Sir Francis Galton and Karl Pearson (the originator of the correlation method). In 1900 the German psychologist and educator, William Stern, published his *Differentielle Psychologie*, which was followed two years later by Thorndike's *Introduction to the Theory of Mental Measurements*. Thorndike introduced statistical methods into educational psychology, and also played a major role in shaping measurement theory in education, especially as applied to the construction of achievement tests. Between 1900 and 1930, education advanced tremendously in the United States as an empirical science. Such universities as Columbia and Chicago became well known for their schools of education. Chicago had its Judd to match Thorndike at Columbia; Judd is best known for his studies on the problems of formal education or the "transfer of training". L. M. Terman, whose name is chiefly associated with the testing of children and adolescents, and with studies of gifted children (*Genetic Studies of Genius*) extending over many years, worked at Stanford. Arthur Gates helped to lay the foundations of modern research into reading.

In Europe, as we have seen, education was closely related to philosophy, and therefore was often a purely speculative or "humanistic" branch of learning. There were several exceptions to this rule, particularly among those researchers who were experimental psychologists.

Recently, greatly increased resources have been placed at the disposal of educational research in a number of countries, reflecting the impact and importance of research and development as a factor of great importance in today's educative society. In consequence more scholars have been recruited into educational research and the quality of work done has improved. This development has been most pronounced in such countries as the United States, England and Sweden. Research programs related to central educational problems have been launched. Problems involved in helping the developing countries have generated a growing interest in comparative education, and the economics of education, a new specialism, has arisen on the borderline between political economy and education. Educational planning has also become a special discipline.

Another trend is the demand for better theory and stricter methods in conducting investigations in the didactic field. Eminent experimental psychologists, such as J. Bruner and B. F. Skinner, have begun to work on fundamental educational problems. Another example is John C. Flanagan's large-scale research project into scholastic ability in the American high school ("project talent").

3. *Summary.* The discipline of education is heterogeneous in its methods. It is unified by its problems; to solve these, education uses methods drawn from many auxiliary disciplines, ranging from the humanistic and historical to the experimental and empirical. The researcher has to identify the historical factors which underlie the present-day nexus of problems. He also has to bring the problems into perspective by observing the aspects they assume in other countries with different historical, social and economic backgrounds. The elective vs. élitist issue can be fully understood only with the aid of studies of how schools differ in the social background of their pupils, and of the attitudes held by parents, teachers and politicians toward the aims and organization of the school. The individual-educational aspect of the grouping or structure problem is best explained by methods derived from developmental and differential psychology. Efforts must be made to map the course of maturation in a certain cultural pattern, and how individual differences manifest themselves at different stages of development. Such a study necessarily involves subtle psychometric and statistical problems. For example, a highly sophisticated method derived from experimental psychology must be designed for a proficient analysis of the reading process.

From the methodological point of view, therefore, education as an academic research discipline is much more heterogeneous than psychology or sociology.

Bibliography: Borg, W.-R.: Educational research: an introduction. New York, 1963. Van Dalen, D.: Understanding educational research. New York, 1962. Ebel, R. (Ed.): Encyclopedia of educational research. 4th ed. New York, 1969. Festinger, L. & Katz, D. (Eds): Research methods in the behavioral sciences. New York, 1953. Gage, N. L. (Ed.): Handbook of research in teaching. Chicago, 1963. Good, C. V. & Scates, D. E.: Methods of research: educational, psychological, sociological. New York, 1954. Kerlinger, F.: Foundations of behavioral research. New York, 1964. Reuchlin, M.: Les méthodes quantitatives en psychologie. Paris, 1962. **Travers, R.**: Introduction to educational research. New York 1963. *T. Husén*

Education, pre-school. The depth psychologists (Freud, Adler, R. A. Spitz, E. H. Erikson, A. Dührssen) have drawn attention to the great importance of pre-school education, particularly for emotional-affective development. On the basis of recent progress in learning psychology, aptitude research and sociolinguistics (J. Mc. Hunt, B. S. Bloom, J. S. Bruner, Bernstein *et al.*) a number of educational measures are being introduced in some countries (e.g. speech training, tuition in reading and modern mathematics, rhythmic exercises) to develop the cognitive and motor capacities of children of pre-school age. The wholly inadequate provision for nursery-school (kindergarten) education to foster individual and social development in a democratic atmosphere is a noticeable feature of some economically advanced countries (e.g. the United Kingdom), where the facilities available tend to be used more by the economically and/or linguistically advantaged than by the disadvantaged, whose children might profit from them at this crucial stage. *H.Ma.*

Educator, personality of. 1. The importance of the educator (parent, teacher, and so on) in the process of education is generally recognized. Ideally, his personality combines a reflection of the system of values which prevails in the culture concerned with pedagogic ability, a mastery of methods and psychological knowledge. His actual personality is determined (apart from wholly individual traits) on the one hand by personal conviction of the validity of dominant societal values (which is unlikely to be complete), and on the other by his personal attitude to the actual process of education (ranging from total commitment to indifference), and his own opinion of the methods used. *H. Schr.*

2. A rough distinction can be made between teachers who adopt a "democratic"

approach and permit their students to participate more in the process of education, and those of a more "authoritarian" personality (q.v.), who interpret leadership as requiring a minimum of consultation and explanation. Aspects of a proficient educational "personality" are: friendliness; consideration for individual and informal as well as official aims in group work; *evident* expertise in, and systematic presentation of, a subject; a mastery of techniques for conveying a sense of enthusiasm; an ability to judge the appropriate ratio of *public* praise and *private* rebuke; and an understanding of the differing requirements of individual personalities in a learning-group (e.g. introversion–extraversion).

Bibliography: Baron, G. & Tropp, A.: Teachers in England and America. In: **Halsey, A. H.** *et al.* (Eds): Education, economy and society. Glencoe, 1961. **Highfield, M. E. & Pinsent, A.**: A survey of rewards and punishments in schools. London, 1952. **Thompson, G. G. & Hunnicutt, C. W.**: The effect of repeated praise or blame on the work achievement of "introverts" and "extraverts". J. educ. Psychol., 1944, *35*, 257–66. *J.C.*

Edwards Personal Preference Schedule. 210 pairs of statements from each of which one has to be chosen; designed to cover fifteen needs from H. A. Murray's list. The statements in each pair are equated in social desirability and this constitutes an advantage over other questionnaires.

Bibliography: Edwards, A. L.: Edwards' Personal Preference Schedule. New York, 1953–59. *R.M.*

EEG. See *Electroencephalogram.*

EEG and personality. Differences between individuals revealed by the electroencephalogram are connected, among other things, with personality characteristics. The significance of this research, which has recently been intensified as a result of electronic EEG evaluation, consists especially in testing hypotheses dealing with personality variables. Results so far obtained are still somewhat contradictory.

Bibliography: Gale, A., Coles, M. & Blaydon, J.: Extraversion—introversion and the EEG. Brit. J. Psychol., 1969, 60, 209–23.   D.B.

Effect, law of. According to E. L. Thorndike, this law, dating from 1898, is the main principle for explaining learning by the method of instrumental conditioning. It states that the effect of any reaction decides whether and to what extent the link between stimulus and reaction occurs. If there is a positive effect from the reaction on the organism (reinforcement, q.v.), the probability of this reaction increases, but, if the effect is negative, the probability that anything will be learnt diminishes (this is known as "extinction"). See *Conditioning*.

Bibliography: Thorndike, E. L.: The psychology of learning. Educational psychology, Vol. 2, New York, 1913.   P.S. & R.S.

Effemination. The state of being, or process of becoming, very effeminate, i.e. displaying woman-like characteristics in mind and/or body. Also used to refer specifically to the female/submissive form of male homosexuality as opposed to the masculine/dominant variety.   G.D.W.

Efference. The term is used in regard to the nerve fibers or tracts conducting potential away from some supply point in a certain direction. It is apparent from the definition that the concept is relative. With respect to the point to which the fibers are leading, the efferent conductors of the source of supply are afferent. Usually it is a case of fibers conducting impulses from the center toward the periphery.

Bibliography: Strong, O. S. & Elwyn, A.: A human neuroanatomy. Baltimore, 1948.   G.A.

Efferent nerves. Efferent nerves conduct electrical currents in the shape of potentials from some source of supply, usually in a direction from the center to the periphery or from major to minor areas. Example: the corticonuclear fibers conduct impulses from the anterior central convolution of the cerebral cortex, etc., into the motor cerebral nerve nuclei of the facial nerve. From here, after crossing the synapses, they run, for example, through the *nervus facialis* (facial nerve, seventh cerebral nerve) into the facial muscles and produce some particular facial expression or cause the eyelids to close. G.A.

Efficiency. A concept and a designation. "Efficiency of statistical assessment or methods" dates back to R. A. Fisher. By that one means a method for quantifying the accuracy of inferential-statistical methods (see *Inference*) of estimation. The criterion (q.v.) for the efficiency of a statistical method of estimation is the variance (q.v.) of its quantities. A procedure giving a narrower scatter of parameter estimations is more efficient than others where estimation quantities have a wider scatter. The efficiency of a significance test can be seen from the size of the random sample which is required for the statistical confirmation of an observed deviation of the coefficients from the parameter (q.v.).

In general, *efficiency* is the ratio of output to effort or energy.   W.H.B.

Ego (syn. *I; Self*). I. A central concept in the psychology of personality. The following are the main interpretations:

1. *In motivation psychology:* the ego is viewed as a source or objective of motivation (examples: "self-assertion" or "egotism"). The meaning is the same in the concept of ego-involvement; this term denotes the extent to which motives centering on the subject's own person (self-assertion, achievement motivation, striving for recognition and influence, etc.) enter into the motivation for a specific behavior.

2. The conception of the ego as the *organizing center for behavior and experience* is related to the above definition. The ego (in accordance with the psychoanalytical concept of the ego as the reality principle; see *Psychoanalysis*) is held responsible for controlling and maintaining the adaptation of the individual to his (physical, mental and social) environment. The term "ego strength" denotes the level of this control over reality (in conflict with competing drives and needs); on the functional level various mechanisms of "ego defense" (e.g. perceptual defense, projection, rationalization) have been described.

3. In empirical personality research the ego is taken to mean the *totality of experiential content and behavior patterns* relating to the subject's own person. The ego is therefore made up of perception of the subject's own personality (self-perception, self-concept) and of trends of action, attitudes and emotions centering on that personality. Self-perception includes, e.g., knowledge of one's own personal development and needs, aims, values, abilities and weaknesses, likes and dislikes, as well as the awareness of living personally in the present. Phenomenological ego-research studies the forms and special characteristics of this ego experience, while behavioral ego-research is confined to the components of self-perception which can be objectivized in tests (including self-esteem and attitude toward the self).

In a mentally sound person, the ego experience is "co-conscious", in the sense defined by H. Rohracher. The entire content of the ego is not continuously present in the consciousness but can be made fully conscious at any time without an effort of memory (e.g. name, marital status, profession, etc.). In a mentally sound individual, the ego experience is also characterized by continuity in space and time; I experience myself always as the same person in spite of changes in time (e.g. from one day to the next) and place (when I travel). On the other hand, various forms of mental illness are characterized

by a disturbed ego experience. For example in schizophrenia (q.v.), continuity in space or time may be limited or completely abolished (the patient may even experience himself simultaneously as several persons), and/or personal orientation is lessened to such an extent that the content of the ego is no longer fully conscious, and can only be reproduced by an effort of memory or in an incomplete or incorrect form.

But less serious behavioral defects, e.g. neuroses (q.v.), are also reflected in the ego experience. Recently the school of client-centered therapy (see *Psychotherapy*) based on the work of C. Rogers has studied the development of neurotic symptoms in this context, and tried to counteract them by psychotherapeutic means. Psycho-diagnostic methods to evaluate self-esteem, ego-ideal discrepancy (q.v.), attitudes to the self, and self-sentiment, etc., are particularly important in this context. Factor-analytical results on these and other objectively testable components of the ego are available, mainly from the school of R. B. Cattell.

On the special significance of the ego in the different strata theories (q.v.) of personality, see Revers (1960).

Bibliography: Cattell, R. B.: Personality and motivation structure and measurement. New York, 1957. **Lersch, P.:** The levels of the mind. In: **David, H. P. & Bracken, H. von** (Eds): Perspectives in personality theory. New York, 1957, 212–7. **Lowe, C. M.:** The self-concept: fact or artifact? Psychol. Bull., 1961, 58, 325–36. Revers, W. J.: Philosophisch orientierte Theorien der Person und Persönlichkeit, in Lersch, P. & Thomae, H. (Eds): Hdb. der Psychol., Vol. 4. Göttingen, 1960. *K. Pawlik*

Ego. II. 1. The term relates primarily to an individual experience. The ego is the most evident content of the consciousness; nevertheless it has been eliminated from experimental psychology, especially of the behaviorist school. Nietzsche defined it as a grammatical illusion. It is extremely difficult to provide an accurate definition of the ego as *individual experience*, because it is present as a component of almost all lived experiences. The characteristics of a central or all-embracing phenomenon are ascribed to the ego. W. Wundt uses the term to denote "the feeling of cohesion of all mental experiences". In the psychic strata theory, it appears as the final, highest layer or as the apex of a pyramid, and is therefore the essential characteristic of the structure of the personality (q.v.). W. James made an important distinction in the sphere of ego experience, when he showed the diversity of experiences comprised in the notion. According to him, there are two aspects of the ego: the knowing ego, i.e. the experience linked with the wide-ranging activities in which the individual sees himself as the subject; and the "self", or empirical ego: the latter covers all the content which the subject experiences in a special manner as belonging to himself.

2. The term acquired a completely new meaning in Freud's theory. In his opinion it is not anchored in self-perception, but in the dynamic mental process, and especially in disturbed mental conditions and conflicts. For Freud, the ego is an area or part of the psychic structure which contrasts with the id (q.v.). To begin with, he considered it to be practically equivalent to the consciousness, until he recognized that functions of the ego may also be unconscious. Originally Freud believed that the ego originated from the id but today psychoanalysis (q.v.) also refers to innate ego-mechanisms, and greater independence is ascribed to the latter (see, e.g., H. Hartmann and E. Kris). The ego permits of adaptation to reality and supports the reality principle (q.v.). Freud has compared it with the rider who "must curb the superior strength of his horse and must borrow the means to do so". Anna Freud has developed the theory of the defense mechanisms of the ego (see *Defense mechanisms*); she states that the ego appears as the decisive component of the psyche to an even greater extent than is postulated in the later writings of Freud himself. But, from the functional as well as from the experiential

aspect, the ego appears to be a very complex phenomenon, and Freud found it necessary to make a distinction between the ego itself and the *super-ego*—as a special structure which is superior to the ego and represents ideals and morality, therefore corresponding broadly to what earlier psychologists had referred to as the *conscience* (q.v.).

3. To the extent that problems of the personality and motivation have been incorporated into empirical psychology primarily in connection with clinical and social psychology, the concept of the ego has again become of interest. However, in order to avoid the arguments which dominated philosophical studies and the psychology of consciousness, the term *ego* has been replaced by the word *self*. One of the classical representatives of learning psychology in the U.S.A., E. R. Hilgard, considers that the mechanisms of adaptation cannot be understood without introducing the concept of the self. Like G. Allport, who suggested the term *proprium* instead of self, Hilgard believes that this concept can establish the link between different phenomena. In this sense, however, the self does not merely denote the unity of the personality. It can best be understood as an individually characteristic centering of the personality. This definition provides the best means of understanding the different ego experiences.

In empirical research the self is now primarily understood as the perception which the subject has of himself. It is apprehended by questionnaire methods which analyze the qualities a person attributes to himself. In a summary of an extensive range of studies, R. Wylie draws attention to the wide margin of uncertainty which still remains.

4. Since the ego can only be studied as a structure, or feature on which the personality centers, research into its development is very difficult, and the results remain hypothetical. No systematic studies seem to have been made of the development of the self-image. This development does not

take place in isolation but as an aspect of the development of the personality structure as a whole. It is not possible to indicate a specific point in time at which the ego is formed. The perception of the subject's own body, which is observed through certain reactions at the end of the first year of life, recognition of his own mirror image, and use of the pronoun "I", defiant attitudes and certain roles played by small children, are initial manifestations which cannot be explained without the "ego" concept (see *Ego discover; Development*). Erikson understands the final stage of ego development as the discovery of one's own identity, and Jung's concept of individuation (q.v.) can be seen as the highest form of ego development: "becoming oneself".

Bibliography: Allport, G. W.: Pattern and growth in personality. New York, 1961. Erikson, E. H.: Identity: Youth and crisis. New York & London, 1968. Freud, S.: The ego and the id. London, ²1962. Hartmann, H.: Ego psychology and the problem of adaptation. New York, 1958. Hilgard, E. R.: Human motives and the concept of the self, Amer. Psychol. 1949, *4*, 374–82. Rogers, C. R.: Client-centered therapy. Boston, 1950. Wylie, R. C.: The self concept. Nebraska, 1961. *R. Meili*

Ego. III. According to Freud, the psychic part system which organizes the primitive and unorganized drives (urges, desires), which are included in the psychic part system known as the id (q.v.), and the drives of the super-ego (q.v.), and then contrives their satisfaction in reality. In doing this it can avail itself of the function of libidinal object cathexis (q.v.) or of object countercathexis; or, in other words, of learning about opportunities for the gratification of a motive and of unlearning about those opportunities which have either proved no longer to lead to the gratification of drives or to be linked to the deprivation of drives. In addition to learning ability, the following must be included (according to Hartmann and Rapaport) among the primary autonomous, i.e. constitutional or innate, characteristics of the ego: ability to react, perception,

intelligence and motor skill, but also frustration tolerance. Different people are distinguished from one another by the degree to which they possess these characteristics. The ego is a construct, but is not identical with the experience and the perception of the self (q.v.).

Bibliography: Freud, S.: The ego and the id. London, ²1962. Hartmann, H., Kris, E. & Löwenstein, R. M.: Comments on the formation of psychic structure. Psychoanalyt. Study of the Child, 1964, *2*, 11–38. Rapaport, D.: The structure of psychoanalytic theory: a systematizing attempt. In: Koch, S.: Psychology: a study of a science, Vol. 3. New York, 1959, 55–183. *W. Toman*

Ego anachoresis. The withdrawal of the ego (e.g.) from non-assimilable contents of the consciousness. This is a defense (q.v.) mechanism in the psychoanalytical sense, which, according to W. T. Winkler, is primarily characteristic of psychotic experience. Ideas lose their "ego-quality" and appear as alien or remotely-controlled. The individual no longer feels responsible for the intolerable content of his consciousness and believes that it is forced upon him by the outside world (connection with projection, q.v.). A whole range of schizophrenic symptoms can be interpreted as ego anachoresis. *W. Sc.*

Ego consciousness. I perceive all that I experience and sense, as well as my memories, etc., as something experienced and sensed *by me*. Knowledge of the self as the subject of experience is ego consciousness. See *Ego*. *V.M.*

Ego discovery. The process by which ego consciousness (q.v.) is acquired, generally during (pre-) puberty. A. Adler (q.v.) has used the term in a narrower sense to denote the awareness of individual existence acquired in the second year of life. *W.Sc.*

Ego function. The activity of the ego (q.v.); intelligence, perception, etc. In psychoanalysis, H. Hartmann makes a distinction between *primary autonomous* ego functions (perception, thought, reality testing, ability to judge) and *secondary autonomous* functions. See *Defense*. *W.Sch.*

Ego ideal. The person, or idea of such a person (or persons), that, on the basis of an individual's subjective experience or knowledge, superlatively embodies the tendencies and motives of his own super-ego (q.v.); the super-ego being the system of desires and motives of persons with whom the individual has identified.
Bibliography: Freud, S.: Introductory lectures on psycho-analysis. London, ³1929. *W.T.*

Ego-ideal discrepancy. According to Rogers, a discrepancy between the (desired) self-image and actual experiences of oneself. This is a situation of tension (e.g. neurotic), because behavior is determined differently by the desire (*a*) of the whole organism, and (*b*) of the self, for fulfillment.
Bibliography: Rogers, C. R.: A theory of therapy, personality and interpersonal relationships, as developed in the client-centered framework. In: Koch, S. (Ed.): Psychology, a study of a science, Vol. 3. New York, 1959. *H.W.*

Ego involvement. A designation introduced by Sherif & Cantril for all those attitudes which determine the status (q.v.) of a person or assign him a role (q.v.) in relation to other individuals, groups or institutions. Behavior can be designated as ego-involved when, in the course of development, acquired attitudes related to one's own ego (q.v.) are brought into play in a certain situation by relevant objects, people or groups, so that either a high degree of participation is produced or attitudes relative to one's own ego, the image of one's ego, etc., are called upon. *W.D.F.*
Bibliography: Sherif, M. & Cantril, H.: The psychology of ego involvements. New York, 1947.

Ego strength. See *Ego*.

Ego(t)ism. Selfish, ego-centered, unsocial behavior. Various psychological theories (see *Psychoanalysis; Reinforcement*) imply that in the last analysis all behavior, even when seemingly altruistic, is actually egoistic. See *Altruism*. *D.B.*

Ehrenfels, Christian von. B. 20/6/1859 in Rodaun (Lower Austria); d. 8/9/1932 in Lichtenau (Lower Austria). Professor of Philosophy at Prague in 1900; discovered the gestalt characteristics of transposability, supersummativity, paradigms: melody), which makes him one of the pioneers of gestalt psychology. See *Ganzheit*.
Works: Uber Gestaltqualitäten, 1890 (Eng. trans.: *Soc. Res.*, 1944, *11*, 78–99). System der Werttheorie, 1898. Grundzüge der Ethik, 1907. Die Religion der Zukunft, 1929.
Bibliography: Petermann, B.: The gestalt theory. London, 1932. Weinhandl, F. (Ed.): Gestalthaftes Sehen. Ergebnisse und Aufgaben der Morphologie. Darmstadt, 1960. *K.E.P.*

Ehrenstein's illusion. An optical illusion in which a given square containing straight radiating lines seems to be distorted into a trapezium. See *Geometrical-optical illusions*.
Bibliography: Ehrenstein, W.: Probleme der ganzheitpsychol. Wahrnehmungslehre. Leipzig, 1947. *P.S.*

Eidesis. According to Hellpach, characteristic of a certain stage in the juvenile's development when imagination predominates.

Eidetic imagery. Vivid visual images of specific objects that are not present in actuality are "seen" by the subject (usually a child), who is generally conscious that these are not directly sensed images of the external world.

Eigenraum. In the psychology of W. Stern, *Eigenraum* is the space required for the dynamic manifestation of the individual body, which through its personal three-dimensionality determines certain qualities (up, down, in front, etc.) of that space, which is thereby differentiated from non-qualitative Euclidean space.   *J.M.*

Eigenzeit. In W. Stern's "personalistic psychology" (q.v.), *Eigenzeit* is the multidimensional or polyrhythmic individual time featuring several modes within mathematical time. The personal past and the future as modes of the present, co-determine, together with the actual present, an individual life as an indivisible whole.   *J.M.*

Einfühlung. See *Empathy*.

Ejaculation. The discharge of sperm during the male orgasm. Today it is no longer assumed that there is any equivalent of ejaculation in the sexual reaction cycle of women. Ejaculation is primarily a reflex process, accompanied by cortical activity. The concept of male potency includes the ability to postpone any ejaculation (see *Circumcision*). As a rule, an ejaculation is followed by a refractory period which varies in length according to the individual and terminates the erection (q.v.) relatively quickly. The object of postponing ejaculation is to avoid too early a conclusion of coitus (q.v.). Such control of ejaculation can be acquired by practice or allegedly be replaced by aphrodisiacs (q.v.). It is usually a consequence of the role (q.v.) which the male partner assumes, and its frequency increases with higher standards of education. An ejaculation which in the opinion of the couple has occurred too quickly is known as *ejaculatio praecox*. To define this concept precisely does not seem possible; in principle an ejaculation could only be diagnosed as premature if it occurred before, during or immediately after the insertion of the penis.   *G.L.*

Elaborated code. See *Restricted code*.

Electra complex. The heroine of the Greek tragedy has given her name to the feminine variant of the Oedipus complex (q.v.). Just as a boy, according to Freud, in the early genital (q.v.) or Oedipal phase begins to love his mother and to compete with his father, so a girl turns from the primary object of her love, the mother, to the secondary object, the father, and competes with the mother for his favor. The Electra complex is overcome in a way similar to that of the Oedipus complex by repressing (q.v.) a part of the love-desires directed at the father and by identification with the mother. If the complex is not completely overcome, there is fixation (q.v.) which under stress (q.v.) at some later date can cause regression (q.v.) to this phase, and neurotic disorders, especially anxiety hysteria and conversion hysteria.

Bibliography: Freud, S.: Introductory lectures on psycho-analysis. London, ²1929.   *W.T.*

Electrocardiogram (abb. EKG). Recording the electric action potential of the heart by the use of electrocardiographs which consist of electrical activators and a writing system working on the galvanometer principle. Depending on the position of the electrode leads, the following are distinguished: W. Eindhoven's lead from the extremities, a Wilsonian lead, or a parietal lead from the chest. An electrocardiogram supplies information about the electrical phenomena in the heart which are associated with some excitation, but only qualified information about the remaining function of the heart. It is used for the diagnosis of disturbances in rhythm and the conduction of excitation, of phenomena due to oxygen deficiency, of cardiac infarcts and of changes in the tissue content.   *E.D.*

Electrodiagnostics. A field of medical diagnostics. Methodologically the following fields can be distinguished: (a) locating and recording currents and voltages in the living organism (e.g. encephalography, q.v.); (b) using electric currents and voltages to test excitability; (c) measuring electrical properties of cells or groups of cells (see *Galvanic skin response*). See also *Electrophysiology*.

K.E.P.

Electroencephalogram. See *Encephalography*.

Electrolytic stimulus. An inadequate stimulus producing a sensory effect by electro-chemical processes.   F.-C.S.

Electrophysiology. The field of physiology which deals with the electrical phenomena in organisms and in studying the latter uses chiefly electrical techniques and methods of measurement. Applied and specialized electrophysiology has as its objects of research: (a) the recording of bioelectrical reactions to the general and reliable demonstration of excitations; (b) the relating of central or peripheral patterns of excitation derived electrically to certain functional states in the living organism. General electrophysiology works in particular on the following: (a) research into the conditions of artificial (especially electrical) stimulation which leads to arousal (q.v.); (b) study of the elementary processes which underlie resting potential as well as the actual process of arousal. ·   K.E.P.

Electroretinography (abb. ERG). The measurement of the electrical processes in the eye. The retina when not exposed to light has a direct voltage potential, as can be shown to be the case with the intact eyeball (cornea positive with respect to the posterior pole of the eye). This direct voltage potential is changed by the influence of light. A distinction is drawn between an a-, b-, c- and d-spike. *Electroretinogram* (ERG): the record obtained.

Bibliography: Müller-Limmroth, W.: Elektrophysiologie des Gesichtssinns. Berlin-Göttingen-Heidelberg, 1959.   R.R.

Electroshock therapy (abb. ECT). Convulsions and unconsciousness produced by an electrical current passing through two electrodes attached to the scalp. If the indications are correctly assessed and possible contraindications considered, complications tend to be more infrequent and harmless than with most other major medical operations. Even today, in many cases—acute catatonia and serious depression—electroshock is still the most reliable and simple treatment and the one least likely to have serious complications.

A.Hi.

Electrotonus. A term in electrophysiology for the change in state of excitable structures (e.g. nerves) when direct current with below threshold voltage is passed through. After local excitation, i.e. after the current has spread out into the region of the locally affected points ("physical electrotonus"), there occurs, simultaneously with the crossing of the threshold (the least possible conditions for intensity, duration and rapidity must be observed), an extension of the change in excitability associated with the passage of current and hence in capacity to transmit ("physiological electronus"). The nerve through which current has passed shows at the anode diminished (anelectrotonus), and at the cathode increased (catelectrotonus), excitability.   F.-C.S.

Elementarism. This term denotes in general the endeavor to describe complex phenomena or totalities as the sums of more simple elements (of which they are thought to be composed). In this sense elementarism is related to reductionism, atomism or molecularism and is used in various academic fields. Historically it denotes in particular the system of W. Wundt (q.v.), where the contents of consciousness are split up into two kinds of elements, those of sensation and those of feeling. The expression is used pejoratively by Wundt's critics. *P.M.*

Elements, psychology of. Those trends in psychology which believed that psychic events could be reduced to small units (elements) such as sensations (q.v.) and associations (q.v.) (see *Psychophysics*, and also *Wundt*). This concept of the psychology of elements is disputed, especially by gestalt psychology. See *Ganzheit*.

Bibliography: Boring, E. G.: A history of experimental psychology. New York, ²1950. Fechner, G. T.: Elemente der Psychophysik. Leipzig, 1860. Wundt, W.: Grundzüge der physiologischen Psychol. Leipzig ⁵1902. *P.S.*

Élite. A term taken from eighteenth-century French, and meaning "the pick". It is a term used in sociology and social psychology when evaluating or analyzing small groups in some existing society who hold an important position with respect to certain activities or offices of power, or from whose ranks future holders of such positions and offices will repeatedly be drawn. Lasswell and others take the view that in the analytical sense there as many élites as there are values in any society.

Starting from Machiavelli, V. Pareto in particular put forward the anti-parliamentarian view of the cycle of élites. Expressed in very simplified terms, Pareto argues that every society has by nature an oligarchical structure. Within a (ruling) élite there are however always two tendencies the strength of which varies: the will to power by force (the "lions") and the desire to use intellectualizing tactics (the "foxes"). After some social change (e.g. a revolution), the group of the "lions" initially takes over the government; gradually, however, tactics and strategies have to be developed in order to be able to hold on to the privileges resting on power. Thus the "foxes" come into their own, and

they may also be drawn from the non-élite. The assumption of power by the "foxes" mobilizes in turn the "lions" in the non-élite (the masses) among whom there are likewise "foxes" who are also joined by the foxes of the élite. These provide the masses with possible tactics and strategy so that a revolution can be initiated, to be followed by a new cycle.

Bibliography: Lasswell, H. D., Lerner, D. & Rothwell, C. E.: The comparative study of élites. Stanford (Calif.), 1952. Pareto, V.: Trattato di sociologia generale, 1918. *W.D.F.*

Emancipation. See *Social psychology*.

Emancipation, sexual. In contrast to sex education (q.v.), sexual emancipation can be understood to mean the endeavor to have sexuality (q.v.) regarded as a matter for purely individual concern, free from any interference by the State or any institution. This includes a critical analysis of the ways in which a society is organized socio-economically and politically and also of its sexual morality (e.g. abstinence, q.v., homosexuality, q.v., form of marriage). Sexual emancipation is usually regarded as a necessary constituent of any political revolution. In the twentieth century a further decisive impetus in this direction was given by Freud, W. Reich, H. Horkheimer and H. Marcuse.

In a narrower sense, sexual emancipation aims at helping those sections of society whose sexual behavior at any given moment is under social pressure (e.g. children, juveniles, women). Thus the sexual emancipation of woman denotes liberation from social constraints (e.g. double standards of morality) as part of a campaign for legal, social and economic equality.

Bibliography: Beauvoir, S. de: The second sex. New York & London, 1952. Horkheimer, M. et al.: Studien über Autorität und Familie. Paris, 1936. Kursbuch No. 17: Frau, Familie, Gesellschaft. Frankfurt, 1969. Marcuse, H.: Eros and civilization. Boston, 1955. Reich, R.: The sexual revolution: toward a self-governing character structure. New York, 1945. *J.F.*

Embedded figures. An experimental arrangement devised by Gottschaldt (1926) for the perception of figures. Simple geometrical figures have to be found in more complex ones. It is of the utmost importance that parts of the complex settings should not correspond to the embedded figures. Exercises set in this way prove very difficult to solve. Gottschaldt's figures were used by R. Meili (1943) and L. L. Thurstone (1944) in factor analyses (plasticity and flexibility of closure) and by H. A. Witkin (1954) for "field independence".
Bibliography: Gottschaldt, K.: Über den Einfluss der Erfahrung auf die Wahrnehmung von Figuren. Psychol. Forsch., 1926, *8*, 261–317.

P.S. & R.M.

Emergency function. Defined by Cannon as a heightened mental-physical activity which is controlled by the sympathetic division of the autonomic nervous system. It includes, e.g., the secretion of adrenaline, liberation of glycogen from the liver, an increase in the blood sugar level and an acceleration of the blood flow to the brain, heart and skeletal muscles. According to Cannon's theory (which has not been empirically confirmed in every detail), the emergency functions are accompanied by emotional reactions and prepare for flight and combat. See *Emotion*.
Bibliography: Cannon, W. B.: The wisdom of the body. New York, 1932.   *W.Sc.*

Emergency theory of the emotions. See *Emergency function*.

Emmert's law or phenomenon. A law named after F. C. Emmert: the apparent size of the afterimage changes proportionally to the change in distance of the projection screen from the observer. Formula: $l' = \dfrac{l\acute{a}}{a}$ (l' = size of afterimage; l = size of stimulus object, a' = distance of eye from afterimage; a = distance of eye from stimulus object).

K.E.P.

Emmetropia. Normal sight in contrast to hyperopia (q.v.) and myopia (q.v.).

Emotion. The term emotion can have many meanings and has been defined in many ways. It is applied to a distinctive category of experience for which a variety of verbal labels is used: fear, anger, love, and so on. Most writers agree that it is a complex state involving heightened perception of an object or situation, widespread bodily changes, an appraisal of felt attraction or repulsion, and behavior organized toward approach or withdrawal. The urge toward action is one of the strongest subjective experiences of emotion, contained in the etymological source (Latin *e* [out] and *movere* [to move]).

Theories of emotion have been offered by existentialists, philosophers, psychiatrists, ethologists and neurophysiologists, and by many psychologists. Methods of study range from pure intuitive understanding (empathy), through the systematic study of subjective experience, to precise quantitative recordings of behavior and physiological change.

Phenomenologists have argued that we must go directly to subjective experience to understand the quality and significance of human emotion. Jaspers (1912) has outlined the method in relation to psychiatry, and there are various modern versions. These attempt to characterize the nature of man's experience of his world and himself, especially in relation to other people. The phenomenological approach has generally been regarded as antithetical to the experimental method: "Essences and facts are incommensurables" (Sartre, 1948).

Behaviorists, on the other hand, have traditionally rejected the subjective ("mentalistic") approach and have argued that the meaning of the term emotion must be limited to outwardly observable events (see Brown & Farber, 1951). Contemporary psychologists, however, are on the whole willing to encompass testimony from many sources, provided an attempt is made to scale or quantify.

1. *Assessment of emotion.* Three main categories of data are recognized: verbal, physiological and overt behavior. Most experimental work has probably been carried out on physiological changes. The role of the autonomic nervous system (q.v.) is seen as of special significance. Cannon (1929) assigned to its parasympathetic division the role of conserver of bodily energies, and to its sympathetic division an "emergency" function. This view has dominated the field. During sympathetic excitation, widespread changes occur which can be readily measured: sweating is increased, the heart beats faster, and blood is redistributed to the muscles. Further adrenergic changes include liberation of sugar into the bloodstream, improved contraction of fatigued muscle, more rapid coagulation of the blood, and so on; in this way the organism is mobilized for prompt and efficient action. Measurement of these changes has given rise to a vast literature on the assessment of emotions.

Such assessment is incomplete without examining overt emotional *behavior* and, in the case of human subjects, emotional *experience*. This latter can be inferred from verbal reports, and increasing use is being made of questionnaires, scales, feeling "thermometers", repertory grids and personal check lists. Studies of overt emotional behavior include facial and vocal expression, gesture and posture.

Approach/avoidance behavior, once linked with a simple instinct mechanism, is being analyzed in terms of subject/object relations, as well as the affective processes ("hedonic tone") which accompany it. Schneirla (1959) has postulated that stimulus intensity basically determines the direction of reaction, low intensity stimulation tending to evoke approach reactions. The attachment behavior of young mammals can be examined in this context (Bowlby, 1969).

The relationship among different measures of emotion has proved to be highly compli-

cated. Even within autonomic changes, individual patterns of reaction occur. Lang (1967) has reported that different measures of fear taken concurrently from phobic subjects do not necessarily yield responses of the same relative strength. A subject might report extremely intense fear yet not necessarily show marked physiological changes, or behavioral avoidance of the feared object. High relationships among measures cannot be assumed. They must be examined empirically. The development of response configurations in individuals is seen to reflect the fact that different components (verbal, physiological, behavioral) are "shaped" (i.e. learned) in accordance with past reinforcement schedules. See *Anxiety*.

2. *Genesis of emotion.* Many authors have postulated the presence at birth of some diffuse excitement, which becomes differentiated and associated with certain situations and motor responses to form the separate emotions. Others have attempted to identify a single specific source of emotion in pleasure/unpleasure, anxiety, love, or a basic pair of opposites such as love and aggression. A single fund of energy capable of endless transformations has been posited repeatedly.

The opposing view is that emotions are inherited and distinct entities, and various numbers of basic passions have been proposed. Earlier instinct theories, as well as modern ethology, tend to subscribe to this view. For them, emotions provide the appropriate driving force for specific instinctual behavior. Through a process of integration and differentiation of primary feelings, an array of derived emotions can be developed.

Numerous developmental mechanisms have been proposed. Various diffuse forms of early experience are known to be relevant. Harlow (1958) has emphasized the role of sensory contact in the infant's early life; Bowlby (1969) has stressed maternal separation. In addition, a number of studies have dealt with the effect of stimulation during infancy on subsequent emotionality. Learning processes, in particular classical conditioning, have been examined by the behaviorists. The role of individual differences in basic neural functioning and ability to learn have been repeatedly stressed (Eysenck, 1967).

No very clear evidence exists for different patterns of physiological reaction in different emotional states (but see studies reviewed by Arnold, 1960, on fear and anger). It seems that human subjects tend to give an emotional label to bodily changes on the basis of prevailing situational factors. It has been suggested that it will only be possible to distinguish one emotional state from another by taking account of specific physiological, specific cognitive and specific behavioral patterns—and then only in conjunction with given eliciting conditions (Lazarus, 1968).

A large number of studies (reviewed by Goldstein, 1968) have sought the neurological structures and circuits involved in emotional behavior. Papez (1937) first proposed a theory of emotion involving the limbic system and this view has persisted. This system may serve as a "visceral brain" which processes internal information rather than external symbols. In man, neocortical-hypothalamic interrelations probably play a role in the fusion of emotional processes with those of perception, memory and learning. The role of the ascending reticular activating system has also been considered in relation to the concepts of arousal (q.v.) and emotion. It has been suggested that emotion falls on the extreme of a single arousal continuum (Duffy, 1962). However, recent authors have differentiated the arousal role of the reticular activating system from that of the limbic system (Eysenck, 1967; Gellhorn & Loufbourrow, 1963; Routtenberg, 1968). They make the point that the two systems, while interrelating physiologically, can be separated conceptually.

3. *The current position.* The shift in emphasis is toward psychological models involving cognition and information processing: the way our vocabulary of feeling is learned and used (Davitz, 1969); the narrowing of cue utilization that occurs in emotion

(Easterbrook, 1959), the comparison of a perceived stimulus with the memory store (Sokolov, 1960), often leading to expectancies and uncertainties (Pribram, 1967), and to assessment and appraisal (Arnold, 1960; Lazarus, 1968).

The theme of emotion as energy, which must be discharged or released if a proper organismic balance is to be maintained, continues to be explored. Current models tend to implicate feedback and cybernetic principles in the regulation of homeostasis. Ways of releasing energy include not only catharsis and abreaction, but perhaps the recently described implosion theory (Stampfl, 1966); Pribram (1967) also suggests that the individual can exert self-control, that is, make internal adjustments that will lead to re-equilibration without recourse to action.

In spite of so much effort, the function of the emotions still remains uncertain. Recently some have asked whether all emotions fit the basic model of the "emergency" reactions, that is, follow a sequence of build-up and discharge of energy. Many have come to feel that too much attention has been concentrated on the energy-mobilizing half of the emotional spectrum, and too little on positive emotional experiences leading to growth, expansion and self-development (Arnold, 1960; Hillman, 1960; Koestler, 1964). In order to reach a more comprehensive account of human emotion, investigators in the next decade will probably give more attention to these positive, often relational properties of emotion, as well as to the more subtle categories of subjective experience.

Bibliography: Arnold, Magda, B.: Emotion and personality. 2 vols. New York, 1960. Bowlby, J.: Psychopathology of anxiety: the role of affectional bonds. Ch. 12. In: Lader, M. H. (Ed.): Studies of anxiety, Brit. J. Psychiat. Special Publication No. 3, 1969. Brown, J. S. & Farber, I. E.: Emotions conceptualized as intervening variables: with suggestions toward a theory of frustration. Psychol. Bull. 1951, *48*, 465–95. Cannon, W. B.: Bodily changes in pain, hunger, fear and rage. New York, ²1929. Davitz, J. R.: The language of emotion. New York, 1969. Duffy, Elizabeth: Activation and behavior.

New York, 1962. **Easterbrook, J. A.**: The effect of emotion on cue utilization and the organization of behavior. Psychol. Rev. 1959, *66*, 183–201. **Eysenck, H. J.**: The biological basis of personality. London & Springfield, 1967. **Gellhorn, E. & Loofbourrow, G. N.**: Emotions and emotional disorders. New York, 1963. **Goldstein, M. L.**: Physiological theories of emotion: a critical historical review from the standpoint of behavior theory. Psychol. Bull. 1968, *69*, 23–40. **Harlow, H. F.**: The nature of love. Amer. Psychol. 1958, *12*, 673–85. **Hillman, J.**: Emotion: a comprehensive phenomenology of theories and their meanings for therapy. London, 1960. **Jaspers, K.**: The phenomenological approach in psychopathology. (Trans. of original article in the Zeitschrift fur die gesamte Neurologie und Psychiatrie, 1912, Vol. 9, 391–408). Brit. J. Psychiat. 1968, *114*, 1313–23. **Koestler, A.**: The act of creation. London, 1964. **Lang, P.**: Fear reduction and fear behaviour: problems in treating a construct. In: **Shlien, J. M.** (Ed.): Research in psychotherapy, Vol. 3, 1967. **Lazarus, R.**: Emotions and adaptation. In: **Arnold, W. J.** (Ed.): Nebraska Symposium on Motivation. Nebraska, 1968. **Papez, J. W.**: A proposed mechanism of emotion. Arch. Neurol. Psychiat. 1937, *38*, 725–43. **Pribram, K. H.**: The new neurology and the biology of emotion. Amer. Psychol. 1967, *22*, 830–38. **Routtenberg, A.**: The two arousal hypotheses: reticular formation and limbic system. Psychol. Rev. 1968, *75*, 51–80. **Sartre, J. P.**: Emotions: outline of a theory. New York, 1948. **Schneirla, T. C.**: An evolutionary and developmental theory of biphasic process underlying approach and withdrawal. In: **Jones, M. R.** (Ed.): Nebraska Symposium on Motivation. Nebraska, 1959. **Sokolov, E. N.**: Neuronal models and the orienting reflex. In: **Brazier, M. A. B.** (Ed.): The central nervous system and behavior. New York, 1960, 187–276. **Stampfl, T. G.**: Implosive therapy: the theory, the subhuman analogue, the strategy, and the technique. In: **Armitage, S. G.** (Ed.): Behavior Modification Techniques in the Treatment of Emotional Disorders. Battle Creek, Michigan: VA Publication, 1966, 12–21.

I. Martin

Emotionality. A collective concept for the individual nature of the emotional life and of the control and processing of affects. In factor-analytical personality research emotionality denotes a factor of the second order in behavioral judgments and personality questionnaires; in the relevant primary factors there are significant differences between neurotics and normal people. See *Neuroticism*.

K.P.

Emotion, transference of. During psychotherapy (q.v.), the patient frequently transfers emotional reactions (which are often unconscious) to the psychiatrist (see *Transference*). He experiences his own feelings as though they originated in the psychiatrist (see *Projection*). While Freud considered that transference involved only wrongly-directed, infantile and repressed emotions, other psychoanalytical authors use the term "transference" to denote any emotional contact between analyst and patient. In the broader sense, the transference of emotions may denote all transference by "infection" (see *Empathy; Ideomotor law*).

W.Sc.

Emotivity. Excessive emotional excitability. Emotivity appears as a symptom of illness in various psychopathological conditions. See *Psychopathology; Psychoses*.

P.S.

Empathy. A term used for the endeavor to add to extraneous behavior with the object of understanding the other person. The way to experience is primarily through linguistic communication, but it can also come through a spontaneous expression of feeling. In psychological practice (*inter alia*, conversation therapy, educational guidance, q.v.), considerable importance is attached to empathy.

P.S.

Empiricism. A philosophical doctrine according to which sensory experience, instead of reason with its organizational principles, is the source of cognition (the memory records repetition by learning, association and induction); the knowledge of things and their structure comes from without to the inquirer (Francis Bacon; Hume; J. S. Mill). In scientific methodology, empiricism no longer denotes the manner of cognition, but the experimental basis of modern science:

a free interchange between the observation of facts and the construction of hypothetico-deductive *models* (q.v.) which proves the explanatory predictive accuracy of the model. For "logical empiricism" see *Positivism*.

M.-J.B.

Encephalitis. Cerebral inflammation. An infectious (viral, bacterial, parasitical) inflammation of the cerebral tissue and frequently also of the meninges (meningoencephalitis) or of the spinal cord (encephalomyelitis), with psychological symtoms (e.g. fatigue, delirium). There is usually permanent organic and mental damage. Numerous clinical sub-forms exist.

Encephalitis, traumatic. An incorrect designation for traumatic *encephalopathy* (q.v.).

Encephalization. Increase in weight of the brain and in anatomical-physiological cerebral differentiation, especially of the cerebrum and its functions in the course of phylogenesis (q.v.) and ontogenesis (q.v.). Encephalization is linked with differentiation and the distinct emergence of the cortical function as against the brain stem (see *Brain*), and during this time there is increasing dependence of sensory and motor functions on the intactness of the cortex (progressive encephalization) and a correspondingly greater predominance of the activity of consciousness in comparison with the deep layers.

The concept of encephalization makes it possible to compare types. E. Dubois describes (1930) encephalization level as the ratio between brain weight and body weight. According to Hofstätter (1957) it is directly proportional to the attainable level of maturation and inversely proportional to the speed of maturation.

Bibliography: Dubois, E.: Die phylogenetische Grosshirnzunahme, Biologia Generalis, 1930, *6*. Hofstätter, P. R.: Psychologie. Frankfurt, 1957.

F.-C.S.

Encephalography. Taking a record of the living brain (q.v.). There are different techniques for recording the function and structure of the brain. In the electroencephalogram (EEG) the electrical voltage fluctuations are registered by electrodes from the undamaged human skull and, when suitably amplified, recorded. This enables the doctor to diagnose how alert the brain is and how it is functioning, whether there are any disturbances and tumors or epileptic foci (Kugler, 1966). With suitable electronic aids, responses to sensory stimuli can be recognized from the encephalogram (Keidel, 1965). Most recently, even the electrical activity of deep brain structures has been recorded by means of suitable needle electrodes (Bechterewa, 1969). With the aid of *pneumoencephalography* the cerebral ventricles can be shown with X-rays if they have previously been filled with air for this purpose (see *Ventricles*). Finally, mechanical changes in the brain such as displacement resulting from hemorrhage and tumors or from liquid in the case of hydrocephalus can be measured supersonically by means of echo-encephalography (Schiefer & Kazner, 1967).

Bibliography: Bechterewa, N. P. *et al.*: Physiologie und Pathophysiologie der tiefen Hirnstrukturen des Menschen. Berlin, 1969. Keidel, W. D.: Neuere Ergebnisse der Physiologie des Hörens. Arch. Ohren-, Nasen- und Kehlkopfheilkunde, 1965, *185*, No. 2. Kugler, J.: Elektroencephalographie in Klinik und Praxis. Stuttgart, 1966. Schiefer, W. & E. Kazner: Klinische Echo-Encephalographie. Berlin & New York, 1967.   E.D.

Encephalon (see *Brain*). It consists of the parts of the central nervous system (q.v.) contained in the skull: cerebrum, diencephalon, etc. Histologically, it is composed of grey (nerve cell bodies) and white (nerve paths) matter. See *Cerebrum*.   E.D.

Encephalopathy. A nosological term for a general cerebral illness or for a condition resulting from some brain damage, the organic basis but not the precise cause of which is obvious enough. While the medical term was already being used in the second half of the nineteenth century by various European specialists, neurologists and psychiatrists, it was not until 1904 that Brissaud and Souques used the concept "*encéphalopathie infantile*" for chronic changes in the infantile brain where the causes could not be understood more precisely.

The cause is damage of the most varied kind to the cells of the ovum and the sperm (gametopathies), to the morula and the blastula (blastopathies), to the embryo (embryopathy), to the fetus (fetopathy), all known collectively as prenatal encephalopathy, and to the brain during birth (perinatal encephalopathy), or until physiological maturity at the age of seven.

The somatic symptoms which may appear are: General retardation of physical development (somatic retardation), deformities (dysplasia), hormonal dysfunctions, autonomic dysregulations, awkward motor activity, motor weakness (nervousness) or restricted movement, slight disorders of coordination, deficient muscular tonus, irregular neural functioning, facial rigidity (hypomimia), bayonet fingers, indistinct speech, etc., together with an irregular encephalogram, albumen irregularity in the cerebral fluid and symmetrical or asymmetrical deformations of the cerebral ventricles.

The following mental and psychic symptoms appear: disturbance of the sense of reality and time; pleasure taken in disturbing, destroying, tormenting and disparaging in the sense of a basic apocritical attitude; excess or deficiency of drive with slowness of response and action; poor social behavior with marked disturbances in conforming to the social situation; incontinence of affect, sudden fluctuations of mood, performance and social behavior with a dysphoric basic mood or vague euphoria; greater irritability with a tendency to violent fits of rage, etc. A distinct disturbance of the ability to learn (as represented in the form of a minimum

peak in the development profile according to C. Bühler and H. Hetzer) can appear as a major symptom. See *Brain pathology*.

Bibliography: Engels, H. J.: Über die Störung der Lernfähigkeit bei frühkindlicher Hirnschädigung. Acta Paedopsychiatrica, 1966, *33*, 67–77.

H. J. Engels

Encephalopathy, traumatic. A condition resulting from traumatic brain damage (e.g. boxer syndrome). There are three stages: slight psychic disturbances (e.g. affective disorders: irritability, lack of self-control or disturbances of the ability to learn); distinct psychopathic phenomena; serious motor and character disturbances. There are almost always autonomic symptoms as well.

F.-C.S.

Encopresis. Involuntary defecation in children even after the age when habits of cleanliness should have been learnt (approximately at the age of three) in contrast to *incontinentia alvi* (weakness of the anal sphincter muscle) due to some organic cause; analogously to enuresis (q.v.), a primary encopresis where habits of cleanliness have not yet been completely acquired is distinguished from a secondary encopresis, renewed incontinence after such habits have been learnt for a year; there are also: *diurnal encopresis* (incontinence during the day) and *nocturnal encopresis* (incontinence during the night); active, voluntary as distinct from passive, involuntary encopresis. There is affinity to psychosomatic symptoms: obstipation, colitis, diarrhea. Treatment: analysis of the supposed underlying conflict (q.v.), play and behavior therapy (q.v.).

Bibliography: Anthony, E. J.: An experimental approach to the psychopathology of childhood: Encopresis. Brit. J. med. Psychol., 1957, *30*, 146–75. Bellmann, M.: Studies on encopresis. Acta Paediatrica Scandinaviae. Stockholm, 1966, Suppl. 170. Biermann, G.: Einkotende Kinder. Psyche, 1951/52, *5*, 618–27.

W.J.S.

Enculturation. An aspect of socialization (q.v.) which can also be described as cultural education. Enculturation denotes the conscious or unconscious acquisition or acceptance of cultural standards and symbols. It differs from acculturation (q.v.) in referring to individuals, not to groups.   *W.D.F.*

End action. The final phase of an instinctive action which is satisfying some urge and proceeding according to some pattern shaped by heredity, e.g. the devouring of prey. See *Instinct.*   *U.H.S.*

Endocrine glands. Thyroid and parathyroid glands, thymus, adrenal glands, pancreas, ovaries, testicles and hypophysis, i.e. glands secreting internally. They represent well-defined cell complexes and are mostly independent organs. Inside their cells they form substances (see *Hormones*) which pass into the blood stream, are distributed by circulation throughout the body, and play an active part in metabolic processes. They chiefly represent part of a humoral feedback system (q.v.) and their function is controlled by the hypophysis (q.v.).   *E.D.*

Endocrine psychosyndrome. This syndrome is in general characterized by anomalies of drive and mood which are not due to diffuse brain damage or some general metabolic disorder. The following symptoms are found: affective dullness and a general slowness of reaction in a case of myedema; indifference and lack of drive in a case of Simmond's cachexia or the Sheehan syndrome (insufficiency of the anterior lobe of the hypophysis, often associated with *anorexia nervosa*; there is no agreement about a possibly identical etiology); a slight tetany (electrolytic imbalance) often shows dysphoric ill humor and a tendency to fatigue; the mood fluctuates from apathy to excitement in the Cushing syndrome (over-production of glucocorticoid); fluctuations of drive and mood in Klinefelter's syndrome (outward form masculine but chromosomal sex feminine); a patient suffering from Basedow's disease is over-excitable, generally restless and experiences fluctuations of mood (over-activity of the thyroid).   *U.H.S.*

Endocrinology. The study of the endocrine (q.v.) glands and the effects of hormones (q.v.).

Endoderm. See *Entoderm.*

Endogamy. A social rule prescribing that the partner in marriage should be sought inside one's own group. An individual may therefore not go too far from his family, either in a horizontal (geographical) or a vertical (in regard to social strata) direction. The rule prescribing endogamy serves, as does the rule prescribing exogamy (q.v.), to perpetuate both the particular family and the wider social structure. With mates from culturally similar groups there are fewer difficulties in mutual adaptation and the chances of a stable family are consequently greater. In addition, the continuity of group culture is maintained because the children receive a social upbringing specific to the particular group.
Bibliography: Goode, W. J.: The sociology of the family. In: Merton, R. K., Broom, L. & Cottrell, L. S. (Eds): Sociology today. New York, 1959.   *S.K.*

Endogenous. Originating from within. The result of natural endowment and not conditioned by environmental influences. Ant. *Exogenous* (q.v.).

Endogenous psychoses. Strictly speaking, this term refers to psychoses which appear to have no precipitating environmental cause but are due to some functional change within the individual. Used chiefly to distinguish between the so-called endogenous depressions which develop "out of the blue" and reactive depressions which have a demonstrable environmental cause. This distinction has been criticized by many authorities who claim that the distinction is one of severity rather than etiology. *R.H.*

Endomorph(ic type). Growth dimension (somatotype). Main characteristics: "round, soft, fat", compact body structure with strongly pronounced digestive and respiratory organs, bones relatively fragile. The psychic correlate is viscerotonia (q.v.). The normal complete endomorphic type resembles the pyknic (q.v.).
Bibliography: Sheldon, W. H.: Varieties of human physique. New York, 1940. *W.K.*

Endopsychic. Psychoanalytical term meaning "within the mind". *Endopsychic structure* refers to the structure of the mind: id, ego, super-ego, conscious, preconscious, unconscious, and so on. *Endopsychic processes* include *endopsychic censorship* (the mechanism by which unacceptable material is prevented from reaching consciousness), and *endopsychic suicide* (mental suicide). See *Intrapsychic*. *G.D.W.*

Endothymic basis. A term from Lersch's personality theory. "Three kinds of experience" are found "in this psychic area", "the stationary states of the vital feelings" (cheerfulness, taciturnity, melancholy, anxiety) "and of self-esteem" (the feeling of one's own value and efficiency), "and the enclosed processes of aspiration" (goal-directive forces) "and emotivity". "Common to all these experiences is that they influence and overcome man." However, they can be governed by the will and mind—by the "personal superstructure" (q.v.) which represents a higher level of the "psychic life".
Bibliography: Lersch, P.: Aufbau der Person. Munich, [10]1966. *W.K.*

End pleasure. Freud's term for the feeling of pleasure accompanying the orgasm, which is followed by a reduction of libido and tension, whereas fore-pleasure creates the desire for constant increase of the intensity of pleasure. *U.H.S.*

Energetics. See *Stimulants*.

Energy, psychic or psychical. Called *libido* (q.v.) by Freud, and conceived as sexual or pleasure seeking energy. With the death instinct (q.v.), the libido (for Freud) is the source of all instinctual desires and motives. According to Freud's earlier views and according to Toman, aggressive motives can be regarded as primitive libidinal motives, and aggression as at least relatively pleasurable. Psychic energy as the source or precondition of all urges and drives, which are only manifested in behavior (q.v.) where they can be observed, would be trivial were it not supposed that a certain amount remains constant over fairly long periods of time, and differs only from one individual to another. For Freud, the amount of psychic energy is synonymous with the strength of the id or with psychic vitality. Toman expresses motive intensities as a proportion of the time since the last gratification t to the median interval of time between successive gratifications $\bar{t}$. The intensity of the motive i, $k_i = \frac{t}{\bar{t}}$. The sum of all motivational intensities k_i at any given moment, according to Toman, is $K = \frac{1}{N} \sum_{i=1}^{N} k_i$.

K corresponds to the total motivation D or the sum of all reaction potentials $\Sigma_s E_R$ (according to Hull). Increments of motivational intensity are represented by Toman as $\varepsilon_i = \frac{1}{\bar{t}_i}$ (first differential coefficient from dy to dt) and the average rate of motive differentiation as $C = f(\sum_{i=1}^{N} \varepsilon_i)$. When

C is constant, and N, the number of motives in any person which can be distinguished from one another grows with its development, the motive intensity increments ε_i are on the average smaller. This was demonstrated experimentally and empirically from samples of N (as independent of one another as possible). C can be considered as a possible operational version of the concept of psychic energy or libido. Since C is an interindividual variable, the following holds good: the greater C is, the less strain given gratification rhythms represent for the person concerned under otherwise comparable conditions (especially in the same objective state of development).

Freud's implicit assumption that libidinal object cathexes occur during motive gratifications corresponds to Hull's theory that motive reduction represents a learning step (i.e. at least a stimulus-reaction association is reinforced).

Toman postulates that there is an inverse proportion between the momentary K of any person and his simultaneous reception of knowledge or data storage. The current data stored are added to the knowledge (concerning opportunities of motive gratification) previously collected and stored, and are also classified. An individual concept of reality is constructed. The individual state of a person's information under average and comparable conditions can be conceived as a function of C and the time he has lived T: $I = f(C, T)$. Knowledge of the world thus reflects past motive gratifications and facilitates progressively the current data storage. The "effort" K_i, i.e., the amount of K which a motive in process of formation demands during its gratification, is a negative growth function with a decreasing increment: $K_i = f$ $(K_{max}e^{-x})$. Here K_{max} is the greatest value of K so far determined for the particular individual in the gratifications of the motive i; e is the euler numeral; and x the number of gratifications so far achieved.

Jung speaks of the desexualization of libido, Freud (with the same object in mind) speaks at first of ego-drives, later of the neutralization of libidinal energy. The meaning of this is that, in the course of development, motives are increasingly "gratified" because of their instrumental gain, no matter what their intensity may be at the time. "Pleasure-seeking energy" becomes "action energy".

Bibliography: Freud, S.: Introductory lectures on psycho-analysis. London, ²1929. Hull, C. L.: Principles of behavior. New York, 1943. Jung, C. G.: The structure and dynamics of the psyche. London, 1960. Toman, W.: Motivation, Persönlichkeit, Umwelt. Göttingen, 1968.   W. Toman

Engram. An enduring structural change in the nervous system resulting from temporary excitation, hypothesized as the physiological basis of memory (and inheritance, according to some writers). Also called *memory trace* and *neurogram*.   G.D.W.

Entelechy. This Aristotelian term denotes either the completed action or the cause determining the actualization of a possibility (*potentia*) (*De Anima* 11. 2, 414 a). Leibniz uses the term to denote all "simple substances or created monads" (*Monadology*, 18); in doing so, he stresses the degree of completeness and self-sufficiency of entelechy which makes it the "source of its internal actions". It is in this sense that H. Driesch (*Philosophie des Organischen*, Leipzig, 1909–28) understands the concept of entelechy as a teleological life factor subordinating physiological processes (which of course are of a physicochemical nature and therefore can be comprehended by means of the experimental sciences) in the organism to its intentions.

P.M.

Enteroceptive. Receiving information about the internal condition of the body. This is usually done through well-defined sensory organs (enteroreceptors) with a specific function, e.g. the *carotis sinus* and aortic depressor for intra-arterial blood pressure, the *glomus caroticum* for the ph-value, osmotic pressure, CO_2- and O_2- content of the blood in the carotid artery, muscle radii for the tension in the sinews. They are contrasted with the exteroreceptors, the sensory organs specifically for stimuli from the outside world. *E.D.*

Entoderm. The inner cell layer produced during gastrulation (see *Gastrula*) and all the tissues and organs which are formed later by the differentiation of this cell layer (e.g. the intestinal system). *H.Sc.*

Entonic proportion. This characterizes most clearly the barykinetic and epileptoid constitution. *Barykinetic:* abrupt (sudden, intensive), constant. *Epileptoid:* explosive (inadequately stimulable), viscous (tenacious, clinging). *W.K.*

Entoptic symptoms. Perception of processes and objects in one's own eye which occur during observation and which normally remain unconscious: e.g. dimness of the refractive media, retinal vessels, movement of the blood corpuscles in the retinal vessels. *R.R.*

Entotic symptoms. Auditory perceptions which can be produced, not by the external effect of sound but by physiological stimulation of the inner ear (e.g. circulation of the blood, muscular tension of the middle ear, etc.). Entotic phenomena are experienced as buzzing or ringing in the ears. This can also occur without any physiological stimulus when, for example, the hair cells of the inner ear are in a permanent state of excitation as a result of pathological changes. Such phenomena need to be distinguished from the buzzing which can be noticed as the aftereffect of protracted aural exposure to sound. *D.V.*

Entropy. 1. In physics, the loss of energy when this is transformed into work. **2.** As used by C. G. Jung, the tendency of psychic energy to pass from a stronger to a weaker value, until a state of equilibrium has been reached. **3.** In information theory H (= entropy) is the degree of chance (and hence, too, the extent of order) which exists in a certain system. *K.E.P.*

Enuresis. Urinating, bed-wetting, involuntary emptying of the bladder after the third year of age, usually bed-wetting at night (nocturnal enuresis), although voluntary control of the bladder function appears at the time to be in order. (Diurnal enuresis = inability to hold one's urine during the day.) Some think the disorder has a psychic cause (defiance, opposition, protest against a withdrawal of affection), i.e. that it results from a neurotic defect or psychopathic tendency, and is rarely the expression of a somatic anomaly. Enuresis can also occur as a symptom when there is a generalized convulsive attack. *H.N.G.*

The relatively low cure rates obtained by psychotherapeutic methods contrast strikingly with the high success rates consistently reported after the use of methods (essentially the urine-pad, electric-circuit and bell, causing the child to wake and complete urination) based on conditioning theory: i.e. enuresis is caused by a failure to learn—to acquire a conditioned response. Mowrer & Mowrer (1938) reported 100% success in their sample. But see *Behavior therapy.*

Bibliography: Lovibond, S.: The mechanism of conditioning treatment of enuresis. Behav. Res. and Ther., 1967, *5*, 11–25. Mowrer, O. H. & Mowrer, W.: Enuresis: a method for its study and treatment. Amer. J. Orthopsychiat., 1938, *8*, 436–59. Turner, R. K. & Young, G. C.: C.N.S. stimulant drugs and conditioning treatment of nocturnal enuresis: a long-term follow-up study. Behav. Res. and Ther., 1966, *4*, 225–8.

Environment. The individual's "life-space"; from the psychological viewpoint, the totality of stimuli affecting an individual from the point of fusion of sperm and ovum to the point of death.

Bibliography: Anastasi, A.: Differential psychology. New York, 1965, 63–7.   *M.A.*

Environment, circumscribed. See *Field theory.*

Envy. The desire to possess specific attributes (or possessions) of another individual. An example is *penis envy* (q.v.), which psychoanalysis (q.v.) considers an element of the personality structure of even adult women. In his socio-psychological theory, Freud takes envy to be the origin of a sense of community, or of the desire for social equality: a person abandons something so that others will not desire the same. *U.H.S.*

Enzygotic twins. See *Monozygotic twins.*

Eonism. See *Transvestism.*

Ephebophilia. Love of youths (see *Homosexuality*).

EPI. See *Eysenck Personality Inventory.*

Epicanthus. A mongolian fold in the skin at the inner edge of the upper eyelid. It is a symptom of mongolism (q.v.), a congenital type of imbecility.   *E.D.*

Epidemic, psychic. A phenomenon of mass psychology: mass hysteria of epidemic proportions which is induced psychologically by a crowd, especially when there is some specially favorable precondition (e.g. in time of crisis). Noteworthy are the heightened emotional states seen and the primitive character

of the phenomenon. Such epidemics occur at all times; they are encouraged by the mass communication media, and are often incited by group interests. Examples are ecstatic rites in primitive tribes; in the Middle Ages, flagellation (q.v.), *danses macabres*, children's crusades, persecution of witches, etc.; today there are the effects of mass suggestion, such as propaganda, advertising, show business; the concept also applies to certain series of crimes. See *Crowd behavior.*   *F.-C.S.*

Epilepsy. See *Absence; Grand mal; Petit mal.*

Epileptoid type. A disputed term for a psychopathic extreme state of entonic proportion (q.v.) (not necessarily connected with epilepsy).   *W.K.*

Epinephrine. See *Adrenalin(e).*

Epiphysis (*Corpus pineale*). The pineal gland. An endocrine gland (q.v.) situated at the base of the brain; its function has not yet been explained. It seems to have some influence on puberty (q.v.). As it usually calcifies in adulthood, it is used by radiologists as an indicator when taking X-ray photographs of the skull.   *E.D.*

Episcotister. An apparatus consisting of a rotating disc with open and closed sectors of adjustable angular width, which may be used to reduce the brightness of a visual field. Placed between the observer and a beam of light, it may also be used in the study of flicker phenomena, and as a device for measuring *critical flicker frequency* (CFF).   *G.D.W.*

Epistemology. A term for a part of cognition theory (q.v.). Epistemology endeavors to investigate cognition in the most varied fields of knowledge by throwing a critical light on the objects of investigation, the principles, methods and results, in order to determine the logical structure and objective value of each science. Epistemology itself can be a science when (in J. Piaget's sense) it is concerned with research into mechanisms of scientific knowledge (such as the "growth of knowledge" or the "historical and epigenetic genesis" of knowledge). In a wider sense the term is often used instead of *cognition theory*, or *theory of knowledge.*

M.-J.B.

Epsilon movement. An expression used to denote an apparent movement (see *Motion, apparent*): it appears when a white line on a black background turns into a black line on a white background (positive-negative movement). *K.E.P.*

Equal appearing intervals method. See *Halving methods.*

Equation, personal. Introduced by the astronomer F. W. Bessel (1784–1846) to denote the different way in which two equally competent observers observe and record the same astronomical event. On the basis of a comparison of the time estimates of a number of observers, Bessel worked out the *error of observation* (personal equation), which remains constant for a considerable length of time. Today the term is used only rarely for the constant individual error of observation recorded during an experiment (in the investigator and in the subject).

Bibliography: Boring, E. G.: A history of experimental psychology. New York, ²1950. *A.Th.*

Equilibrium. The organ of equilibrium is made up of two functionally distinguishable systems: the statoliths (q.v.) respond to

translatory acceleration, the semi-circular canals to angular acceleration (e.g. rapid turning). The sense of equilibrium functions under physiological conditions and is |unaffected by consciousness. *M.S.*

Equivalence of stimuli. The equivalent stimuli method was developed by Kluever: experimental animals which have learned to respond to a specific stimulus are presented with other stimuli. Whether or not the learned response occurs, it is then possible to confirm which characteristics are decisive for the equivalence of stimuli, and to what extent they are decisive.

Bibliography: Kluever, H.: The equivalence of stimuli in the behavior of monkeys. J. genet. Psychol., 1931, 39. *V.M.*

Equivalence, principle of. The visual perception system receives (*inter alia*) signals on the retina regarding the movement of an object, and signals regarding the position of the eye. The system uses the second type in order to eliminate the detrimental effect of one's own eye movement on proficient evaluation. This example serves to illustrate the following definition of the equivalence principle: in general, the fact that the perceptual schema utilizes an equivalent signal in order to eliminate an intrusive signal. *V.M.*

Equivalence theory. The theory that in the appreciation of art, the work of art is not taken as real, but is experienced as a substitute for reality. *V.M.*

Erection. An increase in length and volume of the penis caused by obstruction of the flow of blood in the *corpora cavernis penis.* Some have suggested the use of the term also for the increase in volume of the male and female breasts or of the *glans clitoridis* under sexual stimulation, but its use for the latter is rejected for systematic reasons. Erection is generally a prerequisite for penetration but not necessarily for ejaculation (q.v.). Complete erection usually occurs only just before orgasm (see *Sexual reaction cycle*). When younger men are sexually stimulated, erection is usually quick; with older men the process takes longer but there is generally a sufficient erection (contrary to the stereotyped view of the aging man). In the refractory period after orgasm, the erection disappears in two phases: before the final relaxation there is a stage (varying in duration) of diminished erection when coitus can often still take place. In the case of an older man this period may tend to occur more and more infrequently. There is supposed to be a reflex center for erection in the lumbar region of the spinal cord; case studies suggest the existence of a center inhibiting erection in the temporal regions of the cortex. For erection disturbances, see *Potency*. G.L.

Erethism. Morbid, excessive irritability and restlessness. K.E.P.

ERG. Abb. for *Electroretinography* (q.v.).

Erg. A concept in R. B. Cattell's personality theory (especially in factor-analytical research into motivation), roughly synonymous with *instinct* (q.v.). It denotes a motivation factor, all the features of which are directed toward a certain behavioral goal (object of drive)—independently of the stimuli released by this purposeful behavior and of the means set in train to achieve the goal. It is interpreted by Cattell as innate response readiness independent of cultural influences and directed toward some demanding terminal action (as distinguished from *metanerg*, the concrete expression of an erg under given cultural conditions). Ex-

amples of ergs are: need for sexual gratification, need for security, curiosity, self-assertion. See *Dynamic personality factors; Sentiment; Source traits*.

Bibliography: Cattell, R. B.: Personality and motivation structure and measurement. New York, 1957.

K.P.

Ergometry. Measurement of muscular performance with the aid of appliances. The *ergograph, ergometer* and *ergostat* are used for preference to measure how large sets of muscles move when given work to do. For example, the bicycle ergometer records the behavior of the muscles as they overcome measured resistance from the brakes. The ergograph (Mosso) supplies a work curve by constant recordings of the heights to which a weight has been raised after being pulled by the fingers. Since this curve affords an insight into the behavior of the muscles when working during a given period, the ergograph is also used to study fatigue and performance motivation. P.S. & R.S.

Ergonomics. The science of the relations between man and the world in which he works. An interdisciplinary science still in the process of development and based on the anatomy, physiology and psychology of work. It is subdivided into the ergonomics of the place of work and the whole area consisting of the man–machine and man–machine system (q.v.). Its field of application is the fitting of work to men, the man to the job. Industrial medicine and hygiene, and research and planning agencies play important parts here. Ergonomics is concerned to devise systems which will take account of the human factors in the work situation.

A.W.-F.

Erklärende Psychologie. In 1894, W. Dilthey contrasted "explanatory psychology" with "descriptive and analytical psychology". By *Erklärende Psychologie*, he understood psychology which worked by the natural–scientific causalistic method, as demonstrated, e.g., by G. T. Fechner in psychophysics. Bühler criticized this dualistic interpretation of psychology as an illusory problem. *P.S. & R.S.*

Erogenous. Sexually stimulating. Erogenous zones are regions of the body which can be manipulated with erogenous results. In a favorable situation, the main requirement for which is the necessary degree of harmony, any point of the body surface is suitable for sexual stimulation. Different types of stimulation are subject to taboos. See *Sexual deviations.* *U.H.S.*

Eros. The Greek god of love, defined by Hesiod in his *Theogony* as the creative force from which the world was born and to which the Orphics attributed the origin of the mystic egg laid by Night. Subsequently reduced to a mere winged angel, Eros appears again in psychoanalysis (q.v.) as the primeval, cosmic force contrasted with the death instinct (*Thanatos*). *P.M.*

Erotomania. 1. Excessive interest and desire for love and sexual intercourse. **2.** A delusional state in which the patient is convinced that some person is in love with him. This frequently leads to the person concerned receiving unwelcome attentions and communications from the patient. *P.Le.*

Error. In general the difference between an observed and a "true" or "expected" value. The deviation may be a chance effect (random error) or systematic (bias). One speaks of a *statistical* error if the statistic calculated from a random sample (q.v.) does not tally with the population (see *Expectation*; *Parameter*) where the conditions of observation for sample (q.v.) and population (q.v.) are

identical. The size of the error can be standardized in accordance with the error distribution (standard error). In this context the term "error" is not used for denoting a false observation (error of observation), a false equation (error in equation) or a false conclusion in checking statistical hypotheses. *W.H.B.*

Error, margin of; probability of. See *Probable error.*

Error of estimate. 1. An error in subjective judgment. **2.** A statistical error in the rating (q.v.) of parameters. Whereas subjective errors can be checked only with difficulty, precision is possible in regard to statistical errors. The standard error (q.v.) and probable error (q.v.) are frequently used to measure statistical errors. *A.R.*

Error of the first kind (Type I). In statistical hypotheses, an error of the first kind is determined by means of the choice of the limit of significance α (q.v.). For example, if a choice is made of $\alpha = 0.01$, the null hypothesis (q.v.) is rejected in 1% of all cases where it is true. This false statistical decision is known as an error of the first kind. Unlike the error of the second kind (q.v.), it increases with a rise in α. *W.H.B.*

Error of the second kind (Type II). If, following a test of significance, a hypothesis (H_0) is accepted when it is false, i.e. when it should have been rejected, an error of the second kind is committed. This is also known as a *conservative* error or β-error in classical works on the statistical testing of hypotheses. The probability of an error of the second kind (β-risk) depends upon the choice of the level of significance (q.v.). An error of the second kind is quantifiable when a special alternative hypothesis H_1 exists, and when the characteristics of the distributions (see *Frequency distribution*) expected to result from H_0 and H_1, and the size of the sample are known.   *W.H.B.*

Error of expectation. The individual tends to approach the future with established attitudes and behavior patterns. This anticipation is necessarily hypothetical and must be checked against reality. If the expectation fails to coincide with reality, an error of expectation has occurred.
                                                        P.S. & R.S.

Error variance. The variance (q.v.) of an error component. This variance of the test error (departure of observed values from the "true" value established after repeated tests on the same object) is to be distinguished from the variance of *sampling error* (q.v.). A sampling error denotes that part of the difference between statistic and parameter (q.v.) due to the non-representative character of the chosen sample (q.v.).   *W.H.B.*

Erythrochloropia. Blue–yellow blindness (= tritanopia or tritanomaly, q.v.; see *Color blindness*); the third receptor pigment for blue is absent or present in a reduced quantity in the retinal cones (q.v.). Occurs very rarely.
                                                        K.H.P.

Erythropsin. The visual purple pigment which occurs in the retinal rods (q.v.).
                                                        K.H.P.

Escapism. A major kind of *defense mechanism*, characterized by the tendency to withdraw physically and mentally from the unpleasant aspects of reality. Many neurotic symptoms (e.g. amnesia, hysterical paralysis) are interpreted by psychoanalysts as escape devices.
                                                        G.D.W.

ESP. See *Extrasensory perception.*

ESP cards. A special pack of cards similar to playing cards used for guessing experiments. The pack consists of twenty-five cards, each card bearing one of the five symbols: circle, cross, square, star and wavy-lines; each symbol is represented five times. Hence the probability of a hit (q.v.) on any given trial with a properly shuffled pack is 1/5. Formerly known as Zener cards.   *J.B.*

Many different types of cards have been used for quantitative ESP research. Such experiments can be carried out and evaluated in a relatively simple manner. The special ESP cards have led to good results in many cases. But it is unlikely that the five symbols mentioned above played a major role here. In most cases other variables, e.g. human relationships, were probably of more importance. In recent years playing or office cards as well as, e.g., postcards suitable for a particular group of subjects (e.g. children) have been used. There are also some attempts under way to select symbols and configurations for particular subjects. Further possibilities result from an exploration of the emotional values of symbols and configurations such that the selections become more accurate and meaningful with respect to particular subjects.   *H.H.J.K.*

Esthesiometer. An instrument for investigating cutaneous (skin) sensation, especially sensitivity as indexed by the *two-point threshold.* One common form of esthesiometer is like a fine pair of compasses and is used to measure the minimum distance between the two points which is necessary for them to be perceived tactually as two rather than one. See also *Hair esthesiometer.*
                                                        G.D.W.

Esthetic type. One of E. Spranger's six life-style or world-view types: an individual inclined to style and self-realization without reference to any considerations of utility. Intellectually more theoretical and concerned with personal style. Distance and self-emphasis are features of interpersonal contact. The artist approximates to the esthetic type. *W.K.*

Esthetics. See *Experimental esthetics; Art; Literature; Music.*

Esthetics, psychological. The branch of psychological research founded by G. T. Fechner which studies the general conditions of taste, especially of proportions (e.g. the golden section), of forms, spatial relations, colors and color combinations. See *Experimental esthetics.*
Bibliography: **Fechner, G. T.:** Vorschule der Ästhetik. Leipzig, 1876. *H.-J.A.*

Estrogens. Female sex hormones (q.v.). The most important estrogens formed in the ovaries are estriadol, estrone and estriol.
Bibliography: **Disfalusy, E. & Lauritzen, C.:** Oestrogene beim Menschen. Berlin, 1961. **Zuckerman, S.:** The ovary, Vols 1 & 2. New York, 1962. For further bibliography see *Sex hormones.* *W.J.*

Estrus; estromania. (Eng. spelling: *Oestrus*). *Heat; Rut; Estrum.* The phase in the sexual cycle of female animals which is characterized by sexual receptiveness. Usually this is accompanied by physiological changes in the reproductive organs, e.g. swelling, coloration, etc. The term is usually applied to non-human species since there is no clear analogy in the human female.
Estrogen: Any hormone that stimulates the female animal to estrus.
Estromania: Nymphomania. Abnormally strong heterosexual desire in the female.
G.D.W.

Eta coefficient (syn. *Correlation ratio*). A measure of correlation for curvilinear regression. In the case of a non-linear regression of this kind, the mean values of the Y measurements do not rise uniformly within the X categories. Just as in the case of a

$r < 1$ correlation there are two regression lines, so there are also two expressions for η. The eta coefficient can also be used to test the linearity of a regression. *W.H.B.*

Ether. A narcotic (q.v.) in use since 1846. It has an extended introductory phase, a marked excitation stage (see *Narcosis*), and an extended recovery stage; it stimulates mucous membranes, salivary secretion, bronchial secretion, and laryngospasm. Vomiting is frequently observed. *E.L.*

Ethics. The study of the distinction between good and evil. A branch of philosophy concerned with morals; it systematically examines the characteristics of value judgments such as "good", "bad", "right", "wrong", etc., and the general principles which justify their application to a subject. Ethics as a system of relations and values is the basis of non-religious structures. *M.R.*

Ethnocentrism. An attitude and/or ideology concerning the relationship between an individual's own group and other groups (*egocentrism* concerns the interaction between an individual and other persons).
Positive characteristics of the subject's (sociological or informal) group are strongly emphasized while features and members of other groups are judged in terms of standards applicable to the subject's group, and denigrated. An easy rejection of unfamiliar things is characteristic of ethnocentrism, which therefore becomes a component of general *prejudice* (q.v.).
The *ethnocentrism scale* developed by T. W. Adorno, E. Frenkel-Brunswik and co-workers shows high positive correlations with "authoritarianism", "anti-semitism" and "politico-economic conservatism" and is therefore a central variable in the authoritarian, anti-democratic syndrome. See *Authoritarian personality.*

Bibliography: Adorno, T. W., Frenkel-Brunswik, E., Levinson, D. J. & Stanford, R. N.: The authoritarian personality. New York, 1950.   *H.D.S.*

Ethnography. The description of a natural society on the basis of field research (the distinction between ethnography and ethnology is rather artificial but is maintained by some authors). The discipline began with reports by travelers in modern times, but these generally only have a limited source value. Relatively objective research results have been available since about 1900. This period of monographs on tribes marks the real beginning of ethnographic or ethnological research (see *Ethnology*).   *S.Kr.*

Ethnology. The descriptive and comparative science of human cultures (generally concerned with "primitive" cultures); largely identical with anthropology (q.v.) until the nineteenth century, it became a genuine science with the development of the field method and the objective compilation of tribal studies (*ethnography*). Four areas of study have developed: (*a*) technology and material culture, (*b*) social organization, (*c*) religion and magic, (*d*) games and art. In the initial period of ethnographic collections and museums (starting in about 1850), interest centered on material culture. The representatives of functionalism (q.v.) reacted against this biassed emphasis on formal aspects of culture by drawing attention to the meaningful content of material and conceptual cultural products. Early attempts to compare different cultures generally aimed at a definition of standard laws of development (evolutionary school). G. P. Murdock was the first to compare cultures on a statistical basis. More recently, research has increasingly been carried out into non-primitive cultures. The cultural transformation of the developing countries provided an opportunity to use ethnology as an applied science (ethnologists engaged on development-aid programs).

Bibliography: Benedict, R.: Patterns of culture. New York, 1934. Boas, F. The mind of primitive man, New York, 1938. Id.: Race, language and culture. New York, 1940. Lévi-Strauss, C.: The savage mind. London, 1966. Id.: Le cru et le cuit. Paris, 1964. Lowie, R.: History of ethnological theory. New York, 1937. Malinowski, B.: Culture. In: Encyclopedia of the social sciences. New York, 1951. Mead, M.: From the South Seas. New York, 1939. Murdock, G. P.: Social structure. New York, 1949. White, A.: The evolution of culture. New York, 1959. Wissler, C.: Man and culture. New York, 1923.
                                                                S.Kr.

Ethnopsychology. The psychological aspect of ethnological research, and as such a branch of social psychology (q.v.). The 2,000 or so different cultures can be considered as natural experiments in terms of the changing nature of human adaptations. M. Mead demonstrated this point with reference to sexual behavior. See *Tribal psychology*.

Bibliography: Mead, M.: Cooperation and competition among primitive peoples. New York, 1937. Id.: Male and female: a study of the sexes in a changing world. New York, 1949.   *W.Sc.*

Ethology. Behavior research; study of the laws and causal relationships in the behavior patterns of organisms. Simple behavior patterns are direct reactions to stimuli applied to the organism by the environment. In the case of higher animals, very complex behavior patterns occur which may be inherited or acquired and are often only indirectly (if at all) released by environmental stimuli. See *Comparative psychology*.
                                                                H.S.

Euclidean space. See *Linear space*.

Eugenics. The theory of the improvement of the hereditary characteristics of descendants by promoting the establishment of socially useful families enjoying good physical and mental health, and by eliminating negative hereditary characteristics through appropriate measures (danger: e.g. developments under the Third Reich, such as the murder in concentration camps of individuals deemed socially useless, and so on). See *Euthanasia*.

K.E.P.

Eunochoidism. A form of infantilism (q.v.) in adults caused by hypofunction of the male reproductive glands, characterized by incomplete formation of the genitalia, absence of external sexual features and underdeveloped libido. Caused by congenital subdevelopment or illness, accident, castration or acquired malfunctioning of the testicles, eunochoidism is a hormone deficiency condition which can be improved by repeated replacement of the missing male reproductive gland hormones. It can also occur as a secondary condition through a gonadotropic hormone deficiency in the case of disease affecting the anterior part of the hypophysis. See *Gonads*. *E.D.*

Euphoria. An elevated mood state of extreme elation associated with feelings of well-being which may not be in accord with environmental circumstances. It is characteristically seen in mania and may occur occasionally in schizophrenia. It is often seen in coarse brain disease, especially when the frontal lobes are involved, for example in Pick's disease, presenile dementia, disseminated sclerosis, and may be a feature of intoxications such as morphine. *D.E.*

Eurhythmia. Greek concept meaning "good rhythm". Harmony of bodily movement, especially as developed with the aid of music. See *Music therapy*. *G.D.W.*

Eustachian tubes. The connection between the tympanum (tympanic cavity) and the naso-pharyngeal space is established by the eustachian tubes. The channel, with a length of about 3·5 cm, is lined with a mucous film carrying the ciliated epithelium. The tubal lumen, which is normally closed, is opened to balance pressure when the subject swallows or yawns. *M.S.*

Euthanasia. The shortening of life by suicide (q.v.) or with the assistance of a third party was permitted in antiquity and is not unusual today in non-Christian cultures. Euthanasia was forbidden by the Church but became a subject of discussion again after the publication of More's *Utopia* (1516). The general tendency for man's life span to be increased has brought interest to bear on the subject again. There is a trend to permit euthanasia for patients suffering from incurable, painful illnesses. The only legal code to allow euthanasia is the Swiss criminal code (art. 115) which states that assistance in suicide is only a punishable offence if the motives of the person giving such assistance are selfish. In England and the U.S.A. associations exist to promote the legal recognition of euthanasia.

Bibliography: Williams, G.: The sanctity of life and the criminal law. London, 1958. *P.M.*

Evaluation. The evaluation of raw experimental data is their statistical description and comparison, and can refer to qualitative or quantitative variations. The term is, however, often used generally to describe any form of expert interpretation of samples, scores, observations, results, and even case histories, etc., in order to determine their relative value. *W.H.B.*

Event. Events are results in a random experiment, i.e. they cannot be infallibly predicted in all particulars (apart from the special case of $P = 1$ or $P = 0$). The prediction of the truth of an event can therefore only take the form of a statement of probability. In contrast to a *simple* event—the occurrence

EXCITABILITY

of a previously defined event A in a random experiment—a *complementary* event is each result which is not classed as an event A ("not A", $\bar{A}$). A and $\bar{A}$ are complementary, i.e. the probability (q.v.) of $P(A) + P(\bar{A}) = 1$. A *certain* event is when $P(A) = 1$. In this case the complement $P(\bar{A})$ is an *impossible* event. A conditional event presupposes the occurrence of another event B where A and B may not be mutually exclusive. A *rare* event has a very slight probability of occurrence.
W.H.B.

Evolution. A developmental mechanism by means of which (with the aid of *selection*, q.v., of those suitable for a specific environment, and *mutation*, or spontaneous genetic change) highly-complex forms of life emerge from simple organisms in the course of many generations.
H.S.

Ewald's laws. Two laws discovered by the physiologist J. R. Ewald (1892) to define the relationship between the endolymphic flow and nystagmus (q.v.): (*a*) the eye movement (the slow component of nystagmus) takes place in the direction of the endolymphic flow which triggered the nystagmus; (*b*) the motor effect of the endolymphic flow is *not* ideal in both directions of flow. When the semicircular canal is in the horizontal position, the ampullopetal flow is stronger; in the vertical position, the ampullofugal flow dominates.
P.S.

Ewald types. See *Biotonus.*

Examination anxiety; Test anxiety. The specific individual proneness to anxiety distinguishes neurotic from normal examination anxiety. As a symptom of various neurotic syndromes, neurotic examination anxiety is a specific-situational anxiety of all situations which are experienced as tests or examinations. The accompanying physical and mental symptoms and disorders

of the intellectual function which is to be tested make the test or examination of questionable value. Neurotic examination anxiety is individually and psycho-socially determined in a variety of ways by the complex interaction of the triad of examinee, examiner and form of examination. The individual proneness to anxiety (of the examinee and the examiner) depends on the unconscious equation of the examination with danger situations in the individual's development (particularly in childhood) (separation; temptation from, punishment of instinctive desires; vexation). Psycho-socially, neurotic examination anxiety arises from the neurotic interaction of the examinees, or examinee and examiner (e.g. inducing anxiety in the other in order to obviate one's own anxiety), and from irrational features of the examination (institutionalized neurotic conditions). See *Anxiety.*

Bibliography: Moeller, M. L. Die Prüfung als Kernmodell psychosozialer Konflikte. Z. Soziol, Sozialpsychol., 1969, *21*, 355–61. World University Service: Student mental health. London, 1961.   *M.L.M.*

Excess. A characteristic of distributions defined in terms of *kurtosis* (q.v.).   *W.H.B.*

Excitability. 1. The ability of living beings to be aroused by a change in the level of stimuli. **2.** Susceptibility to irritative stimuli of an affective nature.   *K.E.P.*

Excitable functional units such as nervous and muscular tissues are subject to excitation (stable potential) through the ion concentration difference (caused by metabolic processes) between the internal and external environment of the cell, which is enclosed in a functional membrane (alternating, selective permeability to potassium and sodium ions). Excitability consists in a depolarization of this membrane, which is first dependent on local stimulus intensity in the case of weak stimuli, with a measurable reduction in the stable potential. However, once a given stimulus threshold is exceeded, the cell responds with a rapidly progressing, complete depolarization; the much higher action potential (q.v.) follows the local response, and the excitation processes continue independently of the form, duration and intensity of the stimulus (see *All-or-nothing law*). Excitability is not confined to the locus of the stimulus but generally extends in both directions along a fiber axis (see *Axon*) with a specifically determined velocity. *M.S.*

Excitation. 1. Hypothetical state of stimulation of the organism or nervous system. **2.** Rapid growth of psychic stress in pleasure, enthusiasm, etc. **3.** Process by which physical energy brings about changes in a sense organ. **4.** Process causing stimulation of a nerve or muscle by nervous irritation. *K.E.P.*

Excitement phase. The first phase in the sexual reaction cycle and, achieved by effective sexual stimulation. According to Masters & Johnson, the pulse rate and blood pressure rise in man and woman as a function of the degree of sexual excitement, while voluntary and involuntary muscular tension increase and the "sex flush" occurs. The woman also has the following physiological reactions: vaginal lubrication; swelling of the nipples, clitoris, labia minora and possibly also labia majora; widening and extension of the vagina; erection of the nipples; enlargement of the breasts. In the male, the corresponding phenomena are erection (q.v.) of the penis, partial elevation of the testicles, and sometimes erection of the nipples.
Bibliography: Masters, W. H. & Johnson, V. E.: Human sexual response. Boston, 1966. Sigusch, V.: Exzitation und Orgasmus bei der Frau. Stuttgart, 1970.   *V.S.*

Excitement type. Easily excitable; conditioned reflexes are easily provoked but difficult to countermand; reflex changes are slow. Ant. *Inhibited type.*
Bibliography: Pavlov, I. P.: Lectures on conditioned reflexes, 2 vols. New York, 1928/41.   *W.K.*

Exhaustion. 1. Condition in which an organism is not able to function normally (see *Fatigue*). **2.** Appearance of a raised stimulus threshold, reduction of the frequency and intensity of reaction to stimuli.   *K.E.P.*

Exhaustion threshold. The limiting condition postulated in extreme fatigue: the point at which threshold is heightened for the stimulus, but after which the response of the active system decreases in frequency and extent, or ceases.

Exhibitionism. A sexual deviation which consists in deriving pleasure from exhibiting the genital organs to other persons. In puberty and epileptic conditions, it is not considered to be a perversion (q.v.). The exhibitionist frequently achieves an orgasm through the conjunction of situational factors during exposure. Defense reactions by the involuntary spectators—generally women—are particularly effective; generally the exhibitionist himself has a defensive reaction to sexual appetence—even during an exhibition—although he usually anticipates sexual stimulation in the spectators. Psychoanalysis explains exhibitionism as a fixation in the phallic phase of libido development (see *Libido*); behavioral psychologists stress the importance of social anxieties. Exhibitionism is almost exclusively reported among men.
                                                    G.L.

Existence analysis. Existence analysis as a science of man and as a therapy considers itself to be a further development of the psychoanalysis (q.v.) of Freud (q.v.). It is based principally on the phenomena of human behavior which were first discovered by Freud. However, it no longer explains these "metapsychologically"—pseudo-scientifically—in the manner of orthodox psychoanalytical theory, but endeavors to explain them phenomenologically. It is found that completely different meanings attach to all the phenomena which had been "prejudiced" by previous "metapsychological" concepts such as "transference" (q.v.), the "unconscious" (q.v.), "repression" (q.v.), "psychic projection", "latent and manifest dream images", etc. The new understanding thus obtained compels existence analysis when applied to therapy to deviate from the old psychoanalytical techniques wherever the "metapsychological theoretical superstructure" of Freud has an impact on practice such that the latter ceases to obey Freud's own basic therapeutic rule.

Phenomenological and existence-analytical psychology and therapy take their bearings from the philosophical *phenomenology* (q.v.) of Heidegger, whereas the philosophy of Descartes was authoritative for orthodox psychoanalytical theory. The view of existence analysis explodes above all the previous supposition of a "psyche" conceived primarily as a kind of capsule into which the objects of the outside world are thought to be reflected in the shape of imaginary images. This also puts an end to all the metapsychological concepts relating to libido processes (see *Libido*) which occur within the psyche and are just as hypothetical. Existence analysis understands what is specific about man as he exists as an *"ek-stare"* in the most literal sense, i.e., as standing outside and spanning an area of the world open to the perceptions and capable of responding to the presence of the person confronting it. To be a human being means therefore "always to be outside in the world and confronting it" and primarily to be absorbed together with one's fellow men in perceptional and responsive relationships to them. As a method of investigation, existence analysis does not suppose that there is anything behind phenomena. But it does endeavor to make manifest and increasingly differentiated those meaningful contents and referential relationships which the confronting person has acquired, until he can also move on to the next hidden essential in what has been perceived. The knowledge of the self and the world that can

thus be acquired by psychoneurotic patients is the therapeutically beneficial aspect of existence analysis; it is identical with finding a worthwhile meaning in life.

Bibliography: Boss, M.: Psychoanalyse und Daseinsanalyse. Berne, 1957. Condrau, G.: Daseinsanalytische Psychotherapie. Berne, 1963. Heidegger, M.: Being and time. London, 1962.

M. Boss & Hicklin, A.

Existential analysis. A term introduced by Frankl to designate his anthropological, psychotherapeutic method of treatment and research developed from depth psychology and based on M. Heidegger's theories. Also known as *logotherapy* (q.v.), it is the third Viennese School. In analyzing biographical details, existential analysis attempts to understand individual human existence from the standpoint of its meaning and possible values. Frankl contrasts Freud's "will to pleasure" and Adler's "will to power" with the "will to meaning" which, if it is not fully achieved, is referred to as "existential frustration" and used as the starting-point for therapy. *Meaning* covers not only the positive aspects of life but also suffering and death. Frankl does not radically reject Freud's psychoanalysis, but tries to complete it. The purpose of existential analysis is less to abolish repressed urges than to arouse the "unconscious spirit" (conscience, existence, self), which may lead to neurotic disorders if it is repressed. The term is often used as a synonym for (L. Binswanger's) *Existence analysis* (q.v.).

Bibliography: Frankl, V. E.: Theorie u. Therapie der Neurosen. Vienna, 1956.   F.-C.S.

Existentialist psychology. A school of philosophical psychology which holds that the subject-matter of psychology is limited to the contents of experience (thoughts, feelings, sensations, etc.) which can be observed introspectively. Closely related to *structural psychology* in its emphasis on the analysis and classification of mental events without interpretation.   G.D.W

Existential psychoanalysis. A therapeutic method developed from Sartre's theories which uses existential philosophy for psychotherapy; it differs from Freudian psychoanalysis. On the principle that each individual chooses what he wishes to be and expresses his choice in every aspect of his behavior, behavioral analysis serves to detect the system of values chosen originally and make it accessible to the patient, who can decide to recognize his original choice.
Bibliography: Sartre, J. P.: Being and nothingness. New York, 1956. Misiak, H. & Sexton, V. S.: History of psychology. New York & London, 1966. *F.-C.S.*

Existential psychology. Because M. Heidegger considers existence as a privileged form of access to being, the study of subjectivity is more important than in the psychology of W. Wundt, which is defined as a science of *direct* experience. Reflection on the self and phenomenological observation (see *Phenomenology*) therefore reveal realities in the psyche of the individual which are disregarded or overlooked by scientific psychology: various types of love (M. Scheler), modesty (Scheler), mood (O. F. Bollnow). This movement has led to existential analysis (q.v.) in psychotherapy.
P.M.

Exner's spiral. An illusion of movement named after S. Exner (1846-1926): a spiral figure drawn on a rotating disk induces the impression of contraction or enlargement according to the direction of rotation. When the disk is stopped, the movement appears to be reversed. *K.E.P.*

Exocrine glands. These are all the structures which produce secreta that do not pass into the blood stream (see *Endocrine glands*), e.g. skin glands (*glandulae cutis*); sweat glands (*glandulae sudoriferae*); sebaceous glands (*glandulae sebaceae*); female mammary gland tissue (*glandula mammaria*);

digestive tract glands: stomach glands (*glandulae gastricae propriae*); intestinal glands (*glandulae intestinales*). *G.A.*

Exogamy. Social rule that a marital partner must be found outside the other partner's group. This rule is the positive version of the incest (q.v.) taboo (q.v.). It applies in almost all societies to the members of the nuclear family, and is generally considered to be "natural". It is extended all the more widely to more distant relations as the latter have a functional significance for the society concerned. The rule serves to ensure unambiguous social roles in the family, and therefore the stability and continuity of society. In addition, it prevents sexual competition in the nuclear family which would bring about the latter's disorganization. When the rule applies to a larger group, it helps to extend discoveries and knowledge beyond the small group and maintains a greater social cohesion. See *Endogamy*.
S.Kr.

Exophthalmic goiter. Protrusion of the eyeball with restriction of movement; may occur on one or both sides. Causes: mechanical forward pressure caused by retrobulbar (i.e. behind the eyeball) processes which require space, e.g. inflammation and swelling, arterial (pulsating) or venous vascular enlargement, benign or malignant tumors, parasites; the condition may also be traumatic (caused by accidents) due to lesions of the vessels or tissue, and finally hormonal (in particular, in hyperthyroidism). Hormonal goiter is not caused by the thyroidal hormones, but by an "exophthalmus producing factor" (EPF) which can be isolated from the anterior part of the hypophysis and is physically, chemically and physiologically distinct from thyrotropin(e) (thyrotropic hormone, TSH). EPF can be demonstrated in the blood in hyper- and hypothyroidism, i.e. whenever the thyroid gland regulation is disturbed. After successful treatment of the thyroid gland disorder, the quantity of EPF may remain high and lead occasionally to "malignant exophthalmus" which may even result in the loss of the eye through paralysis of the eye muscle and disturbance of tear secretion, together with corneal ulceration.

K.H.P.

Exopsychic. Descriptive of physical or social effects in the individual's environment which can be traced back to his mental activity.

K.E.P.

Expansive type. Character type which attempts to solve difficulties "outwards" by turning toward the source of the problem. "Definite sthenic character with strong retention capacity", "egotistic", and possibly "unbridled". Primitive, "superficial/egotism" or "a more nuanced ethical sense of right".

W.K.

Expectancy. The expectancy of the occurrence of an event is dependent on attitudes and expectations. It is therefore a subjective notion of probability. Theoretically, expectancy can be defined as the amount which a percipient is prepared to wager on the occurrence of an event. Expectancy is also the *attitude*, or *set*, of one who expects or is attentive.

K.W.

Expectation. "The anticipation and actualization in the imagination of coming events in their relation to the objectives of our aspirations" (Lersch). This "anticipatory target reaction" (D. C. McClelland) is derived from earlier experience. The hypothetical and provisional nature of expectation is expressed in subjective experience as expectation tension. It is a function of attainability or mental distance from the goal and its influence as a motivating factor varies greatly. The expectation tension is closely related to the expectation gradient, i.e. to the difference between the present and

future "real situations" and determines the expectation level.

P.S. & R.S.

Expectation, mathematical. For any discrete random variable X and a function $g(X)$ defined for all possible values of X, the expression $E[g(X)]$ is known as the mathematical expectation value of the function $g(X)$, or the expectation of $g(X)$. In the case of a continuous distribution with density $f(X)$, the expectation of a function $g(x)$ solved for all values of X is given by:

$$E[g(x)] = \int_{\infty}^{\infty} g(x) f(x) d(x).$$

W.H.B.

Expectation value. See *Expectation, mathematical.*

Experience. Believed by many to be the best term to describe the subject-matter of psychology. May be used as a noun: the subjective (conscious) appreciation of stimulus events, or the knowledge resulting from this; or as a verb: to live through, meet with, find, feel, undergo, or be aware of any stimulus object, sensation, or internal event. Hence the term is used in psychology in the same way as in everyday language. G.D.W.

Experience error. Köhler's (q.v.) term for the incorrect supposition that there is a precise *structural* correspondence between an experience and the form of mental organization it evokes.

Experience types. Two response types which occur with the Rorschach test (and other shape interpretation methods). Intraverts tend to interpret movement. Their relationship to the world around them is dependent primarily on intra-mental activity. Extratensive types interpret primarily from the standpoint of color. They are very sensitive to environmental stimuli, and dependent on the latter. Rorschach defines both types solely on the basis of the type of interpretation made by them in the experiment and not on the basis of their behavior in real life, which Jung used to determine his function(al) types. *W.K.*

Experiential experiment. Unlike the normal psychological experiment, this is primarily concerned not with a manifest reaction of the individual but with subjective experiences provoked in the testee by the experimental situation. These subjective experiences must be described by the subject and therefore objectivized. The validity of the experimental data depends on the extent to which the subject is able to make objective self-observations. Quantitative determination of results is possible only to a limited extent. *P.S.*

Experiment. An experiment is the planned manipulation of variables for observation purposes; at least one of the variables, i.e. the independent or experimental variable, is altered under predetermined conditions during the experiment; the variable whose alteration is observed as a function of this change is known as the dependent variable. If an effect on the dependent variable appears possible, the other variables needed in the experiment are either held constant for the duration of observation (controlled variables, experimental parameters) or disregarded as irrelevant variables. Every controlled variable is therefore a possible independent variable for further experiments. The observation must allow a clear identification of the changes in the dependent variables within the limits of accuracy needed for a particular experiment; the observation therefore requires a measurement at least on a nominal scale level.

Experimental methods contrast with empirical methods (differential methods) in which a special set of variables is sought for observational (measurement) purposes. Since none of the variables can be manipulated in a predetermined manner during the observation, the distinction between dependent and independent variables ceases to apply; no direct conclusions can therefore be drawn from the results on the direction of the dependence. The definition of the experiment includes consideration of its purpose. An arrangement used experimentally to determine the direction and nature of relations between variables can also be used for measurement—e.g. for other experiments—as soon as these relationships are known. Experimental methods are therefore frequently also used as empirical methods (tests). See *Test theory.*

The questions asked in an experiment depend on the knowledge already available. If the latter is pre-scientific or consists merely of assumptions, we speak of a *pilot study*; in this case an attempt is often made to determine a relatively large number of variables, if it is impossible to specify adequately which effects are to be expected from the independent variables. In control experiments the results of studies conducted by the same or other workers are already known and an attempt is made to reproduce them for greater security. In generalizing experiments, the range of variation of the independent variables is increased in order to enlarge the validity of a relationship already determined. Test experiments are arranged to relate the results to previous theoretical assumptions in order to determine the range of validity of a theory.

If clear, but conflicting assumptions can be made from different theories regarding the results of an experiment so that it is possible to use it to refute one of the contradictory theories, we speak of a crucial experiment (*experimentum crucis*).

1. *Types of experiment.* In the simplest case, one independent variable is altered and the effect measured on one or more dependent variables; these univariate experiments contrast with planned or multivariate experiments, in which several independent

variables are altered in combination, in such a way that the effects of each variable can be determined separately and their interaction can be examined. Techniques are described in the literature on experimental design and evaluation (generally by analysis of variance). Further classifications of experiments can be derived from the degree of graduation of the independent variables. In bivalent experiments, the independent variable assumes only two values (e.g. dependence of calculability on the appearance or non-appearance of an interfering noise). Although such experiments have only limited value, they are still frequent and sometimes inevitable. They may show whether an effect of the experimental variables can be proved. This demonstration will not be reliable if there is a non-linear or non-monotonous relationship between the independent and dependent variable: an average noise intensity may facilitate performance while performance remains unchanged at higher and lower intensities. Multivariate experiments provide the answer in this case. In the most favorable assumption, non-monotonous relationships with the dependent variables can already be determined with three independent variables. If even more independent variables are taken in the functional experiment, it is possible to show the functional relationship with the dependent variable. The corresponding enlargement can also be made in the multivariate experiment: if the functional dependence of a variable on several independent variables is determined in this way, we speak of a parametric experiment.

In many psychological experiments, we are not so much concerned with the state assumed by the dependent variables after manipulation of the independent variables, as with the time function according to which the dependent variable reacts to changes in the independent variables (response function). Most learning experiments are examples of this. We may speak here of dynamic experiments by contrast with static

forms. Generally the dependent variable changes over from one stable state to another. In the case of this type of experiment, it is necessary to record both dependent and independent variables continuously. For evaluation purposes, we associate time functions for the variables. In systems theory, we find certain well-defined formal expressions for complete analysis of the time characteristic of systems by specific stimulation functions of the independent variables (sine, rise, interval, surge); these can be directly used in some areas of psychology.

2. *History of experimental psychology.* The history of psychology (q.v.) as an independent science begins with the introduction of the experiment in about 1860 (H. L. F. von Helmholtz, W. Wundt, G. T. Fechner). However, the experimental method was never considered to be the sole method of psychology. Empirical observation and descriptive analysis of individual cases (case studies) were also used by some schools of psychology as well as the phenomenological method (philosophical psychology). It is possible to define experimental psychology as a separate discipline. Experimental psychology was first concerned mainly with problems of perception and reaction time. However, its use was rapidly extended: as long ago as 1925, I. P. Pavlov was able to show that general behavioral defects similar to human neuroses can be induced in dogs if the animals are exposed to severe, traumatic experiences (Petersburg flood, 1924) or insoluble problems. Doubts are occasionally cast on this equation of behavioral disturbances (experimental neuroses) with human neuroses. Today the experimental method is used almost universally, when there are no moral objections (damage to subject), practical difficulties (many areas of social psychology) or economic problems (cost).

Experiments were originally conducted on a small group or even on individuals, or sometimes on the research worker himself (H. Ebbinghaus, W. James). As statistical knowledge grew (e.g. "Student's test") the number of Ss needed could be rationally estimated. The development of analysis of variance (q.v.) by Fisher (1925) enabled planned experiments to be carried out; the introduction of non-parametric statistical methods (especially after 1950) simplified analysis of many experimental results, especially when the data clearly departed from the normal distribution. It is often difficult to distinguish between irrelevant and relevant variables. In addition, measurement of the dependent variable generally involves an intervention which may have an effect of its own. The addition of control groups to the experimental group was therefore an important step forward: the subject in the control group undergoes the same measurements as that in the experimental group, but without manipulation of the independent variable. Control groups were first used around 1908; from the early 1950s about half the reported experiments have included control groups.

Our experiments have been influenced by technical as well as psychological developments. The precise mechanical apparatus initially needed for many experiments was expensive to acquire and maintain (e.g. the Hipp's chronoscope for time measurement). Since about 1950, this equipment has been rapidly replaced by electronic devices which allow precise control of the experiment and simple measurement together with reliable recording of the results. The present state of development is characterized by an emphasis on systems theory, which influences both the theory and the test set-up and analysis of results; rapid progress has also been made in electronics, and we have seen the introduction of experiments in which the dependent variable, the behavior of the subject, the further course of the experiment, i.e. the state of the independent variables, can be directly influenced.

3. *Problems of the psychological experiment.* Although the theoretical problems of psychological experimentation have been solved in principle, there remain practical problems which restrict the use of the experimental method and clear interpretation of the results; the main problems concern operational definition of the variables used, the possibility of generalizing experimental results, and limitations of a moral and legal nature.

In experiments involving human beings, the definition of the variables used is partly dependent on the interpretation of the situation by the testee; in spite of careful instruction, this interpretation is often difficult to control adequately. Personal characteristics of the experimenter, and possibly also his expectation of the subject's performance (experimenter effect) influence this interpretation so that corresponding control experiments become necessary by means of blind and double-blind tests (Rosenthal effect). In experiments in animals, attempts are made by manipulating the stimuli (frequently hunger) to determine which variables in the situation will act on the animal subject.

The possibility of generalizing experimental results depends on whether the conditions can be considered representative. There are no serious difficulties here as regards the subjects involved, although many results are based solely on experiments conducted on psychologists and students of psychology. On the other hand, the remaining conditions of psychological experiments are often representative neither of practical (biotic) experiments nor theoretical problems. So far relatively few results have been published which answer both theoretical and practical questions.

Finally, the restrictions caused by moral or legal considerations are very noticeable in the experimental techniques used. Even in relatively simple learning tests it may be necessary to delude the test subject intentionally by the instruction; experiments in schools are hampered by the failure of parents to give their agreement; and simple sociopsychological surveys are impossible to carry out because of the possible undesirable secondary effects on the group studied. Many socially important questions will only be studied experimentally and solved when a substantial section of the population becomes convinced of the value of psychological experiments.

Bibliography: Boring, E. G.: A history of experimental psychology. New York, 1929. Cattell, R. B. (Ed.): Handbook of multivariate experimental psychology. Chicago, 1966. Plutchik, R.: Foundations of experimental research. New York & London, 1968. Sidowski, J. B. (Ed.): Experimental methods and instrumentation in psychology. New York & London, 1966.   F. Merz

Experimental design. The experimental testing of hypotheses in regard to the dependence and interdependence of variables. In a "design" of this kind, it is possible to plot the effects of one or more independent variables on one or more dependent variables. In general, experimental design refers to measures adopted to ensure that the planning and procedure of an experiment use all available appropriate information and as far as possible take into account all the factors implicated. In this sense, experimental design includes selection of the behaviors to be observed, precise formulation of the hypotheses to be tested (choice of the appropriate statistical procedure *before* carrying out the experiment), and selection of the sample size and of control variables in regard to the precision of the statistical tests chosen.   *D.W.E. & W.H.*

Experimental drive diagnosis. L. Szondi's method (1947) of diagnosing dominant drive vectors (sexual, paroxysmal, ego and contact drives) associated in each case with two contrary drive requirements. The two most appealing and least appealing portraits must be selected from six series of eight portraits each, representing eight requirements. Differentiated conclusions are drawn by a complex process of evaluation.   *R.M.*

Experimental esthetics. G. T. Fechner, generally regarded as the father of experimental psychology, was the founder of experimental esthetics. This is the application of the methods of experimental psychology to problems concerning the arts and, more generally, to the study of motivational effects of perceptual forms and qualities. Fechner advocated an esthetics "from below", in contrast to the esthetics "from above" favored by philosophical estheticians. Apart from a number of largely speculative laws, his main contributions consist of his contention that the experimenter should begin with simple stimuli, representative of the most elementary components of works of art, and his advocacy of three methods of investigation, akin to the psychophysical methods that he introduced for the measurement of sensory processes. They comprise: the *method of choice* (in which subjects are presented with several stimuli and indicate their preferences); the *method of production* (in which they perform manipulations giving rise to stimuli illustrative of their preferences); and the *method of application* (the study of artefacts as indicators of the preferences current in a particular society).

Most of the work in experimental esthetics during the century that has since elapsed has used variants of the method of choice. Recent advances in scaling theory have made available a large range of sophisticated methods of measuring preference through ratings, ranking, and so on, and of constructing mathematical models to summarize the data so obtained. Many experiments, beginning with Fechner's own, elicited judgments of visual shapes and of colors. Relatively consistent findings have been a tendency for preferences with regard to rectangles, and divisions of a line segment, to cluster—despite wide variability—around the golden section (the ratio such that $A/B = B/A + B = 0.62$), and a tendency for red and blue to be liked more than other colors. More complex artistic material (reproductions of paintings, pictures of vases, musical passages, verse extracts, and so on) has been used for the investigation of individual differences in taste and of correlations of these with personality traits. Factor analysis has regularly revealed a general factor reflecting overall capacity for esthetic appreciation and a bipolar factor, which has been characterized differently by different writers (e.g. inclination toward simplicity or complexity, sensitivity to color or to form).

The impact of contemporary theoretical developments began to be felt in the 1920s and 1930s and modified the essentially empirical approach that had hitherto prevailed. Psychoanalysts interpreted artistic products, like so many other psychological phenomena, as disguised expressions of unconscious wishes and conflicts. The structural qualities to which the gestalt school attached importance in its research into perception, and especially those qualities that distinguish "good" configurations, have been seen as prime determinants of esthetic enjoyment, particularly by Arnheim. Birkhoff offered an influential mathematical treatment, ascribing esthetic value to the interaction of complexity (C) and order (O) factors.

Recent developments. Advances in psychology and neurophysiology have encouraged a distinct revival of interest in experimental esthetics in the 1960s. Studies of exploratory behavior, psychophysiological changes, and other phenomena, have drawn attention to the motivational importance of stimulus properties such as novelty, surprisingness, complexity, and ambiguity, which could be recognized as the constituents of artistic "form" or "structure". The mathematical concepts introduced by information theory have been used by Attneave, Hochberg & McAlister, and later Garner, for the quantitative treatment of "goodness" of configuration or amount of structure, and by Moles, Frank & Gunzenhäuser for a quantitative theory of esthetic value. Much has been learned about the brain processes that underlie fluctuations in emotion or "arousal", as well as about those that have to do with hedonic processes (reward and punishment, pleasurable and aversive pro-

perties of stimulus patterns). Possibilities of synthesis appeared as it became increasingly apparent that these brain processes are affected by structural or "collative" properties of stimulus patterns (novelty, complexity, and so on) and that these properties are closely related to information-theoretic concepts such as information content and uncertainty. A growing body of experiments indicates that moderate degrees of novelty and complexity tend to be favorably valued and sought out, whereas higher degrees are judged unpleasant and shunned.

In short, experimental esthetics seems to be entering a period of increasing integration with other areas of psychology, particularly motivation theory. It is also coming to rely less exclusively on verbal expressions of preference, seeking correlations between these and non-verbal measures such as spontaneous self-exposure and physiological indices of changes in arousal.

Bibliography: Berlyne, D. E.: Psychobiology and esthetics. New York, 1970. Child, I. L.: Esthetics. In: Lindzey, G. & Aronson, E. (Eds): Handbook of social psychology, Vol. 3. Reading, Mass., ²1969, Fechner, G. T.: Vorschule der Ästhetik. Leipzig. 1876. Frances, R.: Psychologie de l'esthétique. Paris, 1968. Frank, H.: Informationsästhetik. Quickborn, 1959. Moles, A.: Information theory and esthetic perception. Urbana, Illinois, 1966. Valentine, C. W.: The experimental psychology of beauty. London, 1962. Woodworth, R. S.: Experimental esthetics. In: Experimental psychology. New York, 1938.   *D. E. Berlyne*

Experimental group. A sample of individuals who, under experimental conditions, in contrast to a parallel, matched control group (q.v.), feature a dependent variable which forms the object of the experiment.
D.W.E.

Experiment, planning of. See *Experimental design.*

Experimenter. One who conducts an experiment.

Explanatory psychology. See *Erklärende Psychologie.*

Exploration. A distinction can be made between three phases of explorative behavior in psychology: (*a*) a state of excitement brought about by an unsatisfied desire, internal unrest or the search for the unknown, confusion, fear, etc.; (*b*) explorative behavior (as a more or less systematic, oriented, controlled, intellectual process) aiming to discover the object or mental state which could reduce this excitement; (*c*) reduction of the state of excitement if no obstacles are encountered (material impossibility or impossibility of solving the conflict). I. P. Pavlov observed this behavior in its simplest form (orienting reflex). Animals examine their natural surroundings to satisfy their wants as does a child to discover sources of stimulation which may contribute to its development; the same goes for scholars, philosophers and mystics. A person who is unable to solve his professional, marital, educational and other problems with his own resources (exploration) can consult a psychologist who will proceed as follows:

The psychologist first analyzes the circumstances and obvious motives which have led to this request as well as the social, family and inter-human relationships. This phase (on which a written report is rarely prepared) provides guidelines for the search for determining factors and the methods of examination used. It provides the reference framework into which the results of the exploration must be translated for the benefit of the subject so that he can understand the importance of the advice given and act accordingly. The psychologist then explores the personality and its conflicts with the means at his disposal: interview, tests of individual functions (intelligence, motility, etc.), personality tests (questionnaire method, projective method: Rorschach, TAT, etc.). Some psychologists use laboratory situations (H. J. Eysenck) or interaction situations

(stress interview, group situation). Others simply concentrate on psychological discussion (psychological exploration in the narrower sense) during which a subject's experiences are brought to light; this facilitates the creation of awareness and may even lead to an alteration of the personality (C. R. Rogers). Psychoanalysis and hypnosis are special processes of exploration used by depth psychologists.

The notion of exploration coincides to a varying degree with the concepts of study, evaluation, advice and diagnosis.

If we separate the two aspects of diagnosis and treatment, following the example of classical medicine, the therapy and the individual under examination become *objects* of a different kind for which the psychologist uses different methods whose validity is known. He then prepares a prognosis on the basis of an empirical correlation or establishes a clinical model to understand the individual case. However, if we adopt the notion that all exploration includes a degree of treatment then all test results are dependent on the interrelation between the patient and psychologist. By his own attitude and personality, the psychologist becomes the most important instrument of exploration, which then appears as a process of development in the existing relationship with the patient.

The activity of clinical psychologists has often been criticized. Their clinical conclusions are often unreliable and their verbal attitudes, methods and stereotypes lead to distortions which are impossible to eliminate. On the other hand the psychologist's exploratory methods are enriched by critical evaluation of clinical procedures and the use of methods enabling symptoms to be controlled by varying the environmental conditions (behavior control). Exploration is being increasingly analyzed on the pattern of sequential decision strategies. Diagnosis and treatment can therefore be combined in a comprehensive procedure.

Bibliography: Cronbach, L. J. & Gleser, G. C.: Psychological tests and personal decisions. Illinois,

1965. **Fiske, D. W. & Maddi, S. R.**: Functions of varied experience. Homewood, Ill., 1961. **Gathercole, C. E.**: Assessment in clinical psychology. Harmondsworth, 1968. **Kruboltz, J. D. & Thoresen, C. E.**: Behavioral counseling. New York, 1969. **Lesser, D.** (Ed.): Explorations in exploration: stimulation seeking. New York, 1969. **McReynolds, P.** (Ed.): Advances in psychological assessment, Vol. 1, Palo Alto, 1968. **Nahoum, C.**: L'entretien psychologique. Paris, 1952. **Rey, A.**: L'examen clinique en psychologie. Paris, 1958. **Rogers, C. R.**: Client-centered therapy. Boston, 1951. **Sundberg, N. D. & Tyler, C.**: Clinical psychology. London, 1963. **Vernon, P. E.**: Personality assessment. A critical survey. London, 1963.

G. Nahoum

Exploratory drive. Interpreted as a primary, unlearned need which is found particularly in the higher mammals and in man with increasing differentiation of the cerebral cortex. This spontaneous readiness is provoked by specific groups of stimuli expressed in notions such as novelty, surprise, uncertainty, etc. Physiologically, the urge to explore can be described as a typical arousal syndrome (high-frequency EEG waves, heightened vegetative and reticular activity).

P.S. & R.S.

Exploratory experiment (*Pilot experiment*). Psychology arrives at its research results with the help of methods based on statistics. Clear hypotheses (null and alternative hypotheses) are formulated which can be checked statistically. However the development of hypotheses already calls for a certain minimum knowledge of the object under investigation; this knowledge is obtained by preliminary exploratory experiments. *P.S.*

Exponential curve. The graphic representation of the exponential function:

$$Y = A^x = e^{bx}, A > 0$$
$$b = \ln A$$

The function can only have positive values. For $A > 1$ (i.e. $b > 0$) it rises constantly from 0 to ∞ and for $A < 1$ ($b > 0$) it falls constantly from ∞ to 0. The curve passes through the point (0, 1) and approaches the X axis asymptotically. *W.H.B.*

Expression (Ger. *Ausdruck*). The object of the psychology of expression (psychology of modes of expression; Ger. *Ausdruckspsychologie*).

1. *Expression in psychology.* Modern expression research has inherited a number of attempts to define the concept, all of which are demonstrably inadequate in one respect or another (see Kirchhoff 1962b, 1963, 1965b) and are now obsolescent if not obsolete. Examples are tautologies such as "Expression is expression of the psychic", or tautological and pointlessly restrictive postulates such as "Expression is the expression of emotion".

"Expression" always implies that a "who or what" (a subject of expression; also: an essential content of expression, or, more exactly: the subject or essential content of an expressive phenomenon) is made apparent, i.e. becomes accessible to someone (the recipient of the expression). If we apply these considerations to the field of psychological expression, it is clear that a full and proficient definition can be obtained only by thematic analysis of the subject (or essential content) of psychologically relevant expressive phenomena, and of these phenomena themselves (= media of the subject of expression). If one's approach is based on a conception of psychology as the "theory of the being and being-thus of individual existents, in so far as they are scientifically and methodologically accessible in terms of their lived experience and their behavior", psychological expression may be defined primarily as the "apparent individual mode of being of men and animals": i.e. apparent or evident in the sense of being accessible in terms of specific, individual expressions and expressive of media or symptoms. Since there are no good reasons for a conceptual and/or material restriction of the individual subject of expression (e.g. merely to emotions, feelings, affects, etc.; see Kirchhoff, 1965b), in principle all actual states of mind and modes of being in the world, and all relatively enduring personality traits, in so far as they are *expressed*, are "essential contents" of psychologically expressive phenomena; the same is true of psychologically expressive media.

On systematic and practical scientific grounds (above all, conflict with psycho-diagnostics, q.v.), a restriction to the actual, or "how", aspects of physically evident expressions is necessary (see Kirchhoff, 1962b). Consequently, we may define psychologically relevant expression as "the (apparent, or evident) individual mode of being of an expressive individual (man or animal), is so far as it is accessible in the actual aspects of individual phenomena" (pathognomically: *how* someone behaves, e.g. laughs, cries, stands, walks, moves expressively, speaks, and so on). This limitation marks out a further field of research which requires more precise differentiation in itself, and allows certain irrelevant phenomena (such as handwriting—a linguistic-graphic-significative artifact) to be excluded (the error of inclusion may be attributed primarily to L. Klages).

2. *The structure of psychological expression.* With this definition, the two main areas of expression, *pathognomy* and *physiognomy*, may also be precisely delineated. In classical antiquity and the Middle Ages, the two areas were confused and treated uncritically, but from the time of J. C. Lavater and G. C. Lichtenberg came increasingly to be distinguished one from the other, both conceptually and objectively; *both* are now considered to be legitimate component objects of the psychology of expression. In this process, pathognomy has come to include not only the traditional phenomena classed under *mimicry* (the play of the features) and *pantomimicry* (movement of the entire body: expressive movements), but vocal expression (phonognomy), vegetative expressions, the pathognomic elements of pragmatic, symbolic, linguistic behaviors (sound and gesture), microvibrations (q.v.), etc.

3. *The inner structure of psychological expression* comprises the relation of "expression transmitter" and "expression receiver", together with their contexts, and the individual transmitting and receiving systems. Expression exists only in terms of the transmitter-receiver relation; there is no "intrinsic expression", for it is always "by someone for someone" (more precisely: the manifestation of an expressive content peculiar to one individual for the sake of another). For the most part, the connection between transmitter and receiver is not unilinear and unipolar, but consists of interaction and social feedback between transmitter and receiver. A cybernetic model for expressive relations will probably become increasingly important. Socially relevant prototypes in this regard are, e.g., modes of visual contact (the social determination of visual expression). See *Communication.*

The following are the major problems in regard to the *transmitting* system: (*a*) How do specific physiognomic and pathognomic expressions occur under certain (actual-, onto-, and phylogenetic) conditions in the case of certain expressive systems? (*b*) How is the relation of the individual and the expressive medium to be determined? What, in particular, are the proper functional and semiotic terms to describe the relation of expressive signs and their signifieds? (*c*) What are the systematic conditions for the process of expression? What is the nature of the relation between "within" and "without", the individual expressing and the medium of his expression, the "psychic" and the "physical"? (See *Emotion.*)

The restricted nature of the earlier psychology of expression led to repeated, profitless theoretical attempts to find the origin of expressions, and in particular certain expressive movements, in non-expressive phenomena ("mere" purposive movements), and in this way (genetically) to explain the existence of "pure" expressions. Right up to the present there has been much discussion of Darwin's (1872) attempted explanations, and particularly of his first hypothesis (the "principle of serviceable associated habits" which become "mere" expressions: i.e. expressive characteristics may be derived from previous practical functions), as well as of Wundt's quasi-parallel though ultimately non-explanatory theory (see *Wundt*), and of the action theory of expression (deriving from J. J. Engel) which does contain a core of truth. Since the idea of the existence of "pure", "special" expressive phenomena (and movements), which was effective up to F. J. J. Buytendijk (1956), largely gave way to more recent data, the basic problem of a theory of expression as "transmission" has again been generally posed as the question of the (actual-, onto-, and phylogenetic) conditions of an individual system that, by means of expression, makes "subjective" essential contents accessible to a specific receiving system with its own similarly classifiable conditions.

This does not imply a more or less mysterious "transubstantiation" of non-expressive (e.g. "mere", "expressionless") into expressive actions. What is in question is rather the "emergence" of the individual essential contents of a transmission system *for* specific receiving systems, with a degree of awareness that depends on their perceptive, cognitive, and other conditions. Here, too, the constitutive basis shows that there is no such thing as "expression in itself" or "*intrinsic* expression", but only "expression *for*" specific receiving systems with their special conditions. (See Allport & Vernon, 1933.)

In the *receiving* system, the problems are in principle to be systematically arranged, formulated and answered in the same way: (*a*) phenography, (*b*) functional analysis and functional interpretation, (*c*) conditional analysis and conditional interpretation of the reception of expression and of the receiving system, together with actual-, onto-, and phylogenetic delineation of the specific individual problems.

4. *Terminology.* Until quite recently a multiplicity of terms has been in use in the psychology of expression; for the most part they were conceptually inadequate and imprecise. See Kirchhoff 1957, 1962b and 1965b for a discussion of the terminological problem.

5. *Historical outline.* In his *Ausdruckstheorie* K. Bühler (q.v.) provided an admirable survey of the basic positions and main trends of the history of expression theory from Aristotle to P. Lersch. Nevertheless, his hope that it would be possible to show a systematic development was, from the nature of the case, unrealizable. However, an historical synopsis—without reference to the actual informative content of the historical sources as such—can offer pointers for the future.

In terms of the maximal, minimal and median determination of subject and medium of expression, all concepts of expression from antiquity through the Enlightenment and Romantic periods, and the natural-scientific period of expression research in the nineteenth century, up to the present, can be ordered as peaks where expression was broadly conceived, and depressions where it was viewed in a restricted fashion.

A first "high range" of broad concepts runs from the pseudo-Aristotelian *Physiognomika* up to C. G. Carus; another from L. Klages' second, broad notion of expression up to F. J. J. Buytendijk; a third from the concepts of K. Lewin (q.v.) and G. Kafka to the present. Between these three high marks there is an initial trough extending from the beginnings of a "natural-scientific" treatment of expression by C. Bell, by way of W. Wundt, to L. Klages' first, narrow concept. A second trough is indicated by the work of researchers such as C. Landis, A. Flach, and M. Turhan, who were concerned to demonstrate that there was no such thing as an unequivocal correspondence of a specific expression to a specific essential content.

A heuristically valuable axiomatics probably lies *between* the two extremes (see Kirchhoff 1957, 1962, 1965.)

6. *Present position, results and critique.*
"The work of the last few centuries contains some progressive and some static trends"—N. H. Frijda's judgment (1965) applies to expression research as a whole. Decisive progress has been evident in recent years in the conceptual, methodological, terminological and descriptive bases of psychological expression. There has also been progress in phenographic and functional (but not so much in ontogenetic) study of the reception of expressive information; and some achievements in, e.g., factor-analytical treatment of data (dimensional analysis of mimic expression; see N. H. Frijda, 1965).

The as yet incomplete separation of (though not definitive dichotomy between) fundamental scientific research and applied psychological evaluation of expression data has been less satisfactory. The theory that a premature diagnostics of expression (as well as a one-sided consideration of expression from the angle of validity) would be more harmful than helpful has not been universally influential. A pathognomic diagnostics of expression (pathognostics) established on the principles of a "universal psychological diagnostics" will be possible only on the basis of broad and solid fundamental research. The *how* and the *what* of behavior (and its effects) are only two aspects of one and the same thing; therefore neither is diagnostics itself impossible, nor is a diagnostics of expression pure and simple possible.

More than in regard to other disciplines, the existing research toward proficient principles must as yet be judged inadequate. What is lacking is not so much the fundaments themselves, and adequate methods and techniques and large-scale research programs, as the concrete possibilities for their realization. Research is carried out and results are obtained; but as a whole it is too unsystematic, scattered, and more "associative" than "coordinated and integrative". All in all, empirical expression research (and, it must be said, psychological research as a whole in Europe outside Britain) is for the most part still out-of-touch, anachronistic, and redolent of nineteenth-century paternalism. To put it positively, what we need are research centers and institutes (something like the Max Planck Institutes) which, within foreseeable periods of time, and on the basis of circumspect total strategies, would be in a position to advance and produce really significant and coherent work. We can only hope that the growing realization of the importance of science (not only technically utilizable, but individually and socially relevant science) will bring about a change in the attitude to expression research within the foreseeable future. See also *Habit; Personality; Traits.*

Bibliography: Allport, G. W. & Vernon, P. E.: Studies in expressive movements. New York, 1933. Allport, G. W.: Personality and social encounter. Boston, 1960. Andrew, R.: The origin and evolution of the calls and facial expressions of primates. Behavior, 1963, *20*, 1–109. Bell, C.: Anatomy and philosophy of expression. London, 1806. Bühler, K.: Ausdruckstheorie. Jena, 1933, ²1968. Buytendijk, F. J. J.: Allgemeine Theorie der menschlichen Haltung und Bewegung. Utrecht, 1956. Darwin, C.: The expression of the emotions in man and animals. London, 1872. Davitz, J. R. (Ed.): The communication of emotional meaning. New York, 1964. Frijda, N. H.: De betekenis van de gelaatsexpressie. Amsterdam, ²1958. Id.: Mimik und Pantomimik. In: Handbuch der Psychologie, Vol. 5. Göttingen, 1965. Görlitz, D.: Ergebnisse und Probleme der ausdruckspsychol. Sprechstimmforschung. Diss. Tech. Univ. Berlin, 1970. Kafka, G.: Grundsätzliches zur Ausdruckspsychologie. Acta Psychol., 1937, *3*, 273–314. Kirchhoff, R.: Allgemeine Ausdruckslehre. Göttingen, 1957. Id.: Vom Ausdruck des Menschenblicks. Stud. Gen, 1960, *13.* Id.: Die Umfelder des pathognomischen Ausdrucks. Jb. Psychol. Psychother. med. Anthropol., 1962, *9* (a). Id.: Methodologische und theoretische Grundprobleme der Ausdrucksforschung. Stud. Gen., 1962, *15* (b). Id.: Ausdruck: Begriff, Regionen. Binnenstruktur. Jb. Psychol., Psychother. med. Anthropol, 1963, *10.* Id.: Zur Geschichte des Ausdrucksbegriffs. In: Handbuch d. Psychol., Vol. 5. Göttingen, 1965a. Id.: Grundfragen der Ausdruckspsychologie. In: Handbuch d. Psychol., Vol. 5, 1965b. Klages, L.: Grundlegung der Wissenschaft vom Ausdruck. Bonn, ⁷1950. Lersch, P.: Gesicht und Seele. Munich, ⁴1955. Lorenz, K.: Studies in animal and human behaviour, Vol. 1. London, 1970. Rudert, J.: Vom Ausdruck der Sprechstimme. In: Handbuch d. Psychol. Vol. 5. Göttingen, 1965.   *R. Kirchhoff*

Expression in animals. Expression research comprises the analysis of motivation and of the transmission of information. Hence the definition: Expression is the state of a living creature in its behavior and bodily form as apparent to another creature. Animal ethology does not as yet make any distinction between a "what" and a "how" aspect. The statement "A is eating" is thought of as predicating something expressive of A, just as much as the statement "A is a hasty eater", in so far as only B apprehends the eating or mode of eating. A distinction may be made between (a) peripheral expressive structures (optically effective body-build characteristics, olfactory organs, skin characteristics affecting cutaneous sensibility); (b) non-directive expressive processes (hair and feather erection and plumage ruffling, color changes, pupillary reactions, variations in cutaneous gland secretion, changes in respiratory rhythm, sounds [in part], trembling, twitching, fidgeting); and (c) directive expressive actions (threat postures, aggressive displays, invitations to play, contact movements, courtship behavior, etc.).

Typical animal expressions are expressive movements, the evolution of which was favored by the requirement for unequivocal, precise, genotypically codifiable, species-specific communication units.

After 1951, the study of the motivational aspect of animal expression received an impetus from the development of the theory of conflicting impulses. Most studies emphasize expressive movements and the functional aspect of the intraspecific, species-typical expressive mode. Here there is a reflection of the considerable part played by animal expressions in the control of social behavior and the preservation of the species-typical associative and population structure. Nevertheless, future research will have to take more account of undifferentiated expression, relations between arbitrarily selected partners, and individual differences. Only in this way will it be possible to achieve a comprehensive description and causal analy-

sis of animal expression. These viewpoints are also becoming increasingly important in applied ethology. See *Animal psychology; Comparative psychology; Instinct.*

Bibliography: Armstrong, E. A.: A study of bird song. London, 1963. Bastock, M.: Courtship: a zoological study. London, 1967. Eibl, I.: Ausdrucksformen der Säugetiere. In: Kükenthal, W.: Handbuch der Zoologie, Vol. 8. Berlin, 1957, *10* (6), 1–26. Lorenz, K.: Methods of approach to the problems of behavior (The Harvey Lectures, Series 54). New York, 1959. Id.: The function of color in coral reef fishes. Proc. Roy. Inst. of G.B., 1962, *39*, 282–96. Schenkel, R.: Ausdrucksstudien an Wölfen. Behaviour, 1947, *1*, 81–129. Stamm, R. A.: Perspektiven zu einer vergleichenden Ausdrucksforschung. In: Handbuch der Psychologie, Vol. 5. Göttingen, 1965, 255–88. Tinbergen, N.: The study of instinct. London, 1951. Id.: Social behavior in animals. London, 1953. Id.: Comparative studies of the behaviour of gulls. Behaviour, 1959, *15*, 1–70.   R. A. Stamm

Expressiveness; expressivity. 1. Richness of expression, expressive content: the degree to which an object of perception has expressive value, i.e. spontaneously releases emotional attitudes in the perceiver (see *Expression*).

2. Ability to express: the ability and willingness, which differ from individual to individual, to communicate thoughts and ideas in language. This ability is dependent on aptitude factors (divergent thinking: verbal, associative and expressive fluency, imagination) and on temperamental features which are covered by the personality factor *extraversion* (Pawlik, 1968).

3. Genetic expressiveness: the degree to which an inherited feature is phenotypically expressed in an individual (see *Heredity*).

Bibliography: Pawlik, K.: Dimensionen des Verhaltens. Berne & Stuttgart, 1968.   K.P.

Extinction. 1. In biology, the disappearance of a species or life form. **2.** In behavioristic psychology, the elimination or progressive reduction in magnitude or frequency of a *conditioned response* upon the withdrawal of *reinforcement*. The term is used in both *classical conditioning* (q.v.) (in which reinforcement is the unconditioned stimulus) and *operant conditioning* (in which reinforcement is reward or punishment contingent upon the response).

Differential extinction: a process by which one conditioned response is extinguished while one or more others are maintained.

G.D.W.

3. The disappearance of memory content (see *Memory*). An acquired ability is progressively lost through lack of reinforcement (q.v.); if the result of a specific, acquired form of behavior is not achieved, this behavior is gradually lost. *Experimental* extinction: a conditioned reflex is broken down by repeated presentation of the conditioned stimulus without reinforcement.

K.E.P.

Extinction-stimulus method. A method developed by H. von Helmholtz (q.v.) for the extinction of a sense-impression by means of a subsequent, stronger stimulus of the same stimulus class. The procedure is used, especially in tachistoscopic experiments, in order to prevent formation of an afterimage (q.v.).

F.M.

Extirpation. Surgical removal of an organ or part of the tissue of an organ; the injury is allowed to heal spontaneously. Applied, e.g., in animal experiments: extirpation of parts or all of the brain. See *Ablation*.

F.C.S.

Extrapyramidal motor areas. The part of the motor system of the spinal cord and brain outside the pyramidal path and not directly subject to volition. Its task is to regulate the general tone of the muscles, to coordinate movement by interaction between agonists and antagonists and simultaneous limb movement and to monitor body posture. It includes parts of the spinal cord and basal ganglia in the diencephalon and mesencephalon, e.g. striate body, *globus pallidum,*

claustrum, nucleus amygdalae, nucleus ruber and *substantia nigra.*

E.D.

Extrasensory perception (ESP). Paranormal cognition. The acquisition of information from the external environment otherwise than through any of the known sensory channels. In experimental parapsychology the term ESP was employed by J. B. Rhine to embrace such phenomena as telepathy (q.v.), clairvoyance (q.v.) and precognition (q.v.). See also *Paragnosia.*

J.B.

The term ESP, which probably goes back to Pagenstecher (*Aussersinnliche Wahrnehmung,* Halle, 1924), is freely used by writers in various fields as well as by the mass media. From a scientific point of view the choice of this term is perhaps less fortunate. Psychologists may point out with some justification that sensory perception is not fully understood and that consequently the meaning of ESP is rather obscure. However, Schmeidler (*Extrasensory Perception,* New York, 1969) pointed out that similar exclusion conditions (i.e. for ESP "no means of sensing or remembering or inferring") are used in more orthodox fields of psychology. It can also be argued that an operational definition of ESP can be formulated by providing detailed descriptions of the operations which measure ESP and which exclude "sensing, remembering and inferring". Nevertheless, the term ESP has perhaps overemphasized a difference between parapsychological phenomena and related events in orthodox areas of psychology. There is also an obvious scarcity of positive criteria for the description of ESP phenomena, and it may be reasonable to attribute some of this lack to the negative essence of the term. In some countries new expressions have been introduced (bioinformation, q.v., Russia; psychotronics, Czechoslovakia). These new terms suggest a closer association with the orthodox sciences and with monism. Dualism was more often the basic outlook in connection with ESP research. But in recent years this tendency has become less pronounced.

H.H.J.K.

Extratensive type. An experiential type showing "an urge to live outward, excitable motility and weak affectivity" in the Rorschach test (q.v.). Coincides in large measure with C. G. Jung's extraverted type.

W.K.

Extravert (syn. *Extrovert*). An attitude type characterized by "positive movement of subjective interest in the object" or a direct attitude to the objective world in evaluation and intention. Direction of psychic energy outward. Tends toward superficial contact. Shows "an obliging, apparently open and willing nature which easily fits in with any situation, quickly establishes relationships and ventures confidently and unhesitatingly into unknown situations without regard to possible problems". Good "adaptation" (C. G. Jung). H. J. Eysenck considers extraversion to be a statistically-proven personality dimension. The questionnaires used in his factor analysis accord with Jung's description. Close relationship with the cyclothymic (q.v.) type. See *Traits; Type.*
Bibliography: Eysenck, H. J.: The structure of human personality. London, ²1960. Jung, C. G.: Psychological type. London, 1970. *W.K.*

Eye. The organ of sight. The light-refractive section is distinguished from the light-receptive section. The former includes: the cornea; the anterior and posterior chambers, which are divided by the iris and are filled with an aqueous humor; the lens; the vitreous humor. The latter includes the retina and its receptor cells, the rods and cones which transform light energy into nervous impulses, which in their turn are conveyed by the "optic nerves" (*fasciculus opticus*) to the central nervous system (CNS). The optical axis of the eye is distinguished from the visual axis. On the optical axis (*axis oculi geometrica*) are the cardinal points of the optical system (points of union, nodal points, and focal points). It connects the anterior pole of the lens with a point between

the blind spot and the *fovea centralis* and corresponds approximately to the symmetrical axis of the eyeball, which is not quite symmetrical in rotation. The visual axis passes

Fig. 1. Section through the eyeball.

through the middle of the fovea and bisects the optical axis in the posterior third part of the lens. See *Sense organs; Visual perception.*
Bibliography: Davson, H. (Ed.): The eye. London & New York, 1962. Graham, C. H.: Vision and visual perception. London, 1964. Weale, R. A.: From sight to light. London, 1968. *R.R.*

Eyeball. The *bulbus oculi*, situated in the orbital cavity (*orbita*). Its outer wall is formed by the cornea and the sclera, under which are the choroid membrane and the retina. It is surrounded by fatty tissue. Because of the six eye muscles attached to it, it can move on all axes (see *Fusion*). This makes the fixation of any object possible (see *Identical [Retinal] Points*). *R.R.*

Eye-blink reflex. A natural response to a blast of air that can be obtained as a conditioned response and accurately measured. Used in conditioning experiments, especially to measure traits.
Bibliography: Franks, C. M. & Trouton, D.: Effects of amobarbital sodium and dexamphetamine on the conditioning of the eyeblink response. J. Compar. Physiol. Psychol., 1958, *51*, 220–22. *J.M.*

Eyeless sight. The alleged capacity to see when the eyes are covered. Regarded by the

Mesmerists as one of the paranormal concomitants of the deep hypnotic trance (q.v.) and akin to clairvoyance (q.v.). Jules Romains coined the expression "extra-retinal" or "paroptic" vision, and attempted to give it a physiological interpretation. See *Skin vision.* *J.B.*

Eysenck Personality Inventory (abb. EPI). A revision of the Maudsley Personality Inventory (q.v.) scoring neuroticism and extraversion and including a lie scale.

Bibliography: Eysenck, H. J. & Eysenck, S. B. G.: Manual of the Eysenck Personality Inventory, London & San Diego, 1964.   *J.M.*

F

Factor. In general terms, the word factor denotes a component part or a part cause. Since the introduction of factor analysis by C. Spearman, the factor is considered to be a psychological variable which has been defined with the aid of this mathematical method. A factor determines part of the overall variance of a measured characteristic. A characteristic may be determined by one or more factors. The factors are therefore psychological conditions which cause variance and establish individual differentiation. Both characteristics and individuals may be defined by factors. Depending on the method, factors are assumed to be independent of each other (orthogonal), or partially dependent, in which case they can be further analyzed. Factors are interpreted either as psychological conditions (capable of no further analysis) or causes of performance or behavior patterns (L. L. Thurstone *et al.*), or simply as principles of classification (C. Burt). Meili distinguishes between basic, or primary factors, and secondary factors originating from learning processes. The number of defined factors is impossible to evaluate and it would take more than the criteria of factor analysis to determine their general relevance. The factors are usually designated by letters or combinations of letters. See *Intelligence* for L. L. Thurstone's and R. Meili's factors, and *Intelligence, structure of* for J. P. Guilford's factors. *R.M.*

Factor analysis. I. 1. *Origins of factor analysis.* Factor analysis has two independent origins, one in psychology, and one in pure mathematics. Although the two distinct streams, represented by Spearman and Hotelling, have now united, an appreciable number of the difficulties psychologists experience with factor analysis arise from differences of assumption and emphasis between the scientific and mathematical models.

In psychology, factor analysis began as an attempt to get more out of the Galton-Pearson correlational approach than had previously been possible. Spearman developed it initially as the only instrument capable of answering the crucial question of whether there is a single, "monarchic" structure of intelligence (q.v.) or a host of "intelligences". From this concern with examining a correlation matrix for a single factor, it was further developed by Thurstone (and more briefly by Maxwell Garnett) into multiple factor analysis. After Spearman, Burt, Thomson and Thurstone used factor analysis to examine ability problems; since 1930 Cattell, Eysenck, Guilford, Horn, Hundleby, Nesselroade, Pawlik and others have used it for problems of determining structure in personality, motivation and psychological states.

2. *Nature and formulation.* The aim of factor analysis is to explain the correlations obtained among a large number, n, of variables, by variation on a smaller number, k, of underlying abstract or inferred factors. This aim is cognate with that of science generally: to go beyond appearances to a more economical set of basic concepts. In the physical sciences good guesses can be made about these underlying concepts, but in the social and biological sciences, where far

more factors are at work, factor analysis is indispensable as a preliminary concept-generating simplification. As a method, its role is both to generate hypotheses and to test them. Mathematically, the basic equations can best be expressed in matrix algebra (see *Statistics*). One begins with the experimentally given $n \times y$ correlation matrix among the variables. The mathematical process of extracting latent roots and vectors permits us to computerize this experimentally obtained $n \times n$ correlation matrix R_v ("reduced" by having communality estimates instead of unities in the diagonal) and to obtain an $n \times k$ *factor pattern matrix*, V_{fp}, which gives the loadings of each of the factors on the n variables, thus:

$$R_v = V_{fp} R_f V'_{fp} \qquad (1)$$

The R_f is in the middle in the $k \times k$ matrix of correlations among the factors, and in the special case where the factors are orthogonal it will be unity, and vanish from (1). The meaning of the loadings (or correlations in the orthogonal case) in V_{fp} is that they indicate how much the normal variance on each of the k common factors is responsible for the observed variation in each of the variables. As equation (4) below (which is a row from the V_{fp} matrix) shows, the variance of any behavioral variable must be the weighted sum of the variance on these common, broad factors (which operate on many other variables) plus that of a specific factor (F_f in equation (4)) which operates only on that specific variable. However, this "specific factor" may be a fiction stating that we do not know what other common factors to bring in.

3. *Unique resolution in the scientific model.* A major problem has been to determine the unique solution for (1), since, mathematically, there is an infinite series of equivalent solutions, which correspond, in a geometrical plot of the test variables on the coordinate axes given by the factors, to spinning the factor axis to an infinite number of positions. Consequently the problem is commonly referred to as unique rotational resolution.

Deciding on the number of factors (and communalities) and extracting them by the computer nowadays takes very little time. But the rotation, in spite of automatic programs like Oblimax, Promax, Rotoplot and Maxplane, can be long; but it is crucial for subsequent psychological meaning. The essence of rotation is the finding of the transformation matrix, L, that will convert the unrotated orthogonal matrix, V_0, which comes from the computer, into the (typical) oblique reference vector structure, V_{rs}, which has the required simple structure or other properties (see below) of the scientific model. Thus:

$$V_{rs} = V_0 L \qquad (2)$$

In mathematical factor analysis, the correlations discovered between factors and variables are simply measures of "association", and all in the infinite set of equivalents are equally correct; but in the scientific use the unique values indicate that the unique position of the factor corresponds to some influence at work in nature. The hypothesis is no longer that the factor corresponds to "a mere mathematical abstraction", as some clinical critics, unfamiliar with factor analysis, have asserted, but that it is a causal influence or structure, resting on the same basis of observation as an electron or a valency in the physical sciences.

4. *Psychological meaning in the behavioral equation.* From equation (1) it is possible to pass to equations for estimating any individual's score on a given factor (or "source trait") from his performances on the variables, thus:

$$z_f = Z_v V_{fe} \qquad (3)$$

where Z_v is an N (people) $\times n$ score matrix of variables, V_{fe} is an $n \times k$ factor estimation matrix and z_f is the $N \times k$ set of factor scores (not in standard scores until a slight transformation is made). If we know both the factor pattern matrix from (1) (but including now a row for some new variable, a) and the individual's standard scores on the factors, from (2) we proceed to use the *specification* or *behavioral* equation, in which the individual's performance is estimated on the new variable from his factor scores, thus:

$$a_j = b_{j1}F_1 + b_{j2}F_2 + \ldots + b_{jk}F_k + b_jF_j \tag{4}$$

Here the *b*'s are factor loadings from a row of the factor pattern matrix, and may in the psychological sense be called *behavioral indices*, for each expresses how much the given factor (or source trait) enters into the determination of the extent of the particular behavior. When the factors are motivation factors and a_j is a symptom, we have what may be called a "quantitative psycho-analysis". In any case the factor analytic model is a mathematical expression of a conceptual background in psychology that is prepared to recognize (*a*) that behavior is typically multiply determined; (*b*) that both the organism (represented by the *F*'s in (4) above) and the stimulus situation (represented by the *b*'s) must be invoked to determine behavior; and (*c*) that any personality concept can be operationally defined and measured only by a whole *pattern* of variables, not (typically) by any single variable. (See *Source traits*.)

In accordance with the use of factor analysis as a scientific, not only a statistical model, the factor resolution should be free to locate oblique and not merely orthogonal factors. In an interacting universe it would be strange to have factors uncorrelated. Work with plasmodes, i.e. numerical examples of a general model, where the structure is actually known (as in Thurstone's box and Cattell's ball problem), shows that simple structure yields factors corresponding to the scientific concepts in the field—length, breadth, weight, elasticity, temperature—and that an orthogonal rotation is meaningless.

5. *Oblique factors, rotational principles, higher order emergents.* Correlated factor concepts enable higher-order factors to be obtained. These are found by factoring the correlation matrix among primary (first-order factors); they have proved to have good psychological meaning. For example, Horn's factoring of Thurstone's primary abilities and others reveals the existence of two higher-order general ability factors— fluid and crystallized intelligence. The pursuit of higher-order factors has put more demands on the rotation of primaries to truly exact obliqueness. Two principles have directed such rotation: (*a*) simple structure, proposed by Thurstone, and accepting maximum simplicity, in the spirit of Newton's *natura est simplex*; and (*b*) confactor rotation, proposed by Cattell, which requires two co-ordinated factor-analytic experiments and the seeking of "proportional profiles" in the loading patterns of corresponding factors at the critical position. The latter—confactor resolution—achieves directly what simple structure aims at as secondary, namely "factor invariance", i.e. a convergence on the *same* concepts, as matchable factor patterns, from different experiments, as discussed by Meredith, Tucker and others. Lately it has become usual to separate the scientific from the mathematical model more explicitly, by calling only the former *factor analysis*, and referring to the latter as *component analysis*. Component analysis, with orthogonal principal axes, will not give the same factors from one experiment to another, since the axis of the first factor extracted will alter with biases in the choice of variables.

6. *New variants.* In the last twenty years, there have been many variants and special developments of factor analysis, such as factoring covariances and cross products (Nesselroade, 1970) instead of correlations: Guttman's non-parametric factoring; Kaiser's alpha factoring; McDonald's non-linear factor analysis; Tucker's three-way factoring; and the special scientific models called the permissive, expending and modulator models.

The three last are intended to fit the model better to certain psychological conditions. Thus the permissive model says that factor *A* cannot come into action at all until factor *B* has reached a certain level. (It brings interaction terms into equation 4 above.) The expending model, designed for motivation research, says that much discharge of a factor in one performance must reduce its availability for another. The modulator model splits the factor trait into an excitability, which alone is truly fixed for the individual and allows the stimulus situation to "modulate" the factor level itself before it operates. This offers one of the chief links between the individual difference use of factor analysis and its use in the areas of "process psychologists" in perception and learning.

7. *Impact on individual difference concepts.* The greatest impact and best understood operation of factor analysis were at first in the area of individual differences and specifically of human abilities, and soon after in the personality field. In the former it has enormously clarified the structure of primary abilities, as begun by Thurstone, and pursued by Meili, Guilford, Arnold, Horn, French and others. It has also given substantial support to certain higher-order concepts, notably those of fluid and crystallized intelligence as approached independently by Hebb in physiology and Cattell in behavior. In the personality field, operating on questionnaires and rating studies by many psychologists, and on objective, miniature situation measures, specifically in the studies of Cattell and Eysenck, it has led to a rich array of twenty or more concepts, which have proved far more stable and replicable than the numerous dimensions suggested on *a priori* or clinical grounds. They include such new concepts as surgency, independence, presmia, the self-sentiment, regression, general inhibition, parmia, affectothymia, ego strength and super ego strength. Some of these (such as the three last) are old clinical concepts, new only in the sense of being given the new outlines of experimental psychology and a basis for estimation of validity of measurement (see *Construct validity*).

8. *Diverse Referee (R, P, S, T, etc.) Techniques.* A less widely understood impact of factor analysis comes from the use of the Diverse Referee Techniques—such as *P-*, *S-*,

T-, and *dR*-techniques. These vary the referees of measurement in the Basic Data Relation Matrix. The BDRM is a ten-dimensional "data box" having as its edges people, tests, occasions in time, etc., and illustrated as to the first three in the familiar "covariation chart" of Figure 1. The basic *R*-technique correlates tests (as relatives) over people

Figure 1. Possible techniques of relational analysis shown in the simpler context of the three-axis covariation chart

(as referees), while its transpose, *Q*-technique, correlates people (as relatives) over tests (as referees). For mathematical reasons, such transposes lead to essentially the same factors, but there is no reason other than some psychological lawfulness, why, say, *R-* and *P-*techniques should yield the same patterns.

In *P*-technique, as indicated in Figure 1, one factors the single person (hence *P*), by correlating behaviors ("tests") over a long enough time series of repeated measurements. Obviously the unitary dimensions so obtained should be those which describe the states of man (as Wundt attempted by *a priori* analysis), and *P*-technique has been the main means by which psychometrically useful concepts have been obtained for such states as anxiety, the depressions, stress, fatigue, etc. It has been effective in clarifying the number and nature of human drives (see *Drive*) by revealing some nine distinct dimensions of ergic tension (sex, fear, pugnacity, curiosity, etc.) measurable by objective devices (memory, projection [perceptual distortion], GSR, etc.) and varying one level with stimulus and satisfaction conditions. The factor-analytic investigation of the multivariate phenomena of motivation has not only led to clearer concepts of the human drive structures, but also (Delhees, Horn, Sweney and others) has extended to a "dynamic calculus" (see *Motivation*) for quantitatively evaluating conflict and studying the learning growth of emotional attitudes. Another effective referee-varying technique is *dR*-technique (differential *R*-technique), where the correlation matrix is obtained by correlating the *changes* between two stimulus occasions over a sample of people. This, like *P*-technique, yields the dimensions of state change, and has been used especially to define and separate anxiety and stress response patterns.

9. *Critical evaluation of the two main sources of experimental design.* In the debates among psychologists on the properties and research roles of various methods, despite half a century of use, an appropriate understanding of the role of factor analysis is only now emerging. Essentially, correlational analysis and analysis of variance divide the field, and factor analysis is the necessary culmination of any more than elementary use of correlational methods. Both factor analysis and anova are used to evaluate the significance and ultimately the magnitude of relations between variables. But anova does this two at a time (dependent and independent) whereas factor analysis handles a large number at a time. It puts the many relations in perspectives of underlying influences, whereas anova leaves it to the experimenter's unaided memory to piece

together the conclusions for hypotheses and theories for many bivariate relations. Both methods create and test hypotheses, but factor analysis (where enough measures can be gathered) is much more positive and penetrating in suggesting, and more exacting in testing a hypothesis, since it tests for the reality of a whole pattern, not a divergence on a single variable.

It has been objected that factor analysis is restricted to linear relations; that it does not employ the manipulative control of the classical bivariate experiment; that it lacks various necessary checks and tests of significance; and that as a result of this last there is much disagreement among factors analysts in their substantive conceptual conclusions—examined extensively by Cattell (1966). Except for McDonald's non-linear factor analysis, which is quite complete, factor analysis is restricted to linear relations. But anova knows no more when it makes a 2-point curve; and, by a succession of tangents (loadings), a series of factor analyses over successive ranges of variables can approach a description of curvilinear relations. As to manipulation, the criticism rebounds; for there is no intrinsic reason why dependent and independent variables should not be factored together, and only the lack of enterprise of those primarily using manipulative designs is responsible for so few instances in the literature of what Cattell & Scheier (1961) have illustrated as the condition-response factor design.

On the other hand, it is true that until recently there were no effective expressions for such hypothesis-testing decisions as the significance of a primary factor loading, of a factor, of a correlation among factors, of a second-order factor, of a communality, and of a match between factors from two experiments. For the significance of a loading, Harris has suggested:

$$|a_{jf}| > t_z \sqrt{\frac{(1-h^2{}_j)d_{ff}}{N-k-1}} \qquad (5)$$

where d_{ff} is the element in *f*th row and column of $R^{-1}{}_f$, h^2 is the communality, N the number of subjects and k the number of factors. Expressions for other required significances have been developed, notably in the Lawley-Rao tests for significance of a factor. Three approaches to determining the goodness of match of purportedly the same factor in two experiments are available in Burt's congruence coefficient, Cattell's salient variable similarity index, and the configurative matching index.

10. *Factor-analytic education.* Those outside and those in the field see the differences of conclusion among factor analysts very differently. Such a difference as that between Thurstone and Guilford on primary ability structure is due to the latter retaining orthogonal factors. He asks a different question and gets a different answer. That between Cattell and Eysenck on the number and naming of personality factors is due to the latter operating at the second order, relative to the first order, which Cattell considers equally important. But if the concepts and structures which Cattell obtains at the second stage are aligned with what Eysenck obtains in a first operation, the agreement of patterns and scales is far better than between, say, the scales that two clinicians might make up for certain psychoanalytic concepts. Indeed, it must be said that the chief problem in the effective use of concepts from factor analysis in general psychological practice and research is not any inherent lack of precision or potency in the concepts themselves, but the fact that only about one-tenth of doctoral-level psychologists, even today, are trained to competence in factor analysis, conceptually or mathematically. The remaining nine-tenths develop imaginary criticisms as a defense against the unknown.

Nevertheless, the future of factor-analytic methodology in psychology is expanding rapidly. Technical procedures have been remarkably refined and enriched in the last decade, while the areas of application have spread from individual differences to social psychology (group dynamics and the dimensions of cultures; Bereiter, Gorsuch), perception (Hake, Schneewind), human and animal motivation (Delhees, Horn, Royce), physiological psychology (Fahrenberg, Mefferd), genetics (Broadhurst, Thompson), language behavior (Osgood, Miron, Papal), clinical dynamics (Cohen), learning theory (Cattell, Eysenck, Fleishman, Tucker, White) and the longitudinal study of states and processes (Baltes, Nesselroade, Scheier).

Bibliography: Burt, C. L.: Factors of the mind. London, 1940. Cattell, R. B.: The basis of recognition and interpretation of factors. Educ. Psychol. Measmt., 1962, 22, 667–97. Id.: The configurative method for surer identification of personality dimensions, notably in child study. Psychol. Rept., 1965, 16, 269–90. Id.: Handbook of multivariate and experimental psychology. Chicago, 1966. Id.: Confactor rotation: the central problem in structural psychology. Laboratory of Personality and Group Analysis Advance Publication, No. 1, Nov., 1966. Id. & Dickman, K.: A dynamic model of physical influences demonstrating the necessity of oblique simple structure. Psychol. Bull., 1962, 59, 389–400. Cattell, R. B. & Sullivan, W.: The scientific nature of factors: a demonstration by cups of coffee. Behav. Sci., 1962, 7, 184–93. Cattell, R. B. & Scheier, I.: The meaning and measurement of neuroticism and anxiety. New York, 1961. Delhees, K.: The abnormal personality: factor analysis of neurotic and delinquent behavior. In: Cattell, R. B. (Ed.): Handbook of modern personality theory. Chicago, 1970, 560–610. Eysenck, H. J.: The structure of human personality. London, ²1960. Guilford, J. P.: Psychometric methods. New York, 1954. Guttman, L.: Some necessary conditions for common factor analysis. Psychometrika, 1954, 19, 149–61. Horn, J. L.: Motivation and dynamic calculus concepts from multivariate experiment. In: Cattell, R. B.: Handbook of multivariate experimental psychology. Chicago, 1966, 611–41. Hotelling, H.: Analysis of a complex of statistical variables into principal components. J. Educ. Psychol., 1933, 24, 417–41, 498–520. Hundleby, J., Pawlik, K. & Cattell, R. B.: Personality factors in objective test devices. San Diego, Calif., 1965. Nesselroade, J. R.: The theory of psychological states and mood action. In: Cattell, R. B. (Ed.): Handbook of modern personality theory. Chicago, 1970, 200–40. Pawlik, K.: Dimensionen des verhaltens. Berne, 1968. Spearman, C.: The abilities of man. London, 1932. Thomson, G. H.: The factorial analysis of human ability. Boston, 1939. Thurstone, L. L.: Multiple factor analysis. Chicago, 1947. Überla, K.: Faktorenanalyse. Berlin, 1968.

R. B. Cattell

II. *A critical view.* In factor analysis, correlations between series of scores (e.g.

results of different intelligence tests) are traced back to unobserved variables or factors. The level of correlation between pairs of observed variables is determined by the proportion of common factors. To determine rules of calculation for a concrete analysis, an assumption must be made concerning the type of association between the variables; traditionally it is assumed that the observed scores should be considered as the weighted total of the factor loadings. Factor analysis therefore becomes a very restrictive *model*.

1. *Critical study of the model*. The model of the linear combination of factors is convincingly simple, but this prevents its application to living systems by way of factual arguments, e.g. reference to known relationships. The introduction of more complex assumptions on the type of interaction is theoretically feasible but once again the assumption would be arbitrary. Since the number of factors is determined from the corresponding data and is unlimited, it is possible to reproduce accurately any set of data by factor analysis. The basically restrictive model therefore seems so imprecise that the results cannot be tested and are not binding.

2. *Critical study of the technique*. The model could be accepted as a "first provisional" approximation if clear results capable of interpretation could be achieved within its preconditions. This is not the case in theoretical or practical terms. This does not mean that any factor analysis leads to an infinite number of solutions which can be transferred by rotations (linear transformations). The mathematical analysis of observed scores is dependent both on the choice of variables (e.g. tests) and on the selection of the subjects. The choice of variables can be considered as an operational definition of the area under examination, and thus justified; the influence of the selection of the subjects has been wrongly contested (Meredith, 1964). It has been shown that selections which are wholly probable in empirical terms may lead to factor solutions which are not in a linear relationship with the factor

structure prior to selection; in addition we find mathematically insoluble variance-covariance matrices (matrices which have not undergone "positive-semi-definite" reduction) (Kalveram, 1970). Empirically, this is only covered by statistical dispersion and the rating of communalities.

Selections of this kind may also be made for representative samples. Such samples are representative of a population but not of a hypothetical factor structure. It might therefore be argued that factor analysis was not an appropriate research method. However, if an adequate solution is found with a few factors and a large number of variables, it is useful for representing relationships in tables or graphs.

Bibliography: Meredith, W.: Notes on factorial invariance. Psychometrika, 1964, *29*, 177–85. Kalveram, K. T.: Über Faktorenanalyse, Arch. ges. Psychol., 1970, *122*. Id.: Probleme der Selektion in der Faktorenanalyse, Arch. ges. Psychol., 1970, *122*.

F.Merz.

Factorial design. An experimental arrangement for simultaneous testing of the influence of a number of independent variables on a dependent variable; applicable to all possible combinations of variable categories. This eliminates the need for a separate check on the independent variables in individual experiments and also enables possibly significant interactions to be identified. See also *Variance, analysis of*.   *W.H.B.*

Fading. A term used with the same meaning as *vanishing* and *weaning* to denote a contraction technique used in the design of teaching programs; the aids (cues, prompts) contained initially in a sequence of learning units are gradually reduced and finally eliminated altogether.   *L.J.I.*

Failure. In the memory research of the Lewin school, the success/failure dimension was held to be a decisive variable for memory processes. The learning psychology of the nineteen forties described failure as an intervening variable (q.v.) (E.C. Tolman; C. L. Hull). See *Aspiration level*.

False reaction. Responding in an experiment to a stimulus other than that prescribed by the experimenter, or a similar kind of response in a non-experimental situation, e.g. "jumping the gun".   *G.D.W.*

Fall chronometer. An arrangement in which a falling weight is stopped by a testee and his reaction time measured.   *K.E.P.*

Family. The psychological significance of the family and its members for a given person was a major feature of the theories of Freud, Adler and Jung. On the basis of the free thought association of his patients undergoing psychoanalytical treatment, Freud described the roles of the mother and father in relation to the child, and also of the child in relation to the parents during the early stages of its development. In the context of similar observations, Adler discussed the typical behavioral tendencies of a number of brothers and sisters, and objected that Freud's characterization of the family situation in early childhood was valid merely for only children. Jung developed his concept of archetypes (q.v.), including innate images of the father and mother which need not always coincide with the characteristics of the real mother or father.

For these reasons, W. Toman used simple combination rules to develop a model of the effects of family structures; his model had the advantage of being tested against the hard reality of social behavior in daily life; statistical tests were also carried out. In his model, psychological and behavioral effects of family members are dependent on each other and also on the persons making up the families. General characteristics of the persons in family groups are provided by the number of persons in the household and their

age and sex; the duration of life in the household and the termination of this form of group life by the loss of family members are further characteristics.

The term "general effects" covers influences on the social life in the family group founded by the subject himself as well as other long-term relationships such as contacts with friends and acquaintances. Empirical evidence has been provided for a wide range of such effects which make up an important part of the family activity and form a part of the set of influences exerted by the psychological and sociological environment of an individual on his behavior. These effects of the family group on the social behavior of an individual can be roughly generalized in the "duplication theorem". This suggests that, all other conditions being equal, new long-term social relationships have more chance of success if they resemble the earlier and earliest social relationships, particularly between members of the family.

It follows that complementarity of the brother and sister roles of partners in marriage may contribute to the success of that marriage, whereas a lack of complementarity or conflict between the roles may lead to failure. Since partners in marriage are generally of similar age and the relationship between brothers and sisters provides the earliest paradigm for life with persons of similar age, the older brother of a sister $b(s)$ and the younger sister of a brother $(b)s$ could be defined as complementary partners in marriage. Both are accustomed (from their original family) to life with a person of the opposite sex but of much the same age. Both complement each other in age ranking. He is used to leading and taking responsibility while she is used to being led, and leaving responsibility to the partner. The same holds good with reversed leading roles for the marriage of the younger brother of a sister with the older sister of a brother (symbolically: $(s)b/s(b)$).

Extreme examples of non-complementarity or conflict (q.v.) between the brother and sister roles would be the marriage of the older brother of a brother with the older sister of a sister, i.e. $b(b)/s(s)$, or the marriage of the younger brother of a brother with the younger sister of a sister, i.e. $(b)b/(s)s$. In both these marriages the partners are not accustomed (from their original families) to living with persons of the opposite sex but of similar age. In addition the partners have similar age rankings. In the first marriage both will want to lead and take responsibility while in the second case each of the partners will expect the other to lead and be responsible.

Partial complementarity between the brother and sister roles occurs if the marital partners had at least one among several brothers and sisters coinciding with the family position of the marital partner (e.g. $b(bs)/(b)s(b)$, i.e. the eldest brother of a brother and sister married with the middle sister of two brothers). Conflict of ranking without sex conflict would occur, e.g. in a marriage of the elder brother of sisters with the elder sister of brothers, e.g. $b(ss)/s(bb)$, and sex conflict without rank conflict in the case of a marriage between the elder brother of one or more brothers and the youngest sister of several sisters, i.e. $b(bb. .)/(ss. .)s$.

Evidence exists that non-complementarity between the brother and sister roles of marital partners increases the probability of divorce, a smaller number of children, and marital or educational problems in the family. Friendships between persons of the same or of the opposite sex last longer if the partners had complementary brother and sister roles. The relationship of an individual to his parents and the relationship between the parents and their children are also determined to some extent by the brother and sister positions of the parents. Other conditions being equal, a parent will identify most easily with those of his children (of the same sex) who have an identical or similar brother and sister position to that parent (the same applies to the relationship between the child and parent). In addition, a parent will be

able to establish the best direct contact with a child of the opposite sex (and vice versa) whose brother and sister position corresponds to that of a brother or sister of the parent (of the opposite sex). Other factors, such as the extent of the age differences between brothers and sisters, between the parents and between parents and children, differences in the intensity of family life, and the success or otherwise of families founded by the brothers and sisters of the parents, influence the effect of family groups on the social behavior of the persons involved. The same holds good for differences in intelligence, vitality and external appearance, as well as for socio-economic, ethnic or religious factors. All these factors complicate the relationships referred to; they may disturb, but they may also strengthen them.

The loss of persons in the original family results in greater readiness to anticipate further losses. This is expressed in a poorer selection of persons for long-term relationships (the likelihood of the latter breaking up is greater than that of other permanent relationships), but also in the tendency to choose as partners persons who have themselves suffered losses or persons whom the individual can himself leave again or by whom he or she is more likely to be left. The loss of family members is all the more serious psychologically the more recent its occurrence, the earlier it occurs in the life of a person, the older the lost person is, the greater the duration of the previous shared life with the lost person and the greater the disturbance of the balance between the sexes in the family, the smaller the number of direct family members, the greater the number of personal losses already suffered and the longer it takes to find a complete substitute for the person lost. Temporary losses are non-permanent absences of persons from the family group. The extent of their disturbing influence is governed by the same rules but depends on the duration of the absence. Partial losses are losses of certain aspects of a person in a family group (e.g. by the discovery that the father drank heavily or had served a prison sentence). The effects of permanent losses on the social development of the persons affected have been demonstrated statistically (Bowlby; Glueck & Glueck; Toman). Early losses are more likely to lead to educational problems, delinquency and criminality, neurotic disorders, unfavorable choices of marital partners, more frequent divorces and illegitimate births, and also to relatively late motherhood or parenthood.

Bibliography: Adler, A.: The practice and theory of individual psychology. London, ²1929. Bowlby, J.: Maternal care and mental health. London, 1951. Freud, S.: Introductory lectures on psychoanalysis. London, ²1929. Glueck, S. & Glueck, E.: Predicting delinquency and crime. Cambridge, Mass., 1959. Jung, C. G.: The structure and dynamics of the psyche. London, 1960. Nye, F. I.: Family relationships and delinquent behavior. New York, 1958. O'Connor, N. & Franks, C. M.: Childhood upbringing and other environmental factors. In: Eysenck, H. J. (Ed.): Handbook of abnormal psychology. London, 1960. Parsons, T. & Bales, R. F.: Family, socialisation and interaction process. Glencoe, Ill., 1955. Toman, W.: Family constellations. New York, ²1969. Wurzbacher, G. (Ed.): Die Familie als Sozialisationsfaktor. Stuttgart, 1968.   W. Toman

Family group. The communal family is a form of family commonly found in feudal societies and nomadic tribes in which three generations live with their wives and children in a common household. The system is generally that of a strict patriarchate (q.v.). In Europe family groups of this kind existed only among certain Balkan peoples. As industrialization progresses, the communal family group tends to break up because of its rigid authoritarian structure and the central family (parents with dependent children) tends to dominate. One might also use the term "family group" in connection with the "communes", or communities of unrelated young people or intellectuals which have been established recently (experimentally) in certain big cities.

Bibliography: Goode, W. J.: World revolution and family patterns. New York, 1964. Id.: The family. New York, 1964. McKinley, D. J.: Social class and family life. New York, 1964. Rosser, C. & Harris, C.: The family and social change. London, 1965. Shanas, E. & Streib, G. F. (Eds): Social structure and the family: generational relations. Englewood Cliffs, 1965. Willmott, P. & Young, M.: Family and class in a London suburb. London, 1960. Young, M. & Willmott, P.: Family and kinship in East London, 1957.   N.S.-R.

Family planning. Behavior typical of developed societies, and related to their population level. By practising birth control, parents themselves determine the size of their family, bringing it into line with their social and economic standards and with their aspirations. For society as a whole, birth control is made necessary by low mortality rates (threat of population explosion, especially in developing countries). Birth control also reduces the number of abortions. See also *Contraception*.
N.S.-R.

Fanaticism. A narrow-minded, passionate and combative attitude on the part of some who are, e.g., victims of effective propaganda (q.v.), and who emphatically propagate exaggerated ideas that brook no compromise. Some adherents of religious and political sects and cure-all utopian ideologies, those who indulge in endless legal squabbles, and some health cranks and heralds of a perfect world, who zealously propound their often demented ideas and refuse to enter into any form of discussion, can be classed as fanatics.
K.T.

Fantasy. 1. *History.* The term derives from the Greek *phantasia* (making visible, capacity for imaging). Trevisa (1398) records that more fantasies are seen by night than by day. Newton mentions the power of fantasy to see colors in dreams. The term refers to subjective imagining, including waking and sleeping imagery, and hallucination. This may be visual, auditory, tactile, or a composite of these and other sense modes. Hume (1748) distinguishes images from sensations in terms of their lack of force and vivacity, but admits that in sleep, fever, and madness images may approach sensations. Galton's (1883) classic study was the first major research into imagery, and was particularly concerned with memory images, and individual differences. Freud's (1900) study of dreams was partly anticipated by Maury (1861), who also provided the name "hypnagogic" for imagery of the half-asleep state. Silberer (1909) contributed an important investigation of hypnagogic imagery.

Freud deals with fantasy under the heading of primary process, contrasted with the secondary process of goal-directed thinking. The primary process discharges itself in dreams and daydreams through wish fulfillment. An alternative terminology derives from Bleuler's concept of autism. Autistic (as opposed to realistic) thinking "may be a fleeting episode of a few seconds duration, or may fill a life and entirely replace reality" (for instance, in schizophrenia). Autism "does not insist upon testing its conclusions by realistic and logical criticism . . . it is not after truths but after the fulfillment of wishes" (Bleuler, 1922; see Rapaport, 1951). Bleuler adds that ordinary thinking is "a mixture of realistic and autistic thinking". For brevity we may speak of A-thinking, and R-thinking (McKellar, 1957). A-thinking may overwhelm the personality as in psychosis, or may exert temporary dominance in dreaming, the hypnagogic state, under hallucinogenic drug influence, and in sensory deprivation experiments. It also appears in daydreams, mythology, and superstition. Some projective techniques, like Murray's TAT (Thematic Apperception Test) involve standard pictures to stimulate fantasies which are then analyzed as a source of information about the personality. (See *Autism; Dream.*)

In his early studies of imagery, Galton (1883) found a "sufficient variety of cases to prove the continuity between all the forms of visualization, beginning with an almost total absence of it, and ending with complete hallucination". He observed that cultural pressures may discourage visionary activity,

or may stimulate it when "faintly perceived fantasies of ordinary men become invested with the authority of reverend men with a claim to serious regard . . . they increase in definition through being habitually dwelt upon". Some spontaneous, and drug-induced or starvation-provoked, fantasies have been interpreted supernaturally. Moreover, the (British) Society for Psychical Research found that just under 10 per cent of a sample of 15,000 people reported experiences strictly classifiable as hallucinations, at least once in their lives (Sidgwick, 1894).

2. *Recent work.* A major break-through with one kind of A-thinking has followed the discovery that recordable effects, including rapid movement of the eyes (REMs), tend to accompany dreaming (Aserinsky & Kleitman, 1958). With REM studies we can now time dreams, and count the number of dreams in a night's sleep. Dreaming appears to be a near-universal phenomenon, and Kleitman (1963) distinguishes between recallers and non-recallers rather than dreamers and non-dreamers. Singer (1966) has extended the use of REMs to the study of waking fantasy and imagery more generally. Singer & Craven (1961) find a peak for daydreaming in the 18–29 age group, and report daydreaming—images of people and events—daily in 96 per cent of their subjects. (See *Sleep.*)

Commenting on a period of undeserved scientific neglect, Holt (1964) welcomed "the return of the ostracized". In so doing he stressed the relevance of imagery research to certain very practical problems of modern transport and engineering psychology. Rosemary Gordon's (1949) test of flexibility of visual imagery, and the Betts' (1909) test of vividness are coming into use (see Richardson, 1969). Synesthesia has been given intensive study by the Soviet psychologist Luria (1969) in his book about one individual subject to this kind of imagery.

Many substances of botanical origin that stimulate A-thinking processes are now known. Some are associated with Aztec and contemporary South- and Central-American religion and mythology. Research in ethnobotany (Schultes, 1963) suggests numerous largely uninvestigated sources of hallucinogens. This represents a promising area for continued study of chemically stimulated fantasy (Efron, Holmstead & Kline, 1967). In this field, as in sensory deprivation research, the word "hallucination" has been carelessly extended. "Imagery" is a general and more appropriate term for many of the phenomena reported.

Bibliography: Efron, D. H., Holmstedt, B. & Kline, N. S. (Eds): Ethnopharmacologic search for psychoactive drugs. Washington, 1967. Galton, F.: Inquiries into human faculty. London, 1883. Holt, R. R.: Imagery: the return of the ostracized. American Psychologist. 1964, 19, 4. Kleitman, N.: Sleep and wakefulness. Chicago, 1963. Luria, A. R.: The mind of a mnemonist. London, 1969. McKellar, P.: Imagination and thinking. London & New York, 1957. Rapaport, D.: Organization and pathology of thought. New York, 1951. Richardson, A.: Mental imagery. London, 1969. Schultes, R. E.: The widening panorama in medical botany. Rhodora, 1963, 65, 762. Singer, J. L.: Daydreaming: an introduction to the experimental study of inner experience. New York, 1966.

                                                          P. McKellar

Farsightedness. See *Hemeralopia.*

Fascination method. Used to induce hypnosis (q.v.) by staring, or getting a patient to stare, at a glittering object such as a metal or glass ball. First used in 1843 for therapeutic self-hypnosis by J. Braid, an English surgeon to whom we also owe the term "hypnosis". Today the term is usually applied to a technique for inducing hypnosis in which the patient stares fixedly into the eyes of the hypnotherapist.   *H.N.G.*

Fascism. Belief in the authority principle in social relations; in the (spurious) Right-Left continuum, it equals accentuated bourgeois conservatism. The "*F*" scale for assessing the authoritarian personality (q.v.) (developed by T. W. Adorno and others) is well known. Fascism or authoritarianism

involves a number of independent dimensions which are not determinable in terms of political doctrine and correlate negatively with educational level. See *Attitude.*

Bibliography: Eysenck, H. J.: Psychology of politics. London, 1954.   *B.H.*

Father fixation. An unusual, quite unconscious influence exerted by the father image (see *Imago*) throughout puberty, and beyond it, on a daughter or son. Affective or sexual fixations are often important (see *Oedipus complex*) unconscious components of this father–child relationship.

Father protest may be described as the contrary state to father fixation, being a largely unconscious attitude or "guideline" (A. Adler), perpetuated in negative attitudes toward the father, and transferred to all situations which are in any way similar to the father–child relationship (e.g. bourgeois society, a hierarchical Church). This principle of transference (q.v.) applies to father fixation as well.   *W.Sch.*

Fatigue. A condition resulting from previous stress which leads to reversible impairment of performance and function, affects the organic interplay of the functions and finally may lead to disturbance of the functional structure of the personality; it is generally accompanied by a reduction in readiness to work and a heightened sensation of strain. A distinction is made between many forms of fatigue, which can be traced back to two principal areas of fatigue: physical fatigue, in particular muscular fatigue, and mental fatigue (also known as central or nervous fatigue, on account of the fact that the primarily physiological substrate of this form of fatigue is the central nervous system). Monotony and mental saturation are conditions similar to fatigue, but which have specific laws of their own. It is impossible to make a sharp distinction between physical and mental fatigue. Recent research has emphasized the complexity of this whole problem, and the interaction between different forms and causes of fatigue, to the extent that fatigue is generally understood as an alteration of the mental and physical structure of the individual under stress. Fatigue is dependent on the degree of stress or effort and on the characteristics and duration of the latter. Stress (q.v.) must be understood in the broad sense of the word. For example, an individual may be subject to greater stress resulting from tension with his environment during the performance of his work than from the activity in itself. See *Anxiety*.

1. *History of fatigue research.* Systematic research into fatigue, which began early this century, is marked by a profusion of confusing definitions, theories and research results. This is due above all to the following facts: (*a*) Some authors understand fatigue to denote the process, i.e. stress caused by an activity; and others, the state which results from stress. This second interpretation has come to be increasingly widely accepted. (*b*) Many different symptoms are reduced to a common denominator, namely the concept of fatigue, so that the concept itself covers a wide variety of notions. (*c*) The phenomenon of fatigue (interpreted in different ways) has been studied by several branches of science with widely varying theoretical assumptions and methods, and largely in isolation.

Bartley & Chute (1947) clarified the confusion by making the following distinctions: (*a*) experience of fatigue which can only be directly determined by psychological methods; (*b*) impairment of the organic structures which can only be directly determined by physiological or biochemical methods; (*c*) impaired performance. Bartenwerfer (1961) stresses that mental, physiological and performance characteristics, which may alter in the course of activity, are poorly correlated. Experiences of fatigue, changes in physiological state and variations in performance may express a mental activity but they may also express other circumstances. Reduced performance may be the sign of impending

illness, and fatigue may be the consequence of a generally depressed mood. In addition, mental, physiological and performance symptoms show only slight correlation with previous activity, having regard to the difficulty and duration of that activity. There are cases in which, e.g., fatigue only sets in when the limit of exhaustion is reached, whereas in other cases it is already present at the start of an activity.

2. *Symptoms of fatigue* (according to Schmidtke, 1965). Physical fatigue: (*a*) changes in the muscle system; changes in muscular force, colloidal condition of the muscles, and disturbed peripheral coordination; (*b*) effects of muscle fatigue on the whole organism; changes in breathing, in the blood and in heart and circulatory activity. In mental fatigue: receptivity, perception and coordination disturbances, disturbed attention (q.v.) and concentration, as well as thinking, personal drive and control functions, and social relations.

3. *Causes of fatigue.* In the case of muscle fatigue, due to the impaired contractile capacity of the muscles, the cause is seen in metabolic disorders, primarily due to a lack of oxygen in the muscles. In mental fatigue, too, oxygen deficiency and resulting temporary physical and chemical changes in the cells of the CNS are considered a possible cause. In addition, research is currently being conducted to determine the extent to which functional disorders may result from specific functional stress on the brain. The question of the causes of mental fatigue is largely unresolved.

4. *Measurement of fatigue.* Muscle fatigue is measured by an ergograph, static exertion and pulse frequency. Mental fatigue is measured by methods with a physiological basis: flicker fusion frequency, optical reaction times, determination of upper auditory threshold, electroencephalogram (EEG), pulse frequency, galvanic skin response (GSR), rhythm of breathing, measurement of chronaxia, determination of muscle condition, microvibration, energy consumption. Mental fatigue

can also be measured by psychological methods: psychomotor coordination tests, motor tests, capacity tests (Pauli test), projective methods (q.v.) (Rorschach test), self-observation questionnaires, global self-analysis on the basis of comparable activities.

Bibliography: Bartenwerfer, H. G.: Beiträge zum Problem der psychischen Beanspruchung. Cologne & Opladen, 1960–63. Id.: Psychische Beanspruchung. In: Hdb. d. Psychol., Vol. 9. Göttingen, 1961. Bartley, S. H. & Chute, E.: Fatigue and impairment in man. New York, 1947. Bornemann, E. (Ed.): Ermüdung, Ihre Erscheinungsformen und Verhütung. Vienna, 1952. Bracken, H. v: Untersuchung zur Diagnose psychischer Ermüdung. Berlin, 1955. Düker, H.: Untersuchungen über die sogenannte Aufmerksamkeit. Berlin, 1955. Floyd, W. F. & Welford, A. T. (Eds): Symposium on fatigue. London, 1953. Graf, O.: Erforschung der geistigen E. und nervösen Belastung, Cologne & Opladen, 1955. Lehmann, G.: Energetik des arbeitenden Menschen. In: Baader, E. W. (Ed.): Hdb. d. ges. Arbeitsmedizin, Vol. 1. Berlin, 1961. Mierke, K.: Wille und Leistung. Göttingen, 1955. Müller, E. A.: Die physische Ermüdung. In: Baader, E. W. (Ed.): Hdb. d. ges. Arbeitsmedizin, Vol. 1, 1961. Schafer, H.: Physiologie der E. und Erschöpfung, Med. Klin., 1959, *54*, 159; *54*, 1109–19. Schmidtke, H.: Die Ermüdung. Berne, 1965.   *A. Gubser*

Fatigue, measurement of. An attempt quantitatively to determine the reduction in mental and physical powers resulting from continuous stress, by means of standardized test methods. The commonest methods are continuous calculation (Pauli test, q.v.; concentration capacity test) in which fatigue results in more frequent faults and a lower calculating capacity per unit of time; flicker tests in which the reduction in fusion frequency indicates the degree of fatigue, and measurements with a dynamometer (q.v.) or ergograph, in which reduced muscular energy indicates fatigue.
P.S.

Fatigue tests. Fatigue denotes a subjective condition or a reduction in capacity due to prior effort. The causes may be biochemical or psychological. There is therefore no single phenomenon of fatigue and no general fatigue test. There is little correlation between different methods of measuring fatigue. Flicker fusion and sensory threshold determination are often used.   *R.M.*

Fausse reconnaissance. 1. An illusive recognition. **2.** A new experience that seems to reproduce a previous experience; then synonymous with *déjà vu* (q.v.).

F distribution (R. A. Fisher). This serves as the basis of one of the major statistical test distributions (*F test*, q.v.). Samples of sizes N_1 and N_2 are taken repeatedly from a normally distributed population. In the process, the sum of the N_1 test values X_f—normally distributed and independent of each other—follows the χ^2 distribution (see *Chi-square distribution*). The same applies to the sum of X_i from the sample N_2. The probability $dI(F)$ of

$$F < \frac{\frac{\chi_1^2}{N_1}}{\frac{\chi_2^2}{N_2}} < (F + dF)$$

can then be determined from the area lying between F and dF of the F distribution $\varphi(F)$. $\varphi(F)$ is a single-peaked distribution skewed to the left; its skewness increases with N_2. Unlike the χ^2 distribution, it does not change into the normal distribution (q.v.).   *W.H.B.*

Fear. A primitive and often intense emotion characterized by a systematic pattern of bodily changes (those resulting from arousal of the sympathetic nervous system) and by certain types of behavior, particularly flight or concealment. (See *Arousal; Anxiety*).

Fear is normally experienced in the face of threat, i.e. when danger is perceived or pain anticipated. Even normal fear is often unadaptive in humans, but fears which are persistently out of proportion to the real danger involved are called *phobias*. In psychoanalysis, a distinction is made between *real fear* and *neurotic fear;* the latter arises when instinctual urges are felt which are unacceptable to the conscious mind.   *G.D.W.*

Fechner, Gustav Theodor. B. 19/4/1801 in Niederlausitz, d. 18/11/1887 in Leipzig. 1834–40 occupied the chair of physics; from 1840 philosopher, anthropologist and main founder of psychophysics (q.v.). In his philosophical works he combined scientific interests with speculative and literary efforts (pantheism, panpsychism) and rudimentary depth psychology. Fechner made pioneer contributions to psychophysics, especially in his investigations of threshold and differential values of stimuli and sensations. He followed up the findings of E. H. Weber (q.v.) concerning just-noticeable differences in stimulation, and put them into mathematical form. *F.C.S.*

Works: Zend-Avesta, 1851. Über die physikalische und philosophische Atomlehre, 1855. Elemente der Psychophysik, 1860 (Eng. trans., ed. Howes, D. H. & Boring, E. G.: Elements of psychophysics. Vol. 1 Chicago, 1966). Über die Seelenfrage, 1861. In Sachen der Psychophysik, 1877. Revision der Hauptpunkte der Psychophysik, 1882. Über die psychischen Massprinzipien und das Webersche Gesetz, 1887.

Bibliography: Boring, E. G.: A History of experimental psychology. New York & London, ²1957. Hall, S.: Founders of modern psychology. New York, 1912. Misiak, H. & Sexton, V. S.: History of psychology. New York & London, 1966. *F.C.S.*

Fechner's law. The generalization, based on psychophysical experimentation, that the intensity of a subjective sensation (e.g. loudness) is proportional to the logarithm of the physical stimulus (sound intensity). Expressed mathematically, $S = k \log R$ where S is the sensation, k a constant, and R the stimulus (Ger., *Reiz*). This law is closely related to Weber's law, and is sometimes called the *Weber-Fechner law*.

Fechner regarded this principle as the first law of the mind since he believed that it described the exact relationship between physical and mental events. Its discovery is sometimes regarded as marking the birth of psychology as a science separate from philosophy. More recent experimentation by S. S. Stevens and others, however, has suggested that the relationship between subjective and physical intensities is better described as a *power* function, and there is some evidence that if Fechner's law holds at all, it more accurately describes the relationship between the physical stimulus and the physiological receptor response (e.g. rate of nerve firing). *G.D.W.*

Feeblemindedness. See *Mental defect; Oligophrenia.*

Feedback. 1. In computer technology, a process which, for example, enables an electronic system to maintain a constant comparison between a pre-set level (set point) and input data (actual values) (*Homeostasis*, q.v.): e.g. temperature control in a refrigerator (thermostat). **2.** In functional biology (e.g. blood pressure, body temperature): a process which serves similarly to preserve an internal balance: feedback from proprioceptive receptors. See *Reafference principle.* **3.** In the personal sphere (Martin Buber's primitive dialogue situation) the feedback principle is equally effective.

Bibliography: Wiener, N.: Cybernetics, or control and communication in the animal and machine. New York, 1948. *K.E.P.*

Feedback system (syn. *Control circuit; Control system, automatic*). A basic concept of cybernetics (q.v.). A process of automatic control (not requiring human intervention) by which the value of a quantity is continuously obtained by measurement of the actual state of the process and used to modify input and activate the control system. A well-known example is the thermostat, which keeps a temperature constant. If the temperature of a refrigerator or an electric iron is too high, the electrical current input is interrupted by means of a metal strip or a mercury column so that the temperature drops; then the mercury column also drops, and at a certain point switches the current on again, so that the temperature rises and, because of the alternate switching on and off, remains constant within a certain margin. Even without numerical values for the measurements, self-observation provides examples of series of experiences which can be interpreted as automatic (feedback) systems which keep mental states constant. One such process consists of the mental effects of frustration (q.v.), as automatic measures for maintenance of self-esteem: every diminution of self-esteem by one's own failure leads "automatically" to compensatory experiences such as rationalization (q.v.) ("I was very tired"), aggression (q.v.), substitute gratification (q.v.), and so on. Since these individual states are undoubtedly intended to restore self-confidence, it is possible to speak of a psychic feedback system (Rohracher, 1963). There is no doubt about the "automatic" nature of this control system, since the results of frustration can occur without conscious cooperation (see *Consciousness*)—even when they are apprehended as apparent "causes". The problem of "mental feedback systems" is essentially one of the immateriality of conscious lived experience, which is wholly ignored by some cyberneticians. Genuine feedback systems are to be found only in technology and in organic processes such as blood pressure, where there are material "sensing organs" and regulation devices; the mental processes, however, are not material (they do not consist of atoms or elementary particles, or of oscillations resulting from the movements of atoms or molecules; consequently, mental processes cannot be controlled by technical methods. Hence there is a further objection against the cybernetic nature of these processes: they are—in principle—non-simulable. Present knowledge does not allow us to predict that it will ever be possible to simulate conscious experiences in a machine. But cybernetic processes must, at least in prin-

ciple, be technically simulable. Admittedly there are biological regulating circuits in cerebral activation (e.g. for maintenance of body temperature or for regulation of pupillary width in specific light conditions). Since all conscious experiences derive from activation processes in the ganglionic cells of the cerebral cortex (see *Cortex*), it may be assumed that it also contains material bases for the automatic regulations whose non-physical effects we experience, e.g., as the results of frustration. Because of the non-physical nature of mental behavior, it is preferable to speak of "so-called" psychic feedback systems, or of "quasi-cybernetic mental processes". See *Communication; Information theory*.

Bibliography: Aizerman, M. A.: Theory of automatic control. Oxford, 1963. Block, H.: The perceptron. Rev. mod. Phys., 1962, 34. Erismann, T. H.: Zwischen Technik und Psychologie. Berlin & New York, 1968 Feigenbaum, E. A. & Feldman, J. (Eds): Computers and thought. New York, 1963. Günther, G.: Das Bewusstsein der Maschinen; Eine Metaphysik der Kybernetik. Krefeld, 1957. Neumann, J. von: The computer and the brain. New Haven, Conn., 1958. Pask, G.: An approach to cybernetics. London, 1961. Rohracher, H.: Regelprozesse im psychischen Geschehen. Forsch. Fortschr., 1963, 37. Id.: Die Arbeitsweise des Gehirns und die psychischen Vorgänge. Munich, ⁴1967. Uttley, A. M.: A theory of the mechanism of learning based on the computation of conditional probabilities. Proc. 1st Int. Cong. on Cybernetics. Namur, 1956. Wiener, N.: God and golem. New York & London, 1964.   H. Rohracher

Feeling. See *Emotion*.

Feeling function. According to C. G. Jung one of the four basic functions of the psyche. Together with the thinking function (q.v.), it belongs to the rational functions. It furnishes the individual value of the data registered by the sensation function (q.v.) as well as feelings like pain, anxiety, joy and love.

                                                                                        W.L.

Feeling type. A functional type (q.v.) in which the feeling function based on emotion is the dominant factor. Most marked in women.

Feeling is either adapted to external norms (extraverted) and therefore "rational", or subjective (introverted) and concealed so as to achieve adaptation "not extensively but intensively".

Bibliography: Jung, C. G.: Psychological types. In: Contributions to analytical psychology. London, 1928.   W.K.

Fellatio. Oral contact with male genitals. Used as a method of mutual masturbation (q.v.) in homosexual relations (see also *Cunnilingus*). Fellatio is indulged in by many primates as a form of masturbation. For anatomical reasons it is in this form rare among men, although the desire is fairly often reported. A study of history shows that oral-genital contacts were not frowned upon in ancient civilizations as they are in today's Judeo-Christian culture. The spread of oral-genital contacts, especially as a prelude to coitus, increases with the level of education. They are demanded by the male more frequently than his female partner, owing to the taboo, can tolerate or carry out.

Bibliography: Kinsey, A. C. et al.: Sexual behavior in the human male. Philadelphia & London, 1948.
                                                                          G.L.

Femininity. All that is characteristic of women. Questionnaires (e.g. Minnesota Multiphasic Personality Inventory, q.v.) are employed to determine the extent to which the subject's attitudes and interests depart from the norm for his or her own sex. These variables are difficult to interpret because subjects' scores depend on their social environment and occupation. The existence of a bipolar factor (q.v.)—"masculinity-femininity"—has been established by R. B. Cattell and others.   G.K.

Feral child. The feral child legend goes back to antiquity (e.g. Romulus and Remus). Reports of "wolf", "bear", "leopard" children, and so on, are of doubtful provenance and trustworthiness. An essential feature is that the child grows up apart from the members of his own species during the decisive years of life (see *Imprinting*). T. A. L. Singh reported the discovery of two girls of about eighteen months and eight years of age in a termite mound inhabited by wolves in the Midnapur district of India. They lapped water like wolves, ate raw meat and carrion, bared their teeth, crawled on all fours, could neither stand nor walk, would not tolerate clothes, did not cry, and were dumb apart from basic sounds indicating excitement or agitation. The report is full of inaccuracies and contradictions.

Bibliography: Brown, R. W.: Words and things, Glencoe, Ill., 1957. Köhler, O.; "Wolfskinder,'· Affen im Haus und vergleichende Verhaltensforschung. Folia Phoniatrica, 1952, *4*, 29–53. Singh, T. A. L. & Zingg, R. M.: Wolf-children and feral man. New York, 1942.   K.F.

Féré phenomenon. A decrease in electrical resistance (or increase in conductance) of the surface of the skin resulting in emotional arousal or heightened psychological activity of any kind. A similar effect can be obtained simply by placing two electrodes on the skin and recording changes in the potential difference across them. This is called the *Tarchanoff effect*, and is to be distinguished from the *Féré phenomenon* which involves introducing an external source of current to the skin surface. Both effects are, of course, named after the men credited with their discovery.

The Féré phenomenon is also called the *psycho-galvanic reflex* (PGR) and the *galvanic skin response* (GSR), and together the two effects are called the *electrodermal response* (EDR). The mechanism is not yet well understood, but it appears that emotional arousal stimulates sweat-gland activity, producing an increase in cell membrane permeability, which results in a polarization change and thus a change in electrical resistance. The effect is best observed using those areas of the body which are characterized by arousal or anxiety sweating rather than thermoregulation (i.e. the palms of the hands, soles of the feet, and forehead). The response is often used in psychophysiological experiments as an indicator of arousal, and is one of the components of the so-called *lie detector* (q.v.).

G.D.W.

Fetish. A symbol for something regarded with peculiar veneration and awe which the fetish serves to embody. In sexual psychology, fetishism denotes a sexual deviation (q.v.) in which the presence of a special object and/or its handling is a condition of sexual satisfaction. Inanimate objects or parts of the body of the sexual partner can serve as fetishes. In psychoanalysis a fetish is regarded as a substitute and often treated as a cover memory.   *U.H.S.*

Fetishism. 1. *Ethnological:* ritual use of specific objects (*fetishes*) to which, because of their nature·or origin (e.g. the hair of an enemy), magical powers are ascribed. **2.** *Clinicopsychological:* a perversion (q.v.): excitement and satisfaction are associated with parts of the body outside the genital area (breast, hair) or objects, esp. articles of clothing. See *Cultural psychology; Sexuality.*

I.L.

Fiducial interval. See *Limits, fiducial.*

Field. An area, space, or region (physical or metaphorical) having boundaries defined in terms of relevance to a particular problem or orientation. Thus *visual field* refers to the totality of objects which are visible in a particular situation, and the *phenomenal field* refers to everything that is being experienced by an organism at a particular moment in time.

   Field theory (usually associated with K. Lewin) is a general approach to psychological data which employs the notion of *fields of force* by analogy from physics. The central proposition is that the properties, objects and events are not static but are derived from or dependent upon the total field of which they are a part (see *Granzheit*).

   A *field investigation* refers to the collection of data not in the laboratory or clinic, but in the natural environment of the organisms being studied.   *G.D.W.*

Field dependence. A term coined by H. A. Witkin for the degree to which perception of the vertical is influenced by simultaneous perception of the ambient field. In field dependence tests (rod and frame, tilting room, tilting chair, rotating room) the subject is required to judge the vertical chiefly in the light of kinesthetic and tactile stimuli, shutting out as far as possible any irrelevant data derived from the visual sense. A number of relations with other perceptual factors are considered to have been established. Relations with personality traits, however, have not yet been satisfactorily explained.

Bibliography: Witkin, H. A. *et al.*: Personality through perception. New York, 1954.   *M.A.*

Field of experience. A concept developed on the basis of Lewin's field theory (q.v.) which denotes the totality of experiential contents which appear in the context of processes and with differing degree of clarity in the consciousness. The field of experience varies from individual to individual in scope and structure and also with regard to its dynamism within the given framework.

Bibliography: Lewin, K.: A dynamic theory of personality. New York & London, 1935.   *P.S.*

Field theory. A concept of Gestalt theory (esp. as developed by K. Koffka and W. Köhler) taken over and modified by K. Lewin. Individual behavior is assumed to result in every case from the grouping of psychologically relevant forces which can be localized in a mathematically reconstructible environment. Accordingly, all behavior is field behavior. Every analysis of behavior in terms of field theory starts off with the investigation of the circumstances in which that behavior occurs. These circumstances are regarded not in physical terms but exactly as they are experienced by the person concerned.   W.D.F.

Fighting, ritualized. Combat which avoids serious injury, especially between aggressive members of the same species. It varies according to species, but frequently many elements are so similar that partial ritual combat is possible between closely related types. Frequently recurring patterns are advancing the forepart (e.g. bill sparring in birds) or the flank, circling, taking hold of the mouth, butting in the case of reptiles, mammals and fish. The fights end with the exhaustion or surrender of the weaker, who submits to the victor (see *Appeasement gestures*). There is both intraterritorial and boundary combat, the most frequent reason being the determination of territory.

Bibliography: Tinbergen, N.: Social behavior in animals. London, ²1965.   K.F.

Figural aftereffect. A modification in the perceived spatial characteristics of one figure (the *test figure*) following exposure to another (the *inspection figure*). E.g., continued inspection of a bowed line leads to a decrease in its apparent curvature, so that when a straight line is presented subsequently, it is perceived to be curved in the opposite direction.

Figural aftereffects are not retinal fatigue phenomena, like visual afterimages, but have been shown to be a property of the central nervous system. Thus they are more closely related to illusions, but based upon relations between *successive* stimuli rather than *simultaneous* stimulus relationships.   G.D.W.

Figure-ground. A kind of perceptual organization in which some part of the field stands out as a unified object while the rest is rele-

gated to the background. This relationship is not necessarily static; the figure is generally the part or parts of the field which are being attended to, and a shift in attention may result in a change of figure-ground organization (e.g. embedded and reversible figures).

Figure 1.

From: & Pauli Arnold, *Psychologisches Praktikum* (Stuttgart, ⁶1957).

The phenomenon is most clearly manifested in the visual sense modality, but is known to be a general characteristic of perception. Other things being equal, those parts of the field which are regular, familiar, or need-relevant, are more likely to be perceived as figure.   G.D.W.

Film. An audio-visual mass medium whose importance and effectiveness have undergone extensive empirical investigation since the nineteen-twenties. The effect of films appears to be to impart information rather than to alter opinions, attitudes or behavior. The aggressive behavior portrayed in films is imitated only in the presence of other conditions that are also typical of other forms of learning. Information furnished by films (just as by *Television*, q.v.) can often, under the same conditions, be better absorbed and retained than that provided by radio and printed matter. See *Aggression; Communication.*

Bibliography: Hoban, C. F. & van Ormer, E. B.: Instructional film research (Rapid mass learning) 1918–1950. Washington, D.C., 1951. Heinrich, K.: Filmerleben, Filmwirkung, Filmerziehung. Berlin, 1960. Weiss, W.: Effects of the mass media of communication. In: Lindzey, G. & Aronson, E. (Eds): Handbook of social psychology. Vol. 5. Reading, Mass, 1970.   H.D.S.

Film color. Unlike surface color (q.v.), film color is less consistent and compact, can be seen through up to a certain depth, and is absolutely uniform. Typical film colors are the subjective grey of the eye, fog, the hue of a clear sky, and the color of surfaces seen through a reduction screen— hence also *reduced color* (q.v.) or *aperture color* (q.v.).   *G.K.*

Finger painting. A psychotherapeutic technique in which children paint directly with their finger in special colors. Since this presents no technical difficulties, the children can easily express themselves *uninhibitedly.*
                                                          R.M.

Finger spelling (*Dactylology*). A mode of communication among deaf-mutes (see *Deaf-mutism*) of which several systems are in existence. With the *manual alphabet* spoken language is represented letter by letter by successive finger positions. This was how deaf-mutes were at one time familiarized with speech (today by optical means). For blind deaf-mutes (see *Blind deaf-mutism*) use is made of the *tactile alphabet* (H. Lorm) in which letters are symbolized by touching or brushing against certain parts of the palm. The *spell system* widely used in the U.S.A. is a kind of manual alphabet (one-hand manual alphabet) employed as an auxiliary in the training of deaf-mutes, the spelling hand being kept in the region of the mouth. Deaf-mutes also use a specially-developed gesture language to communicate with each other.
Bibliography: Moser, H. M., O'Neill, J. J., Oyer, H. J., Wolfe, S. M., Abernathy, E. A. & Showe, B. M.:

Hand signals. Finger-spelling. USAF Operat. Applications Lab. tech. Rep., 1958, 58–66.   *F.Ki.*

Finger sucking. A habit that usually takes the form of thumb sucking and is generally regarded as harmless in infants and young children. It is particularly common in children of seven months to two years, and often associated with hunger and fatigue. Finger sucking has a soothing function.

An abnormal habit in children of five years and upward and in juveniles, it is often accompanied by nail biting and hair pulling. It is then said to be neurotic, or the outcome of an unsatisfied craving for affection, although there is no evidence to support this notion.   *P.J.*

First impression. Particularly important on first meetings. This importance is due to the effect of novelty and above all the exploratory conduct triggered by the unknown person if he has valence for the observer. In general, the first impression is determined on the one hand by striking features in the expression of the unknown person and on the other by cultural standards and values of the observer. Descriptions of the first impression contain above all psychological judgments (friendly, timid, etc.) and then statements on external appearance. According to P. R. Hofstätter, the validity of the first impression is dependent on three variables: the ability of the observer, the nature of the characteristics observed, and the character of the observed person. Similar characters and members of the same sex are able to gain an impression of one another more easily.   *F.Ki.*

Fisher-Yates test. The use of χ^2 as a test of independence in a double dichotomy has limitations if the cell frequencies are small. A. Yates (1934) proposed a correction for continuity (q.v.) in these circumstances and, following a suggestion by R. A. Fisher, also gave a method for computing the exact probability (q.v.) of any observed set of cell frequencies in a two-by-two table. In testing significance, it is essential to compute the probability of the frequencies observed and the probabilities of all possible extreme frequencies, and to cumulate the results. The test is also known as the *Exact χ² test*.

W.H.B.

Fixation. Used in two different senses: **1.** The strengthening of a tendency or response leading to the establishment of a memory or motor habit; **2.** The process of becoming, or the condition of being, set, rigid, inflexible or compulsive in some particular way of thinking, attitude, feeling, or behavior.

In psychoanalysis, used to refer to an attachment to an early stage of development, or some object at that stage, which persists in immature and neurotic form, interfering with other normal attachments (e.g. mother fixation; smoking interpreted as an oral fixation). *G.D.W.*

A tendency to regress to stages of development and spheres of motivation in which, according to Freud and Fenichel, there was too little satisfaction of certain motives, or too much or too little satisfaction following earlier excessive satisfaction of such motives. Toman considers "too much satisfaction" self-contradictory and only meaningful if neglect of other motives and other spheres of motivation is implied. Fixations are therefore always caused by frustrations, traumas and deprivation of the chance of satisfying motives, i.e. too little satisfaction. Regression (q.v.) occurs in those spheres of motivation—within such a disturbed stage of development—which were not affected by frustration (q.v.), or in the phase immediately preceding the frustrated stage. According to Freud, fixations in the early and late oral or anal phases, and in the early genital phase, can lead to neuroses (q.v.), psychoses (q.v.), perversions (q.v.) and criminality (q.v.), but not as a rule frustrations,

traumas and losses experienced during later stages of development. (See also *Psychopathology*.)

Bibliography: Freud, S.: The ego and the id. London, ²1962. Id.: Introductory lectures on psycho-analysis. London, ²1929. Toman, W.: Introduction to psychoanalytic theory of motivation. London & New York, 1960. Id.: Motivation, Persönlichkeit, Umwelt. Göttingen, 1968. *W.T.*

Fixation, visual. The directing or focussing of the eye toward a particular target or object of regard (the *fixation point*) so that the image falls on the retina. In *binocular fixation* both eyes are directed at the same point, but this is apparently fairly unusual. The fixation point is normally also the center of attention in the visual field, although it is also possible to attend to the periphery of vision. *G.D.W.*

Fixed attention. O. Vollmer, in particular, distinguishes between a person whose attention (q.v.) is *fixed* and one in whom it fluctuates. The first explores the field of attention systematically, step by step, taking particular note of details. The second skims over the salient features of the perceptual field and gets only a blurred impression of details. See also *Attention types*. *W.K.*

Fixed idea. See *Idée fixe*.

Flagellation. An early form of religious penance performed by scourging oneself or others. As such it is now encountered only now and then in small sects. Flagellation has a certain following as a sado-masochist sexual *deviation* (q.v.). In order to arouse or heighten sexual excitement, one partner beats the other with one of an often wide armory of appliances. Cases of reciprocal flagellation are rarer. *U.H.S.*

Flanagan Aptitude Classification Tests (FACT), developed for the USAF during the Second World War. An analysis of skills yielded 21 "critical work elements", of which 19 were embodied in the tests. Various empirically established combinations of the individual results of the tests are used to determine aptitudes for 38 professions.

Bibliography: Flanagan, J. C.: Flanagan Aptitude Classification Tests. Chicago, 1953–59.   R.M.

Flexibilitas cerea (*Catalepsy*). Waxen flexibility, in which the patient's limbs can be made to move passively and to retain for some time the attitude forced upon them by the investigator. Patients' behavior is similar to that of wax dolls. Can be observed in organic psychoses (q.v.), hysterias (q.v.) and above all in schizophrenias (q.v.).   A.Hi.

Flexibility. Pliancy, adaptability; ant. *rigidity* (q.v.). This factor has been studied by means of factorial analysis.

Bibliography: Guilford, J. P.: Personality. London, 1959.   W.K.

Flicker photometry. A psychophysical method for comparing or equating different fields with respect to brightness using as an index the rate of *flicker* necessary to give *fusion* (q.v.) (the *critical flicker frequency;* CFF). This rate is known to increase as a function of both absolute brightness, and the difference in brightness between the two phases of the flicker sequence. One apparatus commonly used in flicker photometry is the *episcotister*, consisting simply of a disc with adjustable sectors which is driven by an electric motor and rotated at variable speed.   G.D.W.

Flight into sickness. An escape, to a greater or less extent subconscious, from a reality that can be neither mastered nor endured, into a state of sickness that frees the sufferer from all responsibility. An incapacity mechanism then comes into operation, and the subject shuts himself off from the world and

experiences feelings of resignation and inferiority and other neurotic complications. Neurotic symptoms are described as a flight into sickness by A. Adler and others.   H.N.G.

Fluctuation of attention. O. Vollmer distinguishes between a person whose attention fluctuates and one in whom it is fixed. (See *Fixed attention; Attention, types of.*)   W.K.

Fluency. A rapid flow of ideas and tendency to change direction and modify information. Measured by tests in which a number of answers that satisfy the same condition must be given. First defined by L. L. Thurstone as a factor of word fluency (*W*). Whether one general factor or several factors of fluency should be postulated is a point of dispute. According to Guilford, fluency belongs to "divergent thinking" (q.v.), for which he defines 24 factors. In the U.S.A., creativity (q.v.) is connected mainly with fluency.

Bibliography: Guilford, J. P.: The nature of human intelligence. New York, 1967.   R.M.

Fluidity. Profile of the dynamic course of affect and movement with respect to intensification, transition and rhythm. In the cyclothymic type (q.v.) the process alternates smoothly, in the barykinetic type (q.v.) it is abrupt, irregular and cumulative.   W.K.

Folk psychology (syn. *National psychology*). W. Wundt (q.v.) conceived of folk psychology as the counterpart of experimental psychology. Whereas the experimental method was to be used for the analysis of "simple psychic processes", Wundt considered that the study of "universally valid cultural products" such as language (q.v.), myth (q.v.), and morals would allow access to "higher mental processes and developments" (1913). This division was the result of Wundt's belief that experimentation was inappropriate to the investigation of "higher" mental processes such as thinking or affectivity. In this field, only "mass psychic phenomena", in contradistinction to individual products (e.g. autobiographies) were suitable objects of research directed toward "objective" findings. Because of the obvious objections against Wundt's restrictive view of experimental method, the folk psychology he proposed as an alternative was neglected. The belief that language, myth and morals were keys to the objective nature of higher intellectual processes laid the method wide open to speculative abuse. Whereas Wundt wholly neglected the social-psychological viewpoint, social psychology (q.v.) played a dominant role from the start in American folk psychology, or *ethnopsychology* (q.v.). The problem of the specific norms and value systems of a culture was preeminent. Whereas Wundt still put forward the theory of a linear evolution in folk psychology by means of which "primitive" thinking and emotions were held to display primeval stages of the same processes in civilized man (see *Cultural anthropology; Magical thought*), this was deemed highly questionable by ethnopsychologists.

A further turning-point came in folk psychology when the post-Hegelian notion of the "folk mind" or "national spirit" ("objectified spirit" for N. Hartmann) gave way to a more realistic study of the individual personality which is influenced by and incorporates the attitudes (see *Attitude*), values and knowledge of a particular culture. The quest for the "character" of a tribe or nation was replaced by that for the *basic personality structure* (A. Kardiner; R. Linton) most frequent in a specific culture (*modal personality*). Many popular hypotheses of folk psychology (e.g. "typical German industry") have become objects of social psychology (see *Prejudice; Stereotype*). At present, comparative ethnography ("ethnographic atlases") makes possible statements backed by evidence of intercultural similarities and differences (e.g. Murdock, 1967).

Bibliography: Cattell, R. B.: The dimensions of cultural patterns. J. abn. soc. Psychol., 1949, *44* **Inkeles, A. & Levinson, D. J.:** National character. In: **Lindzey, G.** (Ed.): Handbook of social psychology. New York, 1954. **Kluckhohn, C.:** Culture and behavior. In: **Lindzey, G.,** *op. cit.* **Murdock, G. P.:** The ethnographic atlas: a summary. Ethnology 1967, *6.*   *W.Sc.*

Forebrain. The nervous system (q.v.) develops from the ectoderm (ectoblast), passing through the neural plate, groove, and tube stages. While the neural plate is forming, the prosencephalon (forebrain) and rhombencephalon appear initially at its anterior end. The telencephalon (q.v.) and diencephalon (q.v.) develop from the forebrain.   *G.A.*

Forensic psychiatry. The application of psychiatric knowledge and medical, psychiatric and psychological research techniques to the appraisal of persons whose behavior departs from social and legal canons and/or who should be confined against their will in a closed psychiatric institution on grounds of self-preservation or for the protection of the community. The subject-matter of forensic psychiatry is highly diversified and includes the assessment of soundness of mind (e.g. the administration of intelligence tests when court cases are referred for assessment of intellectual level), prognoses from the social, psychological and criminological points of view in the case of offenders and therapeutic measures for their rehabilitation, and problems of civil law such as the capacity of persons to transact business or make a will, the case for putting them under guardianship, divorce, etc.

In the legal sphere forensic psychiatry is mainly concerned with pathological disturbances of mental activity, i.e. all derangements of the mind and personality of organic origin, (*a*) based on injuries, diseases and abnormalities of the brain or of the central nervous system (e.g. cranial and brain traumas, symptomatic epilepsies, intoxications, infections, arteriosclerotic atrophy of the brain); or (b) known to be endogenous psychoses of the schizophrenic and manic-depressive group.

Bibliography: Glueck, S.: Law and psychiatry. Cambridge, Mass. & London, 1963. Mayer-Gross, W. *et al*.: Clinical psychiatry. London, 1969. Watson, A. S.: Psychiatry for lawyers. New York, 1968.

H.M.

Forensic psychology (*Legal psychology*) is a branch of applied psychology (q.v.). It seeks to throw light on all psychological problems arising in connection with those involved in court cases. The formulation of questions and subject-matter are governed by the law in force in a particular country or state. The requirements of the administration of justice are therefore the decisive factor. The services of psychiatrists and psychologists are today enlisted in criminal cases (expert opinions on witnesses and offender), civil cases (e.g. family law), industrial cases (e.g. labor disputes), administrative matters (e.g. assessment of aptitude of drivers), and in the execution of sentences (see *Punishment*).

In fact psychology now permeates the entire administration of justice. Almost every sphere of psychology must be taken into account by forensic psychology. The emphasis lies on developmental psychology (q.v.), social psychology (q.v.), the psychology of personality (q.v.), diagnosis, clinical psychology (q.v.), sexual psychology (q.v.), and the depth-psychology aspect.

1. *History*. In its early stages (at the turn of the century) only scant empirical material was available to researchers (e.g. W. Stern, O. Lipmann, K. Marbe). Psychological experts were seldom called upon in court and therefore had little chance of assembling cases on a large scale. If they were called at all it was usually by the defense, so that they were presented with a one-sided selection. Their activity was therefore confined to laboratory investigations of a general psychological nature. In the process the faulty nature of statements made in court became apparent. As W. Stern said in 1902: "Faulty memory is

the exception, not the rule." Scarcely any attempt was made at any stage to establish the credibility of testimonies on scientific lines. In recent years experts have begun to assemble in actual practice a wide range of empirical material. To start with, their work lay mainly in delivering opinions on juvenile witnesses, chiefly in cases of sexual offenses (q.v.). The other fields earlier referred to were gradually added once it was established that psychologists could help a great deal in clearing up the facts of a case. Today both expert opinions on personality and the analysis of verbal statements can play a central role in the work of forensic psychologists.

2. *Methods*. These largely coincide with those of personality diagnosis (see *Psychodiagnostics*). An anamnesis is always carefully compiled and an analysis made of the current situation in terms of social psychology, as well as an investigation using the most effective techniques and a special exploration (q.v.) bearing on the psychology of testimony (since the forensic questions referred to a psychologist are largely bound up with the subjective data of the person on trial). In the process any admission (in the course of any statement, even a confession) must be carefully checked. Both the aspect of performance and that of motivation must invariably be taken into account.

3. *Appraisal of witnesses*. Here the emphasis has shifted from credibility (q.v.) in general terms to credibility in the case being heard. U. Undeutsch in particular described general credibility as an outdated idea of a static human character. Modern personality theories (see *Personality*) embrace all dynamic concepts. In this respect the outstanding authors are in agreement. Nonetheless, an analysis of personality that takes account of behavioral constants is indispensable. The accent lies, however, on testimony, and the psychosocial conditions that govern it.

4. *Criminal responsibility*. All legal systems make provision for diminished responsibility (see *Responsibility*) for a punishable offense. Nowadays, juvenile offenses are not tried

under retaliatory law, which aims at preventing crime in general, but are dealt with by special preventive measures, i.e. the offender is judged in the light of his individual stage of development. In Western Germany, for example, persons aged from 18 to 21 *can*, depending on their degree of maturity, be grouped among punishable juveniles (aged 14 to 18 years), and this is what in most cases happens in court. Practice varies from country to country. The best system would seem to be that the forensic psychologist is required not so much to appraise the maturity of offenders (often enough a questionable business because such assessments have to fit into an artificial idea of a "juvenile") as to put forward individual observations from case to case. At the same time he should be required to take a more active part in suggesting measures likely to lead to social rehabilitation of the individual. Achievements in the field of developmental psychology retain their importance, although the highly flexible social and cultural conditions of maturity (q.v.) should gain still more importance instead of a static and ideologically colored notion of adolescence or puberty (q.v.). This calls for close integration of psychological and criminological research, of which there is little sign today. For this purpose, statistical methods for predicting criminality (q.v.) will have to be improved. There is also a lack of educative techniques for the treatment of criminals. All scientists who have studied the problems of responsibility (q.v.) agree that the essential need is to elucidate what was going on in the wrongdoer's mind at the time of the act, and (H. Thomae) to compare his behavior and experience at that time with the model of normal behavior so often portrayed in works on psychology. In this connection, affective psychogenic disorders of consciousness (q.v.) occupy a central place in psychological assessment, which must take all available information into account. Here, too, the analysis of testimony plays an important role, since one is often thrown back on sub-

jective data furnished exclusively by the offender. Any law which divides capacity for guilt (q.v.) into (*a*) ability to understand and (*b*) self-restraint and will-power, will tend to support differences found in the way of thinking of lawyers, psychiatrists and psychologists.

5. *Infliction of punishment.* Here the efforts of forensic psychology must obviously be directed toward social rehabilitation and special preventive measures. This calls for rational classification of groups of offenders, those needing psychotherapeutic or other treatment receiving it in special institutions. Further tasks are the diagnostic classification of prisoners, their psychological treatment, training of prison staff, occupational and educational measures, forecasts of date of release, and the provision of advice to groups and individuals.

6. *Civil law.* Here the full potential of individual diagnosis should be exhausted. Moreover, the results of research in sociology and social and developmental psychology ought to be applied and be made to embrace also the phases of the middle and later years. See *Criminality; Punishment.*

Bibliography: Blau, G. & Müller-Luckmann, E. (Eds): Gerichtliche Psychologie. Neuwied-Berlin, 1962. Britt, S. H.: The rules of evidence: an empirical study in psychology and law. Cornell Law Quart., 1940, *25*, 556–80. Eysenck, H. J.: Crime and personality. London, 1964. Glueck, S. & Glueck, E. T.: Unraveling juvenile delinquency. Cambridge, Mass., 1950. Id.: Law and psychiatry. Cambridge, Mass. & London, 1963. Müller-Luckmann, E.: Über die Glaubwürdigkeit kindlicher und jugendlicher Zeuginnen bei Sexualdelikten. Stuttgart, ²1963. Id.: Aussagepsychologie. In: Ponsold, A. (Ed.): Lehrbuch der gerichtlichen Medizin. Stuttgart, ³1967. Münsterberg, H.: On the witness stand. New York, 1908. Nau, E.: Die Persönlichkeit des jugendlichen Zeugen. Beitr. z. Sexualforschung. 1965, *33*, 27–37. Reid, J. E. & Inbau, F. E.: Truth and deception. Baltimore, 1966. Trankell, A.: Vittnespsykologins arbetsmetoder. Stockholm, 1963. Undeutsch, U.: Forensische Psychologie. In: Handwörterbuch der Kriminologie. Berlin, 1966. Id.: (Ed.): Forensische Psychologie. Hdb. d. Psychol. Vol. II. Göttingen, 1967 (Deals exhaustively with all the subjects referred to in this article and has an extensive bibliography).

E. Müller-Luckmann

Foreplay. See *Coital foreplay.*

Forepleasure. See *Anticipation; End pleasure.*

Forgetting. In psychoanalysis (q.v.), forgetting is explained by reference to the significance of affective and motivational factors for retention. Particular forms of forgetting (for Freud's disciples, tendencies to generalize originally specific data) are derived from the effect of defense (q.v.) mechanisms (see *Repression*), which inhibit memory contents that appear dangerous to the conscious ego (q.v.). See *Amnesia; Memory; Reminiscence* for non-Freudian aspects.
Bibliography: **Rapaport, D.:** Emotions and memory. New York, 1961.   *H.H.*

Formal. 1. Pertaining to that which constitutes something (rare). **2.** Pertaining to the visible qualities of something. **3.** Regular or symmetrical. **4.** Pertaining to rules rather than essence: approbative or pejorative use, depending on whether the ancient though doubtful principle of moral improvement through discipline (see *Formal discipline; Learning; Child education; Abilities*) is maintained or rejected.

Formal characteristic (syn. *Formal trait*). A dominant characteristic in the sense that it is claimed as determining the degree to which other characteristics are expressed. But see *Traits.*

Formal discipline. A term that corresponds to the notion of formal education broadened to embrace the process of transfer (q.v.). The practice (q.v.) of activities and the development of abilities (q.v.) are advocated not for their own sake but in order to succeed in the practice of other (similar) activities and "acquire" other abilities. The results of empirical investigations are in part con-

tradictory. In the main they do not confirm expectations, which have been set too high.
                                              H.Schr.

Formatio reticularis (*Reticular formation*). A reticular structure of nerve cells and short nerve fibers in the region of the brain-stem and midbrain, reaching to the hypothalamus and forming the prolongation in the spinal cord (q.v.) of the short intermediate neurons to the extrapyramidal system. The *formatio reticularis* is provided with collateral fibers and thus with information from all centrifugal and centripetal conduction paths. By inhibiting and stimulating the thalamus and cortex (q.v.) it controls the individual's state of wakefulness and attention. Destruction of these substances in experiments on animals produces loss of consciousness which can be restored by means of LSD (lysergic acid diethylamide brings about reversible mental changes accompanied by hallucinatory symptoms).   *E.D.*

Formboards. First used on the feebleminded by E. Seguin (1846), then developed as a test by Goddard (1915). A variety of wooden shapes (circles, squares, crosses, etc.) have of be fitted into matching depressions in a board. In the *casuist formboard* designed by R. Pinter & D. G. Paterson the subject is required to fill the depression by inserting into it a number of different shapes. In G. A. Lienert's *formlaying test*, four flat pieces must be put together to form specified figures. In the *Minnesota Paper Form Board* the subject must pick out the figure that can be assembled.   *R.M.*

Form constancy. See *Shape constancy.*

Foster children. Children who are brought up by foster or adoptive parents. A number of studies of adopted children, their natural and their foster-parents have been made to help elucidate the development of intelligence (q.v.) and personality (q.v.) as conditioned by heredity and environment. The data suggest that environment and the methods used by the foster-parents to rear the children do influence their development, but that characteristics found in their own parents are also of some importance. A quite positive interpretation of the results is not possible because it is difficult to avoid methodological defects.

Bibliography: Anastasia, A.: Differential psychology. New York, ³1958.   D.B.

Foucault's law. The velocity of light through water is less than that through air. Jean Léon Foucault (1819–68) carried out the crucial experiments to determine that light passes more rapidly through rarer than denser media, thus finally refuting the emission theory (corpuscular theory), which maintained the opposite, and further confirming wave theory.

Fourier analysis. Based on a mathematical model (q.v.) (see *Fourier's law*) in which complex functions of a variable (e.g. time) are represented as the sum of an (in general) infinite series of sine and cosine terms. The resolution of the function into its components according to this model is known as Fourier analysis. See *Mathematical psychology; Statistics.*

Bibliography: Edwards, R. E.: Fourier series—a modern introduction. Oxford, 1967.   W.H.B.

Fourier's law. A mathematical model (q.v.) of the composition of a complex periodic function (oscillation) from an (in general) infinite series of sine and cosine functions. Such an oscillation is resolved into a series of harmonic functions (see *Fourier analysis*) by means of the polynomial $Y = a_o + a_1 \cos t + b_1 \sin t + a_2 \cos 2t + b_2 \sin 2t + \ldots$
                                                    W.H.B.

Four Picture Test (syn. *Lennep Test*). A projective technique (Lennep, 1930) assumed to reveal an individual's social relations as they affect his personality. It consists of four ambiguous water-color style pictures, each representing an important social situation; S. has to arrange these in a sequence so that they tell a sequacious story. Interpretation is usually qualitative and based on depth-psychological criteria; empirically obtained norms are not available.

Bibliography: Lennep, D. J.: Manual of the four picture test. Utrecht, ²1958.   P.G.

Fovea. A shallow pit (0·5 mm diameter) at the center of the 5 mm-diameter *macula lutea* (see *Yellow spot*). The depression is due to the absence at this point of the retinal ganglionic cell layers (ganglionic *retinae* and ganglionic *fasciculi optici*) below the sensory cells, as a result of which the neuroepithelium, here consisting entirely of cones (q.v.) and permeated with yellow pigment that is soluble in alcohol, lies exposed against the vitreous humor. The macula as a whole contains about 100,000 cones which, without converging, are each connected to a bipolar ganglionic cell and further to an optic ganglionic cell, whose prolongations reach to the *papilla fasciculi optici* (see *Blind spot*). (This contrasts with the outer edges of the retina where many cones or rods (q.v.) converge to an optic fiber, so that resolution is impaired.) Because of this, and the fact that it is unencumbered by cell layers (also refracting), the fovea is the area of the most distinct vision.
                                                    K.H.P.

Fractionation. A method of introspection, associated with the Würzburg School, which involves the concentration of attention, according to the instructions of the experimenter, onto different parts or phases (fractions) of the total process or phenomenon which is being observed. Also, in statistics, the division of data into different groups for separate analysis.   G.D.W.

FREEDOM

Frame. Equivalent to *item, step;* the smallest component in a learning program (q.v.)—originally part of a program strip appearing in the window or frame of a teaching machine. A frame contains as a rule a piece of information (q.v.), a call for a response, a report (q.v.) back to the learner as to the correctness of his response, and—where the program is not computer-controlled—instructions regarding further stages of the program. The size of a frame can range from a single statement to be completed by the learner (*Skinner program*) to several paragraphs (*Crowder program*). *L.J.I.*

Frame of reference. A basis for comparison when perceiving and judging the facts of a case. (*a*) *A lasting frame of reference:* during the course of his development a person forms on the basis of his experience norms to which he unconsciously refers when judging anything. These criteria agree in large measure as between individuals as well as inside any culture, and this is one of the most important prerequisites for communication and mutual understanding. The center (also zero) of the single criteria is often termed the adaptation level (q.v.), according to Helson (1947). (*b*) *A temporary frame of reference.* This is especially constructed in perception by adaptation (q.v.) to the prevailing stimulus situation. If the stimulus factor changes, the new situation will be subject to renewed adaptation. See *Optical illusions; Weber's law.* Reference must be made to more recent investigations by Witte.

Bibliography: Helson, H.: Adaptation-level theory. In: Koch, S. (Ed.): Psychology, a study of a science, Vol. 1. New York, 1959, 565–621. Witte, W.: Zur Struktur von Bezugssystemen. Göttingen, 1956.
H.-J.A.

Fraternal twins. Twins produced by two separate though simultaneously fertilized eggs. Hence they are no more like one another genetically than ordinary siblings. Fraternal twins may be of the same or different sexes.

They are also known as *dizygotic* twins and thus contrasted with *monozygotic*, or one-egg twins.

Free association. See *Association, free.*

Free choice method (ant. *Selection method,* (q.v.). A form of programmed instruction (q.v.) in which the response of the addressee is made up of a sequence of individual responses from a pre-existing repertoire (e.g. a sequence of typewriter strokes). In the *simple* (or *word*) free choice method, an endless number of such sequences is provided for the branches (q.v.) of the learning algorithm (q.v.). In the *real* (or *event*) free choice method, classes of equivalent sequences are defined (and not merely by enumerating their elements in full). *H.F.*

Freedom. Decision and freedom of choice play a central role in the psychology of personality. All modern theories of personality (q.v.) agree as to the existence of relative, but not absolute, free will. Man is independent, and responsible for his acts, within the bounds of his personal constitution (q.v.). Freedom is a factor of special importance at law in establishing guilt and meting out punishment; i.e. in forensic psychology (q.v.).

The individual's margin of freedom is determined first by his psychophysical constitution (see *Traits; Abilities*) and then by sociocultural influences, e.g. his environment (q.v.) and the age he lives in. All physical and mental processes take place within a general ordered system that obeys the rules of cybernetics—the matching of actual and desired values (see *Homeostasis*). The biological and psychological feedback systems (q.v.), like mechanical controls, can be regulated only because they function systematically and are therefore determinable within limits and to some extent predictable (probability principle). Decisions of conscience (see *Conscience*) are also taken within an ordered system. Actual values—deeds, attitudes—have to be brought into line with desired values (commandments, virtues, norms). Degrees of freedom (q.v.) within the framework of the individual constitution vary from person to person, and the capacity for freedom of each is an individual one, i.e. indivisible. Owing to the existence of individual degrees of freedom, a man's character and personality traits are more than a system of purely reactive behavior. He is endowed with a will and the ability to take decisions. To this extent he can also act spontaneously and, within the limits of his capacity for freedom, is responsible for his acts and omissions. See *Type; Will.*

Bibliography: Arnold, W.: Freiheit und Verantwortung in psychol. Sicht. Schweiz. Z. Psychol. Anwend. No. 1/2, 1970. Id.: Über die sozialpsychol. Notwendigkeit der Unterscheidung von selbsttätigen, organischen und mechanischen Regelprozessen. In: Rep. of 12th Ger. Psychol. Cong. in Würzburg. Göttingen, 1963. Eysenck, H. J.: Crime and personality. London, 1964. Kay, W.: Moral development. London, 1968.

W.A.

Freedom, degrees of. See *Degrees of freedom.*

Freedom, reflex of. The reflex by which animals deprived of their usual freedom try to release themselves. Described by Pavlov as a "common trait, a general reaction of animals, and one of the most important of inborn reflexes", and exemplified for him by its unusual persistence in one dog obstinately resistant to any limitation of his freedom of movement.

Frequency. Frequency denotes the number of times that an event of a specific type or size occurs (the number of elements of a population—random sample—belonging to a specific category). Frequency $f(X)$ is brought into relation with the total number of N observations by means of the relative frequency $(pX) = f(X)/N$. See *Frequency distributions.*

W.H.B.

Frequency distributions are systematic (numerical or graphic) compilations of the observed frequencies (f_i) of all categories (X_i) of a (simple or composite) characteristic or score. In the socio-biological sciences they generally represent the first step in processing raw data. Normally, the number (N) of individual observations (on individuals, in situations, etc.) considerably exceeds the number (i) of stages or classes of the observation material. For example, the observational variable "sex" can only be recorded in two stages while "number of syllables noted" can only vary, depending on the extent of the series, in the classes "0·1 . . ." correct reproductions; on the other hand, dozens or even hundreds of cases are observed. Frequency distributions are divided according to the number of variables observed simultaneously into univariate, bivariate and multivariate types; a distinction is also made according to the type of variable (nominal, ordinal, intervening and relation variables, scaling, psychological methods). In the case of nominal variables the sequence of individual classes is immaterial or corresponds to an external convention. The commonest example in psychology is the frequency distribution of an intervening variable, e.g. distribution of points (number of correct solutions) scored by each person in a series of problems.

In the case of intervening variables, and ordinal or relational variables, the classes X_i are ranked by magnitude. If the number of cases is not much larger than the number of classes, a frequency distribution can only be obtained by assembling classes. For example, in the case of age distributions in small samples of adults, the classes (age indication in years) are grouped together in larger ten-year groups, such as 20 to 29, 30 to 39, 40 to 49, etc. If several frequency distributions have to be compared, it is useful to indicate the relative frequencies (probabilities) $p = \dfrac{f_i}{N}$ for the individual classes instead of the absolute frequency values.

Frequency distributions can also be represented in graphic form; the classes of the characteristic are entered on the abscissa and the frequencies on the ordinate.

Each class is defined either by its limits or by the figure X, which represents the class. In empirical distributions, X_i as abscissa values, and f_i as ordinate values, are *discrete* (discontinuous) magnitudes, i.e. they can only assume specific (e.g. whole number) values. Certain theoretical distributions are also discrete functions, e.g. the binomial distribution and Poisson's distribution. On the other hand, many distributions used in mathematical statistics (e.g. the standard distribution, the F distribution, t distribution, etc.) involve a transition from a finite number of cases N to an infinite number, and from a finite number of classes X to an infinite number; these are presented in the general form of a function $y = f(x)$ ($x =$ abscissa value for the dimension scale, $y =$ ordinate value for the "distribution density"). Both parameters therefore become continuously variable.

The cumulative distribution is a special form (assuming at least an ordinal scale). In this case, we do not determine the frequencies of the individual classes but the overall frequency f_i up to a specific class i (or a specific point on the scale such as the central point of each class). The cumulative distribution can also be represented as a probability distribution of the values.

The determination of an empirical frequency distribution has a practical and theoretical significance. Its practical significance is (a) to facilitate a general survey of all available data. Instead of individual figures, we have a frequency table with two columns containing relatively few numerical values which give a provisional impression of the position (central tendency, mean value), dispersion (variability, scatter), and course of the distribution (distribution form). (b) With a frequency distribution it is possible without mechanical aid to calculate much more quickly than from the individual data

the different characteristics (such as mean value, scatter, skew, kurtosis). From the theoretical angle, frequency distributions are important because they enable hypotheses to be established on the occurrence of a specific, formally definable (generally by means of very few parameters) distribution type (e.g. standard distribution, logarithmic standard distribution, exponential function, power function, etc.) and further assumptions to be made on the effective mechanism which determines the processes underlying the characteristic variation.

For example, the occurrence of observed data following a precise standard distribution would show that the observed characteristic (measured in an adequate interval scale) varies as a result of random variation of a large number of independent, individual factors which make up the characteristic additively.

Theoretically recognized frequency distributions occur above all in consideration of the distributions of statistics (sampling scores). The fact that many distributions of sampling scores are theoretically known, allows a quantitative determination of the uncertainty of sample results in research (sampling error, limits of reliability, significance of differences between two or more sample values).

Bivariate frequency distributions occur if associated pairs of observations of two variables can be formed. They are found most commonly in correlational and regression statistics. The formation of observational pairs is frequently based in psychology (a) on the use of two types of measurement on the same individual (e.g. manual skill and performance), (b) on the repetition of measurements on the same individual (e.g. passing of the same intelligence test at three-year intervals).

The shape of the bivariate distribution, or better still the pattern of mean values of the regression lines (curves), gives an initial idea of the nature and degree of statistical association between two features (correlation).

For example, the linear correlation is more accurate the greater the number of values grouped around one of the two diagonals of the distribution. See *Correlational techniques; Factor analysis.* E. Mittenecker

Frequency histogram. This is a form of graphic representation of frequency distributions (q.v.). A rectangle is drawn over each class of score for a variable in such a way that the length of the vertical lines corresponds to the frequencies in the classes. The histogram is mainly used to represent the frequency distributions of qualitative criteria. *W.H.B.*

Frequency polygon. A diagram showing the form of a frequency distribution (q.v.) of a quantitatively recorded characteristic in a two-dimensional system of coordinates. A frequency polygon differs from a frequency histogram (q.v.) in that the frequencies plotted over the class marks are joined together by a line. The area below the frequency polygon corresponds to that shown by a histogram of the same distribution. *W.H.B.*

Freud, Sigmund. B. 6/5/1856, Freiberg, Moravia; d. 23/9/1939, London; psychiatrist. Commenced academic career in 1885; professor in Vienna from 1902. Creator (with J. Breuer) of psychoanalysis. His researches began with an attempt to treat functional psychological disorders (see *Hysteria; Neurosis*) by suggestion (q.v.) and hypnosis (q.v.). In this he was influenced by the works of J. M. Charcot, H. M. Liebault and A. A. Bernheim. Freud's "psychocathartic" treatment is based on bringing back to consciousness repressed emotions, and releasing them by abreaction. The working up of these techniques into the psychoanalytic method led to the replacement of hypnosis by dream (q.v.) interpretation, free association (q.v.)

and the analysis of lapses in behavior (see *Freudian slips*). Freud's insights into the structure of drives and the significance of the unconscious for psychic activity elicited an eager response from his supporters and pupils. Even though his views were later disputed in certain points (see *Adler; Jung*), Freud became the decisive force in depth psychology (q.v.). Nor should one underestimate the influence his life and work had on the development of scientific psychology in the twentieth century. Freud's co-workers and pupils include S. Ferenczi, A. Adler, W. Stekel, P. Federn, O. Pfister, O. Rank, and his daughter Anna Freud. See *Psychoanalysis; Literature.*

Works: The Standard Edition of the Complete Psychological Works of Sigmund Freud, 24 vols, Ed. J. Strachey & A. Freud. London, 1953-70. Gesammelte Werke, London, 1948-.

Some major separate works are: An autobiographical study. London, 1935. Beyond the pleasure principle. London, [2]1959. Civilization and its discontents. London, [2]1963. The ego and the id. London, [2]1962. The interpretation of dreams, London, 1955. Introductory lectures on psycho-analysis. London, [2]1959. Jokes and their relation to the unconscious. London, 1960. New introductory lectures on psycho-analysis. London, 1933. The origins of psycho-analysis. London, 1954. An outline of psychoanalysis. London, [2]1959. Three essays on the theory of sexuality, London, [2]1962. Totem and taboo. London, 1950. Studies on hysteria (with J. Breuer). London, 1956. Dreams in folklore (with D. E. Oppenheim). New York, 1958.

Bibliography: Arlow, J. A.: The legacy of Sigmund Freud. New York, 1956. Binswanger, L.: Erinnerungen an Sigmund Freud. Stuttgart, 1956. Bernfield, S.: Freud's earliest theories and the school of Helmholtz. Psychoan. Q., 1944, *13*, 341-62. Brinkmann, D.: Probleme des Unbewussten. Berne, 1943. Fromm, E.: Sigmund Freud's mission. London, 1959. Jones, E.: Sigmund Freud: life and work, 3 vols. London, 1953-7. Lee, S. G. & Herbert, M.: Freud and psychology. Harmondsworth, 1970. Schraml, D.: Einführung in die Tiefenpsychologie. Stuttgart, 1968. Shakow, D. & Rapaport, D.: The influence of Freud on American psychology. New York, 1964. Wollheim, R.: Freud. London, 1971. *K.E.P.*

Freudian slips. Acts that are out of place, serve ends other than those intended, or are mistakenly left undone, including such inadvertent errors as slips of the tongue (*lapsus linguae*) and slips of the pen (*lapsus calami*). Freud described such cases of mislaying, forgetting, lapses in speech, and so on, and tried to show that they were motivated by an unconscious desire. Examples: "I welcome those present and declare the sitting closed" (for "open, but I wish it were closed"); hostess to guest glancing at his watch: "Don't stay. Can't you go?" Most everyday blunders are commonplace and lack significant motivation for those concerned, e.g. errors in typing, in totting up figures. The possible personal significance of a mistake is first brought out by the improbability of its occurrence and its relatively protracted effects, and only then justifies the time and expense involved in analysis and interpretation.

Bibliography: Freud, S.: Psychopathology of everyday life. New York, 1914. Id.: Introductory lectures on psycho-analysis. London, ²1929.   *W.T.*

Freudian theory embraces the dynamic model of psychic structures (id, ego, super-ego, q.v.), the schema of psychic (libidinal) development of persons (oral, anal and genital stages, q.v.), and the psychoanalytical schema of psychopathology (q.v.). These were the fruit of observation of thoughts and emotions freely expressed during the psychoanalytic treatment of mentally disturbed patients. This treatment includes the temporary transference (q.v.) of the patient's feelings toward persons of his childhood to the psychotherapist, and the overcoming of resistance to the perception and experience of his own unconscious, and often infantile, wishes and motives. See *Depth psychology*.

Bibliography: Toman, W.: Dynamik der Motive. Vienna, 1954. See also *Freud, S.*   *W.T.*

Friedman test. A distribution-free analysis of variance (q.v.) for the simultaneous testing of the significance (q.v.) of the results of correlating samples (q.v.) in the presence of two independent variables (q.v.). Used mainly in evaluating "Kendall designs", repeated measurements carried out on the same sample under varying conditions.   *W.H.B.*

Frigidity. A woman's inability to obtain satisfaction in the performance of the sexual act. Often due merely to a lack of harmony between the partners in regard to sexual wishes and behavior, which prevents adequate stimulation. In all this, cultural rejection of various practices can also play a part. Psychoanalysis attributes frigidity to ill-managed parental love, faultily developed penis envy, and imperfect transfer of capacity for stimulation from the clitoris to the *introitus vaginae*. According to psychoanalytic theory, one can result from the other, and components of aggressive inhibition often also appear. The existence of two types of orgasm, associated respectively with the vagina and clitoris, is rejected as unproven by modern sexual psychology.   *U.H.S.*

Frontal lobes (Lat. sing.: *lobus frontalis*) are among the most complicated parts of the brain (q.v.) to have evolved at a very late stage. In the lower mammals they are still rudimentary, and only in man, in whom they account for 25 per cent of the brain's bulk, are they fully developed.

The cortex of the frontal lobes covers both the premotor area, which is concerned with the functions of movement (Brodmann's areas 6 and 8) and the prefrontal (granular) cortex (Brodmann's areas 9, 10, 11, 46) which carries out the more complex functions and ensures the overall organization, within specific programs, of man's voluntary activities.

Views about the functions of the frontal lobes have changed since the early days of brain physiology and neurology (see *Neurophysiology*) and have to some extent become contradictory; the original belief was that they had no special function, the current belief is that they are the supreme organ of the brain.

Such contradictions are due to the fact that the frontal lobes—and especially their prefrontal sections—do not directly carry out rudimentary functions of feeling and movement, so that damage to them leads neither to disturbance of sensibility nor to impairment of speech or movement. Their function cannot, therefore, be described in terms of elementary neurology.

The frontal lobes, however, are crucial for the course of complicated psychological processes.

As they are closely connected with the *formatio reticularis* (q.v.), they play a vital role in the regulation of the state of activity ("wakefulness") of the cerebral cortex by maintaining the requisite tonus in expectation of information or preparation for activity. Massive damage to the frontal lobes thus leads to reduced activity and the impossibility of carrying difficult intentions into effect. In addition, after such damage the necessary program of activity ceases to play a dominant role, and casual impressions and impulses are no longer inhibited.

Patients suffering from extensive lesions of the frontal lobes are unable to carry out difficult behavioral programs, to switch from one activity to another, or to impart to their behavior a complex purposive character. Their speech is dominated by echolalias (q.v.) or perseverations (q.v.). Difficult forms of intellectual activity become disorganized and give way to uncontrolled associations or inert stereotypes. Damage of this kind also renders the sufferer unable to compare his acts with his original intentions, or to judge the effects of these acts and control their course while correcting any errors that creep in.

All this shows that the frontal lobes play a central role in self-regulation of the complicated forms of conscious psychic activity, and that they are an important component of

that cerebral apparatus called the "acceptor of behavior" (P. K. Anochin) or TOTE (test/operate, text/exit—K. Pribram, J. Miller, E. Galanter). Precisely because of this, extensive damage to the frontal lobes leads to the clinically familiar symptoms of aspontaneity and "disorders of critical faculty". Limited damage to the frontal lobes, on the other hand (because of the high replacement capacity of their nerve tissue), need not cause any marked symptoms.

The latest research points to differentiation of the functions of the various areas of the frontal lobes, the outer areas being closely associated with control of movement, the mediobasal areas with the control of affective processes.

Bibliography: Luria, A. R.: Higher cortical functions in man. New York, 1962. Id. & Pribram, K. (Eds): The behavioral physiology of the frontal lobes. New York, 1970. Warren, J. M. & Akezt, K. (Eds): The frontal granular cortex and behavior. New York, 1964. Id.: Frontal lobe syndromes. In: Vinken, P. J. & Bruyn, G. W.: Handbook of clinical neurology, Vol. 2. Amsterdam, 1969. Id. & Hornskaya, E. D. (Eds): Frontal ideas and regulation of the psychological processes. Moscow, 1966 (in Russian).

A. R. Luria

Frustration. 1. *Terminology.* Three different meanings of the term "frustration" must be distinguished:

(a) *Frustrating situation.* Strict definitions have been used by Maier (1949), for whom the essential characteristics are an insoluble problem situation, impossibility of moving out of the situation, and high motivation to respond; and by Amsel (1958, 1962), for whom a frustrating situation is one in which non-rewarded trials are interspersed with, or follow, rewarded trials. Broader definitions have been summarized by Lawson & Marx (1958) and Brown & Farber (1951) who include as frustrating situations the introduction of partial or complete physical barriers, the omission or reduction of reward, delay between initiation and completion of a response sequence, failure with possibility of success implied, and infliction of punishment.

(b) *Frustration state.* The frustrating situation will induce a state of frustration in the organism, the degree of frustration varying between individuals. Measures of the strength of frustration should not be the same as those used to assess the reaction to the frustration state, otherwise circularity of argument is involved. This requirement has often been neglected. The frustration state may be measured directly (e.g. by GSR activity or pulse rate) or it may be treated as an intervening variable, not directly measurable. The term "frustration tolerance" (Rosenzweig, 1944) refers to individual differences (innate or acquired) in the capacity to tolerate frustrating situations.

(c) *Reaction to frustration.* The principal reactions to the frustration state which have been studied in detail are aggression (q.v.), regression, fixation, and increased or decreased strength of response.

2. *Frustration-aggression hypothesis.* This hypothesis, advanced by Dollard *et al.* (1939) stated that "aggression is always a consequence of frustration" and "the occurrence of aggressive behavior always presupposes the existence of frustration" (p. 1). Aggression was defined as "an act whose goal-response is injury to an organism (or organism-surrogate" (Dollard *et al.*, 1939, p. 8). The theory is circular since frustration is defined in terms of aggression, and vice versa. The strength of instigation to aggression is a function of the strength of instigation to the frustrated response, the degree of interference with the frustrated response, the number of frustrated response sequences, and the number of non-aggressive responses extinguished through non-reinforcement as frustration persists. The instigation to aggression will be inhibited as a function of the amount of punishment anticipated as a consequence of performing the aggressive act. Aggressive behavior will generalize to other objects along a generalization continuum, but may be displaced onto other objects if the behavior toward the primary object of aggression is inhibited. The occur-

rence of an aggressive act will reduce the instigation to aggression (catharsis). The theory has been applied more generally, particularly to the explanation of prejudice. Criticisms of the theory (Yates, 1962) have centered upon problems relating to the measurement of aggressive behavior, the generality of aggressiveness, the relationship between overt and fantasy aggressiveness, and the probability that much aggressive behavior results from learning rather than frustration.

3. *Frustration-regression hypothesis.* Barker *et al.* (1941) stated that frustration leads to regression which is defined as "a primitivation of behavior, a 'going back' to a less mature state which the individual has already outgrown" (p. 1). Regression may occur with respect to the original goal of the person, or other forms of activity. Barker *et al.* studied the constructiveness of play of children who, following a period of free play with toys of differing degrees of attractiveness, were deprived of the more attractive toys which were still visible, however, through a wire-mesh barrier. Regressive behavior was indexed by a decline in constructiveness of play with the less attractive toys, and the appearance of other forms of behavior, such as approach to the barrier. An alternative explanation in terms of competing response tendencies was put forward by Child & Waterhouse (1952). Experimental support for their position may be derived from studies of instrumental act regression (e.g. Whiting & Mowrer, 1943).

4. *Frustration-fixation hypothesis.* Using the Lashley jumping-stand technique, Maier (1949) showed that rats presented with an insoluble problem situation would develop stereotyped forms of behavior indistinguishable from the behavior of rats in a soluble problem situation. However, when the insoluble problem situation was made soluble, the rats were unable to modify their stereotyped behavior, which Maier termed "fixated". Maier considered that such fixated behavior manifested characteristics which could not be accounted for in terms of conventional

learning theory (e.g. the behavior was not modifiable by punishment; was permanent; and highly specific). Fixated behavior could be modified only by a technique known as *guidance*. Alternative explanations of Maier's results were advanced by Farber (1948) (fixations as anxiety-reducing responses); Wilcoxon (1952) (fixations as the result of partial reinforcement schedules of training); and Wolpe (fixations as learned responses reducing primary drive). Maier (1956) has rejected these alternative explanations while significantly modifying his earlier position.

5. *Frustration and learning theory*. Brown & Farber (1951) suggested that frustration

Figure 1. The double runway apparatus for the investigation of frustrative non-reward.

may produce two general effects: an increase in the general level of motivation (drive); and the production of internal drive-stimuli which serve as conditioned cues mediating escape or avoidance responses. Empirical evidence supporting both these propositions stems mainly from the work of Amsel (1958, 1962). That frustration produced drive-increment was demonstrated in the double-runway apparatus (Figure 1). After training in running through G_1 to G_2 (food being available in both goal-boxes) food was omitted in G_1 (frustrating situation defined by non-reward following reward) and an increment in running speed in runway 2 was found. The cue properties of frustration stimulation were demonstrated in a study by Adelman & Maatsch (1955) who argued that frustration as a drive-stimulus (S_f) will elicit several responses, the one which is

strengthened being that which removes the organism from the frustrating situation. This approach has mediated a substantial body of experimentation and theoretical controversy (Longstreth, 1966; Hill, 1968) and has been used to explain children's reactions to non-reward in a variety of experimental situations (Ryan & Watson, 1968).

6. *Reviews of the literature.* Critical analyses of the literature on frustration may be found in Yates (1962), Lawson & Marx (1958) and Lawson (1965), while Amsel (1958, 1962) has critically analyzed the experimental work on frustrative non-reward situations.

7. *Conclusion.* Two distinct approaches to the study of frustration are discernible. First, there is the series of studies of a broad kind relating frustration to aggression, regression and fixation; second, a later series of laboratory-based investigations on the effects of frustrative non-reward producing drive and cue effects. It might have been expected that cross-fertilization would have resulted in a revival of interest in the frustration-aggression/regression/fixation hypotheses. This cross-fertilization has unfortunately not yet occurred. As Lawson (1965) has pointed out, this may be because of a belief that aggression, regression and fixation may be reducible to more fundamental operations.

Bibliography: Adelman, H. M. & Maatsch, J. L.: Resistance to extinction as a function of the type of response elicited by frustration. J.exp.Psychol., 1955, *50*, 61–5. **Amsel, A.:** The role of frustrative nonreward in noncontinuous reward situations. Psychol. Bull., 1958, *55*, 102–19. **Id.:** Frustrative nonreward in partial reinforcement and discrimination learning: some recent history and a theoretical extension. Psychol. Rev., 1962, *69*, 306–28. **Barker, R. C., Dembo, T. & Lewin, K.:** Frustration and regression: an experiment with young children. Univer. Iowa Studies in Child Welfare, 1941, *18*, No. 1. **Brown, J. S. & Farber, I. E.:** Emotions conceptualized as intervening variables—with suggestions toward a theory of frustration. Psychol. Bull., 1951, *48*, 465–95. **Child, I. L. & Waterhouse, I. K.:** Frustration and the quality of performance: I. A critique of the Barker, Dembo and Lewin experiment. Psychol. Rev., 1952, *59*, 351–62. **Dollard, J., Miller, N. E., Doob, L. W., Mowrer, O. H. & Sears, R. R.:** Frustration and aggression. New Haven, 1939. **Farber, I. E.:** Response fixation under anxiety and nonanxiety conditions. J. exp. Psychol., 1948, *38*, 111–31. Hill, W. F.: An attempted clarification of frustration theory. Psychol. Rev., 1968, *75*, 173–6. Lawson, R.: Frustration: the development of a scientific concept. New York, 1965. Id. & Marx, M. H.: Frustration: theory and experiment. Genet. Psychol. Monogr., 1958, *57*, 393–464. Longstreth, L. E.: Frustration and secondary reinforcement concepts as applied to human conditioning and extinction. Psychol. Monogr., 1966, *80*, No. 11 (whole No. 619) (pp. 29). Maier, N. R. F.: Frustration: the study of behavior without a goal. New York, 1949. Id.: Frustration theory: restatement and extension. Psychol. Rev., 1956, *63*, 370–88. Ryan, T. J. & Watson, P.: Frustrative nonreward theory applied to children's behavior. Psychol. Bull., 1968, *69*, 111–25. Rosenzweig, S.: An outline of frustration theory. In: Hunt, J. McV. (Ed.): Personality and the behavior disorders. New York, 1944. Whiting, J. W. M. & Mowrer, O. H.: Habit progression and regression—a laboratory study of some factors relevant to human socialization. J. comp. Psychol., 1943, *36*, 229–53. Wilcoxon, H. C.: "Abnormal fixation" and learning. J. exp. Psychol., 1952, *44*, 324–33. Yates, A. J.: Frustration and conflict. New York, 1962.   *A. J. Yates*

Frustration-aggression hypothesis. The theory that frustration always leads to aggression (although sometimes concealed or indirectly manifested, as in scapegoating), and that aggression is always a result of frustration. See *Frustration*.   *G.D.W.*

Frustration-fixation hypothesis. Refers to the experimental finding that animals often persist in performing inadequate and non-adaptive responses when continually frustrated or placed in a situation of strong avoidance-avoidance conflict (the choice of two unpleasant outcomes). In a well-known experiment using the jumping-stand apparatus, rats were forced by electric shock to jump toward one of two doors. The door marked with one pattern always opened on impact, giving the rat access to a food reward, whereas the door marked with another pattern resulted only in a severe bump on the nose. When this visual discrimination problem was made particularly difficult, some rats

fixated on a non-adaptive response such as jumping always to one side, or between the two doors. See *Frustration*.   *G.D.W.*

Frustration-regression hypothesis. The hypothesis that frustration often gives rise to a reversion to primitive or early-learned responses which are usually less adaptive than other possible alternative modes of behavior (e.g. crying, throwing things around). The hypothesis also implies that regression to relatively immature behavior is normally a result of frustration.   *G.D.W.*

Frustration tests. See *Picture frustration test*.

Frustration tolerance. Capacity for putting up with passing or lasting deprivation (q.v.) (see also *Frustration*) of satisfaction of motives, i.e. the postponement or forgoing of satisfaction. Dependent on constitutional characteristics such as reaction, perception and learning capacity, as well as inborn components of affective development. Under normal conditions, frustration tolerance is also largely dependent on the individual's experience, the way in which his motives have been satisfied or frustrated in the past. Frustration tolerance ranks as one of the most direct indicators of *ego strength* (q.v.). In psychopathological personality disorders, frustration tolerance declines with the severity of the disorder. According to Toman, it is finally defined in terms of (*a*) the different average rates of learning as between individuals (in Estes' sense), which indicate changes in the probability of the reactions in recurrent situations; (*b*) the individual's average rate of motive differentiation (see *Energy, psychic*); and (*c*) the individual's state of knowledge or the extent to which he has been forced by his environment to forgo satisfaction and knowledge. Frustration tolerance can be regarded as an individual's tolerance to variations in K (K = sum of all present motive intensities

K_t). When at any moment a great many motives remain unsatisfied, K is high; when many motives have just been satisfied, K is low. The mean of K,

$$K = \frac{1}{{}^nK^i} = \sum_1^{{}^nK} K_i,$$

obtained from K values of the number ${}^nK$ measured at intervals of time, tends toward unity. When a series of further measurements of K lies clearly above unity, a stress condition exists. When the measurements lie clearly below unity, a state ranging from relaxation to boredom is present. Popular synonyms for frustration tolerance are *strength of will* and *self-discipline*.

Bibliography: Estes, W. K.: Toward a statistical theory of learning. Psychol. Rev. 1950, *57*, 94–106. Freud, S.: The ego and the id. London, ²1962. Toman, W.: Motivation, Persönlichkeit, Umwelt. Göttingen, 1968.   *W.T.*

FSH (*Follicle stimulating hormone*) stimulates the growth of Graafian follicle; secretion is inhibited by LH (luteinizing hormone), also known as ICSH (interstitial cell stimulating hormone)—induced estrogen formation. FSH is secreted in the anterior lobe of the pituitary, secretion being controlled by an FSH-RF (FSH releasing factor), a neurosecretion from the sexual center of the hypothalamus. FSH is a glycoprotein, FSH-RF a polypeptide.   *U.H.S.*

F test. A statistical test for ensuring, with the aid of the variance ratio

$$F = \frac{S^2 1}{S^2 2}$$

that the difference between the variances (q.v.) of two (sample) distributions are not affected by a random event ($df_1 = N_1 - 1$; $df_2 = N_2 - 1$). This variance ratio is known as the *F* value. Its distribution (see *F distribution*) obeys R. A. Fisher's *F*-function and depends on the size of samples N_1 and N_2. Critical *F* values, which correspond to current significance limits, are given in most textbooks for df_1 and df_2. The *F* test is used mainly for testing the significance of mean value variations by analysis of variance.
                                           W.H.B.

Function. 1. In biology, psychology, and sociology, the purpose, role, or reason for the survival of a structure (organic, mental, social, etc.). E.g., the *function* of sex drive is reproduction of the species. Thus a *functional disorder* may refer either to a disorder of some function, or to a disorder which is itself functional (i.e. provides a *secondary gain*).

2. In mathematics, a function is a relationship between two or more variables such that the value of one is dependent upon the value of others. E.g. work performance is a *function* of ability and motivation.   *G.D.W.*

Functional ambivalence. G. E. Müller's term for indefinite phases of conceptual thought which attain to clarity when determinate content becomes available.

Functional area. In Uexküll's sense, the functional area (*Funktionskreis*) is an ethological concept; it comprises the inner and outer, subjective and objective world. The interaction of characteristics and effective characteristics within the functional area conditions the differentiation of the system.

Bibliography: Uexküll, I. J.: Umwelt and Innenwelt der Tiere. Berlin, ²1921.   *K.E.P.*

Functional autonomy. The notion of G. W. Allport that some motives originally acquired in relation to physiological needs tend to function quite independently at a later stage. This concept is used by Allport and others to explain the persistence of certain habits long after the motives which led to their acquisition have ceased to be operative (e.g. continuing to amass money after one has already made a fortune).   *G.D.W.*

Functional defects. Defects of the closely interwoven psychophysical organism as a whole. These are often due to faulty control in the autonomic nervous system (q.v.). The organic system is, however, left intact (in contrast to organic defects, in which a causative organic substrate is always detected). Such defects are mostly neurotic in origin. J. H. Schultz describes neurosis as an "impairment of function of the whole living organism".   *H.N.G.*

Functional drives. A term used by H. Rohracher to characterize certain "drives" featuring the need or compulsion to act in a specific way.

Functionalism. The philosophical doctrine of W. James (q.v.) which considers mental phenomena in their dynamic unity as a system of functions (geared to adapting the organism to its environment) for the satisfaction of needs that are biological in origin. Derived from this is an educational theory that sees in the exercise of these functions the primary condition for their development (J. Dewey; E. Claparède). The term is also applied to a trend, started by B. Malinowski, in Anglo-American ethnology (q.v.): if James's approach is applied to social life, this appears as an organism comprehended through the relationship existing between organs and their functions. A. R. Radcliffe-Brown (1930) lays stress on the unitary character of the social organism (leaving aside biological reduction), in which the parts function for the sake of the whole. This theory leads to structuralism, since Radcliffe-Brown's use of the function approaches that of mathematics.   *M.-J.B.*

Functional pleasure. It is not the goal or the outcome of activity that produces pleasure, but the exercise of the activity itself. This view of Bühler's is an important contribution to game theory (q.v.).

Bibliography: Bühler, K.: Die Krisis der Psychologie. Jena, ²1929. Id.: The mental development of the child. New York & London, 1930.   *K.E.P.*

Functional sexual disorders occur in the course of the sexual reaction cycles, e.g. premature ejaculation (q.v.), difficult ejaculation and erection in man, and vaginism, faulty vaginal lubrication and anorgasmy (q.v.) in woman.   *U.H.S.*

Functions, main. Jung defines as a function of the psyche "an activity which remains identical under different circumstances and is completely independent of given contents". He refers to four main functions: thinking, intuition, feeling, and sensation. Thinking and feeling are said to be rational functions because they both work with "value judgments". Thought proceeds by applying the criterion "true or false", whereas feeling proceeds by means of the emotional criterion of "pleasure—unpleasure". The two other functions (intuition and sensation) are termed "irrational" by Jung because they avoid reason by working with mere perceptions without value judgments or any interpretation of significance. The functional type (e.g. thinking type) of an individual is determined by the functions which predominate in any given case. Assimilation with Jung's two basic personality types, i.e. the introverted type and extraverted type, gives further psychological distinctions such as the introverted thinking type, extraverted thinking type, and so on.   *W.Se.*

Functions, principal. Mental processes as distinct from the contents of experience. Pfahler describes the principal functions as consisting of the following: attention, activity, involvement of feeling, and perseveration. Jungians use the term for the rational functions of thinking and feeling, and irrational intuition and sensation.

Bibliography: Jung, C. G.: Psychological types. London & New York, 1923. Pfahler, G.: System der Typenlehren. Leipzig, 1943.   *B.H.*

Functions, psychic. See *Psychic functions.*

Function types. Named after the four basic mental functions of thinking (q.v.), sensation (q.v.), feeling (q.v.) and intuition (q.v.). The form they assume is determined by attitude types (q.v.).   *W.K.*

Fundamental, or primary, colors are the phenomenologically pure colors; other colors are intermediate. H. von Helmholtz defines red, green and blue as the fundamental (or primary) colors, while E. Hering refers to the four phenomenologically simple colors, red, green, yellow, blue. These are found at the four corners of the color square (q.v.).   *G.Ka.*

Furor (syn. *Fits*). Uncontrolled outbreaks of rage or aggression in epileptics. A result of abnormal cerebral excitation. *Furor epilepticus* can occur in the prodromal stages before an epileptic attack or can replace the attack. The latter is known as an "epileptic equivalent" and may be associated with a drop in the level of consciousness.   *D.E.*

Fusion. Generally, the combination or blending of two or more elements into one whole. For instance, in perception, *binocular fusion* refers to the combination of the images falling on each retina to give a single perceptual experience. In psychoanalysis, fusion refers to the balanced union of life and death instincts which is supposed to characterize the normal adult, whereas psychiatric conditions are usually supposed to involve some degree of *defusion* of the instincts.   *G.D.W.*

Because the two eyes are set at a certain distance apart, only some of the points of an object in the visual field are registered at identical retinal points (q.v.). Most of them are registered at disparate retinal points, so that the image in one eye differs somewhat from that on the other. They are not perceived as double images, however, but are fused into a stereoscopic spatial impression.

Binocular fusion: based on the association of eye movements (q.v.), i.e. as a result of the mixed origin of the oculomotor fibers in the primary cores, which are connected in pairs and to the cores of the fourth (*trochlearis*) and sixth (*abducens*) cranial nerves, the eyes cannot be moved separately.

Tonal fusion: blending of two or more tones so that they appear to fuse when uniformly soft and pleasant to the ear. The result of tonal fusion can be explained largely in terms of accord and harmony.   *K.H.P.*

Fusion of stimuli. Stimuli disparate in either space or time may be fused if the differences are not too great. The fusion of stimuli slightly disparate in space is the basis of depth perception and stereoscopy (see *Horizontal disparity*). The fusion of stimuli disparate in time is the basis of the *critical flicker fusion* test and the two-flash threshold, the latter being the longest interval between two flashes at which they still appear as one. The apparent movement produced by a succession of discrete stimuli, as in the cinema, is also an example of the fusion of stimuli.   *C.D.F.*

G

GABA. See *Gamma-amino-butyric acid.*

Gait. Mode of walking in human and animal locomotion considered from the anatomical and physiological viewpoints. Klemm's work (²1954) on the rhythm and gestalt characteristics of gait is particularly well-known to psychologists. Kietz's studies (²1966) are especially important for the expressive psychological aspects of gait (see *Expression*). Smieskol (1968) summarizes more than 700 publications on the subject.

Bibliography: Kietz, G.: Gang und Seele. Munich, ²1966. Klemm, O.: Leistung. In: Ganzheit und Struktur. Festschrift for F. Krueger. Stuttgart, ²1954. Smieskol, H.: Methoden und Ergebnisse der allg. G. forschung und die Psychol. des menschlichen Ganges (Thesis, Berlin Technical Univ.). Berlin, 1968.
J.M.

Gallup, George Horace. B. 18/11/1901 in Jefferson (Iowa). Founder of the modern opinion poll. Lecturer at the University of Iowa from 1923 to 1929. Appointed professor of journalism at Drake University in 1929 and at the Northwestern University in 1931. He was Director of research in the Young and Rubicam Advertising Agency between 1932 and 1947, and Professor at the Pulitzer School of Journalism at Columbia University from 1935-37. In 1935, Gallup founded the American Institute of Public Opinion in Princeton—the first institute ever to conduct public opinion polls. He gained immediate fame in 1936 by forecasting Roosevelt's victory in the American presidential elections with an error of only 6 per cent. In the same year he also founded the British Institute of Public Opinion. He has been Editor of *The Public Opinion Quarterly* since 1936. *W.W.*

Gallup poll. A social survey or method of measuring public opinion developed by G. H. Gallup in the United States. Data are gathered by systematic sampling; an attempt is made to obtain representative results by means of personal interviews. The general validity of the method has remained unquestioned since 1936.

Bibliography: Berelson, B. & Janowitz, M.: Reader in public opinion and communication. New York, ²1966. Gallup, G.: Public opinion in a democracy. Princeton, 1939. Id. & Rae, S. F.: The pulse of democracy. New York, 1940. Id.: A guide to public opinion polls. Princeton, 1944.
W.N.

Galton, Sir Francis. *Life and work* (other than psychological): B. 16/2/1822 in Birmingham (England); d. 17/1/1911 in London. Galton was a half-cousin of Darwin and is considered by many authors to have been a genius. His IQ has been estimated at 200. His psychological studies were not systematic but extremely varied and significant. After medical training at the Birmingham General Hospital and medical studies at King's College, London, he turned to mathematics, graduating from Trinity College, Cambridge. He spent most of the next ten years up to 1855 on research in South-West and North Africa, publishing a number of reports (*Art of*

Travel, 1855, etc.) for which he was awarded the Medal of the Royal Geographic Society. He then worked on meteorology, and published the first weather maps; he discovered the anticyclone, etc.

Psychological work: Impressed by Darwin's *Origin of Species,* Galton devoted increasing attention from 1860 onwards to anthropological and psychological problems. His studies were far-ranging, including research into various areas of sense phenomena, mental imagery, the origin and measurement of thought associations, free will, and the phenomenon of ability and its inheritance (with particular reference to genius). Galton's major contribution to psychology was in the area of methodology. He is generally considered to have founded the psychometric school of psychology. He invented the first psychological test methods for the measurement of intelligence and ability. These were primarily based on sensory discrimination and were prepared by comparing extreme groups, i.e. highly-gifted and mentally-defective individuals. He founded the first test laboratory in London (in 1882) at which visitors could take a battery of psychological tests on a fee-paying basis.

In his studies of visual imagery, Galton was one of the first authors to use questionnaires in order to study psychological characteristics. He also invented the word association test, which was later taken over by W. Wundt; and he is taken to be the founder of twin studies.

Galton originally believed that psychological traits could be inherited just like physical characteristics. He conducted a number of tests (mainly on public figures) to confirm his assumption; he tried in particular to determine the frequency of outstanding individuals among the ancestors, descendants and relatives of his subjects. Galton made a significant contribution to the development of differential psychology by suggesting— and thus opposing contemporary theories— that human characteristics are extremely varied, so that it is of value to psychologists to study the extent and causes of individual differences.

In statistics, Galton made an important contribution by developing and applying the correlation method. At his suggestion, his pupil, Pearson, later continued his work in this area and developed the product-moment correlation (q.v.) method. Galton founded the first journal of scientific statistics (*Biometrika*). His application of the normal distribution curve (q.v.) to psychological data was a major contribution to the development of psychological methodology. On the basis of his practical studies he concluded that psychological and physical characteristics follow a normal distribution pattern throughout the population.

Major works: The telotype: a printing electric telegraph, 1850. The art of travel, or shifts and contrivances available in wild countries, ⁴1872. Meteorographica, or methods of mapping the weather, 1863. Hereditary genius: the laws and consequences of heredity, 1869. English men of science: their nature and nurture, 1874. Address to the anthropological department of the British Association, 1878. Generic images: with autotype illustrations, 1879. Psychometric experiments, *Brain,* 1879, *2,* 149–62. Inquiries into human faculty and its development, 1883. Record of family faculties, 1884. Measurement of character, *Fortnightly Review,* 1884, *36,* 179–85. Co-relations and their measurement, chiefly from anthropometric data. *Proc. Roy. Soc.,* 1888, *15,* 135–45. Natural inheritance, 1889. Fingerprints, 1892. Finger-print directories, 1895. Index to achievements of near kinsmen of some of the fellows of the Royal Society, 1904. Eugenics: its definition, scope and aims, 1905. **Bibliography: Burt, C.:** Francis Galton and his contributions to psychology. Brit. J. Stat. Psychol., 1962, *15.* **Galton, F.:** Memories of my life. London, 1908. **Pearson, K.:** The life, letters and labours of Francis Galton, Vols 1–4. London, 1914–30. *W.W.*

Galvanic skin response (abb. GSR; syn. *Electrodermal response; Psychogalvanic* *reflex*). The skin activity triggered by a sensory stimulus or motor reaction (coughing, sneezing) can be measured (*a*) as a short (0·5 to 3·5 seconds) amplification of a direct current passed through the skin (exosomatic galvanic skin reflex) due to a reduction in the basal polarization resistance; or (*b*) as a temporary, primarily negative fluctuation in the potential which can be directly derived from the skin (endosomatic galvanic skin reaction).

These electrical processes on the skin start essentially (negative deflection) as changes brought about by differing adsorption of oppositely charged ions on the surface of membranes, or by varying permeation through the membrane into the epidermal layer (in particular the *stratum lucidum*). After a certain latency, a further potential change (positive deflection) is superimposed because of depolarization of the sweat gland membrane, further amplified by incipient secretion and short-term contraction of the sweat gland passages. The epidermal cells and sweat glands may be innervated by separate sympathetic fibers; this would suggest that the galvanic skin response is a phenomenon accompanying first of all a change in the efficiency of somatosensitive receptors, secondly an increase in the motor grasping and holding activities. In psychophysiology the galvanic skin response based on stimuli actuated primarily in subcortical, vegetative centers is a useful measurement method, e.g. for habituation processes, conditioning, vegetative excitability, etc. Good correlation with intensity parameters for sensory stimuli is also reported.

Bibliography: Edelberg, R.: Electric properties of the skin. In: Brown, C. C. (Ed.): Methods in psycho-physiology. Baltimore, 1967. Keller, P.: Elektrophysiologie der Haut. In: Marchioni, A. (Ed.): Handbuch der Dermatologie. Berlin, Göttingen & Heidelberg, 1963. Montagu, J. D. & Coles, R.: Mechanism and measurement of the galvanic skin response. Psychol. Bull., 1966, 65, 261–79. Venables, P. H. & Martin, I.: Skin resistance and skin potential. In: Venables, P. H. & Martin, I. (Eds): A manual of psychophysiological methods. Amsterdam, 1967. Venables, P. H. & Sayers, E.: On the measurement of the level of the skin potential. Brit. J. Psychol., 1963, 54, 251–60.

Wilcott, R. C.: The partial independence of skin potential and skin resistance from sweating. Psychophysiology, 1964, 1, 55.   M.S.

Gametes. Haploid sex cells which combine to form a diploid zygote representing a new individual (unicellular), or from which a new individual may develop (multicellular), which then shows a new combination of characteristics inherited from the parents (gamonts). If the two combining gametes are externally identical the process is *isogamy;* if they differ in size, *anisogamy;* and if the female gamete (then known as the ovum) is not capable of autonomous movement and is much larger than the mobile male gamete, *oogamy*.   H.S.

Game theory. A mathematical theory which serves as a model for decision-making behavior, in so far as the result of the behavior is always determined by several decision units (individuals, groups, societies, and so on).

A "game" occurs if the decisions (or results of decisions) of at least two organisms result in a consequence for each participant, which for at least one of those concerned is not independent of the behavior of at least one of the others. The numerical values of the consequences are known as "payoffs". Those games in which an increased payoff for one participant is linked to a decreased payoff for an opponent enable the theory to serve as a model for certain social conflicts (see *Conflict*).

Bibliography: Shubik, M.: (Ed.): Game theory and related approaches to social behavior. New York London, 1964.   W.H.T.

Gamma-amino-butyric acid (*γ-aminobutyric acid;* abb. GABA). A biogenic amine (q.v.) first detected in the brain in 1950; it is produced from glutamic acid (q.v.) by biosynthesis. The biological role of GABA has not yet been determined; neurophysiological experiments on animals do, however, show that it is a significant factor in inhibiting cortical transmission.

Bibliography: Curtis, D. R. & Watkins, J. C.: The pharmacology of amino acids related to gamma-amino-butyric acids. Pharmacol. Rev., 1965, *17*, 347-91.   *W.J.*

Gamma movement. An apparent movement (q.v.) of expansion and contraction which occurs if the intensity of illumination of a single figure in a dark surrounding area is suddenly increased or reduced. See *Irradiation*.   *W.P.*

Ganglion. Ganglia form a collection of nerve cells (see *Ganglionic cells*) in the form of a circular, oval or irregular structure with a length of one or more millimeters. With the exception of the basal ganglia (q.v.), the ganglia are located outside the central nervous system. The spinal ganglia in the inter-vertebral foramina consist mainly of pseudo-unipolar ganglionic cells, and constitute the cell body of the primary, efferent neurons. The ganglia of the autonomic nervous system (q.v.) are located in the head, sympathetic nerves, and abdominal and pelvic region. In surgery the term "ganglion" is used to describe a cystic tumor of the joint membranes or tendon sheaths.   *G.A.*

Ganglionic blocking agents. Substances which block the transmission of impulses through synapses of the autonomic ganglia primarily by reaction with acetylcholine receptors. This results in a reduction of blood pressure and diminished tonicity of the smooth musculature. Ganglionic blocking agents are antagonists of nicotine (q.v.), which is a ganglionic stimulant.

Bibliography: Volle, R. L. & Koelle, G. B.: Ganglionic stimulating and blocking agents. In: Goodman, L. S. & Gilman, A.: The pharmacological basis of therapeutics. New York, 1965.   *G.D.*

Ganglionic cells. Cells (nerve cells, neurocytes, gangliocytes, neurones) which comprise the cell body (perikaryon), the cell nucleus, and one or more extensions in the form of dendrites—which consist, like the cell body, of cytoplasm and have a receptive function, together with neurites (q.v.) which act as effectors and transmitters. A distinction is made between unipolar, pseudo-unipolar, bipolar and multipolar ganglionic cells on the basis of the configuration of the extensions. There are between 14 and 16 thousand million ganglionic cells in the human nervous system. See *Axon; Synapse*.

Bibliography: Porter, K. R. & Bonneville, M. A.: An introduction to the fine structure of cells and tissues. Philadelphia, 1964.   *G.A.*

Ganser syndrome. Otherwise known as the "syndrome of approximate answers", this was originally described by S. J. M. Ganser. It occurs characteristically in prisoners who give silly approximate answers to questions in order to feign mental illness. An inconsistent lay impression of mental illness is presented. May be viewed as malingering or hysteria. A similar picture sometimes occurs in schizophrenia or after head injury.   *D.E.*

Ganzheit; gestalt; structure. Some confusion surrounds the use of these three terms. Many authors use them as synonyms. Definitions and explanatory comments in dictionaries are also broadly similar. We shall try to distinguish between the notions on the basis of fundamental texts and suggest how they should be used in future. A more rigid distinction will be made between their substantive and attributive use than has been the case in the past.

1. *Ganzheit* (whole, wholeness, completeness, entity) is derived from the notion of "*das Ganze*" (or "the whole"), and was introduced into psychology by F. Krueger. A totality as a function of space, time or both space and time (a complex) is referred to

as *"ein Ganzes"* or "a whole" if the type, location and arrangement of the "components" are not accidental or random (as they are in an aggregate), i.e. if the totality *has a structure*, and provided that there is a real relationship between the component factors. This totality is the combination of all its parts and only exists as a "whole" (i.e. is *"ganzheitlich"*) if none of these parts is lacking and if the relationship between them (as well as the distinction between this interaction and the environment) is not interrupted anywhere; this last point is generally overlooked in the literature.

A whole is only "holistic", or possesses "wholeness", if it satisfies an additional condition, which is best formulated in the following proposition of Wertheimer's (1925): "There are relationships in which all that occurs in the whole is not dependent on the nature and combination of the individual parts, but on the contrary . . . where that which occurs in a part of the whole is determined by inner structural laws of this whole". Objects which have this holistic, total character tend also to possess features which cannot be detected in any of their isolated parts (holistic or total characteristics, or complex qualities, e.g. the expression of a face). To this extent, wholes are also "super-summative".

Such phenomena can only be understood by holistic (*molar*) observation, as opposed to the atomistic (*molecular*) approach proper to non-holistic phenomena. What is the difference between these two modes of observation? In examining an object which is not holistic in the sense defined above, the "analysis" may be based on a factual ("objective") separation of individual parts from the whole, since it is justifiable to assume that these parts will behave in the same way in isolation as they do in their appropriate location in the total unit. In the holistic approach, analysis consists of an investigation of the individual parts and component processes as they are located in the whole, and with regard to their function in the whole. Behavior in isolation cannot be expected to coincide with the

behavior in the whole; in addition, it is probable that local phenomena or processes will be affected both by local factors and by extralocal or translocal factors. Finally, if parts or loci are isolated or separated out, it is probable that information which is essential to the whole will be overlooked or disappear. Comparison of reactions under different conditions may of course afford valuable information; an investigation based on atomistic procedures may therefore also be of heuristic value for the study of a "whole", provided that it is carried out alongside the strictly holistic analysis.

In addition to living and animate beings whose holistic nature is immediately apparent, at least the field phenomena of the inanimate environment also require a holistic approach (Köhler, 1918). A philosophical attitude or world view in which the central notion is the fact of "wholeness" is known as "holism" (Smuts, 1926). Those personality theories which, by contrast with the idea of a multiplicity of more or less independent "factors", stress the unity of the personality and in which groups or communities are considered as supra-individual and real unities or real wholes, and individuals as "we-factors", are also known as holistic. This applies, e.g., to the "individual psychology" founded by Adler (1907).

The holistic psychological theories, in particular those of the Leipzig School (q.v.) and that of Werner (1953), assume a genetic primacy of the non- or insignificantly structured (complex, diffuse, continuous) whole over its structured (differentiated) realizations; this applies both to behavior and individual experience. The unorganized primary forms are defined as "whole" in a narrower, "more specific" sense. Their (affective) holistic characteristics are distinguished, as "complex qualities", from the "gestalt qualities" of sharply defined and (generally) organized, or structured, wholes. It is difficult to make a distinction between the two, and it does not seem fundamentally important to do so.

2. *Structure (Struktur)*. This term originally denoted a *characteristic* of a whole, i.e. its composition, the arrangement of its parts or elements including the orderly totality of the relations between them. The word is also used with this meaning in other sciences: in chemistry, mineralogy or anatomy one may speak of the structure of a molecule, crystal or bone. W. Dilthey, who introduced the notion of structure into psychology, clearly uses it in this attributive sense when he says it is the "arrangement by which psychological facts of differing composition are connected together in the developed mental life by an internal relationship which can be experienced". In the earlier quotation, Wertheimer used the concept to describe the construction of unities of experience and action. Spranger uses it to denote the complex of interests of an individual, while L. Klages, P. Lersch and Wellek speak of the "structure of the person". See *Strata theory*.

Two special meanings have developed in pyschology, of which the second at least is objective: (*a*) in the American expression "structuralism" signifying, e.g. for E. B. Titchener, the totality of the (statically apprehended) contents of consciousness as opposed to the conditional behavioral relationships considered by the *functionalists;* (*b*) in the terminology of the Leipzig School holistic theory. A distinction is made here between two sub-concepts of the general notion of wholeness: "experiential wholes" and "structures". According to Krueger, these are the relatively permanent *premisses for the possibility of developing experiential wholes*. They form the basis of psychic functions, and are essentially "beyond consciousness", or transphenomenal, i.e. intervening variables or constructs in E. C. Tolman's terminology, but also in certain "profound individual experiences" (feelings and value judgments) only rarely accessible to direct experience. Strictly speaking, they do not exist "in themselves" or "as such" but only to the extent that they are effectively expressed in psychic phenomena (individual experiences) (Wellek, 1941). This suggests that what occurs is a hypostatization in the sense of the Platonic "idea" and the neovitalist "entelechy".

3. *Gestalt* (form, configuration). The gestalt concept is a further refinement of the notion of wholeness, which proved useful initially in perception theory, and was then more generally applied, and has tended to come increasingly to the fore in connection with the problem of the order obtaining within the whole.

(*a*) *First stage*. It has been known since classical antiquity that the specific character of the whole can be changed decisively by slight local interventions (removal, addition, alteration, displacement). In 1890, von Ehrenfels added the new notion that when changes occur which affect all the parts of a whole (exchange of material, movement to other sensory or existential areas), the specific character of this whole is maintained if its structure (i.e. the dimensional and positional relationships between the parts; and, in particular, their functions, in the case of behavioral wholes) is retained. Von Ehrenfels referred to wholes which possessed this characteristic as "gestalts" (*Gestalten*), to their supersummative property as "gestalt quality", and to the change which takes place without affecting that quality as "transposability".

(*b*) *Second stage* (Wertheimer, 1912). The whole is not, as von Ehrenfels supposed, the sum of the parts plus the holistic characteristic: $W = \Sigma p + h$, but $W = f\,(\Sigma p, c, l, m, n\,.\,.\,.)$, in which the letters following p stand for, e.g., constitution or disposition, level of development, previous history, expectation, mode of apprehension. In other words, the whole is something other than the sum of its parts. (Example: stimulus a + stimulus b at adjacent points but at a short interval of time do not result in "sensation" A + "sensation" B + movement, but in a "sensation" which moves from position A to position B). In the marginal case, e.g. in visual perception, the dynamic interaction between part-stimuli determines whether and where a whole ends and whether it possesses parts, and what parts these are.

(c) *Third stage.* In addition to the specific characteristics of wholes, there are also specific characteristics of parts. These are characteristics which distinguish a phenomenon as the "part" of a whole from its given mode of existence as an "individual content": the function or "role" of the part in the whole (Köhler, 1918; Wertheimer, 1933).

(d) *Fourth stage.* Because of the dynamic interaction between the part processes, the assumption of a one to one correspondence between the locus of the stimulus and type of stimulus on the one hand, and the locus and type of phenomenon on the other has to be abandoned (the assumption of "constancy") (Köhler, 1913).

(e) *Fifth stage.* The structures which are most likely to develop because of this dynamic procedure are characterized by orderliness (regularity and simplicity), i.e. there is a tendency to pregnance (*Prägnanz*), i.e. to form a "good gestalt". This is not only decisive in spontaneous field formation and three-dimensional distribution in the visual modality (Kopfermann, 1930; Metzger, 1935), but also leads under certain specific conditions to disparities between perceptive and objective form and quality (illusions).

(f) *Sixth stage.* Order can in principle be produced and maintained in two different ways. In addition to mechanical maintenance (the sole form recognized previously) of the order of states and processes through the strengthening of a material or wall ("canalization"), it is also possible to establish order by the interaction of certain part processes, i.e. there is an order which has a "dynamic" foundation. This dynamic order brought about by the interaction of inner forces, differs from mechanical order in various respects: the same forces (i) bring the order into being, (ii) maintain it, (iii) re-establish it (within certain limits) when a disturbing factor is encountered, and (iv) restructure it under certain conditions (as a

correction), e.g. in productive processes. The states of equilibrium which are finally reached also have a distinctly formal nature. The assumption of supporting factors (analogously to the postulate of entelechy) therefore becomes superfluous.

Mechanical and dynamic forms of order are not mutually exclusive; between the two extreme cases of purely dynamic and purely mechanical order, there is a continuous series of possibilities for different involvement of the two principles. The mechanical factor, e.g. in visual perception, consists (i), generally, of the anatomical structure of the receptors and conduction system, and (ii), specifically, of the instantaneous spatio-temporal configuration of stimuli. The extreme case of minimum dynamic maintenance of order, in which the event retroacts upon itself at *one* point at least, is cybernetic automation.

(g) *Seventh stage.* A high degree of automatic dynamic control can be assumed for all the part areas of the psyche. This holds good also for living beings as "open systems" (L. von. Bertalanffy), and for the different kinds of force fields in physics (Köhler, 1924). It is therefore possible to assume an "isomorphy" of mental and the associated physiological (psychophysical) processes. A "gestalt theory" is a psychological method which makes this possibility a psychophysical working hypothesis (Köhler, 1925).

Bibliography: Adler, A.: Organ inferiority. New York, 1907. Ehrenfels, C. v.: On gestalt qualities. Psychol. Rev., 1937, *44*, 521–4. Klix, F. & Krause, B.: Zur Definition des Begriffs Struktur, seiner Eigenschaften und Darstellungsmöglichkeiten in der Experimentalpsychologie. Z. Psychol., 1969, *176*. Koffka, K.: Principles of gestalt psychology, New York, 1935. Köhler, W.: Über umbemerkte Empfindungen und Urteilstauschungen, Z. Psychol, 1913, *66*. Id.: Nachweis einfacher Strukturfunktionen beim Schimpansen und beim Haushuhn. Abhandl. Preuss. Akad. Wiss. Berlin, 1918. Id.: Gestaltprobleme und Anfänge einer Gestalttheorie. Jber. ges. Physiol. exp. Pharmakol. für 1922, 3/1, 1925. Id.: Die physischen Gestalten in Ruhe und im stationärem Zustand. Erlangen, 1924. Id.: The mentality of apes. London, 1925. Id.: Gestalt psychology. New York, 1929. Id.: Dynamics in psychology. New York, 1940. Kopfermann, H.: Psychol. Untersuchungen über die Wirkung zweidimensionaler Darstellung körperlicher Gebilde. Psychol. Forsch. 1930, 13. **Krueger, F.**: Der Strukturbegriff in der Psychologie. Ber. VIII Kong. exp. Psychol. Leipzig & Jena, 1924. **Id.**: Zur Philosophie und Psychol. der Ganzheit. Berlin, 1953. **Metzger, W.**: Tiefenerscheinungen in optischen Bewegungsfeldern, Psychol. Forsch. 1935, *2.* **Petermann, B.**: The gestalt theory. London & New York, 1932. **Popper, K. R.**: The poverty of historicism. London, 1960, 76–93. **Rausch, E.**: Über Summativität und Nichtsummativität, Psychol. Forsch., 1937, *21.* **Sander, F. & Volkelt, H.**: Ganzheitspsychologie. Munich, 1962. **Smuts, J. C.**: Holism and evolution. London, 1926. **Wellek, A.**: Das Problem des seelischen Seins. Leipzig, 1941. **Werner, H.**: Einführung in die Entwicklungspsychologie. Munich, 1953. **Wertheimer, M.**: Experimentelle Studien über das Sehen von Bewegung. Z. Psychol. 1912, *61,* 161–265. **Id.**: Über Schlussprozesse im produktiven Denken. Berlin, 1920 (Productive thinking. New York, 1959). **Id.**: Untersuchungen zur Lehre der Gestalt, I. Psychol. Forsch., 1922, *1*; II. Psychol. Forsch. 1923, *4.* (Part trans.: **Beardsall, D. C. & Wertheimer, M.** (Eds): Readings in perception. Princeton, 1958, 115–35.) **Id.**: Drei Abhandlungen zur Gestalttheorie. Erlangen, 1925. **Id.**: Zum Problem der Unterscheidung von Einzelinhalt und Teil. Z. Psychol., 1933, *129.* **Id.**: On gestalt theory. Soc. Res., 1944, *11,* 78–99. **Witte, W.**: Zur Geschichte des psychol. Ganzheits- und Gestaltbegriffes. Stud. Gen., 1952.   *W. Metzger*

Gargoylism. A genetic disturbance of the metabolism. Metabolic products (mucopolysaccharide) are deposited in the brain and many other organs, whose development is thus impaired. Disproportionate stunted growth with contorted facial features ("gargoyle") and organic disorders result. Generally accompanied by mental deficiency.   *C.S.*

GAS (*General anxiety scale*). See *Manifest anxiety scale* (MAS).

Gastrula. In multicellular animals the blastula—a hollow sphere with a wall formed by a single cell layer—generally develops first from the fertilized ovum by cell division. The double-layered gastrula is then formed from this hollow sphere by invagination. The point of invagination remains as an opening.
                                                        H.Sch.

Gaussian curve (syn. *Gauss's curve; Normal* [*probability*] *curve*). A graphic representation of a symmetrical, bell-shaped, continuous distribution (see *Normal distribution*) with a single peak. Its probability density is determined by the following function:

$$f(x) = \frac{1}{\sigma\sqrt{2\pi}}\, e^{-\frac{1}{2}\left(\frac{x-\mu}{\sigma}\right)^2}$$

The distribution is therefore clearly determined by μ and N. Since many biological characteristics accord with the normal distribution, this form is often used.   *W.H.B.*

Gefüge. See *Structure.*

Gegenstandstheorie. See *Object; Objective theory.*

Geisteswissenschaftliche Psychologie (Eng. *Cultural science psychology; Social science psychology*). French and English positivism (A. Comte, J. S. Mill) led to a general revision of the notion of science which had become widely accepted in Germany too. Either the natural sciences (*Naturwissenschaften*) were accepted as the only true science (Comte) or it was suggested that the social sciences (*Geisteswissenschaften*) were to be based on natural science (Mill), psychology being considered as a branch of biology.

At the end of the nineteenth and in the early twentieth century there was a very active movement in Germany which tried to establish a more balanced attitude by creating an objective, logical foundation for the cultural sciences (which, according to Dilthey, are, e.g., "history, national economy, the sciences of law and of the state, the science of religion, the study of literature and poetry, of art and music, of philosophical worldviews and systems, and finally psychology"), based on cognition theory. Because all "cultural phenomena are associated with mental phenomena" it was thought necessary

405 GEMÜT

to consider psychological thought processes and make a newly conceived psychology the theoretical framework and basic discipline for all the human sciences.

Since Dilthey (1883, ²1957) the term *"Geisteswissenschaft"* had been in general use; accordingly, the term *"Geisteswissenschaftliche Psychologie"* gained currency as a collective designation for the psychological trends which—unlike the empirical research of the natural sciences—concentrated their research on the investigation of meaningful individual experiences, value factors, and purpose. All three aspects are conceivable only in the "mental" or "spiritual" sphere (*das Geistige*). However, nothing could be "explained" *causally* in this sphere (as in the natural sciences), and only the principle of "understanding" (*Verstehen*) was considered valid, the individual experience of the "soul" or "psyche" (*Seele*) being approached indirectly through *"objective mind"* or "intellectual products" (art, culture), which form the external objective expressions of the human spirit in its lived experience. Since the meaning (value) with which cultural science psychology is concerned never appears as an isolated phenomenon but only in a certain *context*, it can only be experienced by means of a "complex psychic structure" (Dilthey, 1894, ²1957). For cultural science psychology, the principle of structure or development and the concept of *Ganzheit* (wholeness) or *gestalt* (configuration) were essential, because the structural tension and interaction of "experienced relationships" could only be described in this way. Dilthey and his followers (especially Spranger) used these notions to understand and describe feelings, aspirations, motives, character, and so on.

Methods. Understanding, re-experiencing (empathy, mimpathy), description, and interpretation are some of the methods used. Just as the natural sciences use the principle of "explanation", or "explication", cultural science psychology uses the principle of "understanding" psychologically to "penetrate" *objective* (meaningfully structured) and

personal life (the ego), and to re-experience the confrontation of the ego with the environment. Instead of explaining mental processes by cause and effect, E. Spranger (1918) defined "understanding" (*verstehen*) as the "basic function of the percipient consciousness", and as "penetration of the value system of a psychic context". According to Scheler (1937), it is an essential aspect of understanding "that we experience the actions (speech and activities) of others from a perceptive mental idea of them as intentionally directed toward a specific end and so far as we and the environment are concerned, and ourselves complete these actions . . . although this form of completion does not entail co-judgment, approval, or other sentiments". Efforts to establish an objective, theoretical foundation for these methods has led to the division of understanding into two main areas: the understanding *of persons* (contact-understanding, intuitive- or perceptive-categorial and conceptual understanding), and the understanding *of objects.*

The further development of psychological research showed that the division between natural and social scientific aspects of psychology was restrictive; nowadays it is rejected by most psychologists.

Geisteswissenschaftliche Psychologie has value mainly in educational and cultural psychology. See *Verstehende Psychologie; General psychology; History of psychology.*

Bibliography: Dilthey, W.: Einleitung in die Geisteswissenschaften. Gesammelte Schriften, Vol. 4. Stuttgart, ²1957. Id.: Ideen über eine beschreibende und zergliedernde Psychologie. Gesammelte Schriften, Vol. 5. Stuttgart, ²1957. Id.: Pattern and meaning in history: thoughts on history and society (Ed. Rickman, H. P.). London, 1961; New York, 1962. Oelrich, W.: Geisteswissenschaftliche Psychol. und Bildung des Menschen. Stuttgart, 1950. Scheler, M.: Der Formalismus in der Ethik und die materiale Wertethik. Frankfurt, ³1937. Spranger, E.: Types of men: the psychology and ethics of personality. Halle, 1928. Id.: Zur Theorie des Verstehens und zur g.P. In: Festschrift für J. Volkelt. Munich, 1918. *F. Novak*

Gemüt (Eng. *Total disposition*). The psychic and spiritual aspect of a person; the totality of emotions, basic dispositions, moods and motivations. Whereas cognitive activity is characterized by knowledge, thought and judgment, *Gemüt* is expressed in feeling and personal lived experience. Education of *Gemüt* as opposed to training of understanding has played an important role in educational theory (especially in the nineteenth century, e.g. in a particularly intense form in F. Fröbel's work). The notion of *Gemüt* acquired major philosophical significance for the German Romantics and in the sect known as "Christian Science". Recently attempts have been made, primarily by Strasser (1956), to develop the fundamentals of a phenomenological philosophy from the concept.

Bibliography: Strasser, S.: Das Gemüt. Freiburg, 1956. *E.U.*

Gene. Term used for the carrier of the hereditary substance (see *De(s)oxyribonucleic acid* = DNA) which, in a simple instance, controls the formation of an individual characteristic (e.g. curly hair in a guinea-pig). In molecular terms, a gene consists of several thousand DNA components (nucleotides), and the development of a characteristic always begins with the formation of a specific simple protein which then acts as a kind of catalyst for the reaction which leads to formation of the specific characteristic. If several genes are responsible for the development of a characteristic, it is known as a "polygenic" characteristic. *H.S.*

General ability. See *Abilities; Intelligence.*

General Aptitude Test Battery (GATB). A series of twelve tests developed by Beatrice J. Dvorak in the U.S.A. (U.S. Employment Service) to determine vocational aptitude. The eight pencil-and-paper tests and four apparatus tests cover a total of nine factors, the scores for which are presented in a profile.

Standard profiles for twenty-two vocational groups are available for comparison. The test battery was determined on the basis of a representative sample of about four thousand testees. According to Cronbach (p. 274), the reliability coefficients for the nine scales vary between 0·65 and 0·68.

Bibliography: Cronbach, L. J.: Essentials of psychological testing. New York, ²1960. Dvorak, B. J.: The General Aptitude Test Battery. Personnel Guid. J., 1956, *35*, 145–54. *P.S.*

General factor (abb. G). If a factor which occurs in all observed variables can be extracted by means of factor analysis (q.v.), it is known as a general factor. E.g., Spearman's "g" factor is a measure of general ability. *W.H.B.*

Generalization is a fundamental concept in learning theory. It denotes the fact that forms of behavior which were coupled with a specific stimulus situation in a learning process can be induced not only by this particular situation but also by other similar stimulus situations. The phenomenon is explained by I. P. Pavlov on the assumption of an irradiation of impulses by the cerebral cortex; C. L. Hull, on the other hand, postulates intermediate stimulus-reaction chains within the organism, while E. R. Guthrie traces the phenomenon back to common elements in stimulus situations. Generalization is used to explain phenomena such as transfer of practice (see *Transfer*), etc. The *generalization gradient* is the ranking of different stimuli according to the degree to which they evoke a response previously coupled with a specific stimulus. The generalization depends on the intensity of this association and has as many dimensions as the stimulus has variables.

Bibliography: Osgood, C. E.: Method and theory in experimental psychology. New York, 1953. *H.Ro.*

Generalized other. G. H. Mead's term for an organized group or community which (beyond relational individuals, or "significant others") endows the individual with a unified ego (q.v.) through group identity. It is assumed that the attitudes of the whole group coincide in the generalized other (e.g. the team in sport) and therefore form part of the experience of the individual group member. The actions of the individual are "controlled" by the fact that he remains himself while at the same time conforming to the attitudes of the others, i.e. is at the same time the "generalized other".

Bibliography: Mead, G. H.: Mind, self and society: from the standpoint of a social behaviorist (Ed. Morris, C. W.). Chicago & London, [13]1965. Rose, A. M. (Ed.): Human behavior and social processes. London, 1962.   *W.D.F.*

General paralysis of the insane. See *Progressive paralysis*.

General psychology. I. The implied emphasis is on general principles as opposed to individual variations (*differential psychology*), species differences (*comparative psychology*), and socio-cultural factors (*social psychology*). The word "general" has been used to refer to principles underlying such processes as learning, remembering, and thinking, and such activities as attention, motivation, and emotion. Some methodologists, e.g. John Stuart Mill (1843), have argued that psychology needs to be complemented by another discipline concerned with the study of individuality. Stern (1921) underlined the same point when he wrote: "the problems set by general psychology and by the psychology of the individual are quite different". G. W. Allport (1938), in arguing for the development of a psychology of personality, adopted a highly critical assessment of the value of general psychology in arguing "to abstract a generalized human mind from a population of active prepossessing well-knit persons is a feat of questionable value. The generalized human mind is entirely mythical; it lacks the most essential characteristics of mind—locus, organic quality, reciprocal action of parts, and self-consciousness". This interest in individuality as opposed to general principles is traditional: it has a long history going back to Empedocles and Plato.

The term *general psychology* is ambiguous. A second usage is given by Chaplin (1968) which refers to "the broad synthesis of all findings and theories in the field as typified by an introductory textbook or course". (Compare the next article by Prof. P. Muller, which refers to this usage.) In this other sense, the term general psychology appears in the syllabus of many university courses, and in textbooks published at different periods of time: e.g. Murphy's *General Psychology* (1933), Valentine's *Experimental Foundations of General Psychology* (1941), Thouless's *General and Social Psychology* (1937), Kimble's *Principles of General Psychology* (1956), Das's *General Psychology* (1964). These and other such textbooks differ in content and do not necessarily exclude differential, social, and comparative psychology.

A distinction between *general* and *differential* psychology is supported by standard dictionary usage. Warren (1958 edition) defines general psychology as "the branch of psychology which seeks to discover what is true of individuals in general rather than of one individual or class of individuals as distinct from others". Warren's criterion is in terms of the goals or purposes of the investigator or writer concerned. English & English (1958 edition) similarly mention goals and purposes in distinguishing *general* from *differential* psychology. They also mention the dichotomy of *nomothetic* (concern to discover general laws) as opposed to *idiographic* (concern to understand particular events or individuals). Drever (1952) similarly defines general psychology as concerned with general principles of mental life "as distinct from peculiarities characteristic of the individual". And Chaplin (1968) similarly distinguishes general from differential psychology.

Illustrations will be taken from the main areas of the science to indicate the orientation of general psychology, and to distinguish it from other possible orientations. A number of opposing theories of learning, associated with such names as Guthrie, Hull and Skinner flourished in the 1930s and 1940s (Hilgard, 1948). These, together with the titles of leading books such as Hull's *Principles of Behavior* (1943), Skinner's *The Behavior of Organisms* (1938), and Hebb's *Organization of Behavior* (1949), exemplify the standpoint of general psychology, by contrast with, for example, Eysenck's application of Hullian theory to the elucidation of individual differences in learning, and perceiving. Within perception, the gestalt psychologists have frequently been criticized for their seemingly exclusive concern with general principles, as opposed to individual variations and personality differences. The title of one such critical paper "Where is the perceiver in perception theory?" illustrates this line of criticism (Klein & Schlesinger, 1949). In relation to memory, the early experiments of Ebbinghaus (1885) represent a significant contribution to general psychology from the standpoint of a single subject; Koffka (1935) attempted to apply general gestaltist principles to the memory field. The tradition of associationism (e.g. Bain, 1863) represents a general psychological approach to thinking as contrasted to the use of association techniques to study individual differences (e.g. Galton, 1883). Within the contributions of Soviet science may be noted the reflexology of Pavlov in its concern with general principles which have made an important impact upon the psychology of learning; this may be contrasted with Pavlov's own interest in typology, and the elaboration of this aspect of differential psychology by B. M. Teplov and his associates.

Historically, general psychology has been closely associated with the method of experiment, in the strict sense of systematic manipulation of experimental variables. By contrast, differential psychology has been historically associated with psychometric methods, and social psychology with observation of a more controlled, or less controlled kind. These connections have been historical, rather than logically necessary ones, and are much less apparent in the contemporary scene. In the early scientific period Wundt, Titchener and others made substantial use of introspective report in developing their general psychology. The classic researches of Sherif on the autokinetic effect have pioneered the by now vigorous use of experiment in social psychology (Sherif, 1936). Experimental methods received early application to personality and clinical research, in for example the study of "how a fear may be removed under laboratory conditions" by Mary Carver Jones (1924). More recent work in this tradition involving "the application of experimental method to the single case" is to be found in, for example, the study by Shapiro & Nelson (1955). Because of these developments, many of which have a long history, any equation of "scientific" psychology with either "experimental" psychology, or "general" psychology, is questionable and misleading.

The distinction between nomothetic (concern with the discovery of general laws), and idiographic (concern with a single event or specific individual), may be noted in connection with general psychology. Of interest is the fact that the size of the population studied is not necessarily a criterion to be used in differentiating the nomothetic from the idiographic. This is particularly apparent if we deal with a population of $N = 1$. Hence Ebbinghaus sought to formulate and test hypotheses, using a single subject, with a view to discovering general principles relevant to understanding, remembering and forgetting. Freud similarly sought to discover the general principles underlying dreaming, using data primarily on himself. With such work may be contrasted studies that have been made of individual cases, with a primarily idiographic orientation. In the early period, Morton Prince (1909) studied the dissociative behavior of Christine Beauchamp in this way; more recently Luria (1968) has studied, over a period of thirty years, a single case involving unusual capacity for remembering, synesthesia of a variety of kinds, and highly limited capacity for forgetting. Individuals who exhibit pain blindness merit idiographic study of a similar kind, but these also may yield information of interest to general psychology, as showing how absence of the sense of pain can affect learning as such (Mowrer, 1950). Similarly Luria's study, though primarily idiographic, may have important implications for the understanding of the general psychology of retention and forgetting.

The notion of general principles or laws of psychology, which are completely or approximately universal, is less widely adhered to than formerly. Individual variations, developmental stages, greater or lesser deviations from the normal, and both species and social differences, are all today fields of intensive, and legitimate, research. Wundtian over-preoccupation with the normal, adult, human, introspective observer, has been modified by the impact of several movements, including Watsonian behaviorism: this staked out a claim for both developmental and comparative psychology. Allport's influential book (1938) firmly established the field of personality-orientated psychology. If McDougall (1908) was concerned with instincts or propensities as generally present motivational variables, H. A. Murray and others have since developed a personality-centered approach to this same field of motivation. The functional perception movement of Bruner and others has sought to correct what the leaders of this group viewed as a narrowly general psychological approach, and to develop the differential psychology lacking in this area. Leading theorists in the field of learning, such as Mowrer (1950) and Skinner (1968), have devoted their recent attention to the study of personality differences in learning on the one hand, and the problems of the individual learner in the classroom, on the other. The concept of general psychology, though perhaps of questionable value today, provides a reference point in terms of which we can view some of these historical, and modern, developments.

Bibliography: Allport, G. W.: Personality: a psychological interpretation. London, 1938. Chaplin, J. P.: Dictionary of psychology. New York, 1968. English, H. B. & English, A. C.: A comprehensive dictionary of psychological and psychoanalytical terms. London, 1958. Klein, G. S. & Schlesinger, H.: Where is the perceiver in perception theory. Journal of Personality. 1949. Koffka, K.: Principles of gestalt psychology. London, 1935. Luria, A. R.: The mind of a mnemonist. (Trans. from the Russian by Solatarff, L.). London, 1969. McDougall, W.: An introduction to social psychology. London, 1908. Mowrer, O. H.: Learning theory and personality dynamics. New York, 1950. Shapiro, M. B. & Nelson, E. H.: An investigation of an abnormality of cognitive function in a co-operative young psychotic: an example of the application of the experimental method to the single case. Journal of Clinical Psychology, 1955, 11. Sherif, M.: The psychology of social norms. New York, 1936. Skinner, B. F.: The technique of teaching. New York, 1968. Warren, H. C.: Dictionary of psychology (1958 edition). New York, 1934.

T. P. H. McKellar

General psychology. II. *The interdisciplinary view.* There are two accepted meanings of the term "general psychology". The first refers to the contents of an introductory course in the subject, the basic knowledge every psychologist should have before specializing in one or other of the different branches of modern psychology; "general psychologies" in this sense are to be found in various manuals (e.g. R. Kimble's *Principles of General Psychology*, New York, 1956; or the large *Handbuch der Psychologie*, I: *Allgemeine Psychologie*, edited by W. Metzger). The second meaning, the one with which this article deals, refers to problems of *method*, to the *interpretation* of psychological data, and to the *cultural* or *philosophical implications* of psychology. To be even more precise, this article is mainly concerned with the relationship between psychology and philosophy (another article discusses methodological problems, see *Philosophy and psychology*).

Psychology is a science which has existed for a long time yet possesses only a brief recorded history (Ebbinghaus, 1885); it has had some difficulty in emerging from the philosophical mold common to all traditional branches of knowledge in the West. It is now becoming apparent that psychological problems are already present in myths (in so far as these are always about man's place in the world); that they are reflected in the earliest philosophical theories; and that they then become increasingly precise in the great traditional systems of thought. Thus the "Psychology" section in Janet & Seailles' *L'Histoire de la philosophie* (1st edition, 1886) includes chapters on the following: animal life, the senses and external perception, consciousness, theories of reason, memory, association of ideas, language, sensitivity, problems of freedom, habit. Each of these chapters traces through the ages the discussion of the problems which experimental psychology, with its laboratory techniques and concern for strict verification, had taken up from 1860 onward.

A similar situation can certainly be found in the other sciences. But whereas the advent of the experimental method in physics, with deductions based on the testing of hypotheses, severed the links between physics and philosophy (at least in principle, if not in the mind of each individual physicist), nothing of the sort has happened in psychology, in spite of the constant efforts of a great number of scholars. In opposition to the earliest scientific psychology of the pioneers (1860–1912) came protests by Bergson, Dilthey, Brentano, Husserl and, finally, Natorp. In the confused era between 1912 and 1930 several psychologists expressly laid claim to philosophical methods (e.g. the "phenomenological psychology" of M. Scheler and of A. Pfänder, continued later in France by J.-P. Sartre and Merleau-Ponty). Finally, even when, from 1930 onward, there was greater unanimity concerning psychology as the "science of behavior", those who thought in depth about psychology continued animatedly to discuss the very possibility of an "objective" science of human behavior.

Philosophy aspires to conscious coherence in the concepts it uses to describe and to understand itself, and thus necessarily *reflects upon itself*. To this extent, somewhere along the line philosophy encounters objective psychology as a rival approach. The reason for this is that objective psychology includes a theory of cognition, and therefore considers the conditions governing knowledge while simultaneously itself claiming to be this knowledge. Is it possible to use concepts of objectivity borrowed from science to construct a subject capable of developing precisely the objective knowledge in question? Can "instrumental" reason of the type used in technology (Pradines) explain itself? Can it do without *dialectical reason?*

Apart from renewing this investigation into the preconditions for psychology (the *critical* question *par excellence*), general psychology should be concerned to describe the factors which make up the three things with which it is primarily concerned: behavior, experience, and other people in so far as they are personal agents. Experimental psychology always assumes that these basic problems have been resolved, whereas it is at this level that the distinction between natural ("physical") science and the various human sciences is worked out.

At a less fundamental level, general psychology describes the social conditions necessary for the birth of psychology, the epistemological limits implied by the three types of psychology (experimental psychology in the third person, clinical psychology in the second person, and phenomenological psychology in the first person), and the existential conditions inherent in any attempt by existence to come to terms with itself. From this point of view, scientific psychology will only become appropriately coherent by raising itself to the level of a "meta-psychology". See *Phenomenology*.

Bibliography: Binswanger, L.: Einführung in die Probleme der allgemeinen Psychologie. Berlin, 1922.

Id.: Grundformen und Erkenntnis menschlichen Daseins. Zürich, ²1953. Id.: Being-in-the-world. New York, 1963. Guillaumin, J.: La dynamique de l'entretien psychologique. Paris, 1965. Merleau-Ponty, M.: The phenomenology of perception. London & New York, 1964. Id.: The structure of behavior. Boston, 1963. Id.: Les sciences de l'homme et la phénoménologie. Bull. de Psychologie, 1964, 18, 141–70. Muller, P.: De la psychologie à l'anthropologie. Neuchâtel, 1946. Id.: La psychologie dans le monde moderne. Brussels, 1966. Piaget, J. (Ed.): Logique et connaissance scientifique. Paris, 1968. Id.: Psychology and philosophy. In: Wolman, B. B. & Nagel, E. (Eds): Scientific psychology: principles and approaches. New York, 1965, 28–43. Pongratz, L. J.: Problemgeschichte der Psychologie. Berne & Munich, 1967. Pradines, M.: Traité de psychologie générale, 3 vols. Paris, 1943. Sartre, J.-P.: Imagination: a psychological critique. Ann Arbor, Mich., 1962. Strasser, S.: Phénoménologie et sciences de l'homme. Louvain & Paris, 1967.   P. Muller

Generation (*Alternation of generations; Metagenesis*). In the biological sense, a generation is the complete life cycle of an organism from the fertilized ovum (zygote) to the sexually mature individual, who himself in turn develops sex cells and produces offspring.

The *alternation of generations* is alternation between generations produced in a different manner. The term *heterogony* means that offspring are produced in different ways from the sex cells, e.g. one generation from normally fertilized ova and the next from unfertilized ova (see *Parthenogenesis*) as is the case, e.g., in water fleas and *Phylloxera vastatrix*. On the other hand, an alternation of one generation produced by a sexual and the other by an asexual process is known as *metagenesis*. E.g.: the *coelenterata*. The jelly-fish produces, by normal sexual processes, zygotes from which polyps develop. The polyp in turn produces the jelly-fish generation by asexual means, through blastogenesis.   *H.S.*

Generation gap. Commonly observed problems and conflicts in the different forms of interaction between young people and mem-

bers of the older generation (youthful protests against rules made by parents and teachers, sometimes also demonstrations against political decisions—which are generally made by members of the older generation). Possible explanations for these phenomena: (*a*) incompatible attitudes in the two age groups: a conservative attitude aiming to maintain the benefits of past achievements on the part of the older generation, and a tendency for the younger generation to be progressive, force changes, and improve traditional patterns by innovation; (*b*) a stereotyped approach on both sides to members of the other group; young people consider their elders to be obstinate, obstructive and outmoded, while they themselves are accused by their elders of showing an inadequate sense of responsibility, lack of experience and idleness, i.e. they are not recognized as adults. See *Authoritarian personality; Prejudice; Stereotype.*

Bibliography: Maccoby, E. E., Newcomb, T. M. & Hartley, E. L. (Eds): Readings in social psychology. New York, ³1958. Shanas, E. & Streib, G. F. (Eds): Social structure and the family: generational relations. Englewood Cliffs, 1965. Wilkins, L. T.: Delinquent generations. London, 1960.   A.S.-M.

Generative glands. See *Gonads.*

Genetic psychology. See *Development; Traits.*

Genetics. The theory of heredity. The physical and mental characteristics formed during the process of individualization of a living being are primarily conditioned by inherited factors (see *Gene*) in the sex cells. A secondary modification of these characteristics through environmental influences can only take place within the framework of modification determined by these inherited factors. Geneticists study both the extent to which characteristics are genetically conditioned, i.e. the extent of the modification range determined by heredity, and the way in which heredity conditions the development of characteristics by chemical and physical means (*molecular genetics*).

Bibliography: Haggis, G. M. (Ed.): Introduction to molecular biology. London, 1964. Srb, A. M., Owen, R. D. & Edgar, R. S.: General genetics. San Francisco & London, ²1965. Wagner, R. P. & Mitchell, H. K.: Genetics and metabolism. New York & London, ²1963. Watson, J. D.: The molecular biology of the gene. New York & Amsterdam, 1965.   H. S.

Geneva scheme. Compilation of main features for work evaluation systems, developed by the ILO (International Labor Organization) in Geneva in 1950.   *G.R.W.M.*

Geneva school. A designation for the branch of developmental psychology founded by J. Piaget and his co-workers (especially B. Inhelder and A. Szeminska). With its studies of the development of intelligence and perception (since 1921) and of genetic epistemology (since 1950), the Geneva school has made one of the most valuable and extensive contributions in this field. J. Piaget's theories can be understood most readily in the light of functionalism (J. Dewey, J. Mc. K. Cattell, E. Claparède).
Bibliography: Flavell, J. A.: The developmental psychology of Jean Piaget. New York, 1963.   H.Z.

Geniology. See *Giftedness; Genius.*

Genital stage (syn. *Genital phase; Genital period*). Divided by Freud into an early and late genital phase. In the early phase, also known as the Oedipal (Oedipus) phase (app. four and five years of age), a child becomes interested (among other things) in his sexual organs. He becomes aware of the anatomical difference between the two sexes, and begins to accept the existence of two sexes and his own sex as a reality. According to Freud, this interest is connected with self-manipulation (of the sexual organs) and, in addition to previous forms of contact, with a desire for specific sexual contact with the parent of the other sex. The boy no longer looks upon his mother merely as a person who cares for him and makes demands on him, but also as a woman. He exhibits his newly discovered "manliness" (see *Phallic stage*); lays claim to his mother's sole attention; and thus comes into conflict with his father. The girl continues to look upon her mother as a person who makes demands and fulfills needs, but turns toward her father with the onset of heterosexual interest— i.e. to a person who is psychologically more novel for her—and therefore comes into conflict with the mother. The conflicts are resolved with increasing adequacy during the early genital phase, usually by partial repression of sexual interest in the parent of the opposite sex, and by identification with the parent of the same sex. These interests are generally repressed less strongly by a girl than by a boy; she remains attached to the father as an object of heterosexual love rather more strongly than a boy remains attached to the mother. The total bond between a son and his mother is, however, often somewhat stronger than a girl's attachment to her mother (or father), because he does not have to give up his primary object of love in the early genital phase as a girl must. Fixation and subsequent regression to the early genital phase may lead to hysteria (q.v.) (anxiety hysteria and phobia on the one hand, conversion hysteria on the other) and to homosexual perversion (see *Homosexuality*); and, in cases of less traumatic attachment in the early genital phase, to impotence or potency problems in the man, and to frigidity and vaginism in the woman. Instead of specific neurotic symptoms, a character change may also occur, i.e. a hysterical personality may develop. This personality type tends to a greater extent than other individuals to look upon social situations as sexual trial situations, and to satisfy his interests in a confused and apparently dishonest manner, or to react with excessive anxiety and defense. In the late genital phase, which begins after the latency phase in puberty, the young person develops an increasingly realistic interest in individuals of the opposite sex, who are generally of much the same age. The late genital phase extends throughout adult life.

Bibliography: Fenichel, O.: The psychoanalytic theory of neurosis. New York, 1945. Freud, S.: Three essays on the theory of sexuality. London, ²1962. Id.: Introductory lectures on psycho-analysis. London, ²1929. Toman, W.: An introduction to psychoanalytic theory of motivation. London & New York, 1960.   W. Toman

Genius. A high level of intellectual ability. Research on the subject generally takes an IQ of 135 or 140 as the lower "limit of genius". This definition would include between 0·5 and 1 per cent of the population, i.e. the most gifted. See *Giftedness; Abilities.*   K.P.

Genome; Genome mutation. "Genome" denotes the totality of genetic material (hereditary substance) present in a cell. Since this material is localized on the chromosomes, in general all the chromosomes present in a cell are defined as the genome.

Genome mutation is the chromosomal alteration which occurs under physical or chemical environmental influences. For example, the whole set of chromosomes, or individual chromosomes, may be doubled.

                                                                                H.S.

Genotype. The totality of hereditary dispositions of an individual (see *Phenotype*). Individuals with the same genotype may show varying features, because of differing environmental influences during their development, but only within the genetically fixed range of variation.   H.S.

Geometric mean. The geometric mean (*G*) of a quantity of *N* values—a measurement of the central tendency of the distribution—is the *N*th root of the product of these values (means):

$$G = \left(\prod_{i=1}^{N} X_i \right)^{1/N}.$$

If a geometric mean exists, it is situated between the harmonic (q.v.) and the arithmetic mean (q.v.).   W.H.B.

Geometrical-optical illusions. Geometrical-optical illusions in the wide sense represent one form of perceptual illusion. They may occur in three-, two- and one-dimensional patterns in the field of vision, in regard to size, shape and position, distance and direction of observation, and may also affect the (metric) relationship between these factors. Illusions of this kind in the narrow sense occur if, in the case of a figure presented on a frontal-parallel plane, the phenomenal distance, angular, directional or curvature characteristics deviate from their original correlates. Illusions in this narrower sense are dealt with in the remainder of this article.

Studies of these phenomena began in the mid-nineteenth century. Initially the various illusions—named after their discoverers (J. J. Oppel, F. Zollner, J. C. Poggendorff, etc.)—were only demonstrated, by means of a drawn figure. Quantitative analyses were added at the turn of the century. A figure which is still generally known as the Müller-Lyer illusion (q.v.), but was in fact developed much earlier by Oppel, was frequently adduced as an example. In figures of this kind, phenomenal equivalence is assumed between the section *i* which "undergoes the illusion" and a variable, isolated comparison value; the difference between *i* and the isolated value which appears equal to *i* ("equivalent" value) is the measure of (absolute) illusion. Hofmann summarized the literature on this subject in 1920. Later on, other figures were added, e.g. a parallelogram-diagonal illusion generally named after F. Sander, but already described previously by M. Luckiesh, which has been studied in particular detail.

Of the many incorrect attempts to explain such illusions, some (*a*) referred to the peripheral sense organ (the structure of the retina, its curvature, functional irregularity, spatial values, eye movements, etc.; and others (b) to previous experience relating in particular to perspective, to confusions, errors of judgment, etc. The hypotheses referred to in (a) above, as well as the perspective theory, are refuted by the fact that they do not also explain the analogous haptic illusions (q.v.). Although contradictory evidence does not prevent the outmoded explanations from being quoted occasionally today, it has become increasingly clear that these illusions are not determined by peripheral conditions or superimposed information from the memory or reasoning, but that their origin lies in central processes of configuration (gestalt formation). This is confirmed by the fact that there are many functional relationships between these illusions and such phenomena as apparent movement which are known to be centrally conditioned.

There has been much research into geometrical-optical illusions in recent decades, and work is still continuing. Research has concentrated on three partially overlapping areas: (a) *Principles* and *methods* of measurement have been developed by introducing the phenogram, i.e. the total-figural equivalent, instead of partial value equivalents; (b) *Functional analysis* has led to the following discoveries: the phenomenal metrics varies with the phenomenal structure; pregnance tendencies and other intra-figural forces may cause illusions; fixation and attention characteristics, contrast and adaptation, are again taken into account for explanatory purposes from new points of view; there are points of relation between geometrical-optical illusions and figural after-effects; excessively long consideration of a single figure leads to a reduction in the degree of illusion; (c) These illusions have been applied primarily in developmental psychology and personality theory, where it has been found that there is no general "illusion characteristic" (whose extent, varying from individual to individual, could be used to indicate a state of development or type). The principles of cognition theory which hold good for perceptual illu-sions are particularly applicable to geometrical-optical illusions (see *Perception, illusions of; Visual perception*).

Bibliography: Gregory, A. H.: Visual perception. London, 1970. Hofmann, F. B.: Die Lehre vom Raumsinn des Auges, Part 1. Berlin, 1920. Oyama, T.: Japanese studies on the so-called geometrical-optical illusions. Psychologia, Int. J. Psychol. Orient., 1960, 3. Piaget, J.: The mechanisms of perception. London, 1969. Rausch, E.: Struktur und Metrik figural-optischer Wahrnehmung, Frankfurt a. M., 1952. Id.: Probleme der Metrik. In: Metzger, W. (Ed.): Hb. der Psychol., Vol. 1. Göttingen, 1966, 776–865. Vernon, M. D. (Ed.): Experiments in visual perception. Harmondsworth, 1966.

E. Rausch

Geopsychology. A scientific discipline and research area, in which the natural environment is studied in its relationship to behavior and mental states. A distinction is made between four principal factors (Hellpach): the influences of weather, climate, soil and landscape. After preparatory work and studies by Montesquieu and C. Lombroso, this subject is becoming increasingly important today in the context of the study of problems of human life under abnormal or atypical conditions: in the polar areas, tropics, bases on the sea-bed, interplanetary space. Some of the work of geopsychology has now been taken over by rhythm research; in biological anthropology, geopsychological problems are considered from the ecological standpoint.

Bibliography: Hellpach, W.: Die geopsychischen Erscheinungen. Leipzig, 1923. Id.: Geopsyche. Die Menschenseele unter dem Einfluss von Wetter und Klima, Boden und Landschaft. Stuttgart, ⁶1950. Sells, S. B. & Berry, C. A. (Eds): Human factors in jet and space travel: a medical-psychological analysis. New York, 1961.   P.M.

Geotaxis. Alignment and movement of lower organisms as a function of gravity as the releasing stimulus. A distinction is made between movement in the direction of the force of gravity (positive geotaxis), and movement in the opposite direction (negative geotaxis). See *Taxis*.   F.C.S.

Geriatrics. Medical research into the phenomena of old age (pathological conditions of old age) is a branch of gerontology (q.v.) and was first elevated into a scientific discipline by the work of M. Burger and E. Abderhalden in the 1930s. It provides valuable information for "social" gerontology, a field of study founded at international level in 1950, in order to help in remedying the increasing social problems encountered by the aged. See *Aging*.   *F.N.*

Gerontology is the science of aging. The term derives from the Greek *geron*—old man, and came into use in the early part of the twentieth century with the increased scientific interest in the processes of aging. The appearance in 1939 of *Problems of Ageing*, edited by E. V. Cowdry, reflected the growing interest in research into aging. Technologically advanced countries now provide conditions in which large numbers of persons survive to old age; hence studies of aging are undertaken from the viewpoint of social science as well as of biology.

Gerontology can be regarded as having three major divisions: biomedical, behavioral, and social. Biomedical problems of aging clearly show the interaction of the biological aging of the organism and its susceptibility to disease. Research on the biology of aging includes the study not only of man but of lower organisms, cells and subcellular components (Comfort, 1964). The behavioral aspects of gerontology include the consideration of man psychologically (as he ages individually), and sociologically (as a member of a group) (Birren, 1959). Social gerontology is concerned particularly with the implications of man's aging in society. The presence of large numbers of retired and older persons in a society has implications for economics, social welfare, and the distribution of health and other services (Tibbitts, 1960).

Most scientists would agree at present that there is no single mechanism of aging—for example, a single *lethal gene* that governs the

length of life. It is probable that the biological processes of aging are controlled by the action of many genes; but the conditions under which the animal is conceived, matures and ages are also important in accelerating or retarding the processes of aging. Important issues in gerontology include: the problem of the identification of the origins of molecular errors or faults that occur in aging cells; discovering the basis of changes in memory with age; identifying the conditions predisposing to alienation and poor life-satisfaction for older persons; and determining the extent to which continuous physical and mental activity retards regressive changes of aging. Many biomedical problems also exist in our limited understanding of the etiology of diseases associated with advancing age. Research and scholarly activity devoted to gerontology will very likely develop as industrial prosperity increases, and as the growing number of older persons in society gives cause for concern about the optimum conditions for human life in the second half of the life span (see *Aging*).

Bibliography: Birren, J. E. (Ed.): Handbook of aging and the individual. Chicago, 1959. Comfort, A.: Aging, the biology of senescence. New York, 1964. Cowdry, E. V. (Ed.): Problems of ageing. Baltimore, 1939. Tibbitts, C. (Ed.): Handbook of social gerontology. Chicago, 1960.   *J. E. Birren*

Gerontophilia. A sexual deviation in which the age of the partner plays a decisive part: sexual attraction to and preference for much older persons. Gerontophilia is the extreme opposite of pedophilia (q.v.), in which the sexual attraction diminishes, and finally ceases altogether, as the partner grows older. Gerontophilia may also occur as a secondary phenomenon in the context of a different sexual deviation, e.g. homosexuality, or may be linked with fetishism (Kronfeld, 1923). Hirschfeld interpreted gerontophilia as an "infantile fixation on older persons". Whether it is pathological, i.e. a sexually "perverse" attitude in the clinical sense, must be determined in each individual case.

Bibliography: Kronfeld, A.: Sexualpathologie. Leipzig & Vienna, 1923. Hirschfeld, M.: Sexual anomalies and perversions. London, ²1952. Giese, H.: Psychopathologie der Sexualität. Stuttgart, 1962. ⁻H.M.

Gesell, Arnold. *Life and works:* B. 21/6/1880, Alma, Wisc.; d. 29/5/1961, New Haven, Conn. He studied psychology at Clark University where he took his Ph.D. in 1906; intermittent teaching work thereafter; in 1911 he founded the Clinic of Child Development at Yale University, New Haven, which he continued to direct until his retirement in 1948. He trained in medicine while assistant professor in Yale and passed his M.D. in 1915; he edited the Journal of Genetic Psychology from 1926.

Gesell is widely considered to be the "father of child psychology". He wrote more than fifteen books on child psychology and helped this branch of psychology to gain wide popularity even among laymen. His research method consisted in simple, accurate observation of children's behavior, generally with the aid of film cameras and one-way mirrors; he also made observations under controlled test conditions. The results of his studies take the form of minute descriptions of widely varying aspects of the behavior of children and young people at different ages. The chronological development summaries prepared in this way imply standards governing the development of children in the areas of behavior under consideration and are intended to help in predicting subsequent mental development. In reality, these aims were not satisfactorily met, particularly because the observational material on which the studies were based was much too narrow (sometimes only eleven cases) for individual age groups, and unrepresentative. Gesell's approach was purely descriptive. It consisted in the description and classification of individual findings without any attempt to lay down a theory of mental development or analyze the factors which influence it. The process of development appears as something mechanical and immutable in his work. He overemphasizes the constitutional aspect and cyclical nature of development, while underestimating the significance of individual variations, and of cultural and social influences on development.

Major works: The mental growth of the pre-school child. New York, 1925. Infancy and human growth. New York, 1928. An atlas of human behavior: a systematic delineation of the forms and early growth of human behavior patterns, Vols. 1 & 2, New York, 1934. The feeding behavior of infants: a pediatric approach to the mental hygiene of early life. Philadelphia, 1937 (with F. L. Ilg). Reciprocal neuromotor interweaving: a principle of development evidenced in the patterning of infant behavior. *J. Comp. Neurol.*, 1939, *70*, 161–80. The first five years of life: a guide to the study of the pre-school child. New York, 1940 (with others). Twins T and C from infancy to adolescence: a biogenetic study of individual differences by the method of co-twin control. *Genet. Psychol. Monogr.*, 1941, *24*, 3–122 (with H. Thompson). Infant and child in the culture of today: the guidance of development in home and nursery school. New York, 1942 (with F. L. Ilg and others). The child from five to ten. New York, 1946 (with F. L. Ilg). Vision, its development in infant and child. New York, 1949 (with others). Child development: an introduction to the study of human growth. New York, 1949 (with F. L. Ilg). Arnold Gesell. In: Boring, E. G., *et al.* (Eds): A history of psychology in autobiography Vol. 4. Worcester, Mass., 1952, 123–42.
W.W.

Gesell Development Schedules (GSCH), also Gesell Development Scales, Gesell Norms of Development, Gesell Tests, Pre-school Child Test, Yale Test of Child Development. The schedules were published by A. Gesell in 1925 as a "general development test" and afterwards substantially modified (Gesell & Amatruda, 1947); they led to the preparation of other development tests (H. Hetzer, C. Bühler, etc.).

Structure: selected items for key age (infants, or pre-school children), maturity and four behavior categories corresponding to the developmental concept: "the young child is as old as his behavior".

Application: GSCH were used for development diagnosis (to estimate the development quotient) of normal and impaired children between the ages of 0 and 6; they were used primarily to determine suitability for adoption and for prediction of atypical and abnormal development processes such as amentia, brain damage, blindness, etc. The *reliability coefficients* are between $r = 0.79$ and $r = 0.88$. *Validity* (correlation with other development tests) is quoted as $r = 0.37$ to $r = 0.74$.

Bibliography: Gesell, A. & Amatruda, C. S.: Developmental diagnosis. Normal and abnormal child development. New York, ²1947.   *F.N.*

Gestalt. See *Ganzheit; Structure.*

Gestalt form, quality. See *Ganzheit.*

Gestogens (syn. *Progestins; Progestogens*). Progestational hormones which prepare the lining of the womb to ensure that the fertilized ovum is implanted (see *Uterus*) and that pregnancy proceeds smoothly (hence known also as "pregnancy hormones"). They provide the developing ovum with optimal protection in the uterus. The most important of these natural (physiological) gestogens is *progesterone* (Micryston progesterone). Gestogens in a wider sense are synthetic hormones. They are administered as oral contraceptives (see *Contraception*) and are also used in the treatment of other disorders, such as acne and excessive menstrual bleeding.   *H.M.*

g factor. A term used in the literature of factor analysis for general factor (q.v.).
                                              W.H.B.

G factor. A personality factor ("superego strength") derived by R. B. Cattell by factor analysis and included in Factor VI of the second order (volitional control and persistence).   *W.H.B.*

Gibson effect. A group of negative aftereffects that set in after prolonged observation of special patterns (field of uniformly curved lines, pattern of oblique lines, etc.) as a result of adaptation (q.v.). The term is used in the literature to distinguish this phenomenon from figural aftereffects (q.v.) and negative aftereffects in Stratton's experiment (q.v.).

Bibliography: Gibson, J. J.: Adaptation, after-effect and contrast in the perception of curved lines. J. exp. Pscyhol. 1933, *16*, 1–31.   *A.H.*

Giftedness, research into. The study of the causes and factors of high intellectual ability (see *Genius*) and its distribution and forms. Studies by L. M. Terman of the development of highly-gifted individuals have shown that these persons are also emotionally more stable (less neurotic). The theory subscribed to by, e.g., Lange–Eichbaum (1928) that genius is accompanied by deficient emotional and social adaptability must therefore be rejected. Family studies have shown that giftedness occurs frequently in several members of a family; both genetic factors and factors connected with the family environment are probably responsible for this. Qualitative research into giftedness (e.g. examination of the factors in thought processes and problem-solving strategy which make possible the creative achievements of genius) is still in the early stages. See *Abilities; Creativity; Intelligence.*

Bibliography: Anastasi, A.: Differential psychology. New York, ³1966. Guilford, J. P.: The nature of human intelligence. New York, 1967. Lange-Eichbaum, W.: Genie, Irrsinn und Ruhm. Munich, 1928. Terman, L. M. *et al.*: Genetic studies of genius,

Vols 1-5. Stanford, 1926-59. Vernon, P. E. (Ed.): Creativity. Harmondsworth, 1970.   K.P.

Gilbreth chronoscope. An instrument fitted with a large dial and used for measuring minute units of time. It finds application in the study of slight movements recorded cinematographically. The time units and the movements are recorded simultaneously on the film, so that the sequence of movements can be plotted against time.   A.Th.

Glandotrop(h)ic hormones. Hormones (q.v.) of the anterior lobe of the pituitary that stimulate hormone production in the endocrine glands. The most important are: *adrenocorticotropic hormone* (ACTH, q.v.), which stimulates production of adrenal hormones (corticosteroids, q.v.); *thyrotropic hormone* (thyrotropine), which stimulates production of thyroid hormones; gonadotropins (q.v.), which stimulate production of sex hormones (follicle stimulating hormone, luteinizing hormone, luteotropic hormone). The production of glandotropic hormones is governed by many factors, especially by the hormones present in the blood and produced in the peripheral glands (negative feedback) and by the releasing factors of the hypothalamus. Bibliography: Harris, G. W.: Neural control of the pituitary gland. London, 1955. Harris, G. W. & Donovan, D. T.: The pituitary gland, Vols 1-3. London, 1966. Szentagthal, J., Flerko, B., Mess, B. & Halasz, B.: Hypothalamic control of anterior pituitary. Budapest, 1962.   W.J.

Glands. Organs of the body which produce special secretions. *Endocrine* glands such as the thyroid gland (q.v.), the adrenal glands (q.v.), the islet cells of the pancreas, the ovaries and the testes discharge hormones into the blood stream, whereas *exocrine* glands such as the sweat, sebaceous, lacrimal, salivary, and digestive glands release their contents to outside the body, or the gastro-intestinal tract. According to their histological structure, glands are divided into the acinous and the tubular, and the latter may themselves be divided into straight, coiled or branched. The masses of lymphatic tissue wrongly called "lymph glands" are more correctly described as *lymph nodes*.   E.D.

Glandula pituitaria. See *Hypophysis*.

Glare effects. A diminution of visual performance (visual acuity, differential, form and color sensitivity, depth vision, etc.) as a result of inadequate lighting, or of a visual environment unfavorable to visual characteristics. In the narrower sense, glare defined by visual performance is called disability glare, or physiological glare, in contrast to discomfort glare, or psychological glare, which is defined by a diminution of the comfort, well-being, etc., of an individual or group of individuals.

Kinds of physiological glare: (*a*) absolute glare: too high light intensities, adaptation to which is impossible; (*b*) adaptation glare: sudden change of the light-intensity level; (*c*) relative glare: too great contrasts relative to the light-intensity level; (*d*) direct glare: glare coming from the light source itself; (*e*) indirect glare: reflection images, e.g., from light sources; (*f*) in-field and (*g*) peripheral field glare: cause of glare central or peripheral; (*h*) simultaneous and (*i*) successive glare: whether the cause of glare operates during or after its presence, and (*j*) fog or haze glare: the result of extensive and illuminated expanding media such as fog, smoke, curtain material, etc. For quantitative relationships see H. Schober (1964). Bibliography: Schober, H.: Das Sehen. Leipzig, 1964.   A.H.

Glial cells. The brain contains about ten times as many glial cells as nerve cells. Glial cells form the non-neural part of the brain tissue.

It is estimated that the human brain contains 100–130 thousand million glial cells, classified by shape into astrocytes, oligodendrocytes and microgliocytes (frequency ratio 60:30:10). Their frequency distribution varies from one region of the brain to another. They are regarded as transmitters in the process of biochemical interchange. It has not yet been determined with absolute certainty to what extent glial cells participate in neural processes. Importance attaches to the glial index $N_{gl}L/N_{neur}$, where N_{gl} is the number of glial cells and N_{neur} the number of neurons. This index is useful for a comparison of the various layers and regions of the brain. Moreover, it provides an indicator for specific physical as well as mental disorders, and changes characteristically in the course of ontogenesis and phylogenesis.   *M.A.*

Global learning consists in mastering the material to be studied, e.g. a poem or piece of music, by tackling it and committing it to memory as a whole. The effectiveness of this method increases with the student's familiarity with it, his intelligence, and the meaningful content of the material and the systematic way in which it is put together. It declines if the material is too lengthy, contains difficult passages, and follows a natural pattern. *G.H.*

Glucagon. A polypeptide hormone secreted in the islands of Langerhans (q.v.) in the pancreas. By breaking down glycogen in the liver it increases blood sugar concentration. Glucagon stimulates the production of insulin (q.v.). It probably exerts only a slight influence on the onset of diabetes. Glucagon is used in the treatment of severe hypoglycemic disorders.

Bibliography: Foa, P. P.: Glukagon. In: Ergebnisse der Physiologie, biologischen Chemie und exp. Pharmakologie, Vol. 60. Berlin, 1968.   *W.J.*

Glutamic acid. A mono-amino-dicarboxylic acid manufactured as needed in the body and supplied to the organism, together with other amino acids, either in dietary albumin or in pure (or synthetic) form. It is of primary importance in the intermediate metabolism, and serves in the organism as a precursor of GABA (gamma-amino-butyric acid, q.v.). Glutamic acid has aroused special interest among psychologists because it is understood to raise mental performance among persons of low intelligence when administered over a protracted period. There have been numerous investigations, but owing to the inadequacy of the methods used, no clear interpretation is possible. No psychological effects are found after a single administration of glutamic acid.

Bibliography: Astin, A. W. & Ross, S.: Glutamic acid and human intelligence. Psychol. Bull., 1960, 57, 429–34. Lingmüller, V.: Biochemie, Physiologie und Linik der Glutaminsäure. Aulendorf, 1955. Vogel, W., Broverman, D. M., Dragus, J. G. & Klaiber, E. L.: The role of glutamic acid in cognitive behaviors. Psychol. Bull., 1966, 65, 367–82.   *W.J.*

Goal gradient. C. L. Hull's term for a regular increase in efficiency while approaching a goal.

Goal orientation. The tendency to orientation toward the goal.   *K.F.*

Goal orientation device. See *Maze learning.*

Golden mean (syn. *Golden section*). An esthetic ratio of division in which the *whole* bears the same proportion to the *larger* part as the latter to the *smaller*.   *W.H.B.*

Gonadodysgenesia. Failure of the sex glands to develop in accordance with genetic constitution, resulting in anomalies such as an individual with XY chromosome structure manifesting female form.   *G.D.W.*

Gonadotrop(h)ic hormones. Active hormonal

substances (albumin compounds) that act directly on male or female gonads (testes, ovaries), stimulating and controlling their growth as well as their endocrine function (production of male or female sex-hormones) and their exocrine function (production of semen, spermatozoa in man; ova and ovaries in woman). They are not sex-specific.

Two groups of gonadotropic hormones are distinguished:

1. *Pituitary gonadotropins*, secreted in the anterior pituitary under the influence of releasing factors of the hypothalamus: (*a*) FSH (*follicle stimulating hormone*) which stimulates the growth of ovarian follicles and, with gonadotropin, brings on the onset of LH maturity and estrogen production of the follicle; and in man the growth of mature sperms in the seminiferous tubules; (*b*) ICSH (*interstitial cell stimulating hormone;* in woman also LH, luteinizing hormone), which controls in particular the secretion of sex hormones in male and female gonads; (*c*) LTH (*luteotropic hormone*), which stimulates the growth and onset of maturity of the female breast (lactogenic hormone).

2. *Placental gonadotropins*, secreted only during pregnancy: (*a*) HCG (*human chorionic gonadotropin*), is produced in bulk in the placenta; (*b*) HPL (*human placental lactogen*), produced in the placenta, supports the action of HCG; (*c*) PMSG (*pregnant mare serum gonadotropin*), which is present in large quantities in the serum of pregnant mares (characterized biologically by a powerful follicle-stimulating effect).

Hormonal regulation mechanisms between primary stimulating centers (anterior pituitary, hypothalamus) and periphery (sex glands) are basically the same in the two sexes. The interaction of gonadotropic and sex hormones proceeds on the lines of a feedback system (e.g. FSH brings on, jointly with LH, the onset of follicular maturity and estrogen production; increasing estrogen production, in turn, slows down FSH secretion in the anterior pituitary). This feedback effect is the basis of hormonal contra-

ception: gonadotropic production is blocked by a constant inflow of estrogens and gestogens, so that the rhythm of the female cycle is interrupted, inhibiting ovulation and, therefore, fertilization.

Bibliography: Suhl, A. M.: Gonadal hormones and social behavior in infrahuman vertebrates. In: Young, W. C. (Ed.): Sex and internal secretions. Baltimóre, 1961. Voigt, K. D. & Schmidt, H.: Sexualhormone. Hamburg, 1968. *H.M.*

Gonadotrop(h)ins. Glandotropic hormones (q.v.) of the anterior pituitary that stimulate production of sex hormones (q.v.). The 3 main gonadotropins are the *follicle stimulating hormone* (FSH, Prolan A), the *luteinizing hormone* (LH), the *interstitial cell stimulating hormone* (ICSH, Prolan B) and the *luteotropic hormone* (LTH, prolactin). The secretory mechanism of gonadotropins is largely unaccounted for. The often alleged reduction of gonadotropins under stress has not been confirmed by recent investigations.

Bibliography: Albert, A. (Ed.): Human pituitary gonadotropins. Springfield, Ill., 1961. Apostolakis, M. & Voigt, K. D.: Gonadotropine. Stuttgart, 1964. Giuliani, G.: Studies on gonadotropin release during stressful situations and the role of the central nervous system. In: Bajusz, E. (Ed.): Physiology and pathology of adaptation mechanisms. Oxford, 1969. *W.J.*

Gonads. *Sex glands:* in man the testis, which produces the male sex hormone (androgen); in woman the ovary, which produces the female sex hormone (estrogen and *corpus luteum* hormone). The testis also produces spermatozoa (sperm), while in the female ovary an ovum ripens every four weeks. The gonadal hormones exert considerable influence on the formation of secondary sex organs, the physique structure of both sexes, and the individual's behavior as a male or female.

E.D.

Goodenough Test (*Draw-a-Man test*, DAM). A non-verbal intelligence test for children of 3–13 years. The child is required to draw a man. The simple evaluation technique, intelligence-age norms, and a satisfactory degree of reliability, assure the test widespread use. The existence of significant relationships with general intelligence and social adaptation factors has been established.

E.F.-K.

Gosset chart. The tabling of "Student's" t distribution of critical probability α and sample size N. With its aid the t test (q.v.) for the statistical testing of significance can be speeded up.   *W.H.B.*

Gottschaldt's figures (*Embedded, hidden figures*). Complex sets of figures in which part-figures of the simplest kind can be isolated, recognized or perceived only with difficulty because of their structural embedding in the overall figure, in whose structure they lie concealed. Test figures of this kind characterize the factor "flexibility of closure".

H.H.

Gradient, approach-avoidance. According to N. E. Miller's goal gradient theory, approach and avoidance gradients are *curvilinear* functions of the *proximity of the goal* and *drive strength*. Approach and avoidance tendencies, which arise in typical conflict situations and under ambiguous stimuli, and are measured, for example, by answers in the Thematic Apperception Test (TAT), and by skin resistance, can be represented graphically as gradients. The point at which the gradients intersect is that of the maximum degree of conflict and, depending on the type of conflict, is known as *labile* or *stable* equilibrium. See *Conflict*.   *F.N.*

Grammar. In general, the *linguistic competence* of the speaker of a natural language (q.v.), and in particular a regulative system by which relations are established between particular sound systems (see *Phonemics*), sound sequences (see *Morphemics*), rules of syntax (rules for forming sentences), and the associated meanings of sound sequences (see *Semantics*).

Every theory of grammar must try to account for the fact that a competent language user can understand, or produce in a way intelligible to others, an unlimited number of sentences never before heard. The principles that enable sentences of unlimited number or length to be assembled from a finite repertoire of elements and rules are known as *recursive rules*.

Structural description provides data on the constituents of sentences, their interrelation and sequence (*phrase-structure rules*), and on the grammatical information needed for interpreting sentences. Various grammatical models exist for structural description, e.g. *generative* (*transformational*) *grammar* (Chomsky, 1957, 1965, 1968), whose analysis in accordance with "immediate constituents" (first level: e.g. subject-predicate), or analysis by means of "transformational rules" (or rules for re-ordering and recombining sentence constituents), is concerned with the generative properties of the *basic* or *deep structure* which corresponds to the "meaning", or fundamental semantic relations, of the sentence. Actual utterances can assume other, at times more complicated, structures (*surface structure*, or structural relations between elements of a sentence) which can be formed in linguistic analysis from the basic structure by using transformational rules to re-order the fundamental constituents. In speech (q.v.) surface structures undergo phonological interpretation and are expressed phonetically (see *Phonemics*). (For the analysis of deep structure, see Chomsky, 1965.)

Language acquisition (grammar acquisition) is explained variously. The empiricist view (e.g. Skinner, 1957) is that language is mastered exclusively by *learning*. Rationalist-nativist theories (e.g. Chomsky, 1968; Chomsky & Halle, 1968) assume that language acquisition also depends on specific *predispositions*. The speed with which basic rules are derived and applied in ontogeny from preexisting language, suggests the existence of preformed (possibly universal) formal principles of grammatical structuralization. Analyses of spoken language appear to show that linguistic competence, e.g. between the ages of 24 and 29 months (age of two- and three-word utterances), draws on only a few grammatical classes which are embodied in simple hierarchic rules:

$$S_1 \rightarrow N + N$$
$$S_2 \rightarrow P + N$$
$$S_3 \rightarrow P + NP$$
$$NP \rightarrow \{P_N\} + N$$
$$N = \text{noun}$$

P = pivot word class (containing adjectives and modifiers)

NP = noun complex

$\begin{Bmatrix} X \\ Y \end{Bmatrix}$ = either X or Y

These rules correspond to the *basic*, or *deep*, *structures* of adult competence. Derived, transposed structures do not yet make their appearance. Children thus seem to begin their *grammatical development* with the syntactical forms immediately associated with semantic interpretation. From the behaviorist point of view it might be expected instead that the child would first learn from the surface structures used by adults (see Braine, 1963; Brown & Bellugi, 1964; Brown & Hanlon, 1970; Miller & McNeill, 1969).

This use of Chomsky's notion of competence is criticized on the ground that it takes account only of what is systematic in speech, of *grammaticality* (q.v.), and not of the context in which utterances are made. For the competence value that verbal utterances acquire through their position in the verbal and situational context, Campbell & Wales (1970) would like to substitute "communicative competence". Consequently, the observational basis of the speech acquisition theory of McNeill (1968) also appears to

be inadequate, as it includes no situational parameter. Other reasons could be adduced for the fact that children do not at first make use of any "derived" sentence structures. Brown & Hanlon (1970) try to incorporate the communicative milieu in the observation of speech development, in order to find out whether speech acquisition is partly determined by specific selections of the child from the supply of information available to it (see also Bernstein, 1961, 1965; Brown, 1965; Irwin, 1960). See *Language; Psycholinguistics; Speech; Verbal behavior; Concept.*

Bibliography: Bernstein, B.: Social class and linguistic development: a theory of social learning. In: Halsey, A. H. et al. (Eds): Education, economy and society. New York, 1961. Id.: A socio-linguistic approach to social learning. In: Gould, J. (Ed.): Penguin survey of the social sciences. Harmondsworth, 1965. Braine, M. D. S.: The ontogeny of English phrase structure: the first phrase. Language, 1963, 39, 1–13. Brown, R.: Social psychology. New York, 1965. Brown, R. & Bellugi, U.: Three processes in the child's acquisition of syntax. Harv. educ. Rev., 1964, 34, 133–51. Brown, R. & Hanlon, C.: Derivational complexity and order of acquisition in child speech. In: Hays, J. R. (Ed.): Cognition and the development of language. New York, 1970. Campbell, R. & Wales, R.: The study of language acquisition. In: Lyons, J. (Ed.): New horizons in linguistics. Harmondsworth, 1970. Chomsky, N.: Syntactic structures. The Hague, 1957. Id.: A review of B. F. Skinner's verbal behavior. Language, 1959, 35, 26–58. Id.: Aspects of the theory of syntax. Cambridge, Mass., 1965. Id.: Language and mind. New York, 1968. Chomsky, N. & Miller, G. A.: Introduction to the formal analysis of natural languages. In: Luce, R. D., Bush, R. R. & Galanter, E. (Eds): Handbook of mathematical psychology, Vol. 2. New York, 1963. Chomsky, N. & Halle, M.: The sound pattern of English. New York, 1968. Irwin, O. C.: Language and communication. In: Mussen, P. H. (Ed.): Handbook of research methods in child development. New York, 1960. McNeill, D.: Developmental psycholinguistics. In: Smith, F. & Miller, G. A. (Eds): The genesis of language. Cambridge, Mass., 1968. Miller, G. A. & McNeill, D.: Psycholinguistics. In: Lindzey, G. & Aronson, E. (Eds): Handbook of social psychology, Vol. III. Reading, Mass., 1969. Skinner, B. F.: Verbal behavior. New York, 1957. W. Abraham

Grammaticality. A language structure is grammatically correct when grammar (q.v.)

allows it a structural description. This presupposes that this structure can also be interpreted semantically, and if so, that the possibility of so interpreting an utterance (i.e. pragmatically) need not of itself imply proficient grammatical form. The boundary line between "correct" grammar (grammaticality) and deviant grammar (caused by sociological and redundancy factors—obvious errors where the context is situatively adequate) is a fluid one. A further distinction must be made between grammaticality and *acceptability*.

Bibliography: Halliday, M. A. K.: Categories of the theory of grammar. Word, 1961, *17*, 241–92. Jespersen, O.: Philosophy of grammar. London, 1924. Leech, G. N.: English in advertising. London, 1966. Palmer, F.: Grammar. Harmondsworth, 1971. Sebeok, T. A. (Ed.): Style in language. Cambridge, Mass., 1960. Warburg, J. F.: The best-chosen English. London, 1961. Id.: Verbal values. London, 1966.   *W.A.*

Grandeur, delusion of. A false belief which qualifies as a delusion, that the person has a social position or ancestors of importance and renown, or great wealth, possessions, abilities or powers.   *B.B.*

Grand mal. *Major* epileptic attack. Clinically subdivided into pre-convulsive, convulsive and post-convulsive phases. The first is characterized by prodromes (premonitory symptoms) which may take the form of irritability, moodiness, tension, or minor attacks. Alongside these general symptoms are frequently found peculiar sensations which immediately precede the onset of the fit, and to which the term *aura* is applied. This is the patient's last experience, generally accompanied by acute anxiety, before unconsciousness sets in. The seizure itself consists of a tonic contraction, then a clonic (tumultuous) spasm followed by a series of clonic convulsions of varying intensity. In the post-convulsive phase the patient remains for some minutes in a profound coma (q.v.). This is followed by a deep sleep lasting a few hours, in some cases by a state of semi-consciousness. The attack is followed by amnesia in regard to the entire event. The spasms can be recorded objectively by EEG (electroencephalogram, q.v.) observation of correlative electrical currents developed by the cerebral cortex. Even between attacks there are often typical indications. So far there has been no satisfactory explanation for the onset of an epileptic fit. It may be assumed that in a general way all CNS substance is spasm-prone, and that in epilepsy the normal properties of the CNS are present on an exaggerated scale. Treatment consists largely in the administration of anti-convulsant drugs. To a limited extent, recourse may be had to stereotactic (q.v.) methods, which also often have a favorable effect on the attendant psychic behavior, e.g. aggressiveness, moodiness, and so on.

Bibliography: Janz, D.: Die Epilepsien. Spezielle Pathologie und Therapie. Stuttgart, 1969. Penfield, W. & Jasper, H.: Epilepsy and the functional anatomy of the human brain. Boston, 1954.   *M.Ad.*

Graph. A diagrammatic representation of variables by points joined in a straight, curved or broken line which shows their relative values.

Graphology. I. 1. *Terminology; concept.* "Graphology" is a technical term from the Greek *graphein* = to write, and *logos* = account. The word was first used by Abbé Jean-Hippolyte Michon, and is to be found in his *Système de graphologie* (1875). More recently, the expression "psychology of handwriting" has been used with the same meaning. In the U.S.A., usage varies between "grapho-analysis" and "handwriting analysis". Graphology claims to be a scientific diagnostic method for learning about the writer's personality from his handwriting. In contrast to most "psycho-technical" tests, graphology attempts to apprehend the whole personality and not merely individual characteristics. It is not itself a science, but a scientific aid in psychological diagnosis. The graphologist must be trained in psychological charactero-logy and have some knowledge of psychiatry and neurology.

Graphology uses handwriting as its objective starting-point. No two people write in exactly the same way.

Writing represents motor activity. As such, it resembles mimicry in being a movement of the body, an individual expression (q.v.) of the personality (q.v.) in movement which writing fixes. Writing is learnt in school according to "national" models. And yet, even in the lowest class, exercise books reveal great individual differences in writing, although the collective "national" pattern may remain recognizable. It is the task of graphology to discover what each person's hand-writing expresses. Some claim that inherited characteristics and those acquired later on can be recognized, and usually differentiated. Everyone's handwriting changes as he grows older and his personality develops. This is due in part to the constitution of his body and brain. A graphologist requires little equipment: an ordinary magnifying-glass and a rule are sufficient. A framed fluorescent screen can also be useful, and the work may be facilitated if a good projector is available.

In addition to establishing the details of the handwriting by analysis, a graphological diagnosis of character structure requires the use of an irrational factor—intuition (q.v.) or empathy. It is indispensable, as in all productive scientific work which is more than a mere collection of facts; however, it cannot alone justify any claim to be a science or support the reliability (q.v.) of graphology, which has been suggested in many experi-

mental studies. Anyone who sets out to interpret handwriting by using only intuition or particularly keen "extrasensory perception" may have some success (R. Schermann), but his work can hardly be called graphology. An analytical approach must be combined with a synthetic picture of the whole, if the task is to be solved and sources of error are to be avoided.

2. *Historical survey.* By nature all people share, and indeed cannot do without, a direct understanding of what is expressed in all living movement. For that reason there was, even in antiquity, a non-scientific (or *pre-scientific*) interpretation of handwriting (e.g. Suetonius in the second century A.D.; in China since A.D. 1000). The first systematic approach dates from the Italian doctor C. Baldi (1622). But not until 150 years later did the Swiss pastor J. C. Lavater (1741–1801) in his *Physiognomische Fragmente zur Beförderung der Menschenkenntnis und Menschenliebe* (1775–81), make the decisive advance which was to lead to a more thorough systematic treatment of the subject. His own interpretations, however, owed too much to surmise, intuition and impression, and were often wide of the mark. But his work was widely read and proved a source of inspiration to others, especially in France (Abbé Flandrin). About a hundred years later Abbé Michon (1806–8) laid the foundations of modern graphology. He had no psychology to work on. His interpretative method was exclusively the study of individual charac-teristics (*signes*) of handwriting specimens. Precisely this apparent simplicity of approach awakened an almost passionate but super-ficial interest in large numbers of people in the nineteenth century. More responsible scientists soon attacked this frivolity. In France, for instance, J. Crépieux-Jamin (1858–1940) taught that many character traits cannot be directly established from simple graphological signs, but must be seen as combining several characteristics ("resultant theory"). Similar work was carried out in Germany by the doctors W. Preyer,

G. Meyer, etc., and above all the chemist L. Klages (1872–1956). Through his own discoveries and ideas, and those of his predecessors, he succeeded in raising graphology to a higher level. He recognized that *all handwriting characteristics had many meanings.* He sought a justifiable standpoint from which they could be judged and thought it could be found in studying the impression produced by the whole complex expression of handwriting, which he called "form level". The difficulty and relative unreliability of a study based solely on intuition caused others to split up, refine and simplify his basic concept of "form level". R. Wieser introduced the very important concept of "basic rhythm" into graphology. The Swiss M. Pulver (1889–1962), like E. Flatow-Worms and A. Mendelsohn-Teillard, introduced fundamentally psychoanalytic elements into the interpretation of handwriting. In place of "form level", as used by Klages, he endeavors to reach an integrative standpoint by the use of intuitive understanding (*Wesensschau*). Important and promising progress was made in the work of R. Pophal, Professor of Graphology at the university of Hamburg. He relates handwriting to physiological cerebral types. In so doing he creates the possibility of justifying and enriching by psychosomatic study graphological findings about personality.

3. *The present state of graphology.* At present, graphological work in the main follows the lines taken by Klages (1956), Wieser (1969) and Pophal (1965, etc.). Both mental and physiological factors are considered. Most recently, influenced by the quantifying approach of Anglo-American psychology, there has been a counter-current known as graphometry (T. Wallner, G. Gruenewald). In its practical training of graphologists, the Zürich Graphological Institute recognizes the particular significance of a psychological foundation. Graphology is also taught at some German and Dutch universities as a branch of academic psychology. A number of associations in Germany, Switzerland, Hol-

land and Italy, some of them representing rival views, seek to further the progress of graphology by their teaching and by publishing journals.

Bibliography: Becker, M.: G. der Kinderschrift. Hamburg, 1949. Grünewald, G.: Graphologische Studien. Zürich, 1954. Heiss, R.: Die Deutung der Handschrift. Hamburg, ³1966. Klages, L.: Handschrift und Charakter. Bonn, ²⁴1956. Müller, W. & Enskat, A.: Graphologie. Berlin, 1961. Pfanne, H.: Lehrbuch der Graphologie. Berlin, 1961. Pokorny, K.: Psychologie der Handschrift. Munich, 1968. Pophal, R.: G. in Vorlesungen, 3 Vols. Stuttgart, 1965, 1966, 1968. Pulver, M.: Symbolik der Handschrift. Zürich, ⁴1945. Teillard, A.: Handschriftendeutung. Berne, ²1963. Wieser, R.: Grundriss der G. Munich, 1969. Wittich, B.: Angewandte Graphologie. Berlin, 1951.   *R. R. Pokorny*

II. *Recent developments.* The more recent trend in graphological research is seen in the endeavor to do away with the confusion of pathognomy and graphology for which L. Klages and others were responsible, and to assign graphology as a diagnostic discipline to *psychodiagnostics* and not to the psychology of expression. The endeavor to objectify graphology and give it a statistical justification may be approved, if one considers the limitations of graphological diagnosis (J. P. Guilford called graphology a "useless method"; see also Müller & Enskat (1965, 562). Writing can lose its authenticity because of external factors. Other errors can be caused by inaccurate appraisal, ambiguity of characteristics, personal prejudice and systems of reference of the particular graphologist. See Allport & Vernon, 1933; Wells, 1946.

The critical justification and analysis of the basis of graphology are concerned with two sets of problems:

1. Checking the basic hypotheses (axioms) of graphological diagnostics, e.g. that the individuality of the handwriting is in essence psychologically conditioned, and that it is possible to draw conclusions from handwriting about the psyche of the writer. See *Graphology I.*

2. Studying the basic problems of the interpretation of handwriting: objectivity (q.v.), reliability (q.v.) and validity (q.v.). Graphometry, which Groffmann (1960) called the basic discipline of graphology, deals with this problem; up to now it has succeeded in objectifying the recording of graphic characteristics (more than 80 variables), grouping these with the aid of factor analysis (q.v.), and using correlational statistics to check them for stability, reliability and validity. Work in this field has so far been published by Timm (1967), Fahrenberg & Conrad (1965), Fischer (1964), Wallner (1963, 1965) and others.

The abovementioned authors all agree in the preliminary finding that, while there are quite *significant* correlations between certain characteristics found in handwriting and certain mental traits, these are nevertheless so slight that a more *critical* use of graphology is called for and that it can scarcely be recommended as the *sole test* method. This finding is largely confirmed by Eysenck's experimental work (1945, 1948). Eysenck confirmed the supposition that a personality diagnosis (e.g. of neuroticism, q.v.) is possible on the basis of a handwriting analysis (correlations with objective tests were low but significant, $v = 21$; with the psychiatric assessment, $r = 02$), but is nevertheless too time-consuming in view of the low level of accuracy. A diagnosis of intelligence with the aid of graphology hardly seems useful (Michel, 1969). A judgment on personality based on handwriting alone can rarely be justified since such fundamental dimensions as extraversion-introversion cannot be accurately diagnosed; control, irritability, etc., being the only components which can be elicited with relative certainty (Timm, 1967).

Bibliography: Allport, G. W. & Vernon, P. E.: Studies in expressive movements. New York, 1933. Eysenck, H. J.: Graphological analysis and psychiatry: an experimental study. Brit. J. Psychol., 1945, 35, 70–81. Id.: Neuroticism and handwriting. J. Abnorm. Psychol., 1948, 43, 94–6. Fahrenberg, J. & Conrad, W.: Eine explorative Faktorenanalyse graphometrischer und psychometrischer Daten. Z. exp. angew. Psychol., 1965, 12, 223–38. Fischer, G.: Zur faktoriellen Struktur der Handschrift. Z. exp. angew. Psychol., 1964, 11, 254–80. Groffmann, K. J.: Aus der Geschichte der Graphologie. Ciba-Zeitschrift, 1960, 98, 3244–58. Michel, L.: Empirische Untersuchungen zur Frage der Übereinstimmung und Gültigkeit von Beurteilungen des intellektuellen Niveaus aus der Handschrift. Arch. ges. Psychol., 1969, 121, 31–54. Müller, W. H. & Enskat, A.: Grundzüge der Graphologie. In: Kirchhoff, R. (Ed.): Hdb. d. Psychol., Vol. 5. Göttingen, 1965. Timm, U.: Graphometrie als psychol. Test. Psychol. Forschung, 1967, 30, 307–56. Wallner, T.: Über die Validität graphologischer Aussagen. Diagnostica, 1963, 9, 26–35. Id.: Graphologie als Objekt statistischer Untersuchungen. Psychol. Rdsch., 1965, 16, 282–98. Wells, F. L.: Personal history, handwriting, and specific behaviour. J. Personality, 1946, 14, 295–314. *F. Novak*

Grasp; grasping. 1. To stretch out one's hand; a series of (purposive) simple movements of the hand and arm to grasp an object (see *Time and motion study*). **2.** Way in which an object is grasped, e.g. with the finger tips or the whole hand (see *Handedness; Manual dexterity; Work-factor system*). **3.** To understand something.

Bibliography: Mausolff, A.: Der Weg zum richtigen Griff. Berlin-Cologne-Frankfurt, 1969. *G.M.*

Grasping reflex (syn. *Palmar response; Tonic grasping reflex*). A baby grasps objects which touch the hollow of its hand. The energy expended is such that the baby can be lifted up. This involuntary reflex can normally be easily demonstrated in the first two months of life, after which it then gradually begins to disappear with the increasing myelinization of the voluntary motor pathways. If the intensity of the grasp increases after the third month, or if the reflex persists longer than the fourth, it is regarded as pathological.

Bibliography: Halverson, H. M.: Studies of the grasping responses of early infancy. J. Genet. Psychol., 1937, 51, 371–449. *K.H.P.*

Grasping stage (syn. *Near space stage*). A baby begins to grasp objects at about the age of five to six months and this activity is the first indication that it is becoming aware of space. The child is now learning to control by motor maneuvers the small area within its grasp. Hence this phase of its development has been called the grasping stage or "near space stage" (Bühler). During this period visual and tactile space are combined; afterwards the visual component gradually predominates.

Bibliography: Bühler, K.: The mental development of the child. New York & London, 1930.   M.Sa.

Gratification. See *Depth psychology*.

Graves' disease. See *Basedow's disease*.

Gravimeter. Appliance for testing sensitiveness to weights. The testee has to lift and give an estimate of various weights which look alike but are not all equally heavy.
                                                    A.Th.

Gravity chronometer. A device used in the last century for measuring reaction time by the distance travelled by a falling weight between the time of the stimulus and the time of the response. Superseded today by precise electronic timers.   *G.D.W.*

Graz school. See *Austrian school*.

Gregariousness. See *Sociability*.

Grey scale. The series of achromatic neutral colors lying between white and black. The different gradations of the scale are represented by elements between which there is a *constant* difference of brightness.   *G.Ka.*

Ground; Figure-ground problem. This concerns the laws of perception which E. Rubin

(1921) was the first to study systematically in the field of optics. The question why a part of the entire field takes over the role of ground, and another part that of figure, and when and why figure-ground distributions constantly vary, were investigated by W. Ehrenstein, K. Koffka, M. Metzger (in particular). See *Figure-ground*.

Bibliography: Hebb, D. O.: The organization of behavior. New York, 1949.   *I.M.D.*

Group. Groups are not distinguished by fundamentally changing laws. There is no Group. A collection of objects or individuals capable of being classed together.

A *typological* approach classifies groups according to their changing combinations of *characteristics* which can be identified operationally, such as, for example, size, density of interpersonal activity (cohesiveness), degree of formalization of roles (institutionalization); they can also be classified according to their goals: e.g. socio-emotional (R. Bales, 1953) (leisure), achievement or performance (work groups), religious, social, or racial groups, or special forms such as therapeutic groups. This mode of classification is also found in group concepts, represented by *polarities* such as big-small, institutional-autonomous, casual-lasting, etc. In spite of such differences, however, they are subject to comparable laws.

Some group concepts have proved especially useful. A genetic criterion is employed to distinguish the *primary* group (C. Cooley, 1909) from the *secondary*. The *primary group*, usually the family, is necessarily, and by the mere fact of its existence, a face-to-face group, i.e. it acts through the direct physical contact of the members. It provides the first personality-formative social experiences, impressions (see *Imprinting*), and learning processes (see *Socialization*). The *secondary group* can also result from direct contact, and is usually only one among several to which an individual belongs (school, club, work team). *Formal groups* are regulated by laws and institutions. *Informal groups* owe their continued existence to voluntary, personal and emotional relations. They are not mutually exclusive, but complementary (E. Mayo, 1933; F. Roethlisberger; W. Dickson, 1939). The concept of the *reference group* (H. Hyman, 1942) implies the identification of the individual with the standards and objects of some group. It is not necessarily identical with *membership group;* if there is agreement, the reference group is also the "ingroup"; otherwise, as an "outgroup", it is often the occasion of conflicts.

Bibliography: Cartwright, D. & Zander, A.: Group dynamics. New York, ²1960. Secord, P. & Backman, C.: Social psychology. New York, 1964.   *P.B.*

Group dynamics. An important object of psychological theory and practice in social, industrial, and occupational psychology (q.v.), psychotherapy (q.v.), and educational psychology (q.v.). Lewin (1936) used the term "group dynamics" to denote this field. The theory deals with groups of two or three (families), with educational, work or leisure groups, and with larger units such as schools, factories or military structures. It is also applied in sociology, educational and political theory, etc.

Group dynamics is *basically related to the socio-cultural context of a society* (q.v.), which helps the individual and a possible group to come together by providing given patterns of feeling, evaluating, thinking and acting. Such correspondences between the demands of the individual and the dynamic activity of the group are among the group-forming factors. They are primary determinants of reciprocal dynamic interaction between individuals who create and regulate social structures. Necessary though insufficient conditions of this kind are *"spatial proximity"* (L. Festinger, S. Schachter & K. Back, 1950) and a certain *"minimum of contacts"* (Homans, 1950; M. Sherif, 1951, 1953). In addition to external opportunities, there must be an *internal agreement* among

the individuals forming the group, which transcends the above mentioned socio-cultural norms. C. B. Broderick (1956) formulated the following variables: (*a*) the nature of the area of agreement, (*b*) the degree of agreement, (*c*) the importance of the area of agreement, (*d*) the extent and number of the areas of agreement. Similarities in values and norms ("similarity of orientations") (Newcomb, 1943, 1956, 1961), and affinities of attitudes and personality traits ("similarity of attitudes") (H. M. Richardson, 1939; Winch, 1958) are reasons why certain persons are preferred to others as partners. In addition, special abilities related to the group's goals as well as intelligence increase eligibility (M. E. Bonney, 1944; B. Grossmann, J. Wrighter, 1948). Opposites, too, according to the theory of "complementary needs" (Winch & Ktsanes, 1955), favor relationships between individuals when, for example, needs felt by both are reciprocally gratified in the interaction. Secord & Backmann (1964) have combined the aspects of agreement and contrast to formulate the theory that the person is selected who will help to maintain a congruence (continuity, confirmation) of existing attitudes. The "exchange theory" (J. W. Thibaut & H. Kelley, 1959; Homans, 1961) emphasizes the outcome of cost and reward in relationships between individuals.

Groups persist when the primary conditions responsible for the grouping become a *more stable, positive interpersonal attraction.* The attraction is the measure of *group cohesiveness,* which finds expression in the frequency of contacts and the emotional and rational closeness of interpersonal relationships. *Equilibrium theories,* for example, are concerned with such processes. That of F. Helder (1946, 1958) states that in a triangular constellation of two persons who are concerned with some common object there will be a balance when (*a*) all three relationship values are positive, or (*b*) two of them are negative. But groups are determined not only by relationships between individuals but by those between dynamic processes. According to a thesis put forward by Bales (1953), group cohesion disintegrates when there are *activities in the field of performance*, whereas it increases when there is *co-operation in the socio-emotional field*.

Group cohesiveness and the structure of interpersonal relationships can be represented quantitatively as well as by graphs; this is done by using the methods of sociometry (q.v.) (J. Moreno, 1953). The so-called Q technique makes it possible to calculate a cohesiveness quotient (Hofstätter, 1965), and the measurement of "social distance" (E. S. Bogardus, 1928) throws light on efforts to establish a similar scale.

In addition to the relatively stable structure of social bonds, group dynamics determines fundamentally the actions of group members. Festinger's (1951) theory of "cognitive dissonance" (q.v.) states that activities begin when, in the cognitive field (perception, imagination, memory, thought), a decision has to be taken in regard to two simultaneous, incompatible elements (e.g. discordant items of information, irreconcilable standards). The cooperative interactions thus provoked, such as orienting behavior (gathering information, discussion), judgments and decisions, planning, differentiation of roles, checking, and actions to restructure the situation within and without, are included in the concept of *"problem-solving"* (*q.v.*) *behavior*, which culminates in the goal of the *self-preservation* of the group. There are two main phases in this process: (*a*) *the analysis of the situation* (consideration of group relationships, with feedback control of goal-attainment, etc.); and (*b*) *organizing and concluding a appropriate performance*. Observation (in the laboratory or the social field) is an example of the analytical processes. Bales (1950) suggests a list of observational categories for analyzing group processes: (*a*) the socioemotional field: (i) positive: e.g. release of tension, (ii) negative: e.g. shows antagonism; (*b*) task area: (i) questions: e.g. asks for suggestions, (ii) answers: e.g. gives information.

The analysis of group dynamic processes is of central importance in group therapy (q.v.). Interpersonal relationships are discussed or represented in dramatic form, and it is hoped that as a result social behavior will be clarified and adjusted (J. Moreno, 1953). This method has also been successful in improving the emotional elements of interaction in group learning (Brocher, 1967).

Group leadership uses methods which vary from the autocratic model to the integrative sessions directed by the group itself, in which appropriate problems are put forward for discussion. Studies designed to elucidate the connection between leadership variables (conceived as direction or education), and modifications of behavior in the group, were reported by Lewin, Lippitt & White in 1939, and recently by Tausch & Tausch (1970). Changes in group dynamics brought about by these different kinds of *leadership* (q.v.) apply to the fields of *achievement, performance, social behavior* and *personality traits*. In spite of initial difficulties of method (determining operationally valid rating categories, practicability, and authenticity of various styles of leadership, etc.), a satisfactory uniformity was achieved in the results. The autocratic (authoritarian) style of leadership is distinguished from the socially integrative (democratic) kind by the degree of *direction and emotional aloofness* involved. The *laissez-faire* style was also examined later. As contrasted with the autocratic (authoritarian) style, the socially-integrative style brings about the following changes: (*a*) *achievement:* the amount remains the same or decreases slightly; the quality improves distinctly, becomes more creative, there is greater variety, greater keenness and independence in tackling the work; (*b*) *social behavior:* the atmosphere among group members becomes more friendly, there is less tension and aggression, more mutual appreciation, a more natural relationship with the leader is established; after six months the group members show more adaptability.

Research into leadership characteristics

has dealt with the connection between *personality and leader behavior*. In a survey of the literature (1948), Stogdill found a consensus regarding: intelligence, scholarship, reliability, sense of responsibility, activity and social sympathy (see *Leader*). Hofstätter (1957), referring also to Carter & Nixon (1949), reports three factors: competence, individual distinction, and group sociability. The leader's involvement in the group is shown in the concept of the "leadership function", which expresses group effectiveness in terms of the set goal. Krech *et al.* (1962) mention the following as functions of leadership: executive, planning, expertise, external group representation, control, reward and punishment, arbitration, example (image), ideology, etc. The specialist's role suggests that a leader's functions can also be exercised by non-leaders. In this case, leadership function and group function coincide. This type stresses the integrative running of the group by the group itself according to the criterion of self-preservation (e.g. the cybernetic growth model: Deutsch, 1949; Mills, 1969). A prominent group function is the improvement in quality of the interaction taking place in the group as, for example, success with contacts. A. Bavelas (1951) and D. D. Barrett (1951) took groups of five for examination as networks of contacts, and examined them from the point of view of possible contacts, and the importance of a central position for mediation between partners; they considered these groups as (*a*) a circle, (*b*) a chain, (*c*) a star. In the "circle", speed and accuracy of work are on a low level, but on a high level in the "chain" and the "star". In the "circle", the organization of contacts is unstable; it is more stable in the "chain", and unmistakable in the "star". Partner satisfaction is greatest in the "circle", less in the "chain", and least in the "star". The results depend on the nature of the activity. The degree of freedom of action which the group possesses, and which is related to organization, is a variable of the power relationships.

Power is manifested in very varying degrees of intensity, which may be visible or subliminal. M. Sherif (1935), using the term "autokinetic phenomenon" (q.v.), showed that individual judgment tends clearly to converge with group judgments when the individual judging is aware in advance of the others' assessments. S. E. Asch (1956) specified the following conditions for conformity of judgment: (*a*) the nature of the stimulus situation, e.g. its structural clarity; (*b*) the nature of the group forces, e.g., unanimity; (*c*) characteristics of the individual, e.g. social behavior. A more rational factor of conformity is the degree of knowledge possessed about the object of judgment. Hence those who wield power commonly resort to censorship, or the "slanting" or suppression of information. Moral defamation can also be a means of exercising power, as can sanctions and corporal punishment. Direct manifestations of power can easily lead to a state of affairs where a split or dissociation is apparent, as, e.g. on the one hand a popular leader, and on the other a leader in the field of action and authority (Hofstätter, 1965). This probably also applies to the hierarchy of motives. The exploitation of constraint to ensure group conformity, and the use of moral stereotypes and mass media, frequently combined with irrelevant appeals to the emotions, constitute some of the more subtle techniques for exerting influence, as do certain forms of propaganda and publicity. But group behavior is not always the outcome of a multiplicity and hierarchy of different goals open to the group. Situational stress (q.v.) is tolerated in order to allow achievement of more important and distant goals, which may be impracticable goals which have only been promised; if the stressful situation lasts too long, the price is not infrequently mental disorder.

The exercise of power shows that the relations between the claims of the individual and the group or society have become *one-sided*, and have resulted in displacement toward a single individual, or toward society. This unilaterality leads to conflicts and confrontations (not always immediately but, in time, inevitably), which can only be avoided by exchanging members. It disturbs the autonomous development of the natural forces at work in social structures. According to internal and external conditions, the group is either an *instrument for misuse* to gratify individual or social demands, or else an admirable means to develop and maintain mature individuals in beneficial interaction with society. Such is the danger and such the opportunity offered by group dynamics. In a positive sense it favors an (active) agreement between: (*a*) individual desires which cannot, or can only less easily, be gratified without the group; (*b*) demands and restrictions imposed by society on the individual, which are necessary in practice to achieve an equal distribution of the greatest benefits derivable from interaction.

Group dynamics is the essence of all problem-solving interaction processes which are developed by individuals conscious of relatively stable structures (e.g. norms, roles, attitudes, habits), and relatively changing forces (e.g. identified goals, cooperative actions, realization of drives, and motives) which may be subjective or standardized by society; the goal is to achieve continuous integrative development and the differentiation of social relationships. Group dynamics is not restricted to the internal working of a group; and it is not necessarily bound up with the concrete presence of a group; but the group is its primary location. See *Group formation; Attitude; Prejudice.*

Bibliography: Bales, R. F.: The equilibrium problem in small groups. In: Parsons, T., Bales, R. F. & Schils, E. A. (Eds) Working papers in the theory of action. New York, 1953, 111–61. Bales, R. F. & Strodtbeck, F. L.: Phases in group problem solving. J. abnorm. soc. Psychol., 1951, *46*, 485–95. Brocher, T.: Gruppendynamik und Erwachsenenbildung. Brunswick, 1967. Carter, L. & Nixon, M.: An investigation of the relation between four criteria of leadership ability for three different tasks. J. Psychol., 1949, *27*, 245–61. Cartwright, D. & Zander, A.: Group dynamics. New York, ²1960. Festinger, L. A.: A theory of social comparison processes. Hum. Relat., 1954, *7*, 117–40. Id.: A theory of cognitive dissonance. New York, 1957. Id., Schachter, S. & Back, K.: Social pressures in informal groups. New York, 1950. Hofstätter, P.: Gruppendynamik. Munich, 1965. Homans, G. C.: The human group. New York, 1950. Id.: Social behaviour: its elementary forms. New York, 1961. Krech, D., Crutchfield, R. S. & Ballachey, E. L.: Individual in society. New York, 1962. Lewin, K.: A dynamic theory of personality. New York, 1935. Id.: Principles of topological psychology. New York, 1936. Lewin, K., Lippitt, R. & White, R. K.: Patterns of aggressive behavior in experimentally created social climates. J. soc. Psychol., 1939, *10*, 271–99. McGrath, J. E. & Altmann, I.: Small group research. New York, 1966. Moreno, J. L.: Who shall survive? New York, 1953. Newcomb, T. M.: The predication of interpersonal attraction. Amer. Psychologist, 1956, *11*, 575–86. Id.: The acquaintance process. New York, 1961. Secord, P. F. & Backmann, C. W.: Social psychology. New York, 1964. Stogdill, R.: Leadership, membership and organisation. Psychol. Bull., 1950, *47*, 1–14. Id.: Personal factors associated with leadership. A survey of the literature. J. of Psychol., 1948, *25*, 25–71. Tausch, R. & A.: Erziehungspsychologie. Göttingen, ³1970. Winch, R. F., Ktsanes, T. & Ktsanes, V.: Empirical elaboration of the theory of complementary needs in mate selection. J. abnorm. soc. Psychol., 1955, *51*, 508–14. (See also *Social psychology*.)

P. Braun

Group factor. The group factor model is a predecessor of the model of several common factors (see *Factor analysis*): apart from the general factor (q.v.), and the specific factors, there are also intermediate general factors— these are group factors which influence some of the items.   *W.H.B.*

Group formation. A process in the course of which a group is formed from a plurality or a mere collection of individuals. Prerequisites for the formation of groups are: (*a*) individual motivation for joining a group (it may be positive, facilitating the gratification of personal needs, or negative, providing a defense against some threat to the individual concerned); (*b*) communication or contact between individuals (facilitated by spatial proximity or insignificant social distance); (*c*) mutual recognition of individuals.

As a group comes into being, the following processes can be observed: common goals appear, roles are differentiated, and taken over by individual members; common rules of behavior and norms develop, with which the behavior of the individual members begins increasingly to conform; a certain group atmosphere or special climate is engendered; auto- and hetero-stereotypes develop, i.e. a positive estimation of one's own or "our" group with reference to its capabilities, the attractiveness of its members, etc., and a rejection or disparagement of the other or "those" groups. See *Group dynamics*.

Bibliography: Hare, A. P.: Handbook of small group research. New York, 1962. Sherif, M., Harvey, O. J., White, B. J., Hood, W. R. & Sherif, C.: Intergroup conflict and cooperation: The robber's cave experiment. New York, 1961. *A. Schmidt-Mummendey*

Group instruction. Group instruction is education in, through, and for the group. It is the primary method used in the democratic style of education. Pupils are activated not by tasks and suggestions coming from the teacher, but by impulses originating in the members of the group. Individual behavior is determined by what the group expects from the activity and how it evaluates it. The group-dynamic forces at work are dealt with in social psychology (q.v.).

Bibliography: Fiedler, F. E.: Leader attitudes and group effectiveness. Urbana, 1958. *H.Schr.*

Group measurements. The term denotes either (a) the observation of a characteristic in some group (sample) with that characteristic, (b) the simultaneous measurement (testing) of a group of subjects (group experiment), or (c) the observation (quantification) of modes of behavior (performances, decisions, etc.) of a group in a socio-psychological experiment, in contrast to the modes of behavior of individuals in conditions which are otherwise similar. See *Correlational techniques*.

Group sexuality. This exists when there is equally privileged interaction of more than two persons with the goal of sexual pleasure. The activity of several directed at a single individual who responds preferentially could only be included under this head as an extreme case of sado-masochism. Promiscuity (q.v.) and the exchange of partners ("group sex") are distinct from group sexuality.
U.H.S.

Group tests. Tests which are constructed so that a fairly large number of testees can take them at the same time. The most varied tests, e.g. certain intelligence tests, tests of skills and abilities, and personality tests, have been developed as group tests. They are more economical to conduct and evaluate, and frequently more global in their results than individual tests. *E.F.-K.*

Group therapy. Psychotherapeutic methods in which several patients (usually six to twelve, half of them where possible being male, the other half female) are treated in the presence of one (or possibly several) therapists using group dynamics (q.v.). The analytical group provides opportunities, both therapeutic and diagnostic, not available in the traditional analytical situation (patient alone with psychotherapist). "Closed" groups are usually maintained for a fairly long period, but sometimes "open" groups are formed (the members of which change more or less frequently). In addition to this analytical method, other group therapies are used by psychotherapists either selectively or exclusively; for example, directive-suggestive treatment could consist of autogenic training (q.v.), psychodrama (q.v.), music therapy (q.v.) and similar methods.

Physiotherapeutic methods used in a group often achieve particularly good results because the participants spur one another on.
Bibliography: Battegay, D.: Der Mensch in der Gruppe, Vols 1-3. Berne & Stuttgart, 1968-9. Foulkes, S. H.: Therapeutic group analysis. London, 1964. Id. & Anthony, E. J.: Group psychotherapy:

the psycho-analytic approach. Harmondsworth, 1957. Jones, M.: Social psychiatry. London, 1952. Id.: Social psychiatry in practice. Harmondsworth, 1968.

H.N.G.

Group work. 1. *In industrial theory:* the direct co-operation of several workers whose efforts are interdependent in the joint execution of some task. **2.** *In education:* a method in which a given subject is not dealt with directly by the teacher standing in front of the class but by the pupils in small groups (a transition from authoritative to co-operative leadership) (see *Leadership*). Especially a form of university teaching in small tutorial or seminar groups. It has been opined that methods used in universities for lectures and discussions will be used later in public life for negotiations, speeches and conferences.   *G.Ma.*

GSR. Abb. for *Galvanic skin response* (q.v.).

Guilford factors. In regard to temperament, these are fifteen primary characteristics isolated by factorial analysis from data taken from inventories; they are not wholly independent; systematized by Guilford using three areas of behavior (general, emotional, social), and five basic polar dimensions (positive-negative, controlled-uncontrolled, active-passive, etc.). For example: immaturity-maturity, confidence-inferiority, social intro-version-extraversion, etc. See *Traits*.

Bibliography: Guilford, J. P.: Personality. New York, 1959.   *H.H.*

Guilford-Zimmermann Aptitude Survey. A test battery for intellectual aptitudes, with separate tests for verbal comprehension, general reasoning, numerical operations, perceptual speed, spatial orientation, spatial visualization and mechanical knowledge. Devised 1947–56; standardized for testees from the age of sixteen.

Bibliography: Guilford, J. P.: The nature of intelligence. New York, 1967.   *R.M.*

Guilford-Zimmermann Temperament Survey. On the basis of extensive factor analyses Guilford & Zimmermann produced a questionnaire for personality assessment in which the following independent characteristics are measured with thirty items each: general activity, restraint, ascendance, emotional stability, sociability, objectivity, friendliness, thoughtfulness, personal relations, masculinity. Prepared and standardized for college students and adults.   *R.M.*

Bibliography: Guilford, J. P. & Zimmermann, W. S.: Fourteen dimensional temperament. Psychol. Monogr., 1956, 70, 1–26.

Guilt. One can speak of guilt as *culpability* only on the assumption that such a thing is ascertainable in human beings within certain fixed limits. The concept and nature of guilt, when not restricted to the empirical psychological or psychopathological phenomenon of a consciousness, feeling, or sense of guilt (a subjective awareness of having offended against personal, familial, religious, or societal norms, which offense may be actual or imaginary), are defined according to philosophical anthropology, ethics and the law.

"Man is the being that is capable of guilt, and capable of perceiving his guilt" (M. Buber). The capability of guilt, or moral responsibility, implies that an individual is capable of free self-determination, responsible behavior, and the assumption of responsibility. The notion of a criminal law basing its conception of criminal responsibility on the criterion of voluntary action implies the freedom of will of the "normal" citizen as a principle. "Freedom" in this sense (as a prerequisite for all legal codes) is not the freedom that philosophers of the most varied schools have been unable to agree upon throughout the centuries. The fact that, e.g., a "normal" citizen "can" stop when the traffic light shows red, that it is impossible for him to "have to" ignore the stop signal, is assumed to be an adequate ground for postulating the "freedom" of a citizen as an inevitable and scientifically unassailable prerequisite for every legal code. Admittedly, the citizen's behavior, considered as acceptable or un-acceptable in regard to the flow of traffic, is causally and finally motivated—but in the same sense as any human behavior, decision or volition. As far as the confirmation of legal responsibility is concerned, it is im-material whether one views freedom of will as a metaphysical premiss or as an ontological prerequisite. What is in question is always no more than the empirically de-tectable conditions for the possibility of unfreedom. The legal code lays down the conditions beforehand in its requirement of *understanding* of the nature of an action, or of the difference between right and wrong. A psychiatrist to whom a case is referred for assessment of understanding of right or wrong, or of normality, may try to assess the determinants of the subject's behavior by physical and psychological examination and tests, even with particular reference to the action in question, but inevitably in regard to the social and criminal prognosis. Ulti-mately, the procedure he adopts must always be empirical. Existing ethical and legal norms permit social evaluation of a specific behavior, and to that extent form the yardstick for guilt. Ethical and legal norms enable one to confirm that a behavior does not accord with the norm. The question of *why?*, of the condi-tions for the abnormal behavior, is on an-other plane, and has to be answered by means of empirical, biological and psycholo-gical criteria. Hence, in most English-speaking countries, clinical psychologists and/or psychiatrists are hampered by the obtaining socio-legal norm. For example, the so-called McNaughten rules (which date back to a successful plea of insanity in Britain

in 1843) directly involve the notions of free will, intent and moral responsibility, and, basically, hold an individual to be responsible for his socially criminal action (e.g. murder), unless he suffered from defective reason or mental disease such as to impair his under-standing of the nature, quality or wrong-ness of the act he committed. Essentially, the law does not provide for refinements of psychological theory or evidence essentially contrary to the basic notion of free will. See also *Abnormal psychology; Alcoholism; Con-science; Criminality; Forensic psychology; Mental defect; Punishment.*

Bibliography: Burton, R. V.: The generality of honesty reconsidered. Psychol. Rev., 1963, *70,* 481–99. **Ehrhardt, H.:** Psychiatrie. In: Sieverts, R. (Ed.): Handwörterbuch der Kriminologie, Vol. 2. Berlin, ²1971. **Id.** & **Villinger, W.:** Forensische und adminis-trative Psychiatrie. In: **Gruhle** *et al.* (Eds): Psychiatrie der Gegenwart, Vol. 3. Berlin, 1961. **Eysenck, H. J.** (Ed.): Handbook of abnormal psychology. London, 1960; New York, 1961. **Id.:** Crime and personality. London, ²1970. **Frey, E. R.** (Ed.): Schuld, Verantwor-tung, Strafe. Zürich, 1964. **Glueck, S.:** Law and psychiatry. Baltimore, 1962. **Id.** & **Glueck, G.:** Unravelling juvenile delinquency. New York, 1950. **Gough, H. C.:** A sociological theory of psychopathy. Amer. J. sociol., 1948, *53,* 359–66. **Guttmacher, M. S.:** The role of psychiatry in law. Springfield, Mass., 1968. **Kaufmann, A.:** Schuld und Strafe. Cologne, 1968. **Ricoeur, P.:** Philosophie de la volonté, Vol. 1, Paris, 1949. **Willett, T.:** Criminal on the road. London, 1964.   *H. Ehrhardt*

Guthrie's contiguous conditioning. See *Post-remity theory.*

Gynadogy. Schaetzing uses the term for psychagogy as specially designed for the gynecologist during consulting hours.
Bibliography: Schaetzing, E.: Die verstandene Frau. Munich, ⁸1963.   *W.Sch.*

Gynandromorph. An abnormal individual with some tissues genetically and structurally male, and others genetically and structurally female, as can occur through disturbance of the sex determination mechanism during

embryonic development. See *Intersexuality;*
Hermaphroditism.   *G.D.W.*

Gynandromorphism. A type of sexual aberration in which both male and female characters are present in the same organism. The
cause in man is either genetic, because of an
excess of X chromosomes, or secondary,
because of some psychic disorder (see *Trans-*
vestism); in the latter case those affected try
to acquire a female shape by taking female
sex hormones (*apparent hermaphroditism*).
Occasionally, but not necessarily, found
together with homosexuality (q.v.).   *W.Sc.*

Gynandry. The tendency in a female to possess
male characteristics. (*Viraginity:* the tendency
for a female to exhibit masculine mental
characteristics.) The parallel condition in
males, i.e. possessing female characteristics,
is called *androgyny.*   *G.D.W.*

Gynecocracy. See *Matriarchy.*

Gynecomastia. The formation of one or two
breasts in a man (a *gynecomast*); in special
circumstances there may be secretion of milk.
It is not a disease but a symptom which has
widely differing causes. The following need to
be distinguished: (*a*) Puberal gynecomastia is
a normal, non-morbid variant of maturation
between the ages of twelve and fourteen;
there is swelling of one or both mammary
glands, and while this is usually transient, it
can be irreversible and require an operation;
occasionally puberal gynecomastia is accompanied by negative psychic effects. (*b*)
Gynecomastia resulting from hormone therapy (e.g. testosterone therapy in cancer of the
prostate gland). (*c*) Gynecomastia as a
symptom of disease of the endocrine glandular system (e.g. estrogen-producing tumors
of the adrenal glands or testicles). (*d*) Gynecomastia as a symptom of congenital
intersexual conditions (real and apparent
hermaphroditism). (*e*) Gynecomastia as a
concomitant symptom in non-endocrine diseases (e.g. cirrhosis of the liver).

Bibliography: Jores, A. & Nowakowski, H.: Praktische Endokrinologie. Stuttgart, 1964. Monje, J.:
Körperlichsexuelle Fehlentwicklungen. Hamburg,
1969.   *H.M.*

Gyrus. *Gyri cerebri* (cerebral and cerebellal
convolutions): irregularly shaped folds 1 cm.
wide and several cm. long, separated by the
cerebral fissures or *sulci cerebri.* Special
terms denote position: e.g. *gyrus temporalis*
medius. Some gyri have an important functional significance, as for example the
gyrus frontalis inferior, area 44, which coordinates the muscles used in speech and
is therefore known as the motor speech
center (*Broca's area,* q.v.).   *G.A.*

H

Haab's pupillary reflex. An ideomotor or cortical pupillary reflex (q.v.): the contraction of the pupils of both eyes when looking at a bright object in a darkened room.   *K.H.P.*

Habit. The term "habit" derives from the Latin noun *habitus*, from the verb *habere*, to have. Modern dictionaries describe at least four usages, all referring to the characteristic external appearance, manner or bearing by which we may recognize an individual or class of individual: human, animal or plant. Thus one special usage refers to dress or attire, especially in relation to religious orders and other functional groups. More relevant to the present context is the usage referring to the customs or practices characteristic of a social group. Closest, however, to the technical usage within psychology is the use of the word to refer to an individual's tendency to act in customary or automatic ways, especially when these are acquired by practice or experience.

Even in this last sense, the term is used in popular language in a variety of ways. It covers many different forms of behavior, including the following:

(*a*) Mechanical, semi-automatic series of movements involved in routine actions such as dressing oneself.

(*b*) Actions related to recurrent acquired physiological cravings, e.g. the "habit" of smoking.

(*c*) Mannerisms such as "tics" and other "nervous habits".

(*d*) Characteristic modes and manners of speech.

(*e*) Characteristic ways of thinking as reflected in predictable points of view and attitudes expressed about issues and events.

(*f*) Actions evaluated on ethical grounds by others, or by society in general; that is, "good" or "bad" habits such as acts of courtesy, stealing or swearing, distinctive of an individual.

The term is also used loosely and in many different ways by psychologists. It may refer to molecular aspects of behavior such as a specific measurable component of a simple conditioned reflex or an acquired association between a pair of words, or to very broad molar patterns of behavior extended over considerable periods of time. In either case, the reactions are predictable or customary. Emphasis may be placed on the actual behavior evoked by a certain set of conditions, or on the underlying "set", disposition or readiness to respond in this way to those conditions. Habits may be seen as possessing autonomous motivating properties or as requiring appropriate motivational states for their activation. Invariably, however, habit is contrasted with pre-programmed innate reflexes or instinctual reactions in that one essential characteristic of a habit is that it is acquired, an end-product of a process of learning. Hence, an acceptable general definition of habit might be: *A customary pattern of behavioral, cognitive or emotional response, predictable according to the conditions operating at the time of response, and acquired by a process of learning* or *the underlying acquired "set" or tendency toward that pattern of response.*

1. *History*. Historically, the modern concept of habit stems from Descartes's (1596-1650) dualistic view of body and mind and his insistence on the mechanical nature of bodily events. Habit, for him, was a consequence of the easing, through usage, of the passage of "animal spirits" through the pores of the hydraulic system he proposed as a model of physiological functioning. Next, in the doctrine of association (q.v.), the English empiricist philosophers provided a central principle for a psychology of learning and placed fruitful emphasis on the importance of sensory processes. Hobbes (1588-1679) claimed that all our ideas stem from sensory experience and that association depends upon the coherence of these ideas. John Locke (1632-1704) took Hobbes's arguments further with his famous and bold assertion that the mind at birth is a "*tabula rasa*". He explained the apparent given quality of many of our ideas by the early inculcation of habits through the teaching of nurses, parents and other mentors. Hume's (1711-1776) entire philosophical system was based on the association of ideas. For him, all perceptions and experiences, even belief in relationships of cause and effect, were explained by habits established by consistencies between experiences. Habit was his universal law of mind.

The biological observations and writings of Charles Darwin (1809-1882) and, in particular, his emphasis on the adaptive nature of behavior, represent the next major relevant influence. In his *Origin of Species* (1859) Darwin discusses the effects of domestication upon animals, especially the resultant suppression of "natural instincts". While recognizing that deliberate selective breeding plays a part, he also argues that imposed habits become fixed reflexes which are then transmitted by genetic mechanisms. Later (1872) Darwin employs similar arguments to account for the acquisition of expressive characteristics from originally voluntary movements subserving practical functions. (See *Expression; Instinct*.)

These trends of thought culminated in William James's (1842-1910) brilliant exposition of psychology as an empirical science in his *Principles of Psychology* (1890). His thinking was dominated by concepts of biological utility, and he saw the function of consciousness (q.v.) as steering a highly evolved and therefore complex but plastic nervous system. James (q.v.) devotes a celebrated chapter to habit. Increased neural plasticity, it is argued, facilitates the establishment of habits whose major function is to allow the performance of routine actions with little or no attention, thus freeing the higher mental processes for more important and difficult tasks. Habit, according to James, is "the enormous fly-wheel of society, its most precious conservative agent". At the same time, James did not deny the importance and biological utility of instinctive, unlearned behavior patterns, but saw them merely as providing the opportunity for progressive, adaptive modification in the light of experience. Thus instincts become overlaid by habits which ultimately replace them. Modern views do not deviate greatly from this doctrine but phenomena such as *imprinting* (q.v.), much studied in animal species by contemporary ethologists, suggest that the relationship between instinctual and learned behavior may sometimes be of a different and equal nature. By imprinting is meant the firm linkage of an innate tendency to a specific environmental object at a critical period in the early life history of the organism, and the generalization of this linkage to other objects of the same class.

Neuro-anatomical and physiological knowledge was sufficiently advanced when James was writing for him to postulate that the neural basis of habit-formation might be the establishment of "connections" to form fixed neural "pathways" in the central nervous system (q.v.). This was an early stage in the still-continuing search for a "memory-trace". James envisaged complex pathways of this nature such that, in the execution of a complex habitual act, each new muscular contraction is instigated by the sensation evoked by the preceding contraction. Such a system would now be described as a "chain-reflex". Unfortunately, this attractively simple account of habit-formation has not survived experimental tests. Even the simplest of motor-habits do not preserve an identical form: the same strategic end may be achieved by a variety of tactical means. Similarly, ablation (q.v.) experiments demonstrate quite clearly that the preservation of a habit does not depend upon the integrity of any particular region of the brain.

Dewey and other members of the American "functionalist" school, following similar Darwinist arguments, acquired views on habit-formation very close to those of James. At about the same time, Thorndike (q.v.) (1898) was carrying out his classic experiments upon trial and error learning in which hungry cats, over a series of trials, gradually acquired the ability rapidly to unlatch the door of their specially designed "puzzle-box" cages in order to secure food placed outside. Thorndike made the point that repetition alone was insufficient to account for his findings. There is also a process of selection among the acts performed so as to increase the likelihood of those acts which yielded access to the food and resulted (so Thorndike postulated) in a state of satisfaction, and decrease the likelihood of those acts which resulted in dissatisfaction. This principle is now known as the *Law of Effect* and the rewards and punishments affecting the process of learning are now generally referred to as *reinforcements*. The Law of Effect has been subjected to much criticism but it remains clear, as argued forcibly by Skinner (1938) and his followers, who describe this type of learning as *operant conditioning* (q.v.), that behavior is modified according to its consequences, and that appropriate reinforcement is an important factor in habit formation. The recent discovery by Olds & Milner (1954) of reinforcing effects produced by electrical stimulation of the septal area of the brain suggests a neuro-physiological basis for this process.

Of equal importance to the work of Thorndike were Pavlov's (1927) investigations into the nature of *conditioned reflexes*. He showed that if a neutral stimulus, such as the sound of a bell, is presented at a very brief interval before a natural or *unconditioned stimulus* (e.g. food), evoking a natural or *unconditioned reflex* (salivation), and this pairing is repeated a number of times, presentation of the sound alone (now a *conditioned stimulus*) will evoke salivation. The latter *conditioned reflex* is qualitatively and quantitatively different from the original unconditioned response and therefore no simple stimulus-substitution theory is tenable. All the evidence points to the anticipatory nature of the conditioned reflex, and therefore suggests that what is learned is an expectancy with clear biological adaptive value. Pavlov was a physiologist, and interested in the light his experiment threw on brain functioning. He was opposed to attempts made by contemporary psychologists to build an entire systematic theory of learning upon his work. Nevertheless, J. B. Watson (q.v.) (1919), the founder of *behaviorism* (q.v.), established an entire system of psychology on this basis. For him, habits were integrated systems of conditioned reflexes built around available innate patterns of movement. Language habits were special cases in that, to some extent, speech could become "implicit", implicit speech being the behaviorist equivalent of thought. Personality, even, was considered to be merely the end-product of hierarchical habit-systems. Man was set apart from other animals only by his greater capacity for developing three of these habit-systems: laryngeal or verbal habits; manual habits; visceral or emotional habits. (See *Conditioning, classical and operant*.)

2. *Recent views*. Despite the cult-like excesses of some of Watson's arguments, a modified behaviorism has remained prominent throughout the recent history of

psychology and has yielded valuable research findings. Particularly important among the contributions of the neo-behaviorists in relation to the concept of habit are the work and theory of C. L. Hull (q.v.) (1943). He laid stress on the distinction between the actual performance of a learned act and the internalized tendency to perform the act when appropriately stimulated. He reserved the term "habit" for the latter. Those consistencies in behavior which indicate learning are only observable in appropriate stimulus conditions which may recur at long intervals. Hull inferred that some theoretically observable modification of the central nervous system, some form of "memory-trace", remains potentially active during the interval. Thus Hull's habit concept has the status of a *hypothetical construct*. It is also an *intervening variable* in his formal theory in which *habit strength* (S H R) represents the compounded effects of various antecedent variables such as the number of reinforced trials, and interacts with other intervening variables such as *drive* (D) to determine a *reaction potential* (S E R). Hence, in his quasi-mathematical presentation of the theory, Hull's fundamental equation is:

$$S E R = f(S H R) \times (D)$$

This equation was further elaborated to include intervening variables representing inhibitory and other factors, but represents, as it stands, the important distinction drawn by Hull between learned habit and performance, and his view that the habit must be energized by a drive state in the presence of appropriate stimulation if an actual response is to occur.

Skinner and his co-workers are atheoretical in their approach to learning, restricting themselves entirely to observable relationships between observable events. This is entirely adequate for their aim of developing a behavioral technology, but Hull's argument concerning a modified state of the organism which persists between learning trials remains valid. Other learning theorists

have elaborated aspects of Hullian theory, e.g. Spence (1956), while others, notably Tolman (1938) with his "purposive behaviorism", have presented alternative systems, stressing cognitive factors. Yet others, such as Osgood (1953), attempt to reconcile these two points of view by postulating cognitive mediating processes within a Hullian framework. All these refer to habit formation of one type or another, based on acquired associative relationships between one stimulus and another, or between stimuli and responses, brought about by appropriate conditions of contiguity and/or reinforcement. The same principles can be extended to account for higher forms of learning, such as concept learning, but the application of the term "habit" to these realms is a matter of choice. Motives can also be acquired in these ways, and there is evidence to suggest that any well-established habit can become functionally autonomous and acquire motivational properties such that the opportunity for its exercise can be used to reinforce new learning. (See *Motivation*.)

Current research and theory take many directions. One of great interest and importance is the search for a physical basis for the "memory-trace". Interesting and influential, if speculative, suggestions concerning the development of complex functional interconnections between cerebral neurons were advanced by Hebb (1949). Recently, however, considerable interest has been aroused and research stimulated by Hyden's (1959) suggestion that ribonucleic acid (RNA) might be a complex chemical mediator for memory functions. The exciting possibilities raised by the location of a "pleasure center" in the brain have already been mentioned. This is likely to give strength to already emerging hedonistic theories. The strategic context within which habits operate has also been mentioned. Miller, Galanter & Pribram's (1960) theoretical account of "plans and the structure of behavior" promises new advances in this area. (See *Memory*.)

Finally, the topic of habits should not be

left without mention of the application of planned re-educational habit-formation and habit-breaking by means of counter-conditioning carried out by the behavior therapists, and by behavior modifiers working in the field of clinical psychology (Eysenck, 1960; Ullmann and Krasner, 1965). (See *Aversion therapy; Behavior therapy.*)

Bibliography: Darwin, C.: The origin of species. London, 1859. Id.: Expression of the emotions in man and animals. London, 1872. Descartes, R.: Principles of philosophy (in Latin). Amsterdam, 1644. Eysenck, H. J. (Ed.): Behaviour therapy and the neuroses. London, 1960. Hebb, D. O.: The organization of behavior. New York, 1949. Hobbes, T.: Leviathan. London, 1651. Hull, C. L.: Principles of behavior. New York, 1943. Hume, D.: Enquiry concerning human understanding. London, 1751. Hyden, H.: Biochemical changes in glial cells and nerve cells at varying activity. Proc. of the Fourth int. Congr. of Biochemistry, Vol. III. London, 1959. James, W.: Principles of psychology. New York, 1890. Locke, J.: Essay concerning human understanding. London, 1690. Miller, G. A., Galanter, E. & Pribram, K. H.: Plans and the structures of behavior. New York, 1960. Olds, J. & Milner, P. M.: Positive reinforcement produced by electrical stimulation of septal area and other regions of rat brain. J. comp. physiol. Psychol, 1954, *47*, 419–27. Osgood. C. E.: Method and theory in experimental psychology. New York, 1953. Pavlov, I. P.: Conditioned reflexes. New York, 1927. Skinner, B. F.: The behavior of organisms. New York, 1938. Spence, K. W.: Behavior theory and conditioning. New Haven, 1956. Thorndike, E. L.: Animal intelligence: an experimental study of the associative processes in animals. Psychol. Rev. Monogr. Suppl., 1898, *2*, No. 4. Tolman, E. C.: The determiners of behaviour at a choice-point. Psychol. Rev., 1938, *45*, 1–41. Ullmann, L. P. & Krasner, L. (Eds.): Case studies in behavior modification. New York, 1965. Watson, J. B.: Psychology from the standpoint of a behaviorist. Philadelphia, 1919. *G. Jones*

Habitat. An ecological term: the entire geographical environment of an organism (species; plant or animal), possibly at a certain stage in its development. The habitat consists of inanimate (biotope) and animate environmental factors. See *Biocenosis*. *H.S.*

Habitual. 1. Pertaining to, or of the nature of a *habit* (q.v.). **2.** Established by habit. **3.** Customary, regular, lasting. Pertaining to that which remains relatively the same over fairly long periods of time (e.g. *traits*, q.v.) in contrast to, e.g., states. *D.B.*

Hair esthesiometer. A hair (from human or horse) used as a fine tactile stimulus in the study of cutaneous sensation. One classical experiment is supposed to demonstrate that different points on the surface of the skin are sensitive to heat, cold, pain and pressure respectively, so that stimulation with a fine point will result in one or other of these four experiences depending upon the exact locus at which the stimulus is applied. *G.D.W.*

Half-length illusion. The phenomenon that the subjective and objective mid-points of a line do not coincide. This illusion occurs in both vision and touch. See *Kundt's bisection test.* *C.D.F.*

Hall, Granville Stanley. B. 1844 in Ashfield (Mass.); d. 1924, Worcester (Mass.). After graduating from Williams College, he studied theology at Union Theological Seminary in New York, and went on to read physiology, physics, theology and philosophy in Bonn and Berlin; he was the first person to obtain a degree in psychology proper in the USA with his doctoral thesis on "The Muscular Perception of Space" (1878). He then again studied physiology in Berlin and was Wundt's first American student in Leipzig. He also worked with Helmholtz in Berlin. He became a lecturer in 1881, and in 1884 was appointed Professor of psychology and pedagogics at Johns Hopkins University. In 1888 he became the first President of the newly-founded Clark University in Worcester, and held this post until 1920, when he resigned.

Hall was the first great organizer of

HALOPERIDOL

American psychology and made a substantial contribution to the expansion of psychology in the USA. In 1884 he founded what was probably the first American psychological laboratory—at Johns Hopkins University. In 1887 he established the first American journal of psychology (*American Journal of Psychology*), followed by the *Pedagogical Seminary* (later the *Journal of Genetic Psychology*) in 1891, the *Journal of Religious Psychology* in 1904, and the *Journal of Applied Psychology* in 1917. In July 1892 he was instrumental in founding the American Psychological Association (APA) of which he was the first President. In 1893, he established the National Association for the Study of the Child to foster research into child psychology.

Hall also made a major contribution to the advancement of psychoanalysis (q.v.) in America. In 1909 he invited Freud and Jung to the USA and arranged a symposium at Clark University during which he introduced leading American psychologists to the European giants.

The theory of evolution is fundamental to Hall's work. His interest in evolution was great enough to earn him the title of "Darwin of the mind". He applied, for example, the "recapitulation theory" to child development, i.e. he assumed that the individual in his ontogenetic development passes through the same stages of development as the race as a whole in its phylogenetic development ("ontogeny recapitulates phylogeny"). Hall's interest in evolution led him to consider in great detail problems of child and developmental psychology. His studies, in which he made use of Galton's questionnaire method, aroused considerable public interest and led to the "child study" movement. In addition, they played a decisive role in the development of educational psychology (q.v.), which investigates the psychological bases of child education. (See *Child psychology; History of psychology*.)

Main works: Content of children's minds. *Princeton Review*, 1883, *11*, 272–94. Adoles-

cence: its psychology and its relations to physiology, anthropology, sociology, sex, crime, religion and education. New York, 1904. Founders of modern psychology. New York, 1912. Jesus, the Christ, in the light of psychology (2 vols.). New York, 1917. Senescence: the last half of life. New York, 1922. Life and confessions of a psychologist. New York, 1923.

: Burnham, J. C.: Sigmund Freud and G. Stanley Hall: exchange of letters. Psychoanal. Quart., 1960, *29*, 307–16. Cattell, J. M.: The founding of the association and of the Hopkins and Clark laboratories, Psychol. Rev., 1943, *50*, 61–4. Dennis, W. & Boring, E. G.: The founding of APA. Amer. Psychologist, 1952, *7*, 95–7. Starbuck, E. D.: G. Stanley Hall as a psychologist. Psychol. Rev., 1925, *32*, 103–20.   W.W.

Hallucinations. Perceptions without corresponding external stimuli, or the absence of perception when external stimuli are presented (*negative* halucinations). Depending on the type of sensory illusion, there are: *olfactory, visual* or *acoustic* hallucinations. As regards etiology, the spectrum ranges from organic psychoses (frequently with elementary hallucinations), by way of exceptional psychogenic conditions, to schizophrenia (q.v.). See *Mental imagery; Psychoses, functional.*
                                                       A.Hi.

Hallucinogens. See *Psychotomimetic Drugs.*

Halo effect. A source of error in personality assessment first described by F. L. Wells (1907) and given its name by Thorndike (1920). The observer (e.g. a teacher) tends to be guided by a specific impression or an outstanding trait in rating an individual.

Bibliography: Thorndike, E. L.: A constant error of psychological ratings. J. appl. Psychol., 1920, *4*, 25–9.   H.Ma.

Haloperidol (*Haldol; Serenase*). The most important minor tranquilizer of the butyrophenone type (neuroleptic group). Haloperidol has a strong neuroleptic action and often has dyskinetic extrapyramidal effects in high doses. In psychological studies of healthy individuals performance and general sensation of well-being were improved rather than impaired with doses of up to 2 mg, but alcohol reinforced negative effects. See *Differential psychopharmacology.*

Bibliography: Janke, W. & Debus, G.: Experimental studies on antianxiety agents with normal subjects; methodological considerations and review of the main effects. In: Efron, D. (Ed.): Psychopharmacology, 1957–1967. Washington, 1968. For other literature see *Butyrophenones.* G.D.

Halving method. In psychophysics, a method for constructing a ratio scale of subjective magnitude. The subject is required to judge when a stimulus is perceptually half the value of a previously presented standard on the dimension being scaled, without knowledge of the relevant physical values: e.g. for scaling perceived brightness, S. is required to indicate when he thinks a variable light is half as bright as the standard (or to adjust it to this position himself). This procedure is repeated for many points along the physical scale until a stable ratio scale of subjective magnitude is achieved. *G.D.W.*

Hand. The "universal tool", an important human organ of sensation (tactile, pressure, temperature, vibratory and pain sensations), expression, communication (sign and finger language, writing), and contact (touching, stroking, gripping). Man's development into his present advanced form would have been impossible without the hand; this is reflected in the expression "*homo faber*". Industrial psychology and occupational psychology study the use of the hand in work (manual skills, motor skills, etc.)

Bibliography: Alpenfels, E. J.: The anthropology and social significance of the human hand. Artificial Limbs, 1955, *2*, 4–21. Kiener, F.: Hand, Gebärde und Charakter. Munich, 1962. Rensch, B. (Ed.): Handgebrauch und Verständigung bei Affen und Frühmenschen. Stuttgart, 1968.

Handedness. A spontaneous or acquired preference for using the right or left hand, associated with corresponding differences in dexterity. Right hand dominance corresponds to a dominance of the left half of the brain, and vice versa. Handedness, which Greene's studies (1943) show to be a special factor in the psychomotor system, can be determined in the simplest instance by questions, or tests such as throwing a ball, pointing, etc. See *Laterality; Motor skills.*

Bibliography: Grant, D. A. & Kaestner, N. F.: Constant velocity tracking as a function of S's handedness and the rate and direction of the target course. J. exp. Psychol., 1955, *49*, 203–8. Greene, E. B.: An analysis of random and systematic changes with practice. Psychometrika, 1943, *8*, 37–52. Simon, J. R., *et al.*: Effects of handedness on tracking accuracy, Percept. mot. Skills Res. Exch., 1952, *4*, 53–7. M.A.

Handicapped children. The psychological and educational problems of handicapped children include on the one hand the child's difficulty in reconciling himself with his obtrusiveness in his habitual surroundings, and his impaired physical movement, and on the other hand attempts by the child, despite his handicap, to maintain a positive development of personality. Care for handicapped children concentrates on strengthening self-reliance, avoiding a succession of failures, and bringing about a positive mental attitude to the handicap. See *Child psychology; Mental defect.* *H.Schr.*

Handicapped person. An individual with innate or acquired impairment of physical or mental function. See *Mental defect; Rehabilitation.* *G.R.W.M.*

Handlines. These lines appear on the palm of the hand and generally form an M-shaped pattern; they are studied in chirology (q.v.). A distinction must be made between the handlines and the papillary lines; fingerprints are taken from the papillary lines on the finger tips (dactyloscopy). The handline patterns of the palm and the lines on the sole of the foot are attracting growing attention in medicine, anthropology and genetics, and also to some extent in psychology (constitutional psychology). Chromosomal anomalies affect both the handline patterns and the psyche.

Bibliography: Penrose, L. S.: Dermatoglyphics. Scientific American, 1969, *22* (6), 72–84.   *F.Ki*

Handwriting. See *Graphology*.

Haploid. By contrast with diploid (q.v.) and polyploid cells, haploid cells contain only one simple chromosome set. *Polyploid* = containing more than two chromosome sets (e.g. many cultivated plants). All the sex cells are haploid, as are many *protozoa*, lower plants and mosses.   *H.S.*

Haploscope. Apparatus constructed by H. Hering for his experiments in binocular vision. The haploscope consists of two cylindrical tubes, the axes of which coincide with the line of vision of both eyes. In contrast to experiments with the *stereoscope* (q.v.), those using the haploscope are aimed not at creating effects in depth but at determining retinal orientation ratios. See *Identical retinal points*.   *F.Ma.*

Haptics; haptic illusions. Haptics is the science relating to cutaneous sensation: that is, the modality of touch. There are many different types of sense organ in the skin, including receptors for pressure, temperature and pain. An example of a haptic illusion is Aristotle's illusion, in which two fingers are crossed and a small object is placed between them. Two objects are perceived since the skin on the outside of the two fingers is stimulated: normally this would result from two objects. Many of the visual illusions, e.g. *Müller-Lyer* and *tau effect*, also occur in the touch modality.   *C.D.F.*

Harmonic. 1. An *overtone*, or upper partial, with a wave vibration frequency which is an integral multiple of that of the fundamental. **2.** Capable of expression in sine or cosine functions. **3.** (syn. *harmonical; harmonious*) Congruous, agreeable, pleasing.

Harmonic mean (*H*). An expression for the central tendency of a distribution: the reciprocal of the arithmetic mean of the reciprocals of a sample (series of values).

$$H = \frac{1}{\frac{1}{N}\Sigma\frac{1}{X_i}} = \frac{N}{\Sigma\frac{1}{X_i}}$$

for discrete variables, and:

$$H = \frac{1}{\int\limits_{-\infty}^{\infty}\frac{f(x)}{x}\,d_x}$$

for continuous variables. In the case of positive x values, *H* is smaller than the geometric mean or arithmetic mean.

W.H.B.

Hashish. Cannabis (q.v.) resin: the strongest of the hemp products used as euphoriants. Hashish is normally smoked but may also be eaten. The use of hashish and other cannabis derivatives such as marihuana (q.v.) has risen constantly in recent years, especially among young people. According to Bewley (1968) consumption in England rose more than 700% in the years 1960 to 1965. The widely held opinion that persons who are labile or show other psychological anomalies are the main users of hashish could not be confirmed by Lennertz (1970) in a questionnaire study of young hashish smokers. The latter differed from a control group in their high level of tolerance, which Lennertz believes to be connected with the entire social and moral outlook of this group.

Few controlled studies have been made of the psychological effects of hashish. Evaluation of the effects is complicated by the fact that the pharmacological effectiveness of hashish varies widely while the effects are also dependent on individual experience with the substance and on the technique of smoking. In normal doses inexperienced testees generally note no subjective changes when hashish is taken, while the experienced persons report slightly euphoriant and stimulating effects. The performance of naïve testees tended to be impaired, whereas experienced marihuana smokers reported improved performance in some cases.

Hallucinogenic effects (primarily visual hallucinations linked with real perceptual objects) only occur with high doses or chronic use. See *Drug dependence; Psychotomimetic drugs*.

Bibliography: Bewley, T. H.: Recent changes in the pattern of drug abuse in London and in the United Kingdom. In: C. W. A. Wilson (Ed.): Adolescent drug dependence. Proceedings of the Society for the Study of Addiction. Oxford, 1968, 197–220. Jones, R. T. & Stone, G. C.: Psychological studies of marijuana and alcohol in man. Psychopharmacologia, 1970, 18, 108–17. Lennertz, E.: Zur Frage der antisozialen Persönlichkeit jugendlicher Hashischraucher. Z. für Sozialpsychol., 1970, 1, 48–56. Weil, A. T., Zinberg, N. E. & Nelson, J. M.: Clinical and psychological effects of marihuana in man. Science, 1968, 162, 1234–42. G.E.

Haunt. House or other locale that has become the scene of apparitions (q.v.) or similar manifestations associated with former inhabitants since deceased. *J.B.*

Hawthorne experiments. Generic name for a series of experiments to analyze conditions maximizing industrial output, proceeding from purely physiological to psychological and sociological questions. The experiments were organized in 1927–32 under E. Mayo and his colleagues T. N. Whitehead, F. J. Roethlisberger, W. J. Dickson, *et al.*, in the Hawthorne Works of the Western Electric Company.

The first series of experiments (first and second Relay Assembly Test Room, Mica Splitting Test Room) showed no clear correlation between productivity and the controlled variables, i.e. wage system and general working conditions. The results of the Mass Interviewing Program (starting in 1928) led to experimental studies of human relations in the Bank Wiring Observation Room (1931–32) and to the discovery of the "informal group" (q.v.) and its significance in determining individual productivity.

Bibliography: Argyle, M.: The relay assembly test room in retrospect. Occ. Psychol., 1963, 27, 98–103. Roethlisberger, F. J. & Dickson, W. J.: Management and the worker, Cambridge, Mass., 1939. W.F.N.

Hearing. See *Auditory perception; Sense organs*.

Hearing, localized. The localization of sound depends on the difference in time taken by the sound to reach the two ears (see *Differential running time*). Because of this, localization of sound sources lying in a vertical plane at right angles to, and in the middle of, a line joining the two ears is very poor, since from all points in this plane the sound will reach both ears at the same time. *C.D.F.*

Heart rate (syn. *Heart beat*). The number of heart beats per minute. The normal value is 60 per minute. Various regulating mechanisms allow the rate to rise during physical activity (greater volume of blood supplied to the heart) up to a possible maximum of 220 beats per minute. The heart rate is determined by measuring the pulse or ECG impulses per minute (cardiochronograph, cardiograph, electrocardiograph, etc.). Recording of heart rhythms is an important part of any examination of circulatory function, and enables conclusions to be drawn on the functional condition of the heart. The rate is faster in abnormal metabolic conditions (Basedow's disease, q.v.), and slower in the case of trained athletes.

E. D.

Hebb's theory of perceptual learning. Hebb's theory (see *Attention*) that (mature) learning is dependent on interacting central neural organizations, or "cell assemblies", which form the neural basis of complex, enduring patterns required for, e.g., concept formation. The structure by which individual assemblies are related to one another is called a "phase sequence". Practice builds up these highly coordinated groups of cells in the cerebral cortex.

Bibliography: Hebb, D. O.: The organization of behavior: a neuropsychological theory. New York, 1949. Id.: A neuropsychological theory. In: Koch, S. (Ed.): Psychology: a study of a science. New York, 1959, 622–43.

Hebephilia. An abnormally passionate interest in adolescents.

Hebephrenia. One of the schizophrenic syndromes. Originally described by Hecker in 1871 as an illness of puberty which led to a silly deterioration of intellect. Hence it was similar to *dementia praecox* (q.v.) and was grouped with it by Kraepelin in 1893. The syndrome is characterized by youthful onset, affective symptoms of blunting with lability, silliness, inappropriateness, irritability, thought disorder and disturbances of volition. Poorly organized delusions and hallucinations are usually present, but motor symptoms are not. The onset is insidious and the prognosis poor.   *B.B.*

Hedonism. The theory that sensual pleasure is the sole objective of all behavior. Today hedonism is mainly considered in psychoanalysis (q.v.) (the *pleasure principle*). In ethics, hedonism is contrasted or combined with *eudaemonism*, according to which the desire for happiness is the end of all (right) action.

Bibliography: James, W.: The principles of psychology, Vol. 2. New York, 1890.   *M.R.*

Height disparity. See *Horizontal disparity.*

Helmholtz, Hermann von. *Life and works.* B. 31/8/1821 in Potsdam; d. 8/9/1894 in Charlottenburg, Berlin. Graduated in 1842 with a study of the origin of nerve fibers in the ganglionic cells. He then worked as an army surgeon in Potsdam. In 1847 he read his famous paper to the Physical Society of Berlin on the principle of the conservation of energy. In 1849, Helmholtz became Professor of physiology in Königsberg, where he remained until 1855. Between 1855 and 1858 he was Professor of anatomy and physiology in Bonn, and then Professor of physiology in Heidelberg until 1871. In 1871 he was appointed Professor of physics at Berlin University, and in 1887 he was appointed first Director of the newly established Imperial Institute of Physics and Technology in Charlottenburg (Berlin).

Helmholtz published more than two hundred articles and monographs in which he made a fundamental contribution to anatomy, medicine, physiology, physics and psychology. In the psychological sphere, his work on the physiology and psychology of sensation is of most interest. By far his most important works are the three volumes of his *Treatise on Physiological Optics* (1856–1867) and his study of the *Theory of Sensations of Tone as the Physiological Basis of the Theory of Music* (1862). In the first work he presents his own findings and offers a survey of the German literature on the anatomical, physiological and physical bases of visual perception; the second study contains his contribution to physiological acoustics, and in particular to the study of problems of the auditory discrimination of timbre and pitch.

Physiological psychology. Helmholtz's first important work in this sphere was the determination of the transmission velocity of nervous excitation in the sensory and motor nerve fibers (i.e. the speed of the neural impulse) by examining the "nerve-muscle preparation" of frogs and carrying out reaction-time experiments on humans. He refuted the previously held opinion that the speed of conduction in the nerve is many time greater than the speed of light. In the sphere of optics and sensory physiology Helmholtz invented the ophthalmoscope, and the ophthalmometer—a device to determine the corneal curvature of the eye. Working independently of the Dutch physiologist Cramer, Helmholtz reached the same conclusions in his description and explanation of the process of accommodation (q.v.) in the eye. In his theory of color perception he developed the view of the British physiologist T. Young. Starting from the law of specific energy of nerves (Müller), Helmholtz assumed the existence of three color-sensitive nerve substances whose excitation leads in each case to a specific color sensation (red, green, blue), while all the other color sensations are obtained by mixing these three primary colors.

Helmholtz's assumptions on space perception (q.v.) and object perception are based on Lotze's local sign theory, which he tried to harmonize with Müller's principle of specific energies. He believed that perception is a two-stage process. The basis of perception is represented by the sensations, whose quality and intensity are inborn, and which are conditioned by specific characteristics of the sense organs. Sensations themselves, however, have no significance for space and object perception but are merely "signs", which only acquire significance in the course of development by association through experience. The acquisition of meaning consists, in Helmholtz's opinion, of judgment processes which may be conscious to begin with but become automatic after repeated association—as "unconscious inferences" which, because of their compulsive character, appear as evident perceptions. Helmholtz adopted a distinctly empirical standpoint in the empiricism vs. nativism debate in perception theory (see *Perception*).

As regards audition (see *Auditory perception*), Helmholtz acquired importance primarily through his resonance theory (q.v.), in which he explained, e.g., the discrimination of pitch by assuming that the variously long fibers in the basilar membrane of the inner ear are made to vibrate by wavelengths corresponding to their natural frequency: i.e. the different hair cells vibrate in tune with the sound wave frequencies.

Main works: Treatise on physiological optics, 3 vols. Ed. J. P. C. Southall. Rochester, N.Y., 1924–5. On the rate of transmission of the nerve impulse. In: Dennis, W. (Ed.): Readings in the history of psychology. New York, 1948, 197–8. On the sensations of tone. New York, 1954.

Bibliography: Boring, E. G.: A history of experimental psychology. New York, 1950. Gruber, H. & V.: Hermann von Helmholtz: nineteenth century polymorph. Sci. Mon, 1956, *83*, 92–9. Lenzen, V. F.: Helmholtz's theory of knowledge. In: Montague, M. F. A. (Ed.): Studies and essays in the history of science and learning. New York, 1946, 299–320. McKendrick, J. G.: Hermann von Helmholtz. London, 1899. Müller, J.: Elements of physiology. London, 1837–42. Warren, R. M. & R. P.: Helmholtz on perception: its physiology and development. New York, 1968. Young, T.: Miscellaneous works. London, 1855.   *W.W.*

Helmholtz squares. This illusion principally demonstrates the effect whereby filled spaces

look larger than empty spaces, for the two squares composed of many parallel lines appear to have a larger surface area than the one consisting of a simple outline. However, the ends of the parallel lines give the illusion of straight edges not actually drawn so that the figure also provides an example of *closure*.   *C.D.F.*

Helson-Judd effect. See *Adaptation level.*

Hemeralop[s]ia (syn. *Night-blindness*).A defect of vision at night or in twilight caused by partial or complete absence of scotopic rod vision. It may be an innate and recessive (in some case also a dominant) inherited characteristic (Trendelenburg, 1961), but is generally acquired through an alimentary deficiency of vitamin A, which is necessary for synthesis of the retinal rod pigment rhodopsin (q.v.).

Bibliography: Trendelenburg, W.: Der Gesichtssinn. Berlin, ²1961.   *K.H.P.*

Hemianopsia (syn. *Hemiopia*). Failure of the visual field on one side, which may occur in lesions of the central optical pathways between the intersection of the optic nerves (*chiasma opticum*) and the occipital lobe. Depending on the location of the lesion, hemianopsia may be homonymous (on the same side), or heteronymous (e.g. bitemporal), complete or incomplete.   *C.S.*

Hemiparesis. Unilateral (motor or sensory), incomplete paralysis due to failure of the central nervous centers or pathways. Since these paths intersect, the lesion is situated on the side opposite the diseased side.   *C.S.*

Hemiplegia. Paralysis of one side of the body generally caused by a stroke (see *Hemiparesis*).

Hemispheres. The two halves of the cerebrum (right and left cerebral hemispheres), which are joined together by the *corpus callosum*.   *C.S.*

Hereditary characterology. A trend in psychology which developed in the nineteen twenties with the object of determining the degree to which character (q.v.) was inherited rather than dependent on environment (q.v.). The most reliable results came from twin studies (q.v.). See *Traits*.   *W.K.*

Heredity, theory of. A hypothesis based on C. Darwin's *Origin of Species* (see *Darwinism*), according to which all animal and plant species have developed by evolution (q.v.) from simpler organisms. This hypothesis also implies that today's wealth of species has developed by division of species from a few organisms and ultimately, perhaps, from a single species. The essentials of heredity theory are generally recognized nowadays by serious scientists, since all the evidence is in its favor, and no refutation is available.

                                    H.S.

Hering, Ewald. *Life and works.* B. 5/8/1834 in Altgersdorf (Saxony); d. 27/1/1918 in Leipzig. Studied medicine in Leipzig where he was influenced by G. T. Weber and G. T. Fechner. After publishing his five-part work on space perception (q.v.), he was appointed Professor of physiology at Vienna University, where he took over C. Ludwig's post. Five years later he went to Prague as Z. Purkinje's successor, and after twenty-five years there he once again replaced C. Ludwig, this time as Professor of physiology in Leipzig.

Hering was a physiologist specializing in sensation who played a very important part as one of the pioneers of experimental physiological psychology. He was a contemporary of H. Helmholtz's (q.v.); the two shared similar interests but differed in their theoretical approaches, which led to constant controversy between them. Helmholtz was an empiricist and Hering a nativist. In his theory of space perception (published in his *Contributions to Physiology*, 1861–64), by stating that the capacity for space perception is innate and does not need to be learnt, Hering stood out against the opinion expressed by Helmholtz one year later in the third volume of *Treatise on Physiological Optics*.

Hering also differed from Helmholtz in the basis of his phenomenological studies. The observation and description of subjective, sensory experience were among his primary objectives. His nativist orientation and methodical, phenomenological approach had a strong influence on C. Stumpf, and above all on later gestalt psychology.

Hering also became important by reason of his famous theory of color vision, which was opposed to Helmholtz's three-color theory. Hering asserted that there were three color-sensitive substances in the retina (q.v.) (red/green—yellow/blue—black/white) which are in a constant state of dissimilation and assimilation, and that one of the two color sensations corresponds to each of these two processes in a substance. All possible color impressions were said to result from the combination of these fundamental colors.

Main works: Beiträge zur Physiologie, 5 vols., 1861–5, Die Lehre vom binokularen Sehen, 1868. Über das Gedächtnis als eine allgemeine Funktion der organisierten Materie, 1870. Grundzüge der Lehre vom Lichtsinn, 1920.

Bibliography: Boring, E. G.: Sensation and perception in the history of experimental psychology. New York, 1942. Hillebrand, F.: Ewald Hering. Leipzig, 1918.

W.W.

Hering fall test. A method for studying monocular and binocular vision in depth. In the simplest case, S. looks through a tube at a point of fixation on which the eye is focussed (see *Accommodation*). The experimenter drops small balls in front of and behind the point of fixation. S. is required to estimate the distance of the balls. *F.M.*

Hering's illusion. One of the geometric

illusions. The two parallel horizontal lines are perceived as bending outwards.

C.D.F.

Hermaphrodite. An individual who has the physical characteristics (particularly sex organs) of both male and female. *Hermaphroditism* is extremely rare in humans, and only one set of sex organs is fully functional, but apparently a shift in dominance through either natural or artificial means is possible.

Hermaphroditism (syn. *Intersexuality*). Disturbed, incomplete physical sex differentiation, characterized by ambiguity or lack of agreement between external and/or internal sex characteristics (male/female). The causes of this abnormal development or malformation vary. Today a distinction is made between three principal forms of hermaphroditism: *pseudohermaphroditismus femininus* (female pseudohermaphroditism), *pseudohermaphroditismus masculinus* (male pseudohermaphroditism), and *hermaphroditismus verus* (genuine hermaphroditism). Whereas in the pseudohermaphroditisms, the genetic sex (chromosomal sex) coincides with the gonadic sex (i.e. either purely male or purely female), the external and internal sex organs are either hybrid (bisexual) or seem to belong to the other sex, in genuine hermaphroditism both sex-gland sexes are present (testicular and ovarian tissue), and the external and internal sex organs represent a mixture of male and female forms or, in external appearance, all stages from the male to the female type. The diagnosis "hermaphroditism" does not, therefore, necessarily involve specific external sex organs; the ambiguity may also be internal. The main problem of hermaphroditism lies in the psychological and psychopathological effects of the physical sexual development, above all from the angle of sex role identification and sex education.

1. *Pseudohermaphroditismus femininus:* genetically female individuals with internal

female sex organs (ovaries, fallopian tubes, uterus, vagina) and intersexual external genital organs, generally in the form of a greatly enlarged clitoris (clitoral hypertrophy), which may resemble a penis in appearance and size and is already visible at birth; the differentiation between the vagina and urethral opening is inadequate. Causes: usually a genetically conditioned overproduction of (masculinizing) androgens (q.v.); also known as the *andreno-genital syndrome* (AGS). Treatment consists in administering the hormone cortisol, which is not formed in the diseased adrenal gland. Money (1968) states early diagnosis is vital, ideally at birth. A girl can then grow up without ever knowing that she has had a special problem. The need for special sexual education is then correspondingly reduced.

2. *Pseudohermaphroditismus masculinus:* persons who are clearly male genetically and in gonadic sex; a distinction is made between two main groups, depending on the external appearance of the sex organs and the phenotype, i.e. (*a*) testicular feminization, as a relatively rare form in which the external genitalia and appearance are feminine—apart from the absence of pubic hair (hairless woman). Female development of the internal sex organs (uterus, ovaries, fallopian tubes) is not present, however. The genetic sex, sex glands and sex hormone production are male. Testicular feminization is not usually diagnosed until adolescence, when a doctor is consulted in the absence of menstrual bleeding. Cause: disturbance of all the androgen-dependent organs and tissues; clearly a hereditary defect by which the male hormones cannot influence the development of the sex organs either in the embryonic stage or in later life. Treatment: surgical extension of the vagina in or after puberty, and adequate psychological explanation of the cause of the condition and of infertility (Money, 1968). The main group of masculine pseudohermaphroditisms consists of (*b*) externally hybrid cases which come somewhere between the male and female pheno-

type, and which are difficult to distinguish externally from apparent female hermaphrodites. The true causes of these malformations cannot generally be explained in the individual case. Psychological and psychopathological problems are frequently encountered because (i) the external genitalia are ambiguous, and in extreme cases the patient himself has doubts about his sex role; (ii) in cases which are diagnosed at a late stage, sex characteristics may develop at puberty (e.g. breast development, absence of the secondary male sex characteristics) which do not correspond to the sex role to which the subject has become accustomed (e.g. male); (iii) certain genital malformations may prevent normal sexual behavior (failure of the erection mechanism), or make it more difficult, or alternatively—e.g. in *hypospadia scrotalis*—prevent sexually specific urination. For these and other reasons, an individual, medicopsychological treatment program must be prepared in each case of masculine hermaphroditism, as in the case of genuine hermaphroditism. There are certain basic criteria and rules for treatment (Wilkins, 1965; Money, 1968; Wallis, 1967).

3. *Genuine hermaphrodites:* the testicles and ovaries may be combined in a single organ (= ovotestes) or present separately (= lateral hermaphrodites) and both may reach fully functional maturity (sperm formation or ovulation and menstruation). The external and internal genitalia may present many different characteristics: all kinds of transitional forms from male to female types are possible (usually mixed forms). Genuine hermaphrodites may be genetically male-female or male or female (sex chromosomes XX or XY or XY/XO). Cause: probably due to disturbed nucleus division during early embryonic development. Occurrence: relatively rare. In all cases of hermaphroditism, early diagnosis is vital because medical treatment and adequate sexual education are dependent on it. The decisive factor in sexing a newly born hermaphrodite should be the anatomical appearance of the external

genitalia, even if the sex-gland sex and genetical sex do not coincide with it. Sex changes should be made at the earliest possible time (before the age of two years), and only if there is no clear phenotype. If hermaphroditism is diagnosed later on, i.e. after the fourth year of age, special medical and psychological treatment as defined by Wilkins (1965) and Money (1968) is indicated.

Bibliography: Money, J.: Cytogenetic and psychosexual incongruities with a note on spaceform blindness. Am. J. Psychiat., 1963, *119*, 820–7. Id. (Ed.): Sex research: new developments. Chicago, 1968. Wilkins, L.: The diagnosis and treatment of endocrine disorders in childhood and adolescence. Springfield, Ill., 1965. Jores, A. & Nowakowski, H.: Praktische Endokrinologie. Stuttgart, 1964. Voigt, K. D. & Schmidt, H.: Sexualhormone, Hamburg, 1968. Wallis, H.: Katamnestische Erhebungen bei Hermaphroditen. Jahrb. f. Psychiat., 1967, *5*, 104–111. *H. Maisch*

Heroin. A semi-synthetic morphine derivative (diacetylmorphine) with highly analgesic and euphoriant action (see *Analgesics*). With chronic use there is a risk of habituation in the sense of psychological and physiological dependence. See *Drug dependence.* *G.E.*

Hertz. A unit of wave frequency equivalent to one cycle per second, especially in electricity.

Heterogamete; homogamete. The male and female differ chromosomally. They are either homogametic or heterogametic from the standpoint of the sex chromosomes. Frequently, e.g. in man and in the fruit fly *drosophila*, the female sex is of the XX and the male of the XY type (heterogamete). Some butterflies, fishes and birds have heterogametic females and homogametic males; there is also the XO type, e.g. in bed bugs. Sex, however, is not determined solely by the ratio of X:Y chromosomes but by the ratio of the number of autosome sets to the number of X chromosomes. *K.Fi.*

Heterogeneous variance. The dissimilarity of two or more sample distributions is so marked that they probably do not originate from the same basic group. See *Variance, analysis of.* *W.H.B.*

Heterohypnosis. Generally referred to simply as *hypnosis* (q.v.): a hypnotic state brought about in a subject by the suggestive influence of another person (the hypnotist) (ant. *autohypnosis*, q.v. = self-hypnosis, i.e. a state of hypnosis brought about by autosuggestion, q.v.). *H.-N.G.*

Heterosensorial (syn. *Heterosensory*). From a different sense area. Ant. *homosensorial* = from the same sense area. E.g. heterosensorial association or reproduction. See *Homosensorial reproduction.*

Heterosexual. 1. Pertaining to sexual relationships with members of the opposite sex. **2.** One who is sexually attracted to members of the opposite sex. In both cases, overt sexual behavior may or may not be involved, and the opposite is *homosexual.* *G.D.W.*

Heterosexuality, compulsive. Abnormally strong desire for heterosexual contact. Called *nymphomania* or *estromania* in females; *satyriasis, satyromania,* or *priapism* in males. Needless to say, the criteria for employing these diagnostic labels are ill-defined and arbitrary. *G.D.W.*

Heterostereotype. By analogy with the term as used in printing, the word *stereotype* (q.v.) denotes a relatively rigid concept of persons or groups which is resistant to change and usually simplified. *Heterostereotypes* are similar concepts of other persons or groups; *autostereotypes* are the ideas a person has of himself or of a reference, and/or membership, group. Examples: heterostereotype: "miserly Scots"; autostereotype: "self-sacrificing scientist."   *H.D.S.*

Heterozygote. In a diploid (q.v.) cell, the two genes (see *Allele*) for a given feature may be identical, i.e. condition the same degree of emphasis of the feature, or different, in which case the emphasis of the feature will also differ. In the first instance, the cell or organism is said to be *homozygotic* in regard to the feature concerned, and in the second case *heterozygotic*. In heterozygotic organisms, the degree of emphasis of the feature is dependent on whether the latter is inherited by dominant-recessive or intermediary means.
                                                            H.S.

Hexis. A term used by Guilford (in his hierarchical model of personality) for the lowest plane of habit (q.v.). Hexis designates a constant disposition, which means that an individual behaves in a similar manner in a given range of situations.   *G.K.*

Hierarchy (syn. *Hierarchical structure*). **1.** A ranking of elements (e.g. persons, things, concepts, constructs) so that each rank is subordinate to the next higher rank. The subordination may be based on widely varying factors (e.g. degree of generality, level of abstraction, dominance), but must remain the same within a hierarchical system. In personality (q.v.) psychology a number of attempts have been made to describe personality as a hierarchical system of, e.g., motives or traits (q.v.). In personality research based on factor analysis the distinction between first, second and higher order factors represents a hierarchical personality model. See *Motive*.   *D.B.*

2. Hierarchy of centers; hierarchy of moods. Behavioral structures are based on central coordination mechanisms with differing degrees of integration; the highest

levels have been defined by Tinbergen as *instincts*. Each instinct influences the motor units and competes with other instincts for control over the latter. Tinbergen assumes a linear arrangement of centers of different orders in the hierarchy of centers, ranging from the superimposed main instinct to the end action. With the exception of the highest center, the centers are generally blocked; the lower centers are charged by higher ones and must be disinhibited by key stimuli. In Baerends' hierarchy of moods, moods of differing order influence the duration of specific behavioral spectra. A specific stimulus situation does not always release the same behavior; the mood prevailing at a given time tends to be the decisive factor. Leyhausen's relative hierarchy of moods does not include a linear arrangement of moods in order of precedence. He assumes the appetence of the final action to be the dominant factor and not the last link in the chain. Cats, for example, do not have a uniform prey-catching impulse, but specific stimuli for lying in wait, creeping, pouncing, killing, etc. Each part action may become the desired final action, and suppress the others. See *Instinct*.

Bibliography: Baerends, G. P.: Fortpflanzungsverhalten und Orientierung der Grabwespe Ammophila campestris. Jur. Tijdschr. Entom., 1941, *84*, 71–275. Leyhausen, P.: Über die Funktion der relativen Stimmungshierarchie. Z. Tierpsychol., 1965, *22*, 412–94. Tinbergen, N.: The study of instinct. Oxford, 2969.   *K.Fi.*

Hierarchy, industrial. An historically conditioned form of authority with power distributed on several different levels and a strictly defined, permanent system of command and subordination. It is undecided to what extent there are tendencies toward elimination of the hierarchical structure as a result of technical progress (automation), and to what degree an approximation to "circular" (democratic) authority structures is possible. See *Industrial psychology*.

Bibliography: Blau, P. M. & Scott, W. R.: Formal organizations: a comparative approach. San Francisco, 1962. Simpson, R. L.: Vertical and horizontal communication in formal organizations. Admin. Sci. Quart., 1959, 4, 188–9. C.B.

Hillebrand's alley. An experimental technique for studying one aspect of the perception of three-dimensional space. Parallel lines, e.g. railway lines, appear to come together in the distance. Hillebrand constructed an alley of hanging threads and people were asked to adjust these until the two rows appeared parallel as they went into the distance. He could then measure the resulting discrepancies from true parallelism, thus discovering some of the properties of subjective space as opposed to objective space. C.D.F.

Hippocampus. A part of the temporal lobe which belongs to the hindbrain (see *Cerebrum*) and forms the medial wall of the inferior horn of the lateral ventricle. It consists of white and grey matter. Its functional significance has not been fully clarified; it is sometimes assumed to play a part in the ability to detect odors (olfactory processes), and sometimes to influence the function of the *formatio reticularis* (q.v.) and the development of conditioned responses. See *Neuroanatomy*. E.D.

Hippocratic types. The four *temperaments* (q.v.) wrongly attributed to the followers of Hippocrates and in fact described first in the Middle Ages. See *Type*. W.K.

Hirsutism. Abnormal growth of body hair in women (hair on the limbs, stomach, breasts; growth of a beard). Various causes: (*a*) heightened production (pathologically conditioned) of male sex hormones by the adrenal cortex (e.g. adrenogenital syndrome of female hermaphroditism, or Cushing's syndrome), or defective ovaries (e.g.

Stein-Leventhal syndrome); (*b*) non-pathological excess production of male sex hormones (androgens) in the adrenal glands or ovaries; also known as idiopathic or "common" hirsutism. Psychological disturbances (e.g. uncertainty about sexual role) almost always occur after the development of the abnormal hair. Incidence: 3 to 4%.

Bibliography: Zerssen, D. von, Meyer, A. E. & Ahrens, D.: Klinische, biochemische und psychologische Untersuchungen an Patienten mit gewöhnlichem Hirsutismus. Dt. Arch. klin. Med., 1960, 206, 234. H.M.

Histamine. Neurohormone or tissue hormone; a biogenic amine (q.v.) obtained by biosynthesis from histidine (decarboxylation). Histamine occurs naturally in many organs (intestine, lungs, liver, skin, central nervous system, etc.). The main physiological effects are: dilatation of the capillary blood vessels with a substantial drop in blood pressure, contraction of the smooth musculature (uterus, intestines, bronchial muscles), and strong stimulation of the secretion of gastric acid. Histamine is assumed to be important in the pathogenesis of allergies, and in the origin and conduction of pain. In antigen-antibody reactions, and in particular in anaphylactic shock, large quantities of histamine are released. Smaller amounts are released in sensory pain. The role of histamine in the central nervous system has not yet been definitively explained. Its concentration distribution is similar to that of the catecholamines. A fairly large number of centrally effective drugs block the effect of histamine (see, e.g., *Antihistamines; Neuroleptics*). See *Psychosomatics*.

Bibliography: Green, J. P.: Histamine and the nervous system. Feder. Proceed., 1964, 23, 1095–102. Handbuch der experimentellen Pharmakologie: Vol. 18, Pt. 1. Histamine. Its chemistry, metabolism and physiological actions. Berlin, 1966. Kahlson, G. & Rosengren, E.: Histamine. Ann. Rev. Pharmacol., 1965, 5, 305. W.J.

Histogram. A histogram is a graphic representation of the frequency distribution (q.v.) for a discrete variable. The frequency for each class is shown as a vertical bar.   *W.H.B.*

Historical psychology. For this school (founded by J. H. van den Berg), the objects of psychological research can be determined only from their history, since they develop in the course of time. This applies in particular to the higher mental processes (needs, will, operations of the intellect, personality). This approach has led to the study of "mentalities" (L. Febvre) and recently to research into the archeology of knowledge (M. Foucauld).   *P.M.*

History of psychology. I. The roots of psychology go back thousands of years and reach into many areas of knowledge. Folkways, magic, religion, philosophy and science have all contributed to the origin of psychology. It is likely that every culture had its own psychology in order to postulate causes for certain human thoughts, actions and events. But the early history of psychology, like the early history of Western thought in general, is primarily known to us through the writings of the Greek philosophers.

1. *Early Greek naturalists.* While speculating on the nature of the universe, the Greek philosophers of the sixth century B.C. were already discussing certain psychological problems. As pointed out by Esper (1964), they considered all nature as animate. Matter, animals and men were thought to be alive because they moved. Thales (c. 625 B.C.), for instance, allowed a magnet a soul because it moved iron. Anaximander (c. 610–c. 547 B.C.) proposed an evolutionary theory, suggesting that life arose from sun-heated mud. He also thought that water was basic to all substance, because it was universal, appeared in many forms, and produced movement when changing its aggregate state. Heraclitus (c. 535–c. 475 B.C.) considered

fire as the primary force and "soul-substance", because it moved and transformed matter. All matter was thought to be in a constant state of flux, and only the orderliness in which change occurred presented constancy, rationality or "logos". Heraclitus also believed that all knowledge must come through the senses, a notion that formed the basis for the psychological thinking of the British empiricist philosophers of the eighteenth century, and in turn the basis for present-day methods of conditioning, reconditioning, and behavior modification.

Democritus (c. 460–c. 370 B.C.) presented the first atomic view of the universe, when he said that matter, like humans, was composed of small, mobile atoms which entered the body to give it life or soul. Different parts of the body were thought to be formed by different types of atoms responsible for a variety of functions. Democritus described the brain as the organ of thought, the heart as that of anger, and the liver as that of disease. He did not distinguish sensing from thinking, since both were based on atomic motion (Diels, 1934).

2. *Early Greek anti-naturalists.* Not all pre-Socratic philosophers believed that mind and matter, or body and soul, had equal properties and were subject to one and the same natural law. Nor did they all agree on the reliability of the senses as indicators of reality. Pythagoras (c. 582–c. 500 B.C.) and his followers were fascinated by numbers, and explained many abstract concepts by them. The Pythagoreans did not consider the soul and the body as one entity, but postulated that the soul leaves the body after death to undergo a possible succession of reincarnations. This division of body and soul was much elaborated by the Christian philosophers, who thus prepared psychology for the dualistic approach of mentalism and mechanism.

Protagoras (c. 480–c. 410 B.C.), an older contemporary of Plato, recognized the subjective value of the human senses and doubted their objectivity. He pointed out that sensations and perceptions differ between and within individuals, being subject to a constant flux of biological and social influences. Hence his famous saying, "Man is the measure of all things" (Diels, 1934).

Anti-naturalism reached its peak with Plato. He thought the senses were unreliable, because one could perceive, for instance, triangles of all shapes and sizes and still maintain an idea of triangularity. It is therefore the idea, the form, or the abstract thought which yields true knowledge. Sense perception, Plato believed, yields only probabilities and approximations. He had so much faith in reason that he preferred it to observation, a viewpoint that has often hindered the future accumulation of psychological knowledge.

The Greek philosophers established two more or less discrete philosophical approaches to psychology. One approach emphasized reason, logic, thought, theory, innate knowledge, and a mind distinct from the body. The other approach emphasized observation, experimentation, environmental learning, and unity of body and soul. Much of all future psychology has fallen into one of these two camps.

3. *Aristotle*. The views of Aristotle (384–322 B.C.) cannot be assigned to either camp. Aristotle was a theorist as well as an observer. Watson (1968) considers him to have been the first psychologist because he tried to present a systematic and integrated view of the function of the human mind. The many topics he wrote about are very similar to the titles of chapter headings in modern general psychology texts.

Unlike Plato, Aristotle thought that form cannot be separated from matter—that a bronze statue, for instance, must have matter in order to have form, and vice versa. This unifying concept is also present in Aristotle's view of the "psyche", often interpreted as "soul" or "mind". Aristotle's soul includes matter as well as the functioning of the mind. Its development is based on evolutionary principles—on a vegetative soul attributed to plants, a sensory soul attributed to animals,

and a rational soul belonging to man. Aristotle's "psyche" did not have any religious or supernatural properties. Religious and supernatural properties were added over a thousand years later by the scholastic philosopher St Thomas Aquinas.

Aristotle wrote about the five senses and postulated a sixth one necessary to combine the functions of any two or more senses. He thought that we must rely on the senses to make factual observations, but warned that empirical data, no matter how correct, are useless if interpreted with false logic or wrong premisses. He also warned that correct logic is misleading if based on faulty observations. He thought knowledge was a combination of sense experience and thinking.

Many of Aristotle's hypotheses on the nature of remembering and forgetting have given rise to much experimentation in the area of learning. His doctrine of association (q.v.) stated that memory is facilitated by either similarity or dissimilarity of a present and past event, or by their close relationship in time and space. Later these hypotheses became known as the laws of similarity, contrast, and contiguity.

Aristotle formed theories about desires, appetites, pain and pleasure, reactions, and emotions. His doctrine of catharsis suggested, for instance, that fears can be transferred to the hero in a tragedy—an idea which much later formed one of the tenets of psychoanalysis and play therapy.

4. *Early Christian period and the Middle Ages*. There was little inquiry into psychology during the early Christian period and during the Middle Ages. St Augustine's (354–430) teachings were accepted for hundreds of years. He emphasized the introspective method, believing that "self-knowledge," subjective reflecting upon one's own mind, is more exact than knowledge gained through sense perception. The main force of the mind or the "self" was the power of the "will," which in turn, was responsible for habits, actions, and faith. Involuntary bodily functions, however, were not considered part of

the "self" and were to be neglected and ignored—an attitude which has remained in Western culture where autonomic functions such as sex, and gastro-intestinal activities are still preferably conducted in privacy.

St Thomas Aquinas (1225–74) accepted Augustine's concept of "faith" and "will" as well as Aristotle's "reason." In this amalgamation Augustine's "will" became subordinated to Aristotle's "reason," and Aristotle's "rational soul" became immortal and resurrectable. Aquinas also modified Aristotle's hierarchical concept of "souls" or "psyche." He postulated that there was only one soul, but that this soul was composed of a rational faculty which was non-physical and deathless, and of sensory and vegetative faculties which were physically dependent and perished with the body.

5. *Beginnings of modern psychology.* Aquinas' definitions of reason, mind, soul and body were not challenged until Descartes (1596–1650) introduced his dualistic concept of man. He held that the mind or soul is located in the brain, though it has no substance. The body, on the other hand, was thought to have substance, or "extended" qualities which, like machines, followed mechanical laws. Descartes further believed that the mind can influence the body and the body the mind, and he attempted to describe the physiological mechanisms of this interaction. Descartes is often called the first modern psychologist, because psychology would have remained speculative without the introduction and the recognition of physiological factors.

After Descartes's introduction of the concept of interaction, philosophers began to debate about the qualities and the quantities of the body's influence on the mind. They were primarily interested to know whether such mental qualities as knowing, thinking, and ideation arise within the mind, or come to the mind via the body's senses. John Locke (1632–1704) took a radical environmental view. He maintained that the mind is a "blank tablet" (*tabula rasa*), that all knowledge must enter the mind through the senses, and that ideas are, in turn, combinations and reflections of sensory impressions. Locke and other British philosophers such as Hume, Hartley, the Mills, and Bain, who held similar views, became known as the "British empiricists." They are also called "associationists," because they believed that Aristotle's principles of association play a major role in the selection, storage, and composition of all mental content such as knowledge, thought, images, and ideas.

Not all philosophers agreed with the empiricists. Berkeley (1685–1753) pointed out that the mind, as in the case of depth perception, for instance, needs to process information from retinal size differences, clearness of the image, tension from certain eye muscles, and so on—information or stimuli not directly related to depth perception. Berkeley argued that the ultimate reality lies in the mind and not in the matter found in the environment.

Psychology's major problem had been that of "body and soul." The nineteenth century superimposed on it that of "nativism vs. empiricism," or that of heredity vs. environment—a problem which still causes much discussion in the measurement and definitions of such psychological factors as temperament and intelligence.

6. *Physiology and the mind.* The physiologists of the nineteenth century gave much to the philosophers who theorized about the content and functions of the mind. Pierre Flourens (1794–1867) demonstrated that certain parts of the brain are directly responsible for certain behavioral functions. When he extirpated the cortex of a bird, for instance, he found that it could no longer fly "voluntarily," but only if thrown into the air. Paul Broca (1824–1880) attempted to locate the brain area responsible for speech, and in 1870 Fritsch and Hitzig discovered the area of the cerebral cortex related to motor functions (Boring, 1950, pp. 61–79).

The studies of sensory receptors, nerves, and muscles also contributed much to the understanding of human feelings, thoughts, and activities. Du Bois-Raymond demonstrated in 1849 that neural activity is measurable, and that it is accompanied by an electrical impulse; and Helmholtz (q.v.) showed in 1850 that neural conduction requires a specified time. Sechenov (1863) examined reflexes and found that some animals can perform "purposive" acts by means of spinal reflex actions which do not require the activity of the brain.

Physiological discoveries such as the above were important psychological "breakthroughs" because the nativists—the dominant majority—insisted that the functions of the mind had no physical correlates in space or time. Sechenov, for instance, was not allowed to publish his findings about the nature of reflexes under the title: "An attempt to establish physiological bases of psychic processes." The censorship committee of St Petersburg thought that the juxtaposition of "physiological" and "psychic" would corrupt the mores of society.

7. *Experimental psychology.* Psychology has been defined as the "product of the union of philosophy and physiology" (Keller, 1936, p. 21). Physiology brought not only physiological data but the scientific method in general to psychology, and scientists from non-physiological disciplines began to make important contributions. The physicist Gustav Fechner (q.v.) (1801–87), who was also a medical doctor and a philosopher, spent much of his lifetime investigating the relationship between the objective, physical world and the subjective, personal one. He measured the physical energy needed to produce various intensities of sensation. He found, for instance, that ten times as much energy is required to produce a tone which is heard twice as loud as before, a hundred times as much energy to hear the tone three times as loud, etc. Fechner's method became known as "psychophysics" (q.v.), and has found much use in apparatus design and human engineering.

The Dutch physician F. C. Donders

(1862) attempted to measure mental activities through reaction-time experiments. To obtain a time measure for thought he deducted the reaction time required for simple from that required for more complicated tasks.

Another scientific, but non-physiological method of exploring the mind was pioneered by Hermann Ebbinghaus (q.v.) (1850–1909). He investigated rates of learning and of forgetting, such as, for instance, the relationship between number of repetitions and length of memory. Ebbinghaus created and used the "nonsense syllable". He theorized correctly that the use of meaningful words would interfere with objectivity in learning experiments.

8. *Academic psychology.* In 1879 the first psychological laboratory was founded by Wilhelm Wundt (q.v.) (1832–1920) at the University of Leipzig. Wundt was trained in medicine, physiology and philosophy. He was a prolific writer "producing a total of 491 publications ranging from one-page articles to books 2,353 pages long" (Boring, 1950, p. 345). Wundt tried to investigate the mind by studying its conscious content, and more specifically the elements of sensation, such as intensity, duration, and locality. Wundt's preferred method was that of "introspection" (q.v.), in which an individual describes his sensations and feelings in discrete, technical terms. Wundt's laboratory became the center of psychological activities. Students came to him from all over the world to investigate problems related to visual perception, hearing, touch and taste, reaction time, word associations, and so on. The variety and the volume of Wundt's contributions to psychology are unique. Boring & Boring (1948) surveyed the background of American psychologists and found that a large majority were trained by teachers who in turn were pupils of Wundt. However, Wundt's influence in his own country was less pronounced (Wesley, 1965).

9. *Diversification of psychology.* Unity in psychology was short-lived and existed

perhaps only *in statu nascendi* in the early days at Wundt's laboratory. Other psychological schools were soon to follow which emphasized different methods for studying the mind. Oswald Külpe (q.v.) (1862–1915) founded a psychological laboratory in Würzburg in 1896. He and his students examined such complex tasks as thinking, remembering, and judging. They used a more molar type of introspection, believing that the Wundtian approach was too atomistic.

The principle of "wholeness" was later stressed again by the founders of "gestalt" psychology. In 1912 Max Wertheimer (q.v.) demonstrated that two stationary lights, lit in a certain succession, will give an observer the sensation of movement. Hence, Wertheimer and the gestalt psychologists maintain that the product, the experience, is not equal to the sum of the stimuli. The gestalt school has continued to oppose atomism and elementarism in psychological research, especially in the areas of sensation and learning. (See *Ganzheit*.)

In Russia, Pavlov (q.v.) (1849–1936) followed Sechenov's work in "reflexology." His work on the conditioned reflex has given many basic rules about the nature of learning, especially those which pertain to time relationships, generalization, discrimination, extinction, reward and punishment, etc., during the process of association between stimuli and responses.

Certain psychological schools and systems which evolved around the turn of the century differed not only in methodology, but about the purpose of psychology itself. Influenced by the writings of William James (q.v.) (1842–1910), psychology in America became "functionalistic." Its research method as well as its purpose became broader. Data from animals, children, and mental patients were admitted for research, and psychologists began to make practical recommendations for child care, education, industry, and living systems in general.

John B. Watson (q.v.) (1878–1958), the behaviorist, used the Pavlovian method of conditioning to show that certain fears and desires of human infants can be conditioned by direct or indirect associations with physical pain or pleasures. Watson published experimental findings as well as much practical advice on child care (Watson, 1919, 1928). (See *Behaviorism*.)

There were other applied systems of psychology which contributed to its great diversification. The historical roots of Freud's psychoanalysis (q.v.) can be found in Greek literature, and in hypnosis and psychopathology (q.v.). Freud's practical task, the cure of neurotic and psychotic patients, produced his theories about the content and the functions of the "unconscious" (q.v.) mind.

Mental testing (q.v.), a psychological area of the most widespread and practical influence, began with the work of Francis Galton (q.v.) (1869), who tabulated the accomplishments of famous men and their offspring. The useful IQ test was developed by Binet (q.v.) & Simon (1905) to provide the Paris Schools Commission with an instrument which could predict whether or not a pupil would benefit from public instruction. In spite of revisions and modifications, the IQ tests, as used today, are essentially like the original ones designed by Binet & Simon.

Applied areas such as conditioning, psychoanalysis, and mental testing have provided, perhaps as by-products, many psychological theories. In some areas, the theories may have overshadowed experimental verification. Some psychologists feel that their science has been "oversold to an overwilling public" (Miller, 1962, p. 4).

10. *Approaches*. Three major historical works, by E. G. Boring, Gardner Murphy, and W. B. Pillsbury respectively, were published in 1929. Boring's book has been the most systematic and influential. Several historical writers (Watson, 1968; Miller, 1962) have dedicated subsequent books to Boring. Boring's approach to history was the description of an individual's accomplishment in relation to the "*Zeitgeist*." Other

texts by R. S. Woodworth (1931), Edna Heidbreder (1933) and J. C. Flugel (1933) followed soon. They described the history of psychology chronologically through the development of psychological schools and systems. More recent chronological approaches are those of Mueller (1960) and Kantor (1963).

There are also biographical, autobiographical or "great men" approaches, such as the works of Pillsbury (1929), Murchison (1930), Garrett (1951) and Watson (1968). A different approach is the doxographic or problem approach, where the histories of a number of basic and recurring problems such as body—soul, consciousness, association, intelligence, and soon, are separately discussed. Works representing this type of approach have been written by Spearman (1937), v. Schiller (1948), Pongratz (1967), and others.

Esper (1964) presents a history guided by a biophysiological theme. Histories from geographical and/or ideological viewpoints have also been written. Hearnshaw (1964) described the history of British psychology, and Roback (1964) the history of American psychology. Brožek (1969) reviewed the work of Petrovskii (1967) which centers upon the theme of the fundamental reconstruction of Russian psychology on a Marxist-Leninist basis; and that of Yaroshevskii (1966), which discusses the birth of psychological thought in Egypt, China, and India, and—in the Marxist spirit—views psychology as having developed from the practical needs of society. A useful bibliography for all major works on the history of psychology published after 1900 is given by Misiak & Sexton (1966, pp. 469-70).

11. *Past, present and future.* More than half a century ago, in his first sentence of his *Abriss der Psychologie*, Ebbinghaus (1908) said that psychology had a long past but only a short history. By "long past" he meant philosophy, by "short history," the experimental method. Much of psychology's history has been written in retrospect. In many instances the writers of psychological ideas did not show historical continuity. Esper (1964, p. 176) points out that associationism, for instance, was first discussed by Plato, later by Aristotle, millennia later by Hobbes in 1650, and again in 1695 by Locke, who thought that the principles of association had not been "hitherto considered." Esper also compares passages from the writings of William James (1890) and Hull (1930) with passages from Aristotle's *On Memory and Reminiscence* and finds many new terms, but few new ideas. He believes that psychology has led other sciences in its neglect of history.

At present the history of psychology seems no longer neglected. In the sixties there has been much renewed interest in its teaching and research. In France a history course has been included in the basic psychology curriculum. Miller (1962) has written a text to teach introductory psychology through a historical theme, and Lyman (1970) has reported on the success of such an approach. The following events have strengthened the history of psychology on the American scene:

The *Archives of the History of American Psychology* were established at the University of Akron (Ohio) in 1961 under the directorship of J. A. Poppletsone. The first volume of the *Journal of the History of the behavioral Sciences* appeared in Jan. 1965 under the editorship of R. I. Watson. The Division of the History of Psychology was established as the 26th division of the American Psychological Association in 1966. The first Summer Institute in the Teaching of the History of Psychology was held at the University of New Hampshire under the directorship of Josef Brožek in 1968. The first meeting of the International Society for the History of the Behavioral and Social Sciences (ISHOBSS) founded by Julian Jaynes was held at Princeton University in May 1969.

Research continues and certain parts of the history of psychology are still being written. For instance, Mountjoy *et al.* (1969) have recently described the falcon training techniques used by Frederick II (1194–1250). They found some striking similarities between medieval falconry and contemporary operant animal psychology.

Psychology has broadened in scope and method. Future accounts will probably include more of the histories of other disciplines, such as anthropology, chemistry, mathematics, medicine, and sociology. This diversification will make the future history of psychology more difficult, but also more obviously necessary, since the history may become the only meaningful link between the various divisions, and the basis for evaluating the many specialties which will arise.

Bibliography: Binet, A. & Simon, T.: Méthodes nouvelles pour le diagnostic du niveau intellectuel des anormaux. Année Psychologique, 1905, *11*, 191–244. Boring, E. G.: A history of experimental psychology. New York, [2]1950. Boring, Mollie D. & Boring, E. G.: Masters and pupils among the American psychologists. American Journal of Psychology, 1948, *61*, 527–34. Brozek, J.: Soviet contributions to history. Contemporary Psychology, 1969, *XIV* (8), 432–4. Diels, H.: Fragmente der Vorsokratiker (W. Krantz, Ed.). Berlin, [5]1934–1938. Donders, F. C.: Die Schnelligkeit psychischer Processe. Archiv. Anatomie & Physiologie, 1862, 657–81. Ebbinghaus, H.: Abriss der Psychologie. Leipzig, 1908. Esper, E. A.: A history of psychology. Philadelphia, 1964. Flugel, J. C.: A hundred years of psychology. London, 1933. Garrett, H. E.: Great experiments in psychology. New York, [3]1951. Hearnshaw, L. S.: A short history of British psychology, 1840–1940. New York, 1964. Heidbreder, Edna: Seven psychologies. New York, 1933. Kantor, J. R.: The scientific evolution of psychology. Vol. 1. Chicago & Ohio, 1963. Keller, F. S.: The definition of psychology. New York, 1937. Lyman, B.: Performance of introductory psychology students in an historical foundations course. J. Hist. Behav. Sci., 1970, *6*, (4), 354–7. Miller, G. A.: Psychology: the science of mental life. New York, 1962. Misiak, H. & Sexton, V.: History of psychology: an overview. New York, 1966. Mountjoy, P. T., Bos, J. H., Duncan, M. O. & Verplank, R. B.: Falconry: neglected aspect of the history of psychology. J. Hist. Behav. Sci., 1969, *5* (1), 59–67. Mueller, F. L.: Histoire de la psychologie de l'antiquité à nos jours. Paris, 1960. Murchison, C. (Ed.): A history of psychology in autobiography. 3 vols. Worcester, Mass., 1930–1936. Murphy, G.: An historical introduction to modern psychology. New York, 1929. Petrovskii, A.: Istoriya sovetskoi psikhologii. Moscow, 1967. Pillsbury, W. B.: The history of psychology. New York, 1929. Pongratz, L. J.: Problemgeschichte der Psychologie. Berne, 1967. Roback, A. A.: A history of American psychology (Rev. ed.). New York, 1964. Schiller, P. v.: Aufgabe der Psychologie. Eine Geschichte ihrer Probleme. Vienna, 1948. Sechenov, I. M.: Reflexes of the brain. Meditsinski Vestnik (Nos. 47 & 48) 1863. (English ed.: Cambridge, Mass., 1965.) Spearman, C.: Psychology down the ages, 2 vols. London, 1937. Watson, J. B.: Psychology from the standpoint of a behaviorist. Philadelphia, 1919. Id.: Psychological care of infant and child. New York, 1928. Watson, R. I.: The great psychologists from Aristotle to Freud. Philadelphia, [2]1968. Wesley, F.: Master and pupils among the German psychologists. J. Hist. Behav. Sci., 1965, *1* (3), 252–8. Woodworth, R. S.: Contemporary schools of psychology. New York, 1931. Yaroshevskii, M. G.: Istoriya psikhologii. Moscow, 1966.   *F. Wesley*

II. *Contemporary psychology*. A study of the history of contemporary psychology shows one significant feature, namely the gradual break-up of the major systems and schools such as gestalt psychology (see *Ganzheit*), behaviorism (q.v.), and, to a much lesser extent, psychoanalysis (q.v.). S. Koch, the editor of *Psychology: A Study of a Science*, noted (1959): ". . . a far more open and liberated conception of the task of psychology, the role of its investigators and systematists, than we have enjoyed in recent history." (See also the general survey of contemporary psychology in *Handbuch der Psychologie*, 1959–70.)

If we inquire more specifically into the nature of this "open and liberated conception", we see with reference to the basic assumptions and positions of psychology, as Marx observed (1963), a greatly increased interest in positivist and empirical science. As regards methods, we find that they are used eclectically and pragmatically, substantial progress having been achieved by more advanced methods of data acquisition and processing (e.g. electronic test apparatus, use of computers). The conventional areas of research in psychology are becoming more and more narrowly circumscribed, e.g. the role of motivation psychology in perception and learning. At the same time, links with neighboring disciplines such as physiology and sociology are becoming increasingly complex. New applications of psychology result from technological projects (e.g. space travel) and the more complex demands of modern social life.

While noting the growing objective and methodological diversity of psychology, the question of its theoretical unity must not be overlooked; indeed it must be stressed, as Foppa has recently suggested (1970), if psychology is to be brought closer to the aim of becoming a science of experience.

The above observations are concerned primarily with psychological research; however, it is also desirable to consider psychology as a theory and profession. As regards psychology as a theory, it has come to acquire a dual role through progressive developments in the universities: on the one hand its form and content are being questioned like other university disciplines while on the other it is called upon to remedy this unsatisfactory state of affairs. In this practical context, psychology seems not so much to lack the necessary means, when we consider the achievements of ability diagnosis, intelligence and creativity research, learning psychology (e.g. programmed learning), socio-dynamics, counseling and psychotherapy, as the ability to use the available means in an organized manner in a given practical problem situation. As regards psychology as a profession, it has taken over a wide range of social functions in the USA and become firmly established in these areas (the American Psychological Association has more than 26,000 members in some thirty sections). Professional representation in other countries is far less developed; Britain, Germany and Japan are among the few countries which approach the American example.

Bibliography: Foppa, K.: Über die Angemessenheit psychologische Beobachtungsweisen. Schweiz. Z. Psychol., 1970, 29, 34–40. Gottschaldt, K., Lersch, Ph., Sander, F. & Thomae, H. (Eds.): Handbuch der Psychologie, 12 vols. Göttingen, 1959–70. Koch, S. (Ed.): Psychology: a study of a science, 6 vols. (Vol. 7 in preparation). New York, 1959. Marx, M. H. (Ed.): Theories in contemporary psychology. New York, 1963.   E. G. Wehner

Hit. In parapsychology: a trial in which the call (q.v.) matches the target (q.v.). Every trial is either a "hit" or a "miss". Displaced hit = trial on which the call matches the target intended for a different trial either earlier than the given trial (= backward or negative displacement) or later (= forward or positive displacement). Cf. retrocognition (q.v.) and precognition. (q.v.)   J.B.

Höfler's illusion. This illusion demonstrates the distortion induced in the perception of

straight lines if they cross a field of radiating lines, and is thus in principle identical to Hering's illusion. (q.v.)   C.D.F.

Holism. J. C. Smuts' theory that whole entities (and, above all, living beings) have specific characteristics which differ from those of their individual parts (entelechy). Holism is an integral part of biological research associated with mutationism (H. de Vries) which considers evolution as a consequence of intermittent variation that can be traced back to sudden restructuring. Against this background, the cause of evolution is to be found in internal characteristics of the organism interpreted as a structure, and in an organizational principle inherent in living matter (by comparison with chemical and physical properties). A correlation can be established between these theoretical notions and the concepts of gestalt psychology. See Ganzheit.

Bibliography: Smuts, J. C.: Holism and evolution. London, 1926.   M.J.B.

Holmgren test. A method of determining anomalies in color vision by classifying threads of colored wool.   G.Ka.

Homeostasis. The term homeostasis was used by the American physiologist Cannon (1932) to characterize the totality of effects responsible for maintaining a certain (relative) physiological constancy (e.g. body temperature, blood sugar). Cannon made a distinction between different hierarchical, homeostatic levels: reflex and instinctive behavior, acquired habits and adaptations, and willed actions, which serve the self-regulating system intent upon maintaining a "fluid" equilibrium (Bertalanffy, 1968). This extension of the concept made it possible to move forward from a study of organic need (deviation of an actual physiological value from the reference, or desired, value) to experimental analysis of psychological requirements within the framework of a motivational and behavioral psychology.

In cybernetics, a distinction is made between two forms of homeostasis (Ashby, 1952). In the simpler case the organic system has control of regulation circuits. But there are also complex organic systems whose mechanisms allow a transition to be made from states within which the desired value can no longer be reached, to other states, until the stability of the corresponding physiological parameters can be assured again ("ultrastability"). A technical model of this form of homeostasis is provided by the *homeostat*, whose feedback systems can compensate any slight deviation of the actual from the desired values. See *Cybernetics; Feedback system; Machine learning*.

Bibliography: Apter, M. J.: Cybernetics and development. Oxford, 1966. Ashby, W. R.: Design for a brain. London, 1952. Bertalanffy, L. von: General system theory. New York, 1968. Cannon, W. B.: The wisdom of the body. New York, 1932, ²1939.   D.Vo.

Homoeroticism. Erotic interest in members of one's own sex. Usually taken as being more general than *homosexuality*.   G.D.W.

Homogeneity; homogeneity index. Similarity. The term is used in psychology primarily to characterize samples of group members, and test methods. A test manifests homogeneity if it covers only a single, narrowly defined dimension of personality. The index of homogeneity (e.g. Loevinger's homogeneity index, 1947) determines this factor quantitatively on the lines of a correlation coefficient (q.v.).

Bibliography: Loevinger, J.: A systematic approach to the construction and evaluation of tests of ability. Psychol. Monogr., 1947, 64, 285.   P.S.

Homogeneous. The term has the same meaning in statistics as in general usage. If two sample distributions have roughly similar statistics (originating from the same population) they are considered to be "homogeneous" (e.g. with reference to the mean values of their variance).

In test theory (q.v.), test problems in a sub-test are described as homogeneous if they have (*a*) a high degree of correlation (intercorrelation) in relation to items of other sub-tests and/or (*b*) retain their relative position with reference to the other items in terms of probable resolution on confrontation with varying degrees of intensity of a given feature (gradual differences).   W.H.B.

Homogeneous grouping. See *Ability grouping*.

Homogeneous variance. The term is used when samples originate from the same basic group. In other cases heterogeneous variance is said to occur. Homogeneous variance is assumed in using certain parametric test methods (e.g. analysis of variance).   W.H.B.

Homology. Behavior patterns can be homologized in the same way as organs, i.e. they may be derived from common basic forms (K. Lorenz). A. Remane has compiled the homology criteria for morphological structures. According to G. P. Baerends, such behavioral elements are homologous if they have the *same neuromuscular pattern*, even if the motivation superimposed on them has changed. Behavior patterns are dependent on time, and as such are certainly the more homologous (identical) the more special features they have in common (criterion of special quality), and the more they accord in their sequence of action (criterion of position in the structural system). A distinction must be made between hereditary homology and traditional homology (Wickler, 1967).

Bibliography: Lorenz, K.: Studies in animal and human behaviour, vol. 2. London, 1971. Wickler, W.: Vergleichende Verhaltensforschung und Phylogenetik. In: Heberer, G. (Ed.): Die Evolution der Organismen, 1967, *1*, 420–508.　　　　　　　　*K.Fi.*

Homophony, mnemic. "Consonance." A term introduced by Semon (1908): *mnemic* excitation (memory) and *actual* excitation (sensation) coincide. Recognition and discrimination occur as a parallel response.

Bibliography: Semon, R.: Die Mneme als erhaltendes Prinzip im Wechsel des organischen Geschehens. Leipzig, ²1908.　　　　　　　　*H.W.*

Homoscedasticity. The equality of sample variability. Equal variability is a prerequisite of *t* tests (q.v.) for homogeneous variance, and of analyses of variance (see *Variance, analysis of*).　　　　　*D.W.E.*

Homosensorial reproduction. A term proposed by Ziehen to describe reproduction from the same sensory area as that which originally received the material, as opposed to heterosensorial (q.v.), reproduction.　　*C.D.F.*

Homosexuality. Sexual attraction by and sexual contact with persons of the same sex; in the narrower sense: continuous, preferred sexual attraction by such persons ("genuine homosexuality").

Attitude to homosexuality. It is socially rejected in Western societies, but for the most part accepted in tribal cultures with no written codes of conduct (64% according to Ford & Beach, 1952); homosexuality among adult males is punishable today only in a minority of countries, primarily for ideological reasons. In international, scientific discussions, proponents of the acceptance of adult homosexuality have long been in a clear majority.

Incidence. In the USA, about 4% of adult white males have *only* homosexual contacts; after puberty about 37% had at least one homosexual experience leading to orgasm. The incidence was much rarer among women (Kinsey, 1948). Temporary homosexual contacts are widespread among young males (developmental or occasional homosexuality). As yet there is no empirical evidence of an increase in homosexuality in recent decades (cf. Kinsey).

Educational and social background. Studies conducted up to now in the USA, Czechoslovakia and West Germany show a concentration of male homosexuality in the middle to upper middle social and educational stratum; in regard to socio-economic level, the lower social stratum dominates in the USA, and the middle social stratum in Europe (Giese, 1967).

Psychological–psychopathological aspects. While some studies of homosexual males revealed no neurotic symptoms (Hooker, 1957; Dean & Richardson, 1964), others have recorded slight or considerable neurotic reactions in the form of schizoid and psychasthenic character traits, mistrustful attitudes, hypochondriac, depressive and hysterical reactions, as well as approximations to neurotic test profiles in the sense of extremely labile, sensitive, dependent and anxious and uncertain (Doidge & Holtzmann, 1960; R. B. Cattell, 1962; Morony, 1962). In many homosexual groups, in particular of intelligent and "bisexual" subjects, there is no striking frequency of neurotic maladjustment (summary: Schmidt, 1968).

Social and psychological aspects. Only a minority (less than 5%) of homosexuals identify themselves with the disagreeable impression held by the general public of the male homosexual (soft, impulsive, weak, emotional, modern, light, unbalanced, unsympathetic, sick, confused, disgusting). The majority have a positive view of their own character which differs from the heterosexual male's idea of himself (Schmidt, 1967; Sigusch, 1967); although these findings are not based on a representative study of male homosexuals, they suggest that the identity and self-acceptance of many male homosexuals are less disturbed than might be expected in view of the strong prejudices held by the public at large.

Research into causes. The causes of homosexuality are still open to question. At present there are three theories concerning the origins of homosexuality. (*a*) Biologically oriented theory: homosexuality is dependent on biological factors which are not influenced by experience. (*b*) Psycho-socially oriented theory: homosexuality is conditioned by the environment, i.e. dependent on experience, and acquired (psychoanalytical theory and learning theory); (*c*) Convergence theory: homosexuality stems from a biological (learning) disposition; its occurrence in an individual is, however, dependent on environmental influences (summary: Freund, 1960).

Therapy. Many modern theorists believe that homosexuality is a variant of normal sexuality which can be treated by helping the homosexual to accept his own condition and not by attempting to convert him to heterosexual forms of conduct. On the other hand, when a homosexual wishes to change the direction of his attachment, those who consider it to be a parasympathetic response which is the chance product of conditioning, would recommend conditioning techniques that teach the homosexual to associate members of his own sex with unpleasant rather than pleasant erotic sensations. See *Aversion therapy; Behavior therapy; Sexuality.*

Bibliography: Feldman, M. P. & McCulloch, M. J.: The application of anticipatory avoidance learning to the treatment of homosexuality. Behav. Res. and Ther., 1965, *2*, 165–83. Ford, C. S. & Beach, F. A.: Patterns of sexual behaviour. London, 1952. Freund, K.: Some problems in the treatment of homosexuality. In: Eysenck, H. J. (Ed.): Behaviour therapy and the neuroses. Oxford, 1960. Giese, G. (Ed.): Homosexualität. Hamburg, 1967. Kinsey, A. C. *et al.*: Sexual behavior in the human male. Philadelphia & London, 1948. Max, L.: Breaking a homosexual fixation by the conditioned reflex technique. Psychol. Bull., 1935, *32*, 734. McCulloch, M. J., Feldman, M. P. & Pinshoff, J. M.: The application of anticipatory avoidance learning to the treatment of homosexuality. Behav. Res. and Ther., 1965, *3*, 21–43. McGuire, R. J., Carlisle, J. M. & Young, B. G.: Sexual deviations as conditioned behaviour: a hypothesis. Behav. Res. and Ther., 1965, *2*, 185–90. Schmidt, G.: Empirisch-psychologische Ergebnisse zur Sexualforschung. In: Giese, H. (Ed.): Die Sexualität des Menschen. Stuttgart, 1968. West, D. J.: Homosexuality. Harmondsworth, 1968.   *H.M.*

Honesty. The degree to which truth and respect (for others) determine behavior. Of particular practical importance in interpreting data furnished by questionnaires. In spite of largely positive correlations between various honesty tests, only Brogden has succeeded in isolating a honesty factor (q.v.) (characterized by behavior in which higher marks can be scored only by cheating, lying and exaggerating, as detected by the experimenter). See *Conscience; Child psychology; Traits.*

Bibliography: Brogden, H. E.: A factor analysis of forty character tests. Psychol. Mon., 1940, *234*, 35–55. Hartshorne, H. & May, M. A.: Studies in deceit. New York, 1928. Kay, W.: Moral development. London, 1968. Maller, J.: General and specific factors in character. J. soc. Psychol., 1934, *5*, 97–102. Piaget, J.: The moral judgement of the child. New York & London, 1960.   *M.A.*

Honi phenomenon. When a person is very well-known to S., he or she may fail to appear distorted in size or shape in the (Ames) distorted room (q.v.).

Horde. The primitive form of human association consisting, according to Charles Darwin and Freud, of an extended family dominated by a strong "father." Modern ethnographic field research makes it impossible to accept this reconstruction of a primitive society. Erect primates such as chimpanzees and gorillas live in loose groups (J. Goodall, G. Schaller, I. De Vore). This also applies to the remaining tribes of hunters and food gatherers, whose groups are never based on a strictly patriarchal structure and have a very flexible membership. The short life expectancy of paleolithic hunters (twenty to twenty-six years) in itself makes it difficult to believe that the younger generation was ever repressed by the "fathers." Recent field research into the various societies of Australian aborigines, which were considered for a long time to be examples of the "horde", has revealed a far more complex pattern.

Bibliography: De Vore, I. (Ed.): Primate behavior. New York, 1965. Lévi-Strauss, C.: The elementary structures of kinship. New York, 1967. Lee, R. B. & De Vore, I. (Eds.): Man the hunter. Chicago, 1968.

W.Sc.

Horizontal disparity. Because our eyes are about two inches apart, there are slight discrepancies in the two pictures of the world that they receive. These discrepancies can be used to calculate the distances of the various objects seen by the observer. The discrepancies can occur in any of the three spatial dimensions. There may be *height disparity, longitudinal disparity*, and *horizontal disparity*. Experiments have shown that horizontal disparities give rise to depth perception, and this, of course, is the normal disparity produced by the horizontal separation of our eyes. C.D.F.

Hormic psychology. In order to break with the exaggerated concern with cognitive phenomena, perceptions, ideas, cognitive development and thinking processes, many psychologists have concerned themselves since the turn of the century with research into the motivations and aims of the organism. W. McDougall (1871–1938), for example, stressed the dynamic aspects of behavior and studied the fundamental needs of the organism. This school of thought has aligned itself with psychoanalysis (q.v.) in its emphasis on the teleological aspects of all behavior(s).

Bibliography: McDougall, W.: The hormic psychology. In: Murchison, C. (Ed.): Psychologies of 1930. Worcester, Mass., 1930, 3–36. Id.: The energies of men. London, 1932.

P.M.

Hormones. 1. *Definition, formation and general effects.* Hormones are substances formed in the body in the internally secreting glands (*glandular hormones*) or in specific cell systems (*tissue* or *cell hormones*). The glandular hormones are discharged directly into the bloodstream by the corresponding gland systems, and take effect in certain organ systems or stimulate the secretion of other hormones in specific glands (see *Glandotropic hormones*). Tissue and cell hormones are generally active only at their points of formation; cell hormones are usually active only in the cell in which they are formed. Tissue or cell hormones, which are formed in the central nervous system or autonomic nervous system and act as transmitter substances (q.v.) to the synapses (q.v.) or effectors, are referred to as *neurohormones* (in particular, acetylcholine and noradrenalin, q.v.). This category is also often taken to include substances which play a decisive part in the metabolism of the nervous system (see *Biogenic amines*). The main hormone-producing glands are the anterior pituitary (adenohypophysis), posterior pituitary (neurohypophysis), pineal gland (epiphysis), thyroid gland, parathyroid gland, thymus, pancreas (Langerhans' islets), adrenal gland and adrenal cortex, ovaries and testes. The hypothalamus (q.v.) is another production center; it generates the releasing factors. These are substances whose nature has not been entirely explained; they are conveyed to the endocrine glands (q.v.) through the nerves. Several hormones are formed not only in special glands but in other systems, e.g. the catecholamines (q.v.). All known hormones are steroids, proteins or amino-acid derivatives. All the major hormones can be synthesized and introduced into the circulatory system or brain from outside (locally if necessary). Many hormones do not pass the blood–brain barrier (q.v.), or liver barrier. Hormones regulate the equilibrium of many different organ systems and perform the following main functions: (a) regulation of the metabolism (e.g. carbohydrate metabolism regulated by insulin); (b) morphogenesis, i.e. growth and maturation; (c) stimulation and depression of the CNS and ANS; (d) regulation of the inner environment for adaptation to external conditions.

2. *Effective mechanisms of hormones and interaction between different hormone systems.* Hormones have a profound influence on physiological and psychological processes. The biochemical mechanisms of these effects have been elucidated only in part. It is generally believed that hormones act locally and in the cells by altering cell permeability or by influencing the synthesis or breakdown of enzymes. Analysis of the biochemical mechanisms is made difficult by many methodological problems. Many theories are based solely on animal experiments (sometimes *in vitro*), and often merely on indirect manipulations in human beings (e.g. with pharmaceutical compounds), or on pathological symptoms occurring with under- or overproduction of specific hormones. The study of hormone effects is complicated by interaction between different hormone systems. The various hormones are sometimes *antagonistic* (e.g. adrenalin—insulin), *synergistic* (glucagon—adrenalin), or form simple or complex regulating circuits. The relation-

ship between the glandotropic hormones and the peripherally secreted hormones can be explained on the negative feedback principle. The secretion of glandotropic hormones leads to secretion of peripheral gland hormones, which in turn block the further formation of glandotropic hormones. Several hormone systems function (in part, at least) synergistically (e.g. adrenal gland—thyroid gland).

3. *Hormones and the nervous system.* Close, though as yet incompletely explained, relationships exist between the CNS, ANS and hormone systems, and form the object of neuroendocrinological research. So far only the relationship between the hypothalamus and pituitary has been explained in any detail: vasopressin (an antidiuretic) and oxytocin are formed in certain neuron(e)s of the hypothalamus, and conveyed by the nervous system to the neurohypophysis and thence into the bloodstream. Secretion of glandotropic hormones also probably occurs with the participation of the hypothalamus (releasing factors). Electrical stimulus tests in animals have shown that localized hypothalamic stimulation leads to the secretion of specific glandotropic hormones. In addition, stimulation and elimination tests show that the peripheral secretion of catecholamines is associated with nervous excitation in the reticulo–thalamic and limbic system (e.g. *nucleus amygdalae*). The previously held assumption that the hypothalamus and pituitary are the sole links between hormones and the nervous system is therefore false. The influence of cerebral electrical activity by the peripheral and centrally localized supply of hormones, or by hormonal disturbances, may be considered certain; the mechanism on which these changes are based is, however, still unexplained. The relationship between the nervous system and hormones is particularly clear in the effective action of the neurohormones, noradrenalin(e), dopamine, acetylcholine, etc. Neurohormones are liberated when the central neuron(e)s on the synapses are stimulated (see

The most important hormones, their functions, associated disorders, and some psychologically significant findings derived from healthy individuals.

Produced by		Hormone	Most important functions	(a) Psychol. & physiol. effects of low doses administered *exogenously* to healthy Ss. (b) Change in hormone activity in healthy Ss under stimulus variation
Anterior pituitary		Growth hormone (somatotropic hormone = STH = somatotropine)	Promotion of growth, protein synthesis and fat oxidation (together with testosterone, thyroid gland hormones, insulin), RNA synthesis	(a) increased activity (?) (b) increased production in hypoglycemia, muscular effort
		Thyrotropic hormone (= TSH = thyrotropin(e))	Growth of thyroid gland, promotion of biosynthesis and stimulation of thyroid gland hormone secretion	
	Glandotropic hormones	Adrenocorticotropic hormone (= ACTH = corticotropin(e))	Stimulation of production of cortical hormones in the adrenal cortex (exception, e.g., aldosterone)	(a) euphoric reactions (?) (b) increased release under all forms of trauma (stress) ("adaptation hormone")
		Gonadotropic hormones (= gonadotropins: (a) follicle stimulating hormone (= FSH)	Growth and maturation of the follicle, estrogen formation; in the male: promotion of spermatogenesis	
		(b) luteinizing hormone (= LH = interstitial cell stimulating hormone = ICSH)	Ovulation. Induction of follicular development and corpus luteum formation, stimulation of estrogen formation. In male: formation of testosterone, potentiation of effect of FSH	
		Luteotropic hormone (= LTH = prolactin)	Increases progesterone formation in corpus luteum; effect on lactation; shares in initiation of breeding behavior	
Posterior pituitary		Oxytocin	Contractions of uterus (induction of labor), lactation (release of milk in response to sucking)	(a) decreased blood pressure, contraction of uterus
		Antidiuretic hormone = ADH = vasopressin	Antidiuresis, neurohormone; assists release of ACTH	(a) increased blood pressure, decreased diuresis (b) increased production under stress

Gland		Hormone	Main function	Psychological / other effects
Intermediate (?) pituitary lobe		Melanotropin (melanocyte-stimulating hormone = MSH)	Skin pigmentation, assists regulation of dark adaptation of eye	(a) Increased skin pigmentation
Thyroid gland	Thyroid gland hormones	Thyroid gland hormones: triiodothyronine, tetraiodothyronine (= thyroxin)	Promotion of oxydative processes; assistance in regulation of protein synthesis, and in thermoregulation	(a) subjective and objective activation, excitation (b) increased secretion under stress, cold stimuli
		Thyrocalcitonin (calcitonin)	Lowers blood calcium (antagonizes parathormone = parathyroid hormone)	
Parathyroid gland		Parathormone (PTH) (= para-thyroid hormone)	Raises blood calcium (antagonizes thyrocalcitonin)	
Pancreas (islands of Langerhans)		Insulin	Lowers blood sugar (antagonizes adrenalin) by conversion into glycogen, influences protein, fat and carbohydrate metabolism, and hence growth	(a) tiredness, dizziness, hunger, affects performance
		Glucagon	Raises blood sugar	(a) reduces hunger
Sex glands; testes	Sex gland hormones	Sex gland hormones: androgens, e.g. testosterone	Promote maturation and growth of primary and secondary sexual characteristics; promotion of general growth synergistically with growth hormone, insulin and thyroid gland hormones	(a) no specific psychol. effects in healthy Ss. Increased performance in exhausted Ss. (b) Reduced excretion in urine under stress
Ovaries		(a) Estrogens, e.g. estradiol, estrone, estriol	Promote maturation and growth of primary and secondary sexual characteristics in puberty; induction of menopause, regulation of cycle. Promotion of general growth	(a) no specific psychol. effects in healthy women, increased performance in exhausted women
		(b) Gestogens, e.g. progesterone (progestins)	Preparation for and maintenance of pregnancy; together with estrogenic regulation of cycle	(a) impaired performance, subjective de-activation; reduced noradrenalin in CNS
Placenta		Choriongonadotropin (human chorionic gonadotropin = HCG)	Gonadotropic hormone, formed only during pregnancy. Assists effect of LH	

Produced by		Hormone	Most important functions	
Adrenal medulla	Catecholamines	Adrenalin (epinephrin)	As antagonist of insulin, releases glycogen (blood sugar). "Ergotropic" regulation of organism	(a) with small amounts: non-specific excitation (b) increased excretion under psychol. stress (anxiety)
		Noradrenalin (norepinephrin)	Ergotropic regulation of organism	(a) administration of small amounts has slight or no psychol. effects (b) increased excretion under physical stress
Adrenal cortex *Zona fasciculata*	Corticoids (corticosteroids)	(a) Glucocorticoids, e.g. cortisol (hydrocortisone), cortisone, corticosterone	Regulation of carbohydrate content	(a) improvement of mood (?) (b) increased excretion under physical and psychol. stress
Zona glomerulosa		(b) Mineralocorticoids, e.g. aldosterone, 11-desoxycorticosterone	Regulation of sodium-potassium content	(a) increased blood pressure, excitation (b) increased excretion under stress
Zona reticularis		(c) Androgenic cortical hormones, e.g. androsterone, androstenedione,	Synergistic effect with male sex gland hormones	As for androgens
Central nervous system and vegetative nervous system (ANS)	Neurohormones or tissue hormones	(a) Acetylcholine	Transmitter substance in ANS (preganglionic fibers of the sympathetic, pre- and post-ganglionic fibers of the parasympathetic) and CNS	
		(b) Serotonin	Transmitter substance in CNS ((transmitter of central parasympathetic system (?)). Regulation of mood; assists sleep-waking rhythm	(a) small quantities (precursor of S.); can be stimulating. Antagonizes LSD (b) reduction of S. concentration in brain during sleep
		(c) Tryptamine	Biogenic amine	(a) Sympathicomimetic effects, subjectively stimulating (b) Reduced excretion in urine in moody periods

The heading of the last column (appearing above Adrenalin row):

(a) Psychol. & physiol. effects of low doses administered *exogenously* to healthy Ss.
(b) Change in hormone activity in healthy Ss under stimulus variation

	Substance	Function	Effects
Neurohormones or tissue hormones	(d) γ-amino-butyric (= GABA)	Biogenic amine, derived from glutamic acid, inhibition of nervous excitation (?)	
	(e) Histamine	Transmitter substance in CNS, assists in genesis of pain	(a) drop in blood pressure, nausea, tiredness (b) liberation under anaphylactic shock and sensory pain
	(f) Tyramine	Biogenic amine	(a) sympathicomimetic effects, e.g. increased blood pressure, subjectively stimulating
	(g) Noradrenalin	Transmitter substance in CNS and ANS	(b) increased secretion under stress
	(h) Dopamine	Transmitter substance in CNS, synergistic to noradrenalin, intermediate substance in biosynthesis of noradrenalin	(b) increased excretion in urine with increased activation
	(i) Angiotensin II	Assists in blood pressure regulation; increases release of aldosterone	(a) rise in blood pressure—increased excretion of catecholamines in urine
	(j) Substance P	Transmitter substance in CNS (?), plays part in the conduction of sensory stimuli	
	(k) Melatonin	Antagonizes melanotropin (inhibition of pigmentation), assists in regulation of light-dependent day–night rhythm	(b) reduced production under permanent lighting (animal tests)
Hypothala-mus	"Releasing factors" (e.g. TRF = thyreotropic hormone releasing factor; LRF = luteotropic hormone releasing factor; CRF = corticotrophic hormone releasing factor)	Stimulate release of anterior pituitary hormones	

Nervous system). They transmit this stimulation to other neuron(e)s or effectors, and therefore act as transmitter substances. With the liberation of the neurohormones, characteristic changes occur in the electrical activity of the nerve cell. Therefore the nervous system can also be considered as a hormone system.

4. *Hormones and psychological disorders.* Over- or under-functioning of the peripheral hormone glands are linked almost without exception not only with physiological but with psychological disorders. On the other hand, it has not been possible to show clear endocrine variations for the majority of mental disorders on the basis of hormones excreted in the urine or blood. In general, endocrine disorders do not lead to specific psychological changes. Yet relatively clear psychological changes occur in the dimension of activation (see *Arousal*) in some endocrine disorders. Promising hypotheses and theories have been put forward in the past twenty years by neuroendocrinologists and psychopharmacologists. Even if the details remain largely obscure, it may be assumed that psychiatric disorders such as schizophrenia (q.v.) and depression (q.v.) are linked with disorders of the metabolism of biogenic amines (q.v.) or neurohormones. These metabolic disorders possibly result from incorrect "programming" in the genetic code. Recent research into depression, in particular, has shown that endogenous depressions result from disorders in the metabolism of endogenous catecholamines or indolamines (see *Serotonin*).

5. *Hormones and behavior.* It is not possible to conclude from the sometimes drastic behavioral changes which occur with hormonal disorders that there is a clear relationship between hormones and normal behavior. Two methods may be followed by the endocrinological psychologist: the study of behavioral changes after the administration of hormones, or the analysis of the occurrence of specific hormones in the urine or blood as a function of systematically varied stimuli.

Both methods are problematical for theoretical reasons. Hormones administered orally or intravenously do induce replicable behavior changes, but it is doubtful whether this can offer anything more than hypotheses on the relationship between natural hormones and behavior. The effective mechanisms and concentration conditions are probably not comparable for externally administered hormones and internal hormone formation. It must be remembered that most hormones introduced into the bloodstream do not pass the blood-brain barrier. Many of the observed behavioral changes probably result in part from peripheral changes. Studies using hormone secretion as a dependent variable have been conducted, in particular for the catecholamines and corticosteroids. Both hormone groups can be determined relatively easily in the urine or blood plasma with good reliability. Stress stimuli increase the excretion of catecholamines and corticosteroids. All other hormones have not yet been studied sufficiently for their significance as indicators of psychological states. Even where a correlation has been shown between hormones and behavior, generalization is difficult because only small proportions of the biologically active hormones can be detected with conventional methods, i.e. the quantity detected does not allow conclusions on the level active in the organism. In addition, the origin of the hormones detected cannot be explained with any certainty.

Bibliography: 1. *General introductions, articles and surveys:* Bajusz, E.: An introduction to clinical neuroendocrinology. Basle, 1967. **Bleuler, M.:** Endokrinologische Psychiatrie. Stuttgart, 1963. **Coppen, A.:** The biochemistry of affective disorders. Brit. J. Psychiatr., 1967, *113*, 1237–64. **Danowski, T. S.:** Clinical endrocrinology, Vols. 1–4. Baltimore, 1962. **Dorfman, R. I.:** Methods in hormone research, Vol. 2. New York, 1969. **Gabe, M.:** Neurosecretion. Oxford, 1969. **Hoagland, H.:** Hormones, brain function and behavior. New York, 1957, **Jores, A. & Nowakowski, N.:** Praktische Endokrinologie u. H. therapie nichtendokriner Erkrankungen. Stuttgart, 1968. **Martini, L. & Ganong, W. F. (Eds.):** Neuroendocrinology, Vols. 1 und 2. New York, 1966–67. **Pincus, G., Thiman, K. V. & Astwood, E. B. (Eds.):**

The hormones: physiology, chemistry, and applications. New York, 1964. **Reiss, M.**: Neuroendocrinology and psychiatry. Int. J. Neuropsychiatr., 1967, *3*, 441–63. **Scharrer, E. & Scharrer, B. V.**: Neuroendocrinology. Columbia, 1963. **Tausk, M.**: Pharmakologie der Hormone, Stuttgart, 1970. **Waelsch, H. & Weil-Malherbe, H.**: Neurochemistry and Psychiatry. In: **Gruhle, H. W.** *et al.* (Eds.): Psychiatrie der Gegenwart. Berlin, 1967. **Wigglesworth, V. B.**: Insect hormones. Edinburgh & London, 1971. **Williams, R. H.**: Textbook of endocrinology. Philadelphia, 1968. **Williams, R. J.**: Biochemical individuality. New York, 1956.

2. *Hormones and psychology:* **Bajusz, E.** (Ed.): Physiology and pathology of adaptation mechanisms. Oxford, 1969. **Bleuler, M.**: Psychische Funktionen u· vegetatives Nervensystem: Endokrine Wirkungen auf die Psyche. In: **Monnier** (Ed.): Physiologie und Pathologie des vegetativen Nervensystems, Vol. 2. Stuttgart, 1963. **Dewhurst, W. G.**: J. Psychosomatic Research, 1965, *9*, 115–27. **Eiduson, S.**, *et al.*: Biochemistry and behavior. Princeton, 1964. **Harlow, H. F. & Woolsey, C. N.**: Biological and biochemical bases of behavior. Madison, 1965. **Mandell, A. J. & Mandell, M. P.**: Psychochemical research in man. New York, 1969. **Meng, H.**: Psyche und Hormon. Berne, 1960.   *W. Janke*

Hormone types. Individuals featuring temperamental dispositions which occur as a function of the heightened or diminished effects of a hormone. Classification according to specific endocrine glands is possible only to a limited extent, e.g. in the case of the thyroid gland: hyperthyroidism = overexcitability; hypothyroidism = underexcitability. Otherwise the general term "endocrine psychosyndrome" is sometimes used.

Bibliography: **Kretschmer, E. & Kretschmer, W.**: Medizinische Psychologie. Stuttgart, ¹³1970. *W.K.*

Hormopathy. According to R. Brun, a primary motivational or emotive disturbance ("anergia" or "anhormia"), which may have essentially organic (endocrine or cerebral) origins or psychofunctional causes (actual neuroses [see *Actual anxiety*] and psychoneuroses, q.v.).   *W.Sc.*

Horner's law. J. F. Horner, a Zürich ophthalmologist (1831–86), first suggested that (most)

color vision defects, like the blood disease "hemophilia", are transmitted by inheritance through apparently unaffected female "carriers", i.e. from the affected man through his apparently healthy daughter to her male descendants.   *K.H.P.*

Horopter. The geometrical locus of those points in the field of vision which are reproduced on corresponding (identical) retinal points. A distinction is made between *geometrical* (derived) and *empirical* (calculated) horopters. If the correspondence is complete (both longitudinally and horizontally), there is a total, point, or full horopter. With a disparation in one of the main axes, there is a partial horopter: a longitudinal or vertical horopter; or, alternatively, a transverse or horizontal horopter.

The total geometrical horopter is the Vieth–Müller circle, which passes through the fixation point and the two optical points of rotation. The empirical total horopter differs substantially from the geometrical equivalent, and already becomes a straight line in the finite range; as the fixation distance increases, it becomes a line which is convex in relation to the observer.   *A.H.*

Horoscope. An astrological concept; in the static sense, a summary of the personality, based on specific constellations of the sun, moon and planets at the moment of birth; in the dynamic sense, the influence of changing constellations at specific moments in time ("astral influence"). The horoscope is based on the assumption that man and the earth have a central position in the universe. In spite of complete rejection by scientists, astrology still has many proponents, who believe in aspects or trends of destiny determined by cosmic factors. The fact that many horoscopes are accurate is due not to astrology but to the diagnostic intuition of some perceptive astrologers. J. P. Guilford found that there are about 10/13 personality factors which to some extent correspond to the signs of the zodiac. A horoscope may be interpreted as an attempt to apply long-confirmed experience to the problem of reducing the wide range of individual characteristics to a relatively small system of basic qualities (P. R. Hofstätter). A distinction is to be made between the astrology of horoscope-makers and the complex cosmosophies of such figures as Paracelsus.

Bibliography: Bender, H.: Astrologie und Aberglaube. Neue Wissenschaft, 1964, *12*. Gauquelin, M.: Der Einfluss der Gestirne und die Statistik. Z. fur Parapsychol. u. Grenzgebiete der Psychol., 1957/58, *1–3*. Jacobi, J. (Ed.): Paracelsus: selected writings. New York & London, 1951.   *E.U.*

Hospitalism. Generic term for all the psychological and physical disorders caused by a long stay in a hospital, clinic, or institution.

1. Hospitalism in the psychological sense is a syndrome of negative mental secondary effects which is particularly marked in small infants and other children who undergo institutional treatment for a long time or grow up in special homes. This is a progressive psychophysical process, intimately connected with development, which is explained by the failure to obtain satisfaction of the need for emotive exchange and human relations with a mother, the lack of emotional warmth and affective-emotional concern, and the absence of a family environment ("nest warmth"). Symptoms observed uniformly in the infant: tendency to cry, apathetic-depressive states, motor inhibitions or unrest, substitute satisfactions (spasmodic hand and head movements, thumb sucking, nail biting), retarded physical (standing, running) and mental development (speech, thought), and a poor state of health (susceptibility to infection, nutritional disorders) which may even lead to death. According to R. Spitz, hospitalized children in homes have a mortality rate of up to 40%. Irreversible damage occurs if the child is isolated from its mother for more than 5 months. R. Mathis has found that 75% of 1400 hospitalized children showed psychological or intellectual dis-

turbance. The predominant characteristics are low frustration tolerance, poor ability to establish contacts and low social adaptativeness, sometimes with aggressive reactions. In puberty, hospitalism may lead to regressive and criminal behavior. The first systematic descriptions of hospitalism were given by Pfaundler (1925) (cachectic treatment damage). Spitz's and Wolf's studies ("anaclitic depression") (1945–6) have become much better known; their observations were confirmed and expanded by Bowlby (1951) and Dührssen (1958). These studies show that for a normal psychophysical development, a good mother–child relationship is more important than good hygienic conditions (cf. Harlow's experiments with monkeys). Attempts are now made to counteract hospitalism by creating closer and more stable relationships between nurses and children (small groups), and by establishing children's villages in which the children live in house communities in small groups of different age and sex, and are cared for by permanent house mothers. Arrangements are now often made to allow the mother of a hospitalized baby or small child to stay with it in the hospital. The psychological neglect of children in the family (e.g. because both parents are working), or attendance at day nurseries has been seen to lead to a "family hospitalism". Even in adult patients, hospitalism may develop after long hospitalization: i.e. in the form of increased dependence and an unwillingness to make a quick recovery. See *Child psychology*.

2. In the narrower, medical sense, "hospitalism" is a term sometimes used to denote all the damage resulting from the frequent occurrence of infection during a stay in hospital: infection either by contagion (staff, inadequate hygiene) or by resistant bacteria and viruses.

Bibliography: Bowlby, J.: Maternal care and mental health. Bull. WHO, 1951, *3*, 355–533. Id.: Child care and the growth of love. Harmondsworth, 1965. Dührssen, A.: Heimkinder und Pflegekinder in ihrer Entwicklung. Göttingen, 1958. Harlow, H. F.: On the meaning of love. Amer. Psychologist, 1958, *13*, 673–85. Id. & Zimmermann, R. R.: Affectional

473   HULL, CLARK LEONARD

responses in the infant monkey. Science, 1959, *130*, 421–32. **Pfaundler, M. v.:** Klinik und Fürsorge. Gesundheitsfürsorge für das Kinderalter, 1925, *1*, 3. **Robertson, J.:** Young children in hospital. London, 1965. **Spitz, R.:** Hospitalism. Psychoanal. Stud. Child, 1945, *1*, 53. **Id. & Wolf, K. M.:** Anaclitic depression. Psychoanal. Stud. Child, 1946, *2*, 113–17.

F.-C. S.

House-Tree-Person Test (Nbb. HTP). A thematic projective test in which S. is asked to draw a house, a tree and a human being. Reliability values are satisfactory. The test is intended to supply information on intelligence, affectivity and degree of maturity, especially in children.

Bibliography: **Hammer, E. F.** (Ed.): The clinical application of projective drawings. Springfield, Ill., 1958.   *E.F-K.*

HPL. See *Human placental lactogen.*

H test. The H test is a distribution-free test method (significance test) for the simultaneous comparison of several groups of a classification variable with reference to the central tendency: i.e. differences between data are tested for statistical significance when the observations are ranked. A useful test when the conditions for a simple analysis of variance are not present. See *Variance, analysis of.*   *W.H.B.*

Hue. A basic property on the basis of which a color is given a specific name. Yellow, for example, is distinguished from orange, red and blue, and in general from any other shade or tint. The phenomenon is associated with narrow wavelength bands but can also be produced by fusing two or more variations of different wavelengths. The normal human eye can distinguish 200–250 hues.   *G.Ka.*

Hull, Clark Leonard. B. 25/5/1884 in Akron (N.Y.); d. 10/5/1952 in New Haven (Conn.).

Hull graduated from the University of Wisconsin in 1918. He was appointed Professor of psychology at Yale University in 1929. He concentrated initially on research into abilities (q.v.) and the development of statistical methods and psychological test methods; he then devoted ten years to the study of hypnosis (q.v.) and suggestibility, on which he published thirty-two articles and a book. Through his extensive studies of learning and motivation, and because of his systematic behavioral theory, which was unique in its stringent approach to the development of psychological theories, he became the most prominent representative of neo-behaviorism (see *Behaviorism*).

Systematic theory of behavior. Hull's theory of behavior can be considered as an S–O–R theory. In addition to the objectively measurable input (stimulus) and output (response) variable, he postulates a series of hypothetical parameters in the organism, known as intervening variables (q.v.), which establish the relationship between the stimulus and response values, and whose functional interrelationship and relationship with the observed parameters Hull explained in verbal terms, and generally also in equation form, through seventeen postulates and seventeen assumptions (corollaries) derived from the postulates (hypothetico–deductive framework).

Hull's central postulate of primary reinforcement (q.v.), which is closely related to E. L. Thorndike's law of effect, states that: "Whenever an effector activity (R) is closely associated with a stimulus afferent impulse or trace (S) and the conjunction is closely associated with the rapid diminution in the motivational stimulus (S_D or S_G), there will result an increment (Δ) to a tendency for that stimulus to evoke that response." Primary reinforcement is important in the learning process; it consists of a reduction of the motivational stimulus generated by a drive (q.v.).

Hull also refers to a secondary reinforcement which occurs when a previously neutral stimulus trace is frequently and regularly associated with the rapid diminution in the motivational stimulus (S_D) and in this way takes over the function of the reinforcing agent. But a stimulus-response association through contiguity under the influence of reinforcement always forms the qualitative prerequisite for the production and reinforcement of habits (see *Habit*).

Habit strength ($_sH_R$) (tendency of a stimulus trace to evoke an associated response) is dependent on the number of reinforcements, and increases as a rising, negatively accelerated function of this reinforced stimulus-response association. The probability of the occurrence of a response, however, depends not only on habit strength, but on additional, non-associative factors included, in addition to the habit potential ($_sH_R$), in the reaction potential ($_sE_R$). Whereas habit potential is an expression of associative intensity, the intensity of the reaction potential indicates the actual tendency of a stimulus to elicit a specific reaction. Reaction potential can be determined from the speed, intensity and resistance to extinction of the reaction, but cannot be identified with the reaction, since it may either be located below a threshold value (and therefore not lead to the reaction), or may interact with competing tendencies (inhibitory potential; see *Inhibition*) (and therefore lead only to an incomplete reaction).

Assuming that the conditions remain constant during the learning process and reaction formation, reaction potential is determined (*a*) by habit strength $_sH_R$; (*b*) by the drive D obtaining during the learning process; (*c*) by the magnitude of intensity, i.e. the stimulus value V; and (*d*) by the incentive motivation K of the reinforcement. The interaction of these factors is multiplicative: $_sE_R = {_sH_R} \times D \times V \times K$.

Reaction potential, on the other hand, is counteracted by the inhibitory potential ($_sI_R$), which is made up of the reactive (I_R) and conditioned inhibition ($_sI_R$) and, as a function of the resulting effective reaction potential ($_s\bar{E}_R = {_sE_R} - {_sI_R}$), may weaken or

neutralize the tendency to carry out specific action.

Main works: Aptitude testing. New York, 1928. Knowledge and purpose as habit mechanisms. Psychol. Rev., 1930, *37*, 511–25. Goal attraction and directing ideas conceived as habit phenomena. Psychol. Rev., 1931, *38*, 487–506. Hypnosis and suggestibility. New York, 1933. Mind, mechanism, and adaptive behavior. Psychol. Rev., *44*, 1–32. Mathematico-deductive theory of rote learning: a study in scientific methodology (with others). New Haven, 1940. Principles of behavior: an introduction to behavior theory. New York, 1943. Essentials of behavior. New Haven, 1951. Autobiography. In: Boring E. G., *et al.* (Eds.): A history of psychology in autobiography, Vol. 4. Worcester, Mass., 1952, 142–63. A behavior system: an introduction to behavior theory concerning the individual organism. New Haven, 1952.

Bibliography: Koch, S.: Clark L. Hull. In: Estes, W. K., *et al.* (Eds.): Modern learning theory: a critical analysis of five examples. New York, 1954, 1–176. Spence, K. W.: Clark Leonard Hull: 1884–1952. Amer. J. Psychol., 1952, *65*, 639–46.

                                                        W.W.

Hull's law. The central proposition in Clark L. Hull's theory of learning, that habit strength accumulates as a direct function of the number of reinforced stimulus-response occurrences.   *G.D.W.*

Human engineering. A branch of engineering science and applied psychology. Special emphasis is placed on ergonomics (q.v.) and industrial science, and above all on occupational psychology (q.v.) and industrial psychology (q.v.). Such problems as optimal working conditions, organization of men and machines, operator skills, and so on, are to the fore. See *Practice; Motor skills; Instructional technology.*   *G.R.W.M.*

Human ethology is the study of the phylogenetic (innate) and ontogenetic (acquired) components of human behavior in natural situations. Particularly valuable information can be obtained from the observation (e.g. by filming) of behavioral development in infants and children born deaf and blind, etc. See *Ethology; Comparative psychology.*

Bibliography: Lorenz, K.: Die angeborenen Formen möglicher Erfahrung. Z. Tierpsychol., 1943, 235–409. Prechtl, H. F. R.: Die Entwicklung der frühkindlichen Motorik, Inst. wiss. Film, Göttingen: Films Nos. C 651, C 652, C 653 (1955).   K.Fi.

Humanistic psychology. I. Humanistic psychology does not set itself up as a new school, still less as "a school to end schools". It does not deny the validity of any psychological work with sound credentials, in theory and method. It insists, however (and this is its distinctive feature), that a comprehensive psychology of man cannot be delimited by particular methods (experimental or statistical), any more than a cartographer can omit oceans or mountain. ranges merely because he cannot traverse the former or scale the latter.

While recognizing, on the basis of evolution, man's kinship with animals, humanistic psychology acknowledges man's essential properties: his subjectivity and selfhood; his sense of past and future which makes him at once a creature of history and a dreamer; and his universal tendency to categorize in the form of moral and other value judgments. If all this evades the method of the laboratory it nevertheless claims the utmost precision of analysis, which does justice to the *phenomena* as such. The humanistic psychologist feels that neo-positivist insistence on methodological rigor is open to suspicion, and that all too often it is indistinguishable from *rigor mortis.*

Finally, humanistic psychology asks for a reappraisal of the division of labor, as between the sciences and humanities. Such a reappraisal should serve to show that psychology can profit equally from its affiliation with history, literature, comparative religion

and the arts, and from its links with neurophysiology and computer science.

Bibliography: Cohen, J.: Humanistic psychology. London, 1958.   J. Cohen

II. Humanistic psychology is the name of a new school of psychology whose main founder was A. Maslow. In 1962 the American Association for Humanistic Psychology started with a nucleus of sponsors. A year before a *Journal of Humanistic Psychology* was edited by A. Sutich.

The main reasons for the initiating of what in a few years developed into a big movement, were originally purely scientific and theoretical. Those who joined in the foundation of what Maslow called the "third force" besides the then prevailing psychoanalysis and behaviorism, felt that none of these other schools did justice to the understanding of a healthily and creatively functioning person. They felt that such a person pursued goals and values not because of a need for "homeostasis", as the more recent psychoanalysis taught, but for the purpose of what Fromm and Horney called *self-realization,* or what K. Goldstein and A. Maslow called *self-actualization,* or C. Bühler called *self-fulfillment,* which she demonstrated in studies of courses of human life.

The school, which began with a small group of sponsors, developed and spread in a very short time to become a great movement. One reason was that Carl Rogers, one of the early sponsors, demonstrated the application of humanistic psychological ideas to *psychotherapy.* He showed a completely new type of relationship between therapist and patient, in which both related as persons, instead of one being an authority and the other a sick individual who had necessarily to transfer his early emotional conflicts with his parents, as psychoanalysis had taught. Of course, this problem is still partly in discussion, and there are different concepts and many experiments in which the handling of this relationship is developed. Rogers has also the historical merit of having insisted on making tape records of psychotherapy sessions which could be made available to other therapists for inspection, comparison with their own work, and other studies. Up to then, the psychoanalysts had handled the process of therapy like an occult science which only the initiated were allowed to know about.

The opening-up of the therapy procedure to those who wanted to study it undoubtedly had many undesirable side-effects in that unqualified or semi-qualified people tried to conduct the process, and some extremists went very far in what they allowed to happen. These procedures occurred mostly in *group therapies*, which, since their early beginnings with Slavson and Moreno, had developed into the biggest movement of our time. The author considers group therapy and the related *"sensitivity training"*, a group process in which people of all walks of life are assembled in groups learning to speak frankly with each other and trying to understand each other, one of the most hopeful cultural processes to take place in the present cultural crisis. Leading figures in the sensitivity training area are L. P. Bradford, J. Gibb, F. Massarik, and others who developed the procedure with industrialists, business men, administrators, educators and others.

This, as all that C. Rogers initiated, goes to show that psychotherapy is no longer considered exclusively or even primarily as a psychiatric procedure with the purpose of curing the mentally ill. Although a humanistic psychologist must be trained (and should be licensed by a supervising board) to treat neurotics, his main—and more frequent—task today is *educational* rather than curative. Together, the patient and therapist work on an understanding of themselves as *persons* and of *human life as a whole*.

Much work is just now being done in this area of educational psychotherapy. Important, however, is that humanistic psychology has gained a scientific foundation which *validates* its approach to the person as a whole, with more scientific reliability than previous psychologies were able to. A recent first international congress, in Amsterdam, was devoted to this double issue of humanistic psychology's offering a new scientific approach to the study of the person as a whole (Maslow, Rogers, C. Bühler), and help in the renewal of our Western civilization so that it offers a better self-understanding and mutual understanding of people.

Bibliography: Bühler, Charlotte & Massarik, F. (Eds.): The course of human life. A study of goals in the humanistic perspective. New York, 1968. Maslow, A. H.: Motivation and personality. New York, 1954. Id.: The psychology of science. A reconnaissance. Chicago, 1966. Rogers, C. R.: Client-centered therapy. Its current practice, implications and theory. Boston, 1951. *C. Bühler*

Humanity. Traditionally, this term denotes a concept which covers both the totality of all characteristics innate in man and those which distinguish him from other living beings. It is used in particular to denote a moral-ethical attitude which is made up of altruism, love for one's fellow men and human understanding; it is the opposite of coercion and brute force. Since the eighteenth century, it has come to designate the revolutionary ideal of a reconciled mankind—a standard for the development of moral and political life (Declaration of Human Rights). *A.T.*

Human management. See *Management; Manipulation.*

Human nature, understanding of. A pre-scientific form of psychodiagnosis (q.v.), i.e. one lacking in objectivity, reliability, validity, and proficient standards. In popular language, a person who "understands human nature" is considered able to sum up an individual's personality, with particular reference to specific features—often on the basis of a first impression (q.v.). Experience is thought to be important in this "intuitive" process. *W.L.*

Human placental lactogen (abb. HPL). A recently discovered extrahypophyseal gonadotropic hormone which is formed—like choriongonadotrophin(e) (q.v.)—in the placenta during pregnancy, and is similar in its effects to the hypophyseal gonadotropin: luteotropic hormone (LTH). In conjunction with other gonadotropins, HPL promotes the formation of hormones (estrogens and progesterone) in the *corpus luteum* of the ovaries and—like other placental gonadotropins—is most active in early pregnancy (second and third months). *H.M.*

Human relations. A term for interpersonal relations in work or industrial organizations. Human relations research was founded in the nineteen thirties by E. Mayo, who conducted experiments in the Hawthorne Works (USA) in the course of which informal (unplanned) structures were "discovered" in industrial concerns, and the significance of psychological and social factors (satisfaction, group standards) for productivity was shown for the first time. The human relations movement attempts to increase productivity by improving the working atmosphere; it exaggerates, however, the importance of informal structures and disregards the conflict of interests between employers and employees. See *Hawthorne experiments; Occupational psychology; Industrial psychology.* *C.B.*

Human rights. The inalienable fundamental rights of every human being: e.g. the rights to life, freedom and equality. *H.J.A.*

Humor. 1. It would not be too extreme to claim that before Freud a real interest in the phenomenon of humor and the use of the term "wit" were not met with in psychology. Before the publication of Freud's *Der Witz und seine Beziehung zum Unbewussten* (Vienna, 1905; Eng. trans., 1960), despite a few attempts to define the term (in particular,

those of T. Lipps and K. Fischer), it had no precise psychological connotation.

For Freud, everything that saves psychic or muscular effort is a source of pleasure. Pleasure *sui generis*, conditioned by a joke or witticism, corresponds to an economizing on mental effort. This saving is realized on two distinct levels: that of "matter" or background, and that of "form". In terms of "matter", the pleasure afforded by the joke corresponds to a saving of psychic effort resulting either from a moderation of the censorship exercised by reason on cognitive activity (when the adult becomes a "real child" once more, he plays quite freely with words and ideas without any concern for logical constraint), or from a moderation of moral censorship over our instincts (humor allows the satisfaction of a prohibited impulse). Another source of pleasure connected with the sense of humor and the exercise of wit is to be found at the formal level. Although accessory, this is by no means a negligible source, consisting as it does in (the study of) techniques for eliciting laughter or appreciation of humor. On the basis of a large number of famous jokes and witticisms, Freud provided a detailed list of various techniques: condensation (with or without substitute-formation), repeated use of the same verbal material, punning, logical inconsistency, representation by means of the contrary, unification, allusion, omission, etc. The only factor common to all these procedures is, according to Freud, a tendency to an economy of expenditure of semantic material.

Although interested mainly in *wit*, Freud in fact represents his theory in the form of the threefold complex of *wit* (jokes), the *comic*, and *humor*. This division relies on the different underlying genetic processes: "The pleasure of wit seems to me" to arise from "an economy of expenditure of inhibition; that of the comic from an economy of expenditure of representational thought; and that of humor from an economy of expenditure of feeling."

However, as far as the last two terms are concerned, no consensus of opinion is as yet available among psychologists on their precise denotations. For Freud, humor corresponds to the economy of expenditure of a painful emotion, and therefore constitutes a means of defense against pain. For Bergson, humor is defined in contradistinction to *irony*: I am humorous when I pretend to believe that things are not as they really are, but instead as they ought really to be. "Humor" is, of course, generally used in a less precise way, and as a global term, in English: i.e. something humorous is something in any way laughable or amusing.

Bergson defines the basis of the comic as arising from the contrast between the mechanical and the organic ("*le vivant*"); he believed that comedy "is not disinterested as genuine art is. By organizing laughter, comedy accepts social life as a natural environment, it even obeys an impulse of social life. And in this respect it turns back upon art, which is a breaking away from society and a return to pure nature." Despite Bergson's insistence that all comic incongruities are examples of mechanization, the word "comic" is still without any precise psychological connotation, and has a different signification for each author. Victoroff (1953) suggests that the comic should be defined in contradistinction to the *ridiculous*, or laughable: one may elicit laughter quite intentionally, or, on the contrary, involuntarily—even bringing it upon oneself. In the first case, the comic is in question, and in the second case the ridiculous (ridicule).

Bibliography: Bergler, E.: Laughter and the sense of humor. New York, 1956. Bergson, H.: Laughter: an essay on the meaning of the comic. London & New York, 1911. Eastman, M.: The sense of humor. New York & London, 1921. Id.: Enjoyment of laughter. New York, 1936. Freud, S.: Jokes and their relation to the unconscious. London, 1960. Victoroff, D.: Le rire et le risible: introduction à la psychosociologie du rire. Paris, 1953.

D. Victoroff

2. The concept of humor is derived from C. Galenus' theory of temperaments (tempera-

ment as a mixture of "humors") and is used today: (*a*) in the sense of a cheerful and comprehensive attitude to life or a basic mood and (*b*) as a generic term for verbal, graphic or pantomimic expressions designed to provoke mirth and laughter (sense of humor). Factor analyses of opinions regarding humorous material showed that the sense of humor consists of at least six factors which are partly correlated with personality traits. Associations of this kind form the basis of the IPAT Humor Test of Personality (R. B. Cattell). *D.B.*

3. A distinction is sometimes made between *personal* or *orectic* (affective, conative: e.g. sex) and *impersonal* or *cognitive* (formal) aspects of humor (e.g. Kambouropoulou, 1926, 1930). Williams (1945) and Eysenck (1947) found evidence of a correlation between extraversion and preferences for orectic humor, and between introversion and preferences for cognitive humor.

Bibliography: Eysenck, H. J.: Dimensions of personality. London, 1947. Guilford, J. P.: Personality. New York, 1959. Kambouropoulou, P.: Individual differences in the sense of humor. Amer. J. Psychol., 1926, 37, 288–97. Id.: Individual differences in the sense of humor and their relation to temperamental differences. Arch. Psychol., 1930, 121, 79. Williams, J. M.: An experimental and theoretical study of humour in children, unpubl. Ph.D. thesis. London, 1945.

Humphrey's paradox (syn. *Arpeggio paradox*). The tendency of organisms to react to specific categories of stimuli in an identical manner, even though the objective characteristics of the stimuli vary; or the tendency of individuals, who would otherwise react differently to a specific tone, to respond identically when that tone is produced not simultaneously but in sequence, e.g. in an arpeggio. See *Generalization; Stereotype.* *H. Ro.*

Hunger. Normally refers to the desire to eat (which may or may not be associated with food deprivation), but is also used in a metaphorical sense to refer to a craving for anything, e.g. sex or affection.

Hunger drive: a hypothetical state operationally defined in terms of food deprivation, which is found to give rise to increased general activity as well as specific food-seeking behavior. (See *Instinct*.)

Hunger pangs: unpleasant sensations in the stomach associated with the need for food, and believed to be associated with contractions of the stomach wall.

Hunger-strike: refusal to eat as a means of bringing political pressure to bear upon an authority, e.g. prisoners attempting to gain improved conditions.   *G.D.W.*

Husserl. See *Phenomenology.*

Hybridization. Crossing or interbreeding. In diploid (q.v.) organisms, a distinction can be made between the phenotype (q.v.) and genotype (q.v.). Individuals with pure heredity (homozygotes) have one identical allele on each (the maternal and paternal) side. Mixed hybrids (heterozygotes) differ in one gene (monohybrid), or in two (dihybrid), or three genes (trihybrid), etc. Depending on the phenotype, hybrids may be intermediate or dominant/recessive.   *K. Fi.*

Hydrazines. Amine oxidase inhibitors which over a period of a week or more have a stimulant effect on mood, which would seem to correspond to the MAO inhibiting effects of the substances. Some toxic side-effects reported. Hydrazines are quite successful with some depressions.

Bibliography: Garattini, S. & Dukes, M.: Antidepressant drugs. Amsterdam, 1967.

Hydrocephalus. An increase of cerebrospinal fluid (csf) within the skull, usually associated with an increase in pressure. It may result from an obstruction to the flow of csf within the ventricular system, or a decreased absorption of the fluid. When it occurs in children an increase in the size of the head may follow, but in the adult this cannot occur, so that neurological and mental symptoms develop as a result of intracranial pressure. In the past, mental deficiency was a common complication in untreated cases in children, although nowadays drainage operations are possible.   *D.E.*

Hydrocortisone (*Cortisol; 17-hydroxycorticosterone,* abb. *71-OHCS; Cortef; Cortril; Efcortesol;* etc.). The most important hormone (q.v.) in the adrenal cortex; belongs to the group of glucocorticoids. Hydrocortisone is very important in psychophysiological emotion research because it can be detected relatively easily and accurately (e.g. by chromatography) in the blood plasma and urine. Many studies in animals and in diseased and healthy testees have shown that all kinds of stress stimuli are associated with increased hormone secretion. Because of the high inter- and intra-individual variance, fairly large samples are often necessary to inform on significant effects. Adequate reliability can only be achieved if many factors are observed (e.g. time of day, age, sex, weight, nourishment, etc.). If these factors are taken into consideration, hydrocortisone is a sensitive indicator even for light and short-term stressors. The administration of hydrocortisone in physiological doses has only a slight effect, but experimentally induced emotions are heightened. The basal values of hydrocortisone secretion are relatively constant in a given individual. Correlation studies with personality traits show that male and anxious testees have higher values than female and non-anxious subjects. In depressive patients, hydrocortisone secretion increases with the severity of the disorder, but negative results have also been observed. See *Corticosteroids.*   *W.J.*

5-hydroxytryptamine. An abbreviation for the chemical composition of serotonin (q.v.).

5-hydroxytryptophan(e). The chemical precursor of serotonin (q.v.). The conversion of 5-hydroxytryptophane into serotonin in the organism takes place under the influence of the enzyme 5-hydroxytryptophane-decarboxylase. This conversion can be blocked by specific substances, such as P-chlorophenylalanine. 5-hydroxytryptophane, unlike serotonin, passes the blood-brain barrier (q.v.). It is therefore of considerable importance for experimental or therapeutic manipulation of the serotonin concentration in the brain. See *Biogenic amines*. *W.J.*

Hygiene, mental. See *Mental hygiene.*

Hypalgesia. Hypalgesia denotes a raising of the pain threshold. This phenomenon may be explained, e.g., by the degeneration of certain nerve fibers in the affected skin area. Once the raised threshold is exceeded, the pain experienced is often even greater than normal (hyperpathy). See *Pain*. *M.S.*

Hyperacusis. Abnormally raised sensitivity to loud sounds: may be due to paralysis of the stapes muscle, which should normally raise the base of the stapes slightly above the oval window of the cochlea on exposure to extreme sound energy (protective function). Hair cell damage at high intensities is sometimes accompanied by hyperacusis. *M.S.*

Hyperal(ges)ia. If the pain threshold is lowered, even light contact may be experienced as painful. In general, the damage is confined to a limited area and the pain is described as "burning". *M.S.*

Hyperbolic type. Ant. hypobolic type or litotes type (see *Speech types*). The hyberbolic type uses drastic and exaggerated language, while the litotes type tends to underemphasize. *W.K.*

Hyperemia. Excess of blood in some part of the body, due to reactive capillary dilatation under mechanical, thermal or chemical excitation, as part of an inflammation, or in a case of venous obstruction, etc. *E.D.*

Hyperesthesia. Increased cutaneous sensitivity due to peripheral or central changes. See *Hyperalgesia*. *M.S.*

Hyperesthetic type. An extreme variant of the schizothymic character: "fickle sensitivity . . . fanatic enthusiasm for nature and art (or) persons . . . easily influenced and hurt . . . reacts oversensitively to ideas with a strong emotional coloring, tends to stick to them vehemently and for a long time." Ant. *Anesthetic type*.

Bibliography: Kretschmer, E. & Kretschmer, W.: Medizinische Psychologie. Stuttgart, [13]1970. *W.K.*

Hyperfunction(ing). The overfunctioning of organs. Often pathological and referred to by specific medical terms. The commonest condition of this kind is a hyperfunctioning of the endocrine glands. The thyroid gland is responsible for Basedow's disease (q.v.) with accelerated metabolic processes, exophthalmus and nervousness, while the adrenal gland may cause the Cushing syndrome with the following symptoms: "moon face", facial reddening, striae (pregnancy marks) and blood pressure crises. The pituitary may cause acromegaly or gigantism. Treatment is generally only possible by partial destruction of the glandular tissue. *E.D.*

Hypergeometric distribution. A hypergeometric distribution of sample values for a discrete variable is obtained by extracting X_1 elements from a finite population *without* replacement. The probability (anticipated relative frequency) of a result of exactly X occurrences of a given alternative ("successes") in a population of N elements— including M "successes"—with a sample size of n, is obtained from:

$$p(x) = \frac{\binom{M}{x}\binom{N-M}{n-x}}{\binom{N}{n}}; \quad \text{for } x = 0, 1, \ldots N.$$

The hypergeometric distribution plays the same part in samples without replacement as the binomial distribution (q.v.) for samples with replacement. It has the mean value:

$$\mu = n \cdot \frac{M}{N},$$

and the standard deviation:

$$\sigma = \frac{n \cdot M(N-M)(N-n)}{N^2(N-1)}.$$

W.H.B.

Hypergonadism; hypogonadism. In general: over- (hyper-) or under- (hypo-) functioning of the male or female sex glands with various causes. Hypogonadism is far more frequent than hypergonadism (ratio 8:1). Hypergonadism occurs very rarely when the gonadotropins (extremely uncommon) or sex gland hormones are produced in excessive quantities because of a tumor, so that there is a strong development of the secondary sexual characteristics (this does not, however, include premature puberty = see *Pubertas praecox*).

Hypogonadism plays a much more important part in clinical practice, clinical psychology, and psychopathology. A distinction is made between two main groups according to the dominant effect:

1. *Primary, hypergonadotropic hypogonadism.* Primary failure of the terminal organ (testicles, ovaries) while the regulating organs (hypophysis, hypothalamus) remain intact; also excessive production of gonadotropic hormones because of impaired functioning of the sex glands. Causes: in both sexes, chromosomal anomalies are the principal cause. Main forms: (*a*) in the male: Klinefelter syndrome; other hereditary testicular malformation syndromes, e.g. Reifenstein and male Turner syndrome are relatively uncommon; (*b*) in the female the prototype is the Turner syndrome; (*c*) special case of failure to mature in persons with external female characteristics, but primarily male sex, and failure of testicles to descend: testicular feminization syndrome.

2. *Secondary, hypogonadotropic hypogonadism.* Diminished formation of gonadotropin caused by factors in the hypophysis (q.v.) or hypothalamus (q.v.) which results in failure of the sex gland functions or even to failure of these functions to develop. Much rarer than forms of primary gonadic hypofunction. Main forms: (*a*) idiopathic eunuchoidism = failure of FSH and ICSH formation, with the result that puberty does not occur even though the testicles are essentially intact; (*b*) fertile eunuchoidism (Pasqualini syndrome); probably isolated disturbance of ICSH production with intact FSH production; so that a eunuchoidal physique with infantile genitalia develops, while the testicles reach almost normal size with well-developed spermiogenesis; hypogenitalism without marked hypogonadism (a very rare condition); (*c*) pituitary dwarfism. In all these forms puberty fails to occur and—unless treated—the patient remains sexually infantile. In addition, there is a secondary form of hypogonadism which is not innate but is acquired during the course of life (=postpuberal hypogonadism) as a partial symptom of complete failure of pituitary functions, generally caused by tumors of the hypophysis.

Chronic failure to reach puberty is more common in men than women. The psychological problem consists essentially in the need as far as possible to avoid any discrepancy between chronological age and social maturity, in spite of biological and physical retardation (childishness and immature appearance). Clinical-psychological and sexual guidance—especially in cases of infertility—are urgent necessities in such cases.

Bibliography: Wilkins, L.: The diagnosis and treatment of endocrine disorders in childhood and adolescence. Springfield, Mass., 1965.   *H.M.*

Hyperkinesis. Abnormally excessive motility of limbs and parts of the body, caused by continuous (tonic) or intermittent (clonic) muscular contractions, which are sometimes painful; the contractions often take the form of cramp. They are due to pathological changes in the brain areas controlling movement: e.g. *nucleus niger, ruber* or the cerebellum (q.v.).   *E.D.*

Hypermetropia. Long sight. Incident light rays are reflected only behind the retina. (*a*) *Axial hypermetropia:* the bulbus is too short. (*b*) *Refractive hypermetropia:* refraction of the light rays is insufficient. The condition can be corrected by means of convex lenses.   *R.R.*

Hypermnesia. An unusually good memory (q.v.), often due to abnormal mental states of excessively acute awareness. In hypnosis (q.v.) the subject may often recall events which occurred in the distant past, but only to the extent of a heightening of the possibilities which are already present in the normal state. *Hypomnesia* = poor memory, impaired ability to recall events.   *H.-N.G.*

Hypermotility. Compulsive movement, motor unrest, or exaggerated mobility of the limbs and joints, e.g. in many forms of mental deficiency.   *E.D.*

Hyperopia. See *Hypermetropia.*

Hyperosmia. An extremely acute sense of smell, especially as a pathological heightening of sensitivity, e.g. in pregnancy, neurasthenia (q.v.), epilepsy (q.v.); generally due to a central cause; the mechanism is not, however, clear.   *K.H.P.*

Hyperplasia. An abnormal increase in the number of cells in organs or parts of the body, sometimes associated with hyperfunctioning (q.v.). Hyperplasia is sometimes pre-cancerous and is generally caused by excessive stress or strong stimuli.   *E.D.*

Hypertension. Abnormally high tension, generally used to denote high blood pressure. See *Hypertonicity.*   *E.D.*

Hyperthymia. A personality trait or type characterized by cheerfulness, high activity and industry. Distinguished from *hypomania* (q.v.) by a lack of social complications and of any necessity for medical or legal restraint. The opposite pole from *dysthymia* (q.v.); together they constitute the cyclothymic personality type, which changes from one state to the other. Manic depressive patients as a group have an excess of hyperthymic or cyclothymic personalities when assessed retrospectively. Prospective studies of hyperthymic personalities who develop the psychosis are not available, and there is no evidence of any alarming relationship.   *B.B.*

Hyperthyroidism. See *Basedow's disease.*

Hypertonicity (or *Hypertension,* q.v.). High blood pressure due to a variety of causes. A distinction is made between several forms of hypertonicity. Genuine red high pressure (red facial coloring) is based on constitutional factors with neural components. Pale renal high pressure (white facial coloring) is due to vascular contraction with hormonal causes, deriving mainly from kidney damage. Thyrotoxicosis, Cushing syndrome (hyperfunction of the adrenal cortex), or adrenogenic symptoms (overfunctioning of the adrenal medulla) are other possible causes. All forms of hypertonicity eventually lead to hypertrophy (q.v.) and damage to the cardiac muscle, as well as vascular sclerosis.   *E.D.*

Hypertrophy. Excessive development of overloaded organs, e.g. the muscular system in athletes, the heart in cases of high blood pressure, or the uterus in pregnancy, without an increase in the cell count. These are all conditions of physiological or activity hypertrophy. On the other hand, the various pathological forms of hypertrophy, e.g. hypertrophy of the prostate gland or tonsils, are disease conditions. See *Hyperplasia*.
                                                           E.D.

Hypnagogic hallucination. See *Sleep*.

Hypnoic mechanisms. Involuntary "functional forms" of the imagination which do not have a logical or objective basis but an emotional or subjective foundation and are reflected in (internal) "images" and in acts of expression (spheric dependence, blurring of the ego boundary, change in time and space relationships, heightened density, displacement, stylization, "picture strip" imagination, etc.).
                                                           W.K.

Hypnolepsy. A state of abnormal sleepiness. The term is usually employed as a synonym for narcolepsy (q.v.).   *J.P.*

Hypnopedia. In hypnopedia (from the Greek = education in sleep) the pupil is taught and given behavioral instructions in a hypnotic state in order to avoid difficulties in absorbing information and controlling behavior while he is awake. Experimental results confirm the possibility of teaching and learning in sleep, but precise data on increased effectiveness obtainable through hypnopedia are not available as yet.   *H. Schr.*

Hypnophobia. An undue fear of sleep.

Hypnosis. "A temporary condition of altered attention in the S. which may be induced by another person and in which a variety of phenomena may appear spontaneously or in response to verbal or other stimuli. These phenomena include alterations in consciousness and memory, increased susceptibility to suggestion and the production in the S. of responses and ideas unfamiliar to him in his usual state of mind. Further, phenomena such as anaesthesia, paralysis, and rigidity of muscles, and vasomotor changes can be produced and removed. . . ." (B.M.A., 1955, p. 191).

Hypnosis, hypnotic state, hypnotic trance, and *hypnotism* are often used interchangeably, but hypnotism may also refer specifically to *hypnotic induction* by a *hypnotist* or *operator*. *Susceptibility* is the degree to which a S. is affected by induction, and determines the *depth* of hypnosis achieved. *Hypnoidal* refers to states having at least some of the characteristics of light hypnosis.

Posthypnotic suggestions (and instructions) are made during hypnosis in order to influence the S. after hypnosis, whereas *posthypnotic phenomena* are consequences of hypnosis arising after its termination, including those resulting from posthypnotic suggestions. There may be spontaneous or induced failure of the S. to remember some or all of the events which took place during hypnosis (*posthypnotic amnesia*), and even having been hypnotized. In so far as a S. can hypnotize himself, we have *auto-hypnosis*.

Hypnosis derives from "neuro-hypnotism", a term introduced by Braid (1843) to denote a trance-like state he observed to result from prolonged visual fixation or from prolonged concentrated attention of other kinds (*mono-ideism*), and resembling the *sleeping-trance* described by de Puységur (1785) as resulting from the prolonged use of mesmeric passes. The fully-developed trance resembled very deep sleep, with the S. stuporous and unresponsive to stimuli. Somewhat similar states have been reported from ancient times as arising in man, often following prolonged exposure to repetitive stimuli such as rhythmical drumming and chanting. Possibly analogous states are observed in many higher animals after exposure to repetitive stimuli such as stroking and flashing lights, and to sudden inversion, forcible restraint, and pressure on body parts; hence the terms *hypnosis* and *hypnotic trance* are sometimes applied to all such trance-like states in animals and men. However, the important characteristics of sleeping trance and neurohypnosis were that if the operator started speaking to the S. while the trance was still very light, and continued to talk at frequent intervals as it deepened, a selective *rapport* developed, the S. remaining responsive to the operator's verbal suggestions yet becoming progressively less responsive to all other stimuli. The term hypnotic trance is best reserved to denote sleeping trance and similar states as modified by the effects of verbal suggestion, in which sense the hypnotic trance can be induced only in humans with at least a rudimentary command of language.

In his later work, Braid increasingly stressed the power of monoideism (resulting from concentrated attention to the operator's suggestions) to induce hypnotic trance without the help of such techniques as visual fixation. He showed that the operator's suggestions and the S.'s expectations both exerted a profound effect on the phenomena elicited during hypnosis. Liébeault and Bernheim stressed the role of such purely psychological determinants of hypnosis to the virtual exclusion of all others: "If you use suggestibility to suggest suggestibility, the result is hypnotism." But some modern work supports Braid's original view that visual fixation can lead to increased suggestibility even in the absence of suggestion or expectation.

The development of hypnosis as a field of study in the context of medicine and psychology dates from Mesmer's claims of therapeutic effects resulting from a form of convulsive seizure (*crisis*) apparently induced by magnets or (later) by mesmeric passes, and from the observations and experiments of those who sought to prove or disprove these claims. The deliberate use of direct verbal suggestion played no part in the early practice of Mesmerism, or in Mesmer's own theories.

1. *Induction and termination.* Detailed descriptions of a wide variety of induction procedures are readily available (e.g., Weitzenhoffer, 1953). The essential characteristic of most is continuous repetitive verbal suggestions, directed by the operator to the S., and normally at first designed to produce relaxation, attention to the operator's voice, drowsiness and eye closure. Subsequently, some degree of response having been observed, the operator may invite the S. to try moving his limbs gently, while at the same time confidently asserting that he will experience great disinclination and difficulty in doing so. Suggestions that the limbs, fingers, and so on, will move in specified ways without the volition of the S., and that sensations such as warmth or numbness will be experienced, may follow. Most operators believe that a crucial stage in increasing depth of hypnosis is reached when *challenge suggestions* are made, e.g. by telling S. that he will be unable to open his eyes no matter how hard he tries, and that the more he tries to open them, the more tightly they will close. Beyond this stage, the hypnosis may be said to be firmly established, and responses to further suggestions may be almost immediate, without the need for repetition; but there is no clearly marked stage at which induction can be said to terminate and the elicitation of the phenomena of hypnosis to

begin. Induction is normally a process of eliciting a continuing series of responses which themselves also constitute the phenomena, to a succession of suggestions of steadily increasing "difficulty". In a proportion of Ss., suggestions that the lethargy of the early stages is to give place to an active state with eyes open, in which strong rapport and hypersuggestibility are nevertheless retained, may be successful (*somnambulism*, q.v.). Most operators combine visual and/or auditory fixation with verbal suggestions in the initial phases of induction, but this is not essential and it is not known how much it influences rate or depth of hypnosis. Termination usually occurs when the operator commands S. to return to his normal state, specifically countermands suggestions judged to merit this, and suggests that feelings of alertness and well-being will follow the "awakening". Some Ss. may complain of disorientation and feelings of unreality, and perhaps drowsiness, for a period in which it will be exceptionally easy to re-hypnotize them. Suggestions made during hypnosis, that it will be easy to induce hypnosis again, are normally so effective, that subsequent inductions may be made almost instantaneously on an agreed signal from the operator.

2. *Susceptibility*. Suggestions can be arranged approximately along a scale of "difficulty" in the sense that if a person responds to a suggestion with any particular difficulty he is likely to respond also to all easier suggestions, whereas if he fails to respond it is unlikely that he will respond to any that are more difficult. Lists of suggestions in order of difficulty are available for measuring the depth of hypnosis achieved with any particular S. Depth tends to increase throughout the duration of any single hypnosis, and with each subsequent hypnosis, up to a maximum which differs markedly from one S. to another. Most research suggests that this maximum is not usually greatly influenced by the personality or technique of a particular operator, or by a variety of environmental factors, but there

is also clear evidence that it sometimes may be. Many investigators report that about ten per cent of European adults are insusceptible, and that somnambulism can be achieved with between twenty and thirty per cent. Above-average susceptibility is more frequently found in women, and is positively correlated with high intelligence, some kinds of waking suggestibility (e.g. Eysenck's primary and tertiary suggestibilities) but not others, a tendency to vivid day-dreams and states of self-absorption, a capacity for vivid imagery, a positive attitude to the idea of being hypnotized, and addiction to narcotic drugs. A variety of relationships between susceptibility and a number of personality characteristics (particularly extraversion) have been reported, but the results of one investigation have seldom been confirmed by another: therefore it has been suggested that relationships are different for high-drive and low-drive (or high anxious and low anxious) subjects, and for men and for women. In children, susceptibility increases with the mastery of language and at about eight to ten years reaches a maximum before declining somewhat to a stable value maintained throughout maturity. Some forms of psychoneurosis may be associated with above average susceptibility, and most psychotic illness with low susceptibility, but the naturally occurring differences between normal Ss. are much larger than those between averages for groups of neurotics and normals.

3. *Phenomena*. A distinction can in principle be made between phenomena resulting from induction of itself, and those depending on specific suggestions to the hypnotized S. There is, however, ample evidence that the expectations of the S. and unintended indirect suggestions from the operator profoundly influence response to induction, so that the intrinsic characteristics of the state are difficult to elucidate. Orne has referred to the *demand characteristics* of the hypnotic situation, being the totality of the intended and unintended cues which influence the S.'s responses. He believes that the essential

characteristics of hypnosis reside in the experience of the S., rather than in his directly observable responses, and that they relate to the distortions of normal logic and normal perceptual organization which have to take place before the operator's suggestions can be accepted.

Success in demonstrating phenomena resulting from specific suggestions varies markedly from one S. to another. Among the well attested phenomena which have survived careful experimental investigation are: *responses of voluntary musculature*, inception and inhibition of contraction; paralysis resulting from simultaneous activation of opposing muscle pairs; increased tolerance of fatigue and discomfort arising from muscular activity, and thus sometimes apparently increased strength (e.g. grip) and/or work capacity; improved muscular control in relatively simple motor skills, but probably not in more complex ones; *physiological phenomena*, increased metabolic rate in relaxed S. during suggestions that muscular work was being undertaken; inhibition of hunger contractions and increased gastric acidity following suggestions that food was being eaten; changes in pepsin, trypsin, lipase and maltose production appropriate to suggested ingestion of protein, fat and carbohydrate respectively; *hallucination of sense*, absence of startle reflex and psychogalvanic reflex (PGR) on exposure to sudden loud noises or flashes following suggested deafness or blindness; appropriate changes in response to Ishihara test cards following suggestions of color-blindness; abolition of normal reactions (including PGR) to painful stimuli (including surgical operations) following suggested anesthesia or analgesia, and interruption of withdrawal reflex at level of first spinal synapse on application of noxious stimulus to hypnotically anesthetized skin; appearance of nystagmus following suggested hallucinations of rotation in a centrifuge.

4. *Memory*. Appropriate specific suggestions can often produce a post-hypnotic amnesia for material learned, or events experienced at any time before or during the hypnosis; and some degree of amnesia for the events of the hypnosis may also arise spontaneously. In so far as conditioned reflexes constitute a form of memory, it should be noted that they seem not to be abolished by direct suggestions, although the conditioned response may fail to appear after suggestions that the conditioned stimulus cannot be perceived. Hypnotic hypermnesia may involve (a) enhanced capacity to recall previous experiences (particularly those with strong emotional content) extending to complete recovery of repressed traumatic memories, or (b) improved recall of learned material, but probably only if it is meaningful, e.g. a poem or logical argument rather than an arbitrary list of words.

5. *Revivification* seems to involve the partial re-establishing of the complete psychophysiological state existing at some time in the Subject's past. Thus in *age regression* the S. may be told that he is again an infant and may then spontaneously exhibit neo-natal reflexes such as reversed Babinski, defecation when startled, together with appropriate alterations in peripheral chronaxie; however, many responses to suggested hypermnesia and revivification are no more than plausible dramatizations of fantasy; *personality alterations*, simple changes in mood and emotions are readily induced but are often difficult to sustain post-hypnotically. Habit changes (e.g. smoking) are often short-lived but may be extended by frequent hypnosis (e.g. daily) over prolonged periods. There are reliable reports of successful experiments in the development of multiple personalities. *Organic changes* are particularly difficult to explain, but there is fair evidence for the occasional production by specific hypnotic suggestion of a variety of allergic and psychosomatic skin changes, and of skin blisters in Ss. of hysteric personality. There are also reports of such phenomena during or following abreaction, under both hypnosis and drugs. Some investigators believe that stigmata may also be produced.

6. *Hypnotherapy* is a term used rather loosely to denote several different therapeutic applications, e.g. (*a*) prolonged hypnotic "sleep" used sometimes for gastric and duodenal ulcers, hypertension, cardiac disease, and other conditions where prolonged periods free from stress might be beneficial; (*b*) *hypnoanalysis*, where classical psychoanalytic techniques are modified and shortened by using hypnosis to facilitate the emergence of memories and associations which are being repressed; (*c*) the production of cathartic abreactions, usually during revivification, as part of the treatment of post-traumatic neuroses in an attempt to relieve conversion and other symptoms such as paralysis; (*d*) direct suggestions oriented toward the relief of specified physical or mental symptoms without attempting to influence any possible underlying causes. Among the most frequently used applications, this is also the most controversial, as many psychiatrists claim that symptoms which can be removed by suggestion serve unconscious needs and help preserve the patients' psychological equilibrium. If removed without regard to etiology, substitute symptoms may soon be generated or, if not, the stability of the personality may be threatened. An influential body of psychiatric opinion, however, regards symptom removal as beneficial. Among conditions treated with apparent success have been addictions, asthma, excessive appetite, eczema, irritable bladder, stress incontinence, homosexuality, impotence, menstrual disturbances, vaginismus, headaches, stammering, warts, phobias, and conversion neuroses. There has been little success with psychosis. In Mason's celebrated case of congenital ichtysosiform erythrodermia of Broq, the photographic and clinical evidence showed that skin characteristics improved only in the limb to which the hypnotic suggestions were specifically directed.

7. *Other medical and dental applications.* The most common is probably the production of analgesia and relaxation during childbirth; the duration of labor may be reduced when this is done. Some practitioners, particularly in dentistry, use hypnosis for the alleviation of anxiety before and during treatment, and for the production of analgesia or anesthesia where using chemical agents would be difficult, inconvenient or dangerous. With some patients suffering intractable pain (e.g. in terminal cancer) hypnosis affords substantial alleviation without the side effects of chemical agents.

8. *Theories.* It is tempting to impose a classification of theories of hypnosis into two types—(*a*) those which explain the phenomena as a consequence of a special state of the central nervous system (or more generally, of the subject's condition of neuropsychological organization) usually generated by the induction, and (*b*) those which explain them as examples of the organism's normal functioning under unusual conditions of motivation, attention, expectation, and attitude, these last being influenced by the induction but by no means essentially dependent on it.

Theories of the first kind include the long established explanations of hypnosis as a form of sleep. However, in respect of a variety of measures of physiological indices such as reflexes, blood-pressure, electrical activity of the brain, oxygen consumption, etc., hypnosis has been shown to resemble wakefulness far more than sleep. There is however some evidence, particularly from electro-encephalographic studies, that it may be a specialized form of very light sleep, clearly distinguishable from both wakefulness and deep sleep. From his work on conditioned reflexes, Pavlov explained hypnosis as a state of generalized cortical inhibition within which the existence of islands of continuing excitation makes it possible to evoke responses whose bizarre characteristics result from the absence of control and modification by the cortex as a whole. Rather more vague theories speak of an inhibition of activity in the white matter of the cerebrum (Bennett), an inhibition of ganglionic cells, and a state of anemia of the frontal lobes (Völgyesi).

Janet viewed hypnosis as a state of simple or multiple dissociation in which the stream of consciousness splits into components functioning relatively independently of one another. It is tempting to see this as the psychological analogue of Pavlov's physiological explanations.

Theories of the second kind include the formulations of Bernheim and Liébeault, who saw the phenomena as special examples of waking suggestibility, produced by suggestion. Such formulations indicate the need for a theory of suggestion rather than, or as well as, of hypnosis. It is known that if the normal waking S. just thinks about certain forms of muscular activity, including speech, then very attenuated nervous impulses, appropriate to the production of that activity, are automatically generated. Such *ideomotor action* is held by some to be a sufficient basis for a theory of motor suggestibility, but it is obviously insufficient to explain the whole range of hypnotic phenomena. Conditioned reflex theories assert that the links between words and the subject's responses in hypnosis are of the same kind, and obey the same law, as those between the conditioned stimulus and the conditioned response in Pavlovian reflexology. Other theories stress the relational aspects of hypnosis. Ferenczi viewed the phenomena as resulting from a psychological regression to the infantile state of dependence on and conflict with the parents, while Freud emphasized the importance of submission, and spoke of the hypnotic relationship as the devotion of someone in love to an unlimited degree, but with sexual satisfaction excluded. More recently, Sarbin has suggested that hypnosis is a highly motivated form of role-playing. The steadily increasing evidence that most if not all kinds of hypnotic phenomena can also be demonstrated with Ss. who have not undergone induction, emphasizes the importance of theories of this kind, though not necessarily of these particular theories.

While all the formulations direct attention to interesting analogies which might help in the generation of hypotheses, none really merits the status of a theory or seems substantially explanatory or predictive. The hypnotized S. functions in modes at least as complex as does the waking S., and it is doubtful if an all-embracing "theory of hypnosis" is possible. When more is known about the determinants of normal waking activity, it should be possible to establish how these are modified in hypnosis, and in particular whether there is a specific "hypnotic state".

Bibliography: Bernheim, H.: Hypnosis and suggestion in psychotherapy. New York, 1964. **Braid, J.:** Neurypnology or the rationale of nervous sleep considered in relation with animal magnetism. London, 1843. **Chertok, M. D.:** Hypnosis. London & Edinburgh, 1966. **Ferenczi, S.:** Introjection and transference. First contributions to psychoanalysis, 1952, 39–93. **Freud, S.:** Introductory lectures on psycho-analysis. London, 1922. **Furneaux, W. D.:** The prediction of susceptibility to hypnosis. J. Pers., 1946, *14*, 281–94. **Liébeault, A.:** Du sommeil et des états analogues, etc. Paris, 1866. **Puységur, A. M. de:** Mémoires pour servir à l'histoire et à l'établissement du magnétisme animal. London, 1785. **Sarbin, T. R.:** Mental age changes in experimental regression. J. Pers., 1950, *19*, 221. **Völgyesi, F. A.:** Hypnotherapie und psychosomatische Probleme. Stuttgart, 1950. **Id.:** Schutz-, Hypnose-, Schlaf-Hemmungen und die zunehmenden Perspektiven der aktiven Psychotherapie. In: **E. Speer** (Ed.): Die Vorträge der 2. Lindauer Psychotherapiewoche 1951. Stuttgart, 1952, 210–6. **Weitzenhoffer, A.:** Hypnotism, an objective study in suggestibility. New York, 1953. For further literature, see **Stokvis, B.:** Hypnose. In: **V. E. Frankl** *et al.* (Eds.): Handbuch der Neurosenlehre und Psychotherapie. Munich & Berlin, 1959, 71–122.   *W. D. Furneaux*

Hypnosis research, experimental. The experimental study of hypnosis promises not only to explain a phenomenon which is interesting in itself, but also to give new insight into hitherto unsolved general psychological problems, since hypnosis allows experimental access to human experience and behavior at different levels of consciousness (see Ullmann *et al.*, 1968; Ullmann, 1971). The progress obtainable through research into hypnosis extends to such general psychological themes as cognition, perception, emotion, motivation, interpersonal relations (Barber, 1969; Orne, 1970, etc.), personality and social adaptability (McGuire, 1968), pain (Hilgard, 1967) and placebo effect (McGlashan *et al.*, 1967), and leads into central problems of psycholinguistics (q.v.) (Sarbin & Coe, 1971).

Experiments conducted by Orne (1959, 1962) have not only given useful information on problems of hypnosis as such, but have demonstrated the general influence of the experimental situation on the testee; a distinction must be made between general behavior and the specific behavior studied in a given experiment. The methodological developments of modern hypnosis research therefore go beyond the narrower subject of study (Gordon, 1967). This also applies to study of the problem of hypnotic trance. The conflicting interpretations of altered states of awareness as legitimate or impermissible constructs express the basic scientific positions of contemporary psychology (Barber, 1969, 1970; Hilgard, 1969, 1970; Sarbin, 1968; Spanos & Chaves, 1970; H. Thomae, 1962; Ullmann & Ullmann, 1966) and form the bases of paradigms of hypnosis experiments.

Sarbin and co-workers have tried to explain the phenomenon of hypnosis exclusively with the aid of social and psychological theorems; hypnotic behavior is considered in the context of a psychology of communicative influences (Sarbin & Coe, 1971), and examined empirically. In Sarbin's opinion, the experience of a trance state is not necessarily based on an objective equivalent as the cause of hypnotic phenomena. Barber adopts a similar approach; in his opinion there is no special hypnotic state of consciousness; that would be a superfluous construct which would not help one to arrive at a more comprehensive appraisal of the problem. Efforts to analyze hypnotic behavior (dependent variables), and the objective parameters which condition such behavior (independent variables), as well as the laws governing relationships between these two sets of variables in

quantitative terms, are characteristic of the procedure adopted. The forms of hypnotic behavior which are to be explained, such as (a) behavior in response to direct suggestions, e.g. hallucinations, analgesia, amnesia, etc., (b) the verbal statements of the testee, and (c) symptoms resembling a state of trance (lack of spontaneity, retarded motor behavior), are analyzed quantitatively with the help of a standardized scale (BSS: Barber, 1965). As regards the antecedents which play a significant part in the occurrence of hypnotic behavior, Barber and co-workers have identified a number of variables which are classified as (a) instruction-suggestion variable, (b) subject variable, (c) hypnotizer variable, and (d) relationship variable (Barber, 1969). It has frequently been found that individual phenomena which occur in hypnosis can be brought about even without hypnotic induction. Barber views this result as supporting his rejection of a special hypnotic state of trance.

According to Hilgard (1965, 1969, 1970), hypnotic phenomena can in part be considered in a different light. From his standpoint of modern functionalism, subjective conditions are a legitimate object of scientific study. Referring to sleep research (see *Sleep*), Hilgard considers it desirable to distinguish between different states of consciousness. He considers that objective indicators should exist for the state of hypnosis as they do for the sleeping state. Apart from trance problems, Hilgard and co-workers have not only studied the use of hypnosis to lessen pain (Hilgard, 1967), but have developed their own scales to examine hypnotic suggestibility as an individual trait, especially from the genetic angle. In Hilgard's opinion, this characteristic can be modified by a series of variables, e.g. by expectancy attitudes of the test subject, or by adjusting the test suggestion (Barber, 1969), but results obtained so far show that this feature is relatively stable in a substantial number of cases. Like Hilgard, P. London (1970) considers the persistent proportion of individual differences in hypnotic performance to be important and attempts—as a basis for a theory of hypnosis —to find appropriate correlates. London considers that there is an empirical basis for the relationship with motivation and EEG (q.v.) patterns. Hilgard believes that the justification for abandoning the normal paradigm and examining a parameter considered in it as a dependent variable, i.e. hypnotic suggestibility, as an independent variable, lies in the additional information likely to be obtained, which can help to define important parameters in more detail.

To sum up, it can be stated that modern experimental hypnosis research is characterized by a high level of experimental plans and techniques. Some representatives of different theoretical schools have tried to determine the validity of their methods in a logical manner; it seems that the validity of the different individual positions will be clarified in the next phase of experimental activity. After the identification of several significant variables and analyzing the relationship between a number of such variables, hypnosis appears as an extremely interesting phenomenon in the broader context of general psychological studies.

Bibliography: Barber, T. X.: Hypnosis: a scientific approach. New York, 1969. Id.: LSD, marihuana, yoga and hypnosis. Chicago, 1970. Gordon, J. E. (Ed.): Handbook of clinical and experimental hypnosis. New York, 1967. Hilgard, E. R.: Hypnotic susceptibility. New York, 1965. Id.: Altered states of awareness. J. nerv. ment. Dis., 1969, *149*, 68–79. Orne, M. T.: On the social psychology of the psychological experiment: with particular reference to demand characteristics and their implications. Amer. Psychol., 1962, *17*, 776–83. Sarbin, T. R. & Coe, W. C.: Hypnotism: a social-psychological analysis. New York, 1971. Spanos, N. S. & Chaves, J. F.: Hypnosis research: a methodological critique of experiments generated by two alternative paradigms. Amer. J. Clin. Hypn., 1970, *13*, 108–27. Thomae, H.: Das Bewusstseinsproblem in der modernen Psychologie. Der Nervenarzt, 1962, *33*, 447–83. Ullmann, J. F., Ullmann, I. M. & Klapp, W. H.: Perspektiven psychologisch-experimenteller Hypnoseforschung bis zum Einsetzen grundsätzlicher methodischer Kritik. Arch. Ges. Psychol., 1968, *120*, 247–300. Ullmann, J. F. (Ed.) (with Ullmann, I. M. & Klapp, W. H.: Hypnose und Suggestibilität, Vol. 1: Empirische Grundlagen. Berne & Stuttgart, 1971/72; Vol. 2: Theoretische Modelle und Konzepte (in preparation).

J. F. Ullmann, I. M. Ullmann & W. H. Klapp

Hypnotics. Natural or synthetic substances which lead directly to a condition similar to sleep or facilitate its occurrence. Desirable properties: generation of a state which resembles natural sleep as closely as possible without secondary and aftereffects (hangover); no cumulative effect, habituation, or development of dependence; large therapeutic range to prevent serious risk in the event of an overdose. The hypnotics include various groups of chemical substances (some of which are no longer in use today) such as the alcohols and aldehydes (ethyl alcohol, chloralhydrate, paraldehyde), sulfones (sulfonal, methylsulfonal), urethanes (ethylurethane, ethinamate), monoureides (Bromisoval, Carbamal), cycloureides (barbiturates) and piperidine derivatives (gluthethimide, thalidomide). It is difficult to draw a clear distinction between the hypnotics and the tranquilizers (q.v.) and narcotics (q.v.). The opinion that there are only quantitative differences (Irwin, 1968) contrasts with the assertion of qualitative differences of effect (Berger). Munoz distinguishes among psychopharmaceutical drugs promoting sleep, one group with euhypnic (hypnogenic) effects, and another with hypnotic (compulsive) action. He assumes that the transition from the euhypnics to the tranquilizers, and that from the hypnotics to narcotics, are fluid. While the euhypnics facilitate sleep by anxiolytic means, the hypnotics progressively— depending on the dose—influence consciousness by general, central inhibition (primarily of the *formatio reticularis*) with a relatively fixed latency period; they lead to sedation with impaired performance, confusion, sleep, narcosis. They have a clear influence on the vegetative functions (pulse, blood pressure, temperature, respiration) and frequently lead to tolerance (also cross-tolerance), and dependence with withdrawal symptoms. The extent of a "hangover" caused by a substance (heaviness in the limbs, reduced performance) is largely dependent on the duration of action and the concentration of the substance which conditions the hypnogenic and hypnotic effect. The absence of a feeling of relaxation is accompanied by reduced body movements in sleep. In doses insufficient to induce sleep, the hypnotics are thought to bring about reversible personality changes in the sense of increasing extraversion (H. J. Eysenck). They reduce performance in many tests (Kornetsky et al., 1957). However these effects on performance are difficult to demonstrate because of compensatory counter-regulation. Among the other secondary effects, the alcohol-potentiating effect and influence on driving capacity have been studied in detail.

Bibliography: Holm, E.: Der pharmakologisch induzierte Schlaf. In: Baust, W. (Ed.): Ermüdung, Schlaf und Traum. Stuttgart, 1970. Irwin, S.: Antineurotics: practical pharmacology of the sedative-hypnotics and minor tranquilizers. In: Efron, D. H. (Ed.): Psychopharmacology 1957–1967. Washington, 1968. Kornetsky, C., Humphries, O. & Evarts, E. V.: Comparison of psychological effects of certain centrally acting drugs in man. A. M. A. Arch. Neurol. Psychiat., 1957, 77, 318–24. Maynert, E. W.: Sedatives and hypnotics. In: Di Palma, J. R.: Drill's pharmacology in medicine. New York, 1965, 169–209. Othmer, E.: Persönlichkeit und Schlafverhalten. Meisenheim, 1965. E.L.

Hypnotism. See *Hypnosis*.

Hypobulic mechanisms. Automatic, i.e. unintentional, reflex and standardized forms of movement. They occur when the higher mental (volitional) functions are disturbed, and earlier, lower psychomotor functions come to the surface and take control (rhythmic movements, violent uncontrolled movements, hysterical stupor and attacks, catalepsy, motor negativism). W.K.

Hypochondria. It has sometimes been suggested that hypochondria in men corresponds to hysteria (q.v.) in women. Nowadays the term is used simply to denote a syndrome encountered primarily in states of anxiety (q.v.) and depression (q.v.). The subject feels pains not only in his stomach, as the etymology of the word suggests, but in his whole body. In fact the "corporality", the "animate" body, is affected in its entirety, and perception continuously manifests unpleasant sensations, so that the patient suffers greatly. The fear and depression at the root of every hypochondriac condition have endogenous rather than reactive origins. J.L.I.

Hypoesthesia. Diminished cutaneous sensitivity due to peripheral or central changes. See *Hypalgesia*. M.S.

Hypofunction(ing). The underfunctioning of organs or parts of the body. The term is generally used in connection with the endocrine glands. Depending on the organ affected, a distinction is made between pituitary dwarfism with normal intelligence, cretinism (q.v.) caused by a thyroid condition, dwarfism accompanied by feeblemindedness, Addison's disease in the event of an adrenalin deficiency indicating underfunctioning of the adrenal medulla, and diabetes mellitus in the event of an insulin deficiency indicating underfunctioning of the pancreas, or eunuchoidism (q.v.). E.D.

Hypokinesis. Impaired movement of the skeletal muscular system, which occurs locally in paralysis but generally as a systemic disorder, e.g. in *paralytis agitans*, accompanied by a "mask face", and involuntary movements. E.D.

Hypomania. A lesser degree of *mania* (q.v.) as part of a manic depressive psychosis. It

may precede or follow mania or it may constitute an episode of the illness. Hypomanic
patients may be able to function for some
time in some or all of their usual social
activities and in fact may be very productive.
Eventually, grandiose or excessive actions or
decisions lead to social complications. Like
mania, it has a descriptive use and overlaps
with *hyperthymia* (q.v.).   *B.B.*

Hypomanic type. See *Diathetic proportion.*

Hypomnesia. Weak memory: a typical symptom of organic psychoses (q.v.) and senile
degeneration of the intelligence. Initially, it
affects events from the recent past rather than,
e.g., memories of youth ("the new dies before
the old").   *W.Sc.*

Hypophysis (syn. *Glandula pituitaria; Pituitary
gland*). A structure with a diameter of about
1.5 cm located in the *sella turcica* at the base
of the brain. As one of the most important
endocrine glands it consists of the anterior
lobe (adenohypophysis), central lobe (*pars
intermedia*), posterior lobe (neurohypophysis)
and the *infundibulum* as a connection with
the brain. The adenohypophysis originates
in the ectodermal vault of the pharynx;
histologically it consists of typical glandular
tissue and forms several hormones (q.v.)
which regulate the function of the other
glands. These hormones include: growth
hormone (see *Acromegaly*); gonadotropic
hormones (q.v.), which influence the male
and female genital glands; thyrotropic and
parathyrotropic hormones, which act on
the thyroid and accessory thyroid glands;
corticotropic hormone, which promotes the
secretion of cortisone in the adrenal medulla;
the lactation hormone prolactin, and the
pancreotropic hormone which influences
Langerhan's cells in the pancreas. The central
lobe originates in the base of the third
ventricle, and consists of brain tissue

(neuroglia); it forms oxytocin, which causes
the uterus to contract, as well as vasopressin,
which is mainly responsible for regulating
the reabsorption of water in the kidney (in
tubulus contortus II). The absence of vasopressin is responsible for diabetes insipidus;
in this condition the subject may produce up
to twenty liters of urine a day.   *E.D.*

Hypoplasia. In general, innate or hereditary
underdevelopment of an organ. It almost
always leads to a reduction in, or failure of,
the function of the part of the body affected.
                                                              E.D.

Hypostasis. A process of the intellect by which
an abstraction is endowed with an independent and quasi-material existence. The
concept of hypostasis was developed in
detail in the philosophy of Plotinus, who
described the three absolute values: goodness
(the infinite), intelligence, and the soul.
In psychology, it is often difficult not to
ascribe a material reality to the objects,
terms and functions referred to (e.g. the will,
ego, or superego).   *M.R.*

Hypotaxia. Defective coordination of voluntary movements (see *Ataxia*). In hypnosis
(q.v.), a medium state in which cataleptic
rigidity and automatism are present without
subsequent amnesia (q.v.).   *W.Sc.*

Hypothalamus. The section of the brain
belonging to the diencephalon, and situated
below the thalamus, whose function consists
primarily in the coordination of vegetative
body functions, such as hormone functions,
respiration, circulation, heat and water
regulation. Close links therefore exist between the hypothalamus and the hypophysis
(q.v.) and deeper parts of the brain.   *E.D.*

Hypothesis. In general, a hypothesis is a
statement which is assumed to be correct and
is used as the basis for a discursive structure.

The word is used with the following three specific meanings: (a) a hypothesis is a means for logical classification of a situation: specific statements are used as the initial principles for a deductive theory (hypothetico-deductive theories); (b) a hypothesis is a plausible explanation preceding stringent (experimental) verification of an assumption; (c) a hypothesis is a heuristic means of discovering the truth. In formal systems, the terms hypothesis, axiom (q.v.) and postulate (q.v.) are equivalent. *M.J.B.*

Hypothesis testing. Statistical hypotheses refer to parameters of population distributions. By referring back to specific assumptions (degree of chance in selecting samples, distribution of random error), the chance distribution of sample values is determined numerically. See *Construct validity; Test theory.* *W.H.B.*

Hypothetical construct. A term for an assumption, i.e. of a phenomenon or process as existent even when not observable, or not observable as assumed. Hypothetical constructs have a heuristic value, i.e. they allow investigations to be made which would otherwise be virtually impossible. See *Construct validity; Test theory.* *R.Hä.*

Hypotonia. Excessively low blood pressure as a sign of defective regulation in the vegetatively labile, or in conditions of cardiac weakness. Hypotonia is reflected in weakness, fatigue and fainting. Ant. *Hypertonia.* *E.D.*

Hypotrophy. Contraction of organs as a result of inactivity. Occurs in the skeletal muscle, capsular ligaments and bones, when the limbs concerned are prevented from moving; also observed in the hearts of those who do not take enough exercise. Hypotrophy mainly affects all organs which are kept motionless, but is fully reversible, unlike hypoplasia (q.v.). *E.D.*

Hysteria. A psychogenic disorder with mental and/or physical symptoms: a reaction to experiences with a strong emotional content which are not processed normally because of an innate or acquired disposition. The following—not necessarily in conjunction—are symptoms of hysteria: semi-consciousness, hallucinations, amnesia, emotional outbursts of weeping or shouting (always in the presence of other persons), pseudo-dementia, disturbances of the senses (e.g. blindness or deafness, anesthesia), paralysis, tremor, tics and motor coordination defects (inability to stand or walk, etc.). The boundary between hysteria and simulated hysteria is often fluid. Treatment is possible by environmental therapy or psychotherapy. See *Defense; Psychopathology; Neurosis; Psychoses, functional.*

Bibliography: Kretschmer, E.: Hysteria, reflex and instinct. London, 1961. *M.A.*

Hysterical type. A term often used to denote the opposite of the dysthymic type (q.v.): extraverted; stresses are processed rapidly, although with exaggerated emphasis, as a violent reaction. This type is described by Kretschmer: impressionable with low active retentive capacity for emotions, exaggerated reaction to stress, rapid elimination of stimuli, demonstrative façade.

Bibliography: Kretschmer, E.: Hysteria, reflex and instinct. London, 1961. *W.K.*

Hysteromania. 1. State of excessive activity in patients suffering from hysteria (q.v.). 2. An archaic synonym for *nymphomania*, which is an excessive desire in women for sexual intercourse. *P.Le.*

I

IA. Abb. for *Intelligence age* (q.v.).

Ich (Ger.). See *Ego*.

ICSH (*Interstitial cell stimulating hormone*). A gonadotropic hormone (q.v.) formed in the anterior pituitary (syn. LH, q.v., in women), which induces or maintains the formation of hormones in the male/female sex glands. In man: in the testicles: (*a*) maintenance of interstitial cells and their production of androgens (q.v.); (*b*) interaction with gonadotropic hormone FSH in spermatogenesis. In woman: (*a*) together with gonadotropic hormone FSH, induces formation of estrogens (q.v.) in the ovum, which in their turn stimulate LH secretion; (*b*) induces ovulation and the onset of the second phase in the female cycle; (*c*) conversion of the former ovum into *corpus luteum*, which produces estrogens and progesterone (q.v.) under the influence of LH and LTH (q.v.).

Bibliography: Fridhandler, L. & Pincus, G.: Pharmacology of reproduction and fertility. Ann. Rev. Pharmacol., 1964, *4*, 177. Friesen, H. & Astwood, E.: Hormones of the anterior pituitary body. New Eng. J. Med., 1965, *272*, 1216. Voigt, K.-D. & Schmidt, H.: Sexualhormone. Hamburg, *1968*.   *H.M.*

Id (Ger. *Es*). A number of psychological theories assume that the whole personality contains a separate, relatively independent area in addition to the conscious "personality". This area is thought to comprise the unconscious "drives" ("impulses", "instincts") and emotions. In the strata theory (q.v.) of personality, the conscious area rests on this unconscious layer. It is sometimes suggested that ontogenetically and phylogenetically ordered structures are involved. By a vague analogy with the findings of brain physiology, we find references to "upper" and "lower" areas, the midbrain representing the second part of the personality and the cerebrum the first. F. Kraus spoke in this context of a "depth person", and based his conclusion on medico-physiological considerations. Nietzsche referred to this dark, mysterious area of the personality as the "id" (though, of course, he used the term "*Es*", properly translated as "it"; "id", however, has come to be the accepted English term). Using the layer theory of the personality, Rothacker took over Nietzsche's term and spoke of the "id" as the unconscious depth, or fundamental ground, of the person. Similarly, P. Lersch makes a distinction between an endothymic infrastructure and a noetic superstructure.

The concept of the "id" acquired its greatest importance in the context of Freud's depth-psychological interpretation of the personality (see *Depth psychology*). Freud referred to G. Groddeck's theories in using the notion of the "id". Freud developed his concept of the tripartite division of the personality into the *id*, *ego* (q.v.) and *superego* (q.v.) in *The Ego and the Id*, and later in *New Introductory Lectures on Psycho-Analysis*. The structural-topological aspect was added to the dynamic concepts of the "conscious"

495

IDEA

and "unconscious". According to Rapaport, the id, ego and superego trichotomy is the most adequate structural theory of the personality in depth psychology, and therefore of importance for psychoanalytic theory. Rapaport does not, however, view it as an independent model; for him it is merely an alternative formulation of earlier theoretical concepts of Freud regarding the nature of the conscious and the unconscious.

All processes in the id are said to be unconscious. On the other hand, the ego is not claimed to be the locus of consciousness. According to the principles of psychoanalysis, the ego also contains unconscious elements. The id is the center of the passions, extends far into the somatic, and may threaten the ego in the same way as the outside world. The ego normally controls access to motility, but frequently has to implement impulses from the id. Freud describes the relationship between the ego and the id by speaking of the ego as a rider and the id as a horse: "Just as a rider, if he does not wish to leave his mount, often has no option but to give it free rein, so the ego converts the will of the id into action as though it were itself responsible for that action." (*Werke*, Vol. 13, p. 253.) Ontogenetically, the id is the older structure; the ego arises directly from the id. The superego as the "heir of the Oedipus complex" (q.v.) also derives from the id. The id contains repressed ideas (images) and inherited "drives". Freud stresses that his concept of the id has nothing in common with C. G. Jung's "collective unconscious" (q.v.). For Freud, the ego is above all the locus of the eros and the death instinct (q.v.). The boundaries between the id and ego are fluid, and the aim of psychoanalysis is to strengthen the ego and thus to make it able to resist the dangers of the surrounding world, the punitive striving of the superego, and the temptations of the id. Psychoanalytical therapy is said to remove some of the energy (libido) from the id, by means of interpretation, "working through" and resistance analysis. Freud compares this work with the

reclamation of the Zuidersee: "The ego must replace the id". (*Werke*, Vol. 15, p. 86.)

The id is one of the most often cited hypothetical constructs of psychoanalysis. It lacks precise definition, is not related to any specific behavior, and is said to be recognized only in the therapeutic process. It is, therefore, a hypothesis largely alien to the methods of modern non-psychoanalytical psychology; its theoretical value for any scientific approach is, to say the least, questionable. The use made of the "id" as a psychoanalytic concept may best be illustrated by citing Freud: "The id . . . has no means of demonstrating love or hatred to the ego. It cannot say what it wants; it has not created a uniform will. Eros and the death instinct are at odds in it; we know the means used by one instinct to combat others. We might say that it is as if the id were ruled by the silent but powerful death instincts, which are at rest and try to still the troublemaker, eros, when it seeks to obey the pleasure principle; but even then we tend to underestimate the role of eros." (*Werke*, Vol. 15, p. 289.)

Bibliography: Freud, S.: Werke, Vols. 13, 15. London, 1940. Id.: New introductory lectures on psychoanalysis. London, 1933. Id.: The ego and the id. London, ²1962. Rapaport, D.: The structure of psychoanalytic theory: a systematizing attempt. In: Koch, S. (Ed.): Psychology: a study of a science, Vol. 3. New York, Toronto & London, 1959.

G. Lischke

Idea. 1. Even in modern times there is an immense number of diverse uses of the term (see 2, below). From the Cartesian viewpoint, an idea is an individual human mental concept; for Locke, an object of conscious thinking; for Berkeley, a sensory percept; and for Hume, an image of a sense impression. For Kant (very roughly summarized), however, an idea of reason is a concept which transcends all experience and cannot be represented sensuously. In general usage, an "idea" is usually that which is perceived mentally or intellectually, and not "by the senses". In any approximation to scientific psychology the term requires precise contextual definition. See *Logical reasoning; Mental imagery; Thinking.* J.C.

2. "Ideas" can be concepts, attitudes, intentions, notions, images or basic models. The idea is always a product of thinking (q.v.). In philosophical usage, a distinction may be made between three principal categories: (*a*) As a model or regulating principle, the idea denotes the universal or all-embracing: a degree of perfection in which things participate and which is a measure of their reality or cohesion; (*b*) as a concept or general idea, an idea denotes an abstract class determined by its elements and also by limiting conditions; this class can only be understood in terms of its logical significance; (*c*) as a phenomenon of intellectual activity, an idea is a product or content of an intellectual process, and may be an innate form devoid of content, or an impression received from the environment. *M.J.B.*

Ideal colors. An ideal color is one obtained through a reflecting surface with a remission curve or through a color filter with a transmission curve (see *Absorption*) having values of only 1 and 0 and at most two points of discontinuity (illumination: sunlight or standard light). Example of an ideal color: a color which has the full intensity of the spectrum by mixing all wavelengths between 490 nm and 520 nm. *A.H.*

Idealized image (syn. *Guiding fiction*). See *As if; Adler, A.*

Ideal type. A complex of characteristics posited as normative and intended to be generally binding, by which individual phenomena are classified, or from which they are derived: e.g. E. Spranger's "forms of life". In a wider sense, every natural complex

arrived at through correlational statistics is an "ideal type" in that, as a conceptual construct, it serves as a yardstick for classifying individual phenomena. *W.K.*

Ideation. Idea formation; cognition; thinking. See *Concept; Inner speech; Mental imagery; Psycholinguistics; Thinking.*

Idée fixe (syn. *Fixed idea*). An idea, or a series of related ideas, which dominates the mental life of a person. Occurs in certain states such as obsessional neurosis. When it occurs in a more developed form in psychotic states it is known as *monomania* (q.v.) or paranoia. See *Schizophrenia.* *R.H.*

Identical direction, law of. The law of identical direction in binocular vision was formulated by E. Hering. When an object is fixated in the field of vision, the visual axes of the two eyes are aligned so that they intersect at the fixation point; they do not terminate there, but continue after intersection. If the fixation point is defined in an appropriate experimental arrangement—a red bar for the visual axis of the right eye and a blue bar for the axis of the left eye—the bars do not appear next to each other but are fused into a single image on an imaginary median line between the two eyes. The two bars are situated "in identical visual directions", and their images are therefore received at identical (retinal) points (q.v.). *R.R.*

Identical elements, theory of. A theory of the transfer of training which supposes that the learning of one task transfers to a second task to the extent that the new task contains elements identical with those of the original task. *C.D.F.*

Identical (retinal) points (syn. *Corresponding retinal points*). If the two foveae and equivalent quadrants of the retinas of both eyes are made to coincide, an inserted needle would pass through identical retinal points; non-identical retinal points of both eyes are known as *disparate* (retinal) points. An object point whose reflected rays fall on disparate retinal points produces a double image. If the retinal points involved in the disparate image are not too far apart, the two images are fused by central coordination into a single spatial impression (see *Fusion*). This results in a three-dimensional impression (see *Depth perception*). Good spatial vision is possible in the fovea (q.v.) with a disparation of 20′ (it increases from the fovea toward the periphery), but the impression of depth disappears with a 25′ disparation: double images are then seen as such. Under normal circumstances this is not realized, because the eye constantly adjusts its accommodation (q.v.) and convergence (q.v.). Only objects fixated by the eye are seen clearly and consciously. In addition, not all the points of the object can be reflected at identical points, since the visual axes of the two eyes are in an angular relation to one another; no double images are formed: instead a spatial impression of the object appears.

Depth perception is only possible with disparation in the horizontal axis of the eye. Disparation in the vertical axis of the eye leads to double images rather than perception in depth.

The points whose reflective rays contact identical points on the two retinas are situated on the horopter (q.v.). All points which do not lie on the horopter result in a disparate image. If the disparate images are displaced in the temporal direction (i.e. outward) on the retina (bitemporal horizontal disparation), the impression appears "closer" than the horopter; but if the displacement is in the nasal direction (i.e. inward; binasal horizontal disparation) the impression appears "more distant". The horopter is always the point of reference.

The spatial impression is dependent on the distance of the objects, i.e. on the angle between the visual axes of the two eyes (convergence). Depth perception therefore diminishes as range increases.

In many oblique positions, simple vision may exist—contrary to what might be expected. New identity relations may develop, so that the fovea of one eye is not identical with that of the other, but corresponds with a point situated in the vicinity of the fovea. However, simple vision is frequently simulated in a squint because the image of one eye is suppressed in perception. See *Amblyopia*.

R.R.

Identical twins (syn. *Monozygotic*, or *monovular*, or *monochorionic twins*). Twins that develop in one chorionic sac from one split fertilized ovum (zygote). See *Twin studies*.

Identification. 1. A postulated (internal) defense (q.v.) mechanism by which a motive deprivation or motive frustration not previously experienced in its present intensity is diminished by adopting (see *Introjection*) one or more motives of other persons. The assumed motives may be substantially similar to the previous motives. Often the process centers on the person in whom the motive deprivation or frustration originated (identification with the aggressor). The direct *subjective benefit* of identification is the feeling of being at least in part the obstructive or exemplary person. The purpose of identification is to reduce the state of anxiety (q.v.) and temporary regression caused by the motive deprivation or frustration, and ultimately to forgo the opportunity for instinctual satisfaction which has been withdrawn or is threatened with punishment. The complexity of identification varies widely as a function of the frustrated motives. It ranges from thumb-sucking as a substitute for the mother's breast (identification with the mother's wish to still the child), to identification of the young girl with her mother (e.g. by playing at cooking as a substitute for direct contact with the mother), identification of the boy with his polite and reserved father (as an answer to the failure of many of his attempts to establish contact with his mother), identification of a pupil with his schoolmaster or mistress, and identification of a great pianist's pupil, a professor's assistant, or a head of government who had an outstanding or popular predecessor with the individual model. Diagnosis of the defense mechanism of identification is therefore generally meaningless without additional information on the motives which are withdrawn or assumed. Short-term identification is also possible, e.g. with an athlete, a team, or a film star; this process may be controlled by earlier identifications but its long-term effects are frequently insignificant. In social psychology (see *Socialization*), *social learning* (as identification) is a research subject in its own right (A. Bandura, 1963). The transition from imitation to identification is not clear. Continuing imitation, in particular of forms of behavior based on longer established and more complex motives, becomes identification (Miller & Dollard, 1941). Earlier forms of identification determine later identification. The totality of identifications constitutes the superego (q.v.), which includes the more primitive environmental motives which arose as reward or punishment motives in answer to individual obedience or disobedience, and were taken over by the individual as his own motives. See *Conscience*.

Bibliography: Bandura, A. & Walters, R. A.: Social learning and personality development. New York, 1963. Freud, A.: The ego and the mechanisms of defence. London, 1937. Freud, S.: Introductory lectures on psychoanalysis. London, ²1929. Miller, N. E. & Dollard, J.: Social learning and imitation. New Haven, 1941. Toman, W.: Motivation, Persönlichkeit, Umwelt. Göttingen, 1968. *W.T.*

2. Ach used the term "identification" for the process in which both retinal images are combined and the new phenomenon of depth perception is produced. In auditory perception the analogous result is directional discrimination. Ach also suggested that (in general) the fusion of two different psychic contents leads to a new content (production principle of identification).

Identification, social. A broad approximation of the action and thought of an individual to those of a model (e.g. father—son), frequently discussed in the context of imitation (q.v.); explained in terms of the greater attention given by the model individual. Bandura refers to a generalization of the cognitive aspects of imitation. See *Identification; Socialization.* *W.D.F.*

Ideology. 1. Any set of (e.g. political, religious or philosophical) beliefs. **2.** An ineffectual, moribund set of beliefs or program. **3.** A set of beliefs acquired (e.g. by indoctrination, q.v.) and held uncritically, to the exclusion of new (or contradictory) ideas.

Ideomotor idea (syn. *Ideomotor image*). An idea or image controlled emotionally or affectively which leads involuntarily to certain motor reactions. See *Ideomotor law.* *A.Th.*

Ideomotor law (syn. *Carpenter effect; Ideoreal law*). A phenomenon described by the English physiologist W. B. Carpenter in 1879: perceptual and imaginative contents, in particular those relating to perceived and/or imagined movements, may be accompanied by partial or complete involuntary drive impulses which correspond to the motor embodiment of those contents; i.e. ideas produce motor responses by innervation of muscle groups corresponding to those ideas. *H.H. & H.Ro.*

Ideomotor reflex. Haab's reflex (q.v.): the two pupils contract when a bright object is fixated in a dark room. The term *ideomotor* (= idea of movement) denotes all movements which are elicited involuntarily by emotionally colored ideas, especially in absentminded persons, who may, e.g., involuntarily imitate others. The physiological mechanism has not been explained.   *K.H.P.*

Ideo-real law. See *Ideomotor law.*

Idiocy. In non-English-speaking Europe the term is still used for a serious form of mental deficiency which is either innate or acquired through brain damage in very early childhood (e.g. birth trauma, encephalitis), characterized by an almost complete condition of ineducability (no development of speech or techniques of defense against physical danger). According to the British Mental Deficiency Act (1927) idiots were defined as representing one grade of mental deficiency (see *Deficiency, mental*), i.e. those unable to guard themselves against common physical dangers. The term has not been used other than clinically since the British Mental Health Act (1959), when "idiocy" was subsumed under "severe subnormality". See *Imbecility; Mental defect.*   *M.A.*

Idiographic. According to W. Windelband, the idiographic sciences are those which, unlike the nomothetic (q.v.) natural sciences, deal with unique events and conditions (historical sciences). The aim of idiographic personality (q.v.) research is to understand and describe as fully as possible the unique nature of an individual in the totality of his forms of expression and at the same time in the unity of his determining forces.   *D.B.*

Idiosyncrasy. 1. Psychological. a reaction which deviates from the norm in the form of an intense dislike for or oversensitivity to specific persons, animals, things, dishes, odors, etc. **2.** Medical: an innate or sometimes acquired hypersensitivity to certain substances (e.g. proteins, etc.) (see *Allergy; Psychosomatics*).   *F.C.S.*

IEM. See *Intromission-copulation-ejaculation mechanism.*

Illusion. An alteration of actuality in subjective perception: a mistaken perception of a given object. A distinction is made between illusions and hallucinations (q.v.), in which non-existent things are perceived. Illusions induced by social perception may facilitate orientation to specific requirements. Illusions occur frequently in general and specific social spheres. Psychotherapy (q.v.) may center on different combinations of illusions. See *Fantasy; Mental imagery; Schizophrenia.*   *U.H.S.*

Illusions, acoustic, optical. In the case of sense perception, an illusion is a subjective distortion of the objective content of the sense data. The many optical and acoustic illusions are experienced by most people and are not a special feature of abnormal states. Piaget has divided illusions into two classes: those in which the subjective distortion increases with age and those in which it decreases. Examples of illusions: *Müller-Lyer illusion, Hering's illusion* (q.v.). See *Geometrical-optical illusions.*   *C.D.F.*

Image. 1. A mental representation: i.e. one of the senses of "idea" (q.v.). **2.** Any representation, copy, likeness, imitation or similitude. **3.** A mental copy of a sensory quality or experience in the absence of any sensory stimulus. **4.** An attitude (q.v.) toward, e.g., a national type. See *Stereotype; Mental imagery.*

Image types (syn. *Ideational types; Idea types*). In Charcot's typology these are individuals whose mental imagery (q.v.) (or ideation) is oriented to a specific sensory modality. See *Fantasy*.

Bibliography: Kiefer, T.: Der visuelle Mensch. Munich & Basle, 1956.   *W.K.*

Imagination is the ability to call to mind, or "picture forth", situations, processes, objects and individuals which are not present. It includes, according to Jung, images of elementary situations, processes, objects or persons which appear as "collective human experience", supposedly without specific human experience. "Creative imagination" is the artistic or scientific combination of such elements into novel unities: e.g. as works of art, philosophic systems, or scientific hypotheses and planned experimentation. See *Fantasy; Archetypes; Imago; Literature, psychology of*.   *W.T.*

Imago ("image"). A wax portrait mask placed on a corpse displayed in the forum in ancient Rome. Freud used the term "imago" to denote the idealizing or de-idealizing distortion of personality which may occur in the course of transference (q.v.): the analyst, for example, may become a father-image. Jung used the term to denote the subsequently effective "image" of a reference person. A psychoanalytical journal took the name *Imago* (later *American Imago*) from C. Spitteler's novel of that title; it deals with literary, mythological and historical subjects from a psychoanalytical standpoint.
W.Sc.

Imbecility. The British Mental Deficiency Act (1927) defined imbeciles as "persons in whose case there exists mental defectiveness which, although not amounting to idiocy, is yet so pronounced that they are incapable of managing themselves or their affairs or, in the case of children, of being taught to do so". The term is no longer in use and since the introduction of the British Mental

Health Act (1959) has been replaced by the terms "subnormality" and "severe subnormality".   *V.K.J.*

Imipramine (*Tofranil;* G22355). A dibenzazepine derivative: one of the group of tricyclic antidepressants. Imipramine was used as the first tricyclic antidepressant and is generally used as a comparison substance for the effectiveness of other antidepressants. In healthy persons there are subjective symptoms of sedation with therapeutic and relatively small individual doses of imipramine. Performance changes in the form of reduced visual motor ability appear when higher therapeutic doses are administered. According to Di Mascio *et al.* (1964; 1968) the mood of healthy, depressed persons is improved, but a contrary effect is evident in some depressed patients.

Bibliography: Bättig, K. & Fischer, H.: Die Wirkung von Pharmaka auf psychische Leistungsfähigkeit und Persönlichkeitsfaktoren. Schweiz. Z. für Psychol. u. ihre Anwendung, 1964, *23*, 26–38. Di Mascio, A., Heninger, G. & Klerman, G.: Psychopharmacology of imipramine and desipramine. A comparative study of their effects in normal males. Psychopharmacologia, 1964, *5*, 361–71. Di Mascio, A., Meyer, R. E. & Stifer, L.: Effects of imipramine on individuals varying in levels of depression. Amer. J. Psychiat., 1968, *124*, 55–8. Ideström, C.-M. & Cadenius, B.: Imipramine–Desmethylimipramine. A pharmacological study of human beings. Psychopharmacologia, 1964, *5*, 431–39.   *P.D.*

Imitation. 1. Experiments in animals, children and adults have shown that the observed behavior of a model may provoke more or less similar behavior in the observing subject (O), even when the latter did not show similar behavior patterns before (learning by imitation). The extent and nature of the imitation are dependent on features of the model, the traits and experience of the observer, and the observed reward or punishment for the model behavior ("representative reinforcement"). The acquisition of, e.g., aggressive behavior as well as standards and value scales is substantially influenced by imitation. See *Socialization; Aggression; Identification*.

2. Behavior is said to be imitative if (*a*) there is a similarity between the behavior of the model and of the imitator; and (*b*) the behavior of the model and not other stimuli is the determining factor in the behavior of the imitator. The instinct (q.v.) theory of imitation has been replaced since about 1920 by various conclusions of learning theory. Allport (1924), Piaget (1951), O. H. Mowrer (1960) emphasized the importance of associative and classical conditioning mechanisms, while N. E. Miller & J. Dollard (1941) as well as B. F. Skinner (1953) stressed instrumental mechanisms. For imitative learning, the contiguity of sensory events is essential (according to Bandura, 1968), and for imitative behavior the nature of the reinforcement. See *Conditioning, classical and operant; Imprinting; Learning*.

Bibliography: Bandura, A.: Social learning theory of identificatory processes. In: **Goslin, D. A.** (Ed.): Handbook of socialization theory and research. Chicago, 1968. **Ervin, S. M.**: Imitation and structural change in children's language. In: **Lenneberg, E. H.**: New directions in the study of language. Cambridge, Mass., 1966, 163–89. **Id. & Walters, R. H.**: Social learning and personality development. New York, 1968. **Flanders, J. P.**: A review of research on imitative behavior, Psychol. Bull, 1968, *69*, 316–37. **Foss, B. M.**: Imitation. In: **Foss, B. M.** (Ed.): Determinants of infant behavior, Vol. 3. London & New York, 1965.   *D.B. & C.M.*

Immediate memory (syn. *Short-term memory*). Momentary storage (duration not exceeding 30 sec. approximately) of information items and their reproduction, as compared with long-term storage (retentive or real memory). This is a genuine function of memory (q.v.). Immediate memory is very liable to disturbance; the matter is very frequently forgotten; the amount depends on the material and the particular sensory modality, and can be extended by verbal coding (Dornič, 1970). In consequence of the unusual conditions operating when the information items were acquired (e.g. a single presentation), immediate memory is treated in some research projects as a unique phenomenon, but is thought to be governed by the same processes as long-term memory (Postman, 1964). Clinical (retrograde amnesia, q.v.), neurophysiological (electric shock), cybernetic, and factor-analytical observations nevertheless suggest that an independent process (and system) is at work. Broadbent (1958) is of the opinion that the immediate memory acts as a selective filter and distributes information.

Bibliography: Broadbent, D. E.: Perception and communication. Oxford & New York, 1958. **Dornič, K.** (Ed.): Visuelles Wahrnehmen. Bratislava, 1970, 81–94. **Postman, L.**: Short-term memory and incidental learning. In: **Melton, A. W.** (Ed.): Categories of human learning. New York, 1964.

Immorality. 1. Dishonesty. **2.** Contrariety to that which a particular moral, religious, legal, political, or social system conceives as virtuous or binding behavior.

Imperceptible given. All those things which at the moment cannot be perceived by some persons and yet are experienced as being really present. For example, all the parts of a perceived object and not merely its visible aspect are experienced as being directly present. Completion phenomena, which have been closely studied by gestalt psychologists, represent an important aspect of the imperceptible given, which must be distinguished from what is only represented in the mind.   *F.Ma.*

Implosive therapy. A form of "learning therapy" developed by Stampfl (1968). Taking as his starting-points the two-factor theory (q.v.) of learning (q.v.) and the concept of secondary motivation (q.v.), Stampfl assumes that neurotic symptoms represent avoidance responses which are produced and maintained by a complex pattern of conditioned aversive stimuli. (See *Neurosis*.)

In contrast to other forms of therapy based

on learning theory (see *Behavior therapy*), implosive therapy makes use of suggestions from depth psychology (q.v.). Implosive therapy does not set out to inhibit neurotic symptoms directly but endeavors to remove the symptoms by extinguishing the conditioned aversive stimuli which motivate the neurotic behavior. In order to do this, the maximum number of stimuli of the original conditioning, with the exception of the unconditioned aversive stimulus, are reproduced verbally or in some other form. On the principle of extinction generalization (see *Extinction; Generalization*), this diminishes the "aversiveness" if the conditioned stimuli are removed from those avoidance responses which constitute the neurotic behavior. Special attention is given to "concealed" stimuli, i.e. stimuli of which the patient cannot give an account (see *Unconscious*). Hence implosive therapy takes into account determinants of neurotic behavior neglected by other learning therapies. See *Aversion therapy*.

Bibliography: Stampfl, T. G. & Lewis, D. J.: Implosive therapy—a behavioral therapy? Behav. Res. Therapy, 1968, 6, 31–6.   *F.Ma.*

Impotence. 1. Inability of the male to achieve or maintain sufficient penile erection to complete sexual intercourse. Often regarded as resulting from psychological factors, e.g. sex guilt, unfortunate early experiences, feelings of inadequacy, and so on. **2.** Inability of the male to produce offspring (*sterility*). **3.** A feeling of helplessness (inability to control events).   *G.D.W.*

Impression. An overall picture of some object, say a landscape or a person, as the product of a relatively complete process of cognition or perception. In the psychology of expression (q.v.), an impression is constitutive in so far as there is no expression as such, but only an expression for someone who apprehends it as a (valid) impression. There are three main approaches:

1. *Phenography.* Study of the sensory channels by which the impression of someone's personal "thusness" is transmitted. The emphasis is on visual (see *Physiognomy; Pathognomy*) and auditory (phonognomy) access; less regard is paid to the tactile (manual pressure) or olfactory aspects of impression.

2. *Analysis of function and interpretation.* This approach deals with the question of how expressive phenomena are apperceived and interpreted. Social perception (q.v.) research is important in this regard (Graumann, 1955/56; Tajfel, 1969; Tagiuri, 1969). There are four main (in part socially conditioned) perceptive factors which go to form an impression: (*a*) *selectivity*, which, in addition to attitude (q.v.) and attention (q.v.), includes the concepts of sensitivization and perceptual defense (q.v.); (*b*) the *organizing act of perception*, underlying which are the gestalt tendencies of perceptual cognition; (*c*) *accentuation*, which modifies the impression by emphasizing a certain point of view; and (*d*) *fixation*, concentrating on points in the stimulus field selected by reason of attitude, prejudice, anxiety, etc. Research into these perceptive factors coincides in large measure with the actual-genetic aspect. From the ontogenetic angle, maturation and learning processes form part of the socio-cultural background (attitudes, stereotypes).

3. *Conditional analysis and interpretation.* This approach examines impressionability and the means by which human or animal expressions become impressions for the recipient. (*a*) The theory of association (q.v.) assumes that, when certain expressions are presented to the recipient, similar ideas (images) and emotions are (associatively) set in train; (*b*) the analogy (q.v.) theory maintains that the observer of an extraneous expression draws conclusions about it on the basis of his own behavior; (*c*) the theory of empathy (q.v.) (T. Lipps) assumes that an impression of another psyche comes about by means of "mimpathic" and "copathic" experience of others' expressions; (*d*) the

theory of rudiments—a version of "empathy"—is based on the assumption that sympathetic micro-movements (ideomotor law, q.v.) during the perception of an extraneous expression produce the elements of a corresponding inner state. Each of these theories is seriously inadequate. The problem of "impressionability" (understanding expression) is still unresolved. Interesting approaches to the phylogenetic aspect are to be found in ethology, which connects the "innate releasing mechanism" (q.v.) with the phylogenetic development of impressionability (Leyhausen, 1967). See *Emotion; Instinct.*

Bibliography: Ewert, O. M.: Zur Ontogenese des Ausdrucksverstehens. Handbuch d. Psychologie, Vol. 5. Göttingen, 1965, 289–308. Graumann, C.-F.: Social Perception. Z. exp. angew. Psychol., 1955/56, *3*, 605–61. Leyhausen, P.: Biologie von Ausdruck und Eindruck. Psychol. Forsch., 1967, *31*, 113–227. Tagiuri, R.: Person perception. Handbook Soc. Psychol., Vol. 3, 1969. Tajfel, H.: Social and cultural factors in perception. Handbook Soc. Psychol., Vol. 3, 1969.   *F. Kiener*

Imprinting. Many animals attach themselves only to members of their own species. But some can prefer creatures of another species if they are encountered first; they follow them about, pair with them when fully grown, and try to copulate with them: "imprinting" has taken place.

1. *Definition.* (*a*) According to Lorenz (1935), imprinting is learning (q.v.) restricted to certain periods in life (sensitive or critical phases); (*b*) only the releaser, or key stimulus (q.v.), of a certain reaction (i.e. characteristics of an object in a specific functional area) is imprinted by differentiation of releasing mechanisms with—initially—low selectivity; (*c*) imprinting is *irreversible*; (*d*) not individual but species characteristics are learned; (*e*) imprinting can take place even before readiness for the corresponding responses has matured; (*f*) *readiness to learn is extinguished* when something definite has been learned, or because of internal processes

of change at the termination of the critical period—even when there has been no learning.

Hess (1959) agrees with Lorenz in emphasizing that imprinting differs from associative learning: in imprinting, the animal achieves more success if practice is restricted to a short period of time; in addition, in choice situations what was learned *first* prevails over what was learned *later*. With learning by association exactly the opposite holds good. Moreover, in the latter case aversive stimuli bring about a rejection of the associated stimulus, whereas they reinforce imprinting. A further difference is the effect of the tranquilizer meprobamate on learning achievement: in hens the solution of color-discrimination tasks is not impaired, whereas imprintability drops almost to zero.

Since the concept of imprinting is based on an "injunctive definition" in Hassenstein's (1954) sense (i.e. ". . . to define the concept of life it is necessary to enumerate a number of constituent characteristics, none of which, taken by itself, constitutes life, but which taken all together, in their summation and interaction, do indeed represent the essence of life". Lorenz, 1966), continuous transitions to related and similar phenomena may be expected. Hence Eibl-Eibesfeld (1967) points to the fact that the criteria (*a*) and (*d*) are also valid for other learning processes Since the requisite basis has still not been found for statement (*e*), what remains as the distinguishing feature of imprinting is only "primacy of experience" (*c*) = irreversibility (Hess, 1959; Lannoy, 1967). However, according to Smith (1969), it cannot be generalized: the presence of an imprintable phase must be considered the crucial difference from associative learning. That such a phase does in fact exist is denied by Hinde (1955, 1962), Thorpe (1963) and Bateson (1963). Lannoy (1967) suggests a new approach: he would prefer a distinction to be made between imprinting and learning on the basis of the "facility in learning certain interactions dependent on the transmutation time", in which operation a "certain transmutation time-limit prevents animals from reaching all response levels".

2. *Incidence.* The dominance of early experience with members of a different species over later experience with members of the same species has so far been established in fish, birds and mammals (in particular). Among fish, certain mouth-breeders (*hemichromis bimaculatus*) prefer alien young to their own if, when they breed for the first time, eggs of an alien species are given them as substitutes (Myrberg, 1964). The fact that mammals reared by humans become attached to them instead of to members of their own species has been observed, e.g., by Grzimek (1949), F. Darling (1938), Hediger (1955), P. Leyhausen (1967) and L. Wilson (1966). According to Gray (1958), Thorpe (1961) and Hampson (1961) man, too, is probably imprintable. There is as yet no experimental proof; the psychoanalytical theory of childhood dreams and various ethnological observations (M. Mead) support this view, but both have only limited validity.

3. *Experimental investigations.* There are numerous accounts of experiments carried out into object imprinting (following responses and behavior toward sexual partners) and motor imprinting (learning the song of parents of an alien species) in birds.

(*a*) *Part areas and methodology.* The following were studied: beginning and end of learning ability, learning time required, influence of learning conditions on learning performance, nature of the learned phenomenon, effect of the learning processes and the matter learnt on the form of actions and their relation to objects, and the degree to which the success of later learning processes depends on earlier learning. The findings are based on comparisons of the responses of test animals when either members of the same or different species or certain objects are presented to them at time intervals or simultaneously.

(*b*) *Results.* In following experiments with a one-hour learning period, ducks are most susceptible to imprinting thirteen to sixteen hours after birth (critical period). Until they are five hours old, chicks react unspecifically; after twenty-four hours they react less and less well, until finally flight occurs (end of the sensitive period) (Fabricius, 1964; Hess, 1959). Changes in the duration of contact can have an effect on the extent to which following and sexual behavior can be released: after remaining for at least forty-eight hours with the imprinting object, two-day-old chickens prefer this in copulation experiments; shorter contact periods produce only following responses (Andrew, 1966). Apart from the *duration of contact*, successful imprinting depends, too, on the *frequency of contact:* a contact of twenty minutes repeated on five successive days produces better following imprinting with a turkey than if five contacts are arranged in the course of a single day (Hale, 1969).

Apart from time factors, successful imprinting depends on properties of the object characteristics; it can be enhanced by movement and the combination of qualitatively different stimuli and the simultaneous presentation of the imprinting characteristic and the gratification of a need. (Immelmann, 1967; Klopfer, 1968; Smith & Nott, 1970; Gottlieb, 1965; Boyd & Fabricius, 1965).

Responses to combinations of characteristics in choice experiments show that imprinting is possible on certain colors, patterns, body shapes and movements, sounds, kinds of odor and combinations of all these (Smith & Bird, 1963; Goodwin & Hess, 1969; and others). But, according to Klopfer (1968), the results of experiments can turn out differently when the same pairs of characteristics are presented; this may depend on the nature of the reward, the arrangement selected for the experiment, and the animal's innate preference for certain stimulus qualities as its internal condition varies. The strengthening or weakening of imprinting by subsequent experiences can also influence results (Schutz, 1965; Sluckin, 1964).

Imprinting always affects only the *orientation*

505   IMPRINTING AND LACTATION

and never the form of the action: imprinted animals mate with members of
different species but use movements peculiar
to their own species (Schutz, 1965; Lannoy,
1967; von Frisch, 1957).

Subsequent learning processes can follow
independently of any previous ones and
produce imprinting on different objects in
different functional areas (Lorenz, 1935;
Schutz, 1965).

Similar conditions apply to song imprinting as to object imprinting (Thorpe,
1958; Nicolai, 1959; Immelmann, 1965).

No characteristics which might exclusively
distinguish imprinting have so far been obtained from investigations based on behavioral comparisons, but there are two
which stand out: the imprinting phase and
the preference of what was learned first to
what was learned subsequently (Lannoy,
1967; Eibl-Eibesfeld, 1967). The exact nature
of the processes leading to these features is
still an open question; if they were known it
could perhaps be shown whether imprinting
differs fundamentally from other forms of
learning (Smith, 1969). See *Instinct; Animal
psychology; Comparative psychology; Conditioning, classical and operant.*

Bibliography: Andrew, R. J.: Precocious adult
behaviour in the young chick. Anim. Behav., 1966,
14, 485–500. Bateson, P. P. G.: Filial and avoidance
behaviour in chicks. Unpublished Ph.D. thesis.
Cambridge, 1963. Boyd, H. & Fabricius, E.: Observations on the incidence of following of visual and
auditory stimuli in naïve mallard ducklings (Anas
platyrhynchos). Behaviour, 1965, *25*, 1–15. Eibl-
Eibesfeld, I.: Grundriss der vergleichenden Verhaltensforschung. Munich, 1967. Fabricius, E.: Zur Ethologie
junger Anatiden. Acta Zool. Fenn., 1951, *68*, 1–178.
Id.: Crucial periods in the development of the following response in ducklings. Z. Tierpsychol., 1964,
21, 326–37. Frisch, O. von: Mit einem Purpurreiher
verheiratet. Z. Tierpsychol., 1957, *14*, 233–37.
Goodwin, E. B. & Hess, E. H.: Stimulus generalization and responses to "supernormal" stimuli in the
unrewarded pecking behaviour of young chicks.
Behaviour, 1969, *34*, 223–37. Gottlieb, G.: Imprinting
in relation to parental and species identification by
avian neonates. J. comp. physiol. Psychol., 1965, *59*,
345–56. Gray, P. H.: Theory and evidence of imprinting in human infants. J. Psychol., 1958, *46*

155–60. Grzimek, B.: Ein Fohlen, das kein Pferd
kannte. Z. Tierpsychol., 1949, *6*, 391–405. Hale,
E. B.: Stages in the process of visual imprinting.
Eleventh International Ethological Conference, 1969.
Hampson, J. L. & Hampson, J. G.: The ontogenesis
of sexual behaviour in man. In: Young, W. C. (Ed.):
Sex and internal secretion. London, 1961. Hassenstein, B.: Abbildende Begriffe. Verh. d. Deutsch.
Zool. Ges., 1954, 197–202. Hediger, H.: Studies of
the psychology and behaviour of captive animals in
zoos and circuses. London, 1955. Hess, E. H.:
Imprinting. Science, 1959, *130*, 133–41. Hinde, R. A.:
The following response of moorhens and coots. Brit.
J. Anim. Behav., 1955, *3*, 121–22. Id.: Some aspects
of the imprinting problem. Sym. Zool. Soc. London,
1962, *8*, 129–38. Immelmann, K.: Prägungserschein-
ungen in der Gesangsentwicklung junger Zebrafinken.
Die Naturwiss., 1965, *52*, 169–70. Id.: Zur onto-
genetischen Gesangsentwicklung bei Prachtfinken.
Zool. Anz. Suppl., 1967, *30*, 320–32. Klinghammer,
E.: Factors influencing choice of mate in altrical
birds. In: Stevenson, H. W. (Ed.): Early behavior.
New York, 1967, 5–42. Klopfer, P. H.: Stimulus
references and discrimination in neonatal Ducklings.
Behaviour, 1968, *32*, 309–14. Lannoy, J. de: Zur
Prägung von Instinkthandlungen. Z. Tierpsychol.,
1967, *24*, 162–200. Lorenz, K.: Der Kumpan in der
Umwelt des Vogels. J. f. Ornith, 1935, *83*, 137–213.
Id.: On aggression. London, 1966. Myrberg, A. A.:
An analysis of preferential care of eggs and young
by adult cichlid fishes. Z. Tierpsychol., 1964, *21*,
53–98. Nicolai, J.: Familientradition in der Gesangs-
tradition des Gimpels (Pyrrhula pyrrhula, L.) J. f.
Ornithol., 1959, *100*, 39–46. Schutz, F.: Sexuelle
Prägung bei Anatiden. Z. Tierpsychol., 1965, *22*,
50–103. Sluckin, W.: Imprinting and early learning.
London, 1964. Smith, F. V. & Bird, M. W.: The
relative attraction for the domestic chick of combinations of stimuli in different sensory modalities.
Anim. Behav., 1963, *11*, 300–5. Smith, F. V.:
Attachment of the young, imprinting and other
developments. Edinburgh, 1969. Smith, F. V. &
Nott, K. H.: The "critical period" in relation to the
strength of the stimulus. Z. Tierpsychol., 1970, *27*,
108–15. Thorpe, W. H.: Further studies on the process
of song learning in the chaffinch (Fringilla coelebs).
Nature, 1958, *182*, 554–57. Id.: Sensitive periods in
learning of animals and men: a study of imprinting
with special reference to the introduction of cyclic
behaviour. In: Thorpe, W. H. & Zangwill, O. L.
(Eds.): Current problems in animal behaviour.
Cambridge, 1961. Id.: Learning and instinct in
animals. London, ²1963.   *B. Tschanz*

Imprinting and lactation. The concept of
"imprinting" (q.v.) was first used in animal

psychology. As applied to human beings it was used to express the long-lasting, "imprinted" effect of impressions received in the early months of life. In this connection the following was observed: if a baby is given a wet-nurse for the first weeks and months after birth, when the infant is weaned subsequently, it remains for a time more attached to the nurse than to its mother. It can be seen from this that the breast-feeding period has an emphatic "imprinting" effect from foster-mother to child.   *M.S.*

Impulse. See *Impulsiveness; Drive; Instinct; Motivation.*

Impulsiveness (syn. *Impulsivity*). A temperamental factor classifiable as extraversion. Impulsiveness is characterized by spontaneous direct action with little regard for the consequences. There is a slight correlation between impulsivity and the intelligence factors of fluency of thought and expression.   *G.K.*

Impulsive neuroses are mental disorders in which the person affected follows irresistible impulses, e.g. to start fires, wander, steal or commit certain crimes. The impulsive neurotic is often similar to the "psychopathic personality" in his behavior. See *Psychopathology.*   *W.T.*

Inadequate stimuli are significant changes in the environment which do not occur under normal conditions; these changes affect excitable biological substrates and evoke reactions in them (excitation). Electrical or mechanical stimuli are inadequate for the eye whereas thermic stimuli are inadequate for the vestibular apparatus (ear); nevertheless they react with a corresponding sense impression or response if the inadequate stimulus is sufficiently strong. The threshold (minimum successful stimulus strength) is substantially higher with inadequate than with adequate stimuli.   *E.D.*

Inanition. This term denotes the psychological aftereffects of the withdrawal of affective attention in early childhood. After a stay in hospital or in a children's home where the child has to do without affectionate interest, there may be a significant retardation of psychomotor development, or some regression to earlier behavior patterns, accompanied by a physical susceptibility to illness. See *Hospitalism.*

Bibliography: Yarrow, L. J.: Maternal deprivation: toward an empirical and conceptual revaluation. Psychol. Bull., 1961, *58*, 459–90.   *M.Sa.*

Inbreeding. The mating of closely related animals, usually resulting in the magnification of certain traits. These traits may be regarded as favorable (e.g. intelligence) or unfavorable (e.g. deafness), but deleterious effects are apparently more likely because of the increased manifestation of recessive and mutated traits. Also, for some unknown reason, inbreeding tends to reduce the fertility of the offspring. The *coefficient of inbreeding* for an individual is calculated as the likelihood that he will possess identical genes at any pair of loci as a result of inheritance from both mother and father.

In sociology, *inbreeding* refers to the process by which a group or institution may tend toward stagnation or even extinction through failure to enlist new elements.   *G.D.W.*

Incentive. 1. Something which incites to action (particularly higher productivity). 2. An incidental reward. 3. A motive (q.v.).

Incest. Sexual relations (coitus) between related individuals. Infringement of one of the oldest sexual taboos, which stems from magical and religious sources; considered as a serious sexual offence in most societies. The extent of the prohibition and the penalty threatened vary widely. There is no legal penalty in some countries (e.g. Luxembourg, Belgium,

Portugal, Turkey). The commonest forms are father-daughter and stepfather-stepdaughter incest. The proportion of concealed cases is thought to be high. Cases disclosed: primarily from the lower social strata (80%–90%); in the middle and higher social groups the "zone of secrecy" is greater. Recidivism: less than 5%. Male offenders are on average forty to forty-one years old on committing their first offense; they are primarily of average or above average intelligence (60%–85%); half of them are socially and psychopathologically unobtrusive; they are rarely psychotic (3%–6%), and in very few cases "hypersexual". The main features of offenders with striking social and psychopathological characteristics are lack of control over aggressive, oral (alcohol), and/or sexual impulses (in all about 40%), and/or maladjusted careers or lives (approximately 35%). The female "victims" are generally at the age of puberty when the offenses begin (around thirteen years old); they are of average or above-average intelligence (approximately 80%), and frequently show disturbed personality symptoms (about 70%) —but these characteristics are no more frequent after incest than before. Incestuous relationships are conditioned by many different factors. The main predisposing factor is a disturbed psychosocial relationship in the family. Incest is not a cause but a consequence of disorganized family life (approx. 80–90%).

The origin of the taboo has as yet resisted all historico-anthropological and psychological attempts at elucidation (degeneration theory, theory of instinctive incest-defense, theory of acquired disinclination, politico-economic cooperation theory, the phylogenetic theory of the incest taboo. See Maisch, 1968, for survey and summary). One sociological theory holds that in modern industrial society the incest taboo has lost any vital social significance, but nevertheless views it as an integrative element of the bourgeois family structure which may well fulfill important psychological and social functions in the development of the individual personality (Parsons' structural-functional theory).

Bibliography: Freud, S.: Totem and taboo. New York, 1918. Maisch, H.: Inzest, Hamburg, 1968. Parsons, T. & Bales, R. F.: Family, socialization and interaction process. New York, ⁴1954. *H.M.*

Inclination. 1. A leaning or sloping. An angle measured from the vertical. **2.** A motivational tendency (non-technical usage).

G.D.W.

Incontinence. Inability to retain stool or urine. Can be caused by, e.g., paraplegia (lesion of the spinal cord) after an accident; damage to the lumbar region of the spinal cord, caused by a slipped disc or carcinomal metastasis. Apart from such physiologically explicable cases, modern approaches to most forms of enuresis (q.v.) or encopresis (q.v.) treat them as faulty conditioning, variously amenable to behavior therapy (q.v.).

E.D.

Incubation. In the study of anxiety (q.v.) and fear (q.v.), the term "incubation" has been used to describe two related phenomena. The first usage refers to "a growth of fear over a time interval which follows some aversive stimulus. The increase in fear is assumed to be spontaneous in the sense that the time interval is free of further exposure to the aversive stimulus" (McAllister & McAllister, 1967, p. 180). In a review of studies dealing with this concept of incubation of anxiety, McAllister & McAllister (1967, p. 189) conclude that "the phenomenon has yet to be convincingly demonstrated". Eysenck (1968) suggests that incubation in this sense does not deserve a special title, and can be explained in terms of a reminiscence-type theory based on consolidation of memory traces.

More recently, the term incubation has been used to refer to an increment in conditioned response (CR) over a number of trials when the conditioned stimulus (CS) is applied but without reinforcement (UCS). This second concept Eysenck (1968) prefers to call the "Napalkov phenomenon" in honor of the Russian investigator who first drew attention to it. Evidence for the Napalkov phenomenon from both animals and human Ss. is reviewed by Eysenck (1968). In these studies the CRs increase in strength over trials where the original aversive UCS was withheld. The effects are clearly in evidence and are difficult to fit into any existing learning paradigm. In the usual conditioning paradigm the CR gradually extinguishes when the CS is presented in the absence of the UCS. In the studies under discussion, the CR increased. Thus, in the first series of experiments, the CR increased over *time* without further conditioning trials; in the second series the CR increased over *unreinforced trials*.

Eysenck (1968) proposes a theory to explain the second phenomenon, laying stress on the CR being, in itself, an aversive stimulus in a feedback cycle which interferes with the usual extinction processes. He argues that an unreinforced CS will always provoke a decrement in the CR, but will also provoke an increment. The observed CR will be the resultant of these two opposing tendencies. Extinction will occur when the decrement exceeds the increment, incubation when the opposite occurs. The increment in strength of the CR is explained in the following way: in aversive conditioning, a CS is followed by a UCS which produces a variety of unconditioned responses (UCRs). After a number of pairings of CS and UCS, the CS either alone or accompanied by the UCS will produce a variety of CRs, and some of these CRs will be physiological in nature (arousal, q.v., which is termed anxiety or fear). The CS has thus acquired the function of signaling danger and impending pain. The emotional responses of fear or anxiety thus elicited are themselves aversive stimuli which, by classical conditioning, come to be associated not only with the reinforced CS but

also with the unreinforced CS. By a feedback system, even unreinforced CSs are actually reinforced and tend to evoke more fear on the subsequent trials. The stimulus value of the emotional responses is in most cases small, and the resultant of the increments and decrements of unreinforced CSs will usually produce extinction. But under certain conditions, possibly when the UCS is exceptionally strong, the resultant effect will be incubation of the conditioned emotional response. A number of parametric studies are required to ascertain the conditions under which incubation instead of extinction occurs, and some hypotheses are proposed by Eysenck (1968) and Ramsay (1969).

Incubation of anxiety as seen in the laboratory has important implications for the study of neurotic behavior. The view of the development of neurosis in learning terms has long been considered inadequate to cover what the clinician observes in his patients. In humans, the processes of verbal conditioning, covert sensitization, imaginal behavior rehearsal, and cognitive factors probably play an important role in the incubation of anxiety, and the behaviorally-oriented theoretician and clinician have yet to integrate these concepts in their approaches. It is possible that a fuller investigation of the processes involved in incubation will bring theory and clinical practice more into line in the understanding and treatment of neurosis (q.v.).

Bibliography: Eysenck, H. J.: A theory of the incubation of anxiety/fear responses. Behav. Res. & Therapy, 1968, 6, 309–21. McAllister, D. E. & McAllister, W. R.: Incubation of fear: an examination of the concept. J. exp. res. Person., 1967, 2, 180–90. Ramsay, R. W.: Incubation of emotional responses. Unpubl. MS., Univ. of Amsterdam, 1969.

R. W. Ramsay

Incubation processes. 1. Processes during a phase of apparent rest in which a covert development takes place after which there is a distinct alteration in the general condition. **2.** Medical: processes during the time between infection and the outbreak of an illness. **3.** Psychology of thought: several "phasic" models of productive thinking use the categories (*a*) preparation, (*b*) incubation, (*c*) illumination, and (*d*) verification. *H.W.*

Incubus. A nightmare. In medieval demonology, an evil spirit which was supposed to lie upon and oppress sleeping persons, especially a male spirit which copulated with sleeping women. Cf. *Succubus*: a female spirit which seduced men during sleep, thus causing nocturnal emissions. *G.D.W.*

Independent variable. See *Variable*.

Index. Indices are ratios characteristic of a body-build and summarized in a mathematical formula; they facilitate the determination of a type (e.g. body-build indices according to H. J. Eysenck, E. Kretschmer, G. Kühnel, W. Plattner, I. Pignet, E. Strömgren, K. Westphal). See *Body-build index*. *W.K.*

Indicators, motivational. A term used to denote variables of stimuli which arouse motivation (q.v.) to a specific behavior, and those which follow some motivation, i.e. variables of motivated responses, motivated behavior. *R.Hä.*

Indifference point; indifference zone. The point of transition between opposites in experience, the neutral point in any series having positive and negative values. This point has been called the *Adaptation level* (q.v.) (Helson), since it varies with its context. A slightly more specific definition applies in the context of psychophysics (q.v.) experiments, in which the indifference point is that stimulus in a graded series which is reproduced or recognized correctly, whereas smaller ones are overestimated and larger ones underestimated. *C.D.F.*

Individual. 1. A single unit, theme, case, etc. **2.** A single, distinct organism. **3.** A person (q.v.), especially as conceived by psychoanalysis (q.v.) or individual psychology (q.v.). Adler drew specific attention to the difficulty of harmoniously integrating the individual into society (socialization, q.v.). He suggested that the child had to overcome a natural feeling of inferiority, and the way in which he managed this was dependent on the environment (parents). He considered this to be the starting point for education. See *Adler, Alfred*. *M.S.*

Individualism is the tendency to attribute independent reality to a single individual (implying nominalism) and to conceive of him as the sole basis of all values and the sole source of social achievements. The individual is both the highest value and the ultimate objective: groups, institutions and the state are simply means to allow the individual to develop. The attitude of the individualist leads to a pattern of behavior which is independent of collective standards. *M.R.*

Individuality. The unique nature of the personality (q.v.). Representatives of idiographic (q.v.) personality research (such as G. W. Allport) understand individuality as the unique *qualitative* characteristic of the individual, whereas representatives of the nomothetic variety (such as J. P. Guilford) consider it as the unique *quantitative* characteristic (in the sense of a uniqueness of the individual configuration of factor values in the relevant ability and personality factors). Apart from twin studies, no reliable empirical research data is available on the subject of individuality. But see *Abilities; Traits; Type*. *K.P.*

Individual psychology. 1. See *Differential psychology*.
2. The psychological theory of Alfred Adler

(q.v.): "The fundamental fact in human development is the dynamic and purposive striving of the psyche.... The unity of personality is implicit in each human being's existence. Every individual represents both a unity of personality and the individual fashioning of that unity." An approach based on the existence of an inferiority complex (q.v.), especially in neurotic individuals, and on a reaction to this complex in the form of compensation. In addition to its influence on the methods of certain psychotherapists who follow Adler's theory, "individual psychology" has had a considerable influence in some educational circles.

Bibliography: Adler, A.: The education of children. New York & London, 1930. *J.L.I.*

Individuation. Jung uses the term "individuation" to characterize the process of reaching maturity and developing the individual personality. The collective unconscious (q.v.) which is composed of archetypes (q.v.), is said gradually to change through individuation into the self (see *Ego*). In immature personalities the process of individuation is delayed. Some Jungian psychotherapeutic methods attempt to foster individuation by analyzing the symbols which appear in dreams and visions. *J.L.I.*

Indoctrination. Instruction in ideas or beliefs which requires their complete acceptance.

Induction. An intellectual procedure which consists of working through a finite number of given propositions in order to arrive at one proposition (the conclusion) which implies them all. In most cases the given assertions are inferred from observed facts. The induction then leads to a law which summarizes them. If the law is able to account for more than the observed facts, we speak of *ampliative induction* (or inference), and in other cases of *perfect induction*; in this case we have a deduction based on the laws

of logic: what is true for each individual entity of a class is true for all other instances. On the problematical nature of the assumption of a measure of uniformity in nature (an assumption made in all inductive reasoning), see Ayer, 1956.

Bibliography: Ayer, A. J.: The problem of knowledge. Harmondsworth, 1956, 71-5. *J.B.G.*

Induction coil. An apparatus based on the principle of electro-magnetic induction which can be used to provide a variable but controlled amount of electric current as an aversive stimulus, usually for experiments on learning or conditioning. *G.D.W.*

Inductor. See *Token object*.

Industrial engineer. An engineer who has to solve industrial problems (systems, working times, personnel management, etc.) by analytical methods. See *Time and motion study*. *G.R.W.M.*

Industrial engineering. The work of industrial engineers in planning, implementing and supervising measures to increase productivity. This work is based not only on technical and business experience but primarily on ergonomic principles. *G.R.W.M.*

Industrial psychology. That branch of applied psychology (q.v.) which is concerned with work and economics. Its aim has often been stated as maximizing *efficiency* in the production and distribution of goods and services through the study and manipulation of "*human factors*"—the approach of *ergonomics* (q.v.)—but there is an increasing tendency for the satisfaction of workers and consumers to be regarded as an end in itself (Smith & Cranny, 1968). Though the industrial psychologist may orientate his work from the viewpoint of the individual worker, management, the organization, or the consumer, it is widely recognized that efficiency is usually best served if the interests of all parties are taken into account. There follows a brief outline of some of the problems and areas with which industrial psychologists may be concerned.

1. *Vocational guidance*. Since the choice of an occupation is one of the most critical decisions any person has to face in the course of a lifetime, he may seek the advice of a psychologist. The aims of vocational guidance are to bring the individual to a realistic awareness of his own potential, and to point out those of the various possibilities open to him which are compatible with both his talents and interests. To supplement his skill as an interviewer, the vocational counselor will probably use *objective tests* (q.v.) of general *intelligence* (e.g. Wechsler Adult Intelligence Scale, Raven Matrices), specific *aptitudes* (e.g. Differential Aptitude Test, q.v., Battery, General Aptitude Test Battery, q.v.), and *occupational interests* (e.g. Strong Vocational Interest Blank, q.v., Kuder Preference Record, q.v.). For a detailed description of these tests, see Cronbach (1960). The final decision is, of course, left with the client, and he may be so keenly motivated to attempt a particular career that he will accept as little as an estimated 10% chance of success.

2. *Employee selection and placement*. If there is a surplus of applicants for a particular job, the industrial or *personnel psychologist* may be called upon to develop a *selection program*, so that the best possible use can be made of the available talent. In this case he must take the view of the management or organization rather than that of the individual applicant. Since it is essential for the psychologist to know exactly what is entailed in the job concerned, and the skills and attributes which are relevant to effective performance, it may be necessary to start with a detailed *job analysis*. Then, in addition to the well-known tests of general intelligence and aptitudes referred to above, new tests specific to the particular situation may have to be developed and standardized for purposes of selection.

Once an applicant has been accepted by an organization, it may still have to be decided exactly what job he will do, in which department, and so on. This task of *placement* within an organization has elements of both vocational guidance and selection, remembering that work satisfaction is directly related to *productivity* and inversely related to staff *turnover*.

3. *Training*. Psychologists may also assist with the training of new employees, the retraining of old employees for new jobs, or the training of instructors in methods of instruction. Here, all the general *laws of learning* are applicable, e.g. the importance of motivation, knowledge of results, distribution of practice, etc. With *automation* has come a particular need to study methods of retraining and the variables which affect acceptance of, and resistance to change.

An effective training program presupposes a knowledge of the best and most efficient methods of work. *Time and motion study* (q.v.), associated with the names of F. W. Taylor and F. Gilbreth who introduced it into the USA in 1911, involves observing the worker at his job and carefully analyzing all his movements and the time taken to execute them with a view to reducing them and thus increasing efficiency. Although this means that with payment on the basis of productivity the worker can increase his earnings, naïve attempts to apply the method in the past have resulted in a great deal of resentment from workers who fear invasion of privacy, exploitation by management, redundancies, and loss of the freedom to do things their own way. This provides a good example of the complex psycho-social problems involving workers' attitudes, which are encountered by the industrial psychologist in his attempts to increase efficiency.

4. *Motivation, morale, and conditions of work*. Motivation is, of course, most directly manipulated by wage incentives such as piece rates and productivity bonuses, but

there is an increasing tendency for psychologists to regard the maintenance of morale (i.e. favorable attitudes) in the work situation as equally important. Morale may be facilitated in a variety of ways, e.g. by providing an avenue of communication between workers and management so that complaints can be registered, ensuring that work groups are compatible and that adequate social and recreational facilities are available. Improving the environmental conditions, e.g. by increasing illumination, reducing ambient noise, installing air conditioning, careful planning of color and decorations, provision of music, and so on, may increase productivity, depending on the personality and other characteristics of the workers concerned and the kind of work that they are doing. While this may sometimes result from direct improvement in physiological functioning, the effect more often results from the positive attitude engendered by pleasant surroundings (Maier, 1955). In the famous "Hawthorne studies" with female relay assembly workers at the Western Electric Company in the USA, it was found that the mere fact of studying workers' conditions was sufficient to exert a beneficial effect upon morale, and thus output, irrespective of the particular changes in physical conditions that were made (Roethlisberger & Dixon, 1940). (See *Hawthorne experiments*.)

5. *Fatigue.* One of the most important factors which interferes with work efficiency is *fatigue* (q.v.), which may be defined as that decrement in work performance occurring as a function of effort and time spent on the job which is recoverable through rest. The effects of fatigue upon psychomotor performance were studied in a well-known experiment conducted at Cambridge University using a simulated aeroplane cockpit. Subjects were required to sit in the "Cambridge Cockpit" for many hours at a time, making prescribed responses to signals which were complicated in their sequence, color, location, etc. The manifestations of fatigue were various, beginning with a

widening indifference to signals which required action, slow reactions, and lapses in judgment, and culminating in complaints of tiredness, bodily discomfort, and emotional outbursts. Among the factors which have been found to forestall or alleviate fatigue are motivation, knowledge of results, rest pauses, and certain drugs such as caffeine (q.v.) and benzedrine (Munn, 1958).

6. *Equipment design.* However high the individual's level of aptitude, training, motivation, morale, and so on may be, his efficiency is also a function of the machines with which he works. Whereas training is concerned with adapting the man to suit the machine, the industrial psychologist may also help in designing the machine to suit the operator. This is one of the central concerns of the field sometimes called *engineering psychology*. For example, finding the best possible spatial arrangement for the controls and instruments in a motor car, aeroplane cockpit, or space craft, designing legible and unambiguous traffic signs, and so on, requires a knowledge of the perceptual and motor capabilities of human beings. Left to their own devices, engineers too often design equipment for appearance or mechanical convenience, without regard to the limitations of the persons who have to work with it.

7. *Organizational processes.* Another area which may be considered part of industrial psychology, although it overlaps the domain of *industrial sociology*, is the study of efficiency in industrial organizations (e.g. Katz & Kahn, 1966). It is now well established that large organizations have functional requirements for growth and survival which create problems of efficiency of their own, independently of the individuals and equipment which comprise the organization, e.g. problems of communication, leadership and authority. Different kinds of organizational structure have been identified (e.g. "tall" versus "flat", "rational" versus "irrational") and these have been related to the characteristic attitudes and behavior to be found within them (Smith & Cranny, 1968).

8. *Consumer research and advertising.*
Finally, there is the branch of industrial
psychology in which interest is focussed on the
product or service itself, and its acceptability
to the consumer (sometimes called "business
psychology"). Consumer research is concerned with discovering the needs and motives
of the public with a view to providing
products and services which are appropriate
to them, whereas marketing and advertising
are concerned with the distribution of
established commodities, e.g. by promoting
public awareness of them and persuading
potential consumers of their desirability. As
with many other areas of applied psychology
(and applied science generally) this field
presents some ethical problems concerning
which little agreement has been reached, e.g.
the use of deliberate deception in research
and advertising.

Some of the tasks frequently undertaken
by consumer psychologists include: assessing
the acceptability of a proposed new product,
its brand name, package design, etc.; discovering the primary factors which determine
brand preferences and purchasing decisions
within a particular product field; assessing
the public image of an established company,
politician, entertainer, etc.; investigating the
most effective media of communication for
promoting a particular commodity; and the
testing of advertising copy. Characteristic
methods include: rating scales,questionnaires,
extended ("depth") interviews, group discussions, panel tests, "in-home" product
tests, controlled observation and actuarial
studies of consumer behavior. For a review
of recent trends in consumer psychology, see
Perloff (1968). See *Marketing; Occupational
psychology.*

Bibliography: Cronbach, L. J.: Essentials of psycho-
logical testing. New York, ²1960. Katz, D. & Kahn,
R. L.: The social psychology of organizations. New
York, 1966. Maier, N. R. F.: Psychology in industry.
Boston, 1955. Munn, N. L.: Psychology: The funda-
mentals of human adjustment. London, ³1958.
Perloff, R.: Consumer analysis. Ann. Rev. Psychol.,
1968, *19*, 437–66. Roethlisberger, F. J. & Dixon,
W. J.: Management and the worker. Cambridge,
Mass., 1940. Smith, P. C. & Cranny, C. J.: Psychology
of men at work. Ann. Rev. Psychol., 1968, *19*,
467–96.   G. D. Wilson

Industrial relations. 1. Human relations
between all the members of staff of an industrial concern as well as their relations with
the management and their own work; sometimes defined in legal and tariff provisions
(labor regulations); 2. Less commonly used
to denote the relations between an industrial
concern and the public (See *Public relations*).
Not to be confused with *labor relations*, i.e.
the relations between an industrial concern
and the trade union organizations.

Bibliography: Kerr, C., Dunlop, J. T., Harbison, F. H.
& Myers, C. A.: Industrialism and industrial man.
New York, 1964.   G.R.W.M.

Infancy. 1. *General.* Usually the period during
which the child cannot yet speak, from birth
till twelve or thirteen months. Characteristic
signs of this period are: development of the
body and posture, development of the
sensorimotor apparatus; the initial learning
of emotional attitudes (attraction to the
mother, anxiety); an inability to move from
place to place of one's own accord, voluntarily to control behavior, to speak, or to
achieve an autonomous adaptation (q.v.).
This period lasts longer in human beings than
in other creatures.

The *maturation* of the nervous system, as a
continuation of the biological development
of the embryo, determines the course of the
following advances: (*a*) the reduction of
sleep periods (from six to seven periods in
twenty-four hours to one to three periods at
the age of one year); (*b*) bent and floppy
limbs become straight and firm; (*c*) disappearance of the "archaic reflexes" through the
development of the cerebral cortex; (*d*)
sitting with support at about four months,
without support at about seven months;
standing with help in the eighth month,
without help in the thirteenth month; walking

holding on at about eleven months, walking alone at about fifteen months.

At first the infant holds a thing just in the palm of his hand, then the thumb is bent sideways over it in about the fourth month. Binocular vision is fully attained in about the sixth month, when turning the head toward a sound source also develops. In the second month the infant can fixate moving objects, the first conditioned responses appear in connection with suckling, and he smiles at faces; in the third month he recognizes people. From three to six months he learns to watch his hands moving, to grasp things which he sees and which arouse his curiosity. At about four months he makes noises directed at other people (social noises), and, at about five months, he begins to "complain". From the sixth to the eleventh month he begins to explore objects: at first impulsively, and then to relate their different sensuous and spatial qualities (surface, relative position); shyness at strangers and the joyful recognition of members of the family, as well as involuntary imitations, begin at about seven months. From ten to thirteen months, after the infant has developed a concept of objects and discovered their "permanence" (he will look for them when they have disappeared behind a curtain), he arranges objects in relation to one another, and organizes his movements in accordance with the findings he remembers. "Instrumental (practical) intelligence" develops; he voluntarily imitates sounds and movements, and at about thirteen months can play "let's pretend"—the first sign that he is approaching the stage of symbolic imitations.

2. *Developmental mechanisms.* The important aspects here are the combined operation and significance of the *instincts, bodily maturation, learning* and interpersonal relationships. Sucking, walking, grasping and posture all have an instinctive component, but require practice in adaptation and social encouragement, and can therefore take very different forms (e.g. in "feral" children, q.v.). It used to be held that smiling at someone and certain echopraxias in the first month indicated a *social instinct.* But it is difficult to distinguish between the influences of the instincts, of maturation and of conditioning (q.v.). Conditioning can begin in the second month: situations which are associated with pleasant feelings (contentment) are reinforced; those which have aroused unpleasant feelings are feared.

Recognition of objects and persons, exploration, the realization of wishes, and the earliest form of understanding are founded upon this mechanism. However, one must also take into account the role of *circular reactions* (J. M. Baldwin, 1906): The infant is excited when he observes that his movements have caused something to happen and therefore repeats the movements. At the age of six months, even complex reactions obey this law of circularity (J. Piaget). Initiatory behavior develops in accordance with the same principle, and by playing noise and movement games with the parents. Circular reactions constitute an important source of differentiations and of discovery in the infant's exploration of his environment.

Affectivity plays a dynamogenic (i.e. initiating or changing motor responses through sensory activity) and regulating role. It develops in interpersonal reactions, principally between the infant and his mother. (See *Hospitalism*; A. Freud, R. A. Spitz, J. Bowlby). The mother appeases or gratifies urgent needs, stimulates activity by showing him things and playing with him, arouses expectations, impatience and laughter (at six months); she requires "goal-directed" behavior by teaching and showing him how (at about nine months). But she also frustrates, forbids and provokes. From the sixth month onward, strangers cause shyness, then anxiety. Psychoanalysts (N. Hartman, E. Kris) hold that object cathexis takes over from the narcissism (q.v.) of the first three months in two major phases: interest in persons (and in situations which announce these "objects"), followed by attraction to and communication with others. These object cathexes are

515

essential to the formation of a balanced ego (q.v.) distinct from the world. The reactions of the first ten months are basic to the formation of permanent behavior patterns: e.g. (a) the desire to "make things happen" is strengthened by its connection with the suckling relationship, and later with motor skills; (b) the infant's increasing interest in sensorimotor experience leads him after ten months to regard his own image in the glass without clearly understanding the significance of what he sees; (c) his dependence upon his mother can turn through frustration (q.v.) to aggression (q.v.); (d) the affirmation of the self (q.v.) in opposition to another in the form of protests (and—after ten months— intentional provocations) is the precursor of speech.

The formation of and part played by these modes of behavior vary from infant to infant (Meili 1957; Escalona, 1968). Differences in activation (q.v.) level determine a bold or fearful approach to the environment, and therefore elicit different responses to the familiar environment: in this way definite character traits are formed. See *Arousal*.

The behavior of the person responsible for bringing the child up, and the methods used, depend upon culture and tradition. A. Kardiner, M. Mead, J. W. M. Whiting and E. H. Erikson indicate the personality (q.v.) differences caused by strict or relaxed methods of early care. The factors which determine the infant's behavior are numerous; they may be complementary or conflicting. On the one hand there is bodily (neurological) maturation (Gesell, 1934), and on the other the influence of emotional relationships. But conditioning (q.v.) (see *Learning theory*) and the active initiatives of the child, either in motor behavior (Piaget, 1952) or in emotive expressions (Wallon, 1934), must be taken into account. The interaction of these factors has still to be clarified. See *Child psychology; Development; Instinct; Traits*.

Bibliography: Baldwin, J. M.: Mental development in the child and the race: methods and processes. New York, ³1906. **Escalona, S. K.:** The roots of individuality. Chicago, 1968. **Fantz, R. L.,** *et al.*: Maturation of pattern vision in infants during the first six months. J. comp. physiol. Psychol., 1967, 55, 907–17. **Foss, B. M.** (Ed.): Determinants of infant behavior, 4 vols. London & New York, 1961, 1963, 1965, 1968. **Gesell, A. & Thompson, H.:** Infant behavior. New York, 1934. **Gouin Decarie, T.:** Intelligence et affectivité. Neuchâtel, 1962. **Gregoire, A.:** L'apprentissage du langage. Paris, 1937. **Lewin, K.:** A dynamic theory of personality, New York, 1935. **Lipsitt, L. P. & Spiker, C. C.** (Eds.): Advances in child development and behavior, 2 vols. New York, 1963–5. **Meili, R.:** Anfänge der Charakterentwicklung. Berne, 1957. **Piaget, J.:** The origins of intelligence in children. London, 1952. **Pratt, K. C.:** The neonate. In: **Carmichael, L.** (Ed.): Manual of child psychology. New York, ²1954, 215–91. **Spitz, R.:** The first year of life. New York, 1965. **Wallon, H.:** Les origines du caractère. Paris, 1934. **Weir, R. H.:** Language in the crib. The Hague, 1962. **Whiting, J. W. & Child, I. L.:** Child training and personality. New Haven, Ill., 1953. *P. Malrieu*

Infantile sexuality. Freudian psychoanalysis (q.v.) divides sexual expression in both sexes in early childhood into various phases: the oral phase (first year of life), the anal-urethral stage (second to fourth year—bowel training, q.v.; see *Anal stage*) and the phallic stage (q.v., fourth to seventh year) characterized by the development and overcoming of the Oedipus complex (q.v.). This early expression of infantile sexuality is said to become latent again with the maturation of the superego, until puberty—when the adolescent usually seeks heterosexual partners outside his own family.

Developmental biology might be thought to confirm certain aspects of psychoanalytical theories: in the "larval stage" of infancy there is already a hormonal difference between boys and girls. Sucking, and erection in the boy, arouse pleasure. Early childhood curiosity includes sexual questions, and children (especially in the third and fourth years) examine their genitals as part of the general process of self-exploration and understanding. Attempts at coitus are not uncommon in play. Subsequent psychosexual health depends in large measure on the examples given to children and on the security of a harmonious marriage and family environment. See *Child psychology; Sexuality.*

K.T.

Infantile type. An individual in whom physical development has been arrested altogether (or more frequently, in part) at a childish stage of development (see *Retardation*). The term is also used in characterology since mental immaturity often goes hand in hand with physical retardation. See *Infantilism.*

W.K.

Infantilism (syn. *Juvenilism*). **1.** If an individual fails to attain that degree of somatic growth and sexual development appropriate to his age, infantilism is said to be present. This condition is not to be confused with *dwarfism*, in which a failure of somatic growth may be accompanied by normal sexual development. Due to endocrine hypofunction (particularly of the pituitary or its connections), chronic infection, coeliac disease, renal disease, cyanotic heart disease, or is idiopathic. Intellect is not impaired, although emotional development and behavior patterns commonly retain childish characteristics.

2. The term also has psychoanalytical connotations, meaning the state of infancy.

J.P.

Infantilism, psychosexual. A distinction is sometimes made between general *infantilism* (q.v.), which affects the whole organism, and partial or *psychosexual* infantilism: nondevelopment of the secondary sexual characteristics, or immaturity of the sexual organs compared with the development of the rest of the body.

J.L.I.

Infant tests. Methods which attempt to describe behavioral development as a whole or specific areas of behavior from the first month of life onward, e.g. Bühler-Hetzer tests (q.v.) for children of 0 to 6 years. See *Development tests; Gesell Development Schedules.*

E.F.-K.

Infection, psychic. A sociopsychological phenomenon: stimuli are transmitted directly from individual to individual; in the simplest case this involves ideomotor reflexes, but opinions and attitudes may also be concerned. On a larger scale "psychic epidemics" may occur, e.g. rapidly propagated excitement as a reaction to music with a strong beat. See *Ideomotor law; Crowd behavior; Attitude; Stereotype.*

H.W.

Inference. 1. A conclusion drawn from antecedent arguments or propositions accepted as true, which may be deductive or inductive. See *Deduction; Induction.* **2.** The process of drawing such a conclusion.

Inferential statistics. The theory and methods of statistics (q.v.) as applied to the "inferring" of population parameters from sample values and distributions.

W.H.B.

Inferiority complex; inferiority, feeling of. Adler (q.v.) bases his psychotherapy on the concept of the inferiority feeling. The self-realization of any human being is already colored in childhood by universal feelings of inferiority which favor or motivate a compensatory trend toward superiority. More precisely, "inferiority complex" denotes neurotic symptoms arising from failure to cope with normal feelings of inferiority.

J.L.I.

Infertility. 1. The temporary or permanent inability of an organism to produce offspring (*sterility*). **2.** The tendency for an individual or group to produce very *few* offspring.

G.D.W.

Infibulation. The stitching together of the external female genitalia (vulva or prepuce), usually in order to prevent copulation.

Inflation. The personality is "flooded" with unconscious factors or identifies with them (C. G. Jung). The clinical consequence is generally an acute psychosis. See *Psychoses, functional.*

W.Sc.

Influence. 1. That which produces an effect. **2.** Directive or modifying power (e.g. in interpersonal relations). **3.** To exert influence.

Informal group. See *Group.*

Information. The general term "information" (a synonym for news, communication) has been developed through the analysis of technical data transmission systems and communications networks into one of the basic concepts of information theory (q.v.) and cybernetics.

Starting from the principle of information transferal through technical devices with an information source (transmitter or sender), transmission channel, and receiver, problems of maximum utilization and development of foolproof codes have been examined. Information measurement according to C. E. Shannon and N. Wiener (after preliminary studies by Nyquist, Gabor and Küpfmüller) measures the invariant aspect of telecommunications in codings and signal transmissions (e.g. conversion of acoustic into electrical signals). The information of a communication, sign or event defines its news or novelty content, or more precisely its *improbability.* A sign with the probability p has the information:

$$i(p) = 1d \frac{1}{p}.$$

The mean information is the mean of a repertoire of r signs weighted with the individual probabilities:

$$H = \sum_{i=1}^{r} p(i) \, {}^{1}d \frac{1}{p(i)}.$$

In stochastic dependence, calculations are made with the limited probabilities.

Information can be interpreted as the length of the communication with optimal coding in a binary code. The information contained in one bit (q.v.) corresponds to a binary code sign or a selection process from two (equally probable) alternatives.

Because of the formal similarity with the expression for thermodynamic entropy, the mean information is frequently referred to as *entropy* (q.v.), or *negentropy.* Thermodynamic entropy is a measure of the state of order of, or degree of randomness in, a physical system, and indicates the proportion of thermal energy which cannot be converted into mechanical work at a given temperature difference in a thermal or caloric engine.

The concept of information is used not only in communications and regulation technology, but whenever the function of complex systems or the interaction between several systems implies informational processes. See *Cybernetics and psychology; Information, psychology of; Cybernetic education.*

Statistical information, objective information, syntactic(al) information and *selective information* are synonymous terms. Statistical information emphasizes the derivation from statistical characteristics; objective information the possibility of determination by external observers; syntactic(al) information the exclusion of the semantic aspect; and selective information the function of the source in generating sign sequences by selection from an ensemble of signs.

Structural information, metric information: depending on the structure of the signals (q.v.), different aspects of information dominate. Data can be conveyed in an equivalent manner by continuous signals, e.g. current fluctuations in the telephone, or by discrete signals, e.g. current impulses in a telex. In discrete signal sequences the information consists of the number of signals and their mean information. Similarly, in continuous signal sequences, the information consists of the number of distinguishable temporally sequacious signal values, and the stages distinguishable at a given degree of measurement accuracy (i.e., to a certain extent, the repertoire) of disjunctive signal values. According to D. M. McKay, the number of distinguishable signals in a signal sequence is referred to as *structural information*, whereas the information of the individual signal value is known as *metric information*.

Topological information: the information of three- or two-dimensional arrangements which can be converted into temporal signal sequences by scanning during information transferal. In topological information, a distinction is again made between structural information as the number of distinguishable grid cells and metric information derived from the intensity values of the individual cells.

Subjective information: the information content of a message for the receiver can be determined only in relation to the internal state of the receiver. In principle, this rule applies to technical receivers. In psychology, the transition to the concept of subjective information is important (K. Steinbuch, H. Frank, A. Charkewitsch, K. Weltner). It implies a change in the theoretical premisses, to the extent that information is now derived from the expectancy probabilities of the receiver which are determined with the help of guessing tests (Shannon, Attneave, Weltner). They enable the subjective information of given complex linguistic and other data to be studied as a function of their context, situation, attitude of the receiver, linguistic and factual understanding, and other psychological parameters.

The transition to the concept of subjective information enables not only the statistical but the *semantic* (the "information of meanings") and the *pragmatic* aspects (the information of behavioral changes elicited by data) to be analyzed. Differentiation therefore enables the semantic component of linguistic data to be isolated from the total information content by measuring the subjective information for two states of the percipient class: (*a*) significance of the unknown information; (*b*) significance of the known information.

Didactic information: in educational cybernetics: the total semantic information in the matter to be learnt; the matter must be available in verbalized form as a basal text. The information remaining when the meaning of the basal text is known is referred to as "esthetic information", which is therefore defined negatively as "non-didactic information", and constitutes a measure of the uniqueness of a particular presentation.

Theoretically precise analysis of *semantic information* is possible only on the basis of unambiguously defined language systems. Appropriate methods are to be found in the theory of logical-semantic information developed by R. Carnap and Y. Bar Hillel. See *Communication; Information theory; Instructional technology; Semantics.*

Bibliography: Attneave, F.: Applications of information theory to psychology. New York, 1959. **Bar-Hillel, Y.:** Language and information. New York, 1964. **Carnap, R.:** What is probability? Scient. Amer., 1953, *189*, 128.   *K. Weltner*

Information analysis, multidimensional (syn. *Multivariate information transmission*). A method described by McGill for analyzing the relationship between multidimensional (multivariate) stimulus-response sequences with the aid of information theory (q.v.), and dividing the information content of the responses into transinformation of stimuli and random components. Multidimensional information analysis may be interpreted as non-parametric analysis of variance.

Bibliography: McGill, W. J.: Multivariate information transmission. Psychometrika, 1954, *19*, 97–116.
                                                        K.W.

519 INFORMATION PROCESSING SYSTEMS

Information capacity of the sense organs. The upper limit of the information flow between the receptors and the projection center of the cerebrum is determined by the specific information capacity of the sense organ concerned. The following values (in bits/sec.) have been determined: optical channel: 3.10^6; acoustic channel: 2.10^4 to 5.10^4; tactile channel (with reference to the whole body surface): 2.10^5; olfactory channel: 10–100; gustatory channel: 10.

Bibliography: Gibson, J. J.: The senses considered as perceptual systems. New York, 1966. Rosenblatt, F.: The perceptron: a probabilistic model for information storage and organization in the brain. Psychol. Rev., 1958, *65*, 386–408. Uttley, A. M.: The classification of signals in the nervous system. EEG clin. Neurophysiol., 1954, *6*, 479–94. *H.R.*

Information, density of. If data are not transmitted as a sequence of signals in time, the quantity of transmitted data is indicated not as an information "flow" (q.v.), but as an information "density" which shows the number of code elements required for coding on a line, a surface, or in a given space. The density of information is measured in signals/cm (cm^2 or cm^3). The density must be determined, e.g., when adapting pictorial material to the capacity of the eye. *H.R.*

Information, esthetics of. The esthetics of information is a branch of esthetics which makes use of the concepts of information theory (q.v.) and information psychology (q.v.). The informational aspect of esthetic processes is subjective and may be described as a process of gradual acquisition; the object of esthetic perception must contain elements of surprise (information) and initially unknown as well as known organizational structures. For a summary of the field, see Bense (1969); for the basic semiological inspiration, Barthes (1967); for the psycholinguistic basis, Chomsky (1957).

Bibliography: Alsleben, K.: Ästhetische Redundanz. Quickborn, 1962. Barthes, R.: Elements of semiology.

London, 1967. Bense, M.: Einführung in die informationstheoretische Ästhetik. Hamburg, 1969. Chomsky, N.: Syntactic structures. The Hague, 1957. Garnier, P.: Spatialisme et poésie concrète. Paris, 1968. Uhr, L. (Ed.): Pattern recognition. New York, 1966. Wathen-Dunn, W. (Ed.): Models for the perception of speech and visual form. Cambridge, Mass., 1967. *K.W.*

Information flow. Information flow is determined as the quantity of information transmitted through an information channel per unit of time. It is measured in "bits/sec." The upper limit is determined by the channel capacity. The concept of information flow has been adopted by information psychology (q.v.) and applied to communication (q.v.), learning, and perception. *H.R.*

Information processing (syn. *Data processing*). Any process by which received data are modified or associated with other data on the basis of specific laws so that new data are available as a result. In control, regulating or adaptation processes, this may lead to changes in the receiver's behavior. Information processing also includes the reception and transmission of data. The term "data processing" is often used only to refer to methods involving the use of a computer. When *all* the procedures in a system are bound up with a computer, the term "integrated data processing" (IDP) is applicable.

Bibliography: Feigenbaum, E.: An information processing theory of verbal behavior. Santa Monica, Calif., 1959. Id. & Feldman, J. (Eds.): Computers and thought. New York, 1962. *P.B.H.*

Information processing systems. A general term for all systems in which data are processed. A system of this kind can associate several different items of data on the basis of rational laws and obtain new information as the result. In general, organisms which absorb information from the environment (stimuli) and derive behavioral changes from that information can be considered as information processing systems.

P.B.H.

Bibliography: Hunt, E. B.: Concept learning: an information processing problem. New York, 1962. Norman, D.A.: Memory and attention: an introduction to human information processing. New York, 1969.

Information psychology. Information psychology represents an attempt to use cybernetic approaches, methods, measurements (in particular that of information) and models in psychology with a view to developing a complete theory.

Information psychology—originally conceived as a psychological basis for the esthetics of information—uses introspection as an indicator of phenomena which are arranged in an (initially qualitative) scheme (an "organogram") appropriate to the psychologically relevant aspect of the human information process. Cybernetic concepts and models (see *Cybernetics and psychology*) are also employed for descriptive ends, and the parameters used are determined quantitatively in experiments. Beyond this *descriptive* stage, the models also allow of quantitative or qualitative, empirically testable conclusions: the explanatory stage. The ultimate stage of the program of information psychology is an abstraction of all "inessential" details, and therefore the restriction of all assertions to a general cybernetic "psychostructural" model. The criterion for the "essential" is appropriateness to the proposed application (which occurs, in particular, within the framework of cybernetic education, q.v.). A series of increasingly complex psychostructural models is used in (largely programmatical) exact information psychology to obtain an approximation to man as a psychologically apprehensible existent.

Various experiments have shown (at least on average) an approximately linear relationship between reaction or perception times and the information content of stimuli. This allows the inference of a maximum reception speed ("apperception speed") of approximately 16 bits/sec. (achieved only at app. twenty years of age) for new consciously apprehended data. At the same age, the information absorption speed of the memory reaches a maximum of about 0.7 bits/sec. Several experiments have also shown that after habituation to a given probability distribution of a repertoire of signs, the subjective receptivity to a symbol reaches a peak at an occurrence probability of $p = 1/e$ (app. 37%). This "maximum effect" is explained by information psychology with the maximum of the function $p \cdot i = p \cdot 1 d \frac{1}{p}$, i.e. with a value proportional to the apperception time. The resulting measurement for incidence has proved accurate both in the quantitative interpretation of the results of frequency ratings and in predictions of the statistical influence of examples on apparently free behavior patterns. So far, however, the approaches of information psychology have proved unsatisfactory for determining the repertoire of signs and probabilities (accommodation of information), and for constructing memory models in regard to the learning of semantic information. Above all, the suggested methods for incorporation of motivation in the model have proved inadequate.

Information psychology is, of course, essentially concerned with *models* of psychological events that are of more or less practical value. See *Instructional technology; Machine learning; Simulation.*

Bibliography: Frank, H.: Kybernetische Grundlagen der Pädagogik. Baden-Baden, ²1959. (See also *Information theory.*) *H. Frank*

Information reduction. The reduction of subjective information into processing data on the basis of informational accommodation and superordination by forming classes or complexes. Information reduction can help to reduce reaction times. *H.R.*

Information system. All the connected means of communication employed within an organism, group or organization.

Information test. A test to estimate an individual's general or specific knowledge.

Information theory. 1. *Development.* Information theory came into being because of problems arising in connection with the transmission of information by technical systems (telegraphy, telephone, wireless). As early as 1924, H. Nyquist (1932) and K. Küpfmüller showed that for electrical transmission systems there was a quantitative connection between the band width of the transmission channel and the maximum speed of the signal. Further developments by C. E. Shannon (1948) led to information theory in its present form, which, as a part area of cybernetics as established by N. Wiener (1948) (see *Cybernetics and psychology*), is also formally connected with the inferential statistics (q.v.) of R. A. Fisher (1925). The fundamental problems are the transmission of signals, news and measurement values and the control of interference.

Shannon & Weaver (1962) deal with the problem of the optimal exploitation of communication chains and networks featuring interference, and base their theory on the objectively observable properties of signal (q.v.) or sign (q.v.) sequences. Relevant areas are the development of interference-free codes, the theory of signal transformation, and the accurate estimation of reductions in channel capacity for idealized degrees of interference.

Information theory is equivalent in many of its aspects to R. A. Fisher's inferential statistics, in so far as Fisher deals with the exclusion of interference (causal disturbances, or "noise") from measurements. Starting from the calculation of probable error (normal probability curve), inferential statistics made it possible to exclude interference

from measurement data (division of disturbances into—arbitrary—classes of random and systematic errors which then become observational variables), and extended the field of relevant empirical research in education, psychology and sociology.

N. Wiener (1948) took as his starting-point the interaction, adaptation and stability of systems coupled to an unstable environment (see *Cybernetics and psychology*; *Feedback system*; *Homeostasis*). The exclusion of interference from measurements and information processing were seen as prerequisites. The result was cybernetics, which has information theory as one of its components.

2. *Theory.* The basic idea is information (q.v.) as a quantitative measure for signs (q.v.) or signals (q.v.) which are exchanged between a sender (source, transmitter, emitter) and a receiver (recipient). Sign sequences are selected by various processes from a repertoire (ensemble) available to the sender. The sign sequence can be transmitted by different physical signals (q.v.). From the repertoire of signs used, their frequency, and the selection-restrictive, statistically expressible links between the signs (*stochastic processes*, q.v.; *Markoff processes*, q.v.; grammatical rules: see *Grammar*) a measurement value is obtained for the information; it remains valid for any number of recodings (see *Code*) and signal transformations (q.v.).

In the restricted sense in which it is used in information theory, information—as a *logarithmic measure of infrequency*, or negative value of the (conditioned) probability of occurrence—is a measure for the novelty or "news" value of the sign. It is arbitrary but useful to take the two as a basis of the logarithm. Then the unit—one bit—is the amount of information of a choice of two equally probable outcomes (tossing a coin). Accordingly one bit in data processing denotes a point of a binary data medium which gives the maximum storage capacity (q.v.) of a store.

The structural content of continuous signals can also be measured. A prerequisite of mathematical information theory is the *ergodicity* of the source, i.e. its statistical properties must remain constant and independent of the point at which a sample is taken.

It is of particular interest that *unequivocal and reversible codings without loss of information* are possible not only from discrete into discrete signs (words into letters, letters into teleprinter code), from continuous into continuous signs (sound vibrations into electrical vibrations, brightness values into current values), but from discrete into continuous and from continuous into discrete sign sequences. The continuous course of a temporal (electrical oscillation) or spatial function can be replaced by a sequence of discrete numerical values if these reproduce the functional values at equidistant intervals. The distance of the intervals must be reduced in proportion to the speed at which the value of the function changes (quantal theory). Conversely, the continuous curve can be recovered from the sequence of numerical values.

Important as it is for its technical uses, this system of transfer opens up new prospects for the marginal conditions of stimulus perception and processing in biological and physiological systems (psychophysics, q.v.). In these, too, continuous physical stimuli are coded into impulse and discharge sequences of neuron(e) networks (see *Decision processes*).

When there is no interference with information transmission, an unequivocal relationship is established between the signal as it is sent and as it is received. When there is interference in the channel, the signal as it is received does not always correspond to the signal as it was sent. The information correctly received—transinformation (T)—is smaller than that which was sent. The difference—the information lost—is "*equivocation*". The information produced by interference is "*irrelevance*". Channel capacity (C) (q.v.) is determined by band width (B) (difference between the highest and lowest transmissible frequency). With a disturbed channel (almost always present), the channel capacity diminishes with an intensity proportional to that of the noise compared with the intensity of the signal.

An unexpected result of information theory is that, even in a disturbed channel, any required degree of transfer reliability can be obtained by suitable coding; then transmission speed can reach almost full channel capacity. This is surprising, since the known technical methods of interference exclusion relied on the use of control signs and, in the most trivial case, on the repetition of the data, thus producing redundancy (q.v.) artificially, and reducing transfer speed.

3. *Tasks and applications.* The measurement units and methods of information theory form the bases of data technology, data processing, theoretical optics and picture transmission (Gabor, 1950, 1963), cybernetics (Frank, 1970; Steinbuch, 1965; Wiener, 1948), and technical automation.

In addition, information theory opens up new prospects in fields in which coupling and interaction between complex systems can be regarded as a whole or in part as informational coupling. When stimuli are perceived, conducted and processed, signals are coded and decoded. Sign recognition of signs and gestalt perception may be treated as interference- and irrelevance-exclusion. Learning may be regarded as the construction of internal models by way of informational links (see *Cybernetic education*). Social processes are apprehended by measuring the entropy (information) of groups (Cube & Gunzenhäuser, 1962).

In its purely mathematical form, information theory excludes the semantic and pragmatic aspects of communication, which have to be considered when analyzing interference which has disturbed vocal or optical human intercommunication chains or networks. Such analysis requires a transition from the concept of statistical analysis to that of subjective information, which is concerned with the internal state of the receiver. In this transition, information measurement now refers not to an objective statistics (q.v.) of sign sequences which can be determined by an external observer, but to the empirically determinable probabilities expected by the percipient (Weltner, 1970). This opens up new areas of application for information theory in the analysis of the linguistic aspects and content of perception processes, and in the analysis of cognitive and learning processes, using a combination of empirical methods and the theoretically grounded measurement and relational system of information theory. In this process certain problems arise which cannot yet be treated in isolation: e.g. relevance, or the repertoire of possible references available to the perceiving recipient. See *Communication; Instructional technology.*

Bibliography: Attneave, F.: Applications of information theory to psychology. New York, 1959. Beer, S.: Decision and control. London, 1966. Bellman, R. & Kalaba, R.: Mathematical trends in control theory. New York, 1964. Borko, H. (Ed.): Computer applications in the behavioral sciences. Englewood Cliffs, N.J., 1962. Brillouin, L.: Science and information theory. New York, 1956. Clapp, L. C. & Yilmas, H.: Optical information processing. In: Colborn, R. (Ed.): Modern science and technology. New York, 1965. Cube, F. v. & Gunzenhäuser, R.: Die Entropie von Gruppen. Quickborn, 1962. Frank, H.: Kybernetik-Brücke zwischen den Wissenschaften. Frankfurt, 1970. Gabor, D.: Communication theory and physics. Phil. Mag., 1950, *41*, 1161. Id: Inventing the future. London, 1963. Gibson, E. J.: Principles of perceptional learning and development. New York, 1969. Langer, D.: Informationstheorie und Psychologie. Göttingen, 1962. Loehlin, J. C.: Computer models of personality. New York, 1968. Mackay, D. M.: Quantal aspects of scientific information. Phil. Mag., 1950, *41*, 289. Meyer-Eppler, W.: Grundlagen und Anwendungen der Informationstheorie. Berlin & New York, [2]1969. Minsky, M. (Ed.): Semantic information processing. Cambridge, Mass. & London, 1968. Nyquist, H.: Regeneration theory. Bell Syst. tech. J., 1932, *11*, 126. Peters, J.: Einführung in die allg. Informationstheorie. Berlin—Heidelberg—New York, 1967. Pierce, J. R.: Symbols, signals and noise. London, 1962. Quastler, H. (Ed.): Information theory in psychology; problems and methods. Glencoe, Ill., 1955. Rose, J.: Survey of cybernetics. London, 1970. Rosenblatt, F.: Principles of neurodynamics. New York, 1961. Shannon, C. & Weaver, W.: The mathematical theory of communication. Urbana, [9]1962. Stachowiak, H.: Denken und Erkennen im kybernetischen Modell. Berlin & New York, 1965. Steinbuch, K.: Automat und Mensch. Berlin & Heidelberg, [3]1965. Tomkins, S. S. & Messik, S.: Computer simulation of personality. New York, 1963. Weltner, K.: Informationstheorie und Erziehungswissenschaft. Quickborn, 1970. Wiener, N.: Cybernetics. New York, 1948.   *K. Weltner*

Information transmission (syn. *Information transfer*; *Information transferal*). The transfer of information with the help of an information medium (see *Signal*) from a transmitter to a receiver. Information (or data) transmission follows the pattern below (communication chain):

An information source generates data consisting of a sequence of signs (symbols). The latter are converted into transferable signals in a transducer. The signals pass through a data channel or transmission medium to a retransducer which reconverts the received signals and conveys them to the receiver. The noise source comprises all the interference to which the signal is subject on transmission.

Bibliography: Fano, R. M.: The transmission of information. M.I.T. Tech. Rep. 65. Cambridge, Mass., 1949. Hartley, R. V. L.: Transmission of information. Bell Syst. tech. J., 1928, *7*, 535.

                                              P.B.H.

Information transmission, multivariate. See *Information analysis, multidimensional.*

Infrared. Electro-magnetic radiations of a frequency just below that of red (103–106 mμ) and therefore outside the visible spectrum. Radiant heat is transmitted in this frequency range.   *C.D.F.*

Infrasonic. Sounds below the frequency range detected by the ear (1/1000—16 Hz). These sounds can sometimes be detected by other senses as tremors or rhythmic beats. They may be produced by winds, earthquakes, and so on.   *C.D.F.*

Inheritance. The combination of genes resulting from the fusion of the parents' cells during fertilization; in a wider sense the totality of the genetic factors which determine the structure and development (q.v.) of the individual in conjunction with environmental (q.v.) influences. See *Abilities; Differential psychology; Traits; Type.*   *M.A.*

Inhibition. I. Curtailment, constraint, prevention. A characteristic of central nervous systems which is ultimately a major factor in recognition. The *spatial* extension and *temporal* sequence of excitation (nerve impulses) released by stimuli are influenced by inhibition as well as facilitation and summation processes.

1. *Local (lateral) inhibition.* The specific path originating at the receptors and running to the projection cortex is interconnected collaterally to adjacent synergistic synapses (see *Synapse*) so that an impulse tends to heighten a strong adjacent impulse, whereas a strong impulse inhibits the weak adjacent impulse. This locally effective contrast system steepens the local excitation gradient by comparison with the stimulus intensity gradient. In general, the organism is governed by the principle that a nucleus of excitation in the information transmission system of the sense organs is always accompanied by an environment with lateral inhibition. Lateral inhibition is primarily important for contrast in the eye (spatial system), and is used only in the higher central nervous layers in the ear (temporal system); in the case of the eye, lateral inhibition of neuronal "on" elements and lateral activation of neuronal "off" elements are essential for contrast recognition.

2. *Temporal inhibition.* Two parallel information channels within the specific pathway from the receptor to the cortex are so interconnected that the channel with the stronger excitation, or—after coding—with the faster action-potential sequence and shorter latency, blocks both channels through an inhibition control neuron, allowing only the first signal of the faster action potential sequence to pass; the remaining signals and above all those in the information channel which is not so strongly energized are completely suppressed.

In the acoustic sense-organ system, temporal inhibition is used, e.g., to suppress a succession of two sound stimuli in a time range in which the time difference is used for a spatial stimulus characteristic, namely the direction of the sound source.

Similarly, temporal inhibition is observed in the acoustic sense-organ system in the sense that specific action-potential intervals in a more or less completely irregular sequence can be suppressed.   *M. Spreng*

II. In *neurophysiology*, inhibition is the prevention of specific nervous processes; inhibition may also denote the processes which give rise to such suppression, and which are frequently considered to be among the basic activities of the central nervous system and are interpreted as the opposite factors to excitation. In *psychology* the term is used to denote certain phenomena or the processes on which they are (hypothetically) based, above all in the psychology of memory, in the psychology of learning (see, e.g., Pavlov, 1928; Hull, 1943; Harlow, 1959; Eysenck, 1970), and in clinical psychology (q.v.) with a depth-psychological (see, e.g., Freud, 1936; Schultz-Hencke, 1951) or behavior-therapeutic orientation (see e.g. Salter, 1949; Wolpe, 1958; see *Behavior Therapy*). Although the shades of meaning sometimes vary considerably, inhibition is always the prevention or curtailment of a behavioral process by an activity of a different kind; it is generally assumed that the inhibited function may continue when the inhibiting factor has been removed.

The significance given to inhibition processes in the social or performance (achievement) context differs widely from author to author, and sometimes even within a given system. Harlow and, in certain cases (primarily differential inhibition), Pavlov attach considerable importance to the notion of inhibition, e.g. as the basis of all higher mental processes.

Reciprocal inhibition, according to Wolpe, is an essentially neutral mechanism, while internal inhibition, according to Pavlov, and reactive inhibition, according to Hull, are close to the concept of fatigue and also emphasize a possible protective function. Inhibitions of memory are generally considered to be performance-reductive influences on learning processes. In clinical psychology the need to acquire specific inhibitions in the socialization (q.v.) process is stressed, while at the same time (and more frequently) attention is drawn to the high probability of negative personality development through excessive inhibition of spontaneous impulses (Schultz-Hencke, 1951; Salter, 1949).

Studies of the associations between neurophysiological and behavioral "inhibitions" are still in their infancy. See *Arousal*; *Behaviorism*; *Conditioning, classical and operant*.

Bibliography: Eysenck, H. J.: The biological basis of personality. Springfield, Ill., ²1970. Freud, S.: Inhibitions, symptoms and anxiety. London, ²1936. Harlow, H. F.: Learning set and error factor theory. In: Koch, S. (Ed.): Psychology: A study of a science, Vol. 2. New York, 1959. Hull, C. L.: Principles of behavior. New York, 1943. Pavlov, I. P.: Lectures on conditioned reflexes, Vol. 1. New York, 1928. Salter, A.: Conditioned reflex therapy. New York, 1949. Schultz-Hencke, H.: Lehrbuch der analytischen Psychotherapie. Stuttgart, 1951. Wolpe, J.: Psychotherapy by reciprocal inhibition. Stanford, 1958.

L. Blöschl

Inhibition, internal (syn. *Inner inhibition*).

In I.P. Pavlov's behavioral theory "internal inhibition" is a term for a group of inhibition phenomena characterized in that they are caused by changes in the conditioned association itself and, unlike the various forms of unconditioned inhibition, are acquired in learning processes. "Internal inhibition develops when the conditioned stimulus is not attended by the unconditioned, whether this be once or always, but in the latter event, only under certain circumstances. Thus come about extinction, retardation, conditioned inhibition, and differential inhibition. We see then that the same conditions are necessary for the development of sleep as for the development of internal inhibition." (Pavlov, 1928.) The following are the most important forms of internal inhibition:

1. *Extinction:* if a conditioned stimulus is not applied repeatedly, the conditioned response gradually ceases to occur. That this is inhibition and not elimination proper is shown by the results of many experiments (spontaneous restoration of the extinguished conditioned reflex after a long delay, etc.).

2. *Differential inhibition:* if one of two similar stimuli, but not the other, is applied repeatedly, the second stimulus is (differentially) inhibited as a special case of extinctive inhibition. See *Conditioning, classical and operant; Inhibition; Orienting reflex*.

Bibliography: Pavlov, I. P.: Lectures on conditioned reflexes, Vol. 1. New York, 1928.   L.B.

Inhibition potential. See *Conditioned inhibition*.

Inhibition, social. A term for the absence (or presence in a modified form) of certain—usually aggressive—modes of behavior toward members of the same species. E.g. rats when *feigning* combat do not bite or display the threat gestures which precede serious fighting. See *Appeasement gestures; Aggression*.   *V.P.*

Inhibition type (syn. *Inhibitory type*). More difficult to excite and less capable of achieving high performance than the excitatory, or excitement type (q.v.); conditioned reflexes are weak and unstable; changeable. "There stand out three well-defined types of nervous systems; the central or equilibrated, and the two extreme types, the excitatory and inhibitory. . . . The melancholic is evidently an inhibitory type of nervous system" (Pavlov, 1928). See *Type*.

Bibliography: Parlov, I. P.: Lectures on conditioned reflexes, Vol. 1. New York, 1928.   *W.K.*

Inhibitory potential (cumulative). See *Conditioned inhibition*.

Initiation. A term taken from the Latin *initiatio*: a beginning, and used in ethnology (q.v.) to denote *rites* performed when a juvenile is received into the adult community. "Puberty rites" is another term with the same meaning. In many tribal cultures where there is no knowledge of writing, initiation rites are of greater significance than marriage. In our culture "confirmation", parties after a school-leaving examination, etc., are feeble reflections of initiation ceremonies (Hofstätter, 1963). In contrast to the vestiges of initiation rites we possess, which all relate to some achievement, the authentic rites in their highly-developed forms also perform such functions as heterosexual "education" and confirmation of sex roles by means of, e.g., circumcision (q.v.) ceremonies (e.g. the removal of the girl's clitoris or the boy's foreskin). Initiation and initiation rites emphasize the break between childhood and adulthood, and at the same time link the two chief periods in life (Chapple & Coon, 1942).

Instruction in tribal knowledge and certain skills (tribal history, mythology, mysteries, dances, pipe playing, etc.), tests of courage and self-control (piercing the nostrils, frightening experiences, etc.) serve to show whether the young member of the tribe is suitable for adult status, and at the same time to prepare him for the concomitant rights and duties.

Symbolic representations and magico-religious actions play a significant part (death and rebirth) in initiation. In general, initiation does not necessarily coincide with biological sexual maturity, and can extend over several weeks or months.

Bibliography: Chapple, E. D. & Coon, C. S.: Principles of anthropology. New York, 1942. Hofstätter, P.: Einführung in die Sozialpsychologie. Stuttgart, 1963. Mead, M.: Coming of age in Samoa. New York, 1928. Id.: Growing up in New Guinea. New York, 1930.   *H.M.*

Innate (syn. *Inborn*). 1. That which is present at birth. 2. Some difference between individuals which is not attributed to environmental influence. See *Differential psychology; Drive; Instinct; Traits*.

Innate releasing mechanism (abb. IRM). The instinctive, selective readiness of an animal to respond to a "releaser", or specific sign- or key-stimulus (q.v.), with a specific reaction. This hypothetical physiological (neurosensory) mechanism works as a "stimulus filter" by checking the reaction in inadequate situations. See *Imprinting; Instinct*.

Bibliography: Tinbergen, N.: An objectivistic study of the innate behaviour of animals. Biblioth. biotheor., 1942, *I*, 39–98. Id.: The study of instinct. Oxford, ²1969.   *I.L.*

Inner speech (syn. *Internal speech; Inner language*). Inner speech is unvoiced speech, a function in itself, and the basic form of thinking in words. The philosophers of antiquity had already noted that "thinking is speaking to oneself in silence". Plato was the first of many philosophers, linguisticians and psychologists who have tried to develop this judgment, some even going so far as to assert (unjustifiably) that thought and spoken language are one, or (in one version of behaviorism) that thinking may be defined as "subvocal" processes in the larynx (Watson, 1920; ³1929).

Early studies of the phenomenon of inner speech were grounded on introspection (q.v.) and clinical observations of speech disorders (i.e. different forms of aphasia, q.v.). On the basis of these observations, inner speech was conceived as "verbal images" of various modalities (acoustic, motor and visual), a deficit in which could be explained in terms of aphasic dysfunctions of thought processes (disturbances of speech comprehension in sensory aphasia and of verbal memory in motor aphasia). Several theories were put forward: a motor basis for inner speech (G. Stricker, 1880); an acoustic basis (Egger, 1881); or a mixed basis (G. Ballet, 1886). In addition, visual forms were characterized as optical images of letters and schematic visual images of objects (A. Lemaitre, 1905). The Würzburg psychologists (K. Bühler, 1907–8), however, argued that perceptual mental images and verbal images did not play any essential role in thinking, and were mere sporadic phenomena.

Experimental research into inner speech is obviously very difficult because of the covert nature of all its processes. The most advantageous course would seem to be an investigation of the motor (kinesthetic) components. At first (1900–25), inadequately sensitive pneumatic and mechanical devices were used in attempts to record the micro-movements of vocal organs (Curtis, Wyczoikowska, Thorson, et al.). In addition, some researchers used various methods of suppressing or inhibiting external and internal articulation (A. Binet, E. Meumann, Pintner). The results of these experiments allowed of more than one interpretation; hence covert articulation was viewed not only as a general but as an individual factor in thought. The use of more sensitive recording devices (at first the string galvanometer, and later the electromyograph) made possible more exact results which indicated an increase in the tonus of the vocal musculature during all verbal functions involving difficult thinking. It was also shown that the EMG (electromyograph) potentials recorded under such conditions are local

speech potentials and not merely the result of diffuse irradiation of muscular tonus. These investigations were pioneered by E. Jacobson (1929–32). The EMG method was used afterwards to study the thinking of the deaf (Max, 1937), thinking in acoustic schizophrenic hallucinations (Gould, 1948–9), in attentive hearing (Smith, Malmo & Shagass, 1954; Wallerstein, 1954), in silent reading (Faaborg-Andersen & Edfeldt, 1957–9; Hardyck et al., 1966), and in verbal and perceptual problem-solving (Sokolov, 1957–68).

The results of these more recent investigations show a considerable variation in linguistic EMG reactions, which is independent of the difficulty and novelty of the conceptual problems to be solved, the degree of automatization of the thought operations to be carried out, the introduction of images (percepts and mental imagery) into mentation, and the individual inclination to a specific memory type. Vocal motor impulses are detectable not only in verbal-abstract but in "visual" thinking, even though they are weaker, or even inhibited or reduced during phases of intensive visual object-analysis. Subsequently, however, there is the phase of covert vocal motor reactions, which neither conclude nor correct the thought process. On the basis of electromyographic data it may be assumed that the main function of vocal motor (proprioceptive and tactile) afference in thinking is probably motor reinforcement or "activation" of the speech mechanisms of the brain in accordance with the "feedback" (q.v.) principle. This accords with Pavlov's (1941) conception of kinesthetic stimulations of the speech organs as the bases or fundamental components of speech, which is a second system of signalization in humans, signaling the first unified signaling system of the animal, and primarily the human, organism.

In Soviet psychology (q.v.), the problem of inner speech has been exhaustively examined in connection with a critique of the Würzburg and the behaviorist conceptions of thought. A general survey of this problem and of relevant experimental findings is available in Sokolov (1968, 1969). See also *Language; Mental imagery; Psycholinguistics; Vygotsky.*

Bibliography: Ballet, G.: Le langage intérieur. Paris, 1886. Edfeldt, A.: Silent speech and silent reading. Stockholm, 1959. Jacobson, E.: Progressive relaxation. Chicago, ²1956. Luria, A. R.: The role of speech in the regulation of normal and abnormal behavior. New York, 1961. Pavlov, I. P.: Lectures on conditioned reflexes, Vol. 2. New York, 1941. Sokolov, A. N.: Internal speech and thought. Moscow, 1968. Id.: Studies of speech mechanisms of thinking. In: A handbook of contemporary Soviet psychology. New York & London, 1969. Vygotsky, L. S.: Thought and language. Cambridge, Mass., 1962. Watson, J. B.: Is thinking merely the action of language mechanisms? Brit. J. Psychol., 1920, *11*, 87–104. Id.: Psychology from the standpoint of a behaviorist. Philadelphia, ³1929.   *A. N. Sokolov*

Innervation. 1. Anatomical: the development of nerve fibers in the organism. **2.** Physiological: the provision of nervous stimuli, in particular the conduction of central impulses to the effectors through (innervating) nerve fibers. In general, a distinction can be made between innervation by afferent (centripetal), efferent (centrifugal) and vegetative (sympathetic and parasympathetic) nerves. Exteroceptors and interoceptors are involved in innervation, which is regulated by the central nervous system (q.v.)   *F.-C.S.*

Input. 1. The energy flowing into a system. **2.** The actual stimulus or signal received. In information theory (q.v.), a living being can be considered as an information channel (communication channel) or as a complex information system. Stimuli comprise the input and responses the output. Information theory models are frequently used to represent and interpret cognitive behavioral patterns (e.g. thought, speech). One such model is the TOTE unit (Miller, Galanter & Pribram, 1960), which includes the feedback concept. Plans (e.g. expectations) are constantly compared with environmental data. If the "plans" are considered as system states and environ-

mental data as (information) input, the environmental influence is compared with the system state. If the two coincide a response is made (output). "Stimulus and response must be seen as phases of the organized, coordinated act . . . Stimulus and response must be considered as aspects of a feedback loop." The stimulus is seen not as preceding but as guiding the response.

Bibliography: Miller, G. A., Galanter, E. & Pribram, K. H.: Plans and the structure of behavior. New York, 1960. Rosenblith, W. A. (Ed.): Sensory communication. New York, 1961.   *H.W.*

Insanity. This term is *not* now used as a synonym for psychosis but is reserved for a medico-legal condition, namely a mental disorder which results in the patient not being responsible for his actions, or in his being unaware of the consequences of his actions. See *Mental defect; Psychoses, functional; Schizophrenia.*   *R.H.*

Insects, state-forming (syn. *Social insects*). With the aid of very complex instinct (q.v.) patterns, a highly sophisticated form of social behavior has developed in certain groups of insects (hymenoptera, termites); a convergence of behavior is observed between certain species. The selective advantage for these social species consists, as in a human culture, in the possibility of answering the demands of life more rationally through the division of labor, which is determined by external influences: according to the mode of nurture, insects develop as sexually mature or retarded workers and soldiers. State-forming bees possess an unusual learning capacity and highly complex modes of exchanging information. See *Dancing language.*

Bibliography: Chauvin, R.: Animal societies from bee to gorilla. London, 1968. Id.: The world of ants. London, 1971. Frisch, K. von: Bees: their vision, chemical senses and language. London, 1968.
                                                        H.Sch.

Insight. 1. An individual's conscious knowledge or understanding of himself or others. See *Empathy; Introspection.* **2.** An immediate understanding of a real or logico-mathematical relationship. Gestalt psychology conceives the process of insight as an organization of events such that structural relationships in the phenomenal *field* (q.v.) change in accordance with the particular phenomenon. The result of such a process is often the familiar "inspiration" or "sudden idea". (See *Aha experience.*)

Bibliography: Köhler, W.: The mentality of apes. New York, 1925.   *P.T.*

Insomnia (syn. *Agrypnia*). Chronic sleeplessness. First investigated by K. von Economo (1917) after an outbreak of epidemic encephalitis in Europe during World War I, which led to a reversal of the normal sleep-waking rhythm. Those suffering from the affliction are awake at night but sleep during the day. Insomnia is to be distinguished from difficulty in getting to sleep and disturbances of sleep. It is neurophysiologically conditioned by hyper-activation of neuron(e) complexes located in the reticular formation. Insomnia frequently occurs in healthy individuals as a disorder of diverse causation (over-arousal, hyper-stimulation from optical and acoustic sources, effects of caffeine ingestion). It often accompanies depressive and schizophrenic states, but can also occur in internal disorders, e.g. cardiac insufficiency, angina pectoris, high blood pressure, hyperthyroidism, etc. In old age, the sleep-waking rhythm becomes irregular; after approximately age fifty, arteriosclerotic changes can induce insomnia in about fifty per cent of individuals. See *Sleep.*   *D.V.*

Inspiration. Originally a theological term: a divine influence, or a condition in which God manifests himself to man in a supernatural manner. Some psychologists have described inspiration as the manifestation of a "secondary personality" concealed in the unconscious. This personality is said to have great creative potential and to allow certain sensitive, intraverted individuals to proceed to unique achievements. Sometimes used as a synonym for genius (q.v.). See *Abilities; Creativity; Meditation.*   *E.U.*

Instinct. Instinct as a word derives from the Latin *instinctus*, from *instinguere*—to incite. In some uses, the word has referred to particular behavior patterns and coordination, but it is in the sense of a basic biological urge that the concept has had greatest influence. All animals maintain themselves by ingestion, digestion and elimination, and all species survive by means of reproduction. Fundamentally, the concept of instinct merely states this. Attempts to elaborate the concept, in particular the incorporation of ideas concerning innateness and subjective, purposive phenomena, have been considered controversial. Indeed the concepts of innateness and purpose are themselves as complex and confused as that of instinct.

1. *History.* The concept of biological urge or inner drive, for which the word instinct is generally used, has a history in classical antiquity. In post-Wundtian psychology the most influential instinct theorists were James (q.v.), Morgan and McDougall (q.v.), who wrote in the early part of this century, but their general influence did not extend beyond its first two decades. Freud (q.v.), the founder of psychoanalysis, is an exception, but his influence as an instinct theorist has continued only outside the mainstream of psychology.

A swing away from instinct and a preoccupation with behaviorism (q.v.) and the problem of drive (q.v.) occurred in psychology during the 1930s and 1940s. Apart from Tolman (q.v.), no influential theorist wrote on instinct, and even Tolman's following was achieved in the context of drive rather than instinct theory.

During its period of decline in psychology, work on instinctive behavior in animals was still being undertaken, mostly on the continent of Europe. The term ethology (q.v.) is now used to describe this work, carried out independently of psychology in a tradition of biology and natural history. Through the influence of this ethological work, a revival of interest in the concept of instinct occurred in comparative psychology during the 1950s. Ethologists and psychologists took renewed interest in each other's work, and the cross-fertilization of ideas has generated new research in comparative psychology (q.v.), but without, however, any widespread revival of interest in the concept in general psychology. (See *Animal psychology*.)

2. *Scientific use of the instinct concept.* Since the theory of evolution is common to all biologically oriented sciences, it is convenient to consider the scientific use of the concept as starting with Darwin. He, and others after him, have used the concept of instinct to account for behavior which is usually complex, adaptive, and often finely attuned to particular environmental conditions. Such behavior is often performed with an appearance of intelligence and aimed, with what appears to be purposiveness, toward particular goals, even though the capacities of the organism concerned make it impossible to attribute such intelligence.

No fully adequate explanation can yet be offered, in terms of physico-chemical events or known biological mechanisms, for much of this kind of behavior, particularly as it occurs in insects, fish and birds. Until research has filled obvious gaps in our knowledge, the concept of instinct will continue to be used to meet these deficiencies.

Three major scientific trends in the literature on instinct are the psychoanalytic, psychological and ethological. All have proposed models in attempts to account for instinctive behavior. Ethological models are most specific and closely linked to empirical phenomena, whereas the psychoanalytic model is more general and difficult to test empirically.

3. *Psychoanalytic views of instinct.* Ac-cording to Freud, an instinct has a particular force or impetus to action. The aim of the action is to abolish the source stimuli creating the impulse, and this can be achieved in or through some object, which can vary according to its satisfying properties. Central to much of Freud's theorizing were the concepts of conflict (q.v.) and equilibrium, representing dynamic forces whereby aims and objects of instinctive behavior could be altered by repression, or sublimation. Although this represents a model of behavior, its link with reality lies in observations of clinical patients. It has proved difficult, though not impossible, to test these ideas empirically. Also, such motivational ideas as are present in Freud's scheme, in so far as they have been incorporated into general psychology, have been considered as drives rather than instincts. (See *Drive*.)

4. *Psychological views of instinct.* Psychological theorists have proposed that instinct involves some internal state disposing an organism to respond selectively to certain kinds of environmental objects or events. This basic impulse is alleged to be innate and to involve subjective, purposive excitement directed toward the ends or goal of the behavior. According to this view, an instinct is an inborn, conative-affective system.

Because of the general acceptance of the concept of evolutionary continuity existing between animals and man, it has been held that the instincts, which form an obvious part of the behavior of animals such as insects, must exist also in man. In man, however, expression of the instinct is considered to be infinitely variable.

McDougall (q.v.) was undoubtedly the most influential psychologist to write on instinct, and his books, written early in this century, were widely used in its early decades and continued in print as late as the 1950s. His system of instincts and their associated sentiments had greatest appeal to social psychologists, among whom, until relatively recently, ideas concerning social interaction seemed less amenable to empirical tests,

531   INSTINCT

probably because his ideas seemed simple and direct. McDougall was, however, and not without justification, criticized as confusing description with explanation.

With the hardening of behaviorist attitudes in psychology (see *Behaviorism*), the use of the concept of innateness was avoided as an inferior substitute for detailed behavioral analysis and subjective phenomena ruled out of scientific analysis. Most phenomena previously considered instinctual were redefined as drive (q.v.). The term drive was relatively free from the related concepts of innateness and purpose, yet covered many of the essential features of instinct. Apart from some areas of comparative and developmental psychology, where psychoanalytic and ethological ideas are influential, the concept of instinct is now largely ignored in psychology.

5. *Ethological views of instinct.* Ethological views of instinct, whilst owing much to the theory of evolution and to early American and European naturalists and zoologists, derive principally from the integrative work of Lorenz and Tinbergen.

Two important organizing influences stem from this work. The first is that rigid, stereotyped behavior patterns, characteristic of much instinctive behavior in animals, are potentially of equal value in taxonomy, as are structural and other factors. The second is that behavior is caused by energy specific to particular instinctive acts of fixed action patterns. When an organism, through the agency of search-like appetitive behavior, meets appropriate environmental stimuli for which the animal has special receptor and perceptual releasing mechanisms, the act is released and specific energy is dissipated. A special appeal of the energy model was that by distinguishing between appetitive behavior and the instinctive act, it could account for achievement of a set goal by variable means without incorporating the idea of purpose, because performance of the act itself was considered to be the goal.

If an animal does not meet with appropriate environmental stimuli, the energy builds up until it results in spontaneous performance of the act despite the absence of appropriate stimuli. This has been called vacuum activity and, in the examples of this kind of behavior which ethologists have described, it has the appearance of behavior performed inappropriately. Another form of inappropriate behavior has been called displacement activity. In an animal prevented from performing some instinctive act in a normal way, energy appropriate to that act is displaced, resulting in behavior inappropriate to the animal's current needs. This ethological model and attendant concepts have generated a large body of research in the field of animal behavior. The model has been severely criticized, in particular the vacuum and displacement activities, important empirical evidence for the energy model being increasingly accounted for in other terms. Concepts associated with the energy model, however, such as sensory and perceptual releasers, displacement activities and fixed action patterns, in revised form, are likely to continue to be used in behavioral analysis.

6. *Current status of the instinct concept.* A dispassionate appraisal of the current status of the concept of instinct is difficult. Considerable research activity is taking place on problems which could be described as proper to instinct, though use of the concept as such is not much in evidence. In particular, recent ideas on and research into critical periods in early behavior, whether imprinting (q.v.), primary socialization or early experience, have direct antecedents in psychoanalytic, psychological and ethological views of instinct.

Bibliography: Birney, R. C. & Teevan, R. C.: Instinct, New York, 1961. Drever, J.: Instinct in man. Cambridge, 1917, Fletcher, R.: Instinct in man. London, 1968. McDougall, W.: An introduction to social psychology. London, 1908. Schiller, C. H.: Instinctive behaviour. London, 1957. Thorpe, W. H.: Learning and instinct in animals. London, [2]1963. Tinbergen, N.: The study of instinct. Oxford, [2]1969. Wilm, E. C.: The theories of instinct. New Haven, 1925.

P. L. Broadhurst & J. Wilcock

Instinctive action; instinctive behavior. See *Instinct; Innate releasing mechanism.*

Instinct-taxis association (syn. *Instinctive motor co-ordination*). According to Lorenz, an instinctive action consists of innate co-ordination (a relatively rigid pattern of muscular contractions) and the taxis (q.v.) components which direct the action.

Bibliography: Lorenz, K.: Über den Begriff der Instinkthandlung. Folia biotheor., 1937, *2*, 17–50. Id.: Studies in animal and human behaviour, Vols. 1, 2. London, 1970–1. *K.Fi.*

Institutes of psychology. When psychology asserted its independence as an empirical and predominantly experimental discipline in its own right, a great number of university institutes and departments of psychology were established as research and teaching centers: e.g. 1879 (a milestone in the history of psychology) Leipzig, by W. Wundt (q.v.); 1881, Göttingen, by G. E. Müller (q.v.); 1883, Johns Hopkins, by G. S. Hall (q.v.); 1888, Pennsylvania, by J. McK. Cattell (q.v.); 1889, the Sorbonne, by H. Beaunis and A. Binet (q.v.); 1886, Kazan, by V. M. Bekhterev (q.v.). Important schools of psychology developed at several of these institutes (e.g. the Berlin, Leipzig and Würzburg Schools). At present, individual university institutes of psychology tend to feature a wide variety of psychological specialisms. Other institutes without any direct university connections are making an increasingly large contribution to research (e.g. the Max Planck Institutes in Germany).

Bibliography: Misiak, H. & Sexton, V. S.: History of psychology. New York, 1966. *E.G.W.*

Institution; institutionalization. A sociological concept used by H. Spencer to denote, e.g., ideas and establishments which take into account the interests or value judgments of a large cultural group through special forms of social interaction, e.g. education, marriage, property, etc. A distinction may be made between, e.g., domestic, sacred, political, professional, economic and other institutions which cover the means and activities considered necessary by a larger group to achieve specific ends. Parsons works on the basis of the internalization of values and standards with which several groups conform. If this conformity leads to satisfaction and causes others to accept these standards, this value or system of standards can be defined as "institutionalized". According to Parsons, an institution is therefore a complex of institutionalized role characteristics or status relationships which is structurally significant for the given social system and its maintenance. See *Group; System, social.*

Bibliography: Caplow, T.: Principles of organization. New York, 1964. Feibleman, J. K.: The institutions of society. London, 1956. Parsons, T.: The social system. New York, ⁴1963. Spencer, H.: The study of sociology. London, ²¹1894. *W.D.F.*

Institutionalized children. Institutionalization (in the sense of the substitution of a state or voluntary home for the natural or foster parents) can have a particularly harmful effect on young children (see *Hospitalism; Inanition*). Some studies have shown clear differences between children raised in institutions and those brought up in a family environment; these differences apply at the level of intellectual development, or that of the degree of voluntary cooperation and school progress; some children raised in institutions experience considerable difficulty in establishing and maintaining social contacts. *M.Sa.*

Instruction. 1. Directions given to the testee regarding his behavior in the experimental or test situation; he should also be motivated to conform to these indications. Even minor changes in initial instruction can lead to statistically certain differences in the test results. The tone of voice and gestures of the psychologist or experimenter during instruction can also affect results to some extent.

2. Authoritative teaching; indoctrination (q.v.). **3.** Systematic teaching. See *Instructional technology.*

Instructional technology. The study of learning should provide knowledge that can be used in designing an instructional environment and in the educational process. However, scientific findings and theories are rarely available immediately for practical use; translation and development are required for their possible application. As the study of learning becomes increasingly relevant to educational problems, an understanding is required of the relations between basic and applied science, and development, that lead to the methods and technology which can be used by the practicing educator to design conditions for learning.

The recent history of the experimental psychology of learning displays a cyclical progress toward contact between scientific endeavors and technological development. In the nineteen twenties and thirties, the work of L. Thorndike (q.v.) showed an exemplary concern with the implications of psychology for educational science (q.v.). In addition to his basic studies on the law of effect and on verbal learning, Thorndike wrote extensively on educational psychology (q.v.) and the psychology of school subjects. Following Thorndike and his associates, the psychology of learning entered a period (1940–45) of decreasing emphasis on school learning, and increasing attention to laboratory experiments and theoretical elaborations based upon them (Melton, 1941; Estes, 1960). But, beginning in the late 'fifties, experimental psychologists have been turning their thinking and their enterprises to the analysis and investigation of the educational, instructional process (Skinner, 1958; Bruner, 1960; Lumsdaine & Glaser, 1960; Bugelski, 1964; Hilgard, 1964; Suppes, 1964; Gagné, 1965; Gibson, 1965; Gilbert, 1965; Glaser, 1965;

Groen & Atkinson, 1966; Moore & Anderson, 1968).

At the present time, an instructional technology based upon an underlying science of learning is emerging. Technology in this sense does not necessarily mean hardware and instrumentation, but rather an applied discipline like engineering or medicine. The techniques and procedures used by the practitioners of these technological disciplines grow out of the findings in their underlying sciences, and also develop by informing science of their needs. The major impetus for the emergence of this field of instructional technology was provided by B. F. Skinner (1954, 1958), who recognized the work of Sidney L. Pressey in the 'twenties (Pressey, 1926). While both Pressey and Skinner thought and conceptualized in terms of the broad application of behavioral science to education, their initial developments centered upon self-instructional devices as a way of making concrete certain principles of learning, and as a way of providing tools and instrumentation around which instructional innovation could take place. It is often mistakenly believed that the devices themselves, and the specifics of the early crude apparatuses, formed the major contribution. In his 1958 article, Skinner emphasized the importance of the principles of programming and the possibility of a scientific technology for instruction. Whereas an important contribution of the field of programmed instruction and instructional technology is the development of materials and instrumentation to extend the capabilities of a teacher as an instructor and the student as a learner, the field is not restricted to these products. Work in instructional technology is extended to the general design of educational environments, including teacher practices, classroom organization, and so forth (Skinner, 1968; Bruner, 1960; Hilgard, 1964).

1. *Psychological bases for instructional design.* At the present time, research and development in the field of instructional technology can be characterized in terms of the following areas: analysis of the behavior to be learned; diagnosis of the characteristics of the learner; specification of the conditions for learning; and the assessment and optimization of the outcomes of learning.

2. *Analysis of the behavior to be learned.* A body of knowledge consists of information and of processes: information includes data, facts, concepts, and rules; processes refer to the cognitive abilities and intellectual skills by which this information is manipulated and transformed for the purposes of acquiring new knowledge and carrying out intellectual performances. From the viewpoint of instructional theory and practice, the presence of competence is inferred by reference to the behavior of an individual. For example, we infer that a student knows certain principles of physics because he can describe them, identify their application, and recall and use them where appropriate. The informational content of a body of knowledge, the ways in which this information is interrelated and structured, and the ways in which it can be processed must be analyzed and understood before the conditions involved in the acquisition of this knowledge can be meaningfully studied and implemented. As a consequence, an increasingly prominent feature of the psychology of learning is the analysis and classification of the behavior to be learned.

A particularly prominent technique for the analysis of structures of knowledge has been presented by Gagné (1962). This analysis begins with a desired instructional objective, stated in terms of student behavior, and asks in effect, "to perform this behavior, what prerequisite or component behavior(s) must the learner be able to perform?" For each behavior identified, the same question is asked, thus generating a hierarchy of behaviors based on identifiable and measurable prerequisites. Analysis of this kind attempts to provide an ordered set of tasks for inclusion in an instructional sequence. Such analyses observe the basic constraint that no objective is taught to the learner until he has met the prerequisites which facilitate learning and

transfer to the next objective. These prerequisite learnings can be achieved in a variety of ways; some individuals can learn them one at a time, and others learn a number of them in larger steps. The instructional process is optimized by continuous identification of the furthest skill along the hierarchy that a student can perform at any moment; or, if a student is unsuccessful in performing a particular task objective, by determining the most immediate sub-objective at which he is successful. These hierarchies indicate transfer relationships between the elements of increasing knowledge or task competence, and make explicit what behaviors are to be observed and tested for.

The relationships between units of learning establish the subject-matter structures that are learned, e.g. concepts, rules, principles, and strategies. With increasing knowledge and with the increasing maturity of the learner, these units of behavior become progressively larger. At certain phases in the acquisition of knowledge, a structure can become a unit of a higher structure. For example, consider the progression of phases in a child learning to read. Assuming that the child has learned to speak, the first phase in the process is the discrimination of graphic symbols (printed letters). In the second phase, these discriminated objects are encoded, or mapped onto language, so that spelling-to-sound (grapheme-phoneme) correspondences are acquired. At this point, relationships are established between the discriminated symbols and speech units. In later phases, the student learns to read not letter-by-letter, but by words and paragraphs, and the previously learned units become part of higher-order structures. Such structures determine the content of a subject-matter learning that is manifested in competent subject-matter behavior; and psychological research in instruction has as a basic requirement the identification of the units and structures involved in subject-matter performance (Gagné & Gephart, 1968; Gibson, 1965, 1969). In addition to analyzing the structures of advanced knowledge, one must also determine those units and structures which serve optimally to facilitate learning for the novice (Bruner, 1964). This means that a technology of instruction must specify the ways in which a body of knowledge can be organized so that it can be most readily grasped by the learner as he progresses to more advanced competence.

3. *Diagnosis of the characteristics of a learner.* Detailed diagnosis of the initial state with which a learner comes into a particular instructional situation is necessary to further his education. In the early stages of instruction, teaching procedures adapt to the findings of this initial assessment. In this concern with initial measurement and diagnosis, an important distinction must be noted: traditional measurement practices have assumed, essentially, a "selection model" of instruction in which the aptitudes of a student are measured and used to predict his success in a relatively uniform instructional environment. In contrast, the present concern in educational technology and programmed instruction is to establish different conditions and procedures for learning, depending upon the initial state of the learner. The direction necessary to take for this purpose has been pointed to by Cronbach (1957) and by Cronbach & Gleser (1965), i.e. to move toward decision-making procedures based upon relationships between the entering behavior of a learner and the variables manipulated in instruction. Measures are taken on the basis of which a decision can be made as to what instructional environment an individual should select in order to optimize his attainment of learning outcomes.

For the most part, measures of general aptitude and general intelligence measures do not seem likely to be the most useful bases for differentiating and adapting instruction because they correlate with success in most instructional methods. As a result, psychologists are now very actively investigating the interaction between entering behavior (aptitude) measures and learning variables.

Fleishman (1965, 1967) carefully studied the learning of psychomotor skills. Fleishman compared the contribution of the various abilities tested at the beginning of learning to performance scores on successive learning trials during practice and showed that the particular combinations of abilities change as practice continues, and that the different abilities existing before entering a learning task influence learning at different learning stages. The implication is that individuals with different patterns of abilities require different learning experiences at different stages of learning. In the area of verbal learning, Jensen (1966, 1967, 1968) suggested certain variables of human performance that appear to interact with the learning of verbal tasks. General reviews and analyses of the field of aptitude-method interactions have been reported by Bracht & Glass (1968), and Cronbach & Snow (1969). (See *Abilities.*)

4. *Specification of the conditions for learning.* In attaining subject-matter knowledge and intellectual skill, the learner proceeds through a novitiate and then on to relative expertise; he learns to be a good reader, a competent mathematician, a deep thinker, a quick learner, a creative person, an inquiring individual, and so on. These activities are learned according to criteria of expertise established by the school and intellectual community; more specifically by subject-matter requirements, peer group expectations, and the general social and professional criteria for what determines low, average, and high levels of competence. The educational and social community adjusts its expectations to the competence level of the learner, so that initially very awkward and incorrect performances are acceptable whereas later they are not; a young child or a novice is frequently rewarded for rather uninteresting behavior but as competence grows, his performance is attended to only in the presence of an appropriate audience or in an appropriate situational context. The process of going from ignorance to competence, from novice to expert, establishes a useful way of looking

at the processes and characteristics of instruction.

Four general properties of behavior appear to distinguish the performance of the beginner from that of the expert: (a) The responses of the learner move from variable, awkward, and crude to consistent, relatively fast, and precise. Responses develop from simple unitary acts into large response integrations and overall strategies. (b) Subject-matter stimuli change from specific instances to members of response classes, and the invariance of these classes becomes the major stimulus event. Stimulus contexts change from simple ones to complex patterns in which relevant must be distinguished from irrelevant aspects, and information must be abstracted from a context of events which are not all appropriate. (c) Behavior becomes increasingly symbolic and covert in the form of mediational responses and information-manipulating processes. The learner responds increasingly to internal representations of an event, to internalized standards and to internalized strategies for thinking and problem solving, all of which are manifested in terms of his behavior as an expert. (d) This behavior of the expert becomes increasingly self-sustaining, increasingly masterful in terms of his skillful use of the rules when they are applicable, and subtle bending of them in appropriate situations. Increasing reliance is placed on one's own ability to generate the events by which one learns and the criteria by which performance is judged and valued.

The process of instruction is concerned with implementing this growth from ignorance to competence, and the characteristics of the course of this growth determine the design of the instructional environment. As the learner interacts with the environment, certain lawful psychological processes influence the way in which this interchange (e.g. Hilgard & Bower, 1966; Skinner, 1968; Hilgard, 1964; Glaser, 1970). The conditions provided for instruction are determined by the properties of the behavior to be learned, the characteristics of the learner, and the

nature of subject-matter competence. The task of an instructional technology is to design conditions for learning based upon knowledge of the learning process and upon techniques of instruction. As appropriate behavior is learned, new conditions are set up to maintain it, and use it to develop more competent and subtle behavior. A complex repertoire is taught through a series of environmental changes, during each stage of which the learner responds to extend his present competence and to prepare himself to respond at a later, more complex stage. The particular properties of the competent behavior acquired depend upon the details of the instructional environment provided in an educational setting, such as teacher practices, textbook design, teaching machines and instructional materials, peer-student interactions, and the learning skills of the student himself.

5. *Assessment and optimization of learning outcomes.* With knowledge of learner characteristics and with alternate instructional procedures available, adaptation is made to the student's performance, i.e. his mastery of prerequisites, rate of learning, requirements for amount of practice, degree of structure and prompting, scheduling of reinforcement, and so on. Different individuals are assigned to (or the student may assign to himself) different instructional conditions. These initial placement decisions reflect only initial assignment, and are corrected by further assignments as learning proceeds, so that allocation to instructional procedures becomes a multi-stage decision process defining an individual instructional path. As a student proceeds to learn, his performance is assessed at appropriate intervals, and measures of this performance are summarized and indexed. The kinds of measures of learning progress one usually obtains, and on which instructional decisions are made, consist of test-score information which measures the frequency of correct responses, errors in relation to some performance standard, and the speed of

performance. The use of measures of transfer and generalization are particularly to be encouraged. Of special interest are measures which can be obtained in the course of learning and may be predictive of future learning requirements. Work along these lines has been reported by Jensen (1966, 1967, 1968), Zeaman & House (1963), Rohwer & Levin (mimeo), and Judd & Glaser (1969).

An adaptive instructional process employs a reiterative pattern of assessment and instructional prescription where decisions are made sequentially, and decisions made early in the process affect decisions made subsequently. The task of instruction is to prescribe the most effective sequence of learner-environment interactions. Problems of this kind in other fields of endeavor have been tackled by optimization procedures (e.g. Wilde & Beightler, 1967). The optimization problem of major concern is finding a decision procedure (to be implemented by the student, teacher, and/or a teaching device, see: Atkinson & Wilson, 1969; Holtzman, 1970) for deciding which instructional alternatives to present at each stage of instruction: given the instructional alternatives available, the set of possible student responses to the previous lesson unit, and specification of the criteria to be optimized for the judgment of competence. For this, two research and development tasks are essential: First, obtain rigorous knowledge of how the system variables interact; second, obtain agreed measures of system effectiveness. The first task is to determine the kinds of experimental studies and learning theory that are most useful for discovering the relationships between individual differences and learning variables. The second task refers to the fact that criterion measures of what is to be optimized become critical. In this regard, extensive work is in progress in measurement theory and technique as related to the instructional process and learned achievement (Glaser & Nitko, 1971; Cronbach, 1963; Bormuth, 1969). This work involves techniques for the development of criterion-referenced measures of achievement in contrast to the more commonly used norm-referenced measures (Glaser, 1963; Ebel, 1962; Flanagan, 1951; Popham & Husek, 1969). Criterion-referenced measures are tests constructed to yield measurements that can be directly interpreted in terms of specified performance standards, rather than relative standards such as percentile scores or normal-curve standard scores. Serious attempts are also being made to measure what has been heretofore so difficult—those aspects of learning and knowledge that are basic to an individual's capability for continuous growth and development, including transfer of knowledge to new situations, problem solving, and self-direction.

Bibliography: Atkinson, R. C. & Wilson, H. A.: Computer-assisted instruction: A book of readings. New York, 1969. Bormuth, J. R.: On achievement test item theory. Chicago, 1969. Bracht, G. H. & Glass, G. V.: The external validity of experiments. Amer. Ed. Res. J., 1968, 5, 437–74. Bruner, J. S.: The process of education. Harvard, 1960. Id.: Some theorems on learning and instruction illustrated with reference to mathematics. In: Theories of learning and instruction, 63rd Yearbook, Part I, NSSE, U. of Chic., 1964, 306–35. Bugelski, B. R.: The psychology of learning applied to teaching. Indianapolis, 1964. Cronbach, L. J.: The two disciplines of scientific psychology. Amer. Psychologist, 1957, 12, 671–84. Id.: Course improvement through evaluation. Teach. Col. Rec., 1963, 64, 672–83. Id. & Gleser, G. C.: Psychological tests and personnel decisions. Urbana, Ill., ²1965. Cronbach, L. J. & Snow, R. W.: Individual differences in learning ability as a function of instructional variables (Final Report Stanford U., School of Education), Maine, 1969. Ebel, R. L.: Content-standard test scores. Educ. psychol. Measmt., 1962, 22, 15–25. Estes, W. K.: Learning. In: Harris, C. W. (Ed.): Encyclopedia of Educational Res. New York, ³1960, 752–70. Flanagan, J. C.: Units, scores, and norms. In: Lindquist, E. F. (Ed.): Educational measurement. Washington, D.C., 1951, 695–763. Fleishman, E. A.: The description and prediction of perceptual-motor skill learning. In: Glaser, R. (Ed.): Training research and education. New York, 1965, 137–76. Id.: Individual differences in motor learning. In: Gagné, R. (Ed.): Learning and individual differences. Columbus, O., 1967, 165–91. Gagné, R. M.: The acquisition of knowledge. Psychol. Rev., 1962, 69, 355–65. Id.: The analysis of instructional objectives for the design of instruction. In: Glaser, R. (Ed.):

Teaching machines and programmed learning, II: Data and directions. Washington, D.C., 1965, 21–65. **Id. & Gephart, W. J.** (Eds.): Learning research and school subjects. Itasca, Ill., 1968. **Gibson, E. J.:** Learning to read. Science, 1965, *148*, 1066–72. **Id.:** Principles of perceptual learning and development. New York, 1969. **Gilbert, T. F.:** A structure for a coordinated research and development laboratory. In: **Glaser, R.** (Ed.): Training research and education. New York, 1965, 559–78. **Glaser, R.:** Instructional technology and the measurement of learning outcomes. Amer. Psychologist, 1963, *18*, 519–21. **Id.** (Ed.): Teaching machines and programmed learning, II: Data and directions. Washington, D.C., 1965. **Id.** (Ed.): The nature of reinforcement. Columbus, O., 1970. **Id. & Nitko, A. J.:** Measurement in learning and instruction. In: **Thorndike, R. L.** (Ed.): Educational measurement. New York, 1971. **Groen, G. J. & Atkinson, R. C.:** Models for optimizing and learning process. Psychol. Bulletin, 1966, *66*, 309–20. **Hilgard, E. R.** (Ed.): Theories of learning and instruction. 63rd Yearbook, Part I, NSSE. Chicago, 1964. **Holtzman, W.** (Ed.): Computer-assisted instruction, testing, and guidance. New York, 1970. **Jensen, A. R.:** Individual differences in concept learning. In: **Klausmeier, H. J. & Harris, C. W.** (Eds.): Analyses of concept learning. New York, 1966, 139–54. **Id.:** Varieties of individual differences in learning. In: **Gagné, R. M.** (Ed.): Learning and individual differences. Columbus, O., 1967, 117–40. **Id.:** Social class and verbal learning. In: **Deutsch, M.** *et al.* (Eds.): Social class, race, and psychological development. New York, 1968, 115–74. **Judd, W. A. & Glaser, R.:** Response latency as a function of training method, information level, acquisition, and overlearning. J. educ. Psychol. Monogr., 1969, *60*, Part 2. **Lumsdaine, A. A. & Glaser, R.** (Eds.): Teaching machines and programmed learning: a source book. Washington, D.C., 1960. **Melton, A. W.:** Learning. In: **Monroe, W. S.** (Ed.): Encyclopedia of educational research. New York, 1941, 667–86. **Moore, O. K. & Anderson, A. R.:** The responsive environments project. In: **Hess, R. D. & Bear, R. M.** (Eds.): Early education: Current theory, research, and action. Chicago, 1968, 171–89. **Popham, W. J. & Husek, T. R.:** Implications of criterion-referenced measurement. J. educ. Measmt. 1969, *6*, 1–9. **Pressey, S. L.:** A simple apparatus which gives tests and scores—and teaches. School and Society, 1926, *23*, 373–6. **Rohwer, W. D. & Levin, J. R.:** Elaboration preferences and differences in learning proficiency. Institute of Human Learning, U. of California, Berkeley. (Mimeo). **Skinner, B. F.:** The science of learning and the art of teaching. Harvard Educ. Rev., 1954, *24*, 86–97. **Id.:** Teaching machines. Science, 1958, *128*, 969–77. **Id.:** The technology of teaching. New York, 1968. **Suppes, P.:** Modern learning theory and the elementary school

curriculum. Amer. Educ. Res. J., 1964, *1*, 79–93. **Wilde, D. J. & Beightler, C. S.:** Foundations of optimization. Englewood Cliffs, N.J., 1967. **Zeaman, D. & House, B. J.:** The role of attention in retardate discrimination learning. In: **Ellis, N.** (Ed.): Handbook of mental deficiencies. New York, 1963, 159–223.

R. Glaser

Instrumental conditioning. See *Conditioning, classical and operant*.

Insufficiency. 1. Inadequateness to some end or purpose. **2.** A want of some ability, value, substance, etc. **3.** An individually felt inadequacy or feeling of *inferiority* (q.v.) is described by Adler (q.v.) in the context of individual psychology (q.v.) as an important factor in the origin of neuroses. Such convictions of personal inferiority are said to occur in the neurotic personality, even in the absence of organic or mental insufficiency, and to lead to "inferiority complexes". See *Neurosis*.

K.Pa.

Insula (syn. *Island of Reil*). The insula forms part of the cerebral cortex. Originally it was situated on the free surface. In the course of development it has moved downward and is covered by parts of the anterior, superior and temporal lobes. It has been suggested that the insula is an association center for acoustic thinking.

G.A.

Insulin. A hormone (polypeptide) formed in the Langerhans islet cells (beta cells) of the pancreas with the main effect of blood sugar maintenance and control. Whereas adrenalin (epinephrine) mobilizes the stored sugar and introduces it into the blood as glucose, insulin—as an antagonist of adrenalin—promotes the development and storage of blood sugar as glycogen. Insulin deficiency leads to hyperglycemia (diabetes mellitus), and an increase in insulin secretion to hypoglycemia. Since 1963, insulin has been synthesized and can be administered intravenously. Few experimental psychologico-physiological studies have been carried out. Low doses of insulin lead to increased heart rate, higher systolic blood pressure and higher respiration frequency, and also reduce diastolic blood pressure. Subjective effects: fatigue, dizziness, hunger. Performance (calculations) is generally impaired. In higher doses, insulin causes hypoglycemic shock, and was used as a means of therapy, e.g. in schizophrenia (q.v.).

Bibliography: Davidoff, F.: Oral hypoglycemic agents and the mechanism of diabetes mellitus. New Eng. J. Med., 1968, 278, 148. Ferner, H.: Das Inselsystem des Pankreas, Stuttgart, 1952. Geller, M. R.: The treatment of psychiatric disorders with insulin, 1936–60: a selected, annotated bibliography. Washington, 1962. Silverman, A. J., McGough, W. E. & Bogdonoff, M. O.: Perceptual correlates of the physiological response to insulin. Psychosom. Med., 1967, 29, 252–64. Sussman, K. E., Cront, J. R. & Marble, A.: Failure of warning in insulin-induced hypoglycemic reactions. Diabetes, 1963, 12, 38–45.   W.J.

Insulin shock (syn. *Insulin coma; Insulin therapy*). A state of hypoglycemic shock or coma (in which the patient is unconscious) induced by administering insulin parenterally until the blood sugar is reduced to a certain level (hypoglycemia). The method has been replaced by drug therapy, primarily because the same therapeutic objective can be achieved by neuroleptics with less risk of complications.

Bibliography: Ackner, B. & Oldham, A. J.: Insulin treatment of schizophrenia. A three year follow-up of a controlled study. Lancet, 1962, i, 504–6. Bourne, H.: The insulin myth. Lancet, 1953, ii, 964–8. Kalinowsky, L. B. & Hoch, P. H.: Somatic treatments in psychiatry. New York, 1961.   A.Hi.

Integrated type. According to E. R. Jaensch, this type is characterized by a holistic attitude and wide-ranging attention; he thinks holistically and organically and is capable of change. Ant.: *disintegrated type*. The integrated type had three further sub-groups, depending on whether the orientation is directed more strongly inward or outward.   W.K.

Integration. In the *central nervous system* (q.v.) stimuli are processed by various means: enormous numbers of neuron(e)s of a few morphological types form synaptic networks. No less than 300,000 synapses converge at a Purkinje('s) cell in the cerebrum. Information is conveyed to chemical synapses (q.v.) through transmitter substances (noradrenalin [norepinephrine], acetylcholine, serotonin, GABA); electrical synapses function directly. Nerve cell bodies (soma) and dendrites integrate on the analogue principle through algebraic, electronic summation while nerve fibers integrate digitally on the all-or-nothing principle with pulse frequency coding. Chemical and electrical fields influence the statistical characteristics of large cell groups. A flow of stimuli with enormously high redundancy (in the order of a million bits/sec) is filtered and grouped (convergence and divergence networks); the frequencies are raised or lowered while feedback loops have a throttling effect. Plasticity is dependent on the reserve of neurons which can be physiologically activated. Hormones influence the stimulus thresholds of neurons. Neuronal excitation circuits store data for a short time while the long-term memory functions with chemical engrams (proteins, nucleotides, amino-acid sequences).

Bibliography: Gerard, R. W.: Neurophysiology: an integration (molecules, neurons, and behavior). Handbook Physiol. Neurophysiol. Vol. 3 (1919–65). Washington, 1960. Horridge, G. A.: Interneurons. London & San Francisco, 1968. Quarton, G. C., Melnechuk, T. & Schmitt, F. O. (Eds.): The neurosciences. A study program. New York, 1967.   K.Fi.

Integration of the personality. 1. The consistency, or degree of coincidence, with which diverse individual processes or actions, and in particular the decisions of a human being, prove effective in functional dependence on each other; or the coordination of characteristics in a given situation or in contact with the environment. If we adopt A. H. Witkin's theory that the personality is an open system, i.e. closely related to the environment, integration denotes the functional relations between the system components. This integration is attributed to a complex system and therefore presupposes differentiation of the system. 2. The making whole of the personality, either through one's own efforts (i.e. in individual development or in self-therapy, or under psychotherapy (q.v.). See *Person; Personality; Type.* *W.D.F.*

Integration, social. A general term for part processes which are necessary to complete or establish a consistent social structure. These processes include (especially in Talcott Parsons' theory): *cultural integration* as the essential consistency of normative factors; *normative integration* as the essential correlation between standards and requirements; *communicative integration* as the essential smooth transmission of standards from one individual to another; and *functional integration* as the essential harmony of requirements, expectations and actual behaviors. *W.D.F.*

Intellect. 1. The perceiving, cognizing, understanding mind. **2.** The power of understanding. **3.** Comprehension. **4.** Whatever that mental ability may be which enables man to think. **5.** High-level abstract or conceptual thought. See *Intelligence.*
Intellection: The act of understanding; using (the) intellect. *H.W.*

Intellect, structure of. The structure of intellect (i.e. intelligence) can be determined from a number of different standpoints (see *Intelligence*). In the factor-analytical sphere, the concept of the structure of intellect has acquired a special meaning as a system of factors which determine intellectual performance. A particularly well-known model for the structure of intellect or intelligence has been suggested by Guilford (1959, 1967). He distinguishes between three aspects of every act of the intelligence: operation,

product and content, and also describes various modes of variation, or categories, of each dimension. In addition to the categories "figural", "symbolic", "semantic", Guilford posits a fourth category (purely theoretical) along the dimension of content, designated as "behavioral" and representing the general area of "social intelligence. Guilford's theoretical model represents (i.e. predicts) 120 distinct abilities in a cube, each cell containing a kind of problem and the corresponding factor. "If education has the general objective of developing the intellects of students, it can be suggested that each intellectual factor provides a particular goal at which to aim." (1959.)

OPERATION:
Evaluation
Convergent production
Divergent production
Memory
Cognition
PRODUCT:
Units
Classes
Relations
Systems
Transformations
Implications
CONTENT:
Figural
Symbolic
Semantic
Behavioral

Bibliography: Guilford, J. P.: Three faces of intellect. Amer. Psychologist, 1959, *14*, 469–79. **Id.**: The nature of human intelligence. New York, 1967. *R.M.*

Intelligence. However clearly we may seem to understand what is meant by intelligence, e.g. in connection with an intelligence test, there is as yet no generally recognized definition of the term. Admittedly intelligence denotes an "ability", i.e. a condition or a complex of conditions for specific performances or achievements. But the specific types of performance which require intelligence have not yet been unambiguously defined, except to the extent that the term covers cognitive problems. Ideas on the essential, "inner" nature of this ability are even more divided. The definition of intelligence as the ability to overcome difficulties in new situations (proposed almost simultaneously by E. Claparède and W. Stern) is most widely accepted today. Since animals too can adapt to new situations for which they have no instinctive solution (W. Köhler's "intelligence tests on anthropoid apes"), thought cannot be considered to be an essential criterion for the exercise of intelligence.

1. *Research into intelligence.* There are close links between research into intelligence and the psychology of thought (processes) inasmuch as intelligence is considered as a prerequisite for individual variations in thinking; nevertheless, the two branches of research have developed separately. The aim of intelligence research is to use statistical comparisons to determine the conditions underlying various types of performance. The degree of similarity between the conditions for two types of performance is determined by correlative techniques. After 1900, Spearman (1927) was the first to develop on this basis a method of analyzing the relations between performances; his method of factor analysis (q.v.) has since been used in almost all intelligence research. These studies need not be confined to typical intellectual performance. It is largely a matter of linguistic convention which of the factors is defined as intellectual. The main problem in this research was to determine the number and nature of the factors involved. Spearman developed the two-factor theory, according to which all intellectual (in the broad sense) operations involve a single, common factor (general factor, or *g*) and a specific factor for each performance. This general factor can therefore be defined as "general intelligence", although Spearman interpreted it hypothetically as general mental energy. Since research eventually showed, however, that there are certain common features between certain types of performance which are not dependent on "g", the "hierarchical theory" of intelligence was adopted by

Spearman's school. This theory assumes that there are also factors of ever-decreasing effect in the hierarchical order down to Spearman's specific factors (Vernon, 1961).

Thurstone (1938) offered a new factor model in the nineteen thirties: this provides, in addition to the specific factors, for *group factors* (but no general factor) each of which is responsible for one class of performance. Thurstone defined seven primary factors (verbal comprehension, numerical, spatial, reasoning, perceptual speed, verbal fluency, memory). With the widespread development of factor analysis, a very large number of factors have been defined (more than two hundred), which are not always wholly distinct. Guilford, who has carried out the largest number of very extensive factor analyses, suggested a three-dimensional system of one hundred and twenty factors, some eighty-two of which he considered he had defined appropriately before 1967.

Since 1946 Meili has maintained that there are only a few fundamental intellectual factors, and has so far defined four of them (complexity, plasticity, globalization and fluency), which he has verified in many experiments on subjects from the age of seven onward. These factors have been defined similarly by others; according to Meili, at least the first three of these factors play a part in all "acts of the intelligence", even though they do not always significantly determine variance in performance. Meili does not deny the possibility of defining other factors (verbal, numerical, etc.), but believes with Spearman that these are less fundamental, and arise in measure large from practice in dealing with specific types of problem. A decision for one or other of these different models cannot be made by the factor-analytical method, because every correlation matrix can be interpreted in different ways and from different approaches to the psychology of thought.

2. *Intelligence and personality.* In general, intelligence is considered today to be a characteristic, aspect or area of (the)

personality (q.v.). In the first instance, this simply implies that the personality is not completely characterized if intelligence is overlooked. But this is merely an aid toward a definition; it is more important to decide whether there are relations between cognitive and non-cognitive phenomena, the latter including primarily motivational and affective phenomena. The problem must be viewed on different levels: (a) Significant correlations are seldom found between performance in intelligence tests and other personality characteristics determined by means of tests or questionnaires. On the other hand, it is known that test performance may be influenced by motivation, anxiety and certain other personality characteristics. However, since these influences do not apply to all individuals to the same extent and are dependent on the test situation (i.e. are not constant) there is generally no correlation. (b) There seem to be correlations between personality types and forms of intelligence. Kretschmer, for example, has shown affinities between his temperament types and forms of scientific thought and literary production. On the basis of other observations, American psychologists have come to speak of "cognitive styles" (Gardner et al., 1959; Gardner, 1959). They are not concerned with the level of performance but with qualitative characteristics of that performance. As yet it is impossible to decide empirically whether these characteristics can be explained by specific factor constellations, or whether they are based on the influence of non-cognitive conditions. It seems fairly certain that certain factor constellations are associated with interests (Wälti, 1970), and it can be assumed that fluency in solving certain types of problem, or ease of performance in some intellectual activities, may stimulate interest in them. In general, an interaction between the cognitive and non-cognitive spheres must be assumed. (c) On the factor level, therefore, factors obtained by the analysis of operations of intelligence cannot be definitely viewed as wholly intellectual: the possibility that they are interactive products (Hürsch, 1971) must be considered.

3. *Development of intelligence.* Here a distinction may be made between two lines of research: the quantitative and the qualitative. For a long time there was little doubt that the intelligence or ability required for cognitive performance was innate, and varied from individual to individual. Even if the observable ability for achievement in a given age group was thought of as acquired through learning processes, a varying ability to learn was (with a few exceptions) assumed, and defined as intelligence. This assumption of an initially given disposition or *anlage* (q.v.) then led to the question of the constancy of intelligence during development, and many studies have been made of this problem. In longitudinal studies, the intelligence of the same children was measured at various intervals after the first year of life and it was found that the IQ values (considered measures of intelligence) began to show a certain constancy only from the age of three to four. The results of different studies vary fairly widely, but it can be stated that it is only from the age of eight or nine that the intelligence level achieved at sixteen or seventeen can be anticipated with some accuracy (correlations of more than 0.80). However, since the problems used for measurement in the different age groups sometimes vary widely, this lack of consistency can be explained at least in part by the variations in the test method. Another reason for the poor correlation between IQs at different ages is the irregularity often noted in individual development. It has been found that the development (q.v.) of intellectual performance as reflected in test results, may be modified by environmental influences as by affective and physical factors. The development of intelligence must therefore be considered to be only in small measure a simple process of "growth". It tends rather to be a highly complex process of alteration of the bases of performance.

4. *Nature and nurture.* The old problem of the respective influences of innate traits and

environmental influences has still not been finally solved. The clearest answer (which still leaves certain problems) is provided by twin studies (q.v.). The correlation for intelligence between identical twins is rather more than 0.90. But if the two subjects grow up in a different environment it falls to about 0.75. The correlation for non-identical twins, or brothers and sisters, is still lower (0.54 to 0.62); and if the children grow up in different environments the correlation falls to 0.40 (Butcher, 1968). These figures suggest that variance in the level of intelligence measured in adults is due to environment to an extent of not more than one third.

In conjunction with the differentiation of different factors, the question of the constancy of the factorial structure has been raised. H. E. Garrett (1946) formulated a differentiation hypothesis which was converted by G. Lienert (1961) into a divergence hypothesis. According to these hypotheses, an originally unified factor (generally identified with Spearman's "g") becomes differentiated in the course of development, and an increasing number of other factors is formed. In only about one half of some thirty studies of this problem was it possible to confirm this hypothesis. It does seem clear that certain factors associated with the school, such as "v" and "n" occur only later, but a distinction between several factors must already be made at a very early stage. This leads to a distinction between basic or primary and acquired or secondary factors. The structure of the former appears to be relatively constant (Meili, 1970).

5. *Qualitative studies.* The dominant orientation here comes from Piaget. On the basis of research over several decades, Piaget distinguishes between four main stages: (a) the stage of sensorimotor intelligence, up to the age of eighteen months; (b) the stage of preoperational thought, up to the age of about seven years; (c) the stage of concrete operational thought, up to eleven years; and (d) the stage of formal logical operations (or formal operational thought). By "intelligence",

Piaget (1950, 1952) understands a mental structure which, in the course of development, achieves an increasingly comprehensive and perfect state of *equilibrium.* The different stages correspond to structures which Piaget has tried to define accurately (in the case of the two final stages, in the terminology of logistics and group theory). See *Abilities; Differential psychology; Traits; Type.*

Bibliography: Burt, C.: The factors of the mind. London, 1940. **Butcher, H. J.:** Human intelligence: its nature and assessment. London, 1968. **Gardner, R. W.:** Cognitive control principles and perceptual behavior. Bull. Meuninger Clin., 1959, *23,* 241–8. **Id.** *et al.:* Cognitive controls: a study of individual consistencies in cognitive behavior. Psychol. Issues, 1959, *1* (4), 1–186. **Garrett, H. E.:** A developmental theory of intelligence. Amer. Psychol. 1946, *1,* 372–8. **Guilford, J. P.:** The nature of human intelligence. New York, 1967. **Hürsch, L.:** Der Einfluss von Versuchsbedingungen auf die Faktorenstruktur von Intelligenzleistungen. Berne, 1971. **Köhler, W.:** The mentality of apes. New York, 1925. **Lienert, G. A.:** Überprufung und genetische Interpretation der Divergenzhypothese von Wewetzer. Vita Humana, 1961, *4,* 112–24. **Meili, R.:** L'analyse de l'intelligence. Arch. de Psychol., 1946, *31,* 1–64. **Id.:** Faktorenstruktur und Intelligenzentwicklung. Schweiz. Z. f. Psychol., 1970, *29,* 404–16. **Oléron, P.:** Les composants de l'intelligence, Paris, 1957. **Piaget, J.:** The psychology of intelligence. New York & London, 1950. **Id.:** The origins of intelligence in children. New York & London, 1952. **Spearman, C.:** The abilities of man. London, 1927. **Thurstone, L. L.:** Primary mental abilities. Chicago, 1938. **Vandenberg, S. G.:** Contribution of twin research to psychology. Psychol. Bull., 1966, *66,* 327–52. **Vernon, P. E.:** The structure of human abilities. London, 1961. **Wältl, U.:** Persönlichkeitszüge im Spiegel der Intelligzenstruktur. Berne, 1970.   *R. Meili.*

Intelligence age (Ger. *Intelligenzalter;* abb. *IA*). The difference between the IA and chronological age (CA) of a subject is the criterion for his advance on, or lag behind, the average intellectual development of other individuals of his age. The "intelligence age" is therefore what is usually known as *mental age* (q.v.).   *A.L.*

Intelligence quotient (abb. *IQ*). Suggested by W. Stern in 1912: IQ $= \dfrac{MA}{CA} \times 100$ (MA = mental age; CA = chronological age). The IQ is a measurement of the intellectual development of a testee in relation to the average value for persons of the same age group. See *Abilities; Intelligence; Intelligence tests*. *A.L.*

Intelligence, structure of. See *Intellect, structure of*.

Intelligence-structure test (abb. IST). A method of determining the general intellectual achievement level applicable to the 13–60 age group. Amthauer, the author of the test, understands intelligence as "a configuration of mental and psychological abilities"; he believes that his method helps to explain this phenomenon. The decisive feature is the test profile determined from the results of nine subtests each of which in the author's opinion represents a center of gravity in the structured totality of intelligence. The reliability (according to the halving method) of the test is r = 0.969, in the author's opinion, i.e. significantly high. In determining the validity of the method, correlations were found with teachers' opinions and school marks of r = 0.623 or r = 0.455.

Bibliography: Amthauer, R.: Intelligenz-Struktur-Test. Göttingen, ²1955. *P.S.*

Intelligence tests. The term "intelligence tests" covers psychological test methods designed to determine interindividual differences in the sphere of human intelligence (q.v.). The testee is required to solve a series of different problems of varying complexity; the number of correct solutions gives a quantitative idea of his intellectual (performance) level by comparison with other persons of the same age. Intelligence is generally measured by the intelligence quotient (IQ) which indicates—in its commonest form—the position of S. in relation to the population as a whole on a normally divided scale (mean value 1001; dispersion 15). Normally, the designation "intelligence test" implies that the method concerned is assumed to measure "general intelligence" and not partial aspects of the latter. Psychologists are not, however, of one mind as to the performance areas covered by "g", or its structure; accordingly, the different intelligence tests are sometimes based on highly divergent models of intelligence.

The earliest attempts at a psychological diagnosis of intelligence were made in the nineteenth century. Galton (q.v.) was the first to organize relatively large-scale systematic experiments to detect interindividual differences in the sphere of intelligence. He postulated the standard distribution of intelligence generally accepted today. Pioneering work was done by Binet (q.v.) who published (with T. Simon) in 1905 the first procedures to justify the use of the term "intelligence test" in its present sense. While Binet's method was designed for educational purposes as an intelligence test for children, the first intelligence tests for adults were developed by military psychologists in America during World War I (see *Army Alpha Test; Army Beta Test*). These methods were suitable for use as group tests and were designed as test batteries; they therefore already possessed two major characteristics typical of most modern intelligence tests. The diagnostic possibilities of test batteries were subsequently extended by adding the psychological profile (test profile) formulated by the Russian psychiatrist G. J. Rossolimo. Going beyond the quantitative determination of a complex of characteristics and the various component parts of the complex (as in the case of a test battery), the psychological profile evaluated the interrelationship between individual subtests on a differential diagnostic basis.

The intelligence diagnosis method owes most of the qualitative improvements it has undergone to the use of statistical methods. These enabled the tests to be designed scientifically and standardized as measuring instruments. With the help of a statistical method, i.e. factor analysis (q.v.), it proved possible to obtain direct empirical access to the problem of intelligence, and to base intelligence tests on experimental findings.

Despite the progress made primarily through statistics, the intelligence tests in general use today are not so perfected as one would expect of precise measuring instruments. The main reason is that the extent and structure of intelligence are not as yet sufficiently well defined, while the conditions of the test situation (above all S.'s motivation) remain rather imprecise in intelligence testing as in other psychodiagnostic methods. Nevertheless, modern intelligence tests are among the most sophisticated methods available for psychological diagnosis. See *Abilities; Objective tests; Test theory; Child psychology*.

Bibliography: Anastasi, A.: Psychological testing. New York, ²1961. Id.: Testing problems in perspective. New York, 1966. Buros, O. S.: Tests in print. New York, 1961. Cronbach, L. J.: Essentials of psychological testing. New York, ²1964. Daniels, J. C. & Diack, H.: The standard reading tests. London, 1960. Doll, E. A.: The Vineland social maturity scale. Princeton, N.J., 1947. Field, J.: Two types of tables for use with Wechsler's intelligence. J. Clin. Psychol., 1960, *16*, 3–7. Frostig, M.: Testing as a basis for educational therapy. Oxford, 1967. Littell, W. M.: The Wechsler intelligence scale for children: a review of a decade of research. In: Savage, R. D.: Readings in clinical psychology. Oxford, 1966. Maxwell, A. E.: A factor analysis of the Wechsler intelligence scale for children. B. J. Educ. Psychol., 1959, *32*, 119–32. Savage, R. D.: Psychometric assessment of the individual child. Harmondsworth, 1968. Schonell, F. S. & E.: Scholastic diagnostic and attainment testing. London, 1960. Terman, L. & Merrill, M. H.: A Stanford-Binet intelligence scale: manual for form L–M. Boston, ³1960. Vernon, P. E.: Intelligence and attainment tests. London, 1960. Wechsler, D.: Manual for the Wechsler intelligence scale for children. New York, 1949. Id.: The measurement and appraisal of adult intelligence. New York, ⁴1965. Id.: The Wechsler preschool and primary intelligence scale. New York, 1966.   *P. Steck*

Intensification. 1. The phenomenon that certain impressions when remembered seem greatly distorted: e.g. terrible, horrific, dangerous, amazing. Artistic representation often lays considerable stress on such distortion. **2.** Reinforcement (q.v.).   *H.W.*

Intensity. 1. Great attention (q.v.) **2.** The state of being forced, strained or increased. **3.** The strength of, or increase of degree of, e.g. an emotion, stimulus or response.

Intention. 1. The orientation of the mind or self toward something. **2.** Goal, purpose, objective. **3.** Close attention.

Intentional psychoses. A psychiatric term which has now gone out of general use. Inhibitions or anxieties prevent the completion of certain intended actions. The cause may be psychotic (e.g. ambivalence, negativism) or neurotic (e.g. compulsion, phobia). See *Neurosis; Psychoses, functional.*   *C.Sch.*

Intention movements (syn. *Intentional responses*). Movements which are incomplete in form, intensity or frequency and show the partner or informed observer what the animal intends to do, i.e. indicate the growing motivation of an instinct. Frequently noted in conflict (q.v.) situations.   *K.Fi.*

Bibliography: Heinroth, O.: Beiträge zur Biologie, namentlich Ethologie und Psychologie der Anatiden. Verh. V. Kongr. Int. Orn. Berlin, 1911. Tinbergen, N.: The study of instinct. Oxford, ²1969.

Interaction. 1. A reciprocal or mutual influence between two characteristics, persons, systems, etc. **2.** In statistics (q.v.) the term *interaction* is primarily used in connection with test designs for analysis of variance. In these designs the effect of several multiple, multiclass, independent variables can be observed simultaneously. Interaction is then a measurement of the extent to which the effect of one (or more) independent variable(s) is (are) dependent on one (or more) other independent variable(s). Interactions are sometimes more interesting than the "main effects". See *Variance, analysis of.* *W.H.B.*

Interaction, psychophysical. The observable reciprocal influence of physical and mental or psychological processes, e.g. the influence of emotions (q.v.) on such functions as heart and pulse rate, respiration, and so on, or the fluctuation of performance caused by fatigue (q.v.). The theory of psychophysical interaction (E. von Hartmann, W. James, H. Lotze, E. Becher), according to which body and mind can have a causative effect upon one another, seeks to explain such phenomena in postulating that the mind can precipitate physical, and the body mental, processes. As a theory it can be traced back to Descartes's separation of mind (*res cogitans*) and body (*res extensa*), and ultimately forms part of the subject-matter of philosophy (see *Mind-body problem*). As a dualistic, causal construct it does not accord with the empirically grounded conception of relations between psychological and physiological processes. See *Physiological psychology; Psychosomatics.* *F.-C. S.*

Interaction, social (syn. *Social intercourse*). The reciprocal influence of individuals or groups through the medium of communication (q.v.). The more specific term "symbolic interaction" is used when the communicative process is specially emphasized in the context of social interaction. "Social interaction" can also denote specific phenomena in social contacts, e.g. gestures, mimicry, reading another person's letter, etc. *W.D.F.*

Interbrain. The *diencephalon* (q.v.).

Interest. 1. Concern, advantage, good, profit. **2.** A tendency to behaviors oriented toward certain objects, activities or experience, which tendency varies in intensity (and generality) from individual to individual. Factor-analytical studies of the structure of interests have shown about fifteen independent dimensions (directions of interest), e.g. for music, politics and economics, technology and natural science, art, etc. The association between interests and personality or performance tests (with the exception of tests centering purely on knowledge) is generally slight. See *Attitude; Creativity.*

Bibliography: Todt, E.: Differentieller Interessen-Test (DIT). Berne & Stuttgart, 1967. *M.A.*

Interest test (syn. *Interest inventory; Interest blank*). A test which measures interests or a questionnaire which elicits a range of interests. See *Kuder Preference Record; Strong Vocational Interest Blank.*

Interference tube. A complex sound conducting tube designed in such a way that certain components of a sound can be eliminated by a wave cancellation process, i.e. the trough of one wave being opposed to the crest of another. In this way it is possible to obtain a sound wave of increased purity. *G.D.W.*

Interindividual. Between different individuals. *Interindividual variability:* the variability of measured values observed in measurements on different individuals. *B.H.*

Intermenstrual pain. Pain occurring between successive periods of menstruation.

Intermodal qualities. Qualities of perception or imagination which are not confined to a single sensory modality. E.g. the quality "warm" is an attribute not only of sensed temperature but of visual and auditory perception; we speak of a "warm" color and of a "warm" voice. *P.T.*

_## 547 INTERSUBJECTIVITY

Internalization. The adoption of attitudes, norms, prejudices, etc., by an individual.

Internal secretion. The release of glandular products directly into the bloodstream from glands without an outlet channel. The products are hormones (q.v.), which influence growth, development and metabolic (hormonal control) as well as psychological processes.   *F.-C.S.*

Interoceptor. See *Enteroceptor.*

Interpretation. An activity as a result of which a physical or psychological datum is related to a conceptual model which assigns place and significance to the datum.   *F.B.*

Interquartile range. The interquartile range takes as its "positional parameters" the measured values in a distribution between which the middle 50% of all observed cases are located. The interquartile range is therefore the interval between the first (25%) and third (75%) quartile.   *W.H.B.*

Interrogation of suspects. In its psychological aspects, the examination of suspects forms part of forensic psychology (q.v.). The methods of psychology are used in an attempt to determine the subjective accuracy of verbal evidence. The methods used may be divided into two classes: (*a*) Association tests (q.v.) and other verbal reaction methods. In most cases the reaction time and word are evaluated diagnostically. These techniques were used even in the early stages of work in this area, by C. G. Jung (q.v.) and M. Wertheimer (q.v.). (*b*) Methods for recording physical side-effects during interrogation. Such techniques usually consist of questioning the suspect with a mixture of directly relevant

and irrelevant questions, and of registering simultaneous physical symptoms. This latter aspect can, of course, be restricted to a mere intuitive interpretation of expressions (see *Expression*), but objective techniques for measuring physical symptoms (e.g. measurement of pulse, respiration, skin resistance, muscular activity; see *Polygraph; Lie detector*) are more sensitive. The relation between the measured physiological processes and simultaneous psychological processes allows the tester to assume a correlation between measurements and the accuracy or inaccuracy of a statement. The legal acceptability of such findings varies from country to country. See *Credibility; Criminality; Objective tests.*

_Bibliography: **Bibliography: Davis, R. C.:** Physiological responses as a means of evaluating information. In: **Biderman, A. D. & Zimmer, H.** (Eds.): The manipulation of human behavior. New York, 1961. **Inbau, F. E. & Reid, J. E.:** Lie detection and criminal interrogation. Baltimore, ³1953. **Jung, C. G.:** Zur psychol. Tatbestandsdiagnostik. Arch. Krim., 1939, *100*, 123–30. **Tent, L.:** Psychologische Tatbestandsdiagnostik. In: **Undeutsch, U.** (Ed.): Handbuch der Psychol., Vol. 11. Göttingen, 1967. **Wertheimer, M.:** Tatbestandsdiagnostik. In: **Abderhalden, E.** (Ed.): Handbuch der Biologischen Arbeitsmethoden, Section VI. Berlin, 1933.   *F.M.*

Interrupted action. See *Zeigarnik effect.*

Intersexuality. The condition of being intermediate between the two sexes, especially with respect to the secondary sex characteristics (see *Hermaphroditism*).

Intersex: Abnormal individual intermediate between male and female, that has identical genetic form throughout all its cells (see *Gynandromorph*).   *G.D.W.*

Interstitial cell stimulating hormone. See *ICSH*.

Intersubjectivity. 1. In E. Husserl's phenomenology (q.v.): the association of subjectivities which is necessary for an objective world to exist. **2.** Subjective experience (e.g. perception) becomes intersubjectivity when several individuals experience the same thing, e.g. report the same experience, or experimental results.   *B.H.*

Interval. 1. The range of time between two events, etc. **2.** The distance between two assignable points or values. **3.** The difference in pitch between any two tones (notes). **4.** Remission of a disorder (e.g. delirium).

Interval estimate (syn. *Interval rating*). In an interval estimate two values are indicated on the basis of samples; a given parameter is situated with a known probability between these two values. An interval estimate indicates the fiducial interval (see *Limits, fiducial*) to be taken into account when a statistical index is substituted for an (unknown) parameter. It is therefore a measure of the accuracy of a sample. See *Statistics*. *W.H.B.*

Interval of uncertainty (abb. *IU*). The range of stimuli between thresholds obtained using different methods, especially ascending and descending series in the *limits method* (q.v.).
                                                       G.D.W.

Interval scale. A unit of measurement whose multiple represents the interval magnitude necessary to quantify an interval (defined as the distance between two values). Unlike ordinal scales, interval scales have identical distances between the scale units, but no genuine (i.e. absolute) zero point. *W.H.B.*

Intervariation characterizes the extent of differences in measured values between individuals. The opposite is the case with *intravariation*, i.e. the variability of measured values in a given individual during repeated observations. With the increasing application

of statistical methods in psychology, these terms have tended to disappear from the literature. The modern equivalents represent standards of statistical variability. For the diagnosis of individual cases, *ipsative* (deviation from average value for a single person) or *normative* (deviation of one person from the average for a sample) values take over this function.   *W.H.B.*

Intervening variable. A hypothetical variable and not a statistical concept, the intervening variable cannot be observed directly even though an operational definition can be given of its effect; it has an "intervening" function in the stimulus-response process, and may be considered as the *expression of a relationship* between stimulating conditions and responses (the dependent variable).   *W.H.B.*

Interview. The most important of the various techniques of data collection is questioning or interviewing; a prominent factor is the use of language as a means of communication (which, of course, creates certain problems). In general, the interview is a means of obtaining verbal (and written) information. Despite the use of early, crude techniques of questioning (e.g. by ethnologists, cultural anthropologists, sociologists and psychologists), the systematic development of the interview into a research instrument and a methodically controlled observation technique occurred only in the early years of the present century. The appearance of market and public opinion research (q.v.) in the USA was followed by the gradual development of sociological research (see *Attitude; Social psychology*) dependent on planned questioning—especially for checking hypotheses. Psychology and psychoanalysis (q.v.) also use interviews in conjunction with observation, tests, experiments, etc., to obtain statements from subjects which will enable conclusions to be drawn about attitudes, actions, circumstances, conflicts, self-interpretations of a person's position in life, etc. In this sense, the interview is a planned procedure with a scientific objective, in which verbal information is elicited from testees by means of a series of deliberate questions or communicated stimuli; it can be a means (in diverse practical fields) of elucidating the situation of entire populations, or groups within a population, or merely the condition (in a wide sense) of an individual patient.

The standardized interview is the technique most often used when dealing with single persons. It allows the greatest degree of comparison. The wording, sequence of questions, possible answers, and *interviewer's behavior* are fixed in advance. Only the standardized questionnaire supplies *fully comparable data*. However, comprehensive knowledge about the subject under review is assumed. More important than the identical wording of the questions is that they should mean the same thing to all the testees. This can be achieved by standardizing the meaning in the partly standardized interview, or by "filter" questions which eliminate Ss. who do not seem to be suitable for a certain range of questions.

In the semi-standardized interview a series of questions is used which enables the interviewer to react at certain points, and to conduct a comparatively free exploration by changing the wording and explaining the questions, omitting or adding others and continuing the questioning. Such interviews (structured or semi-structured interviews, and formal questionnaires or inventories) have a detailed plan; in contrast, the *depth interview* (unstructured, open, exploratory, intensive or qualitative) leaves the shaping and development of the questioning in large measure to the discretion of the interviewer, who works to a general plan consisting especially of interview objectives, some groups of subjects, and possibly *ad hoc* questions. This type of interview is more like a free but guided conversation, with or without written note-taking or tape recording. It is suitable in various psychological disciplines, especially

for obtaining a more complete account of individual cases (flexibility and more comprehensive information—more difficult quantitative evaluation).

Sets of data obtained by unstructured and intensive questioning are not comparable since standardization of significance during the course of the interview is impossible. In contrast to the form of the personal interview, the written interview consists usually of standardized questionnaires which are sent out to the testees (these may be useful in collecting more objective data, but there is not sufficient checking and possibly few replies may be received). *Group interviews* are also carried out in a written or personal form, in natural or experimental groups.

Questions vary very widely in form. The closed question allows the interviewee to give only set answers: in the alternative question these are Yes or No, in the choice question there are several possibilities to be selected from a list which is either printed or read out. The open question, on the other hand, allows free answers; other "half-open", questions allow for answers which are not prescribed but nevertheless admissible. The direct question makes the meaning and purpose of the question clear from the start; the indirect question, sometimes in conjunction with projective techniques (q.v.), conceals the orientation in order to exclude wrong and/or socially standardized answers. Batteries of questions, i.e. a number of individual questions, are useful in an optimally comprehensive investigation of a thematic complex separated from other themes by introductory and bridging questions. Follow-up questions complete the picture; filter questions are used to find out which main questions do not apply to a particular testee; control questions enable answers to be checked.

The interviewer's behavior can have considerable influence on the interview and its results. In the neutral interview the interviewer must adhere strictly to his instructions, and refrain from giving any help or making any comment. On the other hand, the interviewer has to play an active part in the "hard" interview (a "cross-examination"), or the "soft" interview (in which an atmosphere of confidence is created). In both cases the object is to get the testee to give the right answers, to prevent evasion, to detect contradictions, etc. Even an adequate training in interviewing will certainly not prevent any negative influence due to prejudice, to influencing the test subject by showing agreement, to the way in which answers are received, the interviewee classified and his responses written down. The following are some of the points which need watching in the interviewee: readiness, fluctuations of mood, alertness, education and training, expressiveness, knowledge, retention, social class, taboo subjects, evaluation of self and intimate environment, and attitude to the role of the interviewer as a stranger. How much anyone will be prepared to disclose varies considerably according to culture, class, club and other social groups. Special problems arise in depth interviews (e.g. in clinical interviewing). In research, such methods are used mainly for pilot studies (q.v.).

Reliability is the degree of consistency with which a result is obtained when the same technique is repeated. With regard to the reliability of interview data, results are available which show a value of 90% for personal interviews in the form of repeated questionings of the same persons—the panel method. The degree of reliability depends on the time lapse between the two interrogations, the groups interrogated and the subjects inquired into. There is more stability when the questions deal with more subjective matters, whereas opinions and attitudes (q.v.) are subject to varying degrees of fluctuation. Validity depends on whether the results obtained by the use of a certain technique really represent what is supposed in the interpretation. As regards the validity of interview data, only isolated material has so far been published and no comprehensive study of the subject is available. Validity

may be verified by, say, comparison of the results of a questionnaire with official figures (e.g. in regard to elections and statistics of electoral behavior). The validity of interview data is no higher than their reliability; on the other hand, a high degree of reliability does not necessarily indicate an equivalent degree of validity. See *Questionnaires; Intelligence tests; Objective tests.*

Bibliography: Anastasi, A.: Psychological testing. New York, 1961. Argyle, M.: The scientific study of social behaviour. London, 1957. Blum, R. H.: Management of the doctor-patient relationship. New York, 1960. Cronbach, L. J. & Gleser, C. C.: Psychological tests and personnel decisions. Chicago, 1957. Maier, N. R. F.: The appraisal interview. New York, 1958. Merton, R. K. *et al.*: The focused interview. Glencoe, Ill., 1956. Sidney, E. & Brown, M.: The skills of interviewing. London, 1961.

A. Bellebaum

Interviewer bias. An intruding variable to be taken into account when evaluating an interview: the effects of the interviewer's attitudes and prejudices.

Interviews, drugs in. Certain psychotropic substances with a beneficial influence on verbal behavior are used in interrogations or interviews. Hypnotic drugs, tranquilizers, antidepressants, stimulants, and hallucinogens or psychotomimetic drugs are used both for diagnostic-therapeutic purposes and also to obtain important information from potential sources. These substances may make an interrogation more productive by inducing (in various ways) some weakening of the resistance of a potential informant. Nevertheless, the validity and accuracy of the knowledge obtained are doubtful and can be confirmed only by extrinsic criteria. Not to give information does not signify that the person interrogated is not in possession of it. Facts disclosed under the influence of such drugs are usually not admissible as evidence in a court of law.

Bibliography: Gottschalk, L. A.: The use of drugs in information-seeking interviews. In: Uhr, L. & Miller,

J. G. (Eds.): Drugs and behavior. London, 1960; New York, 1964. *E.L.*

Intimacy. 1. Coitus (q.v.). 2. In gestalt psychology (usually "intimacy principle"): the interdependence of the "parts" of a gestalt, none of which may be removed or added to without changing the whole, and therefore all other parts. See *Ganzheit*.

Intimate sphere. A pre-scientific term for areas of private behavior supposedly withdrawn from social influence. *J.F.*

Intolerance. See *Tolerance; Authoritarian personality; Prejudice.*

Intonation. Speech melody: aspects of pitch (q.v.) in speech.

Intoxication. 1. Poisoning. 2. A temporary psychological condition resulting from poison or drugs (especially ethyl alcohol) and manifested in a variety of behaviors and symptoms ranging from exhilaration and loss of personal and social responsibility to depression, stupor or coma. See *Alcoholism; Drug dependence* (as chronic states). 3. Usage is sometimes extended metaphorically to include similar behavioral effects of purely psychological origin, e.g. "intoxicated with joy".
Intoxicant: An agent producing the state of intoxication. *G.D.W.*

Intraindividual. Within an individual. *Intraindividual fluctuations:* fluctuations of values (e.g. body temperature) observed during repeated measurements of a particular characteristic in a given individual. *B.H.*

Intramural nervous system. A term sometimes used to describe the majority of the nerve fibers and ganglionic cells in the various layers of the intestinal wall. The most important are the *plexus myentericus* (L. Auerbach), between the intestinal musculature, and the *plexus submucosus* (G. Meissner) below the mucous membrane layer. The intramural nervous system forms part of the autonomic nervous system (q.v.) and regulates intestinal movement and secretion. The blood vessel walls also contain elements of the autonomic nervous system which affect the smooth musculature of the vessels, and thus regulate the hemodynamically effective cross-section as well as tonus.

Bibliography: Leonhardt, H.: Histologie und Zytologie des Menschen. Stuttgart, 1969. *G.A.*

Intrapsychic. Within the mind (endopsychic, q.v.), or the self as a whole.

Intrinsic. That which is inward, fixed in the nature of the person or thing, and therefore not dependent on external influences or accident. Ant. *extrinsic:* that which is outward and does not belong to the essential nature of the person or thing.

Intrinsic-extrinsic. A distinction of H. Heckhausen's in regard to two components of *learning motivation. Intrinsic motivation* consists of achievement motivation (q.v.); stimuli from a specialism; task stimuli (related to the degree of difficulty of the task); attainability (calculation of the probable success in performing a task); and the degree of novelty possessed by a thing or task, or attributable to it. All other motivations are extrinsic, i.e. come from without, and are posited, not with the thing or task, but by the teacher, his personality, his style of teaching, and his sanctions. Extrinsic stimuli, rewards and punishments are thought to be less effective in the long run than those deemed intrinsic. *M.H.*

Introception. The inclusion of social standards (e.g. customs, conventions, ideals) in the individual's own system of motivation; introception is not identical with socialization, where conformity (especially in behavior) is not necessarily emphasized in the dynamic structure. *B.H.*

Introjection. 1. The term is generally used with the same meaning as identification (q.v.): an individual's incorporation into his ego of an object-image representing the object as he thinks it is. The most primitive form of intro-jection is "oral incorporation" which is alleged to consist of fantasized incorporation of the primary love-object (the mother) by the child when in a state of oral frustration; according to Freud, Abraham and Fenichel, this is a significant factor in psychotic depression.
2. The epistemological theory that the conscious mind apprehends the external world (only) by means of (the) images (the mind generates).

Bibliography: Abraham, K.: Selected papers on psychoanalysis. London, 1927. Fenichel, O.: The psychoanalytic theory of neurosis. New York, 1945. Freud, S.: Collected papers, Vol. 4. London, 1924–5.
W.T.

Intromission-copulation-ejaculation mechanism. A concept which occurs in comparative psychology (q.v.) and sex research. The two- or three-mechanism theory attempts to explain sexual behavior patterns in the male animal, and draws on the results of experiments in mammals (mice, rats, hamsters, guinea pigs). It is suggested that at least two or three mechanisms are involved in male sexual behavior: (*a*) an *arousal mechanism* (AM), which leads to sexual excitement, followed by erection and copulation; (*b*) a *copulatory mechanism* (CM), which is activated by the first intromission (introduction) of the penis, and leads to repeated intromission which maintains the full excitement of the CM until the critical threshold of ejaculation is reached (Beach *et al.*, 1956, 1959); (*c*) the *ejaculatory mechanism*, which is triggered by ejaculation (neurologically: the "ejaculation reflex") and prevents sexual excitement (by inhibiting the AM) until a certain recovery of "drive" has taken place (McGill, 1965). AM, CM and EM, defined by certain behavioral characteristics and duration times, vary not only from one species of animal to another but (as a function of the genotype) within a given species. For a critical summary, see Bolles (1967).

Bibliography: Beach, F. A.: Characteristics of masculine sex drives. In: Jones, M. R. (Ed.): Nebraska symposium on motivation. Lincoln, 1956, 1–32. Beach, F. A. & Whalen, R. E.: Effects of ejaculation on sexual behavior in the male rat. J. comp. physiol. Psychol., 1959, 52, 249–54. Bolles, R. C.: Theory of motivation. New York & London, 1967, 167–72. McGill, T. E.: Studies of sexual behavior of male laboratory mice: effects of genotype, recovery of sex drive, and theory. In: Beach, F. A. (Ed.): Sex and behavior. New York & London, 1965, 76–88. *H.M.*

Introspection. Self-observation. The contemplation of one's own experiences; sometimes, though not necessarily, implying a morbid preoccupation with one's inner thoughts and feelings. In *structural psychology*, the reporting of thought processes and sensations (either during—*simultaneous introspection*—or immediately after—*retrospective introspection*—the process) as a technique for generating psychological data. *Beschreibung* (*Ger.*): such reporting of the direct experience of the individual. *G.D.W.*

Introspective psychology. A branch of psychology which uses introspection (q.v.) as a preferred method for obtaining data. The basic assumption is that subjective elements are objectified (see *Phenomenology*). In its theoretical and experimental aspects, the school has developed several different models, e.g. for processes of the will (see *Külpe*). *B.H.*

Introversion. Jung (1971) maintained that mental or psychic energy (libido) may be directed outward (extraversion) or inward (introversion). Hence there are two opposed reaction types determining the nature of behavior, subjective experience, and even compensation by the unconscious. Introversion (like extraversion) is rooted (according to Jung) in the biological constitution of the individual and is therefore difficult to alter. The definition of an individual as introverted or extraverted may be considered as remaining constant throughout his life. See *Traits; Type*.

Bibliography: Jung, C. G.: Psychological types (Collected Works, Vol. 6). London & New York, 1971.   *W.S.*

Introversive type. An individual who in the Rorschach test shows a "predominance of introverted behavior, intensive relationships, stabilized affectivity and motility, inadequate adaptability to reality, and inadequate extensive relationships." Partly identical with the introvert.   *W.K.*

Introvert (syn. *Introverted type*). A character type defined by Jung, and having a deficient or negative relationship between the ego and object as its main feature. Tendency to distance and depth. An individual in whom "a subjective attitude is inserted between perception of the object and his own behavior which prevents behavior from assuming a character corresponding to the given objective structure." Introverts "if normal, are characterized by a hesitant, reflective, withdrawn nature; they are reserved, frightened by objects, always on the defensive and likely to hide behind mistrustful observation"; they are therefore not very adaptable. Eysenck also defines the introvert as the opposite of the extravert, but as a statistically determined personality factor (see *Type*).

Bibliography: Jung, C. G.: Psychological types. London & New York, 1971. Eysenck, H. J.: The structure of human personality. London, ³1970.   *W.K.*

Intuition. A mode of operation of intelligence (q.v.) and its product. As a mode of operation, intuition denotes a form of direct cognition characterized by its direct and sudden nature. It is based on spontaneous internal organization, on a perception, or on an idea or image. Intuition as "sympathy" with the object (H. Bergson) may amount to nonconceptual cognition, but may also be a rapid analytical understanding of a reference system whose actual analysis would require long discursive development (E. Brunswik). Intuition is concerned with an externally (empirical) or internally (metaphysical) perceptible phenomenon. In every case the existential nature of the object is apprehended by the mind.   *M.J.B.*

Intuitive type. A functional type in whom the "basic function" of intuition dominates, and judgment is only secondary. As an extravert, the intuitive type constantly seeks new possibilities and is guided by confidence in his perception. As an introvert, however, the intuitive type appears as an "imaginative, artistic person" or as a "dreamer and visionary", internal perception being directed to the esthetic or moral sphere.   *W.K.*

Intuitive understanding, psychology of. See *Verstehende Psychologie*.

Invariance. A parameter or trait is said to be invariant in relation to a transformation if it remains unchanged on application of the latter. E.g. the length of a rod is an invariant factor when it is rotated in space.   *K.-D.G.*

Invariance, problem of. Any problem associated with the constancy, i.e. independence, of stimuli in regard to changes in external conditions. Invariance is dealt with under terms such as "generalization of learning", "concept formation", "constancy of perception". E.g. constancy of perception is the easiest type of invariance to examine. The resulting perceptual content is independent of all changes brought about by interference. A distinction is made between: color constancy, brightness constancy, gestalt constancy, size constancy, and direction and movement constancy.   H.W.

Inventories. See *Questionnaires*.

Inversion. A reversal of poles, e.g. top to bottom, right to left, e.g. inversion of the retinal image. In mathematics, a transform which achieves reversal of a variable or matrix.   G.D.W.

Inversion, sexual. Assumption of the characteristics and role of the opposite sex, e.g. *transves(ti)tism* (q.v.). Has also been loosely used as a synonym for *homosexuality* (q.v.) (especially in psychoanalysis), and even *hermaphroditism* (q.v.). *Invert:* An individual with homosexual inclinations.   G.D.W.

Inverted figures. See *Reversibility*.

Involution. On reaching maturity, the psychological development of man continues at a slower rate, and finally enters a phase of involution. At the climacteric (about the age of forty-eight), biological involution sets in as a transition to a way of life in which mental activity is more highly emphasized. Old age is a further period of involution. See *Aging; Gerontology*.   M.Sa.

IPAT Anxiety Scale. The Ipat (Institute for Personality and Ability Testing) Anxiety Scale was developed by Cattell and Scheier on the basis of factor-analytical principles (1957). The subjective questionnaire comprises forty items which represent the secondary factor "anxiety"; anxiety, in turn, consists of five primary factors. The test—retest reliability is between r = 0.87 and 0.93 (1–2 weeks) and the split-half reliability between r = 0.84 and 0.91. The construct validity (q.v.) of the items is r = 0.92, and that of the primary factors r = 0.85. The criterion validity (correlations with other anxiety tests) is between r = 0.72/0.85.

Bibliography: Cattell, R. B. & Scheier, I. H.: Handbook for the IPAT Anxiety Scale. Champaign, Ill., 1957; ²1963.   P.G.

IPAT (O-A) Anxiety Battery. The Objective-Analytic (O-A) Anxiety Battery was designed by Cattell and Scheier (1960) on the basis of factor-analytical principles. The objective questionnaire with its two hundred and sixty-two items represents the primary factor "anxiety", and measures mainly the trait anxiety. The split-half reliability of the verbal subtests is between r = 0.56 and 0.90 (average: r = 0.75). The construct validity (q.v.) of the overall battery is indicated by Cattell as r = 0.94. The criterion validity (other anxiety tests) is greater than 0.80.

Bibliography: Cattell, R. B. & Scheier, I. H.: Handbook for the A-O Anxiety Battery. Champaign, Ill., 1960.   P.G.

IPAT Objective-Analytic (O-A) Personality Test Batteries. The representative test battery in factor-analytical personality research, with objective tests by Cattell. The version for adults measures fourteen objective personality factors, with fifty-six objective tests (q.v.) (for children: eight [six to ten years], or eleven [eleven to twelve years] personality factors). Reliability coefficients are not given in the manual. The factor loadings are described by Hundleby, Pawlik & Cattell (1965). In the present state of development, the test is primarily a research instrument.

Bibliography: Cattell, R. B. *et al*.: Handbook for the O-A. Personality Test Batteries, Champaign, Ill.,

555   ISLAND OF REIL

1955. Hundleby, J. D., Pawlik, K. & Cattell, R. B.: Personality factors in objective test devices. Champaign, Ill., 1965, 339–406.   P.G.

Ipsation (syn. *Ipsism*). Masturbation (q.v.) or autoeroticism with reference to some particular part of the body, e.g. anal ipsation, mammary ipsation, and so on.   G.D.W.

IQ. Abb. for *Intelligence quotient* (q.v.).

Iris. An opaque regulable diaphragm in the form of an 0.5 mm thick disk of connective tissue with a variable internal diameter, separating the anterior from the posterior chamber of the eye (see *Eye; Sense organs*). The iris is continuous peripherally with the ciliary body; its aperture is the contractile pupil, whose width can be varied between about 8 and 2 mm by the smooth *sphincter pupillae* (sphincter) and *dilatator pupillae* (dilator) muscles located in the iris. The pigmentation of its posterior pigmented surface is wholly absent in the condition of albinism. The anterior colored surface represents the "color of a person's eyes". K.H.P.

IRM. Abb for *Innate releasing mechanism* (q.v.).

Irradiation. 1. The influence exerted by one field on another. **2.** Physiologically: the extension of stimuli in certain regions of the brain to neighboring areas of the CNS. **3.** Psychologically, and in the sense of an optical illusion: bright objects on a dark background appear larger than dark objects of the same size on a bright background. According to T. Ziehen, irradiation occurs when neutral conscious material is influenced by emotional experiences which are present at the same time or have some associative connection with it.   K.E.P.

Irrational. Any assertion based not on the laws of reason but on intuition is irrational, as are theories regarding an object (life, existence, will, etc.) outside reality. This is particularly true of Freud (in his late phase).   M.R.

Irrelevant actions (syn. *Comfort movements*). Inappropriate behaviors such as stretching, yawning, scratching one's head, preening (see *Allopreening*). Although these "occur easily" (e.g. insects cleaning their antennae), by no means all such movements are autochthonous; in conflicts they often tend to be displacement activities (q.v.). As derived and ritualized movements they play a great part in the evolution of displays.

Bibliography: Bilz, R: Zur Psychophysik des Verlegenheitskratzens. Zentralbl. Psychother. u. Grenzgeb., 1941, *13*, 36–50. Tembrock, G.: Verhaltensforschung. Jena, 1964.   K.Fi.

Irritability. 1. Stimulability; excitability; the characteristic property of living matter to respond to stimuli by movement, etc. **2.** Contractability of a muscle. **3.** Affective response; emotional changeability; oversensitivity to stimulation: a strongly emotional response is given to normally acceptable stimuli. See *Arousal; Emotion*.   H.W.

Irritation. 1. The effect of stimuli. **2.** Inflammation.

Ishihara test (syn. *Ishihara chart; Ishihara color plate*). A test for color blindness: figures are printed in varying hues against backgrounds of varying saturations and brightness. The color-blind or color-defective individual does not see the figure, or sees it imperfectly.

Island of Reil. See *Insula*.

Isolation. A hypothetical internal defense (q.v.) mechanism in which a motive which can no longer be satisfied or is forbidden can only be "abandoned" by partially satisfying it in thought or symbolically, and is therefore experienced as alien to the individual. The unsuccessful attempt at repression is reinforced by repression (q.v.) of the connection between the questionable motive and the individual. Isolation is said to occur frequently in compulsion neuroses.   *W.T.*

Isolation of variables. In experiments: the intentional alteration of a condition (independent variation) in order to observe a dependent variable, while all other conditions are kept "constant", or are not altered systematically. The effect of individual conditions which are otherwise closely bound up with the phenomenon or process can then be observed in isolation.   *W.H.B.*

Isolation, social. Minimal social contact or maximum social distance between individuals and/or groups. The aftereffects of social isolation in the early years of life have been described in particular by Harlow (1958) and Spitz (1958) as hospitalism (q.v.). Voluntary or planned isolation of one group in relation to alien groups is frequently used as a means of heightening the internal cohesion of the isolated group. See *Group dynamics*.

Bibliography: Harlow, H. F.: The nature of love, Amer. Psychol., 1958, *13*, 573–685. Spitz, R. A.: Hospitalism: an enquiry into the genesis of psychiatric conditions in early childhood. New York, 1958.
          A.S.M.

Isomorphism. The theory of *isomorphy*, or correspondence of gestalts: i.e. between what is experienced perceptually and the central-physiological correlate. It is assumed that the physiological processes correspond, not in their geometrical forms, but in their dynamic structures, with the contents of experience. See *Ganzheit; Psychophysics*.   *P.T.*

Item. A single exercise in a test. See *Objective tests; Test theory*.

Item analysis. The various processes used to select items for tests. See *Test theory*.

Iteration tests. Statistical test methods for checking the randomness of a sample selection.

Ixothymia. A viscous temperament (q.v.).

J

Jackson's law. After John Hughlings Jackson, English neurologist (1834–1911). The generalization that when intellectual functions are lost through disease of the nervous system, those which appeared latest in evolution are the first to disappear, that is deterioration retraces evolution in reverse. The phylogenetically developing, "stratified" structure of the CNS corresponds to a distribution of functions in the sense that the higher systems always exercise an inhibiting influence on the lower ones. The function of the higher, phylogenetically younger centers is more labile than that of the deeper, older centers. In brain damage the mental and intellectual functions (orientation, perceptual ability, memory and thought) are the most sensitive and most easily injured, and are the first to be impaired or lost. *G.D.W. & C.S.*

James-Lange theory of emotion. A theory concerned with the relationship between the physiological changes that occur with emotional arousal (q.v.) and the accompanying experience of the emotion (q.v.). The Danish philosopher C. G. Lange had argued that emotion is identical with changes in the circulatory system. The American psychologist William James (q.v.) elaborated this theory, arguing that the emotional experience results from the perception of the various bodily changes that occur in response to emotive stimuli. Thus he held that the bodily changes are neither the outcome nor the concomitants of the emotional experience, but its *cause*. It would therefore be more true to say that we are afraid because we run away, than that we run because we are afraid.

Bibliography: Lange, C. G. & James, W.: The emotions (Ed. Dunlap, K.). Baltimore, 1922. *G.D.W.*

James, William. B. 1/11/1842 in New York City; d. 16/8/1910 at Mount Chocorua, New Hampshire. In 1861 James enrolled at Harvard University in the Lawrence Scientific School. He first studied chemistry, then comparative anatomy, biology and physiology, and entered the Harvard Medical School in 1864. His interest in psychology was heightened by a visit to Germany in 1867–8. In Berlin he attended lectures by Du Bois-Reymond, the famous physiologist, and in Heidelberg courses given by Helmholtz and Wundt. His academic career continued at Harvard: M.D. in 1869, Instructor, 1872, and Assistant Professor of physiology in 1876, Assistant Professor of philosophy in 1880, and then Professor of philosophy in 1885; in 1889, Professor of psychology, and Professor of philosophy again from 1897 to 1907. He set up one of the first psychological laboratories in the world, in 1875. His main psychological study, *Principles of Psychology* (1890), is one of the basic works of modern psychology. James was a pioneer of American psychology and is sometimes compared with Wundt. He was a co-founder of the functionalist movement and a supporter of evolutionism; he was a friend of C. Stumpf and worked with H. Münsterberg. He was an independent thinker and not a proponent of systems or a laboratory psychologist but a man of many ideas and an intelligent critic who remained close to reality; his style was highly original. In his psychology of emotion (q.v.) and expression he represented an extreme type of physiologism but was nevertheless on the way to "a phenomenological psychology" (J. Linschoten); he advocated an experimental psychology which he did not himself practice; he stood for "radical empiricism" and also developed a pragmatic religious philosophy and psychology. Among his contributions to psychology, his theory of consciousness (q.v.) and the self (see *Ego*) deserve especial mention. James saw consciousness as a result of adaptation helping man toward species- and self-preservation. As regards the self, he made a distinction (still discussed) between the "discriminated aspects and not separate things" of "I" (the self as knower) and the social "Me" (the self as known: material, social and spiritual). He represented consciousness ("stream of consciousness") as processual rather than static (structured), and emphasized the dynamic nature of human psychology. "Consciousness, as a process in time, offers the paradoxes which have been found in all continuous change. There are no 'states' in such a thing, any more than there are facets in a circle. . . . Yet how can we do without 'states', in describing what the vehicles of our knowledge seem to be?"

Main works: Principles of psychology. New York, 1890; London, 1891. Text-book of psychology. New York & London, 1892. The will to believe. London, 1897. Human immortality. Boston & London, 1898; ²1917. Talks to teachers on psychology, and to students on some of life's ideals. New York & London, 1899. The varieties of religious experience: a study in human nature. London, 1902. Pragmatism, London, 1897. The meaning of truth. London, 1909. A pluralistic universe. London, 1909. Some problems of philosophy. London, 1911. Essays in radical empiricism. London, 1912.

Bibliography: Allport, G. W.: The productive paradoxes of William James. Psychol. Rev., 1943, *50*, 95–120. **Id.:** William James and the behavioral sciences. J. Hist. beh. Sci., 1966, *2*, 145–7. **Boring, E. G.:** Human nature vs. sensation: William James and the psychology of the present. Amer. J. Psychol., 1942, *55*, 310–27. **Harper, R. S.:** The laboratory of William James. Harvard Alum. Bull., 1949, *52*, 169–73. **Knight, M.:** William James. London, ²1954. **Linschoten, J.:** Auf dem Wege zu einer phänomenologischen Psychologie: die Psychologie von W. James. Berlin, 1961. **Perry, R. B.:** The thought and character of William James, 2 vols. Boston & London, 1935.

                                                   L.J.P.

Janet, Pierre. B. 29/5/1859, in Paris; d. 24/2/1947, in Paris. Studied philosophy and medicine at the University of Paris; in 1889 he gained his doctorate for philosophy with a thesis on the psychology of automatic activities; in 1890 Charcot appointed him Director of the psychological laboratory at the Salpêtrière hospital. In 1892 he received his doctorate in medicine with a thesis on the mental state of hysterics, in which he attempted a systematic classification of the different forms of hysteria, and tried to establish a concordance between hysterical symptoms and psychological theories; he taught at the Sorbonne from 1895 to 1902 and then replaced Ribot in the chair of psychology at the Collège de France, where he remained until his retirement in 1936. In 1904 Janet and G. Dumas founded the *Journal de psychologie normale et pathologique*, which Janet edited until 1937.

Janet's "psychologie de la conduite". In his behavioral theory, Janet works from the assumption that a scientific study of psychology can be meaningful only if all mental processes are interpreted as behaviors. He was one of the first to place special emphasis on the dynamic characteristics and unity of psychological phenomena. Although he had much in common with Freud (q.v.), their relationship was strained, partly because Janet claimed that Freud's psychoanalysis (q.v.) was based on his own work and that of Charcot. Janet conceived personality as a totality of tendencies which he arranged in a hierarchy on the basis of their phylogenetic and ontogenetic origins (strata theory), from the lower (reflex actions, etc.) to the higher tendencies (rational, etc.). By "tendency", Janet understood a disposition of the organism to complete a specific action; he included both external and internal or secondary actions (e.g. emotions) under the notion of action. A human being generally has access to tendencies which correspond to all the diverse stages and are normally present in a latent form. All these tendencies have specific energy loadings, which Janet derived from hereditary, physiological and psychological processes, and whose activation is manifested in behavior (actions). The lower tendencies generally have higher energy charges than the higher tendencies; they are also easy to arouse, and discharge more completely than the higher tendencies, which are only discharged successively (in this context Janet, like Freud, allows for the possibility of the inhibition and transference of instinctive[drive] energies). In general, the overall behavior of a given individual corresponds to a certain hierarchical level ("psychological or mental tension") determined both by the rank order of behaviors in the hierarchy of tendencies and by the degree of activation of those behaviors. An individual's mental tension is high if he can easily perform, frequently and accurately, actions with a high ranking in the hierarchy. The tension level is not constant but subject to continuous fluctuation. Janet emphasizes the degree of reduction of mental tension as the criterion for a classification of personality disorders. Reductions in tension which relate only to the stage of the highest tendencies are still normal; if mental tension drops below the stage of considered behavior (medium tendencies), Janet speaks of *neuroses*. If the tension falls to the level of elementary intellectual behavior, he speaks of *psychoses*; and if it drops to the level of perception and reflex actions, organic disorders of the CNS are in question.

Main works: L'automatisme. Paris, 1889. L'état mental des hysteriques. Paris, 1892

(Eng. trans. The major symptoms of hysteria. New York, [2]1920; facsimile ed., N.Y., 1965). Les obsessions et la psychasthénie. Paris, 1903. Névroses et idées fixes. Paris, [2]1904. Les névroses. Paris, 1909. De l'angoisse à l'extase. Paris, 1926. Psychological healing: a historical and clinical study, 2 vols. London, 1925. Psychological analysis. In: Murchison, C. (Ed.): Psychologies of 1930. Worcester, 1930, 369–73. Pierre Janet. In: Murchison, C. (Ed.): History of psychology in autobiography, Vol. 1. Worcester, 1930, 123–33.

Bibliography: Mayo, E.: Some notes on the psychology of Pierre Janet. Cambridge, Mass., 1948. Zilboorg, G. & Henry, G. W.: A history of medical psychology. New York, 1941.   W.W.

J curve. A hypothesis put forward by F. H. Allport (1934) according to which the frequency of the behavioral characteristics of a group exposed to pressure to conform—unlike groups without such pressure—follows a J distribution rather than a standard distribution (e.g. punctuality of workers in a company with fixed working hours as opposed to punctuality in a company in which the starting time may vary; or varied behavior at traffic lights). The curve of varying degrees of conformity often approximates an inverted capital J.

Bibliography: Allport, F. H.: The J-curve hypothesis of conforming behavior. J. soc. Psychol., 1934, 5.
                                            A.S.-M.

Jargon. 1. Incomprehensible speech. **2.** Language, vocabulary or style specific to a particular profession, political party, branch of learning, etc.

Jastrow's illusion. One of the geometric illusions. Although they are identical in size the lower of the two curved figures appears larger. *C.D.F.*

Job. 1. A task. **2.** An occupational activity performed in return for (a monetary) reward.

Job analysis. A detailed study of all the requirements and conditions of a particular occupation. Often used in management training and the preparation of interview programs. See *Industrial psychology.*

Job enlargement. Adding to an occupational activity by the inclusion of new operations (previously performed by others) in order to make the work more interesting, rational and/ or responsible. *G.R.W.M.*

Job rotation. A planned change in activities and/or functions for training and vocational advancement of executives. *G.R.W.M.*

Jost's law(s). 1. The older of two associations of identical intensity diminishes less with the the passage of time. **2.** Practice is of greater benefit to the older of two associations of identical intensity. See *Association.*

Bibliography: Jost, A.: Die Assoziationsfestigkeit in ihrer Abhängigkeit von der Verteilung der Wieder-holungen. Z. Psychol., 1897, *14*, 436–72. *H.H.*

Judgment. 1. The power or process of discerning the relations between one object, or concept, or term, or proposition, and another; or a propositional statement of those relations. See *Logical reasoning; Perception; Thinking.* **2.** A critical evaluation. **3.** The discernment of stimuli and their intensities (see *Psychophysics*).

Bibliography: Abercrombie, M. L. J.: The anatomy of judgment. London, 1960. Bruner, J. S., Goodnow, J. J. & Austin, G. A.: A study of thinking. New York, 1962.

Judgment, change of. A process of social suggestion or influence in which relatively simple verbal of symbolic "more or less" decisions on specific objects (e.g. perceptual objects) are altered: for instance, such basic judgments as "long" or "short", "positive" or "negative", "sympathetic" or "unsym-pathetic". A term sometimes used to charac-terize changes of opinion or attitude where there is no conceptual qualification beyond the basic term. See *Psychophysics.* *H.D.S*

Judicious learning. See *Learning, mechanical.*

Jung, Carl Gustav. B. 26/7/1875 in Kesswil (Switzerland); d. 6/6/1961 in Küssnacht. After obtaining his medical degree from the Uni-versity of Basle in 1900, Jung was appointed assistant, and later lecturer, under Eugen Bleuler at Zürich. He gave up his university post in 1913 in order to devote himself to private practice and to research. From 1906 he corresponded regularly with Freud, whom he met for the first time in 1907, in Vienna. This was the beginning of a short-lived friend-ship, during which Freud for a time saw Jung as his successor. In 1909 they traveled to-gether to Worcester, USA. In 1907 Jung founded the Freud-Gesellschaft in Zürich. In 1908 he organized the first International Psychoanalytic Congress in Salzburg. In 1911, with Freud's support, Jung was elected first president of the International Psycho-analytic Society; soon afterwards, the diffi-culties in his relations with Freud (primarily arising from Jung's rejection of the libido theory) increased. Their correspondence ceased in 1913; and in 1914 Jung resigned his presidency (and later his membership) of the International Psychoanalytic Society. Be-tween 1921 and 1926 he made field expeditions to study primitive cultures in Arizona, Mexico, North Africa, and Kenya, and pursued his interest in mythology, alchemy, religion, occult practices, and so on. From 1933 to 1942 he was Professor at the Zürich

Polytechnic; and in 1944 he was appointed Professor of medical psychology at the University of Basle.

In contradistinction to Freud's more natural-scientific, mechanistic theory of personality, Jung's analytical conception of personality represents an attempt to interpret human behavior from a philosophic, religious and mystical viewpoint. Jung's theory is also distinguished from psychoanalysis (q.v.) by its stronger emphasis on teleology (q.v.) (not only causality, q.v.) as a determinant of behavior, a stress on racial and phylogenetic bases of personality, and much less emphasis on sexuality as a significant factor in the development of personality.

In explaining the dynamics of personality, Jung—like Freud—uses the concept of libido (q.v.) but—unlike Freud—does not see it as a collective concept for human sexual tendencies, but as an *undifferentiated* energy at the basis of the most varied mental processes (thinking, feeling, sensing, drive). The regulation of psychic activity is not determined by the pleasure-pain principle, but occurs autonomously by way of libido, and is determined primarily by the principles of the conservation of energy and of entropy (q.v.).

The whole personality (psyche) consists of three interacting systems: the conscious, the personal unconscious, and the collective unconscious. The midpoint of the *conscious* is constituted by the ego (q.v.), which comprises the conscious perceptions, memory contents, thoughts and feelings, and permits the individual to adapt to the environment. The *personal unconscious* consists of the personal experiences, wishes and impulses which were once conscious but were then repressed or forgotten, but are essentially capable of being once again brought to consciousness. The *collective unconscious*, the most influential psychic system, operates wholly without the conscious awareness of the individual. It is the inherited racial foundation of the structure of personality and manifests the influence of the cumulative experiences of all previous generations, and

even the animal past of the human species. The structural components of the collective unconscious are the *archetypes* (q.v.), which are universal, inherited dispositions of the human imaginative faculty, which dispose the individual to experience and behave in eternally recurrent situations (birth, death, danger, fatherhood) as his ancestors experienced and behaved in them. Some archetypes are so developed that they constitute autonomous personality systems: the persona, anima, animus, and shadow.

The *self*, an archetype which is responsible for the integration and stability of the personality, occupies a central position in the Jungian theory of personality. It is expressed in the inborn striving of the human individual toward psychic wholeness, a central process which Jung calls *individuation* (q.v.), or striving toward self-realization. Since neurosis (q.v.) is said to represent a disturbance of the process of individuation, Jung's analytical therapy aims at a restoration of this natural process of development.

Jung's typology (see *Type*) is based on a distinction between function and reaction types. Whereas function types are divided into the four basic functions of thinking, intuition, feeling and sensation, the reaction type characterizes the direction of libidinous energy. According to whether libido is oriented more inwardly or outwardly, Jung distinguishes between *introversion* and *extraversion*.

Works: The Collected Works of C. G. Jung, 17 vols. Ed. Read, H., Fordham, M. & Adler, G. London & New York, 1953–.

Some major individual works are: Studies in word association. London, 1918; New York, 1919. Contributions to analytical psychology. London, 1928. Modern man in search of a soul. London & New York, 1933. Psychiatric studies (Works, Vol. 1, pt. 1), London & New York, 1957. Psychological types (vol. 6). London & New York, 1971. The structure and dynamics of the psyche (Vol. 8). London & New York, 1960. The archetypes and the collective unconscious

(Vol. 9, pt. 1). London & New York, 1959. Psychology and alchemy (Vol. 12). London & New York, ²1969. The development of personality (Vol. 17). London & New York, 1954. The interpretation of nature and the psyche (with W. Pauli). London, 1955.

Bibliography: Clark, R. A.: Jung and Freud: a chapter in psychoanalytic history. Amer. J. Psychother., 1955, 9, 605–11. Fordham, F.: An introduction to Jung's psychology. Harmondsworth, ²1966. Fordham, M. (Ed.): Contact with Jung. Essays on the influence of his work and personality. London, 1963. Gray, H. & Wheelwright, J. B.: Jung's psychological types, including the four functions. J. Gen. Psychol., 1945, 33, 265–84. Hochheimer, W.: Psychotherapy of C. J. Jung. New York, 1969. Jacobi, J.: Complex, archetype, symbol in the psychology of C. G. Jung. New Haven & London, 1959. Id.: The psychology of C. G. Jung. An introduction. New Haven & London, ⁷1969. Munroe, R. L.: Schools of psychoanalytic thought. New York, 1955. Progoff, I.: Jung's psychology and its social meaning. New York, ²1969. Schaer, H.: Religion and the cure of souls in Jung's psychology. London, 1951. Serrano, M.: C. G. Jung and Herman Hesse. A record of two friendships. London, 1966. Wehr, G.: Portrait of Jung. New York, 1971.

W.W.

Just-noticeable difference (abb. j.n.d.). A minute difference between stimuli which is just barely above threshold: i.e. an only just perceptible physical change in stimuli. See *Psychophysics.*

Just-not-noticeable difference (abb. j.n.n.d.). The largest difference between two stimuli which is only just imperceptible.

Juvenile delinquency. The most common offenses committed by juveniles are theft and embezzlement. In the twentieth century, and especially after World War II, juvenile crime increased far more quickly than adult crime and became an ever greater social problem. Juvenile psychology (q.v.) and criminal psychology (q.v.) investigate the causes of this development. In the practical field, child psychology (q.v.), educational counseling (q.v.), forensic psychology (q.v.), and clinical psychology (q.v.) deal with the problem of juvenile delinquency. See *Aggression; Criminality; Drug dependence.*

Bibliography: Conger, J. J. & Miller, W. C.: Personality, social class and delinquency. New York, London & Sydney, 1966. Glueck, S. & Glueck, E. T.: Unraveling juvenile delinquency. Cambridge, Mass., 1950. Gottlieb, D. & Reeves, J.: Adolescent behavior in urban areas. New York, 1963. Mays, J. B.: Growing up in a city. Liverpool, 1956. Sheldon, W. H., Hartl, E. & McDermott, E.: Varieties of delinquent youth. New York, 1949. F.Ma.

Juvenile psychology. A part field of developmental psychology (see *Development*). Juvenile psychology studies the psychological situation and developmental processes of juveniles in pre-puberty (q.v.), puberty (q.v.), and adolescence (q.v.). The principal areas of research are psychobiological (bodily changes, personality development) and psychosocial problems (socialization, q.v.) of youth (q.v.). Special attention is given to adaptive disorders (see *Adjustment, social*) and juvenile delinquency (q.v.). See *Child psychology; Differential psychology; Educational psychology; Infancy sexuality.*

Bibliography: Gesell, A., Ilg, F. & Ames, L. B.: Youth. New York, 1956. F.Ma.

Juvenilism. See *Infantilism.*

K

Kallikak. A pseudonym for a much-studied family with two lines of descendants: one socially respectable, the other variously defective.

Bibliography: Goddard, H. H.: The Kallikak family: a study in the heredity of feeble-mindedness. New York, 1912. Id.: In defense of the Kallikak study. Science, 1942, *95*, 574.

Kappa effect. If two stimuli are presented separated by a fixed temporal interval, the experienced temporal interval depends on the spatial separation of the stimuli, larger separation giving the appearance of a longer interval. This effect, which is small, occurs in both vision and touch. *C.D.F.*

Kaspar-Hauser. See *Caspar Hauser*.

Kendall's rank correlation method (syn. *Kendall tau coefficient*). A non-parametric correlation method whose use presupposes ordinal variables. The calculation is made according to

$$\tau = \frac{2S}{n(n-1)},$$

where S is the number of rank pairs of the second variables which are in the correct sequence when the first rank series is placed in its natural order. τ is not algebraically comparable with the Spearman's correlation coefficient. See *Correlational techniques*.

Bibliography: Kendall, M. G.: A new measure of rank correlation. Biometrika, 1938, *30*, 1–15. Id.: Rank correlation methods. London, ³1962. *G.Mi.*

Kendall's W (syn. *Coefficient of concordance*). A non-parametric method to determine the degree of concordance of more than two rankings. The calculation is made according to:

$$W = \frac{11 \, \Sigma \, D_1^2}{k^2(N^3 - N)},$$

in which k is the number of rank series and D_1 the deviations of the summed rankings of the individual components from the mean of the group rankings.

Bibliography: Kendall, M. G.: Rank correlation methods. London, ³1962. *G.Mi.*

Kent-Rosanoff Test. A free word-association test on Jungian principles developed by G. H. Kent and A. J. Rosanoff in 1910 for psychiatric clinics. The frequencies of reaction words for the one hundred stimulus words of the test were determined in one thousand testees, and the interpretation objectivized. Other authors standardized the answers for specialized groups.

Bibliography: Buros, O. K.: The sixth mental measurement yearbook. New Jersey, 1965. *R.M.*

Keratoscope. Also known as a Placido disk after A. Placido (1882), a keratoscope is used for qualitative determination of irregular corneal curvature (see *Astigmatism*). It is a circular disk with concentric white and black rings, and a central aperture. If the cornea of a patient is viewed through the aperture, in astigmatism the reflected circles are distorted. *K.H.P.*

Keynote (syn. *Tonic*). **1.** The main, lowest note of the scale from which the passage is constructed: i.e. the first degree of the (major or minor) key, which gives the key its name. **2.** In acoustics, the lowest, overtone-free partial of a clang (q.v.) *B.S.*

Key stimulus. (syn. *Releasing stimulus; Releaser*). A trigger for an instinctive action operating through an IRM. The relevant characteristics of the stimulus object are determined in dummy sign stimuli (q.v.) experiments. E.g.: In spring the stickleback attacks rivals only when they are brilliantly colored (red belly). Although realistic stickleback dummies with no red coloration do not elicit an attack, the response occurs if a model only remotely resembling a fish but with a red base is sighted. See *Innate releasing mechanism; Instinct.* *I.L.*

Kinesiotherapy. Various kinds of movement therapy: relaxation exercises, breathing practice, rhythmic movement, gymnastics; also individual and group sports for relaxation, development of social ease, and the acquisition of new, or the recovery of previously repressed, somatic aspects of the individual personality. See *Autogenic training.* *W.T.*

Kinesthesia (syn. *Kinesthesis*). The perception of movements of parts of the body mediated by receptors in the joints, muscles and tendons. A *kinesthetic hallucination* would thus be the experience of a bodily movement which did not actually occur. Such a hallucination is sometimes experienced after traveling a long time on a boat. *C.D.F.*

Kinesthesiometer. An instrument for checking the accuracy of sensations of movement. Without visual checks, either passive movements are repeated actively or active movements of a specific type are directed to previously agreed points in space. The accuracy with which the movements are repeated or the points reached is measured. *A.T.*

Kinesthetic type (syn. *Motor type*). An ideational or one of the imagination types in whom tactile and movement images predominate. Described by Stern in 1911. *W.K.*

Kinsey report. The studies known as the Kinsey Report (Kinsey *et al.*, 1948; 1953) were conducted at the Institute for Sex Research in Bloomington (Indiana, USA) founded by A. Kinsey, and were the first comprehensive, empirical scientific studies of sexual behavior. Kinsey and his colleagues conducted surveys among 5300 white males and 5490 white females over a period of fifteen years; their subjects were of widely varying age and educational groups, social strata and religious affiliations; they were questioned about their sexual behavior: e.g. masturbation (q.v.), marital and extramarital intercourse (see *Coitus*), petting (q.v.), homosexuality (q.v.). Criticism (excluding moral rejection of the findings) has primarily been directed at the allegedly unrepresentative nature of the sample (Cochran *et al.*, 1953) and (e.g. Trilling, 1952) at the "worship of the factuality of the fact ... the effect of suggesting a most ineffectual standard of social behavior—that is, social behavior as it exists." Beyond the results and their exemplary multivariate evaluation, the importance of the Kinsey report lies in the fact that it opened a new phase in empirical studies of sexual behavior—some of which have come from the Institute, which was continued by Gebhard after Kinsey's death. See *Sexuality.*

Bibliography: Cochran, W. G. *et al.*: Statistical problems of the Kinsey Report. J. Am. Statist. Ass., 1953, *48*, 673–716. Gebhard, P. H., Gagnon, J. H., Pomeroy, W. B. & Christenson, C. V.: Pregnancy, birth and abortion. New York, 1958. Id.: Sex offenders. New York, 1965. Himmelhoch, J. & Fava, S. F. (Eds.): Sexual behavior in American society. New

York, 1955. Kinsey, A. C., Pomeroy, W. B. & Martin, C. E.: Sexual behavior in the human male. Philadelphia, 1948. Id. & Gebhard, P. H.: Sexual behavior in the human female, Philadelphia, 1953. Trilling, L.: The Kinsey Report. Perspectives USA, 1952, *1*, 193–206.   *J.F.*

Kirschmann's law of contrast. In simultaneous color contrast, if there are no differences in brightness the induced color saturation is proportional to the logarithm of the saturation of the color inducing the contrast.
                                                                        W.P.

Kjersted-Robinson law. The proportion of material learned during equal fractions of learning time is relatively constant for different lengths of material.

Klages' types. Three basic attitudes: (*a*) ego emphasis: close relationship between the ego and id; (*b*) elimination of the feeling of self: the ego and id are split apart (dissolution); (*c*) cult of images and ecstasy.

Bibliography: Klages, L.: Grundlagen der Charakterkunde. Bonn, [13]1966.   *W.K.*

Klang (Ger.). See *Clang*.

Kleptomania. Compulsive pathological stealing. The objects stolen often appear to be of little value to the thief and therefore are often viewed as being of symbolic value. To a Freudian the objects would have sexually satisfying qualities. To others the thefts are seen as acts of aggression against society, to assert authority, or as a revenge against material and emotional deprivation in childhood.   *D.E.*

Klinefelter's syndrome. A syndrome described by the American physician H. F. Klinefelter in 1942. Symptoms: hypogona-dism with testicular atrophy, underdevelopment of the secondary sex characteristics, gynecomastia (q.v.), absence of spermiogenesis, and (frequently) eunuchoidal physique. The cause is a chromosomal anomaly with trisomia of the sex chromosomes—generally XXY.   *E.D.*

Knee-jerk reflex. See *Patellar reflex*.

Knowledge. 1. *Simple knowledge:* apprehension (q.v.); perception (q.v.). **2.** *Complex knowledge:* understanding (q.v.). **3.** Certain (i.e. indubitable) apprehension or understanding. "I conclude . . . that the necessary and sufficient conditions for knowing that something is the case are first what one is said to know be true, secondly that one be sure of it, and thirdly that one should have the right to be sure. This right may be earned in various ways . . ." (Ayer, 1956). **4.** Accurate information. **5.** The relation between object and subject (see *Epistemology; Cognition*).

Knowledge, theory of: see *Cognition theory*.

Bibliography: Ayer, A. J.: The problem of knowledge. London, 1956. Wittgenstein, L.: Philosophical investigations. London, [2]1958.

Knowledge of results. In psychotherapy, education (especially programmed instruction), etc.: confirmation of the accuracy or inaccuracy of a response.

Koffka, Kurt. B. 18/3/1886 in Berlin; d. 22/11/1941 in Northampton, Mass. Received his doctorate in 1908 under C. Stumpf in Berlin, with a thesis on experimental studies of rhythm theory; was an assistant of J. von Fries in Freiburg (Breisgau) in 1908/09, and of O. Külpe and K. Marbe in Würzburg, in 1909/10. As research assistant to F. Schumann in Frankfurt in 1910, he met Wertheimer and Köhler, and with them founded the Berlin school of gestalt psychology. In 1919 Koffka became a private lecturer and in 1918 Extraordinary Professor in Giessen, where he remained until 1924. He left Germany in 1924 and taught at Cornell University in 1924/25, Clark University in 1925, the University of Wisconsin in 1926/27, and at Smith College from 1927 until his death.

Works: Koffka, Wertheimer and Köhler are considered to be the founders of gestalt psychology. Apart from his experimental work, Koffka's main contribution was his systematic presentation and application of gestalt principles to a wide range of phenomena from perception, learning, memory and development to social psychology.

Unlike Wertheimer and Köhler, Koffka formulated his gestaltist viewpoint at a relatively early stage, i.e. when, in 1923, he published the first of a series of twenty-five "Contributions to gestalt psychology". In 1915 he answered the critics of gestalt theory in his *Fundamentals of the Psychology of Perception: a Debate with V. Benussi,* and in 1919 with an article on the influence of experience on perception. In his *Principles of Psychological Development: An Introduction to Child Psychology* (1921), for the first time Koffka applied gestalt principles to child psychology. He believed that the development process is essentially the result of the interaction of internal and external conditions (convergence hypothesis), and consists of an increasing differentiation of originally diffuse, qualitatively holistic experience.

Koffka's most important work, his *Principles of Gestalt Psychology* (1935), was the most comprehensive attempt yet to represent and integrate the results of gestalt psychological research in various fields (including the work of Lewin). His treatment of learning and memory may be considered the most systematic presentation of gestaltist ideas on the subject. (See *Ganzheit.*)

Koffka's learning theory is based on the assumption that learning, like other areas of behavior, can be explained by the gestalt principles of organization. New learning consists in the formation of "memory traces": i.e. of specific excitatory gestalts in the brain which result from previous processes (physiological correlates of direct percepts) and therefore represent past experience in the present. The memory process consists of the activation of memory traces by present processes on the basis of mutual similarity. The trace system is organized in accordance with the conventional gestalt laws and is subject to pregnance. Its time-conditioned changes do not therefore consist of a weakening of memory traces (forgetting) but in a qualitative change toward a "good gestalt" with increasing regularity and sharper accentuation of special features. The typical form of learning is learning by insight, even though this may be preceded by a testing stage. Practice brings about a consolidation and strengthening of the trace system. The "law of effect" is basically acknowledged, but reinterpreted: attainment to the goal influences learning (on the basis of the gestalt law of closure) through the completion of the action gestalt. The transfer of successful solutions to new situations (transposition) is possible if the principle of solution (i.e. the dynamic structural relation) is similar.

Main works: Perception: an introduction to the *Gestalttheorie.* Psychol. Bull., 1922, *19,* 631–85. The growth of the mind: an introduction to child psychology. London & New York, ²1928. Principles of gestalt psychology. New York, 1935.   *W.W.*

Köhler, Wolfgang. B. 21/1/1887 in Reval, Estonia; d. 11/6/1967, Lebanon, New Hampshire. Köhler received his doctorate in 1909 under C. Stumpf in Berlin; he then went to Frankfurt as an assistant to F. Schumann and became a private lecturer in 1911; he met Wertheimer and Koffka in Frankfurt and with them carried out the historic experiments that established gestalt psychology; he later became a co-founder of the Berlin school; from 1913 to 1920 he worked as director of the anthropoid station of the Prussian Academy of Sciences at Teneriffe, where he conducted his famous investigations into the "intelligence" of apes. In 1921 he took over from Stumpf as director of the Berlin psychological laboratory, and was appointed Professor of psychology and philosophy in 1922. In 1935 he left Germany because of the Nazi dictatorship and emigrated to the United States; he became Professor at Swarthmore College, where he remained until his retirement in 1955. He was President of the A.P.A., a member of the National Academy of Sciences, and in 1956 received the A.P.A.'s Distinguished Scientific Contribution Award.

Works. Together with Wertheimer and Koffka, Köhler founded gestalt psychology. His major contributions on the psychology of perception include treatises on the assumption of constancy in earlier psychology, and studies of figural aftereffects. He believed that he could use the existence of figural aftereffects indirectly to prove the existence of the cortical tension fields assumed in his neurophysiological theory of dynamic "self-distribution". In his studies of constancy, Köhler was able to show that (contrary to previous ideas) there is no constant correspondence between local sensory stimuli and experimental impressions, and that a perception is influenced not only by the local stimulus but, primarily, by the organization of the visual reference system and by the stimulus constellation of the other sense organs.

In the sphere of the psychology of learning and memory, Köhler criticized the learning theories of association psychology, and in particular the principle of association (q.v.) by contiguity; his own opinion was that associations occur under the influence of gestalt organizational tendencies: the associated contents become parts of a gestalt. Spatial and temporal contiguity was important in associations only in favoring the organization of a gestalt by sheer proximity.

Köhler's most famous works are his studies of the intelligent behavior of chimpanzees. Departing from the theory of E. L. Thorndike (who reduced animal behavior to trial-and-

error learning), Köhler showed that animals are already able to act with insight, and even to use or manufacture tools to achieve their objectives.

In his gestalt theory of brain physiology, Köhler started from the assumption of a dynamic self-distribution in the physical sphere (physical gestalts) and arrived at the notion that physiological activation processes in the brain are also subject to dynamic self-distribution, and that there is a formal, topological correspondence between perceived space and the underlying physiological brain processes. See *Isomorphism; Ganzheit.*

Main works: Intelligence in apes. In: Murchison, C. (Ed.): Psychologies of 1925. Worcester, [2]1927, 145–61. The mentality of apes. New York, [2]1927. Gestalt psychology. New York, 1929. The place of value in a world of facts. New York, 1938. Dynamics in psychology. New York, 1940. On the nature of associations. Proc. Amer. phil. Soc., 1941, *84*, 489–502. Gestalt psychology: an introduction to new concepts in modern psychology. New York, [3]1957. Relational determination in perception. In: Jeffress, L. A. (Ed.): Cerebral mechanisms in behavior. New York & London, 1951, 200–43. The present situation in brain physiology. Amer. Psychologist, 1958, *13*, 150–4. Perceptual organization and learning. Amer. J. Psychol., 1958, *71*, 311–5 Gestalt psychology today. Amer. Psychologist, 1959, *14*, 727–34.

Bibliography: Murchison, C. (Ed.): The psychological register, Vol. 2, Worcester, 1929.   *W.W.*

Kolmogoroff-Smirnoff test. A non-parametric method for testing the extent to which two independent distributions match. These may be one empirical and one theoretical distribution, or, alternatively, two empirical distributions. The greatest observable difference between the two summed distributions is determined as the index for matching.

Bibliography: Kolmogoroff, A. N.: Sulla determinazione empirica di une legge di distribuzione. Giornale Istituto Italiano Attuari, 1933, *4*, 83–91.

Smirnoff, N. W.: On the estimation of the discrepancy between empirical curves of distribution for two independent samples. Bull. Univ. Moscow. Ser. Internat., Sect. A2 (2), 1939, 3–8.   *G.M.*

Korsakov's syndrome (syn. *Korsakov's psychosis*). An amnesic psychosyndrome described for the first time by K. S. Korsakov in alcohol-deranged individuals. The term was subsequently extended and is often now applied to all organic psychoses in which memory disorders are a dominant factor. The characteristic feature is a marked disturbance of perception and immediate memory, whereas long-term memory often remains adequate; there is a tendency to perseverations and confabulation. See *Alcoholism; Psychoses, functional.*   *A.Hi.*

Korte's laws. Korte's laws concern apparent motion, i.e. stroboscopic motion produced by the intermittent presentation of stationary objects in different positions. If two objects are presented in this way, but appear successive, then apparent motion can be induced either by increasing the distance between the objects (Korte's first law) or by decreasing the time between presentations (Korte's second law). The third law states that an increase in separation of time can be compensated for by an increase in time or separation without regard to the quantitative relationship.   *C.D.F.*

Koster's phenomenon. In artificially induced myopia (dispersion lines in front of the eyes) the colors of all (reduced) objects perceived appear fuller and more distinct.   *F.C.S.*

Kraepelin, Emil. B. 15/2/1856 in Neustrelitz; d. 7/10/1926 in Munich. Kraepelin qualified as a doctor in Würzburg in 1878, then worked in the municipal mental hospital in Munich. He moved to Leipzig in 1882 in order to work with Wundt, whose friend he became while still a student, but Wundt advised him against devoting himself entirely to psychology. After a short period as a private lecturer at the university clinic in Leipzig, he was appointed Professor in Dorpat in 1885, and in Heidelberg in 1891. In 1894 he edited the periodical *Psychologische Arbeiten.* From 1903 until his death in 1926 he was Professor of psychiatry and Director of the psychiatric clinic in Munich.

Works: Kraepelin became famous mainly for his contribution to psychiatric nosology, and in particular for his classification of mental disorders. He subdivided psychoses into two main groups: dementia praecox (q.v.) and manic-depressive psychosis (q.v.); his classification is fundamentally maintained by modern authors.

Despite his friendship with Wundt, Kraepelin's standpoint on the etiology of mental disorders was primarily somatic in orientation (i.e. psychological factors play no part). He considered them to result from organic brain damage, metabolic disorders, endocrinal disturbances, or hereditary factors.

Kraepelin was also important in being the first to use the methods of psychological investigation and experimentation in psychiatry. He was the first to use objective tests (q.v.) and measurements to elucidate mental disorders. He was interested in psychological time measurements, choice reactions, associations and ergography. His studies on the work process and its forms anticipated some significant features of modern learning psychology (reactive inhibition, q.v., etc.) whose discovery (according to H. J. Eysenck) was wrongly attributed to later psychologists. Eysenck believes that Kraepelin ought to be recognized as the "father of clinical psychology".

Kraepelin's third major contribution consisted in his pioneering work in psychopharmacology (q.v.), which he virtually founded. He was the first to use experimental methods to study the effects of drugs, alcohol, nictotine, etc., on human behavior.

Main works: Compendium der Psychiatrie,

4 vols. Jena, 1883. Einführung in die psychiatrische Klinik, 3 vols. Jena, 1901. Über die Beeinflussung einfacher psychischer Vorgänge durch einige Arzneimittel. Jena, 1892. Die Arbeitskurve. Leipzig, 1902. Über geistige Arbeit. Leipzig, 1903. Lectures on clinical psychiatry. New York, 1904 (facsimile ed., N.Y., 1967).

Bibliography: Braceland, F. J.: Kraepelin: his system and its influence. Amer. J. Psychol., 1957.   *W.W.*

Krause end bulb (syn. *Krause ending; Krause's corpuscle*). A rounded neuronal receptor occurring in, e.g. the conjunctiva and genitals, and thought to be a sensory end organ for cold stimuli. See *Sense organs.*

Kretschmer, Ernst. B. 8/10/18 in Wüstenrot; d. 8/2/1964, in Tübingen. Kretschmer studied medicine in Munich (where he came under the influence of Kraepelin) and at the Eppendorf Hospital in Hamburg. He received his doctorate in 1914 with a dissertation on mania and manic-depressive symptoms; he then enlisted, and was responsible for establishing a neurological department at the Bad Mergentheim military hospital. In 1918 he left Bad Mergentheim and became a private lecturer in Tübingen; in 1926 he was appointed Professor of psychiatry and neurology at Marburg University, and between 1946 and 1959 he was Director of the neurological clinic at Tübingen University.

Although Kretschmer was a highly prolific author, his name is primarily linked to his *Physique and Character* (*Körperbau und Charakter,* 1921), in which he presented his constitutional typology. After 1946 he carried out detailed studies of constitutional and developmental physiology, and of child and adolescent psychopathology, as well as research into constitutional biology. He also tried to develop new psychotherapeutic methods and hypnotic techniques. He carried out basic research in the field of criminal behavior and made recommendations for modifications of the penal law that would allow for adequate treatment.

Constitutional typology. Kretschmer's type theory has a morphological bias and is based on human physique. He makes a distinction between the leptosomic-asthenic type and the pyknic type. His major contribution in this field, beyond the distinction between physical types, was a classification of the relationship between these types and the three main forms of endogenous psychosis. On the basis of studies of two hundred and sixty mentally ill subjects, which have now been validated by examination of more than nine thousand cases, he was able to show that schizophrenic individuals are primarily leptosomic, manic-depressives are pyknic, and epileptics athletic.

Starting from the assumption that there is only a gradual, non-qualitative distinction between mental disorders and normality, Kretschmer established the existence of three character types (temperaments) with the same essential features (though in a much reduced form) as the corresponding psychoses from which they were derived. The schizothymic (split character, introversion, etc.) temperament (type) corresponds to the leptosomic physique (type); the cyclothymic (sudden changes of moods, affective responses, etc.) to the pyknic; and the viscous (cautious, slow) temperament (type) to the athletic type.

While the correlations between physique and psychosis postulated by Kretschmer appear relatively certain, there has not yet been any decisive confirmation of his assumptions concerning physique and character in normal psychology. See *Traits; Type.*

Main works: Der sensitive Beziehungswahn: ein Beitrag zur Paranoiafrage und zur psychiatrischen Charakterlehre. Berlin, ⁹1950. Körperbau und Charakter, Berlin, ²⁴1961 (Eng. trans.: Physique and character, New York & London, 1925). Medizinische Psychologie. Stuttgart, ¹¹1956. Geniale Menschen. Berlin, ⁴1948 (Eng. trans.: The psychology of men of genius. London, 1925). Hysterie, Reflex und Instinkt. Stuttgart, ⁵1948 (Eng.

trans.: Hysteria, reflex and instinct. London, 1961). Über gestufte aktive Hypnoseübung und den Umbau der Hypnosetechnik. D. med. Wochenschrift, 1946, 71, 29-31.

Bibliography: Eysenck, H. J.: Cyclothymia and schizothymia as a dimension of personality, I: historical review. J. Personal., 1950, 19, 123-52. Id.: The structure of human personality. London, ²1960.

W.W.

Kruskal–Wallis test. A non-parametric method for comparing several independent samples in regard to their central trend. The observations are ranked, and the rankings of all k samples arranged in one rank order; the rank sums (Rj) of the individual samples are compared. The critical value H is determined according to

$$H = \frac{12}{N(N+1)} \left(\sum_j \frac{R_j^2}{n_j} \right) - 3(N+1).$$

It is distributed at $n > 5\chi^2$ with $k-1$ degrees of freedom.

Bibliography: Kruskal, W. H. & Wallis, W. A.: Use of ranks in one-criterion variance analysis, J. Amer. Stat. Ass., 1952, 47, 583-621.

G.Mi.

Kuder Preference Record. A questionnaire designed to show the relative interest for individual, comprehensive areas of vocational interest. S. has to state most pleasant and most disagreeable of three activities. The test consists of ten scales presented in an interests profile, and one scale to detect dishonest answers. Standardized versions exist for children and adults.

F.G.

Kuder-Richardson Formula 20. A formula developed by Kuder & Richardson (1937) for estimating the coefficient of consistency (see Reliability) on the basis of item difficulty (p) and test value dispersion (s_x):

$$r_{tt} = \frac{n}{n-1} \left(\frac{s_x^2 - \Sigma pq}{s_x^2} \right).$$

It presupposes that the item-intercorrelations are approximately identical. See Test theory.

Bibliography: Kuder, G. F. & Richardson, M. W.: The theory of the estimation of test reliability. Psychometrika, 1937, 2, 151-60.

G.Mi.

Külpe, Oswald. B. 3/8/1862 in Candau (Courland); d. 30/12/1915 in Munich. Külpe began by studying history; he went on to psychology under Wundt in Leipzig, and Müller in Göttingen. He received his doctorate in 1887 (under Wundt) with a dissertation on the theory of sensory feeling. He then remained eight years in Leipzig, where he prepared a study of the "theory of will in modern psychology", and worked as a lecturer and as Wundt's assistant. In 1893 he published his *Outlines of Psychology*, a systematic presentation of psychology on Wundtian principles. He was appointed Professor at Würzburg University in 1894. In 1896 he established a psychological laboratory which, as the center of the Würzburg school (q.v.), became the most celebrated after that at Leipzig. In 1909 he was appointed Professor at Bonn. In 1913, he went to Munich.

The Würzburg school. Külpe founded the Würzburg school, which grounded the experimental psychology of thought processes. Apart from a short article "On the modern psychology of thought", Külpe wrote nothing else on this subject, but concerned himself primarily with philosophical questions in his publications: *Contemporary Philosophy in Germany* (1902), *Natural Science and the theory of Knowledge* (1910), *Realization; A Contribution to the Theory of the Realistic Sciences* (1912-1923). Külpe did, however, inspire the experimental studies of thought processes on which fifty of his Würzburg pupils published monographs. Other members of the Würzburg school (chronologically) were: A. Mayer, J. Orth, K. Marbe, H. J. Watt, N. Ach, A. Messer and K. Bühler.

The Würzburg school owed its foundation to Külpe's belief (in contrast to Wundt's) that the higher thought processes also can be studied experimentally. Külpe's approach was "systematic experimental introspection", a fractionated, retrospective account of the mental processes occurring in the course of a complex task. The main result of the Würzburg school's research work was a refutation of the previously dominant idea that thinking was a combination of quasi-perceptual images.

Külpe was able to demonstrate that thought is for the most part "imageless" and "sensation-free", and takes place with only a minimum degree of conscious awareness—so that the individual stages of the thought process are hardly "experienced". On the other hand, he showed that thought is, in general, non-associative and non-mechanical, yet directed and meaningful. The "determining tendencies" (N. Ach, 1905) which allow thought a specific orientation are either conscious *tasks* and experientially perceived *objectives*, or "conscious sets" ("*Bewusstseinslagen*": A. Messer, 1906)—attitudes, habits, long-term decisions, etc.—which may be non-perceptual or unconscious. See *Thinking*.

Main works: Grundriss der Psychologie. Leipzig, 1893 (Eng. trans.: Outlines of psychology: based upon the results of experimental investigation. New York, 1895). Vorlesungen über Psychologie. Leipzig, 1922. Die Realisierung, 3 vols. Leipzig, 1912–23.

Bibliography: Boring, E. G.: History of experimental psychology. New York, ²1950. Humphrey, G.: Thinking: an introduction to its experimental psychology. London & New York, 1951. Ogden, R. M.: Oswald Külpe and the Würzburg school. Amer. J. Psychol., 1951, *64*, 4–19. Titchener, E. B.: Experimental psychology, 2 vols. New York, 1901–5.
                                                          W.W.

Kundt's bisection test. When bisecting a horizontal line monocularly, there is a tendency to place the middle toward the nasal side. This phenomenon is also known as *Kundt's rule.*   C.D.F.

Kundt's illusion. The illusion whereby divided distances appear greater than objectively equal undivided distances. This phenomenon is sometimes known as *Kundt's rule.* C.D.F.

Kundt's rule. See *Kundt's bisection test; Kundt's illusion.*

Kurtosis (Ku). The degree of flatness or peakedness (excess) about the mode of a frequency distribution (curve). If a curve has a sharper peak than the normal frequency distribution, the divergence is said to be positive (*leptokurtosis*); in the opposite case it is negative (*platykurtosis*). (An average divergence is *mesokurtosis*.)   A.R.

Kymograph. A device consisting of a blackened drum or a moving strip of (smoked) paper used to record variations in the intensity of relatively protracted reaction processes (movements; muscular, pressure and temperature processes; electrophysiological processes: e.g. EEG, EKG, EMG). Since the drum or the paper strip moves at a constant speed, the graphic record obtained (kymogram) will indicate fluctuations.   A.Th.